West Interactive Casebook Series™
eBook KeyCode - Required for entry into eBook

This keycode enables access to an online version of this Interactive Casebook. If you purchased a used, unsealed copy of this book access to the electronic version of this book may not be available.

The **Interactive Casebook Series** eBook:

- **Links to Black's Law Dictionary® & Westlaw®**
- **Allows for highlighting portions of your ebook**
- **Provides the functionality to take and add notes**

Please register for your online version at our Interactive Casebook Series website.

Registration is fast and easy. Here's how:

Step 1: Go to **interactivecasebook.com**

Step 2: Click on **"Create a New Account"**

Step 3: On the "Create a New Account" page, enter in all required data

Step 4: Enter the **KeyCode** printed below

Step 5: Read the **End User License Agreement** and click on the **"I Accept"** radio button

Step 6: Click **"Submit"**

Step 7: On the next page, select the appropriate title and click on **"View eBook"**

Access to this electronic book will expire on August 31, 2010.

KeyCode: CCB1R-KRRZX-GK51S-GQURU-SD5PA

D1156027

THE INTERACTIVE CASEBOOK SERIES™

EVIDENCE

A Contemporary Approach

By

Sydney A. Beckman

DEAN AND PROFESSOR OF LAW
DUNCAN SCHOOL OF LAW AT LINCOLN MEMORIAL UNIVERSITY

Susan Crump

PROFESSOR OF LAW
SOUTH TEXAS COLLEGE OF LAW

and

Fred Galves

PROFESSOR OF LAW
UNIVERSITY OF THE PACIFIC MCGEORGE SCHOOL OF LAW

WEST®

A Thomson Reuters business

Mat #40730425

Interactive Casebook Series is a trademark registered in the U.S. Patent and Trademark Office.

© 2009 Thomson Reuters
      610 Opperman Drive
      St. Paul, MN 55123
      1–800–313–9378

Printed in the United States of America

ISBN: 978–0–314–19105–2

 TEXT IS PRINTED ON 10% POST CONSUMER RECYCLED PAPER

Editor's Note

The cases in this book have been edited and with regard to certain cases heavily edited. Traditional standards have not always been followed either to enhance clarity or readability. Footnotes have largely been removed from cases or edited into cases when the editors felt the footnote enhanced a case.

This book is intended to enhance your learning experience with a difficult subject. We value your input and feedback. If you have any comments, questions, notations of error or otherwise, please send your feedback to us at EvidenceCasebook@gmail.com.

Preface

This book is designed to be different than traditional textbooks in a number of ways. Those differences are detailed in Chapter 1. Importantly, the authors have attempted to cover the subject of Evidence both thoroughly and yet with enough brevity to keep the experience as interesting and complete as possible.

The authors would like to thank Louis Higgins and all of the individuals at West and Red Line Editorial for their assistance in the creation of this book.

Syd Beckman would like to thank his wife, Allyson, for all of her support through this and all of his projects.

Susan Crump would like to thank her husband, Les, for his wise counsel, insight and endless patience, as well as her daughter Catherine and son John, for their keen law student perspective and suggestions.

Fred Galves would like to thank his wife, Christine, and his two sons, Anthony and Johnston, for all of their love, support, and understanding in all endeavors.

General Table of Contents

Detailed Table of Contents

CHAPTER SEVEN *Hearsay and Constitutional Considerations*

CHAPTER EIGHT *A Return to Relevance I: Limits Based on Policy*

Table of Cases

The principal cases are in bold type.
Cases cited or discussed in the text are roman type. References are to pages.
Cases cited in principal cases and within other quoted materials are not included.

CHAPTER 1

Overview

"... if I can't introduce something in court it doesn't exist, legally ..."

– Ted Crawford played by Anthony Hopkins in the motion picture "Fracture"

A. What is Evidence?

Evidence is the bedrock of litigation. While the Federal Rules of Evidence do not define the term, "evidence" refers to witness testimony and physical items presented by a party and admitted during trial to prove an element of that party's case or to refute an element of an opponent's case. "Evidence" is also "[t]he body of law regulating the admissibility of what is offered as proof into the record of a legal proceeding." Black's Law Dictionary. In other words, evidentiary rules restrict admissibility and govern the way in which witness testimony and physical items can be introduced in court. Unless evidence is legally admissible under the rules, it may as well not exist. Judges and juries cannot consider what is not properly admitted.

1. The Study of the Rules of Evidence

Knowing the rules of evidence, therefore, is critical to a successful litigation practice. Even attorneys in a non-litigation practice should have a solid understanding of the admissibility of evidence in the event litigation should arise from their representation.

Evidence is regularly taught and learned in law school by studying the rules of evidence themselves and their application through the review of appellate cases. However, the academic study of evidence is frequently disconnected from use of the rules in the courtroom. As a result, students too often come away without a full appreciation of the depth, flexibility, and interplay of the rules and without a full understanding of their strategic and tactical uses. This text therefore seeks to marry the academic study of evidence with the practical application of the rules by a clear and concise discussion and analysis of "real world" evidentiary problems.

2. Evidence "Logic Maps."

Throughout this text, you will find diagrams which help illustrate certain rules or sets of rules. These logic maps are designed to provide a visual representation of the evidentiary issues discussed and to put those issues in a larger context. In Chapter 3, for example, you will study the concept that all relevant evidence is admissible under Rule 402. You will also study other rules that exclude relevant evidence, such as the rule against admitting hearsay under Rule 801, or against admitting evidence that is unfairly prejudicial, confuses the issues or misleads the jury, creates undue delay waste of time or needless presentation of cumulative evidence under Rule 403. A diagram of this concept might be illustrated as follows:

Overview: Admission or Exclusion of Evidence

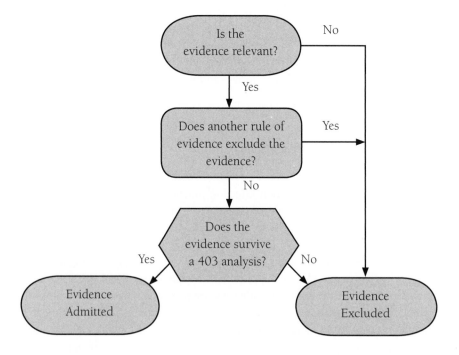

3. Scope of the Text

This book covers the rules of evidence which are most commonly used, most commonly found to be challenging and most commonly tested. No course in evidence can successfully cover each and every rule of evidence. This book is designed to present a breadth and depth of coverage that the student will find most useful. The Federal Rules of Evidence are provided in the appendix in two forms. First, the bare rules by themselves may be found in complete form in Appendix A. The complete Federal Rules of Evidence with the Advisory Committee Notes may be found in Appendix B. Advisory Committee Notes are explanatory notes written by the drafters of the rules and frequently used by courts as guidance in their interpretation.

4. Features of this Casebook

This casebook is designed to make the understanding of evidence easier. An understanding of evidence requires more than merely rote memorization; it requires recognition of the rules and an understanding of how and why those rules interact as applied in a litigation setting. As you progress through this book you should be able to begin to effectively assess the admissibility of evidence under the rules. For example, when assessing the admissibility of a photograph, you should be able to reach the point where you know what questions to ask and the likely answers to assess whether a photograph would be admissible in a given case. In many cases, there is not a definitive answer as to admissibility. To the contrary, many people will disagree as to the likelihood of admissibility. Given that fact, you may wonder how you can effectively "learn" evidence. The answer lies in the analysis. The critical understanding is what questions to ask and how those questions are analyzed under a given set of facts. A photograph might be relevant but, given its size, it might be unfairly prejudicial. As a student, you should learn to ask the question as to whether it is unfairly prejudicial. Specifically, you will be taught to analyze the picture under Rule 403. Understanding that you must examine the evidence in light of Rule 403 is, at least in part, "half of the battle."

The format of this casebook was designed in an effort to strike a balance between presenting the information in a way that is understandable and gently nudging you to delve into the material to discover many of the important principles yourself with sufficient guidance along the way. Toward that end, this casebook departs from the approach and appearance of traditional casebooks you will likely experience in other courses. Every innovation has been designed with one purpose in mind: the facilitation of student learning. Here are the main features of this book.

Logic Maps

Throughout this book you will find some *logic maps*. An example is the one you reviewed above that shows the general course of an evidentiary analysis. These Logic Maps are designed to give you a visual representation of the evidentiary issue discussed. As you proceed, you should expand these maps and create your own.

Electronic Casebook with Hyperlinks

One of the more unique features of this series of casebooks is the availability of an accompanying electronic version containing hyperlinked text. This entire casebook is available electronically in a format that you can highlight and search with ease. Additionally, the electronic version of this book is fully hyperlinked to many different resources.

Cases, Statutes and Articles

Case citations, statutes, rules, constitutional provisions and most law review articles are hyperlinked to Westlaw. Simply click on the link and students with Westlaw accounts will be able to view the complete versions of the linked source.

FYI

Law review articles that do not appear on Westlaw will be linked to PDF versions at HeinOnline (http://heinonline.org/front/front-index)

Legal Terminology

When you see legal terms that are hyperlinked (example: hearsay), that is an indication that clicking on the term will take you to the Black's Law Dictionary definition of the term. This is useful to do as you read through cases because your complete understanding of a case will often depend on knowing the meaning of key legal terms used in the case.

Online Materials

As you see in the text box above, whenever a Website is referred to in the text, it will be presented as a live hyperlink that you can click in order to visit the indicated site online.

Text Boxes

Throughout this book you will find various text boxes on either side of the page that are intended to provide useful information that will aid in your understanding of a case, draw your attention to important or noteworthy matters that deserve special attention, or cause you to think more deeply about an issue or question arising from the material. The categories of text boxes are as follows:

For More Information

These boxes point you to additional resources to consult for more information on a subject.

Food for Thought

These boxes will appear to pose questions that prompt you to think about various issues raised by the material.

Take Note!

Here you will be prompted to take special notice of what is being discussed in a case or something interesting that deserves further thought or attention.

Major Themes

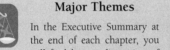

In the Executive Summary at the end of each chapter, you will find here a discussion of some of the deeper themes and issues pertaining to the topic covered in that chapter.

FYI

A self-explanatory category that shares useful or simply interesting information relevant to material in the text.

See It

These boxes point you to visual information that is relevant to the material in the text.

Hear It

These boxes point you to an audio file that is relevant to the material in the text.

Go Online!

If there are relevant online resources that are worth consulting in relation to any matter being discussed, these boxes will direct you to them.

Make the Connection

When concepts or discussions that pertain to information covered in other law school courses appear in a case or elsewhere in this text, often you will find this text box to indicate the course in which you can study those topics. Here you may also be prompted to connect information in the current case to material that you have covered elsewhere in this course.

It's Latin to Me

The law is fond of Latin terms and phrases; when you encounter these in the text for the first time, this box will explain their meaning.

Practice Pointer

Here you will find advice relevant to legal practice typically inspired by the actions (or inactions) of legal counsel in the cases or simply prompted by an important issue being discussed.

What's That?

These boxes will explain the meaning of special legal terms that appear in the main text. *Black's Law Dictionary* definitions may be accessed by clicking on the hyperlinked term in the text.

Name of Justices and Other Judges

The names of Supreme Court Justices and, on occasion, lower court judges, are hyperlinked to biographical information about them when their names appear as authors of or signatories to an opinion in a case (example: ROBERTS). If you take time to look at this information, you will gain valuable insight into the background of each Justice; this information will often prove useful in understanding a Justice's perspective, style, or jurisprudence. When other names are highlighted, such as influential individuals, the link will take you to websites which illustrate their biographical information.

Court Websites

Whenever a court is referenced in a case its name will be hyperlinked to that court's website. (example: U.S. Court of Appeals for the Fifth Circuit). You can visit these sites to get a better idea of the court's place within the judicial system or its geographical location, which can be important to understanding some cases. Both federal and state courts will be hyperlinked throughout the text.

Organizational and Government Websites

There will be times when organizations of various kinds (governmental, corporate, and non-profit) will appear in the text as litigants or third-parties or as agencies that previously handled the case (example: Securities and Exchange Commission). When appropriate, these will be hyperlinked to their respective websites so that you can learn more about the particular organization, either to aid in your understanding of a case or simply to obtain additional information that will broaden your view of the parties that are involved in a dispute.

Internal Cross-References

When other sections or chapters are referred to in the text, they will be hyperlinked so that clicking on them will immediately take you to that portion of the casebook (example: Chapter 7). Additionally, the table of contents is hyperlinked so that you can easily access portions of the book by clicking on the page number of interest.

FLEX Cases

When a case of some significance to an issue is mentioned or discussed, but is not included as a principal case in this text, you may find a hyperlink to a "FLEX Case." This hyperlink will take you to an edited version of the case that your professor may assign as additional reading or that you may choose to read on your own to gain additional insight into the matters raised.

Case Excerpts

Cases that appear in this text have been edited. Some have been substantially edited. Unedited versions may be accessed by clicking on the hyperlink to the case, which you will find in the caption.

Because cases and other third-party material included in this text are heavily edited, it should be noted that material included in this text is considered important. You should not omit anything in this text if assigned by your professor. Every effort was made to reduce or eliminate unneeded material. This is particularly true of footnotes. Most students completely skip over footnotes. Footnotes are included in this text for a reason. Read them. The same goes for concurring and dissenting opinions. If they are in here, read them. They are designed to help with your understanding of the material.

Statutes and Rules

Evidence is a course based on rules. A complete set of the Federal Rules of Evidence may be found in Appendix A. A complete set of the Federal Rules of Evidence with Advisory Committee Notes may be found in Appendix B. Throughout the book you will find hyperlinks to the complete rules to aid you in quickly reviewing the rules and navigating your way around the text. Within each discussion of a particular rule, you will find a box which sets out all or a portion of the rule being studied. For example:

Take Note!

This casebook was designed to eliminate extraneous information. Contrary to many casebooks, this text only contains information the authors deemed significant to the concepts addressed. Therefore, it is critical you do not skip – or skim – material contained herein. If it's in here – it's important.

Rule 403. Exclusion of Relevant Evidence on Grounds of Prejudice, Confusion, or Waste of Time.

Although relevant, evidence may be excluded if its probative value is substantially outweighed by the danger of unfair prejudice, confusion of the issues, or misleading the jury, or by considerations of undue delay, waste of time, or needless presentation of cumulative evidence.

The purpose is to focus your attention on the rule being addressed without distracting you from the main text.

Points for Discussion, Hypotheticals, and Perspective and Analysis

At various points in this book there will be a Points for Discussion section that will feature focused questions that you should consider and be able to answer. These will permit you to assess your understanding of material previously covered. You may also find hypotheticals to test your understanding of the rules addressed and assess your ability to apply the rules to new factual situations.

Finally, when a topic has been the subject of scholarly discussion or debate, there may be a shaded area entitled Perspective and Analysis. Under this heading you will find the presentation of an issue followed by an extended excerpt from a scholarly writing on the matter. The purpose of this Perspective and Analysis is designed to deepen your knowledge of a topic and enhance your appreciation of its significance to larger concerns.

Executive Summaries

At the end of each chapter there will be an executive summary that summarizes the main points addressed in the chapter. Use these summaries to confirm that you take away from each chapter what you were supposed to have learned. If you discover gaps in your understanding, either refer back to the relevant section of the chapter for review, meet with your professor, or consult additional resources to read more about the topic.

CHAPTER 2

The Process of Proof and the Structure of Trial

A. Introduction

Going to trial is sometimes equated to a roll of the dice in Vegas – a gamble. No one can predict a trial's outcome, whether the fact finder is a jury or a judge. However, while trial outcomes are not amenable to forecast, neither are trials random processes. The process of trial is structured and made somewhat predictable by the application of rules of evidence and procedure. The rules allow attorneys and their clients to form reasonable expectations and define the tasks necessary to present a case in an orderly, efficient, and reliable manner.

> **FYI**
>
> In federal civil cases, a fact finder may be a judge or a jury. In federal criminal cases, although a defendant's guilt or innocence may be decided by a judge or jury, the judge always determines punishment. Trials to a judge are typically called "trials to the bench," or "bench" trials. Note: a defendant is never actually found "innocent." He may, however, be found "not guilty".

Trials are mainly fights over facts and factual inferences. The Federal Rules of Evidence are designed to allow admission of facts that are relevant and reliable while excluding information that is tangential, confusing, speculative, and unrelated to the issues in the case. The trial judge is the arbiter in the application of these rules and enjoys a fair amount of discretion in making sure that they are "construed to secure fairness in administration, elimination of unjustifiable expense and delay, and promotion of growth and development of the law of evidence to the end that the truth may be ascertained and proceedings justly determined." Rule 102, Federal Rules of Evidence.

1. Witnesses and Physical Evidence

Facts are proved at trial through the introduction of evidence. There are generally two types of evidence a lawyer may introduce in court. The first is the testimony of live witnesses answering questions under oath before the fact finder. The second is tangible physical evidence relating to the case. Tangible physical evidence can be divided into two categories: <u>*real* evidence</u>, which is the evidence generated by the case, such as the knife used in the murder in question or the written contract that is the basis of the lawsuit, and <u>*demonstrative* evidence</u>, such as maps, photographs, charts, experiments, or computer simulations, which are used to illustrate and explain other evidence in the case. Tangible physical evidence is called an "<u>exhibit</u>," must be given an exhibit number or letter, and must be shown to be authentic (often through questioning of a witness with knowledge of its accuracy) before it may be admitted into evidence.

Trial lawyers present evidence in a step-by-step fashion by crafting questions for a witness so as to give meaning to discrete or disparate facts which permits the fact finder to comprehend the totality of his case. The lawyer wants the fact finder to see the facts and circumstances of his case as a coherent whole, "in living color." In this sense, the process of proving a party's case is much like painting a landscape, one stroke and one color at a time. As in painting, technique is important, and some techniques become routine. There are, for instance, usual and expected methods for questioning an eyewitness to an event or admitting tangible physical evidence, such as a gun or scene photograph. Below are examples of these techniques in a murder trial.

> **For More Information**
>
> There are a number of excellent resources available to students and lawyers that demonstrate how to introduce evidence in a question and answer format and that give the reader basic information about the federal rule in question. One such resource is "Evidentiary Foundations," by Edwin Imwinkelried, Matthew Bender, 2008; another is the Federal Trial Objections Quick Reference Card published by the National Institute for Trial Advocacy (<u>www.NITA.org</u>).

Example of Live Witness Testimony:

Q. State your name for the jury.

A. Adam Jones.

Q. Do you know the defendant in this case, Mike Sutton?

A. I do.

Q. Do you see him in the courtroom?

A. Yes, he is sitting at counsel table, wearing a blue tie.

Q. May the record reflect that the witness has identified the defendant, Mike Sutton.

Q. How do you know him?

A. Mike has been my neighbor for fifteen years.

Q. Directing your attention to May 13, 2008, did you see the defendant on that evening?

A. Yes.

Q. Where was the defendant?

A. On the lawn in front of his house.

Q. What was he doing when you first saw him?

A. Shooting his wife, Laura Sutton, with a gun. . . .

Example of the Introduction of Tangible Physical Evidence: Real

Q. State your name, please.

A. Tommy Thompson

Q. How are you employed?

A. I am a homicide detective here in the city of Madison.

Q. What are your duties as a police officer?

A. I investigate suspected homicides in Madison.

Q. Were you called to the scene at 113 Main Street on the evening of May 13, 2008 to investigate a homicide?

A. Yes.

Q. Whose residence is that?

A. The defendant, Mike Sutton's.

Q. As you were conducting your investigation at 113 Main, did you find any weapons relevant to this case?

A. Yes, we found a .44 caliber Smith and Wesson pistol in the defendant's pants pocket when we searched him.

Q. I want to show you what has been marked as State's Exhibit 1 [a pistol]. Can you identify it?

A. Yes. This is the .44 caliber pistol I found on the defendant immediately after the shooting.

Q. How do you know this is the same pistol you found on that evening?

A. Immediately after I took it from the defendant, I bagged it, sealed and labeled the bag with my initials and the date, and put it in the police evidence room under the defendant's name. Yesterday, I retrieved it from the evidence room in the same sealed and unaltered condition.

Q. Your honor, I offer State's Exhibit 1 into evidence.

Example of the Introduction of Tangible Physical Evidence:

Demonstrative

Q. Officer Thompson, please explain the layout of the front yard where the homicide took place.

A. The yard is basically a rectangle. The driveway is in the middle of the rectangle.

Q. Where was the victim, Laura Sutton, when you first observed her on the evening of May 13, 2008?

A. She was face down about twenty feet from the front door, with her head pointed toward the street.

Q. Would it aid your testimony today if you could draw a diagram of 113 Main Street and the position of Mrs. Sutton?

A. Yes, it would.

Q. Your honor, may Officer Thompson step down from the witness stand and draw a representation of the scene at 113 Main on the white board?

[Judge]

He may.

[Officer complies].

Q. Your honor, I would like to have this diagram labeled as State's exhibit 2, for demonstrative purposes only.

[Judge]

It will be so labeled.

Q. Officer Thompson, is State's exhibit 2 a fair and accurate representation of 113 Main Street on May 13, 2008, the scene of the homicide we've been discussing?

A. Yes.

Q. Your honor, I offer State's exhibit 2 into evidence for demonstrative purposes only.

2. Direct and Circumstantial Evidence

Evidence may be categorized as to whether it directly or circumstantially establishes a fact at issue in the lawsuit.

(a) *Direct evidence* is evidence based on a testifying witness's personal knowledge gained through the witness's senses which, if true, proves a fact without an inference or presumption. In the above dialogue, when witness Jones testifies that he saw the defendant shoot the defendant's wife with a gun, this statement, if believed, is direct evidence to support the proposition that the defendant killed her and does not require the fact finder to draw inferences from the statement in order to make it relevant to the case.

(b) *Circumstantial evidence* is evidence from which a fact-finder must make inferences to reach a factual conclusion in the case. The inferences may be weak, moderate, or strong. For instance, the fact that the officer in the above dialogue found the murder weapon on the defendant soon after the shooting is strong circumstantial evidence that the defendant was the person who shot his wife.

> **FYI**
> To quote Henry David Thoreau, "Some circumstantial evidence is very strong, as when you find a trout in the milk."

It is often said that direct eyewitness testimony is more reliable than circumstantial evidence in proving a case, but this is not always true. Eyewitness testimony is only as good as the witness's powers of observation, recall, sincerity and narration. For instance, if the witness has poor eyesight or a strong bias in the case, he may not be credible. However, the fact that the murder weapon was found in the defendant's possession soon after the shooting may be a more convincing indicator of the defendant's guilt.

B. The Role of the Judge

Although lawyers provide information to the jury through the use of witnesses, documents, other exhibits, and argument, the trial judge controls the trial process by setting limits on lawyers in order to achieve justice and efficiency. Federal Rule of Evidence 102 allows the trial judge to use the Federal Rules of Evidence to "secure fairness" and "eliminate undue expense and delay." Rule 403 permits the judge to exclude evidence that would otherwise be admissible if it confuses the issues, misleads the jury, causes undue delay, waste of time, or is a needless presentation of cumulative evidence. Rules 611 and 614 give judges the power to regulate the order and presentation of the evidence, call and interrogate witnesses, and make comments to the jury about the evidence that has been presented. The trial judge must, however, implement these rules in an impartial manner. The following cases illustrate the tension between these two concepts: control vs. impartiality.

1.   The Time Limits of Presenting Evidence

Rule 102. Purpose and Construction

These rules shall be construed to secure fairness in administration, elimination of unjustifiable expense and delay, and promotion of growth and development of the law of evidence to the end that the truth may be ascertained and proceedings justly determined.

One of the powers granted trial judges under the Federal Rules of Evidence is to set reasonable time limits on the various stages of the trial. In the following case, notice the court's description of the tension between the goal of the judge and the goal of the attorney in this regard.

> **Rule 403. Exclusion of Relevant Evidence on Grounds of Prejudice, Confusion, or Waste of Time**
>
> Although relevant, evidence may be excluded if its probative value is substantially outweighed by the danger of unfair prejudice, confusion of the issues, or misleading the jury, or by considerations of undue delay, waste of time, or needless presentation of cumulative evidence.

> **Rule 611. Mode and Order of Interrogation and Presentation**
>
> **(a) Control by court.** The court shall exercise reasonable control over the mode and order of interrogating witnesses and presenting evidence so as to (1) make the interrogation and presentation effective for the ascertainment of the truth, (2) avoid needless consumption of time, and (3) protect witnesses from harassment or undue embarrassment. . . .

United States v. Reaves

U.S. District Court for the Eastern District of Kentucky
636 F. Supp. 1575 (E.D. Ky. 1986)

BERTELSMAN, DISTRICT JUDGE:

Both the prosecution and the defendants in this criminal tax fraud case have challenged the authority of this Court to curtail the presentation of cumulative and time-wasting evidence by placing time limits on various stages of the trial. . . .

Make the Connection

Federal Rule of Evidence 1006 allows a party to present the contents of voluminous writings, recordings, or photographs in summary form if those contents cannot be conveniently examined in court, as long as the originals or duplicates are made available to the opposing party to allow the opposing party to check the accuracy of the summary.

Initially, the United States estimated the trial would take a month. Upon further inquiry, the court was convinced that this time was excessive. It was apparent to the Court that the prosecution intended to introduce numerous tax returns of various individuals and partnerships page by page, making little effort to organize the voluminous evidence into a meaningful pattern or streamline the presentation of the case by the use of charts or summary exhibits. Fed. R. Evid. 1006.

* * *

It would seem that early in the career of every trial lawyer, he or she has lost a case by leaving something out, and thereupon resolved never again to omit even the most inconsequential item of possible evidence from any future trial. Thereafter, in an excess of caution the attorney tends to overtry his case by presenting vast quantities of cumulative or marginally relevant evidence. In civil cases, economics place some natural limits on such zeal. In a criminal case, however, such fiscal constraints, and the attorney's enthusiasm for tautology is virtually unchecked.

* * *

The scheduling order was designed to give the United States ten days to present its case-in-chief and to impose proportionate limits on the other phases of the trial. The order worked well in practice. Actually, it was more than generous, the prosecution's case still being overlong. It was refreshing to see, however, how things started to move along as the prosecution's time

> **FYI**
>
> The scheduling order, attached as an appendix to the opinion, allowed the government sixty hours of trial time to present its evidence, the defendant thirty hours, and the government six hours for rebuttal, if necessary, excluding recesses and bench conferences.

began to run out. Suddenly, the prosecutors quickly reached the point with each witness and stuck to the issues, thus eliminating many objections, and the case became intelligible and interesting. Unfortunately, it ended in a mistrial because of the conduct of a witness.

* * *

Fed.R.Evid. 403 recognizes the power and duty of the court to exclude cumulative evidence or evidence which consumes more time than its probative value justifies. Rule 611 *commands* the court to "exercise reasonable control over the mode and order of interrogating witnesses and presenting evidence, so as to (1) make the interrogation and presentation effective for the ascertainment of the truth, [and] (2) avoid needless consumption of time."

It is fundamental that a court has the power and duty to manage its docket and the individual cases before it to "secure fairness in administration, [and] elimination of unjustifiable expense and delay." Fed.R.Evid. 102. Modern courts recognize that the court's time is "a public commodity which should not be squandered." D. Louisell and C. Mueller, *2 Federal Evidence* § 128 (1985). There is an unnamed party in every lawsuit-the public. Public resources are squandered if judicial proceedings are allowed to proliferate beyond reasonable bounds. The public's right to a "just, speedy, and inexpensive determination of every action"

public resources

is infringed, if a court allows a case, civil or criminal, to preempt more than its reasonable share of the court's time.

A court cannot rely on the attorneys to keep expenditures of time in trying a case within reasonable bounds. The perspectives of the court and the attorneys in trying a case differ markedly. A judge wants to reach a just result in the case and to do so expeditiously and economically. An attorney's primary concern is to WIN the case. If he believes he can win that case by proliferating the evidence of the favorable, but relatively uncontested matters so that the weaker aspects of the case will be camouflaged, it is asking too much of our fallen nature to expect him voluntarily to do otherwise.

* * *

Setting a reasonable time limit forces counsel to conform their zeal to the need of the court to conserve its time and resources. But, subject to the time limits imposed, counsel remain in control of the case. It is still counsel's case, although it must now be presented in a reasonable time. It is counsel rather than the court who decide what evidence is to be admitted and what is to be pruned. Numerous objections or *sua sponte* interruptions by the court to debate what evidence is repetitious or cumulative are avoided. Thus, the goal of preserving the court's resources is achieved while the traditional autonomy of counsel to present their own case, subject to the exigencies of that goal, is preserved. Properly stream-lined, the case is more effective for the ascertainment of truth, as mandated by Fed.R.Evid. 611(a).

* * *

holding)

This court holds that it has the power to impose reasonable time limits on the trial of both civil and criminal cases in the exercise of its reasonable discretion. Of course, the court must analyze each case carefully to assure that the time limits set are not arbitrary.

—————————

Points for Discussion

a. Crossing the Line.

Reaves was a case involving tax fraud. The prosecution had asked for a month to present its evidence but was only given approximately 10 days. Once the prosecution's allotted time started to run out, the judge remarked that "the prosecutors quickly reached the point with each witness and stuck to the issues, thus eliminating many objections, and the case became intelligible and interesting." Perhaps the case was initially uninteresting to the judge because he had tried similar tax fraud cases before. But, is it possible that a jury, upon attempting to wade through technical and complex facts and law, may have needed more time to absorb and process the information?

b. Trials as a Public Resource.

The court observes that "[m]odern courts recognize that the court's time is 'a public commodity which should not be squandered,' and that '[p]ublic resources are squandered if judicial proceedings are allowed to proliferate beyond reasonable bounds.'" It is true that trying a case, as opposed to settling or dismissing it, often takes up a larger percentage of available judicial resources. Is this a sufficient justification to allow the trial judge in *Reaves* to reduce substantially the time period allowed for the prosecution to present its case? Is the trial judge in a better position than the lawyers to judge how long their case should take?

---

2. The Order of Witnesses and Their Testimony

Normally, the lawyers determine the order in which they will call witnesses at trial. However, as the following case illustrates, federal trial judges have some discretion in this area.

Stone v. Peacock

U.S. Court of Appeals for the 11th Circuit
968 F.2d 1163 (1992)

PER CURIAM:

Plaintiff [sued three] officers of the Georgia Department of Corrections claiming they terminated his employment in retaliation for his speaking out about the improper use of public property and funds. . . . At the beginning of trial, the district court required Stone to testify first so that some chronology would be laid out at the beginning of the case. This initial testimony was not subject to cross-examination at that time. Stone's counsel protested the court's reordering of the witnesses. Federal Rules or Evidence Rule 611(a), however, gives courts reasonable control over the order and presentation of evidence. There may have been some error, but perhaps harmless in this case, if the court did not give Stone proper notice. The court's witness order requirement alone, however, is not reversible error absent some showing of harm. Although it does not appear that Stone has shown harm, we need not make this determination. If there is a retrial,

[handwritten margin note: must show harm]

the plaintiff will be on notice that he may be required by the court to testify at the beginning of the case.

Reversed and Remanded (on other grounds).

————————

Points for Discussion

a. The Trial Judge's Objective.

The nature of the case and the brevity of the *Stone* decision suggest that the case may not have been as complex or difficult for a jury to follow as other types of federal cases, such as those involving antitrust, tax, or securities fraud claims. While it might be helpful to the jury to require that a witness be called out of order to present a chronology of events at the beginning of trial, do you think a trial judge should be allowed to do this as a matter of course? Why do you think the trial judge did not allow the cross-examination of witness Stone at this time? Was it because the witness or the opposing attorney might not be ready for cross?

b. Showing Harm.

How would Stone's attorney show harm in a case such as this where the client is suddenly called to the witnesses stand without warning? Is there anything Stone's attorney could have argued to convince the appellate court that there was reversible error?

3. Comments on the Evidence.

Federal judges may comment on the evidence presented at trial. Often, this opportunity arises when the judge charges the jury. In such a case, "[it] is within his province, whenever he thinks it necessary, to assist the jury in arriving at a just conclusion by explaining and commenting upon the evidence, by drawing their attention to the parts of it which he thinks important; and he may express his opinion upon the facts, provided he makes it clear to the jury that all matters of fact are submitted to their determination." *Quercia v. United States*, 289 U.S. 466,

Make the Connection

After the lawyers give closing arguments, the trial judge reads written instructions to the jury. These instructions contain the substantive and procedural law the jurors must follow and apply during jury deliberations before reaching a verdict. It is during the reading of jury instructions that federal judges are allowed to comment on the evidence that has been presented at trial. To understand where the reading of jury instructions fits into the order of proceedings at trial, see Section C of this chapter.

469, 53 S.Ct. 698, 77 L.Ed. 1321 (1933). In other words, the judge may analyze and dissect the evidence for the jury, as long as she does not distort or add to it. Federal judges may also comment on the evidence as it is presented during the trial itself. However, in doing so, the judge should use great care to not prejudice the litigants or their cases.

United States v. Yates

U.S. Court of Appeals for the Sixth Circuit
553 F.2d 518 (6th Cir. 1977)

ENGEL, Circuit Judge.

[Yates appealed from his jury conviction of bank robbery. He had signed a confession but maintained he did not know what he was signing, did not rob the bank, thought he was under investigation for writing bad checks, and wanted to cooperate with the FBI].

The last witness to testify for the government in its case-in-chief was FBI Agent Rogers who testified at length concerning the circumstances of the interview with Yates on January 6 and of the preparation and execution of the purported confession. At the conclusion of Rogers' testimony, the Assistant United States Attorney offered and the court admitted as government's Exhibit No. 2 the document which had been identified as Yates' confession. The colloquy which then ensued before the jury and which forms the basis of defendant's objection is reprinted [below]:

> MR. BROWN (Assistant United States Attorney): Your Honor, I would request that Exhibit No. 2 [the confession] be published to the jury, however, to avoid any unnecessary time delay I would request that it be read in open court by some suitable person, either myself or the Clerk.
>
> THE COURT: Mr. Dersom?
>
> MR. DERSOM (Yates' counsel): Is that as to Exhibit 2?
>
> MR. BROWN: Yes, sir.
>
> MR. DERSOM: Your Honor, respectfully, I submit if the exhibit is in evidence that the jury will have time to look at it themselves. It need not be read at this time.
>
> THE COURT: That's true, Mr. Brown.
>
> MR. BROWN: Yes, Your Honor.

THE COURT: The written statement of the admissions or confession, or whatever you want to call it, as made by this Defendant is in evidence and the jury will have an opportunity to read it, so it will not be read to or by the jury at this time. It is clear in the record from the testimony of Mr. Gableman and Mr. Rogers that this Defendant did admit his participation in this bank robbery, so call your next witness, Mr. Brown.

D argues

The defendant strongly urges that the district judge's remark that defendant admitted his participation in the bank robbery exceeds the scope of permissible judicial comment on the evidence and is reversible.

gov't argues

The government, however, asserts that remarks are within the broad traditional powers of a trial judge to control the progress of the case and to comment on the evidence . . . . Further, the government urges that the remarks, in their context, amounted not to a comment upon the evidence but rather were simply an observation that the document introduced was self-explanatory and did not need to be published to the jury as requested by the prosecution. The government contends that this interpretation logically explains the failure of the defense to object to the statement at the time or to request any curative instruction then or later.

Ct. says

. . . . While the government urges that "the jury would not have interpreted said comment as having any bearing whatsoever upon the veracity of the defendant, in that at the time the comment was made, the defendant had not yet testified . . .", it is nevertheless clear that the court's comment struck directly at the heart of Yates' defense; it negated Yates' claim that he did not make the confession, that he signed the paper without realizing its contents and that he did not rob the bank. While it is true, of course, that Yates had not yet testified at the trial, he had testified fully at the suppression hearing and thus the trial judge had to be aware of his position. Essentially Yates had no other defense.

* * *

Ct. holds

The impression was clearly created before the jury that the Court considered certain necessary elements of the Government's case had been proved, thereby infringing upon the rights of the defendant to have the jury weigh the evidence as to proof of guilt. . . .

Reversed and remanded for a new trial.

———————————

Points for Discussion

a. Counsel's Dilemma.

Do you agree with the court in *Yates* that the trial judge's remarks were so egregious that the case should be reversed even though the defense attorney did not object when the statements were made? What dilemma does trial counsel face when deciding whether to object to this kind of remark?

b. Is Reversible Error Less Likely in Trials to the Court?

If the *Yates* case had been tried to the judge instead of a jury, do you think these remarks would have reversed the case?

---

4. Questioning Witnesses

> **Rule 614. Calling and Interrogation of Witnesses by Court**
>
> **(a) Calling by court.** The court may, on its own motion or at the suggestion of a party, call witnesses, and all parties are entitled to cross-examine witnesses thus called.
>
> **(b) Interrogation by court.** The court may interrogate witnesses, whether called by itself or by a party.
>
> **(c) Objections.** Objections to the calling of witnesses by the court or to interrogation by it may be made at the time or at the next available opportunity when the jury is not present.

Rule 614 of the Federal Rules of Evidence expressly grants judges the right to call and question witnesses, even repeatedly and aggressively, to clear up confusion and manage trials whenever necessary. This authority, however, has its limits. Judges may not ask questions that signal their belief or disbelief of witnesses ~limits~ because that determination is part of the jury's role in a case.

The line between appropriate and inappropriate judicial questioning of witnesses is not always clear because appellate records do not convey the demeanor or tone of judicial questioning. Generally, however, a judge's overly aggressive questioning of witnesses will not result in reversal unless it affects the substantial rights of a party.

Crandell v. United States

U. S. Court of Appeals for the Fourth Circuit
703 F.2d 74 (4th Cir. 1983)

SPROUSE, Circuit Judge:

[Scott and Linda Crandell brought suit for medical malpractice against medical personnel at Quantico Marine base for failure timely to diagnose their 6 month old daughter Jennifer with spinal meningitis. They claimed that as a result, Jennifer became severely retarded. The Crandells lost in a trial to the court. On appeal, they contend that that the trial judge had predetermined their case.]

Make the Connection

A trial to the bench, or "bench trial" means a trial in which the judge is the fact-finder rather than the jury.

As evidence of his prejudgment, the Crandell's point specifically to the judge's remarks concerning (a) their refusal to settle and (b) financial considerations extraneous to the issues. They further point to (c) the judge's badgering of their expert witnesses and (d) his interference with the Crandell's counsel's attempts to cross-examine the key defense witness, as demonstrations of the judge's determination to prevent them from developing their evidence. [The court first determines that the first two allegations are correct].

* * *

The trial judge's interference with the Crandells' expert witnesses is even more clearly a demonstrable error. The judge on one occasion ridiculed one of plaintiffs' experts while contorting his testimony.

THE COURT: This doctor says it was, there was growth deficiency prior to the meningitis, isn't that what you just said?

THE WITNESS: No. He is saying that from a review of the history-

THE COURT: (Interposing) Certainly, you couldn't exist without history, could you, Doctor?

THE WITNESS: No.

THE COURT: Well, I didn't think you could. You couldn't diagnose any thyroid without having a very complete history.

THE WITNESS: We could, yes.

THE COURT: You could? Could you tell me now if I have got a headache, Doctor?

THE WITNESS: A headache is a symptom not a disease.

THE COURT: Could you tell me whether I have a thyroid deficiency without asking questions-my, my, my, Doctor, you are the first doctor in all my 80 years that ever told me substantive symptoms, which is history, didn't mean a thing to you.

MR. SNEAD: He didn't say that.

THE WITNESS: I didn't say that.

THE COURT: I know what he said. I know what he means. He said he didn't need the history.

THE WITNESS: To make a diagnosis of hypothyroidism in an infant.

THE COURT: That's what he said. He didn't need the history.

THE WITNESS: Yes, sir. I can explain why.

THE COURT: Well, that's your opinion.

MR. SNEAD: Could he explain it?

THE COURT: Let him explain it. I don't want you to testify. You brought him over here as an expert.

THE WITNESS: You can make the diagnosis of hypothyroidism in an infant because they are now screened and we get a laboratory test. In addition, where a child comes in untreated there are certain physical findings you can see that you do not need a history for, and I can list a large number of diseases that can make the diagnosis, I can make the diagnosis by merely looking at the patient without a word being uttered because it is so characteristic.

THE COURT: Well, I am sure if I had my right arm cut off you can tell me I am missing my right arm. I am conscious of that.

Although the issues were tried to the judge alone, the possible inhibitive effect on witnesses and counsel presented as much a danger as it would have in a jury trial.

Finally, the trial judge prevented effective cross-examination of the most important defense witness. At the conclusion of the trial, the judge based his opinion almost exclusively on the testimony of the government's expert, Dr. Lehman. All of the findings in the court's memorandum opinion, on the issue of whether the Naval Hospital personnel breached the standard of care and on the issue of medical causation, were lifted virtually verbatim from a report prepared by Dr. Lehman.

The court precluded the Crandells' counsel, however, from effectively cross-examining Dr. Lehman on facts in evidence, including the records which Dr. Lehman relied on in forming his opinion.

Question: You don't know, then-you don't have an opinion for this Court about-

Answer: (Interposing) Not without being given information that is reliable on what happened between the 28th and the 1st, no.

Question: All you know is it happened sometime-

THE COURT: (Interposing) He says he doesn't even know it happened.

MR. SNEAD: If it happened. Doctor, let's assume that this child did develop, sometime between the 28th and the 1st, a very fulminating viral bacterial meningitis. And further assume that there were frank indications of this on the 1st, that there was a bulging fontanelle, that the left eye was turned inward-

THE COURT: (Interposing) Doctor, you are not assuming that, are you, in your findings?

THE WITNESS: I am listening to him. These are not my assumptions at the moment.

MR. SNEAD: Your Honor, it's in evidence.

THE COURT: What's in evidence?

MR. SNEAD: The fact that the child-

THE COURT: (Interposing) But he doesn't accept it. Next question. He doesn't have to accept everything you say.

MR. SNEAD: He certainly doesn't, and I don't expect him to. But I would expect him to accept the facts in evidence.

THE COURT: You are not the judge of the sole facts in evidence. Next question. If you have something in the record, pick it out of the record. You can show it to him. Ask him how he reconciles his opinion with this exhibit.

MR. SNEAD: I'm trying to understand-this Court asked this witness about his feelings about the adequacy of the care of the infant on the 1st of July.

THE COURT: Based solely, nothing hypothetical, based solely upon what he discovered from these records that he looked at.

MR. SNEAD: Yes.

THE COURT: I didn't ask him to make any hypotheses, period.

MR. SNEAD: If I told you that the evidence in this case is that there was a significant neurological sign, the left eye was turned inward-

THE COURT: (Interposing) Next question. I'm not going to let him with this (sic). We will be here the rest of the night.

MR. SNEAD: Your Honor, I believe that is material to the-

THE COURT: (Interposing) Well, I'm sorry.

MR. SNEAD: It's material to the material the gentleman reviewed.

THE COURT: I'm not going to let you-you asked eleven hypotheses and hypotheticals, but I really want to find out what the facts are and not hypotheses.

This action by the trial judge was particularly glaring since the defendant's counsel never objected to the form or appropriateness of the questions-the court simply assumed the role of an advocate.

* * *

It is true that a trial judge functions not merely as an umpire, but as a governor to see that justice is done. The judge, for example, is entitled to propound questions pertinent to a factual issue which requires clarification. He may intercede because of apparent inadequacy of examination or cross-examination by counsel, or to draw more information from relevant witnesses or experts who are inarticulate or less than candid. This privilege or duty, however, is subject to reasonable limitations.

A trial judge must assiduously perform his function as governor of the trial dispassionately, fairly, and impartially. He must not predetermine a case, and we must condemn any conduct before or during the course of a trial which indicates predisposition. It is important that a litigant not only actually receive justice, but that he believes that he has received justice.

* * *

An impartial observer could well conclude from the record in the case *sub judice* that the trial judge predetermined the outcome before the Crandells fully presented their case. The record reveals numerous judicial interjections indicating hostility toward the plaintiffs and their experts, and also reveals an over-solicitous acceptance of the testimony of defendant's expert. The trial judge precluded plaintiffs from developing important evidence at trial. Some of the judge's remarks could only lead an impartial observer to conclude that his decision was influenced by concerns irrelevant to the issues-the price of malpractice insurance and that "taxpayers" may ultimately bear the burden of paying any damages. No litigant can rightfully expect a favored status before a judge or jury, but all must be assured that their cause will be presented, reviewed, and judged impartially and fairly. We are cautious not to fetter unduly the necessary governing function of trial court judges, but the conduct of the judge in the present case again fell far short of the standards requiring him to govern the trial dispassionately. We do not express any opinion on the substantive merits of the malpractice claim, but we conclude that the trial judge's conduct deprived the Crandells of a fair trial. We, therefore, reverse the judgment of the district court and remand with instructions to the Chief Judge of the Eastern District of Virginia to reassign the case to a different trial judge.

Reversed and Remanded.

———————————

Points for Discussion

a. Is It What a Judge Says or How He Says It?

It is clear from the questions, answers and judge's comments in *Crandell* that the trial judge was extremely skeptical of the plaintiffs' expert's testimony. But, how does the appellate court know that the trial judge had already determined that the plaintiffs should lose by the time he questioned plaintiffs' expert? Do you think that trial judges frequently know how they are going to decide before all the evidence has been presented?

b. The Appearance of Justice.

Do you agree with the statement in the case that the appearance of justice is as important to a litigant as justice itself? If so, why?

C. The Order of Proceeding

The rules of evidence permeate every level of litigation, both civil and criminal. Competent counsel, from the very onset of a case, will gather facts and anticipate how to present them in ways that the rules will allow to support a claim or defense. Long before trial, consideration of whether evidence is admissible guides counsel in evaluating how to draft pleadings in civil matters and indictments or complaints in criminal matters. Discovery in civil cases extends only to matters that are "reasonably calculated to lead to admissible evidence" and allows counsel to preserve evidence for later use at trial. Motions for matters such as summary judgment or other judgments as a matter of law require the motion drafter to show facts that are admissible in evidence. It is at trial, however, that the evidentiary rules take center stage, as the following description of the stages of trial illustrates.

Basic Stages of Trial

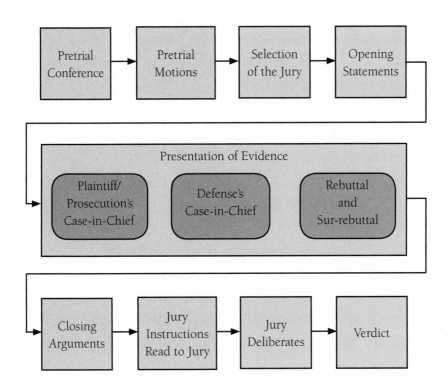

1. *Pretrial Conferences.* As the date of a trial draws near, federal procedural rules require that the judge hold a pre-trial conference with lawyers for each party in order to narrow the legal and factual issues that will be raised at trial and to identify witnesses and documents that will be offered as evidence. Once determined, these matters are drawn up in a pre-trial order which controls the presentation of each party's case at trial.

2. *Pretrial Motions.* Before the trial begins, the parties may attempt to control the admissibility of evidence at trial by filing what are called *motions in limine* requesting that the judge keep from the jury certain designated

It's Latin to Me

Non constat
ex temporal hora
jus civile
a posteriori

"In limine" (pronounced "lim-in-ee") is Latin for 'at the threshold."

testimony or documents which a party anticipates her opponent will attempt to offer. For example, a defendant in a product liability case may make a *motion in limine* to prevent the plaintiff from referring to, or introducing evidence of, other instances where the defendant's product caused similar accidents. If the motion is granted, the opposing party is ordered not to raise the matter ruled inadmissible *in limine,* on pain of contempt and possible mistrial, until the jury is excused and final admissibility of the evidence can be determined. If a motion *in limine* is not granted, the party making the motion has another chance to object and keep the jury from hearing the evidence when it is offered at trial.

What's That?

The term "voir dire" (pronounced "vwahr deer") is French for "to speak, to say." It refers to any trial process by which a person's qualifications are determined by questioning. For example, prospective jurors are "voir dired" to determine if they are biased or there is cause to not allow them to serve in the case. The term is also used during trial when a party wants to question a witness in order to determine if that witness is qualified to be testifying in accordance with the rules of evidence.

3. *Selection of the Jury.* When the parties decide not to use a jury or neither side has a right to a jury trial, the judge sits as both judge and finder of fact in what is called a *bench* trial. Most serious cases, however, involve jury trials. Juries are picked by a process called "voir dire," where the judge and the attorneys in turn ask questions of a panel of prospective jurors to determine whether they are qualified to be selected to hear the case. During this process, lawyers must have a thorough knowledge of not only the law but also the facts in order to ask questions that might reveal a juror's bias in the type of case at issue. Once the requisite number of jurors has been selected, they take an oath to "a true verdict render," and the trial begins.

4. *Opening Statements.* Opening statements provide an opportunity for lawyers to tell the jury in summary form about their theory of the case and to describe evidence the jury will hear at trial in support of that theory. Lawyers need to make certain that the facts they describe in opening statement are admissible; if they are not, the jurors are liable to remember what was promised and hold the failure to produce the evidence against that lawyer's client. Plaintiff/prosecution gives the first opening statement, followed by the defendant. Or, the defendant may waive opening statement and present it later in the trial before the defense presents its case-in-chief. (See Step 7, infra).

5. *Presentation of the Evidence: Plaintiff/Prosecution's Case-in-Chief.* After opening statements, the party with the burden of proof presents evidence in her case-in-chief by calling witnesses to the witness stand, questioning them under oath, and sometimes introducing physical evidence through the witness or otherwise.

<u>Direct Examination</u> The questioning by the lawyer who calls a witness to testify is called "direct examination." The goal during direct examination is to question the witness so as to elicit facts favorable to the party who has called the witness. The lawyer conducting the direct examination is generally required to ask the witness questions that are short, open-ended, non-leading, such as "What happened next?" Witnesses are also required to give relatively short, non-narrative answers, such as, "The next thing I saw was the defendant running the red light." When the lawyer is finished asking questions on direct, he "passes the witness" for cross-examination.

What's That?

Non-leading questions are those that do not suggest a particular answer. Asking a witness "What happened next? is a non-leading question. Asking a witness "Didn't you then call the police?" is a leading question.

Take Note

Although leading questions during direct examination are generally prohibited, Rule 611(a) gives the trial judge discretion to allow a lawyer to lead a witness on direct or ask narrative questions in federal court to control the mode or order of interrogating witnesses to further ascertaining the truth, avoid needless consumption of time, and protect witnesses from harassment or undue embarrassment.

<u>Cross-Examination:</u> Questioning by the lawyer of an adverse witness is called cross-examination. It is through cross-examination that the accuracy and completeness of a witness's testimony is tested. Rule 611(b) embodies the "American" or "restrictive" rule by limiting cross-examination to the scope of the matters asked on direct examination and to witness credibility. By limiting cross-examination, the rule allows an orderly presentation of evidence at trial. For example, if the defense in a murder case calls a witness to testify about the defendant's insanity, it would be inappropriate, absent permission from the court, to allow the prosecution to question the witness about what she learned as an eye-witness to the crime. If the prosecution wanted to question the witness about the crime itself, she would be required to call the witness during presentation of the prosecution's rebuttal case.

<u>Redirect Examination:</u> After cross-examination has been completed, the direct examiner may conduct a re-direct examination. The scope of re-direct is theoretically limited to matters raised during cross-examination and is not an opportunity for the direct examiner to repeat questions previously asked or raise matters that were not initially addressed on direct. The trial judge may also allow re-cross by the opposing party to respond to matters raised anew on re-direct. The trial judge

Compare the more restrictive American rule of cross-examination to the English rule, which allows "wide-open" cross-examination of a witness about any matter that is relevant to the case, not just the subject matter of direct and matters affecting the witness's credibility. Two advantages of the English rule, which is followed in many state courts, are that the (1) the trial judge is not required to determine whether certain cross-examination questions are within the scope of direct examination (which, at times, can be problematic); and (2) there is no need for the cross-examiner to call the witness later and question her in a non-leading manner, thus making the presentation of evidence more efficient.

may permit this back and forth questioning for some time until the witness is excused. Once all witnesses have been questioned, physical evidence has been introduced, and objections made and determined, the lawyer will then "rest" her case-in-chief.

<u>Objections:</u> During the presentation of evidence, lawyers may make objections. They do so for two basic reasons: (1) to prevent the introduction of evidence; and (2) to preserve error for appeal when such evidence is admitted over objection in admission of that evidence for appeal. A lawyer most often will make objections to questions or answers of a testifying witness, although objections may also be made to the admission of physical evidence.

To be timely, objections must be made before the witness answers the question. Thus a lawyer has very little time to determine whether the question is objectionable, whether it is worth making, and how to phrase the objection. The failure to object will often waive evidentiary error on appeal.

Once an objection is made, a trial judge will either *sustain* the objection, thus agreeing that the evidence is not admissible, or *overrule* the objection, thus finding that the evidence is admissible. At times, the judge may ask for further clarification or argument from counsel before deciding how to rule.

Take Note

If a question is not objectionable but an answer contains inadmissible evidence, the opposing lawyer makes a "motion to strike" the inadmissible portion of the answer rather than an "objection."

> **Rule 103. Rules on Evidence**
>
> (a) Effect of Erroneous ruling. Error may not be predicated upon a ruling which admits or excludes evidence unless a substantial right of the party is affected, and
>
> (1) Objection. In case the ruling is one admitting evidence, a timely objection or motion to strike appears of record, stating the specific ground of objection, if the specific ground was not apparent from the context; or
>
> (2) Offer of proof. In case the ruling is one excluding evidence, the substance of the evidence was made known to the court by offer or was apparent from the context within which questions were asked.
>
> Once the court makes a definitive ruling on the record admitting or excluding evidence, either at or before trial, a party need not renew an objection or offer of proof to preserve a claim of error for appeal.
>
> * * *

Offers of Proof: When an objection is sustained, the party whose evidence has been excluded may decide to preserve the ruling for appellate review. In order to appeal an erroneous ruling excluding evidence, Rule 103 (a)(2) provides that a party must make "the substance of the evidence known to the court" unless the substance "was apparent from the context in which the questions were asked." This process is called making an "offer of proof." Lawyers may make their offers of proof either by asking the witness in *question and answer form* what they would have asked had the

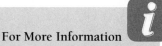

For More Information

See Stephen A. Saltzburg, *Offers of Proof: The Basic Requirement,* (2002).

objection been overruled, or by summarizing the evidence for the record. For obvious reasons, offers of proof must be made outside the hearing of the jury.

6. *Motions for Judgment as a Matter of Law.* After the plaintiff/prosecution concludes her case-in-chief, the defendant may move for a judgment as a matter of law. To grant the motion, the judge must conclude that no rational jury could find that the plaintiff/prosecution's evidence satisfies the applicable standard of proof, such as beyond a reasonable doubt in a criminal case or by a preponderance in a civil case. To support or oppose this motion, lawyers must be able to marshall the

evidence, argue reasonable deductions from it, and apply those deductions to the substantive law in the case.

7. *Defendant's Case-in-Chief.* If the defendant's motion for a judgment as a matter of law (or "directed verdict") is denied by the judge, as they often are, it is now the defendant's turn to present its case-in-chief. If the defendant's lawyer did not make an opening statement at the beginning of the trial, he or she may do so at this point. The defendant's attorney will then call to the stand defense witnesses and question them through direct examination; and the plaintiff/prosecution will question the defense witness through cross examination. Redirect and re-cross are also usually allowed for each defense witness, within the discretion of the judge. The defense may also offer its own physical evidence if relevant to the case. When the defense finishes presenting witnesses and physical evidence, he too will "rest" his case.

8. *Rebuttal and Surrebuttal.* After the defendant's case is concluded, the plaintiff/prosecution is often allowed to present more evidence as long as it contradicts or clarifies evidence that has been presented in the defendant's case-in-chief. This process is called *rebuttal.* For example, if the defendant raises the defense of alibi in his case-in-chief, the prosecution may call witnesses to show the alibi defense is not credible. On occasion, judges may allow the defense to present witnesses in response to rebuttal evidence through a process called *surrebuttal.* Whichever party calls the witness to the stand during *rebuttal* or *surrebuttal* will conduct a direct examination, the opposing party will conduct a cross-examination, and the original party will conduct a redirect examination.

9. *Closing Argument.* Once all parties rest, the lawyers for each side make their closing arguments telling jurors in a lengthy speech why the evidence they presented should allow them to win the case. The plaintiff/prosecution usually makes an introductory argument, the defense attorney goes next, and the plaintiff/prosecution then closes the argument.

10. *Jury Instructions.* Based upon the law and the evidence admitted at trial, the judge will draft a set of instructions to the jury, also called the "charge of the court." The charge tells jurors how to conduct themselves and what to do and not do when deciding the case. It explains the law of the case and gives the jury specific questions they must answer by applying the law to the facts as they have found them to be. In federal court, the charge is read after lawyers make their closing arguments; in many state courts, the charge is read before argument.

11. *Deliberations, Verdict, Judgment.* The jury now retires to consider its verdict. They gather in private to select a presiding juror, read the charge, and determine the facts in light of the law the judge has given them in the charge. Once they

have made their determinations, their decision is announced in open court, the judge accepts their conclusions and, if necessary, applies the law to the facts that the jury has found to reach a verdict. The judge then issues a judgment based on the verdict.

Executive Summary

Evidence: Testimony and Exhibits.

Evidence is the bedrock of all trials. There are two general forms of evidence. The first type is testimony of witnesses answering questions under oath ("direct examination" is where witnesses have the opportunity to tell their story, while "cross-examination" is where the opposing attorney tests/attacks their credibility). The second type is exhibits, or tangible physical evidence, consisting of "real evidence" (actual items involved in the case), and "demonstrative evidence" (items created for trial to help clarify testimony).

Direct and Circumstantial Evidence.

Direct evidence is eyewitness testimony which, if true, does not require the fact-finder to make an inference to reach a factual conclusion in the case; while circumstantial evidence, if true, requires the fact-finder to make an inference to reach a factual conclusion in the case. Neither is necessarily stronger or better evidence.

Power and Discretion of the Trial Judge.

Trial judges have a great deal of power and discretion to run their courtrooms, rule on objections and motions, and set limits on lawyers, provided such power and discretion is exercised fairly and efficiently. (*Reaves*). Judges also have much power and discretion to control the mode and order of (1) interrogating witnesses and (2) presenting exhibits at trial. (*Peacock*). Judges also have the power and discretion to comment on the evidence presented at trial, as long as such commentary is impartial. (*Yates*). They also can question witnesses, but again, only if they do so impartially (*Crandell*).

Events at Trial.

The following events constitute the basic steps and order of proceedings in most state and federal trials:

1. Pretrial Conferences: There are several hearings in the weeks preceding the trial where the judge and lawyers meet and confer to narrow issues for trial, discuss witnesses and exhibits, and draft a "Pre-Trial Order" that serves to organize and govern the trial.

2. Pretrial Motions: Before trial, the judge will consider pretrial matters raised by the attorneys, such as "motions in limine," where the attorneys request that certain evidence be admitted or excluded and that such decision be made now, instead of at trial.

3. Jury Selection: Judge and counsel engage in questioning ("voir dire") of potential witness to ensure the jury picked is impartial and unbiased.

4. Opening Statements: Each side presents an introductory "road map" of what they think they evidence will show during trial.

5. Presentation of Evidence/Plaintiff or Prosecution Case-in-Chief: This is where plaintiff (civil) or prosecution (criminal) presents their case, using their witnesses and exhibits. They do a direct examination of their witness, and the defense gets to cross-examine them. Sometimes there is a re-direct ("rehabilitation") of the witness, and a re-cross.

Attorneys make "objections" during the questioning process if opposing counsel's question is improper and/or calls for inadmissible evidence. Attorneys will also make a "motion to strike" if a witness answers a question by referring to inadmissible evidence. If an objection is "sustained" (upheld), then the attorney asking the question can make a Rule 103 "offer of proof" outside the hearing of the jury in order to preserve the evidence for appeal. An objection that is "overruled" is rejected, so that the question or evidence presented is deemed proper.

6. Motions for Judgment as a Matter of Law. If the plaintiff/prosecution fails to provide sufficient evidence upon which a rational jury could base a finding of guilt or liability, then the defense is granted a favorable judgment as a matter of law.

7. Presentation of Evidence/Defense Case-in-Chief: This is the opportunity for the defense to present its case (its witnesses and exhibits) in the exact same manner as set forth in Step #5, above.

8. Rebuttal and Surrebuttal. After the defendant's case-in-chief, additional witnesses can be called by either side to rebut (clarify or contradict) any testimony presented by either side in their case-in-chief. The "close of evidence" is after the last witness testifies.

9. Closing Arguments. Each side has an opportunity to summarize the evidence and argue how the fact-finder should make findings and inferences based on the evidence provided during trial.

10. Jury Instructions. The judge reads general admonitions to the jury about their deliberation process and the applicable law and legal elements to be applied in their deliberations.

11. Deliberations, Verdict, Judgment. The jury deliberates, renders a verdict and the judge enters a legal judgment based on the verdict, or on the judge's factual findings in a bench trial.

CHAPTER 3

Relevance–A Primer

A. Introduction

Not all evidence a party may wish to offer at trial is useful in resolving a disputed issue. Some evidence may be too tangential, confusing, cumulative, or unfairly prejudicial to a fair determination of the facts. The process of sorting through evidence that will assist a judge or jury in resolving a dispute is known as determining relevancy, and it is done as a threshold matter before a court considers any other evidentiary barriers to admission.

The rules regarding relevancy are found in Federal Rule 401, which contains the definition of relevancy, Rule 402, which provides that all relevant evidence is (presumptively) admissible, and Rule 403, which describes exclusionary principles that weigh against admissibility. This chapter will focus on these rules, that is, how relevancy is determined and how discretionary factors may keep such evidence from being admitted.

B. Definition of Relevant Evidence

Rule 401. Definition of "Relevant Evidence"

"Relevant evidence" means evidence having any tendency to make the existence of any fact that is of consequence to the determination of the action more probable or less probable than it would be without the evidence.

Rule 402. Relevant Evidence Generally Admissible; Irrelevant Evidence Inadmissible

All relevant evidence is admissible, except as otherwise provided by the Constitution of the United States, by Act of Congress, by these rules, or by other rules prescribed by the Supreme Court pursuant to statutory authority. Evidence which is not relevant is not admissible.

Rule 401 embodies two concepts. First, the rule requires that evidence must bear upon a "fact that is of consequence to the determination of the action." Whether a fact is of consequence to a case turns upon the requirements of the underlying substantive law. For example, in a statutory rape case where consent of the underage victim is not at issue, the fact that the defendant believed that the victim had consented would not be of consequence to the case because legally, consent does not matter. The victim's consent would be of consequence to the case, however, if the defendant were charged with raping an adult victim.

> **FYI**
>
> It is not necessary that the "fact that is of consequence" be in dispute in the case. Evidence offered as an aid to understanding other evidence, such as a witness's biographical information that is not in dispute, might be relevant to shed light on the witness's substantive testimony.

> **FYI**
>
> The drafters of Rule 401 considered two possible models of relevance. The Wigmore model rejected an approach that depended upon multiple chains of reasoning when the evidentiary value was slight. The Thayer approach allowed admission of evidence that had "any tendency" to make a fact at issue more or less probable and did not require the evidence to have any minimum probity. The Thayer Theory was incorporated in Rule 401.

Second, evidence a party seeks to offer must be probative, that is, have a "tendency to make the existence of a fact . . . more probable or less probable than it would be without the evidence." Sometimes, this is called determining "logical relevance." Probative value is not an inherent charactersitic of any item of evidence. It exists as a relation between evidence and a proposition sought to be proved or disproved by that evidence. Furthermore, any increase or decrease in the probablility of a fact of consequence will suffice, no matter how small. The fact that the defendant (along with others) was found two blocks from the crime scene might slightly increase the probability that he committed the crime and thus have probative value under Rule 401, even though it would never be a sufficient basis for a guilty verdict by itself. To have probative value, therefore, evidence need not by itself prove the fact at issue. It can be combined with other evidence to prove or disprove a fact. Or, as famously stated by Professor McCormick, "a brick is not a wall." In other words, each brick of

> **Food for Thought**
>
> It might be helpful to think of pieces of evidence as puzzle pieces. A single puzzle piece or even several of them will not make a complete picture. All of them are required. Or, to put a more modern spin on it, each piece of evidence is like a pixel in a digital image that goes into making up a complete photograph.

evidence need not, in and of itself, prove a fact completely before it is relevant; it can be one of many bricks in a wall of proof.

Once a trial judge has determined evidence has probative value in proving or disproving a fact under Rule 401, Rule 402 deems that evidence presumptively admissible.

C. Determining Relevant Evidence

People v. Adamson

Supreme Court of California
165 P.2d 3 (1947)

TRAYNOR, Justice.

The body of Stella Blauvelt, a widow 64 years of age, was found on the floor of her Los Angeles apartment on July 25, 1944. The evidence indicated that she died on the afternoon of the preceding day. The body was found with the face upward covered with two bloodstained pillows. A lamp cord was wrapped tightly around the neck three times and tied in a knot. The medical testimony was that death was caused by strangulation. Bruises on the face and hands indicated that the deceased had been severely beaten before her death.

The defendant does not contend that the evidence does not justify a finding that murder in the first degree had been committed... The sole contention of fact that he makes is that the evidence is not sufficient to identify him as the [D argues] perpetrator. The strongest circumstance tending to so identify the defendant was the finding of six fingerprints, each identified by expert testimony as that of the defendant, spread over the surface of the inner door to the garbage compartment of the kitchen of the deceased's apartment... Counsel for defendant questioned witnesses as to the possibility of defendant's fingerprints being forged, but the record does not indicate that any evidence to that effect was uncovered. The theory of the prosecution was that the murderer gained his entrance through the garbage compartment, found the inner door thereof latched from the kitchen side, and forced the door from its hinges. It was established that defendant could have entered through the garbage compartment by having a man about his size do so. The fact that the key to the apartment could not be found after search and the testimony of a neighboring tenant as to sounds heard indicate that the murderer left the apartment through the door thereof and made his exit from the building down a rear stairway.

The tops of three women's stockings identified as having been taken from defendant's room were admitted in evidence. One of the stocking tops was found on a dresser, the other two in a drawer of the dresser among other articles of apparel. The stocking parts were not all of the same color. At the end of each part, away from what was formerly the top of the stocking, a knot or knots were tied. When the body of the deceased was found, it did not have on any shoes or stockings. There was evidence that on the day of the murder that the deceased had been wearing stockings. The lower part of a silk stocking with the top part torn off was found lying on the floor under the body. No part of the other stocking was found. There were other stockings in the apartment, some hanging in the kitchen and some in drawers in a dressing alcove, but no other parts of stockings were found. None of the stocking tops from defendant's room matched with the bottom part of the stocking found under the body...

What's That?

The term "material" at common law meant that evidence would be offered to help prove or disprove a matter in dispute in the lawsuit. The drafters of Rule 401 thought the term too narrow and legalistic. They discarded it in favor of requiring the evidence to be "of consequence to the determination of the action," a much broader concept based upon common sense that does not require the evidence be directed to matters in controversy.

To be admissible, evidence must tend to prove a material issue in the light of human experience. The stocking tops found in defendant's room were relevant to identify defendant because their presence on his dresser and in a drawer thereof among other articles of wearing apparel with a knot or knots tied in the end away from what was formerly the top of the stocking indicates that defendant had some use for women's stocking tops. This interest in women's stocking tops is a circumstance that tends to identify defendant as the person who removed the stockings from the victim and took away the top of one and the whole of the other. Although the presence of the stocking tops in defendant's room was not by itself sufficient to identify defendant as the criminal, it constituted a logical link in the chain of evidence. Evidence that tends to throw light on a fact in dispute may be admitted. The weight to be given such evidence will be determined by the jury... The admission of such evidence must be regulated by the sound discretion of the court.

jury determines weight of evidence

Food for Thought

Try to identify each step in the chain of inferences in *Adamson* which connects the stocking tops found in the defendant's room and his identity as the perpetrator of the crime. Would this chain of logic be persuasive to a jury?

It is contended that the admission of the stocking tops deprived defendant of a fair trial and therefore denied him due process of law. Defendant states that their admission could serve no purpose except to create prejudice against him as a Negro by the implication of a fetish or sexual degeneracy. No implication of either was made by the prosecutor in his brief treatment of the evidence in oral argument. Moreover, except in rare cases of abuse, demonstrative evidence that tends to prove a material issue or clarify the circumstances of the crime is admissible despite its prejudicial tendency…

Make the Connection

Counterweights, such as unfair prejudice, that may exclude logically relevant evidence are discussed in section D. below.

The judgments and the order denying a new trial are affirmed.

Perspective and Analysis

Rule 401 makes information relevant if it has "any tendency" to make a fact at issue more or less probable, implying that relevancy can be shown by an infinitely long chain of questionable inferences. After considering Rule 401 and its expansive definition, can it be said that there is such a thing as "irrelevant evidence?" At least one commentator has argued there is not.

"Given Rule 401, it takes real ingenuity to come up with an example of evidence that seems truly irrelevant. One of my favorites comes from Dean Newell H. Blakley, who was a great classroom teacher. Imagine that the defendant is on trial in Chicago for theft. The indictment charges that he stole a television set from the owner's home. The prosecutor offers testimony of an eyewitness, along with other evidence that is "of consequence" to the elements of the crime. This evidence sounds relevant, and under the Federal Rules it undoubtedly is.

But after the prosecution rests, the defense lawyer—with great fanfare, let us suppose—calls a witness to offer testimony that it was raining in Utah on the day in question. Isn't this evidence "irrelevant?"

The paradoxical answer is, not by the definition in the Federal Rules. One can construct chains of experiential and logical propositions—long chains, admittedly—that connect [this] evidence to the issues in the case. Rainfall in Utah has at least some statistical correlation to weather in Chicago, the site of the alleged crime. We can prove this proposition, if it is doubted, by producing an expert who will testify that precipitation in the Rockies correlates with weather systems elsewhere so that, ever so slightly, it is more probable that the weather was bad in Chicago given this fact than if we did not know it. And this inference, in turn, affects the credibility of eyewitness testimony identifying the defendant, thereby influencing the probability of existence of a fact that is of consequence."

David Crump, *On the Uses of Irrelevant Evidence*, 34 Hous. L. Rev. 1, 9 (1997).

Hypo 3.1

Police stop the defendant for driving while intoxicated. One of the officers takes a half-pint bottle about two-thirds full of an unknown liquid from the defendant's car. The contents of the bottle are never tested. How would the prosecution argue that this bottle has probative value in the case? What would the defendant argue to the contrary? (Remember, in making your analysis, do not confuse determining probative value with determining admissibility).

Points for Discussion

a. Flight as Evidence of Guilt. Admission by Conduct.

If the defendant in *Adamson* fled the state shortly after the crime, what would be the probative value of this flight evidence if offered by the prosecution? Is this chain of inferences excessively long? Is it necessarily reliable? Would it be relevant to his innocence if he did NOT flee the state? Can you think of any other type of evidence that might constitute an admission by conduct?

b. The Probative Value of Statistics.

A witness to a hit-and-run accident testifies that the car that struck the plaintiff was a white Ford Mustang. There is testimony that the defendant drives a white Ford Mustang. The plaintiff's attorney wishes to offer statistical evidence from the Department of Motor Vehicles that only 2% of all car owners in the city drive white Ford Mustangs. Is this evidence relevant? How persuasive is this evidence in proving the identity of the defendant as the driver of the car that hit the plaintiff?

Make the Connection

The admissibility of statistical evidence is discussed in more detail in Chapter 12.

D. Exclusion of Relevant Evidence

> **Rule 402. Relevant Evidence Generally Admissible; Irrelevant Evidence Inadmissible**
>
> All relevant evidence is admissible, except as otherwise provided by the Constitution of the United States, by Act of Congress, by these rules, or by other rules prescribed by the Supreme Court pursuant to statutory authority. Evidence which is not relevant is not admissible.

Two of the most basic principles of evidence law are that relevant evidence should be admitted, and irrelevant evidence should be excluded. Rule 402 embodies both of these concepts. With regard to irrelevant evidence, this is the end of the inquiry. Irrelevant evidence is never admissible. With regard to relevant evidence, however, Rule 402 also contains an "except as otherwise provided" clause that allows the trial judge to prevent its admissibility by considering other sources of legal authority that may outweigh any relevancy. For instance, the government in a federal criminal case may have compelling relevant evidence, but if it were obtained through an unreasonable search and seizure, it must be excluded. A basic map of Rule 402 looks like this:

Rule 402 Logic Map

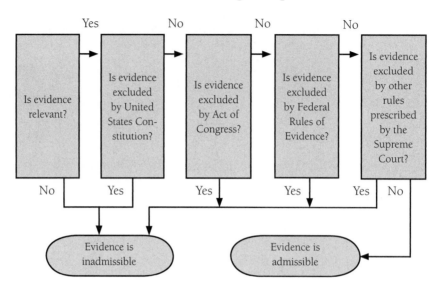

Although several sources of the law are named by Rule 402 as providing possible exclusions of relevant evidence, one of the most frequently used exclusions is contained in Rule 403.

Rule 403. Exclusion of Relevant Evidence on Grounds of Prejudice, Confusion or Waste of Time

Although relevant, evidence may be excluded if its probative value is substantially outweighed by the danger of unfair prejudice, confusion of the issues, or misleading the jury, or by consideration of undue delay, waste of time, or needless presentation of cumulative evidence.

The exclusions listed in Rule 403 are called "counterweights," and the process of balancing the strength of the relevancy of evidence against the "counterweights" listed in Rule 403 is called determining "legal relevance." These counterweights range from those that might influence a decision on a non-logical (often emotional) basis to those that merely waste time at trial.

Unfair Prejudice. Of all the counterweights, the one most frequently argued to exclude relevant evidence is that of "unfair prejudice." Most evidence offered by a party is prejudicial in the sense that it is harmful to an opponent. However, to exclude relevant evidence, the prejudice must be "unfair," that is, it must distort the fact finding function of the trial by allowing the jury to draw inferences that are improper. For example, even though relevant, courts on occasion refuse to admit autopsy photos in a homicide case because of their tendency to arouse the jury's sense of outrage or horror and to encourage the jurors to convict the defendant solely on the basis of their emotional reaction.

Other Less Frequently Used Counterweights. The remaining counter-weights are less frequently urged. Confusion of the issues and misleading the jury refer to a tendency of the evidence to distract the jury from deciding the case on a proper basis by placing too much emphasis on matters that are not essential to a proper determination. For example, it might confuse or mislead the jury if evidence was introduced showing subsequent changes to an allegedly defective product or its design because such evidence would divert the jury's attention from whether the product was defective at the relevant time. Counterweights such as undue delay, waste of time, or needless presentation of cumulative evidence allow the trial court to keep the trial streamlined and the fact-finder focused. It might be proper, for example, for a trial judge to exclude the testimony of additional witnesses to prove facts as to which five witnesses have already testified. Many of these counterweights overlap each other to ensure that the trial judge has broad discretion to manage the trial.

Conducting the Balancing Test. There are several steps a judge must take when conducting a Rule 403 balancing test. First, she must determine whether the evidence has probative value under Rule 401, that is, she must determine if it has any possibility of making a fact at issue more or less probable than it would be without the evidence. If so, the evidence is presumptively admissible under Rule 402. Second, the judge will estimate the strength of that probative value. In making this assessment, the judge looks at the extent to which the evidence will sway the jury in the proponent's favor on a contested issue of fact taking into account her own experience, knowledge and general understanding of the human thought process, as well as the extent to which the facts at issue are established by other evidence, stipulation, or inference. Third, the judge then determines the strength of any counterweights under Rule 403 and decides whether they substantially outweigh the probative value of the evidence. In the case of unfair prejudice, the judge will estimate the likelihood that a jury will make improper inferences from the evidence as opposed to proper inferences. Nowhere in the rule or the Advisory Committee Notes to the rule is "substantially" outweighed defined. It has been generally interpreted, however, to mean that in a case where the probative value and countervailing factors are close, the judge should admit the evidence. See Saltzburg, Martin, and Capra, <u>Federal Rules of Evidence Manual</u> (9th ed. 2006). In other words, if the probative value is simply outweighed by the danger of unfair prejudice, then the evidence is still admissible. It is therefore only when the probative value is *"substantially"* outweighed by the 403 dangers, or the counter-weights, that the evidence is inadmissible.

To begin moving through the Rule 403 logic map, you must have already made a determination that the evidence in question is relevant. The Rule 403 logic map looks as follows:

Rule 403 Basic Map

No	No	No	No	
Is the probative value substantially outweighed by the danger of unfair prejudice?	Is the probative value substantially outweighed by the danger of confusion of issues?	Is the probative value substantially outweighed by the danger of misleading the jury?	Is the probative value substantially outweighed by considerations of undue delay?	Is the probative value substantially outweighed by the needless presentation of cumulative evidence?
Yes	Yes	Yes	Yes	Yes / No

Evidence is inadmissible

Evidence is admissible

Carter v. Hewitt

U.S. Court of Appeals for the Third Circuit
617 F.2d 961 (3rd Cir. 1980)

GARTH, Circuit Judge:

issue

We are called upon to determine whether a letter written by the plaintiff Reginald Carter, a prison inmate, violated the Federal Rules of Evidence when it was read and admitted into evidence at the trial of a §1983 action brought by Carter against prison authorities. We determine that it did not, and therefore affirm the judgment of the district court in favor of the defendants.

Reginald Carter is an inmate at the Pennsylvania State Correctional Institution at Huntingdon. He claims that he was severely beaten in the course of a routine "shakedown," or search, of his cell on September 22, 1977 by three prison guards, defendants John Fuiek, Duane Pyles, and Gilbert Levi...

What's That?

The court here is referring to <u>42 U.S.C.A. §1983</u>, which gives plaintiffs a federal cause of action against defendants who deprive them of their constitutional rights while acting under color of law, i.e. pursuant to ostensible legal authority.

[Defendants filed a motion for summary judgment which was heard by a Magistrate. During the hearing, a number of witnesses testified, including plaintiff Carter]. The incident giving rise to this appeal occurred during Carter's cross-examination. Carter was shown a letter written by one "Abdullah" to a fellow inmate at Huntingdon. Carter admitted that he had written the letter, and also admitted that he had denied writing this same letter when he had been questioned as to its authorship in an earlier prison disciplinary proceeding. Defense counsel asked Carter to read the letter. Carter objected on the grounds of relevance, claiming that the letter had been written six months after the alleged beating. The Magistrate then ordered Carter to read the letter but expressly reserved ruling on whether the letter was admissible. Complying with the Magistrate's direction, Carter read the letter aloud. The letter, which was undated, generally described to its unidentified recipient how to file a complaint charging prison guard brutality. In its most significant portion, the letter reads:

> This is a set up my brother — compile complaints to be use for bullshit courts, possibility news media, and a radio program in Pittsburg [sic] & W.D.A.S. down Philly. We want to establish a pattern of barbaric brutal harrassment [sic] and turn it on these chumps to the max.

Defense counsel suggested that this letter was a direction to file a false brutality complaint. Carter claimed that he was only encouraging the filing of a legitimate complaint... We believe, quite simply, that the letter is admissible, substantive evidence because it bears on the central factual issue in the case—whether Carter was beaten by prison guards on September 22, 1977. The standard of relevance established by the Federal Rules of Evidence is not high: evidence is relevant if it has "any tendency to make the existence of any fact that is of consequence to determination of the action more probable or less probable than it would be without the evidence." Fed. R. Evid. 401 (emphasis added). A fact finder could reasonably interpret this letter as reflecting a plan on Carter's part to promote the filing of false complaints. A fact finder could further draw the inference that Cart-

Ct. holds

relevant if:

Food for Thought

What are the two contrary inferences that could be made by reading the letter? Why does the court disregard the defendant's interpretation in favor of the prosecution's interpretation? If these inferences are equally likely, does this mean the evidence is not relevant? Do opposite inferences cancel out one another, or do they merely show that the evidence is relevant and admissible for two possible reasons?

er's own complaint about being beaten on September 22, 1977 had been filed pursuant to that plan. Thus, the letter is relevant: it has some tendency to make Carter's assertion that he was beaten less likely to be true than it would be without the evidence. Since the letter is relevant, it is also admissible, unless its admission is otherwise restricted. Fed. R. Evid. 402…

Carter finally contends that the letter should have been excluded under Fed. R. Evid. 403. Again, we are constrained to disagree.

Rule 403 provides:

Although relevant, evidence may be excluded if its probative value is substantially outweighed by the danger of unfair prejudice, confusion of the issues, or misleading the jury, or by considerations of undue delay, waste of time, or needless presentation of cumulative evidence.

This rule cannot help Carter. It does not offer protection against evidence that is merely prejudicial, in the sense of being detrimental to a party's case. Rather, the rule only protects against evidence that is unfairly prejudicial. Evidence is unfairly prejudicial only if it has "an undue tendency to suggest decision on an improper basis, commonly, though not necessarily, an emotional one." It is unfairly prejudicial if it "appeals to the jury's sympathies, arouses its sense of horror, provokes its instinct to punish," or otherwise "may cause a jury to base its decision on something other than the established propositions in the case." A classic example of unfair prejudice is a jury's conclusion, after hearing a recitation of a defendant's prior criminal record, that, since the defendant committed so many other crimes, he must have committed this one too. This is an improper basis of decision, and the law accordingly prohibits introduction of prior convictions to demonstrate a propensity to commit crime.

unfairly prejudicial

Carter's letter, while undoubtedly prejudicial to his case in that it resulted in the district court ruling against him, presents no danger of unfair prejudice. The letter was offered by the defendants to suggest that no beating

Food for Thought

The court claims that admission of the letter presents no danger of unfair prejudice to Carter. Do you agree? Assuming the letter contains unfair prejudice, is it possible that the court could still admit it?

occurred on September 22, 1977 and that Carter was lying when he testified to the contrary. This, of course, was the central issue at trial. In a case such as the one here where the witnesses on each side take diametrically opposed positions, the fact finder's task is to determine which witnesses are more credible. If the Magistrate, after hearing the letter read, drew the inference that Carter was lying, it cannot be claimed that this was an improper basis of decision. It was, rather, a use of properly admitted evidence which, together with other evidence in the case, resulted in a decision on a proper basis. Thus, Carter has made no showing of unfair prejudice: he cannot demand exclusion of the letter under rule 403.

Old Chief v. United States

Supreme Court of the United States
519 U.S. 172 (1997)

Justice SOUTER delivered the opinion of the Court.

Subject to certain limitations, 18 U.S.C. § 922(g)(1) prohibits possession of a firearm by anyone with a prior felony conviction, which the Government can prove by introducing a record of judgment or similar evidence identifying the previous offense. Fearing prejudice if the jury learns the nature of the earlier crime, defendants sometimes seek to avoid such an informative disclosure by offering to concede the fact of the prior conviction. The issue here is whether a district court abuses its discretion if it spurns such an offer and admits the full record of a prior judgment, when the name or nature of the prior offense raises the risk of a verdict tainted by improper considerations, and when the purpose of the evidence is solely to prove the element of prior conviction.

In 1993, petitioner, Old Chief, was arrested after a fracas involving at least one gunshot. The ensuing federal charges included not only assault with a dangerous weapon and using a firearm in relation to a crime of violence but violation of 18 U.S.C. § 922(g)(1). This statute makes it unlawful for anyone "who has been convicted in any court of, a crime punishable by imprisonment for a term exceeding one year" to "possess in or affecting commerce, any firearm..."

The earlier crime charged in the indictment against Old Chief was assault causing serious bodily injury. Before trial, he moved for an order requiring the Government "to refrain from mentioning-by reading the Indictment, during jury selection, in opening statement, or closing argument-and to refrain from offering into evidence or soliciting any testimony from any witness regarding the prior criminal convictions of the Defendant, except to state that the Defendant has been convicted of a crime punishable by imprisonment exceeding one (1) year." He said that revealing the name and nature of his prior assault conviction would unfairly tax the jury's capacity to hold the Government to its burden of proof beyond a reasonable doubt on current charges of assault, possession, and violence with a firearm, and he offered to "solve the problem here by stipulating, agreeing and requesting the Court to instruct the jury that he has been convicted of a crime punishable by imprisonment exceeding one (1) yea[r]." He argued that the offer to stipulate to the fact of the prior conviction rendered evidence of the name and nature of the offense inadmissible under Rule 403 of the Federal Rules of Evidence, the danger being that unfair prejudice from that evidence would substantially outweigh its probative value.

① argued

The Assistant United States Attorney refused to join in a stipulation, insisting on his right to prove his case his own way, and the District Court agreed, ruling orally that, "If he doesn't want to stipulate, he doesn't have to." At trial, over renewed objection, the Government introduced the order of judgment and commitment for Old Chief's prior conviction. This document disclosed that on December 18, 1988, he "did knowingly and unlawfully assault Rory Dean Fenner, said assault resulting in serious bodily injury," for which Old Chief was sentenced to five years' imprisonment. The jury found Old Chief guilty on all counts, and he appealed.

[The Ninth Circuit affirmed and the Supreme Court granted certiorari on the basis that the Courts of Appeals were divided on the issue.]

II

A

relevancy

As a threshold matter, there is Old Chief's erroneous argument that the name of his prior offense as contained in the record of conviction is irrelevant to the prior-conviction element, and for that reason inadmissible under Rule 402 of the Federal Rules of Evidence. Rule 401 defines relevant evidence as having "any tendency to make the existence of any fact that is of consequence to the determination of the action more probable or less probable than it would be without the evidence." Fed. Rule Evid. 401. To be sure, the fact that Old Chief's prior conviction was for assault resulting in serious bodily injury rather than, say, for theft was not itself an ultimate fact, as if the statute had specifically required proof of injurious assault. But its demonstration was a step on one evidentiary route to the ultimate fact, since it served to place Old Chief within a particular sub-class of offenders for whom firearms possession is outlawed by §922(g)(1). A documentary record of the conviction for that named offense was thus relevant evidence in making Old Chief's §922(g)(1) status more probable than it would have been without the evidence.

Was relevant

Nor was its evidentiary relevance under Rule 401 affected by the availability of alternative proofs of the element to which it went, such as an admission by Old Chief that he had been convicted of a crime "punishable by imprisonment for a term exceeding one year" within the meaning of the statute. The 1972 Advisory Committee Notes to Rule 401 make this point directly:

> "The fact to which the evidence is directed need not be in dispute. While situations will arise which call for the exclusion of evidence offered to prove a point conceded by the opponent, the ruling should be made on the basis of such considerations as waste of time and undue prejudice (see Rule 403), rather than under any general requirement that evidence is admissible only if directed to matters in dispute."

If, then, relevant evidence is inadmissible in the presence of other evidence related to it, its exclusion must rest not on the ground that the other evidence has rendered it "irrelevant," but on its character as unfairly prejudicial, cumulative or the like, its relevance notwithstanding.

B

1

The term "unfair prejudice," as to a criminal defendant, speaks to the capacity of some concededly relevant evidence to lure the factfinder into declaring guilt on a ground different from proof specific to the offense charged. So, the [Advisory] Committee Notes to Rule 403 explain, " 'Unfair prejudice' within its context means an undue tendency to suggest decision on an improper basis, commonly, though not necessarily, an emotional one." *unfair prejudice*

Such improper grounds certainly include the one that Old Chief points to here: generalizing a defendant's earlier bad act into bad character and taking that as raising the odds that he did the later bad act now charged (or, worse, as calling for preventive conviction even if he should happen to be innocent momentarily). As then-Judge Breyer put it, "Although… 'propensity evidence' is relevant, the risk that a jury will convict for crimes other than those charged-or that, uncertain of guilt, it will convict anyway because a bad person deserves punishment-creates a prejudicial effect that outweighs ordinary relevance." *United States v. Moccia, 681 F.2d 61, 63 (C.A.1 1982)*. Justice Jackson described how the law has handled this risk:

> "… The state may not show defendant's prior trouble with the law, specific criminal acts, or ill name among his neighbors, even though such facts might logically be persuasive that he is by propensity a probable perpetrator of the crime. The inquiry is not rejected because character is irrelevant; on the contrary, it is said to weigh too much with the jury and to so overpersuade them as to prejudge one with a bad general record and deny him a fair opportunity to defend against a particular charge. The overriding policy of excluding such evidence, despite its admitted probative

value, is the practical experience that its disallowance tends to prevent confusion of issues, unfair surprise and undue prejudice."

Rule of Evidence 404(b) reflects this common-law tradition by addressing propensity reasoning directly: "Evidence of other crimes, wrongs, or acts is not admissible to prove the character of a person in order to show action in conformity therewith." Fed. Rule Evid. 404(b). There is, accordingly, no question that propensity would be an "improper basis" for conviction and that evidence of a prior conviction is subject to analysis under Rule 403 for relative probative value and for prejudicial risk of misuse as propensity evidence.

As for the analytical method to be used in Rule 403 balancing, two basic possibilities present themselves. An item of evidence might be viewed as an island, with estimates of its own probative value and unfairly prejudicial risk the sole reference points in deciding whether the danger substantially outweighs the value and whether the evidence ought to be excluded. Or the question of admissibility might be seen as inviting further comparisons to take account of the full evidentiary context of the case as the court understands it when the ruling must be made. This second approach would start out like the first but be ready to go further. On objection, the court would decide whether a particular item of evidence raised a danger of unfair prejudice. If it did, the judge would go on to evaluate the degrees of probative value and unfair prejudice not only for the item in question but for any actually available substitutes as well. If an alternative were found to have substantially the same or greater probative value but a lower danger of unfair prejudice, sound judicial discretion would discount the value of the item first offered and exclude it if its discounted probative value were substantially outweighed by unfairly prejudicial risk. As we will explain later on, the judge would have to make these calculations with an appreciation of the offering party's need for evidentiary richness and narrative integrity in presenting a case, and the mere fact that two pieces of evidence might go to the same point would not, of course, necessarily mean that only one of them might come in. It would only mean that a judge applying Rule 403 could reasonably apply some discount to the probative value of an item of evidence when faced with less risky alternative proof going to the same point. Even under this second approach, as we explain below, a defendant's Rule 403 objection offering to concede a point generally cannot prevail over the Government's choice to offer evidence showing guilt and all the circumstances surrounding the offense.

The first understanding of the Rule is open to a very telling objection. That reading would leave the party offering evidence with the option to structure a trial in whatever way would produce the maximum unfair prejudice consistent with relevance. He could choose the available alternative carrying the greatest threat of improper influence, despite the availability of less prejudicial but equally probative evidence. The worst he would have to fear would be a ruling sustaining a Rule 403 objection, and if that occurred, he could simply fall back to offering substitute evidence. This would be a strange rule. It would be very odd for the law of evidence to recognize the danger of unfair prejudice only to confer such a degree of autonomy on the party subject to temptation, and the Rules of Evidence are not so odd.

Rather, a reading of the companions to Rule 403, and of the commentaries that went with them to Congress, makes it clear that what counts as the Rule 403 "probative value" of an item of evidence, as distinct from its Rule 401 "relevance," may be calculated by comparing evidentiary alternatives. The [Advisory] Committee Notes to Rule 401 explicitly say that a party's concession is pertinent to the court's discretion to exclude evidence on the point conceded. Such a concession, according to the Notes, will sometimes "call for the exclusion of evidence offered to prove [the] point conceded by the opponent…".

2

In dealing with the specific problem raised by § 922(g)(1) and its prior-conviction element, there can be no question that evidence of the name or nature of the prior offense generally carries a risk of unfair prejudice to the defendant. That risk will vary from case to case, for the reasons already given, but will be substantial whenever the official record offered by the Government would be arresting enough to lure a juror into a sequence of bad character reasoning. Where a prior conviction was for a gun crime or one similar to other charges in a pending case, the risk of unfair prejudice would be especially obvious, and Old Chief sensibly worried that the prejudicial effect of his prior assault conviction, significant enough with respect to the current gun charges alone, would take on added weight from the related assault charge against him.

* * *

Old Chief's proffered admission would, in fact, have been not merely relevant but seemingly conclusive evidence of the element. The statutory language in which the prior-conviction requirement is couched shows no congressional concern with the specific name or nature of the prior offense beyond what is necessary to place it within the broad category of qualifying felonies, and Old Chief clearly meant to admit that his felony did qualify, by stipulating "that the Government has proven one of the essential elements of the offense." As a consequence, although the name of the prior offense may have been technically relevant, it addressed no detail in the definition of the prior-conviction element that would not have been covered by the stipulation or admission. Logic, then, seems to side with Old Chief.

3

There is, however, one more question to be considered before deciding whether Old Chief's offer was to supply evidentiary value at least equivalent to what the Government's own evidence carried. In arguing that the stipulation or admission would not have carried equivalent value, the Government invokes the familiar, standard rule that the prosecution is entitled to prove its case by evidence of its own choice, or, more exactly, that a criminal defendant may not stipulate or admit his way out of the full evidentiary force of the case as the Government chooses to present it. The authority usually cited for this rule is *Parr v. United States*, 255 F.2d 86, in which the Fifth Circuit explained that the "reason for the rule is to permit a party 'to present to the jury a picture of the events relied upon. To substitute for such a picture a naked admission might have the effect to rob the evidence of much of its fair and legitimate weight.' "

gov't argues

This is unquestionably true as a general matter. The "fair and legitimate weight" of conventional evidence showing individual thoughts and acts amounting to a crime reflects the fact that making a case with testimony and tangible things not only satisfies the formal definition of an offense, but tells a colorful story with descriptive richness. Unlike an abstract premise, whose force depends on going precisely to a particular step in a course of reasoning, a piece of evidence may address any number of separate elements, striking hard just because it shows so much at once; the account of a shooting that establishes capacity and causation may tell just as much about the triggerman's motive and intent. Evidence thus has force beyond any linear scheme of reasoning, and as its pieces come together a narrative gains momentum, with power not only to support conclusions but to sustain the willingness of jurors to draw the inferences, whatever they may be, necessary to reach an honest verdict. This persuasive power of the concrete and particular is often essential to the capacity of jurors to satisfy the obligations that the law places on them. Jury duty is usually unsought and sometimes resisted, and it may be as difficult for one juror suddenly to face the findings that can send another human being to prison, as it is for another to hold out conscientiously for acquittal. When a juror's duty does seem hard, the evidentiary account of what a defendant has thought and done can accomplish what no set of abstract statements ever could, not just to prove a fact but to establish its human significance, and so to implicate the law's moral underpinnings and a juror's obligation to sit in judgment. Thus, the prosecution may fairly seek to place its evidence before the jurors, as much to tell a story of guiltiness as to support an inference of guilt, to convince the jurors that a guilty verdict would be morally reasonable as much as to point to the discrete elements of a defendant's legal fault.

But there is something even more to the prosecution's interest in resisting efforts to replace the evidence of its choice with admissions and stipulations, for beyond the power of conventional evidence to support allegations and give life to the moral underpinnings of law's claims, there lies the need for evidence in all its particularity to satisfy the jurors' expectations about what proper proof should be. Some such demands they bring with them to the courthouse, assuming, for example, that a charge of using a firearm to commit an offense will be proven by introducing a gun in evidence. A prosecutor who fails to produce one, or some good reason for his failure, has something to be concerned about. "If [jurors'] expectations are not satisfied, triers of fact may penalize the party who disappoints them by drawing a negative inference against that party." Expectations may also arise in jurors' minds simply from the experience of a trial itself. The use of witnesses to describe a train of events naturally related can raise the prospect of learning about every ingredient of that natural sequence the same way. If suddenly the prosecution presents some occurrence in the series differently, as by announcing a stipulation or admission, the effect may be like saying, "never mind what's behind the door," and jurors may well wonder what they are being kept from knowing. A party seemingly responsible for cloaking something has reason for apprehension, and the prosecution with its burden of proof may prudently demur at a defense request to interrupt the flow of evidence telling the story in the usual way.

In sum, the accepted rule that the prosecution is entitled to prove its case free from any defendant's option to stipulate the evidence away rests on good sense. A syllogism is not a story, and a naked proposition in a courtroom may be no match for the robust evidence that would be used to prove it. People who hear a story interrupted by gaps of abstraction may be puzzled at the missing chapters, and jurors asked to rest a momentous decision on the story's truth can feel put upon at being asked to take responsibility knowing that more could be said than they have heard. A convincing tale can be told with economy, but when economy becomes a break in the natural sequence of narrative evidence, an assurance that the missing link is really there is never more than second best.

4

This recognition that the prosecution with its burden of persuasion needs evidentiary depth to tell a continuous story has, however, virtually no application when the point at issue is a defendant's legal status, dependent on some judgment rendered wholly independently of the concrete events of later criminal behavior charged against him. As in this case, the choice of evidence for such an element is usually not between eventful narrative and abstract proposition, but between propositions of slightly varying abstraction, either a record saying that conviction for some crime occurred at a certain time or a statement admitting the same thing without naming the particular offense. The issue of substituting one statement for the other normally arises only when the record of conviction would not be admissible for any purpose beyond proving status, so that excluding it would not deprive the prosecution of evidence with multiple utility; if, indeed, there were a justification for receiving evidence of the nature of prior acts on some issue other than status (i.e., to prove "motive, opportunity, intent, preparation, plan, knowledge, identity, or absence of mistake or accident," Fed. Rule Evid. 404(b). Rule 404(b) guarantees the opportunity to seek its admission. Nor can it be argued that the events behind the prior conviction are proper nourishment for the jurors' sense of obligation to vindicate the public interest....Congress, however, has made it plain that distinctions among generic felonies do not count for this purpose; the fact of the qualifying conviction is alone what matters under the statute.... The most the jury needs to know is that the conviction admitted by the defendant falls within the class of crimes that Congress thought should bar a convict from possessing a gun, and this point may be made readily in a defendant's admission and underscored in the court's jury instructions. Finally, the most obvious reason that the general presumption that the prosecution may choose its evidence is so remote from application here is that proof of the defendant's status goes to an element entirely outside the natural sequence of what the defendant is charged with thinking and doing to commit the current offense. Proving status without telling exactly why that status was imposed leaves no gap in the story of a defendant's subsequent criminality, and its demonstration by stipulation or admission neither displaces a chapter from a continuous sequence of conventional evidence nor comes across as an officious substitution, to confuse or offend or provoke reproach.

Given these peculiarities of the element of felony-convict status and of admissions and the like when used to prove it, there is no cognizable difference between the evidentiary significance of an admission and of the legitimately probative component of the official record the prosecution would prefer to place in evidence.... In this case, as in any other in which the prior conviction is for an offense likely to support conviction on some improper ground, the only reasonable conclusion was that the risk of unfair prejudice did substantially outweigh the discounted probative value of the record of conviction, and it was an abuse of discretion to admit the record when an admission was available. What we have said shows why this will be the general rule when proof of convict status is at issue, just as the prosecutor's choice will generally survive a Rule 403 analysis when a defendant seeks to force the substitution of an admission for evidence creating a coherent narrative of his thoughts and actions in perpetrating the offense for which he is being tried.

The judgment is reversed, and the case is remanded to the Ninth Circuit for further proceedings consistent with this opinion.

Justice O'CONNOR, with whom THE CHIEF JUSTICE, Justice SCALIA, and Justice THOMAS join, dissenting.

The Court today announces a rule that misapplies Federal Rule of Evidence 403 and upsets, without explanation, longstanding precedent regarding criminal prosecutions....

I

Rule 403 provides that a district court may exclude relevant evidence if, among other things, "its probative value is substantially outweighed by the danger of unfair prejudice." Certainly, Rule 403 does not permit the court to exclude the Government's evidence simply because it may hurt the defendant. As a threshold matter, evidence is excludable only if it is "unfairly" prejudicial, in that it has "an undue tendency to suggest decision on an improper basis." The evidence tendered by the Government in this case-the order reflecting petitioner's prior conviction and sentence for assault resulting in serious bodily injury, in violation of 18 U.S.C. § 1153 and 18 U.S.C. § 113(f) (1988 ed.)-directly proved a necessary element of the § 922(g)(1) offense, that is, that petitioner had committed a crime covered by § 921(a)(20). Perhaps petitioner's case was damaged when the jury discovered that he previously had committed a felony and heard the name of his crime. But I cannot agree with the Court that it was unfairly prejudicial for the Government to establish an essential element of its case against petitioner with direct proof of his prior conviction.

...The structure of § 922(g)(1) itself shows that Congress envisioned jurors' learning the name and basic nature of the defendant's prior offense.... The statute excludes from § 922(g)(1)'s coverage certain business crimes and state misdemeanors punishable by imprisonment of two years or less. § 921(a)(20). Within the meaning of § 922(g)(1), then, "a crime" is not an abstract or metaphysical concept. Rather, the Government must prove that the defendant committed a particular crime. In short, under § 922(g)(1), a defendant's prior felony conviction connotes not only that he is a prior felon, but also that he has engaged in specific past criminal conduct.

* * *

The Court never explains precisely why it constitutes "unfair" prejudice for the Government to directly prove an essential element of the § 922(g)(1) offense with evidence that reveals the name or basic nature of the defendant's prior conviction. It simply notes that such evidence may lead a jury to conclude that the defendant has a propensity to commit crime, thereby raising the odds that the jury would find that he committed the crime with which he is currently charged...

Yes, to be sure, Rule 404(b) provides that "[e]vidence of other crimes, wrongs, or acts is not admissible to prove the character of a person in order to show action in conformity therewith." But…[i]n a prosecution brought under § 922(g)(1), the Government does not submit evidence of a past crime to prove the defendant's bad character or to "show action in conformity therewith." It tenders the evidence as direct proof of a necessary element of the offense with which it has charged the defendant…

mitigating

Any incremental harm resulting from proving the name or basic nature of the prior felony can be properly mitigated by limiting jury instructions. Federal Rule of Evidence 105 provides that when evidence is admissible for one purpose, but not another, "the court, upon request, shall restrict the evidence to its proper scope and instruct the jury accordingly." Indeed, on petitioner's own motion in this case, the District Court instructed the jury that it was not to " 'consider a prior conviction as evidence of guilt of the crime for which the defendant is now on trial.' "…

II

The Court also holds that, if a defendant charged with violating § 922(g)(1) concedes his prior felony conviction, a district court abuses its discretion if it admits evidence of the defendant's prior crime that raises the risk of a verdict "tainted by improper considerations."…

Why, precisely, does the Court think that this item of evidence raises the risk of a verdict "tainted by improper considerations"? Is it because the jury might learn that petitioner assaulted someone and caused serious bodily injury? If this is what the Court means, would evidence that petitioner had committed some other felony be admissible, and if so, what sort of crime might that be? Or does the Court object to the order because it gave a few specifics about the assault, such as the date, the location, and the victim's name? Or perhaps the Court finds that introducing the order risks a verdict "tainted by improper considerations" simply because the § 922(g)(1) charge was joined with counts charging petitioner with using a firearm in relation to a crime of violence, in violation of 18 U.S.C. § 924(c), and with committing an assault with a dangerous weapon, in violation of 18 U.S.C. § 1153 and 18 U.S.C. § 113(c) (1988 ed.)? Under the Court's nebulous standard for admission of prior felony evidence in a § 922(g)(1) prosecution, these are open questions.

More troubling still is the Court's retreat from the fundamental principle that in a criminal prosecution the Government may prove its case as it sees fit. The Court reasons that, in general, a defendant may not stipulate away an element of a charged offense because, in the usual case, "the prosecution with its burden of persuasion needs evidentiary depth to tell a continuous story." The rule has, however, "virtually no application when the point at issue is a defendant's legal status, dependent on some judgment rendered wholly independently of the concrete events of later criminal behavior charged against him."...

On its own terms, the argument does not hold together. A jury is as likely to be puzzled by the "missing chapter" resulting from a defendant's stipulation to his prior felony conviction as it would be by the defendant's conceding any other element of the crime. The jury may wonder why it has not been told the name of the crime, or it may question why the defendant's firearm possession was illegal, given the tradition of lawful gun ownership in this country.

Confuse jury.

III

...Like it or not, Congress chose to make a defendant's prior criminal conviction one of the two elements of the § 922(g)(1) offense. Moreover, crimes have names; a defendant is not convicted of some indeterminate, unspecified "crime." Nor do I think that Federal Rule of Evidence 403 can be read to obviate the well accepted principle, grounded in both the Constitution and in our precedent, that the Government may not be forced to accept a defendant's concession to an element of a charged offense as proof of that element. I respectfully dissent.

Points for Discussion

a. Stipulations and Limiting Instructions.

Lawyers often use offers to stipulate strategically. For example, if there is a gruesome photograph in a murder case showing the location of the bloody bodies of the victims, the defense may offer to stipulate as to the location of the bodies, and thus render the photo inadmissible because the probative value of the photo is already contained in the stipulation, but without the unfair prejudice contained in the gruesome photo. Similarly, the prosecution might offer a Rule 105 limiting instruction to be given by the judge directing the jury to consider the photo only for purposes of showing the location of the bodies, and thus render the photo admissible

What's That?

The term stipulation merely means "agreement". Lawyers will often stipulate or offer to stipulate which means they agree with their opponent about a matter thereby avoiding a decision by the judge. For example, the lawyers may stipulate to the admission of a piece of evidence or its authenticity or the like.

because any unfair prejudice will now be ignored by the jury.

b. The Balancing of Unfair Prejudicein a Trial to the Court

In *Gulf States Utilities Co. v. Ecodyne Corp.*, 577 F.2d 1031 (5th Cir. 1978), the court stated that the exclusion of relevant evidence on the basis that it is unfairly prejudicial has no application to non-jury trials and is a "useless procedure" because a trial judge can "exclude those improper inferences from his mind in reaching a decision." Is this argument persuasive?

What's That?

Rule 105 provides that evidence may be admissible for one purpose but not for another. Therefore, in a jury trial, the judge may give the jury a 'limiting instruction' which instructs the jury that such evidence is only admissible for the purpose given by the judge. This allows some flexibility for evidence that may be critical but may be excluded as to certain purposes. Rule 105 eliminates the concept of "all or nothing" with regard to admissibility.

c. Review of the Trial Court's Rule 403 Decision on Appeal

Rule 403 decisions are discretionary and once made, will seldom be reversed on appeal unless the decision cannot be supported by reasonable arguments. *United States v. Awadallah,* 436 F.3d 125 (2d Cir. 2006). Appellate courts recognize that trial judges are in a unique position to assess the jury's need for the evidence and its likely affect on the jury. But a judge's discretion is not unlimited. See *McQueeney v. Willington Trust Co.*, 779 F.2d 916 (1985) (reversing a Rule 403 decision to exclude evidence that the plaintiff committed perjury in a related deposition because there was no particularized showing of unfair prejudice, and the evidence did not have the obvious potential for such a showing).

Hypo 3.2

Three robbery suspects are stopped by the police at gunpoint. According to an officer, one of the suspects made a quick movement with his hand into his coat as if he were going to reach for a weapon, after which the officer shot and killed him. In a civil rights action against the officers by the suspect's survivors, the survivors wish to offer evidence that the suspect was unarmed when he was shot. The law of self-defense allows defenders to use deadly force against apparent danger as well as actual danger as long as their actions are reasonable under the circumstances. Is evidence that the suspect was unarmed admissible under Rule 403? If the trial court admits this evidence, do you think this ruling would be upheld on appeal? See *Sherrod v. Berry,* 856 F.2d 802 (7th Cir. 1988) (en banc).

3. Judicial Determination of Preliminary Questions

Rule 104 Preliminary Questions

(a) **Questions of admissibility generally.** Preliminary questions concerning the qualification of a person to be a witness, the existence of a privilege, or the admissibility of evidence shall be determined by the court, subject to the provisions of subdivision (b). In making its determination it is not bound by the rules of evidence except those with respect to privileges.

Under Rule 104(a), the trial judge determines the admissibility of proposed evidence except for matters involving conditional relevancy as discussed below. In making that decision, the judge may hold a hearing outside the presence of the jury where each side presents evidence relevant to whether the legal requirements for admissibility have been met. These legal requirements often require that the judge act as a trier of fact. For example, if the competency of a child-witness is challenged, the judge would need to determine from the facts whether the child knows the difference between right and wrong and can coherently narrate events, the legal requirements for witness competency. In the same manner, if a party seeks to prevent the admission of evidence allegedly protected by the attorney-client privilege, the judge might need to ascertain from the facts whether an attorney-client relationship ever existed, and if so, whether communications between the attorney and the client were made in confidence. A judge's findings as to these preliminary questions must be made by a preponderance of the evidence in both civil and criminal cases.

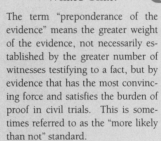

What's That?

The term "preponderance of the evidence" means the greater weight of the evidence, not necessarily established by the greater number of witnesses testifying to a fact, but by evidence that has the most convincing force and satisfies the burden of proof in civil trials. This is sometimes referred to as the "more likely than not" standard.

Rule 104(a) also provides that the judge is not bound by the rules of evidence in determining evidence admissibility, except for those with respect to privileges. It is based on the assumption that the judge, unlike the jury, is legally trained to consider only reliable portions of evidence that is offered and to disregard those

Food for Thought

Can you think of an instance where the judge might be allowed to consider privileged material to determine the admissibility of evidence? How about when determining whether the statements themselves are privileged?

that are unreliable. While the rule appears straightforward, its application can be problematic. What if the only evidence a party offers to lay a foundation for admission of written hearsay statement is the content of the written statement itself? If the statement alone is allowed to satisfy its own foundation for admissibility, it would in essence "bootstrap" itself into evidence. This "bootstrapping" problem has been resolved by an amendment to Rule 801(d)(2), which permits the proponent of the evidence to offer the hearsay contents of the statement itself as proof of the statement's admissibility as long as the proponent also offers evidence other than the statement's contents. Prior to the rule's amendment, however, the "bootstrapping" issue was rigorously debated and unresolved. See *United States v. Bourjaily*, 483 U.S. 171 (1987).

4. Judicial Determination of Conditional Relevancy

Rule 104. Preliminary Questions

(b) Relevancy Conditioned on Fact. When the relevancy of evidence depends upon fulfillment of a condition of fact, the court shall admit it upon, or subject to, the introduction of evidence sufficient to support a finding of the fulfillment of the condition.

Occasionally, the relevancy of a piece of evidence depends upon proof of other facts. For example, the relevancy of a contract may depend upon whether the defendant's agent who signed the contract had authority to do so, a fact issue that may be hotly contested by the parties. Or, proof that a particular automobile was speeding before the accident may be relevant only if it can be shown that the automobile was being driven by the defendant in the case.

To avoid interference with the functioning of the jury, the drafters of Rule 104(b) provide that both the judge and the jury share the responsibility of determining admissibility for evidence whose admission is conditioned upon another fact. The judge's role is to decide whether a reasonable juror could find the contested fact to be true. If so, the judge admits the evidence, and the jury is instructed to disregard it if they find the contested fact does not exist.

Rule 104(b) issues are usually entwined with the admissibility of evidence under other evidentiary rules such as Rule 404(b), as the following case illustrates.

Huddleston v. United States

Supreme Court of the United States
485 U.S. 681 (1988)

Chief Justice REHNQUIST delivered the opinion of the Court:

* * *

Petitioner, Guy Rufus Huddleston, was charged with one count of selling stolen goods in interstate commerce, one count of possessing stolen property in interstate commerce. The two counts related to two portions of a shipment of stolen Memorex videocassette tapes that petitioner was alleged to have possessed and sold, knowing that they were stolen.

The evidence at trial showed that a trailer containing over 32,000 blank Memorex videocassette tapes with a manufacturing cost of $4.53 per tape was stolen from the Overnight Express yard in South Holland, Illinois, sometime between April 11 and 15, 1985. On April 17, 1985, petitioner contacted Karen Curry, the manager of the Magic Rent-to-Own in Ypsilanti, Michigan, seeking her assistance in selling a large number of blank Memorex videocassette tapes. After assuring Curry that the tapes were not stolen, he told her he wished to sell them in lots of at least

> ### Make the Connection
>
> Rule 404(b) of the Federal Rules of Evidence allows admission of evidence of a person's prior acts that are relevant to show a fact at issue in the case. For example, evidence that the defendant possessed cocaine on another occasion might be relevant to prove the defendant knew that the substance for which he was arrested was cocaine, if he denies such knowledge. This rule will be examined later in this book as a special application of Rules 401-403.

500 at $2.75 to $3 per tape. Curry subsequently arranged for the sale of a total of 5,000 tapes, which petitioner delivered to the various purchasers-who apparently believed the sales were legitimate.

There was no dispute that the tapes which petitioner sold were stolen; the only material issue at trial was whether petitioner knew they were stolen. The  District Court allowed the Government to introduce evidence of "similar acts" under Rule 404(b), concluding that such evidence had "clear relevance as to [petitioner's knowledge]." The first piece of similar act evidence offered by the Government was the testimony of Paul Toney, a record store owner. He testified that in February 1985, petitioner offered to sell new 12" black and white televisions for $28 apiece. According to Toney, petitioner indicated that he could obtain several thousand of these televisions. Petitioner and Toney eventually traveled to the Magic Rent-to-Own, where Toney purchased 20 of the televisions. Several days later, Toney purchased 18 more televisions.

The second piece of similar act evidence was the testimony of Robert Nelson, an undercover FBI agent posing as a buyer for an appliance store. Nelson testified that in May 1985, petitioner offered to sell him a large quantity of Amana appliances-28 refrigerators, 2 ranges, and 40 icemakers. Nelson agreed to pay $8,000 for the appliances. Petitioner was arrested shortly after he arrived at the parking lot where he and Nelson had agreed to transfer the appliances. A truck containing the appliances was stopped a short distance from the parking lot, and Leroy Wesby, who was driving the truck, was also arrested. It was determined that the appliances had a value of approximately $20,000 and were part of a shipment that had been stolen.

Petitioner testified that the Memorex tapes, the televisions, and the appliances had all been provided by Leroy Wesby, who had represented that all of the merchandise was obtained legitimately. Petitioner stated that he had sold 6,500 Memorex tapes for Wesby on a commission basis. Petitioner maintained that all of the sales for Wesby had been on a commission basis and that he had no knowledge that any of the goods were stolen.

limiting instruction

In closing, the prosecution explained that petitioner was not on trial for his dealings with the appliances or the televisions. The District Court instructed the jury that the similar acts evidence was to be used only to establish petitioner's knowledge, and not to prove his character. The jury convicted petitioner on the possession count only.

* * *

issue

We granted certiorari to resolve among the Courts of Appeals as to whether the trial court must make a preliminary finding before "similar act" and other Rule 404(b) evidence is submitted to the jury. We conclude that such evidence should be admitted if there is sufficient evidence to support a finding by the jury that the defendant committed the similar act.

Federal Rule of Evidence 404(b)-which applies in both civil and criminal cases-generally prohibits the introduction of evidence of extrinsic acts that might adversely reflect on the actor's character, unless that evidence bears upon a relevant issue in the case such as motive, opportunity, or knowledge. Extrinsic acts evidence may be critical to the establishment of the truth as to a disputed issue, especially when that issue involves the actor's state of mind and the only means of ascertaining that mental state is by drawing inferences from conduct. The actor in the instant case was a criminal defendant, and the act in question was "similar" to the one with which he was charged. Our use of these terms is not meant to suggest that our analysis is limited to such circumstances.

Before this Court, petitioner argues that the District Court erred in admitting Toney's testimony as to petitioner's sale of the televisions. The threshold inquiry a court must make before admitting similar acts evidence under Rule 404(b) is whether that evidence is probative of a material issue other than character. The Government's theory of relevance was that the televisions were stolen, and proof that petitioner had engaged in a series of sales of stolen merchandise from the same suspicious source would be strong evidence that he was aware that each of these items, including the Memorex tapes, was stolen. As such, the sale of the televisions was a "similar act" only if the televisions were stolen. Petitioner acknowledges that this evidence was admitted for the proper purpose of showing his knowledge that the Memorex tapes were stolen. He asserts, however, that the evidence should not have been admitted because the Government failed to prove to the District Court that the televisions were in fact stolen.

[handwritten margin note: 1) argues]

[handwritten margin note: threshold issue]

Petitioner argues from the premise that evidence of similar acts has a grave potential for causing improper prejudice. For instance, the jury may choose to punish the defendant for the similar rather than the charged act, or the jury may infer that the defendant is an evil person inclined to violate the law. Because of this danger, petitioner maintains, the jury ought not to be exposed to similar act evidence until the trial court has heard the evidence and made a determination under Federal Rule of Evidence 104(a) that the defendant committed the similar act. Rule 104(a) provides that "[p]reliminary questions concerning the qualification of a person to be a witness, the existence of a privilege, or the admissibility of evidence shall be determined by the court, subject to the provisions of subdivision (b)." According to petitioner, the trial court must make this preliminary finding by at least a preponderance of the evidence.

* * *

[The Court rejects the petitioner's position that the language of Rule 404(b) requires a preliminary showing that the Rule 404(b) act occurred before admitting the act into evidence].

[Q]uestions of relevance conditioned on a fact are dealt with under Federal Rule of Evidence 104(b).

> "When the relevancy of evidence depends upon the fulfillment of a condition of fact, the court shall admit it upon, or subject to, the introduction of evidence sufficient to support a finding of the fulfillment of the condition."

In determining whether the Government has introduced sufficient evidence to meet <u>Rule 104(b)</u>, the trial court neither weighs credibility nor makes a finding that the Government has proved the conditional fact by a preponderance of the evidence. <u>The court simply examines all the evidence in the case and decides whether the jury could reasonably find the conditional fact-here, that the televisions were stolen by a preponderance of the evidence.</u> The trial court has traditionally exercised the broadest sort of discretion in controlling the order of proof at trial, and we see nothing in the Rules of Evidence that would change this practice. Often the trial court may decide to allow the proponent to introduce evidence concerning a similar act, and at a later point in the trial assess whether sufficient evidence has been offered to permit the jury to make the requisite finding. If the proponent has failed to meet this minimal standard of proof, the trial court must instruct the jury to disregard the evidence.

Take Note!

The Court states that the trial judge, in making a Rule 104(b) determination, should not weigh witness credibility. What do you think is the policy behind this requirement? Is it realistic to think that a judge will be able to put aside her own beliefs as to witness credibility in making this decision? Is it humanly possible for a judge to consider something and then be able to ignore it, even though it is still in the back of her mind? Can anyone ever "unring a bell"?

We emphasize that in assessing the sufficiency of the evidence under <u>Rule 104(b)</u>, the trial court must consider all evidence presented to the jury. Individual pieces of evidence, insufficient in themselves to prove a point, may in cumulation prove it. The sum of an evidentiary presentation may well be greater than its constituent parts. In assessing whether the evidence was sufficient to support a finding that the televisions were stolen, the court here was required to consider not only the direct evidence on that point-the low price of the televisions, the large quantity offered for sale, and petitioner's inability to produce a bill of sale-but also the evidence concerning petitioner's involvement in the sales of other stolen merchandise obtained from Wesby, such as the Memorex tapes and the Amana appliances. Given this evidence, the jury reasonably could have concluded that the televisions were stolen, and the trial court therefore properly allowed the evidence to go to the jury.

Affirmed.

Points for Discussion

a. Is There Really a Distinction Between Rule 104(a) and 104(b)

Rule 104(a) governs procedures for the admission of all evidence except evidence that is conditionally relevant under Rule 104(b). While this division may appear to be straightforward, this may be an illusion. For example, in a negligence case the admissibility of testimony that the plaintiff was struck by a speeding red car does not appear to require a conditional relevance evaluation because it simply describes how the accident occurred. However, it can be argued that such testimony is only relevant if the plaintiff can prove that it was the defendant who was the driver of the red car. In the same manner, a chemist's expert opinion that the contents of a particular baggie contained cocaine is only relevant if the police took the baggie from the possession of the defendant. For reasons such as these, many scholars agree that all cases of relevancy are cases of conditional relevance.

b. Is the Distinction Between Rule 104(b) and 104(b) Significant in Practice?

Despite scholarly criticism and call for reform, Rule 104 (a) and (b) have not been amended, perhaps because attorneys seldom make conditional relevance objections at trial, so there is no real world pressure for a change in the rules.

---

5. The Reverse Balancing Portion of Rule 403

Normally, evidence that has probative value is presumptively admissible unless substantially outweighed by a Rule 403 counterweight. In two rules which we have yet to consider, (Rules 412 and 609) however, the balancing test is reversed. For evidence to be admissible under these rules, the proponent must show that the probative value of the evidence substantially or otherwise outweighs any counterweights. This creates a presumption of inadmissibility for this evidence, but allows it to come in when it is strongly important to the case.

Executive Summary

Relevant/Irrelevant Evidence

The initial inquiry into any evidentiary issue is relevance. It is a very low threshold: under Rule 401, if the proposed evidence has "any tendency" to make a disputed fact more or less probable (it has "logical relevancy"), and if it relates to a legal issue in the case (it has "legal relevancy"), then the proposed evidence is considered relevant. (*Adamson*). Relevant evidence is admissible, provided that it does not violate any other rule of evidence. However, irrelevant evidence is always inadmissible under Rule 402.

Exclusion of Relevant Evidence

Rule 403 gives the judge the discretion to exclude otherwise relevant evidence if the "danger of unfair prejudice" of the evidence *substantially outweighs* its probative value. Simply because an item of evidence may be "prejudicial" does not mean it should be excluded. In fact, all relevant evidence is "prejudicial" in the sense that it has a tendency to make a factual issue more or less likely. Thus, the proposed evidence must contain so much *"unfair"* prejudice that it substantially outweighs the probative value. (*Carter*). Note that the Rule 403 discretionary balancing test requires the danger of unfair prejudice to *substantially* outweigh the probative value, meaning that even if the danger of unfair prejudice merely outweighs its probative value, the proposed evidence will still be admissible.

A strategic move to exclude evidence under Rule 403 is to offer to "stipulate" to a matter and thereby remove the justification for offering the evidence containing the unfair prejudice. A stipulation is a way to maintain some or all of the probative value of the evidence, yet still remove the unfair prejudice, because the evidence is not used. A judge should consider an offer to stipulate, but should not necessarily require the parties to accept it, because parties should be able to use the evidence they choose, without it being "sanitized" or overly diluted by the stipulation. (*Old Chief*). Rule 403 does not means all emotional, or powerful, or even graphic evidence should be excluded. Such evidence has a place in trials and often will form part of the legitimate probative value of the evidence, instead of its unfair prejudice.

A strategic move to overcome a Rule 403 objection is to request that the judge offer a Rule 105 "limiting instruction," where the evidence is admissible only for a limited (legitimate) purpose, but not for an illegitimate (unfair prejudice) purpose ("limited admissibility").

Unfair prejudice in not the only "counterweight" that should be balanced against probative value; there are also the concerns for confusion of the issues, misleading the jury, or considerations of undue delay, waste of time, or needless presentation of cumulative evidence.

Preliminary Questions

Rule 104 allows the judge to make preliminary findings regarding the admissibility of evidence.

Rule 104(a) allows the judge to consider any underlying evidence (admissible or not) in order to make a legal finding about the admissibility of an item of evidence in issue. This includes having a conference with counsel outside the hearing of the jury.

Rule 104(b), on the other hand, requires the judge to allow the jury to decide whether certain underlying *factual conditions* exists in order to make an item of evidence relevant. Because the determination of whether the factual condition exists is an inquiry for the jury, the judge will admit the item of evidence and allow the jury to give it whatever weight and relevance it sees fit during deliberations. However, the judge will allow this to occur only where there has been an initial showing that reasonable jury could find by a preponderance of the evidence that the factual condition at issue exists. (*Huddleston*).

CHAPTER 4

Qualification of a Fact Witness

A. Introduction

A fact witness is someone who testifies as to what she saw or otherwise perceived about the events underlying a case. Historically, the common law deemed a number of fact witnesses incompetent to testify for fear they would lie under oath. These witnesses included atheists, agnostics, convicted felons, parties to the case and their spouses, persons with an interest in the case, children and the mentally ill. As might be expected, these common law limitations often had the consequence of preventing witnesses with the most knowledge of the case from testifying.

> **Make the Connection**
>
> 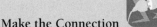 Fact witnesses, who are also called lay witnesses, are required by Federal Rule of Evidence 602 to testify from personal knowledge. Expert witnesses may testify from personal knowledge as well but per Rule 703 may also base their opinions on facts made known to them by others. The personal knowledge requirement for fact witnesses is covered later in this chapter; the basis for an expert's testimony is covered in Chapter 12 of this book.

The Federal Rules of Evidence have largely eliminated common law witness incompetency. Most of these former disqualifications, such as having a felony conviction or an interest in the case, are now only usable to attack a witness's credibility. In their place, Rule 601 presumes all witnesses competent to testify. Rules 602 and 603 require testifying fact witnesses to have personal knowledge of the facts and be willing to take an oath or affirmation to tell the truth. Despite these fairly low witness qualification standards, competency challenges remain.

B. The General Rule of Competency

> **Rule 601. General Rule of Competency**
>
> Every person is competent to be a witness except as otherwise provided in these rules. However, in civil actions and proceedings, with respect to an element of a claim or defense as to which State law supplies the rule of decision, the competency of a witness shall be determined in accordance with State law.

C. Mentally Incapacitated Witnesses

Although Rule 601 presumes all witnesses competent, there is authority under the rule that allows a federal judge to find that an individual witness's ability to testify is so impaired that he cannot give meaningful testimony. Exercise of that authority is within the broad discretion of the trial court. However, as stated by the Advisory Committee Note to Rule 601, "A witness wholly without capacity is difficult to imagine."

United States v. Roach

U.S. Court of Appeals for the Fifth Circuit
590 F.2d 181 (5th Cir. 1979)

GEE, Circuit Judge:

The evidence tended to establish that Roach and Stewart, wearing masks and carrying guns, robbed a bank in Dallas, Georgia. Bank personnel soon discovered that the robbers had swallowed . . . a security package containing a dye bomb designed to emit a red, tear-gas-like substance within minutes after removal. They reported this to police, along with a general description of the robbers and their getaway car, and the opinion that a third person had been waiting outside.

Brenda Jackson, Stewart's girlfriend, testified that Roach and Stewart had robbed the bank and that she was driving the getaway car when the dye bomb exploded, making it difficult for them to see. Roach switched places with Jackson and began driving. Stewart threw the shotgun out of the car and, after a bit, fled with the stolen money.

Minutes later a county deputy sheriff, alerted to the car description by radio, stopped Roach and Jackson and asked them to get out of the car. After they had exited, the deputy noticed a large red stain on the car's front seat, some gloves on the floorboard, and a white print shirt on the back seat, all in plain view through the car windows. Roach and Jackson were placed in the police car, and before any interrogation had begun Jackson asked the deputy, "Why are you arresting us?" Roach immediately cut in, "Shut up, you know why." After FBI agents arrived, the car was towed to the police station, where it was searched and the stained parts removed for laboratory analysis. The stain was found to contain the same chemicals used in the bank's security packs.

Stewart was apprehended a month later in Baton Rouge, Louisiana. In a statement admitted into evidence at trial, he told interrogating agents that Jackson was his girlfriend and that he had resided in Dalton, Georgia, until March 1977, when he heard from friends that he was wanted for bank robbery.

* * *

About three months before trial, Brenda Jackson received a psychiatric examination and was judged competent to stand trial. She was also found to have used drugs intermittently. Questioning Jackson's competence to be a witness against his client, Roach's attorney was given access to the psychiatric report, and the court granted his request for a preliminary examination into Jackson's current mental state. Though Jackson had been emotionally troubled during the previous three months and admitted using drugs on two occasions in that time, her answers to questions by government and defense attorneys were lucid and discriminating. The trial judge asked no questions, nor were expert witnesses employed. At the end of the hearing, the judge declared Jackson competent to testify.

> **What's That?**
>
> Competency to stand trial in a criminal case requires that the defendant have the capacity to understand the proceedings, to consult meaningfully with counsel, and to assist in his defense. It is a related but different inquiry from Rule 601 Competency to testify as a witness in a case.

Roach complains that these procedures were insufficient guarantees of a fair trial: another psychiatric examination should have been ordered; experts should have testified; the judge should have personally questioned Jackson since Rule 104 of the Federal Rules of Evidence requires him to decide preliminary questions regarding the "qualification of a person to be a witness . . . or the admissibility of evidence."

O argue)

As to the necessity of a psychiatric examination, we have held that the district court has broad discretion in determining whether to order such examinations. Given the earlier examination and the further preliminary hearing, there can be no serious claim of abuse of discretion. Moreover, under the new Federal Rules of Evidence it is doubtful that mental incompetence would even be grounds for dis-

Food for Thought

Is the court saying that there is no such thing as a witness who is so mentally incapacitated that he is not competent to testify? How about witnesses who are so severely delusional they cannot tell right from wrong? Of what value might their testimony be to a jury?

qualification of a prospective witness. Rule 601 provides that "(e)very person is competent to be a witness except as otherwise provided in these rules," and nowhere is mental competence mentioned as a possible exception. The Notes of the House Committee on the Judiciary state that one effect of Rule 601 is to abolish mental capacity as a ground for rendering a person incompetent as a witness. The Advisory Committee in their Notes on the Proposed Rules took a similar view, observing that the question of capacity was one "particularly suited to the jury as one of weight and credibility, subject to judicial authority to review the sufficiency of the evidence."

If these views are to be rigorously adhered to, there seems no longer to be any occasion for judicially-ordered psychiatric examinations or competency hearings of witnesses—none, at least, on the theory that a preliminary determination of competency must be made by the district court. If the court finds the witness otherwise properly qualified, the witness should be allowed to testify and the defendant given ample opportunity to impeach his or her perceptions and recollections. That the court here went further and allowed the preliminary hearing into Jackson's competence is an added ground for affirming the jury's verdict rather than a reason to set it aside.

————————

Points for Discussion

a. The Trial Court's Discretion in Evaluating Witness Competency.

As *Roach* illustrates, appellate courts will seldom overturn a trial court's competency determination. For example, in *United States v. Blankenship*, 923 F.2d 1110 (5th Cir. 1991), the trial court decision to allow a witness to testify was upheld, even though evidence in the record showed she was an admitted drug addict and incarcerated felon who occasionally hallucinated and whose testimony on direct examination was confused and inconsistent with her testimony on cross-examination. Reversals occur most frequently when the trial court has found a witness incompetent. See, e.g., *United States v. Lightly*, 677 F.2d 1027 (4th Cir. 1982), reversing a trial court's determination that a witness, who had been adjudicated insane and incompetent to stand trial in a previous criminal case, was not competent to testify. There was evidence in the record that she could remember events, understand the oath, and communicate what she saw.

b. Psychological Examinations and Expert Testimony.

A substantial number of narcotics users end up testifying in federal court as prosecution witnesses in drug cases. Defense attorneys have attempted to disqualify those witnesses on the basis that their memory of events is unreliable due to their drug use at the time of the crime or afterwards. Tactics have included requesting that the trial judge order psychiatric examinations of these witnesses and that defense experts be allowed to testify to their lack of competence. These defense efforts have met with little success. Generally, courts cannot order non-party witnesses to be examined by a psychiatrist, although they can condition admissibility of their testimony on such an examination. See *United States v. Gutman*, 725 F.2d 417 (7th Cir. 1984). Additionally, there is a great reluctance to admit expert testimony as to issues of competence or credibility. See *United States v. Ramirez*, 871 F.2d 582 (6th Cir. 1989). What do you think is the reason for this reluctance?

D. Child Witnesses

Child witnesses can present challenging competency issues. Sometimes very young children confuse fact with fantasy or are highly susceptible to adult suggestions. As a result, it may be difficult to show that a child three years of age or younger is competent to testify. When the child is between four and six years of age, trial judges have more discretion to admit their testimony because in a courtroom, as in life, every child is unique.

> **FYI**
>
> For example, a three-year old child may want to go to New York to visit the sewers where he believes the Teenage Mutant Ninja Turtles live.

Wheeler v. United States

Supreme Court of the United States
159 U.S. 523 (1895)

Mr. Justice BREWER delivered the opinion of the court.

On January 2, 1895, George L. Wheeler was by the circuit court of the United States for the Eastern district of Texas adjudged guilty of the crime of murder, and sentenced to be hanged; whereupon he sued out this writ of error. . . .

The . . . objection is to action of the court in permitting the son of the deceased to testify. The homicide took place on June 12, 1894, and this boy was five years old on the 5th of July following. The case was tried on December 21, at which time he was nearly five and a half years of age. The boy, in reply to questions put to him on his *voir dire*, said, among other things, that he knew the difference between the truth and a lie; that if he told a lie, the bad man would get him, and that he was going to tell the truth. When further asked what they would do with him in court if he told a lie, he replied that they would put him in jail. He also said that his mother had told him that morning to 'tell no lie,' and, in response to a question as to what the clerk said to him when he held up his hand, he answered, 'Don't you tell no story.' Other questions were asked as to his residence, his relationship to the deceased, and as to whether he had ever been to school, to which latter inquiry he responded in the negative. . . .

Take Note

In this case, the five year old boy is being "voir dired" to determine whether he is competent to testify.

That the boy was not by reason of his youth, as a matter of law, absolutely disqualified as a witness is clear. While no one should think of calling as a witness an infant only two or three years old, there is no precise age which determines the question of competency. This depends on the capacity and intelligence of the child, his appreciation of the difference between truth and falsehood, as well as of his duty to tell the former. The decision of this question rests primarily with the trial judge, who sees the proposed witness, notices his manner, his apparent possession or lack of intelligence, and may resort to any examination which will tend to disclose his capacity and intelligence, as well as his understanding of the obligations of an oath. As many of these matters cannot be photographed into the record, the decision of the trial judge will not be disturbed on review, unless from that which is preserved it is clear that it was erroneous. These rules have been settled by many decisions, and there seems to be no dissent among the recent authorities. In *Brasier's Case*, 1 Leach, Crown Cas. 199, it is stated that the question was submitted to the 12 judges, and that they were unanimously of the opinion 'that an infant, though under the age of seven years, may be sworn in a criminal prosecution, provided such infant appears, on strict examination by the court, to possess a sufficient knowledge of the nature and consequences of an oath; for there is no precise or fixed rule as to the time within which infants are excluded from giving evidence, but their admissibility depends upon the sense and reason they entertain of the danger and impiety of falsehood, which is to be collected from their answers to questions propounded to them by the court.'

These principles and authorities are decisive in this case. So far as can be judged from the not very extended examination which is found in the record, the boy was intelligent, understood the difference between truth and falsehood, and the consequences of telling the latter, and also what was required by the oath which he had taken. At any rate, the contrary does not appear. Of course, care must be taken by the trial judge, especially where, as in this case, the question is one of life or death. On the other hand, to exclude from the witness stand one who shows himself capable of understanding the difference between truth and falsehood, and who does not appear to have been simply taught to tell a story, would sometimes result in staying the hand of justice.

We think that, under the circumstances of this case, the disclosures on the *voir dire* were sufficient to authorize the decision that the witness was competent, and therefore there was no error in admitting his testimony. These being the only questions in the record, the judgment must be affirmed.

Points for Discussion

a. Determining Competency of a Child Witness.

Generally, to be competent, a child witness must be able to tell the difference between the truth and a lie and be able to remember and coherently narrate events. What questions should a judge ask of a child to determine whether these standards are met? How should a judge question a child witness to make certain the child has not been influenced by others in recalling events? Can a criminal defendant be constitutionally excluded from being present when this questioning occurs? See *Kentucky v. Stincer*, 482 U.S. 730 (1987) (the Due Process Clause of the Fifth Amendment and the Confrontation Clause of the Sixth Amendment were not violated by excluding the defendant from a hearing to determine the competency of two child witnesses because neither girl was asked about the substantive testimony she would give at trial).

b. The Rights of Child Victims and Child Witnesses.

Although trial judges have a great deal of discretion in making competency determinations, Congress has enacted special rules regulating child testimony in federal court. See 18 U.S.C.A. §3509. This statute contains a presumption that children are competent witnesses and permits the exclusion of child testimony only for "compelling reasons" other than the age of the child. In addition, the statute allows a child to give live testimony in court through a closed circuit television if the trial judge finds the closed circuit procedure necessary in the case. See

Maryland v. Craig, 497 U.S. 836 (1990). See generally Graham, *Indicia of Reliability and Face to Face Confrontation: Emerging Issues in Child Sexual Abuse Prosecutions*, 40 U. Miami L. Rev. 19 (1985).

E. Previously Hypnotized Witnesses

Should witnesses who have had their memories hypnotically refreshed be considered competent? Put another way, does hypnotically refreshed testimony produce truthful results?   Hypnosis is a state of inner absorption, focused attention and diminished peripheral awareness which bypass the censor of the mind.

FYI

"[S]ome researchers believe that hypnosis can be used by individuals to the degree they possess a hypnotic trait, much as they have traits associated with height, body size, hair color, etc. Other professionals who study and use hypnosis believe there are strong cognitive and interpersonal components that affect an individual's response to hypnotic environments and suggestions. Recent research supports the view that hypnotic communication and suggestions effectively change aspects of the person's physiological and neurological functions." See www.asch.net.

It has been suggested that there are several problems inherent in the use of hypnosis. First, hypnotized subjects are in a state of hyper-suggestibility and are often highly motivated to please, which means they may fabricate. Second, they may have pseudo-memories of facts they did not experience but which were suggested consciously or unconsciously by the hypnotist. If hypnotically refreshed testimony is at all unreliable, and experts differ as to whether this is the case, should there be a *per se* rule excluding all hypnotically refreshed testimony? If such a rule excluded the testimony of a defendant in his own criminal case, would it be constitutional?

Rock v. Arkansas

Supreme Court of the United States
483 U.S. 44 (1987)

Justice BLACKMUN delivered the opinion of the Court.

[Petitioner was charged with manslaughter for shooting her husband. In order to refresh her memory as to the precise details of the shooting, she underwent hypnosis by a trained neuropsychologist on two occasions. These sessions were tape recorded. After hypnosis, she was able to recall that during the shooting, her gun had misfired, which was corroborated by a defendant expert's testimony. However, the trial court ruled that under Arkansas law, no hypnotically refreshed testimony was admissible and limited petitioner's testimony to a reiteration of statements she had made prior to hypnosis.]

Petitioner's claim that her testimony was impermissibly excluded is bottomed on her constitutional right to testify in her own defense. At this point in the development of our adversary system, it cannot be doubted that a defendant in a criminal case has the right to take the witness stand and to testify in his or her own defense. This, of course, is a change from the historic common-law view, which was that all parties to litigation, including criminal defendants, were disqualified from testifying because of their interest in the outcome of the trial. . . .

The question now before the Court is whether a criminal defendant's right to testify may be restricted by a state rule that excludes her posthypnosis testimony. This is not the first time this Court has faced a constitutional challenge to a state rule, designed to ensure trustworthy evidence, that interfered with the ability of a defendant to offer testimony. In *Washington v. Texas*, 388 U.S. 14, 87 S.Ct. 1920, 18 L.Ed.2d 1019 (1967), the Court was confronted with a state statute that prevented persons charged as principals, accomplices, or accessories in the same crime from being introduced as witnesses for one another. The statute, like the original common-law prohibition on testimony by the accused, was grounded in a concern for the reliability of evidence presented by an interested party. [The court held the statute unconstitutional under the Sixth Amendment].

Just as a State may not apply an arbitrary rule of competence to exclude a material defense witness from taking the stand, it also may not apply a rule of evidence that permits a witness to take the stand, but arbitrarily excludes material portions of his testimony. In *Chambers v. Mississippi*, 410 U.S. 284, 93 S.Ct. 1038, 35 L.Ed.2d 297 (1973), the Court invalidated a State's hearsay rule on the ground that it abridged the defendant's right to "present witnesses in his own defense."

Of course, the right to present relevant testimony is not without limitation. The right "may, in appropriate cases, bow to accommodate other legitimate interests in the criminal trial process." But restrictions of a defendant's right to testify may not be arbitrary or disproportionate to the purposes they are designed to serve.

In establishing its per se rule, the Arkansas Supreme Court simply followed the approach taken by a number of States that have decided that hypnotically enhanced testimony should be excluded at trial on the ground that it tends to be unreliable. Other States that have adopted an exclusionary rule, however, have done so for the testimony of witnesses, not for the testimony of a defendant.

The Arkansas Supreme Court failed to perform the constitutional analysis that is necessary when a defendant's right to testify is at stake.

Although the Arkansas court concluded that any testimony that cannot be proved to be the product of prehypnosis memory is unreliable, many courts have eschewed a per se rule and permit the admission of hypnotically refreshed testimony. Hypnosis by trained physicians or psychologists has been recognized as a valid therapeutic technique since 1958, although there is no generally accepted theory to explain the phenomenon, or even a consensus on a single definition of hypnosis. The use of hypnosis in criminal investigations, however, is controversial, and the current medical and legal view of its appropriate role is unsettled.

Responses of individuals to hypnosis vary greatly. The popular belief that hypnosis guarantees the accuracy of recall is as yet without established foundation and, in fact, hypnosis often has no effect at all on memory. The most common response to hypnosis, however, appears to be an increase in both correct and incorrect recollections. Three general characteristics of hypnosis may lead to the introduction of inaccurate memories: the subject becomes "suggestible" and may try to please the hypnotist with answers the subject thinks will be met with approval; the subject is likely to "confabulate," that is, to fill in details from the imagination in order to make an answer more coherent and complete; and, the subject experiences "memory hardening," which gives him great confidence in both true and false memories, making effective cross-examination more difficult. Despite the unreliability that hypnosis concededly may introduce, however, the procedure has been credited as instrumental in obtaining investigative leads or identifications that were later confirmed by independent evidence.

The inaccuracies the process introduces can be reduced, although perhaps not eliminated, by the use of procedural safeguards. One set of suggested guidelines calls for hypnosis to be performed only by a psychologist or psychiatrist with special training in its use and who is independent of the investigation.

The more traditional means of assessing accuracy of testimony also remain applicable in the case of a previously hypnotized defendant. Certain information recalled as a result of hypnosis may be verified as highly accurate by corroborating evidence. Cross-examination, even in the face of a confident defendant, is an effective tool for revealing inconsistencies. Moreover, a jury can be educated to the risks of hypnosis through expert testimony and cautionary instructions. . . .

We are not now prepared to endorse without qualifications the use of hypnosis as an investigative tool; scientific understanding of the phenomenon and of the means to control the effects of hypnosis is still in its infancy. Arkansas, however, has not justified the exclusion of all of a defendant's testimony that the defendant is unable to prove to be the product of prehypnosis memory. . . .

[The] circumstances present an argument for admissibility of petitioner's testimony in this particular case, an argument that must be considered by the trial court. Arkansas' per se rule excluding all posthypnosis testimony infringes impermissibly on the right of a defendant to testify on his own behalf.

Chief Justice REHNQUIST, with whom Justice WHITE, Justice O'CONNOR, and Justice SCALIA join, dissenting.

In deciding that petitioner Rock's testimony was properly limited at her trial, the Arkansas Supreme Court cited several factors that undermine the reliability of hypnotically induced testimony. . . .

In the Court's words, the decision today is "bottomed" on recognition of Rock's "constitutional right to testify in her own defense." While it is true that this Court, in dictum, has recognized the existence of such a right, the principles identified by the Court as underlying this right provide little support for invalidating the evidentiary rule applied by the Arkansas Supreme Court. . . .

[T]he Court candidly admits that the increased confidence inspired by hypnotism makes "cross-examination more difficult," thereby diminishing an adverse party's ability to test the truthfulness of defendants such as Rock. Nevertheless, we are told, the exclusion of a defendant's testimony cannot be sanctioned because the defendant "above all others may be in a position to meet the prosecution's case."

In conjunction with its reliance on broad principles that have little relevance here, the Court barely concerns itself with the recognition, present throughout our decisions, that an individual's right to present evidence is subject always to reasonable restrictions. . . . Surely a rule designed to exclude testimony whose trustworthiness is inherently suspect cannot be said to fall outside this description.

Points for Discussion

a. The Balancing Test in *Rock*.

Rock holds that questionably reliable evidence, such as hypnotically refreshed testimony, when offered by a criminal defendant cannot be excluded because it "infringes impermissibly on the right of a defendant to testify on his own behalf." Would this same logic apply to a situation where a criminal defendant wanted to offer evidence that he had passed a polygraph test, even though polygraph results are routinely held inadmissible because they are unreliable? After all, there is some contrary evidence that polygraph results are reliable. Also, they are frequently used by some police departments, businesses and government agencies in certain contexts.

b. Is *Rock* applicable to Witnesses Other Than Criminal Defendants?

Should witnesses other than criminal defendants who have had their memories refreshed be allowed to testify as a matter of policy? Different jurisdictions take different approaches. Some have determined that hypnotically refreshed testimony, other than testimony given by a criminal defendant, is not scientifically reliable enough to be admitted. See, e.g., *State ex rel. Collins v. Superior Court,* 644 P.2d 1266 (Ariz. 1982); *Commonwealth v. Nazarovitch,* 436 A.2d 170 (Pa. 1981). Some jurisdictions have adopted a *per se* rule of inadmissibility, except for testifying criminal defendants. See, e.g., *Beck v. Norris,* 801 F.2d 242 (6th Cir. 1986); *United States v. Awkard,* 597 F.2d 667 (9th Cir.) cert. denied, 444 U.S. 885 (1979). Others admit hypnotically refreshed testimony on a case-by-case basis, after balancing the probative value of the evidence against its prejudicial effect under Federal Rule of Evidence 403. See, e.g., *Wicker v. McCotter,* 783 F.2d 487 (5th Cir. 1986) cert. denied, 478 U.S. 1010 (1986). Still others admit such testimony if procedures designed to safeguard reliability were followed. See *Sprynczynatyk v. General Motors,* 771 F.2d 1112 (8th Cir. 1985). Which do you think is the better approach?

———————

F. A Witness's Religious Beliefs

The common law deemed atheists and agnostics incompetent to testify, reasoning that only religious witnesses who believed in a deity who punishes false testimony would testify truthfully. Even under the common law, however, that deity need not be a Christian one; all religious sect members were viewed as competent. Modern law has not only repudiated this religious disqualification but has also made a witness's religious beliefs inadmissible for the purpose of bolstering or attacking that witness's credibility under Rule 610. Cases make a distinction, however, between using a witness's religious beliefs to show that the witness is truthful or untruthful (usually an inadmissible offering), and using evidence of religious affiliation with a party in a case to show bias (usually an admissible offering).

> ### Rule 610. Religious Beliefs or Opinions
>
> Evidence of the beliefs or opinions of a witness on matters of religion is not admissible for the purpose of showing that by reason of their nature the witness' credibility is impaired or enhanced.

Firemen's Fund Insurance Company v. Thien

U.S. Court of Appeals for the Eighth Circuit
63 F.3d 754 (8th Cir. 1995)

MAGILL, Circuit Judge.

[This case arises out of a small plane crash where Charles Benedict died, and his survivors sued the air courier service which owned the plane in question. Michael Thien was the director of the defendants' operations. Richard Lund, *ad litem* for the deceased defendant pilot, was also sued by the

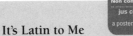

It's Latin to Me

An *ad litem* is someone who represents another in a lawsuit who, because of infancy, incapacity, or disability, cannot represent herself.

Benedicts. Because Thien and Lund were sued in the wrongful death action, they sought liability coverage from their insurance carrier, Fireman's Fund, in order to defend them and pay any liability they might incur in the wrongful death suit.]

[Witnesses Martina and Chris Benedict testified in favor of Thien in the case. The Benedicts argued that the district court erred in excluding evidence of their religious beliefs, offered to show that they were biased because they were both members of "Zion's Endeavor," a religious group of which Thien was the pastor.]

Under Rule 610 of the Federal Rules of Evidence, "[e]vidence of the beliefs or opinions of a witness on matters of religion is not admissible for the purpose of showing that by reason of their nature the witness' credibility is impaired or enhanced." However, [w]hile the rule forecloses inquiry into the religious beliefs or opinions of a witness for the purpose of showing that his character for truthfulness is affected by their nature, an inquiry for the purpose of showing interest or *allowed* bias because of them is not within the prohibition. Thus disclosure of affiliation with a church which is a party to the litigation would be allowable under the rule." Fed.R.Evid. 610 advisory committee's notes. The court admitted testimony that the church consisted of "a group of folks who met in [Thien's] basement, about 30 people...." The court further admitted testimony that Chris and Martina were members of the church of which Thien was the pastor, and that Chris worked for a company owned by Thien and was "close" to Thien. This evidence was properly admitted for the purpose of showing that Chris and Martina may have been biased in favor of Thien through their religious affiliation with him.

The evidence excluded by the court, however, was not probative of Martina's and Chad's bias in favor of Thien. All of the evidence cited in appellant's brief as improperly excluded under Rule 610 concerns a specific tenet of Zion's Endeavor that participation in civil litigation is in violation of biblical law. The Benedicts proposed to introduce testimony regarding this specific tenet as the reason why Martina and Chris were not parties to the state court wrongful death action brought by the Benedicts, and why Chad delayed in joining that action. We fail to see the relevance of this issue to the instant case, and we fail to see how showing that Martina and Chris had religious reasons to decide not to join the wrongful death action shows that they were biased witnesses in the insurance action. The fact that Martina and Chris were members of a small religious group led by Thien, and that met regularly in Thien's basement, was before the jury. This fact is probative of bias, and was admitted. The reasons why Martina and Chris did not join the wrongful death action, and why Chad was late in joining, do not add to a showing of bias, and appear to us to be an attempt to undermine Martina's and Chris's credibility, and to prejudice the jury against them, by painting them as religious extremists.

The district court did not abuse its discretion in excluding detailed examination of the nature of Martina and Chris Benedict's religious beliefs.

————————

Points for Discussion

a. Religious Beliefs to Show Bias of a Witness.

The court held that Martina and Chad's religious beliefs that participating in civil litigation was wrong were not sufficiently relevant to show their bias against the plaintiffs for bringing the lawsuit. Do you agree? Could it not be argued that if their religion disfavored those who brought lawsuits, they might slant their testimony against the plaintiffs?

b. What is a Religious Belief?

The *Fireman's Fund* case makes it clear that Rule 610 is not only designed to protect mainstream religious beliefs but also those that are unconventional. But what if a government witness claims that the defendant and the defendant's testifying witness all belong to a "religious" prison group whose basic tenets are to lie, steal and murder for each other. Could such tenets be classified as "religious beliefs," and would Rule 610 prohibit such testimony to show the witness's bias? See *United States v. Abel*, 469 U.S. 45 (1984).

————————

G. Judges and Jurors as Witnesses

Rule 605. Competency of Judge as Witness

The judge presiding at the trial may not testify in that trial as a witness. No objection need be made in order to preserve the point.

Rule 606. Competency of Juror as Witness

(a) **At the trial.** A member of the jury may not testify as a witness before that jury in the trial of the case in which the juror is sitting. If the juror is called so to testify, the opposing party shall be afforded an opportunity to object out of the presence of the jury.

(b) **Inquiry into validity of verdict or indictment.** Upon an inquiry into the validity of a verdict or indictment, a juror may not testify as to any matter or statement occurring during the course of the jury's deliberations or to the effect of anything upon that or any other juror's mind or emotions as influencing the juror to assent to or dissent from the verdict or indictment or concerning the juror's mental processes in connection therewith. But a juror may testify about (1) whether extraneous prejudicial information was improperly brought to the jury's attention, (2) whether any outside influence was improperly brought to bear upon any juror, or (3) whether there was a mistake in entering the verdict onto the verdict form. A juror's affidavit or evidence of any statement by the juror may not be received on a matter about which the juror would be precluded from testifying.

Federal Rule of Evidence 601 provides that all witnesses are competent to testify "except as provided in these rules." Two of those exceptions are contained in Rule 605 and 606(a), which deem judges and jurors incompetent to testify in a trial where they sit. This is not because their testimony would be unreliable; rather it is because it would carry too much weight with the fact-finder and because opposing counsel might be reluctant to cross-examine them or object to their testimony for fear of giving offense.

Rule 606(b) recognizes a third exception that occurs when a losing party files a motion for new trial based upon jury misconduct. This portion of the rule renders jurors incompetent to give affidavits or testify concerning their mental processes or emotions that may have played a role in their verdict. For example, Rule 606(b) would prohibit a juror from testifying that he did not understand the term "reasonable doubt" in a criminal case, or that he was voting against the plaintiff because he did not like the way she looked. There are two exclusions from this exception. Juror affidavits and testimony may be received if "extraneous prejudicial information" was improperly brought to the attention of the jury, for example, if a juror reads a newspaper article about the trial, or if an "outside influence" was brought to bear upon any juror, such as if a juror was bribed. Although this rule may have unjust results in some cases, there are at least two primary policy reasons for such a prohibition: (1) verdict stability and (2) prevention of juror harassment. Sometimes, however, the cost of refusal to consider egregious juror misconduct can be very high.

Tanner v. United States

Supreme Court of the United States
483 U.S. 107 (1987)

Justice O'CONNOR delivered the opinion of the Court.

[After his conviction for mail fraud, Petitioner filed a motion for new trial and sought leave to interview the jurors in his case on the basis that one juror told petitioner's counsel that the jurors in the trial acted as if they were on "one big party." The juror claimed that he and three other jurors consumed between them "a pitcher to three pitchers" of beer during various recesses, that two other jurors had one or two mixed drinks during the lunch recess, and that one other juror, the presiding juror, consumed a liter of wine on three occasions. He also stated that one juror sold a quarter pound of marijuana to another during the trial, and took marijuana, cocaine, and drug paraphernalia into the courthouse. He noted that some of the jurors were falling asleep during the trial, and that one of the jurors described himself to the juror as "flying."]

[The trial judge refused to conduct an evidentiary hearing to determine whether there was juror misconduct and denied a new trial. The Eleventh Circuit Court of Appeals agreed. The Supreme Court granted certiorari to determine whether an evidentiary hearing during which jurors would testify as to juror alcohol and drug used was barred by Federal Rules of Evidence Rule 606(b) prohibiting juror impeachment of jury verdict, or whether such conduct constituted an "improper outside influence" or "extraneous prejudicial information" as an exception to the rule.]

Lower [common law] courts used [an] external/internal distinction to identify those instances in which juror testimony impeaching a verdict would be admissible. The distinction was not based on whether the juror was literally inside or outside the jury room when the alleged irregularity took place; rather, the distinction was based on the nature of the allegation. Clearly a rigid distinction based only on whether the event took place inside or outside the jury room would have been quite unhelpful. For example, under a distinction based on location a juror could not testify concerning a newspaper read inside the jury room. Instead, of course, this has been considered an external influence about which juror testimony is admissible. Similarly, under a rigid locational distinction jurors could be regularly required to testify after the verdict as to whether they heard and comprehended the judge's instructions, since the charge to the jury takes place outside the jury room. Courts wisely have treated allegations of a juror's inability to hear or comprehend at trial as an internal matter.

Most significant for the present case, however, is the fact that lower federal courts treated allegations of the physical or mental incompetence of a juror as "internal" rather than "external" matters. . . . [Otherwise,] [j]urors would be harassed and beset by the defeated party. [T]he result would be to make what was intended to be a private deliberation, the constant subject of public investigation—to the destruction of all frankness and freedom of discussion and conference." .
. .

There is little doubt that postverdict investigation into juror misconduct would in some instances lead to the invalidation of verdicts reached after irresponsible or improper juror behavior. It is not at all clear, however, that the jury system could survive such efforts to perfect it. Allegations of juror misconduct, incompetency, or inattentiveness, raised for the first time days, weeks, or months after the verdict, seriously disrupt the finality of the process. Moreover, full and frank discussion in the jury room, jurors' willingness to return an unpopular verdict, and the community's trust in a system that relies on the decisions of laypeople would all be undermined by a barrage of postverdict scrutiny of juror conduct.

[P]etitioners argue that substance abuse constitutes an improper "outside influence" about which jurors may testify under Rule 606(b). In our view the language of the Rule cannot easily be stretched to cover this circumstance. However severe their effect and improper their use, drugs or alcohol voluntarily ingested by a juror seems no more an "outside influence" than a virus, poorly prepared food, or a lack of sleep . . . .

Pets argue

In light of these other sources of protection of petitioners' right to a competent jury, we conclude that the District Court did not err in deciding, based on the inadmissibility of juror testimony and the clear insufficiency of the nonjuror evidence offered by petitioners, that an additional post-verdict evidentiary hearing was unnecessary.

SC agreed that no post verdict evidentiary hearing was necessary

Points for Discussion

a. Non-Juror Testimony.

Would non-juror testimony about collective jury intoxication be admissible under Rule 606(b)? See *United States v. Taliaferro*, 558 F.2d 724 (4th Cir. 1977) (the trial court properly considered testimony of a marshal who accompanied jurors to a club as well as club records to show that the jurors were intoxicated during deliberations). Why should it make a difference who testifies to the misconduct?

b. Impeaching the Verdict.

Which, if any, of the following could be used to impeach a jury verdict under Rule 606(b): (1) A juror threatens to assault another juror if the first juror does not agree to a particular verdict; (2) Jurors play "rock, paper, scissors" to determine the verdict; (3) A juror's remark in a criminal case that the juror should "hang him now, so that we can go home"; or (4) a juror's remark to other jurors that he would not follow the judge's instructions and convict the defendant of sexual assault of a minor because he did not believe such conduct should be a crime. As to situation 4, see *United States v. Edwards*, 303 F.3d 606 (5th Cir. 2002).

c. Error in Recording the Verdict.

On December 1, 2006, Rule 606(b) was amended to allow juror testimony to correct any clerical errors and conform the verdict to what was actually decided. According to the Advisory Committee Note, the amendment also specifically rejected the practice of allowing jurors to testify that they misunderstood the consequences of the verdict.

d. Lawyers as Testifying Witnesses.

At common law, if lawyers had a monetary interest in the case they were trying, they were deemed incompetent to testify as would be any witness with such an interest. Of course Rule 601 now renders everyone competent to testify regardless of their interests in the litigation. Nonetheless, Codes of Professional Responsibility and Disciplinary Regulations usually prohibit lawyers from taking a case when they know or should know they will have to testify, unless the testimony relates to an uncontested matter or to the nature and value of legal services the lawyer has rendered in the case, or unless refusal to take the case would work a substantial hardship on the client because of the distinctive value of the lawyer or his firm as counsel in the case. It is generally thought that the role of an advocate and that of a witness are inconsistent, and that lawyers representing parties in the case are more easily discredited as witnesses to the detriment of their clients because of their interest in the lawsuit. See Model Code of Professional Responsibility, EC 5-9 (1980).

H. State Dead Man's Statutes

When state legislatures repealed laws that held persons with an interest in the outcome of a case incompetent to testify, there was still a continuing concern about interested persons testifying and possibly making up facts when a party to the conversation or transaction was deceased. As a result, most states continued to recognize some form of what is called the "Dead Man's" statute, which limits survivor testimony against the deceased in a case where the deceased is a party. The rationale for this limitation, as explained by the common law, was that death has closed the mouth of one party, and the law will close the mouth of the other.

At the federal level, the Advisory Committee to the Federal Rules of Evidence initially proposed that Rule 601 abolish all witness incompetency in federal court, including any federal "Dead Man's" statute. Congress, however, argued that in diversity cases, federal evidentiary law should not override state policies in the area of witness competency. Rule 601 was therefore amended to provide that in a diversity case, the competency law of the state that supplies the rule of decision will control. This means that diversity-based federal trials will recognize state "Dead Man" statutes.

Make the Connection

Recall the famed "Erie" doctrine from Civil Procedure. This doctrine states that in federal court, federal procedural law applies; for federal question cases, federal substantive law applies as well. For diversity cases, however, a federal court applies the substantive law of the state that supplies the rule of decision under the comparative law of the state where the court sits. Rules of competency, like Dead Man Statutes, are considered substantive matters for *Erie* purposes.

The text of Dead Man statutes varies significantly from state to state. Most often, they prohibit the testimony of a party or interested witness concerning any tort, contract, transaction or communication with a decedent even though relevant to the lawsuit. States will occasionally allow such testimony if it is corroborated.

I. Other Prerequisites to Testifying

1. The Oath or Affirmation Requirement

> **Rule 603. Oath or Affirmation**
>
> Before testifying, every witness shall be required to declare that the witness will testify truthfully, by oath or affirmation, administered in a form calculated to awaken the witness' conscience and impress the witness' mind with the duty to do so.

FYI

Normally, a witness is required to swear or affirm that she will "tell the truth, the whole truth, and nothing but the truth." From the authors' trial experiences, this is a promise that is unfortunately broken all too often.

Rule 603 requires that witnesses either take an oath or affirm to tell the truth before testifying. The difference between an oath and an affirmation is that an oath requires swearing to a divine power whereas an affirmation does not. The Advisory Committee Note to this rule states that it is "designed to afford the flexibility required in dealing with religious adults, atheists, conscientious objectors, mental defectives, and children." In any case, the oath or affirmation must be worded so as to impress on the mind of the witness a duty to speak the truth. In other words, some sort of solemn pledge is required.

United States v. Fowler

U.S. Court of Appeals for the Fifth Circuit
605 F.2d 181 (5th Cir. 1979)

GEE, Circuit Judge:

This cause provides eloquent testimony, albeit negative, to the value of counsel's assistance to criminal defendants. Appellant Fowler, a dealer in gravestones and an apparent tax protester among other things, ceased filing federal income tax returns in 1953. A wheel that did not squeak, Fowler's practices at last attracted Revenue's notice in time to result in his indictment for willful failure to file returns for the years 1971-75. During the investigation, he cooperated with investigating revenue agents no further than by providing them with partial records for the years in question. A trial at which the government employed the "bank-deposits" mode of proof resulted in his conviction on all counts, and he appeals.

Fowler, who conducted his own defense at trial but is represented by counsel here, advances seven points of error. Six present little of merit and may be dealt with rather briefly, but the seventh is of slight difficulty. Upon a careful consideration of all, however, we affirm his convictions. . . .

Fowler . . . complains that the court erred in refusing to allow him to testify after he refused either to swear or affirm that he would tell the truth or submit to cross-examination. At one point in their extended colloquy on the point, the judge offered to accept the simple statement, "I state that I will tell the truth in my testimony." Fowler was willing to do no more than laud himself in such remarks as, "I am a truthful man," and "I would not tell a lie to stay out of jail." Rule 603, Federal Rules of Evidence, is clear and simple: "Before testifying, every witness shall be required to declare that he will testify truthfully, by oath or affirmation . . . ." No witness has the right to testify but on penalty of perjury and subject to cross-examination. This contention is frivolous....

We cannot doubt that Fowler has derived substantial financial benefit from a long refusal to carry his share of the common burdens of citizenship. Sad to say, for he is a man no longer young, he must now respond not only in currency but in another coin: incarceration. Counsel's efforts on his behalf are commendable, but they came too late.

AFFIRMED.

Points for Discussion

a. The Flexibility of the Oath or Affirmation.

In *United States v. Looper*, 419 F.2d 1405, 1407 n.4 (4th Cir. 1969), the court remarked that "English courts have permitted Chinese to break a saucer, a Mohammedan to bow before the Koran and touch it to his head and a Parsee to tie a rope around his waist to qualify them to tell the truth." Why, then, was it not sufficient in *Fowler* for the defendant to state that he was a truthful man and would not lie to stay out of jail as an alternative to taking an oath or giving an affirmation?

FYI

A Parsee is a member of a Zoroastrian community based primarily in India.

b. A Witness's Refusal to be Sworn.

If a witness refuses to take an oath or affirmation, may that witness be held in contempt? See Note, *A Reconsideration of the Sworn Testimony Requirement: Securing Truth in the Twentieth Century*, 75 Mich. L. Rev. 1681 (1977), citing state and foreign cases in support of holding a witness in contempt for refusal to be sworn.

——————————

2. The Personal Knowledge Requirement

> **Rule 602. Personal Knowledge**
>
> A witness may not testify to a matter unless evidence is introduced sufficient to support a finding that the witness has personal knowledge of the matter. Evidence to prove personal knowledge may, but need not consist of the witness' own testimony. This rule is subject to the provisions of Rule 703, relating to opinion testimony by expert witnesses.

Rule 602, which requires a fact witness to have personal knowledge of the subject matter of his testimony, is not a rule of competency. Competency refers to the qualification of person to be a witness at all; whereas, a witness's lack of personal knowledge does not generally disqualify him from being a witness. Rather, it limits the scope of his testimony.

What does having personal knowledge mean? Generally, it means knowledge perceived by the physical senses, such as sight, hearing, touch, smell or taste, or is a reasonable inference therefrom. For example in *United States v. Santana,* 342 F.3d 60 (1st Cir. 2003), it was found proper for the trial court to admit lay witness testimony that the contents of a package were marijuana when he smelled it because he was familiar with the smell of marijuana through his work. The requirement of personal knowledge is one of conditional relevance under Rule 104(b). That is, if challenged, the proponent of the witness's testimony must introduce evidence to support a finding by a reasonable juror that the witness had personal knowledge. The evidence may come from the witness herself, other witnesses, or the factual circumstances of the case. For example, in a slip and fall case, a witness may be asked preliminary questions that demonstrate he was coming out of a restaurant when the plaintiff fell and that he observed the fall. Or, other witnesses may testify to his presence.

McCrary-El v. Shaw

U.S. Court of Appeals for the Eighth Circuit
992 F.2d 809 (8th Cir. 1993)

MORRIS SHEPPARD ARNOLD, Circuit Judge.

Appellant Jerry McCrary-El is currently serving a life sentence plus 35 years in Farmington, Missouri (FCC), for assault with intent to kill with malice aforethought, first-degree arson, and carrying a concealed weapon. He claims that correctional center employees used excessive force against him in violation of 42 U.S.C. § 1983. After a three-day trial, the Hon. David D. Noce presiding, the jury found for the officers. McCrary-El filed a motion for a new trial, which was denied, and this appeal followed.

McCrary-El was housed in the administrative segregation wing of FCC, which holds those inmates considered to be especially dangerous, violent, and aggressive. The appellees/officers were operating pursuant to standard FCC policy that requires two or more officers to be present when any cell in that housing wing is being opened. McCrary-El alleges that he was housed in a one-man cell and the officers tried to force him to take a cell-mate, which he refused to do. He claims that the officers grabbed him around the legs, arm, head, and neck and that they picked him up and slammed him onto the concrete floor of the cell, thus injuring his back, shoulders, and neck. He further asserts that appellee Courtney began punching him in the side while Mills held him in a headlock and began twisting his neck. McCrary-El states that he was placed in handcuffs and leg shackles and dragged to another cell.

The officers claim, however, that when they instructed McCrary-El to move to the back of his cell so that his cell-mate could enter, McCrary-El refused and remained in the cell doorway. They assert that McCrary-El shoved Officer Shaw as soon as the cell door was opened, and they therefore entered the cell immediately and restrained McCrary-El by established procedures. The officers assert that McCrary-El did not complain of any pain at the time, but instead cursed the officers. They argue that they used only the force necessary to restrain McCrary-El and remove him from the cell so that another inmate could take up residence with him. It is undisputed that, when the officers returned McCrary-El to his cell during the second cell movement, they wore protective gear including padding, helmets, and visors.

For his first argument, McCrary-El claims that the trial court erred by forbidding him to read Antonio Jones's deposition into evidence. He claims that Jones was in the cell next to his and witnessed the confrontation between the officers and him. McCrary-El argues that, while Jones admittedly could not see everything from his cell, he saw enough to meet the requirements of Fed.Rule of Evid. 602. The trial court ruled, however, that Jones "had an inability to testify about what [was] relevant and at issue in this lawsuit."

Rule 602 states, "A witness may not testify to a matter unless evidence is introduced sufficient to support a finding that he has personal knowledge of the matter. Evidence to prove personal knowledge may, but need not, consist of the testimony of the witness himself ..." The trial court heard Jones testify that there was a crack at the corner of his cell door that was about an inch and a half, through which he witnessed McCrary-El's assault. He also testified that he could see into the cell only until all the officers were inside. The trial court saw a diagram of the cell placement and heard Jones testify as to the space through which he could see, as well as to what he allegedly did see. After weighing the evidence, the trial court had the discretion to determine whether Jones qualified under Rule 602. Rule 602 excludes "testimony concerning matter the witness did not observe or had no opportunity to observe." We cannot say that the trial court abused its discretion in determining that no reasonable person could conclude that Jones was able to see anything of relevance. There was therefore no error in excluding his testimony.

For the reasons stated, the trial court is affirmed in all respects.

Points for Discussion

a. The Personal Knowledge Requirement and Hearsay.

Notice the interplay in *McCrary-El* between the personal knowledge requirement and the rule against admitting hearsay in the case. If witness Jones did not see what occurred when the altercation took place, the opponent should object on the basis that Jones lacked personal knowledge. If the defendant McCrary-El were to testify that Jones told him about what he saw during the altercation, and the defendant wanted to repeat that conversation in court, the proper objection is hearsay. A lack of personal knowledge is also the basis of an objection to a question that "calls for speculation" when the answer is not based on personal perception.

Make the Connection

Hearsay is an out of court statement offered for the truth of the matter alleged in the statement. See Federal Rule of Evidence 801 (a)–(c). The hearsay rule, its exemptions and its exceptions are covered in Chapter 6 of this book.

b. The Basis of Personal Knowledge.

The trial judge must admit a witness's testimony even though the witness is not positive about what he saw as long as he had the opportunity to perceive it. In *United States v. Franklin,* 415 F.3d 537 (6th Cir. 2005), for example, a witness was allowed to testify as to a conversation he overheard even though he was intoxicated when he heard it. The court stated that the threshold for having personal knowledge is very low. If the threshold is so low, why then did the trial court in *McCracy-El* find lack of personal knowledge? Could it be that the trial court believed that Jones' ability to observe was a physical impossibility?

c. Personal Knowledge and Expert Testimony.

The last sentence of Rule 602 recognizes that expert witnesses may testify to facts that they did not perceive with their own senses under Rule 703. Expert witnesses are covered in Chapter 12.

Practice Pointer

Witnesses at trial will sometimes testify that a particular fact occurred or that they "learned" that a fact occurred from their investigation even though they have no personal knowledge of it. The opponent of the witness must take special care to find out whether the witness was told about the fact, in which case the testimony may be hearsay, or whether the witness observed or inferred the fact from personal perception. Even though the witness is otherwise in the middle of testifying when statements such as these occur, the opponent should ask the judge if she can immediately question the witness to determine whether the witness has personal knowledge for purpose of objection. This is also known as "taking the witness on voir dire."

Executive Summary

General Rule of Witness Competency

Under Rule 601, all witnesses are presumed qualified to testify. Therefore, all traditional common law disqualifications have been eliminated, although they are still available to attack a witness's credibility. As a result, competency is now largely a weight, rather than an admissibility, issue. However, in diversity cases, Rule 601 requires the federal court to apply any applicable state law disqualifications during trial, such as state Dead Man's statutes.

Mental Incompetence of a Witness

Mentally incompetent individuals (whether by substance abuse, medical, or psychological infirmity) may be permitted to testify, provided the judge determines that the individual is not so impaired that he cannot understand what the truth is and generally can remember and explain events. (*Roach*).

Child Witnesses

There is no statutory threshold age below which a child is not permitted to testify. Instead, it depends upon the individual child's ability to understand the difference between the truth and a lie ("make-believe") and the ability to remember and explain events. (*Wheeler*).

Previously Hypnotized Witnesses

The viability of these individuals as competent witnesses is not yet clearly defined either by our courts or by our rules. There is a concern that the witness can be easily influenced by the hypnotist's suggestions, and actual memories can be confabulated with unsubstantiated dreams or other various thoughts that never actually occurred. However, there is some constitutional protection for criminal defendant witnesses to use this kind of testimony on their behalf to defend themselves, but such is not necessarily available for a non-criminal defendant witness. (*Rock*).

A Witness's Religious Beliefs

Under Rule 610, a witness's religious beliefs, or lack thereof, cannot be used to attack or bolster the witness's general credibility. This represents the elimination of the common law competency disqualification of atheists or agnostics as witnesses. However, religious beliefs can be used for other purposes, such as possibly exposing a particular bias of a witness. (*Firemen's Fund*).

Judges and Jurors as Witnesses

Under Rules 605 and 606(a), judges and jurors are incompetent to serve as witnesses in a case in which they are serving given that their testimony would carry too much weight and opposing counsel might be reluctant to cross-examine them. However, after a verdict is rendered, a former juror may be called in a later proceeding attacking or supporting the former verdict under Rule 606(b), provided the juror testifies about "extraneous prejudicial information," an "improper influence" on the jury, or a clerical error in transcribing the verdict form. Note that "internal" influences, even seemingly large, illegitimate influences (such as jurors drinking and taking drugs during trial) are still considered "internal;" therefore, in such cases, a former juror would be incompetent to testify and the verdict will not be upset on appeal. (*Tanner*). The policy concern is to preserve verdict stability and prevent harassment of former jurors.

Oath or Affirmation

Under Rule 603, witnesses must be willing to declare that they will testify truthfully by oath or affirmation administered in such a way as to awaken the witness's conscience regarding their duty to tell the truth under penalty of perjury. There is no "official" oath, the witness simply needs to recognize the importance of telling the truth. (*Fowler*). Accordingly, the court has a great deal of discretion in formulating the particular words used for the oath for any witness.

Personal Knowledge

Under Rule 602, a witness is qualified to testify only regarding those matters about which the witness has personal knowledge. Thus, a witness may be competent to testify in general, but that competency is limited by the scope of the witness's personal knowledge. Although there are various exceptions to this rule, such as Rule 702 expert testimony, Rule 404(a) and Rule 608 character testimony, and various Rule 803 and 804 hearsay exceptions; generally a witness can testify only to the extent of their personal knowledge – that is, the extent to which they actually perceived something first hand in the case. (*McCrary-El*).

CHAPTER 5

Witnesses

After opening statement comes the presentation of witness testimony. The party with the overall burden of

Make the Connection

See Chapter 2 for the order of events at trial.

FYI

Generally, direct examination refers to the questioning of a witness who is called by the questioner. This also assumes that the witness will be friendly – or at least not hostile – towards the questioner. When the questioner has called a witness who is hostile – the questioner may ask the court's permission to treat the witness as hostile which will result in the questions falling under the rules of cross-examination.

proof in the case presents witnesses first, the prosecution in a criminal case and almost always the plaintiff in a civil case. The established protocol is for the party calling the witness to conduct a direct examination, the opposing party then to conduct a cross-examination, and the original party thereafter to conduct a redirect examination.

A. Direct Examination and Cross Examination

Rule 611. Mode and Order of Interrogation and Presentation

(a) **Control by the court.** The court shall exercise reasonable control over the mode and order of interrogating witnesses and presenting evidence so as to (1) make the interrogation and presentation effective for the ascertainment of the truth, (2) avoid needless consumption of time, and (3) protect witnesses from harassment or undue embarrassment.

(b) **Scope of cross-examination.** Cross-examination should be limited to the subject matter of the direct examination and matters affecting the credibility of the witness. The court may, in the exercise of discretion, permit inquiry into additional matters as if on direct examination.

> **(c) Leading Questions.** Leading Questions should not be used on the direct examination of a witness except as may be necessary to develop the witness's testimony. Ordinarily leading questions should be permitted on cross-examination. When a party calls a hostile witness, an adverse party, or a witness identified with an adverse party, interrogation may be by leading questions.

1. Direct Examination

The function of a direct examination is to present through witness testimony a mosaic of facts which tells a coherent story in support of a party's case. There are several formalities to observe when conducting a direct examination. Normally, a direct examination requires that a lawyer ask questions that call for short, factual answers. Asking a question that invites a witness to respond with a lengthy answer is called "asking for a narrative response" (for example, "Tell me everything you did that morning"). Narrative responses are discouraged because they often solicit irrelevant evidence, and they do not allow the opponent sufficient time to object, although they may be allowed in the trial judge's discretion.

FYI

Rule 611(c) is, however, is phrased to allow the trial court discretion to permit a lawyer to lead a witness on direct examination on some occasions. These occasions include questioning a witness about preliminary uncontested matters, examining a child witnesses or any witness whose memory is exhausted, or questioning an adverse or hostile witness. An adverse or hostile witness is one who is an opposing party or identified with an opposing party.

Rule 611(c) also generally prohibits a lawyer from leading a witness on direct examination, that is, prohibits asking questions that suggest the answer the witness should give. For example, "Isn't it cold outside?" would be a leading and objectionable question on direct examination. Non-leading questions are those that do not suggest the answer. Most non-leading questions begin with the words, "who," "what," "where," "when," "why," and "how." "What is the weather like today?" would be a permissible non-leading question.

The following example illustrates the direct examination of a witness to an automobile accident. Notice several things about this questioning. (1) How the lawyer sets up and directs the witness and then slowly draws out the story piece by piece, without having the witness tell his story all at once; (2) How the lawyer presents the witness's testimony in a logical, understandable and organized manner and occasionally summarizes important testimony in order to emphasize it; (3) How questions are short and open-ended and often preceded by the words "who," "what," "where," "when," "why," and "how."

Q. Mr. Witness, **where** were you standing when the collision occurred?

A. I was standing on Main and Fifth Streets.

Q. **Why** were you there?

A. I was trying to get to work.

Q. **Where** do you work?

A. At First National Bank, on 5th Street.

Q. **What** direction were you facing when you saw the accident?

A. I was facing Main Street. Fifth Street crosses Main Street to my right.

Q. **What**, if anything, was blocking your view?

A. Nothing was blocking my view.

Q. **What** time was it when the accident occurred?

A. About 10 a.m.

Q. Now let's talk about the automobile collision you saw. **When** did you first see the plaintiff?

A. I saw him when I got to the intersection.

Q. **Where** were you when you saw him?

A. I was facing north, walking on Main Street.

Q. **What** direction was he traveling?

A. From North to South on 5th Street, coming from straight ahead of me, about 100 feet from the intersection.

Q. **When** did you first see the defendant?

A. He was headed east on Main Street, about 200 feet from the intersection.

Q. **What** did you see next?

A. The defendant was approaching the intersection and wasn't slowing down. He had the red light.

Q. **How** do you know he had the red light?

A. I saw it because the cross-walk sign said I could walk, but he wasn't stopping. So I looked carefully to see what color his light was.

Q. So, after you saw the defendant had the red light and saw him speeding toward the intersection, **what** happened next?

A. The defendant kept coming toward the intersection and then finally slammed on his brakes, but it was too late. He ran into the plaintiff's car.

Q. **Where** was the plaintiff's car at the time the defendant hit him?

A. In the middle of the intersection. He had the green light at the time. . . .

2. Cross-Examination

In the words of Wigmore, cross-examination is "the greatest engine ever invented for discovery of truth." 5 J. Wigmore, Evidence § 1367, p. 32 (J. Chadbourn rev. 1974)). From a practicing lawyer's standpoint, it is the means by which she can attack the credibility of a witness, diminish any harmful effect

FYI
John Henry Wigmore was an American jurist and expert in the law of evidence. He was born in 1863 and died in 1943. His rules of evidence are used by many United States courts and his treatise on evidence, originally published in 1904, is often quoted.

of the witness's direct testimony, and obtain information that may be favorable to the cross-examiner. All of these goals are made attainable because Rule 611(c) permits a cross-examiner to use leading questions that allow her to direct the questioning of a witness effectively and press a less than friendly witness into admissions.

a. The Scope of Cross-Examination. The scope of cross-examination is limited by Rule 611(b) to the subject matter of direct examination and matters affecting the credibility of the witness. The Advisory Committee Notes to Rule 611(b) state that the purpose of the limited scope of cross-examination is to "promote orderly presentation of the case." In other words, the rule allows a party to present her case as a whole by producing evidence that supports only those issues on which she has the burden of proof. For example, if the prosecution in a criminal case wants to present a witness who will testify only as to the facts of the crime, the defense attorney should not be permitted to cross-examine the witness concerning the defendant's claim of insanity. If the defense lawyer wants the prosecution's witness to testify as to the defendant's insanity, he must recall the prosecution's witness during the defense's case-in chief and conduct a direct examination of that witness (i.e. he cannot lead the witness).

For More Information

An excellent resource for those interested in honing their cross-examination skills is *Cross-Examination: Science and Techniques, 2d (2004)* by Larry S. Pozner and Roger J. Dodd.

It is difficult at times to determine at what point cross-examination goes beyond the scope of direct. If, on direct examination of an insurance agent, he is asked merely to authenticate certain insurance policies, could the opponent cross-examine by inquiring into the basis for the figures in those policies? In *United States v. Wolfson,* 573 F.2d 216 (5th Cir. 1978), the trial could held that such questioning was beyond the scope of direct, but the appeal court found to the contrary. See also *United States v. Roberts,* 14 F.3d 502 (10th Cir. 1993) (prosecution could cross-examine a defendant as to his ability to direct drug sales during the time period surrounding his arrest because the defendant had testified he was not rational when he was arrested).

b. Strategies of Cross Examination. A witness's credibility may be challenged by focusing on four "targets" so to speak: (a) the witness's perception, (b) memory, (c) communication of the story, and (d) the witness's own truthfulness.

(1) Perception. A witness's credibility may be undermined by casting doubt on the witness's ability to perceive what he claims to have witnessed. Assume in the following that the defendant has been charged with stealing a briefcase from the victim.

Q: The person who stole your briefcase approached you from behind, right?

A: Yes.

Q: You were startled, weren't you, that a stranger grabbed your briefcase?

Make the Connection

Notice that effective cross-examination attempts to limit answers to "yes" and "no."

A: Yes, that's true.

Q: It was after midnight when this theft that startled you took place, wasn't it?

A: Yes.

Q: There wasn't a street light for at least three blocks, was there?

A: No, there wasn't.

Q: After he ran up from behind you and suddenly grabbed the briefcase from your hand, he immediately began running away from you, correct?

A: Yes.

Q: Isn't it true that as he ran away, you saw only the back of his head, not his face?

A: Well, yes.

Q: So late one evening on a dark night, this person came up from behind you, abruptly snatched your briefcase, and then immediately ran away, so that you only saw his face, if at all, for only a split second, right?

A: Yes. But...

Q: Thank you, no further questions.

(2) Memory. If a witness has difficulty remembering an incident, or a particular set of circumstances, then that witness' credibility can be called into question. Although his recollection may be refreshed under Rule 612, the very fact that a witness' recollection of events would need refreshing raises concern about the reliability of the testimony. The next illustration

FYI

The use of Rule 612 to refresh a testifying witness's memory with a writing is discussed in the next subsection of this chapter.

demonstrates an attack on the memory of a police officer witness in a drunk driving case.

Q: Officer, you arrested the defendant for suspicion of drunk driving nearly nine months ago, correct?

A. Yes.

Q. During the last nine months, you have made over two hundred traffic stops of drivers suspected of driving under the influence, right?

A: That's about right.

Q: Now for each of those stops, about half of the time you conduct a field sobriety test, and the rest of the time you do not, is that right?

A: Yeah.

Q: You did not write down whether you gave a test in this case, did you?

A: No. It may not be in the report, but I remember I gave him a test.

Q: You also do not remember which type of test you supposedly gave, do you?

A. No, it was some kind of field sobriety test though.

Q. Then it's your testimony that you don't remember what kind of test you gave him, isn't that correct?

A. Well I guess so.

Q. And isn't it true that you cannot tell us how my client performed on any such test because you can't tell us what kind of test it was?

A. Well, maybe.

Q: Thank you, no more questions.

(3) *Communication.* Even if a witness adequately perceived and can sufficiently recall an event, she may not be able to explain or effectively communicate those events. Similarly, if the witness's "story" does not make sense, is contradictory, logically impossible, or implausible, then she can be impeached on that basis. The following illustration demonstrates this type of impeachment technique. Assume the defendant, Mr. Jones, is charged with illegally accessing child pornography on the internet. The prosecution has submitted authenticated computer records showing all of the illegal child pornography websites visited by the defendant's work computer over a certain period of time and all e-mail activity of that computer for the same period.

Q: Mr. Jones, you have admitted that your computer was used to access various child pornography web sites, is that right?

A: Yes, but someone set me up just to make me look bad.

Q: Isn't it also true that the records contain the list of websites visited, the time of day those sites were visited, and all e-mail messages sent and received by your computer?

A: Yes, I can see that. OK.

Q: So, on January 23, 2009, at 1:01 p.m., the record shoes that computer accessed, "Children Exposed," an illegal website, until 1:07 p.m. I read that correctly, didn't I?

A: Yes, you did.

Q: And don't the records indicate that at 1:07 p.m., you sent an e-mail to your wife, Sally Jones?

A: That's what it says, yes.

Q: And the substance of the e-mail was that you were telling her to call your mother?

A: Yes.

Q: Isn't it true, Mr. Jones, that the very next entry on the computer record at 1:09 p.m., right after the e-mail to your wife, is a search on Google for "naked pics of kids"?

A: OK, alright, it says that, but you still can't prove it was me doing those searches.

Q: But it was you who conducted these searches on your computer, wasn't it?

A: Look, I know it sounds crazy, but I think I remember leaving my office for something, I often do that at work, and then someone must have snuck back into my office and got on my computer.

Q: Your secretary has never reported any strangers going into your office, and then quickly leaving, when you were not there, has she?

A: Well, then, they must have had disguises, as janitors or something; plus, the people in the office are busy, maybe they didn't notice.

Q: No further questions.

(4) *Veracity.* A witness's truthfulness may be challenged (1) by exposing a witness's personal or financial bias, thereby offering a reason for the witness to deceive; (2) by contradicting a witness's testimony by confronting him with his own prior inconsistent statement, thereby revealing at least one, if not both statements, to be false; and (3) by challenging his character for honesty, in effect demonstrating an untruthful nature such that the witness is not worthy of belief because she has a propensity to lie.

c. Cross-Examination Tactics. Although there are as many techniques for cross-examination as there are trial lawyers, there are some basic rules that most follow. A skilled cross-examiner, for example, will usually make an assertion of fact and then ask the witness to respond with a "yes" or "no" answer. These questions are narrowly crafted to avoid a long witness explanation because the more that a witness explains, the more control the cross-examiner loses over the questioning. For example, it is not a good idea to ask a witness, "Why did you go to the plaintiff's house that evening?" It is a better idea to ask, "Didn't you go to the plaintiff's house because you wanted to steal her jewelry?" Questions used on direct examination are generally too open-ended for cross-examination.

Another cross-examination pitfall to avoid, which has (unfortunately) happened to all trial lawyers at some point in their careers, is asking questions to which you do not know the answer, as the following example demonstrates:

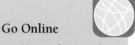

Go Online

Professor Irving Younger has provided trial lawyers with a useful list of "dos" and "don'ts" of cross-examination entitled, *The Ten Commandments of Cross-Examination.* Included in this list is advice to be brief and ask short questions, use simple language, ask only leading questions, know the answer before you ask the question and others. His discussion of these commandments is a must-see for trial lawyers.

> Q. Officer, did you see my client fleeing the scene?
>
> A. No sir, but I subsequently observed a person matching the description of the offender, running several blocks away.
>
> Q. Officer, who provided this description?
>
> A. The officer who responded to the scene.
>
> Q. A fellow officer provided the description of this so-called offender? Do you trust your fellow officers?
>
> A. Yes sir, with my life.
>
> Q. Well, if you trust your officers with your life, why is it that you have locks on your lockers at the police station?
>
> A. You see, sir, we share the building with the court complex and sometimes defense lawyers like yourself have been known to walk through the locker room.

3. Refreshing a Witness's Memory

Rule 612. Writing Used to Refresh Memory

Except as otherwise provided in criminal proceedings by section 3500 of title 18, United States Code, if a witness uses a writing to refresh memory for the purpose of testifying either—

(1) while testifying, or

(2) before testifying, if the court in its discretion determines it is necessary in the interests of justice, an adverse party is entitled to have the writing produced at the hearing, to inspect it, to cross-examine the witness thereon, and to introduce in evidence those portions which relate to the testimony of the witness. If it is claimed that the writing contains matters not related to the subject matter of the testimony the court shall examine the writing in camera, excise any portions not so related, and order delivery of the remainder to the party entitled thereto. Any portion withheld over objections shall be preserved and made available to the appellate court in the event of an appeal. If a writing is not produced or delivered pursuant to order under this rule, the court shall make any order justice requires, except that in criminal cases when the prosecution elects not to comply, the order shall be one striking the testimony of, if the court in its discretion determines that the interests of justice so require, declaring a mistrial.

No matter how extensively a lawyer prepares her witness to testify, the witness may sometime forget facts when being questioned at trial. Often this occurs because the witness is nervous or frightened or because she is trying to remember information that is detailed or voluminous. A lawyer may assist the witness's memory by showing her a writing that contains the facts she has forgotten. Because it is being used only as a memory stimulus, the writing need not have been authored by the witness and need not be admissible in evidence.

In the profession, preparing a witness for testifying is often called "woodshedding" the witness. It consists of talking to the witness before he testifies and instructing him about the proper method of responding to questions while giving testimony. Woodshedding is not the same as the unethical behavior of coaching witnesses which is putting words in their mouths.

Rule 612 of the Federal Rules of Evidence governs the process for refreshing a witness's memory with a written statement. The rule requires that the proponent of the evidence show the writing to opposing counsel and wait for an objection. If there is no objection or all objections are overruled, the proponent then shows the writing to the witness and asks her to read it silently to herself. After reading the document, the proponent instructs the witness to put it face down or return it to the proponent.

Practice Pointer

The opponent should make sure the writing is inaccessible to the witness while testifying, which can be done by insisting the writing be placed face down or out of sight. Some witnesses like to keep the writing in view so they can continually consult it. This increases the risk that the witness will answer questions by referring to facts in the document, not by referring to the witness's own memory. It also harms the credibility of the witness.

If the writing successfully jogs the witness's memory, the witness then testifies from that refreshed memory. If not, the proponent will usually attempt to get the writing into evidence and overcome any hearsay objections by arguing the writing falls under a hearsay exception, most often the one for Past Recollection Recorded, Rule 803(5). The number of times a witness may refresh her memory with a writing is discretionary with the judge and may be allowed to a greater degree when there are a large number of detailed facts for the witness to remember, when considerable time has passed between the event and the testimony, or the witness's age and capacity to relate events is questionable. Rule 612 also requires that the opponent be given an opportunity to cross-examine the witness with the document and "introduce portions that relate to the testimony of the witness."

Doty v. Elias

U.S. Court of Appeals for the Tenth Circuit
733 F.2d 720 (10th Cir. 1984)

LOGAN, Circuit Judge.

Becky Doty, Vicky Doty, David Price, and Roy Price brought this action against Eddy Elias under the Fair Labor Standards Act alleging that Elias violated the Act's minimum wage and overtime compensation provisions. Plaintiffs formerly worked as waitresses or waiters at Eddy's Steakhouse, a restaurant Elias owns and operates. None of the plaintiffs received an hourly wage or salary while working at the restaurant. Instead, Elias permitted plaintiffs to keep all of the tips they received. After a bench trial, the district court found that plaintiffs were Elias' employees within the meaning of the Act and that Elias had violated the Act's minimum wage provisions.

The court awarded plaintiffs unpaid wages and prejudgment interest but refused to award liquidated damages. Both parties appealed. The issues we address are . . . (4) whether the trial court erred in computing the number of hours plaintiffs worked. . .

Elias argues that the trial court committed reversible error by permitting Becky Doty and Vicky Doty to refer to notes during their testimony. Several months after the Dotys stopped working at the restaurant, a representative of the United States Department of Labor asked the Dotys to compile a schedule of the times they had worked for Elias. Using a calendar and relying largely upon memory, they did so. Plaintiffs did not offer the schedules

Food for Thought

Is there anything the opponent could have done to better preserve his error on this point? What if the witnesses were not testifying from their refreshed memory but rather from having memorized the contents of the writing? How could the opponent prove this to the trial judge?

into evidence or read them into the record. However, the trial court permitted the Dotys to refer to the schedules occasionally during their testimony. Elias argues that the Dotys' testimony from the schedules was inadmissible because it constituted hearsay under Fed.R.Evid. 801(c) and did not fall within the hearsay exception for past recollection recorded, Fed.R.Evid. 803(5).

Plaintiffs, on the other hand, contend that the trial court properly permitted the Dotys to refer to the schedules to refresh their memories as Fed.R.Evid. 612 permits.

After carefully reviewing the record, we conclude that the trial court permitted the Dotys to use their notes during their testimony merely to refresh their memories. Thus, the testimony was not hearsay, and we need to consider whether the hearsay exception for past recollection recorded applies. . . . "The primary difference between [refreshed recollection and past recollection recorded] is the ability of the witness to testify from present knowledge; where the witness' memory is revived, and he presently recollects the facts and swears to them, he is obviously in a different position from the witness who cannot directly state the facts from present memory and who must ask the court to accept a writing for the truth of its contents because he is willing to swear, for one reason or another, that its contents are true." . . .

Make the Connection

The hearsay exception for past recollection recorded is discussed in Chapter 6. One of the predicates for the exception is that the witness has insufficient recollection to enable him to testify fully and accurately.

The trial judge enjoys broad discretion in determining whether a witness is using a writing to refresh memory or offering a writing for the truth of something the witness can no longer recall. Both at the time they compiled the schedules and at the time of trial the Dotys apparently recalled the number of weeks they worked for defendant and approximately how many hours per week they worked. The schedules merely helped them recall quickly, without repetition of the mental process of organizing their memories, the approximate dates of specific occurrences. The trial court understood that the schedules were approximations from memory and it treated them as such. Thus, we hold that the trial court did not abuse its discretion in permitting the Dotys to refer to the writings.

———————

Points for Discussion

a. How to Refresh a Witness's Memory.

The following is an illustration of how the plaintiffs' lawyer in *Doty* might have refreshed Mrs. Doty's memory under Rule 612:

Q. Mrs. Doty, how many hours did you work for Eddy Elias during the week of July 10th?

A. Well I just don't remember. That was quite some time ago.

Q. Did you make a schedule listing the days and times you worked for Mr. Elias during the month of July?

A. Yes, I did.

Q. Would seeing that schedule now refresh your memory as to the number of hours you worked that week?

A. Yes, I think it would.

Q. May I approach the witness, your honor?

[Judge] Yes, you may.

Q. May the record reflect that I am showing Plaintiff's Exhibit 5 to opposing counsel for inspection?

[Judge] Any objections?

[Opposing counsel] No, your honor.

[Judge] The record will so reflect.

Q. I am now showing you Plaintiff's Exhibit 5. What is this document?

A. This is a listing of the hours I worked for Eddie during the month of July.

Q. Would you please read this document silently to yourself. When you are finished, place the document face down in front of you.

A. Yes, ok.

Q. Do you now remember how many hours you worked the week of July 10th for Mr. Elias?

A. Yes.

Q. Do you now remember how many hours it was?

A. Yes. I worked 45 hours that week.

Do you think it is credible to a jury that Mrs. Doty's memory was refreshed by this process, or do you think she was testifying from having memorized the document?

b. Is a Witness's Credibility Harmed by Having His Memory Refreshed?

Is the credibility of the witnesses in *Doty* lessened because they needed to refresh their memories in order to recall the dates and hours they worked? Is this an instance where a jury would understand a witness's memory loss? Is forgetting dates and hours worked different than forgetting the important facts of a traffic accident?

c. The Mandatory and Permissive Provisions of Rule 612.

A witness may use a writing to refresh his memory prior to testifying at trial or on the witness stand while testifying. If the writing is used to refresh prior to trial, the opponent has an absolute right to have a copy of the writing, cross-examine the witness regarding it, and introduce portions of it into evidence for impeachment purposes. However, if the witness uses the writing to refresh her memory during questioning at trial, disclosure is discretionary with the judge. Some trial judges exercise that discretion by excluding privileged or work-product materials from being inspected. See *Carter-Wallace, Inc. v. Hartz Mountain Indus., Inc.*, 553 F. Supp. 45 (S.D.N.Y. 1982) (the court refused to allow documents containing privileged and work-product material used to prepare witnesses for a deposition to be disclosed, even though there was a danger that exclusion could create selective memories on the part of the witnesses).

B. Impeachment of a Witness

Impeaching a witness means to discredit him for being untruthful in some manner. There are a number of ways to do this, but the ones covered in this Chapter include impeachment by showing the witness's character for untruthfulness, prior convictions, prior inconsistent statements, and bias. But first, we will discuss several general impeachment concepts.

1. General Impeachment Guidelines: Impeaching a Party's Own Witness

Under the common law, a party who called a witness to testify was understood to vouch for the witness's truthfulness. His lawyer was prohibited from impeaching the witness except when the witness was hostile or adverse, or when his lawyer could claim his side was damaged by unexpected testimony. Rule 607 did away with this common law rule. A lawyer may now impeach any witness, including those she calls to the witness stand. When the common law tradition was abolished by Rule 607, however, the possibility of using the rule as a subterfuge to admit otherwise inadmissible hearsay became an issue.

United States v. Morlang

U.S. Court of Appeals for the Fourth Circuit
531 F.2d 183 (4th Cir. 1975)

Conspiracy to bribe

[Appellant Morlang was convicted for conspiracy to bribe the Director of the Federal Housing Administration in connection with an FHA insured housing project.]

The next issue concerns the prosecution's use of an out-of-court statement which was purportedly made by one of its own witnesses, Fred Wilmoth. Wilmoth was called by the government as its first witness despite the fact that it was fully aware that his testimony would tend to exonerate Morlang from participation in the bribery although damning against Ballard and Barron as well as Wilmoth himself. The real purpose for calling Wilmoth was apparently to elicit from him a denial that he had ever had any conversation with a fellow prisoner in which he implicated Morlang. (The government freely admits that it was in no way surprised when Wilmoth's testimony did not implicate Morlang. It is of more than passing interest that the statement attributed to Wilmoth by Crist did not relate to any of the facts of the case, or to the bribes, which are at the heart of the controversy, but was a conclusory statement from which could only be inferred Morlang's guilt. It was: 'One of us had to take the rap so the other one could stay out and take care of the business.' The 'other one' was first identified by Crist as either Morlang or Haught, and immediately following as both of them. Crist testified the statement was made while he and Wilmoth were fellow prisoners in jail.)

Having obtained such a denial, the prosecution called Raymond Crist, the man to whom the out-of-court statement was allegedly made. Crist was, at that time, an inmate at the federal correctional institution at Ashland, Kentucky, and had spent more than half his adult life in prison for a series of convictions extending back to 1941, which included grand larceny, auto theft, breaking and entering, and Dyer Act. The court permitted the testimony of Crist to be introduced only for the purpose of attacking the credibility of Wilmoth.

testimony to attack credibility of Wilmoth

We are of opinion that the court erred in permitting the prior statement of Wilmoth to be introduced. While it is the rule in this circuit that a party calling a witness does not vouch for his credibility, it has never been the rule that a party may call a witness where his testimony is known to be adverse for the purpose of impeaching him. To so hold would permit the government, in the name of impeachment, to present testimony to the jury by indirection which would not otherwise be admissible. The courts have consistently refused to sanction such a practice.

TC erred in permitting prior statement of Wilson to be introduced.

The government, however, urges that the introduction of this testimony was proper under our holding in *United States v. Lineberger*, 444 F.2d 122 (4th Cir. 1971), where, in a per curiam opinion, we noted that some authorities have permitted a defendant under certain circumstances to impeach his own witness. In so doing, we cited Rule 607 of the then proposed Rules of Evidence. That rule provides, 'The credibility of a witness may be attacked by any party, including the party calling him.' The Federal Rules of Evidence had not been adopted at the time of these proceedings, however, and until such time as they were 'the trial court was bound by the decisions on the subject.' To interpret *Lineberger* as allowing the government in a criminal prosecution to set up a straw man in order to impeach him attaches significance to the opinion beyond its holding, which is that if the district court erred in not allowing impeachment, its error was harmless. . . .

We, of course, recognize that the strict rule against impeaching one's own witness has long been discredited. It is now generally recognized that impeachment may be resorted to where the trial court, in its discretion, determines that it is necessary to alleviate the harshness of subjecting a party to the mercy of a witness who is recalcitrant or who may have been unscrupulously tampered with. The overwhelming weight of authority is, however, that impeachment by prior inconsistent statement may not be permitted where employed as a mere subterfuge to get before the jury evidence not otherwise admissible.

Witnesses may, of course, sometimes fail to come up to the expectations of counsel and in such situations there is an understandable temptation to get before the jury any prior statement made by the witness. And it may be that in certain instances impeachment might somehow enhance the truth-finding process. Yet, whatever validity this latter assertion may have, it must be balanced against the notions of fairness upon which our system is based. Foremost among these concepts is the principle that men should not be allowed to be convicted on the basis of unsworn testimony.

We must be mindful of the fact that prior unsworn statements of a witness are mere hearsay and are, as such, generally inadmissible as affirmative proof. The introduction of such testimony, even where limited to impeachment, necessarily increases the possibility that a defendant may be convicted on the basis of unsworn evidence, for despite proper instructions to the jury, it is often difficult for them

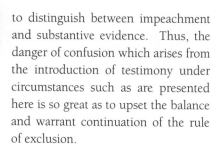

Food for Thought

Is this a candid admission by the court that limiting instructions are often misunderstood or disregarded by juries?

to distinguish between impeachment and substantive evidence. Thus, the danger of confusion which arises from the introduction of testimony under circumstances such as are presented here is so great as to upset the balance and warrant continuation of the rule of exclusion.

In the instant case, the witness Wilmoth, in statements given to the government, consistently adhered to his story that the appellant was not a participant in the bribery. The prosecution admits this. Thus, the only apparent purpose in calling him was to get before the jury the alleged statement made to Crist. Clearly, the introduction of this testimony was damaging. To permit the government in this case to supply testimony which was a naked conclusion as to Morlang's guilt in the name of impeachment would be tantamount to permitting the use of hearsay and would seriously jeopardize the important policies underlying Justice Douglas' opinion in Bridges. Despite the fact that impeachment of one's own witness may be permitted, this does not go so far as to permit the use of the rule as a subterfuge to get to the jury evidence otherwise inadmissible.

We are thus of opinion the judgment of the district court must be vacated and the case reversed and remanded for a new trial.

Points for Discussion

a. Claiming Surprise.

Does *Morlang* bring back the common law ban against impeaching one's own witness unless a party can show he was surprised by the testimony? Perhaps it does, at least when a party calls that witness solely for impeachment purposes.

b. The Viability of *Morlang*.

Morlang was decided before the Federal Rules of Evidence went into effect on July 1, 1975. Nonetheless, the court referenced them anyway, and most courts have subsequently agreed with the *Morlang* decision. See e.g. *United States v. Hogan*, 763 F.2d 697 (5th Cir. 1985) (the prosecution may not call a witness it knows to be hostile for the purpose of eliciting otherwise inadmissible impeachment testimony in order to avoid the hearsay rule). In a criminal case, when impeachment evidence is offered by a defendant, constitutional concerns may add an additional factor to the analysis. See *United States v. Buffalo*, 358 F.3d 519 (8th Cir. 2004) (admissibility of impeachment testimony to discredit a witness called by the defense in a criminal case solely to get into evidence the witness's statement that he, not the defendant, committed the crime is subject to a Rule 403 balancing test because admission of the statement does not endanger the defendant's liberty with a risk of conviction based upon uncross-examined testimony). Would constitutional concerns change the result in *Morlang* if Wilmoth's testimony had been offered by the defendant?

---

2. General Impeachment Guidelines: Bolstering a Witness's Credibility

Once they swear or affirm to tell the truth, all testifying witnesses are presumed to be credible. Because of this presumption, common law practice did not allow a lawyer to strengthen his own witness's testimony by "bolstering" it. "Bolstering" means to offer evidence solely for the purpose of enhancing a witness's credibility before that credibility has been attacked. For example, until a witness's credibility has been attacked, a lawyer may not enhance the witness's credibility by putting on testimony that others think she is a truthful person or that she performs honest deeds.

United States v. Rosario-Diaz

United States Court of Appeals for the First Circuit
202 F.3d 54 (2000)

TORRUELLA, Chief Judge.

Ralph Rosario-Díaz, Wilson Montalvo-Ortiz, Ada Meléndez-García, Juan Báez-Jurado, and Wilfredo López-Morales were each convicted on both counts of a grand jury indictment charging them with (1) aiding and abetting each other in a carjacking that resulted in the death of the victim [Edna]; and 2) conspiring to commit that carjacking. The court sentenced each defendant to life in prison on each count, the sentences to run concurrently. All five defendants now appeal.
. . . .

On June 15, 1995, after being apprehended by Edna's husband, Aponte-Lazú [a co-conspirator] gave the first of several inconsistent statements to law enforcement. Among those statements was the assertion that López-Morales had had nothing to do with the crime, which the government claimed at trial was made in an attempt to gain the release of López-Morales so that López-Morales could murder the government's witnesses. Subsequent to his guilty plea in July of 1995, Aponte-Lazú began to divulge the details of the crime to investigators. . . .

At trial, the prosecution's star witness became Aponte-Lazú, who testified extensively about the details of the crime and the participation of each defendant. Immediately after the testimony of Aponte-Lazú, the United States put FBI agent Daryl Huff on the witness stand. Over the objection of defense counsel, Agent Huff testified at length about his interactions with Aponte-Lazú during the investigation of the carjacking and murder of Edna. Agent Huff testified as to the interrogation techniques used with Aponte-Lazú, as to the statements made by Aponte-Lazú, and even as to how law enforcement evaluated the veracity and reliability of Aponte-Lazú's statements. For example, Agent Huff identified omissions and falsities in Aponte-Lazú's statements specifically with regards to why he traveled to Caguas, one of the lies. And also specifically about the rape. He had not mentioned that. And he also omitted the fact that Wilson Montalvo Ortiz and Ralph Rosario Díaz were involved in the carjacking or conspiracy of the carjacking fully. So, those were three of the lies.

Q: Okay. Now, how were those omissions discovered?
A: Again through interview and through seeing the discrepancies, inconsistencies and just things that didn't make sense in the statement. It became pretty obvious in most cases. . . .
Q: And did you use or need a polygraph in order to do that?
A: No, a polygraph is a last resort technique. There was no need for a polygraph in the particular situation. We were pinning him down without a polygraph. We could tell when he was lying. . . . [and when he was not]

Appellants argue that the testimony of FBI Agent Daryl Huff constituted improper bolstering of the testimony of cooperating witness Aponte-Lazú. . . .

The case law is clear, and the parties agree, that prosecutors may not place the prestige of the United States behind a witness by making personal assurances about the credibility of a witness or by indicating that facts not before the jury support the witness's testimony. It is also undisputed that the prosecution cannot accomplish such improper bolstering of a witness through the testimony of other government witnesses. Government witnesses may of course testify to facts within their personal knowledge that support or corroborate another witness's testimony. Indeed, in a case such as this one, where the bulk of critical testimony comes from a single cooperating coconspirator, the prosecution's principal task is often to convince the jury that the witness's account is credible. The prosecution simply must do so through competent and reliable evidence and not through improper vouching that could invite the jury to find guilt on the basis of something other than the evidence presented at trial.

We have no difficulty concluding that the testimony of Agent Huff was improper. Although Huff could properly have testified as to the actions he took to corroborate Aponte-Lazú's testimony, we think it obvious that he could not properly opine on whether particular statements by Aponte-Lazú were "lies," nor could he represent that the statements not singled out as lies had been "tested" and verified through interrogation techniques. Particularly in light of Huff's testimony concerning his training and experience in interrogation and investigation, the clear purpose and effect of his testimony was to put the prestige of his professional knowledge as a federal agent behind the testimony of Aponte-Lazú. That is the very definition of improper bolstering, and it is impermissible. . . .

[T]he testimony of [the officer] was admitted after [defendant's] testimony, whereas in *Mazza* the agents' testimony came at the opening of trial. Thus we are not faced here with the *Mazza* danger that the agent would testify as to items that would never come into evidence, nor would [defendant's] testimony be bolstered by the law enforcement officer before the jury could evaluate it independently. Furthermore, the government was justified in seeking admission of this testimony because of the defense's attacks on the informant's credibility.

In this case, Aponte-Lazú testified extensively before Agent Huff took the stand, and Aponte-Lazú was subject to vigorous cross-examination. Furthermore, the district court took pains to instruct the jury that they were to judge Aponte-Lazú's credibility on the basis of his testimony alone, and not that of Agent Huff. On these facts, and in light of the other probative evidence admitted in this case, we hold that the improper bolstering solicited by the prosecution from Agent Huff was harmless error not warranting reversal. We nevertheless take this occasion to issue a strong warning against the use of this procedure by government prosecutors and advise that they will tread on thin ice indeed if they continue to practice this technique in the future.

Points for Discussion

a. Bolstering as Harmless Error?

The testimony of Agent Huff seems to imply that everything the witness Aponte-Lazu testified about on the witness stand had to be true because Huff was able before trial to uncover any false statements through various investigative techniques. The court holds that the admission of Huff's testimony was error but harmless. Do you agree? Aponte-Lazu was the prosecution's star witness at trial, and his testimony, which was essential to a guilty verdict, was vouched for by a government agent supposedly knowledgeable in determining the truthfulness of witnesses. How could this be harmless error?

b. Rehabilitation of Discredited Witnesses.

The court states that "the government was justified in seeking admission of [Huff's] testimony because of the defense's attacks on the informant's credibility." Is this a more persuasive ground for the court's decision?

———————————————

Character evidence offered for non-impeachment purposes will be discussed in Chapter 9.

3. Impeaching a Witness's Character for Truthfulness

Character evidence may consist of reputation, opinion or specific act testimony. The admissibility of a person's particular character trait depends upon the purpose for which the evidence is offered. For example, under Rule 404(a), a criminal defendant charged with murder might offer a witness to testify that he is a peaceful man to rebut the charge that he is a murderer. If he is charged with embezzlement, he might offer a witness to testify that he is an honest person. Or in a defamation case, where the plaintiff claims to have been slandered by accusations she is a drunk, either side may offer character evidence to show she is sober or besotted under Rule 405(b). All of these offering have one thing in common; they are offered to show a substantive issue which is in dispute in the case.

Character evidence offered to impeach a testifying witness's credibility under Rules 608 and 609 is different, even though the form of the evidence (reputation, opinion, or specific act testimony) is the same. When a witness testifies, that witness's veracity becomes an issue. Attacking a testifying witness's honesty is called impeaching the witness; supporting that character after impeachment is called rehabilitating the witness.

Rule 608. Evidence of character and conduct of witness.

(a) **Opinion and reputation evidence of character.** The credibility of a witness may be attacked or supported by evidence in the form of opinion or reputation, but subject to these limitations: (1) the evidence may refer only to character for truthfulness or untruthfulness, and (2) evidence of truthful character is admissible only after the character of the witness for truthfulness has been attacked by opinion or reputation evidence or otherwise.

(b) **Specific instances of conduct.** Specific instances of the conduct of a witness, for the purpose of attacking or supporting the witness's character for truthfulness, other than conviction of crime as provided in rule 609, may not be proved by extrinsic evidence. They may, however, in the discretion of the court, if probative of truthfulness or untruthfulness, be inquired into on cross-examination for the witness (1) concerning the witness's character for truthfulness or untruthfulness, or (2) concerning the character for truthfulness or untruthfulness of another witness as to which character the witness being cross-examined has testified.

The giving of testimony, whether by an accused or by any other witness, does not operate as a waiver of the accused's or the witness's privilege against self-incrimination when examined with respect to matters that relate only to character for truthfulness.

a. Reputation and Opinion Evidence.
Rule 608(a) allows a witness to testify that a previous witness is not to be believed by testifying to the witness's reputation in the community for dishonesty, or by stating his own opinion of the witness's untruthfulness, or both. This concept may be illustrated as follows:

Take Note!

Because Rule 608(a) allows attack on the testifying witness's character for truthfulness, this is the only character trait that can be used under the rule. Other character traits such as peacefulness, being law-abiding, or sobriety are irrelevant to questioning under Rule 608(a).

Prosecution's Case-in-Chief

Defendant's Case-in-Chief

Witness # 1 Testifies on Direct Examination:

"The defendant shot the victim for no reason"

Witness #2 Testifies on Direct Examination:

"Witness #1 has a reputation for *dishonesty* in the community."

and/or

"Witness #1 is, in my opinion a *dishonest* person."

Notice that the prosecution in this scenario presents Witness # 1 during his case-in-chief, and the defense attorney presents Witness #2, his countervailing witness, during the defense case-in-chief.

United States v. Whitmore

U.S. Court of Appeals for the District of Columbia Circuit
359 F.3d 609 (C.A.D.C. 2004)

Henderson, Circuit Judge:

Issue

Gerald F. Whitmore was convicted by a jury on firearm and drug charges. He appeals the firearm conviction on the ground that the district court committed reversible error in preventing him at trial from attacking the credibility of the arresting officer. . . .

Viewed in the light most favorable to the government, the evidence at trial established that on the evening of November 1, 2001, Officer Bladden Russell of the District of Columbia Metropolitan Police Department (MPD), while patrolling the Fort Davis neighborhood in Southeast Washington, directed a crowd gathered at a bus stop to disperse. The crowd, with the exception of Whitmore, complied. Russell exited his car to approach Whitmore and Whitmore fled. Russell pursued him on foot and noticed that Whitmore, while running, held his right hand close to his body at his waist and the right side pocket of his jacket.

Whitmore successfully eluded Russell but MPD Officer Efrain Soto, Jr., who was also patrolling the neighborhood in his police cruiser, spotted Whitmore and gave chase, first in his car and then on foot. Soto also noticed Whitmore's right hand holding the right side of his jacket. While still in the cruiser, Soto saw Whitmore throw a gun towards an apartment building next to an alley Whitmore ran into. Shortly thereafter, Soto apprehended Whitmore. Once Russell caught up to assist, Soto found a gun in a window well of the apartment building. The weapon (with four rounds of ammunition, one of which was chambered) showed signs that it had been recently thrown against the building: a piece of brick was stuck in its sight, there were scuff marks on it and it was covered with masonry dust. The police found nothing in the right pocket of Whitmore's jacket but did discover a small bag of cocaine base in his left pocket.

D argued Soto lied about story

At trial Whitmore defended on the ground that Soto had fabricated the story about the gun and had planted the gun in the window well. Soto provided, almost exclusively, the evidence connecting Whitmore to the gun and Whitmore therefore sought to attack Soto's credibility in several ways. He first attempted to call three defense witnesses - Jason Cherkis, Bruce Cooper and Kennith Edmonds

- to testify regarding Soto's "character for truthfulness" under Fed.R.Evid. 608(a). Cherkis, a reporter with the City Paper, wrote an article in January 2000 reporting that Soto and three other MPD officers were the target of multiple complaints from residents of the MPD's Sixth District, the district in which Whitmore was arrested. According to Whitmore, Cherkis would testify, based on conversations he had with his sources for the article, that Soto had a reputation as a liar. . . . Before trial, the court excluded Cherkis's testimony under Fed.R.Evid. 608(a) because Cherkis was not personally acquainted with Soto and because the foundation of Cherkis's testimony - interviews that he conducted for the 2000 article -was too remote in time to be relevant.

Bruce Cooper was a local criminal defense counsel who, Whitmore claimed, would testify regarding both Soto's reputation for untruthfulness within what he called the "court community" and Cooper's own opinion that Soto was untruthful. Whitmore proffered that Cooper would testify that several defense counsel thought Soto was a liar and that Cooper had the same opinion based on having tried many cases in which Soto was a government witness. The district court excluded Cooper's reputation testimony because, even assuming the "court community" constituted a recognized community, Cooper did not know Soto's reputation within the entire "court community" and did not live in Soto's neighborhood. The court also rejected Cooper's opinion testimony under Fed.R.Evid. 403 because it was "inherently biased," and unduly prejudicial in that Cooper's contacts with Soto arose from his representation of criminal defendants against whom Soto testified and because Cooper's testimony would lead to additional delay - that is, the court would have to allow the government to explore the circumstances underlying Soto's testimony in the other cases about which Cooper intended to testify.

Kennith Edmonds, whom Whitmore also sought to call as both a reputation and opinion witness, was an acquaintance of Soto who used to live in the neighborhood where Soto worked and who saw Soto regularly until roughly five years before the trial, when Edmonds moved away. Whitmore proffered that Edmonds would say that he still saw Soto a few times each week when Edmonds returned to his old neighborhood to visit his mother and still maintained contacts with others in the neighborhood who knew Soto. Edmonds's proffered opinion evidence was based on two incidents: (1) Soto had participated in the arrest of a friend of his and, when Edmonds attempted to collect his friend's property from the police, Edmonds was told that there was no property to collect; and (2) Soto and other officers wrongly arrested Edmonds for drug possession in 1995. The court excluded Edmonds's reputation testimony because he had not lived in the neighborhood where Soto worked for some time; it excluded his opinion testimony because it questioned whether Soto was involved in the events on which Edmonds based his opinion. It also excluded Edmonds's testimony in its entirety under Fed.R.Evid. 403, concluding that the minimal probative value of Edmonds's evidence was outweighed by unfair prejudice, including the government's resulting need to examine the events underlying Edmonds's testimony. . . .

The Sixth Amendment guarantees a defendant the right to present a defense by calling witnesses on his own behalf and by cross-examining the witnesses against him. The district court nonetheless has considerable discretion to place reasonable limits on a criminal defendant's presentation of evidence and cross-examination of government witnesses. It must "be cautious," however, "[p]articularly where a party is seeking to impeach a witness whose credibility could have an important influence on the outcome of the trial."

Whitmore makes two challenges: one related to the exclusion of his proposed character witnesses under Fed.R.Evid. 608(a) and the other to the exclusion of his proposed cross-examination of Soto under Fed.R.Evid. 608(b). We review the district court's evidentiary rulings for abuse of discretion.

> **Make the Connection**
>
> The second portion of the opinion concerning the admissibility of evidence under Rule 608(b) is discussed in the next section of this chapter.

Fed.R.Evid. 608(a) allows a party to attack the credibility of a witness through reputation and opinion evidence of his character for truthfulness. Whitmore complains that the district court erroneously excluded the testimony of three character witnesses he sought to call to attack Soto's credibility. As noted earlier, they included: (1) Cherkis, a reporter who had written a newspaper article involving Soto in 2000; (2) Cooper, a local defense counsel who had represented defendants against whom Soto had testified; and (3) Edmonds, an acquaintance who had lived in the neighborhood where Soto worked. Whitmore wanted Cherkis to provide reputation evidence and Cooper and Edmonds both reputation and opinion evidence.

In order to offer reputation evidence under Fed.R.Evid. 608(a), a party must establish that the character witness is qualified by having an "acquaintance with [the witness]," his "community," and "the circles in which he has moved, as to speak with authority of the terms in which generally [the witness] is regarded." With regard to Cherkis, Whitmore relied on the interviews that Cherkis had conducted for the 2000 article and on the holding in *Wilson v. City of Chicago*, 6 F.3d 1233, 1239 (7th Cir.1993), in which the Seventh Circuit reversed a district court's exclusion of a reporter's reputation testimony. The reporter in Wilson, however, had personally interviewed the principal witness while Cherkis had never met Soto. Furthermore, neither Cherkis nor Edmonds had had direct contact with Soto or his community for some time. The district court found the proposed testimony of both Cherkis and Edmonds as to Soto's alleged reputation for truthfulness "too remote" in time from the time of trial. Finally, with regard to Cooper's testimony - and leaving aside the troublesome issue whether the "court community" represents a cognizable community for the purpose of a law enforcement officer's reputation - the district court found the foundation for his testimony weak because it relied on Cooper's conversations with only a few other criminal defense counsel, a subset of the proposed "community."

Food for Thought

If the job of a reputation witness is to report on what the community thinks about the testifying witness's reputation for honesty, why should it matter that Cherkis has never met Soto?

While recognizing that the foundational requirement for opinion evidence regarding a witness's character for truthfulness is less stringent than that for reputation evidence, the district court nonetheless rejected both Cooper's and Edmonds's proposed opinion evidence. It concluded that both opinions lacked sufficiently supportive factual information to be credible and thus would be unfairly prejudicial under Fed.R.Evid. 403. The foundation for Cooper's opinion that Soto was untruthful was limited to his observation that Soto had testified falsely against his clients; the facts underlying Edmonds's opinion did not provide a reasonable basis from which the jury could conclude that Soto was even directly involved in the events, much less indicate that he was untruthful about them.

Whitmore contends that the foundational defects could have been highlighted by the government in cross-examining his character witnesses but were not severe enough to exclude the evidence altogether. The foundation required by Fed.R.Evid. 608(a), however, is designed to keep unreliable evidence from being heard by the jury at all. The district court did not abuse its discretion in excluding this evidence under Fed.R.Evid. 608 - the foundational defects were serious - and Fed.R.Evid. 403, on the ground that its value would have been substantially outweighed by the unfair prejudice to the government and by needlessly occupying the time of the jury and the court. . . .

Points for Discussion

a. The Foundation for Reputation and Opinion Testimony.

Under Rule 608(a), a reputation witness must be sufficiently acquainted with the testifying witness's reputation for honesty in the community where the testifying witness lives. An opinion witness must personally know the testifying witness's character for honesty. As *Whitmore* demonstrates, the trial court has discretion to determine whether these foundations have been met. From how many people from the relevant community must a witness hear before he can testify to a person's reputation? Does this type of testimony not risk elevating gossip into fact?

b. Support of Credibility with Good Opinion or Reputation Testimony.

Reputation and opinion testimony to rehabilitate a testifying witness's character for honesty may be offered after the witness's character for honesty has been attacked. This would be illustrated as follows:

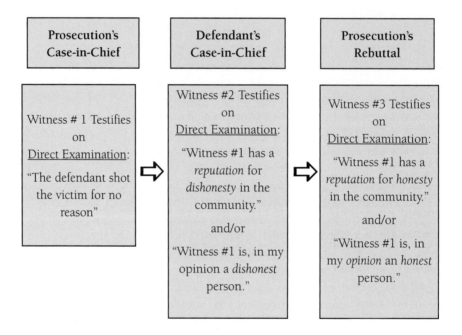

c. The Rule 608(a) Foundation.

The laying of a Rule 608(a) foundation is short, straightforward, and general. It is the same foundation for introducing reputation and opinion under Rule 405(a) for general character traits such as peacefulness or violence. Had the court allowed Cherkis to testify as a character witness in the *Whitmore* case, it might have looked like this:

Q. Mr. Cherkis, are you acquainted with the reputation of Officer Efrain Soto, Jr. for honesty in his community?

A. Yes, I am.

Q. And what is that reputation?

A. It is very bad.

Q. And knowing what you know of that reputation, would you believe Officer Soto under oath?

A. No, I honestly would not.

How do you think a jury would receive this testimony? What would they make of it?

---

b. Specific Acts of Dishonesty. Rule 608(b) provides that a testifying witness may be challenged with the witness's own specific acts of dishonesty by allowing a cross-examiner to question the witness directly about the acts, regardless whether or not they resulted in a conviction. The rule gives the trial judge the discretion to determine whether the acts are sufficiently probative of dishonesty to be admissible. The rule also states that if the witness denies the dishonest acts, the questioner must "take the witness's answer," that is, he cannot bring in other evidence extrinsic to the witness's testimony to refute the denial. Therefore, a questioner can ask about a specific instance of conduct to test the character for truthfulness of a witness but is not permitted to prove that specific instance occurred with extrinsic evidence.

United States v. Whitmore

United States Court of Appeals for the District of Columbia Circuit
359 F.3d 609 (2004)

Henderson, Circuit Judge:

[The facts of this case appear previously in this section. Defendant Whitmore was convicted of unlawful possession of a firearm and ammunition by a felon and of simple possession of a controlled substance. This portion of the opinion deals with whether the trial court erred in refusing to allow the defendant to cross-examine prosecution witness Soto about his past instances of misconduct that involve dishonesty under Rule 608(b).]

Fed..R.Evid. 608(b) allows a party to attack the credibility of a witness by cross-examining him on specific instances of past conduct. Cross-examination pursuant to Fed.R.Evid. 608(b) is not confined to prior criminal convictions - they are governed by Fed.R.Evid. 609 - but the conduct must be probative of the witness's character for truthfulness. It may not, however, be proven by extrinsic evidence.

Whitmore contends that the district court erroneously prevented him from cross-examining Soto under Fed.R.Evid. 608(b) regarding three instances of past misconduct: (1) his testimony before the Superior Court judge in 1999; (2) the 1998 suspension of Soto's Maryland driver's license and his failure to report the suspension to his supervisors; and (3) Soto's failure to make child-support payments. The district court prohibited cross-examination as to the first instance under Fed.R.Evid. 403; with regard to Soto's failure to report his suspended license and his failure to make child support payments, the court concluded that the document on which Whitmore relied to pursue the questioning was itself unreliable hearsay. We disagree.

Under Fed.R.Evid. 403, a court may exclude relevant evidence "if its probative value is substantially outweighed by the danger of unfair prejudice, confusion of the issues, or misleading the jury, or by considerations of undue delay, waste of time, or needless presentation of cumulative evidence." "Rule 403 tilts," however, "as do the rules as a whole, toward the admission of evidence in close cases;" when "performing the balancing test required under Rule 403, ... the balance should be generally struck in favor of admission." We nonetheless recognize that the district court is in the best position to conduct the balancing test and therefore review a Fed.R.Evid. 403 ruling "only for grave abuse."

Here the district court first determined that the probative value of any cross-examination regarding Soto's testimony before the Superior Court judge would be slight because it involved an unrelated and dated matter and fell short of a perjury conviction. It then concluded that cross-examination on the subject presented a "grave risk that the jury might abdicate" its role in weighing Soto's testimony and that both the cross-examination and the government's inevitable rehabilitation of Soto's testimony would "divert the jury from the facts in this case and from the assessment that they need to make in this case."

For his part, Whitmore contends that the proposed cross-examination was strongly probative of Soto's character for untruthfulness and that, given the critical nature of Soto's evidence against Whitmore, the district court should have allowed it. We agree. Nothing could be more probative of a witness's character for untruthfulness than evidence that the witness has previously lied under oath. Indeed, as the Second Circuit observed - in a remarkably similar case (before the enactment of Fed.R.Evid. 608(b)) in which a party sought to cross-examine a "key witness" regarding a finding by another court that the witness had " 'intentionally g[iven] false testimony' ": "the rule seems to be well settled that although the opponent is not permitted to adduce extrinsic evidence that a witness lied on a previous occasion, he may nonetheless ask questions to that end." . . .

[T]the government nevertheless contends that the probative value of the proposed cross-examination was limited because the judge's finding "more closely resembles a mere complaint ... or a ruling that the testimony of opposing witnesses [was] more credible, whose probative value is hard to know." Hardly. The government's attempt to analogize the judge's simple and direct statement - "I think [Officer Soto] lied" - to an unsubstantiated civil complaint, or to a judge's suppression of evidence because he found "defense witnesses more credible than" the government's witness, is strained at best. Furthermore, the government's suggestion that inquiry under Fed.R.Evid. 608(b) should be limited to a prior perjury conviction would make Fed.R.Evid. 609 superfluous. Fed.R.Evid. 608(b) allows a witness's credibility to be attacked based on misconduct that, while not constituting a criminal conviction, nevertheless tends to show that the witness is untruthful. . . .

We also believe the district court erred in excluding the entire line of cross-examination on the ground that its probative value was substantially outweighed by the risk that the jury might blindly follow the prior judge's lead or be otherwise distracted from the substance of Whitmore's trial. . . . The district court here could have adequately guarded against any risk of unfair prejudice or undue delay by limiting cross-examination, by giving limiting instructions to the jury and by setting reasonable parameters on the government's rehabilitation of Soto. Instead, by prohibiting cross-examination of the only witness who testified to Whitmore's unlawful possession of the gun, we believe the district court abused its discretion.

Turning to the district court's denial of cross-examination regarding Soto's suspended driver's license and failure to pay child support, we also find error. The trial court precluded cross-examination on those matters on the ground that there was "no basis" for the cross-examination because Whitmore's only support for them - the record from the Maryland Motor Vehicle Administration - was inadmissible hearsay. Counsel, however, need only have " 'a reasonable basis for asking questions on cross-examination which tend to incriminate or degrade the witness,' " and "the general rule in such situations is that 'the questioner must be in possession of some facts which support a genuine belief that the witness committed the offense or the degrading act to which the question relates.' " The copy of Soto's Maryland driving record provided sufficient basis for such cross-examination and defense counsel readily acknowledged that he did not seek to admit the record itself and would be bound by Soto's answers. The court apparently assumed, however, that Soto would simply deny that his license had been suspended, leaving the jury with a bare denial of a damaging accusation. We pass over the fact that this assumption implied that Soto would intentionally lie under oath. The court lacked a basis for such an assumption, however, because it failed to conduct any voir dire. The knowledge that he could be charged with perjury would encourage

Soto to respond truthfully, even if he thought that Whitmore's counsel could not impeach him further. Accordingly, in excluding cross-examination on these matters as well, the district court abused its discretion.

[The error was not harmless, and the case was reversed].

————————

Points of Discussion

a. Policies Behind the Exclusion of Extrinsic Evidence under Rule 608(b).

Wigmore describes the overall rationale behind the common law ban on extrinsic evidence as preventing confusion of issues through proliferation of testimony on minor matters and preventing unfair surprise arising from false allegations of improper conduct. 3A Wigmore on Evidence §979, at 826-27 (Chadbourn Rev. Ed. 1970). Do these policies outweigh allowing a testifying witness to lie under oath, even about a minor matter such as a Rule 608(b) act of dishonesty?

b. What Happens if the Witness Lies?

If a witness lies about not having committed a prior act involving dishonesty under Rule 608(b), the cross-examiner must "take his answer," that is, the cross-examiner cannot disprove that lie by offering other (extrinsic) evidence to the contrary. Does this mean the witness gets away with perjury? The answer is yes. In most jurisdictions, the crime of perjury requires a material misstatement of fact under oath with the intention to mislead, and Rule 608(b) acts are not considered to be material.

c. An Exception to the Extrinsic Evidence Ban.

What if, on retrial, Officer Soto is cross-examined about his acts of dishonesty, and he admits to them? Does the cross-examiner have any leeway to quiz him further about the details of that conduct or even use other (extrinsic) evidence to question him further? See *Carter v. Hewitt,* 617 F.2d 961 (3d Cir. 1980). *Carter* (discussed in Chapter 3) involved a civil rights case where the plaintiff prisoner wrote a letter to another prisoner allegedly encouraging him to file false prison complaints. The letter was admitted on the issue of whether the plaintiff committed an act of dishonesty by writing the letter, had a dishonest character, and thus should not be believed under oath. The court found that because the plaintiff admitted to authoring the letter, the admission of the letter for purposes of further cross-examination did not violate the Rule 608(b) ban against extrinsic evidence because the questioning did not waste the court's time nor divert the jury's attention from the issues in the case.

4. Impeaching a Witness with Prior Convictions

Rule 609. Impeachment by Evidence of Conviction of Crime.

(a) **General Rule.** For the purposes of attacking the character for truthfulness of a witness.

(1) evidence that a witness other than the accused has been convicted of a crime shall be admitted, subject to Rule 403, if the crime was punishable by death or imprisonment in excess of one year under the law under which the witness was convicted, and evidence that an accused has been convicted of such a crime shall be admitted if the court determines that the probative value of admitting this evidence outweighs its prejudicial effect to the accused; and

(2) evidence that any witness has been convicted of a crime shall be admitted regardless of the punishment, if it readily can be determined that establishing the elements of the crime required proof or admission of an act of dishonesty or false statement by the witness.

(b) **Time Limit.** Evidence of a conviction under this rule is not admissible if a period of more than ten years has elapsed since the date of the conviction or of the release of the witness from the confinement imposed for that conviction, whichever is the later date, unless the court determines, in the interests of justice, that the probative value of the conviction supported by specific facts and circumstances substantially outweighs its prejudicial effect. However, evidence of a conviction more than 10 years old as calculated herein, is not admissible unless the proponent gives to the adverse party sufficient advance written notice of intent to use such evidence to provide the adverse party with a fair opportunity to contest the use of such evidence.

(c) **Effect of Pardon, Annulment, or Certificate of Rehabilitation.** Evidence of a conviction is not admissible under this rule if (1) the conviction has been the subject of a pardon, annulment, certificate of rehabilitation, or other equivalent procedure based on a finding of the rehabilitation of the person convicted, and that person has not been convicted of a subsequent crime which was punishable by death or imprisonment in excess of one year, or (20 the conviction has been the subject of a pardon, annulment, or other equivalent procedure based on a finding of innocence.

(d) Juvenile Adjudications. Evidence of juvenile adjudications is generally not admissible under this rule. The court, may, however, in a criminal case allow evidence of a juvenile adjudication of a witness other than the accused if conviction of the offense would be admissible to attack the credibility of an adult and the court is satisfied that admission in evidence is necessary for a fair determination of the issue of guilt or innocence.

(e) Pendency of Appeal. The pendency of an appeal therefrom does not render evidence of a conviction inadmissible. Evidence of the pendency of an appeal is admissible.

Take Note!

A "conviction" for Rule 609 purposes means any sentence in a criminal case where the defendant is confined or given probation but not where the defendant is placed on "deferred adjudication." "Deferred adjudication is where the defendant is placed on probation but a finding of guilt is deferred and never entered on the record unless the deferred adjudication is revoked.

Under the common law, convicted felons were incompetent to testify. Rule 609 now makes a witness's conviction a matter of impeachment rather than incompetency. The rule divides convictions into two categories: (1) crimes punishable by death or imprisonment (i.e., felony convictions), and (2) crimes whose elements required proof or admission of an act of dishonesty or false statement (i.e. felony or misdemeanor convictions involving dishonesty or false statement).

To admit a felony conviction to impeach a witness under Section (a)(1) of the rule, the trial judge must balance the conviction's probative value for proving dishonesty against its unfair prejudice. This balancing test is different depending on whether the witness being impeached is a criminal defendant. To impeach a witness other than a criminal defendant, the conviction's probative value for dishonesty must not be *substantially* outweighed by the conviction's unfair prejudice. To impeach a criminal defendant, the conviction's probative value for showing dishonesty *must outweigh* the conviction's unfair prejudice to the defendant. Thus, the balancing test is weighed in favor of admissibility for witnesses other than a criminal defendant and weighed against admissibility for criminal defendants.

United States v. Sanders

U.S. Court of Appeals for the Fourth Circuit
964 F.2d 295 (4th Cir. 1992)

PHILLIPS, Circuit Judge:

Carlos Sanders appeals his convictions for assault with a dangerous weapon with intent to do bodily harm and for possession of contraband (a shank used in the assault). Because we believe that the district court erred by admitting evidence of Sanders' prior convictions for assault and possession of a contraband shank and that the error was prejudicial as to his assault conviction, we reverse that conviction and remand for a new trial. But we find the error harmless as to his contraband possession conviction, and affirm it. . . .

Before trial, Sanders filed a motion in limine to exclude evidence of his prior convictions. Although the district court granted this motion in part by prohibiting the government from questioning Sanders about a stabbing for which he was acquitted and an armed robbery for which his conviction was reversed, the court declined to preclude the government from cross-examining Sanders about his prior assault and contraband possession convictions. The court ruled that the assault and contraband convictions were admissible under Federal Rules of Evidence 609(a). . . .

After hearing the evidence, the jury . . . convicted Sanders of possession of a shank. The jury was unable to reach a verdict on the assault count against Sanders, however. The district court accordingly declared a mistrial as to that count and set it for re-trial. . . .

Sanders' convictions for assault and possession of contraband fall under 609(a)(1), and the district court therefore was required to balance the probative value of the evidence against its prejudicial effect in assessing its admissibility. Here, although evidence of the prior convictions may be thought somehow generally probative of Sanders' lack of credibility, they were extremely prejudicial since they involved the exact type of conduct for which Sanders was on trial.

We have recognized the prejudice that results from admitting evidence of a similar offense under Rule 609:

> Admission of evidence of a similar offense often does little to impeach the credibility of a testifying defendant while undoubtedly prejudicing him. The jury, despite limiting instructions, can hardly avoid drawing the inference that the past conviction suggests some probability that defendant committed the similar offense for which he is currently charged. The generally accepted view, therefore, is that evidence of similar offenses for impeachment purposes under Rule 609 should be admitted sparingly if at all.

We think that it is doubtful if this conviction could ever serve as the basis for impeachment. It was remote in time, almost falling within the presumptive bar of Rule 609(b). It was for a similar offense, an odious one likely to inflame the jury and thus prejudice defendant. Moreover, it was an offense that had minimal if any bearing on the likelihood that defendant would testify truthfully. But in any event, defendant was denied the safeguards of Rule 609(a). The district court failed to determine as a prerequisite to use of the evidence that the probative value of the conviction for impeachment purposes outweighed its prejudicial effect to the defendant as required by Rule 609(a).

. . . . It is unclear whether and how the district court may have sought to balance the probative value of this evidence against its prejudicial effect, since at the hearing on Sanders' motion in limine the district judge simply stated, "[t]hey [the government] are entitled to go into that [Sanders' prior convictions] both on the question of intent and impeachment." Even if the district court had explicitly conducted a balancing inquiry before admitting this evidence, we would find the evidence inadmissible under Rule 609(a) because of the high likelihood of prejudice that accompanies the admission of such similar prior convictions. As we stated in Beahm,

> [w]here as here the offense sought to be admitted against defendant had little bearing on his propensity to tell the truth, the district court should have recognized that the substantial likelihood of prejudice outweighed the minimal impeachment value of the evidence, and refused to admit the evidence, ... or at the very least limited disclosure to the fact of conviction without revealing its nature.

We therefore hold that Sanders' prior convictions were not admissible under Rule 609(a).

———————

Points for Discussion

a. The Tendency of a Prior Conviction to Impeach.

The theory behind admitting felony convictions to impeach is that any conviction for a serious crime has probative value to show dishonesty. Such crimes demonstrate that the witness is willing to violate the law, suggesting that the witness may violate the law again by not telling the truth at trial. Nonetheless, a conviction for some felonies is more likely to show dishonesty than a conviction for others. Crimes such as robbery, kidnapping, burglary, or murder are crimes of violence and have only a modest tendency to show dishonesty. Even so, the trial court has discretion to admit them under a Rule 609(a)(1) balancing test. See *United States v. Alexander,* 48 F.3d 1477 (9th Cir. 1995) (the trial judge acted within his discretion when he admitted a testifying defendant's prior drug and robbery convictions). If the trial judge in *Sanders* exercised his discretion not to admit the defendant's prior convictions for assault and possession of a contraband shank, do you think that ruling would be upheld under the facts of the case?

b. Factors Considered in a Rule 609(a)(1) Balancing.

Some of the factors trial courts take into account in making a Rule 609(a)(1) balancing to impeach a testifying witness include:

(1) *The impeachment value of the prior crime.* Convictions for crimes involving violence, such as robbery, burglary, arson, rape, murder, and aggravated assault, have low probative value for showing dishonesty; convictions for crimes such as perjury, fraud, embezzlement or theft by false pretenses, have high probative for showing dishonesty and are automatically admitted under section (a)(2) of the rule. Crimes such as felony drug possession or felony driving while intoxicated involve neither violence nor dishonesty, and their probative value for impeachment is based primarily upon their status as felonies in and of themselves.

(2) *The remoteness of the crime.* The older the crime, the less probative value it has in showing a witness's untruthful character. Convictions that exceed the ten year time limit, however, are presumptively inadmissible under Rule 609(b)—where a "reverse 403" balancing test is used.

(3) *The degree to which the witness's credibility is an issue in the case.* The more essential a witness's credibility is to a party's case, the more likely it is that the felony conviction will be admitted to assist the jury in determining the weight to be given the witness's testimony.

(4) *The importance of a criminal defendant's testimony.* The decision of a criminal defendant to testify in his own case may depend upon whether or not the prosecution is allowed to impeach him with a prior conviction. The degree to which his testimony is important to the defense is the degree to which his prior convictions will be excluded.

(5) *The similarity between the crime for which the defendant was convicted and the crime with which he is being charged.* The greater the resemblance between the impeachment crime and the crime for which the defendant is being tried, the more unfair prejudice the impeachment crime has. Similarity makes it more likely that a jury will use the impeachment crime to conclude that he committed a similar crime and must therefore be guilty of the present one. In other words, the more similar the crime, the less likely it is to be admitted to impeach a testifying criminal defendant.

Hypo

Mark has been indicted for murder. He plans to testify that he was some-where else the night of the murder and could not have committed it. His only other witness is his girlfriend Mary, who will testify that Mark was with her the evening of the murder. Mark and Mary have both been convicted of the felonies of burglary and armed robbery, having committed them together nine years ago. Analyze the admissibility of each of these convictions for each of these witnesses under Rule 609(a)(1).

Rule 609(a)(2) makes the admission of crimes involving dishonesty and false statement automatic. This is because they contain very high probative value for showing dishonesty, regardless of whether they are a felony or misdemeanor. But what qualifies as a crime of dishonesty or false statement?

United States v. Hayes

U.S. Court of Appeals for the Second Circuit
553 F.2d 824 (2nd Cir. 1977)

OAKES, Circuit Judge:

[Appellant was convicted on two counts each of robbery and using a weapon in connection with the robbery of two banks.] Similar act evidence was intro-duced as to another robbery by appellant of the Swiss Bank Corporation in the same general area of New York City on March 24, 1976. A fifth count, for assault on federal agents at the time of appellant's arrest was based on events occurring on April 2, 1976, on the sidewalk in front of a branch of the Irving Trust Company. We affirm on all counts.

Appellant [questions] the court's refusal to suppress evidence of a recent nar-cotics conviction so that he might testify.

We further hold that the court below did not err in refusing to suppress appellant's recent narcotics conviction. Appellant was convicted in early 1976 of one count of importation of cocaine. Under Rule 609(a) of the Federal Rules of Evidence, he sought a ruling in the instant case that the Government would not be permitted to use this conviction in cross-examining him if he should testify in his own defense. He was unsuccessful and accordingly did not take the stand. Rule 609(a) established a two-pronged test of admissibility:

> For the purposes of attacking the credibility of a witness, evidence that
> he has been convicted of a crime shall be admitted if elicited from him

or established by public record during cross-examination but only if the crime (1) was punishable by death or imprisonment in excess of one year under the law under which he was convicted, and the court determines that the probative value of admitting this evidence outweighs its prejudicial effect to the defendant, or (2) involved dishonesty or false statement, regardless of the punishment.

Under the second prong of this rule, evidence of conviction of a certain type of crime one involving "dishonesty or false statement" must be admitted, with the trial court having no discretion, regardless of the seriousness of the offense or its prejudice to the defendant. Because this rule is quite inflexible, allowing no leeway for consideration of mitigating circumstances, it was inevitable that Congress would define narrowly the words "dishonesty or false statement," which, taken at their broadest, involve activities that are part of nearly all crimes. Hence Congress emphasized that the second prong was meant to refer to convictions "peculiarly probative of credibility," such as those for "perjury or subornation of perjury, false statement, criminal fraud, embezzlement, or false pretense, or any other offense in the nature of *crimen falsi*, the commission of which involves some element of deceit, untruthfulness, or falsification bearing on the accused's propensity to testify truthfully." The use of the second prong of Rule 609(a) is thus restricted to convictions that bear directly on the likelihood that the defendant will testify truthfully (and not merely on whether he has a propensity to commit crimes). It follows that crimes of force, such as armed robbery or assault, or crimes of stealth, such as burglary, or petit larceny, do not come within this clause. If the title of an offense leaves room for doubt, a prosecutor desiring to take advantage of automatic admission of a conviction under the second prong must demonstrate to the court "that a particular prior conviction rested on facts warranting the dishonesty or false statement description."

Appellant's conviction was for the importation of cocaine, a crime in the uncertain middle category neither clearly covered nor clearly excluded by the second prong test and thus one as to which the Government must present specific facts relating to dishonesty or false statement. If this importation involved nothing more than stealth, the conviction could not be introduced under the second prong. If, on the other hand, the importation involved false written or oral statements, for example on customs forms, the conviction would be automatically admissible. Because nothing more than the bare fact of conviction is before us, we must conclude that the prosecution has failed to carry its burden of justifying the admission of appellant's conviction under the second prong of Rule 609(a). . . . .

Judgment affirmed.

Points for Discussion

a. Determining Crimes of Dishonesty or False Statement.

In 2006, Rule 609(a)(2) was amended to provide that a conviction may be automatically admitted to impeach a testifying witness if the proponent proves that "the conviction required the factfinder to find, or the defendant to admit, an act of dishonesty or false statement." In other words, acts of dishonesty or false statement must be included in the defining statutory elements that have to be proved beyond a reasonable doubt in order to convict. However, some courts, like the court in *Hayes,* allow the proponent to admit a Rule 609(a)(2) felony by showing that the way in which the crime was committed involved dishonesty or false statement even if the statutory elements of the crime do not require this showing, for example by showing that the defendant committed a robbery by falsely claiming to be a security guard to gain entrance to a bank. Crimes such as perjury, subordination of perjury, criminal fraud, embezzlement, or acts of false statement or false pretense qualify under either test.

b. "Crimen Falsi" Crimes.

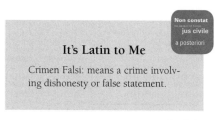

It's Latin to Me

Crimen Falsi: means a crime involving dishonesty or false statement.

There is still some debate on whether larceny qualifies as "crimen falsi." Compare *United States v. Carden,* 529 F.2d 443 (5th Cir. 1976) (petit larceny involves dishonesty), with *United States v. Fearwell,* 595 F.2d 771 (D.C. Cir. 1978) (petit larceny is not a crime of dishonesty or false statement unless it is committed by deceit). From what you know about larceny from criminal law, which approach is better?

c. Stale Convictions.

If the date of the conviction or the release of the defendant from confinement (whichever is more recent) is more than ten years, the conviction is presumptively inadmissible. Stale convictions are thought to no longer reveal anything relevant about the witness's character for truthfulness. However, if the impeachment value of a stale conviction substantially outweighs the risk of unfair prejudice and this "reverse 403" balancing is "supported by specific facts and circumstances," the judge may admit it. Under this formula, a 12-year-old fraud conviction might be admitted if the defendant shows a pattern of more recent offenses demonstrating her lack of rehabilitation. Put another way, if the defendant has a 12-year-old conviction for perjury, an 8-year-old conviction for burglary, and a 4-year-old conviction for fraud, the trial judge could, in her discretion, admit the stale conviction on the theory that the defendant had not changed her criminal ways.

5. Impeaching a Witness With a Prior Inconsistent Statement

Rule 613. Prior Statements of Witnesses

(a) **Examining Witness Concerning Prior Statement.** In examining a witness concerning a prior statement made by the witness, whether written or not, the statement need not be shown nor its contents disclosed to the witness at that time, but on request the same shall be shown or disclosed to opposing counsel.

(b) **Extrinsic Evidence of Prior Inconsistent Statement of Witness.** Extrinsic evidence of a prior inconsistent statement by a witness is not admissible unless the witness is afforded an opportunity to explain or deny the same and the opposite party is afforded an opportunity to interrogate the witness thereon, or the interests of justice other require. This provision does not apply to admissions of a party opponent as defined in rule 801(d)(2).

One of the most common methods of impeachment is to show the witness made a prior written or oral statement that is different from what she is saying now at trial. The fact that there is an inconsistency between the prior statement and in-court testimony may be sufficient to cause the jury to disbelieve either statement. It is not important which statement is true because the witness's credibility has been damaged either way. Because prior inconsistent statements are not offered for the truth of their contents, they are not considered hearsay.

Make the Connection

Use of prior inconsistent statements as non-hearsay is covered in Chapter 6.

Under the common law, as set out in *The Queen's Case*, 129 Eng. Rep. 976 (1820), the witness had to be told of the time, place, and person to whom the alleged inconsistent statement was made, and the witness had to be shown any written statement before impeachment could proceed. Only if the witness denied making the prior statement was the statement admissible in evidence. Neither of the *Queen's Case* requirements is necessary under Rule 613. The rule only requires that the witness at some point in time during the trial be given an opportunity to examine or explain her statement and the opposing party be given an opportunity examine the statement before the statement can be admitted into evidence. These opportunities need not come during cross-examination or even before the introduction of the statement.

United States v. Young

U.S. Court of Appeals for the Ninth Circuit
86 F.3d 944 (9th Cir. 1996)

TASHIMA, Circuit Judge:

[Defendants were charged with various narcotics offenses. Pursuant to a plea bargain, co-defendants Drake and Larsen testified for the government. Through their testimony, the government was able to show that the defendants used Drake as a middleman to distribute kilogram quantities of cocaine to Larsen.]

gov't argues

The government's final contention is that [defense witness] Delfs's testimony, offered as extrinsic evidence of Drake's prior inconsistent statement [that he would falsely accuse someone], would have been inadmissible in any case for lack of a proper foundation. The government asserts that Fed.R.Evid. 613(b) barred admission of Delfs's testimony because the defense did not first provide Drake an opportunity to explain or deny his prior inconsistent statement.

ct. disagrees R.613(b) require

> **FYI**
>
> The trial judge also has the discretion to dispense with the Rule 613(b) requirements in the "interests of justice." The judge might choose to exercise this discretion if a prior inconsistent statement has been admitted, and the witness cannot be recalled to explain or deny it because he has died, disappeared, or is otherwise unavailable.

The government's argument is without merit. We have expressly recognized that the foundational prerequisites of Rule 613(b) require only that the witness be permitted-at some point-to explain or deny the prior inconsistent statement. On cross-examination, Drake denied ever having gone to Flash's (Adams's) house in November 1994, which is where Delfs alleged that Drake made the inconsistent statement. It may have been preferable for Tamez's counsel to question Drake directly whether he ever stated that he intended falsely to accuse a source in the Tri-Cities. However, even absent Drake's flat denial of the statement on cross-examination, Delfs's testimony concerning Drake's prior inconsistent statement would not have been barred[The government would have been free to re-call Drake as a witness and give him an additional opportunity to explain or deny the statement attributed to him.] Thus, the government's objection to Delfs's testimony on the basis of Rule 613(b) is without merit.

————————

Points for Discussion

a. The Virtue of Rule 613.

One advantage Rule 613 has over *The Queen's Case* foundation is that a lying witness is not warned as early in cross-examination about the fact that she previously made a false statement. This is particularly useful in examining several witnesses about a joint statement before the statement is introduced into evidence. Even though Rule 613(b) relaxes the common law foundation required by *The Queen's case*, why does the court in *Young* say that the government, the party opposing admission of the inconsistent statement, is the party who should have re-called the witness to explain or deny making it? Isn't this what the defense should have done?

b. The Dangers of Rule 613.

One of the dangers of allowing a party to impeach a witness with her prior inconsistent statement before she has an opportunity to explain or deny it, is that the lawyer may be bluffing in an attempt to create a false impression with the jury. This possibility is handled in the rule by the requirement that the statement must be shown or its contents disclosed to opposing counsel upon request before the questioning begins. The common law had no such requirement.

c. The Advantages of *The Queen's Case* Foundation.

The Queen's Case foundation required that the witness be alerted to the time, place, and persons to whom the statement was made and be given an opportunity to explain or deny the statement before it could be introduced into evidence. This is not a requirement under Rule 613. If the witness admits having made the statement, laying this foundation saves time because the statement is not then admitted.

d. Extrinsic Evidence is only Admissible to Disprove a Material Statement under Rule 613(b).

Rule 613(b) only admits prior inconsistent statements as extrinsic evidence if the content of that statement is material to the case. If a witness testifies she is 24 years old, and she stated in a prior deposition that she was 26, the cross-examiner may ask the witness about her prior statement, but if she denies making it, the cross-examiner cannot introduce the statement into evidence. The two-year discrepancy in age would be a "collateral matter" and the court need not waste valuable court time by having a mini-trial as to her age. On the other hand, if the witness testifies she saw the defendant rob a liquor store in a prior statement to the police, and she testifies at his trial that the robber was someone else, the cross-examiner may not only ask her if she made a prior inconsistent statement but also introduce that statement into evidence under Rule 613(b) because the issue is considered non-collateral (material).

————

6. Impeaching a Witness by Showing Bias

Bias is a term used to describe a person's tendency to be prejudiced either for or against someone which interferes with that person's ability to be impartial. A witness can be biased in an infinite number of ways, including partiality due to love, hate, financial interest, employment, or even membership in an organization. Often, bias must be proved circumstantially because witnesses seldom directly admit their biases.

United States v. Abel

Supreme Court of the United States
469 U.S. 45 (1984)

Justice REHNQUIST delivered the opinion of the Court.

Respondent John Abel and two cohorts were indicted for robbing a savings and loan in Bellflower, Cal.. The cohorts elected to plead guilty, but respondent went to trial. One of the cohorts, Kurt Ehle, agreed to testify against respondent and identify him as a participant in the robbery.

Respondent informed the District Court at a pretrial conference that he would seek to counter Ehle's testimony with that of Robert Mills. Mills was not a participant in the robbery but was friendly with respondent and with Ehle, and had spent time with both in prison. Mills planned to testify that after the robbery Ehle had admitted to Mills that Ehle intended to implicate respondent falsely in order to receive favorable treatment from the Government. The prosecutor in turn disclosed that he intended to discredit Mills' testimony by calling Ehle back to the stand and eliciting from Ehle the fact that respondent, Mills, and Ehle were all members of the "Aryan Brotherhood," a secret prison gang that required its members always to deny the existence of the organization and to commit perjury, theft, and murder on each member's behalf.

Defense counsel objected to Ehle's proffered rebuttal testimony as too prejudicial to respondent. After a lengthy discussion in chambers the District Court decided to permit the prosecutor to cross-examine Mills about the gang, and

DC allowed rebuttal

if Mills denied knowledge of the gang, to introduce Ehle's rebuttal testimony concerning the tenets of the gang and Mills' and respondent's membership in it. The District Court held that the probative value of Ehle's rebuttal testimony outweighed its prejudicial effect, but that respondent might be entitled to a limiting instruction if his counsel would submit one to the court.

prob > prejudice

At trial Ehle implicated respondent as a participant in the robbery. Mills, called by respondent, testified that Ehle told him in prison that Ehle planned to implicate respondent falsely. When the prosecutor sought to cross-examine Mills concerning membership in the prison gang, the District Court conferred again with counsel outside of the jury's presence, and ordered the prosecutor not to use the term "Aryan Brotherhood" because it was unduly prejudicial. Accordingly, the prosecutor asked Mills if he and respondent were members of a "secret type of prison organization" which had a creed requiring members to deny its existence and lie for each other. When Mills denied knowledge of such an organization the prosecutor recalled Ehle.

*P
recalled
Ehle*

Ehle testified that respondent, Mills, and he were indeed members of a secret prison organization whose tenets required its members to deny its existence and "lie, cheat, steal [and] kill" to protect each other. . . .Respondent's counsel did not request a limiting instruction and none was given.

*1) didn't request
limiting instruction.*

The jury convicted respondent. On his appeal a divided panel of the Court of Appeals reversed. The Court of Appeals held that Ehle's rebuttal testimony was admitted not just to show that respondent's and Mills' membership in the same group might cause Mills to color his testimony; the court held that the contested evidence was also admitted to show that because Mills belonged to a perjurious organization, he must be lying on the stand. This suggestion of perjury, based upon a group tenet, was impermissible. The court reasoned:

> "It is settled law that the government may not convict an individual merely for belonging to an organization that advocates illegal activity. Rather, the government must show that the individual knows of and personally accepts the tenets of the organization. Neither should the government be allowed to impeach on the grounds of mere membership, since membership, without more, has no probative value. It establishes nothing about the individual's own actions, beliefs, or veracity."

The court concluded that Ehle's testimony implicated respondent as a member of the gang; but since respondent did not take the stand, the testimony could not have been offered to impeach him and it prejudiced him "by mere association." . . .

*appeals ct.
said*

Both parties correctly assume, as did the District Court and the Court of Appeals, that the question is governed by the Federal Rules of Evidence. But the Rules do not by their terms deal with impeachment for "bias," although they do expressly treat impeachment by character evidence and conduct, Rule 608, by evidence of conviction of a crime, Rule 609, and by showing of religious beliefs or opinion, Rule 610. Neither party has suggested what significance we should attribute to this fact. Although we are nominally the promulgators of the Rules, and should in theory need only to consult our collective memories to analyze the situation properly, we are in truth merely a conduit when we deal with an undertaking as substantial as the preparation of the Federal Rules of Evidence. In the case of these Rules, too, it must be remembered that Congress extensively reviewed our submission, and considerably revised it.

Before the present Rules were promulgated, the admissibility of evidence in the federal courts was governed in part by statutes or Rules, and in part by case law. This Court had held that a trial court must allow some cross-examination of a witness to show bias. This holding was in accord with the overwhelming weight of authority in the state courts as reflected in Wigmore's classic treatise on the law of evidence. Our decision in *Davis v. Alaska,* 415 U.S. 308, 94 S.Ct. 1105, 39 L.Ed.2d 347 (1974), holds that the Confrontation Clause of the Sixth Amendment requires a defendant to have some opportunity to show bias on the part of a prosecution witness.

With this state of unanimity confronting the drafters of the Federal Rules of Evidence, we think it unlikely that they intended to scuttle entirely the evidentiary availability of cross-examination for bias. One commentator, recognizing the omission of any express treatment of impeachment for bias, prejudice, or corruption, observes that the Rules "clearly contemplate the use of the above-mentioned grounds of impeachment." Other commentators, without mentioning the omission, treat bias as a permissible and established basis of impeachment under the Rules.

We think this conclusion is obviously correct. Rule 401 defines as "relevant evidence" evidence having any tendency to make the existence of any fact that is of consequence to the determination of the action more probable or less probable than it would be without the evidence. Rule 402 provides that all relevant evidence is admissible, except as otherwise provided by the United States Constitution, by Act of Congress, or by applicable rule. A successful showing of bias on the part of a witness would have a tendency to make the facts to which he testified less probable in the eyes of the jury than it would be without such testimony.

The correctness of the conclusion that the Rules contemplate impeachment by showing of bias is confirmed by the references to bias in the Advisory Committee Notes to Rules 608 and 610, and by the provisions allowing any party to attack credibility in Rule 607, and allowing cross-examination on "matters affecting the credibility of the witness" in Rule 611(b). The Courts of Appeals have upheld use of extrinsic evidence to show bias both before and after the adoption of the Federal Rules of Evidence. . . .

Ehle's testimony about the prison gang certainly made the existence of Mills' bias towards respondent more probable. Thus it was relevant to support that inference. Bias is a term used in the "common law of evidence" to describe the relationship between a party and a witness which might lead the witness to slant, unconsciously or otherwise, his testimony in favor of or against a party. Bias may be induced by a witness' like, dislike, or fear of a party, or by the witness' self-interest. Proof of bias is almost always relevant because the jury, as finder of fact and weigher of credibility, has historically been entitled to assess all evidence which might bear on the accuracy and truth of a witness' testimony. The "common law of evidence" allowed the showing of bias by extrinsic evidence, while requiring the cross-examiner to "take the answer of the witness" with respect to less favored forms of impeachment.

bias may be introduced

Mills' and respondent's membership in the Aryan Brotherhood supported the inference that Mills' testimony was slanted or perhaps fabricated in respondent's favor. A witness' and a party's common membership in an organization, even without proof that the witness or party has personally adopted its tenets, is certainly probative of bias. . . . Mills' and respondent's membership in the Aryan Brotherhood was not offered to convict either of a crime, but <u>to impeach Mills' testimony.</u> Mills was subject to no sanction other than that he might be dis-

proof of membership was offered

believed. . . .For purposes of the law of evidence the jury may be permitted to draw an inference of subscription to the tenets of the organization from membership alone, even though such an inference would not be sufficient to convict beyond a reasonable doubt in a criminal prosecution under the Smith Act.

What's That?

The Smith Act is a federal law criminalizing membership in subversive organizations.

Respondent argues that even if the evidence of membership in the prison gang were relevant to show bias, the[District Court erred in permitting a full description of the gang and its odious tenets.]Respondent contends that the District Court abused its discretion under Federal Rules of Evidence 403, because the prejudicial effect of the contested evidence outweighed its probative value. In other words, testimony about the gang inflamed the jury against respondent, and the chance that he would be convicted by his mere association with the organization outweighed any probative value the testimony may have had on Mills' bias.

D argues

Respondent specifically contends that the District Court should not have permitted Ehle's precise description of the gang as a lying and murderous group. Respondent suggests that the District Court should have cut off the testimony after the prosecutor had elicited that Mills knew respondent and both may have belonged to an organization together. This argument ignores the fact that the type of organization in which a witness and a party share membership may be relevant to show bias. If the organization is a loosely knit group having nothing to do with the subject matter of the litigation, the inference of bias arising from common membership may be small or nonexistent. If the prosecutor had elicited that both respondent and Mills belonged to the Book of the Month Club, the jury probably would not have inferred bias even if the District Court had admitted the testimony. The attributes of the Aryan Brotherhood-a secret prison sect sworn to perjury and self-protection-bore directly not only on the fact of bias but also on the source and strength of Mills' bias. The tenets of this group showed that Mills had a powerful motive to slant his testimony towards respondent, or even commit perjury outright.

A district court is accorded a wide discretion in determining the admissibility of evidence under the Federal Rules. Assessing the probative value of common membership in any particular group, and weighing any factors counseling against admissibility is a matter first for the district court's sound judgment under Rule 401 and 403 and ultimately, if the evidence is admitted, for the trier of fact.

Before admitting Ehle's rebuttal testimony, the District Court gave heed to the extensive arguments of counsel, both in chambers and at the bench. In an attempt to avoid undue prejudice to respondent the court ordered that the name "Aryan Brotherhood" not be used. The court also offered to give a limiting instruction concerning the testimony, and it sustained defense objections to the prosecutor's questions concerning the punishment meted out to unfaithful members. These precautions did not prevent all prejudice to respondent from Ehle's testimony, but they did, in our opinion, ensure that the admission of this highly probative evidence did not unduly prejudice respondent. We hold there was no abuse of discretion under Rule 403 in admitting Ehle's testimony as to membership and tenets.

The judgment of the Court of Appeals is reversed.

————————

Points for Discussion

a. Extrinsic Evidence to Prove a Witness's Bias.

Recall there are limits to the admissibility of extrinsic evidence to impeach a witness. Rule 608(b), for example, requires that the questioner "take the answer" of the witness when impeaching with prior specific acts involving dishonesty and prohibits introduction of extrinsic evidence. Why is the law more willing to admit extrinsic evidence of bias than prior acts of dishonest conduct to attack character for truthfulness?

b. Bias and Rule 610.

What if the Aryan Brotherhood argued that it was a religion and that its tenets were an article of faith? Would Rule 610, which prohibits "evidence of the beliefs or opinions of a witness on matters of religion" to prove or disprove the witness's credibility, prevent the prosecution from impeaching Mills for bias? Are the Aryan Brotherhood's tenets the type of beliefs Rule 610 had in mind?

c. The Constitutional Ramifications of Showing Bias.

In *Davis v. Alaska*, 415 U.S. 308 (1974) the defense wanted to show that a juvenile prosecution witness, who had been involved in a crime, feared revocation of his probation and thus had a strong motive to wrongfully incriminate the defendant. The prosecution argued that juvenile records were confidential and should not be used for impeachment. The Court held that the Sixth Amendment Confrontation Clause trumped the confidentiality of juvenile records and their use for impeachment. If the juvenile's testimony had not been so critical to the prosecution's case, would there have been the same result? Does this mean that any time a defense attorney wants to show bias of a prosecution witness that showing is constitutionally required? See *United States v. Renfro*, 620 F.2d 497 (5th Cir. 1980) (evidence that a testifying FBI agent had offered immunity to potential witnesses against the defendant was excluded as unfairly prejudicial).

7. An Extrinsic Evidence Chart

The following chart summarizes what we have learned so far about using extrinsic evidence to refute a witness's denial of impeachment evidence.

Extrinsic Evidence May Be Used If Witness Denies:	Extrinsic May Not Be Used If Witness Denies
1. Prior Convictions Rule 609	1. Character for Truthfulness Rule 608(a) and (b)
2. Prior Inconsistent Statements on a Material Issue	2. Prior Inconsistent Statements as to a Non- Material Issue
3. Bias	

Executive Summary

Direct Examination

Attorneys should ask open-ended, non-leading "who, what, when, where, why, and how" questions when examining a "friendly" witness on direct. That way, the witness can tell her story, in her own words, and build rapport and establish credibility.

Cross-Examination

Cross-examination is the hallmark of the adversarial system. It allows an attorney to challenge the four testimonial capacities of a witness: (1) perception, (2) memory, (3) communication, and (4) veracity. However, under Rule 611(b), the scope of the cross-examination is limited to the scope of the direct examination, unless the judge in her discretion allows the questioning to go beyond that scope. Under Rule 611(c), attorneys should ask leading questions for which they already know the answer when questioning a hostile or adverse witness in order to attack the witness's four testimonial capacities and undermine credibility.

Refreshing Recollection

If a witness forgets something while testifying, then Rule 612 allows the questioning attorney to use a document, on any other item, to refresh the witness's recollection. Once the witness's memory is refreshed, the document should be removed, so that the witness can testify from her "sparked" memory. The document is not admitted into evidence (unless the opposing party submits it) because the document itself is not evidence; only the testimony of the witness, whose memory has just been refreshed, is evidence. (*Doty*) Do not confuse Rule 612 "refreshed recollection," with Rule 803(5) "past recollection recorded," a hearsay exception. Rule 803(5) is used when the witness's recollection cannot be refreshed, but a document contains the witness's past recollection recorded that can be read to the fact-finder in open court as allowable hearsay to prove the truth of the matter asserted in the document.

Impeachment

A party may impeach any hostile or adverse witness, including their own witness, under Rule 607. However, a party cannot call adverse witnesses on direct examination solely to impeach them with a prior inconsistent statement because such a statement used this way would constitute inadmissible hearsay (*Morlang*). Also, a party may not "bolster," or vouch for, the credibility of a witness by putting on a second witness to testify that the first witness is a truthful person and is telling the truth. (*Rosario-Diaz*). Bolstering of a witness is allowed only when that witness's character for truthfulness has first been attacked.

Attacking a Witness's Character for Truthfulness

Do not confuse *character for truthfulness* under Rule 608, with *general* character of a criminal defendant or victim, such as the defendant's or the victim's character for peacefulness or violence, under Rule 404. Rule 608(a) allows either party, in either a criminal or civil case, to attack the character for truthfulness of any witness who takes the stand. Once attacked, that witness's character for truthfulness can be bolstered. When attacking character for truthfulness (or the alleged "propensity" to lie), Rule 608(a) allows a party to offer a second witness to testify that the first witness has a bad *reputation* for being untruthful, or in the *opinion* of the second witness, the first witness has bad character for truthfulness (is a "liar"). (*Whitmore I*).

Rule 608(b) does not allow extrinsic evidence of a specific instance of conduct to prove bad character for truthfulness. However, a lawyer can often *ask about* specific instances of conduct to test the credibility of a witness that is attacking the character for truthfulness of another witness, but because no extrinsic evidence is allowed, the lawyer is "stuck" with whatever answer is given by the witness. (*Whitmore II*). The lawyer must have a "good-faith basis" for asking the question.

However, if that specific instance of conduct – showing the bad character for truthfulness of a testifying witness – is a criminal *conviction of* that witness, then Rule 609 often allows extrinsic evidence of that conviction (testimony and the conviction records) to attack the character for truthfulness of the testifying witness.

Admission of the testifying witness's former conviction under Rule 609 depends on whether the conviction was for a felony, or for a misdemeanor. Under 609(a)(1), the conviction must be of a felony. If it is a felony then we must look to the status of the witness in order to determine which balancing test to apply.

If the witness is the defendant in a criminal case, the conviction's probative value of bad character for truthfulness must outweigh its unfair prejudice. The concern often is that the jury might use the conviction as evidence of bad *general* character under Rule 404 (which is prohibited), instead of as evidence of bad character *for truthfulness* (felony convictions show bad character for truthfulness by definition). If the witness is not a criminal defendant, then the Rule 403 balancing test applies – the conviction is admitted, provided its probative value of bad character for truthfulness is not substantially outweighed by its unfair prejudice. (*Sanders*).

If the conviction is for a crime involving *deceit or false statement*, such as perjury or fraud, or any other such narrowly construed deceit/false statement crime, then that conviction "shall be admitted" – there is no balancing test applied and the witness's status does not matter. This type of conviction will be admissible regardless of whether it was a felony or misdemeanor conviction. (*Hayes*)

If a conviction is over ten years old, then under Rule 609(b), yet another balancing test applies. The probative value of the "old" conviction showing bad character for truthfulness must substantially outweigh its unfair prejudice. Note how this is a "*reverse*" Rule 403 balancing.

Attacking a Witness's Credibility with a Prior Inconsistent Statement and/or Bias

In addition to attacking a witness's veracity by attacking that witness's character for truthfulness – showing them to be a "liar" (see above) – another way to attack veracity is to show that the witness is specifically "lying" about a matter in their testimony. The former is a character/propensity attack, while the latter is not because it does not involve showing that they have a propensity to lie (that they are a "liar") and therefore might lie; instead, it involves catching them in a specific lie while testifying (that they are "lying").

Rule 613 allows an attorney to show that the witness's story is inconsistent, that she says different things at different times, and is therefore not trustworthy. If the attorney is going to submit the prior inconsistent statement in evidence, then under Rule 613(b), that attorney must give the witness an opportunity to explain or deny the prior inconsistent statement at some point in the trial. (*Young*).

Finally, even if a witness is not a "liar" by nature (Rule 608/609 character for truthfulness), nor has changed their story (Rule 613 prior inconsistent statement), an attorney may show that the witness has a specific *incentive or reason to lie* – such as a personal or economic *bias* in the case. (*Abel*).

Chapter 6

Hearsay

A. Introduction – The Idea Behind the Hearsay Rule

The term "hearsay" may seem familiar. Intuitively, one may recognize that statements which are made outside of a courtroom are thought of as hearsay. That is, "hearsay" is generally used to describe what one person "hears" another person "say." Inherent in this doctrine is the possibility that what is ultimately testified to in a court of law may be untrustworthy. Risks associated with hearsay are usually classified into four basic areas: perception (or misperception); recollection (or faulty memory); narration (or ambiguity in the statements) and sincerity (or insin- cerity on the part of the speaker). These risks are more fully discussed below.

To be admitted, evidence which is hearsay must meet an exception or exemption. The following case helps illustrate the significance behind the rules of hearsay:

1. The Trial of Sir Walter Raleigh

The Trial of Sir Walter Raleigh for High Treason
2 How. St. Tr. 1, 27 (1603)

Sir Walter Raleigh was tried for treason. The indictment included the following allegations:

> [T]hat [Sir Walter Raleigh] ... had conspired to kill the King, to raise a rebellion, with intent to change the religion and subvert the government, and, for that purpose, to encourage and incite the king's enemies to invade the realm. ... [It was alleged that] Sir Walter Raleigh had conferred with Lord Cobham about advancing Arabella Stuart [an aunt of the King, James I] to the Crown of England, and dispossessing the King; that it was then arranged that Lord Cobham should go to the King of Spain ... for the purpose of supporting Arabella Stuart's title....

> To this Indictment, Sir Walter Raleigh pleaded Not Guilty....

Defendants in cases of treason did not have a right to counsel and Sir Walter Raleigh represented himself. He repeatedly complained that his alleged coconspirator, Lord Cobham, whose confession led to the indictment of Raleigh, did not appear in court to testify against Raleigh. Instead, his confession was read into evidence and used against Raleigh. Lord Cobham was being held in jail nearby and was available to testify in person.

Lord Cobham's Confession which was read into evidence:

> "He confesseth that he [Cobham] had ... a Passport to go into Spain, and that he intended ... to confer with the Archduke about these practices.... Being shown a note under Raleigh's hand, ... [he] then said, that he [Cobham] had never entered into these courses, but by Raleigh's instigation, and that [Raleigh] would never let him alone ...."

In essence, Cohbam alleged that his involvement was at the instigation and urging of Raleigh. He says but for Raleigh, he would not have been involved. Part of Raleigh's defense was that Cobham had implicated Raleigh in an effort to save his own life. Raleigh consistently expressed his innocence and believed that Cobham, who he alleged fabricated his accusations against Raleigh, would not lie to his face. Therefore, throughout the trial he consistently asked for Cobham to be brought into court so that he may face his accuser. This concept underlies the basis for the hearsay rule.

> *Raleigh: This (Cobham's confession) is absolutely all the evidence can be brought against me;*
>
> *Popham, L.C.J.: [T]he countenance and action of my Lord Cobham much satisfied me that what he confessed was true, and that he surely thought Sir [Walter] Raleigh had betrayed him.*
>
> *Raleigh: ... I claim to have my accuser brought here face to face to speak.... If you proceed to condemn me ... without witnesses, upon a paper accusation, you try me by the Spanish Inquisition....*
>
> *[R]emember too the story of Susannah; she was falsely accused, and Daniel called the judge's 'fools, because without examination of the truth they had condemned a daughter of Israel,' and he discovered the false witnesses by asking them questions.*
>
> *... I beseech you, my lords, let Cobham be sent for, let him be charged upon his soul ... and if he will then maintain his accusation to my face, I will confess myself guilty.*
>
> *Popham, C.J.: ... And of all other proofs, the accusation of one, who by his confession accuseth first himself, is the strongest, for that hath the force of a verdict of twelve men.*

Raleigh: But it is strange to see how you press me still with my Lord Cobham, and yet will not produce him; ... he is [held as a prisoner] and may soon be brought [here into court]. ... [L]et him be produced, and if he will yet accuse me, or avow this confession of his, it shall convict me....

Raleigh: [L]et my accuser come face to face, and be [questioned].

Popham, C. J.: Where no circumstances do concur to make a matter probable, then an accuser may be heard; but so many circumstances agreeing and confirming the accusation in this case, the accuser is not to be produced; for, having first confessed against himself voluntarily, and so charged another person, if we shall now hear him again in person, he may, for favour or fear, retract what formerly he hath said, and the jury may, by that means, be inveigled."

Raleigh: ... I may be massacred by mere hearsay. ... You say, that Brooke told Watson what Cobham told Brooke, that I had said to him;—what proof is this? ...

Raleigh: " The common trial of England is by jury and witnesses."

Chief Justice: "No, by examination; if three conspire a treason, and they all confess it, here is never a witness, yet they are condemned." Justice Warburton.—" I marvel, Sir Walter, that you, being of such experience and wit, should stand on this point; for so many horse stealers may escape, if they may not be condemned without witnesses. ... My Lord Cobham hath, perhaps, been laboured withal; and to save you, his old friend, it may be that he will deny all that which he hath said."

Raleigh: I have already often urged the producing of my Lord Cobham, but it is still denied me. I appeal now once more to your lordships in this: my Lord Cobham is the only one that hath accused me, for all the treasons urged upon me are by reflection from him. ... [L]et him now by word of mouth convict or condemn me.

At the conclusion of the trial the jury deliberated and returned a verdict after only fifteen minutes. The verdict: Guilty of Treason.[1]

———————

The beginning, or starting point, for most "hearsay" evidence is that such statements will generally not be admitted into evidence. This rule of exclusion embodies the fundamental idea of a fair trial, the idea that one should be able to cross-examine one who speaks evidence relevant to the issues before the court; the very point of which Sir Walter Raleigh complained. The rule presumes that we should distrust statements which have been made out-of-court and are merely repeated in the courtroom without the proper opportunity to question the speaker.

———————

[1] Wilson's Remarkable Trials, The Making of the Modern Law: Trials 1600-1926, *Trial and Conviction of Sir Walter Raleigh, for High Treason.* (Gale 2008).

Without a statement falling within an exception to the rule, such statements are excluded on the basis that the fact finder cannot assess the veracity or accuracy of the statement. The Hearsay Rule is exclusionary.

Hearsay creates some unique concerns with regard to the viability of evidence. Admissible evidence is intended to be reliable and accurate. However, the fact finder (judge or jury) is not in a position to assess the accuracy of out of court statements. Therefore, the rules are designed to ensure, in appropriate circumstances, a level of reliability without complete exclusion of relevant evidence. "The primary reason for excluding hearsay is that the trier of fact has no adequate basis for evaluating the declarant's credibility, because the declarant was not subject to cross-examination under oath in the trier's presence."[2]

2. Hearsay Risks

As mentioned above, risks associated with hearsay are often categorized into four areas: (1) perception, (2) recollection, (3) narration, and (4) sincerity.

Illustrative Fact Pattern:

Law students Ashley and John have dated since their first year. John loves ballet; Ashley hates ballet and loves college football. John tells Ashley that he has two tickets to the ballet for Saturday night (which happens to be the evening of her college homecoming game). Ashley apologizes that she will be unable to accompany John to the ballet because she must go home (200 miles away) for the weekend to help with a family problem. John attends the ballet with a friend. On Tuesday John passes his friend Barry between classes. As Barry is walking away he says, "I saw Ashley at the game."

John draws the conclusion from Barry's statement that Ashley has deceived him about the weekend. Would the risks associated with hearsay make John's conclusion erroneous?

> *Perception:* Although there are numerous definitions of perception, one such definition from the Oxford English Dictionary is: "to apprehend through one of the senses, especially sight; to become aware of by seeing, hearing, etc.; to see; to detect." The risk with perception is that the one perceiving may have made an error.
>
> > *Example:* Barry saw someone at the game who resembled Ashley but who was not Ashley. Barry made an error in perception.

---

[2] Park, Roger C., "I DIDN'T TELL THEM ANYTHING ABOUT YOU": IMPLIED ASSERTIONS AS HEARSAY UNDER THE FEDERAL RULES OF EVIDENCE, 74 MNLR 783 (1990).

Recollection: This risk is also known as memory. Even though one may have accurately perceived an event, upon recalling that event an error may be made. The Oxford English Dictionary includes the following in their many definitions: "that which is remembered of a person, object, or event." The risk is that the recollection may be inaccurate.

> *Example:* Barry has seen Ashley at many other games, but Barry did not see Ashley at Saturday's game. Barry's recollection is imperfect. His recollection of last Saturday night's game now has an image of Ashley in it. Barry's perceptions were all accurate when made, but an error of memory has produced an erroneous belief at the time of the statement.

Narration: The risk in narration is that the person communicating the information may make an error in the communication. Note that even though the person communicating the information correctly perceived and recalled the information, the narration may result in an error.

> *Example*: Barry was referring to a different game, such as an intramural (or practice) game on Sunday or Monday evening, not the game on Saturday night. This narration, or poor explanation, led to John's incorrect conclusion.

Narration in the context of hearsay refers to all "accidental" forms of miscommunication, not just those that result from some identifiable misuse of language by the declarant. NOTE: ambiguity and misinterpretation may occur without fault by speaker or writer.

> *Sincerity:* The Oxford English Dictionary defines sincerity as "freedom from falsification, adulteration, or alloy; purity, correctness." Another way to express this risk is the risk of the declarant lying.

> *Example:* Barry may be lying. His motivation may include trying to cause trouble between John and Ashley.

It is difficult to fully explore these issues if Barry is not on the witness stand to be cross-examined.

3. Trial Safeguards

The hearsay rule is designed to help combat the risks associated with hearsay. Additionally, other tools are used to help safeguard against these risks. These safeguards include cross-examination, oath, and assessment of a witness's demeanor. These safeguards are more fully discussed in other sections of this text.

B. Analysis Under the Rules

The rules of evidence approach hearsay by defining what constitutes hearsay (Rule 801), excluding that evidence which is defined as hearsay (Rule 802) and then by providing exceptions to the exclusion of such evidence (Rules 803 and 804).

Rule 802. Hearsay Rule

Hearsay is not admissible except as provided by these rules or by other rules prescribed by the Supreme Court pursuant to statutory authority or by Act of Congress.

Make the Connection

Although evidence may not be excluded because of the hearsay rule, another rule of evidence may result in its exclusion.

Because the rule is exclusionary, it must be determined whether statements offered into evidence fit within the definition. If a particular statement does not fit within the definition, it is not hearsay, and therefore, it is not excluded under the rule. Any hearsay analysis should begin with parts *a* through *c* of Rule 801.

Rule 801. Definitions *(Parts a – c)*

The following definitions apply under this article:

(a) Statement. A "statement" is (1) an oral or written assertion or (2) non-verbal conduct of a person, if it is intended by the person as an assertion.

(b) Declarant. A "declarant" is a person who makes a statement.

(c) Hearsay. "Hearsay" is a statement, other than one made by the declarant while testifying at the trial or hearing, offered into evidence to prove the truth of the matter asserted.

801 (a) Statements

(a) Statement. A "statement" is (1) an oral or written assertion or (2) non-verbal conduct of a person, if it is intended by the person as an assertion.

What is a "statement?"

Regardless of the purpose for which evidence is offered, it is not excluded under the hearsay rule unless it qualifies as a statement. The definition of a statement in this context is provided by the rule. Application of this definition is relatively straight-forward. Both oral and written assertions are included within the definition. Also, non-verbal conduct can constitute a statement if the person demonstrating the non-verbal conduct intends such conduct to constitute an assertion.

Most words spoken are assertive; that is, the words both express and are intended to communicate ideas through the use of language to be heard by a listener. Under Rule 801, it appears that words are not always assertive. Variances of language usage may help illustrate the complexities of these assertions. Here are some examples:

Direct Assertions: Most statements are direct assertions. The words used directly state the meaning that the speaker intends to convey. The statement, "that woman just ran the red light." is a direct assertion which communicates the speaker's perception of the event. The intent behind the words is clear and if later offered at trial, the statement would be hearsay under the definition.

> *Example:* "Jason took the candy from the jar." This is a direct assertion where the speaker conveys her perception.

Hidden Assertions: Some statements are not obvious; rather, they are somewhat hidden. An individual's literal words do not always express what the speaker intends to assert.

> *Example:* "That car is really hot." The speaker may be referring to the car's temperature (a direct assertion) or, the speaker may be using 'hot' in the colloquial term as being very attractive.

Hidden assertions are still assertions and are still subject to the restrictions of the hearsay rules.

Hyperbolic Assertions: A statement that is expressed as hyperbole is still an assertion of the true underlying meaning.

> *Example:* "I'm so hungry I could eat a horse." This is still an assertion of extreme hunger even though the speaker is not asserting that he could eat a real horse.

Indirect Assertions: An indirect assertion is an assertion that is intended with the words spoken but is not reflected in the words spoken.

> *Example #1:* John Doe is charged with burglary of a business that occurred on Thursday at 6:00 p.m. In order to prove that John Doe had the opportunity to burglarize the business, David testifies that he saw John Doe walking outside the business at approximately 6:00 on the night of the burglary.

The context might indicate that John Doe committed the burglary or at least provide some evidence that he had the opportunity to do so.

> *Example #2:* Suppose Jenny is stopped at an intersection and sees James run a red light. Jenny says to her passenger, "No one pays attention to red lights anymore. He could have injured someone. That was foolish."

Here, the context might indicate that James ran the red light. The listener can interpret the statement of Jenny as an implied assertion that James ran the red light.

These examples are indirect statements because the speaker did not likely mean what was indicated by the literal words. Indirect assertions do not escape the application of the hearsay rule. In Example #2 above, if the court determines that Jenny's purpose was to convey that James ran the red light, then the statement is hearsay. It makes no difference that the literal meaning of the words differs from the intended meaning. An indirect assertion is still an assertion and the hearsay rule still applies.

Linked Assertions: Linked assertions require additional information to determine what is being asserted by the declarant. As an example, the assertion "Yes" means nothing unless one knows what question is being asked.

> *Example:* David: Did you rob the business?
>
>   John: Yes.

Without David's question, John's response, which is clearly an assertion, does not have any meaning.

Vicarious Assertions: An assertion which is vicarious is an assertion by a declarant treated as though it had been made by another person.

> *Example:* "John saw the green car run the red light." In this example the statement is attributed to John even though John did not speak the words.

Implied Assertions: An implied assertion is an assertion which is not directly reflected in the words spoken. Rather, the assertion must be implied from the words. Implied assertions can create a number of difficulties. They are often not considered a statement under the rules. Consider the following example.

> *Example:* David calls John at John's house. David asks "Hey John, do you have any Marijuana?" At a subsequent trial, the prosecution seeks to introduce this phone call. David's words could be interpreted to include several implied assertions:

1) David's call could be offered to prove that John could supply Marijuana.

2) David's call could be offered to prove David believed that John could supply Marijuana.

3) The behavior of David in making the call is behavior from which it could be inferred that John could supply Marijuana.

4) The behavior of David in making the call is behavior from which it could be inferred that David believed John could supply Marijuana.

The purpose for which evidence is offered is critical in a hearsay analysis. As reflected in the discussion of 801(c), if not offered for the truth of the matter asserted, then the statement will not be considered hearsay. Under illustration 1, above, the statement offered as an implied assertion fits the definition under 801. Under illustration 3, the question of whether or not the statement is hearsay is more challenging. It is more akin to illustration #1 and, therefore, more likely to be considered an assertion under the definition. Under illustrations 2 and 4 above, the fact that a belief can be ascertained is not likely to be an assertion under the definition.

Conduct Constituting an Assertion

Nonverbal conduct, or a person's actions, may be regarded as a statement for purposes of the hearsay rule. Some nonverbal conduct, such as the act of pointing to identify a suspect in a lineup, is clearly the equivalent of words, assertive in nature, and to be regarded as a statement. Other nonverbal conduct, however, may be offered as evidence that the person acted as he did because of his *belief* in the existence of the condition sought to be proved, from which belief the existence of the condition may be inferred. This sequence is, arguably, in effect an assertion of the existence of the condition and hence properly includable within the hearsay concept.[4]

Evidence which is nonverbal and which constitutes an assertion but is offered for the implied belief behind the assertion is untested with respect to the perception, memory, sincerity and narration (or their equivalents) of the declarant. However, Advisory Committee opined that these risks are minimal and do not justify the loss of the evidence on hearsay grounds.[5] The Advisory Committee pointed out that no evidence is free of the possibility of fabrication but felt that the likelihood of fabrication is less with nonverbal conduct than with assertive verbal conduct.

What about questions? Note that non-verbal questions are not "assertions" because they literally do not assert anything; rather, they simply request information.

Example: John has a bloody nose. Bystander asks John, "who hit you?" John points to David. John's nonverbal conduct clearly was intended to constitute an assertion indicating that David is the one who hit him.

801 (b) Declarant

(b) Declarant. A "declarant" is a person who makes a statement.

---

[4] Advisory Committee Notes to Rule 801
[5] Id.

Rule 801(b). Declarant

Non-Human Declarations

The definition of declarant should leave little room for discussion. Computers (or automated devices) which generate information automatically are not declarants. *United States v. Khorozian*, 333 F.3d 498, 506 (3d Cir. 2003). Statements are not 'said' by a machine. Id. However, situations may arise in which the issue of whether or not evidence from a machine or an animal is hearsay.

Machines:

The key to whether or not hearsay is implicated with machines is found in how the information is created. If the information is automated, it is unlikely hearsay is implicated because the risks associated with hearsay are most likely not present.

Example: A rain gauge is connected to a computer which prints out rainfall records over a period of time. This automated creation of information does not implicate the hearsay rule.

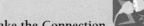

Make the Connection

A computer printout of a business's receipts might be hearsay if the data was entered by a person.

Animals:

The questions of testimony from animals is not usually an issue. In most cases, the evidence relates to a canine tracking or otherwise using its extraordinary abilities to identify scents as evidence. In a Pennsylvania case the Defendant argued that a dog's identification was hearsay. *Com. v. Michaux*, 360 Pa.Super. 452, 520 A.2d 1177 (Pa.Super.,1987). The appellant argued that the trial court erred when it permitted a police officer to testify as to the dog's actions, because such testimony constituted hearsay, that the dog was the real witness, and the officer's testimony regarding the dog's identification was hearsay. The Court of Appeals rejected appellant's contention. "It is the human testimony that makes the [tracking] done by the animal competent; and [the dog's] actions are described by human testimony as it would describe the operations of a piece of intricate machinery." The police officer testified to "his and the dog's training; to the conduct which he observed as the dog [tracked the defendant]; and to his interpretations of this conduct. [The officer] was present in court and was extensively cross-examined by defense counsel." The court held that the testimony which he gave did not constitute hearsay.

On the other hand, not all judges find such testimony reliable or exempt from the hearsay rule. A Montana case found otherwise:

"Dogs and other dumb animals do not qualify as witnesses in the courts of this state. They know not the nature of an oath. They may not be sworn. They cannot be cross-examined. They testify only through professed interpreters whose translations and conclusions are always hearsay.

...

The evidence admitted here is of the same character as hearsay and is, in my opinion, more objectionable and untrustworthy.

'One of the greatest safeguards against falsehood and error is cross-examination. Even that may fail at times to break down a false or mistaken witness, but its efficacy in general is recognized by all Courts. The dogs, of course, could not have been cross-examined, yet their master was permitted to detail (sic) in the witness box what they by their actions had told him." State v. Storm, 238 P.2d 1161, 1176 (Mont. 1951).

Rule 801(c) Hearsay

801 (c) Hearsay

"Hearsay" is a statement, other than one made by the declarant while testifying at the trial or hearing, offered into evidence to prove the truth of the matter asserted.

Understanding part (c) of the Rule is often aided by breaking the sentence into parts:

1) *Statement:* First, hearsay is a statement. If the evidence being offered is not a statement, then the hearsay rule does not apply.

2) *Out of Court:* Second, the statement must be one made *out of court*. It is a common error to believe that if the declarant is restating *in court* something he or she said *out of court*, then the statement does not meet the terms of subpart (c). This belief is misguided. Subpart (c) defines the hearsay statement as "… other than one made by the declarant **while testifying at the trial or hearing**…." This is best illustrated by example.

Example:

1) While testifying, John was asked what color the light was when the car passed through the intersection. John says "The light was red." This is his in court statement referring to what be believes the color the light to have been.

2) While testifying, John was asked, what did you tell Bystander the color the light was when the car passed through the intersection. John says "I said (to the bystander) that the light was red." Here, John is recounting his previous out of court statement.

In Example #1 above, John's statement is not an out of court statement. It is his testimony about an event or memory in the past. He can be examined and cross-examined about this memory, perception, et cetera. In Example #2, John is testifying about a statement which he previously made *out of court*. Even though John is actually in court and testifying, he is testifying about his statement which was made out of court. This statement meets the definition of being a statement which is not one made by the declarant while testifying at the trial or hearing. The statement about which he is testifying was previously made to the bystander and is an out of court statement. It does not matter if the statement was made in a previous court, such as at an earlier trial. It will still be a statement made out of *this* court.

Offered to Prove the Truth of the Matter Asserted

Assuming the declarant has made a hearsay statement, an assertion intended as a communication, either oral or written or by conduct, this is only the first part of the definition. The last part of the rule requires the statement to be "*offered into evidence to prove the truth of the matter asserted.*" Analyzing a statement in light of this part of the definition can be challenging. Think of it this way, is there a match between what the party offering the evidence seeks to prove and what the declarant has asserted in the statement?

It is often helpful to ask two questions to help determine whether or not a statement meets this requirement. One must determine "for what purpose is the statement offered?" A statement could be 'hearsay' in one case and not in another depending upon the purpose for which it is offered. The second question to ask is what the declarant's intent was in making the statement, that is, "what is the matter asserted?" Determination of the purpose for which evidence is offered is critical in determining whether a statement is hearsay or not.

C. Utterances and Conduct That Are Not Hearsay

Take Note!

If a statement is offered for a purpose other than the truth of the matter asserted, this does not mean the evidence is admissible. This only means that the evidence is not excluded under the Hearsay doctrine. It may be excluded under other rules.

If a statement is not offered for the truth of the matter asserted, then it is not hearsay. A statement may be offered for a number of purposes other than the truth of the matter asserted. Although there are many reasons for which evidence may be offered other than for the truth of the matter asserted, typical purposes are included in the following list, which is not exclusive:

- Impeachment of a witness;

- Effect on the listener (or reader);

- Verbal Acts

- Verbal Objects

- Circumstantial evidence of state of mind of the declarant

- Circumstantial evidence of memory or belief of the declarant

Make the Connection

Although use of a prior inconsistent statement is a permissible purpose under the hearsay rule; that is, the statement is not offered for the truth of the matter asserted, numerous rules and case law govern impeachment evidence. Do not assume that because impeachment evidence is not excluded under the Hearsay rule that such evidence will be admissible. Carefully review the section on Impeachment for a thorough discussion of the subject matter.

Impeachment of a witness

The purpose of impeachment arises when a witness has previously made a statement and now, on the witness stand, changes her story. The idea is to

Food for Thought

Although a statement might not be excluded under the hearsay rule, it may raise concerns that the fact-finder might consider it for improper purposes. Under this theory, for example, the statement could be excluded under Rule 403 and its ability to exclude evidence based on the risk of "unfair predice."

"impeach" the witness, that is, challenge her credibility based upon admission of a prior statement that varies from the statement recently offered. The theory behind the admissibility of this evidence is that the purpose for which it is offered is to show the conflict between the previous statement and the current statement. Under this theory, the fact-finder can assess the credibility of the witness without using the statement for purposes excluded under the hearsay rule. One is not trying to prove the truth of either statement; rather, one is simply pointing out that the two statements are inconsistent and therefore the witness's story may not be trustworthy.

Similarly, a witness may be impeached through the use of silence. If she remained silent under circumstances in which a reasonable person would likely respond, the statements to which no response was offered may be offered, not for the truth of the matter asserted, but rather to provide the context for the silence.

Effect on the listener (or reader or viewer of conduct)

A statement which would be inadmissible if offered to prove the truth of the matter asserted may, nevertheless, be admitted to show the statement's effect on the listener, the reader, or viewer of the assertive conduct. The following case illustrates this point.

McClure v. State

Texas Court of Criminal Appeals
575 S.W.2d 564 (Tex. Crim. App. 1978)

ONION, J.: This is an appeal from a conviction for the offense of murder.... Appellant ... contends that ... the court erroneously excluded ... evidence that the deceased (appellant's wife) had been unfaithful to him.... We agree ... and ... reverse the judgment.   *argued*

. . .

Appellant's testimony raised the issue of voluntary manslaughter, and the court instructed the jury thereon. In support of the defensive theory that he was guilty of only this lesser included offense, appellant offered the testimony of [three men]. Each of these witnesses testified outside of the presence of the jury that he had had sexual intercourse with the deceased while she was married to appellant. ... Appellant also offered to testify and was allowed to do so only outside the presence of the jury that one [witness] had told him that the deceased had had sexual relations with [two of these men]. ...

. . .

We think the court erred in rejecting the evidence offered by defendant to prove the adulterous intercourse between his wife and [the three men], and that recently before the homicide he had been informed of this fact. This and any other evidence which tended to show that he had reasonable cause to be excited, troubled, distracted and frenzied, that he had knowledge of facts well calculated to destroy his mental equilibrium, to dethrone his reason, to render it improbable that he could and did act with a cool, sedate and deliberate mind in committing the homicide, was in our opinion admissible.

In order for the evidence of the deceased's infidelity to be admissible, appellant was required to show that he had knowledge thereof.

To prove that he had knowledge of the deceased having had sexual relations with [the remaining two of the three men], appellant offered to testify that [a witness] had so informed him. The court erred in refusing to allow appellant to testify as to what [the witness] had told him on the ground that such testimony would have been hearsay.

"When it is proved that D made a statement to X, with the purpose of showing the probable state of mind thereby induced in X, such as being put on notice or having knowledge, or motive, or to show the information which X had as bearing on the reasonableness or good faith of the subsequent conduct of X, or anxiety, the evidence is not subject to attack as hearsay." *McCormick, Evidence, s 249, pp. 589-90 (2nd ed. 1972).*

"Whenever an utterance is offered to evidence the State of mind which ensued in another person in consequence of the utterance, it is obvious that no assertive or testimonial use is to be made of it, and the utterance is therefore admissible, so far as the hearsay rule is concerned." *6 Wigmore, Evidence, s 1789, p. 314 (Chadbourn rev. 1976).* The court should have allowed appellant to testify as to what [the witness] had told him, since that testimony would have shown he had knowledge of the deceased's indiscretions with [the two men].

Appellant testified that he saw the deceased go on a date with [one of the men] and stay out until 10 a. m. the next day, and it may be inferred that he also had knowledge of her indiscretions with [that man]. Since appellant would have shown ... his knowledge of the deceased's actions with [the three men], the court should have allowed those three witnesses to testify.

The ... testimony ... of the three lay witnesses [was] relevant to appellant's defensive theory that he was guilty of only voluntary manslaughter, and not murder.

The judgment is reversed and the cause remanded.

————————

Points for Discussion

a. The Relevance of Untrue Statements

Why can the challenged evidence in *McClure* be false and still be admissible? How is the defendant's case helped by offering potentially false witness statements? Why do you suppose the prosecution wanted to keep this evidence from the jury? What harm might it do to the prosecution's case?

b. The Admissibility of Hearsay Statements Offered for More Than One Purpose

In *Ferrara v. Galluchio*, 152 N.E.2d 249 (Ct. App. 1958), the plaintiff's wife, who was suffering from bursitis in her right shoulder, received a series of x-ray treatments from the defendant doctor, after which her shoulder became blistered and raw. Two years later, she was referred by her lawyer to a dermatologist, who told her to have her shoulder checked every six months because it might become cancerous. At trial, the plaintiff was allowed to testify to the dermatologist's statement to show a reasonable basis for her mental anguish about contracting cancer. What if the dermatologist's statements were offered to show that her shoulder would become cancerous as a result of the radiation burns? Would the statement be hearsay? What should a trial judge do if testimony is offered for a permissible purpose (to show mental anxiety) but it is likely a jury will use it for an impermissible purpose (to show she would get cancer)? Would a Rule 105 limiting instruction solve the problem? As this case demonstrates, courts will usually admit evidence if it is offered for a non-hearsay purpose that is relevant, even though the jury might take the statement as true and give it an inappropriate significance or meaning.

Verbal Acts

The phrase "verbal acts" is merely a reference to legal significance associated with the words, themselves, being spoken. Examples include words that constitute a contract between parties, defamatory statements, and statements which may constitute a crime.

Words constituting a contract: If Adam and Betty reach a verbal contract, the words spoken can be used to evidence the contract. The intent of the parties is irrelevant; hence, the statements in this context are not offered for the truth of the matter asserted. Rather, just the fact that the words were spoken have independent legal significance. Whether or not the words constitute a contract can be evaluated later in court.

Defamatory statements: Here too, the words being spoken are the critical fact. For example, Shelly says "John is a thief. He embezzled $20,000 from his last employer." At trial, John is trying to prove defamation. He would offer the statement made by Shelly, not for its truth (that he is a thief) but rather merely to prove that is *what* Shelly said. The legally operative fact is Shelly's speaking of the words that John alleges are defamatory.

The following case illustrates the concept of a verbal act:

Hanson v. Johnson

Supreme Court of Minnesota
201 N.W. 322 (1924)

Wilson, C.J.: In proving title to corn in the crib on a farm owned by [Hanson], it is not hearsay ... to prove conduct of parties for the purpose of showing a division; to also show that the tenant pointed to the crib and told [Hanson] that the particular crib of corn was his share, the language under the circumstances being a verbal act.

It is claimed that the court erred in the reception of evidence. [Hanson] owned and leased a farm to [tenant] under a written lease, the terms of which gave [Hanson] two-fifths of the corn grown. The tenant gave a mortgage to defendant bank on his share of the crops. The tenant's mortgaged property was sold at auction by the bank with his permission. At this sale a crib of corn containing 393 bushels was sold by the bank to [Johnson]. If [Hanson] owned the corn it was converted by [Johnson].

In an effort to prove that the corn was owned by [Hanson], and that it was a part of his share, he testified over the objection of hearsay ... that when the tenant ... pointed out the corn in question ... and said:

'Mr. Hanson, here is your corn for this year, this double crib here and this single crib here is your share for this year's corn; this belongs to you, Mr. Hanson.'

A bystander was called, and against the same objection testified to having heard the talk in substantially the same language.

There is no question but that [Hanson] owned some corn. It was necessary to identify it. The division made his share definite. This division and identity was made by the acts of tenant in husking the corn and putting it in separate cribs and then his telling Hanson which was his share, and the later's acquiescence therein.

The language of the tenant was the very fact necessary to be proved. The verbal part of the transaction between plaintiff and the tenant was necessary to prove the fact. The words were the verbal acts. They aid in giving legal significance to the conduct of the parties. They accompanied the conduct. There could be no division without words or gestures identifying the respective shares. This was a fact to be shown in the chain of proof of title. It was competent evidence. It was not hearsay.... As between [Hanson] and the tenant, this evidence would be admissible. ....

Affirmed.

Hypo 6.1

Suppose there is a car accident and a little girl sustains an injury to her vocal cords and cannot speak. However, defendant has a witness who claims to have heard the little girl say "I can speak." Would it be hearsay because the defendant is trying to prove the truth of the matter asserted by the little girl—that she can speak? What if the witness heard her say, "My dress is dirty"? Does it even matter what she asserts?

Points for Discussion

a. The Binding Nature of Verbal Acts

What if Mr. Hanson was lying when he told his tenant he could have the single and double cribs of corn? Would this fact change the court's analysis? What if Hanson later told his tenant he had changed his mind and the tenant he could only have two single cribs? Would this second designation of corn have any legal effect?

b. Assertions that Characterize an Act: Verbal Parts of an Act

One subcategory of verbal acts is what is called "verbal parts of an act." "Verbal parts of an act" are statements which explain an otherwise ambiguous act and are not considered hearsay. In *Anthony v. Dewitt*, 295 F.3d 554 (6th Cir. 2002), for example, threats made against a murder witness in an attempt to silence her were admitted to explain why she was with the defendant and failed to report the murder to the authorities. The verbal threats explained the witness's otherwise ambiguous acts.

Hypo

While conducting recitation during an Evidence class, Professor Smith puts her $300 gold pen down on a student's desk. The student later claims the pen was a gift. The law of gifts requires that the student prove the professor had a donative intent to give the student her pen when the professor transferred it to the student. Which of the following statements by Professor Smith would be considered a verbal part of an act and therefore non-hearsay?

1. Professor Smith's statement made before the pen was put on the student's desk that if the student recited well, Smith would give the student her pen as a gift.

2. Professor Smith's statement that because the student recited well, the pen, which Professor Smith placed on the student's desk, now belonged to the student.

3. Professor Smith's statement made 15 minutes after Smith put the pen on the student's desk that she was giving the pen to the student as a gift.

Circumstantial Evidence of Declarant's State of Mind, Memory or Belief

A written statement may be admitted as circumstantial evidence of a person's state of mind, not to prove the truth of the matter asserted but rather to provide the fact finder a basis upon which could be drawn an inference concerning the person's state of mind. Examples include:

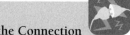

Make the Connection

Under this rule, a statement is offered to show the declarant's own state of mind without accepting the truth of what is asserted in the utterance. Statements offered under Rule 803(3) are offered to show a declarant's state of mind and are offered for the truth of the matter asserted.

- Belief or Fear of Something

- Knowledge or a Lack of Knowledge

- Lack of Predisposition to Commit Crime

- Motive

- Notice

A statement of a declarant is usually intended to express a direct thought or idea as opposed circumstantial evidence of such thought or idea. The statement "I am going to Disney World" stated out of court expresses the declarant's intent and would typically be hearsay if later offered into evidence. Under certain circumstances, however, inferences may be drawn as to a declarant's state of mind by examining the reasons behind the statements as opposed to the direct assertions.

In *Loetsch v. New York City Omnibus Corp.* 52 N.E.2d 448 (N.Y. 1943) the court examined statements in a will made by the wife shortly before she died which left her husband only one dollar. The will made direct assertions regarding her husband that would otherwise be considered hearsay. The court found that these statements were not hearsay because "... the fact that such a declaration was made by the decedent, whether true or false, is compelling evidence of her feelings toward, and relations to, her husband. As such it is not excluded under the hearsay rule..." Id. at 449. The will showed the relationship between the husband and the wife.

The wife stated, in her will, "Whereas I have been a faithful, dutiful, and loving wife to my husband ... and whereas he reciprocated my tender affections for him with acts of cruelty and indifference, and whereas he has failed to support and maintain me in that station of life which would have been possible and proper for him, I hereby limit my bequest to him to one dollar." The words of the wife are not offered for their truth.

The words only prove her state-of-mind. They cannot be offered for their truth. They cannot be used to prove her husband actually was cruel and indifferent, only that she thought or felt that he was.

D. Statements Which Are Not Hearsay by Definition

1. Rule 801. Definitions
(Part d)

Assuming the proposed evidence meets the definition of hearsay under

Food for Thought

It is often difficult to distinguish the difference between those statements which are defined as "not hearsay" under Rule 801(d) and those defined as exceptions under Rules 803 and 804. Either way, both of these types of statements are admissible despite being hearsay.

801(a)-(c), the next step in the analysis is to determine whether or not the statement is defined as "not hearsay" under the rules of evidence or whether the statement meets an exception to the exclusionary rule.

801(d) Statements which are not Hearsay

(d) Statements which are not hearsay. A statement is not hearsay if--

(1) Prior statement by witness. The declarant testifies at the trial or hearing and is subject to cross-examination concerning the statement, and the statement is (A) inconsistent with the declarant's testimony, and was given under oath subject to the penalty of perjury at a trial, hearing, or other proceeding, or in a deposition, or (B) consistent with the declarant's testimony and is offered to rebut an express or implied charge against the declarant of recent fabrication or improper influence or motive, or (C) one of identification of a person made after perceiving the person; or

(2) Admission by party-opponent. The statement is offered against a party and is (A) the party's own statement, in either an individual or a representative capacity or (B) a statement of which the party has manifested an adoption or belief in its truth, or (C) a statement by a person authorized by the party to make a statement concerning the subject, or (D) a statement by the party's agent or servant concerning a matter within the scope of the agency or employment, made during the existence of the relationship, or (E) a statement by a coconspirator of a party during the course and in furtherance of the conspiracy. The contents of the statement shall be considered but are not alone sufficient to establish the declarant's authority under subdivision (C), the agency or employment relationship and scope thereof under subdivision (D), or the existence of the conspiracy and the participation therein of the declarant and the party against whom the statement is offered under subdivision (E).

The drafters of the rules created subpart (d) to define statements which would otherwise be hearsay (that is, they meet the definition under parts (a)-(c)) and define them as "not hearsay." The concept can be confusing.

Food for Thought

To reach this point in the analysis, the statement in question must first be defined as hearsay. If the statement then meets a definition under 801(d), the statement is effectively "transformed" into a statement which is not hearsay by definition.

801(d)(1) - Statements Which Are Not Hearsay – Prior Statement by Witness

Prior Inconsistent Statement (801(d)(1)(A))

Admissibility under this rule requires the prior out-of-court statement to be inconsistent with the testimony given by the witness testifying in court. The judge determines whether or not the inconsistency exists.

must be inconsistent statement

United States v. Barrett

U.S. Court of Appeals
539 F.2d 244 (C.A. Mass. 1976)

LEVIN H. CAMPBELL, Circuit Judge.

Arthur Barrett appeals from his conviction after a jury trial for crimes arising from the theft and sale of a collection of postage stamps .... Barrett and seven others were charged in a three-count indictment with the interstate transportation of stolen postage stamps.... Of the eight indicted, Barrett alone went to trial.

. . .

We turn next to the court's exclusion of the testimony of the defense's two remaining witnesses, Thomas J. Delaney and Jeanne Kelley. We hold such exclusion to have been error.

Ct. holds

Delaney stated that he met with Buzzy Adams ... in a Boston area restaurant. He was then asked to relate their conversation. The Government objected and Barrett offered to prove that "Adams said that he had heard that Barrett had been indicted, or had gotten into trouble on this matter, and that it was too bad because he, Buzzy, knew that Barrett was not involved. "Kelley, a waitress, was prepared to testify that, while waiting on Adams and Delaney at the same restaurant, she overheard Adams say "it was a shame that Bucky got arrested on this matter" because he (Adams) "knew that Bucky didn't have anything to do with it."

Conceding that this evidence was hearsay, ... Barrett argues that it was admissible as a prior inconsistent statement to impeach Adams' credibility. Adams had earlier testified that Barrett admitted to him shortly after his arrest that he had been involved in the stamp transaction. Barrett contends that Adams' subsequent statement to Delaney ... that Barrett was not involved, was contradictory and so admissible to impeach his credibility.

We believe the court erred in excluding this testimony. Counsel for Barrett advised the court, albeit rather succinctly, that the testimony went to the credibility of Adams who had testified. The court ruled it out on the ground that it was a "hearsay opinion by Mr. Adams, that this guy is innocent. That is all this amounts to." The Government now argues, in the same vein, that Adams' purported opinion was too vague and unsupported to be useful. However, the clear purport of Adams' direct testimony was that in late October, 1974, after Barrett's arrest, Adams acquired first-hand knowledge of Barrett's involvement in the stamp affair, and the jury could have inferred from this and other testimony that at all times thereafter Adams remained of the impression that Barrett was involved. The statement to Delaney, therefore, made supposedly in November, 1974, was clearly inconsistent. To be received as a prior inconsistent statement, the contradiction need not be "in plain terms. It is enough if the proffered testimony, taken as a whole, either by what it says or by what it omits to say, affords some indication that the fact was different from the testimony of the witness whom it is sought to contradict." Furthermore, the fact that Adams' belief that Bucky was not involved might be called an "opinion" is immaterial. The important point is the clear incompatibility between Adams' direct testimony and the alleged statement.

· · ·

Vacated and remanded.

————————————

Points for Discussion

a. Towards a Broader Definition of "Inconsistency"

Barrett demonstrates that previous out-of-court statements need not be diametrically opposed to a witness's testimony for them to be deemed "inconsistent." What if the testifying witness cannot remember the subject matter of the prior statement? See *United States v. Gajo*, 290 F.3d 922 (7th Cir. 2002). Or, what if a witness is evasive, silent, or changes his position on a matter during questioning? See *United States v. Matlock*, 109 F.3d 1313 (8th Cir. 1997). Although a determination of inconsistency is within the discretion of the trial court, any divergence of note between a witness's in-court testimony and out-of-court statement can be deemed an inconsistency.

b. Prior Inconsistent Statements and Federal Rule 801(d)(1)(A)

In *Barrett*, if Adams' prior inconsistent statements were offered to show only that they were true, they would be impermissible hearsay. However, at trial, the statements were offered to show that Adams made prior statements contrary to his in-court testimony and thus was not a credible witness. This is a non-hearsay offering. If a witness's prior statement was made under oath at a trial, deposition, or other proceeding, it may be admitted as a hearsay exemption to prove the truth of matters asserted in the statement. Such statements are considered reliable because they were subject to the opportunity for cross-examination and made on the record.

[handwritten margin note: hearsay exception]

To recap, prior inconsistent statements made out-of-court by a testifying witness may be offered for three different reasons:

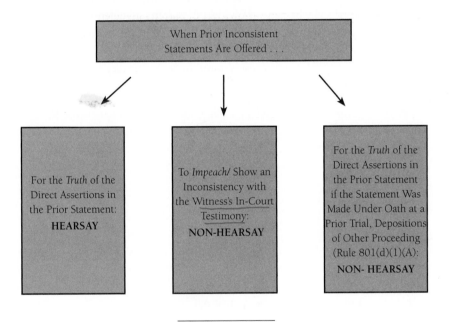

Prior Consistent Statement to Rebut a Charge of Fabrication (801(d)(1)(B))

Tome v. United States

Supreme Court of the United States
513 U.S. 150 (1995)

Justice KENNEDY delivered the opinion of the Court.

… At issue is the interpretation of a provision in the Federal Rules of Evidence bearing upon the admissibility of statements, made by a declarant who testifies as a witness, that are consistent with the testimony and are offered to rebut a charge of a "recent fabrication or improper influence or motive." Fed.Rule Evid. 801(d)(1)(B). The question is whether out-of-court consistent statements made after the alleged fabrication, or after the alleged improper influence or motive arose, are admissible under the Rule.

I

Petitioner Tome was charged in a one-count indictment with the felony of sexual abuse of a child, his own daughter, aged four at the time of the alleged crime. The case having arisen on the Navajo Indian Reservation, Tome was tried by a jury in the United States District Court for the District of New Mexico, where he was found guilty ….

Tome and the child's mother had been divorced in 1988. A … court awarded joint custody of the daughter, A.T., to both parents, but Tome had primary physical custody. In 1989 the mother was unsuccessful in petitioning the … court for primary custody of A.T., but was awarded custody for the summer of 1990. … On August 27, 1990, the mother contacted Colorado authorities with allegations that Tome had committed sexual abuse against A.T.

The prosecution's theory was that Tome committed sexual assaults upon the child while she was in his custody and that the crime was disclosed when the child was spending vacation time with her mother. The defense argued that the allegations were concocted so the child would not be returned to her father. At trial A.T., then 6 1/2 years old, was the Government's first witness. For the most part, her direct testimony consisted of one- and two-word answers to a series of leading questions. Cross-examination took place over two trial days. The defense asked A.T. 348 questions. On the first day A.T. answered all the questions posed to her on general, background subjects.

The next day there was no testimony, and the prosecutor met with A.T. When cross-examination of A.T. resumed, she was questioned about those conversations but was reluctant to discuss them. Defense counsel then began questioning her about the allegations of abuse, and it appears she was reluctant at many points to answer. As the trial judge noted, however, some of the defense questions were imprecise or unclear. The judge expressed his concerns with the examination of A.T., observing there were lapses of as much as 40-55 seconds between some questions and the answers and that on the second day of examination the witness seemed to be losing concentration. The trial judge stated, "We have a very difficult situation here."

After A.T. testified, the Government produced six witnesses who testified about a total of seven statements made by A.T. describing the alleged sexual assaults: A.T.'s babysitter recited A.T.'s statement to her on August 22, 1990, that she did not want to return to her father because he "gets drunk and he thinks I'm his wife"; the babysitter related further details given by A.T. on August 27, 1990, while A.T.'s mother stood outside the room and listened after the mother had been unsuccessful in questioning A.T. herself; the mother recounted what she had heard A.T. tell the babysitter; a social worker recounted details A.T. told her on August 29, 1990, about the assaults; and three pediatricians, Drs. Kuper, Reich, and Spiegel, related A.T.'s statements to them describing how and where she had been touched by Tome. All but A.T.'s statement to Dr. Spiegel implicated Tome....

A.T.'s out-of-court statements, recounted by the six witnesses, were offered by the Government under Rule 801(d)(1)(B). The trial court admitted all of the statements over defense counsel's objection, accepting the Government's argument that they rebutted the implicit charge that A.T.'s testimony was motivated by a desire to live with her mother. ... Following trial, Tome was convicted and sentenced to 12 years' imprisonment.

On appeal, the Court of Appeals for the Tenth Circuit affirmed, adopting the Government's argument that all of A.T.'s out-of-court statements were admissible under Rule 801(d)(1)(B) even though they had been made after A.T.'s alleged motive to fabricate arose. ... We granted certiorari, and now reverse.

II

The prevailing common-law rule for more than a century before adoption of the Federal Rules of Evidence was that a prior consistent statement introduced to rebut a charge of recent fabrication or improper influence or motive was admissible if the statement had been made before the alleged fabrication, influence, or motive came into being, but it was inadmissible if made afterwards. As Justice Story explained: "[W]here the testimony is assailed as a fabrication of a recent date, ... in order to repel such imputation, proof of the *antecedent* declaration of the party may be admitted." Ellicott v. Pearl, 35 U.S. 412, 439 (1836) (emphasis added).

Rule

McCormick and Wigmore stated the rule in a more categorical manner: "[T]he applicable principle is that the prior consistent statement has no relevancy to refute the charge unless the consistent statement was made before the source of the bias, interest, influence or incapacity originated." E. Cleary, McCormick on Evidence § 49, p. 105 (2d ed. 1972) (hereafter McCormick). The question is *Issue* whether Rule 801(d)(1)(B) embodies this temporal requirement. We hold that it does.

A

... Rule 801 defines prior consistent statements as nonhearsay only if they are offered to rebut a charge of "recent fabrication or improper influence or motive." Fed.Rule Evid. 801(d)(1)(B). Noting the "troublesome" logic of treating a witness' prior consistent statements as hearsay at all (because the declarant is present in court and subject to cross-examination), the Advisory Committee decided to treat those consistent statements, once the preconditions of the Rule were satisfied, as nonhearsay and admissible as substantive evidence, not just to rebut an attack on the witness' credibility. ... A consistent statement meeting the requirements of the Rule is thus placed in the same category as a declarant's inconsistent statement made under oath in another proceeding, or prior identification testimony, or admissions by a party opponent. See Fed.Rule Evid. 801.

The Rules do not accord this weighty, nonhearsay status to all prior consistent statements. To the contrary, admissibility under the Rules is confined to those statements offered to rebut a charge of "recent fabrication or improper influence or motive," the same phrase used by the Advisory Committee in its description of the "traditiona[l]" common law of evidence, which was the background against which the Rules were drafted. ... Prior consistent statements may not be admitted to counter all forms of impeachment or to bolster the witness merely because she has been discredited. In the present context, the question is whether A.T.'s out-of-court statements rebutted the alleged link between her desire to be with her mother and her testimony, not whether they suggested that A.T.'s in-court testimony was true. The Rule speaks of a party rebutting an alleged motive, not bolstering the veracity of the story told.

. . .

There may arise instances when out-of-court statements that postdate the alleged fabrication have some probative force in rebutting a charge of fabrication or improper influence or motive, but those statements refute the charged fabrication in a less direct and forceful way. Evidence that a witness made consistent statements after the alleged motive to fabricate arose may suggest in some degree that the in-court testimony is truthful, and thus suggest in some degree that that testimony did not result from some improper influence; but if the drafters of Rule 801(d)(1)(B) intended to countenance rebuttal along that indirect inferential chain, the purpose of confining the types of impeachment that open the door to rebuttal by introducing consistent statements becomes unclear. If consistent statements are admissible without reference to the timeframe we find imbedded in the Rule, there appears no sound reason not to admit consistent statements to rebut other forms of impeachment as well. ... [I]t is clear to us that the drafters of Rule 801(d)(1)(B) were relying upon the common-law temporal requirement.

gov't theory

The underlying theory of the Government's position is that an out-of-court consistent statement, whenever it was made, tends to bolster the testimony of a witness and so tends also to rebut an express or implied charge that the testimony has been the product of an improper influence. Congress could have adopted that rule with ease, providing, for instance, that "a witness' prior consistent statements are admissible whenever relevant to assess the witness' truthfulness or accuracy." ... The narrow Rule enacted by Congress, however, cannot be understood to incorporate the Government's theory.

. . .

B

Our conclusion that Rule 801(d)(1)(B) embodies the common-law premotive requirement is confirmed by an examination of the Advisory Committee's Notes to the Federal Rules of Evidence.

. . .

The Notes disclose a purpose to adhere to the common law in the application of evidentiary principles.... The Notes give no indication, however, that Rule 801(d)(1)(B) abandoned the premotive requirement. The entire discussion of Rule 801(d)(1)(B) is limited to the following comment:

"Prior consistent statements traditionally have been admissible to rebut charges of recent fabrication or improper influence or motive but not as substantive evidence. Under the rule they are substantive evidence. The prior statement is consistent with the testimony given on the stand, and, if the opposite party wishes to open the door for its admission in evidence, no sound reason is apparent why it should not be received generally." Notes on Rule 801(d)(1)(B).

... [W]e do not think the drafters of the Rule intended to scuttle the whole premotive requirement and rationale without so much as a whisper of explanation....

C

Gov't argues

The Government's final argument in favor of affirmance is that the common-law premotive rule advocated by petitioner is inconsistent with the Federal Rules' liberal approach to relevancy and with strong academic criticism, beginning in the 1940's, directed at the exclusion of out-of-court statements made by a declarant who is present in court and subject to cross-examination. This argument misconceives the design of the Rules' hearsay provisions.

Hearsay evidence is often relevant.... Relevance is not the sole criterion of admissibility. ... That certain out-of-court statements may be relevant does not dispose of the question whether they are admissible.

. . .

D

The case before us illustrates some of the important considerations supporting the Rule as we interpret it, especially in criminal cases. If the Rule were to permit the introduction of prior statements as substantive evidence to rebut every implicit charge that a witness' in-court testimony results from recent fabrication or improper influence or motive, the whole emphasis of the trial could shift to the out-of-court statements, not the in-court ones. The present case illustrates the point. In response to a rather weak charge that A.T.'s testimony was a fabrication created so the child could remain with her mother, the Government was permitted to present a parade of sympathetic and credible witnesses who did no more than recount A.T.'s detailed out-of-court statements to them. Although those statements might have been probative on the question whether the alleged conduct had occurred, they shed but minimal light on whether A.T. had the charged motive to fabricate. At closing argument before the jury, the Government placed great reliance on the prior statements for substantive purposes but did not once seek to use them to rebut the impact of the alleged motive....

III

.... Rule [801(d)(1)(B)] permits the introduction of a declarant's consistent out-of-court statements to rebut a charge of recent fabrication or improper influence or motive only when those statements were made before the charged recent fabrication or improper influence or motive. These conditions of admissibility were not established here.

The judgment of the Court of Appeals for the Tenth Circuit is reversed, and the case is remanded for further proceedings consistent with this opinion.

It is so ordered.

Points for Discussion

a. Is the *Tome* Majority Correct?

Do you agree with the majority that only pre-motive statements should be allowed to rebut an improper motive? Is there any language in Rule 801(d)(1)(B) that supports this conclusion? Or does the dissent have it right? Could the term "rebut" require a relevance analysis rather than a rigid pre-motive requirement? Can there ever be a situation where a post-motive statement might be relevant to "rebut" an improper motive?

b. Bolstering and Prior Consistent Statements Offered to Impeach

Generally, a lawyer may not prove that a testifying witness is truthful by offering evidence that the witness made a prior out-of-court statement consistent with her in-court testimony. This is called *bolstering the witness* before her credibility has been attacked and is not allowed. But what if the defense lawyer, through cross-examination, attempts to show that the little girl in *Tome* fabricated the abuse? Could the prosecution then offer her out-of-court statements to rehabilitate her credibility? How is this offering different from the one in *Tome*? Some courts have determined that the offering of a prior consistent statement to rehabilitate a testifying witness's credibility cannot be admitted unless it satisfies the requirements of Rule 801(d)(1)(B). See *United States v. Miller*, 874 F.2d 1255 (9th Cir. 1989). Can you articulate why?

Like prior inconsistent statement, prior consistent statements may be offered for three different purposes:

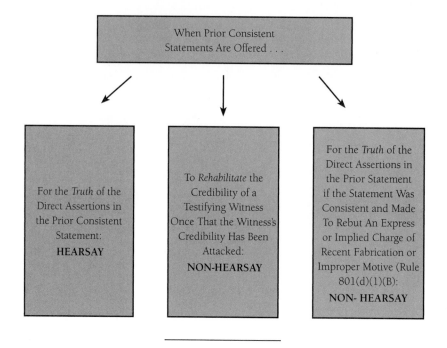

Prior Statement of Identification of a Person (801(d)(1)(C))

United States v. Lewis

U.S. Court of Appeals for the Second Circuit
565 F.2d 1248 (2nd Cir. 1977)

FEINBERG, Circuit Judge: After a jury trial appellant Lewis was convicted of armed bank robbery ... Lewis appeals ....

I. The Facts

There is no claim that the evidence on the bank robbery conviction was insufficient. On the morning of January 3, 1977, appellant and an accomplice robbed the Barclay's Bank.... The robbers operated in style. They were driven to the vicinity of the bank in a chauffeured white Cadillac limousine, and went in pretending to be customers. In short order, both men drew guns and threatened those inside the bank. Appellant threw a woman customer to the ground and fired two shots from his gun. His accomplice disarmed a bank guard and collected about $11,800 from the cash drawers and the employees. The two men then went around the corner to the waiting limousine.

....At trial, the case against appellant was overwhelming. The guns were, of course, strong evidence of guilt. In addition, a bank customer (Norma Sharpe) had identified appellant from photographs after the robbery, and she so testified.

II. The Bank Robbery Conviction

The photographic identification

...The most substantial arguments on appeal stem from Norma Sharpe's pre-trial identification of appellant from a display of photographs. At trial, Mrs. Sharpe was unable to identify appellant in the courtroom and mistakenly picked out a Deputy United States Marshal instead. When Mrs. Sharpe was then shown the photographic display, she testified that she had previously identified one of the bank robbers from the group of pictures, and she then picked out the photograph she had earlier selected. This picture, which was of appellant, was then admitted into evidence. After Mrs. Sharpe's testimony, FBI Agent Leo Farrell testified as to the way in which he had prepared the photographic spread. He also confirmed that Mrs. Sharpe had selected appellant's picture shortly after the bank robbery.

Appellant ... argues that the identification testimony should have been excluded as hearsay, and is not permitted by the ... Federal Rules of Evidence. ... Appellant argues that Agent Farrell's testimony should have been excluded because "identification of a person made after perceiving him" contemplates only corporeal, not photographic, identification; and because it was improper to allow Farrell to testify in the absence of an in-court identification by Mrs. Sharpe. Appellant also claims that Mrs. Sharpe's testimony about her prior identification after she erroneously identified someone else in court amounted to testimony about a prior inconsistent statement not made under oath, rendering it improper under subsection (A), which overrides subsection (C)....

Congress has recognized, as do most trial judges, that identification in the courtroom is a formality that offers little in the way of reliability and much in the way of suggestibility. The experienced trial judge gives much greater credence to the out-of-court identification. ... This court recently pointed out that "(t)he purpose of the rule was to permit the introduction of identifications made by a witness when memory was fresher and there had been less opportunity for influence to be exerted upon him." *United States v. Marchand*, 564 F.2d 983, 996 (2d Cir. 1977).

With these considerations in mind, we turn to appellant's specific contentions. The legislative history makes clear that Congress intended "nonsuggestive . . . photographic," as well as lineup, identifications to be covered by subsection (C). ...We can see no sound principle for construing "identification of a person" to exclude identification by a photograph. True, there are dangers peculiar to photographic identification and these, like the dangers of a lineup or even those of an on-the-spot identification, must be taken into account in assessing reliability. But they do not justify a limiting construction of subsection (C).

Appellant's second argument on this point is that the failure of Mrs. Sharpe to identify appellant in court made inadmissible Agent Farrell's evidence that she had identified appellant a month or two earlier. Appellant may be confusing this situation with that posed by the failure or refusal of the identifying witness to recall in court the earlier identification, which is discussed in Judge Weinstein's treatise from which appellant's brief extensively quotes. In that situation, testimony like Agent Farrell's might well raise questions concerning the adequacy of cross-examination and the right to confront the original identifying witness. In this case, however, Mrs. Sharpe did recall her prior identification and so testified. ... [T]estimony concerning extra-judicial identifications is admissible regardless of whether there has been an accurate in-court identification.

Appellant's final point seems to be that subsection (C) does not apply at all when the identifier has made an erroneous in-court identification because the prior identification is inconsistent with it and was not given under oath, as required by subsection (A). The Government responds that since appellant's appearance had changed significantly by the time of trial, there was no inconsistency. More significantly, even though Rule 801(d)(1) embraces subsection (C), the latter is not limited by the earlier subsections. Subsection (C) represents a legislative decision to admit statements of identification provided the declarant "testifies at . . . trial . . . and is subject to cross-examination concerning the statement." These conditions were met here, and we do not think that subsection (C) is rendered inoperative by Mrs. Sharpe's misidentification in court.

Judgment affirmed.

————————

Points for Discussion

a. The Validity of In-Court Identifications

Why would the court think that an in-court identification of the defendant as the person who committed the crime tends to be perfunctory and unreliable? Is it because witnesses, like the witness in *Lewis*, often fail to identify the defendant in court, or conversely, because it is too easy for a witness to identify a defendant because the defendant always sits at counsel table next to defense counsel? Or, is it because in-court identifications are made so long after the crime occurs? Or is there another reason? See the Advisory Committee Note to Rule 801(d)(1)(C).

b. Constitutional Requirements

Rule 801(d)(1)(C) addresses the hearsay objection to admitting a witness's prior identification by creating an exemption. However, in criminal cases, there is an additional concern. Under the Sixth Amendment, the defendant has a constitutional right to have counsel present at any stage of an adversarial criminal proceeding This right extends to police line-up identifications, *United States v. Wade*, 388 U.S. 218 (1967) and preliminary hearing identifications, *United States v. Ash*, 413 U.S. 300 (1973), but not to identifications made as a result of photo arrays, *Kirby v. Illinois*, 406 U.S. 682 (1972). Failure to permit counsel to be present may be used as a basis for a motion to suppress any out-of-court statements identifying the defendant during a line-up or other proceeding.

c. The Forgetful Witness

Shortly after being attacked and suffering from a skull fracture, a witness picks out the defendant's picture from an array of photographs. At trial, the witness testifies about the attack and his identification of the defendant from the photo array but admits, on cross-examination, that he has no memory of ever seeing his assailant or whether anyone had suggested to him that the defendant was the assailant. Does the witness's forgetfulness deny the defendant the right to confront and cross-examine the witness "concerning his statement" under Rule 801(d)(1)(C)? See *United States v. Owens*, 484 F.3d 1248 (2d Cir. 1977).

2. 801(d)(2) - Admission by a Party Opponent

Generally

An admission by a party opponent is treated as non-hearsay under the Federal Rules. An admission is a statement which was made that amounts to a prior acknowledgment by one of the

Take Note!

The term "admission" is a bit misleading. The statement need not be, and frequently is not a statement of fault. Further, the statement need not be against the party's interest at the time it was made.

parties to the action of one of the relevant facts. This rule, which is an exception to the exclusionary rule (although not called one), is based on the premise that a person cannot argue that her statements cannot be admitted because they were not made under oath, subject to cross-examination, or in the hearing of the trier of fact.

Take Note!

An admission can only be offered by that party's opponent, not by the party who made the admission.

Although many theories support the rule's application, the practical support is common-sense. The declarant is present and able to explain the statements. Parties should not be able to hide from their own statements behind the hearsay rule.

The admission of the statement does not bind the declarant. The declarant may have the opportunity to explain, rebut, or deny the statement. One should always determine *who* is the declarant. If the declarant is one of the parties, determine if 801(d) (1) might apply.

Personal Knowledge Not Required

The lack of personal knowledge does not necessarily exclude a party's admission. An admission may, in fact, be predicated on hearsay. As the Advisory Committee Notes reflect, "[t]he freedom which admissions have enjoyed from ... the rule requiring firsthand knowledge ... calls for generous treatment of this avenue of admissibility."

Personal Admissions

In its simplest form, a personal admission is merely a statement made by a party. That party's opponent in litigation is permitted to offer the statement of the party into evidence. If relevant, and not excluded by some other rule, this statement will not be excluded by the hearsay rule.

No Self-Serving Statements

The rule allows a statement of a party *opponent*. This means a party cannot offer their own previous statement to bolster their own story.

Judicial Admissions

One type of personal admission which can occur during a lawsuit is called a judicial admission. A judicial admission is a formal waiver of proof that relieves an opposing party from having to prove the admitted fact and bars the party who made the admission from disputing it. Judicial admissions are often made in the form of pleadings or affidavits filed in the case in which the admission is offered. For example, if a party to a divorce action puts in her pleading that the date of marriage was December 1, 1976, then the husband would not need to prove the date of the marriage. He could ask the court to consider the wife's pleading which contains the date of marriage as a judicial admission of the date of marriage.

Take Note!

When examining a statement which was "repeated" you must do so within the context in which is was said. For example, if the statement was said sarcastically, then it may not have actually be expressly adopted.

Adoptive Admissions

A party may expressly or impliedly adopt someone else's statement as his own, which results in an "adoptive admission." (801(d)(2)(B)). In these cases, the speaker's statement "becomes" the statement of the declarant. A simple illustration would be a passenger in an automobile telling the driver, "You just ran that stop sign." In response, the driver says "So what?" This effectively "adopts" the statement of the passenger. Although this scenario is fairly straightforward, the rule provides a broader basis for adoptions.

Express

A party may adopt another's statement in a clear manner, thereby "expressly" adopting the statement. Such adoption will be clear if the party orally expresses her agreement with the statement, repeats the statement, or reads and signs a statement prepared by a third party.

Silence

A party may adopt another's statement by her silence. Although this may seem unusual, adoption by silence may occur in certain situations. Adoption by silence may occur when a party:

1) hears the statement;

2) understands the statement;

3) has knowledge of the matter stated; and

4) the circumstances were such that she would have likely replied had she disagreed with the statement.

For example, if the plaintiff tells the defendant, you owe me $1,000 for painting your house, and the defendant remains silent, the plaintiff might be able to offer the defendant's silence as an admission of the debt.

Meeting these elements does not guarantee admission of the statement. If the party had a physical or mental factor that contributed to her failure to respond; the speaker is someone that the party would not likely respond to; or the silence came in response to questioning or comments by law enforcement, a party's silence may not be construed as an admission.

Vicarious Admissions

Admissions can come in the form of those authorized by a third person. When the authorizing person is a party in the case, then the statement from the authorized person may be admissible. The following cases are illustrative of some scenarios.

Party's Own Statement - 801(d)(2)(A)

Jewel v. CSX Transportation, Inc.

U.S. Court of Appeals for the Sixth Circuit
135 F.3d 361 (6th Cir. 1998)

BELL, District Judge.

...

The accident that gave rise to this case occurred in a rural area of Henderson County, Kentucky, where the Anthouston-Frog Island Road crosses the CSX Transportation, Inc. (hereinafter "CSX") railroad grade crossing. The Anthouston-Frog Island Road crosses the tracks at a 45-47 degree angle. As the road approaches the crossing it narrows and goes up an incline to cross the elevated tracks. On the date of the collision the only warning devices were standard cross bucks. There were no lights, bells, or mechanical gates.

At about 6:00 p.m. on March 11, 1990, Greg Jewell was driving his pickup truck west on Anthouston-Frog Island Road with his wife Sheila Jewell, and his six-year old daughter Brittney Jewell. As his truck crossed the tracks it was struck by a southbound CSX train which approached the crossing from Greg Jewell's right. All three passengers were thrown from the truck. Greg Jewell was killed and his wife and daughter were injured.

... [Plaintiffs] alleged that CSX was negligent in failing to sound a warning as the train approached the crossing, that the train crew failed to exercise ordinary care in the operation of the train and that the subject crossing was extra-hazardous.

Prior to trial the district court denied Appellants' Second Amended Motion in Limine to exclude testimony regarding statements made by Brittney concerning an alleged argument between Greg and Sheila immediately before the collision. The case was tried before a jury from July 25, 1994 to August 4, 1994. At the close of Appellants' evidence the district court issued a directed verdict in favor of CSX on the issue of the extra-hazardous crossing. The jury returned a verdict in favor of CSX.

...

III.

Appellants contend the trial court committed reversible error by admitting statements made by Brittney Jewell regarding an alleged argument between Greg and Sheila Jewell immediately before the collision. ... The trial court ... admitted the evidence under the party admission exception to the hearsay rule. Fed.R.Evid. 801(d)(2)(A).

Ps argue here

At trial CSX introduced testimony from six witnesses that Brittney told them that Greg and Sheila had been arguing immediately prior to the accident, and that when she told them a train was coming, she was told to be quiet.

Appellants offered evidence that Brittney suffered permanent brain damage as a result of the accident. Her physicians testified that she had retrograde amnesia and had no memory of the accident. They also testified that patients recovering from a coma have a tendency to grasp onto anything they hear to supplement their memory. They offered testimony from family members that Brittney may have overheard their conversations where they speculated about the cause of the accident, including the possibility of an argument between Greg and Sheila. Even those Brittney told about the argument testified that she simultaneously made statements about the accident that were clearly inaccurate.

R 801(d)(2)(A)

Rule 801(d)(2)(A) provides that a statement is not hearsay if the statement is offered against a party and is "the party's own statement in either an individual or representative capacity." Fed.R.Evid. 801(d)(2)(A).

Appellants contend that because Brittney suffered brain damage and has no "independent" recollection of the accident, her statements about the argument were not made in her "individual" capacity.

Appellants' argument lacks logical consistency. They have confused the terms "independent" and "individual." "Independent" and "individual" are not synonymous. Brittney was the source of the statements. She made the statements in her individual capacity, whether or not she had an independent recollection of the matters she spoke about.

Ct. says

Trustworthiness is not a separate requirement for admission under Rule 801(d)(2)(A). ... The admissibility of statements of a party-opponent is grounded not in the presumed trustworthiness of the statements, but on "a kind of estoppel or waiver theory, that a party should be entitled to rely on his opponent's statements." United States v. DiDomenico, 78 F.3d 294, 303 (7th Cir.1996). As noted in the advisory committee notes to Rule 801(d)(2)(A), admissions by a party-opponent are excluded from the category of hearsay "on the theory that their admissibility in evidence is the result of the adversary system rather than satisfaction of the conditions of the hearsay rule." Evid. 801 advisory committee's note.

No guarantee of trustworthiness is required in the case of an admission. The freedom which admissions have enjoyed from technical demands of searching for an assurance of truthworthiness in some against-interest circumstance, and from the restrictive influences of the opinion rule and the rule requiring firsthand knowledge, when taken with the apparently prevalent satisfaction with the results, calls for generous treatment of this avenue to admissibility.

. . .

For the foregoing reasons we AFFIRM the judgment of the district court in its entirety.

——————————

Points for Discussion

a. The Adversary Theory of Admissions by a Party Opponent.

The appellants in *Jewel* argue that Brittany Jewel's statements should not be admitted as party admissions because she had no independent recollection of the accident when the statements were made. The court dismisses this argument, determining that a party admission need not be trustworthy to be admissible if offered by that party's opponent. However, one of the traditional explanations given for creating exemptions for party admissions is that the declarant, being a party to the litigation, is always free to explain or contradict them at trial. This is not possible for Brittany Jewel, who suffered from brain damage and retrograde amnesia from the accident and cannot testify. Is this a better argument for keeping Brittany's statements from the jury or will the statements eventually come into evidence no matter what the appellants argue?

b. Admissions by a Party Opponent Made in a Representative Capacity.

Rule 801(d)(2)(A) admits party opponent statements made by an individual acting for himself or acting as a representative of another. Representatives include administrators, executors, trustees, and guardians. When a representative makes a statement in his representative capacity, it is admissible when offered against the representative or the person represented. See *In re Special Fed. Grand Jury,* 819 F.2d 56 (3d Cir. 1987) (corporate agent's statement held admissible against the agent and the corporation).

Adopted Statement

United States v. Morgan

U.S. Court of Appeals for the District of Columbia Circuit
581 F.2d 933 (C.A. D.C. 1978)

BAZELON, Circuit Judge: Appellant, William Morgan, was found guilty by a jury of possessing phenmetrazine with intent to distribute.... We agree with his contention that the trial judge erred in excluding certain evidence from the jury.

I

On January 6, 1977, officers of the Metropolitan Police Department obtained a warrant to search for illegal drugs in a single-family dwelling in Northwest Washington, D.C. The warrant was issued upon the affidavit of Detective Mathis, stating that a reliable informant had advised him that a black male, age 22 to 24 and known as "Timmy," was selling drugs from inside the house; that "within the past 48 hours" Mathis had gone to the house with the informant and waited outside while the informant made a "controlled" buy; that upon rejoining Mathis, the informant handed him some pink pills, later identified as phenmetrazine; and that the informant said he had purchased these pills from Timmy.

When the officers arrived at the house at 10 p. m. to execute the warrant, they did not find Timmy but instead came across appellant and four other persons in the front hallway. Appellant was holding the leash on a snarling German shepherd. According to the officers, appellant immediately reached in his pocket with his free hand, grabbed some pink pills, threw them on the floor, and started to mash them with his foot. Detective Mathis managed to recover intact twelve of the pills, which subsequently were determined to be phenmetrazine. A search of the basement resulted in seizure of seventy-seven additional such pills and $30 cash, found in a shaving kit secreted in a hole in the ceiling; $4,280 cash, found in a fuse box; $410 cash, found in a dresser drawer; the birth certificate of a Kelsey Etheridge, found in an unidentified article of clothing on a chair; and Etheridge's school identification, found on top of a television. No fingerprints were taken from any of these particular items, and no fingerprints were introduced at trial. Besides appellant, at least six other persons were in the house when the police arrived, including the four who were in the hallway.

At trial, the government sought to connect appellant not merely with the twelve pills seized from the floor in the hallway but also with the seventy-seven pills and $4,280 cash found in the basement. The owner of the house, Mrs. McKnight, testified that she had known appellant for about two years and that he came to her home daily to feed and exercise her dogs, which were chained in the basement. Appellant, she said, was the only person regularly in the house who was not afraid of the dogs. She also stated, however, that with the exception of Etheridge, who used the basement bathroom, no one had lived in the basement since October 1976.

Appellant testified that he resided in Southeast Washington with his sister and brother. On the evening of the search, he had gone to Mrs. McKnight's house to invite one of the occupants, a William Taylor, to go with him to a party. He denied dropping any phenmetrazine, and claimed to have no knowledge of the drugs or money found in the basement. He admitted that he did take care of the dogs, however, and thus came to the house and entered the basement every other day.

Three times during the trial defense counsel sought to establish that Timmy, Mrs. McKnight's son, lived in the house and was selling drugs. Counsel proffered as evidence of this fact the statements made by the informant to Detective Mathis that are contained in the affidavit supporting the search warrant. The trial judge excluded this evidence on grounds that it was irrelevant and was hearsay.

II

Morgan contends that the informant's statements were neither (a) irrelevant nor (b) hearsay under the Federal Rules of Evidence, and that their exclusion was highly prejudicial.

B. HEARSAY

The Federal Rules of Evidence specifically provide that certain categories of out-of-court statements offered to show the truth of the matter asserted shall not be regarded as "hearsay." Under Rule 801(d)(2)(B) such a statement is not barred as hearsay if a party-opponent "has manifested his adoption or belief in its truth . . . ." This Rule plainly applies to the informant's statements to Detective Mathis. The government manifested its belief in the truth of the informant's statements about Timmy by characterizing them as "reliable" in a sworn affidavit to a United States Magistrate. (We note that the Federal Rules clearly contemplate that the federal government is a party-opponent of the defendant in criminal cases, and specifically provide that in certain circumstances statements made by government agents are admissible against the government as substantive evidence.)

... Clearly, statements in which the government has manifested its "adoption or belief" stand on more solid ground than mere out-of-court assertions by a government agent. We do not decide that just Any statement the informant might have made is admissible against the government. We decide only that where, as here, the government has indicated in a sworn affidavit to a judicial officer that it believes particular statements are trustworthy, it may not sustain an objection to the subsequent introduction of those statements on grounds that they are hearsay.

It is not clear whether these cases survive the Federal Rules. Rule 801(d)(2) (D) provides that statements made by an "agent or servant concerning a matter within the scope of his agency or employment, made during the existence of the relationship" shall be treated as admissions by his principal. As in the case of Rule 801(d)(2)(B), there is no indication in the history of the Rules that the draftsmen meant to except the government from operation of Rule 801(d)(2) (D) in criminal cases. But consider in this connection the possible significance of Rule 803(8).

Reversed and remanded for a new trial.

Points for Discussion

a. Adoptive Admissions by the Government.

Consider the possibility in *Morgan* that the government agent, by signing and swearing to his affidavit, was merely swearing that the informant relayed to him certain facts, which were then passed on to a Magistrate to determine whether those facts constituted sufficient probable cause to issue a search warrant. Under these circumstances, do you think the court was correct in saying the government adopted the informant's statements?

b. Adoptive Admissions by Words or Conduct.

In some cases, a party's words or conduct that allegedly adopts the truth of another's statement maybe be susceptible to more than one interpretation. Assume, for example, that that plaintiff tells the defendant that she knows the defendant ran over her dog, and the defendant responds by saying, "I'm so sorry." Does that mean the defendant is sorry because he is agreeing that he ran over the dog, or he is sorry that the dog is dead? How should a trial judge determine admissibility of the declarant's statement? See also *National Bank of N. America. v. Cinco Investors, Inc.*, 610 F.2d 89 (2d Cir. 1979) (evidence should not be considered when it is unclear whether the party allegedly adopting the statement had made up his mind about the statement's truth). Whether a party has adopted another person's statement is a question of conditional relevance under Rule 104(b)).

c. Adoptive Admission by Silence

When is a party's silence in the face of another's statement sufficient to show that the party adopted the statement's contents? The burden is on the proponent to show that under all the circumstances, a failure of a party to respond is so unreasonable that it supports the inference that the party agreed with the statement. See *Carr v. Deeds*, 453 F.3d 593 (4th Cir. 2006) (a police officer was in a room when a detainee told his family the officer had assaulted him did not adopt the detainee's statement because there was no showing the officer would have responded if the statement were not true).

d. The Constitutional Dimension of Adoptive Admissions by Silence

In criminal cases, there are constitutional limitations on the extent to which the prosecution can show that a defendant's silence in the face of incriminating allegations constitutes an adoptive admission. If the allegations are made by or in the presence of law enforcement officers, the defendant's failure to deny them may be attributable to the protections of the Fifth Amendment and the right of an accused to remain silent. See *United States v. Flecha*, 539 F.2d 874 (2d Cir. 1976), a case where the defendant was under arrest for smuggling marihuana, when another defendant six feet away stated in Spanish, "Why so much excitement? If we are caught, we are caught." The court held that it was natural for the defendant to say nothing because "many arrested persons know that silence is golden" as a result of Fifth Amendment protections. Therefore, even though the defendant was not being questioned by law enforcement, the court held the defendant's silence not to be an adoptive admission.

———————

Statement by Person Authorized - 801(d)(2)(C)

This rule provides that statements made by a person who is authorized by a party to make those statements are admissions and not exempt from hearsay. Whether or not the person (agent) had authority (was authorized) to make the statements must be established at trial. The authority to do so may be express or implied. An example is a president of a corporation who is authorized to speak on behalf of the organization.

Authorization can be determined by examining the acts or the conduct of the principal (person authorizing the agent) or the principal's statements to the agent or to a third party regarding the agent.

A party's books and records fall within this rule and are admissible against the party without regard to whether the party intended to disclose them to a third party.

Kirk v. Raymark Industries

U.S. Court of Appeals
61 F.3d 147 (C.A. 1995)

COWEN, Circuit Judge.

This asbestos-related personal injury action was tried to a jury.... The jury returned a verdict in favor of the plaintiff in excess of two million dollars. ...[W]e are called upon to determine whether the district court committed an error of law by: (1) allowing plaintiff to introduce into evidence the prior testimony of an out of court expert witness from an unrelated state court action; (2) permitting plaintiff to introduce the interrogatory responses of a co-defendant who settled with the plaintiff prior to trial; ...

[handwritten: issue]

...[W]e conclude that the district court erred as a matter of law in allowing the introduction of hearsay evidence ....

[handwritten: held]

I. Factual and Procedural History

Alfred Kirk ("decedent"), a retired painter, died on July 5, 1988 at the age of 65 from malignant asbestos-induced mesothelioma. Mrs. Sarah Kirk ("Kirk"), suing on behalf of herself and her deceased husband's estate, filed this diversity action against eight defendants, including Owens-Corning Fiberglas Corporation ("Owens-Corning"). Kirk alleged that her husband's mesothelioma was caused by exposure to dust from asbestos products during his employment at the New York Shipyard in Camden, New Jersey, during the late 1950's and early 1960's.

[handwritten: wrongful death]

[handwritten: cause of mesothelioma]

On December 13, 1993, the trial (which was reverse-bifurcated) began with issues of medical causation and damages. At the conclusion of this phase of the trial, the jury returned a verdict in favor of the Estate of Alfred Kirk for $1.2 million and in favor of Sarah Kirk for $810,000. The liability phase of the trial commenced several days later before the same jury that had previously heard the damages phase. At the conclusion of the liability trial, the jury returned a verdict against Owens-Corning. The jury also found that the decedent was not exposed to dust emitted by any asbestos-containing product manufactured by co-defendant Garlock, Inc. ("Garlock").

Following the jury verdict, Owens-Corning moved for a new trial, alleging several trial errors including: ... (2) allowing the introduction of hearsay evidence.

III. Prior Testimony of Out of Court Witness

During the liability phase of the trial, Owens-Corning offered the expert testimony of Dr. Harry Demopoulos to prove that the overwhelming majority of asbestos-induced mesotheliomas are caused by crocidolite asbestos fiber. This testimony supported Owens-Corning's defense that its product, Kaylo, which did not contain crocidolite fiber, could not have caused the decedent's mesothelioma. Over Owens-Corning's objection, Kirk was permitted to read to the jury the prior trial testimony of Dr. Louis Burgher from an unrelated New Jersey State Court asbestos action in 1992. In that case, Dr. Burgher had been an expert witness for Owens-Corning and testified on cross-examination that it was possible for mesothelioma to be caused by chrysotile fibers contaminated with tremolite. Kirk was clearly attempting to discredit Owens-Corning's defense offered through Dr. Demopoulos by revealing to the jury that Owens-Corning's expert witness in a previous case voiced a different and contradictory opinion as to which asbestos fibers cause mesothelioma. After the jury returned a verdict in favor of Kirk, Owens-Corning made a post-trial motion for a new trial based in part on the alleged admission of hearsay evidence, i.e., the prior testimony of Dr. Burgher in an unrelated case. The district court denied this motion....

hearsay evidence

Owens-Corning argues that the district court erred in allowing the jury to hear this evidence in light of the fact that it was hearsay. Although the record is at best vague as to what the district court's basis was for allowing such testimony, Kirk attempts to justify its admission under two distinct theories–either the testimony was not hearsay pursuant to Rule 801(d)(2)(C) of the Federal Rules of Evidence or it was hearsay, but subject to an exception pursuant to Rule 804(b)(1).

P argues

A. Rule 801(d)(2)(C) of the Federal Rules of Evidence

Kirk first attempts to justify the district court's admission of the prior trial testimony of Dr. Burgher by arguing it is an admission by a party opponent since it is a statement by a person authorized by Owens-Corning to speak concerning mesothelioma and is thus not hearsay. See Fed.R.Evid. 801(d)(2)(C) see also Precision Piping v. E.I. du Pont de Nemours, 951 F.2d 613, 619 (4th Cir.1991) (authority in the context of 801(d)(2)(C) means "authority to speak" on a particular subject on behalf of someone else). In her brief, Kirk argues that Dr. Burgher was authorized by Owens-Corning to offer his expert opinion about medical literature regarding mesothelioma and fiber type. At oral argument, Kirk suggested that the testimony of any expert that Owens-Corning has previously used in a trial can be used in future litigation against it as an authorized admission.

In support of this proposition, Kirk cites Collins v. Wayne Corp., 621 F.2d 777, 782 (5th Cir.1980), which held that deposition testimony of an expert employed by a bus manufacturer to investigate an accident was an admission under 801(d)(2)(C). However, in that case the court made a finding that the expert witness was an agent of the defendant and the defendant employed the expert to investigate and analyze the bus accident. The court determined that in giving his deposition, the expert was performing the function that the manufacturer had employed him to perform. As such, the court concluded that the expert's report of his investigation and his deposition testimony in which he explained his analysis and investigation was an admission of the defendant....

Kirk misconstrues the entire premise of calling expert witnesses. In theory, *Ct. says* despite the fact that one party retained and paid for the services of an expert witness, expert witnesses are supposed to testify impartially in the sphere of their expertise. Thus, one can call an expert witness even if one disagrees with the testimony of the expert. Rule 801(d)(2)(C) requires that the declarant be an agent of the party-opponent against whom the admission is offered, and this precludes the admission of the prior testimony of an expert witness where, as normally will be the case, the expert has not agreed to be subject to the client's control in giving his or her testimony. Since an expert witness is not subject to the control of the party opponent with respect to consultation and testimony he or she is hired to give, the expert witness cannot be deemed an agent. See Restatement (Second) of Agency § 1 cmt. a (1958) ("The relation of agency is created as the result of conduct by two parties manifesting that one of them is willing for the other to act for him subject to his control, and that the other consents so to act.").

Because an expert witness is charged with the duty of giving his or her expert opinion regarding the matter before the court, we fail to comprehend how an expert witness, who is not an agent of the party who called him, can be authorized to make an admission for that party. ... We are unwilling to adopt the proposition that the testimony of an expert witness who is called to testify on behalf of a party in one case can later be used against that same party in unrelated litigation, unless there is a finding that the expert witness is an agent of the party and is authorized to speak on behalf of that party. Accordingly, we find Dr. Burgher's prior trial testimony to be hearsay in the context of the present trial.

. . .

VI. Conclusion

... Allowing into evidence the prior testimony of a witness in an unrelated state court trial was error.... Accordingly, we will reverse the judgment of the district court and remand the matter to the district court for a new trial. ...

————————

Points for Discussion

a. Expert Witnesses as Rule 801(d)(2)(C) Agents

Why does the court in *Kirk* hold that expert witnesses employed by a party to testify in a case are not authorized to make an admission on behalf of that party, but experts who are employed to investigate and analyze facts are so authorized? Given that testifying experts are often referred to in the legal profession as "hired guns" who will slant their testimony in favor of the party who hired them, should they also be considered authorized agents?

b. Who Is Authorized to Make an Admission for a Party?

Individuals authorized to speak for a party include lawyers, presidents of corporations, the managing partner of a partnership, or even, on occasions, accountants and employees. See *Reid Brothers Logging Co. v. Ketchikan Pulp Co.*, 699 F.2 1292 (9th Cir. 1983) (a report on a business's operations written by an employee of a related company at the request of the party's chairman of the board and distributed by the party to executives, officers, and managers was an authorized admission). The authority to speak can be express or implied. See *United States v. Da Silva*, 725 F.2d 828 (2d Cir. 1983) (statements made by a defendant through an interpreter were considered authorized admissions); *Michaels v. Michaels*, 767 F.2d 1185 (7th Cir. 1985) (statements about the possible sale of a company made by a person authorized by the company to serve as its broker were authorized admissions by the company).

c. Establishing the Authority to Make an Authorized Admission

Rule 801(d)(2) provides that the court may consider the contents of an alleged agent's statements in determining whether the agent was authorized by a party to make a statement concerning the subject matter. For example, a lawyer might tell a journalist he had authority to speak for his client. The lawyer's statement, however, would be insufficient prove his authority. Other independent evidence, such as an employment agreement, is necessary. See *Bourjaily v. United States* reproduced in this chapter under the heading "Statements by Coconspirators."

————————

Statement by Party's Agent - 801(d)(2)(D)

Mahlandt v. Wild Canid Survival & Research Center, Inc.

U.S. Court of Appeals for the Eighth Circuit
588 F.2d 626 (8th Cir.1978)

VAN SICKLE, District Judge. This is a civil action for damages arising out of an alleged attack by a wolf on a child. The sole issues on appeal are as to the correctness of three rulings which excluded ... statements .... Two of them were made by a defendant, who was also an employee of the corporate defendant; and the third was in the form of a statement appearing in the records of a board meeting of the corporate defendant.

On March 23, 1973, Daniel Mahlandt, then 3 years, 10 months ... was sent by his mother to a neighbor's home ... to get his older brother.... Daniel's mother watched him cross the street, and then turned into the house to get her car keys. Daniel's path took him along a walkway adjacent to the Poos' residence. Next to the walkway was a five foot chain link fence to which [the wolf] Sophie had been chained with a six foot chain. In other words, Sophie was free to move in a half circle having a six foot radius on the side of the fence opposite from Daniel.

Sophie ... had been born at the St. Louis Zoo, and kept there until she reached 6 months of age, at which time she was given to the Wild Canid Survival and Research Center, Inc. It was the policy of the Zoo to remove wolves from the Children's Zoo after they reached the age of 5 or 6 months. Sophie was supposed to be kept at the Tyson Research Center, but Kenneth Poos, as Director of Education for the Wild Canid Survival and Research Center, Inc., had been keeping her at his home because he was taking Sophie to schools and institutions where he showed films and gave programs with respect to the nature of wolves. Sophie was known as a very gentle wolf who had proved herself to be good natured and stable during her contacts with thousands of children, while she was in the St. Louis Children's Zoo.

Sophie was chained because the evening before she had jumped the fence and attacked a beagle who was running along the fence and yapping at her.

A neighbor who was ill in bed in the second floor of his home heard a child's screams and went to his window, where he saw a boy lying on his back within the enclosure, with a wolf straddling him. The wolf's face was near Daniel's face, but the distance was so great that [the neighbor] could not see what the wolf was doing, and did not see any biting. Within about 15 seconds the neighbor saw

Clarke Poos, about seventeen, run around the house, get the wolf off of the boy, and disappear with the child in his arms to the back of the house. Clarke took the boy in and laid him on the kitchen floor.

Clarke had been returning from his friend's home immediately west when he heard a child's cries and ran around to the enclosure. He found Daniel lying within the enclosure, about three feet from the fence, and Sophie standing back from the boy the length of her chain, and wailing. An expert in the behavior of wolves stated that when a wolf licks a child's face that it is a sign of care, and not a sign of attack; that a wolf's wail is a sign of compassion, and an effort to get attention, not a sign of attack. No witness saw or knew how Daniel was injured. Clarke and his sister ran over to get Daniel's mother. She says that Clarke told her, "a wolf got Danny and he is dying." Clarke denies that statement. The defendant, Mr. Poos, arrived home while Daniel and his mother were in the kitchen. After Daniel was taken in an ambulance, Mr. Poos talked to everyone present, including a neighbor who came in. Within an hour after he arrived home, Mr. Poos went to Washington University to inform Owen Sexton, President of Wild Canid Survival and Research Center, Inc., of the incident. Mr. Sexton was not in his office so Mr. Poos left the following note on his door:

Owen, would [you] call me at home ...? Sophie bit a child that came in our back yard. All has been taken care of. I need to convey what happened to you. [*note*]

issue   Denial of admission of this note is one of the issues on appeal.

Later that day, Mr. Poos found Mr. Sexton at the Tyson Research Center and told him what had happened. Denial of plaintiff's offer to prove that Mr. Poos told Mr. Sexton that, "Sophie had bit a child that day," is the second issue on appeal. [*statement*]

A meeting of the Directors of the Wild Canid Survival and Research Center, Inc., was held on April 4, 1973. Mr. Poos was not present at that meeting. The minutes of that meeting reflect that there was a "great deal of discussion . . . about the legal aspects of the incident of Sophie biting the child." Plaintiff offered an abstract of the minutes containing that reference. [*minutes*] Denial of the offer of that abstract is the third issue on appeal.

. . .

The jury brought in a verdict for the defense.

TC
excluded
note   The trial judge's rationale for excluding the note, the statement, and the corporate minutes, was the same in each case. He reasoned that Mr. Poos did not

have any personal knowledge of the facts, and accordingly, the first two admissions were based on hearsay; and the third admission contained in the minutes of the board meeting was subject to the same objection of hearsay, and unreliability because of lack of personal knowledge.

. . .

The relevant rule here is:

Rule 801. Definitions.

. . . (d) Statements which are not hearsay. A statement is not hearsay if

. . . (2) Admission by party-opponent. The statement is offered against a party and is

. . . (A) his own statement, in either his individual or representative capacity or

(B) a statement of which he has manifested his adoption or belief in its truth, or

(C) a statement by a person authorized by him to make a statement concerning the subject, or

(D) a statement by his agent or servant concerning a matter within the scope of his agency or employment, made during the existence of the relationship,...

[*Note and Statement Offered Against Mr. Poos*][13]

[The *Note*] is not hearsay, and is admissible against Mr. Poos. [Per Rule 801(d)(2)(A)] It was his own statement, and as such was clearly different from the reported statement of another. It was also a statement of which he had manifested his adoption or belief in its truth. [Per Rule 801(d)(2)(B)]. And the same observations may be made of the [*Statement*] made later in the day to Mr. Sexton that, "Sophie had bit a child . . . ."

[*Offered Against Wild Canid Survival and Research Center, Inc.*]

Are these statements admissible against Wild Canid Survival and Research Center, Inc.? They were made by Mr. Poos when he was an agent or servant of the Wild Canid Survival and Research Center, Inc., and they concerned a matter

---

[13] Editor's Note: Italicized headings have been added for ease of delineating the arguments.

within the scope of his agency, or employment, i. e., his custody of Sophie, and were made during the existence of that relationship. [Per Rule 801(d)(2)(D)].

. . .

As to the entry in the records of a corporate meeting, the directors as primary officers of the corporation had the authority to include their conclusions in the record of the meeting. So the evidence would fall within 801(d)(2)(C) as to Wild Canid Survival and Research Center, Inc., and be admissible. ...

[Minutes Offered Against Mr. Poos]

But there was no servant, or agency, relationship which justified admitting the evidence of the board minutes as against Mr. Poos.

None of the conditions of 801(d)(2) cover the claim that minutes of a corporate board meeting can be used against a non-attending, non-participating employee of that corporation. The evidence was not admissible as against Mr. Poos.

[403 Analysis]

There is left only the question of whether the trial court's rulings which excluded all three items of evidence are justified under Rule 403. He clearly found that the evidence was not reliable, pointing out that none of the statements were based on the personal knowledge of the declarant.

. . .

So here, remembering that relevant evidence is usually prejudicial to the cause of the side against which it is presented, and that the prejudice which concerns us is unreasonable prejudice; and applying the spirit of Rule 801(d)(2), we hold that Rule 403 does not warrant the exclusion of the evidence of Mr. Poos' statements as against himself or Wild Canid Survival and Research Center, Inc.

But the limited admissibility of the corporate minutes, coupled with the repetitive nature of the evidence and the low probative value of the minute record, all justify supporting the judgment of the trial court under Rule 403.

The judgment of the District Court is reversed and the matter remanded to the District Court for a new trial consistent with this opinion.

———————————

Overview of the *Mahlandt v. Wild Canid Survival & Research Center, Inc.*

A visual overview of the *Mahlandt* case may help make the case more understandable. The following illustrates the parties to the dispute visually.

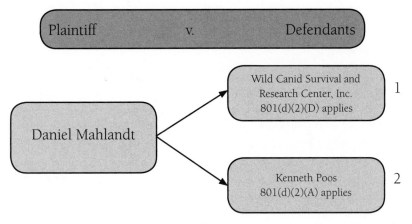

In the first issue the statement is offered against a party (the Wild Canid Survival and Research Center) and is (D) a statement by the party's agent or servant concerning a matter within the scope of the agency or employment, made during the existence of the relationship…. Therefore, 801(d)(2)(D) would apply and the note would be admissible.

In the second issue, the statement is offered against a party (Kenneth Poos) and is (A) the party's own statement in either an individual or a representative capacity. Therefore, 801(d)(2)(A) would apply and the note would be admissible.

Points for Discussion

a. Personal Knowledge

The traditional reason given for abandoning the requirement of personal knowledge for party admissions is that the admissions are likely to be true. The common law assumed an identity of interests between employers and employees such that employees were seen as not likely to make false statements damaging to their employers because they would not want to jeopardize their jobs and were interested in their employers' welfare. Do you think this is true? Can you think of a better reason for doing away with the personal knowledge requirement? See *Grace United Methodist Church v. City of Cheyenne*, 427 F.3d 775 (10th Cir. 2005).

[handwritten margin note: Need not be personal knowledge]

b. Who Is the Agent for Whom?

Why are the corporate minutes of the directors of the Center not admissible against Kenneth Poos, but the statements of Poos are admissible against the Center? For a case resolving a similar issue, see *United States v. Wideyk*, 71 F.3d 602 (6th Cir. 1995).

c. The Distinction Between Rule 801(d)(2)(C) and Rule 801(d)(2)(D) Admissions

Prior to the enactment of Rule 801(d)(2)(D), federal courts applied the traditional agency test to determine whether a statement by an agent or employee was admissible. This test would not admit a statement by an agent unless the agent was authorized by the principle to speak to the public about the subject of the statement. Because agents were seldom authorized to make damaging statements about their principals, such statements were seldom admitted. This led to unfair results, such as courts refusing to admit a statement by a truck driver about his driving that cause the accident with the plaintiff. "Speaking" authority is no longer a concern under Rule 801(d)(2)(D), which only requires that the statements relate to a matter within the scope of the agency or employment and that the agent be employed at the time the statement was made.

d. Establishing the Authority to Make a Vicarious Admission

As with "speaking admissions," the court may also consider the contents of the agent's statement in determining the existence and scope of the relationship between the declarant and the party. However, the contents of the statement itself are not sufficient. See Rule 801(d)(2).

Hypo

A patient died allegedly because a hospital allowed him to bleed to death following surgery. The hospital asked a physician, an independent contractor, to review the patient's medical records and determine whether there was fault. The physician wrote a report determining that the hospital was negligent in the death of the patient. If offered by the patient's widow against the hospital, is this report admissible as an admission by a party opponent? See *Murrey v. United States*, 73 F.3d 1448 (7th Cir. 1996).

Statement by Coconspirator - 801(d)(2)(E)

Before a statement is admissible as a statement by a coconspirator, the court must make certain preliminary factual determinations.

1) Was there a conspiracy?

2) Was the declarant a member of the conspiracy?

3) Was the statement made while the conspiracy was in existence?

4) Was the statement made in *furtherance of* the conspiracy?

In assessing the answers to these questions, the court must consider the contents of the offered statement, but the statement alone is not sufficient to establish the required relationship or authority. These preliminary facts should be decided by the trial court pursuant to the standard set forth in Rule 104(a). The reason is that the statement being offered is almost always relevant whether or not the facts are all true.

The United States Supreme Court in the *Bourjaily* case (below) resolved three evidentiary issues while reserving a fourth for the future.

Issue 1: With regard to the coconspirator exception to the hearsay rule, the question as to whether or not a conspiracy existed at the time the out-of-court statement was made and whether the conspiracy included the declarant was to be decided by the trial judge (as opposed to a jury) under Rule 104(a).

Issue 2: The burden of proof in making this determination was by a preponderance of the evidence.

Issue 3: The statement itself could be used as evidence of the conspiracy and other preliminary facts.

Issue 4: The court did not address whether or not the statement would be admissible if that statement was the only evidence of such preliminary facts.

Bourjaily v. United States

Supreme Court of the United States
483 U.S. 171 (1987)

Chief Justice REHNQUIST delivered the opinion of the Court.

Federal Rule of Evidence 801(d)(2)(E) provides: "A statement is not hearsay if ... [t]he statement is offered against a party and is ... a statement by a coconspirator of a party during the course and in furtherance of the conspiracy." We granted certiorari to answer three questions regarding the admission of statements under Rule 801(d)(2)(E): (1) whether the court must determine by independent evidence that the conspiracy existed and that the defendant and the declarant were members of this conspiracy; (2) the quantum of proof on which such determinations must be based; and (3) whether a court must in each case examine the circumstances of such a statement to determine its reliability.

[handwritten: issues]

In May 1984, Clarence Greathouse, an informant working for the Federal Bureau of Investigation (FBI), arranged to sell a kilogram of cocaine to Angelo Lonardo. Lonardo agreed that he would find individuals to distribute the drug. When the sale became imminent, Lonardo stated in a tape-recorded telephone conversation that he had a "gentleman friend" who had some questions to ask about the cocaine. In a subsequent telephone call, Greathouse spoke to the "friend" about the quality of the drug and the price. Greathouse then spoke again with Lonardo, and the two arranged the details of the purchase. They agreed that the sale would take place in a designated hotel parking lot, and Lonardo would transfer the drug from Greathouse's car to the "friend," who would be waiting in the parking lot in his own car. Greathouse proceeded with the transaction as planned, and FBI agents arrested Lonardo and petitioner immediately after Lonardo placed a kilogram of cocaine into petitioner's car in the hotel parking lot. In petitioner's car, the agents found over $20,000 in cash.

Petitioner was charged with conspiring to distribute cocaine ... and possession of cocaine with intent to distribute.... The Government introduced, over petitioner's objection, Angelo Lonardo's telephone statements regarding the participation of the "friend" in the transaction. The District Court found that, considering the events in the parking lot and Lonardo's statements over the telephone, the Government had established by a preponderance of the evidence that a conspiracy involving Lonardo and petitioner existed, and that Lonardo's statements over the telephone had been made in the course of and in furtherance of the conspiracy. Accordingly, the trial court held that Lonardo's out-of-court statements satisfied Rule 801(d)(2)(E) and were not hearsay. Petitioner was convicted on both counts and sentenced to 15 years. ... We affirm. *[handwritten: SC]*

[handwritten margin notes: gov't introduced; DC found]

Before admitting a co-conspirator's statement over an objection that it does not qualify under Rule 801(d)(2)(E), a court must be satisfied that the statement actually falls within the definition of the Rule. There must be evidence that there was a conspiracy involving the declarant and the nonoffering party, and that the statement was made "during the course and in furtherance of the conspiracy."

[handwritten margin note: Ct. must find (1) (2)]

...

[P]etitioner challenges the admission of Lonardo's statements. Petitioner argues that in determining whether a conspiracy exists and whether the defendant was a member of it, the court must look only to independent evidence-that is, evidence other than the statements sought to be admitted. Petitioner relies on Glasser v. United States, 315 U.S. 60 (1942), in which this Court first mentioned the so-called "bootstrapping rule." ... The question thus presented is whether any aspect of Glasser 's bootstrapping rule remains viable after the enactment of the Federal Rules of Evidence.

[handwritten margin note: D argues]

[handwritten margin note: issue]

Petitioner concedes that Rule 104, on its face, appears to allow the court to make the preliminary factual determinations relevant to Rule 801(d)(2)(E) by considering any evidence it wishes, unhindered by considerations of admissibility. That would seem to many to be the end of the matter. Congress has decided that courts may consider hearsay in making these factual determinations. Out-of-court statements made by anyone, including putative co-conspirators, are often hearsay. Even if they are, they may be considered, Glasser and the bootstrapping rule notwithstanding. But petitioner nevertheless argues that the bootstrapping rule, as most Courts of Appeals have construed it, survived this apparently unequivocal change in the law unscathed and that Rule 104, as applied to the admission of co-conspirator's statements, does not mean what it says. We disagree.

Petitioner claims that Congress evidenced no intent to disturb the bootstrapping rule, which was embedded in the previous approach, and we should not find that Congress altered the rule without affirmative evidence so indicating. It would be extraordinary to require legislative history to confirm the plain meaning of Rule 104. The Rule on its face allows the trial judge to consider any evidence whatsoever, bound only by the rules of privilege. ...

The Advisory Committee further noted: "An item, offered and objected to, may itself be considered in ruling on admissibility, though not yet admitted in evidence." We think this language makes plain the drafters' intent to abolish any kind of bootstrapping rule. Silence is at best ambiguous, and we decline the invitation to rely on speculation to import ambiguity into what is otherwise a clear rule.

Nor do we agree with petitioner that this construction of Rule 104(a) will allow courts to admit hearsay statements without any credible proof of the conspiracy, thus fundamentally changing the nature of the co-conspirator exception. ...

Petitioner's theory ignores two simple facts of evidentiary life. First, out-of-court statements are only presumed unreliable. The presumption may be rebutted by appropriate proof. Second, individual pieces of evidence, insufficient in themselves to prove a point, may in cumulation prove it. The sum of an evidentiary presentation may well be greater than its constituent parts. Taken together, these two propositions demonstrate that a piece of evidence, unreliable in isolation, may become quite probative when corroborated by other evidence. A per se rule barring consideration of these hearsay statements during preliminary factfinding is not therefore required. Even if out-of-court declarations by co-conspirators are presumptively unreliable, trial courts must be permitted to evaluate these statements for their evidentiary worth as revealed by the particular circumstances of the case. Courts often act as factfinders, and there is no reason to believe that courts are any less able to properly recognize the probative value of evidence in this particular area. The party opposing admission has an adequate incentive to point out the shortcomings in such evidence before the trial court finds the preliminary facts. If the opposing party is unsuccessful in keeping the evidence from the factfinder, he still has the opportunity to attack the probative value of the evidence as it relates to the substantive issue in the case. ...

We think that there is little doubt that a co-conspirator's statements could themselves be probative of the existence of a conspiracy and the participation of both the defendant and the declarant in the conspiracy. Petitioner's case presents a paradigm. The out-of-court statements of Lonardo indicated that Lonardo was involved in a conspiracy with a "friend." The statements indicated that the friend had agreed with Lonardo to buy a kilogram of cocaine and to distribute it. The statements also revealed that the friend would be at the hotel parking lot, in his car, and would accept the cocaine from Greathouse's car after Greathouse gave Lonardo the keys. Each one of Lonardo's statements may itself be unreliable, but taken as a whole, the entire conversation between Lonardo and Greathouse was corroborated by independent evidence. The friend, who turned out to be petitioner, showed up at the prearranged spot at the prearranged time. He picked up the cocaine, and a significant sum of money was found in his car. On these facts, the trial court concluded, in our view correctly, that the Government had established the existence of a conspiracy and petitioner's participation in it.

We need not decide in this case whether the courts below could have relied solely upon Lonardo's hearsay statements to determine that a conspiracy had been established by a preponderance of the evidence. ... It is sufficient for today to hold that a court, in making a preliminary factual determination under Rule 801(d)(2)(E), may examine the hearsay statements sought to be admitted. ... The courts below properly considered the statements of Lonardo and the subsequent events in finding that the Government had established by a preponderance of the evidence that Lonardo was involved in a conspiracy with petitioner. We have no reason to believe that the District Court's factfinding of this point was clearly erroneous. We hold that Lonardo's out-of-court statements were properly admitted against petitioner.

...

The judgment of the Court of Appeals is Affirmed.

Points for Discussion

a. The Judge's Role in Admitting a Statement by a Coconspirator

In a conspiracy case, *Bourjaily* requires that the trial judge decide by a preponderance of the evidence whether a statement by an alleged co-conspirator is admissible under Rule 801(d)(2)(E). This means that the court will have to make many of the same factual findings that the jury will be asked to make at the end of the case (that a conspiracy existed, and the declarant and the defendant were a member of the conspiracy). Rulings on the admissibility of most hearsay objections do not require a court to make factual findings before admitting evidence. Why does the Court require them for statements by a coconspirator?

b. Are the Contents of the Statement Alone Sufficient to Prove the Statement Admissible?

The *Bourjaily* Court left open the question whether the statement itself could be considered by a trial court in determining whether there was a sufficient foundation for the statement's admission under Rule 801(d)(2)(D). In December, 1997, Rule 801(d)(2) was amended to provide that the statement alone was not sufficient. The Advisory Committee Note to this amendment counsels that a trial court, in making a Rule 801(d)(2)(E) ruling, should also consider the circumstances surrounding the statement, such as the identity of the speaker, the context in which the statement was made, or evidence corroborating the contents of the statement in making its determination. This amendment also applies to determining an agency relationship for purposes of authorized admissions (801(d)(2)(C)) and vicarious admissions (801(d)(2)(D)).

c. The Order of Proof in a Criminal Conspiracy Case

In a criminal conspiracy case, trial courts in some federal jurisdictions have the discretion to admit a coconspirator's statement without first determining whether the statement is admissible under Rule 801(d)(2)(E), subject to the prosecution's later proof of its admissibility. There is a reason for this. Suppose that the Government in a conspiracy case has a large number of witnesses, each of whom will testify as to what they know about the conspiracy. Suppose further that there are several defendants in the case. If the government must prove each defendant's participation in the conspiracy twice, once at a hearing before the judge and again before the jury, it will substantially increase the time and difficulty of the trial. Thus, several federal courts have indicated that the trial judge may follow whatever order of proof she prefers. See, e.g., *United States v. Smith*, 320 F.3d 647 (6th Cir. 2003). But not all circuits agree. The Fifth Circuit, in *United States v. James*, 1590 F.2d 575 (5th Cir. 1979) (en banc), for example, requires that the trial judge must resolve the admissibility of a conspirator's statement before admitting it. Which do you think is better policy?

E. Hearsay Within Hearsay

Hearsay within Hearsay merely refers to multiple 'levels' or 'layers' of hearsay and is governed by Rule 805 which provides:

> **Rule 805. Hearsay within Hearsay.**
>
> Hearsay included within hearsay is not excluded under the hearsay rule if each part of the combined statements conforms with an exception to the hearsay rule provided in these rules.

Consider the following example: Allen says to Bill, "David ran the red light." Bill says to Cindy, "Allen told me that David ran the red light." Cindy testifies at trial that she was told that David ran the red light. There are two levels of hearsay to consider in this situation:

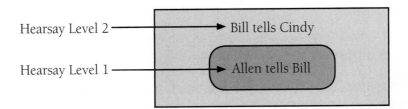

Hearsay Level 2 ──────────► Bill tells Cindy

Hearsay Level 1 ──────────► Allen tells Bill

Under Rule 805 each statement must meet an exception to the hearsay rule for Cindy's testimony to be admitted. Hearsay within hearsay is common. One common example comes in the form of documentary evidence. The documents are hearsay and often contain statements by third parties which are also hearsay. In these cases, each statement must independently meet an exception to the hearsay rule.

> **FYI**
>
> When documents contain multiple levels of hearsay it is often the case that all of the hearsay statements do not meet an exception to the hearsay rule. In those cases, the entire document need not be excluded. If those portions of the document which do not meet an exception are <u>redacted</u> then the document may usually be admitted in its redacted form.

> **Make the Connection**
>
> Do not fall into the trap that because a statement meets an exception it is admissible. Another rule, such as Rule 403, may keep the statement out.

F. Hearsay Exceptions

The Federal Rules of Evidence divide the exceptions to the hearsay rule into two categories. The <u>first</u> ① category (Rule 803) applies to those exceptions set out within the rule regardless of whether the declarant is or is not available; the <u>second category</u> ② (Rule 804) applies only when the declarant is not available. The largest number of exceptions (twenty-three) fall within Rule 803. This rule is often referred to as containing "strong" exceptions because of the fact that they are not dependant upon the availability of the declarant. Conversely, Rule 804 exceptions are referred to as "weak" exceptions because the declarant must be unavailable before they apply. Any statement which fits into one (or more) of the exceptions is not excluded by the hearsay rule.

1. Rule 803. Hearsay Exceptions; Availability of Declarant Immateral

> **803(1) - Present Sense Impression.**
>
> A statement describing or explaining an event or condition made while the declarant was perceiving the event or condition, or immediately thereafter.

A critical requirement of this exception is timeliness. The rule requires that the statement be made while the declarant was perceiving the event or condition or immediately thereafter. Think of a sports announcer's play-by-play description of a football game. The entire game describing the action on the field would qualify as "present sense impressions." The first option – while perceiving the event is pretty straightforward. The second, immediately thereafter, is a bit more difficult. If a person perceives the event and remains in shock for an hour thereafter, and while still in shock from the event explains the event, does this explanation meet the temporal requirement of the rule? The next case examines this exception.

Schindler v. Seiler

U.S Court of Appeals for the Seventh Circuit
474 F.3d 1008 (7th Cir. 2007)

BAUER, Circuit Judge. ... Dr. Schindler ... alleg[ed] that Seiler had defamed him by informing a third party, Dr. Kerry White, that Dr. Schindler was a "bad doctor" who had "paralyzed four patients." Both Seiler and Dr. White deny that Seiler made these statements.

The sole evidence offered by Dr. Schindler to prove that these statements were made was his own testimony that Dr. White had said to him, "Joe Seiler is downstairs right now and just told me that you paralyzed four patients." The district court ruled that Dr. Schindler's testimony about what Dr. White had said to him was inadmissable hearsay.... We affirm.

I. Analysis

Dr. argues

... In his appeal, Dr. Schindler first argues that the district court erred in excluding as inadmissible hearsay his testimony that Dr. White told him that "Joe Seiler is downstairs right now and just told me that you paralyzed four patients."

... Dr. Schindler contends that the district court erred because his testimony is not being offered to prove the truth of the matter asserted, i.e., that Dr. Schindler paralyzed four patients, but rather to prove that the defamatory statements were made.

...

Where a plaintiff attempts to introduce the testimony of an individual who did not personally witness the alleged defamatory statement but was later told by another that the statement was made, such testimony is rejected as hearsay. ... This is precisely what Dr. Schindler is attempting to do through his own testimony.

Seiler testified during his deposition that he had informed Dr. White that he had overheard others making derogatory remarks about Dr. Schindler. Seiler denied, however, that he relayed any specific details of the derogatory statements to Dr. White. Likewise, Dr. White testified that Seiler had not told him that Dr. Schindler had paralyzed four patients or that Dr. Schindler was a bad doctor. Had Dr. White testified to the contrary, that Seiler had said to him that Dr. Schindler was a "bad doctor" who had "paralyzed four patients," Dr. White's testimony would be admissible. Dr. Schindler, however, has failed to present testimony from any individual who personally heard Seiler make the defamatory statements. And Dr. Schindler's own testimony as to what Dr. White said to him is offered precisely to prove the ultimate fact in question and the truth of the matter asserted therein: Seiler said to Dr. White that Dr. Schindler was a "bad doctor" who had "paralyzed four patients." Dr. Schindler has not asserted any other non-hearsay purpose for offering his testimony. The district court properly excluded such evidence as inadmissible hearsay.

impermissible purpose

... Dr. Schindler argues that even if his testimony is hearsay, it is admissible under ... the present sense impression exception to the general rule barring hearsay....

Dr. argues

Under Rule 803(1), hearsay is admissible as a present sense impression if the "statement describing or explaining an event or condition [was] made while the declarant was perceiving the event or condition, or immediately thereafter." There are three criteria for the admission of statements under Rule 803(1): "(1) the statement must describe an event or condition without calculated narration; (2) the speaker must have personally perceived the event or condition described; and (3) the statement must have been made while the speaker was perceiving the event or condition, or immediately thereafter." ..."A declarant who deliberates about what to say or provides statements for a particular reason creates the possibility that the statements are not contemporaneous, and, more likely, are calculated interpretations of events rather than near simultaneous perceptions." ...

3 criteria for admission of evidence under 803(1)

Dr. White testified that he told Dr. Schindler "that Mr. Seiler had brought to my attention that disparaging and derogatory comments were being made at institutions outside of Eau Claire." He also testified that he told Dr. Schindler about the derogatory comments because he was concerned about their impact on Dr. Schindler and his reputation. Additionally, Dr. Schindler claims that Dr. White testified that he immediately went to Dr. Schindler after hearing Seiler's defamatory statement. This claim is untrue. Although Dr. White testified that he conveyed the information that he had received from Seiler to Dr. Schindler, he never testified that he did so immediately after speaking with Seiler. Dr. Schindler relies on his own testimony-that Dr. White told him, "Joe Seiler is downstairs right now and just told me that you paralyzed four patients"-to prove the immediacy of Dr. White's statement. Because Dr. White's statement to Dr. Schindler was a calculated narration, made for a specific reason, and Dr. Schindler has failed to present admissible evidence of the statement's immediacy, the present sense impression exception to the hearsay rule does not apply...

————

Points for Discussion

a. The Reliability of Present Sense Impressions.

The language of Rule 803(1) only requires there be a statement "describing or explaining an event or condition made while the declarant was perceiving the event or condition, or immediately thereafter." Why do you think the court in *Schindler* also required the statement be "without calculated narration?" Think back to the four risks of hearsay discussed earlier in this chapter, those of memory, perception, sincerity and narration. Which of these risks is not present when a present sense impression statement is made?

b. The Time Delay

One of the earliest cases recognizing a present sense impression was *Houston Oxygen v. Davis*, 161 S.W.2d 474 (Tex. 1942). *Houston Oxygen* involved an automobile accident. Several miles before the accident, as the plaintiff's car passed the declarant's car on the road, the declarant stated to her passengers that the occupants of plaintiff's car "must have been drunk" and that they would "find them somewhere on the road wrecked if they kept that rate of speed up." The Texas Supreme Court held this statement to be admissible as a present sense impression because it was made spontaneously and was free from defects of memory or sincerity. Although *Houston Oxygen* was a case in which the statements were made at the time the declarant was observing the event, this is not a requirement under the rule. The rule only requires that the statement, if not made simultaneous with the event, be made "immediately thereafter." The Advisory Committee's Note to Rule

803(a) states that "immediately thereafter" permits only a "slight lapse of time." Try your hand at constructing a brief definition of "immediately thereafter" that takes into account the requirement the statement be free from defects of memory or sincerity.

803(2) – Excited Utterance.

A statement relating to a startling event or condition, made while the declarant was under the stress of excitement caused by the event or condition.

Unlike the temporal requirement of the Present Sense Impression, the Excited Utterance exception has no time limit. Instead, the requirement is that the statement be made while the declarant was under the stress of excitement caused by the event or condition. This could be minutes or, on rare occassions, hours after the event occurred.

City of Dallas v. Donovan

Court of Appeals of Texas
768 S.W.2d 905 (Tex. App. - Dallas, 1989)

BAKER, *Justice.* ... Michael and Victoria Donovan, ... sued the city because of injuries that they suffered in a collision on January 14, 1984. The accident happened at an intersection in the Dallas city limits. A stop sign, which would have controlled traffic moving in the direction of the Donovan's travel, was down at the time of the accident. A governmental unit is immune from liability for damages based on a claim arising from the removal or destruction of a traffic or road sign by a third party unless the governmental unit fails to correct the situation within a reasonable time after actual notice. ... The jury found that a third party had removed the stop sign, that the city did have actual notice that the sign was down, that the city failed to replace the sign within a reasonable time after receiving notice, and that this failure was a proximate cause of the collision.

In its first point of error, the city argues that the trial court erred in admitting certain testimony of ... Backhaus. He testified that a middle-aged woman drove up to the scene of the accident minutes after the collision. She observed the injured children, and Backhaus could tell that she was affected by what she saw, based on her facial expression and tone of voice. He said that she was very excited or

City argues

upset, she was emotional, her hands were shaking, and her voice was "crackling." He said that she volunteered the statement that days prior to the accident she had reported to the city that the stop sign was down.

The city objected to the woman's statement, contending that it was inadmissible hearsay, and the city makes the same argument on appeal. The Donovans contend that the statement was admissible as an excited utterance under rule 803(2) .... The pertinent part of the rule states:

The following are not excluded by the hearsay rule, even though the declarant is available as a witness: .... (2) Excited utterance. A statement relating to a startling event or condition made while the declarant was under the stress of excitement caused by the event or condition.

. . .

The city argues that the woman's statement lacks the necessary relationship to the startling event. The city asserts that the statement bears no relationship to the events immediately preceding the accident, the accident itself, or the resulting injuries. ... In our view, the woman's statement about her report to the city concerning the stop sign does tend to explain or illuminate the accident, and it does relate to happenings causative of the accident. The Donovans argued at trial that the city's failure to restore the stop sign after actual notice was a proximate cause of the collision, and the jury so found. Since the woman's statement is probative of actual notice to the city that the stop sign was down, it does tend to explain the accident, and it relates to happenings causative of the accident. Therefore, we view Coleman as supportive of the Donovans' argument that the statement was admissible as an excited utterance.

. . .

We also observe that the Texas and federal rules on excited utterances are identical, and that Texas adopted the federal rule. ... A number of Texas commentators have considered the advisory committee's notes on the federal rules as persuasive. ... As to the content of statements excepted from the hearsay rule, the advisory committee note states:

Permissible subject matter of the statement is limited under Exception (1) [rule 803(1) on present sense impressions] to description or explanation of the event or condition.... In Exception (2) [rule 803(2) on excited utterances], however, the statement need only "relate" to the startling event or condition, thus affording a broader scope of subject matter coverage.

. . .

In a case applying the federal rule, there was testimony by the plaintiff's father that after the plaintiff fell in the defendant's store, another shopper stated that she had informed "them" about a substance on the floor about an hour and a half ago. The trial court admitted the statement as an excited utterance. The federal appellate court held that the three required conditions for admission had been satisfied: a startling occasion, a statement made before time to fabricate, and a statement relating to the circumstances of the occurrence. The statement was probative of notice of the premises defect, and the court stated that "it is undisputed that [the declarant's] statement directly concerned the 'circumstance' surrounding the occurrence." ...

3 conditions

In the present case, the necessary relationship between the statement and the event is disputed, but we resolve that dispute in favor of the Donovans. We conclude that the statement was clearly related to the event, since it was probative of actual notice and therefore relates to happenings causative of the accident and tends to at least partially explain the accident. We agree with the advisory committee's note that excited utterances are not confined to statements describing or explaining the startling event itself. ...

statement was relevant

The city also argues that the statement was inadmissible because it referred to an incident remote from the startling event in terms of time. We disagree with the premise of this argument. The advisory committee suggests that the time element is important only with respect to the duration of the declarant's state of excitement. ... A statement made while in a condition of excitement theoretically stills the capacity for reflection and prevents fabrication. ... We conclude that the only requirement concerning time with respect to admission of excited utterances is the necessity that the statement be made while in a state of excitement caused by the startling event. ...

city argues

time element

timing

... We hold that it was not error to admit Backhaus' testimony about the woman's statement. The statement was admissible as an excited utterance.

We affirm the trial court's judgment.

———————

Points for Discussion

a. The Stress of the Excitement

The basis for admitting a statement as an excited utterance is that the declarant has no time to fabricate and thus speaks the truth without calculation. This may be the reason the court in *Donovan* only required the content of the excited utterance relate to an issue in the case, rather than the startling event itself. How does this differ from the requirements of a present sense impression under Rule 803(1)?

b. Unidentified Bystander Declarants

In *Donovan*, the declarant was identified by name. What if the bystander who made the excited utterance is unknown? Should the unknown identity of the bystander be a factor in determining whether the statement is an excited utterance? Should it be a bar to admissibility? See *Miller v. Keating*, 754 F.2d 507 (3d Cir. 1985).

c. Factors for Determining Excited Utterances

Some of the factors courts look to in determining whether a statement was an excited utterance include: (1) How exciting was the event? (2) The period of time between the event and the statement; (3) Whether the statement was in response to a question; and (4) Whether the declarant was a participant or bystander to the event. Using these factors, was there an excited utterance when the declarant, after being rendered unconscious for 20 hours as a result of an automobile accident, woke up and stated, "The Headlights closed," before becoming unconscious? See *Chestnut v. Ford Motor Co.*, 445 F.2d 967 (4th Cir. 1971).

———————————

Comparison of 803(1) and 803(2)

Exceptions 803(1) and 803(2) are certainly very similar. Many statements will satisfy both exceptions, but others will not. The following chart compares the two exceptions:

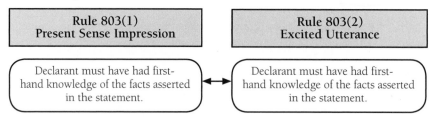

Rule 803(1) Present Sense Impression	Rule 803(2) Excited Utterance
Declarant must have had first-hand knowledge of the facts asserted in the statement.	Declarant must have had first-hand knowledge of the facts asserted in the statement.

To satisfy either 803(1) or 803(2) the party offering the statement must demonstrate that the declarant perceived the event or condition that is the subject matter of the statement. The declarant is not required to participate in the event, only perceive the event. Additionally, courts do not require the offering party to introduce evidence that the event actually occurred. The statement alone is considered sufficient.

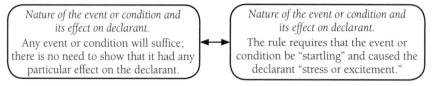

Nature of the event or condition and its effect on declarant. Any event or condition will suffice; there is no need to show that it had any particular effect on the declarant.	*Nature of the event or condition and its effect on declarant.* The rule requires that the event or condition be "startling" and caused the declarant "stress or excitement."

Under the present sense impression exception (803(1), virtually any event or condition may suffice. Alternatively, under the excited utterance exception, (803(2), the event or condition must have been 'startling' and must have caused 'stress' or 'excitement' to the declarant. Some events are necessarily startling, such as an assault or witnessing a crime.

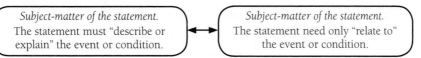

Under 803(1), the statement must be 'closely tied' to the event or condition that prompted it as the rule mandates that the statement describe or explain the event or condition.

Under 803(2), the statement need only 'relate to the startling event or condition.' Statements made under this exception are considered reliable based on the idea that the spontaneous reaction will overcome any thought process that may lead to fabrication.

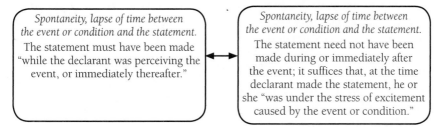

The time element is the critical component of each of these hearsay exceptions. The Advisory Committee Notes state that "[t]he most significant practical difference [between the two exceptions] will lie in the time lapse allowable between event and statement." Time to reflect on the event weighs against the application of the present sense impression. Rule 803(1) requires the statement to be made either "while ... perceiving the event, or immediately thereafter." The time period between the event or condition and the statement can be substantially longer under 803(2) than 803(1). The only requirement under 803(2) is that the statement be made while "under the stress or excitement caused by the event or condition.

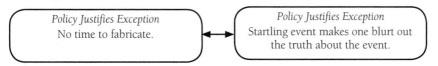

The reliability in both statements rests with the assumption that the declarant does not have the time or the inclination to fabricate details of the event.

> **803(3) – Then Existing Mental, Emotional or Physical Condition.**
>
> A statement of the declarant's then existing state of mind, emotion, sensation, or physical condition (such as intent, plan, motive, design, mental feeling, pain, and bodily health), but not including a statement of memory or belief to prove the fact remembered or believed unless it relates to the execution, revocation, identification, or terms of declarant's will.

The typical risks associated with hearsay are presumed inapplicable when a statement is offered to show a declarant's then existing state of mind, emotion, sensation, or physical condition. These types of statements are considered trustworthy because their spontaneous nature makes them as reliable as declarations made on the witness stand under oath. The exception can be broken down into two basic categories: 1) then existing state of mind, emotion, (or) sensation and 2) then existing physical condition. Much like an 803(1) present sense impression, the declarant is describing something as it is happening, but instead of being an "external" situation, it is an "internal" situation, that of the declarant's own thoughts or physical condition.

Mutual Life Ins. Co. of New York v. Hillmon

Supreme Court of the United States
145 U.S. 285 (1892)

On July 13, 1880, Sallie E. Hillmon, a citizen of Kansas, brought an action against the Mutual Life Insurance Company, a corporation of New York, on a policy of insurance, dated December 10, 1878, on the life of her husband, John W. Hillmon, in the sum of $10,000, payable to her within 60 days after notice and proof of his death. On the same day the plaintiff brought two other [actions],-the one against the New York Life Insurance Company...on two similar policies of life insurance ... for the sum of $5,000 each; and the other against the Connecticut Mutual Life Insurance Company, ... for the sum of $5,000.

In each case the declaration alleged that Hillmon died on March 17, 1879, during the continuance of the policy, but that the defendant, though duly notified of the fact, had refused to pay the amount of the policy, or any part thereof; and the answer denied the death of Hillmon, and alleged that he, together with John H. Brown and divers other persons, on or before November 30, 1878, conspiring to defraud the defendant, procured the issue of all the policies, and afterwards, in March and April, 1879, falsely pretended and represented that Hillmon was dead,

D refused to pay life insurance

[handwritten: D claimed husband faked his death]

and that a dead body which they had procured was his, whereas in reality he was alive and in hiding.

. . .

On February 29, 1888, after two trials at which the jury had disagreed, the three cases came on for trial,... At the trial plaintiff introduced evidence tending to show that on or about March 5, 1879, Hillmon and Brown left Wichita, in the state of Kansas, and traveled together through southern Kansas in search of a site for a cattle ranch; that on the night of March 18th, while they were in camp at a place called 'Crooked Creek,' Hillmon was killed by the accidental discharge of a gun; that Brown at once notified persons living in the neighborhood, and that the body was thereupon taken to a neighboring town, where, after an inquest, it was buried. The defendants introduced evidence tending to show that the body found in the camp at Crooked creek on the night of March 18th was not the body of Hillmon, but was the body of one Frederick Adolph Walters. Upon the question whose body this was there was much conflicting evidence, including photographs and descriptions of the corpse, and of the marks and scars upon it, and testimony to its likeness to Hillmon and to Walters.

The defendants introduced testimony that Walters left his home at Ft. Madison, in the state of Iowa, in March, 1878, and was afterwards ... his family frequently received letters from him, the last of which was written from Wichita; and that he had not been heard from since March, 1879. The defendants also offered the following evidence:

Elizabeth Rieffenach testified that she was a sister of Frederick Adolph Walters, and lived at Ft. Madison; and thereupon, ... the following proceedings took place:

'Witness further testified that she had received a letter written from Wichita, Kansas, about the 4th or 5th day of March, 1879, by her brother Frederick Adolph; that the letter was dated at Wichita, and was in the handwriting of her brother; that she had searched for the letter, but could not find the same, it being lost; that she remembered and could state the contents of the letter.

[handwritten: objection to contents of letter]

'Thereupon the defendants' counsel asked the question, 'State the contents of that letter;" to which the plaintiff objected, on the ground that the same is incompetent, irrelevant, and hearsay. The objection was sustained .... The following is the letter as stated by witness:

Wichita, Kansas, March 4th or 5th or 3d or 4th,-I don't know,-1879.

Dear Sister and All: I now in my usual style drop you a few lines to let you

know that I expect to leave Wichita on or about March the 5th with a certain
Mr. Hillmon, a sheep trader, for Colorado, or parts unknown to me. I expect to
see the country now. News are of no interest to you, as you are not acquainted
here. I will close with compliments to all inquiring friends. Love to all.

I am truly your brother, FRED. ADOLPH WALTERS.'

Alvina D. Kasten testified that she was 21 years of age, and resided in Ft.
Madison; that she was engaged to be married to Frederick Adolph Walters; that
she last saw him on March 24, 1878, at Ft. Madison; that he left there at that time,
and had not returned; that she corresponded regularly with him, and received
a letter about every two weeks until March 3, 1879, which was the last time
she received a letter from him; that this letter was dated at Wichita, March 1,
1879, and was addressed to her at Ft. Madison, and the envelope was postmarked
'Wichita, Kansas, March 2, 1879;' and that she had never heard from or seen him
since that time.

The defendants put in evidence the envelope with the postmark and address,
and thereupon offered to read the letter in evidence. The plaintiff objected to the
reading of the letter. The court sustained the objection....

This letter was dated 'Wichita, March 1, 1879,' was signed by Walters, and
began as follows:

'Dearest Alvina: Your kind and
ever welcome letter was received
yesterday afternoon about an hour
before I left Emporia. I will stay here
until the fore part of next week, and
then will leave here to see a part of
the country that I never expected to
see when I left home, as I am going
with a man by the name of Hillmon,

Go Online

For an interesting forensic investigation into the actual identity of
John Hillmon where the body was
exhumed see www.thehillmoncase.
com.

who intends, to start a sheep ranch, and, as he promised me more wager than
I could make at anything else, I concluded to take it, for a while at least, until I
strike something better. There is so many folks in this country that have got the
Leadville fever, and if I could not of got the situation that I have now I would
have went there myself; but as it is at present I get to see the best portion of
Kansas, Indian Territory, Colorado, and Mexico. The route that we intend to
take would cost a man to travel from $150 to $200, but it will not cost me a
cent; besides, I get good wages. I will drop you a letter occasionally until I get
settled down. Then I want you to answer it.'

. . .

The court, after recapitulating some of the testimony introduced, instructed the jury as follows: 'You have perceived from the very beginning of the trial that the conclusion to be reached must practically turn upon one question of fact, ... whose body was it that on the evening of March 18, 1879, lay dead by the camp fire on Crooked creek? The decision of that question decides the verdict you should render.'

The jury ... returned verdicts for the plaintiff against the three defendants ... for the amounts of their policies ....

Mr. Justice GRAY, after stating the case as above, delivered the opinion of the court.... There is, ... one question of evidence so important, so fully argued at the bar, and so likely to arise upon another trial, that it is proper to express an opinion upon it.

This question is of the admissibility of the letters written by Walters on the first days of March, 1879, which were offered in evidence by the defendants, and excluded by the court. In order to determine the competency of these letters it is important to consider the state of the case when they were offered to be read.

[handwritten margin note: competency of letters]

The matter chiefly contested at the trial was the death of John W. Hillmon, the insured; and that depended upon the question whether the body found at Crooked creek on the night of March 18, 1879, was his body or the body of one Walters.... The evidence that Walters was at Wichita on or before March 5th, and had not been heard from since, together with the evidence to identify as his the body found at Crooked creek on March 18th, tended to show that he went from Wichita to Crooked creek between those dates. Evidence that just before March 5th he had the intention of leaving Wichita with Hillmon would tend to corroborate the evidence already admitted, and to show that he went from Wichita to Crooked creek with Hillmon. Letters from him to his family and his betrothed were the natural, if not the only attainable, evidence of his intention.

The position taken at the bar that the letters were competent evidence ... as memoranda made in the ordinary course of business, cannot be maintained, for they were clearly not such.

But upon another ground suggested they should have been admitted. A man's state of mind or feeling can only be manifested to others by countenance, attitude, or gesture, or by sounds or words, spoken or written. The nature of the fact to be proved is the same, and evidence of its proper tokens is equally competent to prove it, whether expressed by aspect or conduct, by voice or pen. When the intention to be proved is important only as qualifying an act, its connection with that act must be shown, in order to warrant the admission of declarations of the intention. But whenever the intention is of itself a distinct and material fact in a chain of circumstances, it may be proved by contemporaneous oral or written declarations of the party.

The existence of a particular intention in a certain person at a certain time being a material fact to be proved, evidence that he expressed that intention at that time is as direct evidence of the fact as his own testimony that he then had that intention would be. After his death these can hardly be any other way of proving it, and while he is still alive his own memory of his state of mind at a former time is no more likely to be clear and true than a bystander's recollection of what he then said, and is less trustworthy than letters written by him at the very time and under circumstances precluding a suspicion of misrepresentation.

[handwritten margin note: leltes evidence that]

The letters in question were competent not as narratives of facts communicated to the writer by others, nor yet as proof that he actually went away from Wichita, but as evidence that, shortly before the time when other evidence tended to show that he went away, he had the intention of going, and of going with Hillmon, which made it more probable both that he did go and that he went with Hillmon than if there had been no proof of such intention. In view of the mass of conflicting testimony introduced upon the question whether it was the body of Walters that was found in Hillmon's camp, this evidence might properly influence the jury in determining that question.

[handwritten margin note: lelters were competent evidence of intention of walters]

... [W]e are of opinion that the two letters were competent evidence of the intention of Walters at the time of writing them, which was a material fact bearing upon the question in controversy; and that for the exclusion of these letters ... the verdicts must be set aside, and a new trial had.

Points for Discussion

a. The Underpinnings of *Hillmon*

Hillmon appears to contemplate the use of a statement to prove the doing of the intended act by the declarant (Walters) and the doing of the act by a third person (Hillmon), as long as the acts were done in concert. What if Walter's letters were offered to prove it was Hillmon who went with Walters to find a sheep ranch? What if Walter's letters were offered to show Hillmon intended to go with Walters? Would these letters then be admissible?

b. The Breadth of *Hillmon*

Consider the following facts:

The day he disappeared, Larry Adell told two friends he was going to meet Angelo (the defendant) at a restaurant to "pick up a pound of marijuana which

Angelo promised him for free." Both friends saw him walk into the parking lot, after which he never was seen again. The defendant was charged with Adell's kidnapping. *United States v. Pheaster*, 544 F.2d 353 (9th Cir. 1976).

Should the trial judge admit the testimony of the two friends to prove that Adell did not voluntarily disappear or to prove that the defendant was among those who kidnapped Adell from the parking lot? How would the *Hillmon* case and Rule 803(3) evaluate this testimony?

Notes on Hillmon

In 1933, some forty-one years after the Supreme Court handed down Hillmon, the Supreme Court issued its opinion in *Shepard v. United States*, 52 N.E.2d 448 (N.Y. 1943). Writing for the Court, Justice Cardozo suggested that Hillmon may be bad law: "The ruling in [Hillmon] marks the high water line beyond which courts have been unwilling to go."

How can a future event be considered a *present* or *the existing* state of mind? The answer lies in the fact that the future is really a present mental concept of the person who is thinking about the future event that has yet to transpire.

Do not think of the past, present, and future as three separate concepts:

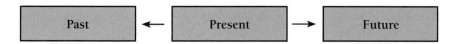

After *Hillmon*, it may be more appropriate to think in terms of two concepts:

The thought of the future is really just a present thought and nothing more.

Why is a future intention relevant? It is relevant as circumstantial evidence of a future intention which eventually transpired into an event that actually occurred. The fact that Hillmon intended to go to Crooked Creek is circumstantial evidence that he actually did go and it was his body that was found there.

Casualty Insurance Co. v. Salinas

Supreme Court of Texas
333 S.W.2d 109 (Tex. 1960).

NORVELL, Justice.

This is a workmen's compensation case in which the Court of Civil Appeals sustained the sole point contained in appellant's brief and reversed the judgment of the trial court because of the exclusion of evidence proffered by the plaintiff, Martin A. Salinas.

... Salinas, while employed by Howel Refining Company was injured when a fellow workman dropped a large bolt upon his right shoulder. ...

Upon the trial, Salinas testified as to his injury, the extent and duration of a disabling pain in his shoulder and back, and maintained that such pain persisted to the date of trial. Two doctors testifying for the insurance carrier stated that Salinas was not seriously injured, had suffered little or no pain except for a short period after the injury, and in effect was malingering. To offset this medical testimony, Salinas called three lay witnesses and tendered proof that Salinas had complained of present existing pain at various times subsequent to his injury. The trial court excluded this testimony.

Upon appeal, Salinas presented one point only, namely:

'The trial court erred in refusing to permit appellant's attorney to introduce evidence of spontaneous oral complaints of present pain and suffering made by the appellant, Martin Salinas.'

The Court of Civil Appeals sustained this point, held that the error was prejudicial, reversed the judgment of the district court and remanded the cause for another trial. ...

...[T]he overwhelming weight of American authority supports the position of the Court of Civil Appeals in holding that Salinas' proffered witnesses should have been permitted to testify as to his complaints of presently existing pain. ...

'The declarations of a party himself, to whomsoever made, are competent evidence, when confined strictly to such complaints, expressions, and exclamations as furnish evidence of a present, existing pain or malady, to prove his condition, ills, pains, and symptoms, whether arising from sickness, or from an injury by accident or violence.'

. . .

'Applied specifically to the present Exception, the judicial doctrine has been that there is a fair necessity for lack of other better evidence, for resorting to a person's own contemporary statements of his mental or physical condition. It is indeed possible to obtain by circumstantial evidence (chiefly of conduct) some knowledge of a human being's internal state of pain, emotion, motive, design, and the like; but in directness, amount, and value, this source of evidence must usually be decidedly inferior to the person's own contemporary assertions of those conditions. It might be argued, however, that the person's own statements on the stand would amply satisfy the need for his testimonial evidence. The answer is that statements of this sort on the stand, where there is ample opportunity for deliberate misrepresentation and small means for checking it by other evidence or testing it by cross-examination, are comparatively inferior to statements made at times when circumstances lessened the possible inducement to misrepresentation.' Wigmore on Evidence (3rd Ed.) § 1714.

... 'It is one of the natural concomitants of illness and of physical injuries for the sick or injured person to complain of pain and distress * * *'

Statements of existing bodily pain need not be made to a physician in order to be admissible, Wigmore (3rd Ed.) § 1719, although this circumstance may have some bearing upon the weight given the declaration by a jury. ...[N]nor is it essential that the expression of pain concerning which testimony is offered be of an involuntary nature such as a scream or a groan or the like. A verbal and articulate statement of complaint comes within the exception to the hearsay rule. Wigmore (3rd Ed.) § 1719.

It is argued in the application for writ of error that objections other than the hearsay nature of the evidence were made to the testimony of the witnesses tendered by Salinas, such as, that the questions propounded to the witnesses were leading and suggestive, called for conclusions and the like. It would serve no useful purpose to set forth in detail the nature and extent of our examination of the statement of facts in connection with these contentions. We agree with the analysis of the record made by the Court of Civil Appeals. The real objection to the proffered evidence was that it was inadmissible because of the hearsay rule.

...[H]ad they been permitted to testify, would have said that upon occasions after his injury Salinas complained of pain and serious bodily discomfort. The record discloses beyond doubt that evidence of such complaints was excluded by the trial judge because of his belief that such statements were proscribed by the hearsay rule.

The judgment of the Court of Civil Appeals is affirmed.

Points for Discussion

a. Statements of Bodily Condition Made to a Physician

What if Mr. Salinas complained to his doctor of past pain from his injury? Would this statement be admissible under Rule 803(3)? Under Rule 803(4)?

b. The Basis for Rule 803(3) Exceptions

Rule 803(3) admits statements concerning a declarant's state of mind, emotion, sensation or physical condition if the declarant is experiencing these matters at the time he makes the statement. The "contemporaneous" requirement of the rule is thought to alleviate any problem with a declarant's memory or perception. Statements such as, "I have a headache," or "I am cold" are admissible under this rule. Statements such as "Yesterday I had a headache," or "Yesterday, I was cold" are not. The rule provides, however, that statements which refer to past maters are admissible if they relate to the execution, revocation, identification, or terms of a declarant's will. Why do you think the rule made an exception for backward-looking statements only for wills? See the Advisory Committee Note to Rule 803(3).

—————————

Statements for Purposes of Medical Diagnosis or Treatment

> **Rule 803(4) – Hearsay Exceptions; Availability of Declarant Im material**
>
> Statements for purposes of medical diagnosis or treatment. Statements made for purposes of medical diagnosis or treatment and describing medical history, or past or present symptoms, pain, or sensations, or the inception or general character of the cause or external source thereof insofar as reasonably pertinent to diagnosis or treatment.

State v. Moen

Supreme Court of Oregon
786 P.2d 111 (Or. 1990)

JONES, Justice.

This is a criminal case in which the defendant seeks reversal of his conviction of the offense of aggravated murder. In the alternative, he requests that his death sentence be vacated.

SUMMARY OF FACTS

Guilt Phase

The bodies of Hazel Chatfield and Judith Moen were found in Hazel Chatfield's residence on Friday, March 14, 1986, by a neighbor and two friends.

Dr. Karen Gunson, the medical examiner, testified that both victims died of gunshot wounds to the head. In addition to the fatal wound to the head, Judith Moen had been shot in the chest after death had occurred. Dr. Gunson also found some bruises and other minor injuries on Judith Moen. ...

The state's theory was that defendant had killed Judith Moen during a domestic quarrel and that he had killed Hazel Chatfield when she became involved in the dispute....

Dr. Daniel Mulkey testified that he treated Hazel Chatfield from August 1985 up to and including visits on February 11 and March 11, 1986. During the latter two visits, Mrs. Chatfield complained of depression and despondency since her daughter and son-in-law (defendant) had moved into her home. Mrs. Chatfield appeared agitated, anxious, nervous, very tearful, and crying. Dr. Mulkey attempted to treat her for a potentially fatal lesion but, because of her situation at home, was unable to convince her that she needed treatment. Dr. Mulkey further testified that Mrs. Chatfield told him that she was upset about her daughter and son-in-law, that her son-in-law had been physically abusive to her daughter, and that "she felt he might kill them both." Dr. Mulkey diagnosed her condition as situational depression and recommended that defendant be removed from the home.

A former husband of Judith Moen testified that defendant was pursuing a dissolution of his marriage with Judith and quoted defendant as saying, "I'm finally going to get rid of the bitch one way or the other."

Brad Barton, Judith Moen's son, described an incident in February 1986, while he was living at Hazel Chatfield's residence, during which defendant and Judith Moen became involved in an altercation. Barton described threats by defendant and a display of a shotgun in a threatening manner....

The evidence then was closed and the jury retired and found defendant guilty of aggravated murder....

ASSIGNMENT OF ERROR II

For his second assignment of error, defendant claims that the trial court erred in allowing Dr. Daniel Davis Mulkey to recite statements of Hazel Chatfield, one of the deceased victims, describing conduct of defendant and fears that defendant might kill both her and her daughter. The court ruled on defendant's objection that the out-of-court statements concerning defendant were hearsay and violated defendant's state and federal constitutional right of confrontation.

D argues

Defendant argues that Dr. Mulkey's testimony concerning Hazel Chatfield's statements should not have been admitted under [Rule of Evidence] 803(4) because: (1) "the declarant's motivation for giving the information is highly suspect," and (2) the doctor "did not specifically rely upon the statement[s] as reasonably pertinent to his diagnosis of depression."

...

Professor Laird Kirkpatrick explains that "[t]he rationale underlying this exception is that the patient's desire for proper treatment or diagnosis outweighs any motive to falsify."

Judge Weinstein, referring to the identical hearsay exception under the Federal Rules of Evidence, FRE 803(4), suggests a second policy ground for the admissibility of these statements, i.e., "a fact reliable enough to serve as the basis for a diagnosis is also reliable enough to escape hearsay proscription." 4 Weinstein & Berger, Weinstein's Evidence 803-146 (1988).

To be admissible under [Rule of Evidence] 803(4), a statement must meet three requirements:

(a) The statement must be "made for purposes of medical diagnosis or treatment";

(b) The statement must describe or relate "medical history, or past or present symptoms, pain or sensations, or the inception or general character of the cause [or] external source thereof";

(c) The statement must be "reasonably pertinent to diagnosis or treatment."

The challenged testimony in this case satisfies these criteria:

a. Were Hazel Chatfield's statements "made for purposes of medical diagnosis [and] treatment "?

Mrs. Chatfield's motive in making the statements at issue must necessarily be determined by reference to the circumstances in which they were made. As explained in 4 Louisell & Mueller, Federal Evidence 593-94, § 444 (1980) (concerning the identical federal provision):

"The principal reason for admitting statements made for purposes of obtaining medical treatment is that they are considered trustworthy. Usually such statements are made by the patient to his physician, and usually they describe the patient's own past and present physical sensations, and things which happened to him personally. Thus, risks of misperception and of faulty memory are minimal. Moreover, the patient will understand that his description is important in determining the treatment he will receive, so he has every reason to speak not only truthfully, but carefully, so that the risks of insincerity and ambiguity are likewise minimal."

On February 11, 1986, Mrs. Chatfield came to her physician's as a patient as "part of a routine follow up for high blood pressure and some other medical problems." She was so "anxious" and "extremely nervous" that Dr. Mulkey could not conduct the planned interview and she "indicated" to him for the first time "that she was suffering from depression or anxiety." When she first referred to her son-in-law's presence in her home, she did so only in response to Dr. Mulkey's question why she was depressed. When he saw her as a patient one month later, she exhibited symptoms "absolutely" associated with extreme depression and was so emotionally distressed that, as before, Dr. Mulkey was unable to talk with her about other medical problems, one of which was "potentially life-threatening." Through his professional training and practice, he knew the symptoms of depression and anxiety and previously had diagnosed her as suffering from situational depression. In this context, Mrs. Chatfield again talked with Dr. Mulkey about defendant's presence in her home, his abusive conduct, and her resulting fears. He determined that she still suffered from the illness of depression and prescribed anti-depressant medication and defendant's removal from the home.

Mrs. Chatfield made these statements as a patient to her treating physician during regularly scheduled visits to his office. The statements related directly to the severe emotional distress that she was suffering at the time of those visits. The depression that she experienced is a medically recognized illness that her physician had the training and experience to diagnose and to treat. Her complaints focused on her feelings of depression. Dr. Mulkey responded to her statements with clinical inquiries, a medical diagnosis, and a prescribed course of treatment.

The trial court was entitled to conclude that the statements in question were "made for purposes of medical diagnosis [and] treatment."

b. Was the subject matter of the statements proper ?

Mrs. Chatfield's statements to her physician quite clearly described "the inception or general character of the cause [or] external source" of her continuing depression. Defendant does not contend otherwise.

c. Were Mrs. Chatfield's statements "reasonably pertinent" to diagnosis and treatment?

[Rule] 803(4) authorizes the admission of a patient's out-of-court statements (made for purposes of diagnosis or treatment) to her physician concerning "the inception or general character of the cause [or] external source " of her condition, to the extent that such information is " reasonably pertinent to [the physician's] diagnosis or treatment." The commentary to the rule confirms the reliability of statements satisfying that condition, i.e.:

"The guaranty [of trustworthiness] also extends to statements regarding causation of a condition, if reasonably pertinent, in accord with the current trend."

In this case, Mrs. Chatfield gave Dr. Mulkey information concerning the cause of her depression and, in doing so, identified defendant. Defendant argues that such statements are "accusations of personal fault" and not reasonably pertinent to diagnosis or treatment. Defendant's argument ignores the wording of [Rule] 803(4). [Rule] 803(4) expressly authorizes the admission of statements concerning the "cause [or] external source" of an illness, provided the statements are "made for purposes of medical diagnosis or treatment" and are "reasonably pertinent" to either endeavor. Mrs. Chatfield's statements concerning defendant communicated to Dr. Mulkey the ongoing cause of her situational depression. He used that information first, to diagnose, and, then, to treat her illness. The information and his professional skills permitted him to distinguish her depression from other forms of that illness and to prescribe specific treatment for it. The requirements of the rule are satisfied. The fact that the continuing cause of her illness was the presence and conduct of a named individual is not a basis for excluding the statements.

In interpreting an identical evidentiary rule, FRE 803(4), the leading federal decision is consistent with our analysis and conclusion. In *United States v. Renville*, 779 F.2d 430 (8th Cir.1985), an 11-year-old child was sexually abused by her stepfather. The defendant claimed that a doctor should not have been permitted to testify to statements of the victim, made during an examination, that identified the defendant as her abuser. He argued that FRE 803(4) did "not encompass statements of fault or identity made to medical personnel." While acknowledging that such statements relating to identity ordinarily are not admissible, the court determined that where such statements were relevant to the physician's diagnosis or treatment, FRE 803(4) authorized their admission. Because the victim's statements were relevant for those purposes, the court held that their admission was proper. That court's analysis is applicable to this case:

"The crucial question under the rule is whether the out-of-court statement of the declarant was 'reasonably pertinent' to diagnosis or treatment. In *United States v. Iron Shell*, 633 F.2d 77 (8th Cir.1980), cert. denied 450 U.S. 1001, this court set forth a two-part test for the admissibility of hearsay statements under rule 803(4): first, the declarant's motive in making the statement must be consistent with the purposes of promoting treatment; and second, the content of the statement must be such as is reasonably relied on by a physician in treatment or diagnosis. The test reflects the twin policy justifications advanced to support the rule. First, it is assumed that a patient has a strong motive to speak truthfully and accurately because the treatment or diagnosis will depend in part upon the information conveyed. The declarant's motive thus provides a sufficient guarantee of trustworthiness to permit an exception to the hearsay rule. Iron Shell, 633 F.2d at 84. Second, we have recognized that 'a fact reliable enough to serve as the basis for a diagnosis is also reliable enough to escape hearsay proscription.'"

...

The testimony of Dr. Mulkey relating statements made to him by his patient, Mrs. Chatfield, concerning defendant's presence and conduct in her home was admissible under [Rule] 803(4) against defendant's hearsay objection.

Points for Discussion

a. Statements of Fault

Statements of fault are not admissible under Rule 803(4). For example, a statement by a declarant to her doctor that she was hit over the head with a baseball bat would be admissible, but a statement that the person wielding the bat was the defendant would not. Why then does the court in *Moen* think that Mrs. Chatfield's statements to her doctor about why she was depressed and anxious were "reasonably pertinent" to her medical diagnosis or treatment? Would the doctor have diagnosed or treated her any differently if the cause of her depression had been the death of her cat or the foreclosure of her home?

b. Statements of Child Victims

Rule 803(4) has increasingly been used to admit statements by child victims in child abuse cases. For example, in *United States v. Iron Shell*, 633 F.2d 77 (8th Cir. 1980), a case where a nine year old girl, the alleged victim of an attempted rape, told a doctor how she was dragged into the bushes, had her clothes removed, and how a man tried to force something into her vagina. The doctor was not only treating her for the abuse but also collecting evidence for the prosecution of the defendant, whom others identified as the rapist. The court held that the girl's answers to the doctor's questions were, in part, reasonably necessary for her diagnosis and treatment and were therefore admissible under Rule 803(4). Nonetheless, the court remarked that had she identified her assailant, it was unlikely her identification would be admissible because his identity would seldom be medically relevant. Not all courts agree. See, e.g., *United States v. Peneaux*, 432 F.3d 882 (8th Cir. 2005), finding that the identity of the child's abuser may be reasonably pertinent if the abuser is a member of the victim's immediate household. Is there a distinction between these two cases? Or are they simply inconsistent?

c. Statements by Someone Other than the Person Needing Diagnosis or Treatment

A mother brings her four year old son to the pediatrician. She tells the doctor that her son has been vomiting ever since he ate a hamburger from a local restaurant at lunch. The son eventually dies. The parents later sue the restaurant for serving their son contaminated meat. The mother is too grief stricken at trial to testify. May the doctor testify about the mother statement? Is there anything in Rule 803(4) that requires a statement made for medical diagnosis or treatment come from the person being diagnosed or treated?

Rule 803(5) – Recorded Recollection

A memorandum or record concerning a matter about which a witness once had knowledge but now has insufficient recollection to enable the witness to testify fully and accurately, shown to have been made or adopted by the witness when the matter was fresh in the witness' memory and to reflect that knowledge correctly. If admitted, the memorandum or record may be read into evidence but may not itself be received as an exhibit unless offered by an adverse party.

One of the human fallacies that the hearsay rule hopes to guard against is poor memory. This exception was created because it is presumed that events recorded at, or near, the time of the event are more reliable than those that are not. Under 803(5), recorded recollections may be admissible if the proponent of the statement can demonstrate that:

Take Note

Under 803(5) the document may only be read to the fact-finder; the document itself is not admissible unless the opponent offers it.

1) the witness once had personal knowledge of the matter;

2) the witness now has insufficient recollection to enable the witness to testify fully and accurately;

3) the memorandum or record is shown to have been made or adopted by the witness when the matter was fresh in the witness's memory; and

Make the Connection

Do not confuse using a writing to refresh memory with this rule. Rule 612 provides the guidelines under which a writing may be used to refresh a witness' memory. This is not the same as admitting a document under the exception to the hearsay rule.

4) the memorandum or record is shown to reflect that knowledge correctly.

This last requirement may be demonstrated if the witness testifies that she remembers making an accurate record of the event in question or, although she no longer sufficiently remembers the facts, the circumstances surrounding the creation of the record ensure the accuracy of the recorded events.

U.S. v. Mornan

U.S Court of Appeals for the Third Circuit
413 F.3d 372 (3rd Cir. 2005)

VAN ANTWERPEN, Circuit Judge.

Appellant Christopher Mornan was charged ... with mail fraud, wire fraud, and conspiracy arising from an alleged telemarketing scheme. A jury found Mornan guilty ....

I. FACTUAL AND PROCEDURAL HISTORY

A. Background

[handwritten margin note: wire + mail fraud]

[handwritten margin note: offered loans to high risk individuals]

Mornan's wire and mail fraud indictment alleged that he ... and his co-conspirators, operating out of Canada, placed newspaper advertisements in the United States offering loans to high-risk borrowers. The advertisements provided a toll-free number to call for details. When a customer called the number, he or she reached one of many telephone sales rooms located in Canada. A telephone sales representative would instruct the customer to complete and return a loan application. Once the application was completed, another individual-a "closer"-would call the customer and represent that the loan had been approved. The customer was then told that he or she would have to purchase a life or disability insurance policy to secure the loan. In many instances, the "closer" would tell the customer that the insurance premiums would be returned upon full repayment of the loan amount....

The telephone representatives would tell customers that they worked on behalf of a number of loan brokerage companies, one of which was Sun Corp. Financial Services ("Sun Corp."). On June 23, 1998, Canadian law enforcement authorities conducted a search of the Sun Corp. offices in Ontario. The police found Mornan and his alleged co-conspirator, Leslie Card, in one of the offices. The police confiscated a list of loan applicants, a list of United States newspapers, and some Sun Corp. loan applications from the desk Mornan was using. The Canadian authorities also interviewed Mornan, who stated that he was an "[a]ssistant manager/closer" and that he and Card shared the role of office manager. He also stated that his job was to answer phones, take customers' information, and tell them that their loan application had been accepted. . . .

[handwritten margin note: Mornan's role]

B. Trial and Sentencing

At Mornan's trial . . . the Government presented the testimony of multiple law enforcement officials who were involved in a "strategic partnership" between the United States and Canada set up to investigate "cross-border frauds." The Government also presented the testimony of 12 individuals who claimed to be victims of the telemarketing scheme.

Also relevant to this appeal was the testimony of Althea Burton, the cousin of Michael Willams, who owned and operated Icon Cheque Cashing Services, Inc. ("Icon") in Ontario. Burton worked for her cousin at Icon from May 2000 to January 2001, and the Government attempted to establish through her testimony that Mornan used Icon to cash money orders that had been made out to various "insurance companies." The Government was permitted to show the jury Burton's testimony in the form of a videotape deposition that she gave in Canada. During

[handwritten margin note: video deposition]

that testimony, Burton indicated that she could no longer remember the particulars of her employment at Icon.

Faced with her purported memory lapse, the Government directed Burton's attention to a statement she made to the prosecutor and United States Postal Inspector Michael Hartman on September 12, 2001, wherein she identified Mornan as the individual who routinely cashed money orders at Icon that were made out to several "insurance companies." However, Burton stated that she did not remember the particulars of the September 2001 statement either. She attributed her memory loss to back and neck injuries suffered during an August 19, 2002, automobile accident.

The Government then attempted to offer the substance of the September 2001 statement into evidence as a past recollection recorded under Fed.R.Evid. 803(5). The District Court initially ruled that the statement did not qualify under Rule 803(5). The Government alternatively argued that the statement was admissible as a prior inconsistent statement under Fed.R.Evid. 801(d)(1)(A), but the court also rejected that argument. However, after reviewing Burton's videotape testimony, the District Court changed its ruling and admitted the statement, over the defense's objection, as a prior inconsistent statement under Rule 801(d)(1)(A). The court reasoned that "it can't be concluded that the memory loss is solely due to the accident as opposed to her own volition...."

At the close of the evidence, the jury found Mornan guilty on 11 counts of mail fraud, three counts of wire fraud, and one count of conspiracy to commit mail fraud and wire fraud. The jury found Mornan not guilty on two counts of mail fraud and one count of wire fraud.

III. ANALYSIS

Although the District Court admitted Burton's September 2001 statement as a prior inconsistent statement under Rule 801(d)(1)(A), both parties seem to agree that Rule 803(5)"is the better of the two proffered grounds for admissibility."...

a. Analysis under Fed.R.Evid. 803(5)

We agree with Mornan that Burton's prior statement did not meet the requirements of Rule 803(5) because Burton neither adopted nor reviewed the statement prior to her purported memory loss.

[Rule 803(5)] requires the witness to have either made the record herself, or to have reviewed and adopted the statement, at a time when the matter it concerned was fresh in her memory. See 5-803 Weinstein's Federal Evidence § 803.07[d] ("A memorandum written by another is admissible as the witness's recorded recollection if the witness can testify (1) that the witness checked the memorandum when the matter it concerned was fresh in his or her memory, and (2) that the witness then knew it to be correct."). Where, as here, the statement was recorded by someone other than the declarant, accuracy may be established through the testimony of the person who recorded the statement....

[handwritten margin note: here statement was recorded by another]

In this case, the recording was made by a typist and attested to by an "official examiner" in Canada, and the Government did not show that Burton either reviewed or adopted the examiner's recording. She testified that she could not remember if she reviewed the statement, and the writing does not bear Burton's signature to indicate that she reviewed it and attested to its accuracy at the time the record was made. Burton also could not attest to the accuracy of her statement during her current testimony. Although she remembered being placed under oath before giving the September 2001 statement, when asked whether the recording was accurate, Burton replied, "I don't know that for certain, but I would hope so." Moreover, the Government did not call the official examiner as a witness to establish that the recording accurately reflected Burton's oral statement.

The Government attempts to establish accuracy in this case by pointing to various indicia of reliability, such as the fact that Burton was under oath and was promised that the statement would not be used against her. The Government relies on ... *United States v. Porter*, 986 F.2d 1014 (6th Cir.1993), and ... *Parker v. Reda*, 327 F.3d 211 (2d Cir.2003), for the proposition that "Rule 803(5) does not specify any particular method of establishing the knowledge of the declarant nor the accuracy of the statement." However, *Porter* and *Parker* are distinguishable from this case because the Government did not show that Burton made, reviewed, or adopted the statement at issue here. In Porter, the witness reviewed and signed the written statement at issue on each page, and in Parker, the witness wrote and signed the statement himself.

[handwritten margin note: distinguished cases]

The indicia of reliability to which the Government points may support the position that Burton spoke truthfully in September 2001, but the Government has not established-through Burton's current testimony, the testimony of the "official examiner," or Burton's signature on the writing-that the written recording read to the jury was either made or adopted by Burton, as is expressly required by Rule 803(5). The District Court therefore correctly held that Rule 803(5) does not apply to Burton's September 2001 statement.

[handwritten margin note: held]

Points for Discussion

a. Attesting to the Accuracy of a Recorded Recollection

What if Ms. Burton signed the statement but later had no memory of doing so, even though she is willing to testify that because she signed it, she knew it must be true because she would not have signed it otherwise? What if she signed the statement and is willing to testify that she never signs anything which does not contain true facts? Is this testimony sufficient to satisfy the accuracy requirement of Rule 803(5)? *See Hodas v. Davis*, 196 N.Y.S. 801 (1922).

b. A Witness with a Selective Memory

Sometimes a witness who gives a statement accusing a defendant of a crime may regret his decision and attempt to claim memory loss as to those parts of the statement that are the most incriminating. Is it still possible for the government to have such a statement admitted as a recollection recorded? *See United States v. Williams*, 571 F.2d 344 (6th Cir. 1978), a case where a man named Mr. Ball, who was a neighbor of the defendant, gave a Secret Service agent a statement implicating the defendant in a forged check scheme. The agent typed up the statement, and the declarant signed it. Later, at trial, Ball claimed lack of memory concerning the most incriminating parts of the statement. The court admitted the entire statement on basis that Mr. Ball still retained sufficient recollection to testify generally about his conversations with the defendant and commented that the witness was exercising selective memory. Do you think Ball's statement would have been admitted if the court believed Ball had suffered a blow to the head that impaired his memory? Should the declarant's good or bad faith memory loss be a factor in admitting a recollection recorded?

c. Admissibility of a Recorded Recollection

You might think that once a foundation has been laid to admit a recorded recollection, the document containing the statement will then be admitted into evidence, as would any document admitted pursuant to other hearsay exceptions. Rule 803(5), however, provides otherwise. The rule states that a recorded recollection may be "read into evidence but not itself received as an exhibit unless offered by an adverse party." Why this difference?

d. Distinguishing Recorded Recollections from Refreshing a Witness's Memory

It is important to distinguish the hearsay exception for recorded recollections from the use of a witness's prior statement to impeach his in-court testimony. Assume a lawyer is cross-examining a witness who has made a prior written statement. Assume further that the statement is hearsay because the lawyer is offering it for the truth of its contents. Normally, this statement would not be admitted;

however, if the witness claims loss of memory about the subject matter, it may be possible to admit the document as a recorded recollection, assuming the other foundational facts of Rule 803(5) can be shown. Then, it may be read into evidence but not admitted as an exhibit, unless the opponent offers it.

On the other hand, if a witness cannot remember details of her testimony, a lawyer may try to refresh that witness's present memory of the events. This can be done in a number of ways, but most often it is done by showing the witness her prior statement to see if it jogs her memory. If it does, the witness then testifies from her memory thus refreshed; if it does not, the statement used to jog her memory will not be admissible because it is hearsay.

refresh memory

Rule 803(6) – Records of Regularly Conducted Activity

A memorandum, report, record, or data compilation, in any form, of acts, events, conditions, opinions, or diagnoses, made at or near the time by, or from information transmitted by, a person with knowledge, if kept in the course of a regularly conducted business activity, and if it was the regular practice of that business activity to make the memorandum, report, record or data compilation, all as shown by the testimony of the custodian or other qualified witness, or by certification that complies with Rule 902(11), Rule 902(12), or a statute permitting certification, unless the source of information or the method or circumstances of preparation indicate lack of trustworthiness. The term "business" as used in this paragraph includes business, institution, association, profession, occupation, and calling of every kind, whether or not conducted for profit.

Rationale and Elements

This exception is commonly known as the "business records exception". This rule assumes that documents created in compliance with its requirements are sufficiently reliable to admit even though they are hearsay. The policy behind this exception is the belief that businesses are unlikely to have faulty business records as reliable

Make the Connection

Even though a record may be admitted under the business records exception, if that record contains multiple levels of hearsay, each level must meet an exception. See rule 805.

records would be required to run their businesses. The rule is not limited to written records. In fact, the rule specifically provides that records in any form may comply with the exception. To comply with the business records exception, the evidence must comply with all of the following:

1) The evidence must be a "memorandum, report, record or data compilation in any form;"

2) The evidence must be proffered by a witness who is the "custodian or other qualified witness;"

3) The record must have been "made by a person with knowledge" of the facts or was "made from information transmitted by a person with knowledge" of the facts;

4) The record must have been "made at or near the time" of the "acts, events, conditions, opinions, or diagnoses" appearing on it;

5) The record must have been made as part of "the regular practice of that business activity;" and

6) The record must have been "kept in the course of a regularly conducted business activity"

Business

Virtually any enterprise can fit the definition of "business." As used in Rule 803(6), a "business" includes any business, institution, association, profession, occupation, and calling of every kind, whether or not conducted for profit.

Form

The form of a "record" is very broad. Although traditionally records were in the form of some written or other paper document, in today's technological age these records are often more broad-based and include a variety of other media, such as electronic database files, word processing documents, photographs, digital photographs, and others.

Entry Made in Regular Course of Business

The reliability standard sought by this exception requires the information recorded be part of the regular activity of that business made by a person with a business duty to make the record.

Business Activity

Hospital and Medical Records

Usually, records kept by hospitals, medical facilities and physicians will fit within the business records exception. Medical records often include multiple levels of hearsay. For example, a doctor's diagnosis is hearsay. This diagnosis will often be based on information reported to the doctor, which she notes on the records.

Take Note!

Even though medical records may fit within the business records exception and, therefore, not be excluded by the hearsay rule, this does not mean the records are admissible. Medical records may be subject to certain privileges and also the Health Insurance Portability and Accountability Act ("HIPPA"), which may mandate its exclusion.

Make the Connection

Look to all of the exceptions in an effort to make multiple levels of hearsay admissible. Statements made to the doctor and notes in the medical records may be admissible under Rule 803(4) - Statements for purposes of medical diagnosis or treatment.

Police Reports

There is frequent disagreement as to whether police reports fall within the business records exception or whether they fall within 803(8), which provides an exception for public records and reports. Often, police reports are not, in fact, public records as defined by the rule and require compliance with the elements of the business records exception as well.

The Rule of *Palmer v. Hofman* - Records Prepared for Litigation

In *Palmer v. Hoffman*, the United States Supreme Court examined the issue of the admissibility of an accident report prepared by the train's engineer which was requested by the railroad that was investigating a railroad crossing accident. 318 U.S. 109 (1943). This report was offered into evidence at trial under the business records exception. On appeal, the United States Supreme Court held that the report was not admissible under the exception because the business of the railroad was running trains, not conducting litigation.

Subsequent decisions have indicated that the *Palmer* decision not be read so narrowly. In fact, some reports prepared for litigation may have a business purpose. It depends on how inherently trustworthy they are.

Personal Knowledge – Not Required

The person making the record can, but is not required to, have personal knowledge of the information recorded. However, if the person recording the information does not have personal knowledge, then the person transmitting the information must have personal knowledge.

Informant Must Be Under Duty to Convey

Although a record may be kept in the course of a regularly conducted business activity, the rule requires more. It must be a regular practice of the business to make that particular type of record.

Entry Made At or Near Time of Event

This rule supports the theory that memories are more accurate the nearer in time to the event recorded. As time passes, memories tend to become less reliable. The rule does not define 'near' relying on particular circumstances to help dictate compliance with the rule.

Entrant Need Not Be Unavailable

This exception falls within the provisions of 803 and, unlike Rule 804, does not require the person making the statements to be unavailable at trial.

Trustworthiness

The final barrier to compliance with this exception is trustworthiness. That is, the records must not indicate a lack of trustworthiness. If the court believes that the source of the information, the method of the preparation or the circumstances of preparation of the information indicates a lack of trustworthiness, then the court may refuse to admit the evidence.

Make the Connection

Many rules of evidence overlap. Rule 803(6) is an example. Documents offered under Rule 803(6) are also subject to the rules regarding authentication and originality. For example, an original may be required under Rule 1002 or a duplicate may suffice under Rule 1003. Under 901(b) a foundation must be laid showing that the record is what it purports to be.

Example of Testimony Designed to Comply with the Business Records Exception

Q: Ms. Doe, what is your occupation?

A: I'm the custodian of records for ABC Company.

Q: What does your job involve?

A: I collect, keep, and maintain all the company financial records.

Q: Ms. Doe, I am showing you what has been previously marked Plaintiff's Exhibit #1. Do you recognize it?

A: Yes.

Q: What is it?

A: It's our general ledger from the last fiscal year.

Q: Was that record made by a person with knowledge of, or made from information transmitted by a person with knowledge of, the acts and events appearing on it?

A: Yes.

Q: Was the record made at or near the time of the acts and events appearing on it?

A: Yes.

Q: Is it the regular practice of the ABC Corporation to make such a record?

A: Yes.

Q: Was that record kept in the course of a regularly conducted business activity?

A: Yes.

Q: Your Honor, we offer Plaintiff's Exhibit #1

Certification Alternative to Live Witnesses

Rule 803(6) also provides that the foundation requirements can be satisfied under certain circumstances without the expense and inconvenience of producing time-consuming (and sometimes expensive) foundation witnesses by certification that complies with Rule 902(11) for domestic records, Rule 902(12) for foreign records in civil cases, or a statute permitting certification. See, for example, 18 U.S.C. § 3505 dealing with foreign records in criminal cases.

Overlap with Other Rules

Rule 803(6) overlaps the hearsay exception for public records contained in Rule 803(8). Where a conflict exists, a public record not meeting the requirements of the more specific rule 803(8) should not be admitted under Rule 803(6). However such public record may be admissible under another hearsay exception such as Rule 803(5), Rule 803(10), or Rule 807.

Keogh v. Commissioner of Internal Revenue

U.S Court of Appeals for the Ninth Circuit
713 F.2d 496 (9th Cir. 1983).

[H]usband ... was employed at the Dunes Hotel & Country Club, in Las Vegas. He worked in the casino, where he dealt blackjack or ran "big wheel" or roulette games and was known as a 21 dealer. The 21 dealers earned regular wages paid semimonthly. In addition, 21 players sometimes gave them tips or "tokes" in the form of coins or casino chips. Players often gave tokes to the dealers directly; at other times, they placed bets for the dealers, with a player determining after a winning bet how much of the winnings was the dealer's to keep.

The tax court found that during the years in question, 1969-1971, all 21 dealers at the Dunes pooled their tokes, and that the pool was divided equally once a day among all the dealers who had worked during that day's three shifts. Dealers who were off work sick for more than three days in a row were paid $20 off the top of the pool, but dealers who worked as temporary supervisors, or "floormen," did not share in the tokes. During the years in question, the dealers earned annual wages ranging from $5,946.52 to $9,113.79. They reported to their employer total annual toke incomes ranging from $632.50 to $1,022.60, and the reported amounts were shown on the employer's W-2 forms and on the dealers' tax returns.

The Commissioner asserted that the Keoghs had underreported tip income in 1969, 1970, and 1971. He calculated Keogh's toke income through a statistical analysis based on entries in a diary kept by one John Whitlock, Jr., not a party to this action, who worked at the Dunes. ... The Commissioner's statistical analysis of the tip entries resulted in an average daily toke income per dealer of between $42.04 and $74.24, depending on the year and the day of the week. ... There were some problems in the Commissioner's analysis. First, Whitlock's diary did not cover the entire period for which the Commissioner alleged income deficiencies in Keogh's reported tokes... Second, Whitlock did not work as a 21 dealer for the entire period covered by his diary; he first was a craps dealer before he switched to 21. It is undisputed that craps dealers generally made more in tokes than 21 dealers, and that craps dealers did not share their tokes with 21 dealers. It is unclear, however, when Whitlock switched from craps to 21. Third, ... the Commissioner's analysis did not reflect consultations with any gaming industry experts outside the I.R.S. and did not consider factors such as the economy, type of game, limits on amounts that could be bet for dealers, amount of money bet, percentage won by the Dunes, season of the year, or holiday periods. Fourth, it is undisputed that Whitlock had, as the tax court found, "a poor reputation for honesty and truthfulness," was dismissed by the Dunes for unsatisfactory work, and had been convicted, with his wife, of receiving stolen property. ...

At trial before the tax court, the principal evidence was a photocopy of the Whitlock diary and testimony by Barbara Mikle, by then Whitlock's former wife. Whitlock, though subpoenaed by the Commissioner, failed to appear. Keogh claimed that he had recorded his daily toke income, but had thrown the records out monthly after reporting toke income to the Dunes each month.

...

II. Evidential Issues.

A. Hearsay.

The Whitlock diary, offered in evidence to prove the truth of its contents as they related to tokes received by Dunes 21 dealers, was hearsay and thus inadmissible unless excepted by one or more rules of evidence. In admitting the diary, the tax court cited the exceptions contained in Rules 803(6) and 804(b)(3). Because we find the diary admissible under Rule 803(6), we do not address the 804(b)(3) exception.

We hold that the tax court did not abuse its discretion in admitting the diary in evidence.

The Keoghs' first argument is that Rule 803(6) does not apply to the diary because it was not a business record. They argue that the diary was Whitlock's personal record, not a record of the business enterprise involved, the Dunes. But

Whitlock's diary, even though personal to him, shows every indication of being kept "in the course of" his own "business activity," "occupation, and calling." "[P]ersonal records kept for business reasons may be able to qualify. A housekeeper's records kept neatly and accurately for purposes of balancing bank statements, keeping strict budgets and preparing income tax returns could qualify under the statute."

The reliability usually found in records kept by business concerns may be established in personal business records if they are systematically checked and regularly and continually maintained. ...

Here, Mikle testified that she saw Whitlock and only Whitlock make entries in the diary; that he usually made them after night shifts of work; that when he made no entries for three to four days, he would copy entries for those days from a record kept in his wallet; that he usually made no entries in the diary on his days off; and that she understood the diary to contain a record of tokes he received from his work as a dealer.

The cases that the Keoghs cite for the proposition that Rule 803(6) applies only to commercial business records that are kept by those under a business duty to do so arose in the commercial context, but in fact stress just the sort of timeliness and regularity of entries that are present here....

More to the point is *Sabatino v. Curtiss National Bank of Miami Springs*, 5 Cir., 1969, 415 F.2d 632, reversing a trial court's refusal to admit in evidence a personal check record. ...[I]ts reasoning is instructive here.... The Sabatino court said, "A man has a direct financial interest in keeping accurate accounts in his personal business. The cases indicate that private records, if kept regularly and if incidental to some personal business pursuit, are competent evidence under ..." It made no difference whether the check account was used for any specific business. "...[I]t is settled that the business 'need not be commercial.' "

The Keoghs dispute the general trustworthiness of the diary entries. They cite *Palmer v. Hoffman*, ... alleging that Whitlock's motives in preparing the diary were never explained. *Palmer v. Hoffman* is not on point because there is no evidence that Whitlock's motives in making the entries were suspect. The diary contained his own personal financial records; there is no reason put forward for him to have lied to himself. The reliability of the tip entries is corroborated by the fact that other entries corresponded with Dunes' payroll records, and that reliability is not tarnished by the fact that Whitlock, as the Keoghs are alleged to have done, reported to the government smaller amounts of tip income than he in fact received and recorded in the diary. Neither is Rule 803(6) made inapplicable by the fact that Mikle, not Whitlock, testified to lay the foundation for the diary. She testified adequately as to the regularity of the entries.

The Keoghs contend that the testimony of Whitlock as custodian of the diary was required because only he could speak to his reliance on the records kept there. But the record gives us no reason to believe that Whitlock did not rely on his personal financial diary; therefore, we do not find that the tax court abused its discretion in admitting it without Whitlock's personal testimony.

——————————

Points of Discussion

a. The Reliability of Personal Records

The hearsay exception for business records is often justified on the grounds that such records are likely to be reliable because they are routinely checked, the persons who record them regularly are likely to careful in their habits, and the business depends on the accuracy of the records to remain in business. The exception also avoids having to produce for trial every witness who contributed to the making of the records, most of whom are likely to have forgotten the details of the records and whose absence is likely to cause the business a substantial inconvenience. Does this reasoning justify extending the business records exception to a private diary created by a single person, as in *Keogh*? See *United States v. Santos*, 201 F.3d 953 (7th Cir. 2000) (finding that an employee's private diary of events was not the business record of his employer).

b. The Custodian of the Records or Other Qualified Witness

In *Keogh*, Barbara Mikle, a person other than the one who made the record, was permitted to testify to the requirements of Rule 803(6) because she was considered a "qualified witness." What was her testimony, and why was it considered sufficient to establish the business record foundation?

c. Hospital Records

Rule 803(6) permits the admission of records of "acts, events, conditions, opinions, or diagnoses." Does this mean that a court will admit all physician opinions found in hospital business records? If so, this might be particularly important to a plaintiff's attorney who is trying a small dollar accident case and needs to prove the cause of his client's injury but cannot afford to pay an expert to testify. On the other hand, if all physician opinions contained in hospital business records are admitted, the opponent of the record loses the chance to cross-examine the physician to determine his qualifications or the accuracy of his findings. Law prior to the enactment of the Federal Rules of Evidence admitted only those opinions on which "competent physicians would not differ." *New York Life Ins. Co. v. Taylor*, 147 F.2d 297 (D.C. Cir. 1944) Rule 803(6) leaves it up to the discretion of the trial court to determine if the records are sufficiently trustworthy to be admitted.

d. Computer Records

Almost all businesses maintain their records in some electronic form. If the proper Rule 803(6) foundation is laid, computer printouts are admissible as business records. But is the printout admissible if it was specifically prepared for litigation and not the running of the business? Most cases hold that as long as the printout contains data that was input into a data storage device at or near the time of the event recorded and does not summarize or other manipulate that data for trial purposes, it will be admissible. See *Sea-Land Service, Inc. v. Lozen Int'l*, 285 F.3d 808 (9th Cir. 2002).

> **Rule 803(7) – Absence of Entry in Records Kept in Accordance with the Provisions of Paragraph (6)**
>
> Evidence that a matter is not included in the memoranda reports, records, or data compilations, in any form, kept in accordance with the provisions of paragraph (6), to prove the nonoccurrence or nonexistence of the matter, if the matter was of a kind of which a memorandum, report, record, or data compilation was regularly made and preserved, unless the sources of information or other circumstances indicate lack of trustworthiness.

The lack of a record may, in itself, be a record. It is a record of no recordation of an event when there would otherwise be a record if the event had actually occurred. So, when a matter is not recorded and such matter normally would be included in the regularly conducted business activity of that entity then that non-recording of a matter may be offered to prove the non-occurrence or nonexistence of the matter and constitutes a hearsay exception under Rule 803(7). The document(s) offered must have been kept in accordance with the provisions of Rule 803(6), and the matter itself must be shown to be of a kind of information which was regularly made and preserved. Just as with 803(6), evidence under 803(7) must be offered by the custodian of the record or other qualified person in order to lay the proper foundation. In addition, either the record from which the matter is absent must be introduced in evidence or someone with personal knowledge must testify that a diligent search failed to disclose the matter in the memorandum, report, record or data compilation.

> **Rule 803(8) – Public Records and Reports**
>
> Records, reports, statements, or data compilations, in any form, of public offices or agencies, setting forth (A) the activities of the office or agency, or (B) matters observed pursuant to duty imposed by law as to which matters there was a duty to report, excluding, however, in criminal cases matters observed by police officers and other law enforcement personnel, or (C) in civil actions and proceedings and against the Government in criminal cases, factual findings resulting from an investigation made pursuant to authority granted by law, unless the sources of information or other circumstances indicate lack of trustworthiness.

This exception assumes that individuals creating records which fall within this rule will do so without motivation to falsify those records and, further, that public inspection will disclose any inaccuracies. If the source of information or the method or circumstances of preparation indicates a lack of trustworthiness, the court may bar admissibility. The individuals furnishing and recording the information must be under an official duty to do so. Without this obligation, an important factor is missing; the assurance of accuracy does not extend to the information itself. An example of this requirement would be a report generated by a police officer. Assume a police officer takes a statement from witness. The police officer would qualify as acting pursuant to an official duty but the witness does not so qualify.

As the next case demonstrates, 803(8) goes beyond 803(6) in that in civil cases, it allows public officials charged with making findings of fact to include their conclusions in the report.

Beech Aircraft v. Rainey

Supreme Court of the United States
488 U.S. 153 (1988).

[This case] address[es] a longstanding conflict among the Federal Courts of Appeals over whether Federal Rule of Evidence 803(8)(C), which provides an exception to the hearsay rule for public investigatory reports containing "factual findings," extends to conclusions and opinions contained in such reports. ...

I

This litigation stems from the crash of a Navy training ... which took the lives of both pilots on board.... The accident took place while Rainey, a Navy flight instructor, and Knowlton, her student, were flying "touch-and-go" .... Their aircraft and several others flew in an oval pattern, each plane making successive landing/takeoff maneuvers on the runway. Following its fourth pass at the runway, [the aircraft] appeared to make a left turn prematurely, cutting out the aircraft ahead of it in the pattern and threatening a collision. After radio warnings from two other pilots, the plane banked sharply to the right in order to avoid the other aircraft. At that point it lost altitude rapidly, crashed, and burned.

Because of the damage to the plane and the lack of any survivors, the cause of the accident could not be determined with certainty. The two pilots' surviving spouses brought a product liability suit against petitioners Beech Aircraft Corporation, the plane's manufacturer, and Beech Aerospace Services, which serviced the plane under contract with the Navy. The plaintiffs alleged that the crash had been caused by a loss of engine power, known as "rollback," due to some defect in the aircraft's fuel control system. The defendants, on the other hand, advanced the theory of pilot error, suggesting that the plane had stalled during the abrupt avoidance maneuver.

At trial, the only seriously disputed question was whether pilot error or equipment malfunction had caused the crash. Both sides relied primarily on expert testimony. One piece of evidence presented by the defense was an investigative report prepared by Lieutenant Commander William Morgan on order of the training squadron's commanding officer and pursuant to authority granted in the Manual of the Judge Advocate General. This "JAG Report," completed during the six weeks following the accident, was organized into sections labeled "finding of fact," "opinions," and "recommendations," and was supported by some 60 attachments. ....

Among his "opinions" Lieutenant Commander Morgan stated . . . that . . . the most probable cause of the accident was the pilots [sic] failure to maintain proper interval."

The trial judge initially determined, at a pretrial conference, that the JAG Report was sufficiently trustworthy to be admissible, but that it "would be admissible only on its factual findings and would not be admissible insofar as any opinions or conclusions are concerned." The day before trial, however, the court reversed itself and ruled, over the plaintiffs' objection, that certain of the conclusions would be admitted. Accordingly, the court admitted most of the report's "opinions," including the first sentence of paragraph 5 about the impossibility

[handwritten margin note: admitted report's opinions.]

of determining exactly what happened, and paragraph 7, which opined about failure to maintain proper interval as "[t]he most probable cause of the accident." On the other hand, the remainder of paragraph 5 was barred as "nothing but a possible scenario," and paragraph 6, in which investigator Morgan refused to rule out rollback, was deleted as well.

This action also concerns an evidentiary ruling as to a second document. Five or six months after the accident, plaintiff John Rainey, husband of the deceased pilot and himself a Navy flight instructor, sent a detailed letter to Lieutenant Commander Morgan. Based on Rainey's own investigation, the letter took issue with some of the JAG Report's findings and outlined Rainey's theory that "[t]he most probable primary cause factor of this aircraft mishap is a loss of useful power (or rollback) caused by some form of pneumatic sensing/fuel flow malfunction, probably in the fuel control unit."

. . .

Following a 2-week trial, the jury returned a verdict for petitioners. A panel of the Eleventh Circuit reversed and remanded for a new trial. ...[T]he panel agreed with Rainey's argument that Federal Rule of Evidence 803(8)(C), which excepts investigatory reports from the hearsay rule, did not encompass evaluative conclusions or opinions. Therefore, it held, the "conclusions" contained in the JAG Report should have been excluded. One member of the panel, concurring specially, urged however that the Circuit reconsider its interpretation of Rule 803(8)(C).... The panel also held, citing Federal Rule of Evidence 106, that it was reversible error for the trial court to have prohibited cross-examination about additional portions of Rainey's letter which would have put in context the admissions elicited from him on direct.

On rehearing en banc, the Court of Appeals divided evenly on the question of Rule 803(8)(C). ...

II

. . .

Controversy over what "public records and reports" are made not excludable by Rule 803(8)(C) has divided the federal courts from the beginning. In the present litigation, the Court of Appeals followed the "narrow" interpretation of *Smith v. Ithaca Corp.*, which held that the term "factual findings" did not encompass "opinions" or "conclusions." Courts of Appeals other than those of the Fifth and Eleventh Circuits, however, have generally adopted a broader interpretation. For example, the Court of Appeals for the Sixth Circuit ... held that "factual findings admissible under Rule 803(8)(C) may be those which are made by the preparer of the report from disputed evidence...."   The other Courts of Appeals that have squarely confronted the issue have also adopted the broader interpretation.   We agree and hold that factually based conclusions or opinions are not on that account excluded from the scope of Rule 803(8)(C).

Because the Federal Rules of Evidence are a legislative enactment, we turn to the "traditional tools of statutory construction," ... in order to construe their provisions. We begin with the language of the Rule itself.   Proponents of the narrow view have generally relied heavily on a perceived dichotomy between "fact" and "opinion" in arguing for the limited scope of the phrase "factual findings." *Smith v. Ithaca Corp.* contrasted the term "factual findings" in Rule 803(8)(C) with the language of Rule 803(6) (records of regularly conducted activity), which expressly refers to "opinions" and "diagnoses."   "Factual findings," the court opined, must be something other than opinions.

For several reasons, we do not agree. In the first place, it is not apparent that the term "factual findings" should be read to mean simply "facts" (as opposed to "opinions" or "conclusions"). A common definition of "finding of fact" is, for example, "[a] conclusion by way of reasonable inference from the evidence." ... [T]he language of the Rule does not compel us to reject the interpretation that "factual findings" includes conclusions or opinions that flow from a factual investigation. Second, we note that, contrary to what is often assumed, the language of the Rule does not state that "factual findings" are admissible, but that "reports... setting forth ... factual findings" (emphasis added) are admissible. On this reading, the language of the Rule does not create a distinction between "fact" and "opinion" contained in such reports.

Turning next to the legislative history of Rule 803(8)(C), we find no clear answer to the question of how the Rule's language should be interpreted. Indeed, in this litigation the legislative history may well be at the origin of the dispute. Rather than the more usual situation where a court must attempt to glean meaning from ambiguous comments of legislators who did not focus directly on the problem at hand, here the Committees in both Houses of Congress clearly recognized and expressed their opinions on the precise question at issue. Unfortunately, however, they took diametrically opposite positions. Moreover, the two Houses made no effort to reconcile their views, either through changes in the Rule's language or through a statement in the Report of the Conference Committee.

...

Clearly this legislative history reveals a difference of view between the Senate and the House that affords no definitive guide to the congressional understanding. It seems clear however that the Senate understanding is more in accord with the wording of the Rule and with the comments of the Advisory Committee.

The Advisory Committee's comments are notable, first, in that they contain no mention of any dichotomy between statements of "fact" and "opinions" or "conclusions." What was on the Committee's mind was simply whether what it called "evaluative reports" should be admissible. Illustrating the previous division among the courts on this subject, the Committee cited numerous cases in which the admissibility of such reports had been both sustained and denied. It also took note of various federal statutes that made certain kinds of evaluative reports admissible in evidence. What is striking about all of these examples is that these were reports that stated conclusions. ... The Committee's concern was clearly whether reports of this kind should be admissible. Nowhere in its comments is there the slightest indication that it even considered the solution of admitting only "factual" statements from such reports. Rather, the Committee referred throughout to "reports," without any such differentiation regarding the statements they contained. What the Committee referred to in the Rule's language as "reports ... setting forth ... factual findings" is surely nothing more or less than what in its commentary it called "evaluative reports." Its solution as to their admissibility is clearly stated in the final paragraph of its report on this Rule. That solution consists of two principles: First, "the rule ... assumes admissibility in the first instance...." Second, it provides "ample provision for escape if sufficient negative factors are present."

. . .

The Advisory Committee proposed a nonexclusive list of four factors it thought would be helpful in passing on this question: (1) the timeliness of the investigation; (2) the investigator's skill or experience; (3) whether a hearing was held; and (4) possible bias when reports are prepared with a view to possible litigation (*citing Palmer v. Hoffman*).

...In the present litigation, the District Court found the JAG Report to be trustworthy. ...

Our conclusion that neither the language of the Rule nor the intent of its framers calls for a distinction between "fact" and "opinion" is strengthened by the analytical difficulty of drawing such a line. ...

We hold, therefore, that portions of investigatory reports otherwise admissible under Rule 803(8)(C) are not inadmissible merely because they state a conclusion or opinion. As long as the conclusion is based on a factual investigation and satisfies the Rule's trustworthiness requirement, it should be admissible along with other portions of the report. As the trial judge in this action determined that certain of the JAG Report's conclusions were trustworthy, he rightly allowed them to be admitted into evidence. We therefore reverse the judgment of the Court of Appeals in respect of the Rule 803(8)(C) issue. ...

TC determined

Points for Discussion

a. The Trustworthy Nature of Investigative Reports

What if the investigator in *Beech Aircraft* relied in part upon hearsay statements in preparing his report? Should the court automatically exclude those portions of the report that are based upon hearsay because they are untrustworthy? In *Miller v. Field*, 35 F.3d 1088, 1091-1092 (6th Cir. 1994), the court found "that factual findings, which are based on inadmissible hearsay, are not admissible under Rule 803(8)(C) because the underlying information is untrustworthy." But see *United States v. Davis*, 826 F.Supp. 617, 623-624 (D.R.I. 1993) (because investigators draw inferences from what they are told, the report is admissible "[a]bsent a specific showing of untrustworthiness, such as multiple lawyers of hearsay"). Which opinion represents the better viewpoint?

b. Government Reports in Criminal Cases

Subdivisions (b) and (c) of Rule 803(8) provide that "matters observed by police officers and other law enforcement personnel" and factual findings from government investigatory reports offered against a criminal defendant are inadmissible. Would these reports be admissible as business records? In *United States v. Oates*, 560 F.2d 45 (2d Cir. 1970), the Second Circuit reversed the trial court's admission, as business records, of a Customs Service chemist's worksheets and lab report which determined that the substance taken from the defendant and analyzed by the lab was heroin. The court found that the chemists of the Customs Service were law enforcement personnel and that the reports were inadmissible because the same limitations in Rule 803(8)(B) and (C) applied to the business records exception of Rule 803(6):

> [I]n view of the articulated purpose behind the narrow drafting of FRE 803 in general and FRE 803(8) in particular, FRE 803(6) must be read in conjunction with FRE 803(8)(B) and (C). Specifically, the pervasive fear of the draftsmen and of Congress that interference with an accused's right to confrontation would occur was the reason why in criminal cases evaluative reports of government agencies and law enforcement reports were expressly denied the benefit to which they might otherwise be entitled under FRE 903(8). *United States v. Oates*, 560 F.2d at 78.

Not all courts agree. See *United States v. Sokolow*, 81 F.3d 397 (listing cases that have criticized *Oates* as an unduly broad interpretation of Rule 803(8) and refusing to apply the restrictions of (B) and(C) to other hearsay exceptions, such as Rule 803(6)).

c. Routine Matters

A number of federal courts have admitted routine non-adversarial police reports. See, e.g., *United States v. Grady*, 544 F.2d 598 (2d Cir. 1976) (admitting routine lists kept by the Irish police of the serial numbers of weapons found in Northern Ireland, some of which the defendant has illegally imported); *United States v. Orozco*, 590 F.2d 789 (9th Cir. 1979) (the recording of license plate number of cars passing through customs at the border was admissible as a government record under Rule 803(8) on the basis that they were "matters observed by law enforcement personnel"); *United States v. Brown*, 9 F.3d 907 (11th Cir. 1993) (admitting a police department's receipt for a gun).

————————

2. Rule 804. Hearsay Exceptions; Declarant Unavailable

Rule 804. Hearsay Exceptions; Declarant Unavailable

804(a) - Definition of unavailability. "Unavailability as a witness" includes situations in which the declarant –

(1) is exempted by ruling of the court on the ground of privilege from testifying concerning the subject matter of the declarant's statement; or

(2) persists in refusing to testify concerning the subject matter of the declarant's statement despite an order of the court to do so; or

(3) testifies to a lack of memory of the subject matter of the declarant's statement; or

(4) is unable to be present or to testify at the hearing because of death or then existing physical or mental illness or infirmity; or

(5) is absent from the hearing and the proponent of a statement has been unable to procure the declarant's attendance (or in the case of a hearsay exception under subdivision (b)(2), (3), or (4), the declarant's attendance or testimony) by process or other reasonable means.

A declarant is not unavailable as a witness if exemption, refusal, claim of lack of memory, inability, or absence is due to the procurement or wrongdoing of the proponent of a statement for the purpose of preventing the witness from attending or testifying.

Definition of Unavailability

As previously discussed, the exceptions to the hearsay rule are divided into those that apply regardless of the availability of the declarant and those that apply only when the declarant is unavailable. Unlike Rule 803 that includes 23 exceptions, Rule 804 includes only five exceptions.

Before one of these exceptions will apply, the declarant must be unavailable. Unavailability is defined by 804(a) and must be determined by the court under Rule 104(a). The term "unavailable" has a specific meaning within the rules of evidence. Do not rely on a "lay" definition or meaning. Rely, instead, on the specific definitions as set out in 804(a). There are five scenarios under the Rule that will constitute unavailability:

1) is exempted by ruling of the court on the ground of privilege from testifying concerning the subject matter of the declarant's statement:

An example of the application of unavailability under this provision would be a criminal defendant who invokes her fifth amendment constitutional privilege against self-incrimination. In this scenario, even though the declarant may be present in the courtroom, the declarant would be unavailable as defined by the rule.

2) persists in refusing to testify concerning the subject matter of the declarant's statement despite an order of the court to do so.

FYI
As an example, a reporter named Sarah Olsen refused to testify in a court-martial about a story she reported concerning a military soldier who allegedly refused to follow orders deploying the soldier to Iraq. The reporter's refusal would fall within F.R.E. 804(a)(2).

Those witnesses who merely refuse to testify would fall within this provision.

(3) testifies to a lack of memory of the subject matter of the declarant's statement; or

(4) is unable to be present or to testify at the hearing because of death or then existing physical or mental illness or infirmity; or

(5) is absent from the hearing and the proponent of a statement has been unable to procure the declarant's attendance (or in the case of a hearsay exception under subdivision (b)(2), (3), or (4), the declarant's attendance or testimony*) by process or other reasonable means.*

(b) Hearsay exceptions. The following are not excluded by the hearsay rule if the declarant is unavailable as a witness:

(1) Former testimony. Testimony given as a witness at another hearing of the same or a different proceeding, or in a deposition taken in compliance with law in the course of the same or another proceeding, if the party against whom the testimony is now offered, or, in a civil action or proceeding, a predecessor in interest, had an opportunity and similar motive to develop the testimony by direct, cross, or redirect examination.

(2) Statement under belief of impending death. In a prosecution for homicide or in a civil action or proceeding, a statement made by a declarant while believing that the declarant's death was imminent, concerning the cause or circumstances of what the declarant believed to be impending death.

(3) Statement against interest. A statement which was at the time of its making so far contrary to the declarant's pecuniary or proprietary interest, or so far tended to subject the declarant to civil or criminal liability, or to render invalid a claim by the declarant against another, that a reasonable person in the declarant's position would not have made the statement unless believing it to be true. A statement tending to expose the declarant to criminal liability and offered to exculpate the accused is not admissible unless corroborating circumstances clearly indicate the trustworthiness of the statement.

(4) Statement of personal or family history. (A) A statement concerning the declarant's own birth, adoption, marriage, divorce, legitimacy, relationship by blood, adoption, or marriage, ancestry, or other similar fact of personal or family history, even though declarant had no means of acquiring personal knowledge of the matter stated;

or (B) a statement concerning the foregoing matters, and death also, of another person, if the declarant was related to the other by blood, adoption, or marriage or was so intimately associated with the other's family as to be likely to have accurate information concerning the matter declared.

(5) [Transferred to Rule 807]

(6) Forfeiture by wrongdoing. A statement offered against a party that has engaged or acquiesced in wrongdoing that was intended to, and did, procure the unavailability of the declarant as a witness.

The last three provisions are fairly self-explanatory. When applying the rule to proposed evidence, the critical factor is to apply the rule specifically to the facts.

804(b)(1) - Former Testimony

This rule creates an exception for prior testimony by an "unavailable" witness when two conditions are met: first, the testimony must have been the same testimony given in a prior proceeding or deposition; second, the party against whom the evidence is now offered must have had an opportunity and similar motive to develop the testimony through either direct, cross, or redirect examination.

Although not a technical requirement, this exception typically applies when the parties and issues from the prior and current proceedings are identical, although changes in the parties or issues would not mandate exclusion from the exception.

The first condition is fairly straight forward: the declarant must have been a "witness" at another trial or hearing or must have been a deponent. The second requirement can be a bit more complex.

U.S. v. DiNapoli

U.S Court of Appeals for the Second Circuit
8 F.3d 909 (2nd Cir. 1993)

On this criminal appeal ...[t]he issue concerns Rule 804(b)(1) of the Federal Rules of Evidence, which provides that testimony given by a currently unavailable witness at a prior hearing is not excluded by the hearsay rule if "the party against whom the testimony is now offered ... had an opportunity and similar motive to develop the testimony by direct, cross, or redirect examination." Fed.R.Evid. 804(b)(1). Our precise issue is whether the prosecution had a "similar motive to develop" the testimony of two grand jury witnesses compared to its motive at a subsequent criminal trial at which the witnesses were unavailable. We hold that the "similar motive" requirement of Rule 804(b)(1) was not met and that the witnesses' grand jury testimony, offered by the defendants, was therefore properly excluded. ...

Background

... Briefly, the case concerns conspiracy and substantive charges under the Racketeer Influenced and Corrupt Organizations Act ("RICO") ... against several defendants accused of participating in a bid-rigging scheme in the concrete construction industry in Manhattan. The trial evidence indicated the existence of a "Club" of six concrete construction companies that ... rigged the bids for concrete superstructure work on nearly every high-rise construction project in Manhattan involving more than $2 million of concrete work. ....

The grand jury investigating the matter returned its first indictment .... That indictment alleged the essential aspects of the criminal activity and named all of the appellants as defendants. The grand jury continued its investigation in an effort to identify additional participants and additional construction projects that might have been victimized by the bid-rigging scheme. In this subsequent phase of the inquiry, the grand jury called ... DeMatteis and ... Bruno as witnesses. They had been principals in Cedar Park Concrete Construction Corporation ("Cedar Park"), a company that other grand jury witnesses had testified had been briefly involved in the scheme. DeMatteis and Bruno, both testifying under grants of immunity, denied awareness of a bid-rigging scheme.

DeMatteis testified in the grand jury on three occasions .... At his third appearance, the prosecutor pointedly asked whether DeMatteis had been instructed not to bid on the Javits Convention Center project and whether he was aware of an arrangement whereby the successful bidder paid two percent of the bid price to organized crime figures. DeMatteis denied both the instruction not to bid and awareness of the two percent arrangement. The prosecutor, obviously skeptical of the denials, pressed DeMatteis with a few questions in the nature of cross-examination. However, in order not to reveal the identity of then undisclosed cooperating witnesses or the existence of then undisclosed wiretapped conversations that refuted DeMatteis's denials, the prosecutor refrained from confronting him with the substance of such evidence. Instead, the prosecutor called to DeMatteis's attention the substance of only the one relevant wiretapped conversation that had already become public-a tape played at a prior trial....

Bruno testified at the grand jury .... Like DeMatteis, Bruno was asked about and denied knowledge of the "Club" and the two percent arrangement for successful bidders. And, like DeMatteis, he was briefly cross-examined and confronted with the contents of the publicly disclosed tape from the [prior] trial but not with any of the information from undisclosed witnesses or wiretaps. After his denials and after giving an answer that sharply conflicted with an answer given by DeMatteis, Bruno was briefly excused from the grand jury room. Upon his return, after the prosecutor had consulted with the grand jury, he was told by the prosecutor of the grand jury's "strong concern" that his testimony had "not been truthful." Four days later, Bruno's lawyer wrote the prosecutor stating that many of Bruno's answers had been inaccurate. The lawyer suggested that the prosecutor should resubmit his questions to Bruno in writing and that Bruno would respond by affidavit. The prosecutor declined the suggestion.

A thirteen-month trial ... commenced ... against eleven defendants and ended ... with the convictions of nine defendants, including the six appellants.... During the trial, the defendants endeavored to call DeMatteis and Bruno as witnesses. Both invoked the privilege against self-incrimination. The defendants then offered the testimony DeMatteis and Bruno had given to the grand jury. ... [T]he District Court ... refused to admit the grand jury testimony as prior testimony under Rule 804(b)(1). Judge Lowe ... ruled generally that the "motive of a prosecutor ... in the investigatory stages of a case is far different from the motive of a prosecutor in conducting the trial" and hence the "similar motive" requirement of Rule 804(b)(1) was not satisfied.

. . .

Discussion

Our initial task is to determine how similarity of motive at two proceedings will be determined for purposes of Rule 804(b)(1). ...[W]e do not accept the position ... that the test of similar motive is simply whether at the two proceedings the questioner takes the same side of the same issue. The test must turn not only on whether the questioner is on the same side of the same issue at both proceedings, but also on whether the questioner had a substantially similar interest in asserting that side of the issue. If a fact is critical to a cause of action at a second proceeding but the same fact was only peripherally related to a different cause of action at a first proceeding, no one would claim that the questioner had a similar motive at both proceedings to show that the fact had been established (or disproved). This is the same principle that holds collateral estoppel inapplicable when a small amount is at stake in a first proceeding and a large amount is at stake in a second proceeding, even though a party took the same side of the same issue at both proceedings. This suggests that the questioner must not only be on the same side of the same issue at both proceedings but must also have a substantially similar degree of interest in prevailing on that issue.

Whether the degree of interest in prevailing on an issue is substantially similar at two proceedings will sometimes be affected by the nature of the proceedings. Where both proceedings are trials and the same matter is seriously disputed at both trials, it will normally be the case that the side opposing the version of a witness at the first trial had a motive to develop that witness's testimony similar to the motive at the second trial. The opponent, whether shouldering a burden of proof or only resisting the adversary's effort to sustain its burden of proof, usually cannot tell how much weight the witness's version will have with the fact-finder in the total mix of all the evidence. Lacking such knowledge, the opponent at the first trial normally has a motive to dispute the version so long as it can be said that disbelief of the witness's version is of some significance to the opponent's side of the case; the motive at the second trial is normally similar.

The situation is not necessarily the same where the two proceedings are different in significant respects, such as their purposes or the applicable burden of proof. The grand jury context, with which we are concerned in this case, well illustrates the point. If a prosecutor is using the grand jury to investigate possible crimes and identify possible criminals, it may be quite unrealistic to characterize the prosecutor as the "opponent" of a witness's version. At a preliminary stage of an investigation, the prosecutor is not trying to prove any side of any issue, but only to develop the facts to determine if an indictment is warranted. Even if the prosecutor displays some skepticism about particular testimony (not an uncommon response from any questioner interested in eliciting the truth), that does not mean the prosecutor has a motive to show the falsity of the testimony, similar to the motive that would exist at trial if an indictment is returned and the witness's testimony is presented by a defendant to rebut the prosecutor's evidence of guilt.

…[W]here the grand jury proceeding has progressed far beyond the stage of a general inquiry, the motive to develop grand jury testimony that disputes a position already taken by the prosecutor is not necessarily the same as the motive the prosecutor would have if that same testimony was presented at trial. Once the prosecutor has decided to seek an indictment against identified suspects, that prosecutor may fairly be characterized as "opposed" to any testimony that tends to exonerate one of the suspects. But, because of the low burden of proof at the grand jury stage, even the prosecutor's status as an "opponent" of the testimony does not necessarily create a motive to challenge the testimony that is similar to the motive at trial. At the grand jury, the prosecutor need establish only probable cause to believe the suspect is guilty. By the time the exonerating testimony is given, such probable cause may already have been established to such an extent that there is no realistic likelihood that the grand jury will fail to indict. That circumstance alone will sometimes leave the prosecutor with slight if any motive to develop the exonerating testimony in order to persuade the grand jurors of its falsity.

Moreover, the grand jury context will sometimes present additional circumstances that render the prosecutor's motive to challenge the exonerating testimony markedly dissimilar to what the prosecutor's motive would be at trial. …

In recognizing these factors that distinguish the grand jury context from the trial context, we do not accept the position … that a prosecutor "generally will not have the same motive to develop testimony in grand jury proceedings as he does at trial." … [T]he inquiry as to similar motive must be fact specific, and the grand jury context will sometimes, but not invariably, present circumstances that demonstrate the prosecutor's lack of a similar motive. We accept neither the Government's view that the prosecutor's motives at the grand jury and at trial are almost always dissimilar, nor the opposing view, apparently held by the District of Columbia Circuit, that the prosecutor's motives in both proceedings are always similar.

…

The proper approach, therefore, in assessing similarity of motive under Rule 804(b)(1) must consider whether the party resisting the offered testimony at a pending proceeding had at a prior proceeding an interest of substantially similar intensity to prove (or disprove) the same side of a substantially similar issue. The nature of the two proceedings-both what is at stake and the applicable burden of proof-and, to a lesser extent, the cross-examination at the prior proceeding-both what was undertaken and what was available but forgone-will be relevant though not conclusive on the ultimate issue of similarity of motive.

[handwritten: assessing similarity in motive]

… We therefore vacate the panel's decision and return the appeal to the panel for further consideration of the appellants' remaining contentions.

Points for Discussion

a. The Opportunity and Motive Test

The "opportunity and motive" test is designed to make certain the party against whom the former testimony is being offered had a meaningful chance to challenge its truthfulness at the first proceeding. In *DiNapoli*, this was interpreted to mean that this party must have "a substantially similar degree of interest in prevailing on [the] issue" as the party questioning the witness at the prior trial, deposition, or other hearing. Despite this holding, most courts have admitted testimony taken during a preliminary hearing when offered by the government, even though defense attorneys traditionally ask few questions of government witnesses at preliminary hearings because they do not want to show the government their trial strategy. See *Glenn v. Dallman*, 635 F.2d 1183 (6th Cir. 1980). Does this seem fair?

b. Party or Predecessor-in-Interest

In a criminal case, the party against whom the testimony is offered at trial must be the one who had the opportunity and motive to cross-examine the witness giving the testimony at the prior proceeding. In a civil case, that person may also be what the rule designates as a predecessor-in-interest. Under the common law, a predecessor-in-interest was defined as persons who had joint or successive legal rights to property. Few courts have interpreted this term so narrowly. In *Lloyd v. American Export Lines*, 580 F.2d 1179 (3d Cir. 1978), for example, the term predecessor-in-interest was held to be someone with a similar motive and opportunity to question the witness in the prior proceeding, thus effectively equating the two requirements. The *Lloyd* case reached this conclusion after reviewing the Congressional history of the rule. But see *IBM Peripheral EDP Devices Antitrust Litig.*, 444 F. Supp. 110 (N.D. Cal. 1978) (equating predecessor-in-interest with someone with similar opportunity and motive negates the intent of Congress in drafting the rule).

Rule 804(b)(2). Statement Under Belief of Impending Death

(b) Hearsay exceptions. The following are not excluded by the hearsay rule if the declarant is unavailable as a witness:

(2) Statement under belief of impending death. In a prosecution for homicide or in a civil action or proceeding, a statement made by a declarant while believing that the declarant's death was imminent, concerning the cause or circumstances of what the declarant believed to be impending death.

Note that in civil cases only, former testimony can be used against a party if that party, or that party's "predecessor-in-interest" had the same opportunity and similar motive to develop the testimony. For example, assume there was a trial in which Company A was a party that developed the testimony of a witness at trial, the former testimony of the witness in the first trial in which Company A was involved might be used against Company B. This would fall within 804(b)(1) provided that (1) witness is now unavailable and (2) Company A is Company B's "predecessor in interest" and (3) Company A had the opportunity and the same motive to develop the witness's testimony as would have Company B.

This rule is informally known as the 'dying declaration.' It is rarely used but is certainly colorful. To fully understand this rule it helps to break it down to its bare elements. The requirements of the exception are as follows:

1) The speaker must be unavailable as defined by Rule 804(a).

2) In criminal cases, this exception applies only to prosecutions for homicide.

3) It applies to all civil cases.

4) The declarant must believe that her death was imminent.

5) The statement must have been made while the declarant believed that her death was imminent.

6) The statement must concern the cause or circumstances of what the declarant believed to be impending death.

7) The declarant must have personal knowledge of the matter asserted.

Take Note!

Do not misinterpret this exception. The declarant need not be dead, just unavailable as that term is defined in Rule 804(a). The status of the declarant is irrelevant to the determination of the application of the exception. The only relevant fact is whether the declarant believed death was imminent.

Analyzing any statement under this exception is more easily accomplished by applying the circumstances in which the statement was made and comparing those circumstances to the elements of the rule. The requirement of personal knowledge is not apparent from the rule. To find this requirement, one must look at the Advisory Committee Notes. The ACN provides that the "continuation of a requirement of first-hand knowledge is assured by Rule 602."

The rationale behind the rule is that a declarant is unlikely to lie or fabricate statements as she is dying. The historical idea is that people would not choose to meet their maker with a "lie on their lips."

Rule 804(b)(3). Statement Against Interest

(b) Hearsay exceptions. The following are not excluded by the hearsay rule if the declarant is unavailable as a witness:

(3) Statement against interest. A statement which was at the time of its making so far contrary to the declarant's pecuniary or proprietary interest, or so far tended to subject the declarant to civil or criminal liability, or to render invalid a claim by the declarant against another, that a reasonable person in the declarant's position would not have made the statement unless believing it to be true. A statement tending to expose the declarant to criminal liability and offered to exculpate the accused is not admissible unless corroborating circumstances clearly indicate the trustworthiness of the statement.

Take Note

Do not confuse this exception with 801(a)(2), a statement of a Party Opponent. Also, parties are usually not unavailable making 804 inapplicable.

This exception embraces the concept that a person would not speak against herself or her own personal or economic interests unless her statements were true. The requirements of this exception are as follows:

1) The declarant must be unavailable as defined by Rule 804(a); and

2) The statement must have been, at the time it was made, so contrary to the declarant's pecuniary or proprietary interest that it would subject her to civil or criminal liability; or

3) The statement would have rendered a claim by the declarant invalid against another; and

4) A person in the declarant's position would not have made the statement unless she believed it to be true.

Note: Elements 1 and 4 are required and either 2 or 3.

If the statement arises in a criminal prosecution and is being used by the defense, then the following additional requirements are added:

5) If the statement is one which would expose the declarant to criminal liability; and

6) The statement is offered to exculpate the accused, then

7) The statement must be corroborated (to prove the declarant is not simply "taking the fall" for someone else).

In the truest sense of the phrase, the requirement is that the statement actually be against the speaker's interest. The problem that may arise in the application of this exception is how to determine what is against one's interest. Generally, interest means self-concern with regard to matters of money, property or criminal consequences. Interests are frequently determined in context and individualized making the determination challenging. Analyzing statements must be done in a broader context which includes facts that extend beyond the statement itself where context and motivation are significant.

It was once thought that related statements which were, in effect, collateral to the statement was against interest would also be admissible. However, the Supreme Court rejected this view in *United States v. Williamson*, 512 U.S. 594 (1994).

Rule 804(b)(4). Statement of Personal or Family History

(b) Hearsay exceptions. The following are not excluded by the hearsay rule if the declarant is unavailable as a witness:

(4) Statement of personal or family history. (A) A statement concerning the declarant's own birth, adoption, marriage, divorce, legitimacy, relationship by blood, adoption, or marriage, ancestry, or other similar fact of personal or family history, even though declarant had no means of acquiring personal knowledge of the matter stated; or (B) a statement concerning the foregoing matters, and death also, of another person, if the declarant was related to the other by blood, adoption, or marriage or was so intimately associated with the other's family as to be likely to have accurate information concerning the matter declared.

The exception found in 804(b)(4) arises frequently in Family Law cases where hearsay abounds.

This exception permits statements from an unavailable declarant in specific situations related to the declarant's personal or family history. Interestingly enough, personal knowledge is not specifically required. As to statements regarding another person's personal or family history, the requirement of personal knowledge is satisfied if the declarant is a member of the family and, therefore, in a position to be familiar with the matter or so intimately associated with the other family as to be reasonably likely to have accurate information as to the matter asserted.

Rule 804(b)(6). Forfeiture by Wrongdoing

(b) Hearsay exceptions. The following are not excluded by the hearsay rule if the declarant is unavailable as a witness:

(6) Forfeiture by wrongdoing. A statement offered against a party that has engaged or acquiesced in wrongdoing that was intended to, and did, procure the unavailability of the declarant as a witness.

This exception is based on a doctrine of fairness. If a party is somehow responsible for a declarant's "unavailability" under Rule 804(a), that party should not then be able to subsequently exclude the declarant's statement as hearsay.

U.S. v. Gray

U.S Court of Appeals for the Fourth Circuit
405 F.3d 227 (4th Cir. 2005)
SHEDD, Circuit Judge:

A grand jury indicted Josephine Gray on five counts of mail fraud and three counts of wire fraud relating to her receipt of insurance proceeds following the deaths of her second husband and a former paramour. Gray was convicted on all counts, and the district court sentenced her to 40 years' imprisonment .... Gray now challenges her conviction, arguing that ... the district court improperly admitted ... hearsay evidence against Gray.

I.

Wilma Jean Wilson met Gray in the late summer of 2000, and the two became friends. They spoke over the telephone, and Wilson sometimes visited Gray's house. During one of those visits…Wilson asked if the reports [that Gray had killed her former husbands] were true, and Gray replied that she was going to tell Wilson something she had never told anyone before and she did not want Wilson to say anything about it. In an emotionless, matter-of-fact manner, Gray then told Wilson that "she had killed both her husbands and another gentleman."

Gray told Wilson that she had killed her first husband, Norman Stribbling, because she was tired of being abused by him. According to Wilson, "[s]he told me that they had gone out for a ride and that she had shot him…. [S]he left the body over on River Road, and it was set up to look like it was a robbery." Gray then confessed to Wilson that she had also killed her second husband, William "Robert" Gray. Although Gray said she was alone with Stribbling when she killed him, "she had help" killing Robert Gray. The help came from Clarence Goode, Gray's cousin and boyfriend. Gray explained to Wilson that Goode "had tried to blackmail her," demanding money in exchange for his silence about the murder of Robert Gray, so "she had to get rid of him too."

Gray's first husband, Stribbling, maintained a life insurance policy through John Hancock Mutual Life Insurance Company and named Gray as the beneficiary. … Shortly after Stribbling's death, Gray made a claim for insurance benefits and later received a check in the amount of $16,000.

Gray had been having an affair with Robert Gray while she was still married to Stribbling. …[T]he couple bought a house … and three months later they married. Robert Gray maintained an insurance policy … that provided for payment of the mortgage on the Grays' house … in the event of his death, with any excess going to his spouse. Robert Gray also maintained an accidental death insurance policy … and designated Gray as his beneficiary.

Robert Gray left the … [home] in August 1990, telling family members that his wife was trying to kill him and that she was having an affair with Goode, who had been living with the Grays. So convinced was Robert Gray that his wife intended him harm that he removed her as his beneficiary under two other insurance policies. He asked relatives and friends for help in avoiding a possible assault by Gray or Goode.

In late August 1990, Robert Gray brought criminal charges against Gray, alleging that Gray had assaulted him at his workplace by swinging at him with a club and lunging at him with a knife. Robert Gray also brought charges against Goode, alleging that Goode had threatened him with a 9-millimeter handgun. Robert Gray appeared in court on October 5, 1990, but the case against Gray and

Goode was continued. Later that same day, Robert Gray was driving home when he noticed his wife's car behind him. She was flashing her lights and signaling her husband to pull over. When Robert Gray did not pull over, Gray drove her car alongside her husband's car. As Robert Gray turned to look toward his wife, Goode sat up (from a reclined position) in the front passenger seat and pointed a gun at him. Robert Gray reported this incident to police, and a warrant was issued for the arrests of Gray and Goode. One week before the November 16, 1990 trial date, Robert Gray was discovered dead in his new apartment, shot once in the chest and once in the neck with a .45 caliber handgun.

...

As a result of Robert Gray's death, Minnesota Mutual paid approximately $51,625 to Perpetual Savings Bank-the named beneficiary-to cover the mortgage on the ... house. Once the mortgage was satisfied, Gray sold the house for a significant profit. The total benefit under Robert Gray's policy exceeded the mortgage payoff amount, so Minnesota Mutual expected to pay the excess benefit to Robert Gray's spouse. Because Gray's whereabouts were unknown to Minnesota Mutual, that benefit was not processed for about ten years.

...

Gray told Wilson that she "had to get rid of" Goode because he was blackmailing her. ... On June 21, 1996, Baltimore City Police officers found Goode's body in the trunk of his car; he had been shot in the back .... Goode had told his sister that he was going to visit Gray at her house, where police later found ... bullets and a large blood stain on the floor of the garage.

Goode maintained a life insurance policy ... and named Gray as his beneficiary under the policy. Shortly after an incident in which Gray pointed a knife at him, Goode closed the bank account from which the premiums for this policy were paid. [The insurance company]... advised Goode by letter in June 1996 that he had a 60-day grace period before the policy would be cancelled for non-payment. Goode's mail was sent to Gray's address, however, and Gray killed Goode shortly after learning that the policy might be cancelled. Gray filed a claim for benefits in September 1996, but [the insurance company] refused to pay because it suspected that Gray was involved in Goode's death. When Gray had not been arrested after two years, [the insurance company] filed an interpleader action to determine the proper beneficiary under Goode's policy. In the course of that litigation, Gray filed pleadings, by mail, in which she flatly denied any involvement in Goode's death. Because Gray's guilt could not be proved at that time, the parties settled the interpleader action and [the insurance company] paid Gray $99,990 in benefits under Goode's policy.

Shortly after Goode's murder, Gray showed her new boyfriend, Andre Savoy, a copy of Goode's insurance policy and told him that she planned to buy him a new Mustang GT with the proceeds. Gray never bought Savoy that car, but she did make inquiries about obtaining life insurance on him. ...

... Gray consistently denied having any involvement in the murders.

II.

... Gray argues that she is entitled to a new trial because the district court erroneously admitted into evidence ... hearsay testimony from Robert Gray.

...

The district court ... admitted into evidence several out-of-court statements made by Robert Gray during the three months preceding his murder:

> Robert Gray's criminal complaint alleging that Goode had tossed a 9-millimeter handgun on the table at his house to provoke an argument;

> Robert Gray's criminal complaint alleging that Gray had tried to stab him with a knife and attack him with a club;

> Statements made by Robert Gray to Darnell Gray and a police detective, claiming that Gray and Goode had assaulted him in October 1990; and

> Statements made by Robert Gray to Rodney Gray claiming that Goode had pulled a gun on him outside a restaurant in September or October 1990.

... [T]he doctrine of forfeiture by wrongdoing allows such statements to be admitted where the defendant's own misconduct rendered the declarant unavailable as a witness at trial. The Supreme Court applied this doctrine in <u>Reynolds v. United States, 98 U.S. 145, 25 L.Ed. 244 (1878)</u>, stating that "[t]he Constitution gives the accused the right to a trial at which he should be confronted with the witnesses against him; but if a witness is absent by [the accused's] own wrongful procurement, he cannot complain if competent evidence is admitted to supply the place of that which he has kept away." By 1996, every circuit to address the issue had recognized this doctrine.

<u>Fed.R.Evid. 804(b)(6)</u>, which took effect in 1997, codifies the common-law doctrine of forfeiture by wrongdoing as an exception to the general rule barring admission of hearsay evidence. ... Under <u>Rule 804(b)(6)</u>, "[a] statement offered

against a party that has engaged or acquiesced in wrong-doing that was intended to, and did procure the unavailability of the declarant as a witness" is admissible at trial. In order to apply the forfeiture-by-wrongdoing exception, the district court must find, by the preponderance of the evidence, that (1) the defendant engaged or acquiesced in wrongdoing (2) that was intended to render the declarant unavailable as a witness and (3) that did, in fact, render the declarant unavailable as a witness. The district court need not hold an independent evidentiary hearing if the requisite findings may be made based upon evidence presented in the course of the trial.

Gray contends that Rule 804(b)(6) should not apply in this case because she did not intend to procure Robert Gray's unavailability as a witness at *this* trial. "Because the Federal Rules of Evidence are a legislative enactment, we turn to the traditional tools of statutory construction in order to construe their provisions. We begin with the language itself." The text of Rule 804(b)(6) requires only that the defendant intend to render the declarant unavailable "as a witness." The text does not require that the declarant would otherwise be a witness at any *particular* trial, nor does it limit the subject matter of admissible statements to events distinct from the events at issue in the trial in which the statements are offered. Thus, we conclude that Rule 804(b)(6) applies *whenever* the defendant's wrongdoing was intended to, and did, render the declarant unavailable as a witness against the defendant, without regard to the nature of the charges at the trial in which the declarant's statements are offered. ...

Our interpretation of Rule 804(b)(6) advances the clear purpose of the forfeiture-by-wrongdoing exception. The advisory committee noted its specific goal to implement a "prophylactic rule to deal with abhorrent behavior which strikes at the heart of the system of justice itself." ... More generally, federal courts have recognized that the forfeiture-by-wrongdoing exception is necessary to prevent wrongdoers from profiting by their misconduct....

Federal courts have sought to effect the purpose of the forfeiture-by-wrongdoing exception by construing broadly the elements required for its application. *See, e.g., Dhinsa, 243 F.3d at 652* (noting that the Rule may apply where the declarant was only a potential witness, *i.e.,*"there was no ongoing proceeding in which the declarant was scheduled to testify"); *Cherry, 217 F.3d at 820* (holding that the declarant's statements may be admitted against a person who participated in a conspiracy to silence the declarant even if that person did not himself engage in witness intimidation or other wrongdoing); *Steele, 684 F.2d at 1201* (stating that "any significant interference" with the declarant's appearance as a witness, including the exercise of "persuasion and control" or an instruction to invoke the Fifth Amendment privilege, amounts to wrongdoing that forfeits the defendant's right to confront the declarant). Although the Rule requires that the wrongdoing was *intended* to render the declarant unavailable as a witness, we have held that a defendant need only intend "in part" to procure the declarant's unavailability.

Like these applications of the forfeiture-by-wrongdoing exception, our interpretation of Rule 804(b)(6) ensures that a defendant will not be permitted to avoid the evidentiary impact of statements made by his victim, whether or not he suspected that the victim would be a witness at the trial in which the evidence is offered against him. A defendant who wrongfully and intentionally renders a declarant unavailable as a witness in any proceeding forfeits the right to exclude, on hearsay grounds, the declarant's statements at that proceeding and any subsequent proceeding. ...

Having rejected Gray's interpretation of Rule 804(b)(6), we need only determine whether the district court properly applied the Rule in admitting Robert Gray's out-of-court statements. Those statements were admissible only if the district court properly found, by a preponderance of the evidence, that (1) Gray engaged in some wrongdoing (2) that was intended to procure Robert Gray's unavailability as a witness and (3) that did, in fact, procure his unavailability as a witness. The district court in this case found that Robert Gray "was killed prior to the court date ... and after the defendant was well aware of his status as a witness, justifies the inference that ... the killing was motivated ... to prevent [Robert Gray] from being available ... at court proceedings." ... Accordingly, the district court did not abuse its discretion in admitting testimony concerning out-of-court statements made by Robert Gray.

Points for Discussion

a. Constitutional Concerns

In *Davis v. Washington*, 547 U.S. 813 (2006) and *Crawford v. Washington*, 541 U.S. 36 (2004), the Supreme Court recognized that a defendant in a criminal case could waive his confrontation rights if the defendant rendered a declarant-witness unavailable for trial. The Court did not say, however, whether the defendant was required to make the witness unavailable for the purpose of not testifying. The difference was considered in *Giles v. California*, 128 S. Ct. 2678, 171 L. Ed.2d 488 (2008),where the Supreme Court struck down a California forfeiture by wrongdoing statute as a violation of the confrontation clause because it allowed the prosecution to present prior incriminating statements of the defendant's former girlfriend, whom he had killed in a domestic dispute for reasons unrelated to his trial.

b. "Acquiescing" in Wrongdoing

What if the party against whom the testimony is offered was only indirectly involved in procuring the absence of a witness in a case? What does Rule 804(b)(6) mean when it says that an absent declarant's statements may be offered against a party who "acquiesced" in wrongdoing resulting in the declarant's absence? Is mere knowledge of someone else's plan to procure the declarant's unavailability sufficient? See *United States v. Cherry*, 217 F.3d 811 (10th Cir. 2000) (waiver may be imputed, under an agency theory of responsibility, to a defendant who participated in a conspiracy but did not engage in the ensuing wrongdoing, if the result was in furtherance of and reasonably foreseeable as a necessary or natural consequence of an ongoing conspiracy); *United States v. Thompson*, 286 F.3d 950 (7th Cir. 2002) (adopting *Cherry*).

G. Residual Exception

807. Residual Exception

A statement not specifically covered by Rule 803 or 804 but having equivalent circumstantial guarantees of trustworthiness, is not excluded by the hearsay rule, if the court determines that (A) the statement is offered as evidence of a material fact; (B) the statement is more probative on the point for which it is offered than any other evidence which the proponent can procure through reasonable efforts; and (C) the general purposes of these rules and the interests of justice will best be served by admission of the statement into evidence. However, a statement may not be admitted under this exception unless the proponent of it makes known to the adverse party sufficiently in advance of the trial or hearing to provide the adverse party with a fair opportunity to prepare to meet it, the proponent's intention to offer the statement and the particulars of it, including the name and address of the declarant.

This exception provides a mechanism through that otherwise inadmissible evidence may be admitted without meeting a specific hearsay exception. This rule provides that such evidence may be admitted if it meets all of the criteria of the rule. These criteria are that the evidence must be reliable, material, probative and serve the interests of justice. Evidence need not be analyzed under Rule 807 unless it does not meet one of the other exceptions. The following case illustrates these criteria.

Dallas County v. Commercial Union Assur. Co.

U.S Court of Appeals for the Fifth Circuit
286 F.2d 388 (5th Cir. 1961)

This appeal presents a single question- the admissibility in evidence of a *issue* newspaper to show that the Dallas County Courthouse in Selma, Alabama, was damaged by fire in 1901. We hold that the newspaper was admissible, and affirm the judgment below.

On a bright, sunny morning, July 7, 1957, the clock tower of the Dallas County Courthouse at Selma, Alabama, commenced to lean, made loud cracking and popping noises, then fell, and telescoped into the courtroom. Fortunately, the collapse of the tower took place on a Sunday morning; no one was injured, but damage to the courthouse exceeded $100,000. An examination of the tower debris showed the presence of charcoal and charred timbers. The State Toxicologist, called in by Dallas County, reported the char was evidence that lightning struck the courthouse. Later, several residents of Selma reported that a bolt of lightning struck the courthouse July 2, 1957. On this information, Dallas County concluded that a lightning bolt had hit the building causing the collapse of the clock tower five days later. Dallas County carried insurance for loss to its courthouse caused by fire or lightning. The insurers' engineers and investigators found that the courthouse collapsed of its own weight. They reported that the courthouse had not been struck by lightning; that lightning could not have caused the collapse of the tower; that the collapse of the tower was caused by structural weaknesses attributable to a faulty design, poor construction, gradual deterioration of the structure, and overloading brought about by remodeling and the recent installation of an air-conditioning system, part of which was constructed over the courtroom trusses. In their opinion, the char was the result of a fire in the courthouse tower and roof that must have occurred many, many years before July 2, 1957. The insurers denied liability.

The case went to the jury on one issue: did lightning cause the collapse of the clock tower?

The record contains ample evidence to support a jury verdict either way. The County produced witnesses who testified they saw lighting strike the clock tower; the insurers produced witnesses who testified an examination of the debris showed that lightning did not strike the clock tower. Some witnesses said the char was fresh and smelled smoky; other witnesses said was obviously old and had no fresh smoky smell at all. Both sides presented a great mass of engineering testimony bearing on the design, construction, overload or lack of overload. All of this was for the jury to evaluate. The jury chose to believe the insurers' witnesses and brought in a verdict for the defendants.

newspaper article

During the trial the defendants introduced a copy of the Morning Times of Selma for June 9, 1901. This issue carried an unsigned article describing a fire that occurred at two in the morning of June 9, 1901, while the courthouse was still under construction. The article stated, in part: 'The unfinished dome of the County's new courthouse was in flames at the top, and soon fell in. The fire was soon under control and the main building was saved.'

. . .

P objected

As a predicate for introducing the newspaper in evidence, the defendants called to the stand the editor of the Selma Times-Journal who testified that his publishing company maintains archives of the published issues of the Times-Journal and of the Morning Times, its predecessor, and that the archives contain the issue of the Morning Times of Selma for June 9, 1901, offered in evidence. The plaintiff objected that the newspaper article was hearsay; that it was not a business record nor an ancient document, nor was it admissible under any recognized exception to the hearsay doctrine. The trial judge admitted the newspaper as part of the records of the Selma Times-Journal. The sole error Dallas County specifies on appeal is the admission of the newspaper in evidence.

In the Anglo-American adversary system of law, courts usually will not admit evidence unless its accuracy and trustworthiness may be tested by cross-examination. Here, therefore, the plaintiff argues that the newspaper should not be admitted: 'You cannot cross-examine a newspaper.' Of course, a newspaper article is hearsay, and in almost all circumstances is inadmissible. However, the law governing hearsay is somewhat less than pellucid. And, as with most rules, the hearsay rule is not absolute; it is replete with exceptions. Witnesses die, documents are lost, deeds are destroyed, memories fade. All too often, primary evidence is not available and courts and lawyers must rely on secondary evidence.

. . .

If they are worth their salt, evidentiary rules are to aid the search for truth. Rule 43(a), notwithstanding its shortcomings, carries out that purpose by enabling federal courts to apply a liberal, flexible rule for the admissibility of evidence, unencumbered by common law archaisms.

We turn now to a case, decided long before the Federal Rules were adopted, in which the court used an approach we consider appropriate for the solution of the problem before us. G. & C. Merriam Co. v. Syndicate Pub. Co., concerned a controversy between dictionary publishers over the use of the title 'Webster's Dictionary' when the defendant's dictionary allegedly was not based upon Webster's dictionary at all. The bone of contention was whether a statement in the preface to the dictionary was admissible as evidence of the facts it recited. Ogilvie, the compiler of the dictionary, stated in his preface that he used Webster's Dictionary as the basis for his own publication. The dictionary, with its preface, was published in 1850, sixty-three years before the trial of the case. Ogilvie's published statement was challenged as hearsay. Judge Learned Hand, then a district judge, unable, as we are here, to find a case in point, for authority relied solely on Wigmore on Evidence (then a recent publication), particularly on Wigmore's analysis that 'the requisites of an exception to the hearsay rule are necessity and circumstantial guaranty of trustworthiness'. Applying these criteria, Judge Hand held that the statement was admissible as an exception to the hearsay rule:

'Ogilvie's preface is of course an unsworn statement and as such only hearsay testimony, which may be admitted only as an exception to the general rule. The question is whether there is such an exception. I have been unable to find any express authority in point and must decide the question upon principle. In the first place, I think it fair to insist that to reject such a statement is to refuse evidence about the truth of which no reasonable person should have any doubt whatever, because it fulfills both the requisites of an exception to the hearsay rule, necessity and circumstantial guaranty of trustworthiness. Besides Ogilvie, everyone else is dead who ever knew anything about the matter and could intelligently tell us what the fact is. As to the trustworthiness of the testimony, it has the guaranty of the occasion, at which there was no motive for fabrication

The Court of Appeals adopted the district court's opinion in its entirety.

The first of the two requisites is necessity. As to necessity, Wigmore points out this requisite means that unless the hearsay statement is admitted, the facts it brings out may otherwise be lost, either because the person whose assertion is offered may be dead or unavailable, or because the assertion is of such a nature that one could not expect to obtain evidence of the same value from the same person or from other sources. Wigmore, § 1421 (3rd ed.). 'In effect, Wigmore says that, as the word necessity is here used, it is not to be interpreted as uniformly demanding a showing of total inaccessibility of firsthand evidence as a condition precedent to the acceptance of a particular piece of hearsay, but that necessity exists where otherwise great practical inconvenience would be experienced in making the desired proof. If it were otherwise, the result would be that the exception created to the hearsay rule would thereby be mostly, if not completely, destroyed.'

The fire referred to in the newspaper account occurred fifty-eight years before the trial of this case. Any witness who saw that fire with sufficient understanding to observe it and describe it accurately, would have been older than a young child at the time of the fire. We may reasonably assume that at the time of the trial he was either dead or his faculties were dimmed by the passage of fifty-eight years. It would have been burdensome, but not impossible, for the defendant to have discovered the name of the author of the article (although it had no by-line) and, perhaps, to have found an eye-witness to the fire. But it is improbable- so it seems to us- that any witness could have been found whose recollection would have been accurate at the time of the trial of this case. And it seems impossible that the testimony of any witness would have been as accurate and as reliable as the statement of facts in the contemporary newspaper article.

The rationale behind the 'ancient documents' exception is applicable here: after a long lapse of time, ordinary evidence regarding signatures or handwriting is virtually unavailable, and it is therefore permissible to resort to circumstantial evidence. Thus, in Trustees of German Township, Montgomery County v. Farmers & Citizens Savings Bank Co., the court admitted as ancient documents newspapers eighty years old containing notices of advertisements for bids relating to the town hall: 'Such exhibits, by reason of age, alone, and unquestioned authenticity, qualify as ancient documents.' The ancient documents rule applies to documents a generation or more in age. Here, the Selma Times-Journal article is almost two generations old. The principle of necessity, not requiring absolute impossibility or total inaccessibility of first-hand knowledge, is satisfied by the practicalities of the situation before us.

The second requisite for admission of hearsay evidence is trustworthiness. According to Wigmore, there are three sets of circumstances when hearsay is trustworthy enough to serve as a practicable substitute for the ordinary test of cross-examination: 'Where the circumstances are such that a sincere and accurate statement would naturally be uttered, and no plan of falsification be formed; where, even though a desire to falsify might present itself, other considerations, such as the danger of easy detection on the fear of punishment, would probably counteract its force; where the statement was made under such conditions of publicity that an error, if it had occurred, would probably have been detected and corrected. These circumstances fit the instant case.

There is no procedural canon against the exercise of common sense in deciding the admissibility of hearsay evidence. In 1901 Selma, Alabama, was a small town. Taking a common sense view of this case, it is inconceivable to us that a newspaper reporter in a small town would report there was a fire in the dome of the new courthouse- if there had been no fire. He is without motive to falsify, and a false report would have subjected the newspaper and him to embarrassment in the community. The usual dangers inherent in hearsay evidence, such as lack of memory, faulty narration, intent to influence the court proceedings, and plain lack of truthfulness are not present here. To our minds, the article published in the Selma Morning-Times on the day of the fire is more reliable, more trustworthy, more competent evidence than the testimony of a witness called to the stand fifty-eight years later.

We hold, that in matters of local interest, when the fact in question is of such a public nature it would be generally known throughout the community, and when the questioned fact occurred so long ago that the testimony of an eye-witness would probably be less trustworthy than a contemporary newspaper account, a federal court, under Rule 43(a), may relax the exclusionary rules to the extent of admitting the newspaper article in evidence. We do not characterize this newspaper as a 'business record', nor as an 'ancient document', nor as any other readily identifiable and happily tagged species of hearsay exception. It is admissible because it is necessary and trustworthy, relevant and material, and its admission is within the trial judge's exercise of discretion in holding the hearing within reasonable bounds.

Judgment is affirmed.

Points for Discussion

a. The Truthworthiness Requirement

Commercial Union, decided in 1961, represents a precursor to the "residual clause" exception of Rule 807. Like the rule, the court required that the newspaper article at issue be sufficiently trustworthy to be admissible. The court found sufficient trustworthiness in the fact that the statement, made in 1901, came from a newspaper in a small town where if it turned out to be false, the reporter and the newspaper would be subject to embarrassment. It this logic is persuasive? If trustworthiness is the only requirement to admit hearsay, does this place too much discretion in the hands of the trial judge? Do you prefer the requirements of Rule 807, which only admit hearsay statements if they are trustworthy, material, more probative than any other evidence the proponent can procure through reasonable efforts, and admissible in the interests of justice?

b. The Notice Requirement

Rule 807 states that a party who wants to offer a hearsay statement under Rule 807 must give notice to her opponent "sufficiently in advance of the trial . . . to provide the adverse party with a fair opportunity to meet it. . ." No other hearsay exception requires such notice. Why, then, does Rule 807?

c. The "Near Miss" Notion

The "near miss" theory is an argument against admissibility of a statement offered under Rule 807 which almost but does not quite qualify for admission under another hearsay exemption or exception. The theory argues that if a statement is excluded under the authority of another hearsay rule, then the statement cannot be admitted under Rule 807, which requires that the statement "not be covered by" other hearsay exceptions. This theory has not been accepted by most circuits. See, e.g., *in re Japanese Electronic Products Antitrust Litig.*, 723 F.2d 238 (3d Cir. 1983) (the "near miss" argument "puts the federal evidence rules back into the straightjacket from which the residual exception [was] intended to free them").

————————

H. Remaining Exceptions

There are a number of additional exceptions contained in Rule 803. These exceptions are either rarely used or are fairly straightforward not requiring substantial explanation. These remaining exceptions are briefly discussed here.

> **803(9). Records of Vital Statistics**
>
> Records or data compilations, in any form, of births, fetal deaths, deaths, or marriages, if the report thereof was made to a public office pursuant to requirements of law.

This exception is justified by the considerations of necessity and reliability. Documents generated that fall within this exception are typically required by an applicable state law. Additionally, it is considered unlikely that one would falsify the information required by these reports.

Issues may arise as to whether this exception is limited to the actual vital statistics (i.e., date and place of birth, name, etc.) or whether the exception encompasses additional details such as in the case of a birth certificate the name of the father, if that information is in dispute. The exception however, does not provide that information admitted pursuant to it must be taken as true. To the contrary, the information may still be disputed and the underlying basis for the recording of the information may be properly challenged.

803(10). Absence of Public Record or Entry

To prove the absence of a record, report, statement, or data compilation, in any form, or the nonoccurrence or nonexistence of a matter of which a record, report, statement, or data compilation, in any form, was regularly made and preserved by a public office or agency, evidence in the form of a certification in accordance with rule 902, or testimony, that diligent search failed to disclose the record, report, statement, or data compilation, or entry.

This exception may be used to provide that a record does not exist or that an event did not occur. To admit a document in compliance with the exception, the proponent of the evidence must:

1) establish that a particular public agency or office regularly made and preserved records of the kind of fact or event in question; and

2) prove that the records of the agency or office do not contain any mention or reference to the occurrence of the event or existence of the fact in question.

The nonexistence of a record may be proved by:

1) testimony that a diligent search failed to locate such a record or entry; or

2) a written certification in accordance with Rule 902 that a diligent search of the office's files failed to locate such a record.

803(11). Records of Religious Organizations

Statements of births, marriages, divorces, deaths, legitimacy, ancestry, relationship by blood or marriage, or other similar facts of personal or family history, contained in a regularly kept record of a religious organization.

This exception comes from a long standing common law exception. The reliability of these records is presumed based on the belief that there is little motivation to fabricate these records.

Take Note!

Documents which are admissible under this exception may also be admissible under the business records exception Rule 803(6).

803(12). Marriage, Baptismal, and Similar Certificates

Statements of fact contained in a certificate that the maker performed a marriage or other ceremony or administered a sacrament, made by a clergyman, public official, or other person authorized by the rules or practices of a religious organization or by law to perform the act certified, and purporting to have been issued at the time of the act or within a reasonable time thereafter.

For evidence to meet the requirements of this exception, the proponent must meet the requirements of the rule:

Make the Connection

If a public official (i.e., a Justice of the Peace) performed the ceremony, an official seal will make the certificate self-authenticating under Rule 902.

1) The person who performed the act in question filled out the certificate;

2) The person was authorized by law or by the rules or practices of a religious organization to perform the act in question; and

3) The certificate was issued at the time of the act or within a reasonable time thereafter.

803(13). Family Records

Statements of fact concerning personal or family history contained in family Bibles, genealogies, charts, engravings on rings, inscriptions on family portraits, engravings on urns, crypts, or tombstones, or the like.

This exception presumes that the location of the information helps to ensure reliability.

803(14). Records of Documents Affecting an Interest in Property

The record of a document purporting to establish or affect an interest in property, as proof of the content of the original recorded document and its execution and delivery by each person by whom it purports to have been executed, if the record is a record of a public office and an applicable statute authorizes the recording of documents of that kind in that office.

This exception assures that records relating to property will be admissible and not subject to exclusion based on a hearsay objection if those records are maintained according to state law.

803(15). Statements in Documents Affecting an Interest in Property

A statement contained in a document purporting to establish or affect an interest in property if the matter stated was relevant to the purpose of the document, unless dealings with the property since the document was made have been inconsistent with the truth of the statement or the purport of the document.

This exception covers statements in documents affecting an interest in property as opposed to records of documents in 803(14) above. This exception has three requirements:

Take Note!

Rule 803(15) does not contain a time requirement, unlike Rule 803(16), which requires the passage of at least twenty years.

1) The statement must be in a document that purports to establish or affect an interest in property;

2) The statement must be relevant to the purpose of the document; and

3) Subsequent dealings with the property must not have been inconsistent with the truth of the statement or the purport of the document.

This exception presumes that those who execute documents that affect an interest in property would make certain that such documents are accurate before execution.

803(16). Statements in Ancient Documents

Statements in a document in existence twenty years or more the authenticity of which is established.

This exception presumes reliability of documents which are at least twenty years old. The exception derives from the probability that there is not likely to be witnesses available with first-hand knowledge of matters contained within the ancient documents. Additionally, documents at least twenty-years old are likely more reliable; the basis for this presumed reliability is that the statements contained in that document were made prior to the controversy in question.

803(17). Market Reports, Commercial Publications

Market quotations, tabulations, lists, directories, or other published compilations, generally used and relied upon by the public or by persons in particular occupations.

Food for Thought

Think about those documents which have their origin based on the internet. The proliferation of web-based "documents" may give rise to some unique challenges, as yet unseen, based on evidence offered under this exception to the hearsay rule.

Documents which fall within this exception are considered inherently reliable.

803(18). Learned Treatises

To the extent called to the attention of an expert witness upon cross-examination or relied upon by the expert witness in direct examination, statements contained in published treatises, periodicals, or pamphlets on a subject of history, medicine, or other science or art, established as a reliable authority by the testimony or admission of the witness or by other expert testimony or by judicial notice. If admitted, the statements may be read into evidence but may not be received as exhibits.

Evidence which relates to specialized fields of knowledge are offered through expert witnesses. Learned treatises are not offered to prove facts through lay witnesses. For example, a lay witness could not use a treatise on psychology to offer evidence of her theory of whether a person has a psychological illness.

This exception requires the following for the admission of evidence through the use of a learned treatise:

1) An expert witness must testify;

2) The treatise offered must be established as a reliable authority;

3) The treatise must be either:

    a) Relied upon by the expert on direct examination; or

    b) Called to the attention of the expert upon cross-examination

4) The statements of the witness may be read into the record but the treatise cannot be admitted as an exhibit.

803(19). Reputation Concerning Personal or Family History

Reputation among members of a person's family by blood, adoption, or marriage, or among a person's associates, or in the community, concerning a person's birth, adoption, marriage, divorce, death, legitimacy, relationship by blood, adoption, or marriage, ancestry, or other similar fact of personal or family history.

The basis for this exception is that information about a person's family status that is widely known is likely to be reliable. This is presumably true even though no one may be available with first-hand knowledge of the information.

To qualify as 'reputation' testimony under this exception, the party offering the testimony must lay the same foundation that would be required to admit reputation testimony under Rules 404(a) through 405(a) or 608(a).

803(20). Reputation Concerning Boundaries or General History

Reputation in a community, arising before the controversy, as to boundaries of or customs affecting lands in the community, and reputation as to events of general history important to the community or State or nation in which located.

This exception is similar to 803(19) above; the information is presumed reliable because the offering party must establish that the information in question is sufficiently well-known to constitute 'reputation.'

803(21). Reputation as to Character

Reputation of a person's character among associates or in the community.

This exception removes the hearsay barrier to reputation evidence that is otherwise admissible under Rules 404, 405 or 608(a).

803(22). Judgment of Previous Conviction

Evidence of a final judgment, entered after a trial or upon a plea of guilty (but not upon a plea of nolo contendere), adjudging a person guilty of a crime punishable by death or imprisonment in excess of one year, to prove any fact essential to sustain the judgment, but not including, when offered by the Government in a criminal prosecution for purposes other than impeachment, judgments against persons other than the accused. The pendency of an appeal may be shown but does not affect admissibility.

This exception provides the following:

1) *The nature of the crime.* Only convictions for crimes punishable by death or imprisonment in excess of one year fit within the exception.

Take Note!

The exception does not require that the defendant receive a death sentence or imprisonment for in excess of one year; it only provides that she could have received such a sentence under the sentencing laws of jurisdiction.

2) *Manner of Conviction.* The conviction fits within the exception only if it came after a trial or plea of guilty. Convictions from pleas of nolo contender do not fall within the exception.

3) *Use of the Conviction.* The exception only applies if the prior conviction is offered to prove any fact essential to sustain the judgment.

4) *Use in Civil Litigation.* Parties to civil litigation may use a conviction under this exception to prove any essential fact to sustain the judgment regardless of who was convicted. The convicted person could have been one of the parties, a witness, or anyone else.

5) *Use in a Criminal Trial:*

   a) *By the Defense.* The defense may use a conviction under this exception to prove any essential fact to sustain the judgment regardless of who was convicted. The convicted person could have been one of the parties, a witness, or anyone else.

   b) *By the Prosecution.* A prosecutor may use a conviction under this exception to prove any essential fact to sustain the judgment only if the person who was convicted in the prior case is also the defendant in the current case.

6) *Pendency of an Appeal.* If an appeal of the conviction is pending, the party adversely affected by the evidence may inform the jury of that fact, but the fact that a case is on appeal does not affect admissibility of the conviction.

> ### 803(23). Judgment as to Personal, Family or General History or Boundaries
>
> Judgments as proof of matters of personal, family or general history, or boundaries, essential to the judgment, if the same would be provable by evidence of reputation.

This exception provides that if litigation in the past (either civil or criminal) resulted in a judgment relating to any of the subjects addressed in Rules 803(19) or 803(20), that judgment is admissible as proof of any fact "essential to the judgment."

Executive Summary

General Rule Against Hearsay

Because cross-examination of a witness is the hallmark of our truth-finding adversarial system, we generally want to hear only from witnesses who are actually in the courtroom and subject to cross-examination, not from individuals who have made previous out-of-court statements when those statements are related in court for their truth. The rule against hearsay makes such statements inadmissible because they are unreliable, they are not subject to the scrutiny of cross-examination (where perception, memory, communication, and veracity can be tested), and they deny litigants the opportunity to confront witnesses against them. (*Sir Walter Raleigh*).

Definition of Hearsay

Under Rule 801(a)-(c), hearsay is defined as an out-of-court "statement" (written, oral, or assertive conduct intended as a communication) made by a "declarant," related in court by a witness (the person who heard, read or saw the declarant's out-of-court statement), and that out-of-court statement is being used to "prove the truth of the matter asserted" by the declarant in the declarant's out-of-court statement.

"Statement." Words that are uttered (oral), or written, constitute a statement as long as those words are *intended as a communication* where the declarant has directly or indirectly "asserted" something. Underlying assumptions of the declarant when making the statement, on the other hand, are not assertions and therefore are not statements. Non-verbal, unwritten conduct can also be a statement as long as the declarant engaging in that conduct is intending her actions as a communication. If the declarant's conduct is not intended as an assertion, then a witness can testify about that conduct as simply observed behavior of someone who did not intend her actions or behavior as a communication or assertion of any kind.

<u>"Declarant"</u> A declarant is a human being who makes an out-of-court statement. Do not be confused by arguments that machines (e.g., a clock, or thermometer, or a radar gun) or animals (a blood hound) make assertions. However, human beings who interpret machines, devices, or animal behavior, may make a hearsay assertion and therefore be a declarant behind the machines, devices, or animal behavior.

<u>"To Prove the Truth of the Matter Asserted" by the Declarant"</u> An out-of-court statement intended as a communication/assertion, and related in court by a witness, may still not be considered hearsay if it is being used for some relevant purpose other than to prove the truth of the matter asserted by the declarant in her out-of-court statement. Examples include: (1) impeachment of a witness with a prior inconsistent statement under Rule 613; (2) effect on the listener, reader, or observer (e.g., to show why they may have felt threatened, put on notice, been misled, etc.) (*McClure*); (3) verbal acts (e.g., where the uttered words themselves have legal consequences, such as defamation, threats, perjury, words constituting a contract, etc.) (*Hanson*); (4) circumstantial evidence of declarant's state of mind or belief (e.g., to show declarant must have been afraid, had or lacked certain knowledge, was or was not on notice, had a certain motive, etc.).

Not Hearsay by Definition

Under Rule 801(d), there are two types of statements which fit the definition of hearsay, but are still defined as not hearsay, and might even better be thought of as hearsay exceptions: 801(d)(1) "Prior Statements" (three kinds, (A)-(C)), and 801(d)(2) "Statements/Admissions of a Party Opponent" (five kinds, (A)-(E)).

Not Hearsay by Definition: Prior Statements

Under Rule 801(d)(1), if the declarant is available at trial and subject to cross-examination as a witness, there are three types of prior statements made by the declarant that are admissible and not considered hearsay.

<u>The first is an 801(d)(1)(A) Prior Inconsistent Statement.</u> If the declarant's prior statement is inconsistent with what she is now saying, and that previous statement was made "under oath," and given at a "trial, hearing, deposition, or other proceeding," then that previous statement can be used, not only to impeach the witness/declarant under 613 for saying different things at different times, but the prior inconsistent statement itself is also admissible to be used for its truth. (*Barrett*).

The second is an 801(d)(1)(B) Prior Consistent Statement. If the declarant's prior statement is consistent with what she is now saying, and that previous statement was made BEFORE a charge of recent fabrication or motive to lie, then the previous statement will be admissible to prove that the witness-declarant's story has been consistent all along despite the suggestion that the witness is now lying. (*Tome*). Note that the previous consistent statement need not be made under oath or given at a trial, hearing, deposition, or other proceeding, like a prior inconsistent statement under 801(d)(1)(A). However, if the prior consistent statement is not used to rebut a charge of recent fabrication or motive to lie, then it is considered inadmissible hearsay.

The third is an 801(d)(1)(C) Prior Identification. If the declarant's prior statement is an identification of a person made after perceiving him, then the prior identification will be admissible to prove that the witness-declarant previously identified the person. (*Lewis*). Note that the requirements of being made under oath, at a proceeding, or to rebut a recent charge of fabrication under 801(d)(1) (A) or (B) are not necessary. Prior identifications are considered reliable and are therefore not considered hearsay under the rule.

Not Hearsay by Definition: Statement/Admission of a Party Opponent

Under Rule 801(d)(2), there are five types of statements/admissions of a party that are admissible and not considered hearsay, provided they are used against that party *by the opposing side*. Thus, a party cannot relate his own previous "self-serving" out-of-court statements because such would be considered hearsay.

Personal knowledge is not required and the party can either personally make the statement, adopt the statement as her own, or be considered to have made it if someone else makes a "vicarious" statement who is standing in the shoes of, or duly representing, the party. Therefore, when considering a hearsay statement, you should always check whether the declarant is a party, or legally standing in the shoes of a party, to see if the statement is admissible as a statement/admission of a party opponent.

The first is an 801(d)(2)(A) Party's Own Statement. If a party personally makes a statement, then that statement can be used against the party. (*Jewel*).

The second is an 801(d)(2)(B) Adopted Statement. Even if the party does not personally make the statement, if the party adopts the statement as her own or does something to show a belief in the statement (even by remaining silent), then that statement can be used against the party as though she personally had made it. (*Morgan*).

The third is an 801(d)(2)(C) Statement by Person Authorized. If the party authorizes someone to make statements on her behalf, like some sort of spokes-person or other authorized person, then that "authorized" statement can be used against the party as though she personally had made it. (*Kirk*).

The fourth is an 801(d)(2)(D) Statement by the Party's Agent. If the party has hired someone or has arranged for someone to act as their agent in employment or some other endeavor, and that agent provides a statement that is (1) made in the scope of his employment/agency and (2) made during the existence of that relationship, then that statement of the agent can be used against the party as though she personally had made it. (*Mahlandt*). Note, however, that a statement by a principal is not attributable to her agent.

The fifth is an 801(d)(2)(E) Statement by a Co-Conspirator. If the party is involved in a conspiracy, and a co-conspirator makes a statement that is (1) made during the course and (2) in furtherance of the conspiracy, then that statement of the co-conspirator can be used against the party as though she personally had made it. (*Bourjaily*). Note that for parts (C)-(E), the "vicarious" statements, there is no pure "bootstrapping" allowed, meaning that although the statements them-selves can be considered when determining whether an authorization, agency, or a conspiracy exists, there must also be corroborating evidence showing the existence of these vicarious relationships with the party in question.

Hearsay within Hearsay

Under Rule 805, each "level" or "leg," of hearsay must have an exception if it is to be admissible.

Rule 803 Exceptions

These exceptions to the rule against hearsay can be used regardless of whether the declarant is now available at trial. The most commonly used 803 exceptions are the first eight:

1. 803(1) Present Sense Impression. If a declarant is simultaneously describing or explaining an event or condition when perceiving it, or immediately thereafter, the statement is admissible. Timing is critical, such a statement is reliable because the declarant has little or no time to fabricate. (*Schindler*).

2. 803(2) Excited Utterance. If a declarant makes a statement under the stress of a startling event or condition, caused by, and relating to, the event or condition, the statement is admissible. Timing is not as critical as 803(1), an excited utterance is reliable because the declarant is unlikely to fabricate when under such stress. (*Donovan*).

3. 803(3) Then Existing Mental, Emotional, or Physical Condition. If a declarant makes a statement explaining her own then existing condition (but not a memory or belief about a past event), then the statement is admissible. It is reliable because the declarant has little or no time to fabricate her description of what she is thinking or feeling. This includes current intentions about a future event because although the event may occur in the future, the intent to do something in the future is really a present, then existing, thought. The declarant's intention can serve as circumstantial evidence that the declarant eventually acted on their intention. (*Hillmon*). The same reliability is found when the declarant makes a statement about a then existing physical condition. (*Salinas*).

4. 803(4) Statements for Medical Diagnosis or Treatment. If a declarant makes a statement to receive a medical diagnosis or treatment, such is reliable because the declarant has an incentive not to lie – receiving a correct diagnosis or appropriate medical treatment. Note that this includes statements about PAST conditions relevant to the treatment or diagnosis. Watch for statements that are not necessary to receive a correct diagnosis or medical treatment, especially those involving legal blame. (*Moen*).

5. 803(5) Past Recollection Recorded. If a declarant's recollection cannot be refreshed under Rule 612, it is possible to use a document that contains the declarant's past recollection if the document contains information about which the declarant once had knowledge, cannot now remember, the document was made or adopted by the witness, when the matter was fresh in the mind of the declarant, and the document accurately reflects that knowledge, then that information is admissible. However, note that the document can only be read in open court and is not itself an admitted exhibit. (*Mornan*).

6. 803(6) Records of Regularly Conducted Activity ("Business Records"). If a declarant keeps "business" records of any kind relating to the operation of the business, they may be admissible if: (1) those records are offered through a witness who is a custodian or other qualified witness, (2) the person who made the record had knowledge of the matter, (3) the record was made at or near the time the events or conditions therein occurred, (4) the person had a business duty to do so that was a regular practice of the organization, and (5) the record was kept in the course of that business activity. However, the record must not lack trustworthiness; for example, it was made with an "eye toward litigation," rather than being a record created that was actually necessary to run the business. (*Keogh*).

7. <u>803(7) Absence of Entry of Business Records.</u> The absence of a reord that otherwise should have been there is itself a business record admissible pursuant to the same policy goals and concerns as set forth in 803(6).

8. <u>803(8) Public Records and Reports.</u> This exception is very similar to 803(6), but it involves records of public agencies instead of business. Although the policy concerns and justifications are the same, there are two key differences: (1) in criminal cases, matters observed and recorded in police reports are excluded; and (2) in civil cases (and against the government in criminal cases), factual findings made pursuant to a duty by law are admissible even if those findings include the "opinions and conclusions" of public agency officials. (*Beech Aircraft*).

Rule 804 Exceptions

These exceptions can be used only when the declarant has been deemed "unavailable" under 804(a), such as an exemption/privilege, refusal, lack of memory, death or illness, or inability to procure attendance through reasonable means.

1. <u>804(b)(1) Former Testimony.</u> If a declarant provided the testimony in a prior proceeding, and the party against whom it is now being used was a party in the previous proceeding, and that party had the same motive and opportunity to develop or confront that testimony, then the former testimony is admissible. (*DiNapoli*). Note that in civil cases, the former testimony can be used against someone who was not a party in the former proceeding, provided that party's "predecessor in interest" was a party in the former proceeding and had the same motive and opportunity to develop and confront that testimony.

2. <u>804(b)(2) Statement Under Belief Of Impending Death ("Dying Declaration").</u> If a declarant made a statement based on personal knowledge while under the *belief that* her own death was imminent, and the statement concerned the cause or circumstances of her impending death, then that statement will be admissible. The declarant need not actually die. Note that the exception applies in civil cases and homicide criminal cases only.

3. <u>804(b)(3) Statement Against Interest.</u> If a declarant makes a statement that when made is against her economic or legal interest such that a reasonable person would not make the statement unless it were true, then that statement will be admissible. Note that if the statement is made to exculpate another person from criminal liability, then the statement must have some corroboration so that the declarant is not merely "taking the rap" for some criminal cohort.

4. <u>804(b)(4) Statement of Personal or Family History.</u> The exception is simple deference to a family member who has made a statement about a family history matter.

6. <u>804(b)(6) Forfieture by Wrongdoing.</u> If a party is involved in, or responsible for, a declarant's unavailability, then any statement the declarant made can be used against that party so the party do not profit from her misdeed. (*Gray*). Parties should not be able to "silence" potential witnesses at trial by procuring their absence and then using the rule against hearsay to exclude their out-of-court statements.

Rule 807 Residual ("Catch-All") Exception

The residual exception allows attorneys to argue for the admission of statements that while "close," do not fall within 803 or 804 but still have equivalent guarantees of trustworthiness, address a material matter, are more probative on the issue than any other evidence, and ought to be admitted in the interest of justice. (*Dallas County*). Pre-trial notice of the intent to use this exception is required.

Remaining Rule 803 Exceptions

See Rules 803(9)-(23) for the remaining less commonly used 803 exceptions and consider why they are considered reliable.

Logic Map: Overview of Hearsay

Is the evidence an oral or written assertion?
801(a)(1) — **Yes**

No

Is the evidence nonverbal conduct of a person intended by the person as an assertion?
801(a)(2)

Yes

No ← Was the statement made by a person [declarant]
(as opposed to an automated report)?
801(b)

Yes

No ← Was the statement made out of court?
(One made by the declarant other than while testifying at the trial or hearing)
801(c)

Yes

No ← Is the statement being offered into evidence to prove the truth of the matter asserted?
801(c)

Yes

No ← Is the statement a *Prior Statement by Witness* as defined by 801(d)(1)

No

Yes ← Is the statement an *Admission by Party Opponent* as defined by 801(d)(2)

No

Yes ← Does the statement meet an exception to hearsay exclusion?
Exceptions set out in 803 and 804 — **No**

Evidence
Not Excluded
Under Hearsay Rule

Evidence
Excluded Under
Hearsay Rule

CHAPTER 7

Hearsay and Constitutional Issues

A. The Sixth Amendment and the Hearsay Rule and Its Exceptions

As you read this material, bear in mind that to be admissible against a defendant in a criminal case, evidence must satisfy the requirements of both the Constitution, the Federal Rules of Evidence, and in this case, the hearsay doctrine.

> ### Confrontation Clause of the Sixth Amendment to the United States Constitution
>
> In all criminal prosecutions, the accused shall enjoy the right ... to be confronted with the witnesses against him.

The Confrontation Clause of the Sixth Amendment guarantees a defendant in a criminal case the right to confront witnesses who have given testimony against him. A literal reading of the Clause would lead one to believe that no hearsay statement is admissible when offered against a criminal defendant, unless the declarant is subjected to a face-to-face cross-examination at trial. Courts, however, have never taken such an extreme position. Rather, they have interpreted the clause in light of its underlying purpose, which is to make certain that any statements used at trial are reliable. Unreliability is also the principal concern of the rule against admitting hearsay as testimony. Does this mean that hearsay reliable enough to be admitted as an exception is reliable enough to satisfy the concerns of the Confrontation Clause? The inter-

Make the Connection

The Sixth Amendment also provides in part that the accused ... "shall have the right to have compulsory process for obtaining witness in his favor, and to have the Assistance of Counsel for his defense." This is a topic that will likely be covered in detail in a course on Criminal Procedure.

relationship between the Clause and the hearsay doctrine has taken decades for courts to resolve and still remains unsettled in some areas.

A Brief History of the Confrontation Clause

The Confrontation Clause may have been inspired, in part, by the injustices stemming from the English trial of Sir Walter Raleigh as discussed in Chapter 3. Cases in the United States addressing the issue date back to 1895. One of the first significant Supreme Court decisions regarding the Confrontation Clause was that of *Mattox v. United States*, 156 U.S. 237, 243 (1895). In *Mattox*, the Court observed that "the primary object of the [Confrontation Clause] was to *prevent* depositions or *ex parte* affidavits ... being used against the prisoner in lieu of personal examination and cross-examination of the witness." The Court recognized, however, that public policy and necessity require that a defendant should not be free from justice where a witness in his prior trial has died because it "would be carrying his constitutional protection to an unwarrantable extent."

It's Latin to Me

Ex parte is Latin meaning "from the part" or from one party only, and is usually the term for a hearing without notice to, or argument from, the adversary party.

Mld

On this basis, the Supreme Court admitted testimony given by an unavailable witness in a former trial against the defendant in a subsequent retrial.

During the Warren Court reforms of the 1960's, application of the Clause was greatly broadened. In *Pointer v. Texas*, 380 U.S. 400 (1965), the Court held that the Fourteenth Amendment made the Clause applicable to the states and that testimony in a preliminary hearing could not be admitted against a defendant at trial because the defendant was not represented by counsel and given a "complete and adequate opportunity to cross-examine." But, was the corollary true? Would prior cross-examination be sufficient to satisfy the Clause in all cases? In *Barber v. Page*, 390 U.S. 719 (1968), the Court excluded cross-examined preliminary hearing testimony because here was no showing the witness was unavailable. A similar result was reached in a companion case to *Pointer*, where a co-defendant read parts of his confession implicating

What's That?

The Warren Court era refers to the time period of 1953-1960 when Earl Warren served as the Chief of the United States Supreme Court. As Chief Justice, his term of office was marked by numerous rulings that, among other things, attempted to dismantle racial segregation, increase the rights of criminally accused and further the separation of church and state. Many consider this era to be the high point in the use of judicial power to effect social progress in the United States.

defendant Douglas at trial but refused to answer defense questions. *Douglas v. Alabama*, 380 U.S. 415 (1965).

In *California v. Green,* 399 U.S. 149 (1970), a juvenile made statements to a police officer and at a preliminary hearing where he was cross-examined by defendant Green's lawyer. Both statements incriminated the defendant. At trial, the juvenile was conveniently forgetful about the defendant's involvement, and as a result, the prosecution was permitted to introduce the prior statements into evidence. The Court found that admission of these statements did not violate the Confrontation Clause because the juvenile admitted making them, and because, in the case of the preliminary hearing statement, the defendant had been able to cross-examine the juvenile at the hearing. In either event, the juvenile was subject to cross-examination at trial as to both statements.

ct. reasoned

In *Dutton v. Evans,* 400 U.S. 74 (1970), the defendant was convicted of first-degree murder following a trial in which a witness testified, over objection, concerning a statement an alleged accomplice had made in the prison that had it not been for Dutton, "we wouldn't be in this now." The Court held that Dutton's right of confrontation was not violated by the admission into evidence of the co-conspirator's statement as related by the witness because the defense had an opportunity to cross-examine the witness on the issue of whether the accomplice actually made the statement, the statement was spontaneous and was against co-conspirator's penal interest to make it, and there was "indicia of reliability" that fully warranted its being placed before the jury. The phrase "indicia of reliability" will return as a talisman in the next case, *Ohio v. Roberts*, 448 U.S. 56 (1980).

B. Hearsay Statements By Non-Testifying Declarants

Ohio v. Roberts

Supreme Court of the United States
448 U.S. 56 (1980)

Mr. Justice BLACKMUN delivered the opinion of the Court.

This case presents issues concerning the constitutional propriety of the introduction in evidence of the preliminary hearing testimony of a witness not produced at the defendant's subsequent state criminal trial.

issue

preliminary hearing testimony of witness not at D's subsequent trial.

I

Herschel Roberts ... was charged with forgery of a check in the name of Bernard Isaacs, and with possession of stolen credit cards belonging to Isaacs and his wife Amy.

[handwritten margin note: forgery of a check + possession of stolen credit cards.]

What's That?

A preliminary hearing is a hearing in a criminal case to determine whether there is sufficient evidence to prosecute a person accused of a crime. If sufficient evidence exists, the case may proceed in the trial court. During the hearing, the prosecution presents witnesses who testify under oath, the defendant is represented by counsel who may engage in cross-examination, and the entire proceeding is recorded by a court reporter.

A preliminary hearing was held in Municipal Court. ... Respondent's appointed counsel had seen the Isaacs' daughter, Anita, in the courthouse hallway, and called her as the defense's only witness. Anita Isaacs testified that she knew respondent, and that she had permitted him to use her apartment for several days while she was away. Defense counsel questioned Anita at some length and attempted to elicit from her an admission that she had given respondent checks and the credit cards without informing him that she did not have permission to use them. Anita, however, denied this...

[handwritten margin note: prelim. hearing held]

[handwritten margin note: D's only witness]

[Five subpoenas for four different trial dates were issued to Anita at her parents' Ohio residence. The last three carried a written instruction that Anita should "call before appearing." She was not at the residence when these were executed. She did not telephone and she did not appear at trial].

[handwritten margin note: witness didn't appear @ trial]

[At trial] respondent took the stand and testified that Anita Isaacs had given him her parent's checkbook and credit cards with the understanding that he could use them. Relying on [an Ohio state evidence law] which permits the use of preliminary examination testimony of a witness who "cannot for any reason be produced at trial," the State, on rebuttal offered the transcript of Anita's testimony.

[handwritten margin note: D's testimony]

[handwritten margin note: Ohio law]

What's That?

In this context the term *voir dire* refers to a preliminary examination of a witness to test her competence as a witness.

Asserting a violation of the Confrontation Clause ... defense objected to the use of the [preliminary hearing] transcript. The trial court conducted a voir dire hearing as to its admissibility. Amy Isaacs, [Anita's mother] the sole witness at voir dire, was questioned by both the prosecutor and defense counsel concerning her daughter's whereabouts. Anita, according to her mother, left home for Tucson, Ariz., soon after the preliminary hearing. About a year before the

[handwritten margin note: use of prelim. hearing transcript]

[handwritten margin note: D argued use of transcript violated conf. clause]

trial, a San Francisco social worker was in communication with the Isaacs about a welfare application Anita had filed there. Through the social worker, the Isaacs reached their daughter once by telephone. Since then, however, Anita had called her parents only one other time and had not been in touch with her two sisters. When Anita called, some seven or eight months before trial, she told her parents that she "was traveling" outside Ohio, but did not reveal the place from which she called. Mrs. Isaacs stated that she knew of no way to reach Anita in case of an emergency. Nor did she "know of anybody who knows where she is." The trial court admitted the transcript into evidence. Respondent was convicted on all counts.

[The Supreme Court of Ohio reversed, holding that "since Anita had not been cross-examined at the preliminary hearing and was absent at trial, the introduction of the transcript of her testimony was held to have violated respondent's confrontation rights."]

* * *

II

A

The Court here is called upon to consider once again the relationship between the Confrontation Clause and the hearsay rule with its many exceptions…

The Sixth Amendment's Confrontation Clause, made applicable to the States through the Fourteenth Amendment, provides: "In all criminal prosecutions, the accused shall enjoy the right … to be confronted with the witnesses against him." If one were to read this language literally, it would require, on objection, the exclusion of any statement made by a declarant not present at trial. But, if thus applied, the Clause would abrogate virtually every hearsay exception, a result long rejected as unintended and too extreme.

The historical evidence leaves little doubt, however, that the Clause was intended to exclude some hearsay…

B

The Confrontation Clause operates in two separate ways to restrict the range of admissible hearsay. First, in conformance with the Framers' preference for face-to-face accusation, the Sixth Amendment establishes a rule of necessity. In the usual case (including cases where prior cross-examination has occurred), the prosecution must either produce, or demonstrate the unavailability of, the declarant whose statement it wishes to use against the defendant. [FN1]

(2) trustworthiness (2)

The second aspect operates once a witness is shown to be unavailable. Reflecting its underlying purpose to augment accuracy in the factfinding process by ensuring the defendant an effective means to test adverse evidence, the Clause countenances only hearsay marked with such trustworthiness that "there is no material departure from the reason of the general rule...".

Food for Thought

If the Confrontation Clause is tied so directly to the hearsay doctrine, would this not mean that Sir Walter Raleigh's accusers could argue that the Raleigh-Cobham conspiracy continued throughout the time of Lord Cobham's questioning, and thus the confession should be admitted under the well-rooted hearsay exception for statements by co-conspirators?

indicia of reliability

In sum, when a hearsay declarant is not present for cross-examination at trial, the Confrontation Clause normally requires a showing that he is unavailable. Even then, his statement is admissible only if it bears adequate "indicia of reliability." Reliability can be inferred without more in a case where the evidence falls within a firmly rooted hearsay exception. In other cases, the evidence must be excluded, at least absent a showing of particularized guarantees of trustworthiness.

III

here 1st issue is whether witness's testimony was reliable

We turn first to that aspect of confrontation analysis deemed dispositive by the Supreme Court of Ohio, and answered by it in the negative--whether Anita Isaacs' prior testimony at the preliminary hearing bore sufficient "indicia of reliability." Resolution of this issue requires a careful comparison of this case to *California v. Green* 399 U.S. 149 (1970).

A.

In *Green*, at the preliminary hearing, a youth named Porter identified Green as a drug supplier. When called to the stand at Green's trial, however, Porter professed a lapse of memory. Frustrated in its attempt to adduce live testimony, the prosecution offered Porter's prior statements. The trial judge ruled the evidence admissible, and substantial portions of the preliminary hearing transcript were read to the jury. This Court found no error. Citing the established rule that prior trial testimony is admissible upon retrial if the declarant becomes unavailable, the Court rejected Green's Confrontation Clause attack. It reasoned:

"Porter's statement at the preliminary hearing had already been given under circumstances closely approximating those that surround the typical trial. Porter was under oath; respondent was represented by counsel-the same counsel in fact who later represented him at the trial; respondent had every opportunity to cross-examine Porter as to his statement; and the proceedings were conducted before a judicial tribunal, equipped to provide a judicial record of the hearings."

These factors, the Court concluded, provided all that the Sixth Amendment demands: "substantial compliance with the purposes behind the confrontation requirement."

It's Latin to Me

The term *de minimus* refers to a fact or thing so insignificant that a court may overlook it in deciding an issue or case.

This passage and others in the *Green* opinion suggest that the opportunity to cross-examine at the preliminary hearing--even absent actual cross-examination satisfies the Confrontation Clause. Yet the record showed, and the Court recognized, that defense counsel in fact had cross-examined Porter at the earlier proceeding.

We need not decide whether the Supreme Court of Ohio correctly dismissed statements in *Green* suggesting that the mere opportunity to cross-examine rendered the prior testimony admissible. Nor need we decide whether *de minimis* questioning is sufficient, for defense counsel in this case tested Anita's testimony with the equivalent of significant cross-examination.

Food for Thought

When it comes to interpreting the policies and goals of Constitutional amendments, the Supreme Court sometimes finds it useful to consider jurisprudence and political considerations beyond our borders and in particular, English history because the concerns of the American Founding Fathers were rooted in the English experience. You will see, however, in *Davis v. Washington*, as reproduced below, that the Court refuses to be confined by such history and diverges from not only previous historical concerns but also its own precedent in *Roberts*. What does this say for the staying power of precedent?

An opportunity to cross-examine @ preliminary hearing satisfies Confrontation Clause

B

Counsel's questioning clearly partook of cross-examination as a matter of form. His presentation was replete with leading questions the principal tool and hallmark of cross-examination...

* * *

We are also unpersuaded that *Green* is distinguishable on the ground that Anita Isaacs--unlike the declarant Porter in *Green* -- was not personally available for questioning at trial. This argument ignores the language and logic of *Green*:

> "Porter's statement would, we think, have been admissible at trial even in Porter's absence if Porter had been actually unavailable... That being the case, we do not think a different result should follow where the witness is actually produced."

* * *

Finally, we reject respondent's attempt to fall back on general principles of confrontation, and his argument that this case falls among those in which the Court must undertake a particularized search for "indicia of reliability." Under this theory, the factors previously cited--absence of face-to-face contact at trial, presence of a new attorney, and the lack of classic cross-examination--combine with considerations uniquely tied to Anita to mandate exclusion of her statements. Anita, respondent says, had every reason to lie to avoid prosecution or parental reprobation. Her unknown whereabouts is explicable as an effort to avoid punishment, perjury, or self-incrimination. Given these facts, her prior testimony falls on the unreliable side, and should have been excluded.

In making this argument, respondent in effect asks us to disassociate preliminary hearing testimony previously subjected to cross-examination from previously cross-examined prior-trial testimony, which the Court has deemed generally immune from subsequent confrontation attack. Precedent requires us to decline this invitation. In *Green* the Court found guarantees of trustworthiness in the accouterments of the preliminary hearing itself; there was no mention of the inherent reliability or unreliability of Porter and his story.

In sum, we perceive no reason to resolve the reliability issue differently here than the Court did in *Green*. "Since there was an adequate opportunity to cross-examine [the witness], and counsel... availed himself of that opportunity, the transcript ... bore sufficient 'indicia of reliability' and afforded "'the trier of fact a satisfactory basis for evaluating the truth of the prior statement."

* * *

We conclude that the prosecution carried its burden of demonstrating that Anita was constitutionally unavailable for purposes of respondent's trial.

The judgment of the Supreme Court of Ohio is reversed, and the case is remanded for further proceedings not inconsistent with this opinion.

[Mr. Justice BRENNAN, with whom Mr. Justice MARSHALL and Mr. Justice STEVENS join, dissenting on the grounds that "reasonable efforts" required that the prosecution do more than it did to locate witness Anita Isaacs].

Points for Discussion

a. The *Roberts* Two-Pronged Approach

Ohio v. Roberts presents a two-pronged approach to identifying which hearsay exceptions are admissible against an accused under the Confrontation Clause. *Roberts* says that an unavailable witness's out-of-court statement may be admitted so long as it has adequate indicia of reliability--i.e., falls within a "firmly rooted hearsay exception" or bears particularized guarantees of trustworthiness." But what exactly is a "firmly rooted" hearsay exception? The *Roberts* Court declined specifically to define it. Under this theory, federal cases have generally held that statements falling within any hearsay exception recognized at common law—such as excited utterances or statements for purposes of medical diagnosis—but not statements against penal interest and those offered under the residual clause, are "firmly rooted." Is this because these exceptions are of long-standing or because they have particular inherent reliability, or both?

b. The Requirement of Declarant Unavailablity After *Ohio v. Roberts*

The language of *Roberts* states that "the Confrontation Clause normally requires a showing that [the declarant] is unavailable" before her out-of-court statements may be admitted into evidence. In United States v. Inadi, 475 U.S. 387 (1986), however, the Court held that the requirement of unavailability did not apply to co-conspirators' out-of-court statements which incriminated the defendant. The Court reasoned that the unavailability rule makes sense in the context of past testimony, which is a poor substitute for live testimony at trial, but not for statements by co-conspirators, which are generally more reliable than a declarant's in-court testimony because conspirators are likely to be more candid when talking to each other about their illegal goals than they would be testifying against a co-conspirator at trial. Based on the reasoning in *Inadi,* the Court, in White v. Illinois, 502 U.S. 346 (1992), went even further by stating that "*Roberts* stands for the proposition that unavailability analysis is a necessary part of Confrontation Clause inquiry only when the challenged out-of-court statements were made in the court of a prior judicial proceeding" and that a hearsay statement that is firmly rooted is "...so trustworthy that adversarial testing can be expected to add little to its reliability."

Thus the Court seemed at this point in time to have recognized that if a hearsay statement is deemed reliable, the Confrontation Clause is satisfied, and this reliability is determined either by reference to traditional hearsay exceptions or a judicial determination of reliability. Is this all the Clause contemplates? Do you agree with the Court's reasoning in *White* that "firmly rooted" hearsay exceptions are so reliable they need little cross-examination? Consider a murder case in which the victim tells her mother she is leaving to meet her boyfriend, and she is found dead two weeks later. If the boyfriend is tried for murder, this statement might be admissible under Rule 803(3) as a statement of her intent to meet her boyfriend to prove her boyfriend had the opportunity to murder her. If you are the boyfriend's attorney, would you agree that this statement is so trustworthy that your cross-examination of declarant, were she alive, would do little to test its reliability? What cross-examination questions might you want to ask her about her statement if you could? Consider statements made by a defendant's accomplice to a police officer that qualify as present sense impressions or excited utterances. How reliable are they without cross-examination?

Crawford v. Washington

Supreme Court of the United States
541 U.S. 36 (2004)

Justice SCALIA delivered the opinion of the Court.

* * *

I

On August 5, 1999, Kenneth Lee was stabbed at his apartment. Police arrested petitioner later that night. After giving petitioner and his wife Miranda warnings, detectives interrogated each of them twice. Petitioner eventually confessed that he and Sylvia had gone in search of Lee because he was upset over an earlier incident in which Lee had tried to rape her. The two had found Lee at his apartment, and a fight ensued in which Lee was stabbed in the torso and petitioner's hand was cut.

[Petitioner thought he saw something in Lee's hands, but he was not positive].

Sylvia generally corroborated petitioner's story about the events leading up to the fight, but her account of the fight itself was arguably different-particularly with respect to whether Lee had drawn a weapon before petitioner assaulted him:

[Handwritten margin notes: "D stabbed Lee + confessed" and "D's wife's testimony regarding fight differed from D's."]

"Q. Did Kenny do anything to fight back from this assault?

"A. (pausing) I know he reached into his pocket or somethin' … I don't know what.

"Q. After he was stabbed?

"A. He saw Michael coming up. He lifted his hand … his chest open, he might [have] went to go strike his hand out or something and then (inaudible).

"Q. Okay, you, you gotta speak up.

"A. Okay, he lifted his hand over his head maybe to strike Michael's hand down or something and then he put his hands in his … put his right hand in his right pocket … took a step back … Michael proceeded to stab him … then his hands were like … how do you explain this … open arms … with his hands open and he fell down … and we ran (describing subject holding hands open, palms toward assailant).

"Q. Okay, when he's standing there with his open hands, you're talking about Kenny, correct?

"A. Yeah, after, after the fact, yes.

"Q. Did you see anything in his hands at that point?

"A. (pausing) um um (no)."

The State charged petitioner with assault and attempted murder. At trial, he claimed self-defense. Sylvia did not testify because of the state marital privilege, which generally bars a spouse from testifying without the other spouse's consent. In Washington, this privilege does not extend to a spouse's out-of-court statements admissible under a hearsay exception, so the State sought to introduce Sylvia's tape-recorded statements to the police as evidence that the stabbing was not in self-defense. Noting that Sylvia had admitted she led petitioner to Lee's apartment and thus had facilitated the assault, the State invoked the hearsay exception for statements against penal interest.

Petitioner countered that, state law notwithstanding, admitting the evidence would violate his federal constitutional right to be "confronted with the witnesses against him." According to our description of that right in *Ohio v. Roberts*, 448 U.S. 56 (1980), it does not bar admission of an unavailable witness's statement against a criminal defendant if the statement bears "adequate 'indicia of reliability.'" To meet that test, evidence must either fall within a "firmly rooted hearsay exception" or bear "particularized guarantees of trustworthiness." The trial court here admitted the statement on the latter ground, offering several reasons why it was trustworthy: Sylvia was not shifting blame but rather corroborating her husband's story that he acted in self-defense or "justified reprisal"; she had direct knowledge as an eyewitness; she was describing recent events; and she was being questioned by a "neutral" law enforcement officer. The prosecution played the tape for the jury and relied on it in closing, arguing that it was "damning evidence" that "completely refutes [petitioner's] claim of self-defense." The jury convicted petitioner of assault.

The Washington Court of Appeals reversed... We granted certiorari to determine whether the State's use of Sylvia's statement violated the Confrontation Clause.

II

The Sixth Amendment's Confrontation Clause provides that, "[i]n all criminal prosecutions, the accused shall enjoy the right ... to be confronted with the witnesses against him." We have held that this bedrock procedural guarantee applies to both federal and state prosecutions. *Ohio v. Roberts.* As noted above, *Roberts* says that an unavailable witness's out-of-court statement may be admitted so long as it has adequate indicia of reliability--i.e., falls within a "firmly rooted hearsay exception" or bears "particularized guarantees of trustworthiness." Petitioner argues that this test strays from the original meaning of the Confrontation Clause and urges us to reconsider it.

[handwritten margin note: unavailable witness's out of ct. statement admissible when]

A

The Constitution's text does not alone resolve this case. One could plausibly read "witnesses against" a defendant to mean those who actually testify at trial, those whose statements are offered at trial, or something in-between. We must therefore turn to the historical background of the Clause to understand its meaning.

The right to confront one's accusers is a concept that dates back to Roman times. The founding generation's immediate source of the concept, however, was the common law. English common law has long differed from continental civil law in regard to the manner in which witnesses give testimony in criminal trials. The common-law tradition is one of live testimony in court subject to adversarial testing, while the civil law condones examination in private by judicial officers.

Nonetheless, England at times adopted elements of the civil-law practice. Justices of the peace or other officials examined suspects and witnesses before trial. These examinations were sometimes read in court in lieu of live testimony, a practice that "occasioned frequent demands by the prisoner to have his 'accusers,' i.e. the witnesses against him, brought before him face to face."

. . .

Through a series of statutory and judicial reforms, English law developed a right of confrontation that limited these abuses. For example, treason statutes required witnesses to confront the accused "face to face" at his arraignment. Courts, meanwhile, developed relatively strict rules of unavailability, admitting examinations only if the witness was demonstrably unable to testify in person. Several authorities also stated that a suspect's confession could be admitted only against himself, and not against others he implicated.

One recurring question was whether the admissibility of an unavailable witness's pretrial examination depended on whether the defendant had had an opportunity to cross-examine him. In 1696, the Court of King's Bench answered this question in the affirmative, in the widely reported misdemeanor libel case of *King v. Paine*, 87 Eng. Rep. 584. The court ruled that, even though a witness was dead, his examination was not admissible where "the defendant not being present when [it was] taken before the mayor ... had lost the benefit of a cross-examination...".

. . .

B

Controversial examination practices were also used in the Colonies. Early in the 18th century, for example, the Virginia Council protested against the Governor for having "privately issued several commissions to examine witnesses against particular men *ex parte*," complaining that "the person accused is not admitted to be confronted with, or defend himself against his defamers."

Many declarations of rights adopted around the time of the Revolution guaranteed a right of confrontation.

* * *

III

This history supports two inferences about the meaning of the Sixth Amendment.

A

First, the principal evil at which the Confrontation Clause was directed was the civil-law mode of criminal procedure, and particularly its use of *ex parte* examinations as evidence against the accused. It was these practices that the Crown deployed in notorious treason cases like Raleigh's; that the Marian statutes invited; that English law's assertion of a right to confrontation was meant to prohibit; and that the founding-era rhetoric decried. The Sixth Amendment must be interpreted with this focus in mind.

Accordingly, we once again reject the view that the Confrontation Clause applies of its own force only to in-court testimony, and that its application to out-of-court statements introduced at trial depends upon "the law of Evidence for the time being." Leaving the regulation of out-of-court statements to the law of evidence would render the Confrontation Clause powerless to prevent even the most flagrant inquisitorial practices. Raleigh was, after all, perfectly free to confront those who read Cobham's confession in court.

Food for Thought

But didn't *Ohio v. Roberts* hold that "firmly rooted" hearsay exceptions would pass Constitutional muster? That is, exceptions which had their roots in centuries of English and American jurisprudence?

This focus also suggests that not all hearsay implicates the Sixth Amendment's core concerns. An off-hand, overheard remark might be unreliable evidence and thus a good candidate for exclusion under hearsay rules, but it bears little resemblance to the civil-law abuses the Confrontation Clause targeted. On the other hand, *ex parte* examinations might sometimes be admissible under modern hearsay rules, but the Framers certainly would not have condoned them.

The text of the Confrontation Clause reflects this focus. It applies to "witnesses" against the accused-in other words, those who "bear testimony." "Testimony," in turn, is typically "[a] solemn declaration or affirmation made for the purpose of establishing or proving some fact." An accuser who makes a formal statement to government officers bears testimony in a sense that a person who makes a casual remark to an acquaintance does not. The constitutional text, like the history underlying the common-law right of confrontation, thus reflects an especially acute concern with a specific type of out-of-court statement.

Various formulations of this core class of "testimonial" statements exist: " *ex parte* in-court testimony or its functional equivalent--that is, material such as affidavits, custodial examinations, prior testimony that the defendant was unable to cross-examine, or similar pretrial statements that declarants would reasonably expect to be used prosecutorially;" "extrajudicial statements ... contained in formalized testimonial materials, such as affidavits, depositions, prior testimony, or confessions;" "statements that were made under circumstances which would lead an objective witness reasonably to believe that the statement would be available for use at a later trial." These formulations all share a common nucleus and then define the Clause's coverage at various levels of abstraction around it. Regardless

[handwritten margin notes: "conf. clause applies to: testimony is"; "ex parte in-court testimony or equivalent"]

of the precise articulation, some statements qualify under any definition -- for example, *ex parte* testimony at a preliminary hearing.

Statements taken by police officers in the course of interrogations are also testimonial under even a narrow standard. Police interrogations bear a striking resemblance to examinations by justices of the peace in England. The statements are not sworn testimony, but the absence of oath was not dispositive. Cobham's examination was unsworn, yet Raleigh's trial has long been thought a paradigmatic confrontation violation. Under the Marian statutes, witnesses were typically put on oath, but suspects were not. Yet Hawkins and others went out of their way to caution that such unsworn confessions were not admissible against anyone but the confessor.

[handwritten margin note: police interrogations are testimonial]

That interrogators are police officers rather than magistrates does not change the picture either. Justices of the peace conducting examinations under the Marian statutes were not magistrates as we understand that office today, but had an essentially investigative and prosecutorial function. England did not have a professional police force until the 19th century, so it is not surprising that other government officers performed the investigative functions now associated primarily with the police. The involvement of government officers in the production of testimonial evidence presents the same risk, whether the officers are police or justices of the peace.

In sum, even if the Sixth Amendment is not solely concerned with testimonial hearsay, that is its primary object, and interrogations by law enforcement officers fall squarely within that class. (We use the term "interrogation" in its colloquial, rather than any technical legal, sense. Just as various definitions of "testimonial" exist, one can imagine various definitions of "interrogation," and we need not select among them in this case. Sylvia's recorded statement, knowingly given in response to structured police questioning, qualifies under any conceivable definition.)

B

The historical record also supports a second proposition: that the Framers would not have allowed admission of testimonial statements of a witness who did not appear at trial unless he was unavailable to testify, and the defendant had had a prior opportunity for cross-examination. The text of the Sixth Amendment does not suggest any open-ended exceptions from the confrontation requirement to be developed by the courts. Rather, the "right ... to be confronted with the witnesses against him," is most naturally read as a reference to the right of confrontation at common law, admitting only those exceptions established at the time of the founding. See *Mattox v. United States*, 156 U.S. 237 (1895). As the English authorities above reveal, the common law in 1791 conditioned admissibility of an absent witness's examination on unavailability and a prior opportunity to cross-examine. The Sixth Amendment therefore incorporates those limitations… (The one deviation we have found involves dying declarations. The existence of that exception as a general rule of criminal hearsay law cannot be disputed. Although many dying declarations may not be testimonial, there is authority for admitting even those that clearly are. We need not decide in this case whether the Sixth Amendment incorporates an exception for testimonial dying declarations. If this exception must be accepted on historical grounds, it is *sui generis*)

We do not read the historical sources to say that a prior opportunity to cross-examine was merely a sufficient, rather than a necessary, condition for admissibility of testimonial statements. They suggest that this requirement was dispositive, and not merely one of several ways to establish reliability…

IV

Our case law has been largely consistent with these two principles. Our leading early decision, for example, involved a deceased witness's prior trial testimony. *Mattox v. United States.* In allowing the statement to be admitted, we relied on the fact that the defendant had had, at the first trial, an adequate opportunity to confront the witness…

Our later cases conform to *Mattox's* holding that prior trial or preliminary hearing testimony is admissible only if the defendant had an adequate opportunity to cross-examine. Even where the defendant had such an opportunity, we excluded the testimony where the government had not established unavailability of the witness. We similarly excluded accomplice confessions where the defendant had no opportunity to cross-examine. In contrast, we considered reliability factors beyond prior opportunity for cross-examination when the hearsay statement at issue was not testimonial.

[handwritten margin note: When not testimonial]

Even our recent cases, in their outcomes, hew closely to the traditional line. *Ohio v. Roberts*, admitted testimony from a preliminary hearing at which the defendant had examined the witness. Lilly v. Virginia, 527 U.S. 116 (1999) excluded testimonial statements that the defendant had had no opportunity to test by cross-examination. And Bourjaily v. United States, 483 U.S. 171 (1987), admitted statements made unwittingly to a Federal Bureau of Investigation informant after applying a more general test that did not make prior cross-examination an indispensable requirement. [FN4]

* * *

Our cases have thus remained faithful to the Framers' understanding: Testimonial statements of witnesses absent from trial have been admitted only where the declarant is unavailable, and only where the defendant has had a prior opportunity to cross-examine.

Rule

Finally, we reiterate that, when the declarant appears for cross-examination at trial, the Confrontation Clause places no constraints at all on the use of his prior testimonial statements. It is therefore irrelevant that the reliability of some out-of-court statements " 'cannot be replicated, even if the declarant testifies to the same matters in court.' " The Clause does not bar admission of a statement so long as the declarant is present at trial to defend or explain it. (The Clause also does not bar the use of testimonial statements for purposes other than establishing the truth of the matter asserted.)

when cross-examined @ trial

V

Although the results of our decisions have generally been faithful to the original meaning of the Confrontation Clause, the same cannot be said of our rationales. *Roberts* conditions the admissibility of all hearsay evidence on whether it falls under a "firmly rooted hearsay exception" or bears "particularized guarantees of trustworthiness." This test departs from the historical principles identified above in two respects. First, it is too broad: It applies the same mode of analysis whether or not the hearsay consists of *ex parte* testimony. This often results in close constitutional scrutiny in cases that are far removed from the core concerns of the Clause. At the same time, however, the test is too narrow: It admits statements that do consist of *ex parte* testimony upon a mere finding of reliability. This malleable standard often fails to protect against paradigmatic confrontation violations.

different rationale

Members of this Court and academics have suggested that we revise our doctrine to reflect more accurately the original understanding of the Clause. They offer two proposals: First, that we apply the Confrontation Clause only to testimonial statements, leaving the remainder to regulation by hearsay law-thus eliminating the overbreadth referred to above. Second, that we impose an absolute bar to statements that are testimonial, absent a prior opportunity to cross-examine-thus eliminating the excessive narrowness referred to above.

In *White v. Illinois*, we considered the first proposal and rejected it. Although our analysis in this case casts doubt on that holding, we need not definitively resolve whether it survives our decision today, because Sylvia Crawford's statement is testimonial under any definition. This case does, however, squarely implicate the second proposal.

A

Where testimonial statements are involved, we do not think the Framers meant to leave the Sixth Amendment's protection to the vagaries of the rules of evidence, much less to amorphous notions of "reliability." Certainly none of the authorities discussed above acknowledges any general reliability exception to the common-law rule. Admitting statements deemed reliable by a judge is fundamentally at odds with the right of confrontation. To be sure, the Clause's ultimate goal is to ensure reliability of evidence, but it is a procedural rather than a substantive guarantee. It commands not that evidence be reliable, but that reliability be assessed in a particular manner: by testing in the crucible of cross-examination. The Clause thus reflects a judgment, not only about the desirability of reliable evidence (a point on which there could be little dissent), but about how reliability can best be determined.

The *Roberts* test allows a jury to hear evidence, untested by the adversary process, based on a mere judicial determination of reliability. It thus replaces the constitutionally prescribed method of assessing reliability with a wholly foreign one. In this respect, it is very different from exceptions to the Confrontation Clause that make no claim to be a surrogate means of assessing reliability. For example, the rule of forfeiture by wrongdoing (which we accept) extinguishes confrontation claims on essentially equitable grounds; it does not purport to be an alternative means of determining reliability.

> **Make the Connection**
>
> The Court here is referring to Rule 804(b)(6), the forfeiture by wrongdoing exception.

The Raleigh trial itself involved the very sorts of reliability determinations that *Roberts* authorizes. In the face of Raleigh's repeated demands for confrontation, the prosecution responded with many of the arguments a court applying *Roberts* might invoke today: that Cobham's statements were self-inculpatory, that they were not made in the heat of passion, and that they were not "extracted from [him] upon any hopes or promise of Pardon." It is not plausible that the Framers' only objection to the trial was that Raleigh's judges did not properly weigh these factors before sentencing him to death. Rather, the problem was that the judges refused to allow Raleigh to confront Cobham in court, where he could cross-examine him and try to expose his accusation as a lie.

Dispensing with confrontation because testimony is obviously reliable is akin to dispensing with jury trial because a defendant is obviously guilty. This is not what the Sixth Amendment prescribes.

B

The legacy of *Roberts* in other courts vindicates the Framers' wisdom in rejecting a general reliability exception. The framework is so unpredictable that it fails to provide meaningful protection from even core confrontation violations.

* * *

The unpardonable vice of the *Roberts* test, however, is not its unpredictability, but its demonstrated capacity to admit core testimonial statements that the Confrontation Clause plainly meant to exclude. Despite the plurality's speculation in *Lilly* that it was "highly unlikely" that accomplice confessions implicating the accused could survive *Roberts*, courts continue routinely to admit them. One recent study found that, after *Lilly*, appellate courts admitted accomplice statements to the authorities in 25 out of 70 cases-more than one-third of the time. Courts have invoked *Roberts* to admit other sorts of plainly testimonial statements despite the absence of any opportunity to cross-examine. [Here, the Court cites cases admitting statements made at plea allocutions, in front of a grand jury, and prior trial testimony]. To add insult to injury, some of the courts that admit untested testimonial statements find reliability in the very factors that make the statements testimonial. As noted earlier, one court relied on the fact that the witness's statement was made to police while in custody on pending charges--the theory being that this made the statement more clearly against penal interest and thus more reliable. Other courts routinely rely on the fact that a prior statement is given under oath in judicial proceedings. That inculpating statements are given in a testimonial setting is not an antidote to the confrontation problem, but rather the trigger that makes the Clause's demands most urgent. It is not enough to point out that most of the usual safeguards of the adversary process attend the statement, when the single safeguard missing is the one the Confrontation Clause demands.

C

Roberts' failings were on full display in the proceedings below. Sylvia Crawford made her statement while in police custody, herself a potential suspect in the case. Indeed, she had been told that whether she would be released "depend[ed] on how the investigation continues." In response to often leading questions from police detectives, she implicated her husband in Lee's stabbing and at least arguably undermined his self-defense claim. Despite all this, the trial court admitted her statement, listing several reasons why it was reliable. In its opinion reversing, the Court of Appeals listed several other reasons why the statement was not reliable. Finally, the State Supreme Court relied exclusively on the interlocking character of the statement and disregarded every other factor the lower courts had considered. The case is thus a self-contained demonstration of Roberts' unpredictable and inconsistent application.

Each of the courts also made assumptions that cross-examination might well have undermined. The trial court, for example, stated that Sylvia Crawford's statement was reliable because she was an eyewitness with direct knowledge of the events. But Sylvia at one point told the police that she had "shut [her] eyes and ... didn't really watch" part of the fight, and that she was "in shock." The trial court also buttressed its reliability finding by claiming that Sylvia was "being questioned by law enforcement, and, thus, the [questioner] is ... neutral to her and not someone who would be inclined to advance her interests and shade her version of the truth unfavorably toward the defendant." The Framers would be astounded to learn that *ex parte* testimony could be admitted against a criminal defendant because it was elicited by "neutral" government officers. But even if the court's assessment of the officer's motives was accurate, it says nothing about Sylvia's perception of her situation. Only cross-examination could reveal that.

The [Washington] State Supreme Court gave dispositive weight to the interlocking nature of the two statements-that they were both ambiguous as to when and whether Lee had a weapon. The court's claim that the two statements were equally ambiguous is hard to accept. Petitioner's statement is ambiguous only in the sense that he had lingering doubts about his recollection: "A. I could a swore I seen him goin' for somethin' before, right before everything happened ... [B]ut I'm not positive." Sylvia's statement, on the other hand, is truly inscrutable, since the key timing detail was simply assumed in the leading question she was asked: "Q. Did Kenny do anything to fight back from this assault?" Moreover, Sylvia specifically said Lee had nothing in his hands after he was stabbed, while petitioner was not asked about that.

The prosecutor obviously did not share the court's view that Sylvia's statement was ambiguous -- he called it "damning evidence" that "completely refutes [petitioner's] claim of self-defense." We have no way of knowing whether the jury agreed with the prosecutor or the court. Far from obviating the need for cross-examination, the "interlocking" ambiguity of the two statements made it all the more imperative that they be tested to tease out the truth.

We readily concede that we could resolve this case by simply reweighing the "reliability factors" under *Roberts* and finding that Sylvia Crawford's statement falls short. But we view this as one of those rare cases in which the result below is so improbable that it reveals a fundamental failure on our part to interpret the Constitution in a way that secures its intended constraint on judicial discretion. Moreover, to reverse the Washington Supreme Court's decision after conducting our own reliability analysis would perpetuate, not avoid, what the Sixth Amendment condemns. The Constitution prescribes a procedure for determining the reliability of testimony in criminal trials, and we, no less than the state courts, lack authority to replace it with one of our own devising.

We have no doubt that the courts below were acting in utmost good faith when they found reliability. The Framers, however, would not have been content to indulge this assumption. They knew that judges, like other government officers, could not always be trusted to safeguard the rights of the people; the likes of the dread Lord Jeffreys were not yet too distant a memory. They were loath to leave too much discretion in judicial hands. By replacing categorical constitutional guarantees with open-ended balancing tests, we do violence to their design.

What's That?

The Court is probably referring to George Jeffreys, the English judge who presided at the Bloody Assizes, a series of trials in 1685 after the Monmouth Rebellion. In one set of trials, more than 1400 prisoners were sentenced to death, although only about 300 were hanged or drawn and quartered. More than 800 other prisoners were transported to the West Indies as a cheap source of brutal labor.

Vague standards are manipulable, and, while that might be a small concern in run-of-the-mill assault prosecutions like this one, the Framers had an eye toward politically charged cases like Raleigh's-great state trials where the impartiality of even those at the highest levels of the judiciary might not be so clear. It is difficult to imagine Roberts' providing any meaningful protection in those circumstances.

* * *

Where nontestimonial hearsay is at issue, it is wholly consistent with the Framers' design to afford the States flexibility in their development of hearsay law-as does *Roberts*, and as would an approach that exempted such statements from Confrontation Clause scrutiny altogether. Where testimonial evidence is at issue, however, the Sixth Amendment demands what the common law required: unavailability and a prior opportunity for cross-examination. We leave for another day any effort to spell out a comprehensive definition of "testimonial." (We acknowledge the Chief Justice's objection that our refusal to articulate a comprehensive definition in this case will cause interim uncertainty. But it can hardly be any worse than the status quo and cases cited. The difference is that the *Roberts* test is inherently, and therefore permanently, unpredictable.) Whatever else the term covers, it applies at a minimum to prior testimony at a preliminary hearing, before a grand jury, or at a former trial; and to police interrogations. These are the modern practices with closest kinship to the abuses at which the Confrontation Clause was directed.

In this case, the State admitted Sylvia's testimonial statement against petitioner, despite the fact that he had no opportunity to cross-examine her. That alone is sufficient to make out a violation of the Sixth Amendment. *Roberts* notwithstanding, we decline to mine the record in search of indicia of reliability. Where testimonial statements are at issue, the only indicium of reliability sufficient to satisfy constitutional demands is the one the Constitution actually prescribes: confrontation.

The judgment of the Washington Supreme Court is reversed, and the case is remanded for further proceedings not inconsistent with this opinion.

[Chief Justice REHNQUIST, with whom Justice O'CONNOR joins, concurring in the judgment but dissenting from the Court's decision to overrule *Ohio v. Roberts* on the basis that the majority's distinction between testimonial and non-testimonial statements "is no better rooted in history than" the current doctrine, that the case could have been decided on the basis of *Idaho v. Wright,* and that the Court's failure to articulate a definition in the case will cause uncertainty in the courts below].

———

Points for Discussion

a. Has the Court totally repudiated *Roberts*?

Rather than recognizing that the Confrontation Clause parallels the hearsay rule and its exceptions, as the Court did in *Roberts,* the Court in *Crawford* attempts to divide hearsay into two groups: testimonial and non-testimonial. Even if a testimonial statement falls within a "firmly rooted" hearsay exception, it may not be admitted against a criminal defendant without her having had a prior opportunity to cross-examine and without a prosecutorial showing that the declarant is unavailable. Whether non-testimonial statements are admissible against a criminal defendant is still an open question under *Crawford.* The Court might decide that *Roberts* still applies to non-testimonial statements, or that the Confrontation Clause need not be considered at all. Based upon what you have read so far, which approach seems more likely?

b. What Exactly Is a Testimonial Statement?

The key to *Crawford's* analysis is the term "testimonial." Does the Court offer its own definition of the word or just quote others? Certainly, at minimum, the term applies to eye-witness statements incriminating the defendant made to a police officer, as was the situation in *Crawford.* The Court also affirms that "*ex parte* in-court testimony or its functional equivalent—that is, material such as affidavits, custodial examinations, prior testimony that the defendant was unable to cross-examine, or similar pretrial statements that declarants would reasonably expect to be used prosecutorially"—would qualify. The Court also declares that "statements that were made under circumstances which would lead an objective witness reasonably to believe that the statement would be available for use at a later trial" is a testimonial one. Under these definitions, would statements made voluntarily to police officers qualify? How about statements made to other government workers, such as probation officers, social workers, teachers, or medical personnel such as doctors conducting a "rape kit" examination? Are these examples any different than statements made to acquaintances or friends where the declarant is aware they made be used against the defendant in a criminal proceeding? The Court criticizes the *Roberts* test as being too subjective. Can the same be said for the test in *Crawford*?

c. Reconciling *Crawford* with Specific Hearsay Statements

The Court in *Crawford* defined statements made by co-conspirators in furtherance of a conspiracy as non-testimonial. Does this mean that in a situation such as *Bourjaily*, where the co-conspirator makes a statement to an undercover government informant, that the statement should be declared non-testimonial? Is it the declarant's lack of knowledge of the informant's identity that prevents the statement from being testimonial? *Crawford* specifically refers to the *Bourjaily* outcome with approval. Why? After *Crawford*, are dying declarations made to police officers claiming the defendant was the cause of the declarant's death testimonial? Would it matter whether the officer questioned the declarant or whether the declarant's statements were spontaneous?

Hypo 7.1

A three year old child tells her mother that her father touched and hurt her in a private place and that she did not like it. She also tells her pediatrician and a social worker the same thing. Would her statements be considered testimonial under *Crawford*? Do you think a three-year-old has a subjective understanding that her statements could be used against her father in a criminal trial? Do you think there should be a blanket exception for incriminating statements made by children under a certain age?

Davis v. Washington

Supreme Court of the United States
547 U.S. 813 (2006)

Justice SCALIA delivered the opinion of the Court.

issue

[There are two cases that the Court considers in this opinion, *Davis v. Washington* and *Hammon v. Indiana*]. These cases require us to determine when statements made to law enforcement personnel during a 911 call or at a crime scene are "testimonial" and thus subject to the requirements of the Sixth Amendment's Confrontation Clause.

I

A

The relevant statements in *Davis v. Washington* were made to a 911 emergency operator on February 1, 2001. When the operator answered the initial call, the connection terminated before anyone spoke. She reversed the call, and Michelle McCottry answered. In the ensuing conversation, the operator ascertained that McCottry was involved in a domestic disturbance with her former boyfriend Adrian Davis, the petitioner in this case:

"911 Operator: Hello.

"Complainant: Hello.

"911 Operator: What's going on?

"Complainant: He's here jumpin' on me again.

"911 Operator: Okay. Listen to me carefully. Are you in a house or an apartment?

"Complainant: I'm in a house.

"911 Operator: Are there any weapons?

"Complainant: No. He's usin' his fists.

"911 Operator: Okay. Has he been drinking?

"Complainant: No.

"911 Operator: Okay, sweetie. I've got help started. Stay on the line with me, okay?

"Complainant: I'm on the line.

"911 Operator: Listen to me carefully. Do you know his last name?"

"Complainant: It's Davis.

"911 Operator: Davis? Okay, what's his first name?"

"Complainant: Adrian

"911 Operator: What is it?"

"Complainant: Adrian.

"911 Operator: Adrian?"

"Complainant: Yeah.

"911 Operator: Okay. What's his middle initial?"

"Complainant: Martell. He's runnin' now."

As the conversation continued, the operator learned that Davis had "just r[un] out the door" after hitting McCottry, and that he was leaving in a car with someone else. McCottry started talking, but the operator cut her off, saying, "Stop talking and answer my questions." She then gathered more information about Davis (including his birthday), and learned that Davis had told McCottry that his purpose in coming to the house was "to get his stuff," since McCottry was moving. McCottry described the context of the assault, after which the operator told her that the police were on their way. "They're gonna check the area for him first," the operator said, "and then they're gonna come talk to you."

The police arrived within four minutes of the 911 call and observed McCottry's shaken state, the "fresh injuries on her forehead and her face," and her "frantic efforts to gather her belongings and her children so that they could leave the residence."

The State charged Davis with felony violation of a domestic no-contact order. "The State's only witnesses were the two police officers who responded to the 911 call. Both officers testified that McCottry exhibited injuries that appeared to be recent, but neither officer could testify as to the cause of the injuries." McCottry presumably could have testified as to whether Davis was her assailant, but she did not appear. Over Davis's objection, based on the Confrontation Clause of the Sixth Amendment, the trial court admitted the recording of her exchange with the 911 operator, and the jury convicted him. We granted certiorari.

B

In *Hammon v. Indiana*, police responded late on the night of February 26, 2003, to a "reported domestic disturbance" at the home of Hershel and Amy Hammon.. They found Amy alone on the front porch, appearing " 'somewhat frightened,' but she told them that 'nothing was the matter.' " She gave them permission to enter the house, where an officer saw "a gas heating unit in the corner of the living room" that had "flames coming out of the ... partial glass front. There were pieces of glass on the ground in front of it and there was flame emitting from the front of the heating unit."

Hershel, meanwhile, was in the kitchen. He told the police "that he and his wife had 'been in an argument' but 'everything was fine now' and the argument 'never became physical.' " By this point Amy had come back inside. One of the officers remained with Hershel; the other went to the living room to talk with Amy, and "again asked [her] what had occurred." Hershel made several attempts to participate in Amy's conversation with the police but was rebuffed. The officer later testified that Hershel "became angry when I insisted that [he] stay separated from Mrs. Hammon so that we can investigate what had happened." After hearing Amy's account, the officer "had her fill out and sign a battery affidavit." Amy handwrote the following: "Broke our Furnace & shoved me down on the floor into the broken glass. Hit me in the chest and threw me down. Broke our lamps & phone. Tore up my van where I couldn't leave the house. Attacked my daughter."

The State charged Hershel with domestic battery and with violating his probation. Amy was subpoenaed, but she did not appear at his subsequent bench trial. The State called the officer who had questioned Amy, and asked him to recount what Amy told him and to authenticate the affidavit. Hershel's counsel repeatedly objected to the admission of this evidence. [T]he trial court admitted the affidavit as a "present sense impression," and Amy's statements as "excited utterances" that "are expressly permitted in these kinds of cases even if the declarant is not available to testify." The officer thus testified that Amy "informed me that she and Hershel had been in an argument. That he became irrate [sic] over the fact of their daughter going to a boyfriend's house. The argument became ... physical after being verbal and she informed me that Mr. Hammon, during the verbal part of the argument was breaking things in the living room and I believe she stated he broke the phone, broke the lamp, broke the front of the heater. When it became physical he threw her down into the glass of the heater. "She informed me Mr. Hammon had pushed her onto the ground, had shoved her head into the broken glass of the heater and that he had punched her in the chest twice I believe."

The trial judge found Hershel guilty on both charges, [and the Indiana Supreme Court also affirmed]. We granted certiorari.

II

The Confrontation Clause of the Sixth Amendment provides: "In all criminal prosecutions, the accused shall enjoy the right ... to be confronted with the witnesses against him." In <u>Crawford v. Washington, 541 U.S. 36 (2004)</u>, we held that this provision bars "admission of testimonial statements of a witness who did not appear at trial unless he was unavailable to testify, and the defendant had had a prior opportunity for cross-examination." A critical portion of this holding, and the portion central to resolution of the two cases now before us, is the phrase "testimonial statements." Only statements of this sort cause the declarant to be a "witness" within the meaning of the Confrontation Clause. It is the testimonial character of the statement that separates it from other hearsay that, while subject to traditional limitations upon hearsay evidence, is not subject to the Confrontation Clause.

Our opinion in *Crawford* set forth "[v]arious formulations" of the core class of "'testimonial'"statements, but found it unnecessary to endorse any of them, because "some statements qualify under any definition." Among those, we said, were "[s]tatements taken by police officers in the course of interrogations." The questioning that generated the deponent's statement in *Crawford*--which was made and recorded while she was in police custody, after having been given Miranda warnings as a possible suspect herself--"qualifies under any conceivable definition" of an " 'interrogation' " We therefore did not define that term, except to say that "[w]e use [it] ... in its colloquial, rather than any technical legal, sense," and that "one can imagine various definitions ..., and we need not select among them in this case." The character of the statements in the present cases is not as clear, and these cases require us to determine more precisely which police interrogations produce testimony.

Without attempting to produce an exhaustive classification of all conceivable statements--or even all conceivable statements in response to police interrogation--as either testimonial or nontestimonial, it suffices to decide the present cases to hold as follows: Statements are nontestimonial when made in the course of police interrogation under circumstances objectively indicating that the primary purpose of the interrogation is to enable police assistance to meet an ongoing emergency. They are testimonial when the circumstances objectively indicate that there is no such ongoing emergency, and that the primary purpose of the interrogation is to establish or prove past events potentially relevant to later criminal prosecution. (Our holding refers to interrogations because, as explained below, the statements in the cases presently before us are the products of interrogations--which in some circumstances tend to generate testimonial responses. This is not to imply, however, that statements made in the absence of any interrogation are necessarily nontestimonial. The Framers were no more willing to exempt from cross-examination volunteered testimony or answers to open-ended questions than they were to exempt answers to detailed interrogation. Part of the evidence against Sir Walter Raleigh was a letter from Lord Cobham that was plainly not the result of sustained questioning. And of course even when interrogation exists, it is in the final analysis the declarant's statements, not the interrogator's questions, that the Confrontation Clause requires us to evaluate.)

II

A

In *Crawford*, it sufficed for resolution of the case before us to determine that "even if the Sixth Amendment is not solely concerned with testimonial hearsay, that is its primary object, and interrogations by law enforcement officers fall squarely within that class." Moreover, as we have just described, the facts of that case spared us the need to define what we meant by "interrogations." The *Davis* case today does not permit us this luxury of indecision. The inquiries of a police operator in the course of a 911 call are an interrogation in one sense, but not in a sense that "qualifies under any conceivable definition." (If 911 operators are not themselves law enforcement officers, they may at least be agents of law enforcement when they conduct interrogations of 911 callers. For purposes of this opinion (and without deciding the point), we consider their acts to be acts of the police. As in *Crawford*, therefore, our holding today makes it unnecessary to consider whether and when statements made to someone other than law enforcement personnel are "testimonial.") We must decide, therefore, whether the Confrontation Clause applies only to testimonial hearsay; and, if so, whether the recording of a 911 call qualifies.

The answer to the first question was suggested in *Crawford*, even if not explicitly held:

> "The text of the Confrontation Clause reflects this focus [on testimonial hearsay]. It applies to 'witnesses' against the accused—in other words, those who 'bear testimony.'" 'Testimony,' in turn, is typically 'a solemn declaration or affirmation made for the purpose of establishing or proving some fact.' An accuser who makes a formal statement to government officers bears testimony in a sense that a person who makes a casual remark to an acquaintance does not."

A limitation so clearly reflected in the text of the constitutional provision must fairly be said to mark out not merely its "core," but its perimeter.

We are not aware of any early American case invoking the Confrontation Clause or the common-law right to confrontation that did not clearly involve testimony as thus defined. Well into the 20th century, our own Confrontation Clause jurisprudence was carefully applied only in the testimonial context.

Even our later cases, conforming to the reasoning of *Ohio v. Roberts,* never in practice dispensed with the Confrontation Clause requirements of unavailability and prior cross-examination in cases that involved testimonial hearsay. Where our cases did dispense with those requirements--even under the *Roberts* approach--the statements at issue were clearly nontestimonial.

Most of the American cases applying the Confrontation Clause or its state constitutional or common-law counterparts involved testimonial statements of the most formal sort--sworn testimony in prior judicial proceedings or formal depositions under oath--which invites the argument that the scope of the Clause is limited to that very formal category. But the English cases that were the progenitors of the Confrontation Clause did not limit the exclusionary rule to prior court testimony and formal depositions. In any event, we do not think it conceivable that the protections of the Confrontation Clause can readily be evaded by having a note-taking policeman recite the unsworn hearsay testimony of the declarant, instead of having the declarant sign a deposition. Indeed, if there is one point for which no case--English or early American, state or federal--can be cited, that is it.

Food for Thought

If the declarant in *Davis* had responded to the 911 operator's question with a statement that defendant Davis had threatened her with a gun on other occasions, would that statement be considered testimonial under the American dictionary definition? What other factors mentioned later by the Court might help decide this issue? If found to be testimonial, should this statement be redacted, and the remainder of the statement admitted?

The question before us in *Davis,* then, is whether, objectively considered, the interrogation that took place in the course of the 911 call produced testimonial statements. When we said in *Crawford* that "interrogations by law enforcement officers fall squarely within [the] class" of testimonial hearsay, we had immediately in mind (for that was the case before us) interrogations solely directed at establishing the facts of a past crime, in order to identify (or provide evidence to convict) the perpetrator. The product of such interrogation, whether reduced to a writing signed by the declarant or embedded in the memory (and perhaps notes) of the interrogating officer, is testimonial. It is, in the terms of the 1828 American dictionary quoted in *Crawford,* " '[a] solemn declaration or affirmation made for the purpose of establishing or proving some fact.' " (The solemnity of even an oral declaration of relevant past fact to an investigating officer is well enough established by the severe consequences that can attend a deliberate falsehood. A 911 call, on the other hand, and at least the initial interrogation conducted in connection with a 911 call, is ordinarily not designed primarily to "establis[h] or prov[e]" some past fact, but to describe current circumstances requiring police assistance.

The difference between the interrogation in *Davis* and the one in *Crawford* is apparent on the face of things. In *Davis*, McCottry was speaking about events as they were actually happening, rather than "describ[ing] past events." Sylvia Crawford's interrogation, on the other hand, took place hours after the events she described had occurred. Moreover, any reasonable listener would recognize that McCottry (unlike Sylvia Crawford) was facing an ongoing emergency. Although one might call 911 to provide a narrative report of a crime absent any imminent danger, McCottry's call was plainly a call for help against bona fide physical threat. Third, the nature of what was asked and answered in *Davis*, again viewed objectively, was such that the elicited statements were necessary to be able to resolve the present emergency, rather than simply to learn (as in *Crawford*) what had happened in the past. That is true even of the operator's effort to establish the identity of the assailant, so that the dispatched officers might know whether they would be encountering a violent felon. And finally, the difference in the level of formality between the two interviews is striking. Crawford was responding calmly, at the station house, to a series of questions, with the officer-interrogator taping and making notes of her answers; McCottry's frantic answers were provided over the phone, in an environment that was not tranquil, or even (as far as any reasonable 911 operator could make out) safe.

We conclude from all this that the circumstances of McCottry's interrogation objectively indicate its primary purpose was to enable police assistance to meet an ongoing emergency. She simply was not acting as a witness; she was not testifying. What she said was not "a weaker substitute for live testimony" at trial, like Lord Cobham's statements in Raleigh's Case, or Jane Dingler's *ex parte* statements against her husband in *King v. Dingler*, 168 Eng. Rep. 383 (1791), or Sylvia Crawford's statement in *Crawford*. In each of those cases, the *ex parte* actors and the evidentiary products of the *ex parte* communication aligned perfectly with their courtroom analogues. McCottry's emergency statement does not. No "witness" goes into court to proclaim an emergency and seek help. (*Roberts* condition[ed] the admissibility of all hearsay evidence on whether it falls under a 'firmly rooted hearsay exception' or bears 'particularized guarantees of trustworthiness.' We overruled *Roberts* in *Crawford* by restoring the unavailability and cross-examination requirements)

* * *

This is not to say that a conversation which begins as an interrogation to determine the need for emergency assistance cannot, as the Indiana Supreme Court put it, "evolve into testimonial statements," once that purpose has been achieved. In this case, for example, after the operator gained the information needed to address the exigency of the moment, the emergency appears to have ended (when Davis drove away from the premises). The operator then told McCottry to be quiet, and proceeded to pose a battery of questions. It could readily be maintained that, from that point on, McCottry's statements were testimonial, not unlike the "structured police questioning" that occurred in *Crawford*. This presents no great problem. Just as, for Fifth Amendment purposes, "police officers can and will

> **Non constat**
> **jus civile**
> a posteriori
>
> ### What's That?
>
> *In limine* is Latin for "at the threshold" and refers to evidentiary issues that are usually raised prior to the onset of trial.

distinguish almost instinctively between questions necessary to secure their own safety or the safety of the public and questions designed solely to elicit testimonial evidence from a suspect," trial courts will recognize the point at which, for Sixth Amendment purposes, statements in response to interrogations become testimonial. Through *in limine* procedure, they should redact or exclude the portions of any statement that have become testimonial, as they do, for example, with unduly prejudicial portions of otherwise admissible evidence. Davis's jury did not hear the complete 911 call, although it may well have heard some testimonial portions. We were asked to classify only McCottry's early statements identifying Davis as her assailant, and we agree with the Washington Supreme Court that they were not testimonial. That court also concluded that, even if later parts of the call were testimonial, their admission was harmless beyond a reasonable doubt. Davis does not challenge that holding, and we therefore assume it to be correct.

B

Determining the testimonial or nontestimonial character of the statements that were the product of the interrogation in Hammon is a much easier task, since they were not much different from the statements we found to be testimonial in *Crawford*. It is entirely clear from the circumstances that the interrogation was part of an investigation into possible criminal past conduct--as, indeed, the testifying officer expressly acknowledged. There was no emergency in progress; the interrogating officer testified that he had heard no arguments or crashing and saw no one throw or break anything. When the officers first arrived, Amy told them that things were fine, and there was no immediate threat to her person. When the officer questioned Amy for the second time, and elicited the challenged statements, he was not seeking to determine (as in *Davis*) "what is happening," but rather "what happened." Objectively viewed, the primary, if not indeed the sole, purpose of the interrogation was to investigate a possible crime--which is, of course, precisely what the officer should have done.

It is true that the *Crawford* interrogation was more formal. It followed a Miranda warning, was tape-recorded, and took place at the station house. While these features certainly strengthened the statements' testimonial aspect--made it more objectively apparent, that is, that the purpose of the exercise was to nail down the truth about past criminal events--none was essential to the point. It was formal enough that Amy's interrogation was conducted in a separate room, away from her husband (who tried to intervene), with the officer receiving her replies for use in his "investigat[ion]." What we called the "striking resemblance" of the *Crawford* statement to civil-law *ex parte* examinations is shared by Amy's statement here. Both declarants were actively separated from the defendant--officers forcibly prevented Hershel from participating in the interrogation. Both statements deliberately recounted, in response to police questioning, how potentially criminal past events began and progressed. And both took place some time after the events described were over. Such statements under official interrogation are an obvious substitute for live testimony, because they do precisely what a witness does on direct examination; they are inherently testimonial. [FN9]

Non constat
ne aliquod et frumen
jus civile
a posteriori

It's Latin to Me

Amici, or "friend of the court," refers to someone who is not a party to a case but who volunteers to offer information on a point of law or some other aspect of the case to assist the court in deciding a matter before it. In this case, the information was in the form of a brief.

Both Indiana and the United States as *amicus curiae* argue that this case should be resolved much like *Davis*. For the reasons we find the comparison to *Crawford* compelling, we find the comparison to *Davis* unpersuasive. The statements in *Davis* were taken when McCottry was alone, not only unprotected by police (as Amy Hammon was protected), but apparently in immediate danger from Davis. She was seeking aid, not telling a story about the past. McCottry's present-tense statements showed immediacy; Amy's narrative of past events was delivered at some remove in time from the danger she described. And after Amy answered the officer's questions, he had her execute an affidavit, in order, he testified, "[t]o establish events that have occurred previously."

Although we necessarily reject the Indiana Supreme Court's implication that virtually any "initial inquiries" at the crime scene will not be testimonial, we do not hold the opposite--that no questions at the scene will yield nontestimonial answers. We have already observed of domestic disputes that "[o]fficers called to investigate ... need to know whom they are dealing with in order to assess the situation, the threat to their own safety, and possible danger to the potential victim." Such exigencies may often mean that "initial inquiries" produce nontestimonial statements. But in cases like this one, where Amy's statements were neither a cry for help nor the provision of information enabling officers immediately to end a threatening situation, the fact that they were given at an alleged crime scene and were "initial inquiries" is immaterial.

V

Respondents in both cases, joined by a number of their *amici* contend that the nature of the offenses charged in these two cases--domestic violence--requires greater flexibility in the use of testimonial evidence. This particular type of crime is notoriously susceptible to intimidation or coercion of the victim to ensure that she does not testify at trial. When this occurs, the Confrontation Clause gives the criminal a windfall. We may not, however, vitiate constitutional guarantees when they have the effect of allowing the guilty to go free. But when defendants seek to undermine the judicial process by procuring or coercing silence from witnesses and victims, the Sixth Amendment does not require courts to acquiesce. While defendants have no duty to assist the State in proving their guilt, they do have the duty to refrain from acting in ways that destroy the integrity of the criminal-trial system. We reiterate what we said in *Crawford*: that "the rule of forfeiture by wrongdoing ... extinguishes confrontation claims on essentially equitable grounds." That is, one who obtains the absence of a witness by wrongdoing forfeits the constitutional right to confrontation.

We take no position on the standards necessary to demonstrate such forfeiture, but federal courts using Federal Rule of Evidence 804(b)(6), which codifies the forfeiture doctrine, have generally held the Government to the preponderance-of-the-evidence standard, State courts tend to follow the same practice. Moreover, [hearsay evidence may be considered, including the declarant's out of court statement]. The *Roberts* approach to the Confrontation Clause undoubtedly made recourse to this doctrine less necessary, because prosecutors could show the "reliability" of *ex parte* statements more easily than they could show the defendant's procurement of the witness's absence. *Crawford*, in overruling *Roberts*, did not destroy the ability of courts to protect the integrity of their proceedings.

We have determined that, absent a finding of forfeiture by wrongdoing, the Sixth Amendment operates to exclude Amy Hammon's affidavit. The Indiana courts may (if they are asked) determine on remand whether such a claim of forfeiture is properly raised and, if so, whether it is meritorious.

* * *

We affirm the judgment of the Supreme Court of Washington in [*Davis*]. We reverse the judgment of the Supreme Court of Indiana [*Hammond*], and remand the case to that Court for proceedings not inconsistent with this opinion.

Justice <u>THOMAS</u>, concurring in the judgment in part and dissenting in part.

In *Crawford v. Washington,* we abandoned the general reliability inquiry we had long employed to judge the admissibility of hearsay evidence under the Confrontation Clause, describing that inquiry as "inherently, and therefore permanently, unpredictable." Today, a mere two years after the Court decided *Crawford*, it adopts an equally unpredictable test, under which district courts are charged with divining the "primary purpose" of police interrogations. Besides being difficult for courts to apply, this test characterizes as "testimonial," and therefore inadmissible, evidence that bears little resemblance to what we have recognized as the evidence targeted by the Confrontation Clause. Because neither of the cases before the Court today would implicate the Confrontation Clause under an appropriately targeted standard, I concur only in the judgment in *Davis v. Washington*, and dissent from the Court's resolution of *Hammon v. Indiana*.

I

A

* * *

The history surrounding the right to confrontation supports the conclusion that it was developed to target particular practices that occurred under the English bail and committal statutes passed during the reign of Queen Mary, namely, the "civil-law mode of criminal procedure, and particularly its use of *ex parte* examinations as evidence against the accused." The predominant purpose of the [Marian committal] statute was to institute systematic questioning of the accused and the witnesses." The statute required an oral examination of the suspect and the accusers, transcription within two days of the examinations, and physical transmission to the judges hearing the case. These examinations came to be used as evidence in some cases, in lieu of a personal appearance by the witness. Many statements that would be inadmissible as a matter of hearsay law bear little resemblance to these evidentiary practices, which the Framers proposed the Confrontation Clause to prevent.

In *Crawford*, we recognized that this history could be squared with the language of the Clause, giving rise to a workable, and more accurate, interpretation of the Clause. " '[W]itnesses,' " we said, are those who " 'bear testimony.' " And " '[t]estimony' " is " '[a] solemn declaration or affirmation made for the purpose of establishing or proving some fact.' " Admittedly, we did not set forth a detailed framework for addressing whether a statement is "testimonial" and thus subject to the Confrontation Clause. But the plain terms of the "testimony" definition we endorsed necessarily require some degree of solemnity before a statement can be deemed "testimonial."

This requirement of solemnity supports my view that the statements regulated by the Confrontation Clause must include "extrajudicial statements ... contained in formalized testimonial materials, such as affidavits, depositions, prior testimony, or confessions." Affidavits, depositions, and prior testimony are, by their very nature, taken through a formalized process. Likewise, confessions, when extracted by police in a formal manner, carry sufficient indicia of solemnity to constitute formalized statements and, accordingly, bear a "striking resemblance," to the examinations of the accused and accusers under the Marian statutes.

Although the Court concedes that the early American cases invoking the right to confrontation or the Confrontation Clause itself all "clearly involve[d] testimony" as defined in *Crawford*, it fails to acknowledge that all of the cases it cites fall within the narrower category of formalized testimonial materials I have proposed. Interactions between the police and an accused (or witnesses) resemble Marian proceedings--and these early cases--only when the interactions are somehow rendered "formal." In *Crawford*, for example, the interrogation was custodial, taken after warnings given pursuant to *Miranda v. Arizona*. Miranda warnings, by their terms, inform a prospective defendant that " 'anything he says can be used against him in a court of law.' " This imports a solemnity to the process that is not present in a mere conversation between a witness or suspect and a police officer.

The Court all but concedes that no case can be cited for its conclusion that the Confrontation Clause also applies to informal police questioning under certain circumstances. Instead, the sole basis for the Court's conclusion is its apprehension that the Confrontation Clause will "readily be evaded" if it is only applicable to formalized testimonial materials. But the Court's proposed solution to the risk of evasion is needlessly overinclusive. Because the Confrontation Clause sought to regulate prosecutorial abuse occurring through use of *ex parte* statements as evidence against the accused, it also reaches the use of technically informal statements when used to evade the formalized process. That is, even if the interrogation itself is not formal, the production of evidence by the prosecution at trial would resemble the abuses targeted by the Confrontation Clause if the prosecution attempted to use out-of-court statements as a means of circumventing the literal right of confrontation. In such a case, the Confrontation Clause could fairly be applied to exclude the hearsay statements offered by the prosecution, preventing evasion without simultaneously excluding evidence offered by the prosecution in good faith.

The Court's standard is not only disconnected from history and unnecessary to prevent abuse; it also yields no predictable results to police officers and prosecutors attempting to comply with the law. In many, if not most, cases where police respond to a report of a crime, whether pursuant to a 911 call from the victim or otherwise, the purposes of an interrogation, viewed from the perspective of the police, are both to respond to the emergency situation and to gather evidence. Assigning one of these two "largely unverifiable motives," primacy requires constructing a hierarchy of purpose that will rarely be present--and is not reliably discernible. It will inevitably be, quite simply, an exercise in fiction.

The Court's repeated invocation of the word "objectiv[e]" to describe its test, however, suggests that the Court may not mean to reference purpose at all, but instead to inquire into the function served by the interrogation. Certainly such a test would avoid the pitfalls that have led us repeatedly to reject tests dependent on the subjective intentions of police officers. It would do so, however, at the cost of being even more disconnected from the prosecutorial abuses targeted by the Confrontation Clause. Additionally, it would shift the ability to control whether a violation occurred from the police and prosecutor to the judge, whose determination as to the "primary purpose" of a particular interrogation would be unpredictable and not necessarily tethered to the actual purpose for which the police performed the interrogation.

B

911 call is non-testimonial

Neither the 911 call at issue in *Davis* nor the police questioning at issue in *Hammon* is testimonial under the appropriate framework. Neither the call nor the questioning is itself a formalized dialogue. [FN10] Nor do any circumstances surrounding the taking of the statements render those statements sufficiently formal to resemble the Marian examinations; the statements were neither Mirandized nor custodial, nor accompanied by any similar indicia of formality. Finally, there is no suggestion that the prosecution attempted to offer the women's hearsay evidence at trial in order to evade confrontation. Accordingly, the statements at issue in both cases are nontestimonial and admissible under the Confrontation Clause.

The Court's determination that the evidence against Hammon must be excluded extends the Confrontation Clause far beyond the abuses it was intended to prevent. When combined with the Court's holding that the evidence against Davis is perfectly admissible, however, the Court's *Hammon* holding also reveals the difficulty of applying the Court's requirement that courts investigate the "primary purpose[s]" of the investigation. The Court draws a line between the two cases based on its explanation that *Hammon* involves "no emergency in progress," but instead, mere questioning as "part of an investigation into possible criminal past conduct," and its explanation that *Davis* involves questioning for the "primary purpose" of "enabl[ing] police assistance to meet an ongoing emergency." But the fact that the officer in *Hammon* was investigating Mr. Hammon's past conduct does not foreclose the possibility that the primary purpose of his inquiry was to assess whether Mr. Hammon constituted a continuing danger to his wife, requiring further police presence or action. It is hardly remarkable that Hammon did not act abusively towards his wife in the presence of the officers, and his good judgment to refrain from criminal behavior in the presence of police sheds little, if any, light on whether his violence would have resumed had the police left without further questioning, transforming what the Court dismisses as "past conduct" back into an "ongoing emergency." Nor does the mere fact that McCottry needed emergency aid shed light on whether the "primary purpose" of gathering, for example, the name of her assailant was to protect the police, to protect the victim, or to gather information for prosecution. In both of the cases before the Court, like many similar cases, pronouncement of the "primary" motive behind the interrogation calls for nothing more than a guess by courts.

II

Because the standard adopted by the Court today is neither workable nor a targeted attempt to reach the abuses forbidden by the Clause, I concur only in the judgment in *Davis v. Washington*, and respectfully dissent from the Court's resolution of *Hammon v. Indiana*.

─────────────

Points for Discussion

a. Determining Whether Statements are Testimonial after *Davis*

The Court in *Davis* characterizes statements to police officers as testimonial or non-testimonial based upon whether their primary purpose is "to meet an on-going emergency," as opposed to establishing past events for the purpose of criminal prosecution. Is this a subjective or objective test and from whose point of view? Consider a situation in which a wife surreptitiously questions her husband on behalf of the police and tapes his responses in which he admits committing crimes. Should the husband's statements be considered testimonial? Does it not appear that the police used the wife in place of an investigator, and they had an expectation that the statements would be used in the husband's trial? See *United States v. Udeozor,* 515 F.3d 260 (4th Cir. 2008) ("[t]he intent of the police officers or investigators is relevant to the determination of whether a statement is 'testimonial' only if it is first the case that a person in the position of the declarant reasonably would have expected that his statements would be used prosecutorially"). What about medical records offered in a criminal case showing that the defendant had illegal drugs in his system where the records were created under police supervision and during an investigation to determine whether a crime was committed? See *United States v. Ellis,* 460 F.3d 920 (7th Cir. 2006 (because the records were made in the ordinary course of business, they were not considered testimonial). Do you agree with these decisions?

b. A Movement Away from the Roots of *Crawford.*

Do you agree with Justice Thomas in his dissent that the majority's analysis of whether a statement is testimonial is not workable and does not target abuses the Confrontation Clause was designed to eliminate, such as the Marian statutes in England? Does the fact that a test is objective mean it is necessarily "workable" in other circumstances? Does the majority's limited application of the Clause give sufficient guidance to courts and attorneys attempting to live with the Court's pronouncements? What do you make of the majority's refusal to restrict its Confrontation Clause analysis to the formal statement-taking procedures of English laws such as the Marian statutes? Is this simply a refusal of the majority to be limited to English precedent, or an about-face from the underpinnings of *Crawford?* Do you agree that "[r]estricting the Confrontation Clause to the precise forms against which it was originally directed is a recipe for its extinction," as the majority claims?

c. A Victim's Testimonial Statements in Domestic Violence Cases

Is the Court right to have refused to give victim statements in domestic violence situations greater admissibility than other testimonial statements? This argument was raised in *Crawford* in an *amicus curie* brief, which cited in support studies showing that abusers threatened their victims in at least half of all domestic violence cases.

Perspective & Analysis

Consider the following excerpt describing the application difficulties *Davis* and *Crawford* present:

The real problem lies in the application of the *Davis* test by courts at future legal proceedings. If the initial cases are any indication, courts are struggling to assess in a uniform manner whether the emergency situation had ended by the time the statement was given, just as Justice Thomas warned in his dissent. The fact-specific nature of the Court's inquiry in *Davis* seems to afford courts broad discretion over defendant's confrontation right, similar to that allowed under the *Roberts* test. Instead of utilizing a subjective, fact-specific inquiry into the reliability of the statement at issue, as was common protocol under *Roberts*, some courts are now taking the same liberty with a subjective, fact-specific inquiry into whether the emergency had ended when the statement was made. Thus, the first impression of the *Davis* effect from lower court decisions is that the defendants' confrontation right is still subject to the same sort of factor-laden analysis that does not tend to yield uniform protection of a constitutional right.

Gregory M. O'Neil, *Davis and Hammon: Redefining the Constitutional Right to Confrontation*, 40 Conn. L. Rev. 511, 535 (2007)

Hypo 7.2

The defendant is accused of burglarizing a house and causing the death of the occupant, who apparently died of a heart attack. At trial, the prosecution presents the testimony of a medical examiner who, in part, bases her opinion of the victim's death on hearsay statements made by a co-defendant. Should these statements be considered testimonial under *Crawford* and *Davis?* See generally, *Howard v. Walker*, 2004 WL 1638197 (W.D.N.Y. 2004).

C. Waiver of Confrontation Rights and Forfeiture By Wrongdoing

Rule 804(b)

(b) The following are not excluded by the hearsay rule if the declarant is unavailable as a witness:

* * *

(6) Forfeiture by Wrongdoing.   A statement offered against a party that has engaged or acquiesced in wrongdoing that was intended to, and did, procure the unavailability of the declarant as a witness.

Rule 804(b)(6) was enacted to admit hearsay statements of a declarant against a party in a civil or criminal case, if that party engages or acquiesces in deliberate wrongdoing that was intended to and did, procure the unavailability of the declarant at trial. In other words, due to her own wrongful conduct a party forfeits the right to object to an otherwise objectionable hearsay declaration. This is a relatively new addition to the Federal Rules of Evidence, having been enacted in 1997, but even before its adoption, virtually all circuits had adopted some type of waiver by misconduct principle in rebuttal either to hearsay or Confrontation Clause objections.

A reading of the rule leaves some questions unanswered. For example, what constitutes engaging or acquiescing in wrongdoing? Must the wrongdoing described by the rule be criminal in and of itself, and can it be proved circumstantially? By what standard must a party prove a Rule 804(b)(6) forfeiture? Many of these issues are addressed in the case below.

United States v. Scott

U.S Court of Appeals for the Seventh Circuit
284 F.3d 758 (7th Cir. 2002)

TERENCE T. EVANS, Circuit Judge.

Robert Scott, along with assorted others, was indicted for conspiracy to possess marijuana and cocaine with intent to distribute. At Scott's first trial, in 1999, the jury failed to reach a verdict, and the judge declared a mistrial. A second trial did not have a happy ending for Mr. Scott--he was convicted. . .

conspiracy to buy drug

[The evidence showed that the defendant, Robert Scott, was in a conspiracy with his brother Billy Scott and Billy's girlfriend Molly Rahar (and sometimes Tim Burnett) to drive to Chicago to buy drugs from a man named Charles Kelsay. After Billy Scott became unreliable because of his heavy drug use and his pocketing of the defendant's money, the defendant replaced him with Shawn Jones and Tim Burnett. Shawn Jones gave grand jury testimony confirming that the defendant was Billy Scott's "money man" during Billy's trips to Chicago and that he also accepted large amounts of money from Scott for the purpose of buying drugs from Kelsay].

jail-house snitch

After he was arrested, the defendant made friends with Billy Chance, who was awaiting sentencing after pleading guilty to armed bank robbery. Chance testified that Scott told him that Billy Scott and Molly Raham had been going to Chicago three or four times a month and buying drugs for him from Kelsay. Scott said that he had Jones take over the drug runs after Billy started ripping him off. Scott also showed Chance a list of phone calls the government was going to use against him. He told Chance the calls were "about the drug transaction that Jones had made." [At trial, other evidence tied the defendant to the drug conspiracies.]

challenged admission of grand jury testimony

On appeal, Scott … challenges the admission of Shawn Jones' December 1995 grand jury testimony… The district judge found him "unavailable" after his refusal to testify at the second trial. Upon the government's motion, the judge admitted the grand jury testimony after holding an evidentiary hearing.

admitting out of ct. statements

There are two independent hurdles to admitting out-of-court statements in federal courts: the Sixth Amendment's Confrontation Clause and the Federal Rules of Evidence. It is, of course, well-established that a defendant forfeits his Confrontation Clause rights by wrongfully procuring the unavailability of a witness. The doctrine was codified with

Take Note!

Why does the court not engage in a Confrontation Clause analysis even though the Jones' out of court grand jury testimony is being admitted in this case?

regard to hearsay in 1997 with the adoption of Federal Rule of Evidence 804(b)(6). We need not worry about any potential differences between the substantive forfeiture standards or standards of review under these two provisions because Scott has not raised a Confrontation Clause issue. He styles his challenge under Rule 804(b)(6). Accordingly, we will review the district court's determination under Rule 804(b)(6) for clear error.

Federal Rule of Evidence 804(b)(6) provides that if the declarant is unavailable, a statement is not excluded as hearsay if it is "offered against a party that has engaged or acquiesced in wrongdoing that was intended to, and did, procure the unavailability of the declarant as a witness." To admit a statement against a defendant under the rule, therefore, the government must show (1) that the defendant engaged or acquiesced in wrongdoing, (2) that the wrongdoing was intended to procure the declarant's unavailability, and (3) that the wrongdoing did procure the unavailability. The district judge required the government to establish these elements by a preponderance of the evidence. Although we have not directly addressed the level of burden to be carried by the government under Rule 804(b)(6), we join the other circuits which have held that the preponderance-of-the-evidence level is correct.

At the evidentiary hearing, the government offered different pieces of evidence regarding Scott's interactions with Jones. First, it submitted transcripts of phone conversations between Scott and Jones occurring in 1998 while Jones was incarcerated and Scott was the target of a grand jury investigation. It also offered prison records showing that Scott and his wife visited Jones in prison in February 1998. Second, it offered testimony that Scott and his wife gave Jones $200 and gave his son a toy laptop computer for Christmas in 1998. Third, it offered the testimony of Mr. Chance, who we recall was in the same cellblock with Jones at Sangamon in the spring of 1999; Chance and Scott were on the same cellblock in the fall of 1999 and shared a cell for a few days. Chance testified to their interactions. As the government seems to concede, only Chance's testimony has much force…

But Chance's testimony reveals that Scott did not think that friendship alone would carry the day. According to Chance, Scott and Jones communicated at Sangamon both in June of 1999, shortly after Scott's indictment, and in the fall of 1999, in the months preceding Scott's first trial. June is useful background. After Scott's arrival, Jones seemed "nervous" and "frightened." Jones identified Scott as the person the government wanted him to testify against and told Chance that "he had a lot to lose and he had to protect himself." Chance observed Jones and Scott communicate through their adjacent cell blocks, out of sight of security cameras, regularly while Scott was there.

In the fall, Scott told Chance that Jones had damaging information. Scott said that "if [Jones] knew what was good for him, he'd keep his mouth shut" and that Jones "better not testify if he knew what was good for him." Scott also told Chance that he learned from his lawyer that the government had approached Jones and told him that it would drop his contempt charges and further reduce his sentence if he testified. Chance had seen Jones in the Sangamon law library, and Scott had Chance tell Jones what his lawyer had told him and ask him whether he was going to testify. When Chance brought up the subject, Jones "looked real nervous and scared." Nonetheless, Jones told Chance (who told Scott) that he was not going to testify. But hearing it from Chance was not good enough for Scott, who asked Chance how to obtain permission to use the law library. He then ventured to the library to "make sure [Jones] was not going to testify again." He did so even though he had told Chance on a few occasions that he was worried the government would use his communication with Jones against him. Chance testified that they talked in a "low tone of voice." Afterwards, Scott was "happy" and "seemed relieved that Jones wasn't going to testify."

Rule 804(b)(6) requires, first, that Scott engage in "wrongdoing." That word is not defined in the text of Rule 804(b)(6), although the advisory committee's notes point out that "wrongdoing" need not consist of a criminal act. One thing seems clear: causing a person not to testify at trial cannot be considered the "wrongdoing" itself, otherwise the word would be redundant. So we must focus on the actions procuring the unavailability. Scott argues his actions were not sufficiently evil because they were not akin to murder, physical assault, or bribery. Although such malevolent acts are clearly sufficient to constitute "wrongdoing," they are not necessary. The notes make clear that the rule applies to all parties, including the government. Although, in the ugliest criminal cases, murder and physical assaults are all too possible on the defendant's side, it seems unlikely that the rule was needed to curtail government murder of potential witnesses. Rather, it contemplates application against the use of coercion, undue influence, or pressure to silence testimony and impede the truth-finding function of trials. We think that applying pressure on a potential witness not to testify, including by threats of harm and suggestions of future retribution, is wrongdoing.

Food for Thought

Would encouraging the witness to invoke the Fifth Amendment at trial constitute "the use of coercion, undue influence or pressure to silence testimony?" How can urging a witness to exercise a Constitutional right be a "wrongdoing?" See *Steele v. Taylor,* 684 F.2d 1193 (6th Cir. 1982).

Scott does not challenge the facts as related by Chance, so what we have is a battle of inferences and, although it is close, we do not believe that the district

(coerced witness)

judge erred by inferring that Scott coerced Jones. First, Scott told Chance what he intended to do in the library; he wanted to "make sure [Jones] was not going to testify again"--this after threatening that Jones should "keep his mouth shut" and "better not testify if he knew what was good for him." The district judge could reasonably infer that Scott did exactly what he told Chance he would do. Second, there is no dispute that Scott had a golden opportunity to coerce Jones. He had a 20-minute conversation with Jones in Sangamon's law library where, likely not out of respect for library policy, they spoke in "low" tones. Third, Scott's reaction to the meeting was positive. He seemed "happy" and "relieved" that Jones would not testify, after previously worrying about it. All of this took place against a backdrop in which Jones was "frightened" by Scott's presence and feared that he had "to protect himself."

In considering this evidence, we are also mindful that there is another potential source of information about the conversation between Scott and Jones: Jones. But Jones gave no testimony at the evidentiary hearing. It seems almost certain that, in a case involving coercion or threats, a witness who refuses to testify at trial will not testify to the actions procuring his or her unavailability. It would not serve the goal of Rule 804(b)(6) to hold that circumstantial evidence cannot support a finding of coercion. Were we to hold otherwise, defendants would have a perverse incentive to cover up wrongdoing with still more wrongdoing, to the loss of probative evidence at trial. We hold that the district judge did not clearly err by finding that Scott had engaged in wrongdoing.

Rule 804(b)(6) requires, second, that Scott's wrongdoing was intended to procure Jones' unavailability. On this point the evidence is clear. Chance testified that Scott threatened that Jones "better not testify if he knew what was good for him." Moreover, Scott wanted access to the law library to "make sure" that Jones would not testify. The district judge properly found that Scott's wrongdoing was intended to procure Jones' unavailability.

Third, the rule requires that Scott's wrongdoing procure Jones' unavailability. This is another close issue. Jones first refused to testify in January 1999 when he appeared again before Scott's grand jury. Thus, it may be difficult for the government to show that Scott's conduct at Sangamon procured Jones' unavailability since Jones had refused to testify over 8 months earlier.

But our task is to measure Jones' refusals to testify at trial and, by that point, Scott ... was no longer a target of an investigation but a criminal defendant. The government had upped the ante on Jones' testimony and Scott knew it. Scott told Chance that he "couldn't believe" the government was going to call Jones to testify. He had assumed the government was going to present Jones' grand jury testimony, which Scott and Jones were trying to have thrown out. Further, Scott thought that the government was applying new leverage. According to what he told Chance, he believed the government was offering to drop Jones' contempt charges and further reduce his sentence in exchange for testimony. This prompted Scott to ask Chance, despite his worries of government surveillance, to find out whether Jones was going to testify. Even after Jones said he was not going to testify, Scott was still worried, so worried that he himself went to the law library to find out if Jones was really going to testify. Only at this point, after which coercion was inferable, was Scott "happy" and "relieved" that Jones would not testify. For his part, Jones alluded to religious and moral reasons for not testifying, which he had not relied upon before. Given his vacillating excuses, we think the district judge did not clearly err in concluding that Scott's influence was the real reason for Jones' unavailability.

403
analysis

Scott argues that, even if Jones' testimony was admissible under Rule 804(b)(6), its probative value was substantially outweighed by unfair prejudice under Federal Rule of Evidence 403. Scott asserts that he was incriminated by unreliable evidence. To the extent this argument depends on the right of cross-examination, the argument is unavailing. The whole point of Rule 804(b)(6) is to admit evidence without cross-examination because, by a defendant's wrongdoing, he forfeits his right to challenge the receipt in evidence of the statements. Moreover, the hearsay statements here were sworn and given before a grand jury. The unfair prejudice to Scott of admitting these statements was, as the district court found, outweighed by its considerable probative value in this case.

The judgment of the district court is Affirmed.

———————————

Points for Discussion

a. The Roots of Rule 804(b)(6)

Rule 804(b)(6) was enacted in response to cases such as *United States v. Houlihan, 92 F.3d 1271 (1996)*, in which the trial judge admitted hearsay statements made by a declarant witness who was eventually murdered by the defendants. The declarant had told both a state trooper and the Boston police that he and another defendant were involved in a drug conspiracy and linked to several murders. The court held that by murdering the witness, the defendants waived their Confrontation Clause and hearsay objections to admission of those statements at least to the extent that they "would have been competent and admissible evidence had the declarant been able to testify in person." Why restrict admissibility to this extent?

b. The Constitutionality of Rule 804(b)(6)

The Supreme Court in both *Crawford* and *Davis* addressed the issue whether forfeiture by wrongdoing is constitutional under the Confrontation Clause. In *Davis*, the Court stated:

> "While defendants have no duty to assist the State in proving their guilt, they do have the duty to refrain from acting in ways that destroy the integrity of the criminal-trial system. We reiterate what we said in *Crawford*: that "the rule of forfeiture by wrongdoing ... extinguishes confrontation claims on essentially equitable grounds. That is, one who obtains the absence of a witness by wrongdoing forfeits the constitutional right to confrontation."

c. Acquiescence in Wrongdoing: Linking *Pinkerton* Theories of Co-Conspirator Liability to Rule 804(b)(6)

What if the defendant does not actively participate in silencing a witness but rather is a member of a conspiracy for that purpose? Is this sufficient to constitute acquiescence under the rule? This issue was addressed in <u>United States v. Cherry, 217 F.3d 811, 820 (10th Cir. 2000)</u> where the court found that by applying the accomplice liability theory of <u>Pinkerton v. United States, 328 U.S. 640 (1946)</u>, the non-active co-conspirator could be found to have acquiesced under Rule 804(b)(6):

> "By recognizing the applicability of agency concepts and permitting admission of the testimony of an unavailable witness against a co-conspirator involved in, but not necessarily immediately responsible for, procuring that witness's unavailability, a Pinkerton [co-conspirator liability] theory strikes a better balance between the conflicting principles at stake.

For More Information

The *Pinkerton* case recognized that the overt act of one partner in crime is attributable to all and that each co-conspirator is liable for all "reasonably foreseeable but originally unintended substantive crimes done by other co-conspirators."

> This is particularly so considering the potential windfall to defendants and the fundamental principle that 'courts will not suffer a party to profit by his own wrongdoing.' We therefore hold that a co-conspirator may be deemed to have "acquiesced in" the wrongful procurement of a witness's unavailability for purposes of Rule 804(b)(6) and the waiver by misconduct doctrine when the government can satisfy the requirements of Pinkerton."

Executive Summary

The Sixth Amendment and Hearsay. In criminal cases only, the Sixth Amendment Confrontation Clause guarantees a defendant the right at his trial to confront the witnesses who have given testimony against him. As a result, out-of-court hearsay statements made by a declarant, and later admitted against the defendant at his trial, can violate the defendant's Sixth Amendment rights, if the criminal defendant had no opportunity to confront that declarant at trial. In effect, if the hearsay statement is used at trial (it satisfies an exception, or is defined as non-hearsay), then the declarant would be a "witness" against the defendant at trial that the defendant did not get to confront. Simply because the declarant's out-of-court statement against the defendant may be defined as non-hearsay, or may fit within an exception to the hearsay rule, does not necessarily mean that it also satisfies the defendant's Sixth Amendment Confrontation Clause rights. However, a Sixth Amendment violation by an otherwise admissible hearsay exception occurs only when the declarant's out-of-court statement was "testimonial in nature" when made. Thus, a "non-testimonial" hearsay statement that fits an exception does not violate the Sixth Amendment (see below).

Traditional Interpretation of the Confrontation Clause and Hearsay. For many years, it used to be that an unavailable witness's out-of-court statement against a criminal defendant would be admitted over any Sixth Amendment challenge, provided the declarant's out-of-court statement against the defendant (1) fell within a "firmly rooted" hearsay exception, and (2) bore "particularized guarantees of trustworthiness." (*Roberts*). In other words, if the declarant's statement was reliable, then, by definition, it did not violate the Confrontation Clause, and "reliability" was determined by whether the statement was within a "firmly rooted" hearsay exception and whether there had been a judicial determination of reliability.

Recent Rulings on the Confrontation Clause. The Supreme Court recently has considered these issues and has "overruled," or at least "clarified," *Roberts*. In so doing, the Court has emphasized the fact that the Confrontation Clause, as a constitutional provision, obviously *supersedes* a rule of evidence, even if that rule represents a "firmly rooted" hearsay exception. However, the Confrontation Clause excludes a declarant's statement only when that statement is "testimonial in nature." (*Crawford*). "Testimonial in nature" is defined by whether the primary purpose of the statement is to meet an ongoing emergency (e.g., a 911 call to have police respond to an ongoing crime) in which case it is *not* testimonial, (*Davis*), as opposed to the declarant relating past events with an eye toward preparing the case for criminal prosecution, in which case it would be testimonial. (*Crawford*). The ambiguity in the application of a criminal defendant's Confrontation Clause rights lies in determining at what point a declarant is merely assisting in an ongoing emergency to stop a crime or apprehend a criminal suspect ("non-testimonial"), (*Davis*), and crosses over into the legal preparation for a criminal prosecution of the defendant ("testimonial") (*Crawford*).

    <u>**Waiver of Confrontation Clause Rights and Forfieture by Wrongdoing**</u>. Recall that Rule 804(b)(6) is a hearsay exception when the declarant is "unavailable" under Rule 804(a) that allows hearsay statements to be used against a wrongdoing party, if that party is the one who procured or was responsible in some way for the declarant's unavailability at trial. The wrongdoing of procuring a witness's absence at trial perpetrated by a criminal defendant acts as a waiver of that criminal defendant's Confrontation Clause rights at trial, in addition to satisfying the Rule 804(b)(6) hearsay exception. The waiver of Confrontation Clause rights applies in the most egregious examples, such as a defendant arranging for the murder of a witness and then attempting to use the rule against hearsay to exclude that witness's previous out-of-court statements. (*Houlihan*). However, the waiver also applies even when the wrongdoing of the defendant is not so clearly "evil," such as "suggesting" the witness not testify against the defendant at trial, and applying "subtle coercion" (providing favors, gifts, "warnings") resulting in the declarant/witness's "voluntary" decision not to testify at trial. (*Scott*).

CHAPTER 8

A Return to Relevance I: Limits Based on Policy

A. Introduction

Even though evidence is relevant and otherwise admissible, it may be excluded for policy reasons, such as preventing unjust results or encouraging parties to settle disputes and remedy harmful or dangerous conditions. Rules 407-411 express these policy concerns in their calculations. As you read each of these rules, think about what policy is being implemented by excluding such evidence. Also notice the common structure of these rules. Each of them (with the exception of Rule 409) begins with a general statement excluding evidence when offered for one purpose but admitting it when offered for different purposes.

Practice Pointer

Whenever evidence is excluded if offered for one purpose but admissible when offered for a different one, the trial judge shall, upon request, give a limiting instruction that will "restrict the evidence to its proper scope and instruct the jury accordingly." Rule 105, Federal Rules of Evidence.

B. Subsequent Remedial Measures

Rule 407. Subsequent Remedial Measures

When, after an injury or harm allegedly caused by an event, measures are taken that, if taken previously, would have made the injury or harm less likely to occur, evidence of the subsequent measures is not admissible to prove negligence, culpable conduct, a defect in a product, a defect in a product's design, or a need for a warning or instruction. This rule does not require the exclusion of evidence of subsequent measures when offered for another purpose, such as proving ownership, control, or feasibility of precautionary measures, if controverted, or impeachment.

Examples of subsequent remedial measures might include ter-
mination of an employee, changes in
the rules of procedure for a business,
warnings, notices or instructions
placed on products, or repair to a
dangerous condition.

A subsequent remedial measure is an action taken after a harm or injury has occurred that in some measure attempts to rectify the cause of the harm or injury. Rule 407 deems these measures inadmissible if they are offered to show a party's negligence, culpable conduct, or a defect in a product, a defect in a product's design, or a need for a warning or instruction. A common example is where the plaintiff slipped and fell by stepping on a rotten grape in defendant's grocery store. The plaintiff may try to offer evidence that after his accident, the defendant instituted a policy that the floors be checked and cleaned every 30 minutes as proof that the defendant was negligent for not having instituted the policy in the first place. Rule 407 would prevent admission when the evidence is offered for this purpose.

There are several reasons for this general exclusion. A defendant may implement subsequent remedial measures for a number of reasons unrelated to an admission of fault. A desire for product improvement or the mandate of subsequent government regulations come to mind. Put another way, Rule 407 rejects the notion that "because the world gets wiser as its gets older, therefore it was foolish before." *Hart v. Lancashine & Yorkshire Ry. Co.*, 21 L.T.R. N.S. 261, 263 (1869). Moreover, if the defendant knows that the plaintiff could offer subsequent remedial measures to show negligence, he might think twice about implementing these measures to the detriment of future customers. Or, more alarmingly, the defendant might engage in a cost/benefit analysis to determine whether it was less expensive to risk occasional lawsuits than to take steps to prevent future injury to persons or property and to have that action used against them at trial.

Nonetheless, subsequent reme-
dial measures may be offered for any relevant purpose other than those prohibited by the rule. Rule 407 provides a non-exclusive list of a number of permissible offerings as examples, including offerings to show ownership, control, or feasibility of precautionary measures, if controverted, or impeachment. The requirement that ownership, control, and feasibility be controverted might seem to allow a party to prevent the operation of these

Examples of unlisted permissible
purposes might also include an
offer to show that a dangerous condition existed, see *Rimkus v. Northwest Colorado Ski Corp.*, 706 F.2d
1060 (10th Cir. 1983), or an offer to
show that defendant was on notice
because of the settlement agreement
that his conduct was wrongful, *Kraft
v. St. John Lutheran Church*, 414 F.3d
943 (8th Cir. 2005).

exceptions by simply refusing to place them at issue through the introduction of facts or argument; however, this strategy can be problematic, as the following case illustrates:

1. The General Rule and the Feasibility Exception

Anderson v. Malloy

U.S. Court of Appeals for the Eighth Circuit
700 F.2d 1208 (8th Cir. 1983)

LAY, Chief Judge.

In January and February of 1979, [Linda and Dariel] Anderson were guests in a motel in the St. Louis area owned and operated by the defendants, Malloy, Zes, and Gibson. On the evening of February 7, 1979, while Linda Anderson was alone in the motel room, an unknown assailant forcibly entered the room and assaulted and raped her.

The Andersons thereupon filed suit alleging diversity jurisdiction in federal district court in St. Louis, alleging that the defendants negligently failed to provide them with reasonably safe lodging, that the defendants breached an express warranty to provide reasonably safe lodging, and that the defendants fraudulently misrepresented the level of security provided to the motel's guests.

P's argued

During the trial, the district court made four evidentiary rulings excluding portions of the plaintiffs' evidence. The court refused to admit . . . evidence that, after Linda Anderson was raped, the defendants installed safety chains and "peep holes" in the entrance doors of the motel rooms.

evidentiary ruling

The motel owners argued in defense that they had done everything reasonably necessary to make their motel secure. The defendants also affirmatively claimed that Linda Anderson's injuries were proximately caused by her own negligence in opening her door in a strange city to a person she did not know.

The jury returned a verdict for the defendants, and the district court entered judgment on the verdict.

* * *

Rule 407 prohibits the admission of evidence of subsequent remedial measures when the evidence is offered to prove negligence or culpable conduct. However, the rule expressly does not require the exclusion of such evidence when offered for another purpose. Of course, to be admissible any evidence not excluded by Rule 407 must still be relevant (Fed.R.Evid. 402) and its probative value must outweigh any dangers associated with its admission (Fed.R.Evid. 403).

P's argue on appeal

The plaintiffs assert on appeal that the defendants controverted the feasibility of the use of peep holes and safety chains. Thus, the plaintiffs argue that the evidence comes within the exception of rule 407. Although the trial court held to the contrary, we find that the defendants did affirmatively controvert the feasibility of the chain locks and peep holes. We conclude that the trial court committed a prejudicial abuse of discretion when it excluded the evidence.

The first witness called by the plaintiffs was the defendant, Malloy, one of the owners of the motel. Malloy was asked by the plaintiffs' counsel about the security measures taken by the defendants since they purchased the motel in 1974, but he was not asked about the absence of peep holes or chain locks on the doors. On cross-examination defense counsel opened up the issue in the following exchange:

Q. We've already talked about the additional lighting that was installed. Did [the village police chief] indicate to you anything about putting these peepholes, as they are called, in the solid core doors?

A. He felt like we had six-foot picture windows right next to the door. If we'd put peepholes in, it would be false security.

Q. Did you follow the officer's recommendation in that regard?

A. Yes. We did not put the peepholes in at that time.

Q. Did he indicate to you anything about these chains you see on doors on occasion?

A. He felt like they were unnecessary, also. False security.

On redirect, in rebuttal, the plaintiffs' counsel then asked:

Q. Do I understand, [the police chief] indicated to you that it wouldn't be feasible to put in peepholes and chain guards on the front doors?

Take Note!

Notice how the plaintiff's lawyer on redirect examination uses the word "feasible" in his question. "Feasible" is a word that has legal meaning under Rule 407, but the witness, being a lay person, probably does not know this. He answers in terms of whether the safety devices were necessary, which is somewhat non-responsive. Why do you suppose that the defense attorney did not object? Why does the majority think that this particular question and answer put feasibility of precautionary measures at issue?

Mr. Malloy replied:

A. At that time he felt like the picture windows were adequate for- that the peephole would be sort of a false security, because they could look out these picture windows and see the door, the step there.

Whether something is feasible relates not only to actual possibility of opera- ~whether~
tion, and its cost and convenience, but also to its ultimate utility and success in ~feasible~
its intended performance. That is to say, "feasible" means not only "possible," but
also means "capable of being ... utilized, or dealt with successfully."

For the defendant to suggest that installation of peep holes and chain locks would provide only a false sense of security not only infers that the devices would not successfully provide security, it also infers that the devices would in fact create a lesser level of security if they were installed. With this testimony the defendants controverted the feasibility of the installation of these devices, because the defendant Malloy in effect testified that these devices were not "capable of being utilized or dealt with successfully."

The defendants' counsel took advantage of the situation and in closing argument to the jury said that the evidence showed that the defendants in providing security "did everything anybody recommended that they do. What more can they do? ... Is there any evidence from any reliable source that [the defendants] could or should have done anything more?" With such a suggestion implanted in the minds of the jurors by Malloy's testimony, the plaintiffs' counsel had every right to rebut that suggestion by showing that the defendants had in fact installed these devices after Linda Anderson was raped.

The plaintiffs were entitled to show affirmatively that these devices were feasible, and furthermore to impeach the credibility of the defendants by showing that, although the defendants testified that they had done everything necessary for a secure motel, and that chain locks and peep holes would not be successful, they in fact took further security measures after Linda Anderson was raped, and in fact installed the same devices that they testified could not be used successfully. Under Rule 407 the evidence could not be used by the plaintiffs to prove the defendants' negligence, and a limiting instruction would ~limiting~
warn the jury of this restriction in its admission. But we think it was an abuse ~instruction~
of discretion for the trial court to refuse to admit the only evidence that would effectively rebut the inferences created by the defendants.

Food for Thought

How would such a limiting instruction be worded?

We find the trial court committed prejudicial error in the ruling discussed above; accordingly, we vacate the judgment of the district court, and remand the case for a new trial.

JOHN R. GIBSON, Circuit Judge, concurring in part and dissenting in part.

* * *

I disagree that the testimony in this case involves a question of feasibility. This line of Malloy's testimony commences:

> Q Did you also, sir, before you went into operation, meet with a representative of the Village of Edmundson Police Department?
>
> A Yes, I did.
>
> Q And did he also make recommendations to you as to what could or should be done insofar as security is concerned?
>
> A Yes, he did. Uh-huh.

Solid core doors, Triple A door locks, and bar pins in sliding doors were all recommended. The witness was asked:

> Q You did follow his recommendations and you did do that?
>
> A We did, yes.

The testimony set out [in] the majority opinion followed. There was then testimony of a recommendation of an additional guard from 11:00 p.m. to 7:00 a.m.

When plaintiffs' offer of proof was made, the district court stated:

> There is no question of feasibility in this situation. He said he went on the recommendation, whether it's good, bad, right or wrong. He hasn't said anything which says it wasn't feasible or would cost too much. . . .

The term "feasible" has been defined by the Supreme Court in *American Textile Mfrs. Inst. v. Donovan*, 452 U.S. 490, (1981) [in a different context]. Justice Brennan in his opinion states:

[margin note: definition of feasible]

> The plain meaning of the word "feasible" supports respondents' interpretation of the statute. According to Webster's Third New International Dictionary of the English Language 831 (1976), "feasible" means "capable of being done, executed,

or effected." Accord, The Oxford English Dictionary 116 (1933) ("Capable of being done, accomplished or carried out") . . . .

The ruling of the district court was consistent with this definition of feasible. While Mr. Justice Brennan's opinion deals with use of the word in 29 U.S.C. § 655(b)(5), his broad treatment of the word "feasible" cannot be limited simply to that statute as opposed to its use in Rule 407, which was presented to Congress and subject to Congressional action . . . .

The majority finds feasibility an issue not from direct testimony that feasibility was involved, but rather by inferring that it is an issue from the testimony concerning false sense of security which was given as the reason for the recommendation of the police chief. My view is that this testimony relates to the question of necessity or desirability and that the majority stretches the chain of inferences too far. . . .

Plaintiffs make no contention with respect to the impeachment exception to Rule 407, neither did they make such contention at trial. I find no testimony in the record that defendants stated that they had done everything necessary for a secure motel, but simply that they had received recommendations from the chief of police and followed these recommendations. I find no testimony of defendants that chain locks and peepholes could not be used successfully, but only that the majority has inferred such statements from the testimony of false sense of security. I think we should not find impeachment of defendants on the basis of inferences the majority draws from the testimony.

Defendants' closing argument stressed the recommendations given by the chief of police. The closing argument certainly cannot be used to justify introduction of evidence during the course of the trial. While defendants posed the question of "what more can they do" the statement, read in context, simply argues that defendants had followed expert recommendations. The following is the omission from the quotation [in] the majority opinion:

Food for Thought

Do you agree that the closing argument cannot be used to justify the introduction of evidence during the course of the trial? Didn't the defendant capitalize on the exclusion by emphasizing that there was really nothing else that the defendants could have done to make the room safer?

You go to the chief of the police or of the area where you're working and you ask him, "What should I do," and he tells you and you do it. You call in Union Electric and they say put in 10 more lights, you put in 10 more lights.

The argument continued:

These gentlemen were concerned about the safety of their guests, concerned enough to seek professional help from Union Electric and from the chief of police, and not only to seek it, but to follow the advice that was given them. What more could they do?

Defendants' argument viewed in its entirety related to the police chief's recommendation and was fully supported by the evidence.

Plaintiffs' attempted introduction of defendants' subsequent remedial measures was an attempt "solely to raise the spectre of negligence under the guise of feasibility." The trial court is entitled to guard against the improper admission of such evidence.

I cannot conclude that the district court abused its discretion in ruling that the testimony involved matters of recommendation rather than feasibility, and in making a ruling that is consistent with the plain meaning of feasible as recognized in the recent decision of the United States Supreme Court. Accordingly, I would affirm.

Points for Discussion

a. Placing Feasibility at Issue.

The language of Rule 407 states that if the defendant denies the feasibility of taking precautionary measures, subsequent remedial measures may be used to show those measures were indeed feasible. How does the majority of the court in *Anderson* read the feasibility requirement of Rule 407? How does the dissent read it? Which view makes more sense in the context of this case and why?

b. The Effectiveness of a Subsequent Remedial Measure.

Rule 407 requires that to be admissible, subsequent remedial measures be ones that "if taken previously, would have made the injury or harm less likely to occur." Does the court in *Anderson* address this issue? If you were the plaintiff or defense attorney in this case, how would you argue this issue to the *Anderson* trial judge? What about a defense argument that if the plaintiff was unwilling to look through a large plate glass window to see who was at the door, it is unlikely she would use a peephole? What might be the plaintiff's response?

c. Applicability of Rule 407 to Product Defect and Defective Design Cases.

A defective product is one that is more dangerous or less fit for its intended use than is reasonable. In 1997, Rule 407 was amended to provide that evidence of a subsequent remedial measure may not be used to prove "a defect in a product or its design, or that a warning or instruction should have accompanied a product." This amendment resolved a conflict in circuits as to this issue prior to the amendment and represents the majority view in those circuits.

d. Pre-Accident Changes.

Also added by the 1997 amendment to Rule 407 were the words "after an injury or harm allegedly caused by an event" to clarify that Rule 407 applies only to changes made after the plaintiff incurs harm or injury. Evidence of measures taken by the defendant prior to harm or injury, however, is not excluded. See *Kelly v. Crown Equip. Co.*, 970 F.2d 1273 (3d Cir. 1992) (excluding evidence of pre-accident repairs in a failure to warn case).

e. The Rule Applies Only to Parties.

What if the subsequent remedial measure was taken by a non-party to the suit? In *TLT-Babcock, Inc. v. Emerson Elec. Co.*, 33 F.3d 397 (4th Cir. 1994), the court held that a non-party's post-accident redesign of a fan shaft was admissible under Rule 407 because "[a] nondefendant . . . will not be inhibited from taking remedial measures if such actions are allowed into evidence against a defendant." Is this ruling consistent with the policies of Rule 407?

2. The Impeachment Exception

Another purpose for which subsequent remedial measures are admissible is to impeach a testifying witness. Courts have generally construed this exception narrowly in an effort to prevent the exception from engulfing the rule.

Harrison v. Sears, Roebuck and Company

U.S. Court of Appeals for the First Circuit
981 F.2d 25 (1st Cir. 1992)

BRODY, District Judge.

Plaintiffs, Benjamin and Rosalind Harrison, appeal from a judgment entered after a jury verdict denying them relief in a personal injury suit against Sears, Roebuck & Company and Emerson Electric Company. . . .

P's account of accident

The precise way in which the accident occurred was heavily disputed at trial. The deposition testimony of the Appellants' decedent stated that while Benjamin Harrison was in the process of shutting off the jointer, his left hand slipped from the on-off switch and entered into an opening allowing his fourth and fifth fingers to make contact with moving cutter blades. Appellants allege that this contact resulted in the partial amputation of the decedent's left ring finger and injury to his left fifth finger. . . . .

D's rebuttal

Appellees presented their engineering expert, Jack Hyde, who testified that the accident could not have occurred as Benjamin Harrison claimed. Hyde gave two reasons for his opinion. First, Hyde testified that because of the design of the jointer, it would be difficult to get one's fingers into the opening unintentionally. In addition, Hyde opined that the injury could not have occurred as Harrison alleged because the angle and location of the cuts on Harrison's fingers, as depicted in the x-ray, were inconsistent with his testimony as to how the fingers were cut. . . . .

P's argue new trial

admit evidence to impeach

new design

Appellants contend that the trial court's denial of their motion for a new trial should be reversed because the court sustained Appellees' objection when Appellants sought to cross-examine Hyde with regard to a subsequent design change which eliminated the opening in the jointer. . . . . Appellants sought to have the evidence of the subsequent removal of the opening in the jointer admitted to impeach Hyde's testimony as well as to diminish his qualifications. Hyde testified on direct examination that, "there [was] no hazardous area left exposed next to the switch where you are going to unintentionally get your hand in there and contact the cutter head." However, after Appellants' claim arose, Hyde participated in designing a new jointer without the opening which allegedly injured Harrison.

In rejecting the use of subsequent remedial measure evidence, it is not clear from the record whether the district court was made aware of the impeachment aspect of Appellants' objection. In any event, the use to undercut qualifications and the use to impeach Hyde's testimony are closely related - in substance Appellants wanted to argue that "you can't trust this witness" - and we will assume that both uses were adequately raised before the trial court. In light of the close connection between these two proposed uses, we will refer to both as impeachment.

Federal Rule of Evidence 407 does not require the exclusion of evidence of subsequent measures when such evidence is being offered exclusively for impeachment purposes. Reversible error has been found when subsequent remedial evidence has been excluded when offered for impeachment purposes. However, cases which have admitted subsequent remedial measure evidence for impeachment purposes tend to involve a greater nexus between the statement sought to be impeached and the remedial measure than the case at bar. For example, in *Anderson v. Malloy*, subsequent remedial measure evidence was admitted to impeach statements that defendants had checked the area prior to the alleged accident and done everything possible to make it safe. A more direct impeachment use of subsequent remedial measure evidence would exist if Appellees' witness stated that he did not change the product after the alleged accident was brought to his employer's attention. Rule 407's impeachment exception must not be used as a subterfuge to prove negligence or culpability.

The leading commentators have noted the difficulty associated with applying the impeachment exception to Rule 407. Professor Wright voices a strong concern that the "exception" has the capacity to engulf the "rule." To guard against the impeachment exception being used as a loophole for bringing in evidence to prove negligence under Rule 407, the commentators advise that trial judges should not abandon their discretionary authority under Federal Rule of Evidence 403 to exclude the use of such evidence.

In this case the trial judge invoked his discretionary power to exclude testimony concerning the subsequent design change to the jointer. It is beyond question that the proffered testimony would have been extremely prejudicial to the Appellees. As impeachment evidence the only available basis for admission of the subsequent design change would have been to impeach Hyde's contention that the accident could not have happened in the manner described by Appellant. To allow Appellants to impeach this statement would in effect enable them to impeach Hyde's claim that the product was not defective and that Appellees were not negligent. If the evidence was admitted to impeach Hyde, Appellants' argument to the jury could have closely paralleled an argument that the subsequent measure could be seen as proof that Appellees were negligent.

It was within the trial judge's discretion under Rule 403 to determine whether this evidence would have prejudiced Appellees contrary to the intent of Rule 407, and to exclude such evidence due to the risk that the jury might improperly infer negligence from it. Because Hyde's statement and qualifications could only have been indirectly impeached by the subsequent remedial measure evidence and because the nature of the evidence was highly prejudicial, the trial judge did not abuse his considerable discretion in excluding such evidence.

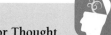

Food for Thought

The court reasoned that the trial judge had Rule 403 discretion to exclude this testimony for impeachment purposes because it was too attenuated. Do you think the court would have reversed the case if the trial judge had exercised her discretion by admitting the evidence?

[handwritten note:] reasoning
→ didn't allow in evidence to impeach

For these reasons, the judgment of the district court is affirmed.

————————

Points for Discussion

a. The Relevance of Impeachment Evidence.

Is the court in *Harrison* simply making a distinction between subsequent remedial measures offered directly to impeach a witness and those offered circumstantially? Is that what is meant when the court says that there must be "a greater nexus between the statement sought to be impeached and the remedial measure?" Is this another way of saying that the measures must have a stronger probative connection to impeachment under Rule 403 than to other impermissible offerings? If so, how much stronger?

b. The Difference Between the Impeachment and the Feasibility Exceptions.

In *Wood v. Morbark Indus., Inc.*, 70 F.3d 1201 (11th Cir. 1995), plaintiff sued a wood chipper company claiming that her husband fell into the chute of one of defendant's chippers because the chute was too short. At trial, the designer of the wood chipper described his product as having the "safest length chute you could possibly put on the machine." The court held that the designer's statement opened the door to allow the plaintiff to impeach his testimony by showing that the chute length was extended in later models. The court rejected plaintiff's argument that the designer's testimony controverted feasibility of a safer design. Has the court ruled correctly? Or should the evidence have been admitted for both purposes?

c. The Ownership and Control Exceptions.

If a defendant repairs a broken sidewalk which allegedly caused the plaintiff to slip and fall, should evidence of this repair be admissible if the defendant denies having ownership or control of the sidewalk? Common sense would say yes, but like all exceptions to Rule 407, the trial judge must conduct a Rule 403 balancing test before admitting the evidence. See *Andres v. Roswell-Windsor Village Apartments*, 777 F.2d 670 (11th Cir. 1985) (landlord's subsequent repairs were excluded from evidence because they did not sufficiently relate to the disputed issue of control). Do close calls under Rule 407 mean that they often get excluded anyway under Rule 403?

————————

C. Settlement Matters

1. When Offered Primarily in a Civil Case

> **Rule 408. Compromise and Offers to Compromise**
>
> **(a) Prohibited Uses --** Evidence of the following is not admissible on behalf of any party, when offered to prove liability for, invalidity of, or amount of a claim that was disputed as to validity or amount, or to impeach through a prior inconsistent statement or contradiction:
>
> **(1)** furnishing or offering or promising to furnish—or accepting or offering or promising to accept—a valuable consideration in compromise or attempting to compromise the claim; and
>
> **(2)** conduct or statements made in compromise negotiations regarding the claim, except when offered in a criminal case and the negotiations related to a claim by a public office or agency in the exercise of regulatory, investigative, or enforcement authority.
>
> **(b) Permitted Uses –** This rule does not require exclusion if the evidence is offered for purposes not prohibited by subdivision (a). Examples of permissible purposes include proving a witness's bias or prejudice; negating a contention of undue delay; proving an effort to obstruct a criminal investigation or prosecution.

Rule 408 excludes evidence of settlement or attempted settlement of a disputed claim when offered to show liability or the amount of the claim. There are several reasons for this ban. Settlements seldom constitute admissions that the opposing claims have merit. Most settlements are attempts to "buy one's peace," that is to avoid the stress, expense, and the time-consuming nature of trial. In addition, settlement is strongly favored by public policy. If parties contemplating settlement knew that their discussions would be admissible at trial should settlement negotiations fail, they would be much less likely to attempt settlement or discuss compromise fully and with candor. Would these policies be served if the party who wants to use an offer of settlement is the party who made the offer? Whose interests are protected by Rule 408?

Pierce v. F.R. Tripler & Company

U.S. Court of Appeals for the Second Circuit
955 F.2d 820 (2nd Cir. 1992)

MESKILL, Circuit Judge:

[Pierce, a former employee, brought suit against his former employer F. R. Tripler & Company, a subsidiary of Hartmarx, on the basis of age discrimination for failure to promote him to a general manager position.]

Pierce's attorney, Debra Raskin, informed Tripler by mail that she believed that Pierce had a meritorious age discrimination claim in the denial of the promotion, but that Pierce was reluctant to litigate the matter. Raskin proposed a meeting with Tripler in order to "work out an amicable resolution of this matter." Carey Stein, General Counsel for Hartmarx Specialty Stores, answered Raskin, stating that while he did not believe that Pierce had a claim, he would be happy to speak to Raskin in order to arrive at "an 'amicable resolution' of any claim he [Pierce] may have."

In early June 1986 Raskin and Stein discussed Pierce's situation but did not come to any agreement. In late July 1986 Pierce filed a complaint with the Equal Employment Opportunity Commission (EEOC) alleging age discrimination. On September 25, 1986, Stein telephoned Raskin offering Pierce a financial position at the Long Island City warehouse of Wallachs, another Hartmarx subsidiary. This conversation engendered some confusion as to whether Pierce would be required to waive his age discrimination claim in order to accept the position.

After this conversation, Raskin wrote Stein stating: "If you are willing to make this offer of employment ... without regard to the settlement of Mr. Pierce's claims, he would, of course, be willing to give it serious consideration." Stein responded by letter, stating that he was confused by Raskin's reference to the offer being "in exchange" for a release. He claimed that he had said that he would not offer the job "just for the purposes of settling the lawsuit," and that he still thought the lawsuit groundless. He further stated that, although the Wallachs' position might already have been offered to someone else, if Pierce were still interested Raskin should call and Stein would check back at Wallachs.

This letter was followed a week later by another from Raskin restating her understanding of the telephone call, which was that the job was conditioned on a release of all claims against the company. Stein wrote back to Raskin, implying that the offer had not been conditioned on such a release, but that they should "agree to disagree about what was said in the phone conversation and get on with the lawsuit if that's what's to be." Pierce then initiated this action in the Southern District of New York.

Hartmarx attempted before trial to have evidence of the subsequent job offer it *evidentiary ruling* made to Pierce ruled admissible. The district judge refused to allow the evidence, *DC* and Hartmarx contends on appeal that this disallowance was reversible error.

Hartmarx argued that the evidence was relevant for two purposes. First, *① D argued* Pierce's rejection of the job offer purportedly showed that Pierce had failed to take reasonable steps to mitigate his damages, thus limiting his claim for back pay. *②* Second, evidence of the job offer made in September 1986 allegedly was relevant to Hartmarx's state of mind in May when it denied Pierce the General Manager position. Pierce opposed the introduction of the evidence, contending that the *P argued* offer took place in the course of settlement negotiations and thus was inadmissible under Fed.R.Evid. 408. The district court held a hearing and determined that, *DC reasoned* because the offer was not "unambiguously unconditional," the evidence was not admissible for either purpose proposed by Hartmarx. The district court did not address the Rule 408 issue.

In order to show a failure to mitigate damages evidence of the failure must first be admissible. . . . Evidence that demonstrates a failure to mitigate damages goes to the "amount" of the claim and thus, if the offer was made in the course of compromise negotiations, it is barred under the plain language of Rule 408. Under Fed.R.Evid. 104(a) preliminary factual questions concerning the admissibility of evidence, such as whether an offer was made in the course of settlement negotiations, are to be determined by the court.

It is often difficult to determine whether an offer is made "in compromising or *whether during negotiated settlement or not* attempting to compromise a claim." Both the timing of the offer and the existence of a disputed claim are relevant to the determination. However, where a party is represented by counsel, threatens litigation and has initiated the first administrative steps in that litigation, any offer made between attorneys will be presumed to be an offer within the scope of Rule 408. Rule 408 does not protect offers to compromise made before a "claim" of some sort is made. But what constitutes making a "claim?" Clearly, sending a demand letter or filing a lawsuit would qualify. But what if the suit was merely

Food for Thought

What if a potential party does not have a lawyer? How would that party go about making a "claim?"

foreseeable? Cases interpreting the rule are not in agreement. See *Affiliated Mfgs., Inc. v. Aluminum Co. of America*, 56 F.3d 521 (3d Cir. 1995) (a clear difference of opinion is required between the parties) with *Deere & Co. v. International Harvester Co.*, 710 F.2d 1551 (Fed. Cir. 1933) (it is not enough that an eventual trial was a probability, Rule 409 is limited to actual disputes). The party seeking admission of an offer under those circumstances must demonstrate convincingly that the offer was not an attempt to compromise the claim.

The district court here did not make an explicit determination as to the admissibility of the evidence of the job offer under Rule 408. However, later . . . the district court stated that the offer was conditioned on the release of Pierce's claims, which is another way of saying that the job offer was an attempt to compromise a claim. Therefore, under the plain language of Rule 408, evidence of the job offer was not admissible to show Pierce's failure to mitigate damages.

d argues

Hartmarx, however, urges us to look behind the language of Rule 408 to its purposes. The Advisory Committee on Proposed Rules stated that the exclusion of evidence of compromise offers "may be based on two grounds. (1) The evidence is irrelevant, since the offer may be motivated by a desire for peace rather than from any concession of weakness of position.... (2) A more consistently impressive ground is promotion of the public policy favoring the compromise and settlement of disputes." Fed.R.Evid. 408, Notes of Advisory Committee on Proposed Rules. Hartmarx contends that neither of these policies would be advanced where, as here, it is the offeror seeking to introduce evidence of the offer. If the offeror is introducing the evidence, according to Hartmarx, we should not worry that the evidence will be unfairly viewed as a concession of weakness of the offeror's position. Similarly, argues Hartmarx, parties will not be discouraged from free and frank settlement discussions by the knowledge that they may introduce their own statements at trial.

Ct. reasons

We believe that admission into evidence of settlement offers, even by the offeror, could inhibit settlement discussions and interfere with the effective administration of justice. As the circumstances under which this issue arose in the district court suggest, widespread admissibility of the substance of settlement offers could bring with it a rash of motions for disqualification of a party's chosen counsel who would likely become a witness at trial.

The issue of admissibility of the job offer here first came before the district court when the defendant's attorney, Hartmarx General Counsel Carey Stein, requested from the court permission to withdraw as trial counsel because he intended to testify as to the substance of the job offer. Under the ABA Code of Professional Responsibility (DR 5-102(A)) and the ABA Model Rules of Professional Conduct (Rule 3.7), an attorney who ought to be called as a witness on behalf of his client must withdraw from representation at trial. Stein's testimony would likely have necessitated rebuttal testimony from Pierce's attorney, Debra Raskin, thus disqualifying her, and perhaps her entire firm, from representing Pierce at trial. Compare DR 5-102(A) (entire firm disqualified) with Rule 1.10 (disqualification of attorney under Rule 3.7 not imputed to members of firm).

It is common for attorneys in pending litigation to be involved in efforts to settle the case before trial actually commences. It is also common that adverse

parties have different memories as to what was said at such a meeting. If the
substance of such negotiations were admissible at trial, many attorneys would be
forced to testify as to the nature of the discussions and thus be disqualified as trial
counsel. Indeed, one commentator has noted that the advocate-witness rule itself
"means that no lawyer in a law firm that a client wished to serve as trial counsel
in threatened litigation could safely attend negotiation sessions designed to avert
trial or to renegotiate a contractual arrangement that had become unravelled, for
fear of becoming a potential witness."

*would Aru
attorneys h
testify at
trial*

This undesirable result is largely avoided by excluding evidence of settlement
negotiations. Hartmarx's interpretation of Rule 408 would discourage settlement
discussions or encourage expensive and wasteful duplication of efforts by "negotiation counsel" and "trial counsel."

We prefer to apply Rule 408 as written and exclude evidence of settlement
offers to prove liability for or the amount of a claim regardless of which party
attempts to offer the evidence from being used against a litigant who was involved
in the settlement, the rule is not limited by its terms to such a situation. Even
where the evidence offered favors the settling party and is objected to by a party
not involved in the settlement, Rule 408 bars admission of such evidence unless
it is admissible for a purpose other than "to prove liability for or invalidity of the
claim or its amount." . . .

hld

Points for Discussion

a. Admission of a Party's Own Offers or Statements.

The court in *Pierce* offers two explanations for its holding that a party may
not waive the protections of Rule 408 to admit its own settlement offers. First, the
policies behind Rule 408 are not advanced when the party making the offer wants
to admit it. Second, if "the substance of such negotiations were admissible at trial,
many attorneys would be forced to testify as to the nature of the discussions and
thus be disqualified as trial counsel." Which argument is more persuasive? What
about the argument that allowing one party to admit its own offer of settlement
would reveal that the opposing party participated in settlement discussions as
well? What harm could this admission cause to the opponent? Would attorneys
participate in settlement negotiations simply to set forth self-serving statements
that later could be used at trial?

b. Immunizing Otherwise Admissible Evidence.

May a party keep otherwise admissible evidence from being admitted by talking about it in settlement negotiations and then claiming it should be excluded

under Rule 408? The answer is no. Only matters prepared solely for settlement purposes are excluded. See *Ramada Development Co. v. Rauch,* 644 F.2d 1097 (5th Cir. 1981) (the trial court did not abuse its discretion by excluding an architect's pre-trial report prepared solely as the basis for settlement negotiations).

c. The Rule 408 Exception in Criminal Cases.

In 2006, Rule 408 was amended (in part) to provide that evidence of statements or conduct made by a party to a government regulatory, investigative, or enforcement agency are admissible in a subsequent criminal case. The amendment precludes a party from making a statement during compromise negotiations with one arm of the government and later contradicting it under oath free from impeachment when testifying in a criminal case brought by another arm of the government. These statements are not admissible, however, in a subsequent civil suit between private parties. The exception is limited to conduct or statements and does not admit any offers or acceptances in compromise of a claim. The statements may still be excluded in the trial court's discretion, however, under Rule 403.

———————

2. The Bias Exception

The last sentence of Rule 408 admits evidence of compromise offers, acceptances or negotiations if they are used to prove something other than the validity of a claim or its amount, such as to prove a witness's bias or prejudice.

John McShain, Inc. v. Cessna Aircraft Company

U.S. Court of Appeals for the Third Circuit
563 F.2d 632 (3rd Cir. 1977)

PER CURIAM:

In May 1969, John McShain, Inc. purchased an aircraft manufactured by Cessna Aircraft Co. from Wings, Inc. for $282,136. In December 1969, several hundred landings and 147 hours of flight later, the main landing gear of the plane collapsed as the plane alighted on the runway in Baltimore. After notifying Cessna, McShain had the aircraft repaired by Butler Aviation-Friendship, Inc. at a cost of $11,734. During the course of the overhaul, Cessna representatives visited the Butler repair facilities. The plane was then returned to McShain.

After 5 hours of further flight, the plane's landing gear once more gave way upon touchdown. The cost of repairs this time totaled $24,681. McShain refused to fly the craft again.

Negotiations between McShain and Cessna regarding a new plane terminated when McShain filed an action in Pennsylvania Common Pleas Court seeking rescission of the original sales contract and the return of the purchase price. *[handwritten: 1st action]*

McShain then instituted the present action against Cessna in district court, alleging defective design in the landing gear and Cessna's failure to correct that design despite knowledge of the defects. McShain requested judgment for (a) the cost of the repairs, (b) consequential damages, and (c) $5,000,000 in punitive damages. Cessna joined Butler as a third party defendant on the theory that the second crash was the result of inept repairs. . . . *[handwritten: 2nd action]*

Before the action was filed in the district court, the plaintiff signed an agreement releasing Butler from any liability for the accident in exchange for $10 and the right to engage as a consultant Ralph Harmon, who was at the time an employee of Butler's sister corporation, Mooney Aircraft Corp. Mr. Harmon was thereupon retained by McShain, and ultimately testified as an expert witness in support of the design-defect contention. Judge McGlynn allowed the release to be entered into evidence and read to the jury for the purpose of impeaching Mr. Harmon's testimony. *[handwritten: signed agreement; allowed release into evidence]*

McShain urges that, under Federal Rule of Evidence 408, agreements in compromise of a claim are generally inadmissible on the issue of liability on such claim. Cessna's reference to the Butler-McShain agreement, McShain insists, is such a proscribed use of evidence, since Cessna's counsel implicitly attempted to shift blame for the second failure from Cessna to Butler. *[handwritten: P argues]*

In response, Cessna maintains that the evidence was in fact admitted for the purpose of establishing the bias of Mr. Harmon, thus falling squarely within the exception to Rule 408. The rule by its terms "does not require the exclusion (of) evidence" when offered for the purpose of "proving bias or prejudice of a witness." *[handwritten: Cessna argues]*

We believe that Judge McGlynn did not commit reversible error in admitting the agreement and in allowing comments upon it. The fact that a sister corporation of Harmon's employer had been released from liability in exchange for Harmon's testimony cast doubt upon Harmon's impartiality. Thus, as counsel for McShain appeared to contend at oral argument, McShain's claim is in reality that the potential prejudice from the admission of the agreement outweighed the agreement's probative value. See Fed.Rule Evid. 403. . . . . The judgment of the court will be affirmed. *[handwritten: Ct. holds]*

Points for Discussion

a. Using Settlements to Show Bias.

Admissibility of settlement agreements to show the bias of a witness depends to a large degree on the terms of the agreement. For example, in *Quad/Graphics, Inc. v. Fass*, 724 F.2d 1230 (7th Cir. 1983), it was held that the trial court properly excluded evidence that the plaintiff settled with one of the defendants who was then dismissed from the suit because the terms of the settlement agreement required the defendant to "testify truthfully." What if the settlement agreement between the witness and a party is silent as to this matter?

b. Using Settlements to Counter Charges of Delay and Obstruction.

Evidence of settlement may be admissible to rebut an allegation of delay. See *Urico v. Parnell Oil Co.*, 708 F.2d 852 (1st Cir. 1983) (the defendant oil company refused to pay for repairs until the plaintiff waived all other claims against it. Testimony as to the defendant's bad faith negotiations was admissible to rebut charges that the plaintiff's failed to mitigate damages). Additionally, settlement offers may be shown if they constitute an attempt to obstruct justice, such as where a company threatens to retaliate against union employees if they pursue grievances against the company. See *Uforma/Shelby Business Forms, Inc. v. N.L.R.B.*, 111 F.3d 1284 (6th Cir. 1997).

What's That?

The term "delay" is not defined by the rules and is more a matter of whether the admission of settlement matters is a relevant response to an allegation of party foot-dragging of any nature.

D. Payment of Medical and Similar Expenses

Rule 409. Payment of Medical and Similar Expenses

Evidence of furnishing or offering or promising to pay medical, hospital, or similar expenses occasioned by an injury is not admissible to prove liability for the injury.

FYI

Medical expenses generally include doctor and hospital bills,
medications, medical equipment,
and possibly even rehabilitation services.

Rule 409 excludes from evidence payments, offers, and attempts to pay medical or similar expenses to prove the offering party's liability. The rule was enacted to encourage what is viewed as humanitarian gestures and because these matters have low probative value for proving fault.

You might be wondering why Rule 409 is necessary when Rule 408 prevents admission of offers, acceptances or payments in compromise in a case. The reason is because Rule 409 does not require that a "claim" precede the offer, unlike Rule 408. Often, it is critical for a party to obtain medical attention following an accident and not wait until the incident ripens into a dispute. Thus, if two people are in an automobile accident and one immediately offers to pay the other's medical bills, Rule 409 would keep this offer out of evidence whereas Rule 408 would not.

Rule 409 does not exclude statements made in connection with a payment, offer, or attempt to pay medical expenses. Communication may be necessary when parties are attempting to reach a settlement but is expected to be "incidental" where medical expense offers are concerned. At times, however, an offer to pay medical expenses may coincide with an admission of liability, for example when a potential defendant says to a potential plaintiff, "Don't worry. Because the accident was my fault, I'll pay your medical bills." Generally, statements of fault are admissible, whereas offers to pay medical expense are not, unless the admission cannot be disclosed without also disclosing the offer (as may be the case in the above example).

Hypo 8.1

Mac and Julian got into a bar room brawl one Saturday night. The next day, Mac feels terrible and visits Julian in the hospital. As he sees Julian's broken jaw, Mac says, "If you will sign a release of liability, I will pay your medical expenses. I know the fight was my fault." Would Rules 408 or 409 keep these statements from being admitted into evidence if a subsequent lawsuit ensues?

E. Plea Bargain Agreements in Criminal Cases

Rule 410. Inadmissibility of Pleas, Plea discussions, and Related Statements

Except as otherwise provided in this rule, evidence of the following is not, in any civil or criminal proceeding, admissible against the defendant who made the plea or was a participant in the plea discussions:

(1) a plea of guilty which was later withdrawn;

(2) a plea of nolo contendere;

(3) any statement made in the course of any proceedings under Rule 11 of the Federal Rules of Criminal Procedure or comparable state procedure regarding either of the foregoing pleas; or

(4) any statement made in the course of plea discussions with an attorney for the prosecuting authority which do not result in a plea of guilty or which result in a plea of guilty later withdrawn.

However, such a statement is admissible (i) in any proceeding wherein another statement made in the course of the same plea or plea discussions has been introduced and the statement ought in fairness be considered contemporaneously with it, or (ii) in a criminal proceeding for perjury or false statement if the statement was made by the defendant under oath, on the record and in the presence of counsel.

It's Latin to Me

"Nolo contendere" is Latin for "I do not wish to contend." It is sometimes called a plea of "no contest" and is used in place of a guilty plea when a criminal defendant does not want his plea to be used against him, usually in a subsequent civil lawsuit arising out of the same facts.

Rule 410 is similar to Rule 408; however, Rule 410 applies only to negotiations in criminal cases. A *plea bargain* is a negotiated agreement between a criminal defendant, his lawyer, and a prosecutor whereby the prosecutor typically agrees to a more lenient sentence or a reduced charge in return for the defendant's plea of guilty or "nolo contendere." In most cases, a defense attorney speaks for her client during plea negotiations; sometimes, however, the prosecution may require that a defendant make candid disclosures regarding his culpability as a condition of negotiation. Once a plea bargain is struck, the trial judge is required to conduct a hearing to determine whether he will accept that plea. During this hearing, the trial judge will most likely question the defendant about his role in the crime to determine whether there is a factual basis for finding the defendant guilty. The admission of a defendant's

The requirements of this hearing are set forth in Rule 11 of the Federal Rules of Criminal Procedure.

factual statements given during plea negotiations or during a plea hearing and offered at a subsequent trial is regulated by Rule 410.

As long as the defendant's Constitutional rights have not been violated, a defendant's written or oral confession is admissible separate and apart from the restrictions of Rule 410, because it is usually made to law enforcement officers or other witnesses.

Guilty pleas that are not later withdrawn are admissible to show the guilt of the defendant. In this respect, they are treated no differently than any other confession by the defendant. However, Rule 410 excludes evidence of pleas that are withdrawn, pleas of "nolo contendere" and statements a defendant makes in the course of discussions with the prosecutor or to the trial judge at the plea hearing. They are excluded when offered against the defendant in both civil and criminal proceedings.

The main purpose of the rule is to encourage the early disposition of criminal cases without the time and expense of trial. To admit a withdrawn guilty plea in a subsequent lawsuit would also be at odds with allowing a defendant to withdraw the plea in the first place and compel him to take the stand to explain that withdrawal. Rule 410 protects parties from having their plea negotiations from being used against them at trial. Should a party be permitted to waive this protection?

United States v. Mezzanatto

Supreme Court of the United States
513 U.S. 196 (1995)

Justice THOMAS delivered the opinion of the Court.

[Respondent Mezzanatto was arrested and charged with possession of methamphetamine with intent to deliver. He and his attorney met with the prosecutor to discuss cooperation with the government. The prosecutor told respondent that if he wanted to co-operate, he would have to be completely truthful and agree that any statements he made could be used to impeach any contradictory statements he made at trial if a plea could not be reached. Eventually the prosecutor ended the discussions because he believed the respondent was lying. At trial, the respondent maintained he did now know the package he delivered contained methamphetamine. The prosecutor was allowed to impeach respondent with a statement he had made to the contrary during plea discussions. Respondent was convicted. The Ninth Circuit reversed, holding that the respondent could not lawfully waive Rule 410].

The Ninth Circuit noted that these Rules are subject to only two express exceptions, neither of which says anything about waiver, and thus concluded that Congress must have meant to preclude waiver agreements such as respondent's. In light of the "precision with which these rules are generally phrased," the Ninth Circuit declined to "write in a waiver in a waiverless rule."

The Ninth Circuit's analysis is directly contrary to the approach we have taken in the context of a broad array of constitutional and statutory provisions. Rather than deeming waiver presumptively unavailable absent some sort of express enabling clause, we instead have adhered to the opposite presumption. A criminal defendant may knowingly and voluntarily waive many of the most fundamental protections afforded by the Constitution.

Our cases interpreting the Federal Rules of Criminal Procedure are consistent with this approach. The provisions of those Rules are presumptively waivable, though an express waiver clause may suggest that Congress intended to occupy the field and to preclude waiver under other, unstated circumstances. . . .

The presumption of waivability has found specific application in the context of evidentiary rules. . . . Indeed, evidentiary stipulations are a valuable and integral part of everyday trial practice. Prior to trial, parties often agree in writing to the admission of otherwise objectionable evidence, either in exchange for stipulations from opposing counsel or for other strategic purposes. Both the Federal Rules of Civil Procedure and the Federal Rules of Criminal Procedure appear to contemplate that the parties will enter into evidentiary agreements during a pretrial conference. During the course of trial, parties frequently decide to waive evidentiary objections, and such tactics are routinely honored by trial judges.

Respondent offers three potential bases for concluding that the Rules should be placed beyond the control of the parties. We find none of them persuasive.

(1) Respondent first suggests that the plea-statement Rules establish a "guarantee [to] fair procedure" that cannot be waived. We agree with respondent's basic premise: There may be some evidentiary provisions that are so fundamental to the reliability of the factfinding process that they may never be waived without irreparably "discredit[ing] the federal courts." But enforcement of agreements like

respondent's plainly will not have that effect. The admission of plea statements for impeachment purposes enhances the truth-seeking function of trials and will result in more accurate verdicts. . . .

Respondent also contends that waiver is fundamentally inconsistent with the ② Rules' goal of encouraging voluntary settlement. Because the prospect of waiver may make defendants "think twice" before entering into any plea negotiation, respondent suggests that enforcement of waiver agreements acts "as a brake, not as a facilitator, to the plea-bargain process."

We need not decide whether and under what circumstances substantial "public policy" interests may permit the inference that Congress intended to override the presumption of waivability, for in this case there is no basis for concluding that waiver will interfere with the Rules' goal of encouraging plea bargaining. The court below focused entirely on the defendant's incentives and completely ignored the other essential party to the transaction: the prosecutor. Thus, although the availability of waiver may discourage some defendants from negotiating, it is also true that prosecutors may be unwilling to proceed without it. . . .

Finally, respondent contends that waiver agreements should be forbidden ③ because they invite prosecutorial overreaching and abuse. Respondent asserts that there is a "gross disparity" in the relative bargaining power of the parties to a plea agreement and suggests that a waiver agreement is "inherently unfair and coercive." Because the prosecutor retains the discretion to "reward defendants for their substantial assistance" under the Sentencing Guidelines, respondent argues that defendants face an " 'incredible dilemma' " when they are asked to accept waiver as the price of entering plea discussions.

The dilemma flagged by respondent is indistinguishable from any of a number of difficult choices that criminal defendants face every day. The plea bargaining process necessarily exerts pressure on defendants to plead guilty and to abandon a series of fundamental rights, but we have repeatedly held that the government "may encourage a guilty plea by offering substantial benefits in return for the plea. "While confronting a defendant with the risk of more severe punishment clearly may have a 'discouraging effect on the defendant's assertion of his trial rights, the imposition of these difficult choices [is] an inevitable'-and permissible-'attribute of any legitimate system which tolerates and encourages the negotiation of pleas.' "

The mere potential for abuse of prosecutorial bargaining power is an insufficient basis for foreclosing negotiation altogether. "Rather, tradition and experience justify our belief that the great majority of prosecutors will be faithful to their duty." Thus, although some waiver agreements "may not be the product of an informed and voluntary decision," this possibility "does not justify invalidating all such agreements." Instead, the appropriate response to respondent's predictions of abuse is to permit case-by-case inquiries into whether waiver agreements are the product of fraud or coercion. We hold that absent some affirmative indication that the agreement was entered into unknowingly or involuntarily, an agreement to waive the exclusionary provisions of the plea-statement Rules is valid and enforceable.

[Justice Ginsburg, joined by Justices O'Connor and Breyer, concurred but argued that had the waivers been used in the government's case-in-chief, a different question would have been presented. Use of such statements "would severely undermine a defendant's incentive to negotiate, and thereby inhibit plea bargaining." Justice Souther, joined by Justice Stevens, dissenting, arguing that the legislative history showed Congress meant to "create something more than a personal right shielding an individual from his imprudence. Rather, [they] are meant to serve the federal judicial system by creating the conditions understood by Congress to be effective in promoting reasonable plea agreements."]

Points of Discussion

a. How Broad Is a Rule 410 Waiver after *Mezzanatto?*

If a defendant does not testify, would a broadly worded waiver allow the prosecution to use his statements to contradict other defense testimony? In *United States v. Velez,* 354 F.3d 190 (2d Cir. 2004), the court found the defendant's express waiver of all Rule 410 protections permitted the prosecution to admit the defendant's plea negotiation statements in order to contradict contrary defense testimony, evidence, and arguments. See also *United States v. Burch,* 156 F.3d 1315 (D.C.Cir. 1998), where the court indicated that Rule 410 can be expressly waived to allow use of a defendant's otherwise inadmissible Rule 410 statements in the prosecution's case-in-chief. Do you think that Justices Ginsburg, O'Connor and Breyer, who were members of the concurrence in *Mezzanatto,* would agree?

b. Exceptions to the General Rule.

There are two circumstances in which Rule 410 admits an otherwise inadmissible plea of guilty which is later withdrawn or a plea of "nolo contentere" and defendant's accompanying statements. If a defendant introduces a statement made during plea negotiations or a plea hearing, other relevant statements that "ought in fairness to be considered contemporaneously" with it are admissible. For example, in *United States v. Doran,* 564 F.2d 1176 (5th Cir. 1977), the prosecutor was allowed to show that the defendant made a counteroffer during plea negotiations to rebut the defendant's testimony that he had refused a plea bargain because he did not commit the crime. Additionally, Rule 410 statements can be used as a basis for a perjury or false statement prosecution if the defendant made them under oath, on the record, and with counsel present.

c. Statements Made to Persons Other than the Prosecuting Attorney.

A defendant's statements must be made to a prosecuting attorney to obtain Rule 410 protection. Otherwise, these statements will not be excluded, even if the defendant believes in good faith he is discussing a plea with someone who has authority to recommend a deal to the prosecution. See *United States v. Olson*, 450 F.3d 655 (7th Cir. 2006) (discussions with an FBI agent).

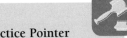

Practice Pointer

Defense attorneys take note. On occasion, prosecutors may make a plea bargain offer contingent upon hearing what a defendant has to say; however, the defendant runs into a real risk of creating adverse statements that can be used to impeach her at trial if negotiations fail and she testifies at trial.

F. Liability Insurance

Rule 411. Liability Insurance

Evidence that a person was or was not insured against liability is not admissible upon the issue of whether the person acted negligently or otherwise wrongfully. This rule does not require the exclusion of evidence of insurance against liability when offered for another purpose, such as proof of agency, ownership, or control, or bias or prejudice of a witness.

Rule 411, which prohibits admission of liability insurance as evidence of negligent or wrongful conduct, is based upon a concern that juries might use evidence of a defendant's liability insurance to compensate a plaintiff without first determining fault. A juror might reason that even though the defendant was not negligent, the plaintiff was truly injured; therefore the defendant's insurance company, with perceived unlimited resources, should pay. Furthermore, Rule 411 is an expression of the social policy of encouraging people to obtain liability insurance to compensate accident victims without such information being used against them at trial.

There are a number of listed exceptions to Rule 411. They include offerings to prove agency, ownership, or control, or bias or prejudice of a witness, and they are usually strictly construed. You will notice in the following case that one lawyer's tactical use of Rule 411 is another lawyer's windfall.

Charter v. Chleborad

U.S. Court of Appeals for the Eighth Circuit
551 F.2d 246 (8th Cir. 1977)

PER CURIAM.

This is a diversity action to recover damages for alleged medical malpractice. In June of 1973, plaintiff was struck by a truck while working as a highway flagman. The accident caused extensive injuries to both of plaintiff's legs. Plaintiff was hospitalized and placed under the care of a general practitioner and defendant, a surgeon. Surgery was performed on both legs. As a result of severe complications plaintiff was transferred to another hospital where both legs were amputated above the knee.

P argues

The trial of the matter resulted in a jury verdict for defendant and the district court denied plaintiff's motion for a new trial. Plaintiff . . . argues that the district court erred in limiting the cross-examination of a rebuttal witness for the defense.

Dr. testified

Plaintiff offered the testimony of Dr. Joseph Lichtor, M.D., a Kansas City, Missouri orthopedic surgeon. Dr. Lichtor testified as to his opinion of the requisite standard of care defendant should have used when treating plaintiff. He compared the treatment given and concluded that defendant had been negligent. Finally, Dr. Lichtor testified that the cause of the complications and subsequent amputations was defendant's negligence.

Food for Thought

Why do you think Alder believes Dr. Lictor to be dishonest? To what degree do you think this opinion is based upon cross-examining Dr. Lictor as a plaintiff's expert witness in other trials, or is it because Alder wants to curry favor with an insurance company that gives him business?

As a part of his rebuttal case, defendant offered the testimony of John J. Alder, an attorney from the Kansas City area. Mr. Alder testified that Dr. Lichtor's reputation for truth and veracity in the Kansas City area was bad. On cross-examination Mr. Alder testified that he did some defense work in medical malpractice cases. He also stated that some of his clients in those cases were insurance companies.

Plaintiff's counsel then asked him to name some of those companies and defendant objected to the relevancy of the matter. After a conference at the Bench the district court refused to allow further questioning on the subject of insurance. As plaintiff stated in his motion for a new trial, Mr. Alder was employed in part by the same liability carrier who represents defendant in this action.

DC refused to allow insurance testimony

It is well established that the existence of a liability insurance policy is not admissible to show one's negligence or other wrongful conduct. This rule has its basis in the belief that such evidence is of questionable probative value or relevance and is often prejudicial. Evidence of the existence of insurance may be offered for other purposes, however.

This Rule does not require the exclusion of evidence of insurance against liability when offered for another purpose, such as proof of agency, ownership, or control, or bias or prejudice of a witness.

Take Note!

A defendant whose insurance companies must pay if a plaintiff recovers a damage award is usually represented by a lawyer hired by defendant's insurance company under the "Duty to Defend" clause of the insurance contract. Nonetheless, the jury is not told of this representation. To a jury, it would appear that the defendant is represented by her own lawyer and that there is no insurance coverage in the case. This is why the jury in *Charter* was probably not aware (although they may have suspected) that the defendant was insured.

In this case the fact that defendant's insurer employed Mr. Alder was clearly admissible to show possible bias of that witness. Defendant does not dispute this obvious import of Rule 411 but urges that for several reasons the district court's exclusion of the evidence was not reversible error. . . .

Show bias of witness

Based upon Rule 403 of the Federal Rules of Evidence defendant also argues that the trial court acted within its discretion in excluding evidence of insurance. This argument is without merit. In our opinion the probative value of the evidence far outweighs any danger of unfair prejudice. Also, there is no indication in the record or briefs of the parties that any particular prejudice was threatened in this case. Rule 403 was not designed to allow the blanket exclusion of evidence of insurance absent some indicia of prejudice. Such a result would defeat the obvious purpose of Rule 411.

D argues

ct says

Defendant's final argument against reversal is that any error was harmless and did not affect a substantial right of the plaintiff. To pass on this argument we must view the total circumstances of the case. Plaintiff's claim rested for the most part on the credibility of his expert witness. When defendant undertook to impeach that witness plaintiff was entitled to attempt to show possible bias of Mr. Alder as

D argues

surrebuttal. Considering the importance of expert testimony in this case we cannot conclude that the trial court's exclusionary ruling was mere harmless error.

Accordingly, the judgment of the district court is reversed and the action is remanded with directions to grant the plaintiff a new trial.

——————

Points for Discussion

a. A Tactical Error?

Do you think defense counsel will use Mr. Alder as a witness at the retrial of this case after reading the appellate court's ruling in *Charter*? What should he consider before making this determination? Certainly, Mr. Alder can discredit the plaintiff's only expert witness, but to what degree will Alder himself be discredited by the revelation that he represents the same insurance company that insures the defendant? How might Alder's testimony potentially harm the defendant? What may a jury do with this information? If the defendant determines that Alder should testify, what type of limiting instruction should the trial judge give that would confine Alder's testimony to a proper purpose? Is such an instruction likely to be effective?

b. Other Exceptions Admitting Insurance.

Rule 411 lists a number of exceptions to the general rule excluding evidence of insurance to show liability. One exception is an offering to prove ownership or control. This exception might arise if the defendant, after an automobile accident, claims he was not driving and does not own the vehicle that struck the plaintiff. The plaintiff can then show the defendant carried insurance on the vehicle. See *Dobbins v. Crain Bros., Inc.*, 432 F.Supp. 1060 (W.D.Pa. 1976). Note, however, that the trial judge has discretion under Rule 403 to exclude such evidence if she thinks that it is too unfairly prejudicial to the defendant or that there is other evidence in the case showing ownership, such as proof of title. Rule 411, like all the rules we have discussed in this chapter, are subject to a Rule 403 balancing test.

——————

Executive Summary

Exclusion of Otherwise Relevant Evidence. Rules 407 - 411 represent specific situations where otherwise relevant evidence is excluded based on various countervailing policy considerations. These exclusions are also referred to as

"Categorical Rules of Exclusion" because certain whole categories of evidence are excluded for policy reasons. In addition to each rule, consider the various exceptions to that rule and look for strategic ways counsel will attempt to admit the evidence, arguing that it is being used for a different, acceptable, and admissible purpose which does not offend the underlying policy concern of the rule.

Rule 407 Subsequent Remedial Measures. Evidence of a remedial measure to "fix" or address a situation, or product, is inadmissible to prove that the person taking the remedial measure did so because the person was negligent or had engaged in culpable conduct in the first place, or that the situation or product remedied had a defect of some kind to begin with, or that there should have been a warning or instruction of some kind all along. The policy reason for the exclusion is so that people will be encouraged to take remedial measures without those actions later being held against them at trial. However, if the measure is offered for *another purpose*, such as to prove that the person had ownership or control over a situation or product, or to refute a claim the there was nothing the person could have feasibly done in order to avoid the problem, (*Anderson*), or to impeach a witness who overstates the defendant's position, (*Harrison*), then the evidence will be admissible.

Rule 408 Settlement Offers and Negotiations in Civil Cases. Evidence of: (1) a settlement agreement, (2) any offer or counter offer to settle, and (3) what is generally said during settlement negotiations, is all inadmissible to prove that a person engaging in such activity is, in effect, admitting or denying, civil liability on a claim that has been disputed as to validity or amount. The policy reason for the exclusion is so that people will be encouraged to engage in frank and open settlement negotiations, and make and accept settlement offers, without those actions later being held against them at trial. However, a party may not submit its own settlement offers and statements in a self-serving way. (*Pierce*). Further, if the settlement negotiations are used for *another purpose*, such as to prove a witness's bias or prejudice, (*McShain*), or to negate a contention of undue delay, or to prove an effort to obstruct a criminal investigation (pay a bribe), then the evidence will be admissible. Note that the rule does not provide protection for otherwise discoverable information, meaning that harmful evidence that is otherwise discoverable through investigation is not rendered inadmissible just because it was mentioned during settlement negotiations.

Rule 409 Offers to Pay Medical or Similar Expenses. Similar to Rule 408 settlement offers and negotiations, evidence of: (1) payment, (2) offers, or (3) attempts to pay medical or similar expenses, is all inadmissible to prove that the person engaging in such activity is, in effect, admitting responsibility for the actions leading up to the need to obtain medical or similar treatment. The policy reason for the exclusion is so that people can make benevolent offers to pay such expenses without those actions later being held against them at trial. Note that unlike Rule 408, Rule 409 does NOT exclude statements or conduct surrounding the offer to pay or act of payment.

Rule 410 Plea Bargain Agreements and Negotiations in Criminal Cases. Evidence of: (1) a plea bargaining agreement, (2) any offer to plea bargain (including guilty pleas and "nolo contendre" pleas later withdrawn), and (3) what is generally said during plea bargaining negotiations, is all inadmissible to prove that the person engaging in such activity is, in effect, admitting or denying criminal liability. The policy reason for the exclusion is so that people will be encouraged to engage in frank and open plea bargaining negotiations, and make and accept offers, without those actions later being held against them at trial. However, a defendant may waive this protection when dealing with a prosecutor just like a defendant can consent to and waive any other constitutional right. (*Mezzanatto*). If the plea bargaining negotiations are used for *another purpose*, such as to give context to other admitted statements from the plea bargaining negotiations that ought if fairness be heard, or in a prosecution for perjury/false statement, if the statement was made under oath, on the record, and in the presence of counsel, then the evidence will be admissible. It is also important for defendants to make sure they are negotiating with someone who has prosecutorial authority to do so, or the rule does not apply. Note that not all detectives or other law enforcement personal have prosecutorial authority.

Rule 411 Liability Insurance. Evidence of liability insurance (or lack thereof) to show: (1) that a person insured has a ready source of funds to pay any judgment for damages, (2) that a person who does not have insurance cannot afford to pay any judgment for damages, (3) that a person insured can afford to act negligently or engage in other wrongful conduct, or (4) that a person is careful in general because they have insurance, is all inadmissible. The policy reason for the exclusion is so that people will be encouraged to obtain and maintain liability insurance without that action later being held against them at trial. However, if the existence of liability insurance is being used for *another purpose*, such as to prove agency, ownership, or control of the insured asset, or to show bias or prejudice of a witness (such as an expert witness hired by the insurance company defending an insured tortfeasor on trial for damages), then the evidence will be admissible (*Chleborad*).

CHAPTER 9

A Return to Relevance II: Character and Habit

A. Introduction

The Federal Rules of Evidence do not define "character evidence." However, the word "character" generally refers to a person's tendency to act consistently with certain mental and ethical traits. People often believe that once they know a person's character, they can predict how that person will act. It is assumed that honest people will tell the truth, and peaceful people will act peacefully. Based upon

A person could also have a trait for being generous or thrifty, drunk or sober, industrious or lazy, law-abiding or criminal. The two types of character traits most often offered at trial, however, are those of honesty or dishonesty and peacefulness or violence.

these assumptions, the prosecution in a theft case might try to offer evidence of the defendant's dishonest character to show circumstantially that he is guilty of the theft. Or, a defendant in an assault case might try to offer evidence of his peaceful character to show circumstantially that she did not commit the assault. In reality, however, character evidence is often a weak predictor of a person's future actions because of its definition as only a "tendency" to act. For example, an otherwise dishonest person may tell the truth when it serves him

For More Information

In fact, some scholars think that character tells us little about human behavior. See Miguel A. Méndez, *Character Evidence Reconsidered: People Do Not Seem to Be Predictable Characters."* 49 HASTINGS L.J. 871 (1998).

better, or a generally peaceful person may react violently when cut off in traffic or when arguing with a spouse. Moreover, human behavior is often messy and complex, making it difficult for anyone to know another person's character completely. Furthermore, evidence offered at trial of a person's poor character carries with it moral overtones that can provoke a jury to react unfairly. In the example above, if the prosecution in a theft case offers evidence that the defendant was convicted of a prior theft, a jury might decide the defendant is guilty on the basis of "once a thief, always a thief"--and, therefore, the defendant deserves to be found guilty because he is a bad person and not because the facts require it.

The admissibility of character evidence is therefore an issue of relevance under Rule 403, which requires a balancing of probative value and unfair prejudice. Over centuries, this balancing has resulted in a general rule excluding character evidence when it is offered to show that a person possessing a particular character trait acted in conformity with that trait. "Once a thief, always a thief" is thus generally an inadmissible inference. The theory behind this exclusion is that people should normally be tried on the basis of what they have actually done and not on their character which only tells us what they are likely to have done. Of course, there are always exceptions to every rule, and character evidence has a number of them. These exceptions, particularly the ones contained in Rules 404 and 405, are often created because of long-standing tradition and policy concerns and are the major concern of this chapter.

Make the Connection

This chapter considers character evidence exceptions when they are offered as evidence of a substantive issue in a case upon which a jury might base its decisions. For example, a defendant in a homicide case might offer evidence that the victim had a violent reputation to prove a factual allegation that the victim was the first aggressor and that the defendant was justified in using self defense. Character evidence may also be offered in another context—to impeach or rehabilitate a testifying witness, that is, to show that a witness who testifies at trial should or should not be believed. See Chapter 5.

When an exception admitting character evidence applies, how does a party prove a person's character trait at trial? The answer is by looking at how that person has acted or is perceived by others to have acted in similar situations. With this in mind, Rule 405 of the Federal Rules of Evidence recognizes that there are three types of character evidence to which a witness may testify at trial when character evidence is admissible:

- A person's reputation in the community for that character trait;

- A witness's opinion as to that person's character trait; or

- A specific act which reveals that person's character trait.

Reputation evidence is testimony about what others in the community think about a person's character trait. Opinion evidence is what a witness personally knows about another person's character trait. Specific act evidence is witness testimony that describes the way a person has demonstrated a particular character trait through that person's actions on particular occasions. Whether evidence is admissible as reputation, opinion, or specific act testimony is determined by the purpose for which the evidence is offered. For example, we will see that witnesses testifying to character evidence exceptions under Rule 404(a) must do so in the form of reputation and opinion testimony, and specific act questions are only allowed on cross-examination. Offerings under Rule 404(b) admit only specific act evidence, and offerings under Rule 405(b) admit evidence in all three forms.

Character evidence is one of the most perplexing areas of evidence law. In large part, this is because the drafters of the Federal Rules of Evidence have written them in short-hand jargon for readers who they assumed already understood them. Because they are based on centuries of archaic, piecemeal, and stylized common law precedent, application of the rules may sometimes seem counter-intuitive and even unfair. In sorting through the confusion of character evidence, you may find it useful to chart answers to the following questions as you think about each rule:

1. Under what circumstances does the rule allow for admissibility of character evidence? To show the person whose trait is at issue acted in accordance with that trait or for some other specific purpose?

2. If admissible, what form must the character evidence take: reputation, opinion or specific act, or a combination of the three?

> **Take Note!**
>
> When thinking about this issue, know that in the federal rules, reputation and opinion evidence go hand in hand; that is, whenever reputation evidence is admissible, so is opinion evidence. See Rule 405(a).

3. Which party is required to present character evidence first at trial, or does it matter which party goes first?

4. What options does an opponent have in response to the presentation of character evidence?

> **Rule 404(a). Character Evidence Not Admissible To Prove Conduct; Exceptions; Other Crimes**
>
> **(a) Character evidence generally.** Evidence of a person's character or trait of character is not admissible for the purpose of proving action in conformity therewith on a particular occasion, except . . .

B. The General Rule Excluding Character Evidence

Think of it this way: If you were going to hire a surgeon to remove your appendix, who would you prefer to hire? A surgeon who had performed 200 appendectomies during which no patients died, or a surgeon who performed 200 appendectomies during which ten patients died? Most people would hire the first surgeon, figuring that either she was a better surgeon or at least very lucky. But why do we think this way? Perhaps we really believe that human behavior, to some degree, is predictable. But this may not be true. The first surgeon might have operated only upon young, healthy adults, while the second surgeon, who may be more skilled, may have only operated on elderly patients with medical complications. Nonetheless, the belief in the predictability of human behavior allows us to guess at a person's future actions when we have limited information, and a guess is required.

But what if a jury is asked to determine, in hindsight, whether the second surgeon was negligent when performing an appendectomy on a specific patient, who then died? Is it fair to allow a jury to consider the second surgeon's mortality rates in making that decision? A surgeon's mortality rates may have some probative value in proving negligence under some circumstance, but admitting them also runs the risk of encouraging the jury to decide against the second surgeon because he caused the death of patients and should be punished, not because of the facts of the case. And is it fair to require the second surgeon to defend against allegations of other wrongful deaths as well as against the allegations of the plaintiff? Remember, we want to judge people on what they actually did in this case, not on what they are likely to have done in past cases.

The following case discusses these issues and explains the rationales behind the general rule of the exclusion of character evidence in a criminal case. Although *Calvert* involves the overall inadmissibility of specific act character evidence, its logic can be extended to the general inadmissibility of reputation and opinion testimony as well.

United States v. Calvert

U.S. Court of Appeals for the Eighth Circuit
523 F.2d 895 (8th Cir. 1975)

HEANEY, Circuit Judge.

[Defendant Ronald Calvert was convicted by a jury of mail fraud and fraud by wire as a result of a scheme in which he entered into a partnership with as unsuspecting businessman, purchased key man and accidental death insurance on him, and then killed him to obtain the benefits. At trial, the Government introduced evidence that the defendant had previously collected on two other insurance policies under similar circumstances. The court determined that this evidence was admissible].

* * *

The admissibility of "other crimes" evidence in accordance with this rule is initially a matter within the sound discretion of the trial judge. In exercising that discretion, the trial court must determine that: (1) the evidence is relevant for a purpose other than showing the character or disposition of the defendant; (2) the proof that the acts were committed by the defendant is "clear and convincing;" and (3) the probative value of the evidence outweighs the danger of prejudice to the defendant.

>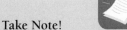
> **Take Note!**
>
> "Clear and convincing" is no longer the standard of proof for admitting evidence of other acts in a case. "Other act" evidence is only admissible if the trial court determines that the jury could reasonably find that the actor committed the act by a preponderance of the evidence. See the discussion of *Huddleston v. United States* in Chapter 3.

The rule is based on three dangers in the presentation of "other crimes" evidence. First, it is feared that . . . a jury might overestimate the probative value of such evidence by assuming that merely because the defendant has committed crimes before, he is likely to be guilty of the offense charged. Second, is the recognized tendency of men to punish a bad man now that he has been caught, even though his guilt on this occasion has not been satisfactorily established. And finally, it is felt that it is unfair to require a defendant to defend against and disprove crimes for which he has never been charged or indicted. Yet there is a tension in the rule, for evidence probative of material facts at issue may incidentally implicate the defendant in other crimes, and to exclude such evidence merely because it tends to show that the defendant is a bad man would "handicap the State in its prosecution of the man of cumulative criminal daring." The true purpose of the rule must thus be "to impel to a greater caution in determining relevancy in a given instance."

Points for Discussion

a. The Unfair Prejudice of Character Evidence.

Make the Connection

Limiting instructions are oral or written statements from the trial judge that order the jury to consider designated evidence only for a particular admissible purpose and not any other. See Federal Rule of Evidence 105.

The court in *Calvert* is concerned about the unfair prejudice that results from use of character evidence to show action in conformity. Could a trial court reduce the unfair prejudice of such an offering by giving a limiting instruction to the jury under Rule 105? How should this instruction be worded? Do you think that such an instruction could be understood and then fairly applied by a jury?

b. The Advantage to the Defendant of Keeping Prior Similar Acts from Being Admitted.

Obviously, a defendant would not want a jury to learn about her prior bad acts, particularly if they resulted in criminal convictions. But does a general exclusion of those bad acts give the defendant an unfair advantage? Jurors in a criminal case may expect to hear evidence about a criminal defendant's prior criminal history and assume, if it is not admitted, that no such evidence exists. Does exclusion of prior bad act evidence give the defendant a presumption of good conduct that she does not deserve?

————————————

C. Exceptions to the General Rule: Character of a Defendant in a Criminal Case

Rule 404(a)(1) and (2) Character Evidence Not Admissible to Prove Conduct; Exceptions; Other Crimes

(a) Character Evidence Generally. Evidence of a person's character or trait of character is not admissible for the purpose of proving actions in conformity therewith on a particular occasion, except:

(1) Character of the Accused. In a criminal case, evidence of a pertinent trait of character offered by an accused, or by the prosecution to rebut the same, or if evidence of a trait of character of the alleged victim of the crime is offered by an accused and admitted under Rule 404(a)(2), evidence of the same trait of character of the accused offered by the prosecution.

(2) Character of the Alleged Victim. In a criminal case, and subject to the limitations imposed by Rule 412, evidence of a pertinent trait of character of the alleged victim of the crime offered by an accused, or by the prosecution to rebut the same, or evidence of a character trait of peacefulness of the victim offered by the prosecution in a homicide case to rebut evidence that the alleged victim was the first aggressor;

Rule 405 Methods of Proving Character

(a) Whenever a trait of character of a person is admissible, proof may be made by testimony as to reputation or by testimony in the form of an opinion. On cross-examination, inquiry is allowable into relevant specific instances of conduct.

Rule 404(a)(1) and (2) contain exceptions that apply only in criminal cases. They admit character evidence to show that a defendant or an alleged victim in a criminal case acted in conformity with certain traits of their character under certain limited circumstances. Rule 405(a) only comes into play when evidence of character is admissible.

1. 404(a)(1): The "Mercy Rule"

Rule 404(a)(1) is divided into two parts: The first clause of the rule, sometimes called the "Mercy Rule," allows the defendant to present evidence of his good character to the degree that it is "pertinent" to the crime with which he is charged. For example, if a defendant is charged with embezzlement, she may present character evidence showing she is an honest person to

Make the Connection

The second clause of Rule 404(a)(1), admitting evidence as to the character of the defendant after the victim's character has been attacked by the defendant, will be considered later in this chapter.

prove circumstantially that she is not guilty of the crime. Under Rule 405(a), "Mercy Rule" witnesses can only testify as to their knowledge of the defendant's reputation or their opinion of the defendant's relevant character trait but not as to any of the defendant's specific acts that form the basis of their testimony. The rule does not allow these witnesses to testify as to specific acts on direct examina-

Take Note!

Rule 404(a)(1) must be read together with Rule 405(a).

tion for fear that proving or disproving them would take considerable time and become the focus of the trial. On the other hand, Rule 405(a) allows the prosecution to cross-examination "Mercy Rule" defense witnesses by asking them about any of the defendant's prior specific acts that demonstrate that his character is contrary to what the witnesses claim. However, the prosecution cannot ask about details of these acts nor imply that those acts are true because to do so would create issues that are collateral to the testimony.

The justification for the "Mercy Rule" is unclear. It may reflect an attempt to counteract a jury's assumption that the defendant is guilty because he has been charged with a crime. Or, perhaps the admission of good character evidence of the defendant is less worrisome in a system where there is a presumption of innocence. For whatever reason, the rule is a well-established one that appears to be a boon to the defendant. A defendant's use of this rule, however, is not without its dangers, as the *Michelson* case—the granddaddy of all "Mercy Rule" cases—illustrates:

Michelson v. United States

Supreme Court of the United States
335 U.S. 469 (1948)

Mr. Justice JACKSON delivered the opinion of the Court.

In 1947 petitioner Michelson was convicted of bribing a federal revenue agent. The Government proved a large payment by defendant to the agent for the purpose of influencing his official action. The defendant, as a witness on his own behalf, admitted passing the money but claimed it was done in response to the agent's demands, threats, solicitations, and inducements that amounted to entrapment. . . .

Defendant called five witnesses to prove that he enjoyed a good reputation [for honesty]. Two of them testified that their acquaintance with him extended over a period of about thirty years and the others said they had known him at least half that long. A typical examination in chief was as follows:

Q. Do you know the defendant Michelson?

A. Yes.

Q. How long do you know Mr. Michelson?

A. About 30 years.

Q. Do you know other people who know him?

A. Yes.

Q. Have you had occasion to discuss his reputation for honesty and truthfulness and for being a law-abiding citizen?

A. It is very good.

Q. You have talked to others?

A. Yes.

Q. And what is his reputation?

A. Very good.

On cross-examination, four of the witnesses were asked, in substance, this question: 'Did you ever hear that Mr. Michelson on March 4, 1927, was convicted of a violation of the trademark law in New York City in regard to watches?' This referred to the twenty-year-old conviction about which defendant himself had testified on direct examination. Two of them had heard of it and two had not. To four of these witnesses the prosecution also addressed the question the allowance of which, over defendant's objection, is claimed to be reversible error: 'Did you ever hear that on October 11th, 1920, the defendant, Solomon Michelson, was arrested for receiving stolen goods?' None of the witnesses appears to have heard of this.

The trial court asked counsel for the prosecution, out of presence of the jury, 'Is it a fact according to the best information in your possession that Michelson was arrested for receiving stolen goods?' Counsel replied that it was, and to support his good faith exhibited a paper record which defendant's counsel did not challenge.

The judge also on three occasions warned the jury, in terms that are not criticized, of the limited purpose for which this evidence was received. (In ruling on the objection when the question was first asked, the Court said: '. . . I instruct the jury that what is happening now is this: the defendant has called character witnesses, and the basis for the evidence given by those character witnesses is the reputation of the defendant in the community, and since the defendant tenders the issue of his reputation the prosecution may ask the witness if she has heard of various incidents in his career. I say to you that regardless of her answer you are not to assume that the incidents asked about actually took place. All that is happening is that this witness' standard of opinion of the reputation of the defendant is being tested. Is that clear?)

Practice Pointer

This rather terse and formulaic method of laying the predicate for admission of reputation testimony comes from the common law and is an attempt to allow the jury to hear the witness's ultimate estimation of the defendant's reputation without getting into the specifics of what the witness heard. We still lay the reputation predicate today in much the same way.

Defendant-petitioner challenges the right of the prosecution so to cross-examine his character witnesses. The Court of Appeals held that it was permissible. The opinion, however, points out that the practice has been severely criticized and invites us, in one respect, to change the rule....

* * *

Practice Pointer

Notice that the prosecution is asking about whether the witness *had heard* about specific acts relating to dishonesty. This *have you heard* formula was required when cross-examining reputation witnesses about prior bad acts under the common law.

When the defendant elects to initiate a character inquiry, another anomalous rule comes into play. Not only is he permitted to call witnesses to testify from hearsay, but indeed such a witness is not allowed to base his testimony on anything but hearsay. What commonly is called 'character evidence' is only such when 'character' is employed as a synonym for 'reputation.' The witness may not testify about defendant's specific acts or courses of conduct or his possession of a particular disposition or of benign mental and moral traits; nor can he testify that his own acquaintance, observation, and knowledge of defendant leads to his own independent opinion that defendant possesses a good general or specific character, inconsistent with commission of acts charged. The witness is, however, allowed to summarize what he has heard in the community, although much of it may have been said by persons less qualified to judge than himself. The evidence which the

Practice Pointer

A jury instruction under Rule 405(a) would look much the same today. Even if the instruction is not a model of clarity, the defense attorney has an opportunity to explain it during final argument and to reinforce the notion that just because the prosecution was allowed to ask about prior specific bad acts of the defendant does not mean those acts are true.

law permits is not as to the personality of defendant but only as to the shadow his daily life has cast in his neighborhood. This has been well described in a different connection as 'the slow growth of months and years, the resultant picture of forgotten incidents, passing events, habitual and daily conduct, presumably honest because disinterested, and safer to be trusted because prone to suspect.

* * *

[T]he witness must qualify to give an opinion by showing such acquaintance with the defendant, the community in which he has lived and the circles in which he has moved, as to speak with authority of the terms in which generally he is regarded. To require affirmative knowledge of the reputation may seem inconsistent with the latitude given to the witness to testify when all he can say of the reputation is that he has 'heard nothing against defendant.' This is permitted upon assumption that, if no ill is reported of one, his reputation must be good. But this answer is accepted only from a witness whose knowledge of defendant's habitat and surroundings is intimate enough so that his failure to hear of any relevant ill repute is an assurance that no ugly rumors were about.

Take Note!

Remember that *Michelson* is a case based upon the common law, which admitted "Mercy Rule" character evidence only in the form of reputation testimony. Federal Rule of Evidence 405(a) now admits opinion evidence whenever reputation evidence is admissible.

Thus the law extends helpful but illogical options to a defendant. Experience taught a necessity that they be counterweighted with equally illogical conditions to keep the advantage from becoming an unfair and unreasonable one. The price a defendant must pay for attempting to prove his good name is to throw open the entire subject which the law has kept closed for his benefit and to make himself vulnerable where the law otherwise shields him.

Food for Thought

Why does the court think that reputation evidence is reliable? Doesn't reputation evidence seem more like gossip, which is notoriously unreliable?

The prosecution may pursue the inquiry with contradictory witnesses to show that damaging rumors, whether or not well-grounded, were afloat--for it is not the man that he is, but the name that he has which is put in issue. Another hazard is that his own witness is subject to cross-examination as to the contents and extent of the hearsay on which he bases his conclusions, and he may be required to disclose rumors and reports that are current even if they do not affect his own conclusion. (A classic example in the books is a character witness in a trial for murder. She testified she grew up with defendant, knew his reputation for peace and quiet, and that it was good. On cross-examination she was asked if she had heard that the defendant had shot anybody and, if so, how many. She answered, 'Three or four,' and gave the names of two but could not recall the names of the others. She still insisted, however, that he was of 'good character.' The jury seems to have valued her information more highly than her judgment, and on appeal from conviction the cross-examination was held proper.) It may test the sufficiency of his knowledge by asking what stories were circulating concerning events, such as one's arrest, about which people normally comment and speculate. Thus, while the law gives defendant the option to show as a fact that his reputation reflects a life and habit incompatible with commission of the offense charged, it subjects his proof to tests of credibility designed to prevent him from profiting by a mere parade of partisans.

* * *

A character witness may be cross-examined as to an arrest whether or not it culminated in a conviction, according to the overwhelming weight of authority.

. . .

Arrest without more may nevertheless impair or cloud one's reputation. False arrest may do that. Even to be acquitted may damage one's good name if the community receives the verdict with a wink and chooses to remember defendant as one who ought to have been convicted. A conviction, on the other hand, may be accepted as a misfortune or an injustice, and even enhance the standing of one who mends his ways and lives it down. Reputation is the net balance of so many debits and credits that the law does not attach the finality to a conviction when the issue is reputation that is given to it when the issue is the credibility of the convict.

The inquiry as to an arrest is permissible also because the prosecution has a right to test the qualifications of the witness to bespeak the community opinion. If one never heard the speculations and rumors in which even one's friends indulge upon his arrest, the jury may doubt whether he is capable of giving any very reliable conclusions as to his reputation.

* * *

The good character which the defendant had sought to establish was broader than the crime charged and included the traits of 'honesty and truthfulness' and 'being a law-abiding citizen.' Possession of these characteristics would seem as incompatible with offering a bribe to a revenue agent as with receiving stolen goods. The crimes may be unlike, but both alike proceed from the same defects of character which the witnesses said this defendant was reputed not to exhibit. It is not only by comparison with the crime on trial but by comparison with the reputation asserted that a court may judge whether the prior arrest should be made subject of inquiry. By this test the inquiry was permissible. It was proper cross-examination because reports of his arrest for receiving stolen goods, if admitted, would tend to weaken the assertion that he was known as an honest and law-abiding citizen. The cross-examination may take in as much ground as the testimony it is designed to verify. To hold otherwise would give defendant the benefit of testimony that he was honest and law-abiding in reputation when such might not be the fact; the refutation was founded on convictions equally persuasive though not for crimes exactly repeated in the present charge.

The inquiry here concerned an arrest twenty-seven years before the trial. Events a generation old are likely to be lived down and dropped from the present thought and talk of the community and to be absent from the knowledge of younger or more recent acquaintances. The court in its discretion may well exclude inquiry about rumors of an event so remote, unless recent misconduct revived them. But two of these witnesses dated their acquaintance with defendant as commencing thirty years before the trial. Defendant, on direct examination, voluntarily called attention to his conviction twenty years before. While the jury might conclude that a matter so old and indecisive as a 1920 arrest would shed little light on the present reputation and hence propensities of the defendant, we cannot say that, in the context of this evidence and in the absence of objection on this specific ground, its admission was an abuse of discretion.

We do not overlook or minimize the consideration that 'the jury almost surely cannot comprehend the Judge's limiting instructions,' which disturbed the Court of Appeals. The refinements of the evidentiary rules on this subject are such that even lawyers and judges, after study and reflection, often are confused, and surely jurors in the hurried and unfamiliar movement of a trial must find them almost unintelligible. However, limiting instructions on this subject are no more difficult to comprehend or apply than those upon various other subjects; for example, instructions that admissions of a co-defendant are to be limited to the question of his guilt and are not to be considered as evidence against other defendants, and instructions as to other problems in the trial of conspiracy charges. A defendant in such a case is powerless to prevent his cause from being irretrievably obscured and confused; but, in cases such as the one before us, the law foreclosed this whole confounding line of inquiry, unless defendant thought the net advantage from opening it up would be with him. Given this option, we think defendants in general and this defendant in particular have no valid complaint at the latitude which existing law allows to the prosecution to meet by cross-examination an issue voluntarily tendered by the defense.

* * *

We concur in the general opinion of courts, text writers and the profession that much of this law is archaic, paradoxical and full of compromises and compensations by which an irrational advantage to one side is offset by a poorly reasoned counter-privilege to the other. But somehow it has proved a workable even if clumsy system when moderated by discretionary controls in the hands of a wise and strong trial court. To pull one misshapen stone out of the grotesque structure is more likely simply to upset its present balance between adverse interests than to establish a rational edifice.

* * *

Points for Discussion

a. What is a "Pertinent Trait?"

Under Rule 404(a)(1), the defendant is allowed to present character evidence only to the extent that it relates to a "pertinent trait" of the crime charged. From *Michelson* we see that a defendant charged with bribery, a crime of dishonesty, may offer evidence under the "Mercy Rule" of his truthful character. A defendant charged with crimes of violence, such as murder, sexual assault, robbery, kidnapping, or assault, may offer evidence supporting his peaceful character. What "pertinent trait" is relevant to a drug crime? Several courts have determined that crimes that involve the illegal possession of drugs raise the character trait of being law-abiding. See, e.g., *United States v. Diaz*, 961 F.2d 1417 (9th Cir. 1992) (holding that the defendant, who was charged with possession of cocaine with intent to distribute, was improperly prevented from calling his pastor to testify to his good character for being law-abiding). Drug crime charges do not, however, raise the character trait of honesty. See *United States v. Jackson*, 588 F.2d 1046 (5th Cir. 1979).

b. Opinion Testimony.

The *Michelson* court follows the older common law prohibiting "Mercy Rule" witnesses from giving their opinion of the defendant's character. The common law reasoned that if a witness was allowed to give his opinion, he should logically be allowed to tell the jury about the defendant's prior instances of good conduct which led him to form his opinion. By the same token, the prosecution should then be allowed to offer evidence of a defendant's past bad conduct so as to contradict the witness's opinion, and the trial would become confusing and lengthy. See *People v. Van Gaasbeck*, 82 N.E. 718 (1907). Rather than exclude opinion evidence altogether, Rule 405(a) allows witnesses to testify as to both opinion and reputation evidence but prohibits them from testifying as to any specific acts, or specific instances of conduct that form the basis of their testimony, except in a limited way on cross-examination.

c. Offering Opinion Testimony.

Assume that *Michelson* was tried under the Federal Rules of Evidence. Construct a brief direct-examination of an opinion witness who will testify that in her opinion the defendant is truthful. As a starting point, look at and modify the questions asked of the defendant's reputation witnesses in *Michelson.*

d. The Character Witness's Foundation for Testifying.

What if the defense offers a witness to testify that the defendant has a reputation for being an honest person because he has heard nothing bad about him from the community? According to *Michelson,* is this a sufficient basis for admitting her testimony? Why or why not?

e. The Prosecution's Options in Response to Presentation of "Mercy Rule" Witnesses.

In *Michelson,* the prosecution has two options for rebutting a defendant's "Mercy Rule" testimony. First, he can cross-examine the defense witness by asking whether he has heard about specific bad acts of the defendant that rebut the positive character testimony on direct examination. Prior bad acts may consist of occurrences, arrests or convictions, but the prosecution may not ask the witness about their details. Second, the prosecution can present its own witnesses to testify that the defendant has a bad reputation for the trait in question. Also keep in mind that the prosecution may only present its own character witnesses after the defendant has "opened the door" by presenting his own "Mercy Rule" witnesses.

f. Cross-Examination of a Reputation or Opinion Witness.

The prosecution in *Michelson* asks the defendant's reputation witnesses on cross-examination if they *have heard* about the defendant's prior bad acts of dishonesty. By using the phrase *have you heard,* the prosecution was testing whether the witnesses were really knowledgeable about what the community was saying about the defendant's character. In the later common law, if the witness had testified about his opinion of the defendant's character, the law would have required the prosecution to ask *do you know* about the defendant's prior acts of dishonesty. It is no longer necessary under the Federal Rules of Evidence to preface specific act questioning during cross-examination in this manner, although it is still permissible.

g. Prosecution Cross-Examination and "Good Faith."

The prosecution must ask its cross-examination questions in good faith; that is, the prosecution may not ask about specific acts that she has reason to believe the defendant never committed. The same holds true when the defense cross-examines the prosecution's reputation or opinion witnesses. If challenged to show good faith, the cross-examiner must convince the judge why he believes the specific act occurred. This might require production of an arrest or conviction record or at least informing the judge about the source and credibility of the specific act information.

h. "Mercy Rule" Risks.

If the defendant chooses not to offer "Mercy Rule" witnesses, the prosecution may not offer witnesses to testify as to the defendant's bad character because Rule 404(a)(1) requires that the defendant make the first offering. Knowing this, a defense attorney should never call "Mercy Rule" witnesses to the stand unless he has checked to make certain his client has no prior bad arrests or convictions that are pertinent to the character trait in question which may be asked about on cross-examination. Such information can usually be found in the defendant's arrest and conviction record, if any, or by asking the defendant about his criminal history, although defendants are not always forthcoming about these matters. Once the "door is open" the prosecution may call witnesses to testify about the defendant's bad character to rebut the defendant's good character witnesses.

Hypo 9.1

The defendant is charged with income tax evasion. Under Rule 404(a)(1), can his wife testify that, in her opinion, he is a peaceful man? An honest man? Can his minister testify that the defendant has a reputation for being a law-abiding citizen? Can a store clerk testify that he gave the defendant too much change and that the defendant returned it?

Hypo 9.2

The defendant, an administrative assistant to the Philadelphia District Attorney's Office, is charged in a criminal case with willfully and knowingly making false declarations to a grand jury. Under the "Mercy Rule," the defense proposes to present the testimony of several character witnesses who will testify that the defendant has a good reputation for truthfulness and veracity. On cross-examination, the prosecution plans to ask these witnesses if they are familiar with an article in the Philadelphia Enquirer that claimed the defendant had attempted to "fix" court cases. If you are the judge, how would you rule on this offering? What if you determined that the article did not actually exist?

2. Rules 413-415: The Defendant's Character in Sexual Assault and Child Molestation Cases

Rule 413. Evidence of Similar Crimes in Sexual Assault Cases.

(a) In a criminal case in which the defendant is accused of an offense of sexual assault, evidence of the defendant's commission of another offense or offenses of sexual assault is admissible, and may be considered for its bearing on any matter to which it is relevant.

(b) In a case in which the Government intends to offer evidence under this rule, the attorney for the Government shall disclose the evidence to the defendant, including statements of witnesses or a summary of the substance of any testimony that is expected to be offered, at least fifteen days before the scheduled date of trial or at such later time as the court may allow for good cause.

(c) This rule shall not be construed to limit the admission or consideration of evidence under any other rule.

(d) For purposes of this rule and Rule 415, "offense of sexual assault" means a crime under Federal law or the law of a State (as defined in section 513 of title 18, United States Code) that involved—

(1) Any conduct proscribed by chapter 109A of title 18, United States Code;

(2) Contact, without consent, between any part of the defendant's body or an object and the genitals or anus of another person;

(3) Contact, without consent, between the genitals or anus of the defendant and any part of another person's body.

(4) Deriving sexual pleasure or gratification from the infliction of death, bodily injury, or physical pain on another person; or

(5) An attempt or conspiracy to engage in conduct described in paragraphs (1)-(4).

Rule 414. Evidence of Similar Crimes in Child Molestation Cases.

(a) In a criminal case in which the defendant is accused of an offense of child molestation, evidence of the defendant's commission of another offense or offenses of child molestation is admissible, and may be considered for its bearing on any matter to which it is relevant.

(b) In a case in which the Government intends to offer evidence under this rule, the attorney for the Government shall disclose the evidence to the defendant, including statements of witnesses or a summary of the substance of any testimony that is expected to be offered, at least fifteen days before the scheduled date of trial or at such later time as the court may allow for good cause.

(c) This rule shall not be construed to limit the admission or consideration of evidence under any other rule.

(d) For purposes of this rule and Rule 415, "child" means a person below the age of fourteen, and "offense of child molestation" means a crime under Federal law of the law of a State (as defined in section 513 of title 18, United States Code) that involved—

(1) Any conduct proscribed by chapter 109A of title 18, United States Code, that was committed in relation to a child;

(2) Any conduct proscribed by chapter 110 of title 18, United States Code;

(3) Contact between any part of the defendant's body or an object and the genitals of the body of a child;

(4) Contact between the genitals or anus of the defendant and any part of the body of a child;

(5) Deriving sexual pleasure or gratification from the infliction of death, bodily injury, or physical pain on a child; or

(6) An attempt or conspiracy to engage in conduct described in paragraphs (1)-(5).

Rule 415. Evidence of Similar Crimes in Civil Cases Concerning Sexual Assault or Child Molestation

(a) In a civil case in which a claim for damages or other relief is predicated on a party's alleged commission of conduct constituting an offense of sexual assault or child molestation, evidence of that party's commission of another offense or offenses of sexual assault or child molestation is admissible and may be considered as provided for in Rule 413 and Rule 414 of these rules.

(b) A party who intends to offer evidence under this Rule shall disclose the evidence to the party against whom it will be offered, including statements of witnesses or a summary of the substance of any testimony that is expected to be offered, at least fifteen days before the scheduled date of trial or at such later time as the court may allow for good cause.

In 1994, Congress enacted Rules 413-415, which allow prosecutors in criminal cases and plaintiffs in civil cases to prove that a defendant committed sexual assault or child molestation by using evidence that the defendant assaulted or molested others. These rules dramatically change the traditional rules of evidence by lifting the ban against use of character evidence to show propensity and by allowing admission of the defendant's prior sexual acts to prove he is the sort of person who would engage in sexual misconduct.

Rules 413-415 resulted from the difficulties involved in prosecuting and convicting defendants of sexual assault and child molestation, especially when the only testifying witnesses were the defendant and the victim. Victims of these crimes are frequently reluctant to file charges and testify in these cases, particularly if they are children. By admitting propensity evidence, the sponsors of the rules hoped that juries would give less weight to a defendant's testimony, more weight to the victim's testimony, and that there would be an increase in the filing and conviction rates for these crimes. Sponsors justified the admission of propensity evidence by arguing that defendants who commit sexual assault and child molestation are much more likely than the average criminal to repeat their crime; thus, evidence of this nature has greater probative value in proving propensity.

The process of enacting these rules generated a great deal of controversy. Unlike other Federal Rules of Evidence, Rules 413-415 were proposed by Congress, not the Advisory Committee of the Judicial Conference. In fact, the Advisory Committee and Judicial Conference recommended that they not be adopted, as did the ABA House of Delegates, which sponsored a resolution opposing them. *criticism*
The basis for their criticism was that the rules unfairly prejudiced defendants

For More Information

For an early unfavorable assessment of these rules see Duane, *The New Federal Rules of Evidence on Prior Acts of Accused Sex Offenders: A Poorly Drafted Version of a Very Bad Idea*, 157 F.R.D. 95 (1994); but see Park, *The Crime Bill of 1994 and the Law of Character Evidence: Congress Was Right About Consent Defense Cases*, 22 FORDHAM URB. L.J. 271 (1995).

and contained drafting ambiguities and possible constitutional infirmities. Nonetheless, after reconsideration, Congress approved Rules 413-415, and they became effective on July 9, 1995.

Since their enactment, defendants have challenged these rules on constitutional grounds and on the basis that they were unfairly prejudicial. The following case illustrates one of those challenges:

United States v. LeMay

U.S. Court of Appeals for the Ninth Circuit
260 F.3d 1018 (9th Cir. 2001)

TROTT, Circuit Judge:

[Fred LeMay, a twenty-four year old Native American and a member of the Fort Peck Indian tribe, was convicted of forcing two of his sister's children, D.R. and A.R, aged five and seven, to orally copulate with him. These crimes occurred in 1997 but his sister never reported them. At trial, the prosecution called A.R. and D.R., who at the time were seven and nine years old, who testified to their sexual assault by the defendant. On cross-examination, LeMay's counsel suggested the boys did not remember events accurately and that they had a motive to lie because they were in foster care and wanted to return home. The prosecution was then permitted to introduce testimony that the defendant had a juvenile rape conviction stemming from two 1989 sexual assaults of the two-year old and eight month old daughters of his aunt, Francine May. After conducting a Rule 403 balancing test, the trial judge admitted the defendant's 1989 acts of molestation under Federal Rule of Evidence 414, an admission which LeMay contends violated his constitutional right to due process.]

FYI

Generally, sexual assault or child molestation cases are prosecuted in state courts. However, if these crimes were committed on federal property, such as in a national park or on an Indian Reservation, they are prosecuted in federal court.

We review de novo a claim that a statute or a rule is unconstitutional. However, a district judge's ruling under Rule 403 that evidence is more probative than prejudicial is reviewed for an abuse of discretion.

Prior to 1994, when Rules 413 through 415 were passed, admission of a defendant's prior crimes or acts was governed by Rule 404(b), which disallows such evidence when used to prove "the character of a person in order to show action in conformity therewith." Rule 414 changes this general rule with respect to child molestation cases. It makes such evidence admissible, providing that in a criminal case in which the defendant is defendant of an offense of child molestation, evidence of the defendant's commission of another offense or offenses of child molestation is admissible, and may be considered for its bearing on any matter to which it is relevant.

LeMay contends that Rule 414 violates due process principles by removing the longstanding ban on propensity evidence in criminal trials. He argues that the traditional rule precluding the use of a defendant's prior bad acts to prove his disposition to commit the type of crime charged is so ingrained in Anglo-American jurisprudence as to be embodied in the due process clause of the Constitution. LeMay has a very high burden in proving this assertion, and we conclude he has not met it.

The Constitution does not encompass all traditional legal rules and customs, no matter how longstanding and widespread such practices may be. The Supreme Court has cautioned against the wholesale importation of common law and evidentiary rules into the Due Process Clause of Constitution. In *Dowling v. United States*, for example, the Court held that a rule or practice must be a matter of "fundamental fairness" before it may be said to be of constitutional magnitude. 493 U.S. 342, 352 (1990). . . . Additionally, "[i]t is not the State which bears the burden of demonstrating that its rule is 'deeply rooted,' but rather [the defendant]." Thus, we must decide if LeMay has shown that the traditional ban on propensity evidence involves a "fundamental conception of justice." We conclude he has not.

The Supreme Court has held that the primary guide for determining whether a rule is so "fundamental" as to be embodied in the Constitution is historical practice. In this case, however, evidence of historical practice does not lead to a clear conclusion. On the one hand, it seems clear that the general ban on propensity evidence has the requisite historical pedigree to qualify for constitutional status.

On the other hand, courts have routinely allowed propensity evidence in sex-offense cases, even while disallowing it in other criminal prosecutions. In many American jurisdictions, evidence of a defendant's prior acts of sexual misconduct is commonly admitted in prosecutions for offenses such as rape, incest, adultery, and child molestation. As early as 1858, the Michigan Supreme Court noted that "courts in several of the States have shown a disposition to relax the rule [against propensity evidence] in cases where the offense consists of illicit intercourse between the sexes." Today, state courts that do not have evidentiary rules comparable to Federal Rules 414 through 415 allow this evidence either by stretching traditional 404(b) exceptions to the ban on character evidence or by resorting to the so-called "lustful disposition" exception, which, in its purest form, is a rule allowing for propensity inferences in sex crime cases. Thus, "the history of evidentiary rules regarding a criminal defendant's sexual propensities is ambiguous at best, particularly with regard to sexual abuse of children."

The historical evidence in this case thus leads to no clear conclusion. In holding that Rule 414 is constitutional, we therefore do not rely solely on the fact that courts have historically allowed propensity evidence to reach the jury in sex offense cases. Because LeMay has the burden of proving that the ban on propensity evidence is a matter of fundamental fairness, the divergence in historical evidence does cut against his position. Yet while we recognize the importance of historical practice in determining whether an evidentiary rule is embodied in the Due Process Clause, in this case, we find it necessary to conduct an independent inquiry into whether allowing propensity inferences violates fundamental ideas of fairness.

We conclude that there is nothing fundamentally unfair about the allowance of propensity evidence under Rule 414. As long as the protections of Rule 403 remain in place to ensure that potentially devastating evidence of little probative value will not reach the jury, the right to a fair trial remains adequately safeguarded.

Although this court has never squarely addressed the issue of whether Rule 414 and its companion rules are constitutional, we have recently held that the balancing test of Rule 403 continues to apply to those rules, and that district judges retain the discretion to exclude evidence that is far more prejudicial than probative. With the protections of the Rule 403 balancing test still in place, LeMay's due-process challenge to Rule 414 loses much of its force. The evidence that he had sexually molested his cousins in 1989 was indisputably relevant to the issue of whether he had done the same thing to his nephews in 1997. The introduction of relevant evidence, by itself, cannot amount to a constitutional violation.

Likewise, the admission of prejudicial evidence, without more, cannot be unconstitutional. All evidence introduced against a criminal defendant might be said to be prejudicial if it tends to prove the prosecution's case. Moreover, evidence that a defendant has committed similar crimes in the past is routinely admitted in criminal prosecutions under Rule 404(b) to prove preparation, identity, intent, motive, absence of mistake or accident, and for a variety of other purposes.

Food for Thought

Is the court saying that without a Rule 403 balancing test, Rule 414 is unconstitutional? If so, do you agree? Can you think of an alternative non-constitutional reason for requiring that Rule 403 should apply to Rule 414?

The introduction of such evidence can amount to a constitutional violation only if its prejudicial effect far outweighs its probative value. [S]uch evidence will only sometimes violate the constitutional right to a fair trial if it is of no relevance, or if its potential for prejudice far outweighs what little relevance it might have. Potentially devastating evidence of little or no relevance would have to be excluded under Rule 403. Indeed, this is exactly what Rule 403 was designed to do. We therefore conclude that as long as the protections of Rule 403 remain in place so that district judges retain the authority to exclude potentially devastating evidence, Rule 414 is constitutional.

* * *

Nor does the admission of even highly prejudicial evidence necessarily trespass on a defendant's constitutional rights. Thus, the claim that Rule 414 is unconstitutional can be reduced to a very narrow question: "whether admission of ... evidence that is both relevant under Rule 402 and not overly prejudicial under 403 may still be said to violate the defendant's due process right to a fundamentally fair trial." "[T]o ask that question is to answer it." Rule 414 is constitutional on its face. *[issue]*

* * *

We also conclude that admitting LeMay's prior acts of molestation was proper in light of the factors we discussed in *Glanzer* and others relevant to this particular case. We begin by noting, as the district judge did, that the evidence of LeMay's prior acts of child molestation was highly relevant. The 1989 molestations were very similar to the charged crimes. Each case involved forced oral copulation. In each case the victims were young relatives of LeMay, and each instance occurred while LeMay was babysitting them.

Moreover, as the district judge suggested, the prior acts evidence was relevant to bolster the credibility of the victims after LeMay suggested they could be fabricating the accusations. The evidence also countered LeMay's claim that there was no evidence corroborating the testimony of D.R. and A.R.

We recognize that this characterization of the evidence is essentially a veiled propensity inference. However, it is also exactly the sort of use of prior acts evidence that Congress had in mind when enacting Rule 414. The case against LeMay rested on testimony of D.R. and A.R. Both children were very young at the time of the incidents, and two years had passed before LeMay was tried. LeMay attacked their credibility and suggested that there was not enough evidence to prove their allegations. That this case made use of the prior acts evidence in precisely the manner Congress contemplated strongly indicates that its admission was not an abuse of discretion.

Additionally, the evidence of LeMay's prior abuse of his cousins was also highly reliable. LeMay had been convicted of at least one of the rape charges arising from the incidents in Oregon. Because LeMay had admitted to abusing his cousins, Francine LeMay's testimony fell within a well-established exception to the hearsay rule. To the extent that allowing the evidence permitted a propensity inference, it was an inference based on proven facts and LeMay's own admissions, not rumor, innuendo, or prior uncharged acts capable of multiple characterizations. Thus, although we do not suggest that district courts may only introduce prior acts of molestation for which a defendant has been tried and found guilty, we hold that the extent to which an act has been proved is a factor that district courts may consider in conducting the Rule 403 inquiry.

Ct. should consider

We must also consider the remoteness in time of LeMay's prior acts of molestation, the frequency of prior similar acts, and whether any intervening events bear on the relevance of the prior similar acts. The "intervening events" factor seems to have little relevance in the present case, and the other two cut in favor of the government. About eleven years had passed between LeMay's abuse of his nieces and his trial for the abuse of D.R. and A.R.. We have held, in the context of Rule 404(b), that the lapse of twelve years does not render the decision to admit relevant evidence of similar prior acts an abuse of discretion. The "frequency of events" factor discussed in *Glanzer* also cuts in favor of the government. Although it was not introduced at trial, the government also had evidence of a third incident in which LeMay had sexually abused his young relatives. True, this incident occurred even before the 1989 abuse of his cousins when LeMay himself was extremely young, and, as the prosecutor noted, was "triple hearsay." However, that there was evidence of a third similar incident suggests that LeMay's abuse of his cousins in 1989 was not an isolated occurrence.

* * *

Finally, Francine LeMay's testimony was necessary to establish that LeMay's 1989 molestations were very similar, and thus relevant, to the charged crimes. We reject the idea that the district court should have limited the prosecution to merely proving that LeMay had been convicted of rape eleven years before. The relevance of the prior act evidence was in the details. Establishing the simple fact of conviction would leave out the information that LeMay had been convicted of sexually abusing his young relatives, by forced oral copulation, while they were in his care. Francine LeMay's testimony was necessary to fill in the details that made the prior rape conviction relevant. Therefore, the "necessity" factor favors the government in all respects.

Several factors do admittedly favor LeMay. LeMay himself was only twelve years old at the time of the 1989 molestations. And foremost, of course, is the emotional and highly charged nature of Francine LeMay's testimony. Although we, as an appellate court, are not in a position to evaluate how great an effect Francine LeMay's testimony had on the jury, we do not doubt that it was powerful. Francine LeMay began her testimony in tears, and certainly, her suggestion that LeMay had raped her infant daughter would have been particularly shocking. However, evidence of a defendant's prior acts of molestation will always be emotionally charged and inflammatory, as is the evidence that he committed the charged crimes. Thus, that prior acts evidence is inflammatory is not dispositive in and of itself. Rather, district judges must carefully evaluate the potential inflammatory nature of the proffered testimony, and balance it with that which the jury has already heard, the relevance of the evidence, the necessity of introducing it, and all the other relevant factors discussed above. The record here shows that the district judge did just that. Therefore, admitting LeMay's prior acts of molestation was not an abuse of discretion.

factors in D's favor

All in all, the record shows that the district judge struck a careful balance between LeMay's rights and the clear intent of Congress that evidence of prior similar acts be admitted in child molestation prosecution.

* * *

Points for Discussion

a. The Applicability of Rule 403.

Caselaw is still developing on the issue of whether evidence admissible under Rules 413-415 is subject to a relevance balancing test under Rule 403 or other rules of exclusion. One argument against subjecting these rules to a Rule 403 balancing test is the observation that the rules themselves state that evidence of other sexual assault offenses "is admissible" rather than "may be" admissible," thus indicating the drafters' preference for automatic admission. On the other hand, admitting any character evidence for use in showing propensity is generally frowned upon and almost certainly guarantees conviction of the defendant. Furthermore, Rules 401-403 are overarching rules that presumptively apply to the admissibility of all evidence. After considering these types of arguments, most circuits require a Rule 403 balancing before sexual misconduct evidence may be admitted. See, e.g., *United States v. Larson* 112 F.3d 600 (2d Cir. 1997) (holding that Rule 414 is subject to a Rule 403 balancing test and observing that the sponsors of the legislative amendment noted that "the general standards of the rules of evidence will continue to apply, including the restrictions on hearsay evidence and the court's authority under evidence Rule 403 to exclude evidence whose probative value is substantially outweighed by its prejudicial effect").

b. Frequency of Defendant's Sexual Misconduct.

It was thought by the Congressional sponsors of Rule 413-415 that sexual offenders frequently repeat their crimes. However, the sexual misconduct in *LeMay* occurred eight years before trial when the defendant was fourteen years old. If LeMay is a frequent sexual offender, why is there no evidence of his sexual misconduct between the alleged abuse of his cousins in 1989 and the alleged abuse that occurred in 1997 in the case? Do you think that this lack of evidence should have weighed more heavily in the court's Rule 403 analysis? The court attempts to overcome this problem by noting that "the government also had evidence of a third incident in which LeMay had sexually abused his young relatives . . . before 1989." This evidence was not introduced at trial and was even labeled "triple hearsay" by the prosecution. Yet, it was cited by the court as suggesting that LeMay's abuse of his cousins in 1989 was not an "isolated occurrence." Do you think it is reasonable for the court to cite such unreliable and inadmissible evidence as support for admitting LeMay's 1989 acts of sexual misconduct?

c. The Form of the Sexual Misconduct Testimony.

Rules 413-415 do not require that sexual misconduct evidence result in a conviction. Thus, courts such as the one in *LeMay* permit the admission of both uncharged acts as well as charged acts and convictions. See *Johnson v. Elk Lake School Dist.*, 283 F.3d 138 (3d Cir. 2002). Witnesses who testify to these offenses are also allowed to testify about the details of the offenses in order to allow the court and jury to determine how relevant they are to the acts at issue in the case. Is there a reasonable argument that by allowing witnesses to testify to the details of sexual misconduct, the unfair prejudice of the evidence is increased to such a degree that it substantially outweighs the probative value of the evidence under Rule 403, and that such evidence should therefore be excluded? How would you make that argument if you were a defense lawyer?

d. Rules 413–415 Were Not Intended to Limit the Admissibility of Sexual Misconduct Evidence Under Other Rules.

Subsection (c) of each of Rules 413-415 states that these rules "shall not be construed to limit admission or consideration of evidence under any other rules." Evidence of a defendant's prior sexual misconduct might be admissible, for example, under 404(b) to show the defendant's criminal intent in a case. Contrast this broad admissibility with Rule 412, the "Rape Shield" rule considered below, which requires that admissibility of a victim's prior sexual behavior or disposition be considered solely under the provisions of Rule 412.

D. Exceptions to the General Rule: Character of the Victim in a Criminal Case

1. Rule 404(a)(2): Victim's Character Generally in Criminal Cases

The second clause of Rule 404(a)(2) provides another exception to the general rule prohibiting the admission of character evidence. It allows the defendant in a criminal case to present evidence concerning the character of a victim as long as it relates to a "pertinent trait." A "pertinent trait" is determined by considering the charges and defenses in the case. A defendant

Make the Connection

This portion of Rule 404(a)(1) provides: "if evidence of a trait of character of the alleged victim of the crime is offered by an accused and admitted under Rule 404(a)(2), evidence of the same trait of character of the accused offered by the prosecution." In other words, if the defendant "opens the door" to the victim's character, the prosecution can put on evidence of the accused's character for the same character trait.

charged with assault, for example, might present evidence to show the victim had a violent character in order to prove that the victim threatened him immediately prior to the assault, thus justifying his use of self-defense. A defendant charged with bribing a judge might present evidence showing that the judge has a reputation for soliciting and extorting bribes to show the judge, not the defendant, was

Make the Connection

The admissibility of evidence of a victim's prior sexual behavior or predisposition, however, is governed solely by Rule 412, which is discussed later in this chapter. A defendant may not, generally, open the door on the victim's character in a sexual assault case.

guilty of bribery and extortion. These offerings, however, always risk unfair prejudice. A jury might conclude that because the victim was violent or corrupt, he deserved what he got and acquit the defendant on that basis. Despite this risk, evidence of a victim's character is admitted out of an attempt to be fair to a defendant and because of its deep roots in the common law.

Make the Connection

This is the same method for presenting reputation and opinion evidence used in presenting character evidence under the "Mercy Rule," Rule 404(a)(1) as discussed earlier in this chapter.

Rule 405(a) governs the method of presenting character evidence under Rule 404(a)(2). In a homicide case, where the defendant claims self-defense, the direct examination of a witness might look like this:

Defense Presentation

Rule 404(a)(2): Defense presents reputation or opinion witness to show victim has a violent character.

Defense Counsel:	How long have you lived in Dayton?
Witness:	About 20 years.
Defense Counsel:	During that time, have you heard people in your community speak about the character of the Victim in this case for being a violent person?
Witness:	Yes I have.
Defense Counsel:	What is the Victim's reputation in this regard?
Witness:	He has a reputation for being a violent person.

The following show the prosecution's four options for responding to Rule 404(a)(2) evidence.

Prosecutor's Option #1

Rule 405(a): Prosecution may cross-examine defendant's character witness above who attacked the victim's character for being violent with specific acts showing the victim's peaceful nature

Prosecution:	You say, Ms. Witness, that you have heard what the community says about the Victim's character for violence, is that true?
Witness:	Yes, that's true.
Prosecution:	Have you also heard that he was attacked last week and refused to fight back?
Witness:	No, I had not heard that.
Prosecution:	Have you heard that the Victim counsels inner city youth on how to avoid violent situations?
Witness:	Yes, I have heard that, but it doesn't change my mind.

Prosecutor's Option #2	
Rule 404(a)(2): Prosecution then presents reputation and opinion witness on rebuttal who testifies that the victim's character is peaceful	
Prosecution:	How long have you lived in Dayton?
Witness:	Ten years.
Prosecution:	Have you ever heard people in the community speak about the Victim's reputation in the community for being peaceful?
Witness:	Yes.
Prosecution:	What is the reputation?
Witness:	The Victim has the reputation as an extremely peaceful person.

The second clause of Rule 404(a)(1) also gives the prosecution a third option.

2. Rule 404(a)(1): Prosecution's Counterattack by Showing the Defendant's Bad Character

Once the victim's character has been attacked under Rules 404(a)(2), the prosecution may counterattack the defendant under Rule 404(a)(1) for having the same bad character trait as the one for which he attacked the victim. For example, if the defendant attacked the victim for having a violent character, the prosecution can attack the defendant for having a violent character.

Prosecutor's Option #3	
Rule 404(a)(1): Prosecution presents reputation and opinion witness who attacks the defendant's character for being violent.	
Prosecution:	How long have you lived in Dayton?
Witness:	All of my life.
Prosecution:	Have you ever heard people in the community speak about the Defendant's reputation in the community for being violent?
Witness:	Yes.
Prosecution:	What is her reputation?
Witness:	The Defendant has a reputation for being a very violent person.

3. Rule 404(a)(2): Character for Peacefulness of the Victim in a Homicide Case

In addition to the previous three options, the prosecution has a fourth opinion, but only in a criminal homicide case. Rule 404(a)(1) allows the prosecution to rehabilitate the character of the victim of a homicide when it has been attacked. In homicide cases, defendants frequently assert self-defense by claiming the victim physically attacked them first. Often, this assertion will be made by defense witnesses or during cross-examination of prosecution witnesses. Once this occurs, Rule 404(a)(2) provides that the prosecution may introduce evidence of the victim's peaceful character to rebut testimony that the victim was the first to attack. Such evidence may be in the form or reputation or opinion testimony under Rule 405(a). Of course, the defense may respond by bringing in its own witnesses to testify that the victim had a bad reputation for being violent or, in the witness's opinion, was a violent person.

Rule 404(a)(2): Prosecution presents reputation and opinion witness who testifies to the peacefulness of a victim of a homicide.	
Prosecution:	How long have you lived in Dayton?
Witness:	All of my life.
Prosecution:	Have you ever heard people in the community speak about the Victim's reputation in the community for being peaceful?
Witness:	Yes.
Prosecution:	What is her reputation?
Witness:	The Victim has a reputation for being a peaceful person.

If this all seems somewhat contrived and confusing, you are not alone. Until these complex and somewhat byzantine character evidence rules change, however, it is necessary to learn them. Such knowledge can give an attorney an advantage at trial that other attorneys do not have.

4. Rule 412: The Victim's Character in a Sex Offense Case

Rule 412. Sex Offense Cases; Relevance of Alleged Victim's Past Sexual Behavior or Alleged Sexual Predisposition

(a) Evidence generally inadmissible.--The following evidence is not admissible in any civil or criminal proceeding involving alleged sexual misconduct except as provided in subdivisions (b) and (c):

(1) Evidence offered to prove that any alleged victim engaged in other sexual behavior.

(2) Evidence offered to prove any alleged victim's sexual predisposition.

(b) Exceptions.--

(1) In a criminal case, the following evidence is admissible, if otherwise admissible under these rules:

(A) evidence of specific instances of sexual behavior by the alleged victim offered to prove that a person other than the accused was the source of semen, injury or other physical evidence;

(B) evidence of specific instances of sexual behavior by the alleged victim with respect to the person accused of the sexual misconduct offered by the accused to prove consent or by the prosecution; and

(C) evidence the exclusion of which would violate the constitutional rights of the defendant.

(2) In a civil case, evidence offered to prove the sexual behavior or sexual predisposition of any alleged victim is admissible if it is otherwise admissible under these rules and its probative value substantially outweighs the danger of harm to any victim and of unfair prejudice to any party. Evidence of an alleged victim's reputation is admissible only if it has been placed in controversy by the alleged victim.

(c) Procedure to determine admissibility.--

(1) A party intending to offer evidence under subdivision (b) must--

(A) file a written motion at least 14 days before trial specifically describing the evidence and stating the purpose for which it is offered unless the court, for good cause requires a different time for filing or permits filing during trial; and

(B) serve the motion on all parties and notify the alleged victim or, when appropriate, the alleged victim's guardian or representative.

(2) Before admitting evidence under this rule the court must conduct a hearing in camera and afford the victim and parties a right to attend and be heard. The motion, related papers, and the record of the hearing must be sealed and remain under seal unless the court orders otherwise.

Rule 412, sometimes called the "Rape Shield" law, makes inadmissible the past sexual behavior and predisposition of a victim of sexual assault or child molestation. The rule represents a substantial departure from the common law rule that allowed a defense attorney to cross-examine a victim extensively about such matters in order to show consent, which had the widespread effect of making sexual assault victims extremely reluctant to report the crime. Exceptions to the rule in criminal cases allow the defendant to offer evidence of a victim's prior sexual acts if he is attempting to show someone else was the source of the semen or injury to the victim; if he claims consent and proposes to show that the victim had previously consented to sexual behavior with him; or, if the Constitution requires admissibility.

A separate provision of Rule 412 applies to civil cases. For civil cases, evidence of a victim's past sexual behavior is admissible if the court determines that its probative value outweighs the prejudicial effect of the evidence to a victim or a party. In other words, although there is a presumption of inadmissibility for sexual behavior evidence in civil cases, there is not the same bar as there would be in criminal cases of the same nature. The reason is that the drafters of this rule did not think it as necessary to bar evidence of a victim's character evidence in a civil case because the victim has already filed suit and would not be as deterred from testifying as in a criminal case.

Judd v. Rodman

U.S. Court of Appeals for the Eleventh Circuit
105 F.3d 1339 (11ᵗʰ Cir. 1997)

BIRCH, Circuit Judge:

Lisa Beth Judd filed this action against Dennis Rodman and alleged that he wrongfully transmitted genital herpes to her. The jury returned a verdict in favor of Rodman. Judd appeals the final judgment on the ground that evidence of her prior sexual history, employment as a nude dancer, and breast augmentation surgery should have been excluded under Rule 412 of the Federal Rules of Evidence. Rodman argues that Rule 412 is not applicable to this case and, in the alternative, that Judd waived her right to appeal the issue by failing to object at trial. We affirm.

I. BACKGROUND

Judd contracted genital herpes following a sexual relationship with Rodman. She subsequently filed a complaint against Rodman alleging several causes of action related to her contraction of genital herpes: tortious transmission of a sexual disease, battery, fraud, and intentional infliction of emotional distress. During discovery, Rodman asked numerous questions about Judd's prior sexual history, employment as a nude dancer, and breast augmentation surgery.

* * *

I. DISCUSSION

We review a district court's ruling on the admissibility of evidence for abuse of discretion. We overturn evidentiary rulings only when the moving party has proved a substantial prejudicial effect. Thus, we review the trial court's admission of evidence under Rule 412 for an abuse of discretion and reverse only when the party asserting error shows that the error prejudiced a substantial right of that party.

Rule 412, as amended in 1994, applies to "any civil ... proceeding involving alleged sexual misconduct." The rule provides that "[e]vidence offered to prove that any alleged victim engaged in other sexual behavior," and "[e]vidence offered to prove any alleged victim's sexual predisposition," are generally inadmissible in civil cases. An exception is provided in Rule 412(b)(2) for evidence of sexual behavior and predisposition which is otherwise admissible if "its probative value substantially outweighs the danger of harm to any victim and of unfair prejudice to any party." To date, Rule 412 has been applied only to civil cases involving rape and sexual harassment. Thus, the applicability of Rule 412 to cases involving transmission of a sexually transmitted disease has not been determined yet by any court. The district court in this case did not issue a conclusive ruling regarding the applicability of Rule 412. Significantly, although the court ordered that the pertinent motions in limine be sealed consistent with the procedural requirements of Rule 412(c)(2), when pressed for clarification as to the applicability of Rule 412 at the beginning of trial, the trial judge stated, "I think Rule 412 does not apply."

Because we find that any error in admitting evidence of Judd's breast augmentation surgery, prior sexual history, and employment as a nude dancer was not substantially prejudicial, we need not analyze the applicability of Rule 412 to cases involving wrongful transmission of a sexually transmitted disease. Thus, we assume, without deciding, that Rule 412 applies to the facts presented in this case and address in turn the admissibility of evidence of breast augmentation surgery, prior sexual history, and nude dancing.

* * *

[The court concludes that Judd waived her objection based on Rule 412 to the admission of evidence regarding her breast augmentation surgery by not properly objecting at trial].

Judd contends that admission of evidence of her prior sexual history warrants a reversal of the judgment against her. To find error warranting reversal, however, we must find not only that Judd made a timely objection, as previously noted, but also that a substantial right was affected.

Food for Thought

If the issue had been properly preserved for appeal, is there any conceivable theory under which the appellate court could have found evidence of Judd's breast augmentation surgery to be admissible under Rule 412?

* * *

To warrant reversal, Judd must establish also that a substantial right was affected by the admission of the evidence. Rule 412(a) provides that "evidence offered to prove that any alleged victim engaged in other sexual behavior" will generally be excluded. Rule 412(b) provides an exception to exclusion when the "probative value substantially outweighs the danger of harm to any victim and of unfair prejudice to any party."

Judd contends that, under the balancing test of Rule 412(b), evidence of her prior sexual history should have been excluded because its probative value failed to outweigh substantially the unfair prejudice toward her. A central issue of the case, however, is whether Judd contracted genital herpes from Rodman. Expert testimony revealed that the herpes virus can be dormant for long periods of time and the infected person can be asymptomatic. Consequently, evidence of prior sexual relationships and the type of protection used during sexual intercourse was highly relevant to Rodman's liability. The court did not abuse its discretion in admitting evidence of Judd's prior sexual history.

Judd contends that evidence of her prior employment as a nude dancer should have been excluded under Rule 412(a)(2) because it was offered to prove her sexual predisposition. Judd objected to the admission of this evidence both in a motion in limine and at trial and, thus, preserved the issue for appeal. She fails, however, to show that a substantial right was affected by the admission of the evidence.

Food for Thought

How does Judd's continued employment as a nude dancer after the herpes infection prove that Judd did not "feel dirty," thus indicating an "absence of change in her body image?"

As discussed above, the district court could have admitted evidence of Judd's nude dancing upon a finding that the probative value substantially outweighed the prejudicial effect. The determination under such a balancing test is necessarily highly fact specific. Judd testified that she felt "dirty" after she contracted herpes. The court determined that Judd's employment as a nude dancer before and after she contracted herpes was probative as to damages for emotional distress because it suggested an absence of change in her body image following the herpes infection. Thus, although we recognize the potentially prejudicial nature of the evidence of Judd's nude dancing, we find that, given the specific facts of this case and the considerable evidence of sexual history and predisposition which were appropriately admitted, the district court could have decided, within its discretion, that the probative value of the evidence substantially outweighed any prejudicial effect. Accordingly, we resolve that Judd has not shown that the court's admission of this evidence constituted reversible error.

Points for Discussion

a. Sexual Behavior.

Rule 412 does not define terms such as "sexual behavior," but it has been generally construed to mean sexual intercourse, contact or even erotic activities. In *Judd*, the court extended the definition far beyond the traditional meaning of the rule in its application to nude dancing, even if the court's consideration of the issue was hypothetical. Perhaps this reasoning is not as far-fetched as it seems.

The Advisory Committee Notes to Rule 412 have suggested that the rule may extend to "activities of the mind, such as fantasies or dreams." For example, the court in *Sheffield v. Hilltop Sand & Gravel Co.,* 895 F. Supp. 105 (E.D.Va. 1995), excluded evidence under Rule 412 that the victim modeled lingerie for two fellow police officers, once had an orgasm while using a sexual device thinking of one of the witnesses, and wanted to get the witness into bed and "hurt" him.

b. Defendant's Constitutional Right to Introduce Evidence.

Under Rule 412 sexual evidence pertaining to the alleged victim cannot be excluded if to do so would violate the defendant's constitutional rights. Does this mean that all evidence the defendant offers to raise reasonable doubt in the case must constitutionally be admitted? This is doubtful, since such an interpretation would engulf the prohibitions of the rule. In situations where the victim's credibility is at issue, however, cases may require admission of the victim's past sexual conduct evidence on constitutional grounds. For example, in *United States v. Begay,* 937 F.2d 515 (10th Cir. 1991), the court found a violation of the Confrontation Clause by the trial court's refusal to allow the defense to cross-examine a child victim about a prior rape by another man in order to challenge a physician's testimony and test the victim's memory.

c. Notice.

If a party intends to offer evidence under an exception to Rule 412, he must, within 14 days of trial, file a written notice describing the evidence to be offered and the purpose for which it is offered. The rule requires that the offering party serve the motion on all other parties, including the victim and his or her guardian or representative, although the trial court can allow notice at other times for good cause shown. If a defendant does not give proper notice in a criminal case, can he be precluded from presenting evidence whose admittance is otherwise constitutionally required? The answer may be yes. See *Michigan v. Lucas,* 500 U.S. 145 (1991) (holding that the defense can be excluded from presenting evidence of his prior relationship with the victim because he did not given the requisite 10 day notice under a state law similar to Rule 412).

————————

E. Character Evidence Offered to Prove a Fact Other Than Character

> **Rule 404(b). Character Evidence Not Admissible To Prove Conduct; Exceptions; Other Crimes**
>
> * * *
>
> (b) Other Crimes, Wrongs, or Acts. Evidence of other crimes, wrongs, or acts is not admissible to prove the character of a person in order to show action in conformity therewith. It may, however, be admissible for other purposes, such as proof of motive, opportunity, intent, preparation, plan, knowledge, identity, or absence of mistake or accident, provided that upon request by the accused, the prosecution in a criminal case shall provide reasonable notice in advance of trial, or during trial if the court excuses pretrial notice on good cause shown, of the general nature of any such evidence it intends to introduce at trial.

> **Rule 403. Exclusion of Relevant Evidence on Grounds of Prejudice, Confusion, or Waste or Time.**
>
> Although relevant, evidence may be excluded if its probative value is substantially outweighed by the danger of unfair prejudice, confusion of the issues, or misleading the jury, or by consideration of undue delay, waste of time, or needless presentation of cumulative evidence.

> **FYI**
>
> A useful way to remember this list is by the acronym "MIAMI COP, which is short for motive, identity, absence of mistake, accident, intent, common plan or scheme, opportunity, and preparation.

Rule 404(b) is a self-contained rule in the sense that it addresses both when character evidence may be admitted into evidence and what form it must take. The first sentence of the rule restates the general principle that character evidence is not admissible to prove action in conformity therewith. However, it then pronounces that specific crimes, wrongs or acts may be admitted for a non-character purpose and gives examples of those purposes, such as to prove motive, opportunity, intent, preparation, plan, knowledge, identity, or absence of mistake or accident, when those issues are raised in the case. The phrase "such as" in the rule indicates that the list of permissible purposes is meant to be illustrative only, not exhaustive. The rule is phrased in terms of "crimes, wrongs, or acts," and thus there is no requirement that any of them result in a final conviction to be admissible.

Theoretically, the rule applies to both civil and criminal cases. As a practical matter, it is used predominantly by the prosecution to introduce other bad act evidence against defendants in criminal cases because fact questions about intent, identity, opportunity, plan and motive are most frequently raised in that context. The rule's use in criminal cases is so prevalent that Rule 404(b) is sometimes referred to as the "Prosecutor's Rule."

Take Note!

Other permissible purposes are determined by the degree to which they are relevant to a fact at issue in the case. For example, in *United States v. Matthews*, 20 F.3d 538 (2d Cir. 1994), evidence that the defendant threatened a former girlfriend was held admissible to rebut a claim by the defendant that his girlfriend falsely testified against him because she was scorned by him.

The party offering Rule 404(b) evidence must satisfy three requirements. First, she must identify a fact at issue to which the specific act is relevant. Second, if the opponent raises an objection based upon Rule 403, she must convince the court that the counterweights listed in the rule do not substantially outweigh the probative value of the evidence. Third, she must introduce evidence that the person whose specific act is in question did, in fact, commit the act.

So how does this Rule 404(b) work in a typical case? Assume for the moment that a defendant is charged with possession of cocaine, but she claims that she did not know the substance she possessed was cocaine because she has never seen it. Assume further that the prosecution has in her possession defendant's arrest sheet, which indicates she was previously arrested for possession of cocaine. If the prosecution offers the prior cocaine arrest, she would first have to articulate a non-character purpose for this offering. In this case, that purpose would be to establish that the defendant knew how to recognize cocaine because she was previously arrested for its possession. No doubt the defense would then claim that the prior cocaine arrest should not be admitted under the balancing test of Rule 403. In response, the prosecution would be required to show that the probative value of the prior cocaine arrest to prove the defendant's knowledge of the drug is not substantially outweighed by any of the Rule 403 counterweights, such as unfair prejudice. If, after conducting a Rule 403 balancing, the trial judge deems the evidence admissible, the prosecution may then introduce witnesses or documentary evidence to show the jury that the arrest occurred, perhaps by presenting the testimony of the arresting officer.

The following diagram of these two possible offerings shows the theoretical difference between a permissible and non-permissible offering:

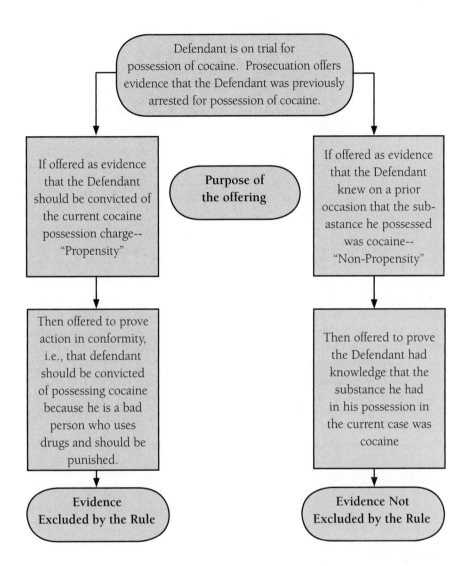

How might a trial judge conduct a Rule 403 balancing test in this situation? In determining probative value, he will most likely take into account factors such as the similarity of the other act evidence to prove knowledge, the reliability of the other act evidence, and the extent to which the factual issue is established by other evidence in the case. In weighing unfair prejudice, he may look to the degree to which the evidence is of a heinous nature, the remoteness of the act, or the strength of the unfair prejudice of the evidence, that is, the degree to which the evidence will be misused or misunderstood by the jury.

Now assume that the trial judge has determined that the defendant's prior cocaine arrest has strong probative value in proving that she can recognize cocaine and that the prior arrest is the only evidence the prosecution can offer to show that knowledge. Also assume that the trial judge does not consider possession of cocaine a heinous crime like murder, the prior arrest was two years ago, and that both the arrest and the crime for which the defendant is charged are identical, increasing the odds that a jury will think the defendant is a bad person who uses drugs and should be punished.

The following illustrates a Rule 403 balancing that might support admission of the defendant's prior cocaine conviction:

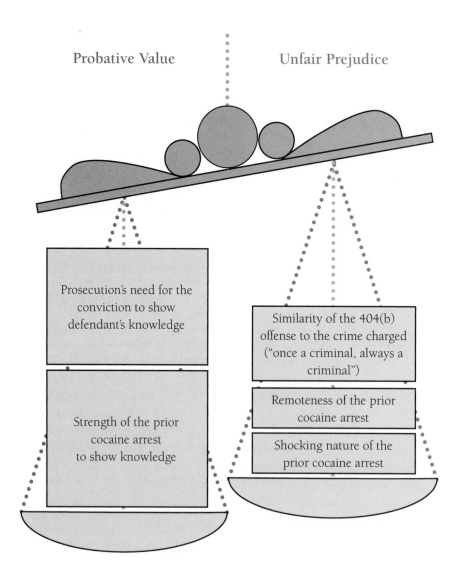

Probative Value

Unfair Prejudice

Prosecution's need for the conviction to show defendant's knowledge

Similarity of the 404(b) offense to the crime charged ("once a criminal, always a criminal")

Strength of the prior cocaine arrest to show knowledge

Remoteness of the prior cocaine arrest

Shocking nature of the prior cocaine arrest

Of course, the trial judge has discretion when making a Rule 404(b) evaluation and may come to a contrary conclusion. His decision depends to a large extent upon his assessment of the strength of the factor he considers. Additionally if a Rule 404(b) other act is admitted, the trial judge must give the jury a Rule 105 limiting instruction, telling the jurors they may only consider the other act for the permissible 404(b) non-propensity purpose and not for the impermissible 404(a) propensity purpose to show criminal propensity.

There are only slight differences between offering the defendant's prior cocaine arrest to show he is a criminal and offering it to show his knowledge of cocaine. If you are having difficulty in sorting out these differences, imagine how much difficulty a jury might have.

1. Acts Offered to Prove Intent

Rule 404(b) specifically lists intent as a fact issue that allows proof of other specific crimes, wrongs, or acts. Other act evidence is said to be relevant in showing intent because repeated occurrences of certain unusual events make it unlikely that any one of those events happened by mistake or accident. If a defendant in a criminal case is charged with homicide and claims he did not know his gun was loaded, for example, evidence that he previously claimed the same defense after he killed another victim would be admissible as proof that his current lack of intent claim was not likely.

Rule 404(b) makes no distinction between specific acts that occurred prior or subsequent to the crime in question as long as they are relevant. Notice in the following case that the Rule 404(b) crimes in question occurred after the robbery for which the defendant was being tried.

United States v. Hearst

U.S. Court of Appeals for the Ninth Circuit
563 F.2d 1331 (9th Cir. 1977)

PER CURIAM:

Appellant [Patty Hearst] was tried under a two-count indictment charging her with armed robbery of a San Francisco bank. The Government introduced photographs and testimony descriptive of appellant's role in the robbery. Appellant raised the defense of duress, contending her co-participants compelled her to engage in the criminal activity. The jury found appellant guilty. . . .

held

We conclude on the basis of well established principles that no reversible error occurred and that the judgment must be affirmed.

During its case-in-chief the government introduced evidence connecting appellant with criminal activity at a sporting goods store and with a kidnapping and theft. These incidents occurred in the Los Angeles area approximately one month after the San Francisco bank robbery. The evidence showed that appellant accompanied William and Emily Harris to Mel's Sporting Goods Store in Los Angeles, that the Harrises entered the store and left appellant outside in a truck, that a store clerk saw William Harris shoplifting and attempted to arrest him, and that appellant discharged an automatic rifle at the store, enabling Harris to escape. The evidence further showed that on the same day appellant and the Harrises stole a van and kidnapped its owner, Thomas Matthews. Matthews testified that during this incident the Harrises were outside the van and appellant had an opportunity to escape or give Matthews a message but did not do so. . . .

Go Online!

The appellant (defendant) in this case, Patty Hearst, was the daughter of Randolf Hearst, owner of the Hearst publishing empire. In 1974, at the age of 19, she was kidnapped by the Symbionese Liberation Army (SLA), a left wing urban guerilla group, in an attempt to trade her for jailed SLA members. At some point she joined her captors, adopted the name "Tania," and committed a number of felonies with her fellow SLA members. At trial, she claimed she was "brainwashed," and denied responsibility for her actions but was nonetheless convicted. http.// en.wikipedia.org/wiki Patty Hearst.

D argued

Appellant . . . asserts the evidence was irrelevant for any purpose except the improper one of convincing the jury that appellant acted in accordance with a criminal disposition. She argues that even if the evidence were relevant to the issue of intent, as the district court held, the incidents were so dissimilar to the bank robbery that its probative value was minimal and outweighed by its prejudicial effect. . . .

Evidence of other criminal acts may be persuasive that the defendant is by propensity a probable perpetrator of the crime charged. Nonetheless, it is excluded when offered for this purpose because it may unduly influence the jury and deny the defendant a fair opportunity to defend against the particular charge.

P argues

Evidence of other criminal acts may be admitted for purposes other than proving criminal predisposition, however. It may be received, for example, to prove knowledge, motive, and intent. Fed.R.Evid. 404(b). The government contends that the evidence of appellant's criminal acts in Los Angeles a month after the bank robbery was relevant to the issue of appellant's intent when she participated in the San Francisco bank robbery, and to whether appellant was acting under duress.

Appellant raised the defense of duress at trial and offered substantial evidence to support it. To convict appellant, therefore, the government was required to show appellant was not acting under duress when she participated in the San Francisco robbery. The evidence of appellant's involvement in the Los Angeles activity was relevant to this issue because it tended to show appellant willingly engaged in other criminal activity with persons of the same group at a time not unduly remote.

Appellant correctly points out that though relevant, evidence of other criminal conduct by the defendant should be excluded if its probative value is outweighed by its prejudicial impact upon the defendant. This determination is largely a matter for the discretion of the district court. Appellant challenges the discretionary determination made by the district court in this instance.

Appellant points out that the Los Angeles offenses were not similar to the San Francisco robbery with which she was charged. Because the events were so dissimilar, she contends, they offer little insight into her state of mind during the robbery. But to justify admission of evidence of other crimes, the crimes must be "similar" to the offense charged only if it is the similarity of the crimes that underlies the relevance of the evidence. Here the relevance of the evidence did not depend on the similarity of the Los Angeles crimes to the bank robbery but

on the circumstances surrounding the occurrence of the Los Angeles crimes, which indicated appellant had not acted under duress when she participated in the bank robbery. The tendency of the evidence regarding the Los Angeles crimes to prove appellant was not coerced when she participated in the San Francisco robbery is not diminished by the lack of similarity between the Los Angeles and San Francisco offenses.

Take Note!

Although the court phrases the Rule 404(b) issue as one of duress, the issue actually involves the appellant's intent when she committed the robbery—did appellant intend to commit the robbery of her own free will or did she do so because she was coerced?

Appellant also argues that the sequence of the San Francisco and Los Angeles events undermines the relevance of the latter to her state of mind during the San Francisco robbery. Absence of duress in the later Los Angeles incidents would not be probative of her state of mind during the San Francisco robbery, she contends, because the robbery itself made her an outlaw and a fugitive. This fact may have caused her to participate willingly in the Los Angeles events, she asserts, even if she were under duress during the earlier robbery.

Appellant's hypothesis does bear upon the probative value of the evidence, and it is an appropriate consideration in determining whether on balance the evidence should have been admitted. It is, however, only a hypothesis, and a highly speculative one. The mere assertion of this hypothesis does not so undermine the probative worth of the evidence of the Los Angeles incidents in establishing appellant's state of mind during the San Francisco robbery as to render admission of the evidence an abuse of discretion. The jury could well reject appellant's theory and conclude that if appellant had been forced to participate in the bank robbery against her will she would have refrained from criminal activity in Los Angeles or seized the opportunity to escape.

The trial judge was called upon to balance the need for the evidence in the search for the truth against the possibility that the jury would be prejudiced against appellant because the evidence revealed she had participated in other conduct that was criminal. The district court acted well within its discretion in admitting the evidence. Appellant's state of mind during the San Francisco robbery was the central issue in the case. State of mind is usually difficult to prove, and the evidence on the issue was sharply divided. The timing and other circumstances of the Los Angeles incidents made evidence of them highly probative on this critical issue. Though criminal, the incidents were not of a kind likely to inflame the jury. The prejudice to appellant arose primarily from the light the evidence cast on appellant's state of mind during the San Francisco robbery and not from the incidental circumstance that it revealed appellant's involvement in other criminal acts.

Affirmed.

Points for Discussion

a. How Much Similarity Is Needed to Show Intent?

In *Hearst,* the court does not require that the prosecution show any similarity between the Rule 404(b) offenses and the robbery with which the defendant is charged in order to rebut the defendant's claim of duress. The reason the court gives is that the relevancy of the subsequent crimes does not depend on their similarity to the robbery in question. What do you think the court means by this? If similarity of the crimes is not required, then what is the basis of admissibility? Compare *Hearst* with *United States v. Beechum*, 582 F.2d 898 (5th Cir. 1978), where the defendant, a substitute mail carrier, was charged with unlawfully possessing a silver dollar that he knew to be stolen from the mail on his route. The defendant's explanation was that he intended to return the dollar after it dropped out of a greeting card, but he could not find his supervisor. To establish the defendant's criminal intent in the case, the prosecution introduced two credit cards found in the defendant's wallet when he was arrested which had been taken from the defendant's mail route ten months earlier. The credit card evidence was admitted, and the defendant was convicted. On appeal, the court stated that relevancy of the Rule 404(b) crime "derives from the defendant indulging himself in the same state of mind in the perpetration of both . . ." crimes. "[B]ecause the defendant had unlawful intent in the [Rule 404(b)] offense, it is less likely that he had lawful intent in the present offense." Are *Hearst* and *Beechum* in conflict, or is the requirement of similarity case specific?

b. The Balancing of Probative Value and Prejudicial Effect in *Hearst*.

There are a number of factors, other than similarity, that often factor into a trial judge's Rule 404(b) decision. They include the reliability of the evidence being offered, see *United States v. Peterson*, 808 F.2d 969 (2d Cir. 1987); the remoteness of the other acts in time, see *United States v. Edelmann*, 458 F.3d 791 (8th Cir. 2006); and the prosecution's need for the evidence, see *United States v. Haywood*, 280 F.3d 715 (6th Cir. 2002). To what degree did these other factors contribute to the court's decision in *Hearst?*

c. The Effect of a Defense Offer to Stipulate.

There is little doubt that other crimes, wrongs or acts admitted under Rule 404(b) against a defendant in a criminal case can be devastating to the defense. Despite limiting instructions and good intentions, it is difficult for juries to put a defendant's prior bad acts out of their minds when considering his guilt. Knowing this, defense attorneys have tried various tactics to take a defendant's intent out of the case. For example, they have argued that their client's intent is not at issue because the defense contends that he did not commit the crime at all. See *United States v. Lampkins*, 47 F.3d 175 (7th Cir. 1995). Others have attempted to take intent out of issue by stipulating to their client's intent. Many, but not all, courts reject these arguments on the basis that the prosecution has a right to prove its entire case, if it so chooses, by whatever evidence it possesses. See *Old Chief,* supra, discussed in Chapter 3.

d. The Effect of a Defendant's Acquittal of a Rule 404(b) Crime.

Logic might dictate that if a defendant is previously acquitted of a crime, it should not be allowed into evidence under Rule 404(b). However, this is not the case. The reason has to do with the difference between the burden of proof in a criminal case (beyond a reasonable doubt), and the burden of

Make the Connection

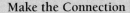

The *Huddleston* case was considered in connection with the issue of conditional relevance in Chapter 3 of this book.

proof in admission of Rule 404(b) misconduct (whether a jury could reasonably conclude that the act occurred and that the defendant was the actor). See *Huddleston v. United States,* 485 U.S. 681 (1988). Merely because the Rule 404(b) crime could not be proven beyond a reasonable doubt in order to obtain a conviction against the defendant does not mean that a jury could not reasonably find the defendant committed it under a lessor standard of proof. See *Dowling v. United States,* 493 U.S. 342 (1990). *Dowling* also held that admission of a Rule 404(b) crime for which the defendant was acquitted was not a violation of the defendant's Due Process rights under the Double Jeopardy Clause of the Fifth Amendment.

e. The Requirement of Notice in Criminal Cases.

Practice Pointer

It is always good practice for the defense in a criminal case to file a motion requesting that the court order the prosecution give notice of its intent to offer Rule 404(b) evidence no less than seven days before trial and update that notice through the time of trial. Otherwise, the defense may not have sufficient time to find witnesses to contradict the prosecution's Rule 404(b) evidence.

In criminal cases, upon defense request, the government is required to provide "reasonable notice" to the defendant of any Rule 404(b) evidence it plans to use at trial. The rule does not define "reasonable notice," but courts have recognized that the degree to which the prosecution, through timely preparation, could have learned of the Rule 404(b) witnesses' availability, the amount of prejudice to the defendant, and the significance of the testimony to the prosecution's case are factors in this determination. *United States v. Perez-Tosta,* 36 F.3d 1552 (11th Cir. 1994).

Hypo 9.3

The defendant is charged with using the mail to attempt to defraud an insurer. He allegedly killed his partner and set fire to their tavern in order to collect on her life insurance policy. The prosecution wants to offer evidence that the defendant previously murdered his wife and collected on her insurance policy. Is this evidence admissible under Rule 404(b), and if so, for what purpose and why?

2. Acts Offered to Prove Plan and Identity

Evidence of other crimes, wrongs or acts may be offered to show they were committed pursuant to the same or a similar scheme as the crime with which the defendant is charged. For example, in a case where the prosecution must prove the defendants used firearms during and in relation to a drug trafficking crime, evidence that the defendants murdered rival gang members might be admissible to prove defendants' plan to use weapons to protect the conspiracy and intimidate competitors and witnesses. Or, plan evidence may be used to show the relationship between the defendant and others in a conspiracy. Under this theory, evidence of prior drug dealings between the defendant and a coconspirator might also be admissible to show why the co-conspirator would trust the defendant to sell other illegal drugs.

Plan evidence may also be admissible to prove that because both the Rule 404(b) offense and the crime in question were committed by such unique and similar methods, there is good reason to believe that the defendant committed both of them. In reality, such an offering is use of plan evidence to show identity. Take, for example, a defendant who commits a murder by stabbing the victim with a fork in the stomach and writing "Death to all pigs" on the wall in red crayon. If a second murder is committed in the exact same manner, a jury could logically assume that one person committed them both pursuant to a unique plan, or what is sometimes called the same *modus operandi*. Thus, if the defendant is identified in the first murder as the person who carried out that plan, he can be identified as the perpetrator of the second murder as well.

It's Latin to Me

Black's Law Dictionary defines modus operandi as Latin for "a manner of operating" or "a pattern of criminal behavior so distinctive that investigators attribute it to the work of the same person."

United States v. Carroll

U.S. Court of Appeals for the Eighth Circuit
207 F.3d 465 (8th Cir. 2000)

BOWMAN, Circuit Judge.

Gerald Carroll was convicted by a jury of armed robbery of a federally insured credit union and a related firearms charge, and was sentenced by the District Court to life in prison plus twenty years. . . . Carroll argues that evidence of a prior conviction was improperly admitted. . . .

Carroll has been convicted of armed robbery previously. In 1988, he robbed a bank using a firearm. He pleaded guilty in 1989 and was sentenced to a substantial prison term. He entered supervised release on September 6, 1996. On July 30, 1998, Carroll and an accomplice, Kevin Carroll, robbed the St. Louis Community Credit Union, the crime at issue in this appeal. During Gerald Carroll's trial, the United States sought to introduce evidence of his prior conviction under Federal Rule of Evidence 404(b), which prohibits the admission of evidence of "other crimes, wrongs, or acts ... to prove the character of a person in order to show action in conformity therewith." But such evidence is admissible "for other purposes," including "plan, knowledge, [or] identity." Like all other evidence, evidence admissible under Rule 404(b) is still subject to analysis under Rule 403, which allows admission unless the evidence's unfair prejudice substantially outweighs its probative value. Over objection, the District Court determined that the evidence of Carroll's prior conviction was "admissible for purposes of showing a plan or pattern ... a melding basically of that, plus identity." The District Court instructed the jury that it could use the Rule 404(b) evidence "to help [it] decide whether the similarity between the acts previously committed and the ones charged in this case suggest that the same person committed all of them." We review for abuse of discretion.

The case law discusses two circumstances in which prior bad acts can be used to show a "plan or pattern." In some circumstances, a defendant's prior bad acts are part of a broader plan or scheme relevant to the charged offense. "For example, when a criminal steals a car to use it in a robbery, the automobile theft can be proved in a prosecution for the robbery." If the evidence merely shows the full context of the charged crime, it is "intrinsic evidence" not governed by Rule 404(b). Evidence of past acts may also be admitted under Rule 404(b) as direct proof of a charged crime that includes a plan or scheme element, or evidence might serve both intrinsic and direct-proof purposes. In other circumstances, where the "pattern and characteristics of the crimes [are] so unusual and distinctive as to be like a signature," evidence of a defendant's prior crimes is admissible to prove that it was indeed the defendant that committed the charged crime. In these cases, the evidence goes to identity. These "plan" and "identity" uses of Rule 404(b) evidence are distinct from each other and from use of prior acts to show knowledge and intent. In drug distribution cases, for example, knowledge and intent are often contested facts proven in part through prior bad acts.

We reject the theory that Carroll's ten-year-old conviction was admissible as part of a broad criminal undertaking including both the prior offense and the charged offense. "The victims were different, and the events were far apart in time. Absent more specific linkage, such evidence is relevant to 'plan' or 'preparation' only insofar as it tends to prove a propensity to commit crimes, which Rule 404(b) prohibits." The fact that Carroll was incarcerated in the interim period only reinforces the conclusion that the events are not part of the same criminal undertaking.

The District Court's jury instruction demonstrates that the evidence was admitted to show identity. If the conduct underlying Carroll's prior conviction and his current charged offense both involved a unique set of "signature facts," then his prior conviction would be admissible to show that the same person committed both crimes. But unless the robberies are "sufficiently idiosyncratic" to make them "clearly distinctive from the thousands of other bank robberies committed each year," evidence of the prior crime is "nothing more than the character evidence that Rule 404(b) prohibits."

In sum, in order to admit Rule 404(b) identity evidence on the signature facts or *modus operandi* theory, the District Court must make a threshold determination that, based solely on the evidence comparing the past acts and the charged offense, a reasonable juror could conclude that the same person committed both crimes. Two factors are relevant in analyzing the question. The first is the distinctiveness of the facts that make the crimes unique and the second is the proximity of the crimes in space and time. After reviewing the evidence in this case, we believe that the prior bank robbery and the credit union robbery charged here are too generic and remote from one another to permit a reasonable inference of identity.

First, the characteristics shared by the two robberies are too common to form a modus operandi that uniquely identifies Carroll as the perpetrator. All the United States can argue is that, in both crimes, the perpetrator wore a nylon stocking mask, carried a gun, and vaulted over the counter to put the bank's money in a bag.

It's Latin to Me

Remember that according to Black's Law Dictionary, a *motion in limine* is a "pretrial request that certain inadmissible evidence not be referred to or offered at trial. Typically, a party makes this motion when it believes that the mere mention of the evidence during trial would be highly prejudicial and could not be remedied by an instruction to disregard."

We must initially determine the frame of reference against which to measure the uniqueness of the crimes. As the question of how often a particular crime is committed in a particular way is ultimately factual, it might be appropriate, in some cases, for the District Court to take evidence on the matter in, for example, deciding a *motion in limine*. In other cases, the *modus operandi* or other characteristics of the prior crime and the crime currently charged may be so distinctive as to self-evidently permit a reasonable inference of identity between the perpetrator of the first and the perpetrator of the second. In the present case, we simply use a set of data readily before us. Based merely on the descriptions of bank robberies available in the published federal appellate reporters, which are incomplete in detail and refer only to a subset of all bank robberies committed, it is amply clear that the signature facts relied upon by the government in this case occur frequently, even in combination. The bank robbery cases finding signature facts have reported much less common features, such as distinguishing costumes or equipment, unusual methods, or distinctive use of a weapon.

Further, examination of the closeness of the robberies, geographically and in time, supports the conclusion that the crimes are not sufficiently related to allow an inference of identity. The two financial institutions here, while not in the same neighborhood, are both in the St. Louis area, relatively close to each other. But the crimes occurred ten years apart. . . .The government . . . asserts that the intervening period is irrelevant because Carroll was incarcerated for most of that time. . . . Perhaps Carroll's incarceration undercuts the significance of the ten-year delay to some extent, but certainly not enough to permit an inference of identity.

Based on the generic nature of the crimes and on the ten years that passed between them, we conclude that the prior conviction was not relevant to prove identity through *modus operandi* because no substantial inference of identity reasonably could be made. Our criminal justice system has long forbidden juries from convicting an individual, not for facts which prove the charged offense, but for prior acts that, at best, show a criminal propensity. It was therefore an abuse of discretion to admit evidence of the prior bank robbery committed by Carroll, for that robbery is not relevant to any question other than Carroll's propensity to rob banks.

The decision of the District Court is affirmed.

Points for Discussion

a. Plan Evidence Offered to Show Identity.

The *Carroll* court held that the characteristics shared by the prior robbery and the robbery with which the defendant was charged were too common to form a method of operation that uniquely identified the defendant as the perpetrator of both crimes. These common characteristics included the fact that both victims were federally insured credit unions and in both robberies the perpetrator wore nylon stocking masks, carried a gun, and vaulted over the counter to put the money in a bag. Perhaps each fact in and of itself is not sufficient, but why are the factors taken together not sufficient to show the robberies are both the handiwork of the defendant? How many bank robbers wear stocking masks, rob federally insured credit unions, carry guns and leap over counters? If these factors are not sufficiently unique, can you think of some that might be?

b. The Time Factor in *Carroll*.

The court cites as a factor for denying admissibility that during most of the ten years separating the prior robbery and the robbery at issue, the defendant was in prison. How important was this ten year gap to the court's analysis? What if the defendant was never in prison, and both robberies occurred within months of each other? Or within days? Might the court have reached a different result?

c. Evidence Offered to Show Motive.

So far, we have seen court decisions concerning evidence offered to show intent, plan and identity. What about motive as a permissible purpose? In *United States v. Cunningham*, 103 F.3d 553 (7th Cir. 1996), the court admitted evidence that the defendant nurse was addicted to Demerol to show her motive in a prosecution for removing Demerol from hospital syringes to feed her addiction. Her motive became relevant in the case because only five nurses, including the defendant, had access to the cabinet where the syringes were kept, and there was no evidence suggesting any of the other four had a motive to steal the drug. How does this differ from offering character evidence to show propensity?

d. Entrapment or Predisposition as a Permissible but Unlisted "Other Purpose."

One unlisted but "permissible purpose" for which Rule 404(b) evidence may be offered is when the defendant in a criminal case alleges the defense of entrapment. The entrapment defense applies when a defendant claims that government action induced the defendant to commit a crime he would not otherwise have committed. To refute this allegation, the prosecution is allowed to show that the defendant committed similar crimes on other occasions and thus was not entrapped. See *United States v. Brand*, 467 F.3d 179 (2d Cir. 2006) (evidence of child pornography found on defendant's computer was admissible to show defendant's intent and predisposition after he raised an entrapment defense to the crime of traveling in interstate commerce for the purpose of engaging in illicit sexual conduct with a minor). On occasion, defendants have been able to bolster their defense of entrapment by showing they have no criminal record and thus no prior intent to commit the crime. See *United States v. Thomas*, 134 F.3d 975 (9th Cir. 1998) (it was reversible error to exclude evidence of a defendant's clean criminal record to show he was entrapped in a case charging him with possession of illegal drugs).

e. Crimes That Are Part of the Offense.

A number of cases have found that some acts are not "other crimes, wrongs, or acts" permitting admission under Rule 404(b), but rather are an integral part of the charged crime. This includes acts that show the chronological line of events that lead to the crime, which complete the crime, or are so connected to the crime that they incidentally involve or explain the circumstances surrounding the crime. For example, in *United States v. Baez,* 349 F.3d 90 (2d Cir. 2003), a prosecution for racketeering, conspiracy and murder, the admission of sixteen uncharged robberies to show the defendant's participation in a criminal enterprise and conspiracy

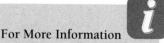

For More Information

To learn more about crimes that are considered part of the offense charged, see Schuster, *Uncharged Misconduct under Rule 404(b): The Admissibility of Inextricably Intertwined Evidence,* 42 U. MIAMI L. REV. 947 (1988).

was determined to be governed by the relevance balancing test of Rule 403, not Rule 404(b). Similarly, in *United States v. Bobb,* 471 F.3d 491 (3d Cir. 2006), the court held that the admissibility of evidence that the defendant assaulted other members of the conspiracy for stealing drugs was not subject to a Rule 404(b) analysis because the assault was intrinsic to the charge that the defendant was an organizer and leader of the conspiracy.

Hypo 9.4

Defendant came into the victim's place of business, grabbed him, propositioned him, put her hands all over him, and when he pushed her away, she pretended to fall down drunk on her way to the restroom. Subsequently, she lifted her dress, and before he could drag her out of the shop, she rubbed her rear end on him. Later, the victim discovered he was missing $150.00 from his wallet.

The prosecution wants to offer evidence of two other instances within the past year in which the defendant performed essentially the same acts on a man in an automobile repair shop and a man in an orthopedic brace shop, after which they too were missing money from their wallets. The only difference is that in these two other incidents, the defendant did not lift her dress or rub her body on these two men. Are these two other instances admissible under Rule 404(b)? If so, for what purpose or purposes? How would a Rule 403 balancing affect admissibility?

Perspective & Analysis

Now that you have discussed and analyzed Rule 404(b), consider whether you agree with this commentator in his assessment of the rule. Is there ever a "propensity-free chain" of logic in the admission of Rule 404(b) acts?

To comply with the plain words of Rule 404(b), courts must refuse to admit any evidence whose relevance depends on propensity reasoning. Even a quick run through the case reports, however, turns up abundant evidence that courts routinely admit such evidence. . . . [In drug cases, for example,] evidence of prior drug activity pours in unexamined on the rationale that, as long as the evidence is probative of "intent," the evidence does not involve the forbidden reasoning . . . . Courts even go so far as to repeatedly generalize that evidence of "the use of prior drug involvement to show plan, motive or intent in a drug trafficking offense is appropriate." Despite the courts' repetition of this principle, it is fatally flawed; its application almost always violates Rule 404(b). What chain of reasoning can link the prior drug history of [a defendant] to the charged crime other than one that infers that the defendant has a drug-related propensity, and that based on this propensity, the jury can disbelieve him when he denies criminal intent as to the latest drug incident? There is no propensity-free chain. The earlier drug use, which is behavior evidence, can be relevant only if we assume that the defendant's behavior forms an unchanging pattern. In the words of Rule 404(b), the drug history is relevant only because it proves the character of the defendant and supports the inference that, in the case at issue, the defendant acted consistent with that character.

Andrew J. Morris, *Federal Rule of Evidence 404(b): The Fictitious Ban on Character Reasoning from Other Crime Evidence*, 17 Rev. Litig. 181, 189-192, 196, 199 (1998).

F. Character Evidence Offered To Prove an Element of a Charge, Claim or Defense

Rule 405. Methods of Proving Character

(a) **Reputation or Opinion.** In all cases in which evidence of character or a trait of character of a person is admissible, proof may be made by testimony as to reputation or by testimony in the form of an opinion. On cross-examination, inquiry is allowable into relevant specific instances of conduct.

All of the character evidence rules we have discussed to this point have involved either using character evidence to prove circumstantially that the person possessing the character trait acted in conformity with it, or to prove circumstantially a specific fact issue in the case, such as intent, motive or the like. We are now going to study instances in which a person's character is a direct issue upon which the jury must make a finding because the substantive law of the case makes it so.

The tort law of defamation is one example. To win a defamation case, the plaintiff must prove that her character has been damaged by the defendant's defamatory remarks. Therefore, evidence of her character both before and after the defamation is relevant to show both her cause of action and the extent of her damages. Both the admissibility of such evidence and the form the evidence must take, are regulated by Rule 405(a).

Notice that 405(b) character evidence can arise in either a criminal, or civil case, no one needs to "open the door" first, and the method of proof is reputation, opinion or specific acts.

Schafer v. Time, Inc.

U.S. Court of Appeals for the Eleventh Circuit
142 F.3d 1361 (11th Cir. 1998)

BIRCH, Circuit Judge:

[Plaintiff Schafer brought suit against the defendant Time Magazine under Georgia's libel laws after he was misidentified in defendant's magazine article as a traitor to United States government and as being involved with the bombing of Pan Am Flight 103].

* * *

Schafer. . . argues that the district court committed reversible error by permitting Time's counsel to question Schafer regarding a number of "specific acts of misconduct" during cross-examination and by excluding from evidence a memorandum discussing the credibility of Time's sources for the Pan Am 103 article. We review the district court's legal decision to apply a

Go Online!

On December 21, 1988, Pan American World Airways Flight 103 left London's Heathrow Airport on its way to New York. It exploded, and the remains were scattered in an 845 miles radius in and around the town of Lockerbie, Scotland. An investigation later revealed that plastic explosives had been detonated in the airplane's forward cargo hold. Two hundred and seventy people from 21 countries lost their lives. Because 180 of the victims were American, the bombing was widely considered an assault on the United States. Eventually, a Libyan intelligence officer and the head of security for Libyan Arab Airlines was convicted in Scotland for his part in the bombing. http.//en.wikipedia.org/wiki Pan Am Flight 103.

particular rule of evidence de novo but its decision to admit or exclude particular evidence under that rule for an abuse of discretion. We will not overturn an evidentiary ruling unless the complaining party has shown a "substantial prejudicial effect."

Specific Acts of Misconduct

Evidence of a person's character is viewed with some suspicion under the law and generally is disfavored in the Federal Rules of Evidence. See Fed. R. Evid. 404 (character evidence generally inadmissible to prove conforming conduct). In an action for defamation or libel, however, the issue of the plaintiff's reputation and character scarcely can be avoided because the plaintiff typically seeks to recover compensation for damage to his or her reputation. Even in such cases, however, the rules of evidence prescribe particular methods for broaching the issue of character. See Fed. R. Evid. 405 ("Methods of Proving Character").

Before trial, the district court instructed the parties that Time would not be permitted to introduce and explore a number of specific acts and events in Schafer's life as they were irrelevant to the issues before the jury. At that time, however, the district court warned both parties that the court would revisit the character issue to the extent that particular acts and events were shown to be relevant to the question of damages or how Schafer's picture might have become associated with the Pan Am case. During the course of the trial, the district court made a preliminary ruling permitting Time to explore selective incidents and acts in Schafer's background but excluding evidence of others. Specifically, the district court ruled that Time would be permitted to question Schafer about a felony conviction, a possible violation of his subsequent parole, convictions for driving under the influence, an arrest for writing a bad check, failure to file tax returns, failure to pay alimony and child support, and evidence concerning Schafer's efforts to change his name and social security number. Schafer attacks the district court's ruling and argues that these specific acts were inadmissible. Character evidence does not constitute an "essential element" of a claim or charge unless it alters the rights and liabilities of the parties under the substantive law. Our determination of whether character constitutes an essential element requires us to examine the "authoritative statutory or common law statement of the elements of the prima facie case and defenses." The advisory committee's notes to the Federal Rules of Evidence provide two examples in which character evidence constitutes such an essential element: "[1] the chastity of a victim under a statute specifying her chastity as an element of the crime of seduction, the use of this evidence has been sharply curtailed by "Rape Shield" law, such as the one found in Rule 412, which prohibits a defendant in a crimi-

Make the Connection

Rule 412 is covered earlier in this chapter.

nal or civil case from introducing evidence of a victim's sexual behavior or disposition except under certain very limited circumstances [2] the competency of the driver in an action for negligently entrusting a motor vehicle to an incompetent driver." Fed.R.Evid. 404(a) adv. comm. note (explaining that Rule 404 does not exclude such evidence because it is not offered to prove conduct consistent with character). In addition to these examples, a charge of defamation or libel commonly makes damage to the victim's reputation or character an essential element of the case. Georgia law confirms that an assertion of damage to reputation in a libel case makes the plaintiff's character an issue under the substantive law. See *Ajouelo v. Auto-Soler Co.,* 6 S.E.2d 415, 419 (1939) ("It is generally held that the foundation of an action for defamation is the injury done to the reputation, that is, injury to character in the opinion of others arising from publication . . ."). Since the plaintiff's character is substantively at issue in a libel case under Georgia law, Rule 405(b) permits the admission of evidence regarding specific instances of the plaintiff's conduct on that issue. Given the plain language of Rule 405(b), Schafer's arguments that specific acts remain inadmissible to prove character in an action for libel are unpersuasive.

Accordingly, we find no error in Time's exploration of these and other issues of character during its cross-examination of Schafer. To the extent that Time strayed from the specific issues of character enumerated in the district court's preliminary ruling, including Time's questions regarding Schafer's work for *Soldier of Fortune* magazine, Time's questions fell within the scope of Federal Rules of Evidence 405(a) . . . . We cannot say that the district court's decisions on these matters rose to the level of an abuse of discretion, nor can we say that Schafer suffered a "substantial prejudicial effect."

Food for Thought

Is this true? Do you think the jury may have found against him, in part, because they did not want to give money to someone with such an unsavory background? Why do you think the court did not consider such an argument in analyzing the admissibility of such evidence?

Points for Discussion

a. Defamation Suits.

Can you articulate why the court in *Schafer* thinks that admission of the plaintiff's prior felony and driving while intoxicated convictions, possible violation of parole, arrest for writing a bad check, failure to file income tax returns, failure to pay alimony and child support, and efforts to change his name and his social security number alter "the rights and liabilities of the parties under the substantive law" of defamation? How do you think the defense attorney made use of this evidence in final argument?

b. Negligent Entrustment Suits.

A negligent entrustment suit is another instance in which a person's character is directly at issue. Negligent entrustment requires that the defendant negligently ". . . permit a third person to use a thing or to engage in an activity which is under the control of the actor, if the actor knows or should know that such person intends or is likely to use the thing or to conduct himself in the activity in such a manner as to create an unreasonable risk of harm to others." RESTATEMENT (SECOND) OF TORTS: Negligence, Chap. 2 (2008). For example, if a father allows his son to drive his car knowing that his son has had numerous accidents and speeding tickets, the father (as well as the son) might be liable for negligence if the son drives through a red light and hits the plaintiff. Under these facts, whose character would then be at issue, the father's or the son's?

c. Crimes Involving Status Issues.

The prime example of a case in which a person's character is at issue is one where a statute makes it a crime for a felon to possess a firearm. To avoid the unfair prejudice that accompanies the prosecution's introduction of the full record of the defendant's prior felony, the defendant will often offer to stipulate to his felony status. Remember that in *Old Chief v. United States,* 519 U.S. 172 (1997), the Supreme Court held that it is an abuse of the trial court's discretion not to allow such a stipulation.

Make the Connection

Old Chief is discussed in Chapter 3 of this book.

G. Making Sense of Rules 404 and 405: A Recap

After reading this chapter, you may agree with the Court in *Michaelson* that character evidence is a "grotesque" structure. Nonetheless, consider Justice Rutledge's dissent in *Michaelson* as an explanation for it:

Make the Connection

The case of *Michaelson v. United States* can be found and discussed earlier in this chapter.

Anomalies [in character evidence] there are, no doubt, with much room for improvement. But here, if anywhere, the law is more largely the result of experience, of considerations of fairness and practicability developed through the centuries, than of any effort to construct a nicely logical, wholly consistent pattern of things. Imperfect and variable as the scheme has become in the application of specific rules, on the whole it represents the result of centuries of common-law growth in the seeking of English-speaking peoples for fair play in the trial of crime and other causes.

It is always gratifying to know that grotesque structures and anomalies have a reason. But, it is another thing altogether to make sense of them. To aid in this attempt, you might find the following chart helpful:

General Rule: Character Evidence is not admissible to show action in conformity, *except*:

Rule	Use	Form of the Evidence	Opponent's Response
404(a)(1) Character of the Defendant ("*Mercy Rule*")	By a criminal defendant to offer evidence of his good character to rebut the charge of bad character implicit in the indictment or information	Reputation and Opinion Can cross-examine with Specific Acts	• Prosecution can cross defense reputation and opinion witnesses by asking about the defendant's specific bad acts relating to the defendant's character. • Prosecution can introduce its own reputation and opinion witnesses to show defendant's bad character.

Rule	Use	Form of the Evidence	Opponent's Response
404(a)(1) Character of the Defendant	By the prosecution to offer evidence to prove the defendant has the same bad character as the victim allegedly has. May be used only after the defendant has attacked the victim's character under Rule 404(a)(2).	Reputation and Opinion Can cross-examine with Specific Acts	• Defense can cross-examine prosecution reputation and opinion witnesses by asking about the defendant's specific good acts relating to the defendant's good character. • Defense can introduce its own reputation and opinion witnesses to show the defendant's good character.
404(a)(2) Character of the Victim	By the defense to offer evidence of the bad character of the victim of a crime.	Reputation and Opinion Can cross-examine with Specific Acts	• Prosecution can cross defense reputation and opinion witnesses by asking about the victim's good acts relating to the victim's good character. • Prosecution can introduce its own reputation and opinion witnesses to show the victim's good character.

Rule	Use	Form of the Evidence	Opponent's Response
404(a)(2) Character of theVictim	By the prosecution to offer evidence that the victim had a good character for being peaceful in a *homicide* case where the defendant has accused the victim of being the first aggressor.	Reputation and Opinion Can cross-examine with Specific Acts	• Defense can cross-examine prosecution reputation and opinion witnesses by asking about the victim's bad acts relating to the victim's character for violence. • Defense can introduce its own reputation and opinion witnesses to show the victim's character for violence.
404(b) (*"Prosecutor's Rule"*)	By either party in a criminal or civil case (usually criminal) to offer specific act evidence to show a factual issue in the case, such as motive, opportunity, plan, intent preparation, knowledge, etc.	Specific Acts	• Opponent can introduce its own witnesses who will testify as to other specific acts in rebuttal concerning the factual issue in question

Rule	Use	Form of the Evidence	Opponent's Response
405(b) ("*Character in Issue Rule*")	By either party in a criminal or civil case (usually civil) to offer evidence when the substantive law places a party's character at issue.	Reputation, Opinion and Specific acts	• Opponent can cross-examine reputation and opinion witnesses by asking about specific acts relating to the person whose character is at issue. • Opponent can introduce its own reputation and opinion witnesses to show the character of the person whose character is at issue.

H. Habit and Routine Practice

Rule 406 Habit; Routine Practice

Evidence of the habit of a person or of the routine practice of an organization, whether corroborated or not and regardless of the presence of eyewitnesses, is relevant to prove that the conduct of the person or organization on a particular occasion was in conformity with the habit or routine practice.

Rule 405 states that in a civil or criminal case, the "habit" of a person or the "routine practice of a business" is relevant in proving that the person or business acted in conformity with the habit. Nowhere does the rule define any of these terms. The language of Rule 406 and the Advisory Committee Note accompanying the rule, however, make it clear that habit refers to actions of an individual, and routine practice refers to the procedures of an organization. But how does habit compare to character evidence? Character evidence is more general. It shows a mere tendency of a person to act in accordance with a particular character trait, such as honesty or peacefulness. Habit evidence is more specific. It shows a stronger likelihood that a person acted in accordance with a particular way of behaving because that person has done so repeatedly, almost automatically, in response to a specific situation that occurs over a period of time. Repetition and uniformity of response give habit evidence its force in proving action in conformity. For example, a person might have a habit of locking her doors before going to bed. She may have done so thousands of times over a period of years. She also might be known as a careful person. If there is an issue in a lawsuit about whether she locked her doors before going to bed, habit evidence will most likely be admissible to prove that she did because habit is a better predictor of conduct than is character evidence of carefulness.

Can a person have a habit for being drunk or is this a character trait? Does the answer to this question depend upon the type of evidence a party offers? These are issues considered below in *Loughan v. Firestone Tire & Rubber Co.*

Loughan v. Firestone Tire & Rubber Co.

U.S. Court of Appeals for the Eleventh Circuit
749 F.2d 1519 (11th Cir. 1985)

HATCHETT, Circuit Judge:

. . . On July 24, 1974, John F. Loughan, the appellant, while employed as a tire mechanic by Slutz-Seiberling Tire Company in Fort Lauderdale, Florida, was mounting and dismounting a Firestone multi-piece rim wheel assembly to a trailer axle. Loughan sustained injuries when, in the process of remounting, a part of the three part rim wheel assembly separated with explosive force, striking Loughan in the head. . . . Loughan asserts that the district court committed reversible error in admitting into evidence prior instances of Loughan's drinking of alcoholic beverages. The district court held that the evidence of Loughan's drinking was sufficiently regular to constitute habit evidence admissible pursuant to Federal Rule of Evidence 406. . . .

An analysis of the admissibility of evidence begins with an examination of the purposes for which the evidence is proffered. The record in this case demonstrates Firestone's intent to establish that Loughan's faculties were impaired due to his consumption of alcoholic beverages at the time of the accident. Such evidence was deemed relevant to support Firestone's defense of assumption of risks and the apportionment of liability under Florida's comparative negligence standard.

Loughan's capacities, both physical and mental, were critical to development of Firestone's arguments.

Our determination of whether the references to Loughan's drinking introduced by the defendant represents evidence admissible to prove habit begins with a review of the Fifth Circuit's decision in *Reyes v. Missouri Railroad Co.*, 589 F.2d 791 (5th Cir.1979). In *Reyes*, a Missouri Pacific railroad train ran over Joel Reyes as he lay on the railroad tracks. Reyes sued the railroad alleging negligence on the part of the railroad's employees in failing to discover him as he lay on the tracks. The district court permitted the railroad to support its defense of contributory negligence by introducing into evidence Reyes' four prior misdemeanor convictions for public intoxication.

The Fifth Circuit reversed the district court and held that the four prior convictions for intoxication were inadmissible under Federal Rule of Evidence 404. The evidence was inadmissible because it was proffered to prove that Reyes acted in conformity with his character on the night of the accident; the court held that the four convictions failed to constitute habit evidence. The court stated: "Although a precise formula cannot be proposed for determining when the behavior may become so consistent as to rise to the level of habit, 'adequacy of sampling and uniformity of response' are controlling considerations." . . .

Loughan asserts that evidence pertaining to his drinking is comparable to the inadmissible evidence in *Reyes* relating to prior misdemeanor convictions for public intoxication. In *Reyes*, the court found that four prior convictions for public intoxication spanning a three and one-half year period are of insufficient regularity to rise to the level of "habit" evidence. Loughan argues that likewise, testimony from Thompson, Loughan's former employer between 1969 and 1971, was too remote in time and insufficient to establish Loughan's

Food for Thought

Would four convictions for public intoxications in one year be sufficient to constitute habit evidence? How about four convictions and three arrests? Is it the number of convictions that concern the *Reyes* court, or is it the absence of evidence concerning the specific circumstances under which these prior incidents took place? Or both? Or something else?

regular routine at the time of the accident in 1974. In Thompson's deposition which was read into evidence, he stated that he fired Loughan because of his drinking. He enumerated the indications that Loughan drank, including Loughan's slurred speech, wobbly walk, alcoholic breath, and complaints from customers. Thompson also testified that Loughan's reputation in the community was a "happy, easy-to-get-along-with guy, but he drank too much." Loughan points out that Thompson's position waivered in his assertions of certainty pertaining to the frequency of Loughan's consumption of alcoholic beverages.

Firestone relied on three separate sources to establish Loughan's habit of drinking between 1968 and July 24, 1974, the date of the accident. Testimony from Thompson, Loughan's previous employer, Orr, Loughan's supervisor, and Loughan himself supports the district court's admission into evidence proof establishing Loughan's drinking habit pursuant to Federal Rule of Evidence 406.

* * *

Evidence adduced from three sources, taken together, demonstrates a uniform pattern of behavior. Loughan admitted that he carried a cooler of beer on his truck while employed by Slutz and that he would drink beer at some time between the hours of 9 a.m. and 5 p.m. Orr, Loughan's supervisor at Slutz, testified that Loughan routinely carried a cooler of beer on his truck and that he was in the habit of drinking on the job. Orr stated that complaints had been made by customers regarding Loughan's drinking while working on their equipment and that Loughan "normally" had something to drink in the early morning hours. Thompson, Loughan's former employer, further corroborated Loughan's habit when he testified that he fired Loughan because, based on his general observations and complaints from customers, he believed Loughan drank beer on the job. Thompson's observations of Loughan while under his employ between 1969 and 1971 are consistent with Orr's testimony regarding Loughan's behavior in Florida between 1971 and 1974. These recounts establish a pattern of drinking over a period of time.

Loughan argues that because no direct evidence was presented that he had anything to drink at the time of the accident, it was improper to admit evidence to establish his "habit" of drinking on the job. We reject this reasoning because proof of habit is through indirect evidence offered to prove that the conduct of a person conformed with his routine practice.

Evidence of the habit of a person or of the routine practice of an organization, whether corroborated or not and regardless of the presence of eye witnesses, is relevant to prove that the conduct of the person or organization on a particular occasion was in conformity with the habit or routine practice.

Fed.R.Evid. 406. Loughan asserts that he did not have anything to drink the day of the injury. Also, Orr, who saw Loughan a couple of hours before the accident, testified that although Loughan may have had a drink in the early morning hours, he had not been drinking after reporting to work. Furthermore, Orr stated that Loughan did not have a cooler in his truck on the day in question.

Evidence of habit or routine is to be weighed and considered by the trier of fact in the same manner as any other type of direct or circumstantial evidence. In this case, as the district court noted, conflicting testimony goes to the weight of the evidence and not to its admissibility. The weight to be given to any testimony depends upon the particular circumstances. Loughan is concerned that the evidence of a habit or routine does not establish conformance with the habit or routine on a particular occasion. To the contrary, such evidence, when substantial, allows the trier of facts to infer that the habit was conformed with on a particular occasion.

Loughan asserts that references to his drinking were inadmissible character evidence. The difficulty in distinguishing inadmissible character evidence from admissible habit evidence is great. Often, the line between the two is unclear:

Character and habit are close akin. Character is a generalized description of one's disposition, or one's disposition in respect to a general trait, such as honesty, temperance, or peacefulness. "Habit," in modern usage, both lay and psychological, is more specific. It describes one's regular response to a repeated specific situation. If we speak of character for care, we think of the person's tendency to act prudently in all the varying situations of life, in business, in family life, in handling automobiles, and in walking across the street. A habit, on the other hand, is the person's regular practice of meeting a particular kind of situation with a specific type of conduct, such as the habit of going down a particular stairway two stairs at a time, or giving the hand signal for a left turn, or of alighting from railway cars while they are moving. The doing of the habitual acts may become semi-automatic. "Although a precise formula cannot be proposed for determining when the behavior may become so consistent as to rise to the level of habit, 'adequacy of sampling and uniformity of response' are controlling considerations." Generally, habit evidence is highly persuasive as proof of conduct on a particular occasion, and its admission depends on the "degree of regularity of the practice and its coincidence with the occasion." Habit evidence is considered to be highly probative and, therefore, superior to character evidence because "the uniformity of one's response to habit is far greater than the consistency with which one's conduct conforms to character or disposition."

* * *

Food for Thought

How much different was the intoxication evidence in *Reyes* from the intoxication evidence in this case? Do you think these two cases stand for the proposition that the appellate courts will give broad discretion to a trial court's finding on a habit issue or is there truly a distinction between them?

We do not attempt here to develop a precise threshold of proof necessary to transform one's general disposition into a "habit"; on a close call, we will find the district court's admission of evidence relating to Loughan's drinking on the job rose to the level of habit pursuant to rule 406. District courts exercise broad discretion in determining the admissibility of evidence and will be reversed only if discretion has been abused. We find no abuse of discretion. . . .

AFFIRMED.

Points for Discussion

a. Habit Evidence as Non-Volitional.

In *Levin v. United States,* 338 F.2d 265 (D.C. Cir. 1964), the defendant, a man of the Jewish faith, was accused of stealing money on the Jewish Sabbath. He attempted to defend by offering testimony from a Rabbi that Orthodox ritual requires members of the Jewish faith to do no work on the Sabbath, much less steal other's money. The trial court refused to admit the Rabbi's testimony, finding that an individual's religious practices are not the type of activities that would involve "invariable regularity," as opposed to a volitional response. Do you agree? Can religious practices ever be deemed a habit? Do you think there would be a different result under Rule 406, which was not in effect until eleven years after the *Levin* opinion?

b. The Routine Practice of Organizations.

Organizations depend to a large extent on creating and following routine practices. These practices save organizations money and time. Because of their repetitive nature, Rule 406 allows an organization's routine be used to prove the routine was followed on a particular occasion. A defendant surgeon might, for example, offer evidence that he always shows patients a video on the risks of surgery to prove the plaintiff saw such a video and knew about the risks of surgury. Another example can be found in *Vining v. Enterprise Fin. Group., Inc.,* 148 F.3d 1206 (10th Cir. 1998), where the plaintiff sued the defendant insurance company for bad faith in denying plaintiff's claims. Evidence of how the same company treated other insureds was admissible to show a routine practice of abuse by the company. Prior to this rule, routine practices of an organization had to be corroborated before they were admissible. This is no longer required under Rule 406.

Hypo 9.5

The plaintiff's and the defendant's cars collided with each other at the intersection of Main and Elm. Plaintiff claims that the defendant ran a stop sign. To disprove the claim, defendant has the following witnesses who are willing to testify at trial: (1) Witness 1, who will testify that she has ridden with the defendant and in her opinion, the defendant is a careful person. (2) Witness 2, who will testify that she has ridden with the defendant and in her opinion, the defendant is a careful driver. (3) Witness 3, who will testify that she has ridden with the defendant and that he always stops at stop signs. (4) Witness 4, who will testify that he rides with defendant to work and that the defendant always stops at the stop sign where the plaintiff and the defendant had the accident. Which of these witnesses is offering character evidence and which is offering habit evidence? Are there any other facts that you would want to know about before making your decision?

Executive Summary

Character Evidence is Generally Inadmissible. Character evidence is evidence of a person's "propensity" to act in conformity with a particular character trait. It is generally excludable because people should be judged in a court of law based on what they *have actually done* in a case, not on a *mere likelihood* of doing something just because they have a particular character trait and *probably acted* in conformity with it. Rule 404(a) excludes such evidence. (*Calvert*).

Character Evidence Exceptions in Criminal Cases. There are two important exceptions to the rule excluding character evidence, and they are both limited to criminal cases. Under Rule 404(a)(1), the defense may raise a *good* character trait of the defendant (the "accused") that is pertinent to the charge or defense at issue in the case (e.g., the defendant's propensity for peacefulness in an assault charge case). Under Rule 404(a)(2), the defense may also raise a *bad* character trait of the victim that is pertinent to the charge or defense at issue in the case (e.g., the victim's propensity for violence in an assault charge/self-defense case).

Defendant Must Be the One to "Open the Door" on Character; The "Mercy Rule." Only the defendant can raise the issue of character under these two criminal case exceptions. Therefore, the prosecution cannot be the first to attack the defendant's character, nor can the prosecution be the first to support the victim's character. This means only the defendant can be the first to "open the door" on character, known as the "Mercy Rule." However, once the defendant opens the door on character, the prosecution can "come through" it by attacking the character of the defendant, or supporting the character of the victim. (*Michelson*). When the defendant opens the door by attacking the victim's character, the defendant not only opens the door on the victim's character, but by doing so the defendant also opens the door on his own character on that issue as well. Note also that in a homicide case only, the defendant is considered to have opened the door on the victim's character simply by putting on evidence that the victim was the "first-aggressor" between them (e.g., that the victim was the first one to throw a punch). So character evidence is inadmissible, unless the defendant decides to bring it up first.

Character for Truthfulness of a Witness. Do not confuse the "general" character traits of a defendant or victim that may be at issue in a criminal case, with the character for truthfulness of any witness, in either a criminal or civil case. Character for truthfulness is a special attack on the credibility of a witness, discussed in Chapter 5, on "Witnesses."

Method of Proof. If general Rule 404(a) character evidence is admissible, then under Rule 405(a), the allowable method of proof is to call a witness who will testify regarding the defendant's, or the victim's, character trait(s). That witness can testify to either the defendant's, or the victim's, (1) *reputation* for the character trait, or that (2) in the witness's *opinion*, the defendant or victim possesses a certain character trait. Such testimony is allowed as long as the character witness limits her testimony to reputation or opinion about a defendant's or a victim's pertinent character traits. However, "extrinsic evidence" of a "specific instance of conduct" is not allowed (e.g., a character witness can state that the defendant has a reputation for being peaceful, or that in the character witness's opinion the defendant is peaceful, but the witness cannot list specific examples of times and places when the defendant did some particular act peacefully). Although no extrinsic evidence of a specific instance of conduct can be used to prove character, an attorney can still "ask about" a specific instance of conduct in order to test the credibility of the character witness. However, the attorney is "stuck" with whatever answer the witness provides because no extrinsic evidence can be used. The attorney can ask about the specific instance of conduct, provided (1) the attorney has a "good-faith basis" for asking the question (she cannot just make up specific instances to ask about), (2) the question addresses a pertinent character trait, and (3) the judge allows the question in her discretion. (*Michelson*).

The Defendant's Character in a Sexual Assault Case. Under Rules 413-415, if the defendant is charged with rape, child molestation, or sexual assault, the prosecution *does not have to wait* for the defendant to open the door on character. Instead, the prosecution can attack the defendant's character by showing evidence of the defendant's commission of another offense or offenses of sexual assault (this means that extrinsic evidence of specific instances of conduct are admissible against the defendant in these circumstances, without the defendant first having to open the door on his own character – no "Mercy Rule" here). (*LeMay*).

The Victim's Character in a Sexual Assault Case. Under Rule 412, in a sex offense case, the defendant *cannot* open the door on the victim's character for "sexual behavior" or "sexual predisposition." So the defendant cannot use the victim's reputation, or use an opinion about the victim, in this regard. However, there are three exceptions in criminal cases. Under 412(b)(1)(A), specific instances of the victim's past are admissible to prove that someone other than the defendant was the source of semen or injury. Under Rule 412(b)(1)(B), past specific instances of the victim's sexual behavior *with the defendant* can be used if the defendant is claiming consent. Under Rule 412(b)(1)(C), evidence can be used if excluding it would violate the Constitution. In civil cases involving any sexual conduct, under Rule 412(b)(2), evidence of sexual behavior and predisposition is admissible against a victim, provided the probative value of the evidence substantially outweighs its unfair prejudice (a "reverse" Rule 403 balancing test). (*Rodman*).

"Other Crimes, Wrongs, or Acts" Used for NON-Propensity Purposes. Under Rule 404(b), past crimes, wrongs, or acts of a person can be used, in either a criminal or civil case, to prove something *other than character or propensity* of that person. Because these acts are, by definition, *not* being used to prove character, but are instead being used to prove something else, they are not subject to Rule 405.

Although these 404(b) past "crimes, wrongs, or acts" of a person (usually of a criminal defendant, but they can also be used in civil cases) are specific instances of conduct, they are, by definition, NOT being used to prove character or propensity, but are instead being used for some other admissible purpose. The pneumonic "**MIAMI COP**," is a helpful way to remember the other non-propensity purposes that can be used under Rule 404(b): **M**otive, **I**dentity (*Carroll*), **A**bsence of mistake/accident, **M**istake/accident, **I**ntent (*Hearst*), **C**ommon plan or scheme, **O**pportunity, **P**reparation.

Character is Admissible in a Criminal Case, or in a Civil Case, If Character Is an "Essential Element" of a Claim, Charge, or Defense. Recall that extrinsic evidence of specific instances of conduct is not allowed, although attorneys can ask about specific instances to test the credibility of a character witness. Recall also that character evidence is generally inadmissible in civil cases. However, when character is an "essential element" of a claim, charge or defense, then under Rule 405(b), character evidence is admissible, and it is admissible using extrinsic evidence in all three forms: reputation, opinion, and specific instances of conduct. (*Shafer*).

Habit and Routine Practice. Under Rule 406, habit evidence of an individual, or the routine practice of an organization, is admissible. However, to be a habit, the action in question has to be a specific, narrow, non-volitional, automatic response to a repeated set of circumstances. Habit or routine practice is admissible because it is considered more reliable than character evidence; and unlike character evidence that can have many possible manifestations (e.g., being "violent" can be exhibited in many differing ways), a habit has only one specific manifestation (e.g., every day a person always drinks a cup of coffee when she first arrives to work in the morning). Watch out for character evidence masquerading as habit in an attempt to make it admissible. (*Loughan*). For example, one cannot be in the "habit" of being careful or violent (really character).

CHAPTER 10

Authentication

A. Introduction

Authentication is the process of proving that a particular piece of evidence is what the proponent of the evidence claims it to be. Federal Rule of Evidence 901 is the basic rule that addresses authentication.

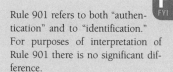

Rule 901 refers to both "authentication" and to "identification." For purposes of interpretation of Rule 901 there is no significant difference.

Rule 901. Requirement of Authentication or Identification

(a) General Provision. The requirement of authentication or identification as a condition precedent to admissibility is satisfied by evidence sufficient to support a finding that the matter in question is what its proponent claims.

Practice Pointer

In practice, the authentication of evidence is rarely challenged because it is often easily satisfied. One should only challenge the authenticity of a document when there is a genuine issue as to its authentication. It should not be used merely as a trial tactic for strategies such as delay or upsetting the opponent's rhythm. This will quickly earn you disfavor with the court.

The issue of authentication applies to non-testimonial evidence and is similar to the requirement of personal knowledge for witnesses. Just as a person must generally have personal knowledge of the facts about which she will testify, non-testimonial evidence must shown to be "authentic" by the offering party because one cannot cross-examine an exhibit; reliability must be tested by some other means. For example, a photograph might meet all other requirements of admissibility but unless it is properly authenticated, it will not be admissible.

Rule 901 sets out three basic requirements:

1) Authentication is a condition precedent to admissibility;

2) This condition is satisfied by evidence which supports the finding; and

3) The finding must be that the matter in question is what the proponent claims it to be.

Because 901 specifically sets out the requirement of authentication as a condition precedent to admissibility, non-testimonial evidence must be excluded if it is not authenticated. To understand where authentication fits into the evidence map, reexamine the General Evidence Logic Map found in Chapter 1 now with the addition of Authentication:

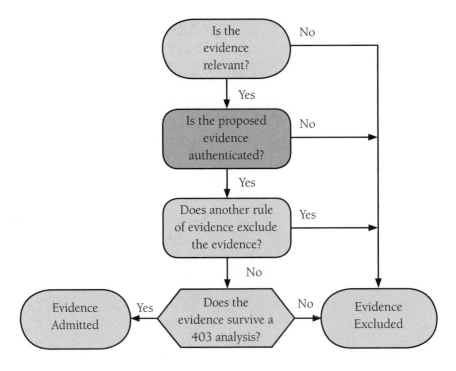

Although the rules do not specifically set out a procedure or time line for challenging authentication, the typical challenge, if any, would be raised prior to its admission.

Non-testimonial evidence may take many forms. Documents involved in a case, such as letters, contracts, photographs, receipts, memos, reports, e-mail messages, and so on, are examples of non-testimonial evidence. Exhibits may also be non-documentary tangible items, such as an alleged murder weapon (gun, knife, poison, etc.), a group of keys, an item of clothing, a set of finger prints, bags of contraband, or hair or fiber samples. Exhibits can also be illustrative diagrams, drawings, or photographs created prior to or during a trial to help clarify the testimony of a witness, such as a map, an organizational chart, a floor plan, a timeline of events, or a computer animation depicting an accident or the inner-workings of a mechanical device. These illustrative types of exhibits are often referred to as "demonstrative" exhibits.

FYI

Exhibits are "marked" for admission into evidence. For example, a photograph might be marked as "Plaintiff's Exhibit #1". This permits the judge, jury, parties and their attorneys to know with certainty which document is being referenced. This marking also makes referencing easier for appellate courts when referring to documents in the record on appeal.

Section (b) of Rule 901 sets out common examples of methods of authentication for selected types of evidence:

> (b) Illustrations. By way of illustration only, and not by way of limitation, the following are examples of authentication or identification conforming with the requirements of this rule:
>
> (1) Testimony of witness with knowledge. Testimony that a matter is what it is claimed to be.
>
> (2) Nonexpert opinion on handwriting. Nonexpert opinion as to the genuineness of handwriting, based upon familiarity not acquired for purposes of the litigation.
>
> (3) Comparison by trier or expert witness. Comparison by the trier of fact or by expert witnesses with specimens which have been authenticated.
>
> (4) Distinctive characteristics and the like. Appearance, contents, substance, internal patterns, or other distinctive characteristics, taken in conjunction with circumstances.

(5) Voice identification. Identification of a voice, whether heard firsthand or through mechanical or electronic transmission or recording, by opinion based upon hearing the voice at any time under circumstances connecting it with the alleged speaker.

(6) Telephone conversations. Telephone conversations, by evidence that a call was made to the number assigned at the time by the telephone company to a particular person or business, if (A) in the case of a person, circumstances, including self-identification, show the person answering to be the one called, or (B) in the case of a business, the call was made to a place of business and the conversation related to business reasonably transacted over the telephone.

(7) Public records or reports. Evidence that a writing authorized by law to be recorded or filed and in fact recorded or filed in a public office, or a purported public record, report, statement, or data compilation, in any form, is from the public office where items of this nature are kept.

(8) Ancient documents or data compilation. Evidence that a document or data compilation, in any form, (A) is in such condition as to create no suspicion concerning its authenticity, (B) was in a place where it, if authentic, would likely be, and (C) has been in existence 20 years or more at the time it is offered.

(9) Process or system. Evidence describing a process or system used to produce a result and showing that the process or system produces an accurate result.

(10) Methods provided by statute or rule. Any method of authentication or identification provided by Act of Congress or by other rules prescribed by the Supreme Court pursuant to statutory authority.

B. Tangible Evidence

Physical tangible exhibits cannot "speak" or testify in court the same way a witness can. Therefore the attorney needs to provide evidence about the exhibit itself before the exhibit can be admitted and considered in the case.

Take Note!

Rule 901(b) specifically provides that the examples are illustrations only. Do not be misled into thinking that the list provided is exclusive.

United States v. Collado

U.S Court of Appeals for the First Circuit
957 F.2d 38 (1st Cir. 1992)

CYR, Circuit Judge.

Appellant … Collado was convicted of possessing cocaine and heroin, with intent to distribute, … and of possessing a firearm during the commission of a drug offense.… Collado contends on appeal that the district court improperly admitted into evidence an incriminating plastic bag he allegedly dropped while attempting to elude arrest in a Providence, Rhode Island, parking lot in the early morning hours of May 24, 1990. We affirm.

I. Background

Providence Police Officer Michael Wheeler saw Collado drop the bag and directed Officer Venditto to seize it. Venditto took the evidence to the police station, completed a seizure report, and turned the evidence over to the Special Investigations Bureau ("SIB"). The bag was found to contain thirty plastic baggies of cocaine, as well as sixteen glassine packets of heroin bound together by an elastic band and bearing the label "Fly High."

Officer Venditto testified that he delivered the evidence to SIB. Detective Purro, the SIB officer responsible for processing drug evidence, testified to the standard operating procedure for depositing seized drugs at the police station between midnight and 8:00 a.m. when the SIB office is closed. The procedure required that Venditto deposit the evidence in a "mail slot" leading into a locked safe, fill out the seizure report, and place the report on top of the SIB safe. Detective Purro further testified that at 9:00 a.m. the following morning, he found Venditto's seizure report on top of the SIB safe, opened the safe, and retrieved a clear plastic bag whose contents precisely matched those described in Venditto's testimony as having been seized from appellant. Other testimony established an uninterrupted chain of custody, commencing with Purro's retrieval of the evidence from the SIB safe and concluding with its presentation at trial. There was no indication that the proffered evidence had been altered in any way.

II. Discussion

The proponent first must authenticate the evidence by demonstrating to the court that there is a reasonable probability that the evidence "is what its proponent claims." Fed. R. Evid. 901(a). …The trial court must be able to determine that it is reasonably probable that there was no material alteration of the evidence after it came into the custody of the proponent. Federal Rule of Evidence 901(b) provides illustrative authentication techniques, among which are rule 901(b)(1) (testimony of witness with knowledge that the evidence is what it is claimed to be) and rule 901(b)(4) (distinctive characteristics, such as "appearance, contents…, taken in conjunction with circumstances"). These two techniques were utilized by the government at trial in the present case.

Officer Wheeler testified that he shouted at Venditto to pick up the bag while Wheeler chased after the defendant on foot. Officer Venditto testified that he seized a clear plastic bag and contents whose descriptions precisely matched the number and labeling of the items offered in evidence by the government. The distinctive characteristics of the contents of the plastic bag that Venditto testified to having seized, and their readily determinable similarity to the proffered evidence, provided a sturdy corroborative basis for the district court's ruling. Moreover, in the circumstances of the present case, the district court was entitled to rely on a presumption of official regularity. United States v. Luna, 585 F.2d 1, 6 (1st Cir.) (trial court "entitled to rely on a presumption of official regularity" where prosecution established chain of custody of heroin "either by official records or by testimony concerning normal police procedure" and where appellant "offered no evidence that the drugs had been altered"), We review the district court's authentication ruling for abuse of discretion.

The government traced custody of the challenged evidence from the moment Officer Wheeler saw Collado drop it, until it was introduced in evidence. Appellant made no effort to undermine the testimony describing the standard police procedure for handling drug evidence seized after SIB office hours. The resulting presumption of official regularity was sufficient in these circumstances to meet the Rule 901(a) authentication requirement. But there was more. Officer Venditto testified that the clear plastic bag, with its distinctively packaged and labeled contents, were the very items seized at the scene. Moreover, Venditto's description of the drugs he seized at the scene was identical to Purro's description of the drugs he retrieved from the SIB safe the next morning. All circumstantial indications suggest that the district court did not drop the ball when it concluded that there was a reasonable probability that Collado dropped the bag and Officer Venditto picked it up. Affirmed.

———————————

Points for Discussion

a. Is a "Chain of Custody" Necessary?

Note that a "chain of custody" was provided for the dropped bag of cocaine exhibit in order to help establish that the cocaine offered in evidence was the actual cocaine taken from defendant at the time he was arrested. Does a break in the chain in custody mean that the tangible item should be inadmissible?

How much of a break in the chain of custody can be tolerated before the attempt at authentication will be found insufficient? Consider the next case. In what circumstances would it still be possible to lay the proper foundation for a tangible item even where there has been a break in the chain of custody of that item?

Lockhart v. McCotter

U.S Court of Appeals for the Fifth Circuit
782 F.2d 1275 (5th Cir. 1986)

JOHNSON, Circuit Judge:

... Lockhart appeals the federal district court's denial of [his] petition for habeas corpus relief. Lockhart contends that he is entitled to habeas corpus relief on the grounds that he was deprived of effective assistance of counsel both at trial and on appeal. Perceiving no reversible error ... we affirm.

I. Background

Lockhart was arrested and ultimately convicted of aggravated robbery in Dallas, Texas. On the day of his arrest, April 2, 1976, Lockhart had worked distributing hand circulars and been paid $18.00. After work, Lockhart spent several hours at the Stop-In Cafe in North Dallas. Lockhart testified at trial that he left the cafe at approximately 11:00 p.m. following an argument with a prostitute.

At approximately the same time that Lockhart left the Stop-In Cafe and in that same neighborhood, James Hall, who had also just left the Stop-In Cafe, was robbed. According to Hall, a man put a knife to Hall's throat and demanded Hall's money. After giving the man his wallet, which contained $30.00, Hall was released. Hall immediately ran to a pay phone and called the police.

When police officers arrived, Hall told the officers that his assailant was about 5 feet, 11 inches tall, weighed 170 pounds, and was wearing a red windbreaker and blue pants. Hall then accompanied the officers to search for the robber. Approximately one block from the Stop-In Cafe, the police encountered Lockhart, who was wearing a red windbreaker and blue trousers, walking along the street. The police officer who spotted Lockhart asked Hall, "Is that him?" In response, Hall identified Lockhart as the robber and, after Lockhart had been stopped and searched, identified a knife taken from Lockhart as the one used in the robbery. Although the police found $12.00 in Lockhart's pants, they could not recall whether they had also discovered Hall's stolen wallet at the time of Lockhart's arrest.

The police took Lockhart to the Dallas City Jail where he was strip searched and booked. After Lockhart was searched, a "purse" [a wallet], keys, two necklaces and $1.06 were inventoried and placed in a personal property envelope to be held for Lockhart. Two knives along with $12.00 in cash which had also been found on Lockhart when he was searched were held by the police as evidence.

Several months after Lockhart's arrest and subsequent transfer to the Dallas County Jail, Dallas County prosecutor Rider Scott asked police investigator William C. Kelley to search Lockhart's personal property envelope. Scott had noticed that a "purse" had been taken from Lockhart and speculated that the inventoried "purse" could be the wallet taken in the robbery. Officer Kelley searched Lockhart's personal property envelope and located a wallet which was in fact later identified at trial as belonging to the robbery victim James Hall.

On May 10, 1976, Lockhart was indicted by a Dallas County Grand Jury for aggravated robbery... At trial, ... Officer Kelley produced the wallet recovered from Lockhart's personal property envelope. The State recalled James Hall who identified the wallet and two pictures, one of Hall's girlfriend and the other of her children, which were contained in the wallet.

Lockhart's attorney ... pointed out to the jury that no State witness had testified that Hall's wallet had actually been recovered from Lockhart at the time of Lockhart's arrest... [thus showing a break in the chair of custody] Lockhart denied having committed the robbery and asserted that the wallet had been planted in his personal property envelope...

B. Failure to Object to Introduction of Hall's Wallet Into Evidence

[Lockhart claims that his trial counsel] failed to object when the State moved to introduce Hall's wallet into evidence at trial. Officer [Kelley] testified that he seized the wallet from Lockhart's personal property envelope at the county jail. Kelley obtained the wallet several months after Lockhart's arrest at the request of the prosecutor...

Lockhart contends that had his trial counsel raised a chain of custody objection to the State's introduction of the wallet, the wallet would have been excluded from evidence. To establish a proper chain of custody as a predicate to introducing the wallet, the State should have introduced testimony (1) tracing the wallet from the arrest to Lockhart's property envelope; (2) establishing the security of and limited access to the envelope; and (3) tracing the wallet from the property envelope to the court. However, the State only introduced testimony tracing the wallet from Lockhart's property envelope to the court. Moreover, the State failed to establish the security of the wallet once it had been removed from Lockhart's personal property envelope.

Recognizing that the State had not established a proper chain of custody, the federal magistrate nevertheless concluded that the failure of Lockhart's attorney to object was not ineffective assistance. The magistrate found that Lockhart's attorney was justifiably surprised at the wallet's appearance given Lockhart's representations that he had disposed of the wallet prior to being arrested. The magistrate also found that because the wallet was "specifically unique and identifiable evidence," … a chain of custody objection would not have barred admission of the wallet. The magistrate concluded that counsel's failure to assert such an objection had not prejudiced Lockhart.

…[T]his Court agrees … that Lockhart was not prejudiced by his counsel's failure to assert a chain of custody objection. Tangible objects involved in a crime, such as the wallet in the instant case, are admissible in evidence only when identified and shown to be in materially the same condition as at the time of the crime. When the object has passed through several hands before being produced in court, it often is necessary to establish a chain of custody in order to prove either identity or lack of alteration.

However, when an object cannot be easily altered or substituted, establishing a continuous chain of custody is not as important. … Absent evidence of substitution or alteration, the failure to establish a chain of custody will generally go only to the weight of the evidence rather than its admissibility. Moreover, when the object is expressly identified at trial as the object involved in the crime, establishing a chain of custody is not necessary for the object to be admissible.

In the instant case, the wallet, containing pictures of the robbery victim's girlfriend and her children, was readily identifiable and not subject to undetectable alteration. At trial, the robbery victim specifically identified the wallet as the wallet which had been taken during the robbery. Moreover, Officer Kelley identified the wallet as the same wallet Kelley had removed from Lockhart's personal property envelope. In these circumstances, a chain of custody objection by Lockhart's attorney would not have resulted in exclusion of the wallet.

Based on testimony at trial, identifying the wallet as that taken from Hall, … the State was not required to establish a chain of custody. However, even if a chain of custody was required, a failure to establish such custody would only go to the weight rather than the admissibility of the evidence. During cross examination of the State's witnesses, Lockhart's attorney pointed out that no one could testify that the wallet was found on Lockhart at the time of his arrest. Whether Lockhart actually had the wallet at the time of his arrest presented a fact issue for the jury. In these circumstances, the attorney's failure to assert a chain of custody objection, which at best only went to the weight of the evidence, cannot be said to have prejudiced Lockhart…

AFFIRMED.

——————

Points for Discussion

a. "Weight" versus "Admissibility"

What did the court mean when it said that "even if a chain of custody was required, a failure to establish such custody would only go to the weight rather than the admissibility of the evidence? What is weight as used in this context?

b. What about "Fungible" Exhibits?

Under what circumstances would the bag of cocaine in *Collado* be properly authenticated with a break in the chain of custody?

c. Criminal versus Civil

Chain of custody requirements tend to be enforced more stringently in criminal cases than civil cases. Why?

C. Writings and Other Documents

United States v. Bagaric

U.S Court of Appeals for the Second Circuit
706 F.2d 42 (2nd Cir. 1983)

[Defendants, including Logarusic, were convicted for violations of Racketeer Influenced and Corrupt Organizations Act [RICO], and they appealed.] Logarusic challenges the admission of … a letter discovered during a consent search of Logarusic's home on April 3, 1981, after his arrest. [Logarusic] claims the letter was not properly authenticated. Fed.R.Evid. 901(a). We disagree. The requirement of authentication "is satisfied by evidence sufficient to support a finding that the matter is what its proponent claims," This finding may be based entirely on circumstantial evidence, including "[a]ppearance, contents, substance … and other distinctive characteristics" of the writing. Here, the letter was addressed to Logarusic and postmarked Asuncion, Paraguay, where Baresic resided. It began with the salutation "Dear Vinko" and ended "your Miro Baresic ... your Miro Toni." "Toni Saric" was the alias Baresic had used in gaining entry into the United States. The letter referred to "our people in Chicago," where four of the defendants lived, and it asked Logarusic to contact "Crni," which the proof showed was Ljubas's sobriquet among his confederates. It also contained references to "Mercedes," a friend of Logarusic who testified on his behalf and admitted knowing Baresic, and to "the Razov family," Logarusic's landlord. Finally, the letter stated that "[t] he Swedes, Americans, and Yugoslavs are requesting expulsion because I am a terrorist and dangerous," a fact confirmed by testimony that Baresic was a fugitive from Sweden where he was sought for the murder of the Yugoslavian ambassador. In sum, as Chief Judge Motley found, there was ample demonstration "that the letter was in fact what the Government claimed, i.e., a letter from Miro Baresic to Vinko Logarusic."

Points for Discussion

a. Rule 901(b)(4): Distributive Characteristics

Can stylistic writing patterns such as grammatical or spelling errors be used to authenticate writings?

b. Recognition of Letterhead

Can a letter be authenticated as a letter from a particular person when it is on that person's letterhead and it appears to be signed by that person? See Rules 901(b)(4) and 901(b)(2).

Assume an attorney in a case would like to introduce as an exhibit a handwritten letter from the defendant to the plaintiff. In order to lay the foundation for the letter, the attorney would have to provide some evidentiary basis for the jury to find that the handwritten letter is actually a handwritten letter from the defendant to the plaintiff. The attorney could provide that foundation in at least four different ways: (1) Call a witness who is familiar with the defendant's handwriting and recognizes it in the letter (Rule 901(b)(2)); (2) Call an expert witness in handwriting analysis who can state that in his expert opinion a handwriting sample of the defendant matches the handwriting in the letter (Rule 901(b)(3)); (3) Present handwriting exemplars of the defendant and the letter itself directly to the jury so that the jurors can compare the handwriting themselves and decide if the letter was written by the defendant (Rule 901(b)(3)); or (4) Call a witness who can identify certain unique aspects of the letter that would prove the letter is what it purports to be; for example, special paper, letterhead, or certain subject matter written about in the letter with which the witness would be familiar, or other circumstances about the letter, making it possible for the witness to recognize and identify the letter as that of the defendant (Rule 901(b)(4)).

Given these options, suppose the attorney calls a witness who is familiar with the defendant's handwriting in order to lay the foundation for the letter. That witness could identify the letter by first establishing that the witness already was familiar with the defendant's handwriting. Once that familiarity with the defendant's handwriting is asserted, the witness could then testify that the letter appears to be written in the handwriting of the defendant. The attorney introducing the letter must do more than merely assert that it is a letter from the defendant to the plaintiff. Instead, the attorney must provide some actual proof – a foundation, here the testimony of the witness – that the letter is what it purports to be, an actual handwritten letter from the defendant to the plaintiff.

Once the foundation is provided, the letter is admitted and it can be weighed and considered in determining the verdict just like any other admitted exhibit. The term "authentication" can be a bit misleading here. Merely providing the foundation for the exhibit does not necessarily mean the letter was actually written by the defendant to the plaintiff and that now the jury must accept and believe that proposition. How the jury (or judge) ultimately weighs the exhibit is still an open question, but the letter would be admissible as an exhibit because it has been properly authenticated. Opposing counsel is still free to argue that the letter is a fraud and that the jury should not believe that it is an actual letter written by defendant to the plaintiff. But again, that argument only goes to the "weight" of the letter, it does not go to its admissibility.

As a result, if the jury finds that the letter is actually the defendant's handwritten letter to the plaintiff, that finding would not merely be a guess on the jury's part, but would be based on the evidentiary foundation provided – the testimony of the witness with knowledge. Again, the jury could always reject the foundation if it so desires because that is its job – to weigh or consider the admitted evidence.

An illustration follows. It involves a cross-examining attorney laying the foundation through an adverse witness for the admission of a receipt for the purchase of a gun:

Defense: Now Witness, you and Willy purchased a Magnum .44 gun on the night of the incident, didn't you?

Witness: No, Willy bought it; I just went along.

Defense: But the two of you used your credit card to make it possible to get the gun, right?

Witness: Yes, I suppose so.

Defense: I show you what has been marked as Defense Exhibit #3 for identification. Do you recognize it?

Witness: Yes I do.

Defense: What is it?

Witness: It's a receipt from "Guns 'R' Us."

Defense: How do you know that?

Witness: Because I recognize the "Guns 'R' Us" logo on the top of the receipt.

Defense: And that is your signature on the bottom of the receipt, correct?

Witness: Yeah, that's right.

Defense: Is the receipt in the same condition as it was on the night you bought the gun?

Witness: Yes, it's the same.

Defense: I offer Defense Exhibit #3 your honor.

Judge: Any objection counsel?

Prosecution: No objections your honor.

Judge: It is admitted.

Defense: Now Witness, directing your attention to Defense Exhibit #3 — you bought more than the gun that night didn't you?

Witness: I didn't buy the gun, like I said before, he did, not me.

Defense: Well, please just look at Exhibit #3 — more than the purchase of the gun is on that receipt, isn't it?

Witness: You mean the bullets in the receipt?

Defense: Yes, I mean the bullets that were also purchased along with the gun that night. They were special "hollow-point" bullets, weren't they?

Witness: That's what the receipt says, but I don't remember buying any bullets.

Defense: But you don't deny that the charges for the gun and the bullets are what is on the receipt, do you?

Witness: No.

D. Voice Identification and Telephone Conversations

Recorded conversations often require authentication. These conversations frequently result from recorded telephone conversations but could be simply taped or digitally recorded live conversations. In either event, a foundation must be laid for proper admissibility of recorded conversations. The rules permit the foundation to be laid by having a witness familiar with the recorded voice testify as to the identity of the speaker. Although not a physical or tangible piece of evidence, the same requirements of authentication, or the laying of a foundation, also apply for voice recognition and/or telephone conversations. Additionally, telephone conversations can be authenticated as to a person by showing that the person answering was the one who was called or with regard to a business that the call was made to that business and the conversation related to the business. See Rules 901(b)(5) and 901(b)(6).

Consider the following case.

United States v. Espinoza

641 F.2d 153 (4th Cir. 1981)

STAKER, District Judge:

[Joseph "Joe" Espinoza was convicted of transporting obscene films and magazines involving children. Espinoza appeals arguing that the court erred in allowing a witness ("Holdren") to testify as to Holdren's telephone conversations with Espinoza. Holdren testified that he communicated by telephone with Espinoza concerning the ordering, pricing and shipping of "kiddie porn." Holdren testified that when he called a certain establishment, a lady would answer the telephone. Holdren would then ask for "Joe." At that point, a man would get on the telephone and say, "This is 'Joe'." In those telephone conversations with "Joe," Holdren ordered the obscene materials. Holdren testified that he had never met

"Joe," and that if he saw him at trial he would not know him.]

The admissibility of Holdren's testimony identifying Espinoza as the person with whom he spoke by telephone is governed to some extent by Rules 901(a) and 104(b).... Under the provisions thereof, it was not requisite to the admissibility of Holdren's testimony that it be sufficient itself to support a finding that it was Espinoza to whom Holdren spoke by telephone; Holdren's testimony was properly admissible, under the provisions of Rule 104(b), "upon, or subject to, the introduction of (other) evidence sufficient to support a finding of the fulfillment of the condition," that is, other evidence which would be sufficient to support a finding that Espinoza was the person to whom Holdren spoke by telephone, the establishment of the identity of Espinoza as that person being requisite to the relevancy of Holdren's testimony.

Testimony of a telephone conversation had between a witness and another person may be conditionally admitted, regardless of which of them initiated or answered the call, even though the witness cannot certainly identify the person with whom he spoke by voice identification, and the identity of the person with whom the witness is alleged to have had the conversation may be established by circumstantial evidence....

Here, the evidence of Espinoza's response to Holdren's telephoned order ... for kiddie porn almost certainly identifies Espinoza as the "Joe" to whom Holdren spoke in that conversation: Holdren communicated ... by speaking with "Joe;" [there is] Holdren's order for kiddie porn, in response to which kiddie porn was shipped ... to Holdren ... along with [an] invoice ... listing the kiddie porn ..., and Holdren paid ... the amount of that invoice by his check. These facts, standing alone, perhaps would not be sufficiently probative of Espinoza's identity, as the "Joe" to whom Holdren communicated the order and as a person involved in ... response to that order, to permit Holdren's testimony to the telephone conversation to be sufficiently relevant to remain before the jury as to Espinoza. But given the additional evidentiary fact that the invoice ... to Holdren for the kiddie porn bore the fingerprint of Espinoza, then compelling evidence existed tending not only to establish that Espinoza had a personal role in the making of [the] response to Holdren's order, thereby sufficiently identifying him as the "Joe" to whom Holdren spoke in the telephone conversation in which he made that order and rendering Holdren's testimony with regard thereto relevant, but also to establish independently that Espinoza was a member of the alleged conspiracy.

In *Davis v. United States*, 279 F.2d 576, 579 (4th Cir. 1960), this court partially relied upon evidence of the response made by Davis, to a telephoned communication to him by an undercover agent who did not then personally know him, to hold Davis thereby to have been sufficiently identified to permit the undercover agent's testimony about the telephone conversation to be admitted. The court committed no error by admitting Holdren's testimony.

————————

E. Photographs

U.S. v. Hyles

479 F.3d 958 (8th Cir. 2007)

MELLOY, Circuit Judge.

In the early morning hours of August 21, 2000, police found … Smith shot to death in his bed. Smith was a private citizen who had been working with law enforcement in the area to make controlled drug purchases from local drug dealers. On August 10, 2000, Smith had testified against Hyles at a preliminary hearing in a state drug case. At the time of Smith's murder, Hyles was being held in … County Jail … pending trial in the state drug prosecution. Co-defendant … Cannon, a close friend of Hyles, lived in Memphis, Tennessee, where he was under parole supervision.…

Following Smith's testimony, David Carter, Hyles's cellmate in the … County Jail, agreed to murder Smith in exchange for having [Hyles' wife] bail him out of jail. [Hyles' wife] bailed Carter out that same day, using a Pontiac … she and Hyles owned as collateral. Carter never killed Smith; instead, Hyles and Cannon agreed that Cannon would drive from Memphis, Tennessee to Caruthersville, Missouri for the purpose of killing Smith. In exchange for Smith's murder, Cannon received the Pontiac Parisienne.

[Hyles was convicted of murder-for-hire and conspiracy to commit murder-for-hire. He appealed]

Hyles … argues that the district court abused its discretion when it admitted writings on the back of photographs … into evidence over Hyles's foundational … objections. Hyles argues that there was no foundation for the admission of the writings because the government did not offer evidence as to when the writings took place, who wrote them, and whether … Hyles knew about the writings.…

…Federal Rule of Evidence 901 requires authentication or identification before evidence can be admitted. This rule is satisfied by providing "evidence sufficient to support a finding that the matter in question is what its proponent claims." Fed.R.Evid. 901(a). We have said that under this standard, the party "need only demonstrate a rational basis for its claim that the evidence is what the proponent asserts it to be." *United States v. Coohey*, 11 F.3d 97, 99 (8th Cir.1993).

The government offered the picture ... and the writing on the back of that picture to demonstrate the importance of the [Pontiac car] to Cannon. According to the government, the car was important enough to Cannon that he kept a picture of it with him in jail. The pictures of Cannon and Hyles together with writing on the back were offered to prove their close relationship. As the government stated at trial, "this is a conspiracy case and [the pictures and writings] establish[ ] a[n] association between" the two. The government expressly stated at trial that it did not matter who put the writing on the back of the pictures.

Keeping in mind the limited purpose the government had for offering the photographs and writings, there was sufficient foundation. The deputy who seized the photographs from Cannon's property at the jail testified that he saw the writing on the back when he seized them. Other officers identified Hyles and Cannon as the people pictured in the photographs, and the car as the same car they had seen Cannon ... driving. The government demonstrated a rational basis for its claim that the pictures were of Cannon and Hyles, that the car was the Pontiac ... and that the writings shed light on the relationship between the co-conspirators. The district court did not abuse its discretion when it admitted the pictures and writings over Hyles's objection as to foundation.

The above case examined the admissibility of a photograph and writings on that photograph. A photograph by itself is not a traditional 'written' document. Nevertheless it is still a document that may be offered as an exhibit. How the photograph is used at trial determines how the foundation must be laid.

For example, suppose an attorney would like to introduce a photograph of a crime scene as an exhibit to show how the crime may have taken place according to a witness. Usually, a witness who is familiar with the crime scene as it appeared around the time the crime occurred would testify that the photograph is a *"fair and accurate representation"* of how the crime scene appeared on the day and time that the crime occurred. With that foundation for the photograph provided, the photograph would then be authenticated and admitted (assuming, of course, the photograph would not violate any other Rule of Evidence).

At that point, the jury could consider and weigh the photograph along with the testimony of the witness referring to it and either reject it or find that it is what it purports to be. If the jurors believe that the photograph of the crime scene is what it purports to be, then they would have something upon which to base that finding – the testimony of the eyewitness who was there.

This is an easy foundation to provide because the photograph is being used only to help clarify an eyewitness' testimony. The eyewitness is there to be cross-examined about the photograph and what she allegedly saw. As a result, the reliability of the photograph really just depends upon the reliability and credibility of the eyewitness. It is not necessary to question the photographer, or the developer of the film, or obtain testimony on how photography, or digital photography works, or even the circumstances under which the photograph was taken.

However, the foundation for a photograph is much more involved when there is no eyewitness to testify about whether the photograph is a fair and accurate representation of the scene on the time and day in question. In such circumstances, an eyewitness cannot be cross-examined, so more qualifying information needs to be provided as to how the photograph was taken, what it depicts, and why it would be reliable.

Consider the next two cases. Pay attention to how the photographs in each of the cases is being used and why in each case the court found that there was a proper foundation for the respective photographs.

United States v. Soto-Beníquez

U.S Court of Appeals for the First Circuit
356 F.3d 1 (1st Cir. 2003)

LYNCH, Circuit Judge.

This massive drug conspiracy case from Puerto Rico involved a six-month trial and resulted in convictions of the eleven defendants who appeal … The government charged this case as involving one overarching conspiracy from January 1990 to March 1994 to distribute drugs … and to protect that distribution through multiple murders…

[Numerous charges were made against all of the defendants and each defendant filed various motions to suppress evidence. One such motion was to exclude a photograph of a gun that was used to show the jury that the gun was the one used by the defendant in the commission of several of the crimes charged. The defendant objected to the admissibility of that the photograph because there was no reliable evidence that the gun in the photograph was the gun actually seized from him].

The district court found that there were sufficient indicia of reliability that the photograph was what it purported to be because specific markings on the gun in the photograph matched the description in the police report. The arresting officer also testified that the photograph depicted the weapon seized from [the defendant]. Under these circumstances, the photograph was properly authenticated. See Fed. R. Evid. 901(a).

This was an easy foundation to lay because the photo was used for demonstration purposes only. It was used simply to help clarify the witnesses' testimony. Compare this foundation to the foundation that is necessary when the photo is being used "substantively."

United States v. Taylor

U.S Court of Appeals for the Fifth Circuit
530 F.2d 639 (5th Cir. 1976)

TUTTLE, Circuit Judge:

Appellants ... Hicks and ... Taylor were convicted by a jury ... for armed robbery of a federally-insured state bank. Briefly stated, the facts surrounding the robbery and their arrests are as follows: at approximately 9 A.M. on February 10, 1975, the Havana State Bank in Havana, Florida, was robbed of about $6,700 at gunpoint by two men wearing masks. The robbers took the money, ordered everyone present into the bank vault, and locked them inside. A bank camera, tripped after the bank personnel were locked in the vault, took pictures of the robbers. A local grocer saw two men pass his storefront window immediately after the robbery, and saw one of the men's faces.

Approximately one hour later, appellants Hicks and Taylor were stopped, questioned, and their car searched by consent in Bainbridge, Georgia by a county sheriff. Two bank tellers present during the robbery then went to Bainbridge but were unable to identify appellants as the perpetrators of the robbery when confronted face to face with them. Appellants were thereupon released, but were arrested the following day in Tallahassee, Florida, by F.B.I. agents, on the strength of some of the bank photographs taken during the robbery. Appellants were indicted ... pleaded not guilty, and trial commenced on June 4, 1975, with the jury returning a guilty verdict on June 6th. This appeal followed.

[The appellants argue] that the district court erred in admitting into evidence contact prints made from the film taken by the bank camera after the tellers and a bank official, Henry Slappey, were locked in the bank vault. Appellant contends that the government failed to lay the proper foundation for admission of these photographs since none of the eyewitnesses to the robbery testified that the pictures accurately represented the bank interior and the events that transpired.

In the case before us it was, of course, impossible for any of the tellers to testify that the film accurately depicted the events as witnessed by them, since the camera was activated only after the bank personnel were locked in the vault. The only testimony offered as foundation for the introduction of the photographs was by government witnesses who were not present during the actual robbery. These witnesses, however, testified as to the manner in which the film was installed in the camera, how the camera was activated, the fact that the film was removed immediately after the robbery, the chain of its possession, and the fact that it was properly developed and contact prints made from it. Under the circumstances of this case, we find that such testimony furnished sufficient authentication for the admission of the contact prints into evidence. Admission of this type of photographic evidence is a matter largely within the discretion of the court and it is clear that the district court did not abuse its discretion here. See _People v. Bowley,_ _382 P.2d 591, 594 (1963)_, where the California Supreme Court recognized that in certain instances photographs may be admissible as probative evidence in themselves, rather than solely as illustrative evidence to support a witness' testimony, provided that sufficient foundation evidence is adduced to show the circumstances under which it was taken and the reliability of the reproduction process.

For the reasons stated above, the judgments of conviction as to both appellants are AFFIRMED.

————————————

Why was it necessary to lay a more elaborate foundation in *Taylor*? I.e., how the film was installed, how the camera was activated, etc., as opposed to the foundation laid in *Soto-Beniquez*?

F. Electronic Mail

The explosive growth of the internet and the use of e-mail is prolific and will only continue to grow as a means by which people communicate. When people communicate using electronic devices they leave "digital footprints" which may become powerful evidence in a case. To the extent e-mail messages are just like traditional notes or letters they are authenticated in much the same way – through witnesses with knowledge. Thus, at first glance, it may appear that this does not provide any special challenges for the law of evidence or for attorneys.

However, there are special issues that arise due to the technology being used. For example, "metadata" that goes along with e-mail messages can be very powerful sources of evidence because the metadata reveals what can be very telling information about the e-mail message itself. Metadata may reveal much more information than a letter or note on a piece of paper reveals because the metadata may contain information such as exactly when and on what computer the e-mail message was created, who or what computers received the e-mail and when, and whether the e-mail or attachment was altered in any way. This can be powerful evidence in a case.

What's That?

Metadata describes other data. For example, a digital photograph may contain metadata that describes the resolution of the picture, the color depth, the size of the picture, what camera took the picture, when the picture was taken and other data. A word processing document may contain metadata that details who the author is, number of times it was edited, when the document was first created and last edited and other data.

Also, people may think that when they delete an e-mail message it is gone forever, like shredding a paper document. However, in many ways, deleting an e-mail message is not that easy. First, the e-mail message may still exist in a "recycle bin" (which is just a different directory on the hard drive). Even if the recycle bin is "emptied," the e-mail message is often still on the computer's hard drive and can be obtained by a computer forensics expert. Frequently, even if the hard drive is re-formatted or destroyed, the e-mail message may still exist on the servers that originally transmitted the e-mail and, of course, on the computers that received the original e-mail or received the e-mail message as forwarded e-mail.

The next case addresses the foundation that was necessary for hundreds of e-mail messages. It is important to think about the foundation and how it follows the same foundation necessary for traditional written hard copies of documents. It is also important to consider the special and different concerns raised by the electronic form of the exhibit.

United States v. Safavian

U.S District Court for the District of Columbia
435 F. Supp. 2d 36 (D.D.C. 2006)

FRIEDMAN, District Judge:

The defendant was an associate of former Washington and indicted lobbyist Jack Abramoff.

[The defendant was charged with making false statements and obstruction of justice during the investigation of Abramoff.] These motions all make arguments regarding the admissibility of approximately 260 e-mails that the government seeks to admit in its case against the defendant.

A. Authentication of E-mails

Authentication is an aspect of relevancy.... The threshold for the Court's determination of authenticity is not high. ... The question for the Court under Rule 901 is whether the proponent of the evidence has "offered a foundation from which the Jury could reasonably find that the evidence is what the proponent says it is." The Court need not find that the evidence is necessarily what the proponent claims, but only that there is sufficient evidence that the jury ultimately might do so...

The question under Rule 901 is whether there is sufficient evidence "to support a finding that the matter in question is what its proponent claims." – in this case, e-mails between Mr. Safavian, Mr. Abramoff, and other individuals. As noted, the Court need not find that the e-mails are necessarily what the proponent claims, only that there is evidence sufficient for the jury to make such a finding. ... Rule 901(b) sets forth illustrations of how evidence may be authenticated or identified; it emphasizes, however, that these are "illustration(s) only" and are not intended to be the only methods by which the Court may determine that the e-mails are what the government says they are. ... For the reasons that follow, the Court finds that there is ample evidence for the jury to find that these exhibits are, in fact, e-mail exchanges between Mr. Safavian, Mr. Abramoff, and other individuals.

One method of authentication identified under Rule 901 is to examine the evidence's "distinctive characteristics and the like," including "[a]ppearance, contents, substance, internal patterns, or other distinctive characteristics, taken in conjunction with circumstances." Fed. R. Evid, 901(b)(4). Most of the proffered exhibits can be authenticated in this manner. The e-mails in question have many distinctive characteristics, including the actual e-mail addresses containing the "@" symbol, widely known to be part of an e-mail address, and certainly a distinctive mark that identifies the document in question as an e-mail. In addition, most of the e-mail addresses themselves contain the name of the person connected to the address, such as abramoffj@ftlaw.com, David.Safavian@mail. house.gov, or david.safavian@gsa.gov. Frequently these e-mails contain the name of the sender or recipient in the bodies of the e-mails, in the signature blocks at the end of the e-mail, in the "To:" and "From:" headings, and by signature of the sender. The contents of the e-mails, also authenticate them as being from the purported sender and to the purported recipient, containing as they do discussions of various identifiable matters, such as Mr. Safavian's work at the General Services Administration ("GSA"), Mr. Abramoff's work as a lobbyist, Mr. Abramoff's restaurant, Signatures, and various other personal and professional matters.

Those e-mails, that are not clearly identifiable on their own can be authenticated under Rule 901(b)(3), which states that such evidence may be authenticated by comparison by the trier of fact (the jury) with "specimens which have been [otherwise] authenticated" – in this case, those e-mails that already have been independently authenticated under Rule 901(b)(4). For instance, certain e-mails contain the address MerrittDC@aol.com with no further indication of what person uses that e-mail address either through the contents or in the e-mail heading itself. This e-mail address on its own does not clearly demonstrate who was the sender or receiver using that address. When these e-mails are examined alongside Exhibit 100 (which the Court finds is authenticated under Rule 901(b)(4) by its distinctive characteristics), however, it becomes clear the MerrittDC@aol.com was an address used by the defendant. Exhibit 100 is also an e-mail sent from that address, but the signature within the e-mail gives the defendant's name and the name of his business, Janus-Merritt Strategies, L.L.C., located in Washington, D.C. (as well as other information, such as the business' address, telephone and fax numbers), thereby connecting the defendant to that e-mail address and clarifying the meaning of both "Merritt" and "DC" in it. The comparison of those e-mails containing MerrittDC@aol.com with Exhibit 100 thereby can provide the jury with a sufficient basis to find that these two exhibits are what they purport to be – that is, e-mails to or from Mr. Safavian. The Court will not perform this exercise with respect to each exhibit. Suffice it to say that the Court has examined each of these e-mails and found that all those that the Court is admitting in whole or in part meet the requirements for authentication under Rule 901.

The defendant argues that the trustworthiness of these e-mails cannot be demonstrated, particularly those e-mails that are embedded with e-mails as having been forwarded to or by others or as the previous e-mail to which a reply was sent. The Court rejects this as an argument against authentication of the e-mails. The defendant's argument is more appropriately directed to the weight the jury should give the evidence, not to its authenticity. While the defendant is correct that earlier e-mails that are included in a chain either as ones that have been forwarded or to which another has replied may be altered, this trait is not specific to e-mail evidence. It can be true of any piece of documentary evidence, such as a letter, a contract or an invoice. Indeed, fraud trials frequently center on altered paper documentation, which, through the use of techniques such as photocopies, white-out, or wholesale forgery, easily can be altered. The possibility of alteration does not and cannot be the basis for excluding e-mails as unidentified or unauthenticated as a matter of course, any more than it can be the rationale for excluding paper documents (and copies of those documents). We live in an age of technology and computer use where e-mail communication now is a normal and frequent fact for the majority of this nation's population, and is of particular importance in the professional world. The defendant is free to raise this issue with the jury and put on evidence that e-mails are capable of being altered before they are passed on. Absent specific evidence showing alteration, however, the Court will not exclude any embedded e-mails because of the mere possibility that it can be done.

The defendant does raise some noteworthy points regarding the limits of what the government can show regarding these e-mails and what they purport to be. The Court notes that it is possible to authenticate these e-mails through examination of the contents, distinctive characteristics, and appearance, and others by comparison to authenticated e-mails, and the jury is free to make its own examinations and conclusions. But the Court has been aided in reaching its conclusions by the proffers of government lawyers. The government will not, of course, be permitted to make such proffers to the jury nor may government witnesses testify to facts beyond their personal knowledge concerning these e-mails. For instance, the F.B.I. agent through whom the government plans to offer these e-mails, cannot testify from personal knowledge as to whether MerrittDC@aol.com is, in fact, Mr. Safavian's e-mail address. He may testify only that Exhibit 100 contains that e-mail address in the From: section of the heading, and that the Exhibit has a signature section that contains Mr. Safavian's name. Similarly, an F.B.I. agent will not be permitted to testify to the meaning of Greenberg Traurig internal e-mail codes (such as the "DIRDC-Gov" designation next to Jack Abramoff's name, which the government proffered at the May 16, 2006 hearing means that Mr. Abramoff was the Director of the Governmental Affairs Division of Greenberg Traurig's D.C. office).

Some of the e-mail addresses do not appear in full in any part of an exhibit. Rather the "To:" and "From:" parts of the heading contain full names with no e-mail address containing the @symbol. Jay Nogle, the official custodian of records for Greenberg Traurig, explained in his Rule 901(11) certification that the "To:" and "From:" sections of these e-mails denoted that a Greenberg Traurig employee had sent or received the e-mail. Certainly, if Mr. Nogle, or another Greenberg Traurigh employee with knowledge of these codes, is called to testify, he or she may testify to their meaning. An F.B.I. agent may not.

In certain e-mails, Mr. Safavian appears to have replied to Mr. Abramoff's e-mails in an atypical manner. Whereas most e-mails chains appear in reverse chronological order, the most recent of the e-mails appearing first, Mr. Safavian's responses to Mr. Abramoff's e-mails sometime come after the email from Mr. Abramoff. Further complicating the matter, this reversal of the order is not designated by the "To:" and "From:" section that normally denotes the start of a separate e-mail. The result is that the text of separate e-mails appears next to one another without a clear division between the end of one and the start of the next. Having examined these e-mails in comparison to one another, the Court has determined that it is apparent that some parts of the text are questions that lead to responses, and therefore the contents and substance serve to identify the exhibit as an exchange of e-mails. A jury, using its own knowledge of how e-mail exchanges work, and considering any testimony that may be offered by those with personal knowledge of these e-mails, may determine which persons, identified in the e-mail through their addresses and names, wrote which portions. No F.B.I. agent, however, may testify to these conclusions nor state which sections of these e-mails have been written by whom. It is beyond his or her personal knowledge and would be wholly speculative.

The jury may draw whatever reasonable conclusions and inferences it chooses to from these e-mails, and determine how to consider them, but the Court will not permit any testimony beyond the bare fact of what words appear on a particular e-mail by a case agent or summary witness who neither composed nor received these e-mails. Should the government choose to call Mr. Abramoff or any other of the authors of these e-mails (other than, of course, the defendant, whom the government is not permitted to call as a witness), that witness may testify as to his or her personal knowledge of any particular e-mail her or she sent or received, and to any personal knowledge of e-mail addresses of persons with whom he or she has exchanged e-mails, even if not the specific ones in evidence…

ORDERED that defendant's motion in limine … DENIED …

The following article provides insight into the authentication of electronic mail.

Internet and Email Evidence

By Gregory P. Joseph, Esq.

[Former chair of the ABA Section of Litigation, and former member of the Judicial Conference Advisory Committee on Evidence Rules].

The explosive growth of the Internet and burgeoning use of electronic mail are raising a series of novel evidentiary issues. The applicable legal principles are familiar – this evidence must be authenticated and, to the extent offered for its truth, it must satisfy hearsay concerns. The novelty of the evidentiary issues arises out of the novelty of the media – thus, it is essentially factual existing principles in a fashion very similar to the way they are applied to other computer-generated evidence and to more traditional exhibits.

I. Internet Evidence

There are primarily three forms of Internet data that are offered into evidence – (1) data posted on the website by the owner of the site ("website data"); (2) data posted by others with the owner's consent (a chat room is a convenient example); and (3) data posted by others without the owner's consent ("hacker" material). The wrinkle for authenticity purposes is that, because Internet data is electronic, it can be manipulated and offered into evidence in a distorted form…

A. Authentication

Website Data. Corporations, government offices, individuals, educational institutions and innumerable other entities post information on their websites that may be relevant to matters in litigation. Alternatively, the fact that the information appears on the website may be the relevant point. Accordingly, courts routinely face proffers of data (text or images) allegedly drawn from websites. The proffered evidence must be authenticated in all cases, and, depending on the use for which the offer is made, hearsay concerns may be implicated.

The authentication standard is no different for website data or chat room evidence than for any other. Under Rule 901(a), "The requirement of authentication is satisfied by evidence sufficient to support a finding that the matter in question is what its proponent claims." <u>United States v. Simpson, 152 F.3d 1241, 1249 (10th Cir. 1998)</u>

In applying this rule to website evidence, there are three questions that must be answered, explicitly or implicitly:

1) What was actually on the website?

2) Does the exhibit or testimony accurately reflect it?

3) If so, is it attributable to the owner of the site?

In the first instance, authenticity can be established by the testimony of any witness that the witness typed in the URL associated with the website (usually prefaced with www); that he or she logged on to the site and reviewed what was there; and that a printout or other exhibit fairly and accurately reflects what the witness saw. This last testimony is no different than that required to authenticate a photograph, other replica or demonstrative exhibit. The witness may be lying or mistaken, but that is true of all testimony and a principal reason for cross-examination. Unless the opponent of the evidence raises a genuine issue as to trustworthiness, testimony of this sort is sufficient to satisfy Rule 901(a), presumptively authenticating the website data and shifting the burden of coming forward to the opponent of the evidence. It is reasonable to indulge a presumption that material on a web site (other than chat room conversations) was placed there by the owner of the site.

The opponent of the evidence must, in fairness, be free to challenge that presumption by adducing facts showing that proffered exhibit does not accurately reflect the contents of a website or that those contents are not attributable to the owner of the site. First, even if the proffer fairly reflects what was on the site, the data proffered may have been the product of manipulation by hackers (uninvited third parties). ... Second, the proffer may not fairly reflect what was on the site due to modification-intentional or unintentional, material or immaterial – in the proffered exhibit or testimony.

Detecting modifications of electronic evidence can be very difficult, if not impossible. That does not mean, however, that nothing is admissible because everything is subject to distortion. The same is true of many kinds of evidence, from testimony to photographs to digital images, but that does not render everything inadmissible. It merely accentuates the need for the judge to focus on all relevant circumstances in assessing admissibility under Fed. R. Evid. 104(a) – and to leave the rest to the jury, under Rule 104(b).

In considering whether the opponent has raised a genuine issue as to trustworthiness, and whether the proponent has satisfied it, the court will look at the totality of the circumstances, including, for example:

The length of time the data was posted on the site.

Whether others report having seen it.

Whether it remains on the website for the court to verify.

Whether the data is of a type ordinarily posted on that website or websites of similar entities (e.g., financial information from corporations).

Whether the owner of the site has elsewhere published the same data, in whole or in part.

Whether others have published the same data, in whole or in part.

Whether the data has been republished by others who identify the source of the data as the website in question.

A genuine question as to trustworthiness may be established circumstantially. For example, more by way of authentication may be reasonably required of a proponent of Internet evidence who is known to be a skilled computer user and who is suspected of possibly having modified the proffered website data for purposes of creating false evidence. See, e.g., <u>United States v. Jackson, 208 F. 3d 633, 637 (7th Cir. 2000)</u> ("Jackson needed to show that the web postings in which the white supremacist groups took responsibility for the racist mailing actually were posted by the groups, as opposed to being slipped onto the groups' web sites by Jackson herself, who was a skilled computer user.")

In assessing the authenticity of website data, important evidence is normally available from the personnel managing the website ("Webmaster" personnel). A webmaster can establish that a particular file, or identifiable content, was placed on the website at a specific time. This may be done through direct testimony or through documentation, which may be generated automatically by the software of the web server. It is possible that the content provider - the author of the material appearing on the site that is in issue – will be someone other than the person who installed the file on the web. In that event, this second witness (or set of documentation) may be necessary to reasonably ensure that the content which appeared on the site is the same as that proffered....

G. Self-Authenticating Exhibits

Some records are considered to be "self-authenticating." Therefore, these types of exhibits do not require extrinsic evidence of authenticity as a condition precedent to admissibility. This means that certain documents already have a foundation "built-in." If the jury wants to believe that the document is what it purports to be, the jury already has a foundation that is intrinsic to the document based on how the document is maintained, or the context in which it is produced. Rule 902 is the authority for self-authenticating documents. The following provides an edited snapshot of the rule. *See Appendix A for the complete Rule.*

Rule 902. Self-authentication

Extrinsic evidence of authenticity as a condition precedent to admissibility is not required with respect to the following:

(1) Domestic public documents under seal.

(2) Domestic public documents not under seal.

(3) Foreign public documents.

(4) Certified copies of public records.

(5) Official publications.

(6) Newspapers and periodicals.

(7) Trade inscriptions and the like

(8) Acknowledged documents.

(9) Commercial paper and related documents.

(10) Presumptions under Acts of Congress.

(11) Certified Domestic Records of Regularly Conducted Activity.

(12) Certified Foreign Records of Regularly Conducted Activity.

These are "self-authenticating" because there is such a low probability of forgery existing in these instances that it is a rule of practical efficiency to think of the foundation as already existing within the document itself. The attorney has to lay no further foundation because there is enough of a basis already for the jury to believe that the document is what it purports to be. Although there is no independent evidence required to show the document is what it purports to be, that is okay because the document itself has indicia that it is what it purports to be given its very official nature.

As with all exhibits, self-authenticating exhibits in no way foreclose the opportunity of the opposing party to challenge the authenticity of these documents should they desire to do so; it is just that the showing by the proponent in the first instance (laying a foundation) is not required because the documents already have a foundation as official documents.

H. Subscribing Witness's Testimony

It is not necessary for the witness who actually wrote the document to authenticate it. It can be identified and authenticated by others if they have personal knowledge (familiarity with handwriting or signature, for example).

Rule 903. Subscribing Witness' Testimony Unnecessary

The testimony of a subscribing witness is not necessary to authenticate a writing unless required by the laws of the jurisdiction whose laws govern the validity of the writing.

I. Demonstrative Evidence

Go Online

For examples of strategic uses of 3-D computer animations with narration and explanations visit: www.fred-galves.com/content/view/110/29/; and www.fredgalves.com/content/view/91/28/. See also www.demon-stratives.com/view-litigation-anima-tions.html.

Demonstrative evidence is typically visual evidence. In reality, it is broader than merely visual and is often referred to as evidence which "appeals to the senses." The types of demonstrative evidence vary greatly and may include such evidence as: photographs, charts, graphs, objects (i.e., a gun), maps, models, simulations, animations, displays, day-in-the-life videos, experiments, re-enactments, et cetera.

Demonstrative evidence is becoming increasingly popular in trial as technology has made its creation easier than it has been historically.

"As computers become more prevalent in society, as jurors obtain more and more information from television images, the Internet, e-mail, and computer programs, and as clients, businesses, and attorneys store, retrieve, and display more and more information on computers, both at home and work, our evidentiary and procedural rules, as well as our actual courtroom practice, will need to keep [in] step with the communication changes brought by time and scientific progress. We can resist the way of the future (either intentionally or by simply failing to adapt to it), or, as set forth herein, we can attempt to recognize all that the future will bring and choose to embrace it...." "Where the Not-So-Wild-Things Are:" By Professor Fred Galves, Harvard Journal of Law & Technology, Volume 13, Number 2 Winter 2000.

New Mexico v. Tollardo

77 P.3d 1023 (New Mexico 2003)

BUSTAMANTE, Judge.

Trial lawyers are acutely aware that one picture is worth a thousand words. Studies show that jurors retain more information from visual presentations or presentations that are both verbal and visual than from verbal presentations alone. A witness can illustrate his or her testimony by drawing diagrams on paper for a jury, as long as the diagram is not misleading. This case concerns the use and admission into evidence of images generated by a computer, rather than drawn by a person. We hold that under the circumstances of this case, the trial court correctly required the proponent of the images to establish the validity of the computer programs used to generate the images. We further hold that the trial court did not abuse its discretion in determining that the programs were valid. Thus, we affirm.

Facts And Proceedings

The events that were the subject of the trial took place in the early morning hours of July 20, 2000, near Taos, New Mexico. Shortly after midnight, Rosalee Kisto, Robert Miera, and Jeremy Trujillo went to Miera's mobile home in a mobile home park outside of Taos. What happened at the mobile home was disputed at trial. The prosecution's theory was that Miera and Kisto had an argument over the proceeds from a drug deal. Kisto's brother, Manuel Tom Tollardo (Defendant), testified that Kisto told him that she had been beaten and raped by Miera. Defendant, Kisto, and a third person drove back to the mobile home park, where they encountered Trujillo, who was driving out of the park to the road. Both cars stopped and their occupants got out. What happened next was the subject of conflicting testimony at trial. However, it was undisputed that Defendant, Kisto, and Trujillo argued loudly, that Miera joined them at some point, and that Miera and Kisto moved away from Defendant and Trujillo. Ultimately, Defendant retrieved a gun from Kisto's car and shot Trujillo and Miera. Both victims died as a result of their wounds. The testimony at trial indicated that at least four shots were fired in rapid succession.

At some point before trial, the State contacted the Federal Bureau of Investigation (FBI) for assistance. Carl Adrian, a visual information specialist examiner in the Investigative, Prosecutive and Graphic Unit ... was assigned to the case. Using information gathered by others investigating the case and computer programs described in more detail below, Adrian set out to determine whether, given the physical evidence found at the scene, a shooter in a fixed location could quickly fire three shots that would create the wounds found in Trujillo's chest, in Miera's chest, and in Miera's thigh. The result was a series of computer images that showed three figures against a checked background. Two of the figures represented the victims, with dotted lines through their bodies indicating the trajectory of the bullets that caused the three wounds. The third figure was a shooter holding a gun. The computer programs allowed Adrian to move the figures of the victims so that the dotted lines of the bullet trajectories intersected with the muzzle of the gun. Using these images, Adrian determined that a person standing in one place could have fired all three shots. Because the images were to scale and were shown against a checked background in which each check represented a square foot, the images also showed the relative distances between the figures. In addition, the images showed Trujillo was crouched down and facing forward and that Miera was turning at the time they were hit by the bullets.

Before trial, Defendant filed a motion in limine asking the trial court to exclude the images....

The trial court held an evidentiary hearing on Defendant's motion. At the hearing, Adrian testified in detail and was subject to cross-examination concerning the information he used to construct the images shown on the exhibit, the nature and accuracy of the application programs he used to create the images, and the process he went through to create the images. At the close of the hearing, the State argued that the images were demonstrative evidence that would be used as visual aids to assist the jury in understanding the evidence. ... The trial court held ... that Adrian's testimony was sufficient to establish the validity of the programs used to generate the images. Accordingly, the trial court held that the exhibit could be admitted into evidence and the images on it shown to the jury during Adrian's testimony, subject, of course, to the requirement that the State lay a proper foundation for the admission of the evidence.

During trial, there was considerable testimony from the various law enforcement personnel involved in investigating the crime. New Mexico State Police Agent Joe Shiel ... testified to what he saw when he first arrived at the scene of the shooting. In addition ... photographs taken at the scene ... were admitted into evidence and shown to the jury. Agent Shiel also made a video of the scene that was admitted into evidence and shown to the jury. Defendant made no objection to the photographs or videotape. Forensic pathologists from the Office of the Medical Investigator testified concerning the autopsies of Miera and Trujillo. Both pathologists made written reports and took photographs that were introduced into evidence. The pathologists testified to the location of the entrance and exit wounds and the path each bullet took through the body. New Mexico State Police Agent Wesley La Cuesta testified that he made a diagram of the scene of the shooting ... took measurements of the various objects found at the scene from a fixed point and noted the measurements on the diagram. Although the diagram was not drawn to scale, La Cuesta testified that the measurements used to locate objects on the diagram were accurate. William Hubbard, an investigator for the district attorney's office, testified about shell ejection and powder residue tests he performed on the weapon used in the shootings. All of these witnesses were cross-examined.

The State's last witness was Adrian. Adrian was recognized as an expert in several areas. First, Adrian was recognized as an expert in crime scene reconstruction, or, as Adrian calls it, "reverse engineering of crime scenes." Reverse engineering

What's That?

CAD is an acronym for "Computer-aided Design." CAD programs aid in the design and particularly the drafting (technical drawing and engineering drawing) of a part or product, including entire buildings. It is both a visual (or drawing) and symbol-based method of communication whose conventions are particular to a specific technical field.

of crime scenes involves using known information, such as the locations of objects at the scene or the trajectory of a bullet as described in an autopsy report, to determine unknown information. Adrian was also recognized as an expert in Computer Assisted Design (CAD) programs, a program referred to as MAYA, and in three-dimensional bullet trajectory analysis in computer systems. Defendant did not object below and does not challenge Adrian's expertise on appeal.

The jury convicted Defendant of voluntary manslaughter for the killing of Miera, and murder in the second degree for the killing of Trujillo. Defendant appeals. On appeal, Defendant argues (1) that the evidence is not sufficient to support the convictions, and (2) that the trial court erred in admitting the exhibit into evidence and allowing the images to be shown to the jury. The use and admission into evidence of computer-generated images is an issue of first impression in New Mexico.

The trial court did not err in admitting the computer-generated evidence.

Defendant and the State dispute the nature of the evidence and the standard used to determine its admissibility. Defendant argues that the images were not demonstrative evidence but real evidence used to prove his guilt. ... The State argues that the images were simply demonstrative evidence used to illustrate Adrian's testimony....

The Computer-Generated Exhibit Must Meet the Alberico Standard.

Evidence used in court is generally broken into three broad categories: testimonial evidence, documentary evidence, and demonstrative evidence. New Mexico cases define demonstrative evidence, also sometimes referred to as real evidence or evidence by inspection, as "such evidence as is addressed directly to the senses of the court or jury without the intervention of the testimony of witnesses, as where various things are exhibited in open court." ... There is no question that the images are demonstrative evidence in this sense.

The fact that something is demonstrative evidence in this sense does not, however, determine the standards for admitting the evidence because "not all tangible exhibits are offered for the same purpose or received on the same theory." In this case, Defendant argues that the images were used as substantive evidence, while the State contends that the images were simply visual aids used to illustrate Adrian's expert opinion. The State points out that visual aids are often used to illustrate the trajectory of a bullet fired into the human body.... Moreover, courts in other jurisdictions have affirmed the use of mannequins and dowel rods as visual aids to illustrate the trajectory of a bullet.

Both parties direct our attention to decisions of other courts that have considered the admissibility of computer-generated evidence. Some courts divide computer-generated exhibits into two categories: computer animations and computer simulations. An "animation" is a computer-generated exhibit that is used as a visual aid to illustrate an opinion that has been developed without using the computer. On the other hand, a "simulation" is a computer-generated exhibit created when information is fed into a computer that is programmed to analyze the data and draw a conclusion from it. When the image is used as a visual aid, the courts do not require a showing that the exhibit was produced by a scientifically or technologically valid method. Instead, the critical issue is often whether the visual aid fairly and accurately represents the evidence or some version of the evidence. On the other hand, before admitting a simulation, in which the computer has been used to analyze data, the courts require proof of the validity of the scientific principles and data. At least one commentator has noted, however, that courts are not always consistent in applying these labels to the particular exhibit at issue. Fred Galves, "Where the Not-So-Wild Things Are: Computers in the Courtroom, the Federal Rules of Evidence and the Need for Institutional Reform and More Judicial Acceptance," 13 Harv. J.L. & Tech. 161, 256 (2000).

The State asserts that the computer-generated evidence in this case was used merely to illustrate Adrian's opinion and thus should be treated as an animation. However, as we understand the testimony, Adrian used the computer to help him form his opinions, not simply to illustrate opinions reached in another manner. On the other hand, the testimony also indicated that the computer did not "analyze" data fed into it; instead it created a visual image based on the same data that would have been used to create paper and pencil drafts on a drafting board. Thus, it does not fall squarely into either category espoused by those cases.

Nevertheless, we think those cases are helpful because they focus attention on the central question: who (or what) is the source of the opinion. When the computer-generated evidence is used to illustrate an opinion that an expert has arrived at without using the computer, the fact that the visual aid was generated by a computer probably does not matter because the witness can be questioned and cross-examined concerning the perceptions or opinions to which the witness testifies. In that situation, the computer is no more or less than a drafting device.... However, when an expert witness uses the computer to develop an opinion on the issue, the opinion is based in part on the computer-generated evidence…. In that situation, the proponent of the evidence must be prepared to show that the computer-generated evidence was generated in a way that is scientifically valid….We think that this approach is consistent with our Supreme Court's opinion in *Alberico*, which emphasizes the importance of making an initial determination of how the evidence will be used. *Alberico*, 116 N.M. at 172, 861 P.2d at 208 (indicating that the initial inquiry for the admissibility of any evidence is the purpose for which it is being offered).

In this case, Adrian used the computer to help him supply missing information based on the physical evidence available. Thus, the images were not visual aids used to illustrate an opinion developed by other means. Instead, they were used to develop the opinion to which Adrian testified. Thus, we agree with the trial court that the *Alberico* standard applies to the images.

The Trial Court Did Not Abuse its Discretion in Determining That the Computer Programs Used Were Valid.

We turn next to the application of the *Alberico* standard to the images at issue in this case….

In *Alberico*, our Supreme Court, following the lead of the United States Supreme Court in *Daubert*, adopted a new test for determining the admissibility of expert opinion evidence…. Before *Alberico*, opinions based on scientific evidence were admissible only if the science was generally accepted in

See It

In order to view the computer animations actually submitted in the *Tollardo* case, please click here. Special thanks to the New Mexico Attorney General's Office for supplying a copy of the animation, Joel Jacobsen, Assistant Attorney General. Consider why the animation seems so simple.

the relevant scientific community. *Alberico* rejected that standard in favor of a more flexible inquiry in which the general acceptance of the theory or technique was considered but was not controlling. Thus, the focus of the inquiry shifted from general acceptance in a particular field to "the validity and the soundness of the scientific method used to generate the evidence." In making this determination, the Court indicated that in addition to considering whether the technique was accepted in a particular field, the courts should examine the relationship between the technique used to generate the evidence and established scientific techniques and the availability of specialized literature addressing the validity of the technique. *Alberico* defined validity as "the measure of determining whether the testimony is grounded in or a function of established scientific methods or principles, that is, scientific knowledge." Thus, the Court opined, a technique grounded in traditional principles of psychology would be considered valid, while a technique grounded in principles of astrology would not. In *Alberico*, the Court held that psychological testimony concerning post-traumatic stress disorder was grounded in valid scientific principle because it was grounded in basic behavioral psychology. "Reliability is akin to relevancy in considering whether the expert opinion testimony will assist the trier of fact." The Court held that testimony that the alleged victim suffers from post-traumatic stress disorder was reliable in this sense because it had a tendency to show that the victim might have been sexually abused. Defendant does not challenge the reliability of the images in this appeal. Thus, we focus on the validity of the method used to generate the images.

Before discussing the scientific validity of a method, we think it is important to identify the specific scientific field involved....

In this case, we are concerned with the techniques used to generate computer images. We agree with the trial court that computer-generated images are more properly characterized as technical rather than scientific.... However, the critical inquiry is whether the method used to generate the images is a valid application of the principles of computer technology.

In the trial court, Defendant argued that the computer applied the laws of physics to the data entered into it. Adrian specifically testified that this was not the case. Thus, the fact that Adrian was not qualified as an expert in physics does not matter. Adrian, however, was qualified as an expert in the use of both computer programs involved as well as an expert in three-dimensional analysis of bullet trajectories using a computer.

Defendant argues that Adrian was not competent to establish the validity of the computer programs he used to create the images. We disagree. As the trial court observed, we are long past the days when computers and computer programs were outside the ordinary experience of jurors. This is particularly true for the types of programs at issue here. We think many jurors have had experience with CAD programs used to design a house, a room, a landscape, or a host of other things. Indeed, at least one court has held that crime scene reconstruction through computer-generated images has become so common that it should be considered generally accepted. Computer-generated figures that move the way a human being moves are also common.

In this case, Adrian used two "off-the-shelf" programs, meaning programs that can be purchased by anyone with the money to buy them and a computer capable of running them. The first was a CAD program. Adrian testified that he had used CAD programs for many years. CAD programs have generally replaced hand drafting. The CAD programs that Adrian uses ... are accurate within 1/100,000 of an inch. Indeed, CAD programs generally are more accurate than drafting by hand. The second off-the-shelf program is referred to as MAYA. MAYA includes a feature called kinemation, which is the feature that Adrian used to animate the figures and move them around. MAYA was developed by the film industry and has been widely used to generate animated figures and special effects. Adrian testified that he had found some discrepancies in other facets of the MAYA program and so he cross-checked the MAYA images against the CAD images. We think this was all that was necessary to establish the validity of the method used to generate the images. Thus, we hold the trial court did not abuse its discretion in determining that the methods used to generate the images were valid uses of computer technology.

Defendant expresses concern about the accuracy of the images because Adrian was not present at the crime scene or the autopsy but used information recorded by others in their reports. We note, however, that the people who created the information used by Adrian testified at trial and were subject to cross-examination concerning the accuracy of their information. In a similar vein, Defendant contends that Adrian interpreted the raw data, thus increasing the margin of error. This contention is not supported by the record. Adrian testified that the process he used did not involve any scientific calculations or procedures; he fed the information into the computer and the computer created images that could have been created by hand-drafting techniques. Defendant argues that the State was required to bring in a witness to testify concerning the range of motion of the human body. However, Defendant did not make this argument below and therefore we will not consider it on appeal. Finally, Defendant argues that the trial court should have given a limiting instruction concerning the computer-generated images shown to the jury. However, Defendant did not ask for such an instruction below and therefore we will not consider the issue on appeal.

...

Conclusion

In summary, we hold that the trial court correctly determined that computer-generated images were required to meet the *Alberico* standard of validity. We further hold that in the circumstances of this case, the testimony of Adrian was sufficient to establish the validity of the computer programs used to generate the images. ...

Defendant's convictions are affirmed....

Executive Summary

What Is "Authentication"? Authentication applies only to "exhibits" – tangible pieces of evidence – such as documents, photographs, timelines, fingerprints, hair samples, a murder weapon, etc. Authentication is the process at trial of providing some type of preliminary proof that the exhibit is what it purports to be (e.g., that it is the document, or the DNA sample, that its proponent claims it to be). Once that preliminary proof is provided, the proponent is considered to have sufficiently "laid the foundation" for the exhibit, and, provided it violates no other rule, the exhibit at that point will be admissible. Once admitted, the fact-finder can then, if it so chooses, base a finding that the exhibit is authentic and genuine and is what it purports to be. Rule 901 sets forth this authentication requirement before an exhibit is admissible and marked as an Exhibit.

Tangible Evidence and a "Chain of Custody." Under Rules 901(b)(1) and 901(b)(4), two common methods to authenticate tangible physical evidence is to call a witness with personal knowledge about the exhibit, or have the witness testify to the exhibit's "distinctive characteristics," such as its "appearance, contents, substance,…taken in conjunction with circumstances." For exhibits that are easily interchangeable, and thus difficult to identify, such as cocaine, often a "chain of custody" will be used to show that the cocaine seized from the defendant can be fully accounted for at all times, from the time of seizure, up to the moment it is introduced at trial. (*Collado*). However, a chain of custody often goes only to its weight, rather than to its admissibility, especially when an exhibit is easily identifiable, such as a personal wallet with family pictures that are easily recognizable by the witness. (*Lockhart*).

Writings and Other Documents. Rule 901(b)(1) is commonly used to authenticate writings such as a letter or a memorandum, where a witness with personal knowledge about the writing testifies about that knowledge of the document. Under Rule 901(b)(2), if the witness is familiar with the handwriting of the person who wrote, or signed, the document, then the witness can authenticate it. The witness need not be an expert to authenticate, but Rule 901(b)(3) allows for that possibility or to show examples to the jury. If the witness recognizes "distinctive characteristics about the wiring, such as its contents, substance, or other distinctive markings on the writing (such as letterhead), Rule 901(b)(4) can be used to authenticate the writing. (*Bagaric*). A chain of custody is not necessary when it comes to easily identifiable writings, still, a chain of custody for the writing might tend to make it a bit more persuasive as genuine or authentic because it has been physically accounted for from the moment it was created or found until introduced at trial.

Like "writings," documents (such as maps, diagrams, photographs, e-mail, etc.) must be authenticated either by someone with personal knowledge about, and sufficient familiarity with, the document, and/or by someone who recognizes certain "distinctive characteristics" within the document that allow the witness to sufficiently identify the document. Such foundation allows the fact-finder to find that the document is what it purports to be.

Voice Identification and Telephone Conversations. Rules 901(b)(5) and 901(b)(6) provide that voice identifications or telephone conversations can be authenticated by someone hearing the voice or making or receiving the telephone call who is familiar with the voice or who has made or received a telephone call at or from a certain telephone number. (*Espinoza*).

Photographs. Like "writings" and "documents," photographs can be authenticated in generally the same manner, either by someone with personal knowledge, and/or by someone who recognizes certain "distinctive characteristics" within the document. (*Hyles*). The foundation that is laid for a photograph, however, depends upon how the photograph is going to be used at trial. If it is going to be used as a demonstrative exhibit – that is, to help clarify the testimony of a witness – then the foundation is fairly simple. The witness merely needs to state that the photograph is a "fair and accurate" depiction of the scene about which she is testifying at the time and date in question. The reliability of the photograph is in the testimony/ cross-examination of the witness whose testimony is being clarified or explained by the exhibit. (*Soto-Beniquez*). The photograph technically is not evidence, only the testimony of the witness is evidence. The photograph is merely being used to clarify that testimony. On the other hand, if the photograph is itself evidence, such as a surveillance camera photograph that captured a crime as it occurred, and there was no eyewitness who can establish that the photograph is a fair and accurate depiction of what they saw, then a more substantial foundation must be laid for such a photograph (how the film was installed, how the surveillance camera was activated, how and when the film was removed, the chain of custody of the film, how it was properly developed, how the content prints were made, and were qualified technicians operating and maintaining the camera, etc.). (*Taylor*).

Internet and E-Mail Evidence. Although many documents today exist electronically on computers, cell phones, flash drives, and other modern devices, the foundation that is required for them can essentially be laid in very much the same manner as traditional writings, documents, and photographs. It can be done either by someone with personal knowledge about the electronic document, and/ or by someone who recognizes certain "distinctive characteristics" about or within the electronic document. E-mail messages are common examples of electronic documents that can contain valuable and extensive information, including revealing "metadata," that can be very helpful evidence in a lawsuit. As long as a witness with knowledge can testify about the e-mail message, and/or can identify distinctive characteristics about the e-mail message, the e-mail can be authenticated. (*Safavian*). The same holds true for website data on the Internet.

Self-Authenticating Exhibits. Under Rule 902, there are twelve specific examples of certain types of certified, or public, or other specialized, formal documents that are considered to have enough foundation to be authentic given the special preparation and official maintenance of the these types of documents. Under Rule 903, additional extrinsic evidence of authenticity is unnecessary.

Demonstrative Evidence. Demonstrative exhibits are usually *visual* exhibits of some sort that are purposefully created for trial in order to help clarify or explain a witness's testimony ("a picture is worth a thousand words"). Typical demonstrative exhibits are PowerPoint lists of elements of a legal claim, a timeline of events, an explanatory diagram, a summary chart, or a photograph that helps to explain a witness's testimony. Some judges allow demonstrative exhibits to go back to the jury deliberation room, while other judges allow them only to be seen and referred to in open court, but not go back to the jury room during deliberations.

In addition to helping to explain or clarify the testimony of eyewitnesses, demonstrative exhibits are often used by expert witnesses in order to help explain or clarify their technical or scientific opinions or their theory about the case. For example, an expert physician might use a wax human skeleton to help explain an injury, or an expert geologist might use a topographical map to help explain an environmental spill. In modern courtrooms, many attorneys use computer animations, re-creations, and simulations to help explain in more vivid detail the testimony of eyewitnesses and/or expert witnesses. If the computer depiction is offered as a demonstrative exhibit, it is much easier to lay the foundation for it because it merely needs to be a "fair and accurate" depiction of the witness's testimony that will help to explain or clarify that testimony. However, if it is offered to help render the expert's own scientific or technical opinion itself, then the foundation is much more elaborate (like that of a surveillance photograph) because now the computer is actually helping the expert to *arrive at* the expert's opinion, it is *not being used merely to help explain or clarify* that expert's opinion. (*Tollardo*).

CHAPTER 11

Best Evidence

A. Best Evidence Rule

Rules 1001-1008 of the Federal Rules of Evidence codify what the common law called the "best evidence rule." The purpose of the rule was to prevent fraud or inaccuracy at trial by requiring that an original writing be produced when the contents of that writing were at issue. Although the common law applied the best evidence rule solely to writings, Rule 1001 expands its coverage to include recordings and photographs (as those terms are defined) in order to reflect technological advances in modern data creation, transmission, and storage.

Rule 1001. Definitions and Basic Rule

For purposes of this article the following definitions are applicable:

(1) Writings and recordings. "Writings" and "recordings" consist of letters, words, or numbers or their equivalent, set down by handwriting, typewriting, printing, photostating, photographing, magnetic impulse, mechanical or electronic record, or other form of data complication.

(2) Photographs. "Photographs" include still photographs, X-rays films, video tapes, and motion pictures.

(3) Original. An "original" of a writing or recording is the writing or recording itself or any counterpart intended to have the same effect by a person executing or issuing it. An "original" of a photograph includes the negative or any print therefrom. If data are stored in a computer or similar device, any printout or other output readable by sight, shown to reflect the data accurately, is an "original."

(4) Duplicate. A "duplicate' is a counterpart produced by the same impression as the original, or from the same matrix, or by means of photograph, including enlargements and miniatures, or by mechanical or electronic re-recording, or by chemical reproduction, or by other equivalent techniques which accurately reproduces the original.

Rule 1002. Requirement of original

To prove the content of a writing, recording, or photograph, the original writing, recording, or photograph is required, except as otherwise provided in these rules or by Act of Congress.

Rule 1003. Admissibility of Duplicates.

A duplicate is admissible to the same extent as an original unless (1) a genuine question is raised as to the authenticity of the original or (2) in the circumstances it would be unfair to admit the duplicate in lieu of the original.

Rule 1004. Admissibility of Other Evidence of Contents

The original is not required, and other evidence of the contents of a writing, recording, or photograph is admissible if:

(1) Originals lost or destroyed. All originals are lost or have been destroyed, unless the proponent lost or destroyed them in bad faith; or

(2) Originals not obtainable. No original can be obtained by any available judicial process or procedure; or

(3) Original in possession of opponent. At a time when an original was under the control of the party against whom offered, that party was put on notice, by the pleadings or otherwise, that the contents would be a subject of proof at the hearing, and that party does not produce the original at the hearing; or

(4) Collateral matters. The writing, recording, or photograph is not closely related to a controlling issue.

The label "best evidence rule" is misleading. There is no requirement in the Federal Rules that a party must always offer the best and most reliable evidence to prove an issue in a case. The drafters of Rule 1002 only require that original writings, recordings and photographs be offered in limited circumstances if their contents are at issue. Further, if the absence of an original can be explained, what is called "duplicate" or "secondary" evidence may, under the proper circumstances, be admitted under Rules 1003 and 1004. Thus, rather than calling it the "best evidence rule," perhaps it is better called the "preference for original writings, recordings or photographs when their content is at issue rule," although that description would be too lengthy to be useful.

In practice, "best evidence" objections are often raised in conjunction with objections based on hearsay, self-authentication, the parole evidence rule, and other evidentiary rules. Nonetheless, "best evidence" rules are self-contained in the sense that a determination of whether they apply does not depend upon consideration of any of any other evidentiary principles that you have learned so far.

1. What is a Writing, Recording, or Photograph?

The Rule 1001(1) definition of a "writing" as "letters, words, or numbers" or their "equivalent" may seem straightforward. However, what constitutes the "equivalent" of a writing can be difficult to determine, as the following case demonstrates:

Seiler v. Lucasfilm, Ltd.

U.S Court of Appeals for the Ninth Circuit
797 F.2d 1504 (9th Cir. 1986)

FARRIS, Circuit Judge:

Lee Seiler, a graphic artist and creator of science fiction creatures, alleged copyright infringement by George Lucas and others who created and produced the science fiction movie "The Empire Strikes Back." Seiler claimed that creatures known as "Imperial Walkers" which appeared in "The Empire Strikes Back" infringed Seiler's copyright on his own creatures called "Garthian Striders." "The Empire Strikes Back" appeared in 1980; Seiler did not obtain his copyright until 1981.

* * *

FACTS

Seiler contends that he created and published in 1976 and 1977 science fiction creatures called Garthian Striders. In 1980, George Lucas released "The Empire Strikes Back," a motion picture that contains a battle sequence depicting giant machines called Imperial Walkers. In 1981 Seiler obtained a copyright on his Striders, depositing with the Copyright Office "reconstructions" of the originals as they had appeared in 1976 and 1977.

Seiler contends that Lucas' Walkers were copied from Seiler's Striders which were allegedly published in 1976 and 1977. Lucas responds that Seiler did not obtain his copyright until one year after the release of "The Empire Strikes Back" and that Seiler can produce no documents that antedate "The Empire Strikes Back."

Because Seiler proposed to exhibit his Striders in a blow-up comparison to Lucas' Walkers at opening statement, the district judge held an evidentiary hearing on the admissibility of the "reconstructions" of Seiler's Striders. . . . On appeal, Seiler contends 1) that the best evidence rule does not apply to his works . . . .

* * *

DISCUSSION

1. Application of the best evidence rule.

> **FYI**
> It is somewhat imprecise to call the "best evidence rule" the "original document rule" since the rule also applies to recordings and photographs.

The best evidence rule embodied in Rules 1001-1008 represented a codification of longstanding common law doctrine. Dating back to 1700, the rule requires not, as its common name implies, the best evidence in every case but rather the production of an original document instead of a copy. Many commentators refer to the rule not as the best evidence rule but as the original document rule.

Rule 1002 states: "To prove the content of a writing, recording, or photograph, the original writing, recording, or photograph is required, except as otherwise provided in these rules or by Act of Congress." Writings and recordings are defined in Rule 1001 as "letters, words, or numbers, or their equivalent, set down by handwriting, typewriting, printing, photostating, photographing, magnetic impulse, mechanical or electronic recording, or other form of data compilation."

The Advisory Committee Note supplies the following gloss:

"Traditionally the rule requiring the original centered upon accumulations of data and expressions affecting legal relations set forth in words and figures. This meant that the rule was one essentially related to writings. Present day techniques have expanded methods of storing data, yet the essential form which the information ultimately assumes for usable purposes is words and figures. Hence the considerations underlying the rule dictate its expansion to include computers, photographic systems, and other modern developments."

Some treatises, whose approach seems more historical than rigorously analytic, opine without support from any cases that the rule is limited to words and figures.

We hold that Seiler's drawings were "writings" within the meaning of Rule 1001(1); they consist not of "letters, words, or numbers" but of "their equivalent." To hold otherwise would frustrate the policies underlying the rule and introduce undesirable inconsistencies into the application of the rule.

In the days before liberal rules of discovery and modern techniques of electronic copying, the rule guarded against incomplete or fraudulent proof. By requiring the possessor of the original to produce it, the rule prevented the introduction of altered copies and the withholding of originals. The purpose of the rule was thus long thought to be one of fraud prevention, but Wigmore pointed out that the rule operated even in cases where fraud was not at issue, such as where secondary evidence is not admitted even though its proponent acts in utmost good faith. Wigmore also noted that if prevention of fraud were the foundation of the rule, it should apply to objects as well as writings, which it does not. 4 Wigmore, *Evidence* § 1180 (Chadbourn rev. 1972).

The modern justification for the rule has expanded from prevention of fraud to a recognition that writings occupy a central position in the law. When the contents of a writing are at issue, oral testimony as to the terms of the writing is subject to a greater risk of error than oral testimony as to events or other situations. The human memory is not often capable of reciting the precise terms of a writing, and when the terms are in dispute only the writing itself, or a true copy, provides reliable evidence. To summarize then, we observe that the importance of the precise terms of writings in the world of legal relations, the fallibility of the human memory as reliable evidence of the terms, and the hazards of inaccurate or incomplete duplication are the concerns addressed by the best evidence rule.

Food for Thought

Does Wigmore's statement that a proponent need not make an allegation of fraud for the best evidence rule to apply sufficiently support the court's conclusion that the equivalent of "writings" should be extended to artistic drawings? How does this square with Wigmore's second observation that the rule does not extend to objects?

Viewing the dispute in the context of the concerns underlying the best evidence rule, we conclude that the rule applies. McCormick summarizes the rule as follows:

"[I]n proving the terms of a writing, where the terms are material, the original writing must be produced unless it is shown to be unavailable for some reason other than the serious fault of the proponent."

McCormick on Evidence § 230, at 704.

The contents of Seiler's work are at issue. There can be no proof of "substantial similarity" and thus of copyright infringement unless Seiler's works are juxtaposed with Lucas' and their contents compared. Since the contents are material and must be proved, Seiler must either produce the original or show that it is unavailable through no fault of his own. Rule 1004(1). This he could not do.

The facts of this case implicate the very concerns that justify the best evidence rule. Seiler alleges infringement by "The Empire Strikes Back", but he can produce no documentary evidence of any originals existing before the release of the movie. His secondary evidence does not consist of true copies or exact duplicates but of "reconstructions" made after "The Empire Strikes Back". In short, Seiler claims that the movie infringed his originals, yet he has no proof of those originals.

The dangers of fraud in this situation are clear. The rule would ensure that proof of the infringement claim consists of the works alleged to be infringed. Otherwise, "reconstructions" which might have no resemblance to the purported original would suffice as proof for infringement of the original. Furthermore, application of the rule here defers to the rule's special concern for the contents of writings. Seiler's claim depends on the content of the originals, and the rule would exclude reconstituted proof of the originals' content. Under the circumstances here, no "reconstruction" can substitute for the original.

Seiler argues that the best evidence rule does not apply to his work, in that it is artwork rather than "writings, recordings, or photographs." He contends that the rule both historically and currently embraces only words or numbers. Neither party has cited us to cases which discuss the applicability of the rule to drawings.

To recognize Seiler's works as writings does not, as Seiler argues, run counter to the rule's preoccupation with the centrality of the written word in the world of legal relations. Just as a contract objectively manifests the subjective intent of the makers, so Seiler's drawings are objective manifestations of the creative mind. The copyright laws give legal protection to the objective manifestations of an artist's ideas, just as the law of contract protects through its multifarious principles the meeting of minds evidenced in the contract. Comparing Seiler's drawings with Lucas' drawings is no different in principle than evaluating a contract and the intent behind it. Seiler's "reconstructions" are "writings" that affect legal relations; their copyrightability attests to that.

A creative literary work, which is artwork, and a photograph whose contents are sought to be proved, as in copyright, defamation, or invasion of privacy, are both covered by the best evidence rule. We would be inconsistent to apply the rule to artwork which is literary or photographic but not to artwork of other forms. Furthermore, blueprints, engineering drawings, architectural designs may all lack words or numbers yet still be capable of copyright and susceptible to fraudulent alteration. In short, Seiler's argument would have us restrict the definitions of Rule 1001(1) to "words" and "numbers" but ignore "or their equivalent." We will not do so in the circumstances of this case.

Our holding is also supported by the policy served by the best evidence rule in protecting against faulty memory. Seiler's reconstructions were made four to seven years after the alleged originals; his memory as to specifications and dimensions may have dimmed significantly. Furthermore, reconstructions made after the release of "The Empire Strikes Back" may be tainted, even if unintentionally, by exposure to the movie. Our holding guards against these problems.

Points for Discussion

a. A "Garthian Strider as a "Writing."

Why does the court think that Seiler's artistic depiction of his "Garthian Striders" is the "equivalent" to a writing? Is it because the court has broadened Rule 1001(1) as a matter of policy to include anything tangible when its contents are at issue? Do you think that the results would have been different if Seiler had built the "Garthian Striders" as models instead of creating them as drawings?

b. Photographs.

Other than snap-shots, photographs include videotapes, motions pictures and x-rays. Rule 1001(2). Most often, photographs are used as demonstrative evidence in a case, that is, as evidence that illustrates or explain a witness's testimony, and Rule 1002 does not require production of the original. A photograph of an intersection where there was an automobile accident, for example, could be used to illustrate the testimony of an eye-witness who claims that a large tree blocked the defendant's view of the plaintiff. On occasion, however, the contents of a photograph may be at issue. As the Advisory Committee Note to Rule 1002 states:

> "Copyright, defamation, and invasion of privacy by photograph or motion picture fall in this category. Similarly as to situations in which the picture is offered as having independent probative value, e.g. automatic photograph of a bank robber."

Suppose that the government in a child pornography case wants to offer the testimony of an investigating officer (who viewed the allegedly pornographic film in question in order to prepare for trial) that the film contained graphic scenes of children having sex with adults. Would this offering be subject to a Rule 1002 objection?

c. Chattel.

Rule 1002 does not usually apply to chattel, like a locket or a tombstone, even if that chattel is inscribed. For example, in *United States v. Yamin*, 868 F.2d 130 (5th Cir. 1989), where the defendants were charged with conspiracy and trafficking in counterfeit watches, the government was not required to produce the original counterfeit watches at trial, even though the writing on the watches was what made them counterfeit. But see *United States v. Duffy*, 454 F.2d 809 (5th Cir. 1972), where the court held that a shirt bearing a laundry mark was both a chattel and a writing but that the judge had the discretion to treat the shirt as either. Would either of these cases impact the results in *Sieler*?

────────────

2. When Are the Contents of a Writing, Recording or Photograph at Issue?

United States v. Bennett

U.S Court of Appeals for the Ninth Circuit
363 F.3d 947 (9th Cir. 2004)

Fisher, Circuit Judge:

This case arises from the boarding and search of defendant-appellant Vincent Franklin Bennett's boat by members of a joint task force targeting smuggling activity from Mexico into Southern California. [An x-ray revealed that the boat contained a large amount of marijuana. To prove the boat had come from Mexico, Chandler, a Customs officer, testified that the global positioning satellite display (GPS) on the boat revealed that the boat had travelled from Mexican waters].

FYI

Federal jurisdiction only applies in this case if the marijuana was imported from outside the United States.

* * *

Bennett's most serious challenge to the evidence supporting his importation conviction relates to Chandler's testimony about the global positioning system he discovered during his search of Bennett's boat. A GPS device uses global positioning satellites to track and record the location of the device and, therefore, the location of any object to which it is attached. The GPS came with a "backtrack" feature that graphed the boat's journey that day. Chandler testified that the backtrack feature mapped Bennett's journey from Mexican territorial waters off the coast of Rosarito, Mexico, to the Coronado Islands and then north to San Diego Bay. Less significantly, Chandler also retrieved "way points"--navigational points programmed into the GPS to assist the captain in navigating to a particular destination. Chandler testified that within the previous year, someone had programmed way points into the GPS that included points in Mexican waters. Chandler acknowledged on cross-examination that he had not taken possession of the GPS device itself or obtained any record of the data contained therein. . . . .

The best evidence rule provides that the original of a "writing, recording, or photograph" is required to prove the contents thereof. Fed.R.Evid. 1002. A writing or recording includes a "mechanical or electronic recording" or "other form of data compilation." Fed.R.Evid. 1001(1). Photographs include "still photographs, X-ray films, video tapes, and motion pictures." Fed.R.Evid. 1001(2). An original is the writing or recording itself, a negative or print of a photograph or, "[i]f data are stored in a computer or similar device, any printout or other output readable by sight, shown to reflect the data accurately." Fed.R.Evid. 1001(3).

. . . . The rule's application turns on "whether contents are sought to be proved." *Fed.R.Evid. 1002* Advisory Committee's note. "[A]n event may be proved by nondocumentary evidence, even though a written record of it was made." *Id.* Accordingly, the rule is inapplicable when a witness merely identifies a photograph or videotape "as a correct representation of events which he saw or of a scene with which he is familiar." *Id.; see also United States v. Workinger,* 90 F.3d 1409, 1415 (9th Cir.1996) ("[A] tape recording cannot be said to be the best evidence of a conversation when a party seeks to call a participant in or observer of the conversation to testify to it. In that instance, the best evidence rule has no application at all."). However, the rule does apply when a witness seeks to testify about the contents of a writing, recording or photograph without producing the physical item itself--particularly when the witness was not privy to the events those contents describe.

That is the nature of Chandler's GPS testimony here and why his testimony violated the best evidence rule. First, the GPS display Chandler saw was a writing or recording because, according to Chandler, he saw a graphical representation of data that the GPS had compiled about the path of Bennett's boat. *See* Fed.R.Evid. 1001(1). Second, Chandler never actually observed Bennett's boat travel the path depicted by the GPS. Thus, Chandler's testimony concerned the "content" of the GPS, which, in turn, was evidence of Bennett's travels. Fed.R.Evid. 1002. At oral argument, the government admitted that the GPS testimony was offered solely to show that Bennett had come from Mexico. Proffering testimony about Bennett's border-crossing instead of introducing the GPS data, therefore, was analogous to proffering testimony describing security camera footage of an event to prove the facts of the event instead of introducing the footage itself.

This is precisely the kind of situation in which the best evidence rule applies. *See, e.g., L.A. News Serv. v. CBS Broad., Inc.,* 305 F.3d 924, 935 (9th Cir.2002) ("We think that Fox's report of what he saw on the label ... was inadmissible under the best evidence rule."), *amended by* 313 F.3d 1093 (9th Cir.2002); *see also* 14 Am.Jur. Proof of Facts 2d 173 § 14 (1977) ("The reported cases show that proponents of computer-produced evidence occasionally founder on the best evidence rule by presenting oral testimony based on the witness' review of computer printouts without actually introducing the printouts themselves into evidence.") Yet the government did not produce the GPS itself-or a printout or other representation of such data, *see* Fed.R.Evid. 1001(3)--which would have been the best evidence of the data showing Bennett's travels. Instead, the government offered only Chandler's GPS-based testimony about an event-namely, a border-crossing-that he never actually saw.

> **FYI**
> "Other evidence," including oral testimony about the contents of a writing, recording or photograph is considered "secondary evidence" and is admissible only if the original cannot be produced. See Rule 1004.

"[O]ther evidence" of the contents of a writing, recording or photograph is admissible if the original is shown to be lost, destroyed or otherwise unobtainable. Fed.R.Evid. 1004. But the government made no such showing. When asked on cross-examination to produce the GPS or its data, Chandler simply stated that he was not the GPS's custodian. He further testified that "there was no need to" videotape or photograph the data and that he had nothing other than his testimony to support his assertions about the GPS's contents. Moreover, the government has not offered any record evidence that it would have been impossible or even difficult to download or print out the data on Bennett's GPS. On the record before us, the government is not excused from the best evidence rule's preference for the original. We therefore hold that Chandler's GPS-based testimony was inadmissible under the best evidence rule.

————————

Points for Discussion

a. What's Really at Issue in *Bennett*?

The court in *Bennett* states that Rule 1002 excludes the oral testimony of Customs Officer Chandler because the GPS recordings themselves should have been admitted into evidence. Why is the content of the GPS recording an issue in the case? Are machine read-outs considered "writings" subject to the requirements of Rule 1002?

b. Writings, Recordings, and Photographs as a Record of the Event.

On occasion, a party may seek to introduce a writing, recording, or photograph as a memorialization of an event that occurred. A birth, marriage, or death may occasion the production of a birth, marriage, or death certificate, for example. If a party offers these certificates as proof that the events took place, their admission is not subject to a Rule 1002 objection because the contents of these documents would not be at issue. These certificates are simply recordations of the events, not the events themselves. Could the GPS recordings in *Bennett* be considered more like recordations of the defendant's trip from Mexican waters, or are the contents of the recordings truly at issue in the case as the court claims?

c. Depositions and Former Testimony.

Suppose a defendant is charged with counseling a client to give perjured testimony before a Senate subcommittee. To prove its case, the government offers the testimony of a witness who heard what the defendant's client told the Subcommittee in its entirety but cannot remember the client's exact words. Is this testimony admissible, or must the government produce a transcript of the testimony in order to satisfy Rule 1002? The defendant in the case might argue that a transcript would be the most reliable evidence of the client's Subcommittee statements, given that the memory or intentions of the testifying witness might be open to dispute. But is an argument about reliability enough to trigger the provisions of Rule 1002? See *Meyers v. United States*, 171 F.2d 800 (D.C. Cir. 1949).

Hypo 11.1

Assume that a federal agent overhears a conversation which was also tape recorded. Would either of the following types of evidence be held inadmissible under Rule 1002 if the original tape recording is not produced? (1) the testimony of a federal agent recounting what he overheard? (2) A copy of the tape recording of the overheard conversation? See *United States v. Howard*, 953 F.2d 610 (11th Cir. 1992).

Hypo 11.2

In a breach of contract case, the defendant offers to prove payment by showing a receipt signed by the plaintiff for the amount due and owing. Would Rule 1002 require production of the original receipt in lieu of the defendant' testimony? Although certainly helpful, does one need a receipt to prove payment?

---

3. Originals, Duplicates and Secondary Evidence

Rules 1001-1004 divide writings, recordings and photographs into three categories: originals, duplicates and secondary evidence.

Originals. The original of writings, recordings and photographs may or may not be the first item of its kind that is created. It must, however, be the item whose content is at issue in the lawsuit for Rule 1002 to apply. You should also be aware that there may also be more than one original, depending upon the intent of the parties. For example, formal contracts, trusts and wills are often created and signed in multiple originals, each one of which is considered an original for Rule 1002 purposes. If a document is created in triplicate form, all three resulting documents would be considered "originals."

Duplicates: A duplicate is defined as "a counterpart produced by the same impression as the original, or from the same matrix, or by means of photograph, including enlargements and miniatures, or by mechanical or electronic re-recording, or by chemical reproduction, or by other equivalent techniques which accurately reproduces the original." In other words, a duplicate is an accurate reproduction of the original. Carbon, Xeroxed, and microfilmed copies qualify as duplicates, as do re-recordings and reprints, enlargements or miniatures of photographs. Duplicates are treated as originals, unless an opponent claims that the original is not authentic or that admission of the duplicate would create unfairness. Rule 1003.

Secondary Evidence. Any evidence other than originals or duplicates that is offered to establish the contents of a writing, recording or photograph is called "secondary evidence." Secondary evidence of a written contract, for example, could consist of the testimony of a party describing the contract's contents, a handwritten copy of the contract, or handwritten notes of the contract's terms. There is no hierarchy of admissibility for secondary evidence. Although a handwritten copy of a written contract may be more reliable than a party's oral testimony as to its contents, the admissibility of one is not preferred over the other. It is thought that to impose such a hierarchy of admissibility for secondary evidence would be too difficult to apply.

Hypo 11.3

Assume a document is typed on a computer and printed out. That document would be an "original." But what if a week later, someone accesses the document file and prints another copy without making alterations? Would that subsequent document be an "original" or "duplicate"? With regard to admissibility, what, if anything, would be the difference at trial?

In this next case, we will see how what appears to be a duplicate can be considered an original document, depending on why it is offered, and how copies of that duplicate may themselves be considered duplicates or secondary evidence, depending on the allegations of the parties.

United States v. Gerhart

U.S Court of Appeals for the Eighth Circuit
538 F.2d 807 (8th Cir. 1976)

GIBSON, Chief Judge.

Defendant, Charles Frederick Gerhart, appeals from his jury conviction for knowingly making a material false statement on a loan application to influence a member bank of the Federal Reserve System to approve and make him a loan. He was sentenced to one year in prison. The sole contention raised by the defendant on this appeal is that the District Court erred in admitting into evidence a photocopy of a document over the defendant's best-evidence objection. The document consisted of a photocopy of a bank check. The proffered exhibit was thus a photocopy of a photocopy.

On January 15, 1973, the defendant applied to the First National Bank of Colfax, Iowa, for a loan in the amount of $56,011.10 and fraudulently listed as a personal asset an account receivable from the Washington Heights Maplenoll Apartments in the amount of $50,000. Previously, in July, 1972, he had terminated a subcontracting agreement on Maplenoll's apartment construction project and accepted a final settlement of $45,079.86 from Maplenoll Construction Company. In payment, defendant had received two checks from Maplenoll: No. 105 in the amount of $40,247.46 payable jointly to the defendant and the Internal Revenue Service (IRS) and No. 106 in the amount of $4,822.40 payable to the defendant alone. In connection with the subsequent loan application, defendant presented the bank with photocopies of the two checks, but the amount on the photocopy of check No. 106 was illegible. The figures were altered or smudged so as to read "$54,822.40" rather than "$4,822.40." In addition, defendant had written across the copy of check No. 105, "the other check is for $54,822.40 Check No. 106", and he told the bank that check No. 106 had mistakenly been sent to the IRS. He also represented falsely that the July, 1972, settlement with Maplenoll had been for $95,079.86 rather than $45,079.86, and presented to the bank a copy of the settlement agreement that had been altered to show $95,079.86 rather than the correct figure of $45,079.86, again demonstrating an unmistakable intent to deceive and mislead.

An officer of the bank, Charles M. Stinson, thereafter contacted the IRS and inquired as to the whereabouts of check No. 106. The IRS answered that no such check had been received. Thereafter, on request of Special Agent Robert Smith of the Iowa Department of Public Safety, Mr. Stinson surrendered the photocopies of both checks, but first, as a precaution, made a second photocopy of each of them. Subsequently, the Iowa agency misplaced the original photocopies. Thus, at trial the Government introduced the second photocopy of check No. 106 that was made by the bank. Bank officer Stinson and Special Agent Smith testified that they had viewed both the first and second photocopies and that, with the exception of some handwriting not seen by the jury, the exhibited copy accurately reproduced the original photocopy of the check.

Under the new Federal Rules of Evidence, though proof of the contents of a writing requires production of the original document, secondary evidence is admissible if the original has been lost. Fed. R. Evid." 1004(1). The defendant does not dispute this principle and does not challenge the adequacy of the Government's showing that the original photocopy had been lost. Rather, he contends that a further prerequisite to the admission of secondary evidence is a clear and convincing showing of its trustworthiness and that no such showing was made.

The Federal Rules of Evidence became effective on July 1, 1975.

The defendant's contentions are entirely without merit. A clear showing of trustworthiness need not be made to admit secondary evidence of the contents of a writing. Rule 1004 of the Federal Rules of Evidence states in relevant part as follows:

Admissibility of Other Evidence of Contents

The original is not required, and other evidence of the contents of a writing, recording, or photograph is admissible if

(1) Originals lost or destroyed. All originals are lost or have been destroyed, unless the proponent lost or destroyed them in bad faith .

This rule, essentially a restatement of the common law, excuses production of the original of a writing if one of the enumerated conditions is satisfied. The rule recognizes no degrees of secondary evidence and in this respect "is probably a departure from the rule found in the majority of American jurisdictions." 5 J. Weinstein, *Evidence* P 1004(01), at 1004-5 (1975). Thus, once an enumerated condition of Rule 1004 is met, the proponent may prove the contents of a writing by any secondary evidence, subject to an attack by the opposing party not as to admissibility but to the weight to be given the evidence, with final determination left to the trier of fact. On the other hand, the new rules allocate to the court preliminary questions such as authenticity, lack of an original and whether the proponent has presented a sufficient foundation so that a "reasonable juror could be convinced" that the secondary evidence correctly reflects the contents of the original. 5 J. Weinstein, Evidence 1004(1)(03), at 1004-11 (1975); see "Fed. R. Evid." 104(a), 901(a), 1008. Contrary to defendant's assertions, no "clear and convincing evidence of authenticity and accuracy" is required for admission.

In the instant case, the Government was merely required to demonstrate preliminarily, to the satisfaction of the court, that the original photocopy was lost, that the proffered photocopy was what it purported to be and that it accurately reflected the contents of the original photocopy. This the Government achieved through the testimony of Mr. Stinson and Special Agent Smith. The District Court's implicit preliminary findings are supported by the record and admission of the exhibit in evidence was by no means an abuse of the District Court's discretion.

The judgment of the District Court is affirmed.

Points for Discussion

a. A Duplicate as an Original Document.

In *Gerhart,* why was a photocopy designated as an original document for Rule 1002 purposes? If the photocopy were instead considered a duplicate in this case, would it still have been admissible? What then would be considered secondary evidence?

b. Loss or Destruction of the Original.

Rule 1004 permits introduction of something other than the original of a writing, recording, or photograph unless the destruction is done in bad faith by the offering party. What if the destruction is done negligently or recklessly? What if production of the original requires extreme expense or inconvenience? Must a proponent attempt to obtain the items by judicial process before the original is not required? See *Merrill v. United States,* 365 F.2d 281 (5th Cir. 1966). Rule 1004 also lists other circumstances under which an original is not required, such as when an original cannot be obtained or is in possession of an opponent who, after notice, does not produce it.

c. The Admissibility of Duplicates.

Duplicates are admissible under Rule 1003 to the same extent as an original document, except where there is a genuine question raised as to the "authenticity of the original" or under circumstances where it would "unfair to admit the duplicate." Consider the following problem: Jane takes her car to Joe, a mechanic, for repairs. They agree that Joe will repair her car for $350.00, and they sign a contract for that amount. After the car is repaired, Jane tries to pay Joe $350 in order to retrieve her car, but Joe produces the original contract which appears to claim Jane owes him $1,350 for the repair. If Jane has a duplicate copy of the contract she received at the time she dropped the car off for repairs, would it be admissible?

d. Computer Records.

All computer print-outs are considered original documents under Rule 1001. That is, if a party wishes to offer a computer print-out of a document, any print-out will suffice as an original document. There are, however, some exceptions. For example, if the print-out is being offered in place of underlying business records, such as sales slips or invoices, then the underlying documents would probably be considered originals, and the print-out may be considered secondary evidence. If there are no underlying documents, then the print-out would be considered an original document.

---

4. The Admissibility of Summaries

Rule 1006 is an exception to the requirement of the original rule. It permits

> ## Rule 1006. Summaries
>
> The contents of voluminous writings, recordings, or photographs which cannot conveniently be examined in court may be presented in the form of a chart, summary, or calculation. The originals, or duplicates, shall be made available for examination or copying, or both, by other parties at reasonable time and place. The court may order that they be produced in court.

a party to present what would otherwise be secondary evidence of voluminous writings, recordings or photographs in the form of charts, summaries, or calculations. For a summary to be admitted, the proponent must establish that the underlying exhibits are too voluminous to be conveniently examined in court, an issue which the trial judge determines within his or her discretion. Although the underlying exhibits upon which a summary is based need not be admitted into evidence, the proponent of a summary must show that they are admissible. The opponent must also be given an opportunity to examine and copy the underlying documents to check for inconsistencies, omissions, or other errors and to use in cross-examination before summaries may be admitted into evidence. For the same reasons, the trial court also has discretion to require the underlying documents be produced in court.

A distinction must be made between summaries as independent evidence pursuant to Rule 1006, and charts, summaries and other devices admitted and used by a proponent to organize and explain testimony or exhibits which have already been admitted at trial under Rule 611(a). Rule 1006 summaries are themselves evidence that will support a verdict. Rule 611(a) summaries are not admitted as substantive evidence, will not support a verdict, and are generally not made available to a jury during their deliberations because they are mere pedagogical devices.

Take Note!

Although usually decided pretrial, the decision whether to use the Rule 1006 summary option may also be made during trial for documents that have already been presented and which proved to be too voluminous to be conveniently examined by the jury. Some courts hold that if the underlying documents have already been admitted, the summary should not be admitted but rather used as an aid to an understanding of the documents. Other courts hold that the summary is evidence in and of itself whether or not the underlying original documents are introduced at trial.

Executive Summary

General Application of the Best Evidence Rule. Whenever the contents of any type of a "writing" or "recording" is to be proved in a case, the best evidence rule requires that the *original* writing or recording must be produced at trial in order to prevent fraud or inaccuracy. For example, a plaintiff suing for breach of contract must produce the "best evidence" of that contract, which would be the actual, original contract in dispute. A copy, or a "duplicate," of an original is generally admissible in place of the original. If an original or duplicate is not produced, then any other evidence about the writing or recording will be inadmissible. However, if the absence of an original or duplicate can be adequately explained (e.g., it was inadvertently lost or destroyed, or is not obtainable, etc.), then "secondary" evidence, such as testimony about the writing or recording, will be allowed in place of the original or duplicate.

What Qualifies as a "Writing" or "Recording" under the Rule? Although the best evidence rule is sometimes referred to as the "original document rule," the best evidence rule actually contemplates a very broad interpretation of "writings" or "recordings," such as diagrams, photographs, computer printouts, or electronic, mechanical, or magnetic data compilations. Although Rule 1001 defines writings or recordings as containing "letters, words, or numbers, or their equivalent," photographs, drawings and even artwork are considered to be writings or recordings under the best evidence rule. (*Lucasfilm*).

When Are the "Contents" of a Writing/Recording to Be Proved? Rule 1002 requires the production of an original at trial "to *prove the content* of a writing, recording or photograph." So when a writing is offered to prove an event (such as a transcript to prove testimony at a former trial), or if a writing itself has legal effect (such as wills, contracts), or if the witness's testimony is reliant on the writing (such as testimony based on the findings of an X-ray or microscope slide), then the "contents" are being proved, making the best evidence rule applicable. (*Bennett*). On the other hand, contents are not in issue, and thus the rule is inapplicable, if personal knowledge of a witness is used to prove that an event occurred, even if a writing or recording about that event exists (e.g., a buyer of goods may testify that she paid for them without having to produce a receipt, or a witness may testify that a birth, marriage, or death occurred without having to produce the corresponding legal certificate). Also, the rule is inapplicable if the contents of a *physical tangible object* are in issue (e.g., a weapon, a beer bottle, a set of keys, shoes, or drugs, etc.), or if the writing is merely collateral to a main issue in the case.

"Originals," "Duplicates" and "Secondary Evidence." There can be more than just one "original" if the parties intend copies of the originals to be considered as originals, such as a document produced in triplicate form. "Duplicates," on the other hand, are accurate reproductions of an original, such as a photocopy, re-recording, reprint, or enlargement or miniature of an original writing or recording, but not intended as an original. Under Rule 1003, duplicates are admissible as if they were an original, provided there is no claim that the original is not authentic, or that it would be unfair under the circumstances to admit the duplicate in lieu of the original.

"Secondary evidence" is any evidence about the writing or recording that is NOT the original writing or recording, or a duplicate, such as witness testimony about the writing or recording that is used to establish the contents of the writing or recording. When the best evidence rule applies (because a party is attempting to prove the contents of a writing or recording), secondary evidence is inadmissible in lieu of the original or duplicate writing or recording. However, under Rule 1004, when the original or duplicate is unavailable, secondary evidence about the writing or recording may still be admissible, provided the original or duplicate is not unavailable because of any bad faith on the part of the offering party. For example, if through no bad faith, the original or duplicate was inadvertently lost or destroyed, or is now not obtainable, then secondary evidence about the writing or recording will be admissible. (*Gerhart*).

Summaries of Originals or Duplicates. A writing or recording that summarizes other voluminous original or duplicate writings or recordings, is not itself an original or duplicate because such a summary is a document that was specially created for trial. However, under Rule 1006, if the writings or recordings upon which the summary is based are original or duplicate writings or recordings, then the summary of those originals or duplicates will be admissible, even though the summary itself is obviously not an original or duplicate.

CHAPTER 12

Opinion Testimony –
Lay and Expert

R. 602

Pursuant to Rule 602, a witness must have personal knowledge about something relevant in the case in order to testify about it. Accordingly, a witness generally may not give her opinion when testifying in a case because "personal knowledge" means that witnesses are supposed to testify only regarding facts about which they have knowledge. The rationale for requiring a witness to testify about facts she has actually witnessed, and not mere personal opinions or conclusions she may have, is so that the jury can make a finding based on what the witnesses actually know.

Generally the only ones in a trial who may form an opinion or conclusion as to what may have actually happened in the case are the jurors. Their conclusion, after weighing all of the evidence offered at trial, becomes the verdict. As such, a witness is not supposed to be a 13th juror. Instead, a witness should simply provide admissible facts for the jury to weigh, and then it is up to the jury to make a conclusion that reflects the truth.

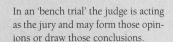

Make the Connection

In an 'bench trial' the judge is acting as the jury and may form those opinions or draw those conclusions.

There are important exceptions, however, allowing a witness to provide opinion testimony. Aside from the permissible use of opinion evidence when proving character evidence under Rules 405(a) or 608(a) allowing reputation and opinion evidence (addressed in Chapter 5 on witnesses and Chapter 9 on Character Evidence), the two main exceptions are: 1) Certain limited types of lay opinions under Rule 701; and, to a much larger extent, 2) opinions given by expert witnesses under Rules 702-706.

A. Lay Opinions

Under Rule 701, a witness can give his or her own general, non-technical opinions or impressions about what happened in the case, but only about certain matters that he or she actually witnessed or perceived first-hand.

Rule 701. Opinion Testimony by Lay Witnesses

If the witness is not testifying as an expert, the witness' testimony in the form of opinions or inferences is limited to those opinions or inferences which are (a) rationally based on the perception of the witness, and (b) helpful to a clear understanding of the witness' testimony or the determination of a fact in issue, and (c) not based on scientific, technical, or other specialized knowledge within the scope of Rule 702.

The proper scope of a lay opinion, which is just a well-founded guess of the witness, includes such perceptions as set forth in the following examples:

- Speed and other measurements ("the car had to be going over 90 miles an hour")

- Physical states such as intoxication or injury ("defendant appeared drunk or hurt to me")

- Personal emotions of others ("defendant was mad, and then he went crazy")

- Sensory descriptions ("it was so hot I was sweating, I'd say it was over 100 degrees")

- Value of one's own land ("my house is worth, about, I'd say, $200,000")

- Sanity of the testator ("he was nuts, he wasn't all there")

These are all examples of proper and acceptable lay opinion testimony. Notice they are opinions or estimates based on what the witness actually perceived or witnessed, and the opinions would be helpful to a jury in determining what actually happened in the case. Imagine how difficult, if not impossible, it would be to explain exactly how hot it was, according to the witness, without the witness being able to give an opinion that it was "over 100 degrees." How could a witness otherwise explain to the jury the heat that the witness believed she experienced if the witness were not allowed to give this type of opinion testimony? A witness would not be able to fully articulate what she experienced if all she could do is just list such things as: "The sun was very bright that day; It was so hot I was perspiring; I was uncomfortable, I overheard a person say that it was very hot," and so on.

The witness being able offer a lay opinion is the best shorthand and most descriptive way for a witness to communicate to the jury just how hot she thought it was on the particular day and time in question. This kind of testimony is a very narrow form of speculation that the Rules permit non-expert witnesses to make. An opinion can often communicate to the jury the witness's "whole" testimony, rather than just the sum of a list of the constituent parts of the witness' testimony.

United States v. Yazzie

U.S. Court of Appeals for the Ninth Circuit
976 F.2d 1252 (9th Cir.1992)

REINHARDT, Circuit Judge.

Johnny Yazzie, Jr., appeals his conviction for sexual abuse of a minor (statutory rape) in violation of 18 U.S.C. §§ 1153, 2243. We have jurisdiction under 28 U.S.C. § 1291. Because we conclude that the district court improperly excluded lay witnesses' testimony that the minor appeared to be at least sixteen years old when the alleged sexual abuse occurred, we reverse.

I.

Johnny Yazzie, Jr., was charged with aggravated sexual abuse (forcible rape) in violation of 18 U.S.C. §§ 1153, 2241(a), and with sexual abuse of a minor (statutory rape) in violation of 18 U.S.C. §§ 1153, 2243. Both charges stemmed from an incident involving Yazzie and a female minor that occurred on a Navajo Indian reservation on July 19, 1989, one month before Yazzie's twenty-first birthday and not quite six months before the sixteenth birthday of the minor.

Yazzie admitted that he had sexual intercourse with the minor on the night in question. His defense to the charge of forcible rape was that the intercourse was consensual. The jurors acquitted Yazzie of forcible rape but convicted him of statutory rape.

Yazzie's sole defense to the statutory rape charge was an affirmative defense permitted under 18 U.S.C. § 2243(c): that at the time of the incident, he reasonably believed that the minor, who was then fifteen-and-a-half years old, was at least sixteen. See 18 U.S.C. § 2243(c) ("[I]t is a defense ... that the defendant reasonably believed that the other person had attained the age of 16 years.").

to prove defense

Make the Connection

In most jurisdictions, statutory rape is a strict liability crime, and the defendant's belief about the age of an underage victim is legally irrelevant. That is why it is "statutory" rape, because even if the underage victim consents to sex, it is still considered to be rape under the law. However, some jurisdictions, as in this case, will allow the defense of the defendant's reasonable mistake that he believed the victim to be over the age of consent. In these circumstances, the defendant's reasonable belief becomes legally relevant.

To establish his belief as to the minor's age, Yazzie testified that on the night of the incident, he believed that the minor was at least sixteen years old. To establish the reasonableness of his belief, he testified that at the time of the incident, the minor smoked cigarettes, drove a car, used makeup, and looked "mature" enough to be at least sixteen. He testified that he knew the minor because he had previously dated her older sister, but that the minor never told him her age.

To further establish the reasonableness of his belief, Yazzie called several witnesses who offered to testify that as of the date of the alleged sexual abuse, their observations caused them to believe the minor to be between sixteen and twenty years old. The district court excluded this testimony, ruling that defense witnesses were permitted to testify to their perceptions of the minor's physical appearance and behavior at the time of the incident but were barred from stating their opinion that the minor was at least sixteen years of age. The reason for the ruling, the court explained, was that a witness' belief as to the minor's age was "subjective and has nothing to do with what [Yazzie] might have believed."

DC excluded this testimony

In accordance with the district court's ruling, Yazzie's witnesses did not testify as to their beliefs regarding the minor's age. Instead, three of Yazzie's witnesses confirmed his claim that the minor smoked cigarettes on the night in question; two testified that they had seen her drive a car before the alleged sexual abuse took place; and two testified that she wore makeup at the time of the incident. Further, three witnesses testified that the minor appeared sexually mature at the time of the alleged sexual abuse. One stated that the minor "was tall and [ ] appeared to be a lady ... a lady like she was full, how do you say, she was fully developed," and that "she was mainly filled out, she was very tall." Another testified that the minor's body shape made her look "[l]ike an older person." A third stated that the minor "was well into her womanhood, well developed ... [and] had her curves and [ ] was into her maturity." In addition, one witness testified that the minor drank beer on the night of the incident.

The minor testified regarding her age and her date of birth, but did not state that she had told Yazzie how old she was or that she had reason to believe that Yazzie knew at the time of the incident that she was not yet sixteen. She did not deny that she occasionally drank beer and smoked cigarettes; indeed, she testified that she did both on the night in question.

To refute Yazzie's claim that he reasonably believed the minor to be at least sixteen years old, the prosecution introduced evidence that Yazzie lived down the street from the minor; that he had dated her sister for several months, up until about ten weeks before the incident occurred; that during the time he dated her sister he went on walks with the minor and helped her with her math homework; and that on the night of the incident, the minor did not wear sophisticated clothing but rather high-top athletic shoes, tube socks, jean shorts over bicycle tights, and a tee shirt. Yazzie denied none of these contentions, but he continued to insist that the minor never said anything to him about her age, that he did not know what school she attended or what grade she was in, and that he thought that she was at least sixteen. When the prosecutor attempted to imply (without offering any supporting evidence) that Yazzie had attended the minor's fifteenth birthday party, which had been held during the time that Yazzie was dating the minor's sister, he denied that he had done so. The prosecution also introduced substantial evidence that people under the age of sixteen commonly drove on the reservation.

II.

Fed.R.Evid. 701 permits a lay witness to give opinion testimony as long as the opinion is "(a) rationally based on the perception of the witness and (b) helpful to a clear understanding of the witness' testimony or the determination of a fact in issue." Fed.R.Evid. 701. ...

701 allows opinions when [handwritten margin note]

We understand Rule 701 to mean that [o]pinions of non-experts may be admitted where the facts could not otherwise be adequately presented or described to the jury in such a way as to enable the jury to form an opinion or reach an intelligent conclusion. If it is impossible or difficult to reproduce the data observed by the witnesses, or the facts are difficult of explanation, or complex, or are of a combination of circumstances and appearances which cannot be adequately described and presented with the force and clearness as they appeared to the witness, the witness may state his impressions and opinions based upon what he observed. It is a means of conveying to the jury what the witness has seen or heard...

Here, the opinion testimony not only meets the requirements of sub-part (a) of Rule 701, but of both the alternative sub-parts of (b). The testimony helps in the understanding of the witnesses' descriptive testimony and in determining a critical fact at issue--whether it was reasonable for Yazzie to believe that the minor was sixteen or older.

In the case before us, the jurors could not themselves assess how old the minor looked at the time of the incident: by the time of the trial, the minor was almost seventeen years old, and her appearance was undoubtedly substantially different than it had been on the night in question, a year and a half earlier. Thus, the jurors were wholly dependent on the testimony of witnesses. Yet the witnesses were permitted to testify only to the minor's describable features and behavior. Their testimony was no substitute for a clear and unequivocal statement of their opinions. It did not tell the jury that these witnesses believed the minor to be at least sixteen years old at the time of the incident.

Our finding that the trial judge erred in not admitting the opinions of Yazzie's witnesses as to the minor's age is supported by all of the considerations that underlie Rule 701's authorization of the use of lay opinion testimony. First, it is difficult to distinguish a fifteen-and-a-half-year-old from a sixteen-year-old, and it is still more difficult to put into words why one believes that a person is one age and not the other. There is a certain intangible element involved in one's conclusions on such a question. We form an opinion of a person's age from "a combination of circumstances and appearances which cannot be adequately described and presented with the force and clearness as they appear[ ]" to us. Mannerisms and facial features are notoriously difficult to describe accurately, and one's reasons for concluding that a person is a particular age are both too complex and too indefinable to set out fully.

. . .

Furthermore, age is a matter on which everyone has an opinion. Knowingly or unknowingly, we all form conclusions about people's ages every day. It is therefore particularly appropriate for a lay witness to express an opinion on the subject.

Here, the witnesses' opinions were especially appropriate for another reason. The issue was whether the defendant held an opinion and if so whether that opinion was reasonable. It is relevant that others having a similar opportunity to observe the minor formed an opinion as to her age that was similar to the opinion the defendant claimed to have formed. Their testimony goes both to Yazzie's credibility and to the reasonableness of his belief. The district court's decision deprived the jury of the most direct evidence available as to the age that the minor reasonably appeared to be on the night of the incident. Thus, the judge's ruling constituted a clear abuse of discretion.

III.

… The excluded testimony of Yazzie's witnesses would have provided important support for his claim that he reasonably believed that the minor was at least sixteen years old on the night of the incident. Because of the trial court's decision, the witnesses were unable to advise the jury of their conclusions. While they were able to describe the minor as mature in some respects, their testimony did not carry the weight it would have if they had been permitted to state that she appeared to be at least sixteen. Indeed, under the court's restriction, the witnesses testified in large part only to facts that the prosecution did not deny: that the minor smoked, drank, and drove a car.

The jury acquitted Yazzie of one of the two charges against him. On the remaining charge, no evidence indicated that Yazzie had actual knowledge of the minor's age. The principal, and determinative, issue was the age the minor appeared to be to a reasonable observer. It is normally a close question whether a young woman of fifteen-and-a-half appears to have reached the age of sixteen. The question of innocence or guilt may well turn on the opinions of witnesses offered by the respective parties. Here, the most probative testimony would have been that of percipient witnesses who were willing to state their conclusions and explain to the extent possible how and why they arrived at them. While it is true that each side may find persons willing to offer opinions helpful to it, the jury is perfectly capable of weighing the veracity and bias of the witnesses. Here, the jury was deprived of that opportunity. It was compelled to resolve the crucial issue in the case before it on the basis of far less direct evidence than could have been provided. Because the evidence supporting the statutory rape charge was inconclusive and the excluded testimony was of considerable importance, we cannot say that a rational jury more probably than not would have convicted the defendant had the testimony not been excluded. We therefore conclude that the error was not harmless and that Yazzie's conviction must be REVERSED.

Gorby v. Schneider Tank Lines, Inc.

U.S Court of Appeals for the Seventh Circuit
741 F.2d 1015 (7th Cir. 1984)

PELL, Circuit Judge.

Dennis Gorby was severely injured when [the] semi-tanker truck [of defen- *accident* dant, Schneider Tank Lines, Inc.] collided with his vehicle at an Indiana highway intersection in the late evening of October 5, 1977. Gorby's wife, acting individually and in her capacity as guardian of her husband's person and estate, brought this diversity action [as plaintiff] seeking compensation for her loss of consortium and for her husband's personal injuries. The case was tried to a jury, which found against [defendant] and awarded [plaintiff] a total of $1,820,000…[Defendant] *D argues* contends that the trial judge improperly prohibited a lay witness from giving opinion testimony…

At trial, [plaintiff] offered the testimony of Carl Highlan, an eyewitness to the accident. On cross-examination, counsel for [defendant] tried to lay a foundation for Highlan's opinion testimony. Counsel elicited from Highlan the facts that Highlan was a licensed driver for twenty-nine years, that he drove approximately 19,000 miles per year, and that visibility was good on the night of the accident. Counsel then asked Highlan: "Do you have an opinion as to whether or not the driver of the semi truck [Welsch] did everything he could to avoid this accident?" [Plaintiff's] counsel objected, and Judge Sharp then permitted the following offer of proof:

> Q. Carl, based on what you saw that night, and on your driving experience, do you have an opinion as to whether or not the driver of the semi would have avoided this accident? ....
>
> A. Yes, I have an opinion .... First of all, keeping in mind I've never been a truck driver, but I have many years of experience driving, I feel that-and this is a sequence of events that happened-that the route he selected, there was insufficient time for him to avoid it.
>
> Q. Now, do you also have an opinion as to whether or not Dennis Gorby could have avoided this accident; he being the driver of the Ford pickup truck?
>
> A. With the route that the semi truck driver took, if Mr. Gorby would have stopped in the driving lane, I feel, in my mind, it could have been avoided.

Counsel for [defendant] argued that Highlan's answers were admissible as lay opinion testimony, but Judge Sharp disagreed and ruled that Highlan could not give the proposed testimony.

... Rule [701], consistent with the modern trend, permits the witness "to resort to inferences and opinions" when, in addition to being helpful to the jury, the opinions are based upon first-hand knowledge or observations...

Highlan was prepared to state two opinions. In our view, Judge Sharp properly excluded the two opinions because neither was based upon first-hand knowledge or observation. First, Highlan was prepared to state that Welsch did "everything he could to avoid [the] accident." Highlan, however, was not present in the truck's cab with Welsch. Highlan could only observe the semi-tanker truck from a car in the opposite lane of traffic and thus could not know the exact measures Welsch took to avoid the accident. More significantly, Highlan could not know when Welsch perceived Gorby's truck. Furthermore, even if Highlan had been present in the cab with Welsch, we would still find that the opinion was not based upon first-hand knowledge or observation. Appellant never established that Highlan was familiar with the Schneider semi-tanker truck. In particular, appellant never established that Highlan was familiar with the safety equipment semi-tanker trucks carry, the distances over which trucks may safely stop, the load the Schneider truck carried, or the brake and steering equipment of such trucks. The mere fact that Highlan was a motorist with twenty-nine years of experience did not give him the personal knowledge necessary to formulate an admissible lay opinion, and Judge Sharp properly exercised his discretion to exclude Highlan's first opinion.

②Highlan was also prepared to state that Gorby could have avoided the accident. The exclusion of this opinion presents a closer question than does the exclusion of the first opinion because a pick-up truck more closely resembles an ordinary car than it does a semi-tanker truck. Our review, however, is limited to identifying an abuse of discretion, and we conclude there was no abuse. There is nothing in the record to indicate that Highlan was familiar with the type of pick-up truck Gorby drove, its safety features, its acceleration and stopping times, or the load it was carrying on the night of the accident. The record fails to disclose that Highlan ever set foot in a pick-up truck, and the district court could well find that Highlan's testimony was based upon speculation rather than upon first-hand knowledge…

AFFIRMED.

Points for Discussion

a. Why Was Lay Opinion Allowed in *Yazzie* but not *Gorby*?

Did the court in *Gorby* commit an analytical error? The witness in the case did perceive the accident first-hand and he rendered a lay opinion based exactly on what he saw. Although the witness was not an accident reconstruction expert, he clearly was not being offered as any kind of expert witness, so his lack of expertise and experience regarding trucks was irrelevant.

b. What Was Helpful to the Jury about the Lay Opinion in *Yazzie* but not in *Gorby*?

Did the witness offer anything to the jury with his opinion that the jury could not have come to on its own based on the evidence? Perhaps the witness's lay testimony in *Gorby* was, in the end, just not all that "helpful to the jury." Recall, if lay testimony is not helpful to the jury, then it is simply another conclusion based on the facts presented. Because the jury can come to a conclusion all on its own, that kind of lay testimony is not helpful to the jury and therefore is improper.

Kostelecky v. NL Acme Tool/NL Industries, Inc.

U.S. Court of Appeals for the Eighth Circuit
837 F.2d 828 (8th Cir. 1988)

HEANEY, Circuit Judge.

P injured his hand

On May 6, 1987, Robert Kostelecky injured his hand and wrist in an accident while working for his employer, Noble Drilling Corporation (Noble).... Gulf Oil Corporation operated the oil venture and hired Noble as a drilling contractor. Gulf had also hired N.L. to perform specialized operations and field service work on the rig. Kostelecky alleges that his injury occurred while working on a Noble crew under the supervision and control of an N.L. representative. . . Kostelecky filed a complaint in federal district court alleging negligence . . . [and] the jury returned a verdict finding N.L. was not negligent. . .

alleged DC erred

Kostelecky contends that the district court erred in admitting into evidence an accident report of Jester Beck, one of Kostelecky's co-workers and an eyewitness to the accident. In particular, Kostelecky objects to statements in the report that the accident was caused by "the injured's own conduct" and that the accident could have been avoided if Kostelecky had listened to warnings and instructions given to him just prior to the accident. He contends that the statements are inadmissible because they are nothing more than the legal conclusions of a lay witness and could not have assisted the trier of fact in determining a factual issue. N.L. argues that the report is admissible because it represents Beck's firsthand observations ... which were therefore helpful to the jury in its deliberations. Moreover, N.L. argues that under Fed.R.Evid. 704(a), testimony in the form of an opinion is not rendered inadmissible merely because it embraces an ultimate issue to be decided by the trier of fact.

... Under the Federal Rules of Evidence, opinion testimony is not inadmissible solely because it embraces an ultimate issue to be decided by the trier of fact. Fed.R.Evid. 704(a). This does not, however, mean that all opinion testimony as to ultimate issues is admissible. In the case of a witness not testifying as an expert, the opinion testimony must be "(a) rationally based on the perception of the witness and (b) be helpful to a clear understanding of the witness' testimony or the determination of a fact in issue." ...

... evidence that merely tells the jury what result to reach is not sufficiently helpful to the trier of fact to be admissible. ...

Although it is not easy to distinguish permissible questions from those that are not permissible, ... we find that the trial court abused its discretion in admitting the accident report. The case was tried on a theory of negligence. Legal causation was very much in dispute. Therefore, in the context of this case, the opinion as to causation served to do nothing more than tell the jury what result it should reach. ... the question was more akin to "Did T have capacity to make a will?" than a request for the specific perceptions of the witness. ... Thus, we find that Beck's accident report was erroneously admitted... Accordingly, we affirm the entry of judgment in favor of N.L. on the jury verdict.

B. Expert Opinions

Although opinion testimony is allowed for lay witnesses, as long as it is based on the witness's perception and is helpful to the jury, opinion testimony provided at trial is actually much more common when it is provided by expert witnesses. As society grows more complex, so do the disputes in which members of society find themselves. Typical jurors often do not have the knowledge, expertise and/or experience to understand what the dispute is really about, let alone how the jury should find in order to resolve the dispute. As a result, attorneys often must rely on expert witnesses to give their opinions in their field of expertise to give the jury the benefit of their knowledge and thereby assist the jury in finding the truth.

This is a very important aspect of trials in the United States. Some observers fear that trials are becoming simply a "battle of the experts," with the side who can afford the best experts often prevailing in the lawsuit -- suggesting that perhaps we may be reducing the integrity of our legal system to a mere "sale" of justice to the highest bidder. Others argue just the opposite. They state that our jury system should be used not only for simple cases, but also for complex cases and that there is great value in requiring experts to make their complex opinions understandable and accessible to the typical juror. In either event, experts are and will continue to be modern staples in trial practice. Thus, it is important for future lawyers to understand the Rules of Evidence regulating the use of experts and the various areas of expertise that are admissible at trial.

An expert who is qualified in a certain field of expertise is allowed to give her expert opinion on a particular issue in the case involving that area of expertise. But unlike lay opinion testimony, personal knowledge of the incident by the testifying expert is not required. For example, even though an expert witness did not actually witness the accident in question, that expert may nevertheless testify that she reviewed the police and accident reports, looked at the measurements of the skid marks, did some physics and mathematical calculations, etc., and now has an opinion as to how fast the cars were going and how the accident must have happened based on the information provided, the Law of Physics, and her "expert analysis" of all the information provided. Rule 702 provides that expert opinion testimony is allowed when scientific, technical or other specialized knowledge will assist the trier of fact in understanding the evidence or determining the fact in issue.

Often an expert is allowed to provide information to the jury as well as a detailed analysis of that information beyond what the ordinary juror can be expected to know from the juror's everyday experience. Indeed the expert often "teaches" the jury in addition to providing the expert's opinion in the case. However, the attorney must first set forth the expert's qualifications before the court can accept them as expert witnesses and allow them to supply the jury with their expert opinion in a certain area.

> **Rule 702. Testimony by Experts**
>
> If scientific, technical, or other specialized knowledge will assist the trier of fact to understand the evidence or to determine a fact in issue, a witness qualified as an expert by knowledge, skill, experience, training, or education, may testify thereto in the form of an opinion or otherwise, if (1) the testimony is based upon sufficient facts or data, (2) the testimony is the product of reliable principles and methods, and (3) the witness has applied the principles and methods reliably to the facts of the case.

The Advisory Committee Note for Rule 702 provides the following:

> An intelligent evaluation of facts is often difficult or impossible without the application of some scientific, technical, or other specialized knowledge. The most common source of this knowledge is the expert witness, although there are other techniques for supplying it. Most of the literature assumes that experts testify only in the form of opinions. The assumption is logically unfounded. The rule accordingly recognizes that an expert on the stand may give a dissertation or exposition of scientific or other principles relevant to the case, leaving the trier of fact to apply them to the facts. . .

1. Qualifications

Expert witnesses have a great deal of credibility with most juries, and therefore, attorneys will often attempt to use them at trial. However, attorneys will sometimes attempt to use the expert witness to give opinions in areas where the witness is not qualified. Accordingly, it is important that an expert witness be allowed to give their expert testimony only in the field in which he is qualified to give an expert opinion. As the next case demonstrates, simply because an expert witness is qualified in one area does not necessarily mean that he is qualified another area, even if that other area is a related area to his expertise.

Polston v. Boomershine Pontiac-GMC Truck, Inc.

U.S. Court of Appeals for the Eleventh Circuit
952 F.2d 1304 (11ᵗʰ Cir. 1992)

PER CURIAM:

. . . In the early morning hours of July 19, 1986, Linda Polston's Pontiac Sunbird and Joyce Banks' Oldsmobile Delta 88 collided head-on on Piedmont Road in Atlanta, Georgia. As a result of this collision, Polston suffered serious multiple injuries. She brought suit against Banks, GMC, and three GMC dealerships. With respect to GMC, Polston argued that her Sunbird was defectively designed in that it was not crashworthy. She maintained that, although the design did not cause the initial collision with Banks, she suffered enhanced injuries that would not have occurred if the car had been crashworthy . . . .

At trial, Polston . . . [called] Murray Burnstine, [to] testify to the existence of *expert* enhanced injuries.

Burnstine was a mechanical engineer with experience as an automobile accident investigator. He gained this experience while employed at Harvard Medical School in the department of legal medicine. During his employment with Harvard, Burnstine was one member of a five member team that investigated the scenes of fatal automobile accidents. As part of his duties, Burnstine consulted with automobile manufacturers concerning safety related problems he discovered in their cars. In addition, Burnstine gained experience in investigating accidents and determining, from the pattern of a person's injuries, what parts of the person's body contacted what part of the automobile. In other words, Burnstine was experienced in determining how certain injuries were caused in a collision and, more specifically, what injuries were caused by the vehicle's lack of crashworthiness.

At trial, Burnstine testified that in his opinion the Sunbird was dangerous in *opinion* a front end collision because there was insufficient crush space and insufficient structure in the front of the car to protect the occupants from having the front of the car intrude into the occupants' space. He testified that some of Polston's lower extremity injuries were due to the Sunbird's lack of crush space and front end structure. After several objections by GMC as to Burnstine's qualifications to give an opinion regarding whether any of Polston's injuries were caused or contributed to by the Sunbird's lack of crashworthiness, [the court limited Burnstine's testimony the lack of crashworthiness of the car and excluded testimony regarding the extent of Polston's medical injuries. . .]

Polston contends that the district court erred in limiting the scope of Burnstine's testimony. Polston's attorney, Mr. Halstrom, attempted to elicit testimony from Burnstine concerning what injuries were caused by, or enhanced by, the alleged defective condition of the Sunbird. Burnstine was asked to base his conclusions on a reasonable degree of medical certainty. GMC objected. The district court sustained the objection based on Burnstine's lack of qualifications to testify about medical probability.

The trial court has broad discretion in the matter of admission or exclusion of expert evidence and his or her decision will be disturbed only if it is manifestly erroneous …The court's decision to exclude Burnstine's testimony was not manifestly erroneous. Burnstine was a mechanical engineer with no medical training. Therefore, he was not qualified to testify to medical probabilities. However, . . . Burnstine was qualified as an expert and was allowed to testify about Polston's injuries based on a reasonable degree of engineering certainty. . .

————————

Points for Discussion

a. Limiting the Scope of Experts

Recall that in the *Polston* case, because the expert witness was a mechanical engineer, and not a medical doctor, the expert was allowed to testify that the lack of crashworthiness of the car contributed to plaintiff's injuries, but he was not qualified as a medical doctor to testify as to which particular medical injuries were caused by the initial crash and those that were caused or enhanced by the lack of crashworthiness. The case demonstrates the importance of defining the precise scope of the expert witness' testimony.

Is the Testimony Helpful to the Jury?

In addition to defining the scope of the expert witness' expertise, it is also critical to determine whether the area of witness' expertise is a legitimate field of knowledge that will be helpful to the jury.

————————

The following is an excerpt written by a practicing trial attorney on how to qualify an expert witness and how to properly question an expert witness on direct examination. The purpose is to demonstrate a real world, practical application of the rules regarding expert witnesses.

DIRECT EXAMINATION OF EXPERTS
How to Make Expert Witnesses Credible
By David Malone[*]

...You have experts testify because you hope that they will move the jury toward your client's position. They can do that only if their testimony is under-standable and persuasive. With these two goals as our guide, let's examine the elements of presenting expert witnesses.

THE INTRODUCTION

Q. What is your full name name, Dr. Jones?

Q. What is your business?

Q. How long have you been a research pathologist?

Q. What is your business address?

... Do not overlook opportunities to use the expert's titles ("doctor" and "research pathologist"); you are trying in every way possible to persuade jurors that this witness's knowledge is so different and better from theirs that they should pay special attention to what he has to say...

THE TICKLER

Q. Have you come to court today, Dr. Jones, prepared to state your expert opinion as a pathologist, on the cause of Harold Good's lung disease?

Prepare the expert to answer, "Yes, I have," to this question. You do not want him inadvertently to blurt out his opinion at this point—the jury is not yet ready for it, and you still have some dramatic interest to build before you reach the climatic moment when he gives his opinion.

... Many lawyers launch right into the expert's qualifications without reflecting on the fact that jurors have little understanding of why the expert is testifying and even less understanding of why they should listen to someone talk about where he went to school when they thought they were going to get evidence about a wrongful death.

---

[*] David M. Malone is the senior litigation partner in the Washington D.C. office of Rivkin, Radler, Dunne & Bayh. He also lectures at the National Institute for Trial Advocacy and consults with law firms and government agencies on trial practice and strategy.

Let them in on the secret. "This guy is here because he has the answer you jurors need." Perhaps this will heighten their interest in his qualifications, since they will now know why you are raising questions about them...

EDUCATIONAL AND WORK QUALIFICATIONS

Q. Before we get to your opinion, Dr. Jones, I would like to give us some information about your qualifications to give that opinion. Let's start with your education. Where did you go to college?

Q. What was your major at Cornell?

Q. What courses did you study that relate particularly to your examination of the cause of Mr. Good's death?

Q. Will you define "Organic Chemistry"?

Q. How does organic chemistry relate to the work you did in determining the cause of Mr. Good's death? (And so forth, highlighting courses that demonstrate his expertise in the area of testimony.)

Q. Let's turn now to your work experience as a pathologist. What was your first position in this field?

Q. How long did you do research for Mercy Hospital in Pittsburgh?

Q. Would you tell us about any responsibilities or experience you had at Mercy Hospital that would relate specifically to identifying the cause of Mr. Good's death? (And so forth, through the relevant work experience.)

Q. Dr. Jones, do you belong to any professional association?

Q. How did you become a member?

Q. Does the American Board of Pathologist have any activities that relate specifically to lung disease?

Q. What was your role in those activities?

Q. How do they relate to your work in this lawsuit?

To permit the expert to testify, the judge need only be persuaded that the witness has specialized knowledge that will help the jury in coming to a decision. As a technical matter, then, the qualifications could end when that minimal presentation has been made. That, however, would ignore the jury's need to develop confidence in the witness, to assess his credibility. If you demonstrate that the expert has had the relevant educational and work experience, jurors will be more willing to rely on the expert.

Again you need not cover all courses or all employment or all associations-just what is needed to meet the threshold requirements for admissibility and to make the expert a persuasive witness to the jury. Ask about associations where membership is by work review and invitation, not about those like the American Medical Association that accept payment of dues as the primary criterion for membership.

RESUME AND PUBLICATIONS

Q. Dr. Jones, let me hand you Plaintiff's Exhibit 47 for identification. Is that your current resume?

Q. Your Honor, I offer Plaintiff's Exhibit 47 in evidence.

Do not call a resume a "curriculum vitae." Few if any jurors are comfortable with written Latin, even fewer with spoken latin. Consider asking, "Is this a summary of your educational and work experience?"…

Do not have the witness read and describe every item on the resume. You have already covered educational and work background. When you get to publication, ask:

Q. Dr. Jones, pages C through H of Plaintiff's Exhibit 47 are a listing of your publications, is that right?

Q. Some of those publications appeared in the *Journal of American Pathologist.* Please tell us what that journal is.

Q. What is a "peer review" journal?

Q. What significance does that have in evaluation the reliability of material published in such a journal.

Q. Who are the readers of that journal?

Q. Which of the publications you have written are particularly relevant to your work in determining the cause of Mr. Good's death?

Q. How does your August 1985 publication relate to the identification of the cause of lung disease? (And so forth, highlighting other relevant publication.)

[… Even if the other side stipulates to your expert's qualifications], you should not dispense with presenting your expert's qualifications to the jury. Remember, [even if there is a stipulation] the court is merely saying that no in-court demonstration of qualifications is required to permit the witness to testify. Jurors still must decide how much weight to give the expert's testimony, [so they should hear something about educational and work background.]

…If your opponent rises during your qualification of an expert and offers to stipulate that the expert is qualified to testify, an effective response is,

> Your Honor, we are happy to accept Mr. Barrister's statement that Dr. Jones is recognized as an expert in pathology and the determination of the cause of death in this type of case, and should be heard by the court and the jury. With the court's permission, we would like to present briefly some of his qualifications so that the jury can determine the weight to give his testimony.

With this, you have emphasized what appears to be opposing counsel's concession of the credentials of your expert, have highlighted your expert's expertise, and have turned aside your opponent's attempt to keep the jury from hearing about your expert's impressive qualifications. Of course, if you tell the court you will be brief, you must be brief…

THE TENDER

> Counsel: Your Honor, I tender Dr. Jones to the court as an expert in the medical specialty of pathology and in the determination of the cause of disease and death in cases involving respiratory failure. Dr. Jones is qualified by reason of his education, experience, and research to provide expert testimony on the cause of the lung disease that resulted in Mr. Good's death.

Some jurisdictions require such a formal tender, others permit but do not require one, and the rest do not permit one. Judges who do not permit a formal tender have two concerns: They do not want to appear to be putting the court's imprimatur on an expert by ruling on the tender, and they do not like lawyers making speeches about evidence or witnesses before the jury. Some judges avoid the "imprimatur" problem by saying, "You may proceed, counsel."

Where permitted, a tender is often greatly appreciated by the court, because it spells out the scope of the expert's experience and testimony, making it easier to rule on admissibility. Also, the tender tolls the time for opposition to the expert; the court will be impatient with an opponent who sits quietly after a tender and later tries to argue that the witness is not qualified. (Of course, testimony that goes beyond the qualifications or tender is subject to challenge and additional voir dire.)…

[Note that opposing counsel is allowed at this point to interrupt the witness' direct examination and "voir dire" the witness, where opposing counsel gets to cross-examine the witness on whether his qualifications are sufficient to be accepted as an expert witness before he provides his expert opinion. If opposing counsel had to wait until the witness completed his direct exam, the judge might later have to ask the jury to disregard an expert witness' entire testimony if the witness is not deemed qualified. This is an exception to the usual practice that opposing counsel must wait to cross-examine a witness until the witness completes direct examination.]

THE OPINION

> Q. Dr. Jones, we have now reviewed your educational, work, research and experience in the medical area of the pathology of lung diseases. Based on that background, do you have an opinion that you hold with reasonable degree of medical certainty on what caused Mr. Good's death?

> Q. What is that opinion?

Now you have arrived at the question you hope the jury has been waiting for: What killed Good? In preparing for trial, caution the expert to answer only "yes" to the first question, so that when he gives the opinion it stands out. The first question of this pair is designed to remind the jury of the reason for going through the credentials and to satisfy the technical requirements that an expert's opinion be based on an appropriate degree of certainty.

The required qualifying language—"reasonable degree of medical certainty"—varies from jurisdiction to jurisdiction (somewhere else, it might be "degree of certainty appropriate in the medical field of pathology"), but always the language must assure the court that the foundation for the expert's opinion is at least as firm as that which pathologist would require for conclusions reached in medical contexts. Thus, the requirement dovetails neatly with that in Rule 703 requiring that the bases of an expert opinion be of a type reasonably relied on by experts in the field. The first requirement goes to the strength with which the opinion is held; the second, to the bases supporting it…

As you complete one major opinion, together with its bases and subordinate opinions, and move to the next, help jurors to organize the testimony in their minds (or their notebooks in enlightened jurisdictions) by using a transitional statement:

Q. Dr. Jones, have we now discussed all the bases for your opinion that Harold Good died of advanced lung disease?

Q. Let's turn then to the question of whether the lung disease was caused by exposure to coal dust from the Carbonblack Mine. Based on your background and on the work you did for this lawsuit, do you have an opinion on that which you hold with a reasonable degree of medical certainty?

This transitional statement also prompts the witness to leave one area and to follow your lead into the next, while allowing you to restate the expert's opinion in an unobjectionable way.

THE BASES

The questions allowing the witness to explain the bases follow a formula: "What did you do? Why did you do this? What did you find? What does that mean to you?" This formula is an attempt to anticipate the order and content of the questions jurors are asking themselves as they listen to the expert.

Q. Will you list for us the bases for your opinion that Harold Good died from lung disease?

Q. Turning to the first of the bases you have stated, the visual observation of the lung tissue during the autopsy: How did you examine the tissue?

Q. Why did you examine the tissue?

Q. What did you observe during the examination?

Q. How doe the observation of blackened lung tissue support your conclusion that lung   disease caused Mr. Good's death?

Q. Now, the second basis that you listed is the chemical analysis of the deposits found in the lung tissue. Why did you have a chemical analysis done?

Q. How was that analysis done?

Q. What were the results of that analysis?

Q. How does the identification of the black deposits as carbon particles support your conclusion that Mr. Good died of lung disease?

If the expert has several bases for a major conclusion, consider presenting them on a chart, a slide, or an overhead projection. You might even want to arrange the exhibit so that one basis at a time can be highlighted for the jury [using computer exhibits].

Do not spring the graphics on the court. At the pretrial, let the court know what chart, slide, or diagram you intend to use, [and make sure to lay a proper foundation for it under Rule 901.]

Under Federal Rule of Evidence 705, the bases need not be disclosed on direct examination. An opinion without articulated bases that are logical and reliable is, however, not very persuasive.

ANTICIPATING THE DEFENSE CASE

Q. Dr. Jones, have we now discussed all your bases for concluding that Harold Good died as a result of lung disease caused by exposure to coal dust that he inhaled during his years as a miner in the Carbonblack Mine?

Q. In coming to your opinion, have you considered the fact that Mr. Good had been a pack-a-day smoker for the last 50 years of his life?

Q. What effect does that fact have on your conclusion that he died because of exposure to coal dust in the mine?

Q. Why?

Q. Did you also consider that Harold Good had lived his entire life in the industrial area of Scranton, Pennsylvania?

Q. Does that fact cause you to change your conclusion that he died because of exposure to coal dust from the mine?

Q. Are you also familiar with the opinions on this question held by Dr. Smith, the pathologist who will be presented by the Carbonblack Mining Company? (Or were you present in court for the testimony of Dr. Smith?)

Q. Does Dr. Smith's opinion cause you to change your expert opinion that Harold Good died as a result of lung disease caused by coal dust from the Carbonblack Mine?

Q. Why not?

Q. Did you have to make any assumptions in coming to your conclusion?

Q. What assumption did you make?

Q. Why did you assume that?

Q. What effect does that assumption have on your analysis?

Q. What effect would an opposite assumption have had on your analysis?

You should know what the likely lines of cross-examination will be. Unless you have some reason to believe that the cross-examiner will avoid or miss certain lines of attack, you are better off raising them on direct. On direct examination your expert can deal with problematic questions in a no adversarial context. If the challenges go to the alleged unreliability of certain bases, deal with those when the particular basis is discussed.

By this approach, you show the jury that your witness is honest and open to considering all the pertinent information, favorable and unfavorable, and you defuse the impact of cross examination. You also boost your own credibility. Redirect examination does provide an opportunity to address problems that developed during cross-examination, but the strictures on redirect limit your opportunity to present the most persuasive and organized answer to the challenges. Anticipating the defense case may save you the time and expense of presenting additional expert testimony on rebuttal.

CONCLUSION

Some lawyers attempt, through their experts, to arm jurors with sufficient expertise to enable them to comprehend and evaluate the evidence relating to the relevant scientific issues. The risk with this approach is that these "newly trained experts" may, in the jury room, evaluate the underlying evidence for themselves without the benefit of the real expert's training and experience.

Other lawyers believe that the best approach is to persuade jurors to trust the expert rather than form their own conclusions. This is the better approach. Jurors need not understand organic chemistry in order to accept expert testimony on chemical tests as significant and consistent with recognized authority.

If expert testimony is well-organized, interesting, and supported by graphic displays that make it more memorable, you will have a better chance to persuade jurors.

One last thing, try to resist the temptation that you, as the attorney, are also now an expert in the expert witness' field of expertise. Lawyers are expert advocates, but they should leave other areas of expertise to the experts. You do not need to become an expert in the field yourself to question an expert effectively. Instead, rely on your own expert to help you understand only those areas that are critical.

In both lay opinion and expert testimony, the opinion given must be "helpful" to the jury. Recall that "helpful to the jury" means that the opinion has to give the jury more than a guess as to what happened – it must be an educated guess based on some key facts or expert analysis beyond the jury's knowledge. This is a decision the judge must make in her discretion, which usually is an easy decision when it comes to lay opinions. The more difficult determination is whether an expert's opinion is helpful to a jury. The problem lies in distinguishing between an expert's "specialized knowledge," which would be helpful to the jury, and what is merely "junk science," designed to manipulate the jury with something that only appears to be specialized or scientific, but really is not. It is where the witness is attempting to pass off a version of the events that is nothing more than just a guess, with no real helpful scientific, technical or specialized knowledge. Courts have been grappling with this issue since at least the beginning of the last century.

2. Reliability of Expert Testimony

Closely related to an expert's qualifications is the issue of reliability. The next two cases paved the way for current jurisprudence on reliability.

Frye v. United States

U.S. Court of Appeals for the District of Columbia
293 F. 1013 (C.A. D.C. 1923)

VAN ORSDEL, Associate Justice.

2nd degree murder

Appellant, defendant below, was convicted of the crime of murder in the second degree, and from the judgment prosecutes this appeal.

A single assignment of error is presented for our consideration. In the course of the trial counsel for defendant offered an expert witness to testify to the result of a deception test made upon defendant. The test is described as the systolic blood pressure deception test [--an early form of a polygraph, or "lie detector" test]. It is asserted that blood pressure is influenced by change in the emotions of

deception test on D

the witness, and that the systolic blood pressure rises are brought about by nervous impulses sent to the sympathetic branch of the autonomic nervous system. Scientific experiments, it is claimed, have demonstrated that fear, rage, and pain always produce a rise of systolic blood pressure, and that conscious deception or falsehood, concealment of facts, or guilt of crime, accompanied by fear of detection when the person is under examination, raises the systolic blood pressure in a curve, which corresponds exactly to the struggle going on in the subject's mind, between fear and attempted control of that fear, as the examination touches the vital points in respect of which he is attempting to deceive the examiner.

In other words, the theory seems to be that truth is spontaneous, and comes without conscious effort, while the utterance of a falsehood requires a conscious effort, which is reflected in the blood pressure.

. . .

Prior to the trial defendant was subjected to this deception test, and counsel offered the scientist who conducted the test as an expert to testify to the results obtained. The offer was objected to by counsel for the government, and the court sustained the objection.

govt objected to testifying expert on D's results

. . .

Rule

'The rule is that the opinions of experts or skilled witnesses are admissible in evidence in those cases in which the matter of inquiry is such that inexperienced persons are unlikely to prove capable of forming a correct judgment upon it, for the reason that the subject-matter so far partakes of a science, art, or trade as to require a previous habit or experience or study in it, in order to acquire a knowledge of it. When the question involved does not lie within the range of common experience or common knowledge, but requires special experience or special knowledge, then the opinions of witnesses skilled in that particular science, art, or trade to which the question relates are admissible in evidence.'

Numerous cases are cited in support of this rule. Just when a scientific principle or discovery crosses the line between the experimental and demonstrable stages is difficult to define. Somewhere in this twilight zone the evidential force of the principle must be recognized, and while courts will go a long way in admitting expert testimony deduced from a well-recognized scientific principle or discovery, the thing from which the deduction is made must be sufficiently established to have gained general acceptance in the particular field in which it belongs.

must have general acceptance

We think the systolic blood pressure deception test has not yet gained such standing and scientific recognition among physiological and psychological

authorities as would justify the courts in admitting expert testimony deduced
from the discovery, development, and experiments thus far made.]

[handwritten: didn't admit expert testimony]

The judgment is affirmed.

————————

For many years, *Frye's* "general acceptance" standard was the standard by
which proffered scientific evidence was judged to see if the area of expertise was a
valid area upon which an expert witness could provide expert opinion testimony.
However, a general acceptance standard necessarily has a built in time lag. By
the time a scientific area or theory is generally accepted in the field, it may be
"old" technology or science. Consequently, "state of the art" or "cutting-edge"
technology or science can never be admitted in court by definition because it
takes a significant amount of time to be vetted and then generally accepted. Also,
the *Frye* standard seemed to hand over the judicial authority and responsibility
for determining admissibility in this area from the judiciary to scientific experts.
Courts began to have trouble with this wholesale relinquishment of a judicial
function and significant delegation of judicial power to scientists and experts in
their various fields of expertise. The next case represents the Supreme Court's
efforts to address both of these concerns.

Daubert v. Merrell Dow Pharmaceuticals, Inc.

Supreme Court of the United States
509 U.S. 579 (1993)

Justice BLACKMUN delivered the opinion of the Court.

In this case we are called upon to determine the standard for admitting expert
scientific testimony in a federal trial.

[handwritten: issue]

. . . Petitioners Jason Daubert and Eric Schuller are minor children born with
serious birth defects. They and their parents sued respondent in California state
court, alleging that the birth defects had been caused by the mothers' ingestion of
Bendectin, a prescription anti-nausea drug marketed by respondent. Respondent
removed the suits to federal court on diversity grounds.

[handwritten: cause of birth defect]

After extensive discovery, respondent moved for summary judgment, contending that Bendectin does not cause birth defects in humans and that petitioners would be unable to come forward with any admissible evidence that it
does. In support of its motion, respondent submitted an affidavit of Steven H.
Lamm, physician and epidemiologist, who is a well-credentialed expert on the
risks from exposure to various chemical substances. Doctor Lamm stated that he

introduced a study

had reviewed all the literature on Bendectin and human birth defects—more than 30 published studies involving over 130,000 patients. No study had found Bendectin to be a human teratogen (*i.e.,* a substance capable of causing malformations in fetuses). On the basis of this review, Doctor Lamm concluded that maternal use of Bendectin during the first trimester of pregnancy has not been shown to be a risk factor for human birth defects.

responded w/ experts

Petitioners did not (and do not) contest this characterization of the published record regarding Bendectin. Instead, they responded to respondent's motion with the testimony of eight experts of their own, each of whom also possessed impressive credentials. These experts had concluded that Bendectin can cause birth defects. Their conclusions were based upon "in vitro" (test tube) and "in vivo" (live) animal studies that found a link between Bendectin and malformations; pharmacological studies of the chemical structure of Bendectin that purported to show similarities between the structure of the drug and that of other substances known to cause birth defects; and the "reanalysis" of previously published epidemiological (human statistical) studies.

DC granted SJ

The District Court granted respondent's motion for summary judgment. The court stated that scientific evidence is admissible only if the principle upon which it is based is " 'sufficiently established to have general acceptance in the field to which it belongs.' " ... The court concluded that petitioners' evidence did not meet this standard. Given the vast body of epidemiological data concerning Bendectin, the court held, expert opinion which is not based on epidemiological evidence is not admissible to establish causation....

9th Circuit affirmed

The United States Court of Appeals for the Ninth Circuit affirmed.... Citing *Frye v. United States* the court stated that expert opinion based on a scientific technique is inadmissible unless the technique is "generally accepted" as reliable in the relevant scientific community... The court declared that expert opinion based on a methodology that diverges "significantly from the procedures accepted by recognized authorities in the field . . . cannot be shown to be 'generally accepted as a reliable technique.' " ...

In the 70 years since its formulation in the *Frye* case, the "general acceptance" test has been the dominant standard for determining the admissibility of novel scientific evidence at trial... Although under increasing attack of late, the rule continues to be followed by a majority of courts, including the Ninth Circuit...

...

The merits of the *Frye* test have been much debated, and scholarship on its proper scope and application is legion. Petitioners' primary attack, however, is not on the content but on the continuing authority of the rule. They contend that the *Frye* test was superseded by the adoption of the Federal Rules of Evidence. We agree. . .

Nothing in the text of...Rule [702] establishes "general acceptance" as an absolute prerequisite to admissibility. Nor does respondent present any clear indication that Rule 702 or the Rules as a whole were intended to incorporate a "general acceptance" standard. The drafting history makes no mention of *Frye,* and a rigid "general acceptance" requirement would be at odds with the "liberal thrust" of the Federal Rules and their "general approach of relaxing the traditional barriers to 'opinion' testimony." ... Given the Rules' permissive backdrop and their inclusion of a specific rule on expert testimony that does not mention "general acceptance," the assertion that the Rules somehow assimilated *Frye* is unconvincing. *Frye* made "general acceptance" the exclusive test for admitting expert scientific testimony. That austere standard, absent from and incompatible with the Federal Rules of Evidence, should not be applied in federal trials.

[handwritten margin note: 702 doesn't require "general acc"]

That the *Frye* test was displaced by the Rules of Evidence does not mean, however, that the Rules themselves place no limits on the admissibility of purportedly scientific evidence. Nor is the trial judge disabled from screening such evidence. To the contrary, under the Rules the trial judge must ensure that any and all scientific testimony or evidence admitted is not only relevant, but reliable.

The primary locus of this obligation is Rule 702, which clearly contemplates some degree of regulation of the subjects and theories about which an expert may testify. "*If scientific,* technical, or other specialized *knowledge will assist the trier of fact* to understand the evidence or to determine a fact in issue" an expert "may testify *thereto.*" The subject of an expert's testimony must be "scientific . . . knowledge." (Rule 702 also applies to "technical, or other specialized knowledge." Our discussion is limited to the scientific context because that is the nature of the expertise offered here.)

The adjective "scientific" implies a grounding in the methods and procedures of science. Similarly, the word "knowledge" connotes more than subjective belief or unsupported speculation.... Of course, it would be unreasonable to conclude that the subject of scientific testimony must be "known" to a certainty; arguably, there are no certainties in science. See, *e.g.,* Brief for Nicolaas Bloembergen et al. as *Amici Curiae* 9 ("Indeed, scientists do not assert that they know what is immutably 'true'—they are committed to searching for new, temporary theories to explain, as best they can, phenomena"); . . . In a case involving scientific evidence, *evidentiary reliability* will be based upon *scientific validity.*)

Rule 702 further requires that the evidence or testimony "assist the trier of fact to understand the evidence or to determine a fact in issue." ... Rule 702's "helpfulness" standard requires a valid scientific connection to the pertinent inquiry as a precondition to admissibility.

That these requirements are embodied in Rule 702 is not surprising. Unlike an ordinary witness, see Rule 701, an expert is permitted wide latitude to offer opinions, including those that are not based on first-hand knowledge or observation. See Rules 702 and 703. Presumably, this relaxation of the usual requirement of first-hand knowledge—a rule which represents "a 'most pervasive manifestation' of the common law insistence upon 'the most reliable sources of information,' "—is premised on an assumption that the expert's opinion will have a reliable basis in the knowledge and experience of his discipline.

Faced with a proffer of expert scientific testimony, then, the trial judge must determine at the outset, pursuant to Rule 104(a), whether the expert is proposing to testify to (1) scientific knowledge that (2) will assist the trier of fact to understand or determine a fact in issue. (Although the *Frye* decision itself focused exclusively on "novel" scientific techniques, we do not read the requirements of Rule 702 to apply specially or exclusively to unconventional evidence. Of course, well-established propositions are less likely to be challenged than those that are novel, and they are more handily defended. Indeed, theories that are so firmly established as to have attained the status of scientific law, such as the laws of thermodynamics, properly are subject to judicial notice under Fed.Rule Evid. 201.)

This entails a preliminary assessment of whether the reasoning or methodology underlying the testimony is scientifically valid and of whether that reasoning or methodology properly can be applied to the facts in issue. We are confident that federal judges possess the capacity to undertake this review. Many factors will bear on the inquiry, and we do not presume to set out a definitive checklist or test. But some general observations are appropriate.

Ordinarily, a key question to be answered in determining whether a theory or technique is scientific knowledge that will assist the trier of fact will be whether it can be (and has been) tested. "Scientific methodology today is based on generating hypotheses and testing them to see if they can be falsified; indeed, this methodology is what distinguishes science from other fields of human inquiry." …

Another pertinent consideration is whether the theory or technique has been subjected to peer review and publication. Publication (which is but one element of peer review) is not a *sine qua non* of admissibility; it does not necessarily correlate with reliability… Some propositions, moreover, are too particular, too new, or of too limited interest to be published. But submission to the scrutiny of the scientific community is a component of "good science," in part because it increases the likelihood that substantive flaws in methodology will be detected…

Additionally, in the case of a particular scientific technique, the court ordinarily should consider the known or potential rate of error ..., and the existence and maintenance of standards controlling the technique's operation... ③

Finally, "general acceptance" can yet have a bearing on the inquiry. A "reli- ④ ability assessment does not require, although it does permit, explicit identification of a relevant scientific community and an express determination of a particular degree of acceptance within that community." ... Widespread acceptance can be an important factor in ruling particular evidence admissible, and "a known technique that has been able to attract only minimal support within the community," ..., may properly be viewed with skepticism.

The inquiry envisioned by Rule 702 is, we emphasize, a flexible one. Its overarching subject is the scientific validity—and thus the evidentiary relevance and reliability —of the principles that underlie a proposed submission. The focus, of course, must be solely on principles and methodology, not on the conclusions that they generate.

[handwritten margin note: 702 is flexible]

... Respondent expresses apprehension that abandonment of "general acceptance" as the exclusive requirement for admission will result in a "free-for-all" in which befuddled juries are confounded by absurd and irrational pseudoscientific assertions. In this regard respondent seems to us to be overly pessimistic about the capabilities of the jury, and of the adversary system generally. Vigorous cross-examination, presentation of contrary evidence, and careful instruction on the burden of proof are the traditional and appropriate means of attacking shaky but admissible evidence... Additionally, in the event the trial court concludes that the scintilla of evidence presented supporting a position is insufficient to allow a reasonable juror to conclude that the position more likely than not is true, the court remains free to direct a judgment, . . . These conventional devices, rather than wholesale exclusion under an uncompromising "general acceptance" test, are the appropriate safeguards where the basis of scientific testimony meets the standards of Rule 702.

Petitioners ... suggest that recognition of a screening role for the judge that allows for the exclusion of "invalid" evidence will sanction a stifling and repressive scientific orthodoxy and will be inimical to the search for truth... It is true that open debate is an essential part of both legal and scientific analyses. Yet there are important differences between the quest for truth in the courtroom and the quest for truth in the laboratory. Scientific conclusions are subject to perpetual revision. Law, on the other hand, must resolve disputes finally and quickly. The scientific project is advanced by broad and wide-ranging consideration of a multitude of hypotheses, for those that are incorrect will eventually be shown to be so, and that in itself is an advance. Conjectures that are probably wrong are of little use, however, in the project of reaching a quick, final, and binding legal judgment—often of great consequence —about a particular set of events in the past. We recognize that in practice, a gatekeeping role for the judge, no matter how flexible, inevitably on occasion will prevent the jury from learning of authentic insights and innovations. That, nevertheless, is the balance that is struck by Rules of Evidence designed not for the exhaustive search for cosmic understanding but for the particularized resolution of legal disputes.

To summarize: "general acceptance" is not a necessary precondition to the admissibility of scientific evidence under the Federal Rules of Evidence, but the Rules of Evidence—especially Rule 702—do assign to the trial judge the task of ensuring that an expert's testimony both rests on a reliable foundation and is relevant to the task at hand. Pertinent evidence based on scientifically valid principles will satisfy those demands.

The inquiries of the District Court and the Court of Appeals focused almost exclusively on "general acceptance," as gauged by publication and the decisions of other courts. Accordingly, the judgment of the Court of Appeals is vacated and the case is remanded for further proceedings consistent with this opinion.

It is so ordered.

Chief Justice REHNQUIST, with whom Justice STEVENS joins, concurring in part and dissenting in part.

… [C]ountless … questions will surely arise when hundreds of district judges try to apply [the majority opinion's] teaching to particular offers of expert testimony… I do not doubt that Rule 702 confides to the judge some gatekeeping responsibility in deciding questions of the admissibility of proffered expert testimony. But I do not think it imposes on them either the obligation or the authority to become amateur scientists in order to perform that role. I think the Court would be far better advised in this case to decide only the questions presented, and to leave the further development of this important area of the law to future cases.

———————

Points for Discussion

a. The "Gatekeeping" Function of the Court after *Daubert*.

In *Daubert*, the Supreme Court attempted to bring a standard of reliability to scientific evidence. This "gatekeeping" function provided one of the most sweeping changes to expert scientific evidence seen in many years. Prior to *Daubert*, most courts followed the *Frye* standard which had a threshold of "general acceptance" in the relevant scientific community. *Daubert* refocused the inquiry to the consideration of multiple factors.

> Rule 702 Advisory Committee note after *Daubert, 2000 Amendment).*
>
> **Rule 702** has been amended in response to *Daubert* . . . , and to the many cases applying *Daubert* . . . *Daubert* set forth a non-exclusive checklist for trial courts to use in assessing the reliability of scientific expert testimony. The specific factors explicated by the *Daubert* Court are (1) whether the expert's technique or theory can be or has been tested--that is, whether the expert's theory can be challenged in some objective sense, or whether it is instead simply a subjective, conclusory approach that cannot reasonably be assessed for reliability; (2) whether the technique or theory has been subject to peer review and publication; (3) the known or potential rate of error of the technique or theory when applied; (4) the existence and maintenance of standards and controls; and (5) whether the technique or theory has been generally accepted in the scientific community. . . No attempt has been made to "codify" these specific factors. *Daubert* itself emphasized that the factors were neither exclusive nor dispositive. Other cases have recognized that not all of the specific *Daubert* factors can apply to every type of expert testimony. . . The standards set forth in the amendment are broad enough to require consideration of any or all of the specific *Daubert* factors where appropriate.

[handwritten margin note: checklist of reliability of scientific expert testimony]

With its new found "gate-keeping" role for the judiciary, the Supreme Court reclaimed for judges the power to assess scientific and technical areas in court, instead of simply ceding that function to experts in their various fields of expertise. Instead of courts holding back and deferring to the experts, judges are supposed to get in the mix and decide if the area of expertise is a valid one for a courtroom. The next case is an example of the Supreme Court exercising that role.

General Electric Company v. Joiner

Supreme Court of the United States
522 U.S. 136 (1997)

CHIEF JUSTICE REHNQUIST delivered the opinion of the Court.

[Respondent Robert Joiner worked as an electrician for the City of Thompsonville, Georgia. In his work, Joiner was exposed to certain fluids in the city's electrical transformers. Some of these fluids contained polychlorinated biphenyls

[handwritten margin note: P was exposed to PCBs & developed small cell lung cancer]

("PCB's"). After he was diagnosed with small-cell lung cancer, Joiner sued General Electric and Westinghouse Electric, the manufacturers of the transformers, and Monsanto, the manufacturer of the PCB's, in Georgia state court. Joiner alleged that his disease was "promoted" by his workplace exposure to chemical "PCBs" and derivative "furans" and "dioxins" that were manufactured by, or present in materials manufactured by, petitioners. Petitioners removed the case to federal court and moved for summary judgment.]

[Petitioners] contended that (1) there was no evidence that Joiner suffered significant exposure to PCBs, furans, or dioxins, and (2) there was no admissible scientific evidence that PCBs promoted Joiner's cancer. Joiner responded that there were numerous disputed factual issues that required resolution by a jury. He relied largely on the testimony of expert witnesses. In depositions, his experts had testified that PCBs alone can promote cancer and that furans and dioxins can also promote cancer. They opined that since Joiner had been exposed to PCBs, furans, and dioxins, such exposure was likely responsible for Joiner's cancer.

The District Court ruled that…[t]heir testimony was…inadmissible.

The Court of Appeals for the Eleventh Circuit reversed…[holding]…that the District Court had erred in excluding the testimony of Joiner's expert witnesses. The District Court had made two fundamental errors. First, it excluded the experts' testimony because it "drew different conclusions from the research than did each of the experts." The Court of Appeals opined that a district court should limit its role to determining the "legal reliability of proffered expert testimony, leaving the jury to decide the correctness of competing expert opinions." . Second, the District Court had held that there was no genuine issue of material fact as to whether Joiner had been exposed to furans and dioxins. This was also incorrect, said the Court of Appeals, because testimony in the record supported the proposition that there had been such exposure. . .

We believe that a proper application of the correct standard of review here indicates that the District Court did not abuse its discretion. Joiner's theory of liability was that his exposure to PCBs and their derivatives "promoted" his development of small cell lung cancer. In support of that theory he proffered the deposition testimony of expert witnesses. Dr. Arnold Schecter testified that he believed it "more likely than not that Mr. Joiner's lung cancer was causally linked to cigarette smoking and PCB exposure." … Dr. Daniel Teitelbaum testified that Joiner's "lung cancer was caused by or contributed to in a significant degree by the materials with which he worked." …

Petitioners contended that the statements of Joiner's experts regarding causation were nothing more than speculation. Petitioners criticized the testimony of the experts in that it was "not supported by epidemiological studies . . . [and was]

based exclusively on isolated studies of laboratory animals." Joiner responded by claiming that his experts had identified "relevant animal studies which support their opinions." He also directed the court's attention to four epidemiological [human population] studies on which his experts had relied.

The District Court agreed with petitioners that the animal studies on which respondent's experts relied did not support his contention that exposure to PCBs had contributed to his cancer. The studies involved infant mice that had developed cancer after being exposed to PCBs. The infant mice in the studies had had massive doses of PCBs injected directly into their peritoneums, or stomachs. Joiner was an adult human being whose alleged exposure to PCBs was far less than the exposure in the animal studies. The PCBs were injected into the mice in a highly concentrated form. The fluid with which Joiner had come into contact generally had a much smaller PCB concentration of between 0-500 parts per million.

...

Rather than explaining how and why the experts could have extrapolated their opinions from these seemingly far-removed animal studies, respondent chose "to proceed as if the only issue [was] whether animal studies can ever be a proper foundation for an expert's opinion."... Of course, whether animal studies can ever be a proper foundation for an expert's opinion was not the issue. The issue was whether *these* experts' opinions were sufficiently supported by the animal studies on which they purported to rely. The studies were so dissimilar to the facts presented in this litigation that it was not an abuse of discretion for the District Court to have rejected the experts' reliance on them.

[handwritten margin note: issue]

[handwritten margin note: DC didn't abuse discretion]

...

Respondent points to *Daubert's* language that the "focus, of course, must be solely on principles and methodology, not on the conclusions that they generate." ... He claims that because the District Court's disagreement was with the conclusion that the experts drew from the studies, the District Court committed legal error and was properly reversed by the Court of Appeals. But conclusions and methodology are not entirely distinct from one another. Trained experts commonly extrapolate from existing data. But nothing in either *Daubert* or the Federal Rules of Evidence requires a district court to admit opinion evidence which is connected to existing data only by the *ipse dixit* of the expert. A court may conclude that there is simply too great an analytical gap between the data and the opinion proffered... That is what the District Court did here, and we hold that it did not abuse its discretion in so doing.

[handwritten margin note: no abuse of discretion]

We hold, therefore, that abuse of discretion is the proper standard by which to review a district court's decision to admit or exclude scientific evidence. We

[handwritten margin note: abuse of discretion standard]

further hold that, because it was within the District Court's discretion to conclude that the studies upon which the experts relied were not sufficient, whether individually or in combination, to support their conclusions that Joiner's exposure to PCBs contributed to his cancer, the District Court did not abuse its discretion in excluding their testimony. . . We accordingly reverse the judgment of the Court of Appeals and remand this case for proceedings consistent with this opinion.

reversed

  It is so ordered.

Justice BREYER, concurring.

  . . . Of course, neither the difficulty of the task nor any comparative lack of expertise can excuse the judge from exercising the "gatekeeper" duties that the Federal Rules impose-determining, for example, whether particular expert testimony is reliable and "will assist the trier of fact," Fed. Rule Evid. 702, or whether the "probative value" of testimony is substantially outweighed by risks of prejudice, confusion or waste of time. Fed. Rule Evid. 403. To the contrary, when law and science intersect, those duties often must be exercised with special care.

  Today's toxic tort case provides an example. The plaintiff in today's case says that a chemical substance caused, or promoted, his lung cancer. His concern, and that of others, about the causes of cancer is understandable, for cancer kills over one in five Americans… Moreover, scientific evidence implicates some chemicals as potential causes of some cancers… Yet modern life, including good health as well as economic well-being, depends upon the use of artificial or manufactured substances, such as chemicals. And it may, therefore, prove particularly important to see that judges fulfill their *Daubert* gatekeeping function, so that they help assure that the powerful engine of tort liability, which can generate strong financial incentives to reduce, or to eliminate, production, points towards the right substances and does not destroy the wrong ones. It is, thus, essential in this science-related area that the courts administer the Federal Rules of Evidence in order to achieve the "end[s]" that the Rules themselves set forth, not only so that proceedings may be "justly determined," but also so "that the truth may be ascertained." Fed. Rule Evid. 102…

—————————

Points for Discussion

a. The Rule Applies to not only Scientific and Technical Knowledge but also "Specialized" Areas of Knowledge.

  The Advisory Committee Note to Rule 702 states the following regarding the scope of knowledge allowed to be testified by an expert under Rule 702

. . . The rule is broadly phrased. The fields of knowledge which may be drawn upon are not limited merely to the "scientific" and "technical" but extend to all "specialized" knowledge. Similarly, the expert is viewed, not in a narrow sense, but as a person qualified by "knowledge, skill, experience, training or education." Thus within the scope of the rule are not only experts in the strictest sense of the word, e.g., physicians, physicists, and architects, but also the large group sometimes called "skilled" witnesses, such as bankers or landowners testifying to land values.

b. How Far Does the Rule Extend Beyond Traditional "Science?"

The next case demonstrates the Supreme Court's decision to apply the *Daubert* case beyond the "novel scientific" context to all areas of knowledge, special experience or technology. In a sense, it is important not to be "elitist" in this context. For example, a non-high school graduate might have special knowledge or experience in a particular area that is beyond that of a typical juror and therefore still qualify as an expert witness in the case in whatever her particular field of expertise may be. Thus, an expert witness' field of expertise might very well extend beyond novel areas of science.

. . .

Kumho Tire Co. v. Carmichael

Supreme Court of the United States
526 U.S. 137 (1999)
Justice BREYER delivered the opinion of the Court.

. . . This case requires us to decide how Daubert applies to the testimony of *issue* engineers and other experts who are not scientists. We conclude that Daubert's *holding* general holding setting forth the trial judge's general "gatekeeping" obligation applies not only to testimony based on "scientific" knowledge, but also to testi- *702* mony based on "technical" and "other specialized" knowledge. See Fed. Rule Evid. 702. We also conclude that a trial court may consider one or more of the more specific factors that Daubert mentioned when doing so will help determine that testimony's reliability. But, as the Court stated in Daubert, the test of reliability is "flexible," and Daubert's list of specific factors neither necessarily nor exclusively applies to all experts or in every case. Rather, the law grants a district court the same broad latitude when it decides how to determine reliability as it enjoys in respect to its ultimate reliability determination. See General Electric Co. v. Joiner, 522 U.S. 136, 143 (1997) (courts of appeals are to apply "abuse of discretion" *abuse of* standard when reviewing district court's reliability determination). Applying these *discretion* standards, we determine that the District Court's decision in this case not to admit *standard of* certain expert testimony was within its discretion and therefore lawful. *review*

On July 6, 1993, the right rear tire of a minivan driven by Patrick Carmichael *tire blew* blew out. In the accident that followed, one of the passengers died, and others *out r* were severely injured. In October 1993, the Carmichaels brought this diversity *caused accident*

claimed tire was defective

suit against the tire's maker and its distributor, whom we refer to collectively as Kumho Tire, claiming that the tire was defective. The plaintiffs rested their case in significant part upon deposition testimony provided by an expert in tire failure analysis, Dennis Carlson, Jr., who intended to testify in support of their conclusion.

P relied on deposition testimony of his expert

Carlson's depositions relied upon certain features of tire technology that are not in dispute....

Carlson's testimony also accepted certain background facts about the tire in question. He assumed that before the blowout the tire had traveled far.... He conceded that the tire tread had at least two punctures which had been inadequately repaired...

Despite the tire's age and history, Carlson concluded that a defect in its manufacture or design caused the blow-out.

...

Carlson added that he had inspected the tire in question. He conceded that the tire to a limited degree showed greater wear on the shoulder than in the center, some signs of "bead groove," some discoloration, a few marks on the rim flange, and inadequately filled puncture holes (which can also cause heat that might lead to separation)... But, in each instance, he testified that the symptoms were not significant, and he explained why he believed that they did not reveal overdeflection. For example, the extra shoulder wear, he said, appeared primarily on one shoulder, whereas an overdeflected tire would reveal equally abnormal wear on both shoulders... Carlson concluded that the tire did not bear at least two of the four overdeflection symptoms, nor was there any less obvious cause of separation; and since neither overdeflection nor the punctures caused the blowout, a defect must have done so.

D moved to exclude experts testimony

Kumho Tire moved the District Court to exclude Carlson's testimony on the ground that his methodology failed Rule 702's reliability requirement. The court agreed with Kumho that it should act as a Daubert-type reliability "gatekeeper," even though one might consider Carlson's testimony as "technical," rather than "scientific." ... The court then examined Carlson's methodology in light of the reliability-related factors that Daubert mentioned, such as a theory's testability, whether it "has been a subject of peer review or publication," the "known or potential rate of error," and the "degree of acceptance within the relevant scientific community." The District Court found that all those factors argued against the reliability of Carlson's methods, and it granted the motion to exclude the testimony....

DC granted motion to exclude

The plaintiffs, arguing that the court's application of the Daubert factors was too "inflexible," asked for reconsideration. And the Court granted that motion... After reconsidering the matter, the court agreed with the plaintiffs that Daubert should be applied flexibly, that its four factors were simply illustrative, and that other factors could argue in favor of admissibility.

…

It consequently affirmed its earlier order declaring Carlson's testimony inadmissible....

What's That?

The term "de novo" means "anew." But what does anew mean? When a court reviews a lower court's decision "de novo" it means it is reviewing the decision as though this is the first trial. It is not limited to errors committed by the lower court. The higher court merely uses the record from the lower court and reaches its own decision.

The Eleventh Circuit reversed... It "review[ed] de novo" the "district court's legal decision to apply Daubert." ... It noted that "the Supreme Court in Daubert explicitly limited its holding to cover only the 'scientific context,' " adding that "a Daubert analysis" applies only where an expert relies "on the application of scientific principles," rather than "on skill- or experience-based observation." ... It concluded that Carlson's testimony, which it viewed as relying on experience, "falls outside the scope of Daubert," that "the district court erred as a matter of law by applying Daubert in this case," and that the case must be remanded for further (non-Daubert-type) consideration under Rule 702...

[handwritten margin note: 11th Circuit reversed]

[handwritten margin note: reasoned]

…

In Daubert, this Court held that Federal Rule of Evidence 702 imposes a special obligation upon a trial judge to "ensure that any and all scientific testimony is not only relevant, but reliable." ... The initial question before us is whether this basic gatekeeping obligation applies only to "scientific" testimony or to all expert testimony. We, like the parties, believe that it applies to all expert testimony...

[handwritten margin note: issue here]

For one thing, Rule 702 itself . . . [m]akes no relevant distinction between "scientific" knowledge and "technical" or "other specialized" knowledge. It makes clear that any such knowledge might become the subject of expert testimony. In Daubert, the Court specified that it is the Rule's word "knowledge," not the words (like "scientific") that modify that word, that "establishes a standard of evidentiary reliability." ... Hence, as a matter of language, the Rule applies its reliability standard to all "scientific," "technical," or "other specialized" matters within its scope. We concede that the Court in Daubert referred only to "scientific" knowledge. But

[handwritten margin note: 702 doesn't distinguish between "scientific" + "technical" knowledge]

as the Court there said, it referred to "scientific" testimony "because that [wa]s the nature of the expertise" at issue…

Neither is the evidentiary rationale that underlay the Court's basic Daubert "gatekeeping" determination limited to "scientific" knowledge. Daubert pointed out that Federal Rules 702 and 703 grant expert witnesses testimonial latitude unavailable to other witnesses on the "assumption that the expert's opinion will have a reliable basis in the knowledge and experience of his discipline." … (pointing out that experts may testify to opinions, including those that are not based on firsthand knowledge or observation). The Rules grant that latitude to all experts, not just to "scientific" ones.

Finally, it would prove difficult, if not impossible, for judges to administer evidentiary rules under which a gatekeeping obligation depended upon a distinction between "scientific" knowledge and "technical" or "other specialized" knowledge. There is no clear line that divides the one from the others. Disciplines such as engineering rest upon scientific knowledge. Pure scientific theory itself may depend for its development upon observation and properly engineered machinery. And conceptual efforts to distinguish the two are unlikely to produce clear legal lines capable of application in particular cases…

We conclude that Daubert's general principles apply to the expert matters described in Rule 702. The Rule, in respect to all such matters, "establishes a standard of evidentiary reliability." … It "requires a valid connection to the pertinent inquiry as a precondition to admissibility." … And where such testimony's factual basis, data, principles, methods, or their application are called sufficiently into question, … the trial judge must determine whether the testimony has "a reliable basis in the knowledge and experience of [the relevant] discipline." …

The District Court did not doubt Carlson's qualifications, which included a masters degree in mechanical engineering, 10 years' work at Michelin America, Inc., and testimony as a tire failure consultant in other tort cases. Rather, it excluded the testimony because, despite those qualifications, it initially doubted, and then found unreliable, "the methodology employed by the expert in analyzing the data obtained in the visual inspection, and the scientific basis, if any, for such an analysis." . . .

Finally, the court, after looking for a defense of Carlson's methodology as applied in these circumstances, found no convincing defense. Rather, it found (1) that "none" of the Daubert factors, including that of "general acceptance" in the relevant expert community, indicated that Carlson's testimony was reliable, …; (2) that its own analysis "revealed no countervailing factors operating in favor of admissibility which could outweigh those identified in Daubert," …; and (3) that the "parties identified no such factors in their briefs," ... For these three reasons taken together, it concluded that Carlson's testimony was unreliable.

Respondents now argue to us, as they did to the District Court, that a method of tire failure analysis that employs a visual/tactile inspection is a reliable method, and they point both to its use by other experts and to Carlson's long experience working for Michelin as sufficient indication that that is so. But no one denies that an expert might draw a conclusion from a set of observations based on extensive and specialized experience. Nor does anyone deny that, as a general matter, tire abuse may often be identified by qualified experts through visual or tactile inspection of the tire. . . . [T]he question before the trial court was specific, not general. The trial court had to decide whether this particular expert had sufficient specialized knowledge to assist the jurors "in deciding the particular issues in the case." ...

The particular issue in this case concerned the use of Carlson's two-factor test and his related use of visual/tactile inspection to draw conclusions on the basis of what seemed small observational differences. We have found no indication in the record that other experts in the industry use Carlson's two-factor test or that tire experts such as Carlson normally make the very fine distinctions about, say, the symmetry of comparatively greater shoulder tread wear that were necessary, on Carlson's own theory, to support his conclusions. .... Of course, Carlson himself claimed that his method was accurate, but, as we pointed out in Joiner, "nothing in either Daubert or the Federal Rules of Evidence requires a district court to admit opinion evidence that is connected to existing data only by the ipse dixit of the expert.". . . .

In sum, Rule 702 grants the district judge the discretionary authority, reviewable for its abuse, to determine reliability in light of the particular facts and circumstances of the particular case. The District Court did not abuse its discretionary authority in this case. Hence, the judgment of the Court of Appeals is Reversed.

—————————

The Advisory Committee Note to Rule702 provide the following in the 2000 to the Rule:

> Courts both before and after Daubert have found other factors relevant in determining whether expert testimony is sufficiently reliable to be considered by the trier of fact. These factors include:
>
> (1) Whether experts are "proposing to testify about matters growing naturally and directly out of research they have conducted

independent of the litigation, or whether they have developed their opinions expressly for purposes of testifying.

(2) Whether the expert has unjustifiably extrapolated from an accepted premise to an unfounded conclusion.

(3) Whether the expert has adequately accounted for obvious alternative explanations.

(4) Whether the expert "is being as careful as he would be in his regular professional work outside his paid litigation consulting."

(5) Whether the field of expertise claimed by the expert is known to reach reliable results for the type of opinion the expert would give.

A review of the caselaw after Daubert shows that the rejection of expert testimony is the exception rather than the rule. Daubert did not work a "seachange over federal evidence law," and "the trial court's role as gatekeeper is not intended to serve as a replacement for the adversary system."...

When a trial court, applying this amendment, rules that an expert's testimony is reliable, this does not necessarily mean that contradictory expert testimony is unreliable. The amendment is broad enough to permit testimony that is the product of competing principles or methods in the same field of expertise...

Nothing in this amendment is intended to suggest that experience alone--or experience in conjunction with other knowledge, skill, training or education--may not provide a sufficient foundation for expert testimony. To the contrary, the text of Rule 702 expressly contemplates that an expert may be qualified on the basis of experience. . .

3. Expert v. Lay Opinions

It is critical not to confuse whether a witness is providing lay opinion testimony or expert opinion testimony. Lawyers who cannot qualify a witness as an expert will sometimes attempt to admit expert testimony as mere lay opinion testimony. Rule 701 is intended for lay witness testimony only. Consider the amendment to the Advisory Committee Note to Rule 701 admonishing the bench and bar not to make this common error.

Rule 701 has been amended to eliminate the risk that the reliability requirements set forth in Rule 702 will be evaded through the simple expedient of proffering an expert in lay witness clothing. Under the amendment, a witness' testimony must be scrutinized under the rules regulating expert opinion to the extent that the witness is providing testimony based on scientific, technical, or other specialized knowledge within the scope of Rule 702... By channeling testimony that is actually expert testimony to Rule 702, the amendment also ensures that a party will not evade the expert witness disclosure requirements set forth in Fed.R.Civ.P. 26 and Fed.R.Crim.P. 16 by simply calling an expert witness in the guise of a layperson...

The amendment does not distinguish between expert and lay witnesses, but rather between expert and lay testimony. Certainly it is possible for the same witness to provide both lay and expert testimony in a single case...

The next case addresses the importance of maintaining a clear analytical distinction between a witness opinion testimony when being allowed under Rule 701 lay opinion and under Rule 702 expert opinion.

The next case addresses this issue.

United States v. Freeman

U.S. Court of Appeals for the Ninth Circuit
498 F.3d 893 (9th Cir. 2007)

JOHN R. GIBSON, Senior Circuit Judge.

Kevin Freeman appeals from his conviction and sentence on one count of conspiracy to manufacture and distribute at least fifty grams of cocaine base and conspiracy to possess with intent to distribute at least five hundred grams of cocaine. Freeman argues that the district court erred in allowing the government's expert witness to testify regarding the meaning of encoded drug language and to testify as a lay witness. Although portions of the expert witness's testimony should have been excluded, we hold that the district court's error was harmless. . . . We affirm.

I. Background

. . . The indictment alleged that as a part of the drug conspiracy, Freeman purchased cocaine from [Mitchell and Brown]. Mitchell and Brown were part of an earlier twenty-three defendant indictment, and since that time Mitchell had been cooperating with investigators. Freeman allegedly converted the cocaine into cocaine base and returned the cocaine to Brown for distribution in the Venice, California area. The Drug Enforcement Administration (DEA) had been investigating Mitchell and Brown as part of the Corey Mitchell drug trafficking organization ... and during their investigation they intercepted telephone calls between Freeman and Brown. ...[Freeman was convicted on one count of conspiracy to distribute cocaine]. . . Freeman now brings the present appeal.

II. Agent Shin's Testimony

D argues

Freeman argues that the district court abused its discretion by allowing Shin to testify as to the meaning of coded drug language used in telephone conversations between Freeman, Mitchell, and Brown. . . Shin offered interpretations regarding the meaning of thirty-six recorded telephone calls. Several of the words he interpreted were part of the jargon commonly used by drug traffickers and were familiar to Shin before the investigation. For instance, he testified that "ticket" signifies a drug price; "iggidy" refers to an ounce; "all gravy" and "straight" both signify that the situation is good; "dove" refers to the number twenty; and the terms "bread," "cheese," and "chips" all refer to money.

interpreted words that that weren't familiar and those that were.

Shin also interpreted a number of words that he was not familiar with before the investigation but, as he explained, are easily decoded based on a manner of speaking common to drug traffickers. Shin testified that Freeman, Brown, and Mitchell altered words by placing "e-z" or some variant thereof in the middle of words. He interpreted "fezone" to mean phone; "teznower" to mean tower; "fezo" to signify four and "fezi" to signify five; "deezove" to mean dove; "peezark" to mean park; and "reezey" to mean ready.

Take Note!

Although this case addresses an expert, a lay witness with appropriate experience could also testify as to the interpretations of these words.

Shin also offered interpretations for drug jargon that he was not familiar with before the investigation, but was able to decipher on the basis of the investigation and his general experience with drug trafficking. For example, Shin explained on the basis of his knowledge of the street value of cocaine that "cuatro-cinco," which are the Spanish words for four and five, signified $450. "Piece," according to Shin, signified ounce, and it was a term that he was able to decipher based on the context of a conversation between Mitchell and Brown. Shin interpreted "diamond" to signify the ten ounces of crack that would be produced by cooking nine ounces of powder cocaine. In this instance, Brown helped to reveal the term's meaning by stating that he was going to "pull ten," and then correcting himself by

stating that he would pull a "diamond." Shin explained that he was familiar with
the process of converting powder cocaine into crack cocaine, and that with skill,
an individual is able to increase the total weight of drugs.

Shin also offered explanations of statements by Freeman, Brown, and Mitchell that were not encoded drug jargon, but instead were phrases that were more
likely to be understood by the jurors without assistance. When Brown instructed
Mitchell to speak with him later so that they "can get all the particulars," Shin
stated that "particulars" was a reference to the "details." Shin explained that when
Mitchell asked Brown during one recorded call how everything had turned out,
this signified that Mitchell was asking Brown how did the "drug deal turn out,
how did everything go?" . . .

A. Standard of Review

On appeal, Freeman argues that the district court committed error by allowing Shin to testify both as a lay witness as well as an expert witness and that
the district court never properly admitted Shin as an expert witness. (Regarding
Shin testifying as an expert, we find no error by the district court. At the time of
trial, Shin had been a police officer for eleven years, with more than four years of
experience as a narcotics detective. Shin also testified that at the time of trial, he
had participated in over one hundred narcotics investigations....)

[handwritten margin note: testifying both lay + expert]

Freeman further contends that the district court, by permitting Shin to testify
as a fact witness, circumvented Fed.R.Evid. 702 and allowed Shin to testify in an
unreliable manner.... The district court's decision to admit expert testimony is
reviewed for abuse of discretion...

[handwritten margin note: abuse of discretion.]

B. Reliability of Agent Shin's Testimony

The Supreme Court has established that Federal Rule of Evidence 702
charges trial judges with the task of ensuring "that any and all scientific testimony
or evidence admitted is not only relevant, but reliable."... The gatekeeping role
exercised by district courts "entails a preliminary assessment of whether the reasoning or methodology underlying the testimony is ... valid and of whether that
reasoning or methodology properly can be applied to the facts in issue."... This
role applies to all expert testimony, not only to "scientific" expert testimony....

[handwritten margin note: reliability]

[handwritten margin note: applies to all testimony]

Our review of the record leads us to conclude that Shin's interpretation of
encoded drug jargon was admissible. Several terms, such as "iggidy," "ticket," and
"all gravy" were familiar to Shin before the investigation. Other terms, such as
"cuatro-cinco" and "diamond" were unfamiliar to Shin before the investigation,
but Shin explained during his testimony how he arrived at his interpretations.
Shin also offered interpretations of altered words such as "fezone" and "teznower,"

[handwritten margin note: Ct. concludes]

[handwritten margin note: Shin's interpretation of encoded jargon was admissible]

which we have acknowledged uses a methodology that satisfies [precedents dealing with expert testimony.] The district court therefore did not err in allowing Shin to testify [as an expert] as to the meaning of encoded drug jargon.

however

Shin's testimony, however, touched on matters far afield from the interpretation of encoded drug jargon when he offered interpretations of ambiguous conversations that did not consist of coded terms at all. For example, in one telephone conversation between Brown and Mitchell, Shin interpreted "long route" to refer to a drug transaction. In several conversations, Shin interpreted ambiguous phrases such as "that," "they," and "one of them," to refer to either money or cocaine. In another conversation, Shin interpreted Brown's statement, "Man, it's done already" to mean "he's given the cocaine to Kevin Freeman and that he's received his money for it." In these and other instances, Shin did nothing more than offer one possible framework for understanding the conversation. When offering this type of testimony, Shin usually explained his reasoning.

testifying as lay witness

However, in these instances Shin ceased to apply his specialized knowledge of drug jargon and the drug trade and began to interpret ambiguous statements based on his general knowledge of the investigation. He was therefore no longer testifying as an expert but rather as a lay witness... A lay witness may provide opinion testimony regarding the meaning of vague or ambiguous statements... But, unlike expert testimony, lay opinion must be "rationally based on the perception of the witness." Fed.R.Evid. 701. It must also be helpful to the jury in acquiring a "clear understanding of the witness's testimony or the determination of a fact in issue." *Id.* We have previously held these requirements were met when a law enforcement investigator testified regarding his understanding of the meaning of a declarant's vague or ambiguous statements....

Freeman argues that it was error for the district court to allow Shin to testify both as an expert witness concerning coded drug terms and as a lay witness.... The appellants argued that the government witness's "dual roles as case agent and expert witness allowed him to serve as a summary witness, improperly testifying as an expert about the general meaning of conversations and the facts of the case."...

when going from expert to lay witness

...[S]everal difficulties ... arise when a case agent goes beyond interpreting code words as an expert and testifies as to the defendant's conduct based upon the agent's knowledge of the case. First, "by qualifying as an 'expert,' the witness attains unmerited credibility when testifying about factual matters from first-hand knowledge." Second, it is possible that "expert testimony by a fact witness or case agent can inhibit cross-examination ... [because a] failed effort to impeach the witness as expert may effectively enhance his credibility as a fact witness." ...

③ Third, "when the prosecution uses a case agent as an expert, there is an increased danger that the expert testimony will stray from applying reliable methodology and convey to the jury the witness's 'sweeping conclusions' about appellants' activities, deviating from the strictures of Rules 403 and 702." ④ Fourth, a case agent testifying as an expert may lead to juror confusion because "[s]ome jurors will find it difficult to discern whether the witness is relying properly on his general experience and reliable methodology, or improperly on what he has learned of the case." ⑤ Finally, "when a case agent/expert strays from the scope of his expertise, he may impermissibly rely upon and convey hearsay evidence."…

… First, we are concerned that a case agent who testifies as an expert receives "unmerited credibility" for lay testimony…. In this case, the line between Shin's lay and expert testimony was never articulated for the jury. This lack of clarity regarding Shin's dual roles created a risk that there was an imprimatur of scientific or technical validity to the entirety of his testimony.

[handwritten margin note: lack of clarity when switched from lay to opinion testimony.]

Second, we are also concerned that Shin was called upon by the government to give his opinion as to the meaning of numerous words and conversations, regardless of whether his testimony, at points, was speculative or unnecessarily repetitive. …[T]his form of expert testimony, "unless closely monitored by the district court, may unfairly provid[e] the government with an additional summation by having the expert interpret the evidence, and may come dangerously close to usurping the jury's function…. Such summarizing also implicates Rule 403 as a needless presentation of cumulative evidence and a waste of time."… District courts have the continuing responsibility of acting as the vigilant gatekeepers of expert testimony to ensure that it is reliable…. The fact that Shin possessed specialized knowledge of the particular language of drug traffickers did not give him carte blanche to testify as to the meaning of other words in recorded telephone calls without regard to reliability or relevance.

Third, as noted, the blurred distinction between Shin's expert and lay testimony may have allowed him to rely upon and convey inadmissible hearsay evidence. Once Shin stopped testifying as an expert and began providing lay testimony, he was no longer "allowed … to testify based on hearsay information, and to couch his observations as generalized 'opinions' rather than as firsthand knowledge."… If Shin relied upon or conveyed hearsay evidence when testifying as a lay witness or if Shin based his lay testimony on matters not within his personal knowledge, he exceeded the bounds of properly admissible testimony.

We agree, however, that the use of case agents as both expert and lay witnesses is not so inherently suspect that it should be categorically prohibited…

Make the Connection

It is not uncommon for a lay witness to also act as an expert witness. Think of the mechanic involved in a divorce case. If one issue was the cost to repair the wife's vehicle, the mechanic/husband could testify as to his expert opinion to repair the vehicle.

Testimony of this kind may save time and expense, and will not necessarily result in juror confusion, provided that the district court engages in vigilant gatekeeping. We think that it is sufficient to emphasize the necessity of making clear to the jury what the attendant circumstances are in allowing a government case agent to testify as an expert. If jurors are aware of the witness's dual roles, the risk of error in these types of trials is reduced.

Turning to the case at hand, Freeman failed to ask the district court to instruct the jury regarding Shin's dual role and did not enter an objection raising that concern... We therefore review Shin's dual role testimony for plain error. Because the distinction between lay and expert testimony in this context is a fine one, we do not fault the district court for failing to intervene sua sponte. Thus there was no plain error. We also note that the opportunity does not lie solely with the district court to clarify in the eyes of the jury the demarcation between lay and expert testimony offered by the same witness. That distinction can also be revealed through direct or cross examination. . .

... It is necessary that a lay witness's "opinions are based upon ... direct perception of the event, are not speculative, and are helpful to the determination" of factual issues before the jury... Some of Shin's testimony, however, consisted of either speculation or repetition of already clear statements. For example, Shin's unnecessary interpretation of "particulars" to signify "details" was not helpful to the jury, thereby violating Rule 701. As well, Shin's opinion as to the reason why Freeman wished to get off of the telephone while driving was speculation and therefore was erroneously admitted. . .

C. Harmless Error

Having concluded that limited portions of Shin's testimony were erroneously admitted, we must now determine whether the error was harmless. For errors that are not of constitutional magnitude, the government must show that the prejudice resulting from the error was more probably harmless than not... This requires a "fair assurance" that the jury was not substantially swayed by the error. We conclude that the errors we have highlighted, when viewed in the context of the entirety of Shin's testimony and other evidence offered by the government, were harmless. . .

Shin's interpretations of the recorded conversations were often corroborated by the extensive surveillance he and other investigators conducted during the course of the investigation... Surveillance by the investigators, combined with Shin's experience with encoded drug jargon and his knowledge of the circumstances surrounding the case, ensured a high degree of reliability for a majority of Agent Shin's testimony. The overwhelming portion of Shin's testimony was therefore properly admitted. This testimony connected Freeman to illegal drug transactions and contradicted his claim that the phone conversations concerned basketball tickets. In light of the evidence as a whole, we conclude that the erroneously admitted testimony was harmless. . .

IV. Conclusion

We conclude that the issues discussed in this opinion do not warrant reversal. Freeman's conviction and sentence are AFFIRMED.

4. Bases of Testimony

Expert opinions under Rule 702 may be based on assumed facts, facts not in evidence, or even inadmissible hearsay, provided the otherwise inadmissible basis for the opinion is a type reasonably relied upon by experts in the field under Rule 703. Because this is a potentially stealthy way to get otherwise inadmissible exhibits admitted as evidence relied upon by the expert witness, the relied upon information is excluded, but that exclusion does not exclude the expert opinion itself. Moreover, the otherwise inadmissible relied-upon information may be admissible, but only if the probative value of that evidence is shown to substantially outweigh its prejudicial value, which may be high since it is otherwise inadmissible evidence.

> **Rule 703. Bases of Opinion Testimony by Experts**
>
> The facts or data in the particular case upon which an expert bases an opinion or inference may be those perceived by or made known to the expert at or before the hearing. If of a type reasonably relied upon by experts in the particular field in forming opinions or inferences upon the subject, the facts or data need not be admissible in evidence in order for the opinion or inference to be admitted. Facts or data that are otherwise inadmissible shall not be disclosed to the jury by the proponent of the opinion or inference unless the court determines that their probative value in assisting the jury to evaluate the expert's opinion substantially outweighs their prejudicial effect.

The Advisory Committee Note for Rule 703 provides the following:

Facts or data upon which expert opinions are based may, under the rule, be derived from three possible sources. The first is the firsthand observation of the witness, with opinions based thereon traditionally allowed. A treating physician affords an example… Whether he must first relate his observations is treated in Rule 705. The second source, presentation at the trial, also reflects existing practice. The technique may be the familiar hypothetical question or having the expert attend the trial and hear the testimony establishing the facts. Problems of determining what testimony the expert relied upon, when the latter technique is employed and the testimony is in conflict, may be resolved by resort to Rule 705. The third source contemplated by the rule consists of presentation of data to the expert outside of court and other than by his own perception. In this respect the rule is designed to broaden the basis for expert opinions beyond that current in many jurisdictions and to bring the judicial practice into line with the practice of the experts themselves when not in court. Thus a physician in his own practice bases his diagnosis on information from numerous sources and of considerable variety, including statements by patients and relatives, reports and opinions from nurses, technicians and other doctors, hospital records, and X rays. Most of them are admissible in evidence, but only with the expenditure of substantial time in producing and examining various authenticating witnesses. The physician makes life-and-death decisions in reliance upon them. His validation, expertly performed and subject to cross-examination, ought to suffice for judicial purposes. . .

If it be feared that enlargement of permissible data may tend to break down the rules of exclusion unduly, notice should be taken that the rule requires that the facts or data "be of a type reasonably relied upon by experts in the particular field." . . .

The ability of an expert to give her opinion without first disclosing the facts or data underlying her opinion is one way to get around the hearsay rule or other Rules of Evidence. For example, because the hearsay rule limits what hearsay evidence can be admitted, an attorney who is having difficulty getting it in evidence may find an expert to base her opinion on the inadmissible hearsay and get it in indirectly. The hearsay is indirectly admitted without going through the hassle of pigeonholing the hearsay into an exception just to get it admitted on its own merit. Many judges dislike this circumvention and will try to find a way to exclude it. Just because the expert relies on it should not mean that the jury gets to rely on it, but the jury may rely on the expert's overall conclusions.

South Central Petroleum, Inc v. Long Brothers Oil Company

U.S. Court of Appeals for the Eighth Circuit
974 F.2d 1015 (8ᵗʰ Cir. 1992)

HEANEY, Senior Circuit Judge.

In this diversity action, Long Brothers Oil Company appeals the district court's grant of summary judgment and order that South Central Petroleum and Jerry Sawyer pay Long Brothers Oil Company $62,627 in exchange for one-half ownership of an oil well. We affirm. . .

[This case involved a very complicated gas extraction contract between the parties. There were various purchases of partial interests in the gas contract between the litigants as well as other parties. The court attempted to severe the interests among the various parties, and as part of a multi-faceted order, determined that plaintiff should receive an offset based on a complex economic calculation] . . . Long Brothers argues that the trial court inappropriately relied on hearsay evidence in making this calculation.

To determine the offset, the district court admitted the expert opinions of witnesses for both parties. The district court admitted this evidence under the evidentiary rule permitting an expert to rely upon hearsay in forming an opinion as long as the hearsay evidence itself remains inadmissible. See Fed.R.Evid. 703. Indeed, the district court recognized that Sawyer's and South Central Petroleum's expert's testimony involved triple hearsay, because the expert based his opinion on information obtained from a commercial production service, which received its information from the state, which in turn obtained its information from the operator of the well, and none of these sources testified at the trial. Sawyer's and South Central Petroleum's expert presented his revenue conclusion in an exhibit, which also listed the production figures on which he based his opinion. As the expert explained, the spreadsheet-like exhibit listed the underlying data and reflected the calculations that formed his opinion. Thus, when the district court accepted the expert's revenue charts, it also allowed the underlying data to be at the court's disposal.

Long Brothers objects to this, and contends that it demonstrates that the district court improperly relied on hearsay evidence. When the district court admitted the exhibit, however, it limited the admission to the expert's opinion, and not to the underlying figures, as required by Federal Rule of Evidence 703. As the district court explained:

I'm going to admit the exhibit. I think that it does qualify under the rule
that experts may testify as to conclusions based on evidence that's not
itself independently admissible.

This statement convinces us that the district court did not blur the evidentiary distinction which Long Brothers argues was violated....

    ... The Federal Rules of Evidence permit experts to rely on inadmissible
information in forming their opinion as long as the underlying information be
"of a type reasonably relied upon by experts in the particular field...." Indeed,
"[a] trial court should exclude an expert opinion only if it is so fundamentally
unsupported that it cannot help the fact finder.... Any weaknesses in the factual
underpinnings of (the expert's) opinion go to the weight and credibility of his
testimony, not to its admissibility." Here, the district court expressly limited the
admission to the expert's opinion and did not admit the information on which
the expert based his opinion. Moreover, Long Brothers does not dispute that their
opponent's expert based his opinion on information reasonably relied upon by
experts in the field. In fact, Long Brothers' expert relied on the same type of production figures on which Sawyer's and South Central Petroleum's expert based his
opinion. We therefore do not believe that the district court abused its discretion
in admitting the contested expert testimony. . .

    Accordingly, we affirm the district court's order.

    The 2000 Amendment to Rule 702 sought to clear up any confusion regard-
ing the overlap between the 702 and 703:

> There has been some confusion over the relationship between Rules
> 702 and 703. [T]he sufficiency of the basis of an expert's testimony
> is to be decided under Rule 702. Rule 702 sets forth the overarching
> requirement of reliability, and an analysis of the sufficiency of the expert's
> basis cannot be divorced from the ultimate reliability of the expert's
> opinion. In contrast, the "reasonable reliance" requirement of Rule 703
> is a relatively narrow inquiry. When an expert relies on inadmissible
> information, Rule 703 requires the trial court to determine whether that
> information is of a type reasonably relied on by other experts in the field.
> If so, the expert can rely on the information in reaching an opinion.
> However, the question whether the expert is relying on a sufficient basis
> of information--whether admissible information or not--is governed by
> the requirements of Rule 702.

5. Opinion on the Ultimate Issue

Pure legal conclusions, by either lay or expert witnesses, are not admissible "opinion" testimony and therefore should be avoided. For example, a witness offering opinion testimony cannot say, "in my opinion, the defendant was not negligent in this case." That statement would be inadmissible because the witness would be applying the law to the facts of the case and arriving at a legal conclusion. Such is a job is for the jury and/or judge to do, not a witness. Remember, the jury finds facts and the judge applies the law to these found facts. Those are not proper roles for a mere witness.

Notwithstanding the fact that a witness's legal conclusions are inadmissible under Rule 704, a witness' opinion sometimes may still embrace the ultimate issue to be decided by the trier of fact. As a practical matter, witnesses should avoid "legal buzz words" in their opinions. For example, a witness should not say: "The defendant is not guilty by reason of insanity." However, that witness could say, "The defendant suffers from a psychological mental disorder where he cannot appreciate the difference between right and wrong." The second statement would be admissible, while the first would not, because the second statement avoids a pure legal conclusion. The first statement that the defendant is not guilty by reason of insanity is for the jury to conclude, not a witness. However, the second statement regarding the existence of a certain psychological disorder by defendant, even though it encompasses the ultimate issue – the defendant's mental state regarding guilt–still properly avoids formal legal terminology and, more importantly, leaves the ultimate legal conclusion of guilt or innocence to the fact finder.

Rule 704. Opinion on Ultimate Issue

(a) Except as provided in subdivision (b), testimony in the form of an opinion or inference otherwise admissible is not objectionable because it embraces an ultimate issue to be decided by the trier of fact.

(b) No expert witness testifying with respect to the mental state or condition of a defendant in a criminal case may state an opinion or inference as to whether the defendant did or did not have the mental state or condition constituting an element of the crime charged or of a defense thereto. Such ultimate issues are matters for the trier of fact alone.

United States v. Lockett

U.S. Court of Appeals for the Ninth Circuit
919 F.2d 585 (9th Cir. 1990)

O'SCANNLAIN, Circuit Judge:

. . . In June 1987, the Portland Police Bureau began investigating cocaine trafficking in the near north and northeast areas of the City of Portland, Oregon. Acting upon information supplied by a confidential informant, the police paid special heed to four individuals, Bradford Lockett, Herbert Lockett, Keith Horsley, and Marcella Manning. Portland police officers began to monitor the activities of Bradford Lockett ("Lockett") and [his girlfriend] Manning, observing Lockett's activities approximately ten to twenty hours per week from October 1987 until his arrest on February 6, 1988.

During this period, Portland police officers observed Lockett engage in numerous suspicious activities. . . During the evening of January 19, 1988, Portland police set up a surveillance of a residence located at 6237 North Montana Street. Manning and another individual were observed through a picture window packaging a controlled substance. . .

On January 25, 1988, Lockett purchased a house for $75,000 from Jo-Ellen Hembree, a real estate broker. At the time of closing, Lockett initially offered $75,000 in cash. When told that this would require the completion of several IRS forms, Lockett left and returned with a number of cashier's checks, which he then used to purchase the house, [although he was unemployed].

On February 6, 1988 . . ., numerous members of the Portland Police Bureau served a search warrant at [another residence] Officer Jacobelli knocked on the door and announced that he was a police officer and that he had a search warrant. After four to five seconds elapsed without a response, the officers pried open the door and entered. Inside, they encountered Lockett, Marcella Manning, and Carla Manning. They also discovered approximately 1,800 grams of cocaine, most of it found either in a bedroom, in a plastic bag resting on the television set, or lying on a large plate on the coffee table in the living room. Some of the cocaine was contained in 80 small baggies, resting on or alongside the coffee table. Also found in the living room was a cooking pot and seven cigarette lighters. The room resembled, according to Officer Brumfield, a cocaine-packaging assembly line. A leather jacket belonging to Lockett was found in a closet. A paging device was discovered on Lockett... A subsequent search of Lockett's residence... revealed currency totaling $25,000.

Lockett was eventually convicted by a jury on four counts: conspiracy to possess cocaine with intent to distribute, conspiracy to distribute cocaine, distri-

CHAPTER 12 *Opinion Testimony –*
Lay and Expert

559

bution of 500 grams or more of cocaine, and possession of 500 grams or more of cocaine with intent to distribute. This timely appeal followed. . .

Lockett contends that the district court erred in allowing Portland Police Officer Derrick Foxworth to testify, as an expert, that only persons intimately involved with a cocaine packaging operation are usually allowed at the packaging site. Lockett does not dispute Foxworth's status as expert witness under Rule 704. By so testifying, Lockett argues, Foxworth was opining as to guilt....

A witness is not permitted to give a direct opinion about the defendant's guilt or innocence. With this caveat, however, an expert may otherwise testify regarding even an ultimate issue to be resolved by the trier of fact... Foxworth's testimony falls in the latter classification rather than the former. Foxworth merely described a typical cocaine packaging operation... The jury was left to determine, on its own, whether there was a cocaine distribution operation in the present case, and whether Lockett's presence was an exception to the general practice of cocaine packaging operations. Foxworth's testimony did not invade the province of the jury....

AFFIRMED.

United States v. Finley

U.S. Court of Appeals for the Ninth Circuit
301 F.3d 1000 (9th Cir. 2001)

BRIGHT, Circuit Judge.

. . . Richard Joseph Finley [was convicted] on one count of making a false claim against the United States ... , one count of attempting to interfere with the administration of the Internal Revenue Service ... , and [two] counts of bank fraud... Finley appeals his conviction... [arguing that] the trial court abused its discretion by excluding the entirety of his psychological expert's testimony...

Finley owned a law bookstore and ran a bar review course for students of non-accredited law schools. In 1992, Finley began looking for investors to assist him in opening a chain of approximately twenty bookstores across the United States. Finley could not obtain traditional bank financing because of a dispute he had with the IRS over a large tax claim. [Finley engaged in various financial transactions to show he was solvent and had the money to pay his debts. The IRS and various banks informed Finley that the financial instruments and transactions were not valid and his case was referred to the FBI and later he was indicted.] . . .

...Finley's counsel filed a notice ... informing the government that it intended to introduce testimony "relating to a mental disease or defect or any other mental condition" relevant to guilt. . . Finley's attorney sent a letter to the government summarizing the expert opinions of Dr. John J. Wicks. Dr. Wicks, a licensed clinical psychologist in California, had examined Finley [and concluded] ... that Finley "has an atypical belief system, a system which is very rigid., ... [and that Mr. Finley did not have the intent to defraud, the requisite mens rea for the crime...]"

It's Latin to Me

The term "mens rea" is the guilty state of mind in a criminal case that the prosecution must prove in order to obtain a conviction.

Thereafter, the prosecution moved ... to preclude Finley from relying on expert mental health testimony at the trial... The government's contention was that [Rule] 704(b) barred the testimony because it addressed an honestly-held "value system."

The court ruled that Dr. Wicks' testimony would be admissible and expressed its understanding that Dr. Wicks could not testify about any element of the crime charged...

The parties proceeded to trial and the defense called Dr. Wicks. Dr. Wicks explained his thirty years of experience in psychology including his extensive experience in conducting psychological evaluations of patients. He stated that he spent two days with Finley, including administering a battery of psychological tests and interviewing him. As a result of the tests and examination, Dr. Wicks testified that Finley has an atypical belief system. Dr. Wicks explained that most people have an open belief system which is subject to change, but some people have closed belief systems. Closed belief systems are more abnormal because they are fixed and rigid. Dr. Wicks then testified how an atypical belief system operates...

... Expert testimony that compels the jury to conclude that the defendant did or did not possess the requisite *mens rea* does not "assist the trier of fact" under Rule 702 because such testimony encroaches on the jury's vital and exclusive function to make credibility determinations. Specifically, Rule 704(b) "limits the expert's testimony by prohibiting him from testifying as to whether the defendant had the mental state or condition that constitutes an element of the crime charged." The "rationale for precluding ultimate opinion testimony applies ... `to any ultimate mental state of the defendant that is relevant to the legal conclusion sought to be proven.'" However, Rule 704(b) allows expert testimony on a defendant's mental state so long as the expert does not draw the ultimate inference or conclusion for the jury. It is, therefore, essential that we distinguish between expert opinions that "necessarily compel" a conclusion about the defendant's *mens rea* and those that do not.

In *Morales* [108 F.3d 1031], we concluded that the district court erred in barring expert testimony under Rule 704(b) because the expert's testimony did not compel the conclusion that Morales lacked the *mens rea* of the crime. Morales, charged with willfully making false bookkeeping entries, wanted an accounting expert to testify that her "understanding of accounting principles" was "weak." We stated:

> Even if the jury believed [the] expert testimony that Morales had a weak grasp of bookkeeping knowledge (and there was evidence to the contrary), the jury would still have had to draw its own inference from that predicate testimony to answer the ultimate factual question — whether Morales willfully made false entries. Morales could have had a weak grasp of bookkeeping principles and still knowingly made false entries.

In *Morales*, we also cited with approval *United States v. Rahm*, in which we reversed the district court's exclusion of a defense expert who was going to testify that Rahm had poor visual perception and consistently overlooked important visual details. In *Rahm*, we drew a distinction between the ultimate issue — whether Rahm knew the bills were counterfeit — and the proffered testimony of the defendant's poor vision, from which the jury could, but was not compelled, to infer that she did not know the bills were counterfeit.

On the other hand, we have applied Rule 704(b) to prohibit certain testimony that does compel a conclusion about *mens rea*. ...[We have] upheld a district court's exclusion of a polygraph expert from testifying that the defendant was truthful when she stated she did not know she was transporting marijuana... We determined that the testimony compelled the conclusion that the defendant did not possess the requisite knowledge to commit the crime because polygraph test results offer an implicit opinion about whether the accused is being deceptive about the very matters at issue in the trial...

Dr. Wicks' expert diagnosis that Finley has an atypical belief system falls into the *Morales / Rahm* line of reasoning.... The jury could have accepted the atypical belief diagnosis and still concluded that Finley knowingly defrauded the banks. If credited, Dr. Wicks' testimony established only that Finley's beliefs were rigid and he would distort or disregard information that ran counter to those beliefs. Dr. Wicks did not, and would not be allowed to, testify about Finley's specific beliefs with regard to the financial instruments. The jury was free to conclude that Finley knew the notes were fraudulent, despite the rigidity of his belief system. [T]he defense was entitled to present evidence so that the jury could infer from the expert's testimony that the defendant lacked the necessary intent to defraud, but such a conclusion was not necessarily compelled by the diagnosis. A psychological diagnosis, unlike a lie detector test, does not automatically entail an opinion on the truth of a patient's statements. Furthermore, the psychological diagnosis can be limited such that it in no way touches upon the specific issues of fact to be resolved by the jury.

We also observe that a jury is free to reject Dr. Wicks' testimony. A jury might decide that Finley was untruthful with Dr. Wicks, as the government so strenuously argues in its brief to this court....

Accordingly, we REVERSE and REMAND for proceedings consistent with this opinion.

---

6. Disclosure of Facts or Data Underlying Expert Opinion

Practice Pointer

Under the Federal Rules of Civil Procedure, Rule 26(a)(2), expert reports are part of mandatory discovery. Rule 26(a)(2)(B) requires an expert report as an early disclosure, 90 days before trial.

An expert opinion may be given, even though the expert does not first disclose the facts or data underlying his opinion. The expert may have to disclose the facts or data underlying his opinion however, if the court requires him to do so or if he is required to during cross-examination. Historically, lawyers avoided the issue by asking experts a long "hypothetical" question which closely mirrored the facts and issues in the actual case. Rule 705 no longer makes this necessary, although some attorneys still use this method for strategic enhancement of the expert's credibility.

Rule 705. Disclosure of Facts or Data Underlying Expert Opinion

The expert may testify in terms of opinion or inference and give reasons therefore without first testifying to the underlying facts or data, unless the court requires otherwise. The expert may in any event be required to disclose the underlying facts or data on cross-examination.

The Advisory Committee Note on Rule 705 states the following:

> The hypothetical question has been the target of a great deal of criticism as encouraging partisan bias, affording an opportunity for summing up in the middle of the case, and as complex and time consuming... While the rule allows counsel to make disclosure of the underlying facts or data as a preliminary to the giving of an expert opinion, if he chooses, the instances in which he is required to do so are reduced. This is true whether the expert bases his opinion on data furnished him at secondhand or observed by him at firsthand...

Marsee v. United States Tobacco Company

U.S. Court of Appeals for the Tenth Circuit
866 F.2d 319 (10th Cir. 1989)

SETH, Circuit Judge.

... The plaintiff, Betty Ann Marsee, brought this products liability action against the defendant, United States Tobacco Company, on behalf of the estate of her late son, Marvin Sean Marsee. Plaintiff alleged that defendant's snuff products caused her son to develop oral cancer which led to his early death. The case was tried to a jury which returned a verdict in favor of defendant...

Plaintiff ... contends that the trial court erred by sustaining defendant's hearsay objection to testimony proffered by Dr. Kent Westbrook, one of plaintiff's experts, on recent cases of oral cancer among young people who dip snuff. Dr. Westbrook was called by plaintiff in her case-in-chief and again in rebuttal to testify on the issue of causation.

During his testimony, Dr. Westbrook expressed his opinion that, in general, the use of snuff is a cause of oral cancer. He also expressed the opinion that Sean Marsee's cancer of the tongue was caused by use of defendant's snuff products. The former opinion was based on Dr. Westbrook's experience in treating oral cancer patients and on his review of the literature on oral cancer. The latter opinion was based on his review of Sean Marsee's case history.

Later, during his redirect examination, Dr. Westbrook testified as follows that he was aware of other young oral cancer patients who had used snuff:

> "Q. ... Do you have any knowledge that would be relied upon generally by people in your field of recent cases of oral cancer in young people who are snuff dippers?

"A. There are some cases that I have talked to doctors about that appear to be oral cancers associated with snuff dipping. These are cases that [plaintiff's counsel] gave me the name of the doctor. I called the doctor and talked with them about the patients."

... Following this exchange, the trial court sustained defendant's hearsay objection to any further testimony by Dr. Westbrook on the details of these conversations. The trial court did not strike the testimony of Dr. Westbrook that he was aware of other oral cancer cases among young snuff dippers. It simply excluded the details of what he had been told over the telephone about these cases...

[Rule] 705 permits inquiry on cross-examination into the facts underlying an expert's opinion even if those facts would be otherwise inadmissible...The substance of Dr. Westbrook's telephone conversations was admitted into evidence. The jury thus heard the doctor testify that he was aware of other cases of oral cancer among young people who chewed tobacco. Only the detailed descriptions of these cases were excluded. Further, a careful review of Dr. Westbrook's testimony reveals that at no time during his lengthy direct and cross-examinations, when his opinions and their bases were extensively explored, did he testify that these cases played any role in the formulation of his opinions. It was only on redirect that Dr. Westbrook mentioned these cases, and even then he did not state that they played a part in forming his opinions. While it can be surmised that these cases helped to reinforce those opinions, the fact that Dr. Westbrook did not mention them in connection with any specific opinion precludes any finding that the trial court's ruling affected a substantial part of plaintiff's case... The judgment of the trial court is AFFIRMED.

---

7. Court Appointed Experts

Although expert witnesses are sought out and hired by the litigants in the case, Rule 706 allows courts themselves to appoint an expert witness who is not associated with either side in the case. It is as though the jury has its own, "neutral" expert. However, the parties can hire and call their own expert witness even if the court appoints one. Most attorneys, however, do not want to appear to be at odds or adverse in any way to the court-appointed expert. Given their perceived "neutrality," a court-appointed expert will almost always have more credibility than an expert witness hired by either side.

Rule 706. Court Appointed Experts

(a) **Appointment.** The court may on its own motion or on the motion of any party enter an order to show cause why expert witnesses should not be appointed, and may request the parties to submit nominations. The court may appoint any expert witnesses agreed upon by the parties, and may appoint expert witnesses of its own selection. An expert witness shall not be appointed by the court unless the witness consents to act. A witness so appointed shall be informed of the witness' duties by the court in writing, a copy of which shall be filed with the clerk, or at a conference in which the parties shall have the opportunity to participate. A witness so appointed shall advise the parties of the witness' findings, if any; the witness' deposition may be taken by any party; and the witness may be called to testify by the court or any party. The witness shall be subject to cross-examination by each party, including a party calling the witness.

(b) **Compensation.** Expert witnesses so appointed are entitled to reasonable compensation in whatever sum the court may allow. The compensation thus fixed is payable from funds which may be provided by law in criminal cases and civil actions and proceedings involving just compensation under the fifth Amendment. In other civil actions and proceedings the compensation shall be paid by the parties in such proportion and at such time as the court directs, and thereafter charged in like manner as other costs.

(c) **Disclosure of Appointment.** In the exercise of its discretion, the court may authorize disclosure to the jury of the fact that the court appointed the expert witness.

(d) **Parties' Experts of Own Selection.** Nothing in this rule limits the parties in calling expert witnesses of their own selection.

Advisory Committee's Note -706

The practice of shopping for experts, the venality of some experts, and the reluctance of many reputable experts to involve themselves in litigation, have been matters of deep concern. Though the contention is made that court appointed experts acquire an aura of infallibility to which they are not entitled. . . , the trend is increasingly to provide for their use. While experience indicates that actual appointment is a relatively infrequent occurrence, the assumption may be made that the availability of the procedure in itself decreases the need for resorting to it. The ever-present possibility that the judge may appoint an expert in a given case must inevitably exert a sobering effect on the expert witness of a party and upon the person utilizing his services....

Subdivision (a) ... provide[s] specifically for the appointment either on motion of a party or on the judge's own motion. A provision subjecting the court appointed expert to deposition procedures has been incorporated. The rule has been revised to make definite the right of any party, including the party calling him, to cross-examine...

C. Scientific Evidence

No specific rule addresses the admissibility of scientific evidence. Rather, scientific evidence is governed by the rules regulating expert testimony generally. Interposed in this framework of rules and their impact on admissibility is a seemingly endless debate on types of scientific evidence. Scientific evidence, it has been suggested, falls into one of two categories: hard sciences and soft sciences. So-called soft sciences are typically considered to be psychology, political science, or those sciences that tend to use more subjective measures and designs as opposed to objective measures and designs.

> We often view hard science as the only type of science. But science (from the Latin *scientia* -- knowledge) is something much more general, which isn't defined by decimal places and controlled experiments. It means the enterprise of explaining and predicting -- gaining knowledge of -- natural phenomena, by continually testing one's theories against empirical evidence. The world is full of phenomena that are intellectually challenging and important to understand, but that can't be measured to several decimal places in labs. They constitute much of ecology, evolution, and animal behavior; much of psychology and human behavior; and all the phenomena of human societies, including cultural anthropology, economics, history, and government.

> *Jared Diamond*

> *Discover (August 1987)*

1. Hard Sciences

This thinking – that hard science is the only type of science – often spills over into our judicial system. When dealing with actual hard sciences, the problem does not seem to be a problem. Hard sciences such as math, physics, and the like usually fit neatly into the *Daubert* models of reliability which make judges more comfortable. As such, admission of evidence based on hard sciences doesn't usually permit much difficulty. However, some areas of seemingly hard sciences do not fit so neatly into the comfort level of the judges. This next case shows this challenge:

Head v. Lithonia Corp., Inc.

U.S. Court of Appeals for the Tenth Circuit
881 F.2d 941 (10th Cir. 1989)

John P. Moore, Circuit Judge.

Defendant Lithonia Corporation, Inc., appeals from a judgment on a jury verdict in favor of plaintiff Barbara Head ... based on products liability. An Oklahoma jury awarded plaintiff $100,000 for the permanent injury she sustained when the reflector in one of defendant's lights fell and struck her on the head. Defendant now complains the court erred as a matter of law in ... allowing plaintiff's expert to testify in an area outside of his expertise, and admitting evidence based on data that is not reasonably relied upon by experts in the field. ... However, because the district court failed to address defendant's objection to the introduction of certain medical testing without a proper foundation, we vacate the judgment and remand for a new trial.

In November 1985, plaintiff was injured at work when the reflector portion of a hanging, fluorescent light fixture manufactured by defendant fell and struck her on the side of her head. Plaintiff was standing under the light while a fellow employee, who had released one end of the shade to remove the bulbs and check on a possible electrical problem, was attempting to fix the light. Though not knocked to the ground or unconscious, plaintiff felt a knot raised on the side of her head. She reported the incident to her employer three weeks later and visited the company doctor for treatment, complaining of headaches, dizziness, and occasional blackouts. Plaintiff was placed on medical leave and later terminated.

Plaintiff initiated this action alleging the quarter-turn fastener on the Lithonia light was defective in design and failed to properly secure the reflector in place in its grooved channel. The defect, she claimed, made the product unreasonably dangerous. Plaintiff sought damages of $1,250,000 for the permanent injuries to her head and neck. Her husband, Ray Head, alleged damages of $100,000 for loss of consortium.

What's That?

Loss of Consortium refers to refers to the deprivation of the benefits of a family relationship due to injuries caused by a tortfeasor.

... Plaintiff's medical expert, Dr. Michael Haugh, her treating neurologist, testified by videotaped deposition and explained his conclusions based on patient's history, clinical exam, and various tests. Although the results of plaintiff's electroencephalogram (EEG), computerized axial tomography (CAT-scan), and clinical exam were normal, one test, topographical brain mapping, apparently pinpointed the location of her injury. On the basis of her history and the topo-graphical brain map, Dr. Haugh concluded plaintiff suffered from post-concussive syndrome and pre-scribed certain medications to alleviate the headaches. ... The jury returned a verdict for plaintiff and awarded her $100,000. Ray Head received no recovery.

During the trial, plaintiff presented evidence of her neck and head injury by introducing the videotaped deposition of her treating neurologist, Dr. Haugh. Dr. Haugh described his clinical examination and findings, explained the neurological tests he administered, and related his observations about plaintiff's condition based on this history. Dr. Haugh described the topographical brain map test he performed which, he explained, was a computerized enhancement of the EEG, using stimulation techniques "to bring out abnormalities on the EEG." When plaintiff attempted to introduce exhibits representing the results of the topographical brain mapping test, defendant objected contending a proper foundation had not been offered for the test. After the jury watched the videotape, defendant renewed its objection to the court. The objection was overruled without explanation. Defendant now contends the court erred in permitting plaintiff to introduce the test results of topographical brain mapping without requiring plaintiff to establish the necessary foundation for the reliability of the test.

Rule 703 of the Federal Rules of Evidence states:

> The facts or data in the particular case upon which an expert bases an opinion or inference may be those perceived by or made known to the expert at or before the hearing. If of a type reasonably relied upon by experts in the particular field in forming opinions or inferences upon the subject, the facts or data need not be admissible in evidence.

Although the rule broadens the basis on which expert opinions may be offered "to bring the judicial practice into line with the practice of the experts themselves when not in court," the advisory notes caution:

If it be feared that enlargement of permissible data may tend to break down the rules of exclusion unduly, notice should be taken that the rule requires that the facts or data "be of a type reasonably relied upon by experts in the particular field." The language would not warrant admitting in evidence the opinion of an "accidentologist" as to the point of impact in an automobile collision based on statements of bystanders, since this requirement is not satisfied.

The limitation that the facts and data "be of a type reasonably relied upon by experts in the field" provides a mechanism by which the court can evaluate the trustworthiness of the underlying data on which the expert relies. This approach does not mean that the expert's opinion must be generally accepted in the scientific community to be "sufficiently reliable and probative to support a jury finding. What is necessary is that the expert arrived at his ... opinion by relying upon *methods* that other experts in his field would reasonably rely upon in forming their own, possibly different opinions, about what caused the patient's disease."

Lithonia asserts that topographical brain mapping is not a method relied upon by other neurologists to establish the disorder of which plaintiff complained. During cross-examination, Lithonia asked Dr. Haugh if the American Academy of Neurology considered topographical brain mapping a medically accepted technique. Dr. Haugh responded: "The technique at the present time has much controversy regarding it. And there have been pros and cons on both sides. And at the present time I'm not aware that the Academy has made a particular position on it."

While recognizing that the procedure may have gotten past the "experimental stage," Dr. Haugh was not able to explain the methodology in the clinical setting: "I do-I don't-I think in some ways it is and other ways it isn't at this time. That's a vague answer and I'm sorry, but that's the best I can do with that."

Dr. Haugh stated that all of his findings based on the clinical examination and test results were normal and did not substantiate plaintiff's complaint. Only when Dr. Haugh coupled plaintiff's topographical brain map with her medical history, was he able to conclude that patient suffered from post-concussive syndrome.

Through cross-examination ... defense counsel elicited testimony that topographical brain mapping remained relatively experimental and was not accepted by other experts in the specialty of neurology or the American Academy of Neurology. Defendant properly placed the inquiry before the court. However, despite Lithonia's objection to the admission of both the hearsay statements, exhibits representing pictures of the brain map, and the statements based on this test, the district court made no inquiry into the reliability of the foundation of the expert's opinion to determine its admissibility.

In *Barrel of Fun, Inc.*, 739 F.2d 1028, the Fifth Circuit vacated a judgment on the ground that expert testimony based solely on the results of a psychological stress evaluation (PSE) was inadmissible because the test itself was flawed. Likening the PSE results to those of a polygraph test, the court noted that plaintiff as the proponent of this scientific evidence "has the burden of showing as a predicate to its admission that the proffered test has achieved scientific acceptability and that the test has a reasonable measure of trust-worthiness."   The Fifth Circuit found defendant State Farm had failed to meet that burden by simply stating the PSE test was used by the fire marshal's office.

In our case, plaintiff's counsel asked Dr. Haugh when he first began using topographical brain mapping. Dr. Haugh explained that he was the first neurologist to use the test in the Tulsa area and maintained the equipment in his office. Over defense objection, Dr. Haugh proceeded to offer his personal opinion of the value of the topographical brain mapping compared to "EEG traditional methods? Is one any better than the other, in your opinion?" Aside from his description of the actual test and this testimony, Dr. Haugh offered no other information on which the trier of fact could understand the reliability of the test, i.e., whether the scientific community has accepted the test.

Under Fed.R.Evid. 703 experts are given wide latitude to testify on facts otherwise not admissible in evidence and "to broaden the acceptable bases of expert opinion." Implicit in the rule, however, is the court's guidance to "make a preliminary determination pursuant to Rule 104(a) whether the particular underlying data is of a kind that is reasonably relied upon by experts in the particular field in reaching conclusions. This determination must be made on "a case-by-case basis and should focus on the reliability of the opinion and its foundation rather than merely on the fact that it was based, technically speaking, upon hearsay." Thus, the district court "may not abdicate its independent responsibilities to decide if the bases meet minimum standards of reliability as a condition of admissibility."

In this case, we believe the court abused its discretion in failing to address defendant's objection to Dr. Haugh's testimony based on topographical brain mapping. Rule 703 contemplates that the court will play some role in the assessment of expert testimony offered to a jury. While the trial process can leverage the probative value of this testimony, the process presupposes the court's guidance. Because the record does not sufficiently establish the trustworthiness of topographical brain mapping or its acceptance in the relevant scientific community, we VACATE the judgment and REMAND for a new trial.

———————

2. Soft Sciences

After *Daubert* and its progeny, the question arose as to how courts must deal with scientific evidence which did not fit into the *Daubert* paradigm. It's easy to analyze scientific evidence with specific tests, criteria, studies, peer review publications, etc. Specifically, although not exclusively, the issue arose as to how a court, in exercising its gatekeeping function, might deal with soft sciences. Soft science refers to those areas of science that rely in large part, if not exclusively, on subjective criteria for evaluation as opposed to objective criteria. Soft sciences can encompass many issues.

Soft sciences, and evidence related to it, creep into many modern trials. In family law cases, psychologists and psychiatrists frequently offer evidence as to parenting abilities, relationships between parents and children, and conclusions as to psychological abuse and neglect. Such experts also provide to fact-finders their opinions as to how certain events will affect children and their relationships with siblings and parents in the future. Psychologists frequently testify in criminal cases with regard to sanity or insanity; the ability for defendants (on a psychological basis) to commit the offense to which they are accused; provide insight as to human perceptions and the like. Psychologists, psychiatrists and other mental health professionals frequently find themselves offering evidence in modern trials in areas called "soft sciences."

Decisions as to the admission or exclusion of evidence related to soft sciences are as varied as the cases that spawn them. Many decisions approve the testimony of soft sciences while criticizing rulings that exclude evidence. Others question its validity. The following case illustrates both questionable "scientific" evidence as well as aspects of psychology as it relates to expert testimony.

United States v. Powers

U.S. Court of Appeals for the Fourth Circuit
59 F.3d 1460 (4th Cir. 1995)

Grady William Powers appeals his conviction for aggravated sexual abuse of a minor. Powers challenges several of the district court's evidentiary rulings....

I.

Powers was accused in 1992 of repeatedly raping his daughter, Brandi Powers, over the course of ten months between November 1989 and September 1990 when she was nine and ten years old. During the time of the alleged rapes, Powers lived with Brandi, her brothers and sisters, and her mother Joyce Powers-now Joyce Powers Gregory (Gregory)-on the Cherokee Indian Reservation in Robbinsville, North Carolina. ... The testimony at trial reflected that Powers repeatedly raped and molested Brandi, often several times a day, and that he would send her brother Brent out of the house so that he could sexually assault her. The record further reflects that, in the fall of 1990, Brandi told her brother Brent that she did not want to be left alone with her father because he had been sexually molesting her. Brent told their mother, who confronted Powers. Powers initially denied Gregory's allegation about the incest, but then admitted to molesting Brandi. Gregory told him to move out of the house. Gregory and Powers were later divorced. Gregory reported the rapes to the authorities in 1992.

Powers was indicted on ten counts of engaging in sexual acts with a person under the age of twelve.... He pled not guilty and went to trial. A jury convicted Powers on all ten counts....

...

IV.

Finally, Powers argues that the district court erred in excluding testimony of two experts who would have testified that Powers did not exhibit the characteristics of a fixated pedophile. Expert testimony explaining scientific evidence is admissible under Fed.R.Evid. 702 if it will assist the jury "to understand the evidence or determine a fact in issue." When determining admissibility under Rule 702, a trial judge must ensure that all scientific testimony or evidence admitted is both relevant and reliable, and that its evidentiary reliability is based upon scientific validity. *Daubert v. Merrell Dow Pharmaceuticals, Inc.* As we recently noted:

> [T]he Daubert Court set forth a two-part test which must be met in order for such expert testimony to be properly admitted under the FRE: (1) the expert testimony must consist of "scientific knowledge"-that is, the testimony must be supported by appropriate validation; and (2) the evidence or testimony must "assist the trier of fact to understand the evidence or to determine a fact in issue."

> *United States v. Dorsey,* 45 F.3d 809, 813 (4th Cir.1995)....

A.

The first question we must confront is whether the results of a penile plethysmograph test meet the scientific validity prong of *Daubert*. Specifically, Powers argues that the district court erred in excluding the testimony of a clinical psychologist who would have testified that the results of a penile plethysmograph test did not indicate that Powers exhibited pedophilic characteristics. The penile plethysmograph, or arousal, test measured Powers' sexual arousal in response to pictures of nude females of various age groups. The district court excluded this evidence because, in its opinion, the test did not satisfy the "scientific validity" prong of *Daubert*.

In *Dorsey*, we enumerated the factors that the Supreme Court directed trial courts to consider when evaluating the scientific validity of proposed evidence:

> (1) Whether the theory or technique used by the expert can be, and has been, tested;

(2) Whether the theory or technique has been subjected to peer review and publication;

(3) The known or potential rate of error of the method used; and

(4) The degree of the method's or conclusion's acceptance within the relevant scientific community.

The evidence produced at trial clearly showed that these factors weighed against the admission of the penile plethysmograph test results. First, the Government proffered evidence that the scientific literature addressing penile plethysmography does not regard the test as a valid diagnostic tool because, although useful for treatment of sex offenders, it has no accepted standards in the scientific community. Second, the Government also introduced evidence before the judge that a vast majority of incest offenders who do not admit their guilt, such as Powers, show a normal reaction to the test. The Government argues that such false negatives render the test unreliable. Powers failed to introduce any indicia, let alone a sufficient level, of reliability to rebut the Government's evidence. Accordingly, in light of extensive, unanswered evidence weighing against the scientific validity of the penile plethysmograph test, we cannot say that the district court abused its discretion.

B.

Next, Powers argues that the district court abused its discretion in excluding the testimony of Dr. Anthony Sciara. Dr. Sciara would have testified that Powers did not demonstrate the psychological profile of a fixated pedophile. The district court ruled that Powers failed to establish either the relevance or the scientific validity of psychological profiling as applied to the facts at issue. The arguments on appeal, however, focus our attention on the second prong of Daubert, namely, whether the evidence is "relevant" to the issue under consideration.

Once again, *Dorsey* provides the analytical framework for our analysis:

In determining whether the evidence meets the second prong of the two part test-that is, whether the evidence will be helpful to the trier of fact-the Supreme Court warned that throughout an admissibility determination, a judge must be mindful of other evidentiary rules, such as FRE 403, which permits the exclusion of relevant evidence "if its probative value is substantially outweighed by the danger of unfair prejudice, confusion of the issues, or misleading the jury."

* * *

[The *Daubert*] Court concluded:

Conjectures that are probably wrong are of little use ... in the project of reaching a quick, final, and binding legal judgment-often of great consequence-about a particular set of events in the past. We recognize that in practice, a gatekeeping role for the judge, no matter how flexible, inevitably on occasion will prevent the jury from learning of authentic insights and innovations. That, nevertheless, is the balance that is struck by the Rules of Evidence designed not for the exhaustive search for cosmic understanding but for the particularized resolution of legal disputes.

Powers argues that Dr. Sciara's psychological profile of him meets the relevancy criteria due to the direct relationship between the subject matter of the test and the crime charged. Counsel for Powers proffered the following evidence concerning Dr. Sciara's psychological profile. Based on numerous interviews with child sex abusers and other research, Dr. Sciara has created a profile of the common characteristics of incest abusers. According to Sciara, the largest common denominator among incest abusers is that forty percent of the time they exhibit the characteristics of fixated pedophiles. Powers' tests, however, revealed that he did not share this characteristic. From this data, Powers argues that "[t]his testimony was clearly relevant for the purpose of demonstrating that [he] was psychologically unlikely to have committed the alleged crimes charged against him." We disagree.

The difficulty with Powers' argument is that he fails to provide a substantial link between the expert testimony and his theory of defense. At most, this evidence would have shown only that Powers did not belong to a group that comprised forty percent of incest abusers. Powers, however, was charged with statutory rape of his daughter-incest abuse-not with being a fixated pedophile. To be relevant, this testimony must show, in a very real way, that because Powers did not share a characteristic common to a large minority of incest perpetrators, he was less likely to be an incest perpetrator himself. The district court clearly understood this fundamental flaw when the testimony was proffered:

THE COURT: [L]et's say that we did allow [Dr. Sciara] now to testify [without basing his opinion on the results of the penile plethysmography test]. And all he's going to say is that this is not the kind of man who has a fixation on children.

[DEFENSE COUNSEL]: Correct, Your Honor.

THE COURT: What does that tell us?

[DEFENSE COUNSEL]: Judge, I don't think it is end all and be all of our defense. I think it's an important piece of evidence for the jury to have.

THE COURT: Why? … [The Court questioned Defense Counsel about whether this evidence would really make it more likely than not that Powers did not commit the offense.]

[DEFENSE COUNSEL]: … I don't think there's any question that some people that aren't fixated pedophiles commit incest. But I think it would be a substantial percentage and I think it is information that is relevant.

If Powers had offered supporting evidence showing that those who are not fixated pedophiles are less likely to commit incest abuse (the crime with which Powers was charged), Dr. Sciara's testimony might have been relevant. However, Powers offered no evidence to link a non-proclivity for pedophilia with a non-proclivity for incest abuse, even after the district court gave Powers ample opportunity to introduce evidence showing the relevance of Dr. Sciara's testimony. Accordingly, we find that the district court did not abuse its discretion in excluding this evidence because Powers failed to prove either its relevancy or "a valid scientific connection to the pertinent inquiry" of whether he committed incest.

…

For the reasons stated above, we affirm the judgment of the district court.

AFFIRMED.

───────────────

Executive Summary

General Rule Against Admissibility of Opinion Evidence. In general, other than when character evidence is allowed either under Rule 404(a) (general character of a criminal defendant or victim), or under Rule 608(a) (character for truthfulness of a testifying witness), opinion testimony is inadmissible. The reason it is inadmissible is because witnesses are called on to give *factual* testimony based on their Rule 602 personal knowledge, not to give their own personal *conclusions or educated guesses* as to what may have occurred in the case. However, there are two important exceptions to this general prohibition and they are set forth in the Rule 700 series. In certain circumstances, (1) a *lay witness* can offer her opinion about the facts she observed, and (2) an *expert witness* can offer her opinion about a legitimate scientific, technical, or other specialized knowledge area in which the expert witness is duly qualified. Both lay and expert opinion testimony must also be "helpful to the fact finder" in order to be admissible.

Lay Opinion Testimony. Under Rule 701, lay opinion testimony is allowed but only when it is rationally based upon the witness's perception (what she actually witnessed or perceived first-hand), and is helpful to a clear understanding of her testimony or to the determination of a fact issue. Lay opinion testimony cannot be based on specialized scientific or technical knowledge. The factors that make up the lay witness opinion, or impression, must be difficult or impossible to articulate such that the opinion is a helpful, and even a necessary, way to relate to the fact finder the sum and substance of a witness' testimony. For example, an opinion as to the age of a person would be helpful far beyond mere factual descriptions of what the person looked like. (*Yazzie*). Other examples can include whether someone was intoxicated, how fast a car was moving, land or personal services values, the identification of voice or handwriting samples under Rules 901(b)(2) or (5) for authentication purposes, etc. However, if the opinion is something that is not helpful to a fact finder and simply amounts to a factual inference or legal conclusion of the witness that the fact finder could make on its own, based upon the evidence presented, then the opinion would be inadmissible. (*Gorby*). Thus, an accident report of an eyewitness that legally concludes fault and negligence is inadmissible because the fact finder already has all the evidence it needs to come to that legal conclusion on its own. (*Kostelecky*).

Expert Opinion Testimony. Under Rule 702, if a witness is a qualified expert in a legitimate scientific, technical, or other specialized knowledge area that would be helpful to the average fact finder to better understand the factual issues in a case (who would not ordinarily be familiar with that area of expertise), then that expert witness can offer her expert opinion testimony. Unlike Rule 701 lay opinion testimony, Rule 702 expert opinion testimony does *not* have to be based on the personal perception of the expert witness.

Qualification of the Expert Witness. Expert witnesses must first be qualified in a particular field or area before they are allowed to give their expert opinion. Just because the expert may be qualified in one area, does not necessarily mean that the expert is also qualified in another, related area. (*Polston*). It is important to inform the fact-finder during this process about the expert's qualifications, not only for admissibility purposes, but also for persuasive purposes.

Reliability of the Underlying Science or Technical Knowledge or Experience of the Expert Witness. The expert witness must be qualified in a "legitimate" or "reliable" area of expertise. Rule 702(2) states that the expert opinion testimony should be "the product of reliable principles and methods." Historically, the test was whether the area of expertise had gained "general acceptance" as a valid area of expertise in the field. (*Frye*). This standard eventually gave way to the "*Daubert*" standard where general acceptance is now merely a factor to be considered. There is no longer such a rigid time lag making all "cutting edge" areas inadmissible.

Even more important, in "*Daubert*" there was a call for the trial judge to take back more of the admissibility decision (to become more of a "gatekeeper") so that admissibility decisions in specialized fields did not, as a practical matter, simply get made by the leading experts in their various fields of expertise. (*Daubert*). The Supreme Court used the *Joiner* case to send a message to all lower courts that they should take their judicial gatekeeper role very seriously (keeping animal studies out of an inquiry into human carcinogens and tort causation). The Court then expanded that gatekeeper role beyond science and technology to apply to areas of "experience" in other "specialized" non-scientific areas, such as a visual tire wear on truck tires. (*Kuhmo Tire*).

Expert vs. Lay Opinion Opinion. Sometimes litigants will try to qualify a lay witness as an expert in order to bolster the witness's credibility and/or allow testimony not based on personal knowledge. Sometimes litigants will try to have a witness testify improperly in both capacities, testifying as a lay witness regarding some issues, and as an expert witness regarding others. For these reasons, it is important to keep these capacities separate and not allow lay witnesses to testify as experts or vice vice-versa, (*Freeman*), unless such a delineation is clear and proper.

Basis of Expert Opinion. Under Rule 703, an expert witness can rely upon any evidence, even inadmissible evidence, in order to arrive at her expert opinion, as long as other experts in the field typically rely on such evidence when rendering an expert opinion. Inadmissible underlying evidence will remain inadmissible, unless it satisfies the "reverse" 403 standard (its probative value substantially outweighs is prejudicial effect), but the expert opinion itself will be admissible in either event (*South Central Petroleum*).

Opinion on the Ultimate Issue. Under Rule 704, a witness's opinion can embrace the ultimate issue in the case, but it cannot be expressed as a pure legal conclusion. For example, a witness cannot state that a defendant is guilty of cocaine trafficking, however, the witness can describe how a typical cocaine packing operation works and then leave it up to the fact finder to determine whether defendant's activities fit the description. (*Lockett*). A psychological diagnosis is allowed under 704(b), as long as there is still room for the fact finder to accept or deny the diagnosis and still determine whether defendant had the *mens rea* to commit the crime. (*Finley*).

Facts or Data Underlying the Opinion. Under Rule 705, an expert witness may provide an expert opinion on a matter, either *before, or after*, disclosing all of the facts or data relied upon in arriving at that expert opinion. It is no longer necessary for an expert to be asked a hypothetical question first. The presentation order is now purely a matter of strategic persuasion. In any event, disclosure of the opinion and its bases are a part of pretrial discovery. However, an expert needs to make it clear that she relied on certain facts or data, even if otherwise inadmissible, because if not, then those underlying facts or data will continue to be inadmissible. (*Marsee*).

Court-Appointed Experts. Under Rule 706, an expert witness may be appointed by the court. As such, a court-appointed expert often is perceived as "neutral," without any specific advocacy agenda for either litigant.

"Hard" Sciences. Although at first glance one might suppose that "hard sciences" like math, physics, orthopedics, etc., present no controversy regarding admissibility as legitimate and reliable areas of expertise upon which an expert witness can offer an expert opinion. While that is largely true, simply because an alleged area of expertise involves what looks like a hard science should not be automatically accepted without the trial judge playing more of a gatekeeper role. (*Head*).

"Soft" Sciences. Soft sciences seem to involve more subjectivity, and room for interpretation, and possible manipulation, than do hard sciences. As a result, many types of sciences that fall victim to the criticism of being "junk science" tend to come more from the "soft sciences" category. (*Powers*). However, soft sciences (sociological and psychological areas, and behavioral science of particular groups, or even political science, etc.) can at times still play a vital role in trials and a fact finder's search for the truth in a complicated case. But it requires the judge, in her engaged gatekeeper role, to apply faithfully the *Daubert* standard and Rule 702 in both soft and hard sciences cases.

CHAPTER 13

Privileges

A. Introduction

> **Rule 501. General Rule**
>
> Except as otherwise required by the Constitution of the United States or provided by Act of Congress or in rules prescribed by the Supreme Court pursuant to statutory authority, the privilege of a witness, person, government, State or political subdivision thereof shall be governed by the principles of the common law as they may be interpreted by the courts of the United States in the light of reason and experience. However, in civil actions and proceedings, with respect to an element of a claim or defense as to which State law supplies the rule of decision, the privilege of a witness, person, government, State or political subdivision thereof shall be determined in accordance with State law.

Privileges generally protect against disclosure of confidential communications between people with certain legally recognized relationships, such as attorneys and clients, husbands and wives, or psychotherapists and patients. They operate like other rules that exclude evidence, except that privileges apply to all stages of judicial proceedings, and persons other than litigants can assert them. Protecting these communications, however, often comes at the price of suppressing relevant facts in litigation. Nonetheless, it is thought that protecting these relationships is more important than disclosing the truth about these facts.

The Federal Rules of Evidence do not contain a specific listing of individual privileges. Originally, the Advisory Committee proposed thirteen privilege rules. Congress, however, was highly concerned about codifying specific privileges that would override state law in diversity cases and lead to forum shopping between state and federal courts depending upon whose privilege rules were more favorable to a party. Congress therefore rejected the proposed rules and left the law

For More Information

This chapter will cover several of the more commonly recognized privileges under federal common law, those of attorney-client, husband-wife, and psychotherapist-patient, as well as some that have not gained universal approval but are still avidly debated, those of journalist-source, clergy-penitent, and parent-child. Other privileges that are not studied in this chapter, such as executive privilege, presidential and congressional privileges, informer's privilege, and trade secret privileges, are discussed and analyzed in PAUL ROTHSTEIN & SUSAN CRUMP, FEDERAL TESTIMONIAL PRIVILEGES (2008).

of privileges in its prior common law state. In their place, Congress drafted Rule 501, which provides that in civil cases, "with respect to an element of a claim or defense as to which state law supplies the rule of decision," privilege is dictated by state law. Thus, in diversity cases, federal courts apply state privilege law; in federal criminal and civil cases, federal courts apply federal privilege law as it "may [be] interpreted by the courts of the United States in the light of reason and experience."

The first privilege we will study is the oldest of the common law privileges, that of the attorney-client privilege.

B. Attorney-Client Privilege

The primary purpose of the attorney-client privilege is to encourage freedom of communication between counsel and prospective or current clients by removing the fear that the contents of their communication will be publically revealed. The privilege is based on the theory that an attorney will be in the best position to evaluate a client's circumstances and give legal advice when the client is free to disclose the good, the bad, and even the ugly about her case.

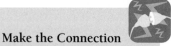

Make the Connection

An attorney is also under an ethical obligation, separate from the attorney-client privilege, to maintain a client's secrets. This obligation applies in all circumstances, not just in judicial proceedings, and is something you will study in a Professional Responsibility course.

Originally, the attorney was the holder of the privilege based on the theory that it would be unethical for an attorney to reveal anything said in confidence by his client. Today, however, the privilege is held by the client whose interests are said to be furthered by its exercise. It may be claimed on behalf of the client by the attorney or others representing the client's interests.

1. Who is the Client?

A client may be a living person. A client may also be any legal entity, public or private, who consults an attorney with a view towards obtaining legal services or is rendered legal services by an attorney. But, who in these organizations are the clients? Potentially, a legal entity may range from a two person partnership to a mega corporation with tens of thousands of officers, directors, employees and agents. But are they all considered clients for purposes of the attorney-client privilege?

Upjohn Co. v. United States

Supreme Court of the United States
449 U.S. 383 (1981)

Justice REHNQUIST delivered the opinion of the Court.

...Petitioner Upjohn Co. manufactures and sells pharmaceuticals here and abroad. In January 1976 independent accountants conducting an audit of one of Upjohn's foreign subsidiaries discovered that the subsidiary made payments to or for the benefit of foreign government officials in order to secure government business. The accountants, so informed

What's That?

"Outside counsel" is an attorney who is hired by a client, but who normally represents other clients. "Inside (or in-house) counsel" is an attorney who works full time for a client.

Practice Pointer

Keeping privileged material confidential is critical for the assertion of any privilege. Without instructions such as those that accompanied the *Upjohn* questionnaires, it is likely that Upjohn would have waived the attorney-client privilege under these circumstances. Labeling material as "confidential" and consistently treating it as such, for example, by limiting access or preventing the inadvertent disclosure in response to large document discovery requests, are several ways to prevent waiver.

petitioner, Mr. Gerard Thomas, Upjohn's Vice President, Secretary, and General Counsel. Thomas is a member of the Michigan and New York Bars, and has been Upjohn's General Counsel for 20 years. He consulted with outside counsel and R. T. Parfet, Jr., Upjohn's Chairman of the Board. It was decided that the company would conduct an internal investigation of what were termed "questionable payments." As part of this investigation the attorneys prepared a letter containing a questionnaire which was sent to "All Foreign General and Area Managers" over the Chairman's signature. The letter began by noting recent disclosures that several American companies made "possibly illegal" payments to foreign government officials and emphasized that the management needed full information concerning any such payments made by Upjohn. The letter indicated that the Chairman had asked Thomas, identified as "the company's General Counsel," "to conduct an investigation for the purpose of determining the nature and magnitude of any payments made by the Upjohn Company or any of its subsidiaries to any employee or official of a foreign government." The questionnaire sought detailed information concerning such payments.

Food for Thought

Given that Upjohn had already submitted a preliminary report to the IRS describing the questionable payments, why do you think the IRS wanted to obtain the questionnaires and the interview notes? Could these materials provide the IRS with any additional information, or was the IRS just fishing?

Managers were instructed to treat the investigation as "highly confidential" and not to discuss it with anyone other than Upjohn employees who might be helpful in providing the requested information. Responses were to be sent directly to Thomas. Thomas and outside counsel also interviewed the recipients of the questionnaire and some 33 other Upjohn officers or employees as part of the investigation. [Upjohn voluntarily submitted its preliminary report to the Securities and Exchange Commission disclosing certain questionable payments, with a copy to the Internal Revenue Service. The IRS immediately began an investigation to determine the tax consequences of the payments. The Service issued a summons demanding production of all responses to the questionnaires and all notes of the interviews. The company refused disclosure on the grounds of attorney-client privilege and work-product privilege. The lower court denied protection].

Federal Rule of Evidence 501 provides that "the privilege of a witness ... shall be governed by the principles of the common law as they may be interpreted by the courts of the United States in light of reason and experience." The attorney-client privilege is the oldest of the privileges for confidential communications known to the common law. Its purpose is to encourage full and frank communication between attorneys and their clients and thereby promote broader public interests in the observance of law and administration of justice. The privilege recognizes that sound legal advice or advocacy serves public ends and that such advice or advocacy depends upon the lawyer's being fully informed by the client. "The lawyer-client privilege rests on the need for the advocate and counselor to know all that relates to the client's reasons for seeking representation if the professional mission is to be carried out." ... This rationale for the privilege has long been recognized by the Court. Admittedly complications in the application of the privilege arise when the client is a corporation, which in theory is an artificial creature of the law, and not an individual; but this Court has assumed that the privilege applies when the client is a corporation ... and the Government does not contest this proposition.

The Court of Appeals, however, considered the application of the privilege in the corporate context to present a "different problem," since the client was an inanimate entity and "only the senior management, guiding and integrating the several operations can be said to possess an identity analogous to the corporation as a whole." The first case to articulate the so-called "control group test" adopted by the court below reflected a similar conceptual approach:

> [I]f the employee making the communication, of whatever rank he may be, is in a position to control or even to take a substantial part in a decision about any action which the corporation may take upon the advice of the attorney, then, in effect, *he is (or personifies) the corporation*.

Such a view, we think, overlooks the fact that the privilege exists to protect not only the giving of professional advice to those who can act on it but also the giving of information to the lawyer to enable him to give sound and informed advice. The first step in the resolution of any legal problem is ascertaining the factual background and sifting through the facts with an eye to the legally relevant.

In the case of the individual client the provider of information and the person who acts on the lawyer's advice are one and the same. In the corporate context, however, it will frequently be employees beyond the control group as defined by the court below--"officers and agents ... responsible for directing [the company's] actions in response to legal advice"--who will possess the information needed by the corporation's lawyers. Middle-level - and indeed lower-level-employees can, by actions within the scope of their employment, embroil the corporation in serious legal difficulties, and it is only natural that these employees would have the relevant information needed by corporate counsel if he is adequately to advise the client with respect to such actual or potential difficulties.

The control group test adopted by the court below thus frustrates the very purpose of the privilege by discouraging the communication of relevant information by employees of the client to attorneys seeking to render legal advice to the client corporation. The attorney's advice will also frequently be more significant to noncontrol group members than to those who officially sanction the advice, and the control group test makes it more difficult to

Food for Thought

Do you really think that Upjohn's employees would not respond frankly to these questionnaires without the protection of a privilege? Do you think that the employees even knew about the attorney-client privilege in a corporate context, or if they did, that they understood its application under the "control group" test? If not, how does this affect the Majority's reasoning?

convey full and frank legal advice to the employees who will put into effect the client corporation's policy.

The narrow scope given the attorney-client privilege by the court below not only makes it difficult for corporate attorneys to formulate sound advice when their client is faced with a specific legal problem but also threatens to limit the valuable efforts of corporate counsel to ensure their client's compliance with the law. In light of the vast and complicated array of regulatory legislation confronting the modern corporation, corporations, unlike most individuals, "constantly go to lawyers to find out how to obey the law," particularly since compliance with the law in this area is hardly an instinctive matter...

The communications at issue were made by Upjohn employees to counsel for Upjohn acting as such, at the direction of corporate superiors in order to secure legal advice from counsel. As the Magistrate found, "Mr. Thomas consulted with the Chairman of the Board and outside counsel and thereafter conducted a factual investigation to determine the nature and extent of the questionable payments *and to be in a position to give legal advice to the company with respect to the payments.*" (Emphasis supplied.) Information, not available from upper-echelon management, was needed to supply a basis for legal advice concerning compliance with securities and tax laws, foreign laws, currency regulations, duties to shareholders, and potential litigation in each of these areas. The communications concerned matters within the scope of the employees' corporate duties, and the employees themselves were sufficiently aware that they were being questioned in order that the corporation could obtain legal advice. The questionnaire identified Thomas as "the company's General Counsel" and referred in its opening sentence to the possible illegality of payments such as the ones on which information was sought. A statement of policy accompanying the questionnaire clearly indicated the legal implications of the investigation. The policy statement was issued "in order that there be no uncertainty in the future as to the policy with respect to the practices which are the subject of this investigation."

The Court of Appeals declined to extend the attorney-client privilege beyond the limits of the control group test for fear that doing so would entail severe burdens on discovery and create a broad "zone of silence" over corporate affairs. Application of the attorney-client privilege to communications such as those involved here, however, puts the adversary in no worse position than if the communications had never taken place. The privilege only protects disclosure of communications; it does not protect disclosure of the underlying facts by those who communicated with the attorney:

> [T]he protection of the privilege extends only to *communications* and not to facts. A fact is one thing and a communication concerning that fact is an entirely different thing. The client cannot be compelled to answer

the question, "What did you say or write to the attorney?" but may not refuse to disclose any relevant fact within his knowledge merely because he incorporated a statement of such fact into his communication to his attorney.

* * *

Our decision that the communications by Upjohn employees to counsel are covered by the attorney-client privilege disposes of the case so far as the responses to the questionnaires and any notes reflecting responses to interview questions are concerned. The summons reaches further, however, and Thomas has testified that his notes and memoranda of interviews go beyond recording responses to his questions. To the extent that the material subject to the summons is not protected by the attorney-client privilege as disclosing communications between an employee and counsel, we must reach the ruling by the Court of Appeals that the work-product doctrine does not apply to [investigative tax] summonses. (The following discussion will also be relevant to counsel's notes and memoranda of interviews with the seven former employees should it be determined that the attorney-client privilege does not apply to them).

* * *

Make the Connection

The "work product doctrine" is a quasi privilege that generally protects materials generated by an attorney when they are made in anticipation of litigation. The doctrine is usually studied as part of discovery materials in a First Year Civil Procedure course.

Government concedes, wisely, that the Court of Appeals erred and that the work-product doctrine does apply to IRS summonses. This doctrine was announced by the Court over 30 years ago in *Hickman v. Taylor*, 329 U.S. 495 (1947). In that case the Court rejected "an attempt, without purported necessity or justification, to secure written statements, private memoranda and personal recollections prepared or formed by an adverse party's counsel in the course of his legal duties." The Court noted that "it is essential that a lawyer work with a certain degree of privacy" and reasoned that if discovery of the material sought were permitted "much of what is now put down in writing would remain unwritten. An attorney's thoughts, heretofore inviolate, would not be his own. Inefficiency, unfairness and sharp practices would inevitably develop in the giving of legal advice and in the preparation of cases for trial. The effect on the legal profession would be demoralizing. And the interests of the clients and the cause of justice would be poorly served."

The "strong public policy" underlying the work-product doctrine ... has been substantially incorporated in Federal Rule of Civil Procedure 26(b)(3).... Rule 26(b)(3) codifies the work-product doctrine, and the Federal Rules of Civil Procedure are made applicable to summons enforcement proceedings by Rule 81(a)(3). While conceding the applicability of the work-product doctrine, the Government asserts that it has made a sufficient showing of necessity to overcome its protections. The Magistrate apparently so found, The Government relies on the following language in *Hickman*:

> We do not mean to say that all written materials obtained or prepared by an adversary's counsel with an eye toward litigation are necessarily free from discovery in all cases. Where relevant and nonprivileged facts remain hidden in an attorney's file and where production of those facts is essential to the preparation of one's case, discovery may properly be had... And production might be justified where the witnesses are no longer available or can be reached only with difficulty.

The Government stresses that interviewees are scattered across the globe and that Upjohn has forbidden its employees to answer questions it considers irrelevant. The above-quoted language from *Hickman*, however, did not apply to "oral statements made by witnesses ... whether presently in the form of [the attorney's] mental impressions or memoranda." As to such material the Court did "not believe that any showing of necessity can be made under the circumstances of this case so as to justify production... If there should be a rare situation justifying production of these matters petitioner's case is not of that type." Forcing an attorney to disclose notes and memoranda of witnesses' oral statements is particularly disfavored [by Hickman] because it tends to reveal the attorney's mental processes.

* * *

Accordingly, the judgment of the Court of Appeals is reversed, and the case remanded for further proceedings.

It is so ordered.

——————————

Points for Discussion

a. The *Upjohn* Test.

The Court criticizes the "control group" test for being too difficult and uncertain, but is it clear what the Court proposes in its place? To the degree you can identify a test in *Upjohn*, is it easier to apply than the "control group" test? After reading *Upjohn,* which, if any, of the following confidential communications are likely to be protected by the attorney-client privilege? (1) An Upjohn bookkeeper consults corporate counsel regarding the legal implications of an accounting error he made? (2) An Upjohn chemist consults corporate counsel to tell him she saw an Upjohn truck run a red light and hit a pedestrian? (3) An Upjohn vice president consults with corporate counsel regarding the legal implications of his divorce?

b. Former Employees of a Corporation.

Upjohn expressly left open the question whether the attorney-client privilege applies to communications between former employees and corporate counsel. The Fourth Circuit, in *In re Allen,* 106 F.3d 582 (4th Cir. 1997), found that the privilege protects these communications as long as the former employees communicate information obtained in the scope of employment and the information is relevant to the attorney's investigation and necessary to develop a legal analysis for the corporate client. Do you agree? Would the *Allen* court's conclusion be supported by *Upjohn*?

c. Does the Attorney-Client Privilege Apply to Government Lawyers?

A government attorney-client privilege generally applies in a civil case to communications made between a public agency's staff and its lawyers concerning agency business. The privilege may also apply to communications between the President and White House Counsel but may not prevent discovery of evidence sought by a grand jury in a criminal case. See

Go Online!

For an overview of the land development scheme known as "Whitewater," visit the Washington Post at http://www.washingtonpost.com/ wp-srv/politics/special/whitewater/ whitewater.htm

*In re Grand Jury Subpoena Duces Tecum,*112 F.3d 910 (8th Cir. 1997), where the court held that a government attorney-client privilege, while generally recognized in civil cases, did not apply to notes from meetings between the President's wife, her attorney and White House counsel regarding her and the President's alleged participation in "Whitewater," a land development scheme. The court justified this civil-criminal distinction by explaining that "the strong public interest in honest government and in exposing wrongdoing by public officials would be ill-served by recognition of a governmental attorney-client privilege applicable in criminal proceedings inquiring into the actions of public officials," and "that to allow any part of the federal government to use its in-house attorneys as a shield against the production of information relevant to a federal criminal investigation would represent a gross misuse of public assets."

d. Legal versus Business Advice.

It is not unusual for an attorney to assume more than one role in a corporation. For example, an attorney may act as an officer or director of a corporation as well as corporate counsel. Some communications between corporate officers and employees and corporate counsel may be relevant to both roles, and determining whether the communications are protected by privilege can be problematic. Generally, these dual purpose communications will only be protected if their primary goal is to facilitate the rendering of legal services. See *In re Ford Motor Co.*, 110 F.3d 954 (3d Cir. 1997) (minutes of a meeting of Ford's Policy and Strategy Committee were privileged even though the ultimate decision reached by the committee was a business one because it was made only after obtaining legal advice).

e. A Distinction: The Work Product Doctrine.

The work product doctrine in federal civil cases is codified in Fed. R. Civ. P. 26(b)(3), and provides that a party may obtain discovery of documents and tangible things prepared in anticipation of litigation by an attorney or the opposing party's agent only upon a showing of "substantial need" and that the party cannot, without undue hardship, obtain the substantial equivalent from other sources. Even when this showing is made, the court must protect against disclosure of an attorney's "mental impressions, conclusions, opinions, or legal theories." The doctrine is based upon public policy considerations designed to protect attorneys, not clients. See *In re Grand Jury Proceedings*, 601 F.2d 162 (5th Cir. 1979). Unlike the attorney-client privilege, however, the work-product doctrine is governed in diversity cases by federal law, specifically, Fed. R. Civ. P. 26(b)(3).

Make the Connection

Generally, a federal court sitting in a diversity case applies federal procedural law but the substantive law of the state which supplies the rule of decision. The application of attorney-client privilege in federal court is usually considered to be a substantive issue. *Baker v. General Motors Corp.*, 209 F.3d 1051 (8th Cir. 2000). You may recall studying the question whether federal or state law applies in a diversity case when you studied the famous *Erie R.R. Co. v. Tompkins*, 304 U.S. 64 (1938) case in your first year Civil Procedure course.

Although the work product doctrine and the attorney-client privilege have much in common, they are distinct in several different ways. First, the work product doctrine only protects materials gathered in anticipation of litigation; the attorney-client privilege has no such limitation. Second, the work product doctrine protects a much broader range of information than does the attorney client privilege. It protects, for example, a statement given to an attorney by a non-client witness, as well as statements given to a party's agent, such as a claims adjuster. The attorney-client privilege only protects confidential communications between the attorney and the client or their representatives. Third, the work product doctrine is a qualified privilege that can be defeated by a showing of substantial need and undue hardship; the attorney-client privilege cannot be defeated by any such showing.

---

2. Who Is an Attorney or an Attorney's Representative?

To be protected, the attorney-client privilege requires confidential communications be made by a client to an attorney. An attorney is defined as someone who is authorized to practice law in a given jurisdiction. The privilege also extends to confidential communications made to an attorney's representatives, such as secretaries, interns, legal assistants and paralegals who assist the attorney in rendering legal services for a client. Attorney representatives may also include those who are specifically hired to provide the lawyer with information and analysis that are outside the attorney's expertise. For example, a probate attorney may hire an accountant to assist in valuing her client's estate. Under these circumstances, confidential communications between an attorney's client and the non-lawyer may be protected by the attorney-client privilege, depending on the attorney's reason and the necessity for seeking a non-lawyer's services.

United States v. Kovel

U.S. Court of Appeals for the Second Circuit
296 F.2d 918 (2nd Cir. 1961)

FRIENDLY, Circuit Judge.

This appeal from a sentence for criminal contempt for refusing to answer a question asked in the course of an inquiry by a grand jury raises an important issue as to the application of the attorney-client privilege to a non-lawyer employed by a law firm...

Kovel is a former Internal Revenue agent having accounting skills. Since 1943 he has been employed by Kamerman & Kamerman, a law firm specializing in tax law. A grand jury in the Southern District of New York was investigating alleged Federal income tax violations by Hopps, a client of the law firm; Kovel was subpoenaed to appear on September 6, 1961, a few days before the date, September 8, when the Government feared the statute of limitations might run. The law firm advised the Assistant United States Attorney that since Kovel was an employee under the direct supervision of the partners, Kovel could not disclose any communications by the client of the result of any work done for the client, unless the latter consented; the Assistant answered that the attorney-client privilege did not apply to one who was not an attorney. [After being questioned by a grand jury and refusing to answer based upon attorney-client privilege, Koval was held in contempt].

* * *

Decision under what circumstances, if any, the attorney-client privilege may include a communication to a nonlawyer by the lawyer's client is the resultant of two conflicting forces. One is the general teaching that "The investigation of truth and the enforcement of testimonial duty demand the restriction, not the expansion, of these privileges." The other is the more particular lesson 'That as, by reason of the complexity and difficulty of our law, litigation can only be properly conducted by professional men, it is absolutely necessary that a man ... should have recourse to the assistance of professional lawyers, and ... it is equally necessary ... that he should be able to place unrestricted and unbounded confidence in the professional agent, and that the communications he so makes to him should be kept secret...' Nothing in the policy of the privilege suggests that attorneys, simply by placing accountants, scientists or investigators on their payrolls and maintaining them in their offices, should be able to invest all communications by clients to such persons with a privilege the law has not seen fit to extend when the latter are operating under their own steam. On the other hand, in contrast to the Tudor times when the privilege was first recognized, the complexities of modern existence prevent attorneys from effectively handling clients' affairs without the help of others; few lawyers could now practice without the assistance of secretaries, file clerks, telephone operators, messengers, clerks not yet admitted to the bar, and aides of other sorts. "The assistance of these agents being indispensable to his work and the communications of the client being often necessarily committed to them by the attorney or by the client himself, the privilege must include all the persons who act as the attorney's agents."

Indeed, the Government does not here dispute that the privilege covers communications to non-lawyer employees with 'a menial or ministerial responsibility that involves relating communications to an attorney.' We cannot regard the privilege as confined to 'menial or ministerial' employees. Thus, we can see no significant difference between a case where the attorney sends a client speaking a foreign language to an interpreter to make a literal translation of the client's story; a second where the attorney, himself having some little knowledge of the foreign tongue, has a more knowledgeable non-lawyer employee in the room to help out; a third where someone to perform that same function has been brought along by the client; and a fourth where the attorney, ignorant of the foreign language, sends the client to a non-lawyer proficient in it, with instructions to interview the client on the attorney's behalf and then render his own summary of the situation, perhaps drawing on his own knowledge in the process, so that the attorney can give the client proper legal advice...

This analogy of the client speaking a foreign language is by no means irrelevant to the appeal at hand. Accounting concepts are a foreign language to some lawyers in almost all cases, and to almost all lawyers in some cases. Hence the presence of an accountant, whether hired by the lawyer or by the client, while the client is relating a complicated tax story to the lawyer, ought not destroy the privilege, any more than would that of the linguist in the second or third variations of the foreign language theme discussed above; the presence of the accountant is necessary, or at least highly useful, for the effective consultation between the client and the lawyer which the privilege is designed to permit. What is vital to the privilege is that the communication be made in confidence for the purpose of obtaining legal advice from the lawyer. If what is sought is not legal advice but only accounting service, or if the advice sought is the accountant's rather than the lawyer's, no privilege exists. We recognize this draws what may seem to some a rather arbitrary line between a case where the client communicates first to his own accountant (no privilege as to such communications, even though he later consults his lawyer on the same matter), and others, where the client in the first instance consults a lawyer who retains an accountant as a listening post, or consults the lawyer with his own accountant present. But that is the inevitable consequence of having to reconcile the absence of a privilege for accountants and the effective operation of the privilege of client and lawyer under conditions where the lawyer needs outside help. We realize also that the line we have drawn will not be so easy to apply as the simpler positions urged on us by the parties-- the district judges will scarcely be able to leave the decision of such cases to computers; but the distinction has to be made if the privilege is neither to be unduly expanded nor to become a trap.

Food for Thought

The court here uses an interpreter analogy in determining whether a client's communications with a non-lawyer hired by an attorney should be protected by the attorney-client privilege. Is this an appropriate comparison? What is the usual function of an interpreter when hired by an attorney? What is the usual function of an accountant? Are there any differences between the two that might affect recognition of the attorney-client privilege?

* * *

The judgment is vacated and the cause remanded for further proceedings consistent with this opinion.

————————

Points for Discussion

a. Persons Necessary to Facilitate Legal Work.

The court in *Koval* states that an attorney-client privilege attaches to a client's communications with an attorney's agents, such as "secretaries, file clerks, telephone operators, messengers, clerks not yet admitted to the bar, and aides of other sorts" who have a "a menial or ministerial responsibility that involves relating communications to an attorney." Based on this statement, do you think that the attorney-client privilege should apply when a law firm's paralegal tells the firm's client about her views of the legal issues in the client's case? See *HPD Lab. v. Clorox Co.*, 202 F.R.D. 410 (D.N. J. 2001). Would your answer be the same if the paralegal had formulated the advice after first discussing it with the client's lawyer? Also, would the privilege apply to a third year law student who was working for a corporation but not supervised by any of the corporate attorneys and who communicated with the corporation's client? See *Dabney v. Investment Corp. of America*, 82 F.R.D. 464 (E.D. Pa. 1979).

b. The Need for Accounting Services.

In *Kovel*, the court extends the attorney-client privilege to accountants who, like foreign language experts, may be necessary to help an attorney "interpret" a client's case. Would a client's communications with an accountant be privileged if the attorney hired the accountant to assist him in rendering legal services that he could have performed by himself? How necessary must another professional's advice be, for it to be protected by the attorney-client privilege? See *J.K. Lasser & Co.*, 448 F. Supp. 103 (E.D.N.Y. 1978).

c. The Need for Psychotherapist Services.

The attorney-client privilege also applies when an attorney refers a client to a psychotherapist to evaluate the client's mental health in preparation for trial. See *Murray v. Board of Educ.*, 199 F.R.D. 154 (S.D.N.Y. 2001). Would a psychotherapist-patient privilege also protect these communications? See *Jaffee v. Redmond*, 518 U.S. 1 (1996) (to be protected by the psychotherapist-patient privilege, the consultation must be for therapeutic purposes).

Make the Connection

Jaffee v. Redmond and the psychotherapist-patient privilege are discussed in Section "D" of this chapter.

3. What is a Communication?

The attorney-client privilege protects "communications" between an attorney and a client. However, anything that an attorney observes while in contact with a client, such as the color of a client's hair or whether the client was inebriated, is not protected on the basis that such facts are observable by anyone. This distinction becomes blurry when an attorney is asked to give an opinion about a client's mental state based in part on observation and in part on a client's communications.

United States v. Kendrick

U.S. Court of Appeals for the Fourth Circuit
331 F.2d 110 (4th Cir. 1964)

PER CURIAM.

This is an appeal from the District Court's decision denying, after hearing, the petitioner's motion ... to vacate an illegal sentence on the grounds that the petitioner was incompetent to stand trial... The substance of his allegations in the present action is that he was adjudicated insane by the North Carolina courts in 1952, and has never

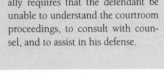

What's That?

Incompetence to stand trial generally requires that the defendant be unable to understand the courtroom proceedings, to consult with counsel, and to assist in his defense.

since then been adjudicated sane; that at his trial in November of 1960 he was insane and suffering from amnesia; that as a result of his disabilities he was not competent to stand trial. He alleged that he lost his memory as the result of a wreck in June 1959 and did not recover it until after psychiatric treatment during his present jail term...

The Government's case consisted of the testimony of counsel appointed by the Court to represent the petitioner at his trial in 1960 and of the F.B.I. Agent who arrested him. Both of these witnesses testified to the extent of their contacts with the petitioner and stated over objection from petitioner's present counsel that in their opinion he was sane and competent to stand trial, and that in their opinion he knew the difference between right and wrong...

We do not agree with the petitioner that the testimony of his trial counsel should have been excluded at the post-conviction hearing on the basis of the attorney-client privilege.

* * *

Food for Thought

What do you think the court means when it says the "substance" of communications is protected? Does the court mean that only the particulars of the communications are protected, or that the general subject matter of the communcations are protected, or both? Would it make a difference?

Communications made in confidence by a client to his attorney are protected by the attorney-client privilege. It is the substance of the communications which is protected, however, not the fact that there have been communications. Excluded from the privilege, also, are physical characteristics of the client, such as his complexion, his demeanor, his bearing, his sobriety and his dress. Such things are observable by anyone who talked with the client, and there is nothing, in the usual case, to suggest that the client intends his attorney's observations of such matters to be confidential. In short, the privilege protects only the client's confidences, not things which, at the time, are not intended to be held in the breast of the lawyer, even though the attorney-client relation provided the occasion for the lawyer's observation of them.

Here the attorney testified to just such nonconfidential matters. Petitioner, the attorney testified, was responsive, readily supplied the attorney with his version of the facts and the names of other people involved, was logical in his conversation and his reasoning, and appeared to know and understand everything that went on before and during the trial. No mention was made of the substance of any communication by client to attorney; the witness testified only about his client's cooperativeness and awareness.

All of the matters to which the attorney testified are objectively observable particularizations of the client's demeanor and attitude. Made at a time when neither client nor lawyer manifested any reason to suppose they were confidential, they were not within the privilege. Certainly, the client was then making no secret of his capacity, or want of capacity to communicate with his attorney and to cooperate in his defense.

* * *

We have not heretofore considered this particular question when it was contested, but we have tacitly assumed that the trial attorney may be examined as to such matters, indeed, that the postconviction court should seek such light as the trial attorney can throw upon the question. Our tacit assumption does not foreclose reconsideration, but after thorough reconsideration in this contested case, we adhere to it.

However persuasive the highly relevant testimony of the attorney, which we now hold properly received, it does not militate against our conclusion that a further hearing should be held to inquire into the petitioner's medical history, diagnosis, treatment and response after his reception in Atlanta. Medical opinion ought to be sought as to whether one suffering from amnesia may appear reasonably oriented in time and place when discussing recent and present occurrences and whether, under such circumstances, apparent reasonableness may be infected with irrationality. Moreover, if the medical testimony should disclose a history of traumatic injury occasioning memory loss before the trial and a subsequent history of successful treatment for it, it might provide weighty evidence, in the light of which the attorney's testimony ought to be weighed. On the other hand, it may confirm all that the attorney has said. The circumstances, we think, require that this source of information be explored.

Take Note!

Is the majority opinion saying here that it tacitly assumed that the attorney-witness could be cross-examined about the substance of his communications with the defendant even though they were made in confidence? Under what theory? If the theory is one of waiver, how did the defendant waive the privilege? By raising incompetence as a defense? The special concurrence takes the court to task on this issue, and the majority never fully explains itself. Can you offer any arguments in its defense?

The judgment is vacated and the case remanded for further proceedings in accordance with this opinion.

SOBELOFF, Chief Judge, and J. SPENCER BELL, Circuit Judge (concurring specially).

... We agree that an attorney may testify as to 'facts observable by anyone,' but we refuse to accept the characterization of the lawyer's testimony here as merely reporting 'facts observable by anyone.' If nothing were involved beyond observations open to anyone, it is doubtful that the attorney would have been called to the stand. His testimony was desired for a purpose more far-reaching. Any expression as to the client's mental competency necessarily embraced more than facts observable by anyone; it comprehended conclusions drawn in the course of an association that is uniquely regarded in the law.

The lawyer's observations were inextricably intertwined with communications which passed between him and his client. It cannot be said that the testimony was confined to nonconfidential matters. This being so, the well-established privilege which protects the client against disclosure was violated.

The fact that a lawyer may be in a position to give enlightening testimony is not itself sufficient reason for relaxing the client's privileges. In many cases the client may have confessed his guilt to the lawyer, who would then be in an excellent position to give effective testimony, but our tradition forbids such disclosure. We know from other areas of the law that often the best evidence is barred from the case for reasons of policy…

Consider the practical difficulty that arises when an attorney is permitted to testify on such an issue… The attorney testifies baldly that his client was 'cooperative' and mentally competent. No meaningful cross-examination is possible without inquiring what his client said to him and what he said to his client. The client finds himself on the horns of a dilemma: Either he must forego raising the issue of his incapacity or he must surrender the protection of the privilege the law accords him--a choice he should not have to make. The lawyer's conclusory opinion thus stands without possibility of effective challenge.

The new hearing which the court awards the appellant will, therefore, do him little or no good.

The appellant was earlier adjudicated insane by a court of competent jurisdiction. The adjudication has not been upset or revised, and no later medical examination was made in an attempt to show that the adjudication should no longer stand. The normal procedure of ordering a psychiatric examination to determine mental capacity to stand trial should have been followed before the case proceeded to trial. There was a similar opportunity, which was not grasped, when the petition was filed. This would seem imperative when there is a background of confinement in a mental hospital, extensive psychiatric treatment, and a formal finding of a lunacy commission. Instead, the mere opinion testimony of a layman, the man's own lawyer at that, is adduced in the hearing to validate the original trial.

The least that the District Court should now do on remand of the case is to order a proper medical inquiry, and the man's lawyer should not be looked to supply the missing link.

Every impeachment the majority so rightly levels against the testimony given by the FBI agent as to appellant's mental condition, on the ground that the witness was a medically untrained layman, applies with equal force to the testimony of the lawyer, likewise a layman in medical matters. Even worse, the lawyer, called to testify outside his professional sphere, did so against his own client. This not only violates the ordinary rule against the admission of expert testimony from inexpert witnesses, but it also undercuts the purpose and policy of the attorney-client relation. It is a procedure we cannot sanction.

* * *

Points for Discussion

a. Information Not Intended as a Communicative Act.

The *Kendrick* court lists a number of observations an attorney may make of a client, such as a client's complexion, demeanor, bearing, sobriety, or dress, all of which fall outside the protection of the attorney-client privilege because they do not involve confidential communications and are observable by anyone. Competency, on the other hand, is a legal term meaning the mental ability to understand the legal proceedings, to consult meaningfully with counsel, and to assist in one's defense. By telling the court that his client "readily supplied the attorney with his version of the facts and the names of other people involved, was logical in his conversation and his reasoning, and appeared to know and understand everything that went on before and during trial," was the attorney partially revealing what his client communicated to him in confidence? Is the court saying that the attorney-client privilege protects only specific factual communications between attorneys and clients but not what was generally discussed? If so, why would a client feel free to communicate with an attorney about her case?

b. Underlying Facts.

As the *Kendrick* case states, the attorney-client privilege protects confidential communications between attorney and client but not the underling facts of the case. A client may therefore be asked "were you speeding before you hit the plaintiff?" but not "what did you tell your attorney about

Make the Connection

Upjohn v. United States is reproduced and discussed in 13.1(A) of this chapter.

whether you were speeding before you hit the plaintiff?" One example illustrating this distinction can be found in *Upjohn v. United States*, 449 U.S. 383 (1981), where the attorneys for the defendant Upjohn sent confidential written questionnaires to Upjohn's corporate subsidiaries asking about bribes allegedly made by Upjohn to foreign governments as the price of doing business in those countries. When the Government sought to discover the questionnaires and employee responses, the Supreme Court determined they were protected by the attorney-client privilege but stated that the "Government was free to question the employees who communicated with [Upjohn's General Counsel] and outside counsel."

c. Information Regarding the Nature of the Attorney-Client Relationship.

The attorney-client privilege normally does not protect information as to the existence, duration, and terms of the attorney-client relationship, nor the identity or address of the client or attorney, fee arrangements or the fees actually paid. Some courts, however, have created exceptions to this rule in circumstances where disclosure of a client's identity or payment of fees would reveal an attorney's legal advice, a client's confidential communications, or be the "last link" in a chain of information that would incriminate the client. One example of an exception can be found in *United States v. Liebman, 742 F.2d 807 (3d Cir. 1984)*, a case in which the IRS sought to obtain the names of a law firm's clients who had paid fees to the firm in connection with their investment in real estate partnerships. The firm conceded that it had told these clients that such fees could be deducted on their tax returns as legal fees rather than non-deductible brokerage charges. The IRS disagreed. It sought the names of the firm's clients because the IRS could not identify them from their tax returns since taxpayers who deduct legal fees are not required to name the recipients. The court held that the client's names were privileged since "so much of the actual communication had already been established, that to disclose the client's name would disclose the essence of a confidential communication." For a summary of the law in various circuits regarding this exception, see *United States v. Sindel, 53 F.3d 874 (8ᵗʰ Cir. 1995)*.

4. Made in Confidence

The requirement that a communication between a client and an attorney be made in confidence can be characterized as the essence of the attorney-client privilege. While it is not necessary for a client to expressly request that an attorney consider a communication confidential for the privilege to apply, the privilege is limited to those communications which the client either expressly made confidential or which he could reasonably assume under the circumstances would be understood by the attorney as confidential. Thus, the presence of a third person when the communication was made usually destroys the privilege, except when the third person was present as the attorney's client's representative to further the rendition of legal services or facilitate the transmission of communications. As the next case will show, the fact that the third person was an attorney does not necessarily guaranty that these exceptions are satisfied.

What's That?

Black's Law Dictionary describes "made in confidence" as "a communication made in trust and not intended for public disclosure."

United States v. Evans

U.S. Court of Appeals for the Seventh Circuit
113 F.3d 1457 (7th Cir. 1997)

CUMMINGS, Circuit Judge.

The trial of Jesse Evans, a Chicago alderman indicted on charges of racketeering (including acts of extortion, accepting bribes, and official misconduct), filing false tax returns, and obstruction of justice, is presently pending in the district court. This interlocutory appeal requires us to review an order of that court granting the government's pretrial motion *in limine* to admit certain testimony by attorney James Koch, which Evans asserts is protected by the attorney-client privilege...

It's Latin to Me

Remember that a motion *in limine* is a pretrial request that certain inadmissible evidence not be referred to or offered at trial.

In early January 1996, news reports revealed that Alderman Evans had been targeted in a federal corruption investigation of City officials ("Operation Silver Shovel"). After learning that his long-time friend and occasional client had been implicated in the investigation, attorney John Holden, who is also a Chicago police officer, contacted Evans and spoke with him about Evans' interviews with FBI agents. In the aftermath of this meeting, Holden arranged for and scheduled Evans to meet with three criminal defense attorneys so that Evans could explain his situation, seek legal advice, and decide which of the three attorneys, if any, to retain. On January 8, 1996, after scheduling an appointment on Evans' behalf with attorney James Koch, Holden took Evans to Koch's office where the three conferred... [It is these discussions about which the government has asked attorney-witness Koch to testify at trial. The defendant claims attorney-client privilege; the government claims waiver by the presence of a third party].

* * *

Koch testified that Holden phoned him early in the morning on Monday, January 8, 1996, informed him that Evans was going to be indicted and needed legal representation, and asked if Evans and he could come and meet with Koch regarding Koch's possible representation of Evans. Koch also stated that Holden informed him that he was a long-time friend of Evans; there was no mention, however, of any business or legal relationship between Evans and Holden. The three men met later that morning. Koch testified that prior to any sort of substantive discussions regarding the nature of the charges against Evans, he expressed concerns about Holden's presence in the room and its consequences as to the confidentiality of the conversation:

> "I told Mr. Evans that, based on what had been represented to me by Mr. Holden, that is that he was there as a personal friend, that this conversation might not be privileged, and for me to ask intimate facts and details and gather information with the idea of either, well, with the idea of preparing a defense, that I had some concerns about its confidentiality, and that was the initial conversation. And I was told that in fact Mr. Holden was a police officer and a friend, that he was there in that capacity, that he was there as a potential character witness should that ever come to light. That was the initial conversation I had with Mr. Evans, and he said he understood the nature of what I was telling him and that he wanted John Holden to be present for the conversation."

* * *

Koch also testified that Holden never indicated that he was there as an attorney for Evans, rather, "he indicated he was there as a friend and, as I said, a potential character witness." Conversely, when asked on cross-examination, "Did Mr. Holden tell you that he was not acting as an attorney for Mr. Evans," Koch answered, "Yes." Koch further testified on cross-examination that Holden never said anything about working on the case as one of Evans' attorneys. To the contrary, Koch testified that Holden stated that he could not represent Evans in the pending matter [because of a potential conflict of interest]...

Holden recounted a very different story. He explained that Evans contacted him and described the situation he was in--namely, that he had been interviewed by the FBI and did not know whether there were any charges, or what was going on. Holden decided that they needed to find competent counsel "to find out whether or not I could represent" Evans. Accordingly, he called Koch, told him that he "represented a prominent client," and scheduled the meeting at Koch's office. When he and Evans met with Koch, Holden introduced Evans by saying, "This is my client, Jesse Evans."

Holden testified that he never told Koch that he was not Evans' lawyer and never stated that he was there as Evans' friend, not his attorney. Holden also denied saying at the meeting that he was there "not as a police officer, not as a lawyer, but as a friend." Furthermore, Holden testified that he never heard Koch say anything to Evans about the attorney-client privilege or that Holden's presence would destroy the attorney-client privilege.

On January 8, 1997, the district judge ruled from the bench that Koch's testimony concerning the conversation he had with Holden and Evans on January 8, 1996, is not privileged. In the course of her oral ruling, Judge Bucklo stated:

"[T]o me, it is a question of credibility, and Mr. Koch is a lot more credible than Holden. The basic question is whether Mr. Holden said, as Mr. Koch testified: I am just here as a friend and maybe a character witness. If so, then it is clear that Mr. Evans could not have thought Mr. Holden was there representing him as an attorney. There is just no reason for Mr. Koch to lie.... [H]e told Mr. Evans and Mr. Holden that in that case the conversation might not be privileged, and Mr. Evans, according to the testimony, said that he wanted Mr. Holden to stay anyway."

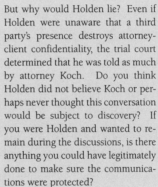

Food for Thought

But why would Holden lie? Even if Holden were unaware that a third party's presence destroys attorney-client confidentiality, the trial court determined that he was told as much by attorney Koch. Do you think Holden did not believe Koch or perhaps never thought this conversation would be subject to discovery? If you were Holden and wanted to remain during the discussions, is there anything you could have legitimately done to make sure the communications were protected?

* * *

... Evans is not aided by cases holding that the presence of a third party at an attorney-client consultation does not defeat the privilege where the third party's presence was needed to make the conference possible or to assist the attorney in rendering legal services. Beyond stating the general rule, Evans has failed to carry his burden of proving that Holden's presence was necessary to accomplish the objective of his consultation. Evans' only showing on this score lies in Holden's discredited testimony that he was present at the meeting in order to advise Evans as to the relative abilities of the several defense attorneys who were to be consulted. Giving effect to the district court's factual findings, we must conclude that Holden was present merely as a friend and potential character witness. This is plainly insufficient to establish the necessity of Holden's presence...

Practice Pointer

This case illustrates why great care must be taken to prevent access by third parties in order to protect confidentiality and preserve the privilege. When in doubt, it is best to err on the side of excluding them.

* * *

For the foregoing reasons, the district court's order granting the government's motion to admit Mr. Koch's testimony is affirmed.

————————————

Points for Discussion

a. Third Party Presence During Confidential Communications.

There can be no confidential intent if a communication is made between an attorney and a client with a third party present, unless that third party is a representative of the attorney or the client. If the trial judge in this case had believed that Holden's role at the meeting was to help the defendant select a defense attorney, would that have been sufficient to qualify Holden as the defendant's representative?

b. Eavesdroppers and Snoops.

There is a trend in federal cases to hold that if a confidential communication otherwise within the attorney-client privilege is overheard by an eavesdropper, the privilege is waived unless reasonable precautions are taken by the privilege holder to prevent this from occurring. In *McCafferty's, Inc. v. Bank of Glen Burnie, 179 F.R.D. 163 (D. Md. 1998)*, for example, the court found no wavier of the attorney-client privilege where the client discarded the draft of a memo sent to her by her attorney, tore it into sixteen pieces and deposited them in her office trash can from where the opponent's investigator retrieved it. See also *Bower v. Weisman, 669 F. Supp. 602 (S.D.N.Y. 1987)*, where the court found the privilege was waived because the document was left on a table in a public room in a suite where another person was staying.

c. The Common Interest Rule.

The common interest rule is an exception to the principle that the attorney-client privilege is waived when privileged information is disclosed to a third party. The rule applies when a client confidentially communicates with his attorney in the presence of a person with whom the client shares a

Make the Connection

For more on this subject, see the waiver discussion in 13.1 (F) of this chapter.

common legal interest regarding a claim or defense whether they both employ the same attorney or separate attorneys to represent them. To prevent waiver, the privilege holder must show that these communications facilitated or advanced the representation regarding the common claim or defense in current or possible later proceedings. The common interest rule extends to partners, makers of mutual wills, joint trustors, and insured and insurer.

Hypo 13.1

An attorney asks a summer associate to sit in on a meeting between her and her client for the purpose of seeing how to discuss legal strategies with a client. The summer associate is not working on the client's case. Does the attorney-client privilege protect these communications?

---

5. To Facilitate Legal Services

Normally, the attorney-client protects confidential communications made by a client to an attorney in order to obtain legal services. Applying the privilege becomes problematic, however, when it is not the client who communicates facts to an attorney but rather another attorney within the law firm.

United States v. Rowe

United States Court of Appeals for the Ninth Circuit
96 F.3d 1294 (9th Cir. 1996)

KOZINSKI, Circuit Judge.

After learning of possible irregularities in attorney W. Lee McElravy's handling of client funds, the senior partner at his San Diego law firm, Charles E. Rowe, asked two young associates to investigate McElravy's conduct. Rowe also wrote to the State Bar, asking it to "take appropriate action" against McElravy. A grand jury investigating McElravy later subpoenaed the associates; the government hoped to question them about their conversations with Rowe. Appellants argued that the conversations were protected by the attorney-client privilege.

The attorney-client privilege can exist only after a client consults an attorney, "for the purpose of facilitating the rendition of professional legal services."

The district judge, although expressing considerable unease about her ruling, held that appellants had not shown these requirements were met. According to the judge, who had spoken to the associates in camera, "Basically, they were trusted young associates [who] were asked to do some leg work and come up with information... [T]hey were ... helping out." The judge noted that the associates were never told they were working as the firm's attorneys; that they didn't bill the firm or record hours expended on the firm's behalf; and that, because they were far less experienced than Rowe, "[t]hey were certainly taking direction from him." The judge issued an order compelling the associates to testify. Rowe and the firm, as probable holders of the privilege, appeal.

The government argues that, in assigning the associates to investigate McElravy, Rowe was not a client consulting an attorney. It further argues that the type of investigative work performed by the associates does not qualify as "professional legal services." We review these mixed questions of fact and law de novo.

1. Attorney-client relationship. Rowe assigned the associates to perform services on behalf of the firm. They were, effectively, in-house counsel. In determining the existence of a privilege, "[n]o attempt [is] made to distinguish between 'inside' and 'outside' counsel..."

What's That?

Remember that "inside (or in-house) counsel" is an attorney who works full time for a client. "Outside counsel" is an attorney who represents more than one client at a time.

Several months after the associates began their investigation, Rowe turned the matter over to outside counsel. The associates thereafter conducted their activities under the direction of this outside counsel. The district court found, and the government now concedes, that the associates' communications with members of the firm after outside counsel was hired were privileged. However, the pre- and post-hiring distinction finds no support in commentary or caselaw. The hiring of outside counsel is, obviously, an indication that litigation is anticipated and, therefore, that legal services are required. In this case, it is clear that litigation was anticipated from day one.

Food for Thought

Why is the court talking about the investigations being in anticipation of litigation? Is the court thinking about the work product doctrine, or does anticipation of litigation also factor into a determination of the attorney-client privilege in this case?

2. Professional legal services. The government also argues that the associates were engaged in fact-finding, rather than the rendering of "professional legal services. It states: "The two associates collected facts for Rowe. They did not render any legal advice..."

Although some commentators ... continue to distinguish between fact-finding and lawyering, federal judges cannot. In <u>Upjohn Co. v. United States, 449 U.S. 383 (1981)</u>, a law firm was retained to investigate wrongdoing within the client corporation. The question on appeal--which has vexed courts before and since--was the definition of "client" in the corporate setting. Whether conversations undertaken in the course of fact-finding can be privileged was never questioned by the Court. In fact, the *Upjohn* Court observed, "The first step in the resolution of any legal problem is ascertaining the factual background and sifting through the facts with an eye to the legally relevant." Thus, "the privilege exists to protect not only the giving of professional advice to those who can act on it but also the giving of information to the lawyer to enable him to give sound and informed advice." ...

Food for Thought

Is this necessarily true? Many businesses have human resource departments who conduct internal investigations before turning the information over to an attorney. Does this possibility undercut support for the court's position here?

3. The government argues that upholding the privilege in this case would reward a law firm just for being a law firm because another type of company that uses its own employees to investigate internal wrong-doing would not get the benefit of the privilege. But a firm whose employees are physicians or computer programmers would probably not use its own employees to investigate legal wrong-doing; they would likely hire lawyers to do the job. Here, the firm happens to have employees who are lawyers, which made it easier for the senior partner to "hire" a lawyer--he needed only walk down the hall. This, however, did not change the fact that he asked lawyers--not secretaries, paralegals, librarians or other of the firm's employees--to conduct the investigation. And, having chosen to hand the job over to lawyers, he is justified in expecting that communications with these lawyers will be privileged. If a doctor, by analogy, consults one of his own partners for diagnosis of a personal health problem, their conversations are protected by the doctor-patient privilege. That patient happens to have easier access to doctors than most people; Rowe had easier access to lawyers. Neither is stripped of the privilege because hiring the professional was convenient...

Make the Connection

Federal law does not recognize a physician-patient privilege, although one is recognized in some states. See the discussion in 13.3 of this chapter.

4. Finally, the government argues that, even if we were to find the existence of communications between a client and an attorney relating to the rendering of professional legal services, the crime or fraud exception may defeat the privilege. In the alternative, it argues, the privilege has been waived by appellants. These are questions for the district court on remand.

REVERSED.

————————————

Points for Discussion

a. The Purpose of the Consultation.

The court in *Rowe* cites the *Upjohn* case for the proposition that attorney fact-gathering "with an eye towards the legally relevant" is covered by the attorney-client privilege; therefore, even if an attorney's only role is to investigate and report, the privilege would attach. Do you agree with this interpretation of *Upjohn?*

b. The Crime-Fraud Exception.

If a client communication to an attorney is to enable the client to commit a crime or fraud, the attorney-client privilege is considered waived by the client. The privilege is lost even if the attorney is unaware of the client's criminal intent. This exception is based on the notion that the use of an attorney's services to further unlawful action undermines the goal of the privilege, which is to promote the proper administration of justice. It also applies in situations where legal advice is sought to cover up a crime or a fraud. *United States v. Edwards, 303 F.3d 606 (5th Cir. 2002).* In *Edwards,* for example, the client used his attorney to cover-up his extortion and perpetuate his tax fraud. In *In re Ryder, 263 F. Supp. 360 (E.D. Va. 1967),* an attorney knowingly accepted stolen money and a weapon used in a robbery from his client. (The attorney was suspended from the practice of law in federal court for 18 months). In both cases, the court held that the crime-fraud exception applied and that there was no attorney-client privilege.

c. Death of the Client.

In *Swidler & Berlin v. United States,* 524 U.S. 399, 407 (1998), the Supreme Court held that except for testamentary situations, the attorney-client privilege survives the death of the client because "knowing that communications will remain confidential even after death encourages the client to communicate fully and frankly with counsel." This case arose out of an investigation conducted by the Office of the Independent Counsel into whether certain

For More Informationa

To learn more about the so-called "Travelgate" scandal, see "The White House Travel Office Controversy" at http://www.wikipedia.org

individuals lied, obstructed justice and committed other crimes in connection with the firing of employees from the White House Travel Office. At the request of the Independent Counsel, a grand jury issued a subpoena to obtain notes taken by an attorney at the law office of Swindler & Berlin during a meeting with Vince Foster, Deputy White House Counsel, during which Foster sought legal advice concerning investigations into these firings. Nine days later, Foster committed suicide. The contents of the note were never disclosed.

6. Waiver of the Privilege

The attorney-client privilege may be expressly waived by the client or the client's representative, such as a client's attorney, if she has authority to do so. Normally if the client is a corporation, the decision to waive the privilege rests with the corporate officers and directors. The privilege may also be impliedly waived in a number of other ways.

1. **Failure to Assert the Privilege:** Waiver will ordinarily be found if the client individually or through his attorney knowingly fails to invoke the privilege where the opportunity arises. See *Dorf & Stanton Comm., Inc. v. Molson Breweries, 100 F.3d 919 (Fed. 1996)* (where the only objection at trial to a privileged communication was hearsay, the privilege was waived). See also *Hawkins v. Stables, 148 F.3d 379 (4th Cir. 1998)* (a client waived the attorney-client privilege by testifying she had never discussed a questioned issue with her attorney).

2. **Waiver by Voluntary Disclosure.** A client waives the attorney-client privilege if he voluntarily testifies or discloses to another person the contents of a confidential communication with his attorney. See *In re Powerhouse Licensing, 441 F.3d 467 (6th Cir. 2006)* (wavier found where client's attorney attached to a motion for summary judgment an affidavit containing facts from and opinions of the client that could only have come from communications between the attorney and client); *In re Grand Jury Proceedings Oct. 12, 1995, 78 F.3d 251 (6th Cir. 1996)* (waiver occurred where the owner and president of a private lab discussed with government investigators advice given by the lab's attorney).

3. **Waiver By Putting the Protected Information at Issue:** When a client sues an attorney, the privilege is often impliedly waived by the client if assertion of the privilege would deny the opposing party access to information important to his case. See *Bieter Co. v. Blomquist, 156 F.R.D. 173 (D. Minn. 1994)* (the privilege was waived when the client sued his attorney for committing wrongful acts involving conflict of interest). Similarly, if an attorney sues a client to collect a fee,

any confidential communications necessary to support the claim are waived to the extent it would be a "manifest injustice" to do otherwise. See *First Fed. Sav. & Loan Ass'n v. Oppenheim*, Appel, Dixon & Co., 110 F.R.D. 557 (S.D.N.Y. 1986).

Waiver may also occur when a client relies upon advice of counsel as an element of a claim or defense. See *In re Grand Jury Subpoena*, 341 F.3d 331 (4th Cir. 2003) (the defendant waived his attorney-client privilege when he told FBI agents that he answered "no" on an immigration form as to whether he had ever been convicted of a crime on advice of counsel), or when a client raises an "adequate investigation" defense in a case. *Peterson v. Wallace Computer Serv.*, Inc., 984 F. Supp. 821 (D. Vt. 1997) (the attorney-client privilege was waived as to materials prepared by the defendant's attorney as part of the sexual harassment investigation).

4. Waiver in a Federal Proceeding or to a Federal Office or Agency

In September, 2008, Rule 502 was enacted by Congress and added to the Federal Rules of Evidence. The rule attempts to resolve a conflict in federal caselaw concerning the effect of disclosing attorney-client or work product matters to federal offices or agencies, and to reduce the costs of protecting against waiver through inadvertent or innocent disclosure. See Advisory Committee Note to Rule 502. Subdivision (a) of the rule provides that a waiver of attorney-client or work product protection extends only to the information disclosed, unless "the waiver was intentional, the disclosed and undisclosed communications or information concern the same subject matter; and they ought in fairness to be considered together." Subsection (b) states there is no waiver if "the disclosure is inadvertent, the holder of the privilege or protection took reasonable steps to prevent disclosure; and the holder promptly took reasonable steps to rectify the error. . ." For a pre-rules case anticipating Rule 502 and discussing the difficulties of attempting to avoid waiver in the face of voluminous electronic discovery, see *Victor Stanley, Inc. v. Creative Pipe, Inc.* 250 F.R.D. 251 (D. Md. 2008).

7. Claiming the Privilege in Court: The Privilege Log

Federal Rule of Civil Procedure 26

(b) (5) Claiming Privilege or Protecting Trial-Preparation Materials.

(A) Information Withheld. When a party withholds information otherwise discoverable by claiming that the information is privileged or subject to protection as trial-preparation material, the party must:

(i) expressly make the claim; and

(ii) describe the nature of the documents, communications, or tangible things not produced or disclosed--and do so in a manner that, without revealing information itself privileged or protected, will enable other parties to assess the claim.

Federal Rule of Civil Procedure 45

(d) When information subject to a subpoena is withheld on a claim that it is privileged ... the claim shall be made expressly and shall be supported by a description of the nature of the documents, communications or things not produced that is sufficient to enable the demanding party to contest the claim.

(d) (2) Claiming Privilege or Protection.

(A) Information Withheld. A person withholding subpoenaed information under a claim that it is privileged or subject to protection as trial-preparation material must:

(i) expressly make the claim; and

(ii) describe the nature of the withheld documents, communications, or tangible things in a manner that, without revealing information itself privileged or protected, will enable the parties to assess the claim.

To guaranty proper consideration of a privilege, attorneys contesting the production of documents must produce a privilege log or document index listing the documents they claim are protected. Producing a privilege log was once regarded as "good practice," but now is required by statute. See Rules 26(5) and 45(d) of the Federal Rules of Civil Procedure. A party who fails to submit a privilege log is deemed to have waived the underlying privilege claim. See *Dorf & Stanton Comm., Inc. v. Molson Breweries*, 100 F.3d 919 (Fed. Cir. 1996).

This privilege log should, at minimum, list each document "by date, all authors and recipients along with their capacities, a statement of the subject matter of the documents and an explanation of the basis for withholding the document from discovery." See *Mold-Masters v. Husky Injection Molding Sys.*, 2001 WL 1558303 (N.D. Ill. 2001). Sufficient detail should be provided to allow a court to determine whether the document is at least potentially protected from disclosure.

As an example, the following is small portion of a privilege log taken from a patent case, *Jack Winter v. Koratron Co.*, 54 F.R.D. 44, 48 (N.D. Cal. 1971), The names of the authors and recipients of the documents were identified elsewhere in the log.

Privilege Schedule I

Number	Date	To	From	Description and Reasons
I-1	9/24/64	White	Weil	Request for advice re how to answer letter in order to obtain rights in newly invented process
I-2	9/16/68	Thompson & Thompson Douglas	Olson	Request to commence trade-mark search
I-3	8/8/60	Singer	White	Bill for professional services
I-4	12/9/63	Koret	White	Bill for professional services
I-5	7/25/66	Greenberg	White	Advice re whether to file foreign applications on 915 patent

C. Spousal Privileges

1. The Adverse Testimonial Privilege

When we speak of marital privileges, we are speaking of two distinct but overlapping ones: the adverse testimonial privilege and the marital communications privilege. The older of the two, the adverse testimonial privilege, sometimes called the "anti-marital facts privilege," is a privilege that allows a witness spouse to refuse to take the stand and testify against the other spouse as to any matters. It applies only in criminal cases and began as a common law rule of incompetency.

In the early common law, all parties to a case were deemed incompetent to testify because of a fear that they might perjure themselves under oath due to their interest in the outcome of the case. Since the common law considered husbands and wife one legal entity, the spouse of a party was also considered incompetent to testify, either for or against the other spouse. Even after the common law deemed parties competent to testify, one spouse could still be prevented from testifying adversely to the other spouse on the basis that to do otherwise would destroy the harmony, privacy and dignity of the marriage. In other words, the non-testifying spouse was the holder of the privilege, at least prior to 1980. But this changed with *Trammel v. United States*.

Trammel v. United States

Supreme Court of the United States
445 U.S. 40 (1980)

Mr. Chief Justice BURGER delivered the opinion of the Court.

We granted certiorari to consider whether an accused may invoke the privilege against adverse spousal testimony so as to exclude the voluntary testimony of his wife. This calls for a re-examination of *Hawkins v. United States*, 358 U.S. 74 (1958).

[Petitioner Trammel was indicted for importing heroin into the United States along with several others, including his wife Elizabeth Trammel. Mrs. Trammel had been caught carrying heroin during a routine custom's search, and she was arrested. In return for leniency, she agreed to testify against her husband. Before trial, Petitioner advised the court that the government intended to call his wife as an adverse witness to Petitioner, and the Petitioner asserted his claim of an adverse testimonial privilege to prevent her from doing so. During a hearing on the motion, Mrs. Trammel described her role and that of her husband in a heroin distribution conspiracy].

After hearing this testimony, the District Court ruled that Mrs. Trammel could testify in support of the Government's case to any act she observed during the marriage and to any communication "made in the presence of a third person;" however, confidential

Make the Connection

The marital communication privilege is covered in 13.2 (B) of this chapter.

communications between petitioner and his wife were held to be privileged and inadmissible.

At trial, Elizabeth Trammel testified within the limits of the court's pretrial ruling; her testimony, as the Government concedes, constituted virtually its entire case against petitioner. He was found guilty on both the substantive and conspiracy charges and sentenced to an indeterminate term of years.

In the Court of Appeals petitioner's only claim of error was that the admission of the adverse testimony of his wife, over his objection, contravened this Court's teaching in *Hawkins v. United States*, and therefore constituted reversible error…

The privilege claimed by petitioner has ancient roots. Writing in 1628, Lord Coke observed that "it hath been resolved by the Justices that a wife cannot be produced either against or for her husband." This spousal disqualification sprang from two canons of medieval jurisprudence: first, the rule that an accused was not permitted to testify in his own behalf because of his interest in the proceeding; second, the concept that husband and wife were one, and that since the woman had no recognized separate legal existence, the husband was that one. From those two now long-abandoned doctrines, it followed that what was inadmissible from the lips of the defendant-husband was also inadmissible from his wife.

Despite its medieval origins, this rule of spousal disqualification remained intact in most common-law jurisdictions well into the 19th century. Indeed, it was not until 1933, in <u>*Funk v. United States*, 290 U.S. 371</u>, that this Court abolished the testimonial disqualification in the federal courts, so as to permit the spouse of a defendant to testify in the defendant's behalf. *Funk*, however, left undisturbed the rule that either spouse could prevent the other from giving adverse testimony. The rule thus evolved into one of privilege rather than one of absolute disqualification.

The modern justification for this privilege against adverse spousal testimony is its perceived role in fostering the harmony and sanctity of the marriage relationship. Notwithstanding this benign purpose, the rule was sharply criticized. Professor Wigmore termed it "the merest anachronism in legal theory and an indefensible obstruction to truth in practice." In its place, Wigmore and others suggested a privilege protecting only private marital communications, modeled on the privilege between priest and penitent, attorney and client, and physician and patient…

In <u>*Hawkins v. United States*</u> … the District Court had permitted petitioner's wife, over his objection, to testify against him. [The Supreme] Court held the wife's testimony inadmissible; it took note of the critical comments that the common-law rule had engendered, but chose not to abandon it. Also rejected was the Government's suggestion that the Court modify the privilege by vesting it in the witness-spouse, with freedom to testify or not independent of the defendant's control. The Court viewed this proposed modification as antithetical to the widespread belief, evidenced in the rules then in effect in a majority of the States and in England, "that the law should not force or encourage testimony which might alienate husband and wife, or further inflame existing domestic differences."

Hawkins, then, left the federal privilege for adverse spousal testimony where it found it, continuing "a rule which bars the testimony of one spouse against the other unless both consent."

The Federal Rules of Evidence acknowledge the authority of the federal courts to continue the evolutionary development of testimonial privileges in federal criminal trials "governed by the principles of the common law as they may be interpreted ... in the light of reason and experience." Fed. Rule Evid. 501. The general mandate of Rule 501 was substituted by the Congress for a set of privilege rules drafted by the Judicial Conference Advisory Committee on Rules of Evidence and approved by the Judicial Conference of the United States and by this Court. That proposal defined nine specific privileges, including a husband-wife privilege which would have codified the *Hawkins* rule and eliminated the privilege for confidential marital communications. See proposed Fed. Rule Evid. 505. In rejecting the proposed Rules and enacting Rule 501, Congress manifested an affirmative intention not to freeze the law of privilege. Its purpose rather was to "provide the courts with the flexibility to develop rules of privilege on a case-by-case basis," and to leave the door open to change.

* * *

Since 1958, when *Hawkins* was decided, support for the privilege against adverse spousal testimony has been eroded further. Thirty-one jurisdictions, including Alaska and Hawaii, then allowed an accused a privilege to prevent adverse spousal testimony. The number has now declined to 24. In 1974, the National Conference on Uniform State Laws revised its Uniform Rules of Evidence, but again rejected the *Hawkins* rule in favor of a limited privilege for confidential communications. That proposed rule has been enacted in Arkansas, North Dakota, and Oklahoma - each of which in 1958 permitted an accused to exclude adverse spousal testimony. The trend in state law toward divesting the accused of the privilege to bar adverse spousal testimony has special relevance because the laws of marriage and domestic relations are concerns traditionally reserved to the states. Scholarly criticism of the *Hawkins* rule has also continued unabated.

Testimonial exclusionary rules and privileges contravene the fundamental principle that " 'the public ... has a right to every man's evidence.' " As such, they must be strictly construed and accepted "only to the very limited extent that permitting a refusal to testify or excluding relevant evidence has a public good transcending the normally predominant principle of utilizing all rational means for ascertaining truth." Here we must decide whether the privilege against adverse spousal testimony promotes sufficiently important interests to outweigh the need for probative evidence in the administration of criminal justice.

It is essential to remember that the *Hawkins* privilege is not needed to protect information privately disclosed between husband and wife in the confidence of the marital relationship-once described by this Court as "the best solace of human existence." Those confidences are privileged under the independent rule protecting confidential marital communications. The *Hawkins* privilege is invoked, not to exclude private marital communications, but rather to exclude evidence of criminal acts and of communications made in the presence of third persons.

No other testimonial privilege sweeps so broadly. The privileges between priest and penitent, attorney and client, and physician and patient limit protection to private communications. These privileges are rooted in the imperative need for confidence and trust. The priest-penitent privilege recognizes the human need to disclose to a spiritual counselor, in total and absolute confidence, what are believed to be flawed acts or thoughts and to receive priestly consolation and guidance in return. The lawyer-client privilege rests on the need for the advocate and counselor to know all that relates to the client's reasons for seeking representation if the professional mission is to be carried out. Similarly, the physician must know all that a patient can articulate in order to identify and to treat disease; barriers to full disclosure would impair diagnosis and treatment.

The *Hawkins* rule stands in marked contrast to these three privileges. Its protection is not limited to confidential communications; rather it permits an accused to exclude all adverse spousal testimony. As Jeremy Bentham observed more than a century and a half ago, such a privilege goes far beyond making "every man's house his castle," and permits a person to convert his house into "a den of thieves." It "secures, to every man, one safe and unquestionable and every ready accomplice for every imaginable crime."

The ancient foundations for so sweeping a privilege have long since disappeared. Nowhere in the common-law world-indeed in any modern society-is a woman regarded as chattel or demeaned by denial of a separate legal identity and the dignity associated with

Take Note!

Is the Court saying that the adverse testimonial privilege applies only to testimony given against a spouse? That is, there is no privilege if a defendant wants a spouse to testify in his favor, or if the non-testifying spouse is not a criminal defendant in a criminal case? The answer appears to be yes. Only testimony that is adverse to the legal interests of an accused is privileged. *United States v. Yerardi*, 192 F.3d 14 (1st Cir. 1999).

recognition as a whole human being. Chip by chip, over the years those archaic notions have been cast aside so that "[n]o longer is the female destined solely for the home and the rearing of the family, and only the male for the marketplace and the world of ideas."

The contemporary justification for affording an accused such a privilege is also unpersuasive. When one spouse is willing to testify against the other in a criminal proceeding--whatever the motivation--their relationship is almost certainly in disrepair; there is probably little in the way of marital harmony for the privilege to preserve. In these circumstances, a rule of evidence that permits an accused to prevent adverse spousal testimony seems far more likely to frustrate justice than to foster family peace. Indeed, there is reason to believe that vesting the privilege in the accused could actually undermine the marital relationship. For example, in a case such as this the Government is unlikely to offer a wife immunity and lenient treatment if it knows that her husband can prevent her from giving adverse testimony. If the Government is dissuaded from making such an offer, the privilege can have the untoward effect of permitting one spouse to escape justice at the expense of the other. It hardly seems conducive to the preservation of the marital relation to place a wife in jeopardy solely by virtue of her husband's control over her testimony.

Our consideration of the foundations for the privilege and its history satisfy us that "reason and experience" no longer justify so sweeping a rule as that found acceptable by the Court in *Hawkins*. Accordingly, we conclude that the existing rule should be modified so that the witness-spouse alone has a privilege to refuse to testify adversely; the witness may be neither compelled to testify nor foreclosed from testifying. This modification-vesting the privilege in the witness-spouse-furthers the important public interest in marital harmony without unduly burdening legitimate law enforcement needs.

Here, petitioner's spouse chose to testify against him. That she did so after a grant of immunity and assurances of lenient treatment does not render her testimony involuntary. Accordingly, the District Court and the Court of Appeals were correct in rejecting petitioner's claim of privilege, and the judgment of the Court of Appeals is

Affirmed.

Points for Discussion

a. The Policy Behind the Adverse Testimonial Privilege.

The Court claims that if one spouse is willing to testify against another spouse, then "their relationship is almost certainly in disrepair" and "there is probably little in the way of marital harmony for the privilege to preserve." Do you agree? Given that Mrs. Trammel agreed to testify in return for leniency, how "voluntary" do you think her testimony actually was? Does her willingness to testify necessarily indicate anything about the state of her marriage prior to her testimony?

Perspective and Analysis

The *Trammel* case did not please everyone. Consider the following excerpt:

> The effect of the Supreme Court's decision in *Trammel* was to declare open season on spouses. Law enforcement has been busy exploiting its new license ever since *Trammel*. The extent and success of federal law enforcement's attempts to turn wives and husbands against each other is difficult to assess. Still, the tip of the iceberg bobs to the surface often enough to cause concern about the mass lurking below the reported opinions. The impact of *Trammel* cuts even deeper into the social fabric. It established a judicial tone that effectively precluded development and recognition of a privilege protecting the parent-child relationship. Today, law enforcement appears to have few qualms about inducing children to inform on their parents.

Michael W. Mullane, *Trammel v. United States: Bad History, Bad Policy, and Bad Law*, 47 ME. L. REV. 105, 110 (1995)

b. When Does the Adverse Testimonial Privilege Apply?

What if Mrs. Trammel and Mr. Trammel were divorced by the time she testified? Since there is no longer any marriage to protect, the privilege would not apply. See *United States v. Fisher*, 518 F.2d 836 (2d Cir. 1975) (the adverse testimonial privilege applies only during the marriage). What if the Trammels were married but separated at the time of trial? Could Mrs. Trammel claim the privilege? Some courts have said no. See *United States v. Cameron*, 556 F.2d 752 (5th Cir. 1977) (there was no adverse testimonial privilege because the marriage was no longer viable, and the couple had no hopes for reconciliation); *United*

States v. Brown, 605 F.2d 389 (8ᵗʰ Cir. 1979) (the marriage was so unstable and of such short duration that it did not deserve to be protected by the privilege); *United States v. Roberson*, 859 F.2d 1376 (9ᵗʰ Cir. 1988) (requiring that the trial court make a detailed factual analysis of the possibility of reconciliation of the spouses at the time of the communication). Do cases like *Cameron, Brown,* and *Roberson* give courts too much power to intrude upon the privacy of a marriage?

c. Sham Marriages

If the marriage is a sham or a fraud on the court, the privilege does not apply. See *United States v. Apodaca*, 522 F.2d 568 (10ᵗʰ Cir. 1975) (after being threatened by the defendant, the primary witness against the defendant married him three days before trial; the court found that under the circumstances, the marriage was "fraudulent, spurious" and "not entered into in good faith"). What if the couple in *Apodaca* had been engaged and lived together for six months prior to the marriage? What if the wife claimed that she did not know that marriage would bar her testimony against her husband? Are these additional facts sufficient to show a marriage is not a sham?

d. Exception: Crimes Against the Spouse or a Child Living in the Home.

The adverse testimonial privilege does not apply when one spouse is prosecuted for a crime against the other spouse or, depending on the jurisdiction, against children of the marriage. See *United States v. Allery*, 526 F.2d 1362 (8ᵗʰ Cir. 1975) (justifying an exception to the adverse testimonial privilege for crimes against spouses and children in the home on the basis that "over ninety percent of reported child abuse cases occurred in the home, with a parent or parent substitute the perpetrator in eighty-seven and one-tenth percent of these cases").

---

2. The Marital Communication Privilege

The common law has long observed a privilege for communications made between spouses during the marriage. This privilege operates much like the attorney-client privilege in that they both protect against the disclosure of confidential communications made between a protected group of people, even after the death of a privilege holder. The justification for the privilege is to encourage full and free communication necessary to a successful marriage. Almost all jurisdictions have recognized the privilege in both civil and criminal cases. The privilege can be defeated, however, if the purpose of the spouses's communications is to commit a crime or fraud.

United States v. Marashi

U.S. Court of Appeals for the Ninth Circuit
913 F.2d 724 (9th Cir. 1990)

CYNTHIA HOLCOMB HALL, Circuit Judge:

In the late summer of 1984, Sharon Smith Marashi ("Smith") learned that her husband, Dr. S. Mohammad Marashi was having an extramarital affair with his secretary, Mrs. Sherrie Danzig. Smith also learned from the secretary's husband, Steve Danzig, that the two had flown off to Europe.... Marashi returned from Europe to discover that his wife was filing for divorce. Several months later, on December 22, 1984, he moved out of their house and into a condominium.

Filing for divorce was not enough for Smith and Danzig. They met several times to discuss how to get even with their unfaithful spouses. At one point, Smith mentioned that Marashi had underreported his federal income tax for some years. Seeing an opportunity to exact revenge upon his rival, Danzig contacted the IRS. Later, he pressured Smith to come forward with information implicating Marashi, [which she did]. In her discussions with the IRS, Smith described how Marashi had enlisted her aid to evade federal income taxes. She explained that daily her husband would bring home slips of paper indicating how much patients had paid him. Marashi would then store the slips in a desk drawer located in his study. Periodically, he would ask Smith to record the information from the slips into either a black ledger for that year or a stenographer's notebook. Marashi would highlight certain items of income and instruct Smith to enter them into the notebook for his own records; this income went unreported to the IRS. Next, he would instruct her to enter the remaining items of income into that year's black ledger, which he kept as an official record for audit purposes. Marashi would then discard the slips of paper.

Smith added that Marashi had employed this double-ledger scheme at least from 1981-84. She estimated that the unreported income contained in the stenographer's notebook ran into the thousands.

* * *

Marashi first appeals the denial of his motion to suppress Smith's testimony... He claims that his statements are covered by the marital communications privilege.

To determine the scope and application of evidentiary privileges in federal criminal cases, we must turn to federal common law. The common law recognizes two separate privileges arising out of the marital relationship. The first, which we have called the "anti-marital facts" privilege, prohibits one spouse from testifying against another during the length of the marriage. Because Smith testified after she divorced Marashi, this privilege does not apply.

The second, so-called "marital communications" privilege, bars testimony concerning statements privately communicated between spouses. The non-testifying spouse may invoke the privilege, even after dissolution of the marriage. Thus, Marashi may attempt to invoke it.

The confines of the marital communications privilege are easy to describe. First, the privilege extends only to words or acts intended as communication to the other spouse. Second, it covers only those communications made during a valid marriage, unless the couple had irreconcilably separated. Third, the privilege applies only to those marital communications which are confidential. That is, the privilege does not extend to statements which are made before, or likely to be overheard by, third parties. Marital communications are presumptively confidential; the government has the burden of demonstrating that they are not.

FYI

Some appellate courts have required trial courts to make a detailed factual analysis into the possibility of reconciliation of the spouses at the time of the communication by looking at the duration and stability of the marriage and whether a divorce petition has been filed. See *United States v. Roberson*, 859 F.2d 1376 (9th Cir. 1988). Not all courts agree. In *United States v. Byrd*, 750 F.2d 585 (7th Cir. 1984), for example, the court found it neither practical nor desirable to require trial courts to determine whether a couple's marriage was sufficiently deteriorated before deciding whether to apply the privilege.

This last presumption notwithstanding, we have emphasized that we will narrowly construe the marital communications privilege because it obstructs the truth-seeking process. Use of the privilege in criminal proceedings requires a particularly narrow construction because of society's strong interest in the administration of justice.

Under this analysis, it is readily apparent that the privilege does not extend to Smith's testimony regarding Marashi's orders to have her erase entries in his appointment books. The presence of a third person, Marya LaSalandra, during the communications destroyed the privilege.

It is also clear that the privilege covers Smith's testimony regarding Marashi's instructions to have her underreport income. Marashi made the statements while the marriage was legally valid. Moreover, because his instructions were made in the privacy of the couple's bedroom, they were confidential.

The government concedes that the privilege extends to the latter testimony. It urges us to adopt a narrow exception to that rule. We consider this point below.

Every circuit addressing the issue has held that the marital communications privilege does not apply to communications having to do with present or future crimes in which both spouses are participants...

This view is consistent with our attitude toward evidentiary privileges in general. We have emphasized that the policies underlying the marital communications privilege pale in the face of public concerns about bringing criminals to justice. Thus we join our sister circuits in holding that the marital communications privilege does not apply to statements made in furtherance of joint criminal activity.

Marashi argues that in any event, the exception should not apply here because the IRS did not prosecute Smith. In rejecting a similar argument, the Fourth Circuit reasoned:

> The policies behind the joint criminal participation exception are concerned with the actual participation by both spouses in a crime, not with their joint prosecution for that crime. The exception arises out of a careful balancing of the policies behind protecting the intimacy of private marital communications and the public policy of getting at the truth and attaining justice... Whether the spouse testifying has been indicted and is being prosecuted for his or her participation is a prosecutorial prerogative that is not material to the policies at issue here.

We agree. The government may well decide, as it has in this case, to forego prosecution of one spouse in order to secure her testimony against the other. The greater public interest is to assure a criminal that if he enlists the aid of his spouse, he is creating a potential witness for the government. Accordingly, the government's decision not to prosecute Smith does not preclude application of the partnership in crime exception.

There is little question that the communications in this case were made in furtherance of a joint criminal venture. Marashi directed Smith to help him underreport income on their joint income tax returns. Smith freely did so, in violation of [federal law]. Accordingly, Marashi's statements in furtherance of these criminal acts were admissible under the partnership in crime exception to the marital communications privilege.

In sum, we hold that the district court did not abuse its discretion by admitting Smith's testimony.

───────────

Points for Discussion

a. Justification for a Marital Communication Privilege.

The purpose of a marital communication privilege is to allow spouses to communicate freely. *United States v. Byrd,* 750 F.2d 585 (7th Cir. 1984) (the communication privilege exists to insure that spouses feel free to communicate their deepest feelings to each other without fear of eventual exposure in a court of law). It is believed that by protecting these communications, marriages will be strengthened. If this is true, then why not extend the privilege to communications between parents and children, or between couples of the same or opposite sex who are in a committed relationship?

b. What is a Communication?

To qualify for a privilege, the marital communication must usually be oral or written. This has been interpreted to mean "utterances or expressions intended by one spouse to convey a message to another." Also protected are gestures that are "intended by one spouse to convey a message to the other," such as pointing or shaking one's head in response to a question. See *United States v. Espino,* 317 F.3d 788, 795 (8th Cir. 2003). Nevertheless, most spousal gestures are characterized as non-communicative. See *United States v. Lofton,* 957 F.2d 476 (7th Cir. 1992) (a wife's testimony about her husband's use of cocaine and her knowledge that a package filled with cocaine belonged to her husband were not considered privileged).

c. Requirement of Confidentiality: Eavesdroppers and Spousal Colluders.

The presence of a third person during marital communications destroys the privilege. In *Marashi,* both husband and wife were aware that a third person was present when they communicated. But, what if the spouses were not aware? At least one case has held that the privilege is not necessary when an eavesdropper overhears an otherwise protected marital communication because neither spouse can blame the other for the breach of confidence and thus will continue to confide in each other. See *United States v. Neal,* 532 F. Supp. 942 (D. Colo. 1982). However, when one spouse connives with the police to overhear a marital communication, the privilege applies because the betrayed spouse's trust in the relationship has ended. *Id.*

d. Exceptions: Crimes Against a Spouse or Other Family Members.

As with the adverse testimonial privilege, the marital communication privilege can be abrogated if one spouse commits a crime against the other spouse. See *Wyatt v. United States,* 362 U.S. 525, 902 (1960) ("The common law has long recognized an exception in the case of certain kinds of offenses committed by the party against his spouse"). A number of courts also recognize an exception where the communication relates to a crime, the victim of which is a minor child who lives in the spouses' household. See, e.g., *United States v. White, 974 F.2d 1135, 1138 (9th Cir. 1992)* ("threats against spouses and a spouse's children do not further the purposes of the privilege and ... the public interest in the administration of justice outweighs any possible purpose the privilege serves in such a case").

e. Summary of Marital Privileges.

In summary, the following represent the significant distinctions between the adverse testimonial privilege and the marital communication privilege.

Adverse Testimonial Privilege	Marital Communications Privilege
1. Applies to all testimony against a spouse on any subject, including marital communications.	1. Applies only to confidential communications between spouses.
2. Spouses must be married to assert the privilege.	2. Spouses need not be married to assert the privilege. Confidential communications are privileged for all time, unless an exception applies.
3. Only the testifying spouse may assert the privilege.	3. Either spouse may assert the privilege in most jurisdictions.
4. Applies only to criminal cases.	4. Applies to both criminal and civil cases.
5. Recognizes an injury to a spouse and children exception.	5. Recognizes an injury to a spouse and children exception.

Hypo 13.2

Defendant murdered the victim before he and his wife married. At the defendant's trial, the prosecution wants to compel the wife to testify that the defendant confided in her after they were married that he killed the victim. Can she be compelled to testify? If so, is this communication nonetheless privileged? Would your answer be different if the wife agreed to testify?

D. Psychotherapist-Patient Privilege

Many people think that federal common law recognizes a physician-patient privilege that protects confidential communications made by a patient to a physician for the purpose of diagnosis or treatment. However, this is not the case.

> The need for a psychotherapist-patient privilege is well supported by professional mental health associations, such as the Group for the Advancement of Psychiatry. For example, in 1960 report, they declared:
>
> Among physicians, the psychiatrist has a special need to maintain confidentiality. His capacity to help his patients is completely dependent upon their willingness and ability to talk freely. This makes it difficult if not impossible for him to function without being able to assure his patients of confidentiality and, indeed, privileged communication. Psychiatrists not only explore feelings and attitudes as well. Therapeutic effectiveness necessitates going beyond a patient's awareness and, in order to do this, it must be possible to communicate freely. Report No. 45, Group for the Advancement of Psychiatry 92 (1960).

A physician-patient privilege was unknown at common law. Beginning in 1928, such a privilege was adopted by statute in a number of states, but these statutes were subject to a great deal of criticism because they unduly restricted judicial fact-finding, and there was little evidence physician-patient communications would be impeded without them. Given this experience, the Advisory Committee to the Federal Rules of Evidence did not propose a physician-patient privilege, and federal courts have generally refused to recognize one. A psychotherapist-patient privilege, however, was another matter.

By 1996, all fifty states, the District of Columbia, and a small but growing number of federal courts recognized a psychotherapist-patient privilege on the basis that communications between psychotherapists and patients typically contain far more personal information than communications with other kinds of doctors, and that unrestrained disclosure might discourage persons from seeking psychological help. Most federal courts were not as convinced. In order to resolve uncertainty in the area, the Supreme Court accepted certiorari in the case of *Jaffee v. Redmond*.

Jaffee v. Redmond

518 U.S. 1 (1996)

Justice STEVENS delivered the opinion of the Court.

issue

After a traumatic incident in which she shot and killed a man, a police officer received extensive counseling from a licensed clinical social worker. The question we address is whether statements the officer made to her therapist during the counseling sessions are protected from compelled disclosure in a federal civil action brought by the family of the deceased. Stated otherwise, the question is whether it is appropriate for federal courts to recognize a "psychotherapist privilege" under Rule 501 of the Federal Rules of Evidence.

* * *

Petitioner filed suit in Federal District Court alleging that Redmond had violated Allen's constitutional rights by using excessive force during the encounter at [an] apartment complex. The complaint sought damages. At trial, petitioner presented testimony from members of Allen's family that conflicted with Redmond's version of the incident in several important respects. They testified, for example, that Redmond drew her gun before exiting her squad car and that Allen was unarmed when he emerged from the apartment building.

During pretrial discovery petitioner learned that after the shooting Redmond had participated in about 50 counseling sessions with Karen Beyer, a clinical social worker licensed by the State of Illinois and employed at that time by the Village of Hoffman Estates. Petitioner sought access to Beyer's notes concerning the sessions for use in cross-examining Redmond. Respondents vigorously resisted the discovery. They asserted that the contents of the conversations between Beyer and Redmond were protected against involuntary disclosure by a psychotherapist-patient privilege. The district judge rejected this argument. Neither Beyer nor Redmond, however, complied with his order to disclose the contents of Beyer's notes. At depositions and on the witness stand both either refused to answer certain questions or professed an inability to recall details of their conversations.

In his instructions at the end of the trial, the judge advised the jury that the refusal to turn over Beyer's notes had no "legal justification" and that the jury could therefore presume that the contents of the notes would have been unfavorable to respondents. The jury awarded petitioner $45,000 on the federal claim and $500,000 on her state-law claim.

* * *

Rule 501 of the Federal Rules of Evidence authorizes federal courts to define new privileges by interpreting "common law principles ... in the light of reason and experience." ...

The common-law principles underlying the recognition of testimonial privileges can be stated simply. " 'For more than three centuries it has now been recognized as a fundamental maxim that the public ... has a right to every man's evidence. When we come to examine the various claims of exemption, we start with the primary assumption that there is a general duty to give what testimony one is capable of giving, and that any exemptions which may exist are distinctly exceptional, being so many derogations from a positive general rule.'

Guided by these principles, the question we address today is whether a privilege protecting confidential communications between a psychotherapist and her patient "promotes sufficiently important interests to outweigh the need for probative evidence... Both "reason and experience" persuade us that it does.

Like the spousal and attorney-client privileges, the psychotherapist-patient privilege is "rooted in the imperative need for confidence and trust." Treatment by a physician for physical ailments can often proceed successfully on the basis of a physical examination, objective information supplied by the patient, and the results of diagnostic tests. Effective psychotherapy, by contrast, depends upon an atmosphere of confidence and trust in which the patient is willing to make a frank and complete disclosure of facts, emotions, memories, and fears. Because of the sensitive nature of the problems for which individuals consult psychotherapists, disclosure of confidential communications made during counseling sessions may cause embarrassment or disgrace. For this reason, the mere possibility of disclosure may impede development of the confidential relationship necessary for successful treatment.FN3 By protecting confidential communications between a psychotherapist and her patient from involuntary disclosure, the proposed privilege thus serves important private interests.

Our cases make clear that an asserted privilege must also "serv[e] public ends." ... The psychotherapist privilege serves the public interest by facilitating the provision of appropriate treatment for individuals suffering the effects of a mental or emotional problem. The mental health of our citizenry, no less than its physical health, is a public good of transcendent importance.

Food For Thought

Can these same arguments about the need for confidentiality also be made for establishing a parent-child privilege? Yet, a parent-child privilege has not been recognized by the federal common law. What does this tell you about whether the parent-child relationship "is a public good of transcendent importance?"

In contrast to the significant public and private interests supporting recognition of the privilege, the likely evidentiary benefit that would result from the denial of the privilege is modest. If the privilege were rejected, confidential conversations between psychotherapists and their patients would surely be chilled, particularly when it is obvious that the circumstances that give rise to the need for treatment will probably result in litigation. Without a privilege, much of the desirable evidence to which litigants such as petitioner seek access-for example, admissions against interest by a party-is unlikely to come into being. This unspoken "evidence" will therefore serve no greater truth-seeking function than if it had been spoken and privileged.

That it is appropriate for the federal courts to recognize a psychotherapist privilege under Rule 501 is confirmed by the fact that all 50 States and the District of Columbia have enacted into law some form of psychotherapist privilege. We have previously observed that the policy decisions of the States bear on the question whether federal courts should recognize a new privilege or amend the coverage of an existing one. Because state legislatures are fully aware of the need to protect the integrity of the factfinding functions of their courts, the existence of a consensus among the States indicates that "reason and experience" support recognition of the privilege. In addition, given the importance of the patient's understanding that her communications with her therapist will not be publicly disclosed, any State's promise of confidentiality would have little value if the patient were aware that the privilege would not be honored in a federal court. Denial of the federal privilege therefore would frustrate the purposes of the state legislation that was enacted to foster these confidential communications...

Because we agree with the judgment of the state legislatures and the Advisory Committee that a psychotherapist-patient privilege will serve a "public good transcending the normally predominant principle of utilizing all rational means for ascertaining truth," we hold that confidential communications between a licensed psychotherapist and her patients in the course of diagnosis or treatment are protected from compelled disclosure under Rule 501 of the Federal Rules of Evidence.

All agree that a psychotherapist privilege covers confidential communications made to licensed psychiatrists and psychologists. We have no hesitation in concluding in this case that the federal privilege should also extend to confidential communications made to licensed social workers in the course of psychotherapy. The reasons for recognizing a privilege for treatment by psychiatrists and psychologists apply with equal force to treatment by a clinical social worker such as Karen Beyer. Today, social workers provide a significant amount of mental health treatment. Their clients often include the poor and those of modest means who could not afford the assistance of a psychiatrist or psychologist, but whose counseling sessions serve the same public goals. Perhaps in recognition of these circumstances, the vast majority of States explicitly extend a testimonial privilege to licensed social workers. We therefore agree with the Court of Appeals that "[d] rawing a distinction between the counseling provided by costly psychotherapists and the counseling provided by more readily accessible social workers serves no discernible public purpose."

We part company with the Court of Appeals on a separate point. We reject the balancing component of the privilege implemented by that court and a small number of States. Making the promise of confidentiality contingent upon a trial judge's later evaluation of the relative importance of the patient's interest in privacy and the evidentiary need for disclosure would eviscerate the effectiveness of the privilege. As we explained in *Upjohn*, if the purpose of the privilege is to be served, the participants in the confidential conversation "must be able to predict with some degree of certainty whether particular discussions will be protected. An uncertain privilege, or one which purports to be certain but results in widely varying applications by the courts, is little better than no privilege at all."

These considerations are all that is necessary for decision of this case. A rule that authorizes the recognition of new privileges on a case-by-case basis makes it appropriate to define the details of new privileges in a like manner. Because this is the first case in which we have recognized a psychotherapist privilege, it is neither necessary nor feasible to delineate its full contours in a way that would "govern all conceivable future questions in this area."

The conversations between Officer Redmond and Karen Beyer and the notes taken during their counseling sessions are protected from compelled disclosure under Rule 501 of the Federal Rules of Evidence. The judgment of the Court of Appeals is affirmed.

Justice <u>SCALIA</u>, with whom THE CHIEF JUSTICE joins as to Part III, dissenting.

The Court has discussed at some length the benefit that will be purchased by creation of the evidentiary privilege in this case: the encouragement of psychoanalytic counseling. It has not mentioned the purchase price: occasional injustice. That is the cost of every rule which excludes reliable and probative evidence - or at least every one categorical enough to achieve its

> **Make the Connection**
>
> The term "Mirandized" comes from the case of *Miranda v. Arizona*, 384 U.S. 436 (1966), which requires police officers to give arrestees notice of their constitutional rights ("You have a right to remain silent; you have a right to an attorney, etc.") before the officers may question them. This is a subject you will learn more about in a course on Criminal Procedure.

Food for Thought

But this is an argument that can be made to prevent the recognition of any privilege, even those of long-standing, such as attorney-client or husband-wife. How does it have particular application to a psycho-therapist-patient privilege? If has no specific application, what is Justice Scalia saying?

announced policy objective. In the case of some of these rules, such as the one excluding confessions that have not been properly "Mirandized," the victim of the injustice is always the impersonal State or the faceless "public at large." For the rule proposed here, the victim is more likely to be some individual who is prevented from proving a valid claim -- or (worse still) prevented from establishing a valid defense. The latter is particularly unpalatable for those who love justice, because it causes the courts of law not merely to let stand a wrong, but to become themselves the instruments of wrong.

I

... I must observe that the Court makes its task deceptively simple by the manner in which it proceeds. It begins by characterizing the issue as "whether it is appropriate for federal courts to recognize a 'psychotherapist privilege,'" and devotes almost all of its opinion to that question. Having answered that question (to its satisfaction) in the affirmative, it then devotes *less than a page of text* to answering in the affirmative the small remaining question whether "the federal privilege should also extend to confidential communications made to licensed social workers in the course of psychotherapy."

... [I]t seems a long step from a lawyer-client privilege to a tax advisor-client or accountant-client privilege. But if one recharacterizes it as a "legal advisor" privilege, the extension seems like the most natural thing in the world. That is the illusion the Court has produced here: It first frames an overly general question ("Should there be a psychotherapist privilege?") that can be answered in the negative only by excluding from protection office consultations with professional psychiatrists (*i.e.*, doctors) and clinical psychologists. And then, having answered that in the affirmative, it comes to the *only* question that the facts of this case present ("Should there be a social worker-client privilege with regard to psycho-therapeutic counseling?") with the answer seemingly a foregone conclusion. At that point, to conclude against the privilege one must subscribe to the difficult proposition, "Yes, there is a psychotherapist privilege, but not if the psychotherapist is a social worker."

II

To say that the Court devotes the bulk of its opinion to the much easier question of psychotherapist-patient privilege is not to say that its answer to that question is convincing. At bottom, the Court's decision to recognize such a privilege is based on its view that "successful [psychotherapeutic] treatment" serves "important private interests" (namely, those of patients undergoing psychotherapy) as well as the "public good" of "[t]he mental health of our citizenry." I have no quarrel with these premises. Effective psychotherapy undoubtedly is beneficial to individuals with mental problems, and surely serves some larger social interest in maintaining a mentally stable society. But merely mentioning these values does not answer the critical question: Are they of such importance, and is the contribution of psychotherapy to them so distinctive, and is the application of normal evidentiary rules so destructive to psychotherapy, as to justify making our federal courts occasional instruments of injustice? On that central question I find the Court's analysis insufficiently convincing to satisfy the high standard we have set for rules that "are in derogation of the search for truth."

When is it, one must wonder, that *the psychotherapist* came to play such an indispensable role in the maintenance of the citizenry's mental health? For most of history, men and women have worked out their difficulties by talking to parents, siblings, best friends, and bartenders--none of whom was awarded a privilege against testifying in court. Ask the average citizen: Would your mental health be more significantly impaired by preventing you from seeing a psychotherapist, or by preventing you from getting advice from your mom? I have little doubt what the answer would be. Yet there is no mother--child privilege.

How likely is it that a person will be deterred from seeking psychological counseling, or from being completely truthful in the course of such counseling, because of fear of later disclosure in litigation? And even more pertinent to today's decision, to what extent will the evidentiary privilege reduce that deterrent? The Court does not try to answer the first of these questions; and it *cannot possibly have any notion* of what the answer is to the second, since that depends entirely upon the scope of the privilege, which the Court amazingly finds it "neither necessary nor feasible to delineate." If, for example, the psychotherapist can give the patient no more assurance than "A court will not be able to make me disclose what you tell me, unless you tell me about a harmful act," I doubt whether there would be much benefit from the privilege at all. That is not a fanciful example, at least with respect to extension of the psychotherapist privilege to social workers.

Even where it is certain that absence of the psychotherapist privilege will inhibit disclosure of the information, it is not clear to me that that is an unacceptable state of affairs. Let us assume the very worst in the circumstances of the present case: that to be truthful about what was troubling her, the police officer who sought counseling would have to confess that she shot without reason, and wounded an innocent man. If (again to assume the worst) such an act constituted the crime of negligent wounding under Illinois law, the officer would of course have the absolute right not to admit that she shot without reason in criminal court. But I see no reason why she should be enabled *both* not to admit it in criminal court (as a good citizen should), *and* to get the benefits of psychotherapy by admitting it to a therapist who cannot tell anyone else...

The Court confidently asserts that not much truth-finding capacity would be destroyed by the privilege anyway, since "[w]ithout a privilege, much of the desirable evidence to which litigants such as petitioner seek access ... is unlikely to come into being." If that is so, how come psychotherapy got to be a thriving practice before the "psychotherapist privilege" was invented? Were the patients paying money to lie to their analysts all those years?...

III

Turning from the general question that was not involved in this case to the specific one that is: The Court's conclusion that a social-worker psychotherapeutic privilege deserves recognition is even less persuasive. In approaching this question, the fact that five of the state legislatures that have seen fit to enact "some form" of psychotherapist privilege have elected not to extend *any form* of privilege to social workers, ought to give one pause. So should the fact that the Judicial Conference Advisory Committee was similarly discriminating in its conferral of the proposed Rule 504 privilege.

...A licensed psychiatrist or psychologist is an expert in psychotherapy - and that may suffice (though I think it not so clear that this Court should make the judgment) to justify the use of extraordinary means to encourage counseling with him, as opposed to counseling with one's rabbi, minister, family, or friends. One must presume that a social worker does *not* bring this greatly heightened degree of skill to bear, which is alone a reason for not encouraging that consultation as generously. Does a social worker bring to bear at least a significantly heightened degree of skill - more than a minister or rabbi, for example? I have no idea, and neither does the Court.. .

Another critical distinction between psychiatrists and psychologists, on the one hand, and social workers, on the other, is that the former professionals, in their consultations with patients, *do nothing but psychotherapy*. Social workers, on the other hand, interview people for a multitude of reasons. Thus, in applying the "social worker" variant of the "psychotherapist" privilege, it will be necessary to determine whether the information provided to the social worker was provided to him in *his capacity as a psychotherapist*, or in his capacity as an administrator of social welfare, a community organizer, etc. Worse still, if the privilege is to have its desired effect (and is not to mislead the client), it will presumably be necessary for the social caseworker to advise, as the conversation with his welfare client proceeds, which portions are privileged and which are not.

Having concluded its three sentences of reasoned analysis, the Court then invokes, as it did when considering the psychotherapist privilege, the "experience" of the States - once again an experience I consider irrelevant (if not counter-indicative) because it consists entirely of legislation rather than common-law decision. It says that "the vast majority of States explicitly extend a testimonial privilege to licensed social workers." There are two elements of this impressive statistic, however, that the Court does not reveal.

First - and utterly conclusive of the irrelevance of this supposed consensus to the question before us -- the majority of the States that accord a privilege to social workers do *not* do so as a subpart of a "psychotherapist" privilege. The privilege applies to all confidences imparted to social workers, and not just those provided in the course of psychotherapy. In Oklahoma, for example, the social-worker-privilege statute prohibits a licensed social worker from disclosing, or being compelled to disclose, " *any information* acquired from persons consulting the licensed social worker in his or her professional capacity" (with certain exceptions to be discussed *infra*).

Thus, in Oklahoma, as in most other States having a social-worker privilege, it is not a subpart or even a derivative of the psychotherapist privilege, but rather a piece of special legislation similar to that achieved by many other groups, from accountants, to private detectives, These social-worker statutes give no support, therefore, to the theory (importance of psychotherapy) upon which the Court rests its disposition.

But turning to those States that do have an appreciable privilege of some sort, the diversity is vast. In Illinois and Wisconsin, the social-worker privilege does not apply when the confidential information pertains to homicide, and in the District of Columbia when it pertains to any crime "inflicting injuries" upon persons. In Missouri, the privilege is suspended as to information that pertains to a criminal act, and in Texas when the information is sought in any criminal prosecution. In Kansas and Oklahoma, the privilege yields when the information pertains to "violations of any law;" in Indiana, when it reveals a "serious harmful act;" and in Delaware and Idaho, when it pertains to any "harmful act," In Oregon, a state-employed social worker like Karen Beyer loses the privilege where her supervisor determines that her testimony "is necessary in the performance of the duty of the social worker as a public employee." In South Carolina, a social worker is forced to disclose confidences "when required by statutory law or by court order for good cause shown to the extent that the patient's care and treatment or the nature and extent of his mental illness or emotional condition are reasonably at issue in a proceeding." The majority of social-worker-privilege States declare the privilege inapplicable to information relating to child abuse. And the States that do not fall into any of the above categories provide exceptions for commitment proceedings, for proceedings in which the patient relies on his mental or emotional condition as an element of his claim or defense, or for communications made in the course of a court-ordered examination of the mental or emotional condition of the patient.

Thus, although the Court is technically correct that "the vast majority of States explicitly extend a testimonial privilege to licensed social workers," that uniformity exists only at the most superficial level. No State has adopted the privilege without restriction; the nature of the restrictions varies enormously from jurisdiction to jurisdiction; and 10 States, I reiterate, effectively reject the privilege entirely. It is fair to say that there is scant national consensus even as to the propriety of a social-worker psychotherapist privilege, and none whatever as to its appropriate scope. In other words, the state laws to which the Court appeals for support demonstrate most convincingly that adoption of a social-worker psychotherapist privilege is a job for Congress…

———————————

Points for Discussion

a. The Need for Confidentiality Between Psychotherapists and Patients.

Do you agree with the opinion that "reason and experience" supports the creation of a psychotherapist-patient privilege because "the mere possibility of disclosure may impede development of the confidential relationship necessary for successful treatment?" Or do you agree with the argument in the dissent that talk-therapy flourished before the Court recognized the privilege? Just how necessary is confidentiality in this context? Can you think of any reason why it may be more crucial to protect communications between psychotherapists and patients than between bar patrons and bartenders, for instance?

Perspective & Analysis

One commentator...argues that the cited studies in the case of *Jaffee v. Redmond* 518 U.S. 1 (1996) which addressed this privilege were not based upon responses from actual patients, or, if they were, did not ask the patients about their attitudes toward court-ordered disclosure and therefore do not support the majority's recognition of the privilege.

> A careful review of the studies cited by the majority leads not only to the conclusion that the recognition of a privilege comes at a cost, the findings in those studies also carry the implication that the cost is excessive. If the only stated justification for the privilege were the instrumental rationale upon which the *Jaffee* majority relied, the Court arguably should have rejected the defendants' privilege claim. The findings in the available studies make Wigmore's classic remark apropos: The "benefits" of the privilege "are . . . speculative; its obstruction is plain and concrete."

> The studies uniformly indicate that the availability of a privilege has little or no influence on the typical patient's decisions to seek therapy and to make disclosures to a therapist. Thus, in the run-of-the-mill case, it does not serve the privilege's instrumental rationale to exclude the statement; contrary to Justice Stevens' assertion, the evidence would have "come into being" even if there had been no privilege.

> However, in that same typical case, the enforcement of the privilege will tend to frustrate the search for truth. If the statement is being proffered at trial and the objection is on privilege--rather than relevance-- grounds, the statement is presumably probative under Federal Rule of Evidence 401. Consequently, to use Justice Stevens' expression, the admission of the statement would further the court's "truth-seeking function." In short, in the typical case the trier of fact will be denied helpful testimony even though the exclusion of the evidence does not effectuate the Court's articulated instrumental rationale

Edward Imwinkelried, *The Rivalry Between Truth and Privilege: The Weakness of the Supreme Court's Instrumental Reasoning in Jaffee v. Redmond, 518 U.S. 1 (1996), 49 Hastings L.J. 969, 982 (1998)*

b. Extending the Privilege to Social Workers.

Was the majority correct in extending the psychotherapist-patient privilege to social workers on the basis that they are, in effect, a "poor man's" psychologist? Or was Justice Scalia correct in arguing that social workers are less trained in psychology and have duties other than counseling, which makes extending the privilege to all confidential communications with their clients overbroad? If the majority is correct, why not extend the privilege to cover physicians dealing with a patient's depression? In fact, this has occurred. See <u>*Finley v. Johnson Oil Co.*, 199 F.R.D. 301 (S.D. Ind. 2001)</u> (extending the psychotherapist-patient privilege to general practitioners at a health clinic to the degree they treat a patient's depression, on the basis that the privilege applies to "more readily accessible social workers"). How about extending the privilege to Alcoholics Anonymous members who counsel and support one another often through life-changing circumstances? See <u>Thomas J. Reed, *The Futile Fifth Step: Compulsory Disclosure of Confidential Communications Among Alcoholics Anonymous Members*, 70 ST. JOHN'S L. REV. 693 (1996)</u>.

c. Is There a "Dangerous Patient" Exception?

The majority in *Jaffee* acknowledged that there would no doubt be "situations in which the privilege must give way, for example, if a serious threat of harm to the patient or to others can be averted only by means of a disclosure by the therapist." A number of states recognize this exception, but lower federal courts are less certain. See <u>*United States v. Glass*, 133 F.3d 1356 (10th Cir. 1998)</u> (the Tenth Circuit acknowledges a "dangerous patient" exception only when the threat was serious when made, and disclosure was the only means of avoiding the harm); but see <u>*United States v. Hayes*, 227 F.3d 578 (6th Cir. 2000)</u> (there is no "dangerous patient" exception in criminal cases because although psychotherapists have a duty to protect third persons who may be victims of the patient's threats, this duty does not extend to testifying against a patient in a case unless those matters are directly related to the patient's involuntary hospitalization).

Hypo 13.3

In a counseling session, a psychotherapist learns that his patient has AIDS (acquired immune deficiency syndrome). Assume that the patient has told the psychotherapist that he had just met someone and their relationship is likely to become sexual. If the psychotherapist knows the name of his patient's sexual partner, should the psychotherapist be allowed to warn him? Or is this information privileged under *Jaffee*?

E. Miscellaneous Privileges

Federal courts have been reluctant to expand existing privileges or create new ones because, in the words of the Supreme Court, "exceptions to the demand for every [person's] ... evidence are not lightly created nor expansively construed." <u>*United States v. Nixon*, 418 U.S. 683 (1974)</u>. Although a number of privileges have been created by statute or decision under state law, federal courts have been slow to follow suit and will not generally infer the existence of a new privilege where Congress has not clearly manifested an intent to create one.

This section discusses several of the more prominent privileges that have been urged at the federal level, occasionally with some success but more often without it.

Clergy-Penitent Privilege.

One of the thirteen privileges proposed by the Advisory Committee but rejected by Congress was the clergy-penitent privilege. When recognized, this privilege operates to preclude the testimony of a clergyman who would disclose a confidential communication made by a person seeking spiritual aid. The policy behind the privilege was explained by the Supreme Court in *Trammel v. United States, 445 U.S. 40, 51 (1980)*, even though *Trammel* was a case dealing with the adverse testimonial privilege for spouses:

> The priest-penitent privilege recognizes the human need to disclose to a spiritual counselor, in total and absolute confidence, what are believed to be flawed acts or thoughts and to receive priestly consolation and guidance in return.

Those supporting recognition of the privilege argue that the nature of a religious confessional may prohibit members of the clergy from disclosing anything said in the confessional, even under the sanction of contempt. Requiring a member of the clergy to testify or face contempt would bring the practice of religion into conflict with the courts under the First Amendment.

Although there is no general recognition of a clergy-penitent privilege in federal common law, several cases have found one where the communication was made to a clergy member in his or her spiritual capacity, and the penitent had a reasonable expectation of confidence. See *In re Verplank, 329 F. Supp. 433 (C.D. Cal. 1971)*; *Grand Jury Investigation, 918 F.2d 374 (3d Cir. 1990)*; *Mullen v. United States, 263 F.2d 275 (D.C. Cir. 1959)*.

The clergy-penitent privilege, if recognized, is held by the penitent, and a third person's presence waives the privilege.

Accountant-Client Privilege:

The common law did not recognize an accountant-client privilege, and neither does the Supreme Court. See *United States v. Arthur Young & Co., 465 U.S. 805 (1984)* (there is no general accountant-client communications privilege, nor is there a general work-product doctrine for an accountant's work). In addition, communications made to an attorney/accountant are not privileged to the degree they are made for the purpose of securing accounting advice or assistance. <u>United States v. Bisanti, 414 F.3d 168 (1st Cir. 2005)</u> (the defendant's attorney was acting as an accountant in representing his client during an IRS audit, and therefore any communications he may have had with his client were not privileged).

In 1998, however, Congress enacted <u>26 U.S.C. §7525</u>, which granted an accountant-client privilege for federally-authorized tax practitioners in any non-criminal tax proceedings in federal court brought by or against the United States. Congress reasoned that clients should not be disadvantaged by obtaining advice from accountants when disclosure of the same information to an attorney would be privileged. The privilege has not been extended beyond the confines of this statute.

Journalist's Privilege.

A privilege protecting the identity of a journalist's source and the information gained from the source is part of the law in a number of states. In those states a journalist's privilege is usually justified on the basis that journalists perform an important service by providing information to the public and that without the privilege, confidential sources will be reluctant to talk. Recognition of a journalist's privilege also avoids problems that are created when journalists refuse to reveal a source, and the court must decide whether to jail the journalist.

On the federal constitutional level, the Supreme Court in <u>Branzburg v. Hayes, 408 U.S. 665 (1972)</u> held in a plurality opinion that a journalist had no constitutional right to refuse to disclose a source in the face of a good faith criminal investigation. Had the criminal investigation not been in good faith, however, Justice Powell, in speaking for the majority, strongly hinted that the court might have been inclined to recognize one. Based upon Justice Powell's opinion, many lower federal court decisions after *Branzberg* have been willing to grant journalists some kind of narrow, qualified right to secrecy, either based upon applicable state privilege law, federal common law, constitutional values or discovery guidelines. See, e.g., <u>In re Madden, 151 F.3d 125 (3d Cir. 1998)</u> (recognizing a journalist privilege in criminal matters); <u>United States v. Cuthbertson, 651 F.2d 189 (3d Cir. 1981)</u> (holding that before a court can compel a journalist to disclose a source, the movant must demonstrate he has made a reasonable effort to obtain the information from other sources). But see <u>In re Grand Jury Subpoena, Judith Miller, 438 F.3d 1141 (D.C. Cir. 2006)</u> ("there is no First Amendment right under *Branzburg* for journalists to refuse to divulge their sources to a grand jury investigating criminal matters; to the extent there may be a common law reporter's privilege, which the court declined to decide, it was overcome by an *ex parte*, in camera governmental showing").

Parent-Child Privilege.

Although federal law does not recognize a privilege protecting confidential communications between parents and children, there have been a few departures from this traditional rule. In *In re Grand Jury Proceedings, Unemancipated Minor Child*, 949 F. Supp. 1487 (E.D. Wash. 1996), the court recognized a privilege not only for parent-child communications but also for any testimony the child might give that would be adverse to a parent in a criminal case. The Fifth Circuit, however, in *Port v. Heard*, 764 F.2d 423 (5th Cir. 1985) refused to find a parent-child privilege on constitutional grounds but acknowledged that had the case involved the federal common law, there might have been a different result. Lastly, the Seventh Circuit, in *In re Grand Jury Proceedings (Greenberg)*, 11 Fed. R. Evid. Serv. 579 (D. Conn. 1982), recognized a parent-child privilege based upon the Free Exercise Clause of the First Amendment where it was shown that the Jewish religion forbids a parent to testify against a child, the witness was a devout Jew, and the communication was between the witness and her daughter.

Moreover, as a result of Prosecutor Kenneth Starr's highly intrusive investigation of former President Bill Clinton's sexual relationship with White House Intern Monica Lewinsky and his questioning of her mother about her conversations with her daughter concerning this relationship, bills proposing a parent-child privilege have been repeatedly submitted to Congress, but they have never been enacted. See Shonah P. Jefferson, Note, *The Statutory Development of the Parent-Child Privilege: Congress Responds to Kenneth Starr's Tactics*, 16 GA. ST. U. L. REV. 429 (1999). Statutes in four states (Connecticut, Idaho, Massachusetts, and Minnesota) and the common law of New York, however, recognize a parent-child privilege.

F. Self-Incrimination

The only privilege recognized in the United States Constitution is the privilege against self-incrimination. This privilege is guaranteed by the Fifth Amendment. Most state constitutions also recognize this privilege, and the United States Supreme Court has held that this privilege extends to states under the Due Process Clause of the 14th Amendment. The Fifth Amendment provides:

> ### United States Constitution – 5th Amendment
>
> No person shall ... be compelled in any criminal case to be a witness against himself....

1. Criminal v. Civil

A reading of the amendment indicates its application to criminal cases. However, such a narrow reading has been rejected by the Supreme Court, and it is now settled that this amendment applies to both criminal as well as civil cases. It also applies in both pretrial hearings as well as trial and may be claimed by witnesses as well as defendants. The privilege has also been recognized in both administrative and legislative proceedings as well as judicial proceedings. The Court has explained the rationale for extending the privilege as follows:

> The privilege against self-incrimination 'registers an important advance in the development of our liberty-one of the great landmarks in man's struggle to make himself civilized.' It reflects many of our fundamental values and most noble aspirations: our unwillingness to subject those suspected of crime to the cruel trilemma of self-accusation, perjury or contempt; our preference for an accusatorial rather than an inquisitorial system of criminal justice; our fear that self-incriminating statements will be elicited by inhumane treatment and abuses; our sense of fair play which dictates a fair state-individual balance by requiring the government to leave the individual alone until good cause is shown for disturbing him and by requiring the government in its contest with the individual to shoulder the entire load, our respect for the inviolability of the human personality and of the right of each individual 'to a private enclave where he may lead a private life,' our distrust of self-deprecatory statements; and our realization that the privilege, while sometimes 'a shelter to the guilty,' is often 'a protection to the innocent.' *Murphy v Waterfront Commission*, 378 U.S. 52, 55 (1964).

2. Persons Protected

The fifth-amendment privilege against self-incrimination belongs only to individuals. It cannot be asserted by corporations, organizations or any other type of associations. The privilege is a personal one and because of its personal nature, a defendant cannot raise the privilege belonging to a co-defendant.

3. Scope of Privilege

The privilege could be read broadly or narrowly. One could interpret the prohibition against self-incrimination so broadly that any action that might produce incriminating evidence would be prohibited. The Supreme Court has adopted a narrower reading holding that the privilege applies only to testimonial evidence.

The Court has held the following not to be considered testimonial and in violation of the privilege:

- The taking of a blood sample

- The requirement of fingerprinting

- The requirement of photographing

- Participation in a line-up

- Submission of a handwriting sample

- The requirement of wearing or removing certain clothing for identification purposes

- The requirement of speaking for identification purposes

- Submission of a hair sample

- Submission of a urine sample

4. Incrimination

What does the privilege protect? The Court has held that the privilege only extends to evidence that could lead to criminal exposure. The disclosure of facts that could lead to civil liability is not subject to the privilege. In evaluating a defendant's allegation of potential incrimination when invoking the privilege the Court has held:

> The privilege afforded not only extends to answers that would in themselves support a conviction … but likewise embraces those which would furnish a link in the chain of evidence needed to prosecute the claimant…. But this protection must be confined to instances where the witness has reasonable cause to apprehend danger from a direct answer. The witness is not exonerated from answering merely because he declares that in so doing he would incriminate himself – his say-so does not of itself establish the hazard of incrimination. It is for the court to say whether his silence is justified, and to require him to answer if 'it clearly appears to the court that he is mistaken.' However, if the witness, upon interposing his claim, were required to prove the hazard in the sense in which a claim is usually required to be established in court, he would be compelled to surrender the very protection which the privilege is designed to guarantee. To sustain the privilege, it need only be evident

from the implications of the question, in the setting in which it is asked, that a responsive answer to the question or an explanation of why it cannot be answered might be dangerous because injurious disclosure could result. The trial judge in appraising the claim 'must be governed as much by his personal perception of the peculiarities of the case as by the facts actually in evidence.' *Hoffman v. U.S.*, 341 U.S. 479 (1951).

Also, the potential for criminal liability must still exist at the time the privilege is raised. If the statute of limitations has run or some other legal barrier exists preventing prosecution, then the privilege may not be invoked.

Make the Connection

The fact that an individual claiming the privilege has already been convicted does not end the entitlement to the protection. If an appeal is still available, then there is the possibility of a reversal and a new trial. Therefore, the protection is still available.

5. Writings

The privilege of against self-incrimination extends to the written word in addition to oral testimony. But how far does the protection extend? The following case looks at one situation.

U.S. v. Doe

465 U.S. 605 (1984).

Justice POWELL delivered the opinion of the Court.

issue

This case presents the issue whether, and to what extent, the Fifth Amendment privilege against compelled self-incrimination applies to the business records of a sole proprietorship.

I

Respondent is the owner of several sole proprietor-ships. In late 1980, a grand jury, during the course of an investigation of corruption in the awarding of county and municipal contracts, served five subpoenas on respondent. The first two demanded the production of the telephone records of several of respondent's companies and all records pertaining to four bank accounts of respondent and his companies.... The third subpoena demanded the production of a list of virtually all the business records of one of respondent's companies for the period between January 1, 1976, and the date of the subpoena. The fourth subpoena sought production of a similar list of business records belonging to another company. The final subpoena demanded production of all bank statements and cancelled checks of two of respondent's companies that had accounts at a bank in the Grand Cayman Islands.

II

Respondent filed a motion in federal district court seeking to quash the subpoenas. The District Court for the District of New Jersey granted his motion except with respect to those documents and records required by law to be kept or disclosed to a public agency. In reaching its decision, the District Court noted that the Government had conceded that the materials sought in the subpoena were or might be incriminating. The court stated that, therefore, "the relevant inquiry is ... whether the act of producing the documents has communicative aspects which warrant Fifth Amendment protection."

The Court of Appeals for the Third Circuit affirmed. It first addressed the question whether the Fifth Amendment ever applies to the records of a sole proprietorship. After noting that an individual may not assert the Fifth Amendment privilege on behalf of a corporation, partnership, or other collective entity ... the Court of Appeals reasoned that the owner of a sole proprietorship acts in a personal rather than a representative capacity....

The Court of Appeals next considered whether the documents at issue in this case are privileged. The court noted that ... that the contents of business records ordinarily are not privileged because they are created voluntarily and without compulsion. The Court of Appeals nevertheless found that respondent's business records were privileged under either of two analyses. First, the court reasoned that ... the business records of a sole proprietorship are no different from the individual owner's personal records. Noting that Third Circuit cases had held that private papers, al-though created voluntarily, are protected by the Fifth Amendment the court accorded the same protection to respondent's business papers. Second, it held that respondent's act of producing the subpoenaed records would have "communicative aspects of its own." The turning over of the subpoenaed documents to the grand jury would admit their existence and authenticity. Accordingly, respondent was entitled to assert his Fifth Amendment privilege rather than produce the subpoenaed documents.

The Government contended that the court should enforce the subpoenas because of the Government's offer not to use respondent's act of production against respondent in any way. The Court of Appeals noted that no formal request for use immunity under 18 U.S.C. §§ 6002 and 6003 had been made. In light of this failure, the court held that the District Court did not err in rejecting the Government's attempt to compel delivery of the subpoenaed records.

sought to quash subpoenas

...

...[T]he Fifth Amendment protects the person asserting the privilege only from compelled self-incrimination. Where the preparation of business records is voluntary, no compulsion is present. A subpoena that demands production of documents "does not compel oral testimony; nor would it ordinarily compel the taxpayer to restate, repeat, or affirm the truth of the contents of the documents sought."

...

Respondent does not contend that he prepared the documents involuntarily or that the subpoena would force him to restate, repeat, or affirm the truth of their contents. The fact that the records are in respondent's possession is irrelevant to the determination of whether the creation of the records was compelled. We therefore hold that the contents of those records are not privileged.

B

Although the contents of a document may not be privileged, the act of producing the document may be. A government subpoena compels the holder of the document to perform an act that may have testimonial aspects and an incriminating effect.

...

The Government did state several times before the District Court that it would not use respondent's act of production against him in any way. But counsel for the Government never made a statutory request to the District Court to grant respondent use immunity. We are urged to adopt a doctrine of constructive use immunity. Under this doctrine, the courts would impose a requirement on the Government not to use the incriminatory aspects of the act of production against the person claiming the privilege even though the statutory procedures have not been followed.

We decline to extend the jurisdiction of courts to include prospective grants of use immunity in the absence of the formal request that the statute requires. ... Congress expressly left this decision exclusively to the Justice Department. If, on remand, the appropriate official concludes that it is desirable to compel respondent to produce his business records, the statutory procedure for requesting use immunity will be available.

V

We conclude that the Court of Appeals erred in holding that the contents *(t. concludes* of the subpoenaed documents were privileged under the Fifth Amendment. The act of producing the documents at issue in this case is privileged and cannot be compelled without a statutory grant of use immunity pursuant to 18 U.S.C. §§ 6002 and 6003. The judgment of the Court of Appeals is, therefore, affirmed in part, reversed in part, and the case is remanded to the District Court for further proceedings in accordance with this decision.

It is so ordered.

Affirmed in part, reversed in part, and remanded.

Justice O'CONNOR, concurring.

I concur in both the result and reasoning of Justice Powell's opinion for the Court. I write separately, however, just to make explicit what is implicit in the analysis of that opinion: that the Fifth Amendment provides absolutely no protection for the contents of private papers of any kind. The notion that the Fifth Amendment protects the privacy of papers originated in *Boyd v. United States*, 116 U.S. 616, 630 (1886), but our decision in *Fisher v. United States*, 425 U.S. 391 (1976), sounded the death-knell for *Boyd*. "Several of *Boyd's* express or implicit declarations [had] not stood the test of time[,]" and its privacy of papers concept "had long been a rule searching for a rationale ...." Today's decision puts a long-overdue end to that fruitless search.

Justice MARSHALL, with whom Justice BRENNAN joins, concurring in part and dissenting in part.

... Contrary to what Justice O'CONNOR contends, I do not view the Court's opinion in this case as having reconsidered whether the Fifth Amendment provides protection for the contents of "private papers of any kind." This case presented nothing remotely close to the question that Justice O'CONNOR eagerly poses and answers. First, as noted above, the issue whether the Fifth Amendment protects the contents of the documents was obviated by the Court of Appeals' rulings relating to the act of production and statutory use immunity. Second, the documents at stake here are business records which implicate a lesser degree of concern for privacy interests than, for example, personal diaries.

Were it true that the Court's opinion stands for the proposition that "the Fifth Amendment provides absolutely no protection for the contents of private pa-pers of any kind," I would assuredly dissent. I continue to believe that under the Fifth Amendment "there are certain documents no person ought to be compelled to produce at the Government's request."

6. Required Records and Reports

As discussed, the compelling or production of writing can raise Fifth Amendment concerns. Are Constitutional protections raised with regard to records or reports required to be kept by law? Many regulations mandate the keeping of records and the submission of certain reports. In Shapiro v. United States, 335 U.S. 1 (1948), the Court upheld the government's right to compel the production of records required to be kept pursuant to statute. Subsequent cases have tilted slightly in favor of the privilege. In 1968 the Court held the following:

The premises of the doctrine … are evidently three: first, the purposes of the United States' inquiry must be essentially regulatory; second, information is to be obtained by requiring the preservation of records of a kind which the regulated party has customarily kept; and third, the records themselves must have assumed 'public aspects' which render them at least analogous to public documents. *Grosso v. U.S.*, 390 U.S. 62 (1968).

Executive Summary

General Rule Against Admissibility or Disclosure of Privileged Information. Rule 501 generally supports and protects certain confidential or trust-based relationships by making the communications of the people in those relationships inadmissible in court and protected from disclosure during discovery. The policy reason for these privileges is to protect certain confidences that are essential in order for these relationships to function properly. Under Rule 501, federal common law privileges apply in federal question cases. However, in diversity cases, or, if there is a supplemental state law claim in a federal question case, federal courts apply state privilege law to the state law claim in order to avoid forum shopping. (*Erie* Doctrine concerns).

Attorney-Client Privilege. The attorney-client privilege is to encourage freedom of full and frank communication between an attorney and client without it being later disclosed. The privilege belongs to the client, not the attorney. So if facts are communicated to the attorney by the client, those communicated facts are privileged from disclosure by the attorney. However, those facts may still be discovered if uncovered through means other than the communication with the attorney.

A "client" is a person, or any legal entity, who consults a lawyer with a view toward being represented, including corporations, and any individual in his or her corporate capacity. (*Upjohn*). Note that the "work product doctrine," under Rule 26(b)(3) of the Fed.R.Civ. Proc., is different from the attorney-client privilege and has more to do with protecting an *attorney's* mental thoughts and impressions about the case or case investigations from disclosure (the attorney's "work product"), than it does with protecting attorney-client communications.

An "<u>attorney</u>" is anyone authorized to practice law in a jurisdiction, but the privilege also extends to communications with that attorney's *representatives and employees* who assist the attorney in providing legal services to the client, as long as the attorney is seeking the non-lawyer's services for representation purposes of the client (*Kovel*).

A "<u>communication</u>" between an attorney and a client does not include "observations" about the client (what the client was wearing, his hair color, or other observable facts).However, an attorney's opinion as to a client's mental state may be protected because only part of the opinion is based on observed facts, while part is based on privileged communications. (*Kendrick*).

"<u>Made in confidence</u>" means communications that are either expressly or impliedly intended to be in confidence, so that a third party being present when the communication was made would show that the communication was *not intended* to be in confidence, unless the third party was necessary or a representative of the attorney. (*Evans*). Such does not apply to eavesdroppers.

"<u>To facilitate legal services</u>" is where a communication between an attorney and client was made in order to render legal services. It can also include another attorney in the firm gathering information and communicating those facts to the attorney. (*Rowe*). The privilege survives even after the death of the client. Note also that the privilege is lost when the client uses an attorney's services to further an on-going crime under the "Crime-Fraud Exception."

Waiver of the Attorney-Client Privilege. The attorney-client privilege can be expressly waived by the client, or if the client is a corporation, by someone with authority to do so. The privilege can also be waived impliedly by: (1) a failure to assert the privilege, (2) voluntary disclosure to a third-party, (3) putting the protected information at issue (such as suing an attorney for malpractice), and (4) inadvertent disclosure resulting in accidental waiver; however, under new Rule 502, if the inadvertent production of documents occurred despite the holder of the privilege taking reasonable steps to prevent the disclosure and rectify the error, the privilege is not waived.

The "Privilege Log." Under Fed. R. Civ. Proc., Rule 26(b)(5) and 45(d), an attorney claiming a privilege for documents or information requested during the discovery phase of the case must produce a "privilege log" listing the documents and information they claim are privileged, instead of not producing such documents at all as if the requested documents and information do not exist. The log should sufficiently identify the document and information, describe the subject matter without waiving the privilege, and explain the basis for the privilege so that the opposing side may contest the existence of the claimed privilege and so that the judge can make a decision on the issue.

Spousal Privileges. There are two different types of spousal privileges.

The first is the "Adverse Testimonial Privilege" where a spouse (if married at the time of trial) is not required to testify against his or her spouse in order to protect the harmony, privacy, and dignity of the marriage. It applies only in *criminal* cases. However, the holder of the privilege is the proposed testifying spousal witness, meaning that if a spouse *wants to testify* against his or her spouse, he or she can do so, because the "relationship is most certainly in disrepair." (*Trammel*). This is why the privilege does not apply if the spouses are no longer married at the time of the trial.

The other spousal privilege is the "Marital Communication Privilege" where communications between spouses during the existence of their marriage is privileged, in both civil and criminal cases, even after the marriage ends or the spouses die. The reason for the privilege is to encourage and protect against the disclosure of full and free communication necessary to a successful marriage. However, if the communications are to commit a crime or fraud, such communications are not privileged. (*Marashi*).

Psychotherapist-Patient Privilege. All states and the District of Columbia recognize this exception because a psychotherapist cannot perform her treatment of patients unless the patients are willing to talk freely and openly without fear of the confidence from being compromised. (*Jaffe*). However, it is unclear whether the privilege is actually necessary to get patients to speak openly and freely, as many patients may not even be aware of the privilege. Further, the privilege has been extended to social workers and even physicians in certain circumstances.

Miscellaneous Privileges. Some of the following privileges have been urged in federal court and in many states, some with success, most without: (1) Clergy-Patient, (2) Accountant-Client, (3) Journalist-Informant, and (4) Parent-Child.

Self-Incrimination. The Fifth Amendment to the US Constitution provides "No person shall…be compelled in any criminal case to be a witness against himself. . ." Despite the reference to criminal cases, it applies in civil cases as well. It applies only to individuals, not corporations, but it applies narrowly only to testimonial evidence, not any physical evidence or observations about the individual, such as fingerprinting, photo lineups, providing physical samples or exemplars, etc. The privilege only extends to testimony that could lead to actual criminal exposure. A defendant need not testify in a criminal case at all and his silence cannot be made the subject or comment or argument. In a civil case, the defendant can be called and must testify but can "plead the Fifth" on the witness stand, if the witness would rather not answer. Finally, the privilege applies not only to oral testimony, but can also apply to written records and reports, especially if they are not private. (<u>Doe</u>).

CHAPTER 14

Judicial Notice

A. Introduction

Rule 201. Judicial Notice of Adjudicative Facts

    (a) **Scope of Rule.** This rule governs only judicial notice of adjudicative facts.

    (b) **Kinds of Facts.** A judicially noticed fact must be one not subject to reasonable dispute in that it is either (1) generally known within the territorial jurisdiction of the trial court or (2) capable of accurate and ready determination by resort to sources whose accuracy cannot reasonably be questioned.

    (c) **When Discretionary.** A court may take judicial notice, whether requested or not.

    (d) **When Mandatory.** A court shall take judicial notice if requested by a party and supplied with the necessary information.

    (e) **Opportunity to be Heard.** A party is entitled upon timely request to an opportunity to be heard as to the propriety of taking judicial notice and the tenor of the matter noticed. In the absence of prior notification, the request may be made after judicial notice has been taken.

    (f) **Time of Taking Notice.** Judicial notice may be taken at any stage of the proceeding.

    (g) **Instructing the Jury.** In a civil action or proceeding, the court shall instruct the jury to accept as conclusive any fact judicially noticed. In a criminal case, the court shall instruct the jury that it may, but is not required to, accept as conclusive any fact judicially noticed.

"Judicial notice" is a court's consideration of an uncontested matter as evidence without formalized proof, either at trial or upon appeal. For example, the fact that a particular street runs North and South in a certain city, or that objects fall toward the earth because of the law of gravity, are both clear examples of propositions that are so indisputable that one need not formally prove them at trial. Instead, the judge will allow the jury to take an evidentiary "shortcut" during trial and accept these types of propositions as true without formal proof. However, Rule 201 specifically states that it governs only notice of "adjudicative facts," which is not to be confused with "evaluative facts," "legislative facts," and notice of the law.

Adjudicative Facts: Adjudicative facts, although not defined in Rule 201, are facts that are decided by a jury in a jury case or by the judge in a trial to the court and which would normally be proved by evidence if judicial notice were not taken. Although many adjudicative facts are contested by parties at trial, there are some whose accuracy cannot be reasonably questioned. For these facts, it would be a waste of the judicial time and resources to determine what is already known. To provide for this possibility, Rule 201 describes two circumstances when judicial notice can be taken. The facts must be either: (1) a matter of general knowledge, or (2) capable of ready determination by sources whose accuracy cannot be reasonably questioned. The simplest example of an adjudicative fact is the fact that a particular date fell on a particular day of the week, e.g., June 5, 2008, was a Thursday. Facts that are personally known to the judge but not generally known or capable of verification do not satisfy Rule 201.

> **FYI**
>
> Indisputable adjudicative facts can include a broad range of other matters: "Historical and geographical/climatological facts are among the most frequent subject of judicial notice. Also noticed are political facts, (such as the identity of office holders), facts relating to practices in business and industry, facts relating to the economy and its condition, sociological facts, and scientific and medical facts, where the question often to be answered is whether the fact in question has achieved sufficient acceptance in the scientific community to be considered indisputable." Louisell & Mueller, FEDERAL EVIDENCE, § 57, Rule 201, p. 437.

Legislative Facts: A legislative fact is information a court uses to interpret a law or statute or make a ruling. It may include the historical, political, economic, and sociological factual background or other non-jurisprudential matters relevant to the legal issue in question. A classic example of a court's use of a legislative fact appears in *Brown v. Board of Education*, 347 U.S. 483 (1954), where the Supreme Court held separate but equal schools unconstitutional on the basis that segregated schools made black students feel inferior and deprived them of an equal education. Legislative facts are distinguishable from adjudicative facts in that they do not have to be indisputable, and they are not regulated by Rule 201. Legislative facts which a party may wish to bring to a court's attention may be proffered by evidence, brief, or memorandum of law, or the court may simply research the matter.

Evaluative Facts: Unlike adjudicative facts, evaluative facts (also called "communicative facts") are information, concepts, and understandings known and shared in common within a society. While "socially" held, evaluative facts are also personal insofar as they operate within an individual's thought process by providing meaning and context to other facts in order to interpret them, make inferences, and draw conclusions. As such, evaluative facts are cognitive constructs of the mind acquired through experience and learning. An inference that a person who is late for an appointment is more likely to have been speeding than a person who is on time is an evaluative fact, for example. Because evaluative facts consist of commonly shared assumptions, they can be mistaken for generally known adjudicative facts. However, a distinction must be made because Rule 201 is not applicable to evaluative facts, no party to a judicial proceeding would seek notice of such facts, and no court will take notice.

Notice of the Law: Part and parcel of judging is actually knowing or being able to ascertain the law in a case. However, "law" is not "evidence," and the Federal Rules of Evidence (including Rule 201) do not address how to determine it. However, there is other federal statutory authority for courts to consider, including the Code of Federal Regulations, the Federal Register and the common law, which permits a court to notice all state statutory and case law. The court's determination of the law of a foreign nation is regulated in civil cases by Federal Rule of Civil Procedure 44.1 and in criminal cases by Federal Rule of Criminal Procedure 26.1.

B. Judicial Notice of Adjudicative Facts

1. The Difference Between Adjudicative and Legislative Facts

One of the first steps in determining whether to take judicial notice of a fact is to classify the nature of that fact. Is it adjudicative or legislative? The distinction between the two is often not well-defined. If the fact is deemed adjudicative, then the standards and procedures of Rule 201 apply, including the requirement that the judge in a criminal case instruct the jury that it may but need not accept the noticed fact as conclusive. If the fact is deemed legislative, the judge may simply instruct the jury on the fact as a matter of law which cannot be contested. The difference is explained in the following case.

United States v. Gould

U.S. Court of Appeals for the Eighth Circuit
536 F.2d 216 (8th Cir. 1976)

GIBSON, Chief Judge.

Defendants, Charles Gould and Joseph Carey, were convicted of conspiring to import and actually importing cocaine from Colombia, South America, into the United States in violation of the Controlled Substances Import and Export Act.

Defendants do not challenge the sufficiency of the evidence but contend that the District Court erred in improperly taking judicial notice and instructing the jury that cocaine hydrochloride is a schedule II controlled substance…

… [D]efendants contend that evidence should have been presented on the subject of what controlled substances fit within schedule II for the purpose of establishing a foundation that cocaine hydrochloride was actually within that schedule. Schedule II controlled substances, for the purpose of the Controlled Substances Import and Export Act, conclude the following:

> Coca leaves and any salt, compound, derivative, or preparation of coca leaves, and any salt, compound, derivative, or preparation thereof which is chemically equivalent or identical with any of these substances, except that the substances shall not include decocainized coca leaves or extraction of coca leaves, which extractions do not contain cocaine or ecgonine.

At trial, two expert witnesses for the Government testified as to the composition of the powdered substance removed from Ms. Kenworthy's platform shoes at the Miami airport. One expert testified that the substance was comprised of approximately 60 percent cocaine hydrochloride. The other witness stated that the white powder consisted of 53 percent cocaine. There was no direct evidence to indicate that cocaine hydrochloride is a derivative of coca leaves. In its instructions to the jury, the District Court stated:

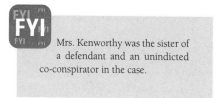

Mrs. Kenworthy was the sister of a defendant and an unindicted co-conspirator in the case.

> If you find the substance was cocaine hydrochloride, you are instructed that cocaine hydrochloride is a schedule II controlled substance under the laws of the United States.

Our inquiry … is twofold. We must first determine whether it was error for the District Court to take judicial notice of the fact that cocaine hydrochloride is a schedule II controlled substance. Secondly, if we conclude that it was permissible to judicially notice this fact, we must then determine whether the District Court erred in instructing the jury that it must accept this fact as conclusive.

The first aspect of this inquiry merits little discussion. In <u>Hughes v. United States</u>, <u>253 F. 543, 545 (8th Cir. 1918)</u> this court stated:

> It is also urged that there was no evidence that morphine, heroin, and cocaine are derivatives of opium and coca leaves. We think that is a matter of which notice may be taken. In a sense the question is one of the definition or meaning of words long in common use, about which there is no obscurity, controversy, or dispute, and of which the imperfectly informed can gain complete knowledge by resort to dictionaries within reach of everybody... Common knowledge, or the common means of knowledge, of the settled, undisputed, things of life, need not always be laid aside on entering a courtroom.

It is apparent that courts may take judicial notice of any fact which is "capable of such instant and unquestionable demonstration, if desired, that no party would think of imposing a falsity on the tribunal in the face of an intelligent adversary." The fact that cocaine hydrochloride is derived from coca leaves is, if not common knowledge, at least a matter which is capable of certain, easily accessible and indisputably accurate verification. See Webster's Third New International Dictionary 434 (1961). Therefore, it was proper for the District Court to judicially notice this fact. Our conclusion on this matter is amply supported by the weight of judicial authority.

Our second inquiry involves the propriety of the District Court's instruction to the jurors that this judicially noticed fact must be accepted as conclusive by them. Defendants, relying upon Fed. R. Evid. 201(g), urge that the jury should have been instructed that it could discretionarily accept or reject this fact.

It is clear that the reach of Rule 201 extends only to adjudicative, not legislative, facts. Fed. R. Evid. 201(a). Consequently, the viability of defendants' argument is dependent upon our characterization of the fact judicially noticed by the District Court as adjudicative, thus invoking the provisions of Rule 201(g). In undertaking this analysis, we note at the outset that Rule 201 is not all-encompassing. "Rule 201 ... was deliberately drafted to cover only a small fraction of material usually subsumed under the concept of 'judicial notice.' "

The precise line of demarcation between adjudicative facts and legisla-

Go Online

According to the Merriam Webster's Online definition, cocaine is a "bitter crystalline alkaloid ... obtained from coca leaves that is used especially in the form of hydrochloride used medically as a topical anesthetic and illicitly for its euphoric effects and that may result in a compulsive psychological need." http://www.merriam-webster.com.

tive facts is not always easily identified. Adjudicative facts have been described as follows:

> When a court … finds facts concerning the immediate parties who did what, where, when, how, and with what motive or intent the court … is performing an adjudicative function, and the facts are conveniently called adjudicative facts…

Stated in other terms, the adjudicative facts are those to which the law is applied in the process of adjudication. They are the facts that normally go to the jury in a jury case. They relate to the parties, their activities, their properties, their businesses.

Legislative facts, on the other hand, do not relate specifically to the activities or characteristics of the litigants. A court generally relies upon legislative facts when it purports to develop a particular law or policy and thus considers material wholly unrelated to the activities of the parties.

Legislative facts are ordinarily general and do not concern the immediate parties. In the great mass of cases decided by courts … the legislative element is either absent or unimportant or interstitial, because in most cases the applicable law and policy have been previously established. But whenever a tribunal engages in the creation of law or of policy, it may need to resort to legislative facts, whether or not those facts have been developed on the record.

Legislative facts are established truths, facts or pronouncements that do not change from case to case but apply universally, while adjudicative facts are those developed in a particular case.

Applying these general definitions, we think it is clear that the District Court in the present case was judicially noticing a legislative fact rather than an adjudicative fact. Whether cocaine hydrochloride is or is not a derivative of the coca leaf is a question of scientific fact applicable to the administration of the Comprehensive Drug Abuse Prevention and Control Act of 1970. The District Court reviewed the schedule II classifications … construed the language in a manner which comports with common knowledge and understanding, and instructed the jury as to the proper law so interpreted. It is undisputed that the trial judge is required to fully and accurately instruct the jury as to the law to be applied in a case. When a court attempts to ascertain the governing law in a case for the purpose of instructing the jury, it must necessarily rely upon acts which are unrelated to the activities of the immediate parties. These extraneous, yet necessary, facts fit within the definition of legislative facts and are an indispensable tool used by judges when discerning the applicable law through interpretation.[1] The District Court, therefore, was judicially noticing such a legislative fact when it recognized that cocaine hydrochloride is derived from coca leaves and is a schedule II controlled substance within the meaning of §812.

Through similar reasoning, this judicially noticed fact simply cannot be appropriately categorized as an adjudicative fact. It does not relate to "who did what, where, when, how, and with what motive or intent," nor is it a fact which would traditionally go to the jury. The fact that cocaine hydrochloride is a derivative of coca leaves is a universal fact that is unrelated to the activities of the parties to this litigation. There was no preemption of the jury function to determine what substance was actually seized from Ms. Kenworthy at the Miami airport. The jury was instructed that, if it found that the confiscated substance was cocaine hydrochloride, the applicable law classified the substance as a schedule II controlled substance.

It is clear to us that the District Court took judicial notice of a legislative, rather than an adjudicative, fact in the present case and Rule 201(g) is inapplicable. The District Court was not obligated to inform the jury that it could disregard the judicially noticed fact. In fact, to do so would be preposterous, thus permitting juries to make conflicting findings on what constitutes controlled substances under federal law.[2]

Food for Thought

How is this any more preposterous than allowing the jury to disregard judicial notice of indisputable adjudicative facts in a criminal case, as Rule 201(g) plainly allows?

The judgment of conviction is affirmed.

---

[1] The Notes of the Advisory Committee to Rule 201 offer support for the proposition that courts utilize legislative facts when they interpret a statute. While judges use judicial notice of "propositions of generalized knowledge" in a variety of situations: determining the validity and meaning of statutes, formulating common law rules, deciding whether evidence should be admitted, assessing the sufficiency and effect of evidence, all are essentially nonadjudicative in nature. (Emphasis added.)

[2] Common sense dictates that the construction urged upon us by defendants is not well-taken. The fact that cocaine hydrochloride is derived from coca leaves is scientifically and pharmacologically unimpeachable. It would be incongruous to instruct the jurors on this irrefutable fact and then inform them that they may disregard it at their whim. It would be similarly illogical if we were to conclude that trial judges could rely upon generally accepted, undisputed facts in interpreting the applicable statutory law, yet obligate them to instruct the jury that it could disregard the factual underpinnings of the interpretation in its discretion.

Perspective and Analysis

One commentator had the following to say about whether the court in *Gould* properly classified the disputed facts as legislative:

> The noticed fact [could have been classified as] adjudicative in nature since the court was finding facts concerning the immediate parties--what *this* defendant had in [her] shoe *was* a derivative of the coca leaf. Whether or not the particular substance in question was a derivative would be a legitimate issue for the jury; thus, it constituted an adjudicative fact. A simple example will illustrate the adjudicative nature of that question. Imagine a case where the thrust of the defendant's entire defense is that the substance found on his person was not a derivative of the banned substance. Would the court take conclusive judicial notice that the substance *was* a derivative? The answer is obviously no. Such action would be an abridgement of the defendant's right to a jury trial. Thus, the question of the substance's classification appears to involve an adjudicative fact.
>
> One could also make a good argument, however, that the decision in *Gould* stands for the proposition that the issue of the substance's classification involves a question of legislative fact. In *Gould*, the defense did not contend that cocaine hydrochloride was unrelated to coca leaves; it merely asserted at the close of all the evidence that the government had failed to show that cocaine hydrochloride was included under the Controlled Substances Import and Export Act. When the issue is framed in this fashion, it can be resolved by determining whether Congress intended to include cocaine hydrochloride on its list of forbidden substances. The Congressional intent is a legislative fact that the court is permitted to judicially notice without complying with the procedural safeguards of F.R.E. 201. The court in *Gould* carefully followed that approach.
>
> It might appear on the surface that the classification of a judicially noticed fact as adjudicative or legislative often depends on how the court poses the question... If the mere rephrasing of the question allows the court to slide easily between the adjudicative and legislative categories, the procedural safeguards of F.R.E. 201 are of minimal value.

<u>Dennis J. Turner, *Judicial Notice and Federal Rule of Evidence 201—Read for a Change*, 45 U. PITT. L. REV. 181, 193-194</u>

Points for Discussion

a. Is *Gould* Really an Example of Notice of Legislative Facts?

The difference between adjudicative facts and of legislative facts is often blurry. Do you agree with the court in *Gould* that whether cocaine hydrochloride is a schedule II controlled substance is a legislative fact? Or do you agree with author Turner that it could also be an adjudicative fact?

b. The Effects of Classification.

If facts in a case are classified as adjudicative, then the court in a criminal case "must instruct the jury that it may, but is not required to, accept as conclusive any fact judicially noticed." Rule 201 (g). Do you think that the court in *Gould* may have classified the facts as legislative to avoid the necessity of allowing the jury to second guess the trial judge on this issue?

Perspective and Analysis

Not all commentators are happy with the unregulated process for taking judicial notice of legislative facts. See if you agree with the following:

> We do not claim that Judges cannot rely on a broad range of facts to force the law forward. We suggest only that the parties should be permitted to participate in the march ... If a fact of set or facts is likely to be critical to a decision on the law to be applied to the parties, there is every reason to want the parties to be heard on the factual question. Evidence need not always be taken. Briefs may work better in many situations. But some chance for the parties to be heard on decisive legislative facts is desirable.

2 Kenneth C. Davis and Richard J. Pierce, Jr., ADMINISTRATIVE LAW TREATISE § 10.5, at 142 (3d ed. 1994).

c. Legislative Fact, Indisputability and the Right to Be Heard.

Because the process is not governed by Rule 201, notice of legislative facts does not require that the facts be indisputable or that the parties be heard on the propriety of taking notice. In *Gould,* the appellate court cited Webster's Dictionary as support for recognizing the classification of hydrochloride as a schedule II controlled substance without giving the parties a chance to be heard on the issue. This illustrates what is usually the case--the taking of notice of legislative facts is often a hidden process. Do you think that the court might have benefited from allowing the parties to brief the issue or call expert witnesses to testify on the matter? Or is the fact so obvious in this case that no inquiry is required? Contrast the *Gould* case with the case of *Trammel v. United States*, 445 U.S. 40 (1980), where the Supreme Court, in effect, took notice of the legislative fact that "[w]hen one spouse is willing to testify against the other in a criminal proceeding—whatever the motivation—their relationship is almost certainly in disrepair. . . " . If you were representing the party opposing the legislative facts in *Gould* and *Trammel*, is there any way to contest them?

Hypo 14.1

Mary, a professional boxer, is charged with aggravated assault with a deadly weapon for striking Jason during an argument. Under the law, the term "deadly weapon is defined as "anything that is likely to cause or does cause serious bodily injury or death." The prosecution wants the trial judge to take judicial notice and instruct the jury that it must find that the fists of a boxer are deadly weapons under the statute. Is the taking of judicial notice in this case appropriate? Is the prosecutor correct in its suggested instruction to the jury?

---

2. Judicial Notice in Civil Cases

Once a court determines that a fact in issue is an adjudicative one, then Rule 201(b) states that judicial notice will only be taken if the matter is beyond dispute because it is (1) generally known in the jurisdiction or (2) generally ascertainable through reasonably undisputable sources. Does this mean that the fact at issue is not actually in dispute or that it is not capable of being disputed, and how is this determined?

Kaggen v. Internal Revenue Service

U.S. Court of Appeals for the Second Circuit
71 F.3d 1018 (2nd Cir. 1995)

FRANK A. KAUFMAN, District Judge:

… This case concerns the propriety of an Internal Revenue Service ("IRS") levy against taxpayers' bank accounts to satisfy a tax deficiency. The issue is whether notice given to taxpayers that funds had been seized complied with 26 U.S.C. § 6335(a). If not, argue plaintiff taxpayers, the levy was not completed before the statute of limitations lapsed, so that the IRS was time-barred from collecting the deficiency.

We held that sufficient notice had been given. In so holding, we observed that "depositors are sent monthly bank statements by banks," which statements, in this case, would have alerted the taxpayers that their bank accounts had been

Section 6335(a) states: "As soon as practicable after seizure of property, notice in writing shall be given by the Secretary to the owner of the property (or, in the case of personal property, the possessor thereof), or shall be left at his usual place of abode or business if he has such within the internal revenue district where the seizure is made… Such notice shall specify the sum demanded and shall contain, in the case of personal property, an account of the property seized…"

levied upon by the IRS well before the limitations period for effecting a seizure of those funds had run. Taxpayers promptly petitioned for rehearing, arguing that we had improperly taken judicial notice of facts not in the record--that depositors receive monthly bank statements--without giving taxpayers an opportunity to be heard…

This Court may appropriately take judicial notice of the fact that banks send customers monthly bank statements, and so doing, continues to conclude that taxpayers' receipt of those statements, in conjunction with receipt of the notices of levy, provided taxpayers all notice required by [the statute].

* * *

[T]he only facts this Court judicially noticed were that 1) banks send customers monthly bank statements, and 2) those statements tell customers to whom their money was paid and in what amounts. Thus, there are two issues relating to judicial notice presently before this Court: 1) whether it was proper for the Court to take judicial notice of those facts, and 2) whether, after judicially noticing those facts, it was proper for the Court to conclude that taxpayers received the notice required by [the statute].

Concerning that first issue, we note that Federal Rule of Evidence 201 states:

A judicially noticed fact must be one not subject to reasonable dispute in that it is either (1) generally known within the territorial jurisdiction of the trial court or (2) capable of accurate and ready determination by resort to sources whose accuracy cannot reasonably be questioned.

Two commentators paraphrase the rule as follows:

In order to take judicial notice under Rule 201, the court must find that the fact is either "generally known" or ascertainable from a source whose accuracy cannot reasonably be questioned; in either case, the court must also find that the fact is not reasonable [sic] subject to dispute." 21 C. Wright and K. Graham, Federal Practice and Procedure: Evidence § 5109 at 519-20 (1977).

Food for Thought

Is the fact that the taxpayers did not contest the taking of judicial notice sufficient in and of itself to allow the court to take judicial notice of any matter of adjudicative fact because it means the facts are not in dispute? Aren't there other procedural mechanisms, such as summary judgments, or judgments as a matter or law that are better suited for this purpose?

That banks send customers monthly statements which inform customers to whom their money was paid and in what amounts is not reasonably subject to dispute, as highlighted by taxpayers' failure to argue that their banks, in fact, do not send their customers such statements. Moreover, those facts are generally known, as also highlighted by taxpayers' failure to argue that banks do not generally send such statements to customers. Thus, in their letter brief, taxpayers were "entitled to contest either the propriety of taking notice or the correctness of the fact to be noticed or both." As noted above, taxpayers did not contest the correctness of the facts noticed. Commenting with respect to the rationale behind Federal Rule of Evidence 201 this Court has previously noted: "Judges are not necessarily to be ignorant in Court of what everyone else, and they themselves out of Court, are familiar with." ... [W]hile the record in the instant case does not indicate that taxpayers received a bank statement or what information the three banks levied upon include in their bank statements, this Court may appropriately take judicial notice of the fact that banks do send monthly statements to customers and that those statements tell customers to whom their money was paid and in what amounts.

* * *

JACOBS, Circuit Judge, dissenting:

...[T]he majority takes judicial notice that bank statements are timely, accurate, timely received and read by depositors, and that they reveal, in accordance with the express statutory purpose, that a particular withdrawal represents a seizure by the IRS. Some of these facts are more intuitively reliable than others, but none meets the judicial notice standard under Rule 201: that facts must be "either (1) generally known ... or (2) capable of accurate and ready determination by resort to sources whose accuracy cannot reasonably be questioned." Fed. R. Evid. 201(b). The majority relies on the general knowledge category.

I do not believe it to be generally known that bank statements are reliably accurate or that they are timely sent and timely examined. It is true that the Uniform Commercial Code furnishes an incentive to read bank statements: after thirty days, a customer is barred (under certain circumstances) from seeking recovery against a bank for an improperly cashed check. U.C.C. § 4-406(d)(2).

Thus, people who choose to ignore their bank statements accept incremental risks of bank error. That choice, however, has nothing to do with the IRS's attempts to collect back taxes.

* * *

Even if we assume that bank statements are accurate, timely sent, and timely read, it is implausible (and certainly not generally known) that all bank statements actually indicate that a particular withdrawal is the result of a seizure by the IRS. Banks may or may not give explanatory information concerning all non-check debits. Depending on what bank regulations provide, banks might understandably conclude that no detailed explanation is needed for funds seized by the IRS, on the assumption that the IRS will follow the statute and provide a Notice of Seizure. After all, the Internal Revenue Code places the burden for notifying taxpayers of a seizure on the tax collector, not the banks.

* * *

The majority takes the plaintiffs to task for two supposed omissions in their papers on rehearing. True, plaintiffs did not say whether their banks sent monthly statements, and do not argue that "banks do not generally" do so. But the judicial notice issue is not affected by whether banks "generally" send statements to their customers, or whether these plaintiffs use a full-service bank. The sending of statements "generally" is insufficient to support

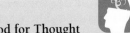

Food for Thought

Is the dissent disputing the taking of judicial notice of the content of normal monthly bank statements in this case or disputing whether a bank statement can substitute for notice of an IRS levy under § 6335(a), or both? Can they both be classified as adjudicative facts?

judicial notice that they are sent invariably, and does not recommend the monthly bank statement as a surrogate for official government notice of the seizure of property.

* * *

Because I adhere to the view that judicial notice was improperly taken, I would hold that the IRS's failure to serve the plaintiffs with a timely notice of seizure makes the collection of the tax assessment invalid.

Points for Discussion

a. Facts "Not Subject to Reasonable Dispute."

The majority in *Kaggen* took judicial notice that 1) banks send customers monthly bank statements, and 2) those statements tell customers to whom their money was paid and in what amounts. Can you tell whether the majority took judicial notice because these facts were "generally known within the territorial jurisdiction of the trial court," or because they were "capable of accurate and ready determination by resort to sources whose accuracy cannot reasonably be questioned?" Or is this just something the majority "knows." If so, how?

b. Was Judicial Notice Proper in *Kaggan*?

Given the requirements of 26 U.S.C. § 6335(a), do you think that the majority is correct in holding that an itemization of withdrawals in a monthly banking statement is sufficient to meet the § 6633(a) notice requirements? Could you make an argument that this involves taking notice of a legislative fact? Or should what constitutes statutory notice always be classified as an adjudicative fact? Compare *United States v. Baker*, 641 F.2d 1311 (9th Cir. 1981) (reversing the trial court for taking judicial notice that non-parties knew of an injunction because of widespread publicity about the injunction, and stating that "the source of publicity referred to by the court, the news media, cannot be said to be unquestionably accurate," and that "nothing was introduced from which widespread knowledge of the order could be inferred"). Is this contrary to *Kaggen*?

c. Notice of Facts in Other Civil Cases.

Judicial notice has been taken in a variety of circumstances in civil cases. See *Rutherford v. Sea-Land Serv. Inc.*, 575 F. Supp. 1365 (N.D. Cal. 1983) (judicial notice that the per diem rate of maintenance in a collective bargaining agreement was unreasonably low in San Francisco); *Barnes v. Bosley*, 745 F.2d 501, 506 n.2 (8th Cir. 1984) (taking judicial notice of the fact that the only real political contests in the City of St. Louis occur at the primary level); *Sinatra v. Heckler*, 566 F. Supp. 1354 (E.D. N.Y. 1983) (many federal employees take their vacations during the holidays at the end of the year when the mails are heavily burdened, resulting in a slow-down of mail delivery); *United Klans v. McGovern*, 453 F. Supp. 836 (N.D. Ala. 1978) (the United Klans is a "white hate group" whose policies are served by terrorism and intimidation). How do the facts of these cases compare to the ones in *Kaggen*? Are they all not subject to "reasonable dispute?"

3. Judicial Notice in Criminal Cases

If a court takes judicial notice in a civil case, Rule 201(g) provides that the court is required to instruct the jury "to accept as conclusive any fact judicially noticed." In a criminal case, Rule 201(g) requires that the court instruct the jury that "it may, but is not required to, accept as conclusive any fact judicially noticed." Why the difference? And does this mean that an appellate court cannot take judicial notice of any adjudicative fact in a criminal case because it has not first been evaluated by a jury? Isn't the whole point of judicial notice to dispose of fact issues "that are not subject to reasonable dispute" during the entire judicial process in order to enhance efficiency?

United States v. Jones

U.S. Court of Appeals for the Sixth Circuit
580 F.2d 219 (6th Cir. 1978)

ENGEL, Circuit Judge.

...William Allen Jones, Jr. was convicted ... of illegally intercepting telephone conversations of his estranged wife and of using the contents of the intercepted communications. The proof at trial showed only that the telephone which Jones had tapped was furnished by South Central Bell Telephone Company. Other than this fact, the government offered no evidence to show that South Central Bell was at the time a "person engaged as a common carrier in providing or operating ... facilities for the transmission of interstate or foreign communications," [which was necessary to prove in order to obtain a conviction].

Following the jury verdict of guilty ... Jones' counsel moved the court for a new trial on the ground that the government had altogether failed to prove that the wire communication which the defendant tapped came within the definition of [a common carrier.] United States District Judge Frank Wilson agreed and entered a judgment of acquittal. The government has appealed.

It is not seriously disputed that an essential element of the crimes charged, and one which the government was obligated to prove beyond a reasonable doubt, was that the conversation which was tapped was a "wire communication" as defined in the Act. Instead, the issue is whether the abbreviated proof offered by the government was minimally sufficient for the *prima facie*

>
> **It's Latin to Me**
>
> A *prima facie* case is the amount of evidence a party with the burden of proof must produce to permit the fact-finder to rule in the party's favor.

case. In other words, was the proof that the tapped telephone was installed and furnished by "South Central Bell Telephone Company," without more, sufficient to enable the jury to find as a matter of fact that South Central Bell was a common carrier which provided facilities for the transmission of interstate or foreign communications? The government contends that, construing that evidence in the light most favorable to it, these facts could be permissibly inferred by the jury without any other proof.

Take Note!

Is the government here contending that South Central Bell's status as a common carrier is an evaluative fact, not an adjudicative fact? If not, what is the government saying?

The government's argument is essentially twofold. First, it urges that South Central Bell's status may reasonably be characterized as a fact within the common knowledge of the jury and that no further record evidence was necessary. Failing that, the government urges that such a fact is the proper subject of judicial notice which may be taken at any stage of the proceeding, including appeal, under Federal Rule of Evidence 201(f).

The government's first argument finds some support in Wigmore. Similarly, the legislative history of the Federal Rules of Evidence indicates that, even in criminal cases, "matters falling within the common fund of information supposed to be possessed by jurors need not be proved." Advisory Committee Note to Federal Rule of Evidence 201(g) (1969 draft). As that Note further indicates, however, such matters "are not, properly speaking, adjudicative facts but an aspect of legal reasoning." Thus, while the jury may properly rely upon its own knowledge and experience in evaluating evidence and drawing inferences from that evidence, there must be sufficient record evidence to permit the jury to consult its general knowledge in deciding the existence of the fact.

While Wigmore notes that "(t)he range of (a jury's) general knowledge is not precisely definable, the scope of this doctrine is narrow; it is strictly limited to a few matters of elemental experience in human nature, commercial affairs, and everyday life." This category of fact is not so much a matter of noticing facts outside the record as it is a matter of the communication value of the words used, which can only be understood in the light of the common experience of those who employ them.

While the issue is not without difficulty, we are satisfied that South Central Bell's status as a "common carrier... providing ... facilities for the transmission of interstate ... communications" is a fact which, if to be established without direct or circumstantial proof, must be governed by the judicial notice provisions of the Federal Rules of Evidence.

The government did not at any time during the jury trial specifically request the district court to take judicial notice of the status of South Central Bell. Nevertheless, it relies upon the provisions of Rule 201(f) which state that "(j)udicial notice may be taken at any stage of the proceeding." It is true that the Advisory Committee Note to 201(f) indicates that judicial notice is appropriate "in the trial court *or* on appeal." (Emphasis added). It is also true that the language of 201(f) does not distinguish between judicial notice in civil or criminal cases. There is, however, a critical difference in the manner in which the judicially noticed fact is to be submitted to the jury in civil and criminal proceedings:

> Instructing jury. In a civil action or proceeding, the court shall instruct the jury to accept as conclusive any fact judicially noticed. In a criminal case, the court shall instruct the jury that it may, but is not required to, accept as conclusive any fact judicially noticed. Fed. R. Evid. 201(g).

Thus under subsection (g) judicial notice of a fact in a civil case is conclusive while in a criminal trial the jury is not bound to accept the judicially noticed fact and may disregard it if it so chooses.

It is apparent from the legislative history that the congressional choice of language in Rule 201 was deliberate. In adopting the present language, Congress rejected a draft of subsection (g) proposed by the Supreme Court, which read: The judge shall instruct the jury to accept as established any facts judicially noticed.

The House Report explained its reason for the change:

> Rule 201(g) as received from the Supreme Court provided that when judicial notice of a fact is taken, the court shall instruct the jury to accept that fact as established. Being of the view that mandatory instruction to a jury in a criminal case to accept as conclusive any fact judicially noticed is inappropriate because contrary to the spirit of the Sixth Amendment right to a jury trial, the Committee adopted the 1969 Advisory Committee draft of this subsection, allowing a mandatory instruction in civil actions and proceedings and a discretionary instruction in criminal cases.

Congress intended to preserve the jury's traditional prerogative to ignore even uncontroverted facts in reaching a verdict. The legislature was concerned that the Supreme Court's rule violated the spirit, if not the letter, of the constitutional right to a jury trial by effectively permitting a partial directed verdict as to facts in a criminal case.

Food for Thought

The Supreme Court of Utah expressed a similar concern in *State v. Lawrence*, 120 Utah 323, 234 P.2d 600 (1951): "If a court can take one important element of an offense from the jury and determine the facts for them because such fact seems plain enough to him, then which element cannot be similarly taken away, and where would the process stop?"

Take Note!

The court appears to be saying that in criminal cases, judicial notice may never be taken on appeal because a jury must first pass on whether to accept a fact that has been judicially noticed by the trial court because of Sixth Amendment constitutional concerns. Notice that neither *Jones* nor the Advisory Committee note cited in *Jones* holds that there is an absolute Sixth Amendment Bar to taking judicial notice in a criminal case on appeal—just that there are concerns. Do you agree those concerns justify the court's conclusion in *Jones*?

As enacted by Congress, Rule 201(g) plainly contemplates that the jury in a criminal case shall pass upon facts which are judicially noticed. This it could not do if this notice were taken for the first time after it had been discharged and the case was on appeal. We, therefore, hold that Rule 201(f), authorizing judicial notice at the appellate level, must yield in the face of the express congressional intent manifested in 201(g) for criminal jury trials. To the extent that the earlier practice may have been otherwise, we conceive that it has been altered by the enactment of Rule 201.

Accordingly, the judgment of the district court is affirmed.

———————

Points for Discussion

a. Evaluative Facts or Adjudicative Facts?

The court in *Jones* first determined that the question whether South Central Bell was "a common carrier providing facilities for the transmission of interstate communications" was not an evaluative fact, that is, it was not a matter within the common knowledge of the jury or "a matter of the communication value of the words used, which can only be understood in the light of the common experience of those who employ them." Is the court's reasoning persuasive? What in particular prevents the definition of a common carrier from being an evaluative fact? The word "facilities?" The phrase "transmission of interstate communications?" Wouldn't most juries know that South Central Bell is a telephone company that services all states and many foreign countries?

b. Taking Judicial Notice on Appeal in Criminal Cases.

Rule 201 specifically states that "judicial notice may be taken at any stage of the proceeding." Theoretically, this would include taking judicial notice for the first time on appeal, even in a criminal case, and courts have so held. See *United States v. Lavender*, 602 F.2d 639 (4th Cir. 1979) (taking judicial notice for the first time on appeal that Blue Ridge parkway was located in federal territory). Most courts follow *Jones*, however, and refuse to take judicial notice in a criminal matter for the first time on appeal. See, e.g. *United States v. Dior*, 671 F.2d 351, 358 n.11 (9th Cir. 1982) (refusing to take judicial notice of the American-Canadian exchange rate and stating, "for a court, however, to take judicial notice of an adjudicative fact after a jury's discharge in a criminal case would cast the court in the role of a fact-finder and violate defendant's Sixth Amendment right to trial by jury"). Do you think that this position encourages courts to waste time and effort on what are basically non-controvertible facts? Why give a jury the ability to disregard the obvious?

c. Judicial Notice in Other Criminal Cases.

See *United States v. Fowler*, 608 F.2d 2 (D.C. Cir. 1979) (it was error, although harmless, for the trial court to take judicial notice of the prosecutor's representations regarding the general social consequences of prostitution since no direct evidence was offered in support); *Harris v. United States*, 431 F. Supp. 1173 (E.D. Va. 1977) (judicial notice taken of activities which constitute a Ponzi or pyramid scheme); *Government of Virgin Islands v. Testamark*, 528 F.2d 742 (3d Cir.1976) (judicial notice taken of the prior convictions of the defendant, even though the better practice would have been to use the records themselves).

d. Notice of Judicial Records.

A court can take judicial notice of its own records regarding the same or prior proceedings. See *United States v. Gordon*, 634 F.2d 639 (1st Cir. 1980) (the defendant was not entitled to an evidentiary hearing on a motion to dismiss his indictment on double jeopardy grounds because the trial court was free to dispose of the motion by taking judicial notice of the proceedings which gave rise to the defense of double jeopardy). Additionally, a court may take judicial notice of the record in another court regarding matters between the same parties. See *Jacques v. U.S. R.R. Retirement Bd.*, 736 F.2d 34 (2d Cir. 1984) (taking judicial notice that the injured plaintiff filed a complaint in a prior related suit). However, courts generally cannot take judicial notice of findings of fact in a separate but related case to prove they are true if these facts were in dispute. See _General Elec. Capital Corp. v. Lease Resolution Corp._, 128 F.3d 1074 (7th Cir. 1997); _United States v. Wilson, 631 F.2d 118 (9th Cir. 1980)_ (a court may not take judicial notice of another court's records that show that the defendant failed to appear for sentencing based solely on certified copies of a release order and court minutes).

e. Scientific Facts.

Courts are somewhat reluctant to take judicial notice of scientific technology because scientific knowledge is always changing. What appears clear and certain to a court at one period of time may be totally refuted at another. For example, consider _Austin v. Tennessee, 179 U.S. 343, 345 (1900)_, where the Supreme Court stated the following when it took judicial notice that use of tobacco does not cause disease, "While [tobacco's] effects may be injurious to some, its use over practically the entire globe is a remarkable tribute to its popularity and value. We are clearly of opinion that it cannot be classed with diseased cattle or meats, decayed fruit, or other articles, the use of which is a nuisance to the health of the entire community."

Nonetheless, many courts currently take judicial notice as to the reliability of DNA analysis. See, e.g. _United States v. Chischilly, 30 F.3d 1144 (9th Cir. 1994)_ (taking judicial notice of the DNA identification analysis theories and procedures adopted by the FBI); _United States v. Beasley, 102 F.3d 1440 (8th Cir. 1996)_ (taking judicial notice of polymerase chain reaction method of DNA analysis). On the other hand, there is no consensus whether fingerprint classification and analysis is a proper subject for judicial notice. Compare _United States v. Mitchell, 365 F.3d 215 (3d Cir. 2004)_ (the court erred in taking judicial notice that human fingerprints were unique and permanent because this is a scientific conclusion which is subject to revision and not a fact) with _United States v. Llera Plaza, 188 F. Supp. 2d 549 (E.D. Pa. 2002)_ (taking judicial notice of the unique and permanent nature of fingerprints).

Make the Connection

While some scientific processes may be judicially noticed, Rule 702 and _Daubert_ still require a proponent to prove that they were properly applied in a given case. See the discussion of Rule 702 and _Daubert_ in Chapter 12.

C. Facts Within the Personal Knowledge of the Judge

United States v. Lewis

U.S. Court of Appeals for the Ninth Circuit
833 F.2d 1380 (9th Cir. 1987)

ALARCON, Circuit Judge:

[On October 21, 1986, shortly after she had returned from surgery and was awakened from general anesthesia, the defendant Lewis, a heroin addict, told Special Agent Michael Degnan of the FBI that she had committed three robberies. The initial interview lasted two minutes. When Degnan questioned her again the next day, October 22, the defendant Lewis signed a waiver of her constitutional rights and again confessed. At trial, Lewis filed a motion to suppress her confessions, claiming in part that "she was a "heroin addict suffering from the effects of drug withdrawal [and] was questioned in her hospital bed hours after she had awakened from a general anesthetic administered during surgery."]

Prior to hearing argument on [the motion to suppress], the court stated that "the first statement was not knowing and voluntary." Before stating its conclusion that the confession was involuntary, the court said: "Now, anybody that has ever been under a general anesthetic following an operation knows that as you come out of a general anesthetic you are not accountable for what you say and do…"

Food for Thought

Would the trial court's statement here be sufficient to support an argument that the court was taking judicial notice under Rule 201 (b) of the fact that people who have just had anesthesia give involuntary statements? The court's conclusion at this point appears to be based upon what the court thinks most people generally know. If so, is it supportable?

[The government argued] that during the first statement on October 21, 1986, Lewis "was at the time aware of what was going on and was able to talk to the agents." … The court then made the following comment:

> Well, you see, I can't go with you on [the first confession being voluntary]. One of the reasons why, and I am frank to say, I am influenced by personal experience. I mean, I represent to you that I have never been a heroin addict and I have never experienced what it is like to come out from under heroin, but I have come out from under an anesthetic. And people have told me that--and I seem to be perfectly all right--and people have

told me that I said the most incredible things during the few first six hours or so after I came out of a general anesthetic. And I have had the same experience related by other people.

You are not accountable for what you do or say for quite a number of hours after you come out of a general anesthetic. So I cannot find that a person who is both withdrawing from heroin and coming out from under a general anesthetic and is under arrest and confronted by FBI agents is in a position to make a voluntary and knowing statement at that time.

Later in the hearing the court observed:

As I said, I think that when agents go into the hospital room of a woman who is coming out from heroin and coming out from a general anesthetic and asks a question on the merits, whether you call it trick or whatever, they are taking advantage of her. They should have never asked the question. It was a clear case of not asking. And I think it was an abuse of the proper procedures in this case. And so I am not saying it was coerced. But I think it was abusive and clearly improper. And I would have to, therefore, treat the first statement as having been voluntary--involuntary. Excuse me.

* * *

The government argues that the district court improperly relied on its personal experience in concluding that the October 21, 1986 admission was not voluntary rather than on the evidence in the record. The government claims that the facts in Degnan's declaration concerning Lewis' condition at the time of the two minute conversation on October 21, 1986 demonstrate that her statements were voluntary. We agree.

The court accepted as true Degnan's sworn statement that Lewis said she was feeling "O.K." The evidence shows that Lewis was alert and her answers to the agent's questions were responsive. She was able to recall past events accurately including the inability of Special Agent Fujita to run as fast as she can. All contradictory statements in Lewis' declaration were rejected by the court as untrue. Degnan's declaration shows that her responses were made knowingly and voluntarily.

There was no evidence in Degnan's declaration that would support an inference that Lewis was withdrawing from heroin addiction on October 21, 1986 or what effect such condition would have on her ability to act voluntarily. There is no evidence in the record showing when she last injected or ingested any narcotic substance. There is no evidence in the record that a person is not accountable for what he or she says for several hours after receiving a general anesthetic.

In making his oral findings, the trial judge candidly acknowledged that his determination the issue of voluntariness was "influenced by his personal experience" and what other people told him about his own behavior after surgery as the result of receiving a general anesthetic.

* * *

Lewis contends for the first time on appeal that the trial judge properly relied on his personal experience based on the court's power to take judicial notice of adjudicative facts under Rule 201 of the Federal Rules of Evidence. This argument is unpersuasive.

A trial judge is prohibited from relying on his personal experience to support the taking of judicial notice. "It is therefore plainly accepted that the judge is not to use from the bench, under the guise of judicial knowledge, that which he knows only as an individual observer outside of court."

In relying on his "personal knowledge" the trial judge did not advise the parties he was taking judicial notice of Lewis' condition at the time she spoke to the agents on October 21, 1986. Furthermore, the trial judge did not rely on facts "generally known within the territorial jurisdiction of the trial court or … capable of accurate and ready determination by resort to sources whose accuracy cannot reasonably be questioned." Fed. R. Evid. 201(b). Instead, he looked solely to his own reaction to an anesthetic. The record is silent concerning the nature of his illness, the surgical procedure performed upon the trial judge, the type and amount of anesthetic administered to him, or its general effect on a patient. Announcement on the record of the fact that a court is taking judicial notice is necessary to accord a party the "opportunity to be heard as to the propriety of taking judicial notice and the tenor of the matter noticed." Fed. R. Evid. 201(e).

Lewis relies on _Bey v. Bolger_, 540 F. Supp. 910 (E.D.Pa.1982) for the proposition that "[c]ourts have also taken judicial notice of commonly known health facts." In *Bey*, the district court took judicial notice in a written memorandum setting forth the basis for its ruling in cross motions for partial summary judgment that a person suffering hypertension is susceptible to stroke, heart attack or other physical ailment. Thus, in *Bey*, the parties were given an opportunity to ask the court to reconsider the propriety of taking judicial notice of the effect of hypertension. Furthermore, the trial judge in *Bey* did not indicate to the parties that he was relying on his personal experience with hypertension.

The trial judge's reliance in the instant matter on facts known to him from his personal experience, denied the government the opportunity to test the basis for the court's opinion concerning the effect of an anesthetic on a person's freedom of choice through the usual methods that assure trustworthiness in our adversarial system of justice. The prosecutor was denied the opportunity to contrast the nature of the illness or injury suffered by the judge with Lewis' abscessed shoulder, the amount of anesthesia administered to each, or the actual statements made by the judge which others characterized as "incredible" with the responses made by the defendant in this matter. Lewis' statements on October 21, 1986 were not "incredible" nor unresponsive. Instead, her answers demonstrated her capacity to understand what was said to her and to respond truthfully.

Reversed and Remanded.

——————

Points for Discussion

a. Judicial Notice and Credibility.

What if the judge in *Lewis* simply concluded that after considering the evidence, he found it credible that Ms. Lewis did not give her statements voluntarily because she was still under the influence of anesthesia? What facts would have to be in the record to support this conclusion? If rephrasing the reason behind the court's decision is enough to keep the case from being reversed on appeal, isn't this tantamount to saying that a judge may base a finding of judicial notice on personal proclivities as long as it is phrased in terms of credibility findings?

Hypo 14.2

In *Jacobellis v. State,* 378 U.S. 184, 197 (1964), a case involving the prosecution of the defendant for possessing and exhibiting an allegedly obscene film, Justice Stewart stated in a concurring opinion:

> "I have reached the conclusion … that … criminal laws in this area are constitutionally limited to hard-core pornography. I shall not today attempt further to define the kinds of material I understand to be embraced within that short-hand description; and perhaps I could never succeed in intelligently doing so. But I know it when I see it, and the motion picture involved in this is not that."

Is Justice Steward taking judicial notice of a matter within his personal knowledge in this instance? Or is he stating an evaluative fact?

——————

Executive Summary

Trial Efficiency and Taking Judicial Notice of Adjudicative Facts. Under Rule 201, judges can take "judicial notice" of certain types of facts, which means judges can accept as true, without formal proof (or in a jury trial, instruct the jury to accept as true without formal proof), certain types of factual propositions. The policy reason for allowing judges to take this "shortcut" process in the presentation of proof at trial is a concern for judicial economy and the promotion of efficient trials.

However, judges can take judicial notice only "adjudicative facts." Adjudicate facts are matters of general knowledge in the jurisdiction (local geography), or matters capable of ready determination by sources whose accuracy cannot be questioned, such as the fact that water freezes at 32 degrees Fahrenheit. On the other hand, "legislative facts" (background facts used by the court to arrive at a legal decision, such as social science propositions), "evaluative facts" (common information, concepts, and understandings in society, such as people late for an appointment are more likely to speed), and "notice of the law" (laws or statutes, such as the holding of an applicable case precedent), are all subjects that are not "adjudicative facts," and therefore are not proper subjects for judicial notice. For example, whether cocaine hydrochloride is a schedule II controlled substance is not an adjudicative fact of which a court can take judicial notice because such is more of a legislative fact. (*Gould*). However, there is an argument that it might be an adjudicative fact after all because it is "capable of ready determination by sources whose accuracy cannot be questioned" – a clear statutory provision/classification.

Judicial Notice in Civil Cases. If the matter is an adjudicative fact, then it is possible to take judicial notice of it, but it must be (1) generally known in the jurisdiction or (2) ascertainable through reasonable undisputable sources. For example, a court can take judicial notice of the fact that banks send customers monthly statements and those statements inform their customers to whom their money was paid and in what amounts. (*Kaggan*). Note that it would have been unnecessary and a waste of judicial resources to require the bank to prove this basic proposition with formally presented evidence. Once the court has taken judicial notice of an adjudicative fact in a civil case, under Rule 201(g), the fact finder is instructed to accept the judicially noticed fact as *conclusive*, meaning it is to be considered established as though proved or as if the parties had stipulated to its truth.

Judicial Notice in Criminal Cases. Judicial notice operates the same way in a criminal case as it does in civil case, with one important difference, under Rule 201(g), the fact finder is instructed that it *may*, but is *not required* to, accept as conclusive (established) any fact that is judicially noticed. Because the jury in a criminal case can either accept or reject the judicially noticed fact, a matter cannot be given judicial notice for the first time on appeal because the jury never would have considered it at the trial level, even though Rule 201(f) states that judicial notice can be taken in the trial court *or on appeal*. (*Jones*).

However, a minority of courts have taken judicial notice of a matter for the first time on appeal in a criminal case. Note also that courts can take judicial notice of their own judicial records regarding the same or prior proceedings. Courts also will sometimes take judicial notice of clear and undisputable scientific facts, but more often will leave the parties to establish these matters through expert opinion testimony under Rule 702 and the requirements of *Daubert*.

Facts Within the Personal Knowledge of the Judge. What if the judge has certain personal experiences that the judge wants to draw upon in ruling upon a factual or legal matter at issue in the case over which the judge is presiding? Such personal judicial experience or knowledge is not a proper matter to be judicially noticed. It therefore was reversible error for a judge to rely on his own experience with being under anesthesia and saying unreliable things, in order to take judicial notice of the fact people say unreliable things in such circumstances when ruling on a case where the defendant, in similar circumstances, made various confessions and was challenging the admissibility of those confessions. (*Lewis*).

CHAPTER 15

Burdens and Presumptions

A. Burden of Proof

Plaintiff sues the defendant for negligence. A jury is selected, and the trial begins. The judge tells the plaintiff that he may present his evidence. The plaintiff, who is new to the world of litigation, thanks the judge for the opportunity but states that he would rather the defense present her evidence first. What should the judge do? The answer is: grant a judgment as a matter of law in favor of the defendant. Why? Because the party with the burden of proof in the case, the plaintiff, has failed to alter the status quo. He has failed to introduce evidence from which the jury could find that he is entitled to win. Why should the plaintiff and not the defendant lose when neither side presents any evidence? In short, because the substantive law of negligence requires the plaintiff to prove duty, breach of duty, proximate causation and damages before he can recover. Otherwise, the status quo is preserved, and the defendant continues to keep her money.

So what does the term burden of proof mean? Generally speaking, it has to do with the risk of losing the case. It guides the judge and jury in determining which side should lose if no evidence or insufficient evidence is presented.

But that is not the end of the matter. The term "burden of proof" also encompasses two separate but related concepts: the burden of production and the burden of persuasion. As a general rule, a party upon whom these burdens are cast must satisfy them both in order to win at trial.

1. Burden of Production

The burden of producing evidence, sometimes called the burden of going forward with the evidence, refers to the amount of evidence sufficient to enable the trier of fact reasonably to find for that party if that evidence is found credible. Of course, the fact-finder may or may not find this evidence credible, but that is not the point. If the plaintiff in our negligence case testifies that the defendant ran a red light, struck him in a cross-walk and broke his arm, this testimony is probably sufficient to allow a jury to consider the issue of defendant's liability, even if the jury eventually concludes that the plaintiff is an unabashed liar. This is true even if the defendant presents no evidence at all, although such a strategy runs the risk that the jury might decide to give an unabashed liar the benefit of the doubt.

On the other hand, what if the plaintiff in our negligence case presents the testimony of three neutral witnesses to the accident who agree with everything that the plaintiff said: that the defendant ran through a red light, struck the plaintiff in a cross-walk and broke his arm? In this instance, not only has the plaintiff satisfied his burden of producing evidence as to all the elements of negligence liability, he has satisfied it so resoundingly that the law shifts the burden of production to the defendant to refute the plaintiff's evidence, by presenting evidence of her own and/or by skillful, creative and vigorous cross-examination of the plaintiff's witnesses. If the defendant fails in her burden of production under these circumstances, the defendant is at risk not only of losing the jury verdict but also of having a partial judgment as a matter of law as to liability granted against her.

Take Note!

For example, through cross-examination, a defense attorney might obtain a plaintiff witness's refutation of her direct testimony, although, *Law and Order* aside, this very seldom occurs.

2. Burden of Persuasion

Once the plaintiff in our negligence case has satisfied the burden of producing sufficient evidence to be considered by the jury, he must now convince the jury that this evidence is of a good enough quality to win on the legal issues. This is called satisfying the burden of persuasion. In a civil negligence case, the plaintiff must convince the fact-finder that all the elements of his claim (i.e. duty, breach of duty, proximate causation and damages) are met by a preponderance of the evidence. Under a preponderance standard, a tie in the evidence goes to the defendant because she does not have the burden of persuasion as to

What's That?

The term "preponderance of the evidence" generally means the greater weight of the credible evidence or a little more than fifty-percent.

Take Note!

There is no universally agreed upon definition of reasonable doubt, although some courts define the term as a doubt based on reason, which is not very helpful. Proof beyond a reasonable doubt in a criminal case is constitutionally required. See *In re Winship*, 397 U.S. 358 (1970).

any of the negligence liability issues. On the other hand, in a criminal case, the prosecution has the burden of proving the defendant guilty of a crime beyond a reasonable doubt. If the proof does not meet this burden, the defendant must be acquitted.

The following logic maps represent a simplified version of what we have just discussed where the plaintiff has sued the defendant for negligence. This illustration does not take into account any defenses or affirmative defenses which the defendant might plead.

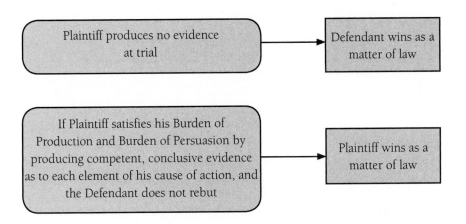

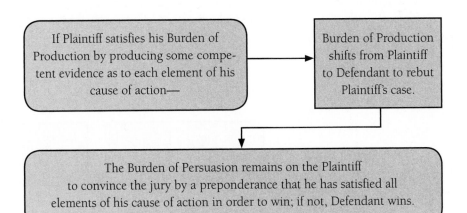

B. Standards of Proof

There are three basic standards of proof. These standards are the level of proof by which the fact-finder must be persuaded in order for a litigant to satisfy her burden of persuasion:

1) Preponderance of the Evidence

This standard is often analogized to just greater than fifty-percent or, "more likely than not." It requires convincing the fact-finder that the existence of a particular fact is more likely than not.

This standard applies to most civil cases and defenses as well as most (but not all) affirmative defenses in criminal cases.

2) Clear and Convincing

This standard would be the rarest among the three. It is more stringent than the Preponderance of the Evidence standard and less stringent than the Beyond a Reasonable Doubt standard. This standard may be required in civil cases involving claims of fraud, in federal criminal cases with defense claims of insanity and in many issues relating to family law in various states.

3) Beyond a Reasonable Doubt

In criminal cases, both federal and state, the prosecution must prove all elements of the charged offense beyond a reasonable doubt. This requirement has its basis in the Due Process Clause of the 14th Amendment to the United States Constitution.

On a continuum, the standards of proof might look something like this:

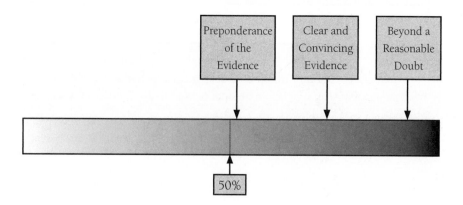

C. Inferences and Presumptions

1. Inferences

When evidence is circumstantial, one of the ways a party may satisfy his burden of proof is by use of inferences and presumptions. Inferences are common sense conclusions deduced from facts. Suppose that a person is walking down the street at night, hears the sound of broken glass and a moment later, a burglar alarm goes off. He then

What's That?

Circumstantial evidence is evidence based upon inferences made from facts that are known, as opposed to direct evidence, which is eyewitness testimony to the event.

Take Note!

Inferences are, of course, only as reliable as the facts from which they are drawn. In our example, the person seen running down the street may have been the homeowner who was out for an evening run and wearing a ski cap because it was cold outside. He saw the actual burglar attempting to break into his house, picked up the burglar's crowbar and chased after him. Direct eyewitness testimony may also be too narrowly focused and inaccurate. See the movie "Rashomon," where the story of a crime is told from the point of view of five different witnesses to the events, each one telling the truth but coming to five different conclusions as to what occurred.

sees a man with a ski hat pulled down around his ears, holding what looks to be a crowbar and running down the street. When he looks at the house, he sees a broken window. From what he saw and heard, he concludes that the man he observed was fleeing after attempting to burglarize the house. Under all the circumstances, the witness has made a rational inference, given that it is common knowledge that burglars tend to operate at night, mask their identity, use tools to gain entrance to structures, are known to break doors or windows to enter, and flee when alarms go off. Attorneys frequently use inferences such as these along with matters of common knowledge to help persuade fact-finders of the truth of their case during closing argument.

2. Presumptions

Presumptions: The law of presumptions is highly complex and murky. This section of the chapter attempts to present a basic overview, leaving a more in-depth discussion for another time.

A presumption is a legal inference. More particularly, a presumption is a rule of law that states that once a certain fact (Fact A) is established, the presumed fact (Fact B) must be taken as established if not disputed by the opposing party. Consider the presumption that a person who has been missing for more than seven years (Fact A) is presumed dead (Fact B). The concluded Fact B flows from Fact A as a logical inference and because the law requires it to do so.

Why create a presumption? Presumptions are created for a number of reasons. They may be created to resolve difficult fact issues in an expedient manner. For example, if a husband and wife die in an aviation accident, there is often no way to determine which of them died first. For probate purposes, the law may create a presumption that both parties died simultaneously, thus allowing their wills to be probated in an orderly and uniform manner. Presumptions are also created in order to further important social policies. Many jurisdictions, for example, recognize a presumption that if a child is born during wedlock, the child is presumed to be the child of the husband. Through this presumption, the law seeks to insure an orderly process of descent and distribution of property, stabilize the family structure, and establish responsibilities for the best interests of the child. On occasion, the law creates a presumption when the ability to introduce proof on an issue is mostly in the hands of the party opposing the presumption. Suppose that the plaintiff in a case is required to prove that the defendant received notice in a case. A defendant might easily claim that she never received the notice even if she actually did, and the plaintiff may be unable to produce any direct evidence to the contrary. The plaintiff might be aided, however, by a presumption stating that if his notice is properly mailed to the defendant, then it is presumed to be received in due course.

> **FYI**
>
> Be aware that there are other ways to classify of presumptions, such as conclusive, irrebutable, or presumptions of law or fact. For the most part, these classifications are confusing, conflicting and occasionally redundant, which is why no time is spent on them in this chapter.

Presumptions may be classified as being permissive or mandatory. Generally, the difference between the two is the effect of the presumption once it has been established, assuming at this point that the opponent of the presumption has not offered evidence in rebuttal. For a permissive presumption, the court will usually instruct the jury that they may but are not required to conclude the presumed fact (Fact B) if the presumption is not contested. For a mandatory presumption, the court will usually instruct the jury that they must find the concluded fact (Fact B) if the presumption is not contested.

D. Presumptions in Civil Cases

Rule 301. Presumptions in General in Civil Actions and Proceedings

In all civil actions and proceedings not otherwise provided for by Act of Congress or by these rules, a presumption imposes on the party against whom it is directed the burden of going forward with evidence to rebut or meet the presumption, but does not shift to such party the burden of proof in the sense of the risk of nonpersuasion, which remains throughout the trial upon the party on whom it was originally cast.

In federal law, the operation of a presumption in a civil case is governed by Rule 301. The rule states that if a party relying on a presumption has the burden of persuasion to prove the presumed fact (Fact B), that burden of persuasion never shifts to the opponent. For example, if the plaintiff has the burden of *persuading* a jury that the defendant received notice in a case, the plaintiff's use of a presumption to establish receipt never shifts the burden of persuading a jury, that notice

FYI

Rule 301 does not, by its own terms, apply to cases governed by state law or those for which Congress otherwise provides. What might these exceptions include? Do they apply to only those federal legislative presumptions that give an effect contrary to the rule or to federal regulations as well? There is nothing in the legislative history of Rule 301 that answers these questions. But see <u>McHenry, *Federal Rules of Evidence 301*</u>

FYI

This theory is named after James Bradley Thayer, a teacher and writer of evidence in the early twentieth century. It is also called the "Bursting Bubble" or the colorful "Bats in the Night" theory because it is said that once the opponent of a presumption presents competent evidence to challenge the presumed fact (Fact B), the presumption should drop out of the case and have no further effect, i.e., the presumption should vanish like a bubble that bursts or like "bats of the law flitting in the twilight, but disappearing in the sunshine of actual facts." <u>*Mackowik v. Kansas City, St. Josephs & Council Bluffs R.R. Co.*, 94 S.W. 256, 262 (1906)</u>.

was not received, to the defendant. However, Rule 301 also instructs that once a presumption is established, the burden of *producing* some evidence to rebut the presumption shifts to the opponent. If the opponent produces no evidence to rebut the presumption, the presumption is established. But what effect does a presumption have in federal court under Rule 301 if the opponent introduces evidence rebutting Fact B? This is an issue that has been subject to some dispute.

Under the most prevalent theory, sometimes called the "Thayer Theory," the only effect of using a presumption is to shift the burden of producing evidence to rebut Fact B to the opponent of the presumption. If the opponent introduces evidence that rebuts Fact B, the presumption disappears. (The "bubble" of the presumption "bursts" and has no effect). As a practical matter, this means that use of a presumption may allow a party to survive a motion for judgment as a matter of law but has no other use at trial.

There are a number of additional theories suggesting that presumptions should have alternate effects. One of the most well-recognized is the "Morgan Theory", which provides that if the facts upon which the presumption is based have probative value, the burden of *production and persuasion* switch to the presumption's opponent to rebut the presumption. This means that once a presumption is established, it continues in a case and may be used by a jury in determining the presumed fact (Fact B) even if it is rebutted by the opponent of the presumption. The Morgan Theory was proposed by the drafters of Rule 301, but ultimately rejected.

How would the Thayer and Morgan Theories work in practice? Assume again that there is a presumption that if a letter is properly mailed, the addressee is presumed to have received it in due course. The plaintiff, who has the burden of proving receipt, testifies that he properly mailed a letter to the defendant, thus establishing Fact A and creating a presumption of receipt (Fact B) in due course. The defendant then testifies that he never received the letter (refuting Fact B). Under the Thayer Theory, the presumption would vanish, and the jury would not be instructed on it, although the facts giving rise to the presumption might be argued as an inference of receipt by the plaintiff's attorney. Additionally, the plaintiff retains his original burden of persuading the jury that the defendant received notice. Applying the Morgan Theory to these facts, the jury would be instructed that there is a presumption of receipt which they must weigh against any contrary evidence to determine whether notice was received. They would also be instructed that the burden of persuading the jury shifts to the defendant to disprove receipt.

In the next case, *Yoder*, the court discusses whether Rule 301 contemplates use of the Thayer Theory of presumptions and how the Thayer Theory works when the issue is whether a party had receipt of notice in a bankruptcy proceeding.

In Re Yoder Co.

United States Court of Appeals for the Sixth Circuit
758 F.2d 1114 (1985)

CORNELIA G. KENNEDY, Circuit Judge.

In this Chapter 11 proceeding the Bankruptcy Court, affirmed by the District Court, held that Mark S. Bratton's products liability claim for the loss of four fingers was barred for failure to timely file a proof of claim. Bratton contends that his claim should not be barred because he did not receive notice of the latest date for filing proofs of claim.

In 1981, Yoder filed a petition requesting relief under Chapter 11 of the Bankruptcy Code. At that time Bratton's products liability suit against Yoder was pending in a Michigan state court. Bratton's claim was listed as a "contingent, unliquidated and disputed" claim in the amended schedule of assets and liabilities filed by Yoder. The Bankruptcy Court issued an order setting July 13, 1981 at the last date for creditors to file proofs of claim against Yoder (the "bar date").

Bratton filed a proof of claim on March 15, 1982, about eight months after the bar date. Yoder applied to the Bankruptcy Court for an order expunging certain products liability claims, including Bratton's. Following a hearing on Yoder's application, at which Bratton was represented, the Bankruptcy Court found that Bratton had been sent sufficient notice of the bar date and that Bratton's failure to file timely proof of claim was not due to excusable neglect. Bratton's claim was therefore barred. The District Court affirmed, and Bratton appeals.

* * *

The Bankruptcy Court heard evidence concerning the procedure used to mail notices of the bar date. An employee of Yoder testified that he supervised a procedure through which an address label was prepared at [the request of] Yoder for each creditor listed in Yoder's amended schedule of assets and liabilities, and that the employee and an accountant proofread the address labels to make sure that all listed creditors were included. The address labels and corresponding notices were taken to the clerk of the Bankruptcy Court. Using labels and envelopes it received from the Bankruptcy Court, the Cleveland Letter Service then prepared and mailed the notices. No record of the address labels actually prepared was kept by Yoder, the Bankruptcy Court clerk, or the Cleveland Letter Service; and neither the clerk's office nor the Cleveland Letter Service checked the labels against any list of creditors. Bratton's name and address did not appear on the matrix of creditors that was filed earlier with the Bankruptcy Court. The courtroom deputy docket clerk testified that she did not know whether the labels sent to the Cleveland Letter Service were the labels prepared by Yoder or labels prepared from the matrix in the court's file.

Bratton's address on the amended schedule of assets and liabilities, the list which Yoder's employee testified was used to prepare the labels, was that of his attorney, A.T. Ornstein. Ornstein testified that he had not received notice of the bar date. Attorneys for two other listed products liability claimants also represented that they and their clients had not received notices of the bar date.

The Bankruptcy Court made a factual finding that notice of the bar date had been sent to Ornstein. The Court did not discuss its reasons for this finding or explain how it weighed the evidence, although the evidence concerning mailing was far from undisputed. Testimony of non-receipt is evidence that the notice was not mailed. We do not need to decide whether the finding that notice was mailed was clearly erroneous, however, because we hold that the Bankruptcy Court abused its discretion in holding that Bratton did not file a late proof of claim as a result of excusable neglect. This holding was based on the closely related finding that Bratton's attorney received the notice, which we hold to be clearly erroneous.

Rule 906(b) of the Rules of Bankruptcy Procedure provides that a time period may be extended if failure to act in time "was the result of excusable neglect…" The parties disagree over the definition of excusable neglect… Under even Yoder's definition, however, nonreceipt of notice would clearly constitute excusable neglect. The Bankruptcy Court's determination that no excusable neglect existed was based entirely on its finding that notice was received at Bratton's attorney's law firm. We thus turn to the question of whether this finding of receipt was clearly erroneous.

The Bankruptcy Court relied mainly on a presumption of receipt that it held arose from evidence that the notice was properly mailed. The common law has long recognized a presumption that an item properly mailed was received by the addressee. The presumption arises upon proof that the item was properly addressed, had sufficient postage, and was deposited in the mail. For purposes of this discussion, we will assume that the presumption of receipt did arise.

The District Court held that the presumption had not been rebutted, reasoning that "testimony amounting to a mere denial that a properly mailed notice was not received is insufficient to rebut the presumption of receipt…" Testimony of non-receipt, standing alone, [however] would be sufficient to support a finding of non-receipt; such testimony is therefore sufficient to rebut the presumption of receipt.

The next question is whether the presumption, once rebutted, retains any effect. The Bankruptcy Court found that it was "entitled to presume that notice has been received once a proper mailing is made, even though the intended recipient testifies that the notice never really came." The Bankruptcy Court reasoned as follows:

> According to the note of the Advisory Committee on Proposed Rules, Federal Rule 301 rejects the so-called "bursting bubble" theory, under which a presumption vanishes upon the introduction of evidence that negates the existence of the presumed fact. According to the Federal Rule, when evidence is put forth negating the fact that the presumption tends to support, the presumption still continues and is evidence to be weighed and considered with all of the other evidence in the case.

* * *

A brief review of the history of [Rule 301] will aid in evaluating the Bankruptcy Court's reasoning. Before adoption of the Federal Rules of Evidence there were two major theories concerning the effect of a presumption once rebuttal evidence is admitted. Under the Thayer or "bursting bubble" theory a presumption vanishes entirely once rebutted, and the question must be decided as any ordinary question of fact. Under a later theory, proposed by Morgan, a presumption shifts the burden of proving the nonexistence of the presumed fact to the opposing party.

The version of Rule 301 that was proposed by the Advisory Committee, accepted by the Supreme Court, and submitted to Congress adopted the Morgan view. That rule, however, was not enacted by Congress. The Advisory Committee notes, on which the Bankruptcy Court relied, that reject the "bursting bubble" theory pertain to the proposed rule, which was not enacted, and are thus of little help in interpreting the final rule.

The House of Representatives adopted a rule espousing an intermediate view, which would allow a rebutted presumption to be considered evidence of the fact presumed. The Senate criticized the House rule on the ground that it made no sense to call a presumption evidence, and adopted the present language of Rule 301, which was adopted by the Conference Committee and enacted into law.

Practice Pointer

Although the Thayer Theory is the most widely recognized theory of presumptions in federal civil cases, this is not always true in every jurisdiction. Therefore, before trying a case, it is always a good idea to make a list of the presumptions that may arise and the legal effect those presumptions have on proving or defending a case.

Most commentators have concluded that Rule 301 as enacted embodies the Thayer or "bursting bubble" approach. At least two other circuit courts have expressly agreed. The Thayer view is consistent with the language of Rule 301, which provides only that a presumption shifts "the burden of going forward with evidence to rebut or meet the presumption." Accordingly, we hold that a presumption under Rule 301 has no probative effect once rebutted. The Bankruptcy Court therefore erred in considering the presumption as evidence of receipt.

The only other evidence of receipt expressly considered by the Bankruptcy Court was that "Mr. Bratton's law firm did receive and respond to the notice setting debtor's objection to his claim for hearing." However, there was no evidence that the notices of the hearing were sent to the same addresses as were the notices of the bar date, which were sent more than a year earlier. The testimony was that no copy of the address labels made up for the bar date notices was kept, so a copy of those labels could not have been used to mail the later notices of the hearing on debtor's objections to claims. That Bratton received notice of the hearing is therefore not evidence that he received notice of the bar date.

The Bankruptcy Court erred in relying upon the presumption and notice of the hearing to establish receipt. Had it properly considered all the evidence it would have had to find that Bratton had not received notice.

Bratton's attorney, to whom the notice was purportedly addressed, testified directly that he did not receive the notice. The only evidence tending to establish receipt of notice is testimony of a Yoder employee that he and employees under his supervision prepared address labels corresponding to all creditors listed in Yoder's amended schedule of assets and liabilities. Bratton was listed on that schedule. These labels were then taken to the Bankruptcy Court by Yoder's attorney. A Cleveland Letter Service employee testified that the notices were mailed using labels received from the Bankruptcy Court.

The evidence in the record, however, does not establish that the labels prepared by Yoder were the ones the Bankruptcy Court sent to the Cleveland Letter Service. The Bankruptcy Court deputy clerk testified that it was possible that labels prepared form the matrix of creditors' addresses already in the file were used, and that she had no record or recollection of whether these labels or the ones supplied by Yoder were sent to the Cleveland Letter Service. The clerk also testified that Bratton was *not* listed on the matrix in the file. Thus, it is equally likely that either set of labels was used.

The evidence in the record, however, does not establish that the labels prepared by Yoder were the ones the Bankruptcy Court sent to the Cleveland Letter Service. The Bankruptcy Court deputy clerk testified that it was possible that labels prepared form the matrix of creditors' addresses already in the file were used, and that she had no record or recollection of whether these labels or the ones supplied by Yoder were sent to the Cleveland Letter Service. The clerk also testified that Bratton was not listed on the matrix in the file. Thus, it is equally likely that either set of labels was used.

Even if the labels supplied by Yoder were used, there is only weak circumstantial evidence that there was a label for Bratton. No record of the actual labels made up was kept. Yoder's employee testified that he checked the labels against the amended schedule, but there were 1,442 labels and a mistake could easily have been made. There was testimony that the matrix of creditors' addresses, which did not include Bratton's, was also supplied by Yoder. Since Yoder mistakenly omitted Bratton from the matrix, it is equally likely to have done the same when preparing the labels for notices of the bar date.

There was also circumstantial evidence that the labels supplied by Yoder were not complete. Only four of twenty scheduled products liability claimants filed proofs of claim. In addition to Bratton's attorney, attorneys for two other claimants testified that they had not received notice. Evidence that one addressee did not receive a notice supports the inference that another addressee did not receive the notice.

The evidence other than Ornstein's testimony that he did not receive the notice is at best neutral. If the Bankruptcy Court had considered all the evidence without relying on a presumption and still found that notice was received, it would have been clearly erroneous. Non-receipt is sufficient ground for excusable neglect, and it is clear from the lower court opinions that had those courts found non-receipt the claim would have been allowed.

Accordingly, the judgment of the District Court is reversed and the case remanded for reversal of the Bankruptcy Court order expunging Bratton's claim.

Points for Discussion

a. Criticisms of the Thayer Theory of Presumptions.

Under the Thayer Theory, a presumption vanishes if rebutted by the opponent. But presumptions are usually created for solid policy reasons. Does this theory give too slight an effect to these policies? Is this concern alleviated by allowing what was once a presumption to be argued as an inference without the benefit of a jury instruction? Does the Morgan Theory have any benefit in this regard? If so, is this benefit sufficient to persuade you that it is a better theory?

b. The Opponent's Responses.

Assume that Yoder has introduced facts that establish a presumption of receipt. Describe the opponent's possible responses. What are the consequences of each response under the Thayer Theory of presumptions? How might a judge instruct a jury as to each possible response?

c. Conflicting Presumptions.

On occasion, more than one presumption might apply to a fact issue in a case. For example, in <u>Legille v. Dann, 544 F.2d 1 (D.C.Cir. 1976)</u>, the parties relied on two different presumptions that gave two different results concerning the dates when the U.S. Patent Officer received the parties' patent applications. The court determined that these presumptions cancelled each other out, and that neither presumption should be given effect. Another approach to the problem of conflicting presumptions has been to give weight only to the presumption that that has the stronger basis in policy or logic. Take, for example, a presumption that a marriage is valid and a presumption that a marriage continues without proof to the contrary. What if a second wife sues for compensation for the wrongful death of her husband, and there is no direct evidence that his first marriage ended in death or divorce? Which presumption is the stronger? Some courts might argue that the presumption of the validity of the marriage trumps the presumption that the first marriage continued because the continuity and stability of a current second marriage is socially more important under these circumstances than determining the continuity of a first marriage. If the court in *Legille* adopted this second approach, what would be the result?

Hypo 15.1

Assume a statute states that a child born during wedlock is presumed to be the child of the husband. Husband and wife file for divorce, and Wife asks for monetary support for Child. At trial, Wife introduces competent evidence that she was legally married to Husband for 10 years, and that Child was conceived and born during this time period. Husband claims in his pleadings that his neighbor Joe is really the father of Child, but he never introduces any evidence to substantiate this claim or to rebut that Child was conceived and born during his marriage to Wife. Under the Thayer Theory of presumptions, is Wife entitled to a judgment as a matter of law that Husband is the father of Child?

E. Presumptions in Criminal Cases

Presumptions in criminal cases are not addressed by the Federal Rules of Evidence. Their use is complicated by the fact that there are several constitutional amendments that protect defendants, which limit the effect of presumptions favoring the prosecution in criminal cases. The Fourteenth Amendment, for example, requires

> The presumption of innocence, however, is enshrined in the Fifth Amendment to the Constitution and is of such importance that it is the only presumption that has a constitutional dimension.

that the prosecution prove its case beyond a reasonable doubt. *In re Winship*, 397 U.S. 358 (1970). The Fifth and Fourteenth Amendments give a defendant the right to trial by jury. Mandatory presumptions that require a jury to accept a presumptive fact once a presumption has been established may conflict with a criminal defendant's constitutional protections.

Additionally, the Supreme Court has held that the Fourteenth Amendment Due Process Clause requires that there be a "rational connection" between facts establishing the presumption in a criminal case (Fact A) and the presumed fact (Fact B). See *Tot v. United States*, 319 U.S. 463 (1943). Normally, to decide whether there is a rational connection courts will scour a presumption's legislative history or findings or, if neither exists, base their determination on common sense inferences and logic. But given the burden of proof in a criminal case, does the Constitution require that this rational connection be proved beyond a reasonable doubt or may it be proved under some lesser standard? These are some of the issues considered by the landmark Supreme Court case of *County Court of Ulster v. Allen*.

County Court of Ulster County v. Allen

Supreme Court of the United States
442 U.S. 140 (1979)

Mr. Justice STEVENS delivered the opinion of the Court.

A New York statute provides that, with certain exceptions, the presence of a firearm in an automobile is presumptive evidence of its illegal possession by all persons then occupying the vehicle...

Four persons, three adult males (respondents) and a 16-year-old girl (Jane Doe, who is not a respondent here), were jointly tried on charges that they possessed two loaded handguns, a loaded machinegun, and over a pound of heroin found in a Chevrolet in which they were riding when it was stopped for speeding on the New York Thruway shortly after noon on March 28, 1973. The two large-caliber handguns, which together with their ammunition weighed approximately six pounds, were seen through the window of the car by the investigating police officer. They were positioned crosswise in an open handbag on either the front floor or the front seat of the car on the passenger side where Jane Doe was sitting. Jane Doe admitted that the handbag was hers. The machine gun and the heroin were discovered in the trunk after the police pried it open. The car had been borrowed from the driver's brother earlier that day; the key to the trunk could not be found in the car or on the person of any of its occupants, although there was testimony that two of the occupants had placed something in the trunk before embarking in the borrowed car. The jury convicted all four of possession of the handguns and acquitted them of possession of the contents of the trunk.

Counsel for all four defendants objected to the introduction into evidence of the two handguns, the machinegun, and the drugs, arguing that the State had not adequately demonstrated a connection between their clients and the contraband. The trial court overruled the objection, relying on the presumption of possession created by the New York statute. Because that presumption does not apply if a weapon is found "upon the person" of one of the occupants of the car, the three male defendants also moved to dismiss the charges relating to the handguns on the ground that the guns were found on the person of Jane Doe. Respondents made this motion both at the close of the prosecution's case and at the close of all evidence. The trial judge twice denied it, concluding that the applicability of the "upon the person" exception was a question of fact for the jury.

At the close of the trial, the judge instructed the jurors that they were entitled to infer possession from the defendants' presence in the car. He did not make any reference to the "upon the person" exception in his explanation of the statutory presumption, nor did any of the defendants object to this omission or request alternative or additional instructions on the subject.

Defendants filed a post-trial motion in which they challenged the constitutionality of the New York statute as applied in this case. The challenge was made in support of their argument that the evidence, apart from the presumption, was insufficient to sustain the convictions.

The Court of Appeals for the Second Circuit affirmed [the convictions].

* * *

Inferences and presumptions are a staple of our adversary system of factfinding. It is often necessary for the trier of fact to determine the existence of an element of the crime-that is, an "ultimate" or "elemental" fact - from the existence of one or more "evidentiary" or "basic" facts. The value of these evidentiary devices, and their validity under the Due Process Clause, vary from case to case, however, depending on the strength of the connection between the particular basic and elemental facts involved and on the degree to which the device curtails the factfinder's freedom to assess the evidence independently. Nonetheless, in criminal cases, the ultimate test of any device's constitutional validity in a given case remains constant: the device must not undermine the factfinder's responsibility at trial, based on evidence adduced by the State, to find the ultimate facts beyond a reasonable doubt.

The most common evidentiary device is the entirely permissive inference or presumption, which allows -- but does not require -- the trier of fact to infer the elemental fact from proof by the prosecutor of the basic one and which places no burden of any kind on the defendant. In that situation the basic fact may constitute prima facie evidence of the elemental fact. When reviewing this type of device, the Court has required the party challenging it to demonstrate its invalidity as applied to him. Because this permissive presumption leaves the trier of fact free to credit or reject the inference and does not shift the burden of proof, it affects the application of the "beyond a reasonable doubt" standard only if, under the facts of the case, there is no rational way the trier could make the connection permitted by the inference. For only in that situation is there any risk that an explanation of the permissible inference to a jury, or its use by a jury, has caused the presumptively rational factfinder to make an erroneous factual determination.

A mandatory presumption is a far more troublesome evidentiary device. For it may affect not only the strength of the "no reasonable doubt" burden but also the placement of that burden; it tells the trier that he or they must find the elemental fact upon proof of the basic fact, at least unless the defendant has come forward with some evidence to rebut the presumed connection between the two facts. (This class of more or less mandatory presumptions can be subdivided into two parts: presumptions that merely shift the burden of production to the defendant, following the satisfaction of which the ultimate burden of persuasion returns to the prosecution; and presumptions that entirely shift the burden of proof to the defendant. The mandatory presumptions examined by our cases have almost uniformly fit into the former subclass, in that they never totally removed the ultimate burden of proof beyond a reasonable doubt from the prosecution. To the extent that a presumption imposes an extremely low burden of production- e. g., being satisfied by "any" evidence-it may well be that its impact is no greater than that of a permissive inference, and it may be proper to analyze it as such.)

In this situation, the Court has generally examined the presumption on its face to determine the extent to which the basic and elemental facts coincide. To the extent that the trier of fact is forced to abide by the presumption, and may

Food for Thought

If a so-called mandatory presumption forces the jury to give effect to the presumed fact, would this also allow the trial judge to find for the prosecution on this issue as a matter of law, and if so, would such a finding be constitutional? See *Sandstrom v. Montana*, 442 U.S. 510 (1979).

not reject it based on an independent evaluation of the particular facts presented by the State, the analysis of the presumption's constitutional validity is logically divorced from those facts and based on the presumption's accuracy in the run of cases. (In...*Leary v. United States* ... Dr. Timothy Leary, a professor at Harvard University, was stopped by customs inspectors in Laredo, Tex., as he was returning from [Mexico]. Marihuana seeds and a silver snuffbox filled with semirefined marihuana and three partially smoked marihuana cigarettes were discovered in his car. He was convicted of having knowingly transported marihuana which he knew had been illegally imported into this country . That statute included a mandatory presumption: "possession shall be deemed sufficient evidence to authorize conviction [for importation] unless the defendant explains his possession to the satisfaction of the jury." Leary admitted possession of the marihuana and claimed that he had carried it from New York to Mexico and then back. Mr. Justice Harlan for the Court noted that under one theory of the case, the jury could have found direct proof of all of the necessary elements of the offense without recourse to the presumption. But he deemed that insufficient reason to affirm the conviction because under another theory the jury might have found knowledge of importation on the basis of either direct evidence or the presumption, and there was accordingly no certainty that the jury had not relied on the presumption. The Court therefore found it necessary to test the presumption against the Due Process Clause. Its analysis was facial. Despite the fact that the defendant was well educated and had recently traveled to a country that is a major exporter of marihuana to this country, the Court found the presumption of knowledge of importation from possession irrational. It did so, not because Dr. Leary was unlikely to know the source of the marihuana, but instead because "a majority of possessors" were unlikely to have such knowledge. Because the jury had been instructed to rely on the presumption even if it did not believe the Government's direct evidence of knowledge of importation (unless, of course, the defendant met his burden of "satisfying" the jury to the contrary), the Court reversed the conviction.) It is for this reason that the Court has held it irrelevant in analyzing a mandatory presumption, but not in analyzing a purely permissive one, that there is ample evidence in the record other than the presumption to support a conviction.

Without determining whether the presumption in this case was mandatory, the Court of Appeals analyzed it on its face as if it were. In fact, it was not, as the New York Court of Appeals had earlier pointed out.

The trial judge's instructions make it clear that the presumption was merely a part of the prosecution's case, that it gave rise to a permissive inference available only in certain circumstances, rather than a mandatory conclusion of possession, and that it could be ignored by the jury even if there was no affirmative proof offered by defendants in rebuttal. ("It is your duty to consider all the testimony in this case, to weigh it carefully and to test the credit to be given to a witness by his apparent intention to speak the truth and by the accuracy of his memory to reconcile, if possible, conflicting statements as to material facts and in such ways to try and get at the truth and to reach a verdict upon the evidence. To establish the unlawful possession of the weapons, again the People relied upon the presumption and, in addition thereto, the testimony of Anderson and Lemmons who testified in their case in chief. Accordingly, you would be warranted in returning a verdict of guilt against the defendants or defendant if you find the defendants or defendant was in possession of a machine gun and the other weapons and that the fact of possession was proven to you by the People beyond a reasonable doubt, and an element of such proof is the reasonable presumption of illegal possession of a machine gun or the presumption of illegal possession of firearms, as I have just before explained to you.") ("Our Penal Law also provides that the presence in an automobile of any machine gun or of any handgun or firearm which is loaded is presumptive evidence of their unlawful possession. "In other words, these presumptions or this latter presumption upon proof of the presence of the machine gun and the hand weapons, you may infer and draw a conclusion that such prohibited weapon was possessed by each of the defendants who occupied the automobile at the time when such instruments were found. The presumption or presumptions is effective only so long as there is no substantial evidence contradicting the conclusion flowing from the presumption, and the presumption is said to disappear when such contradictory evidence is adduced." The presumption or presumptions which I discussed with the jury relative to the drugs or weapons in this case need not be rebutted by affirmative proof or affirmative evidence but may be rebutted by any evidence or lack of evidence in the case.") The judge explained that possession could be actual or constructive, but that constructive possession could not exist without the intent and ability to exercise control or dominion over the weapons. He also carefully instructed the jury that there is a mandatory presumption of innocence in favor of the defendants that controls unless it, as the exclusive trier of fact, is satisfied beyond a reasonable doubt that the defendants possessed the handguns in the manner described by the judge. In short, the instructions plainly directed the jury to consider all the circumstances tending to support or contradict the inference that all four occupants of the car had possession of the two loaded handguns and to decide the matter for itself without regard to how much evidence the defendants introduced.

Food for Thought

Is the Court here using a state presumption to limit a constitutional presumption of innocence? If so, do you think this is a legitimate limitation?

As applied to the facts of this case, the presumption of possession is entirely rational. Notwithstanding the Court of Appeals' analysis, respondents were not "hitchhikers or other casual passengers," and the guns were neither "a few inches in length" nor "out of [respondents'] sight." The argument against possession by any of the respondents was predicated solely on the fact that the guns were in Jane Doe's pocketbook. But several circumstances - which, not surprisingly, her counsel repeatedly emphasized in his questions and his argument made it highly improbable that she was the sole custodian of those weapons.

Even if it was reasonable to conclude that she had placed the guns in her purse before the car was stopped by police, the facts strongly suggest that Jane Doe was not the only person able to exercise dominion over them. The two guns were too large to be concealed in her handbag. The bag was consequently open, and part of one of the guns was in plain view, within easy access of the driver of the car and even, perhaps, of the other two respondents who were riding in the rear seat.

* * *

Under these circumstances, the jury would have been entirely reasonable in rejecting the suggestion -- which, incidentally, defense counsel did not even advance in their closing arguments to the jury -- that the handguns were in the sole possession of Jane Doe. Assuming that the jury did reject it, the case is tantamount to one in which the guns were lying on the floor or the seat of the car in the plain view of the three other occupants of the automobile. In such a case, it is surely rational to infer that each of the respondents was fully aware of the presence of the guns and had both the ability and the intent to exercise dominion and control over the weapons. The application of the statutory presumption in this case therefore comports with the standard laid down in *Tot v. United States* and restated in *Leary v. United States.* For there is a "rational connection" between the basic facts that the prosecution proved and the ultimate fact presumed, and the latter is "more likely than not to flow from" the former.

Respondents argue, however, that the validity of the New York presumption must be judged by a "reasonable doubt" test rather than the "more likely than not" standard employed in *Leary*. Under the more stringent test, it is argued that a statutory presumption must be rejected unless the evidence necessary to invoke the inference is sufficient for a rational jury to find the inferred fact beyond a reasonable doubt. Respondents' argument again overlooks the distinction between a permissive presumption on which the prosecution is entitled to rely as one not necessarily sufficient part of its proof and a mandatory presumption which the jury must accept even if it is the sole evidence of an element of the offense.

In the latter situation, since the prosecution bears the burden of establishing guilt, it may not rest its case entirely on a presumption unless the fact proved is sufficient to support the inference of guilt beyond a reasonable doubt. But in the former situation, the prosecution may rely on all of the evidence in the record to meet the reasonable-doubt standard. There is no more reason to require a permissive statutory presumption to meet a reasonable-doubt standard before it may be permitted to play any part in a trial than there is to require that degree of probative force for other relevant evidence before it may be admitted. As long as it is clear that the presumption is not the sole and sufficient basis for a finding of guilt, it need only satisfy the test described in *Leary*.

The permissive presumption, as used in this case, satisfied the *Leary* test. And, as already noted, the New York Court of Appeals has concluded that the record as a whole was sufficient to establish guilt beyond a reasonable doubt.

[The case was reversed on other grounds].

Points for Discussion

a. Mandatory and Permissible Presumptions as Defined in *County Court of Ulster County*.

Normally a presumption is thought of as a rule of law that requires the existence of a presumed fact when other facts are established, unless the presumed fact is rebutted. An inference, on the other hand, is based in logic and reason and allows the factfinder to draw its own conclusion. Do these definitions agree with definitions of mandatory and permissible presumptions in *County Court of Ulster County*, or is a permissible presumption really more like an inference? If so, has the court created a new class of presumptions in criminal cases?

b. Establishing the "Rational Connection" for a Mandatory Presumption.

In *United States v. Gainey*, 380 U.S. 63 (1965), the Supreme Court held constitutional a presumption that a person's presence at the site of a still was sufficient evidence to authorize a conviction for carrying on the business of the distillery without giving the required bond. The Court found a rational connection between the facts proved and the ultimate fact presumed by reasoning that "almost anyone at the site of a secret still could reasonably be said to be carrying on the business or aiding and abetting it, and that Congress had accorded the evidence of present its natural probative force." Shortly thereafter, in *United States v. Romano*, 382 U.S. 136 (1965), the Court found no rational basis between a person's presence at a secret still and the conclusion that he had care, custody or control of the still. Can these cases be reconciled? And what do they tell you about how to determine whether there is a "rational connection" between the facts giving rise to the presumption and presumed facts in a criminal case?

c. Presumptions that Shift the Burden of Persuasion in Criminal Cases and that Establish Facts Conclusively.

The Court in *County Court of Ulster County* recognized two types of mandatory presumptions: those that shift the burden of production to the defendant and those that shift the burden of persuasion. In *Francis v. Franklin*, 471 U.S. 307 (1985), the Court determined that a mandatory presumption which shifts the burden of persuasion to a criminal defendant is unconstitutional. In *Sandstrom v. Montana*, 442 U.S. 510 (1979), the Court held that conclusive or irrebuttable presumptions in criminal cases are unconstitutional. Would the holdings in *Francis* and *Sandstrom* force the Court to alter some of its reasoning in *County Court of Ulster County*?

Executive Summary

Burden of Proof. The "burden of proof" is the legal responsibility placed on a party to bring and present evidence in court to support that party's legal and factual positions in the case. The burden is usually placed on the party who is trying to change the status quo, that is, the party asking the court for relief, remedy, or punishment (usually it is the plaintiff in a civil case and the prosecution in a criminal case). There are actually two specific burdens that make up the burden of proof: (1) the burden of *production* and (2) the burden of *persuasion*.

The "burden of production" is the responsibility to bring sufficient evidence supporting one's position in the case that, if true, would allow a rational jury to find for the party producing that supporting evidence. The jury is allowed to reject that evidence, but if the jury were to decide for the party, then there must be sufficient evidence upon which the jury could base that finding. If the party with the burden fails to produce that evidence, then the opposing party will be entitled to "summary judgment" if it is raised before trial, or a "judgment as a matter of law" (also known as a "directed verdict") if it is raised during or after trial, or a "judgment notwithstanding the verdict" (also known as a "JNOV") if it is after the jury has rendered its verdict.

Assuming the burden of production is satisfied, the second part of the burden of proof is the "burden of persuasion." The burden of persuasion is the responsibility of the party with the burden to convince, or to persuade, the fact finder, based on the evidence that has been produced, that the party with the burden should ultimately prevail in the case according to that party's version of the facts and the applicable standard of proof.

Three Standards of Proof. There are three standards of proof depending upon whether the case is criminal or civil, or whether there is a special heightened standard (usually in a civil case). The *"preponderance of evidence,"* or the *"more likely than not,"* standard, is the standard in civil cases where the fact-finder must find for the party with the burden if the evidence weighs slightly in favor of that party (e.g., more than 50.01%). The *"beyond a reasonable doubt"* standard is the standard in criminal cases where the prosecution must prove to a very high and stringent standard that the defendant is guilty (e.g., the evidence of guilt must be something like 90% or 95%). The *"clear and convincing evidence"* standard is a standard in special circumstances, usually in civil cases, where the party with the burden must prove the proposition at issue to a "middle" standard – higher than the preponderance standard, but lower than the reasonable doubt standard (e.g., the evidence proving the proposition must be something like 75% or higher).

Presumptions v. Inferences. An "inference" is simply a *logical deduction* from existing facts. The inference is only as good as the facts upon which it is based and the surrounding assumptions that are made about how those facts relate to one another. A "presumption" is an inference that the jury can make as matter of law because the inference is very likely true given the existence of another set of provable facts.

Presumptions in Civil Cases. Under Rule 301, once a presumption has been made, it is proved unless the opposing party can rebut it with evidence to the contrary. So, in the previous example, the opposing party might be able to rebut the presumption of death by supplying evidence that the victim is not really missing or by showing that the victim is actually alive. Metaphorically, if the presumption is a "bubble," the bubble may be "burst" by the opposing side – the "Thayer Theory." Once evidence contrary to the presumption is presented, the original party must still prove her case, but if so, must do so by other means, as the presumption will no longer be available. (*Yoder*). The evidence rebutting the presumption, however, must be very powerful and substantial; otherwise, any presumption could be rebutted with a simple contrary allegation.

Some presumptions cannot legally be rebutted (they are irrefutable presumptions because there is no legal opportunity to rebut them). Note that under Rule 302, in civil cases, presumptions are considered to be "substantive." This means that, in a diversity case, the federal court must apply state presumption law.

Presumptions in Criminal Cases. The rules do not address presumptions in a criminal case. However, although presumptions are deemed to apply in criminal cases, the problem is that there are many constitutional protections for a criminal defendant that often trump the application of certain presumptions or require others. For example, criminal defendants are entitled to a constitutional presumption of innocence, the prosecution must prove guilt beyond a reasonable doubt, defendant has the right to a jury trial on all issues, a right to confront witnesses against him, and, presumptions in a criminal case must have a "rational connection" between the presumption and the underlying facts they are based upon. (*Allen*).

Rules of Evidence for United States Courts and Magistrates

Article I. General Provisions

Rule 101. Scope

These rules govern proceedings in the courts of the United States and before the United States bankruptcy judges and United States magistrate judges, to the extent and with the exceptions stated in rule 1101.

Rule 102. Purpose and Construction

These rules shall be construed to secure fairness in administration, elimination of unjustifiable expense and delay, and promotion of growth and development of the law of evidence to the end that the truth may be ascertained and proceedings justly determined.

Rule 103. Rulings on Evidence

(a) Effect of Erroneous Ruling.--Error may not be predicated upon a ruling which admits or excludes evidence unless a substantial right of the party is affected, and

(1) Objection.--In case the ruling is one admitting evidence, a timely objection or motion to strike appears of record, stating the specific ground of objection, if the specific ground was not apparent from the context; or

(2) Offer of Proof.--In case the ruling is one excluding evidence, the substance of the evidence was made known to the court by offer or was apparent from the context within which questions were asked.

Once the court makes a definitive ruling on the record admitting or excluding evidence, either at or before trial, a party need not renew an objection or offer of proof to preserve a claim of error for appeal.

(b) Record of Offer and Ruling.--The court may add any other or further state-ment which shows the character of the evidence, the form in which it was offered, the objection made, and the ruling thereon. It may direct the making of an offer in question and answer form.

(c) Hearing of Jury.--In jury cases, proceedings shall be conducted, to the extent practicable, so as to prevent inadmissible evidence from being suggested to the jury by any means, such as making statements or offers of proof or asking ques-tions in the hearing of the jury.

(d) Plain Error.--Nothing in this rule precludes taking notice of plain errors affecting substantial rights although they were not brought to the attention of the court.

Rule 104. Preliminary Questions

(a) Questions of admissibility generally. Preliminary questions concerning the qualification of a person to be a witness, the existence of a privilege, or the admis-sibility of evidence shall be determined by the court, subject to the provisions of subdivision (b). In making its determination it is not bound by the rules of evidence except those with respect to privileges.

(b) Relevancy conditioned on fact. When the relevancy of evidence depends upon the fulfillment of a condition of fact, the court shall admit it upon, or subject to, the introduction of evidence sufficient to support a finding of the fulfillment of the condition.

(c) Hearing of jury. Hearings on the admissibility of confessions shall in all cases be conducted out of the hearing of the jury. Hearings on other preliminary matters shall be so conducted when the interests of justice require, or when an accused is a witness and so requests.

(d) Testimony by accused. The accused does not, by testifying upon a preliminary matter, become subject to cross-examination as to other issues in the case.

(e) Weight and credibility. This rule does not limit the right of a party to introduce before the jury evidence relevant to weight or credibility.

Rule 105. Limited Admissibility

When evidence which is admissible as to one party or for one purpose but not admissible as to another party or for another purpose is admitted, the court, upon request, shall restrict the evidence to its proper scope and instruct the jury accord-ingly.

Rule 106. Remainder of or Related Writings or Recorded Statements

When a writing or recorded statement or part thereof is introduced by a party, an adverse party may require the introduction at that time of any other part or any other writing or recorded statement which ought in fairness to be considered contemporaneously with it.

ARTICLE II. JUDICIAL NOTICE

Rule 201. Judicial Notice of Adjudicative Facts

(a) Scope of rule. This rule governs only judicial notice of adjudicative facts.

(b) Kinds of facts. A judicially noticed fact must be one not subject to reasonable dispute in that it is either (1) generally known within the territorial jurisdiction of the trial court or (2) capable of accurate and ready determination by resort to sources whose accuracy cannot reasonably be questioned.

(c) When discretionary. A court may take judicial notice, whether requested or not.

(d) When mandatory. A court shall take judicial notice if requested by a party and supplied with the necessary information.

(e) Opportunity to be heard. A party is entitled upon timely request to an opportunity to be heard as to the propriety of taking judicial notice and the tenor of the matter noticed. In the absence of prior notification, the request may be made after judicial notice has been taken.

(f) Time of taking notice. Judicial notice may be taken at any stage of the proceeding.

(g) Instructing jury. In a civil action or proceeding, the court shall instruct the jury to accept as conclusive any fact judicially noticed. In a criminal case, the court shall instruct the jury that it may, but is not required to, accept as conclusive any fact judicially noticed.

ARTICLE III. PRESUMPTIONS IN CIVIL ACTIONS AND PROCEEDINGS

Rule 301. Presumptions in General in Civil Actions and Proceedings

In all civil actions and proceedings not otherwise provided for by Act of Congress or by these rules, a presumption imposes on the party against whom it is directed the burden of going forward with evidence to rebut or meet the presumption, but does not shift to such party the burden of proof in the sense of the risk of nonpersuasion, which remains throughout the trial upon the party on whom it was originally cast.

Rule 302. Applicability of State Law in Civil Actions and Proceedings

In civil actions and proceedings, the effect of a presumption respecting a fact which is an element of a claim or defense as to which State law supplies the rule of decision is determined in accordance with State law.

ARTICLE IV. RELEVANCY AND ITS LIMITS

Rule 401. Definition of "Relevant Evidence"

"Relevant evidence" means evidence having any tendency to make the existence of any fact that is of consequence to the determination of the action more probable or less probable than it would be without the evidence.

Rule 402. Relevant Evidence Generally Admissible; Irrelevant Evidence Inadmissible

All relevant evidence is admissible, except as otherwise provided by the Constitution of the United States, by Act of Congress, by these rules, or by other rules prescribed by the Supreme Court pursuant to statutory authority. Evidence which is not relevant is not admissible.

Rule 403. Exclusion of Relevant Evidence on Grounds of Prejudice, Confusion, or Waste of Time

Although relevant, evidence may be excluded if its probative value is substantially outweighed by the danger of unfair prejudice, confusion of the issues, or misleading the jury, or by considerations of undue delay, waste of time, or needless presentation of cumulative evidence.

Rule 404. Character Evidence Not Admissible To Prove Conduct; Exceptions; Other Crimes

(a) Character evidence generally.--Evidence of a person's character or a trait of character is not admissible for the purpose of proving action in conformity therewith on a particular occasion, except:

> (1) Character of accused.--In a criminal case, evidence of a pertinent trait of character offered by an accused, or by the prosecution to rebut the same, or if evidence of a trait of character of the alleged victim of the crime is offered by an accused and admitted under Rule 404(a)(2), evidence of the same trait of character of the accused offered by the prosecution;

> (2) Character of alleged victim.--In a criminal case, and subject to the limitations imposed by Rule 412, evidence of a pertinent trait of character of the alleged victim of the crime offered by an accused, or by the prosecution to rebut the same, or evidence of a character trait of peacefulness of the alleged victim offered by the prosecution in a homicide case to rebut evidence that the alleged victim was the first aggressor;

(3) Character of witness.--Evidence of the character of a witness, as provided in Rules 607, 608, and 609.

(b) Other Crimes, Wrongs, or Acts.--Evidence of other crimes, wrongs, or acts is not admissible to prove the character of a person in order to show action in conformity therewith. It may, however, be admissible for other purposes, such as proof of motive, opportunity, intent, preparation, plan, knowledge, identity, or absence of mistake or accident, provided that upon request by the accused, the prosecution in a criminal case shall provide reasonable notice in advance of trial, or during trial if the court excuses pretrial notice on good cause shown, of the general nature of any such evidence it intends to introduce at trial.

Rule 405. Methods of Proving Character

(a) Reputation or opinion. In all cases in which evidence of character or a trait of character of a person is admissible, proof may be made by testimony as to reputation or by testimony in the form of an opinion. On cross-examination, inquiry is allowable into relevant specific instances of conduct.

(b) Specific instances of conduct. In cases in which character or a trait of character of a person is an essential element of a charge, claim, or defense, proof may also be made of specific instances of that person's conduct.

Rule 406. Habit; Routine Practice

Evidence of the habit of a person or of the routine practice of an organization, whether corroborated or not and regardless of the presence of eyewitnesses, is relevant to prove that the conduct of the person or organization on a particular occasion was in conformity with the habit or routine practice.

Rule 407. Subsequent Remedial Measures

When, after an injury or harm allegedly caused by an event, measures are taken that, if taken previously, would have made the injury or harm less likely to occur, evidence of the subsequent measures is not admissible to prove negligence, culpable conduct, a defect in a product, a defect in a product's design, or a need for a warning or instruction. This rule does not require the exclusion of evidence of subsequent measures when offered for another purpose, such as proving ownership, control, or feasibility of precautionary measures, if controverted, or impeachment.

Rule 408. Compromise and Offers to Compromise

(a) Prohibited uses.--Evidence of the following is not admissible on behalf of any party, when offered to prove liability for, invalidity of, or amount of a claim that was disputed as to validity or amount, or to impeach through a prior inconsistent statement or contradiction:

(1) furnishing or offering or promising to furnish--or accepting or offering or promising to accept--a valuable consideration in compromising or attempting to compromise the claim; and

(2) conduct or statements made in compromise negotiations regarding the claim, except when offered in a criminal case and the negotiations related to a claim by a public office or agency in the exercise of regulatory, investigative, or enforcement authority.

(b) Permitted uses.--This rule does not require exclusion if the evidence is offered for purposes not prohibited by subdivision (a). Examples of permissible purposes include proving a witness's bias or prejudice; negating a contention of undue delay; and proving an effort to obstruct a criminal investigation or prosecution.

Rule 409. Payment of Medical and Similar Expenses

Evidence of furnishing or offering or promising to pay medical, hospital, or similar expenses occasioned by an injury is not admissible to prove liability for the injury.

Rule 410. Inadmissibility of Pleas, Plea Discussions, and Related Statements

Except as otherwise provided in this rule, evidence of the following is not, in any civil or criminal proceeding, admissible against the defendant who made the plea or was a participant in the plea discussions:

(1) a plea of guilty which was later withdrawn;

(2) a plea of nolo contendere;

(3) any statement made in the course of any proceedings under Rule 11 of the Federal Rules of Criminal Procedure or comparable state procedure regarding either of the foregoing pleas; or

(4) any statement made in the course of plea discussions with an attorney for the prosecuting authority which do not result in a plea of guilty or which result in a plea of guilty later withdrawn.

However, such a statement is admissible (i) in any proceeding wherein another statement made in the course of the same plea or plea discussions has been introduced and the statement ought in fairness be considered contemporaneously with it, or (ii) in a criminal proceeding for perjury or false statement if the statement was made by the defendant under oath, on the record and in the presence of counsel.

Rule 411. Liability Insurance

Evidence that a person was or was not insured against liability is not admissible upon the issue whether the person acted negligently or otherwise wrongfully. This rule does not require the exclusion of evidence of insurance against liability when offered for another purpose, such as proof of agency, ownership, or control, or bias or prejudice of a witness.

Rule 412. Sex Offense Cases; Relevance of Alleged Victim's Past Sexual Behavior or Alleged Sexual Predisposition

(a) Evidence generally inadmissible.--The following evidence is not admissible in any civil or criminal proceeding involving alleged sexual misconduct except as provided in subdivisions (b) and (c):

(1) Evidence offered to prove that any alleged victim engaged in other sexual behavior.

(2) Evidence offered to prove any alleged victim's sexual predisposition.

(b) Exceptions.--

(1) In a criminal case, the following evidence is admissible, if otherwise admissible under these rules:

(A) evidence of specific instances of sexual behavior by the alleged victim offered to prove that a person other than the accused was the source of semen, injury or other physical evidence;

(B) evidence of specific instances of sexual behavior by the alleged victim with respect to the person accused of the sexual misconduct offered by the accused to prove consent or by the prosecution; and

(C) evidence the exclusion of which would violate the constitutional rights of the defendant.

(2) In a civil case, evidence offered to prove the sexual behavior or sexual predisposition of any alleged victim is admissible if it is otherwise admissible under these rules and its probative value substantially outweighs the danger of harm to any victim and of unfair prejudice to any party. Evidence of an alleged victim's reputation is admissible only if it has been placed in controversy by the alleged victim.

(c) Procedure to determine admissibility.--

(1) A party intending to offer evidence under subdivision (b) must--

(A) file a written motion at least 14 days before trial specifically describing the evidence and stating the purpose for which it is offered unless the court, for good cause requires a different time for filing or permits filing during trial; and

(B) serve the motion on all parties and notify the alleged victim or, when appropriate, the alleged victim's guardian or representative.

(2) Before admitting evidence under this rule the court must conduct a hearing in camera and afford the victim and parties a right to attend and be heard. The motion, related papers, and the record of the hearing must be sealed and remain under seal unless the court orders otherwise.

Rule 413. Evidence of Similar Crimes in Sexual Assault Cases

(a) In a criminal case in which the defendant is accused of an offense of sexual assault, evidence of the defendant's commission of another offense or offenses of sexual assault is admissible, and may be considered for its bearing on any matter to which it is relevant.

(b) In a case in which the Government intends to offer evidence under this rule, the attorney for the Government shall disclose the evidence to the defendant, including statements of witnesses or a summary of the substance of any testimony that is expected to be offered, at least fifteen days before the scheduled date of trial or at such later time as the court may allow for good cause.

(c) This rule shall not be construed to limit the admission or consideration of evidence under any other rule.

(d) For purposes of this rule and Rule 415, "offense of sexual assault" means a crime under Federal law or the law of a State (as defined in section 513 of title 18, United States Code) that involved--

(1) any conduct proscribed by chapter 109A of title 18, United States Code;

(2) contact, without consent, between any part of the defendant's body or an object and the genitals or anus of another person;

(3) contact, without consent, between the genitals or anus of the defendant and any part of another person's body;

(4) deriving sexual pleasure or gratification from the infliction of death, bodily injury, or physical pain on another person; or

(5) an attempt or conspiracy to engage in conduct described in paragraphs (1)-(4).

Rule 414. Evidence of Similar Crimes in Child Molestation Cases

(a) In a criminal case in which the defendant is accused of an offense of child molestation, evidence of the defendant's commission of another offense or offenses of child molestation is admissible, and may be considered for its bearing on any matter to which it is relevant.

(b) In a case in which the Government intends to offer evidence under this rule, the attorney for the Government shall disclose the evidence to the defendant, including statements of witnesses or a summary of the substance of any testimony that is expected to be offered, at least fifteen days before the scheduled date of trial or at such later time as the court may allow for good cause.

(c) This rule shall not be construed to limit the admission or consideration of evidence under any other rule.

(d) For purposes of this rule and Rule 415, "child" means a person below the age of fourteen, and "offense of child molestation" means a crime under Federal law or the law of a State (as defined in section 513 of title 18, United States Code) that involved--

(1) any conduct proscribed by chapter 109A of title 18, United States Code, that was committed in relation to a child;

(2) any conduct proscribed by chapter 110 of title 18, United States Code;

(3) contact between any part of the defendant's body or an object and the genitals or anus of a child;

(4) contact between the genitals or anus of the defendant and any part of the body of a child;

(5) deriving sexual pleasure or gratification from the infliction of death, bodily injury, or physical pain on a child; or

(6) an attempt or conspiracy to engage in conduct described in paragraphs (1)-(5).

Rule 415. Evidence of Similar Acts in Civil Cases Concerning Sexual Assault or Child Molestation

(a) In a civil case in which a claim for damages or other relief is predicated on a party's alleged commission of conduct constituting an offense of sexual assault or child molestation, evidence of that party's commission of another offense or offenses of sexual assault or child molestation is admissible and may be considered as provided in Rule 413 and Rule 414 of these rules.

(b) A party who intends to offer evidence under this Rule shall disclose the evidence to the party against whom it will be offered, including statements of witnesses or a summary of the substance of any testimony that is expected to be offered, at least fifteen days before the scheduled date of trial or at such later time as the court may allow for good cause.

(c) This rule shall not be construed to limit the admission or consideration of evidence under any other rule.

ARTICLE V. PRIVILEGES

Rule 501. General Rule

Except as otherwise required by the Constitution of the United States or provided by Act of Congress or in rules prescribed by the Supreme Court pursuant to statutory authority, the privilege of a witness, person, government, State, or political subdivision thereof shall be governed by the principles of the common law as they may be interpreted by the courts of the United States in the light of reason and experience. However, in civil actions and proceedings, with respect to an element of a claim or defense as to which State law supplies the rule of decision, the privilege of a witness, person, government, State, or political subdivision thereof shall be determined in accordance with State law.

Rule 502. Attorney-Client Privilege and Work Product; Limitations on Waiver

The following provisions apply, in the circumstances set out, to disclosure of a communication or information covered by the attorney-client privilege or work-product protection.

(a) Disclosure made in a Federal proceeding or to a Federal office or agency; scope of a waiver.--When the disclosure is made in a Federal proceeding or to a Federal office or agency and waives the attorney-client privilege or work-product protection, the waiver extends to an undisclosed communication or information in a Federal or State proceeding only if:

(1) the waiver is intentional;

(2) the disclosed and undisclosed communications or information concern the same subject matter; and

(3) they ought in fairness to be considered together.

(b) Inadvertent disclosure.--When made in a Federal proceeding or to a Federal office or agency, the disclosure does not operate as a waiver in a Federal or State proceeding if:

(1) the disclosure is inadvertent;

(2) the holder of the privilege or protection took reasonable steps to prevent disclosure; and

(3) the holder promptly took reasonable steps to rectify the error, including (if applicable) following Federal Rule of Civil Procedure 26(b)(5)(B).

(c) Disclosure made in a State proceeding.--When the disclosure is made in a State proceeding and is not the subject of a State-court order concerning waiver, the disclosure does not operate as a waiver in a Federal proceeding if the disclosure:

(1) would not be a waiver under this rule if it had been made in a Federal proceeding; or

(2) is not a waiver under the law of the State where the disclosure occurred.

(d) Controlling effect of a court order.--A Federal court may order that the privilege or protection is not waived by disclosure connected with the litigation pending before the court--in which event the disclosure is also not a waiver in any other Federal or State proceeding.

(e) Controlling effect of a party agreement.--An agreement on the effect of disclosure in a Federal proceeding is binding only on the parties to the agreement, unless it is incorporated into a court order.

(f) Controlling effect of this rule.--Notwithstanding Rules 101 and 1101, this rule applies to State proceedings and to Federal court-annexed and Federal court-mandated arbitration proceedings, in the circumstances set out in the rule. And notwithstanding Rule 501, this rule applies even if State law provides the rule of decision.

(g) Definitions.--In this rule:

(1) 'attorney-client privilege" means the protection that applicable law provides for confidential attorney-client communications; and

(2) 'work-product protection" means the protection that applicable law provides for tangible material (or its intangible equivalent) prepared in anticipation of litigation or for trial.

ARTICLE VI. WITNESSES

Rule 601. General Rule of Competency

Every person is competent to be a witness except as otherwise provided in these rules. However, in civil actions and proceedings, with respect to an element of a claim or defense as to which State law supplies the rule of decision, the competency of a witness shall be determined in accordance with State law.

Rule 602. Lack of Personal Knowledge

A witness may not testify to a matter unless evidence is introduced sufficient to support a finding that the witness has personal knowledge of the matter. Evidence to prove personal knowledge may, but need not, consist of the witness' own testimony. This rule is subject to the provisions of rule 703, relating to opinion testimony by expert witnesses.

Rule 603. Oath or Affirmation

Before testifying, every witness shall be required to declare that the witness will testify truthfully, by oath or affirmation administered in a form calculated to awaken the witness' conscience and impress the witness' mind with the duty to do so.

Rule 604. Interpreters

An interpreter is subject to the provisions of these rules relating to qualification as an expert and the administration of an oath or affirmation to make a true translation.

Rule 605. Competency of Judge as Witness

The judge presiding at the trial may not testify in that trial as a witness. No objection need be made in order to preserve the point.

Rule 606. Competency of Juror as Witness

(a) At the trial. A member of the jury may not testify as a witness before that jury in the trial of the case in which the juror is sitting. If the juror is called so to testify, the opposing party shall be afforded an opportunity to object out of the presence of the jury.

(b) Inquiry into validity of verdict or indictment. Upon an inquiry into the validity of a verdict or indictment, a juror may not testify as to any matter or statement occurring during the course of the jury's deliberations or to the effect of anything upon that or any other juror's mind or emotions as influencing the juror to assent to or dissent from the verdict or indictment or concerning the juror's mental processes in connection therewith. But a juror may testify about (1) whether extraneous prejudicial information was improperly brought to the jury's attention, (2) whether any outside influence was improperly brought to bear upon any juror, or

(3) whether there was a mistake in entering the verdict onto the verdict form. A juror's affidavit or evidence of any statement by the juror may not be received on a matter about which the juror would be precluded from testifying.

Rule 607. Who May Impeach

The credibility of a witness may be attacked by any party, including the party calling the witness.

Rule 608. Evidence of Character and Conduct of Witness

(a) Opinion and reputation evidence of character. The credibility of a witness may be attacked or supported by evidence in the form of opinion or reputation, but subject to these limitations: (1) the evidence may refer only to character for truthfulness or untruthfulness, and (2) evidence of truthful character is admissible only after the character of the witness for truthfulness has been attacked by opinion or reputation evidence or otherwise.

(b) Specific instances of conduct. Specific instances of the conduct of a witness, for the purpose of attacking or supporting the witness' character for truthfulness, other than conviction of crime as provided in rule 609, may not be proved by extrinsic evidence. They may, however, in the discretion of the court, if probative of truthfulness or untruthfulness, be inquired into on cross-examination of the witness (1) concerning the witness' character for truthfulness or untruthfulness, or (2) concerning the character for truthfulness or untruthfulness of another witness as to which character the witness being cross-examined has testified.

The giving of testimony, whether by an accused or by any other witness, does not operate as a waiver of the accused's or the witness' privilege against self-incrimination when examined with respect to matters that relate only to character for truthfulness.

Rule 609. Impeachment by Evidence of Conviction of Crime

(a) General rule.--For the purpose of attacking the character for truthfulness of a witness,

> (1) evidence that a witness other than an accused has been convicted of a crime shall be admitted, subject to Rule 403, if the crime was punishable by death or imprisonment in excess of one year under the law under which the witness was convicted, and evidence that an accused has been convicted of such a crime shall be admitted if the court determines that the probative value of admitting this evidence outweighs its prejudicial effect to the accused; and

(2) evidence that any witness has been convicted of a crime shall be admitted regardless of the punishment, if it readily can be determined that establishing the elements of the crime required proof or admission of an act of dishonesty or false statement by the witness.

(b) Time limit. Evidence of a conviction under this rule is not admissible if a period of more than ten years has elapsed since the date of the conviction or of the release of the witness from the confinement imposed for that conviction, whichever is the later date, unless the court determines, in the interests of justice, that the probative value of the conviction supported by specific facts and circumstances substantially outweighs its prejudicial effect. However, evidence of a conviction more than 10 years old as calculated herein, is not admissible unless the proponent gives to the adverse party sufficient advance written notice of intent to use such evidence to provide the adverse party with a fair opportunity to contest the use of such evidence.

(c) Effect of pardon, annulment, or certificate of rehabilitation.--Evidence of a conviction is not admissible under this rule if (1) the conviction has been the subject of a pardon, annulment, certificate of rehabilitation, or other equivalent procedure based on a finding of the rehabilitation of the person convicted, and that person has not been convicted of a subsequent crime that was punishable by death or imprisonment in excess of one year, or (2) the conviction has been the subject of a pardon, annulment, or other equivalent procedure based on a finding of innocence.

(d) Juvenile adjudications. Evidence of juvenile adjudications is generally not admissible under this rule. The court may, however, in a criminal case allow evidence of a juvenile adjudication of a witness other than the accused if conviction of the offense would be admissible to attack the credibility of an adult and the court is satisfied that admission in evidence is necessary for a fair determination of the issue of guilt or innocence.

(e) Pendency of appeal. The pendency of an appeal therefrom does not render evidence of a conviction inadmissible. Evidence of the pendency of an appeal is admissible.

Rule 610. Religious Beliefs or Opinions

Evidence of the beliefs or opinions of a witness on matters of religion is not admissible for the purpose of showing that by reason of their nature the witness' credibility is impaired or enhanced.

Rule 611. Mode and Order of Interrogation and Presentation

(a) Control by court. The court shall exercise reasonable control over the mode and order of interrogating witnesses and presenting evidence so as to (1) make the interrogation and presentation effective for the ascertainment of the truth, (2) avoid needless consumption of time, and (3) protect witnesses from harassment or undue embarrassment.

(b) Scope of cross-examination. Cross-examination should be limited to the subject matter of the direct examination and matters affecting the credibility of the witness. The court may, in the exercise of discretion, permit inquiry into additional matters as if on direct examination.

(c) Leading questions. Leading questions should not be used on the direct examination of a witness except as may be necessary to develop the witness' testimony. Ordinarily leading questions should be permitted on cross-examination. When a party calls a hostile witness, an adverse party, or a witness identified with an adverse party, interrogation may be by leading questions.

Rule 612. Writing Used to Refresh Memory

Except as otherwise provided in criminal proceedings by section 3500 of title 18, United States Code, if a witness uses a writing to refresh memory for the purpose of testifying, either--

(1) while testifying, or

(2) before testifying, if the court in its discretion determines it is necessary in the interests of justice, an adverse party is entitled to have the writing produced at the hearing, to inspect it, to cross-examine the witness thereon, and to introduce in evidence those portions which relate to the testimony of the witness. If it is claimed that the writing contains matters not related to the subject matter of the testimony the court shall examine the writing in camera, excise any portions not so related, and order delivery of the remainder to the party entitled thereto. Any portion withheld over objections shall be preserved and made available to the appellate court in the event of an appeal. If a writing is not produced or delivered pursuant to order under this rule, the court shall make any order justice requires, except that in criminal cases when the prosecution elects not to comply, the order shall be one striking the testimony or, if the court in its discretion determines that the interests of justice so require, declaring a mistrial.

Rule 613. Prior Statements of Witnesses

(a) Examining witness concerning prior statement. In examining a witness concerning a prior statement made by the witness, whether written or not, the statement need not be shown nor its contents disclosed to the witness at that time, but on request the same shall be shown or disclosed to opposing counsel.

(b) Extrinsic evidence of prior inconsistent statement of witness. Extrinsic evidence of a prior inconsistent statement by a witness is not admissible unless the witness is afforded an opportunity to explain or deny the same and the opposite party is afforded an opportunity to interrogate the witness thereon, or the interests of justice otherwise require. This provision does not apply to admissions of a party-opponent as defined in rule 801(d)(2).

Rule 614. Calling and Interrogation of Witnesses by Court

(a) Calling by court. The court may, on its own motion or at the suggestion of a party, call witnesses, and all parties are entitled to cross-examine witnesses thus called.

(b) Interrogation by court. The court may interrogate witnesses, whether called by itself or by a party.

(c) Objections. Objections to the calling of witnesses by the court or to interrogation by it may be made at the time or at the next available opportunity when the jury is not present.

Rule 615. Exclusion of Witnesses

At the request of a party the court shall order witnesses excluded so that they cannot hear the testimony of other witnesses, and it may make the order of its own motion. This rule does not authorize exclusion of (1) a party who is a natural person, or (2) an officer or employee of a party which is not a natural person designated as its representative by its attorney, or (3) a person whose presence is shown by a party to be essential to the presentation of the party's cause, or (4) a person authorized by statute to be present.

Rules 616 to 700. Reserved for future legislation

ARTICLE VII. OPINIONS AND EXPERT TESTIMONY

Rule 701. Opinion Testimony by Lay Witnesses

If the witness is not testifying as an expert, the witness' testimony in the form of opinions or inferences is limited to those opinions or inferences which are (a) rationally based on the perception of the witness, (b) helpful to a clear understanding of the witness' testimony or the determination of a fact in issue, and (c) not based on scientific, technical, or other specialized knowledge within the scope of Rule 702.

Rule 702. Testimony by Experts

If scientific, technical, or other specialized knowledge will assist the trier of fact to understand the evidence or to determine a fact in issue, a witness qualified as an expert by knowledge, skill, experience, training, or education, may testify thereto in the form of an opinion or otherwise, if (1) the testimony is based upon sufficient facts or data, (2) the testimony is the product of reliable principles and methods, and (3) the witness has applied the principles and methods reliably to the facts of the case.

Rule 703. Bases of Opinion Testimony by Experts

The facts or data in the particular case upon which an expert bases an opinion or inference may be those perceived by or made known to the expert at or before the hearing. If of a type reasonably relied upon by experts in the particular field in forming opinions or inferences upon the subject, the facts or data need not be admissible in evidence in order for the opinion or inference to be admitted. Facts or data that are otherwise inadmissible shall not be disclosed to the jury by the proponent of the opinion or inference unless the court determines that their probative value in assisting the jury to evaluate the expert's opinion substantially outweighs their prejudicial effect.

Rule 704. Opinion on Ultimate Issue

(a) Except as provided in subdivision (b), testimony in the form of an opinion or inference otherwise admissible is not objectionable because it embraces an ultimate issue to be decided by the trier of fact.

(b) No expert witness testifying with respect to the mental state or condition of a defendant in a criminal case may state an opinion or inference as to whether the defendant did or did not have the mental state or condition constituting an element of the crime charged or of a defense thereto. Such ultimate issues are matters for the trier of fact alone.

Rule 705. Disclosure of Facts or Data Underlying Expert Opinion

The expert may testify in terms of opinion or inference and give reasons therefor without first testifying to the underlying facts or data, unless the court requires otherwise. The expert may in any event be required to disclose the underlying facts or data on cross-examination.

Rule 706. Court Appointed Experts

(a) Appointment. The court may on its own motion or on the motion of any party enter an order to show cause why expert witnesses should not be appointed, and may request the parties to submit nominations. The court may appoint any expert witnesses agreed upon by the parties, and may appoint expert witnesses of its own selection. An expert witness shall not be appointed by the court unless the witness consents to act. A witness so appointed shall be informed of the witness' duties by the court in writing, a copy of which shall be filed with the clerk, or at a conference in which the parties shall have opportunity to participate. A witness so appointed shall advise the parties of the witness' findings, if any; the witness' deposition may be taken by any party; and the witness may be called to testify by the court or any party. The witness shall be subject to cross-examination by each party, including a party calling the witness.

(b) Compensation. Expert witnesses so appointed are entitled to reasonable compensation in whatever sum the court may allow. The compensation thus fixed is payable from funds which may be provided by law in criminal cases and civil actions and proceedings involving just compensation under the fifth amendment. In other civil actions and proceedings the compensation shall be paid by the parties in such proportion and at such time as the court directs, and thereafter charged in like manner as other costs.

(c) Disclosure of appointment. In the exercise of its discretion, the court may authorize disclosure to the jury of the fact that the court appointed the expert witness.

(d) Parties' experts of own selection. Nothing in this rule limits the parties in calling expert witnesses of their own selection.

ARTICLE VIII. HEARSAY

Rule 801. Definitions

The following definitions apply under this article:

(a) Statement. A "statement" is (1) an oral or written assertion or (2) nonverbal conduct of a person, if it is intended by the person as an assertion.

(b) Declarant. A "declarant" is a person who makes a statement.

(c) Hearsay. "Hearsay" is a statement, other than one made by the declarant while testifying at the trial or hearing, offered in evidence to prove the truth of the matter asserted.

(d) Statements which are not hearsay. A statement is not hearsay if--

> (1) Prior statement by witness. The declarant testifies at the trial or hearing and is subject to cross-examination concerning the statement, and the statement is (A) inconsistent with the declarant's testimony, and was given under oath subject to the penalty of perjury at a trial, hearing, or other proceeding, or in a deposition, or (B) consistent with the declarant's testimony and is offered to rebut an express or implied charge against the declarant of recent fabrication or improper influence or motive, or (C) one of identification of a person made after perceiving the person; or

> (2) Admission by party-opponent. The statement is offered against a party and is (A) the party's own statement, in either an individual or a representative capacity or (B) a statement of which the party has manifested an adoption or belief in its truth, or (C) a statement by a person authorized by the party to make a statement concerning the subject, or (D) a statement by the party's agent or servant concerning a matter within the scope of the agency or

employment, made during the existence of the relationship, or (E) a statement by a coconspirator of a party during the course and in furtherance of the conspiracy. The contents of the statement shall be considered but are not alone sufficient to establish the declarant's authority under subdivision (C), the agency or employment relationship and scope thereof under subdivision (D), or the existence of the conspiracy and the participation therein of the declarant and the party against whom the statement is offered under subdivision (E).

Rule 802. Hearsay Rule

Hearsay is not admissible except as provided by these rules or by other rules prescribed by the Supreme Court pursuant to statutory authority or by Act of Congress.

Rule 803. Hearsay Exceptions; Availability of Declarant Immaterial

The following are not excluded by the hearsay rule, even though the declarant is available as a witness:

(1) Present sense impression. A statement describing or explaining an event or condition made while the declarant was perceiving the event or condition, or immediately thereafter.

(2) Excited utterance. A statement relating to a startling event or condition made while the declarant was under the stress of excitement caused by the event or condition.

(3) Then existing mental, emotional, or physical condition. A statement of the declarant's then existing state of mind, emotion, sensation, or physical condition (such as intent, plan, motive, design, mental feeling, pain, and bodily health), but not including a statement of memory or belief to prove the fact remembered or believed unless it relates to the execution, revocation, identification, or terms of declarant's will.

(4) Statements for purposes of medical diagnosis or treatment. Statements made for purposes of medical diagnosis or treatment and describing medical history, or past or present symptoms, pain, or sensations, or the inception or general character of the cause or external source thereof insofar as reasonably pertinent to diagnosis or treatment.

(5) Recorded recollection. A memorandum or record concerning a matter about which a witness once had knowledge but now has insufficient recollection to enable the witness to testify fully and accurately, shown to have been made or adopted by the witness when the matter was fresh in the witness' memory and to reflect that knowledge correctly. If admitted, the memorandum or record may be

read into evidence but may not itself be received as an exhibit unless offered by an adverse party.

(6) Records of Regularly Conducted Activity.--A memorandum, report, record, or data compilation, in any form, of acts, events, conditions, opinions, or diagnoses, made at or near the time by, or from information transmitted by, a person with knowledge, if kept in the course of a regularly conducted business activity, and if it was the regular practice of that business activity to make the memorandum, report, record or data compilation, all as shown by the testimony of the custodian or other qualified witness, or by certification that complies with Rule 902(11), Rule 902(12), or a statute permitting certification, unless the source of information or the method or circumstances of preparation indicate lack of trustworthiness. The term "business" as used in this paragraph includes business, institution, association, profession, occupation, and calling of every kind, whether or not conducted for profit.

(7) Absence of entry in records kept in accordance with the provisions of paragraph (6). Evidence that a matter is not included in the memoranda reports, records, or data compilations, in any form, kept in accordance with the provisions of paragraph (6), to prove the nonoccurrence or nonexistence of the matter, if the matter was of a kind of which a memorandum, report, record, or data compilation was regularly made and preserved, unless the sources of information or other circumstances indicate lack of trustworthiness.

(8) Public records and reports. Records, reports, statements, or data compilations, in any form, of public offices or agencies, setting forth (A) the activities of the office or agency, or (B) matters observed pursuant to duty imposed by law as to which matters there was a duty to report, excluding, however, in criminal cases matters observed by police officers and other law enforcement personnel, or (C) in civil actions and proceedings and against the Government in criminal cases, factual findings resulting from an investigation made pursuant to authority granted by law, unless the sources of information or other circumstances indicate lack of trustworthiness.

(9) Records of vital statistics. Records or data compilations, in any form, of births, fetal deaths, deaths, or marriages, if the report thereof was made to a public office pursuant to requirements of law.

(10) Absence of public record or entry. To prove the absence of a record, report, statement, or data compilation, in any form, or the nonoccurrence or nonexistence of a matter of which a record, report, statement, or data compilation, in any form, was regularly made and preserved by a public office or agency, evidence in the form of a certification in accordance with rule 902, or testimony, that diligent

search failed to disclose the record, report, statement, or data compilation, or entry.

(11) Records of religious organizations. Statements of births, marriages, divorces, deaths, legitimacy, ancestry, relationship by blood or marriage, or other similar facts of personal or family history, contained in a regularly kept record of a religious organization.

(12) Marriage, baptismal, and similar certificates. Statements of fact contained in a certificate that the maker performed a marriage or other ceremony or administered a sacrament, made by a clergyman, public official, or other person authorized by the rules or practices of a religious organization or by law to perform the act certified, and purporting to have been issued at the time of the act or within a reasonable time thereafter.

(13) Family records. Statements of fact concerning personal or family history contained in family Bibles, genealogies, charts, engravings on rings, inscriptions on family portraits, engravings on urns, crypts, or tombstones, or the like.

(14) Records of documents affecting an interest in property. The record of a document purporting to establish or affect an interest in property, as proof of the content of the original recorded document and its execution and delivery by each person by whom it purports to have been executed, if the record is a record of a public office and an applicable statute authorizes the recording of documents of that kind in that office.

(15) Statements in documents affecting an interest in property. A statement contained in a document purporting to establish or affect an interest in property if the matter stated was relevant to the purpose of the document, unless dealings with the property since the document was made have been inconsistent with the truth of the statement or the purport of the document.

(16) Statements in ancient documents. Statements in a document in existence twenty years or more the authenticity of which is established.

(17) Market reports, commercial publications. Market quotations, tabulations, lists, directories, or other published compilations, generally used and relied upon by the public or by persons in particular occupations.

(18) Learned treatises. To the extent called to the attention of an expert witness upon cross-examination or relied upon by the expert witness in direct examination, statements contained in published treatises, periodicals, or pamphlets on a subject of history, medicine, or other science or art, established as a reliable authority by the testimony or admission of the witness or by other expert testi-

mony or by judicial notice. If admitted, the statements may be read into evidence but may not be received as exhibits.

(19) Reputation concerning personal or family history. Reputation among members of a person's family by blood, adoption, or marriage, or among a person's associates, or in the community, concerning a person's birth, adoption, marriage, divorce, death, legitimacy, relationship by blood, adoption, or marriage, ancestry, or other similar fact of personal or family history.

(20) Reputation concerning boundaries or general history. Reputation in a community, arising before the controversy, as to boundaries of or customs affecting lands in the community, and reputation as to events of general history important to the community or State or nation in which located.

(21) Reputation as to character. Reputation of a person's character among associates or in the community.

(22) Judgment of previous conviction. Evidence of a final judgment, entered after a trial or upon a plea of guilty (but not upon a plea of nolo contendere), adjudging a person guilty of a crime punishable by death or imprisonment in excess of one year, to prove any fact essential to sustain the judgment, but not including, when offered by the Government in a criminal prosecution for purposes other than impeachment, judgments against persons other than the accused. The pendency of an appeal may be shown but does not affect admissibility.

(23) Judgment as to personal, family, or general history, or boundaries. Judgments as proof of matters of personal, family or general history, or boundaries, essential to the judgment, if the same would be provable by evidence of reputation.

(24) [Transferred to Rule 807]

Rule 804. Hearsay Exceptions; Declarant Unavailable

(a) Definition of unavailability. "Unavailability as a witness" includes situations in which the declarant--

(1) is exempted by ruling of the court on the ground of privilege from testifying concerning the subject matter of the declarant's statement; or

(2) persists in refusing to testify concerning the subject matter of the declarant's statement despite an order of the court to do so; or

(3) testifies to a lack of memory of the subject matter of the declarant's statement; or

(4) is unable to be present or to testify at the hearing because of death or then existing physical or mental illness or infirmity; or

(5) is absent from the hearing and the proponent of a statement has been unable to procure the declarant's attendance (or in the case of a hearsay exception under subdivision (b)(2), (3), or (4), the declarant's attendance or testimony) by process or other reasonable means.

A declarant is not unavailable as a witness if exemption, refusal, claim of lack of memory, inability, or absence is due to the procurement or wrongdoing of the proponent of a statement for the purpose of preventing the witness from attending or testifying.

(b) Hearsay exceptions. The following are not excluded by the hearsay rule if the declarant is unavailable as a witness:

(1) Former testimony. Testimony given as a witness at another hearing of the same or a different proceeding, or in a deposition taken in compliance with law in the course of the same or another proceeding, if the party against whom the testimony is now offered, or, in a civil action or proceeding, a predecessor in interest, had an opportunity and similar motive to develop the testimony by direct, cross, or redirect examination.

(2) Statement under belief of impending death. In a prosecution for homicide or in a civil action or proceeding, a statement made by a declarant while believing that the declarant's death was imminent, concerning the cause or circumstances of what the declarant believed to be impending death.

(3) Statement against interest. A statement which was at the time of its making so far contrary to the declarant's pecuniary or proprietary interest, or so far tended to subject the declarant to civil or criminal liability, or to render invalid a claim by the declarant against another, that a reasonable person in the declarant's position would not have made the statement unless believing it to be true. A statement tending to expose the declarant to criminal liability and offered to exculpate the accused is not admissible unless corroborating circumstances clearly indicate the trustworthiness of the statement.

(4) Statement of personal or family history. (A) A statement concerning the declarant's own birth, adoption, marriage, divorce, legitimacy, relationship by blood, adoption, or marriage, ancestry, or other similar fact of personal or family history, even though declarant had no means of acquiring personal knowledge of the matter stated; or (B) a statement concerning the foregoing matters, and death also, of another person, if the declarant was related to the

other by blood, adoption, or marriage or was so intimately associated with the other's family as to be likely to have accurate information concerning the matter declared.

(5) [Transferred to Rule 807]

(6) Forfeiture by wrongdoing. A statement offered against a party that has engaged or acquiesced in wrongdoing that was intended to, and did, procure the unavailability of the declarant as a witness.

Rule 805. Hearsay Within Hearsay

Hearsay included within hearsay is not excluded under the hearsay rule if each part of the combined statements conforms with an exception to the hearsay rule provided in these rules.

Rule 806. Attacking and Supporting Credibility of Declarant

When a hearsay statement, or a statement defined in Rule 801(d)(2)(C), (D), or (E), has been admitted in evidence, the credibility of the declarant may be attacked, and if attacked may be supported, by any evidence which would be admissible for those purposes if declarant had testified as a witness. Evidence of a statement or conduct by the declarant at any time, inconsistent with the declarant's hearsay statement, is not subject to any requirement that the declarant may have been afforded an opportunity to deny or explain. If the party against whom a hearsay statement has been admitted calls the declarant as a witness, the party is entitled to examine the declarant on the statement as if under cross-examination.

Rule 807. Residual Exception

A statement not specifically covered by Rule 803 or 804 but having equivalent circumstantial guarantees of trustworthiness, is not excluded by the hearsay rule, if the court determines that (A) the statement is offered as evidence of a material fact; (B) the statement is more probative on the point for which it is offered than any other evidence which the proponent can procure through reasonable efforts; and (C) the general purposes of these rules and the interests of justice will best be served by admission of the statement into evidence. However, a statement may not be admitted under this exception unless the proponent of it makes known to the adverse party sufficiently in advance of the trial or hearing to provide the adverse party with a fair opportunity to prepare to meet it, the proponent's intention to offer the statement and the particulars of it, including the name and address of the declarant.

ARTICLE IX. AUTHENTICATION AND IDENTIFICATION

Rule 901. Requirement of Authentication or Identification

(a) General provision. The requirement of authentication or identification as a condition precedent to admissibility is satisfied by evidence sufficient to support a finding that the matter in question is what its proponent claims.

(b) Illustrations. By way of illustration only, and not by way of limitation, the following are examples of authentication or identification conforming with the requirements of this rule:

(1) Testimony of witness with knowledge. Testimony that a matter is what it is claimed to be.

(2) Nonexpert opinion on handwriting. Nonexpert opinion as to the genuineness of handwriting, based upon familiarity not acquired for purposes of the litigation.

(3) Comparison by trier or expert witness. Comparison by the trier of fact or by expert witnesses with specimens which have been authenticated.

(4) Distinctive characteristics and the like. Appearance, contents, substance, internal patterns, or other distinctive characteristics, taken in conjunction with circumstances.

(5) Voice identification. Identification of a voice, whether heard firsthand or through mechanical or electronic transmission or recording, by opinion based upon hearing the voice at any time under circumstances connecting it with the alleged speaker.

(6) Telephone conversations. Telephone conversations, by evidence that a call was made to the number assigned at the time by the telephone company to a particular person or business, if (A) in the case of a person, circumstances, including self-identification, show the person answering to be the one called, or (B) in the case of a business, the call was made to a place of business and the conversation related to business reasonably transacted over the telephone.

(7) Public records or reports. Evidence that a writing authorized by law to be recorded or filed and in fact recorded or filed in a public office, or a purported public record, report, statement, or data compilation, in any form, is from the public office where items of this nature are kept.

(8) Ancient documents or data compilation. Evidence that a document or data compilation, in any form, (A) is in such condition as to create no suspicion concerning its authenticity, (B) was in a place where it, if authentic, would likely be, and (C) has been in existence 20 years or more at the time it is offered.

(9) Process or system. Evidence describing a process or system used to produce a result and showing that the process or system produces an accurate result.

(10) Methods provided by statute or rule. Any method of authentication or identification provided by Act of Congress or by other rules prescribed by the Supreme Court pursuant to statutory authority.

Rule 902. Self-authentication

Extrinsic evidence of authenticity as a condition precedent to admissibility is not required with respect to the following:

(1) Domestic public documents under seal. A document bearing a seal purporting to be that of the United States, or of any State, district, Commonwealth, territory, or insular possession thereof, or the Panama Canal Zone, or the Trust Territory of the Pacific Islands, or of a political subdivision, department, officer, or agency thereof, and a signature purporting to be an attestation or execution.

(2) Domestic public documents not under seal. A document purporting to bear the signature in the official capacity of an officer or employee of any entity included in paragraph (1) hereof, having no seal, if a public officer having a seal and having official duties in the district or political subdivision of the officer or employee certifies under seal that the signer has the official capacity and that the signature is genuine.

(3) Foreign public documents. A document purporting to be executed or attested in an official capacity by a person authorized by the laws of a foreign country to make the execution or attestation, and accompanied by a final certification as to the genuineness of the signature and official position (A) of the executing or attesting person, or (B) of any foreign official whose certificate of genuineness of signature and official position relates to the execution or attestation or is in a chain of certificates of genuineness of signature and official position relating to the execution or attestation. A final certification may be made by a secretary of an embassy or legation, consul general, consul, vice consul, or consular agent of the United States, or a diplomatic or consular official of the foreign country assigned or accredited to the United States. If reasonable opportunity has been given to all parties to investigate the authenticity and accuracy of official documents, the

court may, for good cause shown, order that they be treated as presumptively authentic without final certification or permit them to be evidenced by an attested summary with or without final certification.

(4) Certified copies of public records. A copy of an official record or report or entry therein, or of a document authorized by law to be recorded or filed and actually recorded or filed in a public office, including data compilations in any form, certified as correct by the custodian or other person authorized to make the certification, by certificate complying with paragraph (1), (2), or (3) of this rule or complying with any Act of Congress or rule prescribed by the Supreme Court pursuant to statutory authority.

(5) Official publications. Books, pamphlets, or other publications purporting to be issued by public authority.

(6) Newspapers and periodicals. Printed materials purporting to be newspapers or periodicals.

(7) Trade inscriptions and the like. Inscriptions, signs, tags, or labels purporting to have been affixed in the course of business and indicating ownership, control, or origin.

(8) Acknowledged documents. Documents accompanied by a certificate of acknowledgment executed in the manner provided by law by a notary public or other officer authorized by law to take acknowledgments.

(9) Commercial paper and related documents. Commercial paper, signatures thereon, and documents relating thereto to the extent provided by general commercial law.

(10) Presumptions under Acts of Congress. Any signature, document, or other matter declared by Act of Congress to be presumptively or prima facie genuine or authentic.

(11) Certified Domestic Records of Regularly Conducted Activity.--The original or a duplicate of a domestic record of regularly conducted activity that would be admissible under Rule 803(6) if accompanied by a written declaration of its custodian or other qualified person, in a manner complying with any Act of Congress or rule prescribed by the Supreme Court pursuant to statutory authority, certifying that the record--

> (A) was made at or near the time of the occurrence of the matters set forth by, or from information transmitted by, a person with knowledge of those matters;

(B) was kept in the course of the regularly conducted activity; and

(C) was made by the regularly conducted activity as a regular practice.

A party intending to offer a record into evidence under this paragraph must provide written notice of that intention to all adverse parties, and must make the record and declaration available for inspection sufficiently in advance of their offer into evidence to provide an adverse party with a fair opportunity to challenge them.

(12) Certified Foreign Records of Regularly Conducted Activity.--In a civil case, the original or a duplicate of a foreign record of regularly conducted activity that would be admissible under Rule 803(6) if accompanied by a written declaration by its custodian or other qualified person certifying that the record--

(A) was made at or near the time of the occurrence of the matters set forth by, or from information transmitted by, a person with knowledge of those matters;

(B) was kept in the course of the regularly conducted activity; and

(C) was made by the regularly conducted activity as a regular practice.

The declaration must be signed in a manner that, if falsely made, would subject the maker to criminal penalty under the laws of the country where the declaration is signed. A party intending to offer a record into evidence under this paragraph must provide written notice of that intention to all adverse parties, and must make the record and declaration available for inspection sufficiently in advance of their offer into evidence to provide an adverse party with a fair opportunity to challenge them.

Rule 903. Subscribing Witness' Testimony Unnecessary

The testimony of a subscribing witness is not necessary to authenticate a writing unless required by the laws of the jurisdiction whose laws govern the validity of the writing.

ARTICLE X. CONTENTS OF WRITINGS, RECORDINGS AND PHOTOGRAPHS
Rule 1001. Definitions

For purposes of this article the following definitions are applicable:

(1) Writings and recordings. "Writings" and "recordings" consist of letters, words, or numbers, or their equivalent, set down by handwriting, typewriting, printing,

photostating, photographing, magnetic impulse, mechanical or electronic recording, or other form of data compilation.

(2) Photographs. "Photographs" include still photographs, X-ray films, video tapes, and motion pictures.

(3) Original. An "original" of a writing or recording is the writing or recording itself or any counterpart intended to have the same effect by a person executing or issuing it. An "original" of a photograph includes the negative or any print therefrom. If data are stored in a computer or similar device, any printout or other output readable by sight, shown to reflect the data accurately, is an "original".

(4) Duplicate. A "duplicate" is a counterpart produced by the same impression as the original, or from the same matrix, or by means of photography, including enlargements and miniatures, or by mechanical or electronic re-recording, or by chemical reproduction, or by other equivalent techniques which accurately reproduces the original.

Rule 1002. Requirement of Original

To prove the content of a writing, recording, or photograph, the original writing, recording, or photograph is required, except as otherwise provided in these rules or by Act of Congress.

Rule 1003. Admissibility of Duplicates

A duplicate is admissible to the same extent as an original unless (1) a genuine question is raised as to the authenticity of the original or (2) in the circumstances it would be unfair to admit the duplicate in lieu of the original.

Rule 1004. Admissibility of Other Evidence of Contents

The original is not required, and other evidence of the contents of a writing, recording, or photograph is admissible if--

(1) Originals lost or destroyed. All originals are lost or have been destroyed, unless the proponent lost or destroyed them in bad faith; or

(2) Original not obtainable. No original can be obtained by any available judicial process or procedure; or

(3) Original in possession of opponent. At a time when an original was under the control of the party against whom offered, that party was put on notice, by the pleadings or otherwise, that the contents would be a subject of proof at the hearing, and that party does not produce the original at the hearing; or

(4) Collateral matters. The writing, recording, or photograph is not closely related to a controlling issue.

Rule 1005. Public Records

The contents of an official record, or of a document authorized to be recorded or filed and actually recorded or filed, including data compilations in any form, if otherwise admissible, may be proved by copy, certified as correct in accordance with rule 902 or testified to be correct by a witness who has compared it with the original. If a copy which complies with the foregoing cannot be obtained by the exercise of reasonable diligence, then other evidence of the contents may be given.

Rule 1006. Summaries

The contents of voluminous writings, recordings, or photographs which cannot conveniently be examined in court may be presented in the form of a chart, summary, or calculation. The originals, or duplicates, shall be made available for examination or copying, or both, by other parties at reasonable time and place. The court may order that they be produced in court.

Rule 1007. Testimony or Written Admission of Party

Contents of writings, recordings, or photographs may be proved by the testimony or deposition of the party against whom offered or by that party's written admission, without accounting for the nonproduction of the original.

Rule 1008. Functions of Court and Jury

When the admissibility of other evidence of contents of writings, recordings, or photographs under these rules depends upon the fulfillment of a condition of fact, the question whether the condition has been fulfilled is ordinarily for the court to determine in accordance with the provisions of rule 104. However, when an issue is raised (a) whether the asserted writing ever existed, or (b) whether another writing, recording, or photograph produced at the trial is the original, or (c) whether other evidence of contents correctly reflects the contents, the issue is for the trier of fact to determine as in the case of other issues of fact.

ARTICLE XI. MISCELLANEOUS RULES

Rule 1101. Applicability of Rules

(a) Courts and judges. These rules apply to the United States district courts, the District Court of Guam, the District Court of the Virgin Islands, the District Court for the Northern Mariana Islands, the United States courts of appeals, the United States Claims Court, and to United States bankruptcy judges and United States magistrate judges, in the actions, cases, and proceedings and to the extent hereinafter set forth. The terms "judge" and "court" in these rules include United States bankruptcy judges and United States magistrate judges.

(b) Proceedings generally. These rules apply generally to civil actions and proceedings, including admiralty and maritime cases, to criminal cases and proceedings, to contempt proceedings except those in which the court may act summarily, and to proceedings and cases under title 11, United States Code.

(c) Rule of privilege. The rule with respect to privileges applies at all stages of all actions, cases, and proceedings.

(d) Rules inapplicable. The rules (other than with respect to privileges) do not apply in the following situations:

> (1) Preliminary questions of fact. The determination of questions of fact preliminary to admissibility of evidence when the issue is to be determined by the court under rule 104.

> (2) Grand jury. Proceedings before grand juries.

> (3) Miscellaneous proceedings. Proceedings for extradition or rendition; preliminary examinations in criminal cases; sentencing, or granting or revoking probation; issuance of warrants for arrest, criminal summonses, and search warrants; and proceedings with respect to release on bail or otherwise.

(e) Rules applicable in part. In the following proceedings these rules apply to the extent that matters of evidence are not provided for in the statutes which govern procedure therein or in other rules prescribed by the Supreme Court pursuant to statutory authority: the trial of misdemeanors and other petty offenses before United States magistrate judges; review of agency actions when the facts are subject to trial de novo under section 706(2)(F) of title 5, United States Code; review of orders of the Secretary of Agriculture under section 2 of the Act entitled "An Act to authorize association of producers of agricultural products" approved February 18, 1922 (7 U.S.C. 292), and under sections 6 and 7(c) of the Perishable Agricultural Commodities Act, 1930 (7 U.S.C. 499f, 499g(c)); naturalization and revocation of naturalization under sections 310-318 of the Immigration and Nationality Act (8 U.S.C. 1421-1429); prize proceedings in admiralty under sections 7651-7681 of title 10, United States Code; review of orders of the Secretary of the Interior under section 2 of the Act entitled "An Act authorizing associations of producers of aquatic products" approved June 25, 1934 (15 U.S.C. 522); review of orders of petroleum control boards under section 5 of the Act entitled "An Act to regulate interstate and foreign commerce in petroleum and its products by prohibiting the shipment in such commerce of petroleum and its products produced in violation of State law, and for other purposes", approved February 22, 1935 (15 U.S.C. 715d); actions for fines, penalties, or forfeitures under part V of title IV of the Tariff Act of 1930 (19 U.S.C. 1581-1624), or under the Anti-Smuggling Act (19 U.S.C. 1701-1711); criminal libel for condemnation, exclusion of imports, or other proceedings under the Federal Food, Drug, and Cosmetic Act (21 U.S.C. 301-392); disputes between seamen under sections 4079, 4080, and 4081 of the Revised Statutes (22 U.S.C. 256-258); habeas corpus under sections 2241-2254 of title 28, United States Code; motions to vacate, set aside or correct sentence under section 2255 of title 28, United States Code; actions for penalties for refusal to transport destitute seamen under section 4578 of the Revised Statutes (46 U.S.C. 679); actions against the United States under the Act entitled "An Act authorizing suits against the United States in admiralty for damage caused by and salvage service rendered to public vessels belonging to the United States, and for other purposes", approved March 3, 1925 (46 U.S.C. 781-790), as implemented by section 7730 of title 10, United States Code.

Rule 1102. Amendments

Amendments to the Federal Rules of Evidence may be made as provided in section 2072 of title 28 of the United States Code.

Rule 1103. Title

These rules may be known and cited as the Federal Rules of Evidence.

Appendix B

Rules of Evidence for United States Courts and Magistrates With Advisory Committee Notes

Rules of Evidence for United States Courts and Magistrates with Advisory Committee Notes

Article I. General Provisions

Rule 101. Scope

These rules govern proceedings in the courts of the United States and before the United States bankruptcy judges and United States magistrate judges, to the extent and with the exceptions stated in rule 1101.

ADVISORY COMMITTEE NOTES

1972 Proposed Rules
Rule 1101 specifies in detail the courts, proceedings, questions, and stages of proceedings to which the rules apply in whole or in part.

1987 Amendments
United States bankruptcy judges are added to conform this rule with Rule 1101(b) and Bankruptcy Rule 9017.

1988 Amendments
The amendment is technical. No substantive change is intended.

1993 Amendments

This revision is made to conform the rule to changes made by the Judicial Improvements Act of 1990.

Rule 102. Purpose and Construction

These rules shall be construed to secure fairness in administration, elimination of unjustifiable expense and delay, and promotion of growth and development of the law of evidence to the end that the truth may be ascertained and proceedings justly determined.

ADVISORY COMMITTEE NOTES

1972 Proposed Rules
For similar provisions see Rule 2 of the Federal Rules of Criminal Procedure, Rule 1 of the Federal Rules of Civil Procedure, California Evidence Code § 2, and New Jersey Evidence Rule 5.

Rule 103. Rulings on Evidence

(a) Effect of Erroneous Ruling.--Error may not be predicated upon a ruling which admits or excludes evidence unless a substantial right of the party is affected, and

(1) Objection.--In case the ruling is one admitting evidence, a timely objection or motion to strike appears of record, stating the specific ground of objection, if the specific ground was not apparent from the context; or

(2) Offer of Proof.--In case the ruling is one excluding evidence, the substance of the evidence was made known to the court by offer or was apparent from the context within which questions were asked.

Once the court makes a definitive ruling on the record admitting or excluding evidence, either at or before trial, a party need not renew an objection or offer of proof to preserve a claim of error for appeal.

(b) Record of Offer and Ruling.--The court may add any other or further statement which shows the character of the evidence, the form in which it was offered, the objection made, and the ruling thereon. It may direct the making of an offer in question and answer form.

(c) Hearing of Jury.--In jury cases, proceedings shall be conducted, to the extent practicable, so as to prevent inadmissible evidence from being suggested to the jury by any means, such as making statements or offers of proof or asking questions in the hearing of the jury.

(d) Plain Error.--Nothing in this rule precludes taking notice of plain errors affecting substantial rights although they were not brought to the attention of the court.

ADVISORY COMMITTEE NOTES

1972 Proposed Rules

Note to Subdivision (a). Subdivision (a) states the law as generally accepted today. Rulings on evidence cannot be assigned as error unless (1) a substantial right is affected, and (2) the nature of the error was called to the attention of the judge, so as to alert him to the proper course of action and enable opposing counsel to take proper corrective measures. The objection and the offer of proof are the techniques for accomplishing these objectives. For similar provisions see Uniform Rules 4 and 5; California Evidence Code §§ 353 and 354; Kansas Code of Civil Procedure §§ 60-404 and 60-405. The rule does not purport to change the law with respect to harmless error. See 28 USC § 2111, F.R.Civ.P. 61, F.R.Crim.P. 52, and decisions construing them. The status of constitutional error as harmless or not is treated in Chapman v. California, 386 U.S. 18, 87 S.Ct. 824, 17 L.Ed.2d 705 (1967), reh. denied id. 987, 87 S.Ct. 1283, 18 L.Ed.2d 241.

Note to Subdivision (b). The first sentence is the third sentence of Rule 43(c) of the Federal Rules of Civil Procedure virtually verbatim. Its purpose is to reproduce for an appellate court, insofar as possible, a true reflection of what occurred in the trial court. The second sentence is in part derived from the final sentence of Rule 43(c). It is designed to resolve doubts as to what testimony the witness would have in fact given, and, in nonjury cases, to provide the appellate court with material for a possible final disposition of the case in the event of reversal of a ruling which excluded evidence. See 5 Moore's Federal Practice § 43.11 (2d ed. 1968). Application is made discretionary in view of the practical impossibility of formulating a satisfactory rule in mandatory terms.

Note to Subdivision (c). This subdivision proceeds on the supposition that a ruling which excludes evidence in a jury case is likely to be a pointless procedure if the excluded evidence nevertheless comes to the attention of the jury. Bruton v. United States, 389 U.S. 818, 88 S.Ct. 126, 19 L.Ed.2d 70 (1968). Rule 43(c) of the Federal Rules of Civil Procedure provides: "The court may require the offer to be made out of the hearing of the jury." In re McConnell, 370 U.S. 230, 82 S.Ct. 1288, 8 L.Ed.2d 434 (1962), left some doubt whether questions on which an offer is based must first be asked in the presence of the jury. The subdivision answers in the negative. The judge can foreclose a particular line of testimony and counsel can protect his record without a series of questions before the jury, designed at best to waste time and at worst "to waft into the jury box" the very matter sought to be excluded.

Note to Subdivision (d). This wording of the plain error principle is from Rule 52(b) of the Federal Rules of Criminal Procedure. While judicial unwillingness to be constructed by mechanical breakdowns of the adversary system has been more pronounced in criminal cases, there is no scarcity of decisions to the same effect in civil cases. In general, see Campbell, Extent to Which Courts of Review

Will Consider Questions Not Properly Raised and Preserved, 7 Wis.L.Rev. 91, 160 (1932); Vestal, Sua Sponte Consideration in Appellate Review, 27 Fordham L.Rev. 477 (1958-59); 64 Harv.L.Rev. 652 (1951). In the nature of things the application of the plain error rule will be more likely with respect to the admission of evidence than to exclusion, since failure to comply with normal requirements of offers of proof is likely to produce a record which simply does not disclose the error.

2000 Amendment

The amendment applies to all rulings on evidence whether they occur at or before trial, including so-called "in limine" rulings. One of the most difficult questions arising from in limine and other evidentiary rulings is whether a losing party must renew an objection or offer of proof when the evidence is or would be offered at trial, in order to preserve a claim of error on appeal. Courts have taken differing approaches to this question. Some courts have held that a renewal at the time the evidence is to be offered at trial is always required. See, e.g., Collins v. Wayne Corp., 621 F.2d 777 (5th Cir. 1980). Some courts have taken a more flexible approach, holding that renewal is not required if the issue decided is one that (1) was fairly presented to the trial court for an initial ruling, (2) may be decided as a final matter before the evidence is actually offered, and (3) was ruled on definitively by the trial judge, See, e.g., Rosenfeld v. Basquiat, 78 F.3d 84 (2d Cir. 1996) (admissibility of former testimony under the Dead Man's Statute; renewal not required). Other courts have distinguished between objections to evidence, which must be renewed when evidence is offered, and offers of proof, which need not be renewed after a definitive determination is made that the evidence is inadmissible. See, e.g., Fusco v. General Motors Corp., 11 F.3d 259 (1st Cir. 1993). Another court, aware of this Committee's proposed amendment, has adopted its approach. Wilson v. Williams, 182 F. 3d 562 (7th Cir.1999) (en banc). Differing views on this question create uncertainty for litigants and unnecessary work for the appellate courts.

The amendment provides that a claim of error with respect to a definitive ruling is preserved for review when the party has otherwise satisfied the objection or offer of proof requirements of Rule 103(a). When the ruling is definitive, a renewed objection or offer of proof at the time the evidence is to be offered is more a formalism than a necessity. See Fed.R.Civ.P. 46 (formal exceptions unnecessary); Fed.R.Cr.P. 51 (same); United States v. Mejia-Alarcon, 995 F.2d 982, 986 (10th Cir. 1993) ("Requiring a party to renew an objection when the district court has issued a definitive ruling on a matter that can be fairly decided before trial would be in the nature of a formal exception and therefore unnecessary."). On the other hand, when the trial court appears to have reserved its ruling or to have indicated that the ruling is provisional, it makes sense to require the party to bring the issue to the court's attention subsequently. See, e.g., United States v. Vest, 116 F.3d 1179, 1188 (7th Cir. 1997) (where the trial court ruled n limine that testimony from defense witnesses could not be admitted, but allowed the defendant to seek leave at trial to call the witnesses should their testimony turn out to be relevant, the defendant's failure to seek such leave at trial meant that it was "too late to reopen the issue now on appeal"); United States v. Valenti, 60 F.3d 941 (2d Cir. 1995) (failure to proffer evidence at trial waives any claim of error where the trial judge had stated that he would reserve judgment on the in limine motion until he had heard the trial evidence).

The amendment imposes the obligation on counsel to clarify whether an in limine or other evidentiary ruling is definitive when there is doubt on that point. See, e.g., Walden v. Georgia-Pacific Corp., 126 F.3d 506, 520 (3d Cir. 1997) (although "the district court told plaintiffs' counsel not to reargue every ruling, it did not countermand its clear opening statement that all of its rulings were tentative, and counsel never requested clarification, as he might have done.").

Even where the court's ruling is definitive, nothing in the amendment prohibits the court from revisiting its decision when the evidence is to be offered. If the court changes its initial ruling, or if the opposing party violates the terms of the initial ruling, objection must be made when the evidence is offered to preserve the claim of error for appeal. The error, if any, in such a situation occurs only when the evidence is offered and admitted. United States Aviation Underwriters, Inc. v. Olympia Wings, Inc., 896 F.2d 949, 956 (5th Cir. 1990) ("objection is required to preserve error when an opponent, or the court itself, violates a motion in limine that was granted"); United States v. Roenigk, 810 F.2d 809 (8th Cir. 1987) (claim of error was not preserved where the defendant failed to object at trial to secure the benefit of a favorable advance ruling).

A definitive advance ruling is reviewed in light of the facts and circumstances before the trial court at the time of the ruling. If the relevant facts and circumstances change materially after the advance ruling has been made, those facts and circumstances cannot be relied upon on appeal unless they have been brought to the attention of the trial court by way of a renewed, and timely, objection, offer of proof, or motion to strike. See Old Chief v. United States, 519 U.S. 172, 182, n.6 (1997) ("It is important that a reviewing court evaluate the trial court's decision from its perspective when it had to rule and not indulge in review by hindsight."). Similarly, if the court decides in an advance ruling that proffered evidence is admissible subject to the eventual introduction by the proponent of a foundation for the evidence, and that foundation is never provided, the opponent cannot claim error based on the failure to establish the foundation unless the opponent calls that failure to the court's attention by a timely motion to strike or other suitable motion. See Huddleston v. United States, 485 U.S. 681, 690, n.7 (1988) ("It is, of course, not the responsibility of the judge sua sponte to ensure that the foundation evidence is offered; the objector must move to strike the evidence if at the close of the trial the offeror has failed to satisfy the condition.").

Nothing in the amendment is intended to affect the provisions of Fed.R.Civ.P. 72(a) or 28 U.S.C. § 636(b)(1) pertaining to nondispositive pretrial rulings by magistrate judges in proceedings that are not before a magistrate judge by consent of the parties. Fed.R.Civ.P. 72(a) provides that a party who fails to file a written objection to a magistrate judge's nondispositive order within ten days of receiving a copy "may not thereafter assign as error a defect" in the order. 28 U.S.C. § 636(b)(1) provides that any party "may serve and file written objections to such proposed findings and recommendations as provided by rules of court" within ten days of receiving a copy of the order. Several courts have held that a party must comply with this statutory provision in order to preserve a claim of error. See, e.g., Wells v. Shriners Hospital, 109 F.3d 198, 200 (4th Cir. 1997)("[i]n this circuit, as in others, a party 'may' file objections within ten days or he may not, as he chooses, but he 'shall' do so if he wishes further consideration."). When Fed.R.Civ.P. 72(a) or 28 U.S.C. § 636(b)(1) is operative, its requirement must be satisfied in order for a party to preserve a claim of error on appeal, even where Evidence Rule 103(a) would not require a subsequent objection or offer of proof.

Nothing in the amendment is intended to affect the rule set forth in Luce v. United States, 469 U.S. 38 (1984), and its progeny. The amendment provides that an objection or offer of proof need not be renewed to preserve a claim of error with respect to a definitive pretrial ruling. Luce answers affirmatively a separate question: whether a criminal defendant must testify at trial in order to preserve a claim of error predicated upon a trial court's decision to admit the defendant's prior convictions for impeachment. The Luce principle has been extended by many lower courts to other situations. See United States v. DiMatteo, 759 F.2d 831 (11th Cir. 1985) (applying Luce where the defendant's witness would be impeached with evidence offered under Rule 608). See also United States v. Goldman, 41 F.3d 785, 788 (1st Cir. 1994) ("Although Luce involved impeachment by conviction under Rule 609, the reasons given by the Supreme Court for requiring the defendant to testify apply with full force to the kind of Rule 403 and 404 objections that are advanced by Goldman in this case."); Palmieri v. DeFaria, 88 F.3d 136 (2d Cir. 1996) (where the plaintiff decided to take an adverse judgment rather than challenge an advance ruling by putting on evidence at trial, the in limine ruling would not be reviewed on appeal); United States v. Ortiz, 857 F.2d 900 (2d Cir. 1988) (where uncharged misconduct is ruled admissible if the defendant pursues a certain defense, the defendant must actually pursue that defense at trial in order to preserve a claim of error on appeal); United States v. Bond, 87 F.3d 695 (5th Cir. 1996) (where the trial court rules in limine that the defendant would waive his fifth amendment privilege were he to testify, the defendant must take the stand and testify in order to challenge that ruling on appeal).

The amendment does not purport to answer whether a party who objects to evidence that the court finds admissible in a definitive ruling, and who then offers the evidence to "remove the sting" of its anticipated prejudicial effect, thereby waives the right to appeal the trial court's ruling. See, e.g., United States v. Fisher, 106 F.3d 622 (5th Cir. 1997) (where the trial judge ruled in limine that the government could use a prior conviction to impeach the defendant if he testified, the defendant did not waive his right to appeal by introducing the conviction on direct examination); Judd v. Rodman, 105 F.3d 1339 (11th Cir. 1997) (an objection made in limine is sufficient to preserve a claim of error when the movant, as a matter of trial strategy, presents the objectionable evidence herself on direct examination to minimize its prejudicial effect); Gill v. Thomas, 83 F.3d 537, 540 (1st Cir. 1996) ("by offering the misdemeanor evidence himself, Gill waived his opportunity to object and thus did not preserve the issue for appeal"); United States v. Williams, 939 F.2d 721 (9th Cir. 1991) (objection to impeachment evidence was waived where the defendant was impeached on direct examination).

GAP Report--Proposed Amendment to Rule 103(a)

The Committee made the following changes to the published draft of the proposed amendment to Evidence Rule 103(a):

1. A minor stylistic change was made in the text, in accordance with the suggestion of the Style Subcommittee of the Standing Committee on Rules of Practice and Procedure.

2. The second sentence of the amended portion of the published draft was deleted, and the Committee Note was amended to reflect the fact that nothing in the amendment is intended to affect the rule of Luce v. United States.

3. The Committee Note was updated to include cases decided after the proposed amendment was issued for public comment.

4. The Committee Note was amended to include a reference to a Civil Rule and a statute requiring objections to certain Magistrate Judge rulings to be made to the District Court.

5. The Committee Note was revised to clarify that an advance ruling does not encompass subsequent developments at trial that might be the subject of an appeal.

Rule 104. Preliminary Questions

(a) Questions of admissibility generally. Preliminary questions concerning the qualification of a person to be a witness, the existence of a privilege, or the admissibility of evidence shall be determined by the court, subject to the provisions of subdivision (b). In making its determination it is not bound by the rules of evidence except those with respect to privileges.

(b) Relevancy conditioned on fact. When the relevancy of evidence depends upon the fulfillment of a condition of fact, the court shall admit it upon, or subject to, the introduction of evidence sufficient to support a finding of the fulfillment of the condition.

(c) Hearing of jury. Hearings on the admissibility of confessions shall in all cases be conducted out of the hearing of the jury. Hearings on other preliminary matters shall be so conducted when the interests of justice require, or when an accused is a witness and so requests.

(d) Testimony by accused. The accused does not, by testifying upon a preliminary matter, become subject to cross-examination as to other issues in the case.

(e) Weight and credibility. This rule does not limit the right of a party to introduce before the jury evidence relevant to weight or credibility.

ADVISORY COMMITTEE NOTES

1972 Proposed Rule
Note to Subdivision (a). The applicability of a particular rule of evidence often depends upon the existence of a condition. Is the alleged expert a qualified physician? Is a witness whose former testimony is offered unavailable? Was a stranger present during a conversation between attorney and client? In each instance the admissibility of evidence will turn upon the answer to the question of the existence of the condition. Accepted practice, incorporated in the rule, places on the judge the responsibility for these determinations. McCormick § 53; Morgan, Basic Problems of Evidence 45-50 (1962).

To the extent that these inquiries are factual, the judge acts as a trier of fact. Often, however, rulings on evidence call for an evaluation in terms of a legally set standard. Thus when a hearsay statement is offered as a declaration against interest, a decision must be made whether it possesses the required against-interest characteristics. These decisions, too, are made by the judge.

In view of these considerations, this subdivision refers to preliminary requirements generally by the broad term "questions," without attempt at specification.

This subdivision is of general application. It must, however, be read as subject to the special provisions for "conditional relevancy" in subdivision (b) and those for confessions in subdivision (d).

If the question is factual in nature, the judge will of necessity receive evidence pro and con on the issue. The rule provides that the rules of evidence in general do not apply to this process. McCormick § 53, p. 123, n. 8, points out that the authorities are "scattered and inconclusive," and observes:

"Should the exclusionary law of evidence, 'the child of the jury system' in Thayer's phrase, be applied to this hearing before the judge? Sound sense backs the view that it should not, and that the judge should be empowered to hear any relevant evidence, such as affidavits or other reliable hearsay."

This view is reinforced by practical necessity in certain situations. An item, offered and objected to, may itself be considered in ruling on admissibility, though not yet admitted in evidence. Thus, the content of an asserted declaration against interest must be considered in ruling whether it is against interest. Again, common practice calls for considering the testimony of a witness, particularly a child, in determining competency. Another example is the requirement of Rule 602 dealing with personal knowledge. In the case of hearsay, it is enough, if the declarant "so far as appears [has] had an opportunity to observe the fact declared." McCormick, § 10, p. 19.

If concern is felt over the use of affidavits by the judge in preliminary hearings on admissibility, attention is directed to the many important judicial determinations made on the basis of affidavits. Rule 47 of the Federal Rules of Criminal Procedure provides:

"An application to the court for an order shall be by motion. * * * It may be supported by affidavit."

The Rules of Civil Procedure are more detailed. Rule 43(e), dealing with motions generally, provides:

"When a motion is based on facts not appearing of record the court may hear the matter on affidavits presented by the respective parties, but the court may direct that the matter be heard wholly or partly on oral testimony or depositions." Rule 4(g) provides for proof of service by affidavit. Rule 56 provides in detail for the entry of summary judgment based on affidavits. Affidavits may supply the foundation for temporary restraining orders under Rule 65(b).

The study made for the California Law Revision Commission recommended an amendment to Uniform Rule 2 as follows:

"In the determination of the issue aforesaid [preliminary determination], exclusionary rules shall not apply, subject, however, to Rule 45 and any valid claim of privilege." Tentative Recommendation and a Study Relating to the Uniform

Rules of Evidence (Article VIII, Hearsay), Cal.Law Revision Comm'n, Rep., Rec. & Studies, 470 (1962). The proposal was not adopted in the California Evidence Code. The Uniform Rules are likewise silent on the subject. However, New Jersey Evidence Rule 8(1), dealing with preliminary inquiry by the judge, provides:

"In his determination the rules of evidence shall not apply except for Rule 4 [exclusion on grounds of confusion, etc.] or a valid claim of privilege."

Note to Subdivision (b). In some situations, the relevancy of an item of evidence, in the large sense, depends upon the existence of a particular preliminary fact. Thus when a spoken statement is relied upon to prove notice to X, it is without probative value unless X heard it. Or if a letter purporting to be from Y is relied upon to establish an admission by him, it has no probative value unless Y wrote or authorized it. Relevance in this sense has been labelled "conditional relevancy." Morgan, Basic Problems of Evidence 45-46 (1962). Problems arising in connection with it are to be distinguished from problems of logical relevancy, e.g., evidence in a murder case that accused on the day before purchased a weapon of the kind used in the killing, treated in Rule 401.

If preliminary questions of conditional relevancy were determined solely by the judge, as provided in subdivision (a), the functioning of the jury as a trier of fact would be greatly restricted and in some cases virtually destroyed. These are appropriate questions for juries. Accepted treatment, as provided in the rule, is consistent with that given fact questions generally. The judge makes a preliminary determination whether the foundation evidence is sufficient to support a finding of fulfillment of the condition. If so, the item is admitted. If after all the evidence on the issue is in, pro and con, the jury could reasonably conclude that fulfillment of the condition is not established, the issue is for them. If the evidence is not such as to allow a finding, the judge withdraws the matter from their consideration. Morgan, supra; California Evidence Code § 403; New Jersey Rule 8(2). See also Uniform Rules 19 and 67.

The order of proof here, as generally, is subject to the control of the judge.

Note to Subdivision (c). Preliminary hearings on the admissibility of confessions must be conducted outside the hearing of the jury. See Jackson v. Denno, 378 U.S. 368, 84 S.Ct. 1774, 12 L.Ed.2d 908 (1964). Otherwise, detailed treatment of when preliminary matters should be heard outside the hearing of the jury is not feasible. The procedure is time consuming. Not infrequently the same evidence which is relevant to the issue of establishment of fulfillment of a condition precedent to admissibility is also relevant to weight or credibility, and time is saved by taking foundation proof in the presence of the jury. Much evidence on preliminary questions, though not relevant to jury issues, may be heard by the jury with no adverse effect. A great deal must be left to the discretion of the judge who will act as the interests of justice require.

Note to Subdivision (d). The limitation upon cross-examination is designed to encourage participation by the accused in the determination of preliminary matters. He may testify concerning them without exposing himself to cross-examination generally. The provision is necessary because of the breadth of cross-examination under Rule 611(b).

The rule does not address itself to questions of the subsequent use of testimony given by an accused at a hearing on a preliminary matter. See Walder v. United States, 347 U.S. 62 (1954); Simmons v. United States, 390 U.S. 377 (1968); Harris v. New York, 401 U.S. 222 (1971).

Note to Subdivision (e). For similar provisions see Uniform Rule 8; California Evidence Code § 406; Kansas Code of Civil Procedure § 60-408; New Jersey Evidence Rule 8(1).

1974 Enactment
Rule 104(c) as submitted to the Congress provided that hearings on the admissibility of confessions shall be conducted outside the presence of the jury and hearings on all other preliminary matters should be so conducted when the interests of justice require. The Committee amended the Rule to provide that where an accused is a witness as to a preliminary matter, he has the right, upon his request, to be heard outside the jury's presence. Although recognizing that in some cases duplication of evidence would occur and that the procedure could be subject to abuse, the Committee believed that a proper regard for the right of an accused not to testify generally in the case dictates that he be given an option to testify out of the presence of the jury on preliminary matters.

The Committee construes the second sentence of subdivision (c) as applying to civil actions and proceedings as well as to criminal cases, and on this assumption has left the sentence unamended. House Report No. 93-650.

Under rule 104(c) the hearing on a preliminary matter may at times be conducted in front of the jury. Should an accused testify in such a hearing, waiving his privilege against self-incrimination as to the preliminary issue, rule 104(d) provides that he will not generally be subject to cross-examination as to any other issue. This rule is not, however, intended to immunize the accused from cross-examination where, in testifying about a preliminary issue, he injects other issues into the hearing. If he could not be cross-examined about any issues gratuitiously raised by him beyond the scope of the preliminary matters, injustice might result. Accordingly, in order to prevent any such unjust result, the committee intends the rule to be construed to provide that the accused may subject himself to cross-examination as to issues raised by his own testimony upon a preliminary matter before a jury. Senate Report No. 93-1277.

1987 Amendments
The amendments are technical. No substantive change is intended.

> ### Rule 105. Limited Admissibility
>
> When evidence which is admissible as to one party or for one purpose but not admissible as to another party or for another purpose is admitted, the court, upon request, shall restrict the evidence to its proper scope and instruct the jury accordingly.

ADVISORY COMMITTEE NOTES

1972 Proposed Rules
A close relationship exists between this rule and Rule 403 which requires exclusion when "probative value is substantially outweighed by the danger of unfair prejudice, confusion of the issues, or misleading the jury." The present rule recognizes the practice of admitting evidence for a limited purpose and instructing the jury accordingly. The availability and effectiveness of this practice must be taken into consideration in reaching a decision whether to exclude for unfair prejudice under Rule 403. In Bruton v. United States, 389 U.S. 818, 88 S.Ct. 126, 19 L.Ed.2d 70 (1968), the Court ruled that a limiting instruction did not effectively protect the accused against the prejudicial effect of admitting in evidence the confession of a codefendant which implicated him. The decision does not, however, bar the use of limited admissibility with an instruction where the risk of prejudice is less serious.

Similar provisions are found in Uniform Rule 6; California Evidence Code § 355; Kansas Code of Civil Procedure § 60-406; New Jersey Evidence Rule 6. The wording of the present rule differs, however, in repelling any implication that limiting or curative instructions are sufficient in all situations.

1974 Enactment
Rule 106 as submitted by the Supreme Court (now Rule 105 in the bill) dealt with the subject of evidence which is admissible as to one party or for one purpose but is not admissible against another party or for another purpose. The Committee adopted this Rule without change on the understanding that it does not affect the authority of a court to order a severance in a multi-defendant case. House Report No. 93-650.

Rule 106. Remainder of or Related Writings or Recorded Statements

When a writing or recorded statement or part thereof is introduced by a party, an adverse party may require the introduction at that time of any other part or any other writing or recorded statement which ought in fairness to be considered contemporaneously with it.

ADVISORY COMMITTEE NOTES

1972 Proposed Rules
The rule is an expression of the rule of completeness. McCormick § 56. It is manifested as to depositions in Rule 32(a)(4) of the Federal Rules of Civil Procedure, of which the proposed rule is substantially a restatement.

The rule is based on two considerations. The first is the misleading impression created by taking matters out of context. The second is the inadequacy of repair work when delayed to a point later in the trial. See McCormick § 56; California Evidence Code § 356. The rule does not in any way circumscribe the right of the adversary to develop the matter on cross-examination or as part of his own case.

For practical reasons, the rule is limited to writings and recorded statements and does not apply to conversations.

1987 Amendments
The amendments are technical. No substantive change is intended.

ARTICLE II. JUDICIAL NOTICE

Rule 201. Judicial Notice of Adjudicative Facts

(a) Scope of rule. This rule governs only judicial notice of adjudicative facts.

(b) Kinds of facts. A judicially noticed fact must be one not subject to reasonable dispute in that it is either (1) generally known within the territorial jurisdiction of the trial court or (2) capable of accurate and ready determination by resort to sources whose accuracy cannot reasonably be questioned.

(c) When discretionary. A court may take judicial notice, whether requested or not.

(d) When mandatory. A court shall take judicial notice if requested by a party and supplied with the necessary information.

(e) Opportunity to be heard. A party is entitled upon timely request to an opportunity to be heard as to the propriety of taking judicial notice and the tenor of the matter noticed. In the absence of prior notification, the request may be made after judicial notice has been taken.

(f) Time of taking notice. Judicial notice may be taken at any stage of the proceeding.

(g) Instructing jury. In a civil action or proceeding, the court shall instruct the jury to accept as conclusive any fact judicially noticed. In a criminal case, the court shall instruct the jury that it may, but is not required to, accept as conclusive any fact judicially noticed.

ADVISORY COMMITTEE NOTES

1972 Proposed Rules
Note to Subdivision (a). This is the only evidence rule on the subject of judicial notice. It deals only with judicial notice of "adjudicative" facts. No rule deals with judicial notice of "legislative" facts. Judicial notice of matters of foreign law is treated in Rule 44.1 of the Federal Rules of Civil Procedure and Rule 26.1 of the Federal Rules of Criminal Procedure.

The omission of any treatment of legislative facts results from fundamental differences between adjudicative facts and legislative facts. Adjudicative facts are simply the facts of the particular case. Legislative facts, on the other hand, are those which have relevance to legal reasoning and the lawmaking process, whether in the formulation of a legal principle or ruling by a judge or court or in the enactment of a legislative body. The terminology was coined by Professor Kenneth Davis in his article An Approach to Problems of Evidence in the Administrative Process, 55 Harv.L.Rev. 364, 404-407 (1942). The following discussion draws extensively upon his writings. In addition, see the same author's Judicial Notice, 55 Colum.L.Rev. 945 (1955); Administrative Law Treatise, ch. 15 (1958); A System of Judicial Notice Based on Fairness and Convenience, in Perspectives of Law 69 (1964).

The usual method of establishing adjudicative facts is through the introduction of evidence, ordinarily consisting of the testimony of witnesses. If particular facts are outside the area of reasonable controversy, this process is dispensed with as unnecessary. A high degree of indisputability is the essential prerequisite.

Legislative facts are quite different. As Professor Davis says:

"My opinion is that judge-made law would stop growing if judges, in thinking about questions of law and policy, were forbidden to take into account the facts they believe, as distinguished from facts which are 'clearly * * * within the domain of the indisputable.' Facts most needed in thinking about difficult problems of law and policy have a way of being outside the domain of the clearly indisputable." A System of Judicial Notice Based on Fairness and Convenience, supra, at 82.

An illustration is Hawkins v. United States, 358 U.S. 74, 79 S.Ct. 136, 3 L.Ed.2d 125 (1958), in which the Court refused to discard the common law rule that one spouse could not testify against the other, saying, "Adverse testimony given in criminal proceedings would, we think, be likely to destroy almost any marriage." This conclusion has a large intermixture of fact, but the factual aspect is scarcely "indisputable." See Hutchins and Slesinger, Some Observations on the Law of Evidence--Family Relations, 13 Minn.L.Rev. 675 (1929). If the destructive effect of the giving of adverse testimony by a spouse is not indisputable, should the Court have refrained from considering it in the absence of supporting evidence?

"If the Model Code or the Uniform Rules had been applicable, the Court would have been barred from thinking about the essential factual ingredient of the problems before it, and such a result would be obviously intolerable. What the law needs at its growing points is more, not less, judicial thinking about the factual ingredients of problems of what the law ought to be, and the needed facts are seldom 'clearly' indisputable." Davis, supra, at 83.

Professor Morgan gave the following description of the methodology of determining domestic law:

"In determining the content or applicability of a rule of domestic law, the judge is unrestricted in his investigation and conclusion. He may reject the propositions of either party or of both parties. He may consult the sources of pertinent data to which they refer, or he may refuse to do so. He may make an independent search for persuasive data or rest content with what he has or what the parties present. * * * [T]he parties do no more than to assist; they control no part of the process." Morgan, Judicial Notice, 57 Harv.L.Rev. 269, 270-271 (1944).

This is the view which should govern judicial access to legislative facts. It renders inappropriate any limitation in the form of indisputability, any formal requirements of notice other than those already inherent in affording opportunity to hear and be heard and exchanging briefs, and any requirement of formal findings at any level. It should, however leave open the possibility of introducing evidence through regular channels in appropriate situations. See Borden's Farm Products Co. v. Baldwin, 293 U.S. 194, 55 S.Ct. 187, 79 L.Ed. 281 (1934), where the cause was remanded for the taking of evidence as to the economic conditions and trade practices underlying the New York Milk Control Law.

Similar considerations govern the judicial use of non-adjudicative facts in ways other than formulating laws and rules. Thayer described them as a part of the judicial reasoning process.

"In conducting a process of judicial reasoning, as of other reasoning, not a step can be taken without assuming something which has not been proved; and the capacity to do this with competent judgment and efficiency, is imputed to judges and juries as part of their necessary mental outfit." Thayer, Preliminary Treatise on Evidence 279-280 (1898).

As Professor Davis points out, A System of Judicial Notice Based on Fairness and Convenience, in Perspectives of Law 69, 73 (1964), every case involves the use of hundreds or thousands of non-evidence facts. When a witness in an automobile accident case says "car," everyone, judge and jury included, furnishes, from non-evidence sources within himself, the supplementing information that the "car" is an automobile, not a railroad car, that it is self-propelled, probably by an internal combustion engine, that it may be assumed to have four wheels with pneumatic rubber tires, and so on. The judicial process cannot construct every case from scratch, like Descartes creating a world based on the postulate Cogito, ergo sum. These items could not possibly be introduced into evidence, and no one suggests that they be. Nor are they appropriate subjects for any formalized treatment of judicial notice of facts. See Levin and Levy, Persuading the Jury with Facts Not in Evidence: The Fiction-Science Spectrum, 105 U.Pa.L.Rev. 139 (1956).

Another aspect of what Thayer had in mind is the use of non-evidence facts to appraise or assess the adjudicative facts of the case. Pairs of cases from two jurisdictions illustrate this use and also the difference between non-evidence facts thus used and adjudicative facts. In People v. Strook, 347 Ill. 460, 179 N.E. 821 (1932), venue in Cook County had been held not established by testimony that the crime was committed at 7956 South Chicago Avenue, since judicial notice would not be taken that the address was in Chicago. However, the same court subsequently ruled that venue in Cook County was established by testimony that a crime occurred at 8900 South Anthony Avenue, since notice would be taken of the common practice of omitting the name of the city when speaking of local addresses, and the witness was testifying in Chicago. People v. Pride, 16 Ill.2d 82, 156 N.E.2d 551 (1959). And in Hughes v. Vestal, 264 N.C. 500, 142 S.E.2d 361 (1965), the Supreme Court of North Carolina disapproved the trial judge's admission in evidence of a state-published table of automobile stopping distances on the basis of judicial notice, though the court itself had referred to the same table in an earlier case in a "rhetorical and illustrative" way in determining that the defendant could not have stopped her car in time to avoid striking a child who suddenly appeared in the highway and that a nonsuit was properly granted. Ennis v. Dupree, 262 N.C. 224, 136 S.E.2d 702 (1964). See also Brown v. Hale,

263 N.C. 176, 139 S.E.2d 210 (1964); Clayton v. Rimmer, 262 N.C. 302, 136 S.E.2d 562 (1964). It is apparent that this use of non-evidence facts in evaluating the adjudicative facts of the case is not an appropriate subject for a formalized judicial notice treatment.

In view of these considerations, the regulation of judicial notice of facts by the present rule extends only to adjudicative facts.

What, then, are "adjudicative" facts? Davis refers to them as those "which relate to the parties," or more fully:

"When a court or an agency finds facts concerning the immediate parties--who did what, where, when, how, and with what motive or intent--the court or agency is performing an adjudicative function, and the facts are conveniently called adjudicative facts. * * *

"Stated in other terms, the adjudicative facts are those to which the law is applied in the process of adjudication. They are the facts that normally go to the jury in a jury case. They relate to the parties, their activities, their properties, their businesses." 2 Administrative Law Treatise 353.

Note to Subdivision (b). With respect to judicial notice of adjudicative facts, the tradition has been one of caution in requiring that the matter be beyond reasonable controversy. This tradition of circumspection appears to be soundly based, and no reason to depart from it is apparent. As Professor Davis says:

"The reason we use trial-type procedure, I think, is that we make the practical judgment, on the basis of experience, that taking evidence, subject to cross-examination and rebuttal, is the best way to resolve controversies involving disputes of adjudicative facts, that is, facts pertaining to the parties. The reason we require a determination on the record is that we think fair procedure in resolving disputes of adjudicative facts calls for giving each party a chance to meet in the appropriate fashion the facts that come to the tribunal's attention, and the appropriate fashion for meeting disputed adjudicative facts includes rebuttal evidence, cross-examination, usually confrontation, and argument (either written or oral or both). The key to a fair trial is opportunity to use the appropriate weapons (rebuttal evidence, cross-examination, and argument) to meet adverse materials that come to the tribunal's attention." A System of Judicial Notice Based on Fairness and Convenience, in Perspectives of Law 69, 93 (1964).

The rule proceeds upon the theory that these considerations call for dispensing with traditional methods of proof only in clear cases. Compare Professor Davis' conclusion that judicial notice should be a matter of convenience, subject to requirements of procedural fairness. Id., 94.

This rule is consistent with Uniform Rule 9(1) and (2) which limit judicial notice of facts to those "so universally known that they cannot reasonably be the subject of dispute," those "so generally known or of such common notoriety within the territorial jurisdiction of the court that they cannot reasonably be the subject of dispute," and those "capable of immediate and accurate determination by resort to easily accessible sources of indisputable accuracy." The traditional textbook treatment has included these general categories (matters of common knowledge, facts capable of verification), McCormick §§ 324, 325, and then has passed on into detailed treatment of such specific topics as facts relating to the personnel and records of the court, Id. § 327, and other governmental facts, Id. § 328. The California draftsmen, with a background of detailed statutory regulation of judicial notice, followed a somewhat similar pattern. California Evidence Code §§ 451, 452. The Uniform Rules, however, were drafted on the theory that these particular matters are included within the general categories and need no specific mention. This approach is followed in the present rule.

The phrase "propositions of generalized knowledge," found in Uniform Rule 9(1) and (2) is not included in the present rule. It was, it is believed, originally included in Model Code Rules 801 and 802 primarily in order to afford some minimum recognition to the right of the judge in his "legislative" capacity (not acting as the trier of fact) to take judicial notice of very limited categories of generalized knowledge. The limitations thus imposed have been discarded herein as undesirable, unworkable, and contrary to existing practice. What is left, then, to be considered, is the status of a "proposition of generalized knowledge" as an "adjudicative" fact to be noticed judicially and communicated by the judge to the jury. Thus viewed, it is considered to be lacking practical significance. While judges use judicial notice of "propositions of generalized knowledge" in a variety of situations: determining the validity and meaning of statutes, formulating common law rules, deciding whether evidence should be admitted, assessing the sufficiency and effect of evidence, all are essentially nonadjudicative in nature. When judicial notice is seen as a significant vehicle for progress in the law, these are the areas involved, particularly in developing fields of scientific knowledge. See McCormick 712. It is not believed that judges now instruct juries as to "propositions of generalized knowledge" derived from encyclopedias or other sources, or that they are likely to do so, or, indeed, that it is desirable that they do so. There is a vast difference between ruling on the basis of judicial notice that radar evidence of speed is admissible and explaining to the jury its principles and degree of accuracy, or between using a table of stopping distances of automobiles at various speeds in a judicial evaluation of testimony and telling the jury its precise application in the case. For cases raising doubt as to the propriety of the use of medical texts by lay triers of fact in passing on disability claims in administrative proceedings, see Sayers v. Gardner, 380 F.2d 940 (6th Cir.1967); Ross v. Gardner, 365 F.2d 554 (6th Cir.1966); Sosna v. Celebrezze, 234 F.Supp. 289 (E.D.Pa.1964);

Glendenning v. Ribicoff, 213 F.Supp. 301 (W.D.Mo.1962).

Notes to Subdivisions (c) and (d). Under subdivision (c) the judge has a discretionary authority to take judicial notice, regardless of whether he is so requested by a party. The taking of judicial notice is mandatory, under subdivision (d), only when a party requests it and the necessary information is supplied. This scheme is believed to reflect existing practice. It is simple and workable. It avoids troublesome distinctions in the many situations in which the process of taking judicial notice is not recognized as such.

Compare Uniform Rule 9 making judicial notice of facts universally known mandatory without request, and making judicial notice of facts generally known in the jurisdiction or capable of determination by resort to accurate sources discretionary in the absence of request but mandatory if request is made and the information furnished. But see Uniform Rule 10(3), which directs the judge to decline to take judicial notice if available information fails to convince him that the matter falls clearly within Uniform Rule 9 or is insufficient to enable him to notice it judicially. Substantially the same approach is found in California Evidence Code §§ 451-453 and in New Jersey Evidence Rule 9. In contrast, the present rule treats alike all adjudicative facts which are subject to judicial notice.

Note to Subdivision (e). Basic considerations of procedural fairness demand an opportunity to be heard on the propriety of taking judicial notice and the tenor of the matter noticed. The rule requires the granting of that opportunity upon request. No formal scheme of giving notice is provided. An adversely affected party may learn in advance that judicial notice is in contemplation, either by virtue of being served with a copy of a request by another party under subdivision (d) that judicial notice be taken, or through an advance indication by the judge. Or he may have no advance notice at all. The likelihood of the latter is enhanced by the frequent failure to recognize judicial notice as such. And in the absence of advance notice, a request made after the fact could not in fairness be considered untimely. See the provision for hearing on timely request in the Administrative Procedure Act, 5 U.S.C. § 556(e). See also Revised Model State Administrative Procedure Act (1961), 9C U.L.A. § 10(4) (Supp.1967).

Note to Subdivision (f). In accord with the usual view, judicial notice may be taken at any stage of the proceedings, whether in the trial court or on appeal. Uniform Rule 12; California Evidence Code § 459; Kansas Rules of Evidence § 60-412; New Jersey Evidence Rule 12; McCormick § 330, p. 712.

Note to Subdivision (g). Much of the controversy about judicial notice has centered upon the question whether evidence should be admitted in disproof of facts of which judicial notice is taken.

The writers have been divided. Favoring admissibility are Thayer, Preliminary Treatise on Evidence 308 (1898); 9 Wigmore § 2567; Davis, A System of Judicial Notice Based on Fairness and Convenience, in Perspectives of Law, 69, 76-77 (1964). Opposing admissibility are Keeffe, Landis and Shaad, Sense and Non-sense about Judicial Notice, 2 Stan.L.Rev. 664, 668 (1950); McNaughton, Judicial Notice--Excerpts Relating to the Morgan-Whitmore Controversy, 14 Vand.L.Rev. 779 (1961); Morgan, Judicial Notice, 57 Harv.L.Rev. 269, 279 (1944); McCormick 710-711. The Model Code and the Uniform Rules are predicated upon indisputability of judicially noticed facts.

The proponents of admitting evidence in disproof have concentrated largely upon legislative facts. Since the present rule deals only with judicial notice of adjudicative facts, arguments directed to legislative facts lose their relevancy.

Within its relatively narrow area of adjudicative facts, the rule contemplates there is to be no evidence before the jury in disproof. The judge instructs the jury to take judicially noticed facts as established. This position is justified by the undesirable effects of the opposite rule in limiting the rebutting party, though not his opponent, to admissible evidence, in defeating the reasons for judicial notice, and in affecting the substantive law to an extent and in ways largely unforeseeable. Ample protection and flexibility are afforded by the broad provision for opportunity to be heard on request, set forth in subdivision (e).

Authority upon the propriety of taking judicial notice against an accused in a criminal case with respect to matters other than venue is relatively meager. Proceeding upon the theory that the right of jury trial does not extend to matters which are beyond reasonable dispute, the rule does not distinguish between criminal and civil cases. People v. Mayes, 113 Cal. 618, 45 P. 860 (1896); Ross v. United States, 374 F.2d 97 (8th Cir.1967). Cf. State v. Main, 94 R.I. 338, 180 A.2d 814 (1962); State v. Lawrence, 120 Utah 323, 234 P.2d 600 (1951).

Note on Judicial Notice of Law. By rules effective July 1, 1966, the method of invoking the law of a foreign country is covered elsewhere. Rule 44.1 of the Federal Rules of Civil Procedure; Rule 26.1 of the Federal Rules of Criminal Procedure. These two new admirably designed rules are founded upon the assumption that the manner in which law is fed into the judicial process is never a proper concern of the rules of evidence but rather of the rules of procedure. The Advisory Committee on Evidence, believing that this assumption is entirely correct, proposes no evidence rule with respect to judicial notice of law, and suggests that those matters of law which, in addition to foreign-country law, have traditionally been treated as requiring pleading and proof and more recently as the subject of judicial notice be left to the Rules of Civil and Criminal Procedure.

1974 Enactment

Rule 201(g) as received from the Supreme Court provided that when judicial notice of a fact is taken, the court shall instruct the jury to accept that fact as established. Being of the view that mandatory instruction to a jury in a criminal case to accept as conclusive any fact judicially noticed is inappropriate because contrary to the spirit of the Sixth Amendment right to a jury trial, the Committee adopted the 1969 Advisory Committee draft of this subsection, allowing a mandatory instruction in civil actions and proceedings and a discretionary instruction in criminal cases. House Report No. 93-650.

ARTICLE III. PRESUMPTIONS IN CIVIL ACTIONS AND PROCEEDINGS

Rule 301. Presumptions in General in Civil Actions and Proceedings

In all civil actions and proceedings not otherwise provided for by Act of Congress or by these rules, a presumption imposes on the party against whom it is directed the burden of going forward with evidence to rebut or meet the presumption, but does not shift to such party the burden of proof in the sense of the risk of nonpersuasion, which remains throughout the trial upon the party on whom it was originally cast.

ADVISORY COMMITTEE NOTES

1972 Proposed Rules

This rule governs presumptions generally. See Rule 302 for presumptions controlled by state law and Rule 303 [deleted] for those against an accused in a criminal case.

Presumptions governed by this rule are given the effect of placing upon the opposing party the burden of establishing the nonexistence of the presumed fact, once the party invoking the presumption establishes the basic facts giving rise to it. The same considerations of fairness, policy, and probability which dictate the allocation of the burden of the various elements of a case as between the prima facie case of a plaintiff and affirmative defenses also underlie the creation of presumptions. These considerations are not satisfied by giving a lesser effect to presumptions. Morgan and Maguire, Looking Backward and Forward at Evidence, 50 Harv.L.Rev. 909, 913 (1937); Morgan, Instructing the Jury upon Presumptions and Burden of Proof, 47 Harv.L.Rev. 59, 82 (1933); Cleary, Presuming and Pleading: An Essay on Juristic Immaturity, 12 Stan.L.Rev. 5 (1959).

The so-called "bursting bubble" theory, under which a presumption vanishes upon the introduction of evidence which would support a finding of the nonexistence of the presumed fact, even though not believed, is rejected as according presumptions too "slight and evanescent" an effect. Morgan and Maguire, supra, at p. 913.

In the opinion of the Advisory Committee, no constitutional infirmity attends this view of presumptions. In Mobile, J. & K. C. R. Co. v. Turnipseed, 219 U.S. 35, 31 S.Ct. 136, 55 L.Ed. 78 (1910), the Court upheld a Mississippi statute which provided that in actions against railroads proof of injury inflicted by the running of trains should be prima facie evidence of negligence by the railroad. The injury in the case had resulted from a derailment. The opinion made the points (1) that the only effect of the statute was to impose on the railroad the duty of producing some evidence to the contrary, (2) that an inference may be supplied by law if there is a rational connection between the fact proved and the fact presumed, as long as the opposite party is not precluded from presenting his evidence to the contrary, and (3) that considerations of public policy arising from the character of the business justified the application in question. Nineteen years later, in Western & Atlantic R. Co. v. Henderson, 279 U.S. 639, 49 S.Ct. 445, 73 L.Ed. 884 (1929), the Court overturned a Georgia statute making railroads liable for damages done by trains, unless the railroad made it appear that reasonable care had been used, the presumption being against the railroad. The declaration alleged the death of plaintiff's husband from a grade crossing collision, due to specified acts of negligence by defendant. The jury were instructed that proof of the injury raised a presumption of negligence; the burden shifted to the railroad to prove ordinary care; and unless it did so, they should find for plaintiff. The instruction was held erroneous in an opinion stating (1) that there was no rational connection between the mere fact of collision and negligence on the part of anyone, and (2) that the statute was different from that in Turnipseed in imposing a burden upon the railroad. The reader is left in a state of some confusion. Is the difference between a derailment and a grade crossing collision of no significance? Would the Turnipseed presumption have been bad if it had imposed a burden of persuasion on defendant, although that would in nowise have impaired its "rational connection"? If Henderson forbids imposing a burden of persuasion on defendants, what happens to affirmative defenses?

Two factors serve to explain Henderson. The first was that it was common ground that negligence was indispensable to liability. Plaintiff thought so, drafted her complaint accordingly, and relied upon the presumption. But how in logic could the same presumption establish her alternative grounds of negligence that the engineer was so blind he could not see decedent's truck and that he failed to stop after he saw it? Second, take away the basic assumption of no liability without fault, as Turnipseed intimated might be done ("considerations of public policy arising out of the character of the business"), and the structure of the decision in Henderson fails. No question of logic would have arisen if the statute had simply said: a prima facie case of liability is made by proof of injury by a train; lack of negligence is an affirmative defense, to be pleaded and proved as other affirmative defenses. The problem would be one of economic due process only. While it seems likely that the Supreme Court of 1929 would have voted that due process was denied, that result today would be unlikely. See, for example, the shift in the direction of absolute liability in the consumer cases. Prosser, The Assault upon the Citadel (Strict Liability to the Consumer), 69 Yale L.J. 1099 (1960).

Any doubt as to the constitutional permissibility of a presumption imposing a burden of persuasion of the nonexistence of the presumed fact in civil cases is laid at rest by Dick v. New York Life Ins. Co., 359 U.S. 437, 79 S.Ct. 921, 3 L.Ed.2d 935 (1959). The Court unhesitatingly applied the North Dakota rule that the presumption against suicide imposed on defendant the burden of proving that the death of insured, under an accidental death clause, was due to suicide.

"Proof of coverage and of death by gunshot wound shifts the burden to the insurer to establish that the death of the insured was due to his suicide." 359 U.S. at 443, 79 S.Ct. at 925.

"In a case like this one, North Dakota presumes that death was accidental and places on the insurer the burden of proving that death resulted from suicide." Id. at 446, 79 S.Ct. at 927.

The rational connection requirement survives in criminal cases, Tot v. United States, 319 U.S. 463, 63 S.Ct. 1241, 87 L.Ed. 1519 (1943), because the Court has been unwilling to extend into that area the greater-includes-the-lesser theory of Ferry v. Ramsey, 277 U.S. 88, 48 S.Ct. 443, 72 L.Ed. 796 (1928). In that case the Court sustained a Kansas statute under which bank directors were personally liable for deposits made with their assent and with knowledge of insolvency, and the fact of insolvency was prima facie evidence of assent and knowledge of insolvency. Mr. Justice Holmes pointed out that the state legislature could have made the directors personally liable to depositors in every case. Since the statute imposed a less stringent liability, "the thing to be considered is the result reached, not the possibly inartificial or clumsy way of reaching it." Id. at 94, 48 S.Ct. at 444. Mr. Justice Sutherland dissented: though the state could have created an absolute liability, it did not purport to do so; a rational connection was necessary, but lacking, between the liability created and the prima facie evidence of it; the result might be different if the basis of the presumption were being open for business.

The Sutherland view has prevailed in criminal cases by virtue of the higher standard of notice there required. The fiction that everyone is presumed to know the law is applied to the substantive law of crimes as an alternative to complete unenforceability. But the need does not extend to criminal evidence and procedure, and the fiction does not encompass them. "Rational connection" is not fictional or artificial, and so it is reasonable to suppose that Gainey should have known that his presence at the site of an illicit still could convict him of being connected with (carrying on) the business, United States v. Gainey, 380 U.S. 63, 85 S.Ct. 754, 13 L.Ed.2d 658 (1965), but not that Romano should have known that his presence at a still could convict him of possessing it, United States v. Romano, 382 U.S. 136, 86 S.Ct. 279, 15 L.Ed.2d 210 (1965).

In his dissent in Gainey, Mr. Justice Black put it more artistically:

"It might be argued, although the Court does not so argue or hold, that Congress if it wished could make presence at a still a crime in itself, and so Congress should be free to create crimes which are called 'possession' and 'carrying on an illegal distillery business' but which are defined in such a way that unexplained presence is sufficient and indisputable evidence in all cases to support conviction for those offenses. See Ferry v. Ramsey, 277 U.S. 88, 48 S.Ct. 443, 72 L.Ed. 796. Assuming for the sake of argument that Congress could make unexplained presence a criminal act, and ignoring also the refusal of this Court in other cases to uphold a statutory presumption on such a theory, see Heiner v. Donnan, 285 U.S. 312, 52 S.Ct. 358, 76 L.Ed. 772, there is no indication here that Congress intended to adopt such a misleading method of draftsmanship, nor in my judgment could the statutory provisions if so construed escape condemnation for vagueness, under the principles applied in Lanzetta v. New Jersey, 306 U.S. 451, 59 S.Ct. 618, 83 L.Ed. 888, and many other cases." 380 U.S. at 84, n. 12, 85 S.Ct. at 766.

And the majority opinion in Romano agreed with him:

"It may be, of course, that Congress has the power to make presence at an illegal still a punishable crime, but we find no clear indication that it intended to so exercise this power. The crime remains possession, not presence, and with all due deference to the judgment of Congress, the former may not constitutionally be inferred from the latter." 382 U.S. at 144, 86 S.Ct. at 284.

The rule does not spell out the procedural aspects of its application. Questions as to when the evidence warrants submission of a presumption and what instructions are proper under varying states of fact are believed to present no particular difficulties.

1974 Enactment

Rule 301 as submitted by the Supreme Court provided that in all cases a presumption imposes on the party against whom it is directed the burden of proving that the nonexistence of the presumed fact is more probable than its existence. The Committee limited the scope of Rule 301 to "civil actions and proceedings" to effectuate its decision not to deal with the question of presumptions in criminal cases. (See note on [proposed] Rule 303 in discussion of Rules deleted). With respect to the weight to be given a presumption in a civil case, the Committee agreed with the judgment implicit in the Court's version that the so-called "bursting bubble" theory of presumptions, whereby a presumption vanishes upon the appearance of any contradicting evidence by the other party, gives to presumptions too slight an effect. On the other hand, the Committee believed that the Rule proposed by the Court, whereby a presumption permanently alters the burden of persuasion, no matter how much contradicting evidence is introduced--a view shared by only a few courts--lends too great a force to presumptions. Accordingly, the Committee amended the Rule to adopt an intermediate position under which a presumption does not vanish upon the introduction of contradicting evidence, and does not change the burden of persuasion; instead it is merely deemed sufficient evidence of the fact presumed, to be considered by the jury or other finder of fact. House Report No. 93-650.

The rule governs presumptions in civil cases generally. Rule 302 provides for presumptions in cases controlled by State law.

As submitted by the Supreme Court, presumptions governed by this rule were given the effect of placing upon the opposing party the burden of establishing the nonexistence of the presumed fact, once the party invoking the presumption established the basic facts giving rise to it.

Instead of imposing a burden of persuasion on the party against whom the presumption is directed, the House adopted a provision which shifted the burden of going forward with the evidence. They further provided that "even though met with contradicting evidence, a presumption is sufficient evidence of the fact presumed, to be considered by the trier of fact." The effect of the amendment is that presumptions are to be treated as evidence.

The committee feels the House amendment is ill-advised. As the joint committees (the Standing Committee on Practice and Procedure of the Judicial Conference and the Advisory Committee on the Rules of Evidence) stated: "Presumptions are not evidence, but ways of dealing with evidence." This treatment requires juries to perform the task of considering "as evidence" facts upon which they have no direct evidence and which may confuse them in performance of their duties. California had a rule much like that contained in the House amendment. It was sharply criticized by Justice Traynor in Speck v. Sarver [20 Cal.2d 585, 128 P.2d 16, 21 (1942)] and was repealed after 93 troublesome years [Cal.Ev.Code 1965 § 600].

Professor McCormick gives a concise and compelling critique of the presumption as evidence rule:

"Another solution, formerly more popular than now, is to instruct the jury that the presumption is 'evidence', to be weighed and considered with the testimony in the case. This avoids the danger that the jury may infer that the presumption is conclusive, but it probably means little to the jury, and certainly runs counter to accepted theories of the nature of evidence." [McCormick, Evidence, 669 (1954); Id. 825 (2d ed. 1972)].

For these reasons the committee has deleted that provision of the House-passed rule that treats presumptions as evidence. The effect of the rule as adopted by the committee is to make clear that while evidence of facts giving rise to a presumption shifts the burden of coming forward with evidence to rebut or meet the presumption, it does not shift the burden of persuasion on the existence of the presumed facts. The burden of persuasion remains on the party to whom it is allocated under the rules governing the allocation in the first instance.

The court may instruct the jury that they may infer the existence of the presumed fact from proof of the basic facts giving rise to the presumption. However, it would be inappropriate under this rule to instruct the jury that the inference they are to draw is conclusive. Senate Report 93-1277.

The House bill provides that a presumption in civil actions and proceedings shifts to the party against whom it is directed the burden of going forward with evidence to meet or rebut it. Even though evidence contradicting the presumption is offered, a presumption is considered sufficient evidence of the presumed fact to be considered by the jury. The Senate amendment provides that a presumption shifts to the party against whom it is directed the burden of going forward with evidence to meet or rebut the presumption, but it does not shift to that party the burden of persuasion on the existence of the presumed fact.

Under the Senate amendment, a presumption is sufficient to get a party past an adverse party's motion to dismiss made at the end of his case-in-chief. If the adverse party offers no evidence contradicting the presumed fact, the court will instruct the jury that if it finds the basic facts, it may presume the existence of the presumed fact. If the adverse party does offer evidence contradicting the presumed fact, the court cannot instruct the jury that it may presume the existence of the presumed fact from proof of the basic facts. The court may, however, instruct the jury that it may infer the existence of the presumed fact from proof of the basic facts.

The conference adopts the Senate amendment. House Conference Report No. 93-1597.

Rule 302. Applicability of State Law in Civil Actions and Proceedings

In civil actions and proceedings, the effect of a presumption respecting a fact which is an element of a claim or defense as to which State law supplies the rule of decision is determined in accordance with State law.

ADVISORY COMMITTEE NOTES

1972 Proposed Rules
A series of Supreme Court decisions in diversity cases leaves no doubt of the relevance of Erie Railroad Co. v. Tompkins, 304 U.S. 64, 58 S.Ct. 817, 82 L.Ed. 1188 (1938), to questions of burden of proof. These decisions are Cities Service Oil Co. v. Dunlap, 308 U.S. 208, 60 S.Ct. 201, 84 L.Ed. 196 (1939), Palmer v. Hoffman, 318 U.S. 109, 63 S.Ct. 477, 87 L.Ed. 645 (1943), and Dick v. New York Life Ins. Co., 359 U.S. 437, 79 S.Ct. 921, 3 L.Ed.2d 935 (1959). They involved burden of proof, respectively, as to status as bona fide purchaser, contributory negligence, and nonaccidental death (suicide) of an insured. In each instance the state rule was held to be applicable. It does not follow, however, that all presumptions in diversity cases are governed by state law. In each case cited, the burden of proof question had to do with a substantive element of the claim or defense. Application of the state law is called for only when the presumption operates upon such an element. Accordingly the rule does not apply state law when the presumption operates upon a lesser aspect of the case, i.e. "tactical" presumptions.

The situations in which the state law is applied have been tagged for convenience in the preceding discussion as "diversity cases." The designation is not a completely accurate one since Erie applies to any claim or issue having its source in state law, regardless of the basis of federal jurisdiction, and does not apply to a federal claim or issue, even though jurisdiction is based on diversity. Vestal, Erie R.R. v. Tompkins: A Projection, 48 Iowa L.Rev. 248, 257 (1963); Hart and Wechsler, The Federal Courts and the Federal System, 697 (1953); 1A Moore, Federal Practice ¶ 0.305[3] (2d ed. 1965); Wright, Federal Courts, 217-218 (1963). Hence the rule employs, as appropriately descriptive, the phrase "as to which state law supplies the rule of decision." See A.L.I. Study of the Division of Jurisdiction Between State and Federal Courts, § 2344(c), p. 40, P.F.D. No. 1 (1965).

ARTICLE IV. RELEVANCY AND ITS LIMITS

Rule 401. Definition of "Relevant Evidence"

"Relevant evidence" means evidence having any tendency to make the existence of any fact that is of consequence to the determination of the action more probable or less probable than it would be without the evidence.

ADVISORY COMMITTEE NOTES

1972 Proposed Rules

Problems of relevancy call for an answer to the question whether an item of evidence, when tested by the processes of legal reasoning, possesses sufficient probative value to justify receiving it in evidence. Thus, assessment of the probative value of evidence that a person purchased a revolver shortly prior to a fatal shooting with which he is charged is a matter of analysis and reasoning.

The variety of relevancy problems is coextensive with the ingenuity of counsel in using circumstantial evidence as a means of proof. An enormous number of cases fall in no set pattern, and this rule is designed as a guide for handling them. On the other hand, some situations recur with sufficient frequency to create patterns susceptible of treatment by specific rules. Rule 404 and those following it are of that variety; they also serve as illustrations of the application of the present rule as limited by the exclusionary principles of Rule 403.

Passing mention should be made of so-called "conditional" relevancy. Morgan, Basic Problems of Evidence 45-46 (1962). In this situation, probative value depends not only upon satisfying the basic requirement of relevancy as described above but also upon the existence of some matter of fact. For example, if evidence of a spoken statement is relied upon to prove notice, probative value is lacking unless the person sought to be charged heard the statement. The problem is one of fact, and the only rules needed are for the purpose of determining the respective functions of judge and jury. See Rules 104(b) and 901. The discussion which follows in the present note is concerned with relevancy generally, not with any particular problem of conditional relevancy.

Relevancy is not an inherent characteristic of any item of evidence but exists only as a relation between an item of evidence and a matter properly provable in the case. Does the item of evidence tend to prove the matter sought to be proved? Whether the relationship exists depends upon principles evolved by experience or science, applied logically to the situation at hand. James, Relevancy, Probability and the Law, 29 Calif.L.Rev. 689, 696, n. 15 (1941), in Selected Writings on Evidence and Trial 610, 615, n. 15 (Fryer ed. 1957). The rule summarizes this relationship as a "tendency to make the existence" of the fact to be proved "more probable or less probable." Compare Uniform Rule 1(2) which states the crux of relevancy as "a tendency in reason," thus perhaps emphasizing unduly the logical process and ignoring the need to draw upon experience or science to validate the general principle upon which relevancy in a particular situation depends.

The standard of probability under the rule is "more * * * probable than it would be without the evidence." Any more stringent requirement is unworkable and unrealistic. As McCormick § 152, p. 317, says, "A brick is not a wall," or, as Falknor, Extrinsic Policies Affecting Admissibility, 10 Rutgers L.Rev. 574, 576

(1956), quotes Professor McBaine, " * * * [I]t is not to be supposed that every witness can make a home run." Dealing with probability in the language of the rule has the added virtue of avoiding confusion between questions of admissibility and questions of the sufficiency of the evidence.

The rule uses the phrase "fact that is of consequence to the determination of the action" to describe the kind of fact to which proof may properly be directed. The language is that of California Evidence Code § 210; it has the advantage of avoiding the loosely used and ambiguous word "material." Tentative Recommendation and a Study Relating to the Uniform Rules of Evidence (Art. I. General Provisions), Cal.Law Revision Comm'n, Rep., Rec. & Studies, 10-11 (1964). The fact to be proved may be ultimate, intermediate, or evidentiary; it matters not, so long as it is of consequence in the determination of the action. Cf. Uniform Rule 1(2) which requires that the evidence relate to a "material" fact.

The fact to which the evidence is directed need not be in dispute. While situations will arise which call for the exclusion of evidence offered to prove a point conceded by the opponent, the ruling should be made on the basis of such considerations as waste of time and undue prejudice (see Rule 403), rather than under any general requirement that evidence is admissible only if directed to matters in dispute. Evidence which is essentially background in nature can scarcely be said to involve disputed matter, yet it is universally offered and admitted as an aid to understanding. Charts, photographs, views of real estate, murder weapons, and many other items of evidence fall in this category. A rule limiting admissibility to evidence directed to a controversial point would invite the exclusion of this helpful evidence, or at least the raising of endless questions over its admission. Cf. California Evidence Code § 210, defining relevant evidence in terms of tendency to prove a disputed fact.

Rule 402. Relevant Evidence Generally Admissible; Irrelevant Evidence Inadmissible

All relevant evidence is admissible, except as otherwise provided by the Constitution of the United States, by Act of Congress, by these rules, or by other rules prescribed by the Supreme Court pursuant to statutory authority. Evidence which is not relevant is not admissible.

ADVISORY COMMITTEE NOTES

1972 Proposed Rules
The provisions that all relevant evidence is admissible, with certain exceptions, and that evidence which is not relevant is not admissible are "a presupposition involved in the very conception of a rational system of evidence." Thayer, Pre-

liminary Treatise on Evidence 264 (1898). They constitute the foundation upon which the structure of admission and exclusion rests. For similar provisions see California Evidence Code §§ 350, 351. Provisions that all relevant evidence is admissible are found in Uniform Rule 7(f); Kansas Code of Civil Procedure § 60-407(f); and New Jersey Evidence Rule 7(f); but the exclusion of evidence which is not relevant is left to implication.

Not all relevant evidence is admissible. The exclusion of relevant evidence occurs in a variety of situations and may be called for by these rules, by the Rules of Civil and Criminal Procedure, by Bankruptcy Rules, by Act of Congress, or by constitutional considerations.

Succeeding rules in the present article, in response to the demands of particular policies, require the exclusion of evidence despite its relevancy. In addition, Article V recognizes a number of privileges; Article VI imposes limitations upon witnesses and the manner of dealing with them; Article VII specifies requirements with respect to opinions and expert testimony; Article VIII excludes hearsay not falling within an exception; Article IX spells out the handling of authentication and identification; and Article X restricts the manner of proving the contents of writings and recordings.

The Rules of Civil and Criminal Procedure in some instances require the exclusion of relevant evidence. For example, Rules 30(b) and 32(a)(3) of the Rules of Civil Procedure, by imposing requirements of notice and unavailability of the deponent, place limits on the use of relevant depositions. Similarly, Rule 15 of the Rules of Criminal Procedure restricts the use of depositions in criminal cases, even though relevant. And the effective enforcement of the command, originally statutory and now found in Rule 5(a) of the Rules of Criminal Procedure, that an arrested person be taken without unnecessary delay before a commissioner or other similar officer is held to require the exclusion of statements elicited during detention in violation thereof. Mallory v. United States, 354 U.S. 449, 77 S.Ct. 1356, 1 L.Ed.2d 1479 (1957); 18 U.S.C. § 3501(c).

While congressional enactments in the field of evidence have generally tended to expand admissibility beyond the scope of the common law rules, in some particular situations they have restricted the admissibility of relevant evidence. Most of this legislation has consisted of the formulation of a privilege or of a prohibition against disclosure. 8 U.S.C. § 1202(f), records of refusal of visas or permits to enter United States confidential, subject to discretion of Secretary of State to make available to court upon certification of need; 10 U.S.C. § 3693, replacement certificate of honorable discharge from Army not admissible in evidence; 10 U.S.C. § 8693, same as to Air Force; 11 U.S.C. § 25(a)(10), testimony given by bankrupt on his examination not admissible in criminal proceedings against him, except that given in hearing upon objection to discharge; 11 U.S.C. § 205(a), railroad reorganization petition, if dismissed, not admissible in evidence; 11 U.S.C. § 403(a), list of creditors filed with municipal composition plan not an admission; 13 U.S.C. § 9(a), census information confidential, retained copies of reports privileged; 47 U.S.C. § 605, interception and divulgence of wire or radio communications prohibited unless authorized by sender. These statutory provisions would remain undisturbed by the rules.

The rule recognizes but makes no attempt to spell out the constitutional considerations which impose basic limitations upon the admissibility of relevant evidence. Examples are evidence obtained by unlawful search and seizure. Weeks v. United States, 232 U.S. 383, 34 S.Ct. 341, 58 L.Ed. 652 (1914); Katz v. United States, 389 U.S. 347, 88 S.Ct. 507, 19 L.Ed.2d 576 (1967); incriminating statement elicited from an accused in violation of right to counsel. Massiah v. United States, 377 U.S. 201, 84 S.Ct. 1199, 12 L.Ed.2d 246 (1964).

1974 Enactment
Rule 402 as submitted to the Congress contained the phrase "or by other rules adopted by the Supreme Court". To accommodate the view that the Congress should not appear to acquiesce in the Court's judgment that it has authority under the existing Rules Enabling Acts to promulgate Rules of Evidence, the Committee amended the above phrase to read "or by other rules prescribed by the Supreme Court pursuant to statutory authority" in this and other Rules where the reference appears. House Report No. 93-650.

> ### Rule 403. Exclusion of Relevant Evidence on Grounds of Prejudice, Confusion, or Waste of Time
>
> Although relevant, evidence may be excluded if its probative value is substantially outweighed by the danger of unfair prejudice, confusion of the issues, or misleading the jury, or by considerations of undue delay, waste of time, or needless presentation of cumulative evidence.

ADVISORY COMMITTEE NOTES

1972 Proposed Rules
The case law recognizes that certain circumstances call for the exclusion of evidence which is of unquestioned relevance. These circumstances entail risks which range all the way from inducing decision on a purely emotional basis, at one extreme, to nothing more harmful than merely wasting time, at the other extreme. Situations in this area call for balancing the probative value of and need for the evidence against the harm likely to result from its admission. Slough, Relevancy Unraveled, 5 Kan.L.Rev. 1, 12-15 (1956); Trautman, Logical or Legal Relevancy--A Conflict in Theory, 5 Van.L.Rev. 385, 392 (1952); McCormick § 152, pp. 319-321. The

rules which follow in this Article are concrete applications evolved for particular situations. However, they reflect the policies underlying the present rule, which is designed as a guide for the handling of situations for which no specific rules have been formulated.

Exclusion for risk of unfair prejudice, confusion of issues, misleading the jury, or waste of time, all find ample support in the authorities. "Unfair prejudice" within its context means an undue tendency to suggest decision on an improper basis, commonly, though not necessarily, an emotional one.

The rule does not enumerate surprise as a ground for exclusion, in this respect following Wigmore's view of the common law. 6 Wigmore § 1849. Cf. McCormick § 152, p. 320, n. 29, listing unfair surprise as a ground for exclusion but stating that it is usually "coupled with the danger of prejudice and confusion of issues." While Uniform Rule 45 incorporates surprise as a ground and is followed in Kansas Code of Civil Procedure § 60-445, surprise is not included in California Evidence Code § 352 or New Jersey Rule 4, though both the latter otherwise substantially embody Uniform Rule 45. While it can scarcely be doubted that claims of unfair surprise may still be justified despite procedural requirements of notice and instrumentalities of discovery, the granting of a continuance is a more appropriate remedy than exclusion of the evidence. Tentative Recommendation and a Study Relating to the Uniform Rules of Evidence (Art. VI. Extrinsic Policies Affecting Admissibility), Cal.Law Revision Comm'n, Rep., Rec. & Studies, 612 (1964). Moreover, the impact of a rule excluding evidence on the ground of surprise would be difficult to estimate.

In reaching a decision whether to exclude on grounds of unfair prejudice, consideration should be given to the probable effectiveness or lack of effectiveness of a limiting instruction. See Rule 106 [now 105] and Advisory Committee's Note thereunder. The availability of other means of proof may also be an appropriate factor.

Rule 404. Character Evidence Not Admissible To Prove Conduct; Exceptions; Other Crimes

(a) Character evidence generally.--Evidence of a person's character or a trait of character is not admissible for the purpose of proving action in conformity therewith on a particular occasion, except:

(1) Character of accused.--In a criminal case, evidence of a pertinent trait of character offered by an accused, or by the prosecution to rebut the same, or if evidence of a trait of character of the alleged victim of the crime is offered by

an accused and admitted under Rule 404(a)(2), evidence of the same trait of character of the accused offered by the prosecution;

(2) Character of alleged victim.--In a criminal case, and subject to the limitations imposed by Rule 412, evidence of a pertinent trait of character of the alleged victim of the crime offered by an accused, or by the prosecution to rebut the same, or evidence of a character trait of peacefulness of the alleged victim offered by the prosecution in a homicide case to rebut evidence that the alleged victim was the first aggressor;

(3) Character of witness.--Evidence of the character of a witness, as provided in Rules 607, 608, and 609.

(b) Other Crimes, Wrongs, or Acts.--Evidence of other crimes, wrongs, or acts is not admissible to prove the character of a person in order to show action in conformity therewith. It may, however, be admissible for other purposes, such as proof of motive, opportunity, intent, preparation, plan, knowledge, identity, or absence of mistake or accident, provided that upon request by the accused, the prosecution in a criminal case shall provide reasonable notice in advance of trial, or during trial if the court excuses pretrial notice on good cause shown, of the general nature of any such evidence it intends to introduce at trial.

ADVISORY COMMITTEE NOTES

1972 Proposed Rules

Note to Subdivision (a). This subdivision deals with the basic question whether character evidence should be admitted. Once the admissibility of character evidence in some form is established under this rule, reference must then be made to Rule 405, which follows, in order to determine the appropriate method of proof. If the character is that of a witness, see Rules 608 and 610 for methods of proof.

Character questions arise in two fundamentally different ways. (1) Character may itself be an element of a crime, claim, or defense. A situation of this kind is commonly referred to as "character in issue." Illustrations are: the chastity of the victim under a statute specifying her chastity as an element of the crime of seduction, or the competency of the driver in an action for negligently entrusting a motor vehicle to an incompetent driver. No problem of the general relevancy of character evidence is involved, and the present rule therefore has no provision on the subject. The only question relates to allowable methods of proof, as to which see Rule 405, immediately following. (2) Character evidence is susceptible of being used for the purpose of suggesting an inference that the person acted on the occasion in question consistently with his character. This use of character is often described as "circumstantial." Illustrations are: evidence of a violent disposition to prove that the person was the aggressor in an affray, or evidence of honesty in disproof of a charge of theft. This circumstantial use of character evidence raises questions of relevancy as well as questions of allowable methods of proof.

In most jurisdictions today, the circumstantial use of character is rejected but with important exceptions: (1) an accused may introduce pertinent evidence of good character (often misleadingly described as "putting his character in issue"), in which event the prosecution may rebut with evidence of bad character; (2) an accused may introduce pertinent evidence of the character of the victim, as in support of a claim of self-defense to a charge of homicide or consent in a case of rape, and the prosecution may introduce similar evidence in rebuttal of the character evidence, or, in a homicide case, to rebut a claim that deceased was the first aggressor, however proved; and (3) the character of a witness may be gone into as bearing on his credibility. McCormick §§ 155-161. This pattern is incorporated in the rule. While its basis lies more in history and experience than in logic an underlying justification can fairly be found in terms of the relative presence and absence of prejudice in the various situations. Falknor, Extrinsic Policies Affecting Admissibility, 10 Rutgers L.Rev. 574, 584 (1956); McCormick § 157. In any event, the criminal rule is so deeply imbedded in our jurisprudence as to assume almost constitutional proportions and to override doubts of the basic relevancy of the evidence.

The limitation to pertinent traits of character, rather than character generally, in paragraphs (1) and (2) is in accordance with the prevailing view. McCormick § 158, p. 334. A similar provision in Rule 608, to which reference is made in paragraph (3), limits character evidence respecting witnesses to the trait of truthfulness or untruthfulness.

The argument is made that circumstantial use of character ought to be allowed in civil cases to the same extent as in criminal cases, i.e. evidence of good (non-prejudicial) character would be admissible in the first instance, subject to rebuttal by evidence of bad character. Falknor, Extrinsic Policies Affecting Admissibility, 10 Rutgers L.Rev. 574, 581-583 (1956); Tentative Recommendation and a Study Relating to the Uniform Rules of Evidence (Art. VI. Extrinsic Policies Affecting Admissibility), Cal.Law Revision Comm'n, Rep., Rec. & Studies, 657-658 (1964). Uniform Rule 47 goes farther, in that it assumes that character evidence in general satisfies the conditions of relevancy, except as provided in Uniform Rule 48. The difficulty with expanding the use of character evidence in civil cases is set forth by the California Law Revision Commission in its ultimate rejection of Uniform Rule 47, id., 615:

"Character evidence is of slight probative value and may be very prejudicial. It tends to distract the trier of fact from the main question of what actually happened on the particular occasion. It subtly permits the trier of fact to reward the good man and to punish the bad man because of their respective characters despite what the evidence in the case shows actually happened."

Much of the force of the position of those favoring greater use of character evidence in civil cases is dissipated by their support of Uniform Rule 48 which excludes the evidence in negligence cases, where it could be expected to achieve its maximum usefulness. Moreover, expanding concepts of "character," which seem of necessity to extend into such areas as psychiatric evaluation and psychological testing, coupled with expanded admissibility, would open up such vistas of mental examinations as caused the Court concern in Schlagenhauf v. Holder, 379 U.S. 104, 85 S.Ct. 234, 13 L.Ed.2d 152 (1964). It is believed that those espousing change have not met the burden of persuasion.

Note to Subdivision (b). Subdivision (b) deals with a specialized but important application of the general rule excluding circumstantial use of character evidence. Consistently with that rule, evidence of other crimes, wrongs, or acts is not admissible to prove character as a basis for suggesting the inference that conduct on a particular occasion was in conformity with it. However, the evidence may be offered for another purpose, such as proof of motive, opportunity, and so on, which does not fall within the prohibition. In this situation the rule does not require that the evidence be excluded. No mechanical solution is offered. The determination must be made whether the danger of undue prejudice outweighs the probative value of the evidence in view of the availability of other means of proof and other facts appropriate for making decision of this kind under Rule 403. Slough and Knightly, Other Vices, Other Crimes, 41 Iowa L.Rev. 325 (1956).

1974 Enactment
Note to Subdivision (b). The second sentence of Rule 404(b) as submitted to the Congress began with the words "This subdivision does not exclude the evidence when offered". The Committee amended this language to read "It may, however, be admissible", the words used in the 1971 Advisory Committee draft, on the ground that this formulation properly placed greater emphasis on admissibility than did the final Court version. House Report No. 93-650.

Note to Subdivision (b). This rule provides that evidence of other crimes, wrongs, or acts is not admissible to prove character but may be admissible for other specified purposes such as proof of motive.

Although your committee sees no necessity in amending the rule itself, it anticipates that the use of the discretionary word "may" with respect to the admissibility of evidence of crimes, wrongs, or acts is not intended to confer any arbitrary discretion on the trial judge. Rather, it is anticipated that with respect to permissible uses for such evidence, the trial judge may exclude it only on the basis of those considerations set forth in Rule 403, i.e., prejudice, confusion or waste of time. Senate Report No. 93-1277.

1987 Amendments
The amendments are technical. No substantive change is intended.

1991 Amendments
Rule 404(b) has emerged as one of the most cited Rules in the Rules of Evidence. And in many criminal cases evidence of an accused's extrinsic acts is viewed as an important asset in the prosecution's case against an accused. Although there are a few reported decisions on use of such evidence by the defense, see, e.g., United States v. McClure, 546 F.2d 670 (5th Cir.1977) (acts of informant offered in entrapment defense), the overwhelming number of cases involve introduction of that evidence by the prosecution.

The amendment to Rule 404(b) adds a pretrial notice requirement in criminal cases and is intended to reduce surprise and promote early resolution on the issue of admissibility. The notice requirement thus places Rule 404(b) in the mainstream with notice and disclosure provisions in other rules of evidence. See, e.g., Rule 412 (written motion of intent to offer evidence under rule), Rule 609 (written notice of intent to offer conviction older than 10 years), Rule 803(24) and 804(b)(5) (notice of intent to use residual hearsay exceptions).

The Rule expects that counsel for both the defense and the prosecution will submit the necessary request and information in a reasonable and timely fashion. Other than requiring pretrial notice, no specific time limits are stated in recognition that what constitutes a reasonable request or disclosure will depend largely on the circumstances of each case. Compare Fla.Stat.Ann. § 90.404(2)(b) (notice must be given at least 10 days before trial) with Tex.R.Evid. 404(b) (no time limit).

Likewise, no specific form of notice is required. The Committee considered and rejected a requirement that the notice satisfy the particularity requirements normally required of language used in a charging instrument. Cf. Fla.Stat.Ann. § 90.404(2)(b) (written disclosure must describe uncharged misconduct with particularity required of an indictment or information). Instead, the Committee opted for a generalized notice provision which requires the prosecution to apprise the defense of the general nature of the evidence of extrinsic acts. The Committee does not intend that the amendment will supercede other rules of admissibility or disclosure, such as the Jencks Act, 18 U.S.C. § 3500, et. seq. nor require the prosecution to disclose directly or indirectly the names and addresses of its witnesses, something it is currently not required to do under Federal Rule of Criminal Procedure 16.

The amendment requires the prosecution to provide notice, regardless of how it intends to use the extrinsic act evidence at trial, i.e., during its case-in-chief, for impeachment, or for possible rebuttal. The court in its discretion may, under the facts, decide that the particular request or notice was not reasonable, either because of the lack of timeliness or completeness. Because the notice requirement serves as condition precedent to admissibility of 404(b) evidence, the offered evidence is inadmissible if the court decides that the notice requirement has not been met.

Nothing in the amendment precludes the court from requiring the government to provide it with an opportunity to rule in limine on 404(b) evidence before it is offered or even mentioned during trial. When ruling in limine, the court may require the government to disclose to it the specifics of such evidence which the court must consider in determining admissibility.

The amendment does not extend to evidence of acts which are "intrinsic" to the charged offense, see United States v. Williams, 900 F.2d 823 (5th Cir.1990) (noting distinction between 404(b) evidence and intrinsic offense evidence). Nor is the amendment intended to redefine what evidence would otherwise be admissible under Rule 404(b). Finally, the Committee does not intend through the amendment to affect the role of the court and the jury in considering such evidence. See Huddleston v. United States, 485 U.S. 681, 108 S.Ct. 1496 (1988).

2000 Amendments
Rule 404(a)(1) has been amended to provide that when the accused attacks the character of an alleged victim under subdivision (a)(2) of this Rule, the door is opened to an attack on the same character trait of the accused. Current law does not allow the government to introduce negative character evidence as to the accused unless the accused introduces evidence of good character. See, e.g., United States v. Fountain, 768 F.2d 790 (7th Cir. 1985) (when the accused offers proof of self-defense, this permits proof of the alleged victim's character trait for peacefulness, but it does not permit proof of the accused's character trait for violence).

The amendment makes clear that the accused cannot attack the alleged victim's character and yet remain shielded from the disclosure of equally relevant evidence concerning the same character trait of the accused. For example, in a murder case with a claim of self-defense, the accused, to bolster this defense, might offer evidence of the alleged victim's violent disposition. If the government has evidence that the accused has a violent character, but is not allowed to offer this evidence as part of its rebuttal, the jury has only part of the information it needs for an informed assessment of the probabilities as to who was the initial aggressor. This may be the case even if evidence of the accused's prior violent acts is admitted under Rule 404(b), because such evidence can be admitted only for limited purposes and not to show action in conformity with the accused's character on a specific occasion. Thus, the amendment is designed to permit a more balanced presentation of character evidence when an accused chooses to attack the character of the alleged victim.

The amendment does not affect the admissibility of evidence of specific acts of uncharged misconduct offered for a purpose other than proving character under Rule 404(b). Nor does it affect the standards for proof of character by evidence of other sexual behavior or sexual offenses under Rules 412-415. By its placement in Rule 404(a)(1), the amendment covers only proof of character by way of reputation or opinion.

The amendment does not permit proof of the accused's character if the accused merely uses character evidence for a purpose other than to prove the alleged victim's propensity to act in a certain way. See United States v. Burks, 470 F.2d 432, 434-5 (D.C.Cir. 1972) (evidence of the alleged victim's violent character, when known by the accused, was admissible "on the issue of whether or not the defendant reasonably feared he was in danger of imminent great bodily harm"). Finally, the amendment does not permit proof of the accused's character when the accused attacks the alleged victim's character as a witness under Rule 608 or 609.

The term "alleged" is inserted before each reference to "victim" in the Rule, in order to provide consistency with Evidence Rule 412.

GAP Report--Proposed Amendment to Rule 404(a)

The Committee made the following changes to the published draft of the proposed amendment to Evidence Rule 404(a):

1. The term "a pertinent trait of character" was changed to "the same trait of character," in order to limit the scope of the government's rebuttal. The Committee Note was revised to accord with this change in the text.

2. The word "alleged" was added before each reference in the Rule to a "victim" in order to provide consistency with Evidence Rule 412. The Committee Note was amended to accord with this change in the text.

3. The Committee Note was amended to clarify that rebuttal is not permitted under this Rule if the accused proffers evidence of the alleged victim's character for a purpose other than to prove the alleged victim's propensity to act in a certain manner.

2006 Amendments
The Rule has been amended to clarify that in a civil case evidence of a person's character is never admissible to prove that the person acted in conformity with the

character trait. The amendment resolves the dispute in the case law over whether the exceptions in subdivisions (a)(1) and (2) permit the circumstantial use of character evidence in civil cases. Compare Carson v. Polley, 689 F.2d 562, 576 (5th Cir. 1982) ("when a central issue in a case is close to one of a criminal nature, the exceptions to the Rule 404(a) ban on character evidence may be invoked"), with SEC v. Towers Financial Corp., 966 F.Supp. 203 (S.D.N.Y. 1997) (relying on the terms "accused" and "prosecution" in Rule 404(a) to conclude that the exceptions in subdivisions (a)(1) and (2) are inapplicable in civil cases). The amendment is consistent with the original intent of the Rule, which was to prohibit the circumstantial use of character evidence in civil cases, even where closely related to criminal charges. See Ginter v. Northwestern Mut. Life Ins. Co., 576 F.Supp. 627, 629-30 (D. Ky.1984) ("It seems beyond peradventure of doubt that the drafters of F.R.Evi. 404(a) explicitly intended that all character evidence, except where 'character is at issue' was to be excluded" in civil cases).

The circumstantial use of character evidence is generally discouraged because it carries serious risks of prejudice, confusion and delay. See Michelson v. United States, 335 U.S. 469, 476 (1948) ("The overriding policy of excluding such evidence, despite its admitted probative value, is the practical experience that its disallowance tends to prevent confusion of issues, unfair surprise and undue prejudice."). In criminal cases, the so-called "mercy rule" permits a criminal defendant to introduce evidence of pertinent character traits of the defendant and the victim. But that is because the accused, whose liberty is at stake, may need "a counterweight against the strong investigative and prosecutorial resources of the government." C. Mueller & L. Kirkpatrick, Evidence: Practice Under the Rules, pp. 264-5 (2d ed. 1999). See also Richard Uviller, Evidence of Character to Prove Conduct: Illusion, Illogic, and Injustice in the Courtroom, 130 U.Pa.L.Rev. 845, 855 (1982) (the rule prohibiting circumstantial use of character evidence "was relaxed to allow the criminal defendant with so much at stake and so little available in the way of conventional proof to have special dispensation to tell the factfinder just what sort of person he really is"). Those concerns do not apply to parties in civil cases.

The amendment also clarifies that evidence otherwise admissible under Rule 404(a) (2) may nonetheless be excluded in a criminal case involving sexual misconduct. In such a case, the admissibility of evidence of the victim's sexual behavior and predisposition is governed by the more stringent provisions of Rule 412.

Nothing in the amendment is intended to affect the scope of Rule 404(b). While Rule 404(b) refers to the "accused," the "prosecution," and a "criminal case," it does so only in the context of a notice requirement. The admissibility standards of Rule 404(b) remain fully applicable to both civil and criminal cases.

Rule 405. Methods of Proving Character

(a) Reputation or opinion. In all cases in which evidence of character or a trait of character of a person is admissible, proof may be made by testimony as to reputation or by testimony in the form of an opinion. On cross-examination, inquiry is allowable into relevant specific instances of conduct.

(b) Specific instances of conduct. In cases in which character or a trait of character of a person is an essential element of a charge, claim, or defense, proof may also be made of specific instances of that person's conduct.

ADVISORY COMMITTEE NOTES

1972 Proposed Rules
The rule deals only with allowable methods of proving character, not with the admissibility of character evidence, which is covered in Rule 404.

Of the three methods of proving character provided by the rule, evidence of specific instances of conduct is the most convincing. At the same time it possesses the greatest capacity to arouse prejudice, to confuse, to surprise, and to consume time. Consequently the rule confines the use of evidence of this kind to cases in which character is, in the strict sense, in issue and hence deserving of a searching inquiry. When character is used circumstantially and hence occupies a lesser status in the case, proof may be only by reputation and opinion. These latter methods are also available when character is in issue. This treatment is, with respect to specific instances of conduct and reputation, conventional contemporary common law doctrine. McCormick § 153.

In recognizing opinion as a means of proving character, the rule departs from usual contemporary practice in favor of that of an earlier day. See 7 Wigmore § 1986, pointing out that the earlier practice permitted opinion and arguing strongly for evidence based on personal knowledge and belief as contrasted with "the secondhand, irresponsible product of multiplied guesses and gossip which we term 'reputation'." It seems likely that the persistence of reputation evidence is due to its largely being opinion in disguise. Traditionally character has been regarded primarily in moral overtones of good and bad: chaste, peaceable, truthful, honest. Nevertheless, on occasion nonmoral considerations crop up, as in the case of the incompetent driver, and this seems bound to happen increasingly. If character is defined as the kind of person one is, then account must be taken of varying ways of arriving at the estimate. These may range from the opinion of the employer who has found the man honest to the opinion of the psychiatrist based upon examination and testing. No effective dividing line exists between character and mental capacity, and the latter traditionally has been provable by opinion.

According to the great majority of cases, on cross-examination inquiry is allowable as to whether the reputation witness has heard of particular instances of conduct pertinent to the trait in question. Michelson v. United States, 335 U.S. 469, 69 S.Ct. 213, 93 L.Ed. 168 (1948); Annot., 47 A.L.R.2d 1258. The theory is that, since the reputation witness relates what he has heard, the inquiry tends to shed light on the accuracy of his hearing and reporting. Accordingly, the opinion witness would be asked whether he knew, as well as whether he had heard. The fact is, of course, that these distinctions are of slight if any practical significance, and the second sentence of subdivision (a) eliminates them as a factor in formulating questions. This recognition of the propriety of inquiring into specific instances of conduct does not circumscribe inquiry otherwise into the bases of opinion and reputation testimony.

The express allowance of inquiry into specific instances of conduct on cross-examination in subdivision (a) and the express allowance of it as part of a case in chief when character is actually in issue in subdivision (b) contemplate that testimony of specific instances is not generally permissible on the direct examination of an ordinary opinion witness to character. Similarly as to witnesses to the character of witnesses under Rule 608(b). Opinion testimony on direct in these situations ought in general to correspond to reputation testimony as now given, i.e., be confined to the nature and extent of observation and acquaintance upon which the opinion is based. See Rule 701.

1974 Enactment
Note to Subdivision (a). Rule 405(a) as submitted proposed to change existing law by allowing evidence of character in the form of opinion as well as reputation testimony. Fearing, among other reasons, that wholesale allowance of opinion testimony might tend to turn a trial into a swearing contest between conflicting character witnesses, the Committee decided to delete from this Rule, as well as from Rule 608(a) which involves a related problem, reference to opinion testimony. House Report No. 93-650.

The Senate makes two language changes in the nature of conforming amendments. The Conference adopts the Senate amendments. House Report No. 93-1597.

1987 Amendments
The amendment is technical. No substantive change is intended.

Rule 406. Habit; Routine Practice

Evidence of the habit of a person or of the routine practice of an organization, whether corroborated or not and regardless of the presence of eyewitnesses, is relevant to prove that the conduct of the person or organization on a particular occasion was in conformity with the habit or routine practice.

ADVISORY COMMITTEE NOTES

1972 Proposed Rules
An oft-quoted paragraph, McCormick, § 162, p. 340, describes habit in terms effectively contrasting it with character:

"Character and habit are close akin. Character is a generalized description of one's disposition, or of one's disposition in respect to a general trait, such as honesty, temperance, or peacefulness. 'Habit,' in modern usage, both lay and psychological, is more specific. It describes one's regular response to a repeated specific situation. If we speak of character for care, we think of the person's tendency to act prudently in all the varying situations of life, in business, family life, in handling automobiles and in walking across the street. A habit, on the other hand, is the person's regular practice of meeting a particular kind of situation with a specific type of conduct, such as the habit of going down a particular stairway two stairs at a time, or of giving the hand-signal for a left turn, or of alighting from railway cars while they are moving. The doing of the habitual acts may become semi-automatic."

Equivalent behavior on the part of a group is designated "routine practice of an organization" in the rule.

Agreement is general that habit evidence is highly persuasive as proof of conduct on a particular occasion. Again quoting McCormick § 162, p. 341:

"Character may be thought of as the sum of one's habits though doubtless it is more than this. But unquestionably the uniformity of one's response to habit is far greater than the consistency with which one's conduct conforms to character or disposition. Even though character comes in only exceptionally as evidence of an act, surely any sensible man in investigating whether X did a particular act would be greatly helped in his inquiry by evidence as to whether he was in the habit of doing it."

When disagreement has appeared, its focus has been upon the question what constitutes habit, and the reason for this is readily apparent. The extent to which instances must be multiplied and consistency of behavior maintained in order to rise to the status of habit inevitably gives rise to differences of opinion. Lewan, Rationale of Habit Evidence, 16 Syracuse L.Rev. 39, 49 (1964). While adequacy of sampling and uniformity of response are key factors, precise standards for measuring their sufficiency for evidence purposes cannot be formulated.

The rule is consistent with prevailing views. Much evidence is excluded simply because of failure to achieve the status of habit. Thus, evidence of intemperate "habits" is generally excluded when offered as proof of drunkenness in accident cases, Annot., 46 A.L.R.2d 103, and evidence of other assaults is inadmissible to prove the instant one in a civil assault action, Annot., 66 A.L.R.2d 806. In Levin v. United States, 119 U.S.App.D.C. 156, 338 F.2d 265 (1964), testimony as to the religious "habits" of the accused, offered as tending to prove that he was at home observing the Sabbath rather than out obtaining money through larceny by trick, was held properly excluded:

"It seems apparent to us that an individual's religious practices would not be the type of activities which would lend themselves to the characterization of 'invariable regularity.' [1 Wigmore 520.] Certainly the very volitional basis of the activity raises serious questions as to its invariable nature, and hence its probative value." Id. at 272.

These rulings are not inconsistent with the trend towards admitting evidence of business transactions between one of the parties and a third person as tending to prove that he made the same bargain or proposal in the litigated situation. Slough, Relevancy Unraveled, 6 Kan.L.Rev. 38-41 (1957). Nor are they inconsistent with such cases as Whittemore v. Lockheed Aircraft Corp., 65 Cal.App.2d 737, 151 P.2d 670 (1944), upholding the admission of evidence that plaintiff's intestate had on four other occasions flown planes from defendant's factory for delivery to his employer airline, offered to prove that he was piloting rather than a guest on a plane which crashed and killed all on board while en route for delivery.

A considerable body of authority has required that evidence of the routine practice of an organization be corroborated as a condition precedent to its admission in evidence. Slough, Relevancy Unraveled, 5 Kan.L.Rev. 404, 449 (1957). This requirement is specifically rejected by the rule on the ground that it relates to the sufficiency of the evidence rather than admissibility. A similar position is taken in New Jersey Rule 49. The rule also rejects the requirement of the absence of eyewitnesses, sometimes encountered with respect to admitting habit evidence to prove freedom from contributory negligence in wrongful death cases. For comment critical of the requirements see Frank, J., in Cereste v. New York, N.H. & H.R. Co., 231 F.2d 50 (2d Cir.1956), cert. denied 351 U.S. 951, 76 S.Ct. 848, 100 L.Ed. 1475, 10 Vand. 447 (1957); McCormick § 162, p. 342. The omission of the requirement from the California Evidence Code is said to have effected its elimination. Comment, Cal.Ev.Code § 1105.

Rule 407. Subsequent Remedial Measures

When, after an injury or harm allegedly caused by an event, measures are taken that, if taken previously, would have made the injury or harm less likely to occur, evidence of the subsequent measures is not admissible to prove negligence, culpable conduct, a defect in a product, a defect in a product's design, or a need for a warning or instruction. This rule does not require

> the exclusion of evidence of subsequent measures when offered for another purpose, such as proving ownership, control, or feasibility of precautionary measures, if controverted, or impeachment.

ADVISORY COMMITTEE NOTES

1972 Proposed Rules

The rule incorporates conventional doctrine which excludes evidence of subsequent remedial measures as proof of an admission of fault. The rule rests on two grounds. (1) The conduct is not in fact an admission, since the conduct is equally consistent with injury by mere accident or through contributory negligence. Or, as Baron Bramwell put it, the rule rejects the notion that "because the world gets wiser as it gets older, therefore it was foolish before." Hart v. Lancashire & Yorkshire Ry. Co., 21 L.T.R. N.S. 261, 263 (1869). Under a liberal theory of relevancy this ground alone would not support exclusion as the inference is still a possible one. (2) The other, and more impressive, ground for exclusion rests on a social policy of encouraging people to take, or at least not discouraging them from taking, steps in furtherance of added safety. The courts have applied this principle to exclude evidence of subsequent repairs, installation of safety devices, changes in company rules, and discharge of employees, and the language of the present rule is broad enough to encompass all of them. See Falknor, Extrinsic Policies Affecting Admissibility, 10 Rutgers L.Rev. 574, 590 (1956).

The second sentence of the rule directs attention to the limitations of the rule. Exclusion is called for only when the evidence of subsequent remedial measures is offered as proof of negligence or culpable conduct. In effect it rejects the suggested inference that fault is admitted. Other purposes are, however, allowable, including ownership or control, existence of duty, and feasibility of precautionary measures, if controverted, and impeachment. 2 Wigmore § 283; Annot., 64 A.L.R.2d 1296. Two recent federal cases are illustrative. Boeing Airplane Co. v. Brown, 291 F.2d 310 (9th Cir.1961), an action against an airplane manufacturer for using an allegedly defectively designed alternator shaft which caused a plane crash, upheld the admission of evidence of subsequent design modification for the purpose of showing that design changes and safeguards were feasible. And Powers v. J.B. Michael & Co., 329 F.2d 674 (6th Cir.1964), an action against a road contractor for negligent failure to put out warning signs, sustained the admission of evidence that defendant subsequently put out signs to show that the portion of the road in question was under defendant's control. The requirement that the other purpose be controverted calls for automatic exclusion unless a genuine issue be present and allows the opposing party to lay the groundwork for exclusion by making an admission. Otherwise the factors of undue prejudice, confusion of issues, misleading the jury, and waste of time remain for consideration under Rule 403.

For comparable rules, see Uniform Rule 51; California Evidence Code § 1151; Kansas Code of Civil Procedure § 60-451; New Jersey Evidence Rule 51.

1997 Amendments
The amendment to Rule 407 makes two changes in the rule. First, the words "an injury or harm allegedly caused by" were added to clarify that the rule applies only to changes made after the occurrence that produced the damages giving rise to the action. Evidence of measures taken by the defendant prior to the "event" causing "injury or harm" do not fall within the exclusionary scope of Rule 407 even if they occurred after the manufacture or design of the product. See Chase v. General Motors Corp., 856 F.2d 17, 21-22 (4th Cir. 1988).

Second, Rule 407 has been amended to provide that evidence of subsequent remedial measures may not be used to prove "a defect in a product or its design, or that a warning or instruction should have accompanied a product." This amendment adopts the view of a majority of the circuits that have interpreted Rule 407 to apply to products liability actions. See Raymond v. Raymond Corp., 938 F.2d 1518, 1522 (1st Cir. 1991); In re Joint Eastern District and Southern District Asbestos Litigation v. Armstrong World Industries, Inc., 995 F.2d 343 (2d Cir. 1993); Cann v. Ford Motor Co., 658 F.2d 54, 60 (2d Cir. 1981), cert. denied, 456 U.S. 960 (1982); Kelly v. Crown Equipment Co., 970 F.2d 1273, 1275 (3d Cir. 1992); Werner v. Upjohn, Inc., 628 F.2d 848 (4th Cir. 1980); cert. denied, 449 U.S. 1080 (1981); Grenada Steel Industries, Inc. v. Alabama Oxygen Co., Inc., 695 F.2d 883 (5th Cir. 1983); Bauman v. Volkswagenwerk Aktiengesellschaft, 621 F.2d 230, 232 (6th Cir. 1980); Flaminio v. Honda Motor Company, Ltd., 733 F.2d 463, 469 (7th Cir. 1984); Gauthier v. AMF, Inc., 788 F.2d 634, 636-37 (9th Cir. 1986).

Although this amendment adopts a uniform federal rule, it should be noted that evidence of subsequent remedial measures may be admissible pursuant to the second sentence of Rule 407. Evidence of subsequent measures that is not barred by Rule 407 may still be subject to exclusion on Rule 403 grounds when the dangers of prejudice or confusion substantially outweigh the probative value of the evidence.

ADVISORY COMMITTEE NOTES

Rule 408. Compromise and Offers to Compromise

(a) Prohibited uses.--Evidence of the following is not admissible on behalf of any party, when offered to prove liability for, invalidity of, or amount of a claim that was disputed as to validity or amount, or to impeach through a prior inconsistent statement or contradiction:

(1) furnishing or offering or promising to furnish--or accepting or offering or promising to accept--a valuable consideration in compromising or attempting to compromise the claim; and

(2) conduct or statements made in compromise negotiations regarding the claim, except when offered in a criminal case and the negotiations related to a claim by a public office or agency in the exercise of regulatory, investigative, or enforcement authority.

(b) Permitted uses.--This rule does not require exclusion if the evidence is offered for purposes not prohibited by subdivision (a). Examples of permissible purposes include proving a witness's bias or prejudice; negating a contention of undue delay; and proving an effort to obstruct a criminal investigation or prosecution.

1972 Proposed Rules

As a matter of general agreement, evidence of an offer to compromise a claim is not receivable in evidence as an admission of, as the case may be, the validity or invalidity of the claim. As with evidence of subsequent remedial measures, dealt with in Rule 407, exclusion may be based on two grounds. (1) The evidence is irrelevant, since the offer may be motivated by a desire for peace rather than from any concession of weakness of position. The validity of this position will vary as the amount of the offer varies in relation to the size of the claim and may also be influenced by other circumstances. (2) A more consistently impressive ground is promotion of the public policy favoring the compromise and settlement of disputes. McCormick §§ 76, 251. While the rule is ordinarily phrased in terms of offers of compromise, it is apparent that a similar attitude must be taken with respect to completed compromises when offered against a party thereto. This latter situation will not, of course, ordinarily occur except when a party to the present litigation has compromised with a third person.

The same policy underlies the provision of Rule 68 of the Federal Rules of Civil Procedure that evidence of an unaccepted offer of judgment is not admissible except in a proceeding to determine costs.

The practical value of the common law rule has been greatly diminished by its inapplicability to admissions of fact, even though made in the course of compromise negotiations, unless hypothetical, stated to be "without prejudice," or so connected with the offer as to be inseparable from it. McCormick § 251, pp. 540-541. An inevitable effect is to inhibit freedom of communication with respect to compromise, even among lawyers. Another effect is the generation of controversy over whether a given statement falls within or without the protected area. These considerations account for the expansion of the rule herewith to include evidence of conduct or statements made in compromise negotiations, as well as the offer or completed compromise itself. For similar provisions see California Evidence Code §§ 1152, 1154.

The policy considerations which underlie the rule do not come into play when the effort is to induce a creditor to settle an admittedly due amount for a lesser sum. McCormick § 251, p. 540. Hence the rule requires that the claim be disputed as to either validity or amount.

The final sentence of the rule serves to point out some limitations upon its applicability. Since the rule excludes only when the purpose is proving the validity or invalidity of the claim or its amount, an offer for another purpose is not within the rule. The illustrative situations mentioned in the rule are supported by the authorities. As to proving bias or prejudice of a witness, see Annot., 161 A.L.R. 395, contra, Fenberg v. Rosenthal, 348 Ill.App. 510, 109 N.E.2d 402 (1952), and negativing a contention of lack of due diligence in presenting a claim, 4 Wigmore § 1061. An effort to "buy off" the prosecution or a prosecuting witness in a criminal case is not within the policy of the rule of exclusion. McCormick § 251, p. 542.

For other rules of similar import, see Uniform Rules 52 and 53; California Evidence Code §§ 1152, 1154; Kansas Code of Civil Procedure §§ 60-452, 60-453; New Jersey Evidence Rules 52 and 53.

1974 Enactment
Under existing federal law evidence of conduct and statements made in compromise negotiations is admissible in subsequent litigation between the parties. The second sentence of Rule 408 as submitted by the Supreme Court proposed to reverse that doctrine in the interest of further promoting non-judicial settlement of disputes. Some agencies of government expressed the view that the Court formulation was likely to impede rather than assist efforts to achieve settlement of disputes. For one thing, it is not always easy to tell when compromise negotiations begin, and informal dealings end. Also, parties dealing with government agencies would be reluctant to furnish factual information at preliminary meetings; they would wait until "compromise negotiations" began and thus hopefully effect an immunity for themselves with respect to the evidence supplied. In light of these considerations, the Committee recast the Rule so that admissions of liability or opinions given during compromise negotiations continue inadmissible, but evidence of unqualified factual assertions is admissible. The latter aspect of the Rule is drafted, however, so as to preserve other possible objections to the introduction of such evidence. The Committee intends no modification of current law whereby a party may protect himself from future use of his statements by couching them in hypothetical conditional form. House Report No. 93-650.

This rule as reported makes evidence of settlement or attempted settlement of a disputed claim inadmissible when offered as an admission of liability or the amount of liability. The purpose of this rule is to encourage settlements which would be discouraged if such evidence were admissible.

Under present law, in most jurisdictions, statements of fact made during settlement negotiations, however, are excepted from this ban and are admissible. The only escape from admissibility of statements of fact made in a settlement negotiation is if the declarant or his representative expressly states that the statement is hypothetical in nature or is made without prejudice. Rule 408 as submitted by the Court reversed the traditional rule. It would have brought statements of fact within the ban and made them, as well as an offer of settlement, inadmissible.

The House amended the rule and would continue to make evidence of facts disclosed during compromise negotiations admissible. It thus reverted to the traditional rule. The House committee report states that the committee intends to preserve current law under which a party may protect himself by couching his statements in hypothetical form [See House Report No. 93-650 above]. The real impact of this amendment, however, is to deprive the rule of much of its salutary effect. The exception for factual admissions was believed by the Advisory Committee to hamper free communication between parties and thus to constitute an unjustifiable restraint upon efforts to negotiate settlements--the encouragement of which is the purpose of the rule. Further, by protecting hypothetically phrased statements, it constituted a preference for the sophisticated, and a trap for the unwary.

Three States which had adopted rules of evidence patterned after the proposed rules prescribed by the Supreme Court opted for versions of rule 408 identical with the Supreme Court draft with respect to the inadmissibility of conduct or statements made in compromise negotiations [Nev.Rev.Stats. § 48.105; N.Mex. Stats.Anno. (1973 Supp.) § 20-4-408; West's Wis.Stats.Anno. (1973 Supp.) § 904.08].

For these reasons, the committee has deleted the House amendment and restored the rule to the version submitted by the Supreme Court with one additional amendment. This amendment adds a sentence to insure that evidence, such as documents, is not rendered inadmissible merely because it is presented in the course of compromise negotiations if the evidence is otherwise discoverable. A party should not be able to immunize from admissibility documents otherwise discoverable merely by offering them in a compromise negotiation. Senate Report No. 93-1277.

The House bill provides that evidence of admissions of liability or opinions given during compromise negotiations is not admissible, but that evidence of facts disclosed during compromise negotiations is not inadmissible by virtue of having been first disclosed in the compromise negotiations. The Senate amendment provides that evidence of conduct or statements made in compromise negotiations is not admissible. The Senate amendment also provides that the rule does not require the exclusion of any evidence otherwise discoverable merely because it is presented in the course of compromise negotiations.

The House bill was drafted to meet the objection of executive agencies that under the rule as proposed by the Supreme Court, a party could present a fact during compromise negotiations and thereby prevent an opposing party from offering evidence of that fact at trial even though such evidence was obtained from independent sources. The Senate amendment expressly precludes this result.

The Conference adopts the Senate amendment. House Report No. 93-1597.

2006 Amendment
Rule 408 has been amended to settle some questions in the courts about the scope of the Rule, and to make it easier to read. First, the amendment provides that Rule 408 does not prohibit the introduction in a criminal case of statements or conduct during compromise negotiations regarding a civil dispute by a government regulatory, investigative, or enforcement agency. See, e.g., United States v. Prewitt, 34 F.3d 436, 439 (7th Cir. 1994) (admissions of fault made in compromise of a civil securities enforcement action were admissible against the accused in a subsequent criminal action for mail fraud). Where an individual makes a statement in the presence of government agents, its subsequent admission in a criminal case should not be unexpected. The individual can seek to protect against subsequent disclosure through negotiation and agreement with the civil regulator or an attorney for the government.

Statements made in compromise negotiations of a claim by a government agency may be excluded in criminal cases where the circumstances so warrant under Rule 403. For example, if an individual was unrepresented at the time the statement was made in a civil enforcement proceeding, its probative value in a subsequent criminal case may be minimal. But there is no absolute exclusion imposed by Rule 408.

In contrast, statements made during compromise negotiations of other disputed claims are not admissible in subsequent criminal litigation, when offered to prove liability for, invalidity of, or amount of those claims. When private parties enter into compromise negotiations they cannot protect against the subsequent use of statements in criminal cases by way of private ordering. The inability to guarantee protection against subsequent use could lead to parties refusing to admit fault, even if by doing so they could favorably settle the private matter. Such a chill on settlement negotiations would be contrary to the policy of Rule 408.

The amendment distinguishes statements and conduct (such as a direct admission of fault) made in compromise negotiations of a civil claim by a government agency from an offer or acceptance of a compromise of such a claim. An offer or acceptance of a compromise of any civil claim is excluded under the Rule if offered against the defendant as an admission of fault. In that case, the predicate for the evidence would be that the defendant, by compromising with the government agency, has admitted the validity and amount of the civil claim, and that this admission has sufficient probative value to be considered as evidence of guilt. But unlike a direct statement of fault, an offer or acceptance of a compromise is not very probative of the defendant's guilt. Moreover, admitting such an offer or acceptance could deter a defendant from settling a civil regulatory action, for fear of evidentiary use in a subsequent criminal action. See, e.g., Fishman, Jones on Evidence, Civil and Criminal, § 22:16 at 199, n.83 (7th ed. 2000) ("A target of a potential criminal investigation may be unwilling to settle civil claims against him if by doing so he increases the risk of prosecution and conviction.").

The amendment retains the language of the original rule that bars compromise evidence only when offered as evidence of the "validity," "invalidity," or "amount" of the disputed claim. The intent is to retain the extensive case law finding Rule 408 inapplicable when compromise evidence is offered for a purpose other than to prove the validity, invalidity, or amount of a disputed claim. See, e.g., Athey v. Farmers Ins. Exchange, 234 F.3d 357 (8th Cir. 2000) (evidence of settlement offer by insurer was properly admitted to prove insurer's bad faith); Coakley & Williams v. Structural Concrete Equip., 973 F.2d 349 (4th Cir. 1992) (evidence of settlement is not precluded by Rule 408 where offered to prove a party's intent with respect to the scope of a release); Cates v. Morgan Portable Bldg. Corp., 708 F.2d 683 (7th Cir. 1985) (Rule 408 does not bar evidence of a settlement when offered to prove a breach of the settlement agreement, as the purpose of the evidence is to prove the fact of settlement as opposed to the validity or amount of the underlying claim); Uforma/Shelby Bus. Forms, Inc. v. NLRB, 111 F.3d 1284 (6th Cir. 1997) (threats made in settlement negotiations were admissible; Rule 408 is inapplicable when the claim is based upon a wrong that is committed during the course of settlement negotiations). So for example, Rule 408 is inapplicable if offered to show that a party made fraudulent statements in order to settle a litigation.

The amendment does not affect the case law providing that Rule 408 is inapplicable when evidence of the compromise is offered to prove notice. See, e.g., United States v. Austin, 54 F.3d 394 (7th Cir. 1995) (no error to admit evidence of the defendant's settlement with the FTC, because it was offered to prove that the defendant was on notice that subsequent similar conduct was wrongful); Spell v. McDaniel, 824 F.2d 1380 (4th Cir. 1987) (in a civil rights action alleging that an officer used excessive force, a prior settlement by the City of another brutality claim was properly admitted to prove that the City was on notice of aggressive behavior by police officers).

The amendment prohibits the use of statements made in settlement negotiations when offered to impeach by prior inconsistent statement or through contradiction. Such broad impeachment would tend to swallow the exclusionary rule and would impair the public policy of promoting settlements. See McCormick on Evidence at 186 (5th ed. 1999) ("Use of statements made in compromise negotiations to impeach the testimony of a party, which is not specifically treated in Rule 408, is fraught with danger of misuse of the statements to prove liability, threatens frank interchange of information during negotiations, and generally should not be permitted."). See also EEOC v. Gear Petroleum, Inc., 948 F.2d 1542 (10th Cir.1991) (letter sent as part of settlement negotiation cannot be used to impeach defense witnesses by way of contradiction or prior inconsistent statement; such broad impeachment would undermine the policy of encouraging uninhibited settlement negotiations).

The amendment makes clear that Rule 408 excludes compromise evidence even when a party seeks to admit its own settlement offer or statements made in settlement negotiations. If a party were to reveal its own statement or offer, this could itself reveal the fact that the adversary entered into settlement negotiations. The protections of Rule 408 cannot be waived unilaterally because the Rule, by definition, protects both parties from having the fact of negotiation disclosed to the jury. Moreover, proof of statements and offers made in settlement would often have to be made through the testimony of attorneys, leading to the risks and costs of disqualification. See generally Pierce v. F.R. Tripler & Co., 955 F.2d 820, 828 (2d Cir. 1992) (settlement offers are excluded under Rule 408 even if it is the offeror who seeks to admit them; noting that the "widespread admissibility of the substance of settlement offers could bring with it a rash of motions for disqualification of a party's chosen counsel who would likely become a witness at trial").

The sentence of the Rule referring to evidence "otherwise discoverable" has been deleted as superfluous. See, e.g., Advisory Committee Note to Maine Rule of Evidence 408 (refusing to include the sentence in the Maine version of Rule 408 and noting that the sentence "seems to state what the law would be if it were omitted"); Advisory Committee Note to Wyoming Rule of Evidence 408 (refusing to include the sentence in Wyoming Rule 408 on the ground that it was "superfluous"). The intent of the sentence was to prevent a party from trying to immunize admissible information, such as a pre-existing document, through the pretense of disclosing it during compromise negotiations. See Ramada Development Co. v. Rauch, 644 F.2d 1097 (5th Cir. 1981). But even without the sentence, the Rule cannot be read to protect pre-existing information simply because it was presented to the adversary in compromise negotiations.

Rule 409. Payment of Medical and Similar Expenses

Evidence of furnishing or offering or promising to pay medical, hospital, or similar expenses occasioned by an injury is not admissible to prove liability for the injury.

ADVISORY COMMITTEE NOTES

1972 Proposed Rules

The considerations underlying this rule parallel those underlying Rules 407 and 408, which deal respectively with subsequent remedial measures and offers of compromise. As stated in Annot., 20 A.L.R.2d 291, 293:

"[G]enerally, evidence of payment of medical, hospital, or similar expenses of an injured party by the opposing party, is not admissible, the reason often given being that such payment or offer is usually made from humane impulses and not from an admission of liability, and that to hold otherwise would tend to discourage assistance to the injured person."

Contrary to Rule 408, dealing with offers of compromise, the present rule does not extend to conduct or statements not a part of the act of furnishing or offering or promising to pay. This difference in treatment arises from fundamental differences in nature. Communication is essential if compromises are to be effected, and consequently broad protection of statements is needed. This is not so in cases of payments or offers or promises to pay medical expenses, where factual statements may be expected to be incidental in nature.

For rules on the same subject, but phrased in terms of "humanitarian motives," see Uniform Rule 52; California Evidence Code § 1152; Kansas Code of Civil Procedure § 60-452; New Jersey Evidence Rule 52.

Rule 410. Inadmissibility of Pleas, Plea Discussions, and Related Statements

Except as otherwise provided in this rule, evidence of the following is not, in any civil or criminal proceeding, admissible against the defendant who made the plea or was a participant in the plea discussions:

(1) a plea of guilty which was later withdrawn;

(2) a plea of nolo contendere;

(3) any statement made in the course of any proceedings under Rule 11 of the Federal Rules of Criminal Procedure or comparable state procedure regarding either of the foregoing pleas; or

(4) any statement made in the course of plea discussions with an attorney for the prosecuting authority which do not result in a plea of guilty or which result in a plea of guilty later withdrawn.

However, such a statement is admissible (i) in any proceeding wherein another statement made in the course of the same plea or plea discussions has been introduced and the statement ought in fairness be considered contemporaneously with it, or (ii) in a criminal proceeding for perjury or false statement if the statement was made by the defendant under oath, on the record and in the presence of counsel.

ADVISORY COMMITTEE NOTES

1972 Proposed Rules
Withdrawn pleas of guilty were held inadmissible in federal prosecutions in Kercheval v. United States, 274 U.S. 220, 47 S.Ct. 582, 71 L.Ed. 1009 (1927). The Court pointed out that to admit the withdrawn plea would effectively set at naught the allowance of withdrawal and place the accused in a dilemma utterly inconsistent with the decision to award him a trial. The New York Court of Appeals, in People v. Spitaleri, 9 N.Y.2d 168, 212 N.Y.S.2d 53, 173 N.E.2d 35 (1961), reexamined and overturned its earlier decisions which had allowed admission. In addition to the reasons set forth in Kercheval, which was quoted at length, the court pointed out that the effect of admitting the plea was to compel defendant to take the stand by way of explanation and to open the way for the prosecution to call the lawyer who had represented him at the time of entering the plea. State court decisions for and against admissibility are collected in Annot., 86 A.L.R.2d 326.

Pleas of nolo contendere are recognized by Rule 11 of the Rules of Criminal Procedure, although the law of numerous States is to the contrary. The present rule gives effect to the principal traditional characteristic of the nolo plea, i.e. avoiding the admission of guilt which is inherent in pleas of guilty. This position is consistent with the construction of Section 5 of the Clayton Act, 15 U.S.C. § 16(a), recognizing the inconclusive and compromise nature of judgments based on nolo pleas. General Electric Co. v. City of San Antonio, 334 F.2d 480 (5th Cir.1964); Commonwealth Edison Co. v. Allis-Chalmers Mfg. Co., 323 F.2d 412 (7th Cir.1963), cert. denied 376 U.S. 939, 84 S.Ct. 794, 11 L.Ed.2d 659; Armco Steel Corp. v. North Dakota, 376 F.2d 206 (8th Cir.1967); City of Burbank v. General Electric Co., 329 F.2d 825 (9th Cir.1964). See also state court decisions in Annot., 18 A.L.R.2d 1287, 1314.

Exclusion of offers to plead guilty or nolo has as its purpose the promotion of disposition of criminal cases by compromise. As pointed out in McCormick § 251, p. 543.

"Effective criminal law administration in many localities would hardly be possible if a large proportion of the charges were not disposed of by such compromises."

See also People v. Hamilton, 60 Cal.2d 105, 32 Cal.Rptr. 4, 383 P.2d 412 (1963), discussing legislation designed to achieve this result. As with compromise offers generally, Rule 408, free communication is needed, and security against having an offer of compromise or related statement admitted in evidence effectively encourages it.

Limiting the exclusionary rule to use against the accused is consistent with the purpose of the rule, since the possibility of use for or against other persons will not impair the effectiveness of withdrawing pleas or the freedom of discussion which the rule is designed to foster. See A.B.A. Standards Relating to Pleas of Guilty § 2.2 (1968). See also the narrower provisions of New Jersey Evidence Rule 52(2) and the unlimited exclusion provided in California Evidence Code § 1153.

1974 Enactment
The Committee added the phrase "Except as otherwise provided by Act of Congress" to Rule 410 as submitted by the Court in order to preserve particular congressional policy judgments as to the effect of a plea of guilty or of nolo contendere. See 15 U.S.C. 16(a). The Committee intends that its amendment refers to both present statutes and statutes subsequently enacted. House Report No. 93-650.

As adopted by the House, rule 410 would make inadmissible pleas of guilty or nolo contendere subsequently withdrawn as well as offers to make such pleas. Such a rule is clearly justified as a means of encouraging pleading. However, the House rule would then go on to render inadmissible for any purpose statements made in connection with these pleas or offers as well.

The committee finds this aspect of the House rule unjustified. Of course, in certain circumstances such statements should be excluded. If, for example, a plea is vitiated because of coercion, statements made in connection with the plea may also have been coerced and should be inadmissible on that basis. In other cases, however, voluntary statements of an accused made in court on the record, in connection with a plea, and determined by a court to be reliable should be admissible even though the plea is subsequently withdrawn. This is particularly true in those cases where, if the House rule were in effect, a defendant would be able to contradict his previous statements and thereby lie with impunity [See Harris v. New York, 401 U.S. 222 (1971)]. To prevent such an injustice, the rule has been modified to permit the use of such statements for the limited purposes of impeachment and in subsequent perjury or false statement prosecutions. Senate Report No. 93-1277.

The House bill provides that evidence of a guilty or nolo contendere plea, of an offer of either plea, or of statements made in connection with such pleas or offers of such pleas, is inadmissible in any civil or criminal action, case or proceeding against the person making such plea or offer. The Senate amendment makes the rule inapplicable to a voluntary and reliable statement made in court on the record where the statement is offered in a subsequent prosecution of the declarant for perjury or false statement.

The issues raised by Rule 410 are also raised by proposed Rule 11(e)(6) of the Federal Rules of Criminal Procedure presently pending before Congress. This proposed rule, which deals with the admissibility of pleas of guilty or nolo contendere, offers to make such pleas, and statements made in connection with such pleas, was promulgated by the Supreme Court on April 22, 1974, and in the absence of congressional action will become effective on August 1, 1975. The conferees intend to make no change in the presently-existing case law until that date, leaving the courts free to develop rules in this area on a case-by-case basis.

The Conferees further determined that the issues presented by the use of guilty and nolo contendere pleas, offers of such pleas, and statements made in connection with such pleas or offers, can be explored in greater detail during Congressional consideration of Rule 11(e)(6) of the Federal Rules of Criminal Procedure. The Conferees believe, therefore, that it is best to defer its effective date until August 1, 1975. The Conferees intend that Rule 410 would be superseded by any subsequent Federal Rule of Criminal Procedure or act of Congress with which it is inconsistent, if the Federal Rule of Criminal Procedure or Act of Congress takes effect or becomes law after the date of the enactment of the act establishing the rules of evidence.

The conference adopts the Senate amendment with an amendment that expresses the above intentions. House Report No. 93-1597.

1979 Amendments
Present rule 410 conforms to rule 11(e)(6) of the Federal Rules of Criminal Procedure. A proposed amendment to rule 11(e)(6) would clarify the circumstances in which pleas, plea discussions and related statements are inadmissible in evidence: see Advisory Committee Note thereto. The amendment proposed above would make comparable changes in rule 410.

Rule 411. Liability Insurance

Evidence that a person was or was not insured against liability is not admissible upon the issue whether the person acted negligently or otherwise wrongfully. This rule does not require the exclusion of evidence of insurance against liability when offered for another purpose, such as proof of agency, ownership, or control, or bias or prejudice of a witness.

ADVISORY COMMITTEE NOTES

1972 Proposed Rules

The courts have with substantial unanimity rejected evidence of liability insurance for the purpose of proving fault, and absence of liability insurance as proof of lack of fault. At best the inference of fault from the fact of insurance coverage is a tenuous one, as is its converse. More important, no doubt, has been the feeling that knowledge of the presence or absence of liability insurance would induce juries to decide cases on improper grounds. McCormick § 168; Annot., 4 A.L.R.2d 761. The rule is drafted in broad terms so as to include contributory negligence or other fault of a plaintiff as well as fault of a defendant.

The second sentence points out the limits of the rule, using well established illustrations. Id.

For similar rules see Uniform Rule 54; California Evidence Code § 1155; Kansas Code of Civil Procedure § 60-454; New Jersey Evidence Rule 54.

1987 Amendments

The amendment is technical. No substantive change is intended.

Rule 412. Sex Offense Cases; Relevance of Alleged Victim's Past Sexual Behavior or Alleged Sexual Predisposition

(a) Evidence generally inadmissible.--The following evidence is not admissible in any civil or criminal proceeding involving alleged sexual misconduct except as provided in subdivisions (b) and (c):

(1) Evidence offered to prove that any alleged victim engaged in other sexual behavior.

(2) Evidence offered to prove any alleged victim's sexual predisposition.

(b) Exceptions.--

(1) In a criminal case, the following evidence is admissible, if otherwise admissible under these rules:

(A) evidence of specific instances of sexual behavior by the alleged victim offered to prove that a person other than the accused was the source of semen, injury or other physical evidence;

(B) evidence of specific instances of sexual behavior by the alleged victim with respect to the person accused of the sexual misconduct offered by the accused to prove consent or by the prosecution; and

(C) evidence the exclusion of which would violate the constitutional rights of the defendant.

(2) In a civil case, evidence offered to prove the sexual behavior or sexual predisposition of any alleged victim is admissible if it is otherwise admissible under these rules and its probative value substantially outweighs the danger of harm to any victim and of unfair prejudice to any party. Evidence of an alleged victim's reputation is admissible only if it has been placed in controversy by the alleged victim.

(c) Procedure to determine admissibility.--

(1) A party intending to offer evidence under subdivision (b) must--

(A) file a written motion at least 14 days before trial specifically describing the evidence and stating the purpose for which it is offered unless the court, for good cause requires a different time for filing or permits filing during trial; and

(B) serve the motion on all parties and notify the alleged victim or, when appropriate, the alleged victim's guardian or representative.

(2) Before admitting evidence under this rule the court must conduct a hearing in camera and afford the victim and parties a right to attend and be heard. The motion, related papers, and the record of the hearing must be sealed and remain under seal unless the court orders otherwise.

ADVISORY COMMITTEE NOTES

1994 Amendments
Rule 412 has been revised to diminish some of the confusion engendered by the original rule and to expand the protection afforded alleged victims of sexual mis-

conduct. Rule 412 applies to both civil and criminal proceedings. The rule aims to safeguard the alleged victim against the invasion of privacy, potential embarrassment and sexual stereotyping that is associated with public disclosure of intimate sexual details and the infusion of sexual innuendo into the factfinding process. By affording victims protection in most instances, the rule also encourages victims of sexual misconduct to institute and to participate in legal proceedings against alleged offenders

Rule 412 seeks to achieve these objectives by barring evidence relating to the alleged victim's sexual behavior or alleged sexual predisposition, whether offered as substantive evidence of for impeachment, except in designated circumstances in which the probative value of the evidence significantly outweighs possible harm to the victim.

The revised rule applies in all cases involving sexual misconduct without regard to whether the alleged victim or person accused is a party to the litigation. Rule 412 extends to "pattern" witnesses in both criminal and civil cases whose testimony about other instances of sexual misconduct by the person accused is otherwise admissible. When the case does not involve alleged sexual misconduct, evidence relating to a third-party witness' alleged sexual activities is not within the ambit of Rule 412. The witness will, however, be protected by other rules such as Rules 404 and 608, as well as Rule 403.

The terminology "alleged victim" is used because there will frequently be a factual dispute as to whether sexual misconduct occurred. It does not connote any requirement that the misconduct be alleged in the pleadings. Rule 412 does not, however, apply unless the person against whom the evidence is offered can reasonably be characterized as a "victim of alleged sexual misconduct." When this is not the case, as for instance in a defamation action involving statements concerning sexual misconduct in which the evidence is offered to show that the alleged defamatory statements were true or did not damage the plaintiff's reputation, neither Rule 404 nor this rule will operate to bar the evidence; Rule 401 and 403 will continue to control. Rule 412 will, however, apply in a Title VII action in which the plaintiff has alleged sexual harassment.

The reference to a person "accused" is also used in a non-technical sense. There is no requirement that there be a criminal charge pending against the person or even that the misconduct would constitute a criminal offense. Evidence offered to prove allegedly false prior claims by the victim is not barred by Rule 412. However, the evidence is subject to the requirements of Rule 404.

Subdivision (a). As amended, Rule 412 bars evidence offered to prove the victim's sexual behavior and alleged sexual predisposition. Evidence, which might otherwise be admissible under Rules 402, 404(b), 405, 607, 608, 609 of some other evidence rule, must be excluded if Rule 412 so requires. The word "other" is used to suggest some flexibility in admitting evidence "intrinsic" to the alleged sexual misconduct. Cf. Committee Note to 1991 amendment to Rule 404(b)

Past sexual behavior connotes all activities that involve actual physical conduct, i.e. sexual intercourse or sexual contact. See, e.g., United States v. Galloway, 937 F.2d 542 (10th Cir. 1991), cert. denied, 113 S.Ct. 418 (1992) (use of contraceptives inadmissible since use implies sexual activity); United States v. One Feather, 702 F.2d 736 (8th Cir. 1983) (birth of an illegitimate child inadmissible); State v. Carmichael, 727 P.2d 918, 925 (Kan. 1986) (evidence of venereal disease inadmissible). In addition, the word "behavior" should be construed to include activities of the mind, such as fantasies of dreams. See 23 C. Wright and K. Graham, Jr., Federal Practice and Procedure, § 5384 at p. 548 (1980) ("While there may be some doubt under statutes that require 'conduct,' it would seem that the language of Rule 412 is broad enough to encompass the behavior of the mind.").

The rule has been amended to also exclude all other evidence relating to an alleged victim of sexual misconduct that is offered to prove a sexual predisposition. This amendment is designed to exclude evidence that does not directly refer to sexual activities or thoughts but that the proponent believes may have a sexual connotation for the factfinder. Admission of such evidence would contravene Rule 412's objectives of shielding the alleged victim from potential embarrassment and safeguarding the victim against stereotypical thinking. Consequently, unless the (b)(2) exception is satisfied, evidence such as that relating to the alleged victim's mode of dress, speech, or life-style will not be admissible.

The introductory phrase in subdivision (a) was deleted because it lacked clarity and contained no explicit reference to the other provisions of the law that were intended to be overridden. The conditional clause, "except as provided in subdivisions (b) and (c)" is intended to make clear that evidence of the types described in subdivision (a) is admissible only under the strictures of those sections.

The reason for extending the rule to all criminal cases is obvious. The strong social policy of protecting a victim's privacy and encouraging victims to come forward to report criminal acts is not confined to cases that involve a charge of sexual assault. The need to protect the victim is equally great when a defendant is charged with kidnapping, and evidence is offered, either to prove motive or as background, that the defendant sexually assaulted the victim.

The reason for extending Rule 412 to civil cases is equally obvious. The need to protect alleged victims against invasions of privacy, potential embarrassment, and unwarranted sexual stereotyping, and the wish to encourage victims to come forward when they have been sexually molested do not disappear because the context has shifted from a criminal prosecution to a claim for damages or injunctive relief. There is a strong social policy in not only punishing those who engage in sexual misconduct, but in also providing relief to the victim. Thus, Rule 412 applies in any civil case in which a person claims to be the victim of sexual misconduct, such as actions for sexual battery or sexual harassment.

Subdivision (b). Subdivision (b) spells out the specific circumstances in which some evidence may be admissible that would otherwise be barred by the general rule expressed in subdivision (a). As amended, Rule 412 will be virtually unchanged in criminal cases, but will provide protection to any person alleged to be a victim of sexual misconduct regardless of the charge actually brought against an accused. A new exception has been added for civil cases.

In a criminal case, evidence may be admitted under subdivision (b)(1) pursuant to three possible exceptions, provided the evidence also satisfies other requirements for admissibility specified in the Federal Rules of Evidence, including Rule 403. Subdivisions (b)(1)(A) and (b)(1)(B) require proof in the form of specific instances of sexual behavior in recognition of the limited probative value and dubious reliability of evidence of reputation or evidence in the form of an opinion.

Under subdivision (b)(1)(A), evidence of specific instances of sexual behavior with persons other than the person whose sexual misconduct is alleged may be admissible if it is offered to prove that another person was the source of semen, injury or other physical evidence. Where the prosecution has directly or indirectly asserted that the physical evidence originated with the accused, the defendant must be afforded an opportunity to prove that another person was responsible. See United States v. Begay, 937 F.2d 515, 523 n. 10 (10th Cir. 1991). Evidence offered for the specific purpose identified in this subdivision may still be excluded if it does not satisfy Rules 401 or 403. See, e.g., United States v. Azure, 845 F.2d 1503, 1505-06 (8th Cir. 1988) (10 year old victim's injuries indicated recent use of force; court excluded evidence of consensual sexual activities with witness who testified at in camera hearing that he had never hurt victim and failed to establish recent activities).

Under the exception in subdivision (b)(1)(B), evidence of specific instances of sexual behavior with respect to the person whose sexual misconduct is alleged is admissible if offered to prove consent, or offered by the prosecution. Admissible pursuant to this exception might be evidence of prior instances of sexual activities between the alleged victim and the accused, as well as statements in which the alleged victim expresses an intent to engage in sexual intercourse with the accused, or voiced sexual fantasies involving that specific accused. In a prosecution for child sexual abuse, for example, evidence of uncharged sexual activity between the accused and the alleged victim offered by the prosecution may be admissible pursuant to Rule 404(b) to show a pattern of behavior. Evidence relating to the victim's alleged sexual predisposition is not admissible pursuant to this exception.

Under subdivision (b)(1)(C), evidence of specific instances of conduct may not be excluded if the result would be to deny a criminal defendant the protections afforded by the Constitution. For example, statements in which the victim has expressed an intent to have sex with the first person encountered on a particular occasion might not be excluded without violating the due process right of a rape defendant seeking to prove consent. Recognition of this basic principle was expressed on subdivision (b)(1) of the original rule. The United States Supreme Court has recognized that in various circumstances a defendant may have a right to introduce evidence otherwise precluded by an evidence rule under the Confrontation Clause. See, e.g., Olden v. Kentucky, 488 U.S. 227 (1988) (defendant in rape cases had right to inquire into alleged victim's cohabitation with another man to show bias).

Subdivision (b)(2) governs the admissibility of otherwise proscribed evidence in civil cases. It employs a balancing test rather than the specific exceptions stated in subdivision (b)(1) in recognition of the difficulty of foreseeing future developments in the law. Greater flexibility is needed to accommodate evolving causes of action such as claims for sexual harassment.

The balancing test requires the proponent of the evidence, whether plaintiff or defendant, to convince the court that the probative value of the proffered evidence "substantially outweighs the danger of harm to any victim and of unfair prejudice of any party." This test for admitting evidence offered to prove sexual behavior or sexual propensity in civil cases differs in three respects from the general rule governing admissibility set forth in Rule 403. First, it Reverses that usual procedure spelled out in Rule 403 by shifting the burden to the proponent to demonstrate admissibility rather than making the opponent justify exclusion of the evidence. Second, the standard expressed in subdivision (b)(2) is more stringent than in the original rule; it raises the threshold for admission by requiring that the probative value of the evidence substantially outweigh the specified dangers. Finally, the Rule 412 test puts "harm to the victim" on the scale in addition to prejudice to the parties.

Evidence of reputation may be received in a civil case only if the alleged victim has put his or her reputation into controversy. The victim may do so without making a specific allegation in a pleading. Cf. Fed.R.Civ.P. 35(a).

Subdivision (c). Amended subdivision (c) is more concise and understandable than the subdivision it replaces. The requirement of a motion before trial is continued in the amended rule, as is the provision that a late motion may be permitted for good cause shown. In deciding whether to permit late filing, the court may take into account the conditions previously included in the rule: namely whether the evidence is newly discovered and could not have been obtained earlier through the existence of due diligence, and whether the issue to which such evidence relates has newly arisen in the case. The rule recognizes that in some instances the circumstances that justify an application to introduce evidence otherwise barred by Rule 412 will not become apparent until trial.

The amended rule provides that before admitting evidence that falls within that prohibition of Rule 412(a), the court must hold a hearing in camera at which the alleged victim and any party must be afforded the right to be present and an opportunity to be heard. All papers connected with the motion must be kept and remain under seal during the course of trial and appellate proceedings unless otherwise ordered. This is to assure that the privacy of the alleged victim is preserved in all cases in which the court rules that proffered evidence is not admissible, and in which the hearing refers to matters that are not received, or are received in another form.

The procedures set forth in subdivision (c) do not apply to discovery of a victim's past sexual conduct or predisposition in civil cases, which will be continued to be governed by Fed. R. Civ. P. 26. In order not to undermine the rationale of Rule 412, however, courts should enter appropriate orders pursuant to Fed. R. Civ. P. 26 (c) to protect the victim against unwarranted inquiries and to ensure confidentiality. Courts should presumptively issue protective orders barring discovery unless the party seeking discovery makes a showing that the evidence sought to be discovered would be relevant under the facts and theories of the particular case, and cannot be obtained except through discovery. In an action for sexual harassment, for instance, while some evidence of the alleged victim's sexual behavior and/or predisposition in the workplace may perhaps be relevant, non-work place conduct will usually be irrelevant. Cf. Burns v. McGregor Electronic Industries, Inc., 989 F.2d 959, 962-63 (8th Cir. 1993) (posing for a nude magazine outside work hours is irrelevant to issue of unwelcomeness of sexual advances at work). Confidentiality orders should be presumptively granted as well.

One substantive change made in subdivision (c) is the elimination of the following sentence: "Notwithstanding subdivision (b) of Rule 104, if the relevancy of the evidence which the accused seeks to offer in trial depends upon the fulfillment of a condition of fact, the court, at the hearing in chambers or at a subsequent hearing in chambers scheduled for such purpose, shall accept evidence on the issue of whether such condition of fact is fulfilled and shall determine such issue." On its face, this language would appear to authorize a trial judge to exclude evidence of past sexual conduct between alleged victim and an accused or a defendant in a civil case based upon the judge's belief that such past acts did not occur. Such an authorization raises questions of invasion of the right to a jury trial under the Sixth and Seventh Amendments. See 1 S. Saltzburg & M. Martin, Federal Rules of Evidence Manual, 396-97 (5th ed. 1990).

The Advisory Committee concluded that the amended rule provided adequate protection for all persons claiming to be the victims of sexual misconduct, and that it was inadvisable to continue to include a provision in the rule that has been confusing and that raises substantial constitutional issues.

[Advisory Committee Note adopted by Congressional Conference Report accompanying Pub.L. 103-322. See H.R. Conf. Rep. No. 103-711, 103rd Cong., 2nd Sess., 383 (1994).]

Congressional Discussion

The following discussion in the House of Representatives of October 10, 1978, preceded passage of H.R. 4727, which enacted Rule 412. The discussion appears in 124 Cong.Record, at page H. 11944.

Mr. MANN. Mr. Speaker, I yield myself such time as I may consume.

Mr. Speaker, for many years in this country, evidentiary rules have permitted the introduction of evidence about a rape victim's prior sexual conduct. Defense lawyers were permitted great latitude in bringing out intimate details about a rape victim's life. Such evidence quite often serves no real purpose and only results in embarrassment to the rape victim and unwarranted public intrusion into her private life.

The evidentiary rules that permit such inquiry have in recent years come under question; and the States have taken the lead to change and modernize their evidentiary rules about evidence of a rape victim's prior sexual behavior. The bill before us similarly seeks to modernize the Federal Evidentiary rules.

The present Federal Rules of Evidence reflect the traditional approach. If a defendant in a rape case raises the defense of consent, that defendant may then offer evidence about the victim's prior sexual behavior. Such evidence may be in the form of opinion evidence, evidence of reputation, or evidence of specific instances of behavior. Rule 404(a)(2) of the Federal Rules of Evidence permits the introduction of evidence of a "pertinent character trait." The advisory committee note to that rule cites, as an example of what the rule covers, the character of a rape victim when the issue is consent. Rule 405 of the Federal Rules of Evidence permits the use of opinion or reputation evidence or the use of evidence of specific behavior to show a character trait.

Thus, Federal evidentiary rules permit a wide ranging inquiry into the private conduct of a rape victim, even though that conduct may have at best a tenuous connection to the offense for which the defendant is being tried.

H.R. 4727 amends the Federal Rules of Evidence to add a new rule, applicable only in criminal cases, to spell out when, and under what conditions, evidence of a rape victim's prior sexual behavior can be admitted. The new rule provides that reputation or opinion evidence about a rape victim's prior sexual behavior is not admissible. The new rule also provides that a court cannot admit evidence of specific instances of a rape victim's prior sexual conduct except in three circumstances.

The first circumstance is where the Constitution requires that the evidence be admitted. This exception is intended to cover those infrequent instances where, because of an unusual chain of circumstances, the general rule of inadmissibility, if followed, would result in denying the defendant a constitutional right.

The second circumstance in which the defendant can offer evidence of specific instances of a rape victim's prior sexual behavior is where the defendant raises the issue of consent and the evidence is of sexual behavior with the defendant. To admit such evidence, however, the court must find that the evidence is relevant and that its probative value outweighs the danger of unfair prejudice.

The third circumstance in which a court can admit evidence of specific instances of a rape victim's prior sexual behavior is where the evidence is of behavior with someone other than the defendant and is offered by the defendant on the issue of whether or not he was the source of semen or injury. Again, such evidence will be admitted only if the court finds that the evidence is relevant and that its probative value outweighs the danger of unfair prejudice.

The new rule further provides that before evidence is admitted under any of these exceptions, there must be an in camera hearing--that is, a proceeding that takes place in the judge's chambers out of the presence of the jury and the general public. At this hearing, the defendant will present the evidence he intends to offer and be able to argue why it should be admitted. The prosecution, of course, will be able to argue against that evidence being admitted.

The purpose of the in camera hearing is twofold. It gives the defendant an opportunity to demonstrate to the court why certain evidence is admissible and ought to be presented to the jury. At the same time, it protects the privacy of the rape victim in those instances when the court finds that evidence is inadmissible. Of course, if the court finds the evidence to be admissible, the evidence will be presented to the jury in open court.

The effect of this legislation, therefore, is to preclude the routine use of evidence of specific instances of a rape victim's prior sexual behavior. Such evidence will be admitted only in clearly and narrowly defined circumstances and only after an in camera hearing. In determining the admissibility of such evidence, the court will consider all of the facts and circumstances surrounding the evidence, such as the amount of time that lapsed between the alleged prior act and the rape charged in the prosecution. The greater the lapse of time, of course, the less likely it is that such evidence will be admitted.

Mr. Speaker, the principal purpose of this legislation is to protect rape victims from the degrading and embarrassing disclosure of intimate details about their private lives. It does so by narrowly circumscribing when such evidence may be admitted. It does not do so, however, by sacrificing any constitutional right possessed by the defendant. The bill before us fairly balances the interests involved--the rape victim's interest in protecting her private life from unwarranted public exposure; the defendant's interest in being able adequately to present a defense by offering relevant and probative evidence; and society's interest in a fair trial, one where unduly prejudicial evidence is not permitted to becloud the issues before the jury.

I urge support of the bill.

Mr. WIGGINS. Mr. Speaker, I yield myself such time as I may consume.

(Mr. WIGGINS asked and was given permission to revise and extend his remarks.)

Mr. WIGGINS. Mr. Speaker, this legislation addresses itself to a subject that is certainly a proper one for our consideration. Many of us have been troubled for years about the indiscriminate and prejudicial use of testimony with respect to a victim's prior sexual behavior in rape and similar cases. This bill deals with that problem. It is not, in my opinion, Mr. Speaker, a perfect bill in the manner in which it deals with the problem, but my objections are not so fundamental as would lead me to oppose the bill.

I think, Mr. Speaker, that it is unwise to adopt a per se rule absolutely excluding evidence of reputation and opinion with respect to the victim--and this bill does that--but it is difficult for me to foresee the specific case in which such evidence might be admissible. The trouble is this, Mr. Speaker: None of us can foresee perfectly all of the various circumstances under which the propriety of evidence might be before the court. If this bill has a defect, in my view it is because it adopts a per se rule with respect to opinion and reputation evidence.

Alternatively we might have permitted that evidence to be considered in camera as we do other evidence under the bill.

I should note, however, in fairness, having expressed minor reservations, that the bill before the House at this time does improve significantly upon the bill which was presented to our committee.

I will not detail all of those improvements but simply observe that the bill upon which we shall soon vote is a superior product to that which was initially considered by our subcommittee.

Mr. Speaker, I ask my colleagues to vote for this legislation as being, on balance, worthy of their support, and urge its adoption.

I reserve the balance of my time.

Mr. MANN. Mr. Speaker, this legislation has more than 100 cosponsors, but its principal sponsor, as well as its architect is the gentlewoman from New York (Ms. Holtzman). As the drafter of the legislation she will be able to provide additional information about the probable scope and effect of the legislation.

I yield such time as she may consume to the gentlewoman from New York (Ms. Holtzman).

(Ms. HOLTZMAN asked and was given permission to revise and extend her remarks.)

Ms. HOLTZMAN. Mr. Speaker, I would like to begin first by complimenting the distinguished gentleman from South Carolina (Mr. Mann), the chairman of the subcommittee, for his understanding of the need for corrective legislation in this area and for the fairness with which he has conducted the subcommittee hearings. I would like also to compliment the other members of the subcommittee, including the gentleman from California (Mr. Wiggins).

Too often in this country victims of rape are humiliated and harassed when they report and prosecute the rape. Bullied and cross-examined about their prior sexual experiences, many find the trial almost as degrading as the rape itself. Since rape trials become inquisitions into the victim's morality, not trials of the defendant's innocence or guilt, it is not surprising that it is the least reported crime. It is estimated that as few as one in ten rapes is ever reported.

Mr. Speaker, over 30 States have taken some action to limit the vulnerability of rape victims to such humiliating cross-examination of their past sexual experiences and intimate personal histories. In federal courts, however, it is permissible still to subject rape victims to brutal cross-examination about their past sexual histories. H.R. 4727 would rectify this problem in Federal courts and I hope, also serve as a model to suggest to the remaining states that reform of existing rape laws is important to the equity of our criminal justice system.

H.R. 4727 applies only to criminal rape cases in Federal courts. The bill provides that neither the prosecution nor the defense can introduce any reputation or opinion evidence about the victim's past sexual conduct. It does permit, however, the introduction of specific evidence about the victim's past sexual conduct in three very limited circumstances.

First, this evidence can be introduced if it deals with the victim's past sexual relations with the defendant and is relevant to the issue of whether she consented. Second, when the defendant claims he had no relations with the victim, he can use evidence of the victim's past sexual relations with others if the evidence rebuts the victim's claim that the rape caused certain physical consequences, such as semen or injury. Finally, the evidence can be introduced if it is constitutionally required. This last exception, added in subcommittee, will insure that the defendant's constitutional rights are protected.

Before any such evidence can be introduced, however, the court must determine at a hearing in chambers that the evidence falls within one of the exceptions.

Furthermore, unless constitutionally required, the evidence of specific instances of prior sexual conduct cannot be introduced at all it if would be more prejudicial and inflammatory that probative.

Mr. Speaker, I urge adoption of this bill. It will protect women from both injustice and indignity.

Mr. MANN. Mr. Speaker, I have no further requests for time, and I yield back the balance of my time.

Mr. WIGGINS. Mr. Speaker, I have no further requests for time, and yield back the balance of my time.

The SPEAKER pro tempore. The question is on the motion offered by the gentleman from South Carolina (Mr. Mann) that the House suspend the rules and pass the bill H.R. 4727, as amended.

The question was taken; and (two-thirds having voted in favor thereof) the rules were suspended and the bill, as amended, was passed.

A motion to reconsider was laid on the table.

Rule 413. Evidence of Similar Crimes in Sexual Assault Cases

(a) In a criminal case in which the defendant is accused of an offense of sexual assault, evidence of the defendant's commission of another offense or offenses of sexual assault is admissible, and may be considered for its bearing on any matter to which it is relevant.

(b) In a case in which the Government intends to offer evidence under this rule, the attorney for the Government shall disclose the evidence to the defendant, including statements of witnesses or a summary of the substance of any testimony that is expected to be offered, at least fifteen days before the scheduled date of trial or at such later time as the court may allow for good cause.

(c) This rule shall not be construed to limit the admission or consideration of evidence under any other rule.

(d) For purposes of this rule and Rule 415, "offense of sexual assault" means a crime under Federal law or the law of a State (as defined in section 513 of title 18, United States Code) that involved--

(1) any conduct proscribed by chapter 109A of title 18, United States Code;

(2) contact, without consent, between any part of the defendant's body or an object and the genitals or anus of another person;

(3) contact, without consent, between the genitals or anus of the defendant and any part of another person's body;

(4) deriving sexual pleasure or gratification from the infliction of death, bodily injury, or physical pain on another person; or

(5) an attempt or conspiracy to engage in conduct described in paragraphs (1)-(4).

Rule 414. Evidence of Similar Crimes in Child Molestation Cases

(a) In a criminal case in which the defendant is accused of an offense of child molestation, evidence of the defendant's commission of another offense or offenses of child molestation is admissible, and may be considered for its bearing on any matter to which it is relevant.

(b) In a case in which the Government intends to offer evidence under this rule, the attorney for the Government shall disclose the evidence to the defendant, including statements of witnesses or a summary of the substance of any testimony that is expected to be offered, at least fifteen days before the scheduled date of trial or at such later time as the court may allow for good cause.

(c) This rule shall not be construed to limit the admission or consideration of evidence under any other rule.

(d) For purposes of this rule and Rule 415, "child" means a person below the age of fourteen, and "offense of child molestation" means a crime under Federal law or the law of a State (as defined in section 513 of title 18, United States Code) that involved--

(1) any conduct proscribed by chapter 109A of title 18, United States Code, that was committed in relation to a child;

(2) any conduct proscribed by chapter 110 of title 18, United States Code;

(3) contact between any part of the defendant's body or an object and the genitals or anus of a child;

(4) contact between the genitals or anus of the defendant and any part of the body of a child;

(5) deriving sexual pleasure or gratification from the infliction of death, bodily injury, or physical pain on a child; or

(6) an attempt or conspiracy to engage in conduct described in paragraphs (1)-(5).

Rule 415. Evidence of Similar Acts in Civil Cases Concerning Sexual Assault or Child Molestation

(a) In a civil case in which a claim for damages or other relief is predicated on a party's alleged commission of conduct constituting an offense of sexual assault or child molestation, evidence of that party's commission of another offense or offenses of sexual assault or child molestation is admissible and may be considered as provided in Rule 413 and Rule 414 of these rules.

(b) A party who intends to offer evidence under this Rule shall disclose the evidence to the party against whom it will be offered, including statements of witnesses or a summary of the substance of any testimony that is expected to be offered, at least fifteen days before the scheduled date of trial or at such later time as the court may allow for good cause.

(c) This rule shall not be construed to limit the admission or consideration of evidence under any other rule.

ARTICLE V. PRIVILEGES

Rule 501. General Rule

Except as otherwise required by the Constitution of the United States or provided by Act of Congress or in rules prescribed by the Supreme Court pursuant to statutory authority, the privilege of a witness, person, government, State, or political subdivision thereof shall be governed by the principles of the common law as they may be interpreted by the courts of the United States in the light of reason and experience. However, in civil actions and proceedings, with respect to an element of a claim or defense as to which State law supplies the rule of decision, the privilege of a witness, person, government, State, or political subdivision thereof shall be determined in accordance with State law.

ADVISORY COMMITTEE NOTES

1974 Enactment
Article V as submitted to Congress contained thirteen Rules. Nine of those Rules defined specific non-constitutional privileges which the federal courts must recognize (i.e. required reports, lawyer-client, psychotherapist-patient, husband-wife, communications to clergymen, political vote, trade secrets, secrets of state and other official information, and identity of informer.) Another Rule provided that only those privileges set forth in Article V or in some other Act of Congress could be recognized by the federal courts. The three remaining Rules addressed collateral problems as to waiver of privilege by voluntary disclosure, privileged matter disclosed under compulsion or without opportunity to claim privilege, comment upon or inference from a claim of privilege, and jury instruction with regard thereto.

The Committee amended Article V to eliminate all of the Court's specific Rules on privileges. Instead, the Committee, through a single Rule, 501, left the law of privileges in its present state and further provided that privileges shall continue to be developed by the courts of the United States under a uniform standard applicable both in civil and criminal cases. That standard, derived from Rule 26 of the Federal Rules of Criminal Procedure, mandates the application of the principles of the common law as interpreted by the courts of the United States in the light of reason and experience. The words "person, government, State, or political subdivision thereof" were added by the Committee to the lone term "witnesses" used in Rule 26 to make clear that, as under present law, not only witnesses may have privileges. The Committee also included in its amendment a proviso modeled after Rule 302 and similar to language added by the Committee to Rule 601 relating to the competency of witnesses. The proviso is designed to require the application of State privilege law in civil actions and proceedings governed by Erie R. Co. v. Tompkins, 304 U.S. 64 (1938), a result in accord with current federal court decisions. See Republic Gear Co. v. Borg-Warner Corp., 381 F.2d 551, 555-556 n. 2 (2nd Cir.1967). The Committee deemed the proviso to be necessary in the light of the Advisory Committee's view (see its note to Court [proposed] Rule 501) that this result is not mandated under Erie.

The rationale underlying the proviso is that federal law should not supersede that of the States in substantive areas such as privilege absent a compelling reason. The Committee believes that in civil cases in the federal courts where an element of a claim or defense is not grounded upon a federal question, there is no federal interest strong enough to justify departure from State policy. In addition, the Committee considered that the Court's proposed Article V would have promoted forum shopping in some civil actions, depending upon differences in the privilege law applied as among the State and federal courts. The Committee's proviso, on the other hand, under which the federal courts are bound to apply the State's privilege law in actions founded upon a State-created right or defense, removes the incentive to "shop". House Report No. 93-650.

Article V as submitted to Congress contained 13 rules. Nine of those rules defined specific nonconstitutional privileges which the Federal courts must recognize (i.e., required reports, lawyer-client, psychotherapist-patient, husband-wife, communications to clergymen, political vote, trade secrets, secrets of state and other official information, and identity of informer). Many of these rules contained controversial modifications or restrictions upon common law privileges. As noted supra, the House amended article V to eliminate all of the Court's specific rules on privileges. Through a single rule, 501, the House provided that privileges shall be governed by the principles of the common law as interpreted by the courts of the United States in the light of reason and experience (a standard derived from rule 26 of the Federal Rules of Criminal Procedure) except in the case of an element of a civil claim or defense as to which State law supplies the rule of decision, in which event state privilege law was to govern.

The committee agrees with the main thrust of the House amendment: that a federally developed common law based on modern reason and experience shall apply except where the State nature of the issues renders deference to State privilege law the wiser course, as in the usual diversity case. The committee understands that thrust of the House amendment to require that State privilege law be applied in "diversity" cases (actions on questions of State law between citizens of different States arising under 28 U.S.C. § 1332). The language of the House amendment, however, goes beyond this in some respects, and falls short of it in others: State privilege law applies even in nondiversity, Federal question civil cases, where an issue governed by State substantive law is the object of the evidence (such issues do sometimes arise in such cases); and, in all instances where State privilege law is to be applied, e.g., on proof of a State issue in a diversity case, a close reading reveals that State privilege law is not to be applied unless the matter to be proved is an element of that state claim or defense, as distinguished from a step along the way in the proof of it.

The committee is concerned that the language used in the House amendment could be difficult to apply. It provides that "in civil actions * * * with respect to an element of a claim or defense as to which State law supplies the rule of decision," State law on privilege applies. The question of what is an element of a claim or defense is likely to engender considerable litigation. If the matter in question constitutes an element of a claim, State law supplies the privilege rule; whereas if it is a mere item of proof with respect to a claim, then, even though State law might supply the rule of decision, Federal law on the privilege would apply. Further, disputes will arise as to how the rule should be applied in an antitrust action or in a tax case where the Federal statute is silent as to a particular aspect of the substantive law in question, but Federal cases had incorporated State law by reference to State law. [For a discussion of reference to State substantive law, see note on Federal Incorporation by Reference of State Law, Hart & Wechsler, The Federal Courts and the Federal System, pp. 491-494 (2d ed. 1973).] Is a claim (or defense) based on such a reference a claim or defense as to which federal or State law supplies the rule of decision?

Another problem not entirely avoidable is the complexity or difficulty the rule introduces into the trial of a Federal case containing a combination of Federal and State claims and defenses, e.g. an action involving Federal antitrust and State unfair competition claims. Two different bodies of privilege law would need to be consulted. It may even develop that the same witness-testimony might be relevant on both counts and privileged as to one but not the other. [The problems with the House formulation are discussed in Rothstein, The Proposed Amendments to the Federal Rules of Evidence, 62 Georgetown University Law Journal 125 (1973) at notes 25, 26 and 70-74 and accompanying text.]

The formulation adopted by the House is pregnant with litigious mischief. The committee has, therefore, adopted what we believe will be a clearer and more practical guideline for determining when courts should respect State rules of privilege. Basically, it provides that in criminal and Federal question civil cases, federally evolved rules on privilege should apply since it is Federal policy which is being enforced. [It is also intended that the Federal law of privileges should be applied with respect to pendent State law claims when they arise in a Federal question case.] Conversely, in diversity cases where the litigation in question turns on a substantive question of State law, and is brought in the Federal courts because the parties reside in different States, the committee believes it is clear that State rules of privilege should apply unless the proof is directed at a claim or defense for which Federal law supplies the rule of decision (a situation which would not commonly arise.) [While such a situation might require use of two bodies of privilege law, federal and state, in the same case, nevertheless the occasions on which this would be required are considerably reduced as compared with the House version, and confined to situations where the Federal and State interests are such as to justify application of neither privilege law to the case as a whole. If the rule proposed here results in two conflicting bodies of privilege law applying to the same piece of evidence in the same case, it is contemplated that the rule favoring reception of the evidence should be applied. This policy is based on the present rule 43(a) of the Federal Rules of Civil Procedure which provides: In any case, the statute or rule which favors the reception of the evidence governs and the evidence shall be presented according to the most convenient method prescribed in any of the statutes or rules to which reference is herein made.] It is intended that the State rules of privilege should apply equally in original diversity actions and diversity actions removed under 28 U.S.C. § 1441(b).

Two other comments on the privilege rule should be made. The committee has received a considerable volume of correspondence from psychiatric organizations and psychiatrists concerning the deletion of rule 504 of the rule submitted by the Supreme Court. It should be clearly understood that, in approving this general rule as to privileges, the action of Congress should not be understood as disapproving any recognition of a psychiatrist-patient, or husband-wife, or any other of the enumerated privileges contained in the Supreme Court rules. Rather, our action should be understood as reflecting the view that the recognition of a privilege based on a confidential relationship and other privileges should be determined on a case-by-case basis.

Further, we would understand that the prohibition against spouses testifying against each other is considered a rule of privilege and covered by this rule and not by rule 601 of the competency of witnesses. Senate Report No. 93-1277.

Rule 501 deals with the privilege of a witness not to testify. Both the House and Senate bills provide that federal privilege law applies in criminal cases. In civil actions and proceedings, the House bill provides that state privilege law applies "to an element of a claim or defense as to which State law supplies the rule of decision." The Senate bill provides that "in civil actions and proceedings arising under 28 U.S.C. § 1332 or 28 U.S.C. § 1335, or between citizens of different States and removed under 28 U.S.C. § 1441(b) the privilege of a witness, person, government, State or political subdivision thereof is determined in accordance with State law, unless with respect to the particular claim or defense, Federal law supplies the rule of decision."

The wording of the House and Senate bills differs in the treatment of civil actions and proceedings. The rule in the House bill applies to evidence that relates to "an element of a claim or defense." If an item of proof tends to support or defeat a claim or defense, or an element of a claim or defense, and if state law supplies the rule of decision for that claim or defense, then state privilege law applies to that item of proof.

Under the provision in the House bill, therefore, state privilege law will usually apply in diversity cases. There may be diversity cases, however, where a claim or defense is based upon federal law. In such instances, federal privilege law will apply to evidence relevant to the federal claim or defense. See Sola Electric Co. v. Jefferson Electric Co., 317 U.S. 173 (1942).

In nondiversity jurisdiction civil cases, federal privilege law will generally apply. In those situations where a federal court adopts or incorporates state law to fill interstices or gaps in federal statutory phrases, the court generally will apply federal privilege law. As Justice Jackson has said:

A federal court sitting in a non-diversity case such as this does not sit as a local tribunal. In some cases it may see fit for special reasons to give the law of a particular state highly persuasive or even controlling effect, but in the last analysis its decision turns upon the law of the United States, not that of any state.

D'Oench, Duhme & Co. v. Federal Deposit Insurance Corp., 315 U.S. 447, 471 (1942) (Jackson, J., concurring). When a federal court chooses to absorb state law, it is applying the state law as a matter of federal common law. Thus, state law does not supply the rule of decision (even though the federal court may apply a rule derived from state decisions), and state privilege law would not apply. See C.A. Wright, Federal Courts 251-252 (2d ed. 1970); Holmberg v. Armbrecht, 327 U.S. 392 (1946); DeSylva v. Ballentine, 351 U.S. 570, 581 (1956); 9 Wright & Miller, Federal Rules and Procedure § 2408.

In civil actions and proceedings, where the rule of decision as to a claim or defense or as to an element of a claim or defense is supplied by state law, the House provision requires that state privilege law apply.

The Conference adopts the House provision. House Report No. 93-1597.

Rule 502. Attorney-Client Privilege and Work Product; Limitations on Waiver

The following provisions apply, in the circumstances set out, to disclosure of a communication or information covered by the attorney-client privilege or work-product protection.

(a) Disclosure made in a Federal proceeding or to a Federal office or agency; scope of a waiver.--When the disclosure is made in a Federal proceeding or to a Federal office or agency and waives the attorney-client privilege or work-product protection, the waiver extends to an undisclosed communication or information in a Federal or State proceeding only if:

(1) the waiver is intentional;

(2) the disclosed and undisclosed communications or information concern the same subject matter; and

(3) they ought in fairness to be considered together.

(b) Inadvertent disclosure.--When made in a Federal proceeding or to a Federal office or agency, the disclosure does not operate as a waiver in a Federal or State proceeding if:

(1) the disclosure is inadvertent;

(2) the holder of the privilege or protection took reasonable steps to prevent disclosure; and

(3) the holder promptly took reasonable steps to rectify the error, including (if applicable) following Federal Rule of Civil Procedure 26(b)(5)(B).

(c) Disclosure made in a State proceeding.--When the disclosure is made in a State proceeding and is not the subject of a State-court order concerning waiver, the disclosure does not operate as a waiver in a Federal proceeding if the disclosure:

(1) would not be a waiver under this rule if it had been made in a Federal proceeding; or

(2) is not a waiver under the law of the State where the disclosure occurred.

(d) Controlling effect of a court order.--A Federal court may order that the privilege or protection is not waived by disclosure connected with the litigation pending before the court--in which event the disclosure is also not a waiver in any other Federal or State proceeding.

(e) Controlling effect of a party agreement.--An agreement on the effect of disclosure in a Federal proceeding is binding only on the parties to the agreement, unless it is incorporated into a court order.

(f) Controlling effect of this rule.--Notwithstanding Rules 101 and 1101, this rule applies to State proceedings and to Federal court-annexed and Federal court-mandated arbitration proceedings, in the circumstances set out in the rule. And notwithstanding Rule 501, this rule applies even if State law provides the rule of decision.

(g) Definitions.--In this rule:

(1) 'attorney-client privilege" means the protection that applicable law provides for confidential attorney-client communications; and

(2) 'work-product protection" means the protection that applicable law provides for tangible material (or its intangible equivalent) prepared in anticipation of litigation or for trial.

ARTICLE VI. WITNESSES

Rule 601. General Rule of Competency

Every person is competent to be a witness except as otherwise provided in these rules. However, in civil actions and proceedings, with respect to an element of a claim or defense as to which State law supplies the rule of decision, the competency of a witness shall be determined in accordance with State law.

ADVISORY COMMITTEE NOTES

1972 Proposed Rules

This general ground-clearing eliminates all grounds of incompetency not specifically recognized in the succeeding rules of this Article. Included among the grounds thus abolished are religious belief, conviction of crime, and connection with the litigation as a party or interested person or spouse of a party or interested person. With the exception of the so-called Dead Man's Acts, American jurisdictions generally have ceased to recognize these grounds.

The Dead Man's Acts are surviving traces of the common law disqualification of parties and interested persons. They exist in variety too great to convey conviction of their wisdom and effectiveness. These rules contain no provision of this kind. For the reasoning underlying the decision not to give effect to state statutes in diversity cases, see the Advisory Committee's Note to Rule 501.

No mental or moral qualifications for testifying as a witness are specified. Standards of mental capacity have proved elusive in actual application. A leading commentator observes that few witnesses are disqualified on that ground. Weihofen, Testimonial Competence and Credibility, 34 Geo.Wash.L.Rev. 53 (1965). Discretion is regularly exercised in favor of allowing the testimony. A witness wholly without capacity is difficult to imagine. The question is one particularly suited to the jury as one of weight and credibility, subject to judicial authority to review the sufficiency of the evidence. 2 Wigmore §§ 501, 509. Standards of moral qualification in practice consist essentially of evaluating a person's truthfulness in terms of his own answers about it. Their principal utility is in affording an opportunity on voir dire examination to impress upon the witness his moral duty. This result may, however, be accomplished more directly, and without haggling in terms of legal standards, by the manner of administering the oath or affirmation under Rule 603.

Admissibility of religious belief as a ground of impeachment is treated in Rule 610. Conviction of crime as a ground of impeachment is the subject of Rule 609. Marital relationship is the basis for privilege under Rule 505. Interest in the outcome of litigation and mental capacity are, of course, highly relevant to credibility and require no special treatment to render them admissible along with other matters bearing upon the perception, memory, and narration of witnesses.

1974 Enactment

Rule 601 as submitted to the Congress provided that "Every person is competent to be a witness except as otherwise provided in these rules." One effect of the Rule as proposed would have been to abolish age, mental capacity, and other grounds recognized in some State jurisdictions as making a person incompetent as a witness. The greatest controversy centered around the Rule's rendering inapplicable in the federal courts the so-called Dead Man's Statutes which exist in some States. Acknowledging that there is substantial disagreement as to the merit of Dead Man's Statutes, the Committee nevertheless believed that where such statutes have been enacted they represent State policy which should not be overturned in the absence of a compelling federal interest. The Committee therefore amended the Rule to make competency in civil actions determinable in accordance with State law with respect to elements of claims or defenses as to which State law supplies the rule of decision. Cf. Courtland v. Walston & Co., Inc., 340 F.Supp. 1076, 1087-1092 (S.D.N.Y.1972). House Report No. 93-650.

The amendment to rule 601 parallels the treatment accorded Rule 501 discussed immediately above. Senate Report No. 93-1277.

Rule 601 deals with competency of witnesses. Both the House and Senate bills provide that federal competency law applies in criminal cases. In civil actions and proceedings, the House bill provides that state competency law applies "to an element of a claim or defense as to which State law supplies the rule of decision." The Senate bill provides that "in civil actions and proceedings arising under 28 U.S.C. § 1332 or 28 U.S.C. § 1335, or between citizens of different States and removed under 28 U.S.C. § 1441(b) the competency of a witness, person, government, State or political subdivision thereof is determined in accordance with State law, unless with respect to the particular claim or defense, Federal law supplies the rule of decision."

The wording of the House and Senate bills differs in the treatment of civil actions and proceedings. The rule in the House bill applies to evidence that relates to "an element of a claim or defense." If an item of proof tends to support or defeat a claim or defense, or an element of a claim or defense, and if state law supplies the rule of decision for that claim or defense, then state competency law applies to that item of proof.

For reasons similar to those underlying its action on Rule 501, the Conference adopts the House provision. House Report No. 93-1597.

Rule 602. Lack of Personal Knowledge

A witness may not testify to a matter unless evidence is introduced sufficient to support a finding that the witness has personal knowledge of the matter. Evidence to prove personal knowledge may, but need not, consist of the witness' own testimony. This rule is subject to the provisions of rule 703, relating to opinion testimony by expert witnesses.

ADVISORY COMMITTEE NOTES

1972 Proposed Rules
" * * * [T]he rule requiring that a witness who testifies to a fact which can be perceived by the senses must have had an opportunity to observe, and must have actually observed the fact" is a "most pervasive manifestation" of the common law insistence upon "the most reliable sources of information." McCormick § 10, p. 19. These foundation requirements may, of course, be furnished by the testimony of the witness himself; hence personal knowledge is not an absolute but may consist of what the witness thinks he knows from personal perception. 2 Wigmore § 650. It will be observed that the rule is in fact a specialized application of the provisions of Rule 104(b) on conditional relevancy.

This rule does not govern the situation of a witness who testifies to a hearsay statement as such, if he has personal knowledge of the making of the statement. Rules 801 and 805 would be applicable. This rule would, however, prevent him from testifying to the subject matter of the hearsay statement, as he has no personal knowledge of it.

The reference to Rule 703 is designed to avoid any question of conflict between the present rule and the provisions of that rule allowing an expert to express opinions based on facts of which he does not have personal knowledge.

1987 Amendments
The amendments are technical. No substantive change is intended.

1988 Amendments
The amendment is technical. No substantive change is intended.

Rule 603. Oath or Affirmation

Before testifying, every witness shall be required to declare that the witness will testify truthfully, by oath or affirmation administered in a form calculated to awaken the witness' conscience and impress the witness' mind with the duty to do so.

ADVISORY COMMITTEE NOTES

1972 Proposed Rules
The rule is designed to afford the flexibility required in dealing with religious adults, atheists, conscientious objectors, mental defectives, and children. Affirmation is simply a solemn undertaking to tell the truth; no special verbal formula is required. As is true generally, affirmation is recognized by federal law. "Oath" includes affirmation, 1 U.S.C. § 1; judges and clerks may administer oaths and

affirmations, 28 U.S.C. §§ 459, 953; and affirmations are acceptable in lieu of oaths under Rule 43(d) of the Federal Rules of Civil Procedure. Perjury by a witness is a crime, 18 U.S.C. § 1621.

1987 Amendments
The amendments are technical. No substantive change is intended.

Rule 604. Interpreters

An interpreter is subject to the provisions of these rules relating to qualification as an expert and the administration of an oath or affirmation to make a true translation.

ADVISORY COMMITTEE NOTES

1972 Proposed Rules
The rule implements Rule 43(f) of the Federal Rules of Civil Procedure and Rule 28(b) of the Federal Rules of Criminal Procedure, both of which contain provisions for the appointment and compensation of interpreters.

1987 Amendments
The amendment is technical. No substantive change is intended.

Rule 605. Competency of Judge as Witness

The judge presiding at the trial may not testify in that trial as a witness. No objection need be made in order to preserve the point.

ADVISORY COMMITTEE NOTES

1972 Proposed Rules
In view of the mandate of 28 U.S.C. § 455 that a judge disqualify himself in "any case in which he * * * is or has been a material witness," the likelihood that the presiding judge in a federal court might be called to testify in the trial over which he is presiding is slight. Nevertheless the possibility is not totally eliminated.

The solution here presented is a broad rule of incompetency, rather than such alternatives as incompetency only as to material matters, leaving the matter to the discretion of the judge, or recognizing no incompetency. The choice is the result of inability to evolve satisfactory answers to questions which arise when the judge abandons the bench for the witness stand. Who rules on objections? Who compels him to answer? Can he rule impartially on the weight and admissibility of his own testimony? Can he be impeached or cross-examined effectively? Can he, in a jury trial, avoid conferring his seal of approval on one side in the eyes of the jury? Can he, in a bench trial, avoid an involvement destructive of impartiality? The rule of general incompetency has substantial support. See Report of the Special Committee on the Propriety of Judges Appearing as Witnesses, 36 A.B.A.J. 630 (1950); cases collected in Annot. 157 A.L.R. 311; McCormick § 68, p. 147; Uniform Rule 42; California Evidence Code § 703; Kansas Code of Civil Procedure § 60-442; New Jersey Evidence Rule 42. Cf. 6 Wigmore § 1909, which advocates leaving the matter to the discretion of the judge, and statutes to that effect collected in Annot. 157 A.L.R. 311.

The rule provides an "automatic" objection. To require an actual objection would confront the opponent with a choice between not objecting, with the result of allowing the testimony, and objecting, with the probable result of excluding the testimony but at the price of continuing the trial before a judge likely to feel that his integrity had been attacked by the objector.

Rule 606. Competency of Juror as Witness

(a) At the trial. A member of the jury may not testify as a witness before that jury in the trial of the case in which the juror is sitting. If the juror is called so to testify, the opposing party shall be afforded an opportunity to object out of the presence of the jury.

(b) Inquiry into validity of verdict or indictment. Upon an inquiry into the validity of a verdict or indictment, a juror may not testify as to any matter or statement occurring during the course of the jury's deliberations or to the effect of anything upon that or any other juror's mind or emotions as influencing the juror to assent to or dissent from the verdict or indictment or concerning the juror's mental processes in connection therewith. But a juror may testify about (1) whether extraneous prejudicial information was improperly brought to the jury's attention, (2) whether any outside influence was improperly brought to bear upon any juror, or (3) whether there was a mistake in entering the verdict onto the verdict form. A juror's affidavit or evidence of any statement by the juror may not be received on a matter about which the juror would be precluded from testifying.

ADVISORY COMMITTEE NOTES

1972 Proposed Rules
Note to Subdivision (a). The considerations which bear upon the permissibility of testimony by a juror in the trial in which he is sitting as juror bear an obvious similarity to those evoked when the judge is called as a witness. See Advisory

Committee's Note to Rule 605. The judge is not, however in this instance so involved as to call for departure from usual principles requiring objection to be made; hence the only provision on objection is that opportunity be afforded for its making out of the presence of the jury. Compare Rule 605.

Note to Subdivision (b). Whether testimony, affidavits, or statements of jurors should be received for the purpose of invalidating or supporting a verdict or indictment, and if so, under what circumstances, has given rise to substantial differences of opinion. The familiar rubric that a juror may not impeach his own verdict, dating from Lord Mansfield's time, is a gross oversimplification. The values sought to be promoted by excluding the evidence include freedom of deliberation, stability and finality of verdicts, and protection of jurors against annoyance and embarrassment. McDonald v. Pless, 238 U.S. 264, 35 S.Ct. 783, 59 L.Ed. 1300 (1915). On the other hand, simply putting verdicts beyond effective reach can only promote irregularity and injustice. The rule offers an accommodation between these competing considerations.

The mental operations and emotional reactions of jurors in arriving at a given result would, if allowed as a subject of inquiry, place every verdict at the mercy of jurors and invite tampering and harassment. See Grenz v. Werre, 129 N.W.2d 681 (N.D.1964). The authorities are in virtually complete accord in excluding the evidence. Fryer, Note on Disqualification of Witnesses, Selected Writings on Evidence and Trial 345, 347 (Fryer ed. 1957); Maguire, Weinstein, et al., Cases on Evidence 887 (5th ed. 1965); 8 Wigmore § 2349 (McNaughton Rev.1961). As to matters other than mental operations and emotional reactions of jurors, substantial authority refuses to allow a juror to disclose irregularities which occur in the jury room, but allows his testimony as to irregularities occurring outside and allows outsiders to testify as to occurrences both inside and out. 8 Wigmore § 2354 (McNaughton Rev.1961). However, the door of the jury room is not necessarily a satisfactory dividing point, and the Supreme Court has refused to accept it for every situation. Mattox v. United States, 146 U.S. 140, 13 S.Ct. 50, 36 L.Ed. 917 (1892).

Under the federal decisions the central focus has been upon insulation of the manner in which the jury reached its verdict, and this protection extends to each of the components of deliberation, including arguments, statements, discussions, mental and emotional reactions, votes, and any other feature of the process. Thus testimony or affidavits of jurors have been held incompetent to show a compromise verdict. Hyde v. United States, 225 U.S. 347, 382 (1912); a quotient verdict, McDonald v. Pless, 238 U.S. 264 (1915); speculation as to insurance coverage. Holden v. Porter, 405 F.2d 878 (10th Cir.1969); Farmers Coop. Elev. Ass'n v. Strand, 382 F.2d 224, 230 (8th Cir.1967), cert. denied 389 U.S. 1014; misinterpretation of instructions, Farmers Coop. Elev. Ass'n v. Strand, supra; mistake in returning verdict, United States v. Chereton, 309 F.2d 197 (6th Cir.1962); interpretation of guilty plea by one defendant as implicating others, United States v. Crosby, 294 F.2d 928, 949 (2d Cir.1961). The policy does not, however, foreclose testimony by jurors as to prejudicial extraneous information or influences injected into or brought to bear upon the deliberative process. Thus a juror is recognized as competent to testify to statements by the bailiff or the introduction of a prejudicial newspaper account into the jury room, Mattox v. United States, 146 U.S. 140 (1892). See also Parker v. Gladden, 385 U.S. 363 (1966).

This rule does not purport to specify the substantive grounds for setting aside verdicts for irregularity; it deals only with the competency of jurors to testify concerning those grounds. Allowing them to testify as to matters other than their own inner reactions involves no particular hazard to the values sought to be protected. The rule is based upon this conclusion. It makes no attempt to specify the substantive grounds for setting aside verdicts for irregularity.

See also Rule 6(e) of the Federal Rules of Criminal Procedure and 18 U.S.C. § 3500, governing the secrecy of grand jury proceedings. The present rule does not relate to secrecy and disclosure but to the competency of certain witnesses and evidence.

1974 Enactment
Note to Subdivision (b). As proposed by the Court, Rule 606(b) limited testimony by a juror in the course of an inquiry into the validity of a verdict or indictment. He could testify as to the influence of extraneous prejudicial information brought to the jury's attention (e.g. a radio newscast or a newspaper account) or an outside influence which improperly had been brought to bear upon a juror (e.g. a threat to the safety of a member of his family), but he could not testify as to other irregularities which occurred in the jury room. Under this formulation a quotient verdict could not be attacked through the testimony of a juror, nor could a juror testify to the drunken condition of a fellow juror which so disabled him that he could not participate in the jury's deliberations.

The 1969 and 1971 Advisory Committee drafts would have permitted a member of the jury to testify concerning these kinds of irregularities in the jury room. The Advisory Committee note in the 1971 draft stated that " * * * the door of the jury room is not a satisfactory dividing point, and the Supreme Court has refused to accept it." The Advisory Committee further commented that--

The trend has been to draw the dividing line between testimony as to mental processes, on the one hand, and as to the existence of conditions or occurrences of events calculated improperly to influence the verdict on the other hand, without regard to whether the happening is within or without the jury room. * * * The jurors are the persons who know what really happened. Allowing them to testify as to matters other than their own reactions involves no particular hazard to the values sought to be protected. The rule is based upon this conclusion. It makes no attempt to specify the substantive grounds for setting aside verdicts for irregularity.

Objective jury misconduct may be testified to in California, Florida, Iowa, Kansas, Nebraska, New Jersey, North Dakota, Ohio, Oregon, Tennessee, Texas, and Washington.

Persuaded that the better practice is that provided for in the earlier drafts, the Committee amended subdivision (b) to read in the text of those drafts. House Report No. 93-650.

Note to Subdivision (b). As adopted by the House, this rule would permit the impeachment of verdicts by inquiry into, not the mental processes of the jurors, but what happened in terms of conduct in the jury room. This extension of the ability to impeach a verdict is felt to be unwarranted and ill-advised.

The rule passed by the House embodies a suggestion by the Advisory Committee of the Judicial Conference that is considerably broader than the final version adopted by the Supreme Court, which embodied long-accepted Federal law. Although forbidding the impeachment of verdicts by inquiry into the jurors' mental processes, it deletes from the Supreme Court version the proscription against testimony "as to any matter or statement occurring during the course of the jury's deliberations." This deletion would have the effect of opening verdicts up to challenge on the basis of what happened during the jury's internal deliberations, for example, where a juror alleged that the jury refused to follow the trial judge's instructions or that some of the jurors did not take part in deliberations.

Permitting an individual to attack a jury verdict based upon the jury's internal deliberations has long been recognized as unwise by the Supreme Court. In McDonald v. Pless, the Court stated:

[L]et it once be established that verdicts solemnly made and publicly returned into court can be attacked and set aside on the testimony of those who took part in their publication and all verdicts could be, and many would be, followed by an inquiry in the hope of discovering something which might invalidate the finding. Jurors would be harassed and beset by the defeated party in an effort to secure from them evidence of facts which might establish misconduct sufficient to set aside a verdict. If evidence thus secured could be thus used, the result would be to make what was intended to be a private deliberation, the constant subject of public investigation--to the destruction of all frankness and freedom of discussion and conference [238 U.S. 264, at 267 (1914)].

As it stands then, the rule would permit the harassment of former jurors by losing parties as well as the possible exploitation of disgruntled or otherwise badly-motivated ex-jurors.

Public policy requires a finality to litigation. And common fairness requires that absolute privacy be preserved for jurors to engage in the full and free debate necessary to the attainment of just verdicts. Jurors will not be able to function effectively if their deliberations are to be scrutinized in post-trial litigation. In the interest of protecting the jury system and the citizens who make it work, rule 606 should not permit any inquiry into the internal deliberations of the jurors. Senate Report No. 93-1277.

Note to Subdivision (b). Rule 606(b) deals with juror testimony in an inquiry into the validity of a verdict or indictment. The House bill provides that a juror cannot testify about his mental processes or about the effect of anything upon his or another juror's mind as influencing him to assent to or dissent from a verdict or indictment. Thus, the House bill allows a juror to testify about objective matters occurring during the jury's deliberation, such as the misconduct of another juror or the reaching of a quotient verdict. The Senate bill does not permit juror testimony about any matter or statement occurring during the course of the jury's deliberations. The Senate bill does provide, however, that a juror may testify on the question whether extraneous prejudicial information was improperly brought to the jury's attention and on the question whether any outside influence was improperly brought to bear on any juror.

The Conference adopts the Senate amendment. The Conferees believe that jurors should be encouraged to be conscientious in promptly reporting to the court misconduct that occurs during jury deliberations. House Report No. 93-1597.

1987 Amendments
The amendments are technical. No substantive change is intended.

2006 Amendments
Rule 606(b) has been amended to provide that juror testimony may be used to prove that the verdict reported was the result of a mistake in entering the verdict on the verdict form. The amendment responds to a divergence between the text of the Rule and the case law that has established an exception for proof of clerical errors. See, e.g., Plummer v. Springfield Term. Ry., 5 F.3d 1, 3 (1st Cir. 1993) ("A number of circuits hold, and we agree, that juror testimony regarding an alleged clerical error, such as announcing a verdict different than that agreed upon, does not challenge the validity of the verdict or the deliberation of mental processes, and therefore is not subject to Rule 606(b)."); TeeVee Toons, Inc., v. MP3.Com, Inc., 148 F.Supp.2d 276, 278 (S.D.N.Y. 2001) (noting that Rule 606(b) has been silent regarding inquiries designed to confirm the accuracy of a verdict).

In adopting the exception for proof of mistakes in entering the verdict on the verdict form, the amendment specifically rejects the broader exception, adopted by some courts, permitting the use of juror testimony to prove that the jurors were operating under a misunderstanding about the consequences of the result that they agreed upon. See, e.g., Attridge v. Cencorp Div. of Dover Techs. Int'l, Inc., 836 F.2d 113, 116 (2d Cir. 1987); Eastridge Development Co., v. Halpert Associates, Inc., 853 F.2d 772 (10th Cir. 1988). The broader exception is rejected because an inquiry into whether the jury misunderstood or misapplied an instruction goes to the jurors' mental processes underlying the verdict, rather than the verdict's accuracy in capturing what the jurors had agreed upon. See, e.g. , Karl v. Burlington Northern R.R., 880 F.2d 68, 74 (8th Cir. 1989) (error to receive juror testimony on whether verdict was the result of jurors' misunderstanding of instructions: "The jurors did not state that the figure written by the foreman was different from that which they agreed upon, but indicated that the figure the foreman wrote down was intended to be a net figure, not a gross figure. Receiving such statements violates Rule 606(b) because the testimony relates to how the jury interpreted the court's instructions, and concerns the jurors' 'mental processes,' which is forbidden by the rule."); Robles v. Exxon Corp., 862 F.2d 1201, 1208 (5th Cir. 1989) ("the alleged error here goes to the substance of what the jury was asked to decide, necessarily implicating the jury's mental processes insofar as it questions the jury's understanding of the court's instructions and application of those instructions to the facts of the case"). Thus, the exception established by the amendment is limited to cases such as "where the jury foreperson wrote down, in response to an interrogatory, a number different from that agreed upon by the jury, or mistakenly stated that the defendant was 'guilty' when the jury had actually agreed that the defendant was not guilty." Id.

It should be noted that the possibility of errors in the verdict form will be reduced substantially by polling the jury. Rule 606(b) does not, of course, prevent this precaution. See 8 C. Wigmore, Evidence, § 2350 at 691 (McNaughten ed. 1961) (noting that the reasons for the rule barring juror testimony, "namely, the dangers of uncertainty and of tampering with the jurors to procure testimony, disappear in large part if such investigation as may be desired is made by the judge and takes place before the jurors' discharge and separation") (emphasis in original). Errors that come to light after polling the jury "may be corrected on the spot, or the jury may be sent out to continue deliberations, or, if necessary, a new trial may be ordered." C. Mueller & L. Kirkpatrick, Evidence Under the Rules at 671 (2d ed. 1999) (citing Sincox v. United States, 571 F.2d 876, 878-79 (5th Cir. 1978)).

Rule 607. Who May Impeach

The credibility of a witness may be attacked by any party, including the party calling the witness.

ADVISORY COMMITTEE NOTES

1972 Proposed Rules

The traditional rule against impeaching one's own witness is abandoned as based on false premises. A party does not hold out his witnesses as worthy of belief, since he rarely has a free choice in selecting them. Denial of the right leaves the party at the mercy of the witness and the adversary. If the impeachment is by a prior statement, it is free from hearsay dangers and is excluded from the category of hearsay under Rule 801(d)(1). Ladd, Impeachment of One's Own Witness--New Developments, 4 U.Chi.L.Rev. 69 (1936); McCormick § 38; 3 Wigmore §§ 896-918. The substantial inroads into the old rule made over the years by decisions, rules, and statutes are evidence of doubts as to its basic soundness and workability. Cases are collected in 3 Wigmore § 905. Revised Rule 32(a)(1) of the Federal Rules of Civil Procedure allows any party to impeach a witness by means of his deposition, and Rule 43(b) has allowed the calling and impeachment of an adverse party or person identified with him. Illustrative statutes allowing a party to impeach his own witness under varying circumstances are Ill.Rev.Stats.1967, c. 110, § 60; Mass.Laws Annot. 1959, c. 233, § 23; 20 N.M.Stats.Annot. 1953, § 20-2-4; N.Y. CPLR § 4514 (McKinney 1963); 12 Vt.Stats.Annot.1959, §§ 1641a, 1642. Complete judicial rejection of the old rule is found in United States v. Freeman, 302 F.2d 347 (2d Cir.1962). The same result is reached in Uniform Rule 20; California Evidence Code § 785; Kansas Code of Civil Procedure § 60-420. See also New Jersey Evidence Rule 20.

1987 Amendments

The amendment is technical. No substantive change is intended.

Rule 608. Evidence of Character and Conduct of Witness

(a) Opinion and reputation evidence of character. The credibility of a witness may be attacked or supported by evidence in the form of opinion or reputation, but subject to these limitations: (1) the evidence may refer only to character for truthfulness or untruthfulness, and (2) evidence of truthful character is admissible only after the character of the witness for truthfulness has been attacked by opinion or reputation evidence or otherwise.

(b) Specific instances of conduct. Specific instances of the conduct of a witness, for the purpose of attacking or supporting the witness' character for truthfulness, other than conviction of crime as provided in rule 609, may not be proved by extrinsic evidence. They may, however, in the discretion of the court, if probative of truthfulness or untruthfulness, be inquired into on cross-examination of the witness (1) concerning the witness' character for truthfulness or untruthfulness, or (2) concerning the character for truthfulness or untruthfulness of another witness as to which character the witness being cross-examined has testified.

The giving of testimony, whether by an accused or by any other witness, does not operate as a waiver of the accused's or the witness' privilege against self-incrimination when examined with respect to matters that relate only to character for truthfulness.

ADVISORY COMMITTEE NOTES

1972 Proposed Rules
Note to Subdivision (a). In Rule 404(a) the general position is taken that character evidence is not admissible for the purpose of proving that the person acted in conformity therewith, subject, however, to several exceptions, one of which is character evidence of a witness as bearing upon his credibility. The present rule develops that exception.

In accordance with the bulk of judicial authority, the inquiry is strictly limited to character for veracity, rather than allowing evidence as to character generally. The result is to sharpen relevancy, to reduce surprise, waste of time, and confusion, and to make the lot of the witness somewhat less unattractive. McCormick § 44.

The use of opinion and reputation evidence as means of proving the character of witnesses is consistent with Rule 405(a). While the modern practice has purported to exclude opinion, witnesses who testify to reputation seem in fact often to be giving their opinions, disguised somewhat misleadingly as reputation. See McCormick § 44. And even under the modern practice, a common relaxation has allowed inquiry as to whether the witnesses would believe the principal witness under oath. United States v. Walker, 313 F.2d 236 (6th Cir.1963), and cases cited therein; McCormick § 44, pp. 94-95, n. 3.

Character evidence in support of credibility is admissible under the rule only after the witness' character has first been attacked, as has been the case at common law. Maguire, Weinstein, et al., Cases on Evidence 295 (5th ed. 1965); McCormick § 49, p. 105; 4 Wigmore § 1104. The enormous needless consumption of time which a contrary practice would entail justifies the limitation. Opinion or reputation that the witness is untruthful specifically qualifies as an attack under the rule, and evidence of misconduct, including conviction of crime, and of corruption also fall within this category. Evidence of bias or interest does not. McCormick § 49; 4 Wigmore §§ 1106, 1107. Whether evidence in the form of contradiction is an attack upon the character of the witness must depend upon the circumstances. McCormick § 49. Cf. 4 Wigmore §§ 1108, 1109.

As to the use of specific instances on direct by an opinion witness, see the Advisory Committee's Note to Rule 405, supra.

Note to Subdivision (b). In conformity with Rule 405, which forecloses use of evidence of specific incidents as proof in chief of character unless character is an issue in the case, the present rule generally bars evidence of specific instances of conduct of a witness for the purpose of attacking or supporting his credibility. There are, however, two exceptions: (1) specific instances are provable when they have been the subject of criminal conviction, and (2) specific instances may be inquired into on cross-examination of the principal witness or of a witness giving an opinion of his character for truthfulness.

(1) Conviction of crime as a technique of impeachment is treated in detail in Rule 609, and here is merely recognized as an exception to the general rule excluding evidence of specific incidents for impeachment purposes.

(2) Particular instances of conduct, though not the subject of criminal conviction, may be inquired into on cross-examination of the principal witness himself or of a witness who testifies concerning his character for truthfulness. Effective cross-examination demands that some allowance be made for going into matters of this kind, but the possibilities of abuse are substantial. Consequently safeguards are erected in the form of specific requirements that the instances inquired into be probative of truthfulness or its opposite and not remote in time. Also, the overriding protection of Rule 403 requires that probative value not be outweighed by danger of unfair prejudice, confusion of issues, or misleading the jury, and that of Rule 611 bars harassment and undue embarrassment.

The final sentence constitutes a rejection of the doctrine of such cases as People v. Sorge, 301 N.Y. 198, 93 N.E.2d 637 (1950), that any past criminal act relevant to credibility may be inquired into on cross-examination, in apparent disregard of the privilege against self-incrimination. While it is clear that an ordinary witness cannot make a partial disclosure of incriminating matter and then invoke the privilege on cross-examination, no tenable contention can be made that merely by testifying he waives his right to foreclose inquiry on cross-examination into criminal activities for the purpose of attacking his credibility. So to hold would reduce the privilege to a nullity. While it is true that an accused, unlike an ordinary witness, has an option whether to testify, if the option can be exercised only at the price of opening up inquiry as to any and all criminal acts committed during his lifetime, the right to testify could scarcely be said to possess much vitality. In Griffin v. California, 380 U.S. 609, 85 S.Ct. 1229, 14 L.Ed.2d 106 (1965), the Court held that allowing comment on the election of an accused not to testify exacted a constitutionally impermissible price, and so here. While no specific provision in terms confers constitutional status on the right of an accused to take the stand in his own defense, the existence of the right is so completely recognized that a denial of it or substantial infringement upon it would surely be of due process dimensions. See Ferguson v. Georgia, 365 U.S. 570, 81 S.Ct. 756, 5 L.Ed.2d 783 (1961); McCormick § 131; 8 Wigmore § 2276 (McNaughton Rev.1961). In any event, wholly aside from constitutional considerations, the provision represents a sound policy.

1974 Enactment
Note to Subdivision (a). Rule 608(a) as submitted by the Court permitted attack to be made upon the character for truthfulness or untruthfulness of a witness either by reputation or opinion testimony. For the same reason underlying its decision to eliminate the admissibility of opinion testimony in Rule 405(a), the Committee amended Rule 608(a) to delete the reference to opinion testimony.

Note to Subdivision (b). The second sentence of Rule 608(b) as submitted by the Court permitted specific instances of misconduct of a witness to be inquired into on cross-examination for the purpose of attacking his credibility, if probative of truthfulness or untruthfulness, "and not remote in time". Such cross-examination could be of the witness himself or of another witness who testifies as to "his" character for truthfulness or untruthfulness.

The Committee amended the Rule to emphasize the discretionary power of the court in permitting such testimony and deleted the reference to remoteness in time as being unnecessary and confusing (remoteness from time of trial or remoteness from the incident involved?). As recast, the Committee amendment also makes clear the antecedent of "his" in the original Court proposal. House Report No. 93-650.

The Senate amendment adds the words "opinion or" to conform the first sentence of the rule with the remainder of the rule.

The Conference adopts the Senate amendment. House Report No. 93-1597.

1987 Amendments
The amendments are technical. No substantive change is intended.

1988 Amendments
The amendment is technical. No substantive change is intended.

2003 Amendments
The Rule has been amended to clarify that the absolute prohibition on extrinsic evidence applies only when the sole reason for proffering that evidence is to attack or support the witness' character for truthfulness. See United States v. Abel, 469 U.S. 45 (1984); United States v. Fusco, 748 F.2d 996 (5th Cir. 1984) (Rule 608(b) limits the use of evidence "designed to show that the witness has done things, unrelated to the suit being tried, that make him more or less believable per se");

Ohio R.Evid. 608(b). On occasion the Rule's use of the overbroad term "credibility" has been read "to bar extrinsic evidence for bias, competency and contradiction impeachment since they too deal with credibility." American Bar Association Section of Litigation, Emerging Problems Under the Federal Rules of Evidence at 161 (3d ed. 1998). The amendment conforms the language of the Rule to its original intent, which was to impose an absolute bar on extrinsic evidence only if the sole purpose for offering the evidence was to prove the witness' character for veracity. See Advisory Committee Note to Rule 608(b) (stating that the Rule is "[i] n conformity with Rule 405, which forecloses use of evidence of specific incidents as proof in chief of character unless character is in issue in the case ... ").

By limiting the application of the Rule to proof of a witness' character for truthfulness, the amendment leaves the admissibility of extrinsic evidence offered for other grounds of impeachment (such as contradiction, prior inconsistent statement, bias and mental capacity) to Rules 402 and 403. See, e.g., United States v. Winchenbach, 197 F.3d 548 (1st Cir. 1999) (admissibility of a prior inconsistent statement offered for impeachment is governed by Rules 402 and 403, not Rule 608(b)); United States v. Tarantino, 846 F.2d 1384 (D.C. Cir. 1988) (admissibility of extrinsic evidence offered to contradict a witness is governed by Rules 402 and 403); United States v. Lindemann, 85 F.3d 1232 (7th Cir. 1996) (admissibility of extrinsic evidence of bias is governed by Rules 402 and 403).

It should be noted that the extrinsic evidence prohibition of Rule 608(b) bars any reference to the consequences that a witness might have suffered as a result of an alleged bad act. For example, Rule 608(b) prohibits counsel from mentioning that a witness was suspended or disciplined for the conduct that is the subject of impeachment, when that conduct is offered only to prove the character of the witness. See United States v. Davis, 183 F.3d 231, 257 n.12 (3d Cir. 1999) (emphasizing that in attacking the defendant's character for truthfulness "the government cannot make reference to Davis's forty-four day suspension or that Internal Affairs found that he lied about" an incident because "[s]uch evidence would not only be hearsay to the extent it contains assertion of fact, it would be inadmissible extrinsic evidence under Rule 608(b)"). See also Stephen A. Saltzburg, Impeaching the Witness: Prior Bad Acts and Extrinsic Evidence, 7 Crim. Just. 28, 31 (Winter 1993) ("counsel should not be permitted to circumvent the no-extrinsic-evidence provision by tucking a third person's opinion about prior acts into a question asked of the witness who has denied the act").

For purposes of consistency the term "credibility" has been replaced by the term "character for truthfulness" in the last sentence of subdivision (b). The term "credibility" is also used in subdivision (a). But the Committee found it unnecessary to substitute "character for truthfulness" for "credibility" in Rule 608(a), because subdivision (a)(1) already serves to limit impeachment to proof of such character.

Rules 609(a) and 610 also use the term "credibility" when the intent of those Rules is to regulate impeachment of a witness' character for truthfulness. No inference should be derived from the fact that the Committee proposed an amendment to Rule 608(b) but not to Rules 609 and 610.

Rule 609. Impeachment by Evidence of Conviction of Crime

(a) General rule.--For the purpose of attacking the character for truthfulness of a witness,

(1) evidence that a witness other than an accused has been convicted of a crime shall be admitted, subject to Rule 403, if the crime was punishable by death or imprisonment in excess of one year under the law under which the witness was convicted, and evidence that an accused has been convicted of such a crime shall be admitted if the court determines that the probative value of admitting this evidence outweighs its prejudicial effect to the accused; and

(2) evidence that any witness has been convicted of a crime shall be admitted regardless of the punishment, if it readily can be determined that establishing the elements of the crime required proof or admission of an act of dishonesty or false statement by the witness.

(b) Time limit. Evidence of a conviction under this rule is not admissible if a period of more than ten years has elapsed since the date of the conviction or of the release of the witness from the confinement imposed for that conviction, whichever is the later date, unless the court determines, in the interests of justice, that the probative value of the conviction supported by specific facts and circumstances substantially outweighs its prejudicial effect. However, evidence of a conviction more than 10 years old as calculated herein, is not admissible unless the proponent gives to the adverse party sufficient advance written notice of intent to use such evidence to provide the adverse party with a fair opportunity to contest the use of such evidence.

(c) Effect of pardon, annulment, or certificate of rehabilitation.--Evidence of a conviction is not admissible under this rule if (1) the conviction has been the subject of a pardon, annulment, certificate of rehabilitation, or other equivalent procedure based on a finding of the rehabilitation of the person convicted, and that person has not been convicted of a subsequent crime that was punishable by death or imprisonment in excess of one year, or (2) the conviction has been the subject of a pardon, annulment, or other equivalent procedure based on a finding of innocence.

(d) Juvenile adjudications. Evidence of juvenile adjudications is generally not admissible under this rule. The court may, however, in a criminal case allow evidence of a juvenile adjudication of a witness other than the accused if conviction of the offense would be admissible to attack the credibility of an adult and the court is satisfied that admission in evidence is necessary for a fair determination of the issue of guilt or innocence.

(e) Pendency of appeal. The pendency of an appeal therefrom does not render evidence of a conviction inadmissible. Evidence of the pendency of an appeal is admissible.

ADVISORY COMMITTEE NOTES

1972 Proposed Rules

As a means of impeachment, evidence of conviction of crime is significant only because it stands as proof of the commission of the underlying criminal act. There is little dissent from the general proposition that at least some crimes are relevant to credibility but much disagreement among the cases and commentators about which crimes are usable for this purpose. See McCormick § 43; 2 Wright, Federal Practice and Procedure: Criminal § 416 (1969). The weight of traditional authority has been to allow use of felonies generally, without regard to the nature of the particular offense, and of crimen falsi without regard to the grade of the offense. This is the view accepted by Congress in the 1970 amendment of § 14-305 of the District of Columbia Code, P.L. 91-358, 84 Stat. 473. Uniform Rule 21 and Model Code Rule 106 permit only crimes involving "dishonesty or false statement." Others have thought that the trial judge should have discretion to exclude convictions if the probative value of the evidence of the crime is substantially outweighed by the danger of unfair prejudice. Luck v. United States, 121 U.S.App.D.C. 151, 348 F.2d 763 (1965); McGowan, Impeachment of Criminal Defendants by Prior Convictions, 1970 Law & Soc.Order 1. Whatever may be the merits of those views, this rule is drafted to accord with the Congressional policy manifested in the 1970 legislation.

The proposed rule incorporates certain basic safeguards, in terms applicable to all witnesses but of particular significance to an accused who elects to testify. These protections include the imposition of definite time limitations, giving effect to demonstrated rehabilitation, and generally excluding juvenile adjudications.

Note to Subdivision (a). For purposes of impeachment, crimes are divided into two categories by the rule: (1) those of what is generally regarded as felony grade, without particular regard to the nature of the offense, and (2) those involving dishonesty or false statement, without regard to the grade of the offense. Probable convictions are not limited to violations of federal law. By reason of our constitutional structure, the federal catalog of crimes is far from being a complete one, and resort must be had to the laws of the states for the specification of many crimes. For example, simple theft as compared with theft from interstate commerce. Other instances of borrowing are the Assimilative Crimes Act, making the state law of crimes applicable to the special territorial and maritime jurisdiction of the United States, 18 U.S.C. § 13, and the provision of the Judicial Code disqualifying persons as jurors on the grounds of state as well as federal convictions, 28 U.S.C. § 1865. For evaluation of the crime in terms of seriousness, reference is made to the congressional measurement of felony (subject to imprisonment in excess of one year) rather than adopting state definitions which vary considerably. See 28 U.S.C. § 1865, supra, disqualifying jurors for conviction in state or federal court of crime punishable by imprisonment for more than one year.

Note to Subdivision (b). Few statutes recognize a time limit on impeachment by evidence of conviction. However, practical considerations of fairness and relevancy demand that some boundary be recognized. See Ladd, Credibility Tests--Current Trends, 89 U.Pa.L.Rev. 166, 176-177 (1940). This portion of the rule is derived from the proposal advanced in Recommendation Proposing in Evidence Code, § 788(5), p. 142, Cal.Law Rev.Comm'n (1965), though not adopted. See California Evidence Code § 788.

Note to Subdivision (c). A pardon or its equivalent granted solely for the purpose of restoring civil rights lost by virtue of a conviction has no relevance to an inquiry into character. If, however, the pardon or other proceeding is hinged upon a showing of rehabilitation the situation is otherwise. The result under the rule is to render the conviction inadmissible. The alternative of allowing in evidence both the conviction and the rehabilitation has not been adopted for reasons of policy, economy of time, and difficulties of evaluation.

A similar provision is contained in California Evidence Code § 788. Cf. A.L.I. Model Penal Code, Proposed Official Draft § 306.6(3)(e) (1962), and discussion in A.L.I. Proceedings 310 (1961).

Pardons based on innocence have the effect, of course, of nullifying the conviction ab initio.

Note to Subdivision (d). The prevailing view has been that a juvenile adjudication is not usable for impeachment. Thomas v. United States, 74 App.D.C. 167, 121 F.2d 905 (1941); Cotton v. United States, 355 F.2d 480 (10th Cir.1966). This conclusion was based upon a variety of circumstances. By virtue of its informality, frequently diminished quantum of required proof, and other departures from accepted standards for criminal trials under the theory of parens patriae, the juvenile adjudication was considered to lack the precision and general probative value of the criminal conviction. While In re Gault, 387 U.S. 1, 87 S.Ct. 1428, 18 L.Ed.2d 527 (1967), no doubt eliminates these characteristics insofar as objectionable, other obstacles remain. Practical problems of administration are raised by the common provisions in juvenile legislation that records be kept confidential and that they be destroyed after a short time. While Gault was skeptical as to the realities of confidentiality of juvenile records, it also saw no constitutional obstacles to improvement. 387 U.S. at 25, 87 S.Ct. 1428. See also Note, Rights and Rehabilitation in the Juvenile Courts, 67 Colum.L.Rev. 281, 289 (1967). In addition, policy considerations much akin to those which dictate exclusion of adult convictions after rehabilitation has been established strongly suggest a rule of excluding juvenile adjudications. Admittedly, however, the rehabilitative process may in a given case be a demonstrated failure, or the strategic importance of a given witness may be so great as to require the overriding of general policy in the interests of particular justice. See Giles v. Maryland, 386 U.S. 66, 87 S.Ct. 793, 17 L.Ed.2d 737 (1967). Wigmore was outspoken in his condemnation of the disallowance of juvenile adjudications to impeach, especially when the witness is the complainant in a case of molesting a minor. 1 Wigmore § 196; 3 Id. §§ 924a, 980. The rule recognizes discretion in the judge to effect an accommodation among these various factors by departing from the general principle of exclusion. In deference to the general pattern and policy of juvenile statutes, however, no discretion is accorded when the witness is the accused in a criminal case.

Note to Subdivision (e). The presumption of correctness which ought to attend judicial proceedings supports the position that pendency of an appeal does not preclude use of a conviction for impeachment. United States v. Empire Packing Co., 174 F.2d 16 (7th Cir.1949), cert. denied 337 U.S. 959, 69 S.Ct. 1534, 93 L.Ed. 1758; Bloch v. United States, 226 F.2d 185 (9th Cir.1955), cert. denied 350 U.S. 948, 76 S.Ct. 323, 100 L.Ed. 826 and 353 U.S. 959, 77 S.Ct. 868, 1 L.Ed.2d 910; and see Newman v. United States, 331 F.2d 968 (8th Cir.1964). Contra, Campbell v. United States, 85 U.S.App.D.C. 133, 176 F.2d 45 (1949). The pendency of an appeal is, however, a qualifying circumstance properly considerable.

1974 Enactment
Note to Subdivision (a). Rule 609(a) as submitted by the Court was modeled after Section 133(a) of Public Law 91-358, 14 D.C.Code 305(b)(1), enacted in 1970. The Rule provided that:

For the purpose of attacking the credibility of a witness, evidence that he has been convicted of a crime is admissible but only if the crime (1) was punishable by death or imprisonment in excess of one year under the law under which he was convicted or (2) involved dishonesty or false statement regardless of the punishment.

As reported to the Committee by the Subcommittee, Rule 609(a) was amended to read as follows:

For the purpose of attacking the credibility of a witness, evidence that he has been convicted of a crime is admissible only if the crime (1) was punishable by death or imprisonment in excess of one year, unless the court determines that the danger of unfair prejudice outweighs the probative value of the evidence of the conviction, or (2) involved dishonesty or false statement.

In full committee, the provision was amended to permit attack upon the credibility of a witness by prior conviction only if the prior crime involved dishonesty or false statement. While recognizing that the prevailing doctrine in the federal courts and in most States allows a witness to be impeached by evidence of prior felony convictions without restriction as to type, the Committee was of the view that, because of the danger of unfair prejudice in such practice and the deterrent effect upon an accused who might wish to testify, and even upon a witness who was not the accused, cross-examination by evidence of prior conviction should be limited to those kinds of convictions bearing directly on credibility, i.e., crimes involving dishonesty or false statement.

Note to Subdivision (b). Rule 609(b) as submitted by the Court was modeled after Section 133(a) of Public Law 91-358, 14 D.C.Code 305(b)(2)(B), enacted in 1970. The Rule provided:

Evidence of a conviction under this rule is not admissible if a period of more than ten years has elapsed since the date of the release of the witness from confinement imposed for his most recent conviction, or the expiration of the period of his parole, probation, or sentence granted or imposed with respect to his most recent conviction, whichever is the later date.

Under this formulation, a witness' entire past record of criminal convictions could be used for impeachment (provided the conviction met the standard of subdivision (a)), if the witness had been most recently released from confinement, or the period of his parole or probation had expired, within ten years of the conviction.

The Committee amended the Rule to read in the text of the 1971 Advisory Committee version to provide that upon the expiration of ten years from the date of a conviction of a witness, or of his release from confinement for that offense, that conviction may no longer be used for impeachment. The Committee was of the view that after ten years following a person's release from confinement (or from the date of his conviction) the probative value of the conviction with respect to that person's credibility diminished to a point where it should no longer be admissible.

Note to Subdivision (c). Rule 609(c) as submitted by the Court provided in part that evidence of a witness' prior conviction is not admissible to attack his credibility if the conviction was the subject of a pardon, annulment, or other equivalent procedure, based on a showing of rehabilitation, and the witness has not been convicted of a subsequent crime. The Committee amended the Rule to provide that the "subsequent crime" must have been "punishable by death or imprisonment in excess of one year", on the ground that a subsequent conviction of an offense not a felony is insufficient to rebut the finding that the witness has been rehabilitated. The Committee also intends that the words "based on a finding of the rehabilitation of the person convicted" apply not only to "certificate of rehabilitation, or other equivalent procedure", but also to "pardon" and "annulment.". House Report No. 93-650.

Note to Subdivision (a). As proposed by the Supreme Court, the rule would allow the use of prior convictions to impeach if the crime was a felony or a misdemeanor if the misdemeanor involved dishonesty or false statement. As modified by the House, the rule would admit prior convictions for impeachment purposes only if the offense, whether felony or misdemeanor, involved dishonesty or false statement.

The committee has adopted a modified version of the House-passed rule. In your committee's view, the danger of unfair prejudice is far greater when the accused, as opposed to other witnesses, testifies, because the jury may be prejudiced not merely on the question of credibility but also on the ultimate question of guilt or innocence. Therefore, with respect to defendants, the committee agreed with the House limitation that only offenses involved false statement or dishonesty may be used. By that phrase, the committee means crimes such as perjury or subornation of perjury, false statement, criminal fraud, embezzlement or false pretense, or any other offense, in the nature of crimen falsi the commission of which involves some element of untruthfulness, deceit or falsification bearing on the accused's propensity to testify truthfully.

With respect to other witnesses, in addition to any prior conviction involving false statement or dishonesty, any other felony may be used to impeach if, and only if, the court finds that the probative value of such evidence outweighs its prejudicial effect against the party offering that witness.

Notwithstanding this provision, proof of any prior offense otherwise admissible under Rule 404 could still be offered for the purposes sanctioned by that rule. Furthermore, the committee intends that notwithstanding this rule, a defendant's misrepresentation regarding the existence or nature of prior convictions may be met by rebuttal evidence, including the record of such prior convictions. Similarly, such records may be offered to rebut representations made by the defendant regarding his attitude toward or willingness to commit a general category of offense, although denials or other representations by the defendant regarding the specific conduct which forms the basis of the charge against him shall not make prior convictions admissible to rebut such statement.

In regard to either type of representation, of course, prior convictions may be offered in rebuttal only if the defendant's statement is made in response to defense counsel's questions or is made gratuitously in the course of cross-examination. Prior convictions may not be offered as rebuttal evidence if the prosecution has sought to circumvent the purpose of this rule by asking questions which elicit such representations from the defendant.

One other clarifying amendment has been added to this subsection, that is, to provide that the admissibility of evidence of a prior conviction is permitted only upon cross-examination of a witness. It is not admissible if a person does not testify. It is to be understood, however, that a court record of a prior conviction is admissible to prove that conviction if the witness has forgotten or denies its existence.

Note to Subdivision (b). Although convictions over ten years old generally do not have much probative value, there may be exceptional circumstances under which the conviction substantially bears on the credibility of the witness. Rather than exclude all convictions over 10 years old, the committee adopted an amendment in the form of a final clause to the section granting the court discretion to admit convictions over 10 years old, but only upon a determination by the court that the probative value of the conviction supported by specific facts and circumstances, substantially outweighs its prejudicial effect.

It is intended that convictions over 10 years old will be admitted very rarely and only in exceptional circumstances. The rules provide that the decision be supported by specific facts and circumstances thus requiring the court to make specific findings on the record as to the particular facts and circumstances it has considered in determining that the probative value of the conviction substantially outweighs its prejudicial impact. It is expected that, in fairness, the court will give the party against whom the conviction is introduced a full and adequate opportunity to contest its admission. Senate Report No. 93-1277.

Rule 609 defines when a party may use evidence of a prior conviction in order to impeach a witness. The Senate amendments make changes in two subsections of Rule 609.

Note to Subdivision (a). The House bill provides that the credibility of a witness can be attacked by proof of prior conviction of a crime only if the crime involves dishonesty or false statement. The Senate amendment provides that a witness' credibility may be attacked if the crime (1) was punishable by death or imprisonment in excess of one year under the law under which he was convicted or (2) involves dishonesty or false statement, regardless of the punishment.

The Conference adopts the Senate amendment with an amendment. The Conference amendment provides that the credibility of a witness, whether a defendant or someone else, may be attacked by proof of a prior conviction but only if the crime: (1) was punishable by death or imprisonment in excess of one year under the law under which he was convicted and the court determines that the probative value of the conviction outweighs its prejudicial effect to the defendant; or (2) involved dishonesty or false statement regardless of the punishment.

By the phrase "dishonesty and false statement" the Conference means crimes such as perjury or subornation of perjury, false statement, criminal fraud, embezzlement, or false pretense, or any other offense in the nature of crimen falsi, the commission of which involves some element of deceit, untruthfulness, or falsification bearing on the accused's propensity to testify truthfully.

The admission of prior convictions involving dishonesty and false statement is not within the discretion of the Court. Such convictions are peculiarly probative of credibility and, under this rule, are always to be admitted. Thus, judicial discretion granted with respect to the admissibility of other prior convictions is not applicable to those involving dishonesty or false statement.

With regard to the discretionary standard established by paragraph (1) of Rule 609(a), the Conference determined that the prejudicial effect to be weighed against the probative value of the conviction is specifically the prejudicial effect to the defendant. The danger of prejudice to a witness other than the defendant (such as injury to the witness' reputation in his community) was considered and rejected by the Conference as an element to be weighed in determining admissibility. It was the judgment of the Conference that the danger of prejudice to a nondefendant witness is outweighed by the need for the trier of fact to have as much relevant evidence on the issue of credibility as possible. Such evidence should only be excluded where it presents a danger of improperly influencing the outcome of the trial by persuading the trier of fact to convict the defendant on the basis of his prior criminal record.

Note to Subdivision (b). The House bill provides in subsection (b) that evidence of conviction of a crime may not be used for impeachment purposes under subsection (a) if more than ten years have elapsed since the date of the conviction or the date the witness was released from confinement imposed for the conviction, whichever is later. The Senate amendment permits the use of convictions older than ten years, if the court determines, in the interests of justice, that the probative value of the conviction, supported by specific facts and circumstances, substantially outweighs its prejudicial effect.

The Conference adopts the Senate amendment with an amendment requiring notice by a party that he intends to request that the court allow him to use a conviction older than ten years. The Conferees anticipate that a written notice, in order to give the adversary a fair opportunity to contest the use of the evidence, will ordinarily include such information as the date of the conviction, the jurisdiction, and the offense or statute involved. In order to eliminate the possibility that the flexibility of this provision may impair the ability of a party-opponent to prepare for trial, the Conferees intend that the notice provision operate to avoid surprise. House Report No. 93-1597.

1987 Amendments
The amendments are technical. No substantive change is intended.

1990 Amendments
The amendment to Rule 609(a) makes two changes in the rule. The first change removes from the rule the limitation that the conviction may only be elicited during cross-examination, a limitation that virtually every circuit has found to be inapplicable. It is common for witnesses to reveal on direct examination their convictions to "remove the sting" of the impeachment. See e.g., United States v. Bad Cob, 560 F.2d 877 (8th Cir.1977). The amendment does not contemplate that a court will necessarily permit proof of prior convictions through testimony, which might be time-consuming and more prejudicial than proof through a written record. Rules 403 and 611(a) provide sufficient authority for the court to protect against unfair or disruptive methods of proof.

The second change effected by the amendment resolves an ambiguity as to the relationship of Rules 609 and 403 with respect to impeachment of witnesses other than the criminal defendant. See, Green v. Bock Laundry Machine Co., 109 S.Ct. 1981, 490 U.S. 504 (1989). The amendment does not disturb the special balancing test for the criminal defendant who chooses to testify. Thus, the rule recognizes that, in virtually every case in which prior convictions are used to impeach the testifying defendant, the defendant faces a unique risk of prejudice--i.e., the danger that convictions that would be excluded under Fed.R.Evid. 404 will be misused by a jury as propensity evidence despite their introduction solely for impeachment purposes. Although the rule does not forbid all use of convictions to impeach a defendant, it requires that the government show that the probative value of convictions as impeachment evidence outweighs their prejudicial effect.

Prior to the amendment, the rule appeared to give the defendant the benefit of the special balancing test when defense witnesses other than the defendant were called to testify. In practice, however, the concern about unfairness to the defendant is most acute when the defendant's own convictions are offered as evidence. Almost all of the decided cases concern this type of impeachment, and the amendment does not deprive the defendant of any meaningful protection, since Rule 403 now clearly protects against unfair impeachment of any defense witness other than the defendant. There are cases in which a defendant might be prejudiced when a defense witness is impeached. Such cases may arise, for example, when the witness bears a special relationship to the defendant such that the defendant is likely to suffer some spill-over effect from impeachment of the witness.

The amendment also protects other litigants from unfair impeachment of their witnesses. The danger of prejudice from the use of prior convictions is not confined to criminal defendants. Although the danger that prior convictions will be misused as character evidence is particularly acute when the defendant is impeached, the danger exists in other situations as well. The amendment reflects the view that it is desirable to protect all litigants from the unfair use of prior convictions, and that the ordinary balancing test of Rule 403, which provides that evidence shall not be excluded unless its prejudicial effect substantially outweighs its probative value, is appropriate for assessing the admissibility of prior convictions for impeachment of any witness other than a criminal defendant.

The amendment reflects a judgment that decisions interpreting Rule 609(a) as requiring a trial court to admit convictions in civil cases that have little, if anything, to do with credibility reach undesirable results. See, e.g., Diggs v. Lyons, 741 F.2d 577 (3d Cir.1984), cert. denied, 105 S.Ct. 2157 (1985). The amendment provides the same protection against unfair prejudice arising from prior convictions used for impeachment purposes as the rules provide for other evidence. The amendment finds support in decided cases. See, e.g., Petty v. Ideco, 761 F.2d 1146 (5th Cir.1985); Czaka v. Hickman, 703 F.2d 317 (8th Cir.1983).

Fewer decided cases address the question whether Rule 609(a) provides any protection against unduly prejudicial prior convictions used to impeach government witnesses. Some courts have read Rule 609(a) as giving the government no protection for its witnesses. See, e.g., United States v. Thorne, 547 F.2d 56 (8th Cir.1976); United States v. Nevitt, 563 F.2d 406 (9th Cir.1977), cert. denied, 444 U.S. 847 (1979). This approach also is rejected by the amendment. There are cases in which impeachment of government witnesses with prior convictions that have little, if anything, to do with credibility may result in unfair prejudice to the government's interest in a fair trial and unnecessary embarrassment to a witness. Fed.R.Evid. 412 already recognizes this and excluded certain evidence of past sexual behavior in the context of prosecutions for sexual assaults.

The amendment applies the general balancing test of Rule 403 to protect all litigants against unfair impeachment of witnesses. The balancing test protects civil litigants, the government in criminal cases, and the defendant in a criminal case who calls other witnesses. The amendment addresses prior convictions offered under Rule 609, not for other purposes, and does not run afoul, therefore, of Davis v. Alaska, 415 U.S. 308 (1974). Davis involved the use of a prior juvenile adjudication not to prove a past law violation, but to prove bias. The defendant in a criminal case has the right to demonstrate the bias of a witness and to be assured a fair trial, but not to unduly prejudice a trier of fact. See generally Rule 412. In any case in which the trial court believes that confrontation rights require admission of impeachment evidence, obviously the Constitution would take precedence over the rule.

The probability that prior convictions of an ordinary government witness will be unduly prejudicial is low in most criminal cases. Since the behavior of the witness is not the issue in dispute in most cases, there is little chance that the trier of fact will misuse the convictions offered as impeachment evidence as propensity evidence. Thus, trial courts will be skeptical when the government objects to impeachment of its witnesses with prior convictions. Only when the government is able to point to a real danger of prejudice that is sufficient to outweigh substantially the probative value of the conviction for impeachment purposes will the conviction be excluded.

The amendment continues to divide subdivision (a) into subsections (1) and (2) thus facilitating retrieval under current computerized research programs which distinguish the two provisions. The Committee recommended no substantive change in subdivision (a)(2), even though some cases raise a concern about the proper interpretation of the words "dishonesty or false statement." These words were used but not explained in the original Advisory Committee Note accompanying Rule 609. Congress extensively debated the rule, and the Report of the House and Senate Conference Committee states that "[b]y the phrase 'dishonesty and false statement,' the Conference means crimes such as perjury, subornation of perjury, false statement, criminal fraud, embezzlement, or false pretense, or any other offense in the nature of crimen falsi, commission of which involves some element of deceit, untruthfulness, or falsification bearing on the accused's propensity to testify truthfully." The Advisory Committee concluded that the Conference Report provides sufficient guidance to trial courts and that no amendment is necessary, notwithstanding some decisions that take an unduly broad view of "dishonesty," admitting convictions such as for bank robbery or bank larceny. Subsection (a)(2) continues to apply to any witness, including a criminal defendant.

Finally, the Committee determined that it was unnecessary to add to the rule language stating that, when a prior conviction is offered under Rule 609, the trial court is to consider the probative value of the prior conviction for impeachment, not for other purposes. The Committee concluded that the title of the rule, its first sentence, and its placement among the impeachment rules clearly establish that evidence offered under Rule 609 is offered only for purposes of impeachment.

2006 Amendments

The amendment provides that Rule 609(a)(2) mandates the admission of evidence of a conviction only when the conviction required the proof of (or in the case of a guilty plea, the admission of) an act of dishonesty or false statement. Evidence of all other convictions is inadmissible under this subsection, irrespective of whether the witness exhibited dishonesty or made a false statement in the process of the commission of the crime of conviction. Thus, evidence that a witness was convicted for a crime of violence, such as murder, is not admissible under Rule 609(a)(2), even if the witness acted deceitfully in the course of committing the crime.

The amendment is meant to give effect to the legislative intent to limit the convictions that are to be automatically admitted under subdivision (a)(2). The Conference Committee provided that by "dishonesty and false statement" it meant "crimes such as perjury, subornation of perjury, false statement, criminal fraud, embezzlement, or false pretense, or any other offense in the nature of crimen falsi, the commission of which involves some element of deceit, untruthfulness, or falsification bearing on the [witness's] propensity to testify truthfully." Historically, offenses classified as crimina falsi have included only those crimes in which the ultimate criminal act was itself an act of deceit. See Green, Deceit and the Classification of Crimes: Federal Rule of Evidence 609(a)(2) and the Origins of Crimen Falsi, 90 J. Crim. L. & Criminology 1087 (2000).

Evidence of crimes in the nature of crimina falsi must be admitted under Rule 609(a)(2), regardless of how such crimes are specifically charged. For example, evidence that a witness was convicted of making a false claim to a federal agent is admissible under this subdivision regardless of whether the crime was charged under a section that expressly references deceit (e.g., 18 U.S.C. § 1001, Material Misrepresentation to the Federal Government) or a section that does not (e.g., 18 U.S.C. § 1503, Obstruction of Justice).

The amendment requires that the proponent have ready proof that the conviction required the factfinder to find, or the defendant to admit, an act of dishonesty or false statement. Ordinarily, the statutory elements of the crime will indicate whether it is one of dishonesty or false statement. Where the deceitful nature of the crime is not apparent from the statute and the face of the judgment -- as, for example, where the conviction simply records a finding of guilt for a statutory offense that does not reference deceit expressly -- a proponent may offer information such as an indictment, a statement of admitted facts, or jury instructions to show that the factfinder had to find, or the defendant had to admit, an act of dishonesty or false statement in order for the witness to have been convicted. Cf. Taylor v. United States, 495 U.S. 575, 602 (1990) (providing that a trial court may look to a charging instrument or jury instructions to ascertain the nature of a prior offense where the statute is insufficiently clear on its face); Shepard v. United States, 125 S.Ct. 1254 (2005) (the inquiry to determine whether a guilty plea to a crime defined by a nongeneric statute necessarily admitted elements of the generic offense was limited to the charging document's terms, the terms of a plea agreement or transcript of colloquy between judge and defendant in which the factual basis for the plea was confirmed by the defendant, or a comparable judicial record). But the amendment does not contemplate a "mini-trial" in which the court plumbs the record of the previous proceeding to determine whether the crime was in the nature of crimen falsi.

The amendment also substitutes the term "character for truthfulness" for the term "credibility" in the first sentence of the Rule. The limitations of Rule 609 are not applicable if a conviction is admitted for a purpose other than to prove the witness's character for untruthfulness. See, e.g., United States v. Lopez, 979 F.2d 1024 (5th Cir. 1992) (Rule 609 was not applicable where the conviction was offered for purposes of contradiction). The use of the term "credibility" in subdivision (d) is retained, however, as that subdivision is intended to govern the use of a juvenile adjudication for any type of impeachment.

Rule 610. Religious Beliefs or Opinions

Evidence of the beliefs or opinions of a witness on matters of religion is not admissible for the purpose of showing that by reason of their nature the witness' credibility is impaired or enhanced.

ADVISORY COMMITTEE NOTES

1972 Proposed Rules
While the rule forecloses inquiry into the religious beliefs or opinions of a witness for the purpose of showing that his character for truthfulness is affected by their nature, an inquiry for the purpose of showing interest or bias because of them is not within the prohibition. Thus disclosure of affiliation with a church which is a party to the litigation would be allowable under the rule. Cf. Tucker v. Reil, 51 Ariz. 357, 77 P.2d 203 (1938). To the same effect, though less specifically worded, is California Evidence Code § 789. See 3 Wigmore § 936.

1987 Amendments
The amendment is technical. No substantive change is intended.

Rule 611. Mode and Order of Interrogation and Presentation

(a) Control by court. The court shall exercise reasonable control over the mode and order of interrogating witnesses and presenting evidence so as to (1) make the interrogation and presentation effective for the ascertainment of the truth, (2) avoid needless consumption of time, and (3) protect witnesses from harassment or undue embarrassment.

(b) Scope of cross-examination. Cross-examination should be limited to the subject matter of the direct examination and matters affecting the credibility of the witness. The court may, in the exercise of discretion, permit inquiry into additional matters as if on direct examination.

(c) Leading questions. Leading questions should not be used on the direct examination of a witness except as may be necessary to develop the witness' testimony. Ordinarily leading questions should be permitted on cross-examination. When a party calls a hostile witness, an adverse party, or a witness identified with an adverse party, interrogation may be by leading questions.

AVISORY COMMITTEE NOTES

1972 Proposed Rules
Note to Subdivision (a). Spelling out detailed rules to govern the mode and order of interrogating witnesses and presenting evidence is neither desirable nor feasible. The ultimate responsibility for the effective working of the adversary system rests with the judge. The rule sets forth the objectives which he should seek to attain.

Item (1) restates in broad terms the power and obligation of the judge as developed under common law principles. It covers such concerns as whether testimony shall be in the form of a free narrative or responses to specific questions, McCormick § 5, the order of calling witnesses and presenting evidence, 6 Wigmore § 1867, the use of demonstrative evidence, McCormick § 179, and the many other questions arising during the course of a trial which can be solved only by the judge's common sense and fairness in view of the particular circumstances.

Item (2) is addressed to avoidance of needless consumption of time, a matter of daily concern in the disposition of cases. A companion piece is found in the discretion vested in the judge to exclude evidence as a waste of time in Rule 403(b).

Item (3) calls for a judgment under the particular circumstances whether interrogation tactics entail harassment or undue embarrassment. Pertinent circumstances include the importance of the testimony, the nature of the inquiry, its relevance to credibility, waste of time, and confusion. McCormick § 42. In Alford v. United States, 282 U.S. 687, 694, 51 S.Ct. 218, 75 L.Ed. 624 (1931), the Court pointed out that, while the trial judge should protect the witness from questions which "go beyond the bounds of proper cross-examination merely to harass, annoy or humiliate," this protection by no means forecloses efforts to discredit the witness. Reference to the transcript of the prosecutor's cross-examination in Berger v. United States, 295 U.S. 78, 55 S.Ct. 629, 79 L.Ed. 1314 (1935), serves to lay at rest any doubts as to the need for judicial control in this area.

The inquiry into specific instances of conduct of a witness allowed under Rule 608(b) is, of course, subject to this rule.

Note to Subdivision (b). The tradition in the federal courts and in numerous state courts has been to limit the scope of cross-examination to matters testified to on direct, plus matters bearing upon the credibility of the witness. Various reasons have been advanced to justify the rule of limited cross-examination. (1) A party vouches for his own witness but only to the extent of matters elicited on direct. Resurrection Gold Mining Co. v. Fortune Gold Mining Co., 129 F. 668, 675 (8th Cir.1904), quoted in Maguire, Weinstein, et al., Cases on Evidence 277, n. 38 (5th ed. 1965). But the concept of vouching is discredited, and Rule 607 rejects it. (2) A party cannot ask his own witness leading questions. This is a problem properly solved in terms of what is necessary for a proper development of the testimony rather than by a mechanistic formula similar to the vouching concept. See discussion under subdivision (c). (3) A practice of limited cross-examination promotes orderly presentation of the case. Finch v. Weiner, 109 Conn. 616, 145 A. 31 (1929). While this latter reason has merit, the matter is essentially one of the order of presentation and not one in which involvement at the appellate level is likely to prove fruitful. See, for example, Moyer v. Aetna Life Ins. Co., 126 F.2d 141 (3rd Cir.1942); Butler v. New York Central R. Co., 253 F.2d 281 (7th Cir.1958); United States v. Johnson, 285 F.2d 35 (9th Cir.1960); Union Automobile Indemnity Ass'n v. Capitol Indemnity Ins. Co., 310 F.2d 318 (7th Cir.1962). In evaluating these considerations, McCormick says:

"The foregoing considerations favoring the wide-open or restrictive rules may well be thought to be fairly evenly balanced. There is another factor, however, which seems to swing the balance overwhelmingly in favor of the wide-open rule. This is the consideration of economy of time and energy. Obviously, the wide-open rule presents little or no opportunity for dispute in its application. The restrictive practice in all its forms, on the other hand, is productive in many court rooms, of continual bickering over the choice of the numerous variations of the 'scope of the direct' criterion, and of their application to particular cross-questions. These controversies are often reventilated on appeal, and reversals for error in their determination are frequent. Observance of these vague and ambiguous restrictions is a matter of constant and hampering concern to the cross-examiner. If these efforts, delays and misprisions were the necessary incidents to the guarding of substantive rights or the fundamentals of fair trial, they might be worth the cost. As the price of the choice of an obviously debatable regulation of the order of evidence, the sacrifice seems misguided. The American Bar Association's Committee for the Improvement of the Law of Evidence for the year 1937-38 said this:

'The rule limiting cross-examination to the precise subject of the direct examination is probably the most frequent rule (except the Opinion rule) leading in the trial practice today to refined and technical quibbles which obstruct the progress of the trial, confuse the jury, and give rise to appeal on technical grounds only. Some of the instances in which Supreme Courts have ordered new trials for the mere transgression of this rule about the order of evidence have been astounding.

'We recommend that the rule allowing questions upon any part of the issue known to the witness * * * be adopted. * * * ' " McCormick, § 27, p. 51. See also 5 Moore's Federal Practice ¶ 43.10 (2nd ed. 1964).

The provision of the second sentence, that the judge may in the interests of justice limit inquiry into new matters on cross-examination, is designed for those situations in which the result otherwise would be confusion, complication, or protraction of the case, not as a matter of rule but as demonstrable in the actual development of the particular case.

The rule does not purport to determine the extent to which an accused who elects to testify thereby waives his privilege against self-incrimination. The question is a constitutional one, rather than a mere matter of administering the trial. Under Simmons v. United States, 390 U.S. 377, 88 S.Ct. 967, 19 L.Ed.2d 1247 (1968), no general waiver occurs when the accused testifies on such preliminary matters as the validity of a search and seizure or the admissibility of a confession. Rule 104(d), supra. When he testifies on the merits, however, can he foreclose inquiry into an aspect or element of the crime by avoiding it on direct? The affirmative answer given in Tucker v. United States, 5 F.2d 818 (8th Cir.1925), is inconsistent with the description of the waiver as extending to "all other relevant facts" in Johnson v. United States, 318 U.S. 189, 195, 63 S.Ct. 549, 87 L.Ed. 704 (1943). See also Brown v. United States, 356 U.S. 148, 78 S.Ct. 622, 2 L.Ed.2d 589 (1958). The situation of an accused who desires to testify on some but not all counts of a multiple-count indictment is one to be approached, in the first instance at least, as a problem of severance under Rule 14 of the Federal Rules of Criminal Procedure. Cross v. United States, 118 U.S.App.D.C. 324, 335 F.2d 987 (1964). Cf. United States v. Baker, 262 F.Supp. 657, 686 (D.D.C.1966). In all events, the extent of the waiver of the privilege against self-incrimination ought not to be determined as a by-product of a rule on scope of cross-examination.

Note to Subdivision (c). The rule continues the traditional view that the suggestive powers of the leading question are as a general proposition undesirable. Within this tradition, however, numerous exceptions have achieved recognition: The witness who is hostile, unwilling, or biased; the child witness or the adult with communication problems; the witness whose recollection is exhausted; and undisputed preliminary matters. 3 Wigmore §§ 774-778. An almost total unwillingness to reverse for infractions has been manifested by appellate courts. See cases cited in 3 Wigmore § 770. The matter clearly falls within the area of control by the judge over the mode and order of interrogation and presentation and accordingly is phrased in words of suggestion rather than command.

The rule also conforms to tradition in making the use of leading questions on cross-examination a matter of right. The purpose of the qualification "ordinarily" is to furnish a basis for denying the use of leading questions when the cross-examination is cross-examination in form only and not in fact, as for example the "cross-examination" of a party by his own counsel after being called by the opponent (savoring more of re-direct) or of an insured defendant who proves to be friendly to the plaintiff.

The final sentence deals with categories of witnesses automatically regarded and treated as hostile. Rule 43(b) of the Federal Rules of Civil Procedure has included only "an adverse party or an officer, director, or managing agent of a public or private corporation or of a partnership or association which is an adverse party." This limitation virtually to persons whose statements would stand as admissions is believed to be an unduly narrow concept of those who may safely be regarded as hostile without further demonstration. See, for example, Maryland Casualty Co. v. Kador, 225 F.2d 120 (5th Cir.1955), and Degelos v. Fidelity and Casualty Co., 313 F.2d 809 (5th Cir.1963), holding despite the language of Rule 43(b) that an insured fell within it, though not a party in an action under the Louisiana direct action statute. The phrase of the rule, "witness identified with" an adverse party, is designed to enlarge the category of persons thus callable.

1974 Enactment
Note to Subdivision (b). As submitted by the Court, Rule 611(b) provided:

A witness may be cross-examined on any matter relevant to any issue in the case, including credibility. In the interests of justice, the judge may limit cross-examination with respect to matters not testified to on direct examination.

The Committee amended this provision to return to the rule which prevails in the federal courts and thirty-nine State jurisdictions. As amended, the Rule is in the text of the 1969 Advisory Committee draft. It limits cross-examination to credibility and to matters testified to on direct examination, unless the judge permits more, in which event the cross-examiner must proceed as if on direct examination. This traditional rule facilitates orderly presentation by each party at trial. Further, in light of existing discovery procedures, there appears to be no need to abandon the traditional rule.

Note to Subdivision (c). The third sentence of Rule 611(c) as submitted by the Court provided that:

In civil cases, a party is entitled to call an adverse party or witness identified with him and interrogate by leading questions.

The Committee amended this Rule to permit leading questions to be used with respect to any hostile witness, not only an adverse party or person identified with such adverse party. The Committee also substituted the word "When" for the phrase "In civil cases" to reflect the possibility that in criminal cases a defendant may be entitled to call witnesses identified with the government, in which event the Committee believed the defendant should be permitted to inquire with leading questions. House Report No. 93-650.

Note to Subdivision (b). Rule 611(b) as submitted by the Supreme Court permitted a broad scope of cross-examination: "cross-examination on any matter relevant to any issue in the case" unless the judge, in the interests of justice, limited the scope of cross-examination.

The House narrowed the Rule to the more traditional practice of limiting cross-examination to the subject matter of direct examination (and credibility), but with discretion in the judge to permit inquiry into additional matters in situations where that would aid in the development of the evidence or otherwise facilitate the conduct of the trial.

The committee agrees with the House amendment. Although there are good arguments in support of broad cross-examination from perspectives of developing all relevant evidence, we believe the factors of insuring an orderly and predictable development of the evidence weigh in favor of the narrower rule, especially when discretion is given to the trial judge to permit inquiry into additional matters. The committee expressly approves this discretion and believes it will permit sufficient flexibility allowing a broader scope of cross-examination whenever appropriate.

The House amendment providing broader discretionary cross-examination permitted inquiry into additional matters only as if on direct examination. As a general rule, we concur with this limitation, however, we would understand that this limitation would not preclude the utilization of leading questions if the conditions of subsection (c) of this rule were met, bearing in mind the judge's discretion in any case to limit the scope of cross-examination [see McCormick on Evidence, §§ 24-26 (especially 24) (2d ed. 1972)].

Further, the committee has received correspondence from Federal judges commenting on the applicability of this rule to section 1407 of title 28. It is the committee's judgment that this rule as reported by the House is flexible enough to provide sufficiently broad cross-examination in appropriate situations in multidistrict litigation.

Note to Subdivision (c). As submitted by the Supreme Court, the rule provided: "In civil cases, a party is entitled to call an adverse party or witness identified with him and interrogate by leading questions."

The final sentence of subsection (c) was amended by the House for the purpose of clarifying the fact that a "hostile witness"--that is a witness who is hostile in fact--could be subject to interrogation by leading questions. The rule as submitted by the Supreme Court declared certain witnesses hostile as a matter of law and thus subject to interrogation by leading questions without any showing of hostility in fact. These were adverse parties or witnesses identified with adverse parties. However, the wording of the first sentence of subsection (c) while generally prohibiting the use of leading questions on direct examination, also provides "except as may be necessary to develop his testimony." Further, the first paragraph of the Advisory Committee note explaining the subsection makes clear that they intended that leading questions could be asked of a hostile witness or a witness who was unwilling or biased and even though that witness was not associated with an adverse party. Thus, we question whether the House amendment was necessary.

However, concluding that it was not intended to affect the meaning of the first sentence of the subsection and was intended solely to clarify the fact that leading questions are permissible in the interrogation of a witness, who is hostile in fact, the committee accepts that House amendment.

The final sentence of this subsection was also amended by the House to cover criminal as well as civil cases. The committee accepts this amendment, but notes that it may be difficult in criminal cases to determine when a witness is "identified with an adverse party," and thus the rule should be applied with caution. Senate Report No. 93-1277.

1987 Amendments
The amendment is technical. No substantive change is intended.

Rule 612. Writing Used to Refresh Memory

Except as otherwise provided in criminal proceedings by section 3500 of title 18, United States Code, if a witness uses a writing to refresh memory for the purpose of testifying, either--

(1) while testifying, or

(2) before testifying, if the court in its discretion determines it is necessary in the interests of justice,

an adverse party is entitled to have the writing produced at the hearing, to inspect it, to cross-examine the witness thereon, and to introduce in evidence those portions which relate to the testimony of the witness. If it is claimed that the writing contains matters not related to the subject matter of the testimony the court shall examine the writing in camera, excise any portions not so related, and order delivery of the remainder to the party entitled thereto. Any portion withheld over objections shall be preserved and made available to the appellate court in the event of an appeal. If a writing is not produced or delivered pursuant to order under this rule, the court shall make any order justice requires, except that in criminal cases when the prosecution elects not to comply, the order shall be one striking the testimony or, if the court in its discretion determines that the interests of justice so require, declaring a mistrial.

ADVISORY COMMITTEE NOTES

1972 Proposed Rules
The treatment of writings used to refresh recollection while on the stand is in accord with settled doctrine. McCormick § 9, p. 15. The bulk of the case law has, however, denied the existence of any right to access by the opponent when the writing is used prior to taking the stand, though the judge may have discretion in the matter. Goldman v. United States, 316 U.S. 129, 62 S.Ct. 993, 86 L.Ed. 1322 (1942); Needelman v. United States, 261 F.2d 802 (5th Cir.1958), cert. dismissed 362 U.S. 600, 80 S.Ct. 960, 4 L.Ed.2d 980, rehearing denied 363 U.S. 858, 80 S.Ct. 1606, 4 L.Ed.2d 1739, Annot., 82 A.L.R.2d 473, 562 and 7 A.L.R.3d 181, 247. An increasing group of cases has repudiated the distinction. People v. Scott, 29 Ill.2d 97, 193 N.E.2d 814 (1963); State v. Mucci, 25 N.J. 423, 136 A.2d 761 (1957); State v. Hunt, 25 N.J. 514, 138 A.2d 1 (1958); State v. Deslovers, 40 R.I. 89, 100 A. 64 (1917), and this position is believed to be correct. As Wigmore put it, "the risk of imposition and the need of safeguard is just as great" in both situations. 3 Wigmore § 762, p. 111. To the same effect is McCormick, § 9, p. 17.

The purpose of the phrase "for the purpose of testifying" is to safeguard against using the rule as a pretext for wholesale exploration of an opposing party's files and to insure that access is limited only to those writings which may fairly be said in fact to have an impact upon the testimony of the witness.

The purpose of the rule is the same as that of the Jencks statute, 18 U.S.C. § 3500: to promote the search of credibility and memory. The same sensitivity to disclosure of government files may be involved; hence the rule is expressly made subject to the statute, subdivision (a) of which provides: "In any criminal prosecution brought by the United States, no statement or report in the possession of the United States which was made by a Government witness or prospective Government witness (other than the defendant) shall be the subject of subpena, discovery, or inspection until said witness has testified on direct examination in the trial of the case." Items falling within the purview of the statute are producible only as provided by its terms, Palermo v. United States, 360 U.S. 343, 351 (1959), and disclosure under the rule is limited similarly by the statutory conditions. With this limitation in mind, some differences of application may be noted. The Jencks statute applies only to statements of witnesses; the rule is not so limited. The statute applies only to criminal cases; the rule applies to all cases. The statute applies only to government witnesses; the rule applies to all witnesses. The statute contains no requirement that the statement be consulted for purposes of refreshment before or while testifying; the rule so requires. Since many writings would qualify under either statute or rule, a substantial overlap exists, but the identity of procedures makes this of no importance.

The consequences of nonproduction by the government in a criminal case are those of the Jencks statute, striking the testimony or in exceptional cases a mistrial. 18 U.S.C. § 3500(d). In other cases these alternatives are unduly limited, and such possibilities as contempt, dismissal, finding issues against the offender, and the like are available. See Rule 16(g) of the Federal Rules of Criminal Procedure and Rule 37(b) of the Federal Rules of Civil Procedure for appropriate sanctions.

1974 Enactment

As submitted to Congress, Rule 612 provided that except as set forth in 18 U.S.C. 3500, if a witness uses a writing to refresh his memory for the purpose of testifying, "either before or while testifying," an adverse party is entitled to have the writing produced at the hearing, to inspect it, to cross-examine the witness on it, and to introduce in evidence those portions relating to the witness' testimony. The Committee amended the Rule so as still to require the production of writings used by a witness while testifying, but to render the production of writings used by a witness to refresh his memory before testifying discretionary with the court in the interests of justice, as is the case under existing federal law. See Goldman v. United States, 316 U.S. 129 (1942). The Committee considered that permitting an adverse party to require the production of writings used before testifying could result in fishing expeditions among a multitude of papers which a witness may have used in preparing for trial.

The Committee intends that nothing in the Rule be construed as barring the assertion of a privilege with respect to writings used by a witness to refresh his memory. House Report No. 93-650.

Rule 613. Prior Statements of Witnesses

(a) Examining witness concerning prior statement. In examining a witness concerning a prior statement made by the witness, whether written or not, the statement need not be shown nor its contents disclosed to the witness at that time, but on request the same shall be shown or disclosed to opposing counsel.

(b) Extrinsic evidence of prior inconsistent statement of witness. Extrinsic evidence of a prior inconsistent statement by a witness is not admissible unless the witness is afforded an opportunity to explain or deny the same and the opposite party is afforded an opportunity to interrogate the witness thereon, or the interests of justice otherwise require. This provision does not apply to admissions of a party-opponent as defined in rule 801(d)(2).

1987 Amendments
The amendment is technical. No substantive change is intended.

ADVISORY COMMITTEE NOTES

1972 Proposed Rules
Note to Subdivision (a). The Queen's Case, 2 Br. & B. 284, 129 Eng.Rep. 976 (1820), laid down the requirement that a cross-examiner, prior to questioning the witness about his own prior statement in writing, must first show it to the witness. Abolished by statute in the country of its origin, the requirement nevertheless gained currency in the United States. The rule abolishes this useless impediment, to cross-examination. Ladd, Some Observations on Credibility: Impeachment of Witnesses, 52 Cornell L.Q. 239, 246-247 (1967); McCormick § 28; 4 Wigmore §§ 1259-1260. Both oral and written statements are included.

The provision for disclosure to counsel is designed to protect against unwarranted insinuations that a statement has been made when the fact is to the contrary.

The rule does not defeat the application of Rule 1002 relating to production of the original when the contents of a writing are sought to be proved. Nor does it defeat the application of Rule 26(b)(3) of the Rules of Civil Procedure, as revised, entitling a person on request to a copy of his own statement, though the operation of the latter may be suspended temporarily.

Note to Subdivision (b). The familiar foundation requirement that an impeaching statement first be shown to the witness before it can be proved by extrinsic evidence is preserved but with some modifications. See Ladd, Some Observations on Credibility: Impeachment of Witnesses, 52 Cornell L.Q. 239, 247 (1967). The traditional insistence that the attendance of the witness be directed to the statement on cross-examination is relaxed in favor of simply providing the witness an opportunity to explain and the opposite party an opportunity to examine on the statement, with no specification of any particular time or sequence. Under this procedure, several collusive witnesses can be examined before disclosure of a joint prior inconsistent statement. See Comment to California Evidence Code § 770. Also, dangers of oversight are reduced. See McCormick § 37, p. 68.

In order to allow for such eventualities as the witness becoming unavailable by the time the statement is discovered, a measure of discretion is conferred upon the judge. Similar provisions are found in California Evidence Code § 770 and New Jersey Evidence Rule 22(b).

Under principles of expression unius the rule does not apply to impeachment by evidence of prior inconsistent conduct. The use of inconsistent statements to impeach a hearsay declaration is treated in Rule 806.

1987 Amendments
The amendments are technical. No substantive change is intended.

1988 Amendments
The amendment is technical. No substantive change is intended.

Rule 614. Calling and Interrogation of Witnesses by Court

(a) Calling by court. The court may, on its own motion or at the suggestion of a party, call witnesses, and all parties are entitled to cross-examine witnesses thus called.

(b) Interrogation by court. The court may interrogate witnesses, whether called by itself or by a party.

(c) Objections. Objections to the calling of witnesses by the court or to interrogation by it may be made at the time or at the next available opportunity when the jury is not present.

ADVISORY COMMITTEE NOTES

1972 Proposed Rules

Note to Subdivision (a). While exercised more frequently in criminal than in civil cases, the authority of the judge to call witnesses is well established. McCormick § 8, p. 14; Maguire, Weinstein, et al., Cases on Evidence 303-304 (5th ed. 1965); 9 Wigmore § 2484. One reason for the practice, the old rule against impeaching one's own witness, no longer exists by virtue of Rule 607, supra. Other reasons remain, however, to justify the continuation of the practice of calling court's witnesses. The right to cross-examine, with all it implies, is assured. The tendency of juries to associate a witness with the party calling him, regardless of technical aspects of vouching, is avoided. And the judge is not imprisoned within the case as made by the parties.

Note to Subdivision (b). The authority of the judge to question witnesses is also well established. McCormick § 8, pp. 12-13; Maguire, Weinstein, et al., Cases on Evidence 737-739 (5th ed. 1965); 3 Wigmore § 784. The authority is, of course, abused when the judge abandons his proper role and assumes that of advocate, but the manner in which interrogation should be conducted and the proper extent of its exercise are not susceptible of formulation in a rule. The omission in no sense precludes courts of review from continuing to reverse for abuse.

Note to Subdivision (c). The provision relating to objections is designed to relieve counsel of the embarrassment attendant upon objecting to questions by the judge in the presence of the jury, while at the same time assuring that objections are made in apt time to afford the opportunity to take possible corrective measures. Compare the "automatic" objection feature of Rule 605 when the judge is called as a witness.

Rule 615. Exclusion of Witnesses

At the request of a party the court shall order witnesses excluded so that they cannot hear the testimony of other witnesses, and it may make the order of its own motion. This rule does not authorize exclusion of (1) a party who is a natural person, or (2) an officer or employee of a party which is not a natural person designated as its representative by its attorney, or (3) a person whose presence is shown by a party to be essential to the presentation of the party's cause, or (4) a person authorized by statute to be present.

ADVISORY COMMITTEE NOTES

1972 Proposed Rules

The efficacy of excluding or sequestering witnesses has long been recognized as a means of discouraging and exposing fabrication, inaccuracy, and collusion. 6 Wigmore §§ 1837-1838. The authority of the judge is admitted, the only question being whether the matter is committed to his discretion or one of right. The rule takes the latter position. No time is specified for making the request.

Several categories of persons are excepted. (1) Exclusion of persons who are parties would raise serious problems of confrontation and due process. Under accepted practice they are not subject to exclusion. 6 Wigmore § 1841. (2) As the equivalent of the right of a natural-person party to be present, a party which is not a natural person is entitled to have a representative present. Most of the cases have involved allowing a police officer who has been in charge of an investigation to remain in court despite the fact that he will be a witness. United States v. Infanzon, 235 F.2d 318 (2d Cir.1956); Portomene v. United States, 221 F.2d 582 (5th Cir.1955); Powell v. United States, 208 F.2d 618 (6th Cir.1953); Jones v. United States, 252 F.Supp. 781 (W.D.Okl.1966). Designation of the representative by the attorney rather than by the client may at first glance appear to be an inversion of the attorney-client relationship, but it may be assumed that the attorney will follow the wishes of the client, and the solution is simple and workable. See California Evidence Code § 777. (3) The category contemplates such persons as an agent who handled the transaction being litigated or an expert needed to advise counsel in the management of the litigation. See 6 Wigmore § 1841, n. 4.

1974 Enactment

Many district courts permit government counsel to have an investigative agent at counsel table throughout the trial although the agent is or may be a witness. The practice is permitted as an exception to the rule of exclusion and compares with the situation defense counsel finds himself in--he always has the client with him to consult during the trial. The investigative agent's presence may be extremely important to government counsel, especially when the case is complex or involves some specialized subject matter. The agent, too, having lived with the case for a long time, may be able to assist in meeting trial surprises where the best-prepared counsel would otherwise have difficulty. Yet, it would not seem the Government could often meet the burden under rule 615 of showing that the agent's presence is essential. Furthermore, it could be dangerous to use the agent as a witness as early in the case as possible, so that he might then help counsel as a nonwitness, since the agent's testimony could be needed in rebuttal. Using another, nonwitness agent from the same investigative agency would not generally meet government counsel's needs.

This problem is solved if it is clear that investigative agents are within the group specified under the second exception made in the rule, for "an officer or employee of a party which is not a natural person designated as its representative by its attorney." It is our understanding that this was the intention of the House committee. It is certainly this committee's construction of the rule. Senate Report No. 93-1277.

1987 Amendments
The amendment is technical. No substantive change is intended.

1988 Amendments
The amendment is technical. No substantive change is intended.

1998 Amendments
The amendment is in response to: (1) the Victim's Rights and Restitution Act of 1990, 42 U.S.C. § 10606, which guarantees, within certain limits, the right of a crime victim to attend the trial; and (2) the Victim Rights Clarification Act of 1997 (18 U.S.C. § 3510).

Rules 616 to 700. Reserved for future legislation

ARTICLE VII. OPINIONS AND EXPERT TESTIMONY

Rule 701. Opinion Testimony by Lay Witnesses

If the witness is not testifying as an expert, the witness' testimony in the form of opinions or inferences is limited to those opinions or inferences which are (a) rationally based on the perception of the witness, (b) helpful to a clear understanding of the witness' testimony or the determination of a fact in issue, and (c) not based on scientific, technical, or other specialized knowledge within the scope of Rule 702.

ADVISORY COMMITTEE NOTES

1972 Proposed Rules
The rule retains the traditional objective of putting the trier of fact in possession of an accurate reproduction of the event.

Limitation (a) is the familiar requirement of first-hand knowledge or observation.

Limitation (b) is phrased in terms of requiring testimony to be helpful in resolving issues. Witnesses often find difficulty in expressing themselves in language which is not that of an opinion or conclusion. While the courts have made concessions in certain recurring situations, necessity as a standard for permitting opinions and conclusions has proved too elusive and too unadaptable to particular situations for purposes of satisfactory judicial administration. McCormick § 11. Moreover, the practical impossibility of determining by rule what is a "fact," demonstrated by a century of litigation of the question of what is a fact for purposes of pleading under the Field Code, extends into evidence also. 7 Wigmore § 1919. The rule assumes that the natural characteristics of the adversary system will generally lead to an acceptable result, since the detailed account carries more conviction than the broad assertion, and a lawyer can be expected to display his witness to the best advantage. If he fails to do so, cross-examination and argument will point up the weakness. See Ladd, Expert Testimony, 5 Vand.L.Rev. 414, 415-417 (1952). If, despite these considerations, attempts are made to introduce meaningless assertions which amount to little more than choosing up sides, exclusion for lack of helpfulness is called for by the rule.

The language of the rule is substantially that of Uniform Rule 56(1). Similar provisions are California Evidence Code § 800; Kansas Code of Civil Procedure § 60-456(a); New Jersey Evidence Rule 56(1).

1987 Amendments
The amendments are technical. No substantive change is intended.

2000 Amendments
Rule 701 has been amended to eliminate the risk that the reliability requirements set forth in Rule 702 will be evaded through the simple expedient of proffering an expert in lay witness clothing. Under the amendment, a witness' testimony must be scrutinized under the rules regulating expert opinion to the extent that the witness is providing testimony based on scientific, technical, or other specialized knowledge within the scope of Rule 702. See generally Asplundh Mfg. Div. v. Benton Harbor Eng'g, 57 F.3d 1190 (3d Cir. 1995). By channeling testimony that is actually expert testimony to Rule 702, the amendment also ensures that a party will not evade the expert witness disclosure requirements set forth in Fed.R.Civ.P. 26 and Fed.R.Crim.P. 16 by simply calling an expert witness in the guise of a layperson. See Joseph, Emerging Expert Issues Under the 1993 Disclosure Amendments to the Federal Rules of Civil Procedure, 164 F.R.D. 97, 108 (1996) (noting that "there is no good reason to allow what is essentially surprise expert testimony." and that "the Court should be vigilant to preclude manipulative conduct designed to thwart the expert disclosure and discovery process") See also United States v. Figueroa-Lopez, 125 F.3d 1241, 1246 (9th Cir. 1997) (law enforcement agents testifying that the defendant's conduct was consistent with that of a drug trafficker could not testify as lay witnesses; to permit such testimony under Rule 701 "subverts the requirements of Federal Rule of Criminal Procedure 16(a)(1)(E)").

The amendment does not distinguish between expert and lay witnesses, but rather between expert and lay testimony. Certainly it is possible for the same witness to provide both lay and expert testimony in a single case. See, e.g, United States v. Figueroa-Lopez, 125 F.3d 1241, 1246 (9th Cir. 1997) (law enforcement agents could testify that the defendant was acting suspiciously, without being qualified as experts; however, the rules on experts were applicable where the agents testified on the basis of extensive experience that the defendant was using code words to refer to drug quantities and prices). The amendment makes clear that any part of a witness' testimony that is based upon scientific, technical, or other specialized knowledge within the scope of Rule 702 is governed by the standards of Rule 702 and the corresponding disclosure requirements of the Civil and Criminal Rules.

The amendment is not intended to affect the "prototypical example[s] of the type of evidence contemplated by the adoption of Rule 701 relat[ing] to the appearance of persons or things, identity, the manner of conduct, competency of a person, degrees of light or darkness, sound, size, weight, distance, and an endless number of items that cannot be described factually in words apart from inferences." Asplundh Mfg. Div. v. Benton Harbor Eng' g, 57 F.3d 1190, 1196 (3d Cir. 1995).

For example, most courts have permitted the owner or officer of a business to testify to the value or projected profits of the business, without the necessity of qualifying the witness as an accountant, appraiser, or similar expert. See, e.g., Lightning Lube, Inc. v. Witco Corp. 4 F.3d 1153 (3d Cir. 1993) (no abuse of discretion in permitting the plaintiff's owner to give lay opinion testimony as to damages, as it was based on his knowledge and participation in the day-to-day affairs of the business). Such opinion testimony is admitted not because of experience, training or specialized knowledge within the realm of an expert, but because of the particularized knowledge that the witness has by virtue of his or her position in the business. The amendment does not purport to change this analysis. Similarly, courts have permitted lay witnesses to testify that a substance appeared to be a narcotic, so long as a foundation of familiarity with the substance is established. See, e.g., United States v. Westbrook, 896 F.2d 330 (8th Cir. 1990) (two lay witnesses who were heavy amphetamine users were properly permitted to testify that a substance was amphetamine; but it was error to permit another witness to make such an identification where she had no experience with amphetamines). Such testimony is not based on specialized knowledge within the scope of Rule 702, but rather is based upon a layperson's personal knowledge. If, however, that witness were to describe how a narcotic was manufactured, or to describe the intricate workings of a narcotic distribution network, then the witness would have to qualify as an expert under Rule 702. United States v . Figueroa-Lopez, supra.

The amendment incorporates the distinctions set forth in State v. Brown, 836 S.W.2d 530, 549 (1992), a case involving former Tennessee Rule of Evidence

701, a rule that precluded lay witness testimony based on "special knowledge." In Brown, the court declared that the distinction between lay and expert witness testimony is that lay testimony "results from a process of reasoning familiar in everyday life," while expert testimony "results from a process of reasoning which can be mastered only by specialists in the field." The court in Brown noted that a lay witness with experience could testify that a substance appeared to be blood, but that a witness would have to qualify as an expert before he could testify that bruising around the eyes is indicative of skull trauma. That is the kind of distinction made by the amendment to this Rule.

GAP Report--Proposed Amendment to Rule 701

The Committee made the following changes to the published draft of the proposed amendment to Evidence Rule 701:

1. The words "within the scope of Rule 702" were added at the end of the proposed amendment, to emphasize that the Rule does not require witnesses to qualify as experts unless their testimony is of the type traditionally considered within the purview of Rule 702. The Committee Note was amended to accord with this textual change.

2. The Committee Note was revised to provide further examples of the kind of testimony that could and could not be proffered under the limitation imposed by the proposed amendment.

Rule 702. Testimony by Experts

If scientific, technical, or other specialized knowledge will assist the trier of fact to understand the evidence or to determine a fact in issue, a witness qualified as an expert by knowledge, skill, experience, training, or education, may testify thereto in the form of an opinion or otherwise, if (1) the testimony is based upon sufficient facts or data, (2) the testimony is the product of reliable principles and methods, and (3) the witness has applied the principles and methods reliably to the facts of the case.

ADVISORY COMMITTEE NOTES

1972 Proposed Rules
An intelligent evaluation of facts is often difficult or impossible without the application of some scientific, technical, or other specialized knowledge. The most common source of this knowledge is the expert witness, although there are other techniques for supplying it.

Most of the literature assumes that experts testify only in the form of opinions. The assumption is logically unfounded. The rule accordingly recognizes that an expert on the stand may give a dissertation or exposition of scientific or other principles relevant to the case, leaving the trier of fact to apply them to the facts. Since much of the criticism of expert testimony has centered upon the hypothetical question, it seems wise to recognize that opinions are not indispensable and to encourage the use of expert testimony in non-opinion form when counsel believes the trier can itself draw the requisite inference. The use of opinions is not abolished by the rule, however. It will continue to be permissible for the experts to take the further step of suggesting the inference which should be drawn from applying the specialized knowledge to the facts. See Rules 703 to 705.

Whether the situation is a proper one for the use of expert testimony is to be determined on the basis of assisting the trier. "There is no more certain test for determining when experts may be used than the common sense inquiry whether the untrained layman would be qualified to determine intelligently and to the best possible degree the particular issue without enlightenment from those having a specialized understanding of the subject involved in the dispute." Ladd, Expert Testimony, 5 Vand.L.Rev. 414, 418 (1952). When opinions are excluded, it is because they are unhelpful and therefore superfluous and a waste of time. 7 Wigmore § 1918.

The rule is broadly phrased. The fields of knowledge which may be drawn upon are not limited merely to the "scientific" and "technical" but extend to all "specialized" knowledge. Similarly, the expert is viewed, not in a narrow sense, but as a person qualified by "knowledge, skill, experience, training or education." Thus within the scope of the rule are not only experts in the strictest sense of the word, e.g., physicians, physicists, and architects, but also the large group sometimes called "skilled" witnesses, such as bankers or landowners testifying to land values.

2000 Amendments
Rule 702 has been amended in response to Daubert v. Merrell Dow Pharmaceuticals, Inc., 509 U.S. 579 (1993), and to the many cases applying Daubert, including Kumho Tire Co. v. Carmichael, 119 S.Ct. 1167 (1999). In Daubert the Court charged trial judges with the responsibility of acting as gatekeepers to exclude unreliable expert testimony, and the Court in Kumho clarified that this gatekeeper function applies to all expert testimony, not just testimony based in science. See also Kumho, 119 S.Ct. at 1178 (citing the Committee Note to the proposed amendment to Rule 702, which had been released for public comment before the date of the Kumho decision). The amendment affirms the trial court's role as gatekeeper and provides some general standards that the trial court must use to assess the reliability and helpfulness of proffered expert testimony. Consistently with Kumho, the Rule as amended provides that all types of expert testimony present questions of admissibility for the trial court in deciding whether the evidence is

reliable and helpful. Consequently, the admissibility of all expert testimony is governed by the principles of Rule 104(a). Under that Rule, the proponent has the burden of establishing that the pertinent admissibility requirements are met by a preponderance of the evidence. See Bourjaily v. United States, 483 U.S. 171 (1987).

Daubert set forth a non-exclusive checklist for trial courts to use in assessing the reliability of scientific expert testimony. The specific factors explicated by the Daubert Court are (1) whether the expert's technique or theory can be or has been tested---that is, whether the expert's theory can be challenged in some objective sense, or whether it is instead simply a subjective, conclusory approach that cannot reasonably be assessed for reliability; (2) whether the technique or theory has been subject to peer review and publication; (3) the known or potential rate of error of the technique or theory when applied; (4) the existence and maintenance of standards and controls; and (5) whether the technique or theory has been generally accepted in the scientific community. The Court in Kumho held that these factors might also be applicable in assessing the reliability of non-scientific expert testimony, depending upon "the particular circumstances of the particular case at issue." 119 S.Ct. at 1175.

No attempt has been made to "codify" these specific factors. Daubert itself emphasized that the factors were neither exclusive nor dispositive. Other cases have recognized that not all of the specific Daubert factors can apply to every type of expert testimony. In addition to Kumho, 119 S.Ct. at 1175, see Tyus v. Urban Search Management, 102 F.3d 256 (7th Cir. 1996) (noting that the factors mentioned by the Court in Daubert do not neatly apply to expert testimony from a sociologist). See also Kannankeril v. Terminix Int'l, Inc., 128 F.3d 802, 809 (3d Cir. 1997) (holding that lack of peer review or publication was not dispositive where the expert's opinion was supported by "widely accepted scientific knowledge"). The standards set forth in the amendment are broad enough to require consideration of any or all of the specific Daubert factors where appropriate.

Courts both before and after Daubert have found other factors relevant in determining whether expert testimony is sufficiently reliable to be considered by the trier of fact. These factors include:

(1) Whether experts are "proposing to testify about matters growing naturally and directly out of research they have conducted independent of the litigation, or whether they have developed their opinions expressly for purposes of testifying." Daubert v. Merrell Dow Pharmaceuticals, Inc., 43 F.3d 1311, 1317 (9th Cir. 1995).

(2) Whether the expert has unjustifiably extrapolated from an accepted premise to an unfounded conclusion. See General Elec. Co. v. Joiner, 522 U.S. 136, 146

(1997) (noting that in some cases a trial court "may conclude that there is simply too great an analytical gap between the data and the opinion proffered").

(3) Whether the expert has adequately accounted for obvious alternative explanations. See Claar v. Burlington N.R.R., 29 F.3d 499 (9th Cir. 1994) (testimony excluded where the expert failed to consider other obvious causes for the plaintiff's condition). Compare Ambrosini v. Labarraque, 101 F.3d 129 (D.C. Cir. 1996) (the possibility of some uneliminated causes presents a question of weight, so long as the most obvious causes have been considered and reasonably ruled out by the expert).

(4) Whether the expert "is being as careful as he would be in his regular professional work outside his paid litigation consulting." Sheehan v. Daily Racing Form, Inc., 104 F.3d 940, 942 (7th Cir. 1997). See Kumho Tire Co. v. Carmichael, 119 S.Ct. 1167, 1176 (1999) (Daubert requires the trial court to assure itself that the expert "employs in the courtroom the same level of intellectual rigor that characterizes the practice of an expert in the relevant field").

(5) Whether the field of expertise claimed by the expert is known to reach reliable results for the type of opinion the expert would give. See Kumho Tire Co. v. Carmichael, 119 S.Ct.1167, 1175 (1999) (Daubert's general acceptance factor does not "help show that an expert's testimony is reliable where the discipline itself lacks reliability, as for example, do theories grounded in any so-called generally accepted principles of astrology or necromancy."), Moore v. Ashland Chemical, Inc., 151 F.3d 269 (5th Cir. 1998) (en banc) (clinical doctor was properly precluded from testifying to the toxicological cause of the plaintiff's respiratory problem, where the opinion was not sufficiently grounded in scientific methodology); Sterling v. Velsicol Chem. Corp., 855 F.2d 1188 (6th Cir. 1988) (rejecting testimony based on "clinical ecology" as unfounded and unreliable).

All of these factors remain relevant to the determination of the reliability of expert testimony under the Rule as amended. Other factors may also be relevant. See Kumho, 119 S.Ct. 1167, 1176 ("[W]e conclude that the trial judge must have considerable leeway in deciding in a particular case how to go about determining whether particular expert testimony is reliable."). Yet no single factor is necessarily dispositive of the reliability of a particular expert's testimony. See, e.g., Heller v. Shaw Industries, Inc., 167 F.3d 146, 155 (3d Cir. 1999) ("not only must each stage of the expert's testimony be reliable, but each stage must be evaluated practically and flexibly without bright-line exclusionary (or inclusionary) rules."); Daubert v. Merrell Dow Pharmaceuticals, Inc., 43 F.3d 1311, 1317, n.5 (9th Cir. 1995) (noting that some expert disciplines "have the courtroom as a principal theatre of operations" and as to these disciplines "the fact that the expert has developed an expertise principally for purposes of litigation will obviously not be a substantial consideration.").

A review of the caselaw after Daubert shows that the rejection of expert testimony is the exception rather than the rule. Daubert did not work a "seachange over federal evidence law," and "the trial court's role as gatekeeper is not intended to serve as a replacement for the adversary system." United States v. 14.38 Acres of Land Situated in Leflore County, Mississippi, 80 F.3d 1074, 1078 (5th Cir. 1996). As the Court in Daubert stated: "Vigorous cross-examination, presentation of contrary evidence, and careful instruction on the burden of proof are the traditional and appropriate means of attacking shaky but admissible evidence." 509 U.S. at 595. Likewise, this amendment is not intended to provide an excuse for an automatic challenge to the testimony of every expert. See Kumho Tire Co. v. Carmichael, 119 S.Ct. 1167, 1176 (1999) (noting that the trial judge has the discretion "both to avoid unnecessary 'reliability' proceedings in ordinary cases where the reliability of an expert's methods is properly taken for granted, and to require appropriate proceedings in the less usual or more complex cases where cause for questioning the expert's reliability arises.").

When a trial court, applying this amendment, rules that an expert's testimony is reliable, this does not necessarily mean that contradictory expert testimony is unreliable. The amendment is broad enough to permit testimony that is the product of competing principles or methods in the same field of expertise. See, e.g., Heller v. Shaw Industries, Inc., 167 F.3d 146, 160 (3d Cir. 1999) (expert testimony cannot be excluded simply because the expert uses one test rather than another, when both tests are accepted in the field and both reach reliable results). As the court stated in In re Paoli R.R. Yard PCB Litigation, 35 F.3d 717, 744 (3d Cir. 1994), proponents "do not have to demonstrate to the judge by a preponderance of the evidence that the assessments of their experts are correct, they only have to demonstrate by a preponderance of evidence that their opinions are reliable.... The evidentiary requirement of reliability is lower than the merits standard of correctness." See also Daubert v. Merrell Dow Pharmaceuticals, Inc., 43 F.3d 1311, 1318 (9th Cir. 1995) (scientific experts might be permitted to testify if they could show that the methods they used were also employed by "a recognized minority of scientists in their field."); Ruiz-Troche v. Pepsi Cola, 161 F.3d 77, 85 (1st Cir. 1998) ("Daubert neither requires nor empowers trial courts to determine which of several competing scientific theories has the best provenance.").

The Court in Daubert declared that the "focus, of course, must be solely on principles and methodology, not on the conclusions they generate." 509 U.S. at 595. Yet as the Court later recognized, "conclusions and methodology are not entirely distinct from one another." General Elec. Co. v. Joiner, 522 U.S. 136, 146 (1997). Under the amendment, as under Daubert, when an expert purports to apply principles and methods in accordance with professional standards, and yet reaches a conclusion that other experts in the field would not reach, the trial court may fairly suspect that the principles and methods have not been faithfully applied.

See Lust v. Merrell Dow Pharmaceuticals, Inc., 89 F.3d 594, 598 (9th Cir. 1996). The amendment specifically provides that the trial court must scrutinize not only the principles and methods used by the expert, but also whether those principles and methods have been properly applied to the facts of the case. As the court noted in In re Paoli R.R. Yard PCB Litig., 35 F.3d 717, 745 (3d Cir. 1994), "any step that renders the analysis unreliable ... renders the expert's testimony inadmissible. This is true whether the step completely changes a reliable methodology or merely misapplies that methodology."

If the expert purports to apply principles and methods to the facts of the case, it is important that this application be conducted reliably. Yet it might also be important in some cases for an expert to educate the factfinder about general principles, without ever attempting to apply these principles to the specific facts of the case. For example, experts might instruct the factfinder on the principles of thermodynamics, or bloodclotting, or on how financial markets respond to corporate reports, without ever knowing about or trying to tie their testimony into the facts of the case. The amendment does not alter the venerable practice of using expert testimony to educate the factfinder on general principles. For this kind of generalized testimony, Rule 702 simply requires that: (1) the expert be qualified; (2) the testimony address a subject matter on which the factfinder can be assisted by an expert; (3) the testimony be reliable; and (4) the testimony "fit" the facts of the case.

As stated earlier, the amendment does not distinguish between scientific and other forms of expert testimony. The trial court's gatekeeping function applies to testimony by any expert. See Kumho Tire Co. v. Carmichael, 119 S.Ct. 1167, 1171 (1999) ("We conclude that Daubert's general holding--setting forth the trial judge's general 'gatekeeping' obligation--applies not only to testimony based on 'scientific' knowledge, but also to testimony based on 'technical' and 'other specialized' knowledge."). While the relevant factors for determining reliability will vary from expertise to expertise, the amendment rejects the premise that an expert's testimony should be treated more permissively simply because it is outside the realm of science. An opinion from an expert who is not a scientist should receive the same degree of scrutiny for reliability as an opinion from an expert who purports to be a scientist. See Watkins v. Telsmith, Inc., 121 F.3d 984, 991 (5th Cir. 1997) ("[I]t seems exactly backwards that experts who purport to rely on general engineering principles and practical experience might escape screening by the district court simply by stating that their conclusions were not reached by any particular method or technique."). Some types of expert testimony will be more objectively verifiable, and subject to the expectations of falsifiability, peer review, and publication, than others. Some types of expert testimony will not rely on anything like a scientific method, and so will have to be evaluated by reference to other standard principles attendant to the particular area of expertise. The trial judge in all cases of proffered expert testimony must find that it is properly grounded, well-reasoned, and not speculative before it can be admitted. The expert's testimony must be grounded in an accepted body of learning or experience in the expert's field, and the expert must explain how the conclusion is so grounded. See, e.g., American College of Trial Lawyers, Standards and Procedures for Determining the Admissibility of Expert Testimony after Daubert, 157 F.R.D. 571, 579 (1994) ("[W]hether the testimony concerns economic principles, accounting standards, property valuation or other non-scientific subjects, it should be evaluated by reference to the 'knowledge and experience' of that particular field.").

The amendment requires that the testimony must be the product of reliable principles and methods that are reliably applied to the facts of the case. While the terms "principles" and "methods" may convey a certain impression when applied to scientific knowledge, they remain relevant when applied to testimony based on technical or other specialized knowledge. For example, when a law enforcement agent testifies regarding the use of code words in a drug transaction, the principle used by the agent is that participants in such transactions regularly use code words to conceal the nature of their activities. The method used by the agent is the application of extensive experience to analyze the meaning of the conversations. So long as the principles and methods are reliable and applied reliably to the facts of the case, this type of testimony should be admitted.

Nothing in this amendment is intended to suggest that experience alone--or experience in conjunction with other knowledge, skill, training or education--may not provide a sufficient foundation for expert testimony. To the contrary, the text of Rule 702 expressly contemplates that an expert may be qualified on the basis of experience. In certain fields, experience is the predominant, if not sole, basis for a great deal of reliable expert testimony. See, e.g., United States v. Jones, 107 F.3d 1147 (6th Cir. 1997) (no abuse of discretion in admitting the testimony of a handwriting examiner who had years of practical experience and extensive training, and who explained his methodology in detail); Tassin v. Sears Roebuck, 946 F.Supp. 1241, 1248 (M.D.La. 1996) (design engineer's testimony can be admissible when the expert's opinions "are based on facts, a reasonable investigation, and traditional technical/mechanical expertise, and he provides a reasonable link between the information and procedures he uses and the conclusions he reaches"). See also Kumho Tire Co. v. Carmichael, 119 S.Ct. 1167, 1178 (1999) (stating that "no one denies that an expert might draw a conclusion from a set of observations based on extensive and specialized experience.").

If the witness is relying solely or primarily on experience, then the witness must explain how that experience leads to the conclusion reached, why that experience is a sufficient basis for the opinion, and how that experience is reliably applied to the facts. The trial court's gatekeeping function requires more than simply "taking the expert's word for it." See Daubert v. Merrell Dow Pharmaceuticals, Inc., 43

F.3d 1311, 1319 (9th Cir. 1995) ("We've been presented with only the experts' qualifications, their conclusions and their assurances of reliability. Under Daubert, that's not enough."). The more subjective and controversial the expert's inquiry, the more likely the testimony should be excluded as unreliable. See O'Conner v. Commonwealth Edison Co., 13 F.3d 1090 (7th Cir. 1994) (expert testimony based on a completely subjective methodology held properly excluded). See also Kumho Tire Co. v. Carmichael, 119 S.Ct . 1167, 1176 (1999) ("[I]t will at times be useful to ask even of a witness whose expertise is based purely on experience, say, a perfume tester able to distinguish among 140 odors at a sniff, whether his preparation is of a kind that others in the field would recognize as acceptable.").

Subpart (1) of Rule 702 calls for a quantitative rather than qualitative analysis. The amendment requires that expert testimony be based on sufficient underlying "facts or data." The term "data" is intended to encompass the reliable opinions of other experts. See the original Advisory Committee Note to Rule 703. The language "facts or data" is broad enough to allow an expert to rely on hypothetical facts that are supported by the evidence. Id.

When facts are in dispute, experts sometimes reach different conclusions based on competing versions of the facts. The emphasis in the amendment on " sufficient facts or data" is not intended to authorize a trial court to exclude an expert's testimony on the ground that the court believes one version of the facts and not the other.

There has been some confusion over the relationship between Rules 702 and 703. The amendment makes clear that the sufficiency of the basis of an expert' s testimony is to be decided under Rule 702. Rule 702 sets forth the overarching requirement of reliability, and an analysis of the sufficiency of the expert's basis cannot be divorced from the ultimate reliability of the expert's opinion. In contrast, the "reasonable reliance" requirement of Rule 703 is a relatively narrow inquiry. When an expert relies on inadmissible information, Rule 703 requires the trial court to determine whether that information is of a type reasonably relied on by other experts in the field. If so, the expert can rely on the information in reaching an opinion. However, the question whether the expert is relying on a sufficient basis of information--whether admissible information or not--is governed by the requirements of Rule 702.

The amendment makes no attempt to set forth procedural requirements for exercising the trial court's gatekeeping function over expert testimony. See Daniel J. Capra, The Daubert Puzzle, 38 Ga.L.Rev. 699, 766 (1998) ("Trial courts should be allowed substantial discretion in dealing with Daubert questions; any attempt to codify procedures will likely give rise to unnecessary changes in practice and create difficult questions for appellate review."). Courts have shown considerable ingenuity and flexibility in considering challenges to expert testimony under Daubert, and it is contemplated that this will continue under the amended Rule. See, e.g., Cortes-Irizarry v. Corporacion Insular, 111 F.3d 184 (1st Cir. 1997) (discussing the application of Daubert in ruling on a motion for summary judgment); In re Paoli R.R. Yard PCB Litig., 35 F.3d 717, 736, 739 (3d Cir. 1994) (discussing the use of in limine hearings); Claar v. Burlington N.R.R., 29 F.3d 499, 502-05 (9th Cir. 1994) (discussing the trial court's technique of ordering experts to submit serial affidavits explaining the reasoning and methods underlying their conclusions).

The amendment continues the practice of the original Rule in referring to a qualified witness as an "expert." This was done to provide continuity and to minimize change. The use of the term "expert" in the Rule does not, however, mean that a jury should actually be informed that a qualified witness is testifying as an "expert." Indeed, there is much to be said for a practice that prohibits the use of the term "expert" by both the parties and the court at trial. Such a practice "ensures that trial courts do not inadvertently put their stamp of authority" on a witness's opinion, and protects against the jury's being "overwhelmed by the so-called 'experts'." Hon. Charles Richey, Proposals to Eliminate the Prejudicial Effect of the Use of the Word "Expert" Under the Federal Rules of Evidence in Criminal and Civil Jury Trials, 154 F.R.D. 537, 559 (1994) (setting forth limiting instructions and a standing order employed to prohibit the use of the term " expert" injury trials).

GAP Report--Proposed Amendment to Rule 702

The Committee made the following changes to the published draft of the proposed amendment to Evidence Rule 702:

1. The word "reliable" was deleted from Subpart (1) of the proposed amendment, in order to avoid an overlap with Evidence Rule 703, and to clarify that an expert opinion need not be excluded simply because it is based on hypothetical facts. The Committee Note was amended to accord with this textual change.

2. The Committee Note was amended throughout to include pertinent references to the Supreme Court's decision in Kumho Tire Co. v. Carmichael, which was rendered after the proposed amendment was released for public comment. Other citations were updated as well.

3. The Committee Note was revised to emphasize that the amendment is not intended to limit the right to jury trial, nor to permit a challenge to the testimony of every expert, nor to preclude the testimony of experience-based experts, nor to prohibit testimony based on competing methodologies within a field of expertise.

4. Language was added to the Committee Note to clarify that no single factor is necessarily dispositive of the reliability inquiry mandated by Evidence Rule 702.

Rule 703. Bases of Opinion Testimony by Experts

The facts or data in the particular case upon which an expert bases an opinion or inference may be those perceived by or made known to the expert at or before the hearing. If of a type reasonably relied upon by experts in the particular field in forming opinions or inferences upon the subject, the facts or data need not be admissible in evidence in order for the opinion or inference to be admitted. Facts or data that are otherwise inadmissible shall not be disclosed to the jury by the proponent of the opinion or inference unless the court determines that their probative value in assisting the jury to evaluate the expert's opinion substantially outweighs their prejudicial effect.

ADVISORY COMMITTEE NOTES

1972 Proposed Rules

Facts or data upon which expert opinions are based may, under the rule, be derived from three possible sources. The first is the firsthand observation of the witness with opinions based thereon traditionally allowed. A treating physician affords an example. Rheingold, The Basis of Medical Testimony, 15 Vand.L.Rev. 473, 489 (1962). Whether he must first relate his observations is treated in Rule 705. The second source, presentation at the trial, also reflects existing practice. The technique may be the familiar hypothetical question or having the expert attend the trial and hear the testimony establishing the facts. Problems of determining what testimony the expert relied upon, when the latter technique is employed and the testimony is in conflict, may be resolved by resort to Rule 705. The third source contemplated by the rule consists of presentation of data to the expert outside of court and other than by his own perception. In this respect the rule is designed to broaden the basis for expert opinions beyond that current in many jurisdictions and to bring the judicial practice into line with the practice of the experts themselves when not in court. Thus a physician in his own practice bases his diagnosis on information from numerous sources and of considerable variety, including statements by patients and relatives, reports and opinions from nurses, technicians and other doctors, hospital records, and X rays. Most of them are admissible in evidence, but only with the expenditure of substantial time in producing and examining various authenticating witnesses. The physician makes life-and-death decisions in reliance upon them. His validation, expertly performed and subject to cross-examination, ought to suffice for judicial purposes. Rheingold, supra, at 531; McCormick § 15. A similar provision is California Evidence Code § 801(b).

The rule also offers a more satisfactory basis for ruling upon the admissibility of public opinion poll evidence. Attention is directed to the validity of the techniques employed rather than to relatively fruitless inquiries whether hearsay is involved. See Judge Feinberg's careful analysis in Zippo Mfg. Co. v. Rogers Imports, Inc., 216 F.Supp. 670 (S.D.N.Y.1963). See also Blum et al., The Art of Opinion Research: A Lawyer's Appraisal of an Emerging Service, 24 U.Chi.L.Rev. 1 (1956); Bonynge Trademark Surveys and Techniques and Their Use in Litigation, 48 A.B.A.J. 329 (1962); Zeisel, The Uniqueness of Survey Evidence, 45 Cornell L.Q. 322 (1960); Annot., 76 A.L.R.2d 919.

If it be feared that enlargement of permissible data may tend to break down the rules of exclusion unduly, notice should be taken that the rule requires that the facts or data "be of a type reasonably relied upon by experts in the particular field." The language would not warrant admitting in evidence the opinion of an "accidentologist" as to the point of impact in an automobile collision based on statements of bystanders since this requirement is not satisfied. See Comment, Cal.Law Rev.Comm'n, Recommendation Proposing an Evidence Code 148-150 (1965).

1987 Amendments
The amendment is technical. No substantive change is intended.

2000 Amendments
Rule 703 has been amended to emphasize that when an expert reasonably relies on inadmissible information to form an opinion or inference, the underlying information is not admissible simply because the opinion or inference is admitted. Courts have reached different results on how to treat inadmissible information when it is reasonably relied upon by an expert in forming an opinion or drawing an inference. Compare United States v. Rollins, 862 F.2d 1282 (7th Cir. 1988) (admitting, as part of the basis of an FBI agent's expert opinion on the meaning of code language, the hearsay statements of an informant), with United States v. 0.59 Acres of Land, 109 F.3d 1493 (9th Cir. 1997) (error to admit hearsay offered as the basis of an expert opinion, without a limiting instruction). Commentators have also taken differing views. See e.g., Ronald Carlson, Policing the Bases of Modern Expert Testimony, 39 Vand.L.Rev. 577 (1986) (advocating limits on the jury's consideration of otherwise inadmissible evidence used as the basis for an expert opinion); Paul Rice, Inadmissible Evidence as a Basis for Expert Testimony: A Response to Professor Carlson, 40 Vand.L.Rev. 583 (1987) (advocating unrestricted use of information reasonably relied upon by an expert).

When information is reasonably relied upon by an expert and yet is admissible only for the purpose of assisting the jury in evaluating an expert's opinion, a trial court applying this Rule must consider the information's probative value in assisting the jury to weigh the expert's opinion on the one hand, and the risk of prejudice resulting from the jury's potential misuse of the information for substantive purposes on the other. The information may be disclosed to the jury, upon objection, only if the trial court finds that the probative value of the information in assisting the jury to evaluate the expert's opinion substantially outweighs its prejudicial effect. If the otherwise inadmissible information is admitted under this balancing test, the trial judge must give a limiting instruction upon request, informing the jury that the underlying information must not be used for substantive purposes. See Rule 105. In determining the appropriate course, the trial court should consider the probable effectiveness or lack of effectiveness of a limiting instruction under the particular circumstances.

The amendment governs only the disclosure to the jury of information that is reasonably relied on by an expert, when that information is not admissible for substantive purposes. It is not intended to affect the admissibility of an expert's testimony. Nor does the amendment prevent an expert from relying on information that is inadmissible for substantive purposes.

Nothing in this Rule restricts the presentation of underlying expert facts or data when offered by an adverse party. See Rule 705. Of course, an adversary's attack on an expert's basis will often open the door to a proponent's rebuttal with information that was reasonably relied upon by the expert, even if that information would not have been discloseable initially under the balancing test provided by this amendment. Moreover, in some circumstances the proponent might wish to disclose information that is relied upon by the expert in order to "remove the sting" from the opponent's anticipated attack, and thereby prevent the jury from drawing an unfair negative inference. The trial court should take this consideration into account in applying the balancing test provided by this amendment.

This amendment covers facts or data that cannot be admitted for any purpose other than to assist the jury to evaluate the expert's opinion. The balancing test provided in this amendment is not applicable to facts or data that are admissible for any other purpose but have not yet been offered for such a purpose at the time the expert testifies.

The amendment provides a presumption against disclosure to the jury of information used as the basis of an expert's opinion and not admissible for any substantive purpose, when that information is offered by the proponent of the expert. In a multi-party case, where one party proffers an expert whose testimony is also beneficial to other parties, each such party should be deemed a "proponent" within the meaning of the amendment.

GAP Report--Proposed Amendment to Rule 703

The Committee made the following changes to the published draft of the proposed amendment to Evidence Rule 703:

1. A minor stylistic change was made in the text, in accordance with the suggestion of the Style Subcommittee of the Standing Committee on Rules of Practice and Procedure.

2. The words "in assisting the jury to evaluate the expert's opinion" were added to the text, to specify the proper purpose for offering the otherwise inadmissible information relied on by an expert. The Committee Note was revised to accord with this change in the text.

3. Stylistic changes were made to the Committee Note.

4. The Committee Note was revised to emphasize that the balancing test set forth in the proposal should be used to determine whether an expert's basis may be disclosed to the jury either (1) in rebuttal or (2) on direct examination to "remove the sting" of an opponent's anticipated attack on an expert's basis.

Rule 704. Opinion on Ultimate Issue

(a) Except as provided in subdivision (b), testimony in the form of an opinion or inference otherwise admissible is not objectionable because it embraces an ultimate issue to be decided by the trier of fact.

(b) No expert witness testifying with respect to the mental state or condition of a defendant in a criminal case may state an opinion or inference as to whether the defendant did or did not have the mental state or condition constituting an element of the crime charged or of a defense thereto. Such ultimate issues are matters for the trier of fact alone.

ADVISORY COMMITTEE NOTES

1972 Proposed Rules
The basic approach to opinions, lay and expert, in these rules is to admit them when helpful to the trier of fact. In order to render this approach fully effective and to allay any doubt on the subject, the so-called "ultimate issue" rule is specifically abolished by the instant rule.

The older cases often contained strictures against allowing witnesses to express opinions upon ultimate issues, as a particular aspect of the rule against opinions.

The rule was unduly restrictive, difficult of application, and generally served only to deprive the trier of fact of useful information. 7 Wigmore §§ 1920, 1921; McCormick § 12. The basis usually assigned for the rule, to prevent the witness from "usurping the province of the jury," is aptly characterized as "empty rhetoric." 7 Wigmore § 1920, p. 17. Efforts to meet the felt needs of particular situations led to odd verbal circumlocutions which were said not to violate the rule. Thus a witness could express his estimate of the criminal responsibility of an accused in terms of sanity or insanity, but not in terms of ability to tell right from wrong or other more modern standard. And in cases of medical causation, witnesses were sometimes required to couch their opinions in cautious phrases of "might or could," rather than "did," though the result was to deprive many opinions of the positiveness to which they were entitled, accompanied by the hazard of a ruling of insufficiency to support a verdict. In other instances the rule was simply disregarded, and, as concessions to need, opinions were allowed upon such matters as intoxication, speed, handwriting, and value, although more precise coincidence with an ultimate issue would scarcely be possible.

Many modern decisions illustrate the trend to abandon the rule completely. People v. Wilson, 25 Cal.2d 341, 153 P.2d 720 (1944), whether abortion necessary to save life of patient; Clifford-Jacobs Forging Co. v. Industrial Comm., 19 Ill.2d 236, 166 N.E.2d 582 (1960), medical causation; Dowling v. L. H. Shattuck, Inc., 91 N.H. 234, 17 A.2d 529 (1941), proper method of shoring ditch; Schweiger v. Solbeck, 191 Or. 454, 230 P.2d 195 (1951), cause of landslide. In each instance the opinion was allowed.

The abolition of the ultimate issue rule does not lower the bars so as to admit all opinions. Under Rules 701 and 702, opinions must be helpful to the trier of fact, and Rule 403 provides for exclusion of evidence which wastes time. These provisions afford ample assurances against the admission of opinions which would merely tell the jury what result to reach, somewhat in the manner of the oath-helpers of an earlier day. They also stand ready to exclude opinions phrased in terms of inadequately explored legal criteria. Thus the question, "Did T have capacity to make a will?" would be excluded, while the question, "Did T have sufficient mental capacity to know the nature and extent of his property and the natural objects of his bounty and to formulate a rational scheme of distribution?" would be allowed. McCormick § 12.

For similar provisions see Uniform Rule 56(4); California Evidence Code § 805; Kansas Code of Civil Procedure § 60-456(d); New Jersey Evidence Rule 56(3).

Rule 705. Disclosure of Facts or Data Underlying Expert Opinion

The expert may testify in terms of opinion or inference and give reasons therefor without first testifying to the underlying facts or data, unless the court requires otherwise. The expert may in any event be required to disclose the underlying facts or data on cross-examination.

ADVISORY COMMITTEE NOTES

1972 Proposed Rules

The hypothetical question has been the target of a great deal of criticism as encouraging partisan bias, affording an opportunity for summing up in the middle of the case, and as complex and time consuming. Ladd, Expert Testimony, 5 Vand.L.Rev. 414, 426-427 (1952). While the rule allows counsel to make disclosure of the underlying facts or data as a preliminary to the giving of an expert opinion, if he chooses, the instances in which he is required to do so are reduced. This is true whether the expert bases his opinion on data furnished him at secondhand or observed by him at firsthand.

The elimination of the requirement of preliminary disclosure at the trial of underlying facts or data has a long background of support. In 1937 the Commissioners on Uniform State Laws incorporated a provision to this effect in their Model Expert Testimony Act, which furnished the basis for Uniform Rules 57 and 58. Rule 4515, N.Y. CPLR (McKinney 1963), provides:

"Unless the court orders otherwise, questions calling for the opinion of an expert witness need not be hypothetical in form, and the witness may state his opinion and reasons without first specifying the data upon which it is based. Upon cross-examination, he may be required to specify the data * * *."

See also California Evidence Code § 802; Kansas Code of Civil Procedure §§ 60-456, 60-457; New Jersey Evidence Rules 57, 58.

If the objection is made that leaving it to the cross-examiner to bring out the supporting data is essentially unfair, the answer is that he is under no compulsion to bring out any facts or data except those unfavorable to the opinion. The answer assumes that the cross-examiner has the advance knowledge which is essential for effective cross-examination. This advance knowledge has been afforded, though imperfectly, by the traditional foundation requirement. Rule 26(b)(4) of the Rules of Civil Procedure, as revised, provides for substantial discovery in this area, obviating in large measure the obstacles which have been raised in some instances to discovery of findings, underlying data, and even the identity of the experts. Friedenthal Discovery and Use of an Adverse Party's Expert Information, 14 Stan.L.Rev. 455 (1962).

These safeguards are reinforced by the discretionary power of the judge to require preliminary disclosure in any event.

1987 Amendment
The amendment is technical. No substantive change is intended.

1993 Amendment
This rule, which relates to the manner of presenting testimony at trial, is revised to avoid an arguable conflict with revised Rules 26(a)(2)(B) and 26(e)(1) of the Federal Rules of Civil Procedure or with revised Rule 16 of the Federal Rules of Criminal Procedure, which require disclosure in advance of trial of the basis and reasons for an expert's opinions.

If a serious question is raised under Rule 702 or 703 as to the admissibility of expert testimony, disclosure of the underlying facts or data on which opinions are based may, of course, be needed by the court before deciding whether, and to what extent, the person should be allowed to testify. This rule does not preclude such an inquiry.

Rule 706. Court Appointed Experts

(a) Appointment. The court may on its own motion or on the motion of any party enter an order to show cause why expert witnesses should not be appointed, and may request the parties to submit nominations. The court may appoint any expert witnesses agreed upon by the parties, and may appoint expert witnesses of its own selection. An expert witness shall not be appointed by the court unless the witness consents to act. A witness so appointed shall be informed of the witness' duties by the court in writing, a copy of which shall be filed with the clerk, or at a conference in which the parties shall have opportunity to participate. A witness so appointed shall advise the parties of the witness' findings, if any; the witness' deposition may be taken by any party; and the witness may be called to testify by the court or any party. The witness shall be subject to cross-examination by each party, including a party calling the witness.

(b) Compensation. Expert witnesses so appointed are entitled to reasonable compensation in whatever sum the court may allow. The compensation thus fixed is payable from funds which may be provided by law in criminal cases and civil actions and proceedings involving just compensation under the fifth amendment. In other civil actions and proceedings the compensation shall be paid by the parties in such proportion and at such time as the court directs, and thereafter charged in like manner as other costs.

(c) Disclosure of appointment. In the exercise of its discretion, the court may authorize disclosure to the jury of the fact that the court appointed the expert witness.

(d) Parties' experts of own selection. Nothing in this rule limits the parties in calling expert witnesses of their own selection.

ADVISORY COMMITTEE NOTES

1972 Proposed Rules

The practice of shopping for experts, the venality of some experts, and the reluctance of many reputable experts to involve themselves in litigation, have been matters of deep concern. Though the contention is made that court appointed experts acquire an aura of infallibility to which they are not entitled, Levy, Impartial Medical Testimony--Revisited, 34 Temple L.Q. 416 (1961), the trend is increasingly to provide for their use. While experience indicates that actual appointment is a relatively infrequent occurrence, the assumption may be made that the availability of the procedure in itself decreases the need for resorting to it. The ever-present possibility that the judge may appoint an expert in a given case must inevitably exert a sobering effect on the expert witness of a party and upon the person utilizing his services.

The inherent power of a trial judge to appoint an expert of his own choosing is virtually unquestioned. Scott v. Spanjer Bros., Inc., 298 F.2d 928 (2d Cir.1962); Danville Tobacco Assn. v. Bryant-Buckner Associates, Inc., 333 F.2d 202 (4th Cir.1964); Sink, The Unused Power of a Federal Judge to Call His Own Expert Witnesses, 29 S.Cal.L.Rev. 195 (1956); 2 Wigmore § 563, 9 id. § 2484; Annot., 95 A.L.R.2d 383. Hence the problem becomes largely one of detail.

The New York plan is well known and is described in Report by Special Committee of the Association of the Bar of the City of New York: Impartial Medical Testimony (1956). On recommendation of the Section of Judicial Administration, local adoption of an impartial medical plan was endorsed by the American Bar Association. 82 A.B.A.Rep. 184-185 (1957). Descriptions and analyses of plans in effect in various parts of the country are found in Van Dusen, A United States District Judge's View of the Impartial Medical Expert System, 32 F.R.D. 498 (1963); Wick and Kightlinger, Impartial Medical Testimony Under the Federal Civil Rules: A Tale of Three Doctors, 34 Ins. Counsel J. 115 (1967); and numerous articles collected in Klein, Judicial Administration and the Legal Profession 393 (1963). Statutes and rules include California Evidence Code §§ 730-733; Illinois Supreme Court Rule 215(d), Ill.Rev.Stat.1969, c. 110A, § 215(d); Burns Indiana Stats.1956, § 9-1702; Wisconsin Stats.Annot.1958, § 957.27.

In the federal practice, a comprehensive scheme for court appointed experts was initiated with the adoption of Rule 28 of the Federal Rules of Criminal Procedure in 1946. The Judicial Conference of the United States in 1953 considered court appointed experts in civil cases, but only with respect to whether they should be compensated from public funds, a proposal which was rejected. Report of the Judicial Conference of the United States 23 (1953). The present rule expands the practice to include civil cases.

Note to Subdivision (a). Subdivision (a) is based on Rule 28 of the Federal Rules of Criminal Procedure, with a few changes, mainly in the interest of clarity. Language has been added to provide specifically for the appointment either on motion of a party or on the judge's own motion. A provision subjecting the court appointed expert to deposition procedures has been incorporated. The rule has been revised to make definite the right of any party, including the party calling him, to cross-examine.

Note to Subdivision (b). Subdivision (b) combines the present provision for compensation in criminal cases with what seems to be a fair and feasible handling of civil cases, originally found in the Model Act and carried from there into Uniform Rule 60. See also California Evidence Code §§ 730-731. The special provision for Fifth Amendment compensation cases is designed to guard against reducing constitutionally guaranteed just compensation by requiring the recipient to pay costs. See Rule 71A(l) of the Rules of Civil Procedure.

Note to Subdivision (c). Subdivision (c) seems to be essential if the use of court appointed experts is to be fully effective. Uniform Rule 61 so provides.

Note to Subdivision (d). Subdivision (d) is in essence the last sentence of Rule 28(a) of the Federal Rules of Criminal Procedure.

1987 Amendment
The amendments are technical. No substantive change is intended.

Article VIII. Hearsay

ADVISORY COMMITTEE NOTES

1972 Proposed Rules
Introductory Note; The Hearsay Problem. The factors to be considered in evaluating the testimony of a witness are perception, memory, and narration. Morgan, Hearsay Dangers and the Application of the Hearsay Concept, 62 Harv.L.Rev. 177 (1948), Selected Writings on Evidence and Trial 764, 765 (Fryer ed. 1957); Shientag, Cross-Examination--A Judge's Viewpoint, 3 Record 12 (1948); Strahorn, A Reconsideration of the Hearsay Rule and Admissions, 85 U.Pa.L.Rev. 484, 485 (1937), Selected Writings, supra, 756, 757; Weinstein, Probative Force of Hearsay,

46 Iowa L.Rev. 331 (1961). Sometimes a fourth is added, sincerity, but in fact it seems merely to be an aspect of the three already mentioned.

In order to encourage the witness to do his best with respect to each of these factors, and to expose any inaccuracies which may enter in, the Anglo-American tradition has evolved three conditions under which witnesses will ideally be required to testify: (1) under oath, (2) in the personal presence of the trier of fact, (3) subject to cross-examination.

(1) Standard procedure calls for the swearing of witnesses. While the practice is perhaps less effective than in an earlier time, no disposition to relax the requirement is apparent, other than to allow affirmation by persons with scruples against taking oaths.

(2) The demeanor of the witness traditionally has been believed to furnish trier and opponent with valuable clues. Universal Camera Corp. v. N.L.R.B., 340 U.S. 474, 495-496, 71 S.Ct. 456, 95 L.Ed. 456 (1951); Sahm, Demeanor Evidence: Elusive and Intangible Imponderables, 47 A.B.A.J. 580 (1961), quoting numerous authorities. The witness himself will probably be impressed with the solemnity of the occasion and the possibility of public disgrace. Willingness to falsify may reasonably become more difficult in the presence of the person against whom directed. Rules 26 and 43(a) of the Federal Rules of Criminal and Civil Procedure, respectively, include the general requirement that testimony be taken orally in open court. The Sixth Amendment right of confrontation is a manifestation of these beliefs and attitudes.

(3) Emphasis on the basis of the hearsay rule today tends to center upon the condition of cross-examination. All may not agree with Wigmore that cross-examination is "beyond doubt the greatest legal engine ever invented for the discovery of truth," but all will agree with his statement that it has become a "vital feature" of the Anglo-American system. 5 Wigmore § 1367, p. 29. The belief, or perhaps hope, that cross-examination is effective in exposing imperfections of perception, memory, and narration is fundamental. Morgan, Foreword to Model Code of Evidence 37 (1942).

The logic of the preceding discussion might suggest that no testimony be received unless in full compliance with the three ideal conditions. No one advocates this position. Common sense tells that much evidence which is not given under the three conditions may be inherently superior to much that is. Moreover, when the choice is between evidence which is less than best and no evidence at all, only clear folly would dictate an across-the-board policy of doing without. The problem thus resolves itself into effecting a sensible accommodation between these considerations and the desirability of giving testimony under the ideal conditions.

The solution evolved by the common law has been a general rule excluding hearsay but subject to numerous exceptions under circumstances supposed to furnish guarantees of trustworthiness. Criticisms of this scheme are that it is bulky and complex, fails to screen good from bad hearsay realistically, and inhibits the growth of the law of evidence.

Since no one advocates excluding all hearsay, three possible solutions may be considered: (1) abolish the rule against hearsay and admit all hearsay; (2) admit hearsay possessing sufficient probative force, but with procedural safeguards; (3) revise the present system of class exceptions.

(1) Abolition of the hearsay rule would be the simplest solution. The effect would not be automatically to abolish the giving of testimony under ideal conditions. If the declarant were available, compliance with the ideal conditions would be optional with either party. Thus the proponent could call the declarant as a witness as a form of presentation more impressive than his hearsay statement. Or the opponent could call the declarant to be cross-examined upon his statement. This is the tenor of Uniform Rule 63(1), admitting the hearsay declaration of a person "who is present at the hearing and available for cross-examination." Compare the treatment of declarations of available declarants in Rule 801(d)(1) of the instant rules. If the declarant were unavailable, a rule of free admissibility would make no distinctions in terms of degrees of noncompliance with the ideal conditions and would exact no quid pro quo in the form of assurances of trustworthiness. Rule 503 of the Model Code did exactly that, providing for the admissibility of any hearsay declaration by an unavailable declarant, finding support in the Massachusetts act of 1898, enacted at the instance of Thayer, Mass.Gen.L.1932, c. 233, § 65, and in the English act of 1938, St.1938, c. 28, Evidence. Both are limited to civil cases. The draftsmen of the Uniform Rules chose a less advanced and more conventional position. Comment, Uniform Rule 63. The present Advisory Committee has been unconvinced of the wisdom of abandoning the traditional requirement of some particular assurance of credibility as a condition precedent to admitting the hearsay declaration of an unavailable declarant.

In criminal cases, the Sixth Amendment requirement of confrontation would no doubt move into a large part of the area presently occupied by the hearsay rule in the event of the abolition of the latter. The resultant split between civil and criminal evidence is regarded as an undesirable development.

(2) Abandonment of the system of class exceptions in favor of individual treatment in the setting of the particular case, accompanied by procedural safeguards, has been impressively advocated. Weinstein, The Probative Force of Hearsay, 46 Iowa L.Rev. 331 (1961). Admissibility would be determined by weighing the probative force of the evidence against the possibility of prejudice, waste of time, and

the availability of more satisfactory evidence. The bases of the traditional hearsay exceptions would be helpful in assessing probative force. Ladd, The Relationship of the Principles of Exclusionary Rules of Evidence to the Problem of Proof, 18 Minn.L.Rev. 506 (1934). Procedural safeguards would consist of notice of intention to use hearsay, free comment by the judge on the weight of the evidence, and a greater measure of authority in both trial and appellate judges to deal with evidence on the basis of weight. The Advisory Committee has rejected this approach to hearsay as involving too great a measure of judicial discretion, minimizing the predictability of rulings, enhancing the difficulties of preparation for trial, adding a further element to the already over-complicated congeries of pretrial procedures, and requiring substantially different rules for civil and criminal cases. The only way in which the probative force of hearsay differs from the probative force of other testimony is in the absence of oath, demeanor, and cross-examination as aids in determining credibility. For a judge to exclude evidence because he does not believe it has been described as "altogether atypical, extraordinary. * * * " Chadbourn, Bentham and the Hearsay Rule--A Benthamic View of Rule 63(4)(c) of the Uniform Rules of Evidence, 75 Harv.L.Rev. 932, 947 (1962).

(3) The approach to hearsay in these rules is that of the common law, i.e., a general rule excluding hearsay, with exceptions under which evidence is not required to be excluded even though hearsay. The traditional hearsay exceptions are drawn upon for the exceptions, collected under two rules, one dealing with situations where availability of the declarant is regarded as immaterial and the other with those where unavailability is made a condition to the admission of the hearsay statement. Each of the two rules concludes with a provision for hearsay statements not within one of the specified exceptions "but having comparable circumstantial guarantees of trustworthiness." Rules 803(24) and 804(b)(6). This plan is submitted as calculated to encourage growth and development in this area of the law, while conserving the values and experience of the past as a guide to the future.

Confrontation and Due Process. Until very recently, decisions invoking the confrontation clause of the Sixth Amendment were surprisingly few, a fact probably explainable by the former inapplicability of the clause to the states and by the hearsay rule's occupancy of much the same ground. The pattern which emerges from the earlier cases invoking the clause is substantially that of the hearsay rule, applied to criminal cases: an accused is entitled to have the witnesses against him testify under oath, in the presence of himself and trier, subject to cross-examination; yet considerations of public policy and necessity require the recognition of such exceptions as dying declarations and former testimony of unavailable witnesses. Mattox v. United States, 156 U.S. 237, 15 S.Ct. 337, 39 L.Ed. 409 (1895); Motes v. United States, 178 U.S. 458, 20 S.Ct. 993, 44 L.Ed. 1150 (1900); Delaney v. United States, 263 U.S. 586, 44 S.Ct. 206, 68 L.Ed. 462 (1924). Beginning with Snyder v. Massachusetts, 291 U.S. 97, 54 S.Ct. 330, 78 L.Ed. 674 (1934), the Court began to speak of confrontation as an aspect of procedural due process, thus extending its applicability to state cases and to federal cases other than criminal. The language of Snyder was that of an elastic concept of hearsay. The deportation case of Bridges v. Wixon, 326 U.S. 135, 65 S.Ct. 1443, 89 L.Ed. 2103 (1945), may be read broadly as imposing a strictly construed right of confrontation in all kinds of cases or narrowly as the product of a failure of the Immigration and Naturalization Service to follow its own rules. In re Oliver, 333 U.S. 257, 68 S.Ct. 499, 92 L.Ed. 682 (1948), ruled that cross-examination was essential to due process in a state contempt proceeding, but in United States v. Nugent, 346 U.S. 1, 73 S.Ct. 991, 97 L.Ed. 1417 (1953), the court held that it was not an essential aspect of a "hearing" for a conscientious objector under the Selective Service Act. Stein v. New York, 346 U.S. 156, 196, 73 S.Ct. 1077, 97 L.Ed. 1522 (1953), disclaimed any purpose to read the hearsay rule into the Fourteenth Amendment, but in Greene v. McElroy, 360 U.S. 474, 79 S.Ct. 1400, 3 L.Ed.2d 1377 (1959), revocation of security clearance without confrontation and cross-examination was held unauthorized, and a similar result was reached in Willner v. Committee on Character, 373 U.S. 96, 83 S.Ct. 1175, 10 L.Ed.2d 224 (1963). Ascertaining the constitutional dimensions of the confrontation-hearsay aggregate against the background of these cases is a matter of some difficulty, yet the general pattern is at least not inconsistent with that of the hearsay rule.

In 1965 the confrontation clause was held applicable to the states. Pointer v. Texas, 380 U.S. 400, 85 S.Ct. 1065, 13 L.Ed.2d 923 (1965). Prosecution use of former testimony given at a preliminary hearing where petitioner was not represented by counsel was a violation of the clause. The same result would have followed under conventional hearsay doctrine read in the light of a constitutional right to counsel, and nothing in the opinion suggests any difference in essential outline between the hearsay rule and the right of confrontation. In the companion case of Douglas v. Alabama, 380 U.S. 415, 85 S.Ct. 1074, 13 L.Ed.2d 934 (1965), however, the result reached by applying the confrontation clause is one reached less readily via the hearsay rule. A confession implicating petitioner was put before the jury by reading it to the witness in portions and asking if he made that statement. The witness refused to answer on grounds of self-incrimination. The result, said the Court, was to deny cross-examination, and hence confrontation. True, it could broadly be said that the confession was a hearsay statement which for all practical purposes was put in evidence. Yet a more easily accepted explanation of the opinion is that its real thrust was in the direction of curbing undesirable prosecutorial behavior, rather than merely applying rules of exclusion, and that the confrontation clause was the means selected to achieve this end. Comparable facts and a like result appeared in Brookhart v. Janis, 384 U.S. 1, 86 S.Ct. 1245, 16 L.Ed.2d 314 (1966).

The pattern suggested in Douglas was developed further and more distinctly in a pair of cases at the end of the 1966 term. United States v. Wade, 388 U.S. 218, 87 S.Ct. 1926, 18 L.Ed.2d 1149 (1967), and Gilbert v. California, 388 U.S. 263, 87 S.Ct. 1951, 18 L.Ed.2d 1178 (1967), hinged upon practices followed in identifying accused persons before trial. This pretrial identification was said to be so decisive an aspect of the case that accused was entitled to have counsel present; a pretrial identification made in the absence of counsel was not itself receivable in evidence and, in addition, might fatally infect a courtroom identification. The presence of counsel at the earlier identification was described as a necessary pre-requisite for "a meaningful confrontation at trial." United States v. Wade, supra, 388 U.S. at p. 236, 87 S.Ct. at p. 1937. Wade involved no evidence of the fact of a prior identification and hence was not susceptible of being decided on hearsay grounds. In Gilbert, witnesses did testify to an earlier identification, readily clas-sifiable as hearsay under a fairly strict view of what constitutes hearsay. The Court, however, carefully avoided basing the decision on the hearsay ground, choosing confrontation instead. 388 U.S. 263, 272, n. 3, 87 S.Ct. 1951. See also Parker v. Gladden, 385 U.S. 363, 87 S.Ct. 468, 17 L.Ed.2d 420 (1966), holding that the right of confrontation was violated when the bailiff made prejudicial statements to jurors, and Note, 75 Yale L.J. 1434 (1966).

Under the earlier cases, the confrontation clause may have been little more than a constitutional embodiment of the hearsay rule, even including traditional excep-tions but with some room for expanding them along similar lines. But under the recent cases the impact of the clause clearly extends beyond the confines of the hearsay rule. These considerations have led the Advisory Committee to conclude that a hearsay rule can function usefully as an adjunct to the confrontation right in constitutional areas and independently in nonconstitutional areas. In recognition of the separateness of the confrontation clause and the hearsay rule, and to avoid inviting collisions between them or between the hearsay rule and other exclusion-ary principles, the exceptions set forth in Rules 803 and 804 are stated in terms of exemption from the general exclusionary mandate of the hearsay rule, rather than in positive terms of admissibility. See Uniform Rule 63(1) to (31) and California Evidence Code §§ 1200-1340.

Fed. Rules Evid. Art. VIII, Refs & Annos, 28 U.S.C.A., FRE Art. VIII, Refs & Annos

Amendments received to 02-19-08

Rule 801. Definitions

The following definitions apply under this article:

(a) Statement. A "statement" is (1) an oral or written assertion or (2) nonverbal conduct of a person, if it is intended by the person as an assertion.

(b) Declarant. A "declarant" is a person who makes a statement.

(c) Hearsay. "Hearsay" is a statement, other than one made by the declarant while testifying at the trial or hearing, offered in evidence to prove the truth of the matter asserted.

(d) Statements which are not hearsay. A statement is not hearsay if--

(1) Prior statement by witness. The declarant testifies at the trial or hearing and is subject to cross-examination concerning the statement, and the statement is (A) inconsistent with the declarant's testimony, and was given under oath subject to the penalty of perjury at a trial, hearing, or other proceeding, or in a deposition, or (B) consistent with the declarant's testimony and is offered to rebut an express or implied charge against the declarant of recent fabrication or improper influence or motive, or (C) one of identification of a person made after perceiving the person; or

(2) Admission by party-opponent. The statement is offered against a party and is (A) the party's own statement, in either an individual or a representative capacity or (B) a statement of which the party has manifested an adoption or belief in its truth, or (C) a statement by a person authorized by the party to make a statement concerning the subject, or (D) a statement by the party's agent or servant concerning a matter within the scope of the agency or employment, made during the existence of the relationship, or (E) a statement by a coconspirator of a party during the course and in furtherance of the conspiracy. The contents of the statement shall be considered but are not alone sufficient to establish the declarant's authority under subdivision (C), the agency or employment relationship and scope thereof under subdivision (D), or the existence of the conspiracy and the participation therein of the declarant and the party against whom the statement is offered under subdivision (E).

ADVISORY COMMITTEE NOTES

1972 Proposed Rules

Note to Subdivision (a). The definition of "statement" assumes importance because the term is used in the definition of hearsay in subdivision (c). The effect of the definition of "statement" is to exclude from the operation of the hearsay rule all evidence of conduct, verbal or nonverbal, not intended as an assertion. The key to the definition is that nothing is an assertion unless intended to be one.

It can scarcely be doubted that an assertion made in words is intended by the declarant to be an assertion. Hence verbal assertions readily fall into the category of "statement." Whether nonverbal conduct should be regarded as a statement for purposes of defining hearsay requires further consideration. Some nonverbal conduct, such as the act of pointing to identify a suspect in a lineup, is clearly the equivalent of words, assertive in nature, and to be regarded as a statement. Other nonverbal conduct, however, may be offered as evidence that the person acted as he did because of his belief in the existence of the condition sought to be proved, from which belief the existence of the condition may be inferred. This sequence is, arguably, in effect an assertion of the existence of the condition and hence properly includable within the hearsay concept. See Morgan, Hearsay Dangers and the Application of the Hearsay Concept, 62 Harv.L.Rev. 177, 214, 217 (1948), and the elaboration in Finman, Implied Assertions as Hearsay: Some Criticisms of the Uniform Rules of Evidence, 14 Stan.L.Rev. 682 (1962). Admittedly evidence of this character is untested with respect to the perception, memory, and narration (or their equivalents) of the actor, but the Advisory Committee is of the view that these dangers are minimal in the absence of an intent to assert and do not justify the loss of the evidence on hearsay grounds. No class of evidence is free of the possibility of fabrication, but the likelihood is less with nonverbal than with assertive verbal conduct. The situations giving rise to the nonverbal conduct are such as virtually to eliminate questions of sincerity. Motivation, the nature of the conduct, and the presence or absence of reliance will bear heavily upon the weight to be given the evidence. Falknor, The "Hear-Say" Rule as a "See-Do" Rule: Evidence of Conduct, 33 Rocky Mt.L.Rev. 133 (1961). Similar considerations govern nonassertive verbal conduct and verbal conduct which is assertive but offered as a basis for inferring something other than the matter asserted, also excluded from the definition of hearsay by the language of subdivision (c).

When evidence of conduct is offered on the theory that it is not a statement, and hence not hearsay, a preliminary determination will be required to determine whether an assertion is intended. The rule is so worded as to place the burden upon the party claiming that the intention existed; ambiguous and doubtful cases will be resolved against him and in favor of admissibility. The determination involves no greater difficulty than many other preliminary questions of fact.

Maguire, The Hearsay System: Around and Through the Thicket, 14 Vand.L.Rev. 741, 765-767 (1961).

For similar approaches, see Uniform Rule 62(1); <u>California Evidence Code §§ 225, 1200</u>; Kansas Code of Civil Procedure § 60-459(a); New Jersey Evidence Rule 62(1).

Note to Subdivision (c). The definition follows along familiar lines in including only statements offered to prove the truth of the matter asserted. McCormick <u>§ 225</u>; 5 Wigmore § 1361, 6 *id.* § 1766. If the significance of an offered statement lies solely in the fact that it was made, no issue is raised as to the truth of anything asserted, and the statement is not hearsay. <u>*Emich Motors Corp. v. General Motors Corp.*, 181 F.2d 70 (7th Cir.1950)</u>, rev'd on other grounds <u>340 U.S. 558, 71 S.Ct. 408, 95 L.Ed. 534</u>, letters of complaint from customers offered as a reason for cancellation of dealer's franchise, to rebut contention that franchise was revoked for refusal to finance sales through affiliated finance company. The effect is to exclude from hearsay the entire category of "verbal acts" and "verbal parts of an act," in which the statement itself affects the legal rights of the parties or is a circumstance bearing on conduct affecting their rights.

The definition of hearsay must, of course, be read with reference to the definition of statement set forth in subdivision (a).

Testimony given by a witness in the course of court proceedings is excluded since there is compliance with all the ideal conditions for testifying.

Note to Subdivision (d). Several types of statements which would otherwise literally fall within the definition are expressly excluded from it:

(1) *Prior statement by witness.* Considerable controversy has attended the question whether a prior out-of-court statement by a person now available for cross-examination concerning it, under oath and in the presence of the trier of fact, should be classed as hearsay. If the witness admits on the stand that he made the statement and that it was true, he adopts the statement and there is no hearsay problem. The hearsay problem arises when the witness on the stand denies having made the statement or admits having made it but denies its truth. The argument in favor of treating these latter statements as hearsay is based upon the ground that the conditions of oath, cross-examination, and demeanor observation did not prevail at the time the statement was made and cannot adequately be supplied by the later examination. The logic of the situation is troublesome. So far as concerns the oath, its mere presence has never been regarded as sufficient to remove a statement from the hearsay category, and it receives much less emphasis than cross-examination as a truth-compelling device. While strong expressions are found to the effect that no conviction can be had or important right taken away on the basis of statements not made under fear of prosecution for perjury, *Bridges v. Wixon, 326 U.S. 135, 65 S.Ct. 1443, 89 L.Ed. 2103 (1945)*, the fact is that, of the many common law exceptions to the hearsay rule, only that for reported testimony has required the statement to have been made under oath. Nor is it satisfactorily explained why cross-examination cannot be conducted subsequently with success. The decisions contending most vigorously for its inadequacy in fact demonstrate quite thorough exploration of the weaknesses and doubts attending the earlier statement. *State v. Saporen*, 205 Minn. 358, 285 N.W. 898 (1939); *Ruhala v. Roby*, 379 Mich. 102, 150 N.W.2d 146 (1967); *People v. Johnson*, 68 Cal.2d 646, 68 Cal.Rptr. 599, 441 P.2d 111 (1968). In respect to demeanor, as Judge Learned Hand observed in *Di Carlo v. United States*, 6 F.2d 364 (2d Cir.1925), when the jury decides that the truth is not what the witness says now, but what he said before, they are still deciding from what they see and hear in court. The bulk of the case law nevertheless has been against allowing prior statements of witnesses to be used generally as substantive evidence. Most of the writers and Uniform Rule 63(1) have taken the opposite position.

The position taken by the Advisory Committee in formulating this part of the rule is funded upon an unwillingness to countenance the general use of prior prepared statements as substantive evidence, but with a recognition that particular circumstances call for a contrary result. The judgment is one more of experience than of logic. The rule requires in each instance, as a general safeguard, that the declarant actually testify as a witness, and it then enumerates three situations in which the statement is excepted from the category of hearsay. Compare Uniform Rule 63(1) which allows any out-of-court statement of a declarant who is present at the trial and available for cross-examination.

(A) Prior inconsistent statements traditionally have been admissible to impeach but not as substantive evidence. Under the rule they are substantive evidence. As has been said by the California Law Revision Commission with respect to a similar provision:

"Section 1235 admits inconsistent statements of witnesses because the dangers against which the hearsay rule is designed to protect are largely nonexistent. The declarant is in court and may be examined and cross-examined in regard to his statements and their subject matter. In many cases, the inconsistent statement is more likely to be true than the testimony of the witness at the trial because it was made nearer in time to the matter to which it relates and is less likely to be influenced by the controversy that gave rise to the litigation. The trier of fact has the declarant before it and can observe his demeanor and the nature of his testimony as he denies or tries to explain away the inconsistency. Hence, it is in as good a position to determine the truth or falsity of the prior statement as it is to determine the truth or falsity of the inconsistent testimony given in court.

Moreover, Section 1235 will provide a party with desirable protection against the 'turncoat' witness who changes his story on the stand and deprives the party calling him of evidence essential to his case." Comment, <u>California Evidence Code § 1235</u>. See also McCormick § 39. The Advisory Committee finds these views more convincing than those expressed in <u>People v. Johnson, 68 Cal.2d 646, 68 Cal.Rptr. 599, 441 P.2d 111 (1968)</u>. The constitutionality of the Advisory Committee's view was upheld in <u>California v. Green, 399 U.S. 149, 90 S.Ct. 1930, 26 L.Ed.2d 489 (1970)</u>. Moreover, the requirement that the statement be inconsistent with the testimony given assures a thorough exploration of both versions while the witness is on the stand and bars any general and indiscriminate use of previously prepared statements.

(B) Prior consistent statements traditionally have been admissible to rebut charges of recent fabrication or improper influence or motive but not as substantive evidence. Under the rule they are substantive evidence. The prior statement is consistent with the testimony given on the stand, and, if the opposite party wishes to open the door for its admission in evidence, no sound reason is apparent why it should not be received generally.

(C) The admission of evidence of identification finds substantial support, although it falls beyond a doubt in the category of prior out-of-court statements. Illustrative are <u>People v. Gould, 54 Cal.2d 621, 7 Cal.Rptr. 273, 354 P.2d 865 (1960)</u>; <u>Judy v. State, 218 Md. 168, 146 A.2d 29 (1958)</u>; <u>State v. Simmons, 63 Wash.2d 17, 385 P.2d 389 (1963)</u>; <u>California Evidence Code § 1238</u>; New Jersey Evidence Rule 63(1)(c); N.Y.Code of Criminal Procedure § 393-b. Further cases are found in 4 Wigmore § 1130. The basis is the generally unsatisfactory and inconclusive nature of courtroom identifications as compared with those made at an earlier time under less suggestive conditions. The Supreme Court considered the admissibility of evidence of prior identification in <u>Gilbert v. California, 388 U.S. 263, 87 S.Ct. 1951, 18 L.Ed.2d 1178 (1967)</u>. Exclusion of lineup identification was held to be required because the accused did not then have the assistance of counsel. Significantly, the Court carefully refrained from placing its decision on the ground that testimony as to the making of a prior out-of-court identification ("That's the man") violated either the hearsay rule or the right of confrontation because not made under oath, subject to immediate cross-examination, in the presence of the trier. Instead the Court observed:

"There is a split among the States concerning the admissibility of prior extra-judicial identifications, as independent evidence of identity, both by the witness and third parties present at the prior identification. See <u>71 ALR2d 449</u>. It has been held that the prior identification is hearsay, and, when admitted through the testimony of the identifier, is merely a prior consistent statement. The recent trend, however, is to admit the prior identification under the exception that admits as substantive evidence a prior communication by a witness who is available for cross-examination at the trial. See 5 ALR2d Later Case Service 1225-1228. * * * " 388 U.S. at 272, n. 3, 87 S.Ct. at 1956.

(2) *Admissions.* Admissions by a party-opponent are excluded from the category of hearsay on the theory that their admissibility in evidence is the result of the adversary system rather than satisfaction of the conditions of the hearsay rule. Strahorn, A Reconsideration of the Hearsay Rule and Admissions, 85 U.Pa.L.Rev. 484, 564 (1937); Morgan, Basic Problems of Evidence 265 (1962); 4 Wigmore § 1048. No guarantee of trustworthiness is required in the case of an admission. The freedom which admissions have enjoyed from technical demands of search- ing for an assurance of truthworthiness in some against-interest circumstance, and from the restrictive influences of the opinion rule and the rule requiring first- hand knowledge, when taken with the apparently prevalent satisfaction with the results, calls for generous treatment of this avenue to admissibility.

The rule specifies five categories of statements for which the responsibility of a party is considered sufficient to justify reception in evidence against him:

(A) A party's own statement is the classic example of an admission. If he has a representative capacity and the statement is offered against him in that capacity, no inquiry whether he was acting in the representative capacity in making the statement is required; the statement need only be relevant to represent affairs. To the same effect in California Evidence Code § 1220. Compare Uniform Rule 63(7), requiring a statement to be made in a representative capacity to be admis- sible against a party in a representative capacity.

(B) Under established principles an admission may be made by adopting or acqui- escing in the statement of another. While knowledge of contents would ordinarily be essential, this is not inevitably so: "X is a reliable person and knows what he is talking about." See McCormick § 246, p. 527, n. 15. Adoption or acquiescence may be manifested in any appropriate manner. When silence is relied upon, the theory is that the person would, under the circumstances, protest the statement made in his presence, if untrue. The decision in each case calls for an evaluation in terms of probable human behavior. In civil cases, the results have generally been satisfactory. In criminal cases, however, troublesome questions have been raised by decisions holding that failure to deny is an admission: the inference is a fairly weak one, to begin with; silence may be motivated by advice of counsel or realization that "anything you say may be used against you"; unusual opportunity is afforded to manufacture evidence; and encroachment upon the privilege against self-incrimination seems inescapably to be involved. However, recent decisions of the Supreme Court relating to custodial interrogation and the right to counsel appear to resolve these difficulties. Hence the rule contains no special provisions concerning failure to deny in criminal cases.

(**C**) No authority is required for the general proposition that a statement authorized by a party to be made should have the status of an admission by the party. However, the question arises whether only statements to third persons should be so regarded, to the exclusion of statements by the agent to the principal. The rule is phrased broadly so as to encompass both. While it may be argued that the agent authorized to make statements to his principal does not speak for him, Morgan, Basic Problems of Evidence 273 (1962), communication to an outsider has not generally been thought to be an essential characteristic of an admission. Thus a party's books or records are usable against him, without regard to any intent to disclose to third persons. 5 Wigmore § 1557. See also McCormick § 78, pp. 159-161. In accord is New Jersey Evidence Rule 63(8)(a). Cf. Uniform Rule 63(8)(a) and California Evidence Code § 1222 which limit status as an admission in this regard to statements authorized by the party to be made "for" him, which is perhaps an ambiguous limitation to statements to third persons. Falknor, Vicarious Admissions and the Uniform Rules, 14 Vand.L.Rev. 855, 860-861 (1961).

(**D**) The tradition has been to test the admissibility of statements by agents, as admissions, by applying the usual test of agency. Was the admission made by the agent acting in the scope of his employment? Since few principals employ agents for the purpose of making damaging statements, the usual result was exclusion of the statement. Dissatisfaction with this loss of valuable and helpful evidence has been increasing. A substantial trend favors admitting statements related to a matter within the scope of the agency or employment. *Grayson v. Williams, 256 F.2d 61 (10th Cir.1958); Koninklijke Luchtvaart Maatschappij N.V. KLM Royal Dutch Airlines v. Tuller, 110 U.S.App.D.C. 282, 292 F.2d 775, 784 (1961); Martin v. Savage Truck Lines, Inc., 121 F.Supp. 417 (D.D.C.1954)*, and numerous state court decisions collected in 4 Wigmore, 1964 Supp. pp. 66-73, with comments by the editor that the statements should have been excluded as not within scope of agency. For the traditional view see *Northern Oil Co. v. Socony Mobil Oil Co., 347 F.2d 81, 85 (2d Cir.1965)* and cases cited therein. Similar provisions are found in Uniform Rule 63(9)(a), Kansas Code of Civil Procedure § 60-460(i)(1), and New Jersey Evidence Rule 63(9)(a).

(**E**) The limitation upon the admissibility of statements of co-conspirators to those made "during the course and in furtherance of the conspiracy" is in the accepted pattern. While the broadened view of agency taken in item (iv) might suggest wider admissibility of statements of co-conspirators, the agency theory of conspiracy is at best a fiction and ought not to serve as a basis for admissibility beyond that already established. See Levie, Hearsay and Conspiracy, 52 Mich.L.Rev. 1159 (1954); Comment, 25 U.Chi.L.Rev. 530 (1958). The rule is consistent with the position of the Supreme Court in denying admissibility to statements made after the objectives of the conspiracy have either failed or been achieved. *Krulewitch v. United States,* 336 U.S. 440, 69 S.Ct. 716, 93 L.Ed. 790 (1949); *Wong Sun v. United States,* 371 U.S. 471, 490, 83 S.Ct. 407, 9 L.Ed.2d 441 (1963). For similarly limited provisions see California Evidence Code § 1223 and New Jersey Rule 63(9)(b). Cf. Uniform Rule 63(9)(b).

1974 Enactment

Note to Subdivision (d)(1). Present federal law, except in the Second Circuit, permits the use of prior inconsistent statements of a witness for impeachment only. Rule 801(d)(1) as proposed by the Court would have permitted all such statements to be admissible as substantive evidence, an approach followed by a small but growing number of State jurisdictions and recently held constitutional in *California v. Green,* 399 U.S. 149 (1970). Although there was some support expressed for the Court Rule, based largely on the need to counteract the effect of witness intimidation in criminal cases, the Committee decided to adopt a compromise version of the Rule similar to the position of the Second Circuit. The Rule as amended draws a distinction between types of prior inconsistent statements (other than statements of identification of a person made after perceiving him which are currently admissible, see *United States v. Anderson,* 406 F.2d 719, 720 (4th Cir.), cert. denied , 395 U.S. 967 (1969)) and allows only those made while the declarant was subject to cross-examination at a trial or hearing or in a deposition, to be admissible for their truth. Compare *United States v. DeSisto,* 329 F.2d 929 (2nd Cir.), cert. denied , 377 U.S. 979 (1964); *United States v. Cunningham,* 446 F.2d 194 (2nd Cir.1971) (restricting the admissibility of prior inconsistent statements as substantive evidence to those made under oath in a formal proceeding, but not requiring that there have been an opportunity for cross-examination). The rationale for the Committee's decision is that (1) unlike in most other situations involving unsworn or oral statements, there can be no dispute as to whether the prior statement was made; and (2) the context of a formal proceeding, an oath, and the opportunity for cross-examination provide firm additional assurances of the reliability of the prior statement. House Report No. 93-650.

Note to Subdivision (d)(1)(A). Rule 801 defines what is and what is not hearsay for the purpose of admitting a prior statement as substantive evidence. A prior statement of a witness at a trial or hearing which is inconsistent with his testimony is, of course, always admissible for the purpose of impeaching the witness' credibility.

As submitted by the Supreme Court, subdivision (d)(1)(A) made admissible as substantive evidence the prior statement of a witness inconsistent with his present testimony.

The House severely limited the admissibility of prior inconsistent statements by adding a requirement that the prior statement must have been subject to cross-examination, thus precluding even the use of grand jury statements. The requirement that the prior statement must have been subject to cross-examination appears unnecessary since this rule comes into play only when the witness testifies in the present trial. At that time, he is on the stand and can explain an earlier position and be cross-examined as to both.

The requirement that the statement be under oath also appears unnecessary. Notwithstanding the absence of an oath contemporaneous with the statement, the witness, when on the stand, qualifying or denying the prior statement, is under oath. In any event, of all the many recognized exceptions to the hearsay rule, only one (former testimony) requires that the out-of-court statement have been made under oath. With respect to the lack of evidence of the demeanor of the witness at the time of the prior statement, it would be difficult to improve upon Judge Learned Hand's observation that when the jury decides that the truth is not what the witness says now but what he said before, they are still deciding from what they see and hear in court. [_Di Carlo v. U.S._, 6 F.2d 364 (2d Cir.1925)].

The rule as submitted by the Court has positive advantages. The prior statement was made nearer in time to the events, when memory was fresher and intervening influences had not been brought into play. A realistic method is provided for dealing with the turncoat witness who changes his story on the stand [see Comment, California Evidence Code § 1235; McCormick, Evidence, § 38 (2nd ed. 1972)].

New Jersey, California, and Utah have adopted a rule similar to this one; and Nevada, New Mexico, and Wisconsin have adopted the identical Federal rule.

For all of these reasons, we think the House amendment should be rejected and the rule as submitted by the Supreme Court reinstated. [It would appear that some of the opposition to this Rule is based on a concern that a person could be convicted solely upon evidence admissible under this Rule. The Rule, however, is not addressed to the question of the sufficiency of evidence to send a case to the jury, but merely as to its admissibility. Factual circumstances could well arise where, if this were the sole evidence, dismissal would be appropriate.]

Note to Subdivision (d)(1)(C). As submitted by the Supreme Court and as passed by the House, subdivision (d)(1)(C) of rule 801 made admissible the prior statement identifying a person made after perceiving him. The committee decided to delete this provision because of the concern that a person could be convicted solely upon evidence admissible under this subdivision.

Note to Subdivision 801(d)(2)(E). The House approved the long-accepted rule that "a statement by a coconspirator of a party during the course and in furtherance of the conspiracy" is not hearsay as it was submitted by the Supreme Court. While the rule refers to a coconspirator, it is this committee's understanding that the rule is meant to carry forward the universally accepted doctrine that a joint venturer is considered as a coconspirator for the purposes of this rule even though no conspiracy has been charged. *United States v. Rinaldi,* 393 F.2d 97, 99 (2d Cir.), cert. denied 393 U.S. 913 (1968); *United States v. Spencer,* 415 F.2d 1301, 1304 (7th Cir., 1969). Senate Report No. 93-1277.

Rule 801 supplies some basic definitions for the rules of evidence that deal with hearsay. Rule 801(d)(1) defines certain statements as not hearsay. The Senate amendments make two changes in it.

Note to Subdivision (d)(1)(A). The House bill provides that a statement is not hearsay if the declarant testifies and is subject to cross-examination concerning the statement and if the statement is inconsistent with his testimony and was given under oath subject to cross-examination and subject to the penalty of perjury at a trial or hearing or in a deposition. The Senate amendment drops the requirement that the prior statement be given under oath subject to cross-examination and subject to the penalty of perjury at a trial or hearing or in a deposition.

The Conference adopts the Senate amendment with an amendment, so that the rule now requires that the prior inconsistent statement be given under oath subject to the penalty of perjury at a trial, hearing, or other proceeding, or in a deposition. The rule as adopted covers statements before a grand jury. Prior inconsistent statements may, of course, be used for impeaching the credibility of a witness. When the prior inconsistent statement is one made by a defendant in a criminal case, it is covered by Rule 801(d)(2).

Note to Subdivision (d)(1)(C). The House bill provides that a statement is not hearsay if the declarant testifies and is subject to cross-examination concerning the statement and the statement is one of identification of a person made after perceiving him. The Senate amendment eliminated this provision.

The Conference adopts the Senate amendment. House Report No. 93-1597.

1987 Amendment

The amendments are technical. No substantive change is intended.

1997 Amendment

Rule 801(d)(2) has been amended in order to respond to three issues raised by *Bourjaily v. United States,* 483 U.S. 171 (1987). First, the amendment codifies the holding in *Bourjaily* by stating expressly that a court shall consider the contents of a coconspirator's statement in determining "the existence of the conspiracy and the participation therein of the declarant and the party against whom the statement is offered." According to *Bourjaily*, Rule 104(a) requires these preliminary questions to be established by a preponderance of the evidence.

Second, the amendment resolves an issue on which the Court had reserved decision. It provides that the contents of the declarant's statement do not alone suffice to establish a conspiracy in which the declarant and the defendant participated. The court must consider in addition the circumstances surrounding the statement, such as the identity of the speaker, the context in which the statement was made, or evidence corroborating the contents of the statement in making its determination as to each preliminary question. This amendment is in accordance with existing practice. Every court of appeals that has resolved this issue requires some evidence in addition to the contents of the statement. *See, e.g., United States v. Beckham,* 968 F.2d 47, 51 (D.C.Cir.1992); *United States v. Sepulveda,* 15 F.3d 1161, 1181-82 (1st Cir.1993), *cert. denied ,* 114 S.Ct. 2714 (1994); *United States v. Daly,* 842 F.2d 1380, 1386 (2d Cir.), *cert. denied ,* 488 U.S. 821 (1988); *United States v. Clark,* 18 F.3d 1337, 1341-42 (6th Cir.), *cert. denied ,* 115 S.Ct. 152 (1994); *United States v. Zambrana,* 841 F.2d 1320, 1344-45 (7th Cir.1988); *United States v. Silverman,* 861 F.2d 571, 577 (9th Cir.1988); *United States v. Gordon,* 844 F.2d 1397, 1402 (9th Cir.1988); *United States v. Hernandez,* 829 F.2d 988, 993 (10th Cir.1987), *cert. denied ,* 485 U.S. 1013 (1988); *United States v. Byrom,* 910 F.2d 725, 736 (11th Cir.1990).

Third, the amendment extends the reasoning of Bourjaily to statements offered under subdivisions (C) and (D) of Rule 801(d)(2). In Bourjaily, the Court rejected treating foundational facts pursuant to the law of agency in favor of an evidentiary approach governed by Rule 104(a). The Advisory Committee believes it appropriate to treat analogously preliminary questions relating to the declarant's authority under subdivision (C), and the agency or employment relationship and scope thereof under subdivision (D).

GAP Report on Rule 801. The word "shall" was substituted for the word "may" in line 19. The second sentence of the committee note was changed accordingly.

Rule 802. Hearsay Rule

Hearsay is not admissible except as provided by these rules or by other rules prescribed by the Supreme Court pursuant to statutory authority or by Act of Congress.

ADVISORY COMMITTEE NOTES

1972 Proposed Rules

The provision excepting from the operation of the rule hearsay which is made admissible by other rules adopted by the Supreme Court or by Act of Congress continues the admissibility thereunder of hearsay which would not qualify under these Evidence Rules. The following examples illustrate the working of the exception:

Federal Rules of Civil Procedure

Rule 4(g): proof of service by affidavit.

Rule 32: admissibility of depositions.

Rule 43(e): affidavits when motion based on facts not appearing of record.

Rule 56: affidavits in summary judgment proceedings.

Rule 65(b): showing by affidavit for temporary restraining order.

Federal Rules of Criminal Procedure

Rule 4(a): affidavits to show grounds for issuing warrants.

Rule 12(b)(4): affidavits to determine issues of fact in connection with motions.

Acts of Congress

10 U.S.C. § 7730: affidavits of unavailable witnesses in actions for damages caused by vessel in naval service, or towage or salvage of same, when taking of testimony or bringing of action delayed or stayed on security grounds.

29 U.S.C. § 161(4): affidavit as proof of service in NLRB proceedings.

38 U.S.C. § 5206: affidavit as proof of posting notice of sale of unclaimed property by Veterans Administration.

Rule 803. Hearsay Exceptions; Availability of Declarant Immaterial

The following are not excluded by the hearsay rule, even though the declarant is available as a witness:

(1) Present sense impression. A statement describing or explaining an event or condition made while the declarant was perceiving the event or condition, or immediately thereafter.

(2) Excited utterance. A statement relating to a startling event or condition made while the declarant was under the stress of excitement caused by the event or condition.

(3) Then existing mental, emotional, or physical condition. A statement of the declarant's then existing state of mind, emotion, sensation, or physical condition (such as intent, plan, motive, design, mental feeling, pain, and bodily health), but not including a statement of memory or belief to prove the fact remembered or believed unless it relates to the execution, revocation, identification, or terms of declarant's will.

(4) Statements for purposes of medical diagnosis or treatment. Statements made for purposes of medical diagnosis or treatment and describing medical history, or past or present symptoms, pain, or sensations, or the inception or general character of the cause or external source thereof insofar as reasonably pertinent to diagnosis or treatment.

(5) Recorded recollection. A memorandum or record concerning a matter about which a witness once had knowledge but now has insufficient recollection to enable the witness to testify fully and accurately, shown to have been made or adopted by the witness when the matter was fresh in the witness' memory and to reflect that knowledge correctly. If admitted, the memorandum or record may be read into evidence but may not itself be received as an exhibit unless offered by an adverse party.

(6) Records of Regularly Conducted Activity.--A memorandum, report, record, or data compilation, in any form, of acts, events, conditions, opinions, or diagnoses, made at or near the time by, or from information transmitted by, a person with knowledge, if kept in the course of a regularly conducted business activity, and if it was the regular practice of that business activity to make the memorandum, report, record or data compilation, all as shown by the testimony of the custodian or other qualified witness, or by certification that complies with Rule 902(11), Rule 902(12), or a statute permitting certification, unless the source of information or the method or circumstances of preparation indicate lack of trustworthiness. The term "business" as used in this paragraph includes business, institution, association, profession, occupation, and calling of every kind, whether or not conducted for profit.

(7) Absence of entry in records kept in accordance with the provisions of paragraph (6). Evidence that a matter is not included in the memoranda reports, records, or data compilations, in any form, kept in accordance with the provisions of paragraph (6), to prove the nonoccurrence or nonexistence

of the matter, if the matter was of a kind of which a memorandum, report, record, or data compilation was regularly made and preserved, unless the sources of information or other circumstances indicate lack of trustworthiness.

(8) Public records and reports. Records, reports, statements, or data compilations, in any form, of public offices or agencies, setting forth (A) the activities of the office or agency, or (B) matters observed pursuant to duty imposed by law as to which matters there was a duty to report, excluding, however, in criminal cases matters observed by police officers and other law enforcement personnel, or (C) in civil actions and proceedings and against the Government in criminal cases, factual findings resulting from an investigation made pursuant to authority granted by law, unless the sources of information or other circumstances indicate lack of trustworthiness.

(9) Records of vital statistics. Records or data compilations, in any form, of births, fetal deaths, deaths, or marriages, if the report thereof was made to a public office pursuant to requirements of law.

(10) Absence of public record or entry. To prove the absence of a record, report, statement, or data compilation, in any form, or the nonoccurrence or nonexistence of a matter of which a record, report, statement, or data compilation, in any form, was regularly made and preserved by a public office or agency, evidence in the form of a certification in accordance with rule 902, or testimony, that diligent search failed to disclose the record, report, statement, or data compilation, or entry.

(11) Records of religious organizations. Statements of births, marriages, divorces, deaths, legitimacy, ancestry, relationship by blood or marriage, or other similar facts of personal or family history, contained in a regularly kept record of a religious organization.

(12) Marriage, baptismal, and similar certificates. Statements of fact contained in a certificate that the maker performed a marriage or other ceremony or administered a sacrament, made by a clergyman, public official, or other person authorized by the rules or practices of a religious organization or by law to perform the act certified, and purporting to have been issued at the time of the act or within a reasonable time thereafter.

(13) Family records. Statements of fact concerning personal or family history contained in family Bibles, genealogies, charts, engravings on rings, inscriptions on family portraits, engravings on urns, crypts, or tombstones, or the like.

(14) Records of documents affecting an interest in property. The record of a document purporting to establish or affect an interest in property, as proof of the content of the original recorded document and its execution and delivery by each person by whom it purports to have been executed, if the record is a record of a public office and an applicable statute authorizes the recording of documents of that kind in that office.

(15) Statements in documents affecting an interest in property. A statement contained in a document purporting to establish or affect an interest in property if the matter stated was relevant to the purpose of the document, unless dealings with the property since the document was made have been inconsistent with the truth of the statement or the purport of the document.

(16) Statements in ancient documents. Statements in a document in existence twenty years or more the authenticity of which is established.

(17) Market reports, commercial publications. Market quotations, tabulations, lists, directories, or other published compilations, generally used and relied upon by the public or by persons in particular occupations.

(18) Learned treatises. To the extent called to the attention of an expert witness upon cross-examination or relied upon by the expert witness in direct examination, statements contained in published treatises, periodicals, or pamphlets on a subject of history, medicine, or other science or art, established as a reliable authority by the testimony or admission of the witness or by other expert testimony or by judicial notice. If admitted, the statements may be read into evidence but may not be received as exhibits.

(19) Reputation concerning personal or family history. Reputation among members of a person's family by blood, adoption, or marriage, or among a person's associates, or in the community, concerning a person's birth, adoption, marriage, divorce, death, legitimacy, relationship by blood, adoption, or marriage, ancestry, or other similar fact of personal or family history.

(20) Reputation concerning boundaries or general history. Reputation in a community, arising before the controversy, as to boundaries of or customs affecting lands in the community, and reputation as to events of general history important to the community or State or nation in which located.

(21) Reputation as to character. Reputation of a person's character among associates or in the community.

(22) Judgment of previous conviction. Evidence of a final judgment, entered after a trial or upon a plea of guilty (but not upon a plea of nolo contendere), adjudging a person guilty of a crime punishable by death or imprisonment in excess of one year, to prove any fact essential to sustain the judgment, but not including, when offered by the Government in a criminal prosecution for purposes other than impeachment, judgments against persons other than the accused. The pendency of an appeal may be shown but does not affect admissibility.

(23) Judgment as to personal, family, or general history, or boundaries. Judgments as proof of matters of personal, family or general history, or boundaries, essential to the judgment, if the same would be provable by evidence of reputation.

(24) [Transferred to Rule 807]

ADVISORY COMMITTEE NOTES

1972 Proposed Rules
The exceptions are phrased in terms of nonapplication of the hearsay rule, rather than in positive terms of admissibility, in order to repel any implication that other possible grounds for exclusion are eliminated from consideration.

The present rule proceeds upon the theory that under appropriate circumstances a hearsay statement may possess circumstantial guarantees of trustworthiness sufficient to justify nonproduction of the declarant in person at the trial even though he may be available. The theory finds vast support in the many exceptions to the hearsay rule developed by the common law in which unavailability of the declarant is not a relevant factor. The present rule is a synthesis of them, with revision where modern developments and conditions are believed to make that course appropriate.

In a hearsay situation, the declarant is, of course, a witness, and neither this rule nor Rule 804 dispenses with the requirement of firsthand knowledge. It may appear from his statement or be inferable from circumstances. See Rule 602.

Note to Paragraphs (1) and (2). In considerable measure these two examples overlap, though based on somewhat different theories. The most significant practical difference will lie in the time lapse allowable between event and statement.

The underlying theory of Exception [paragraph] (1) is that substantial contemporaneity of event and statement negate the likelihood of deliberate or conscious misrepresentation. Moreover, if the witness is the declarant, he may be examined on the statement. If the witness is not the declarant, he may be examined as to the circumstances as an aid in evaluating the statement. Morgan, Basic Problems of Evidence 340-341 (1962).

The theory of Exception [paragraph] (2) is simply that circumstances may produce a condition of excitement which temporarily stills the capacity of reflection and produces utterances free of conscious fabrication. 6 Wigmore § 1747, p. 135. Spontaneity is the key factor in each instance, though arrived at by somewhat different routes. Both are needed in order to avoid needless niggling.

While the theory of Exception [paragraph] (2) has been criticized on the ground that excitement impairs accuracy of observation as well as eliminating conscious fabrication, Hutchins and Slesinger, Some Observations on the Law of Evidence: Spontaneous Exclamations, 28 Colum.L.Rev. 432 (1928), it finds support in cases without number. See cases in 6 Wigmore § 1750; Annot. 53 A.L.R.2d 1245 (statements as to cause of or responsibility for motor vehicle accident); Annot., 4 A.L.R.3d 149 (accusatory statements by homicide victims). Since unexciting events are less likely to evoke comment, decisions involving Exception [paragraph] (1) are far less numerous. Illustrative are Tampa Elec. Co. v. Getrost, 151 Fla. 558, 10 So.2d 83 (1942); Houston Oxygen Co. v. Davis, 139 Tex. 1, 161 S.W.2d 474 (1942); and cases cited in McCormick § 273, p. 585, n. 4.

With respect to the time element, Exception [paragraph] (1) recognizes that in many, if not most, instances precise contemporaneity is not possible and hence a slight lapse is allowable. Under Exception [paragraph] (2) the standard of measurement is the duration of the state of excitement. "How long can excitement prevail? Obviously there are no pat answers and the character of the transaction or event will largely determine the significance of the time factor." Slough, Spontaneous Statements and State of Mind, 46 Iowa L.Rev. 224, 243 (1961); McCormick § 272, p. 580.

Participation by the declarant is not required: a non-participant may be moved to describe what he perceives, and one may be startled by an event in which he is not an actor. Slough, supra; McCormick, supra; 6 Wigmore § 1755; Annot. 78 A.L.R.2d 300.

Whether proof of the startling event may be made by the statement itself is largely an academic question, since in most cases there is present at least circumstantial evidence that something of a startling nature must have occurred. For cases in which the evidence consists of the condition of the declarant (injuries, state of shock), see Insurance Co. v. Mosely, 75 U.S. (8 Wall.) 397, 19 L.Ed. 437 (1869); Wheeler v. United States, 93 U.S. App.D.C. 159, 211 F.2d 19 (1953), cert. denied 347 U.S. 1019, 74 S.Ct. 876, 98 L.Ed. 1140; Wetherbee v. Safety Casualty Co.,

219 F.2d 274 (5th Cir.1955); Lampe v. United States, 97 U.S.App.D.C. 160, 229 F.2d 43 (1956). Nevertheless, on occasion the only evidence may be the content of the statement itself, and rulings that it may be sufficient are described as "increasing," Slough, supra at 246, and as the "prevailing practice," McCormick § 272, p. 579. Illustrative are Armour & Co. v. Industrial Commission, 78 Colo. 569, 243 P. 546 (1926); Young v. Stewart, 191 N.C. 297, 131 S.E. 735 (1926). Moreover, under Rule 104(a) the judge is not limited by the hearsay rule in passing upon preliminary questions of fact.

Proof of declarant's perception by his statement presents similar considerations when declarant is identified. People v. Poland, 22 Ill.2d 175, 174 N.E.2d 804 (1961). However, when declarant is an unidentified bystander, the cases indicate hesitancy in upholding the statement alone as sufficient, Garrett v. Howden, 73 N.M. 307, 387 P.2d 874 (1963); Beck v. Dye, 200 Wash. 1, 92 P.2d 1113 (1939), a result which would under appropriate circumstances be consistent with the rule.

Permissible subject matter of the statement is limited under Exception [paragraph] (1) to description or explanation of the event or condition, the assumption being that spontaneity, in the absence of a startling event, may extend no farther. In Exception [paragraph] (2), however, the statement need only "relate" to the startling event or condition, thus affording a broader scope of subject matter coverage. 6 Wigmore §§ 1750, 1754. See Sanitary Grocery Co. v. Snead, 67 App.D.C. 129, 90 F.2d 374 (1937), slip-and-fall case sustaining admissibility of clerk's statement. "That has been on the floor for a couple of hours," and Murphy Auto Parts Co., Inc. v. Ball, 101 U.S.App.D.C. 416, 249 F.2d 508 (1957), upholding admission, on issue of driver's agency, of his statement that he had to call on a customer and was in a hurry to get home. Quick, Hearsay, Excitement, Necessity and the Uniform Rules: A Reappraisal of Rule 63(4), 6 Wayne L.Rev. 204, 206-209 (1960).

Similar provisions are found in Uniform Rule 63(4)(a) and (b); California Evidence Code § 1240 (as to Exception (2) only); Kansas Code of Civil Procedure § 60-460(d)(1) and (2); New Jersey Evidence Rule 63(4).

Note to Paragraph (3). Exception [paragraph] (3) is essentially a specialized application of Exception [paragraph] (1), presented separately to enhance its usefulness and accessibility. See McCormick §§ 265, 268.

The exclusion of "statements of memory or belief to prove the fact remembered or believed" is necessary to avoid the virtual destruction of the hearsay rule which would otherwise result from allowing state of mind, provable by a hearsay statement, to serve as the basis for an inference of the happening of the event which produced the state of mind. Shepard v. United States, 290 U.S. 96, 54 S.Ct. 22, 78 L.Ed. 196 (1933); Maguire, The Hillmon Case--Thirty-three Years After, 38

Harv.L.Rev. 709, 719-731 (1925); Hinton, States of Mind and the Hearsay Rule, 1 U.Chi.L.Rev. 394, 421-423 (1934). The rule of Mutual Life Ins. Co. v. Hillmon, 145 U.S. 285, 12 S.Ct. 909, 36 L.Ed. 706 (1892), allowing evidence of intention as tending to prove the doing of the act intended, is, of course, left undisturbed.

The carving out, from the exclusion mentioned in the preceding paragraph, of declarations relating to the execution, revocation, identification, or terms of declarant's will represents and ad hoc judgment which finds ample reinforcement in the decisions, resting on practical grounds of necessity and expediency rather than logic. McCormick § 271, pp. 577-578; Annot. 34 A.L.R.2d 588, 62 A.L.R.2d 855. A similar recognition of the need for and practical value of this kind of evidence is found in California Evidence Code § 1260.

Note to Paragraph (4). Even those few jurisdictions which have shied away from generally admitting statements of present condition have allowed them if made to a physician for purposes of diagnosis and treatment in view of the patient's strong motivation to be truthful. McCormick § 266, p. 563. The same guarantee of trustworthiness extends to statements of past conditions and medical history, made for purposes of diagnosis or treatment. It also extends to statements as to causation, reasonably pertinent to the same purposes, in accord with the current trend. Shell Oil Co. v. Industrial Commission, 2 Ill.2d 590, 119 N.E.2d 224 (1954); McCormick § 266, p. 564; New Jersey Evidence Rule 63(12)(c). Statements as to fault would not ordinarily qualify under this latter language. Thus a patient's statement that he was struck by an automobile would qualify but not his statement that the car was driven through a red light. Under the exception the statement need not have been made to a physician. Statements to hospital attendants, ambulance drivers, or even members of the family might be included.

Conventional doctrine has excluded from the hearsay exception, as not within its guarantee of truthfulness, statements to a physician consulted only for the purpose of enabling him to testify. While these statements were not admissible as substantive evidence, the expert was allowed to state the basis of his opinion, including statements of this kind. The distinction thus called for was one most unlikely to be made by juries. The rule accordingly rejects the limitation. This position is consistent with the provision of Rule 703 that the facts on which expert testimony is based need not be admissible in evidence if of a kind ordinarily relied upon by experts in the field.

Note to Paragraph (5). A hearsay exception for recorded recollection is generally recognized and has been described as having "long been favored by the federal and practically all the state courts that have had occasion to decide the question." United States v. Kelly, 349 F.2d 720, 770 (2d Cir.1965), citing numerous cases and sustaining the exception against a claimed denial of the right of confrontation.

Many additional cases are cited in Annot., 82 A.L.R.2d 473, 520. The guarantee of trustworthiness is found in the reliability inherent in a record made while events were still fresh in mind and accurately reflecting them. Owens v. State, 67 Md. 307, 316, 10 A. 210, 212 (1887).

The principal controversy attending the exception has centered, not upon the propriety of the exception itself, but upon the question whether a preliminary requirement of impaired memory on the part of the witness should be imposed. The authorities are divided. If regard be had only to the accuracy of the evidence, admittedly impairment of the memory of the witness adds nothing to it and should not be required. McCormick § 277, p. 593; 3 Wigmore § 738, p. 76; Jordan v. People, 151 Colo. 133, 376 P.2d 699 (1962), cert. denied 373 U.S. 944, 83 S.Ct. 1553, 10 L.Ed.2d 699; Hall v. State, 223 Md. 158, 162 A.2d 751 (1960); State v. Bindhammer, 44 N.J. 372, 209 A.2d 124 (1965). Nevertheless, the absence of the requirement, it is believed, would encourage the use of statements carefully pre-pared for purposes of litigation under the supervision of attorneys, investigators, or claim adjusters. Hence the example includes a requirement that the witness not have "sufficient recollection to enable him to testify fully and accurately." To the same effect are California Evidence Code § 1237 and New Jersey Rule 63(1)(b), and this has been the position of the federal courts. Vicksburg & Meridian R.R. v. O'Brien, 119 U.S. 99, 7 S.Ct. 118, 30 L.Ed. 299 (1886); Ahern v. Webb, 268 F.2d 45 (10th Cir.1959); and see N.L.R.B. v. Hudson Pulp and Paper Corp., 273 F.2d 660, 665 (5th Cir.1960); N.L.R.B. v. Federal Dairy Co., 297 F.2d 487 (1st Cir.1962). But cf. United States v. Adams, 385 F.2d 548 (2d Cir.1967).

No attempt is made in the exception to spell out the method of establishing the initial knowledge or the contemporaneity and accuracy of the record, leaving them to be dealt with as the circumstances of the particular case might indicate. Multiple person involvement in the process of observing and recording, as in Rathbun v. Brancatella, 93 N.J.L. 222, 107 A. 279 (1919), is entirely consistent with the exception.

Locating the exception at this place in the scheme of the rules is a matter of choice. There were two other possibilities. The first was to regard the statement as one of the group of prior statements of a testifying witness which are excluded entirely from the category of hearsay by Rule 801(d)(1). That category, how-ever, requires that declarant be "subject to cross-examination," as to which the impaired memory aspect of the exception raises doubts. The other possibility was to include the exception among those covered by Rule 804. Since unavailability is required by that rule and lack of memory is listed as a species of unavailability by the definition of the term in Rule 804(a)(3), that treatment at first impression would seem appropriate. The fact is, however, that the unavailability requirement of the exception is of a limited and peculiar nature. Accordingly, the exception is located at this point rather than in the context of a rule where unavailability is conceived of more broadly.

Note to Paragraph (6). Exception [paragraph] (6) represents an area which has received much attention from those seeking to improve the law of evidence. The Commonwealth Fund Act was the result of a study completed in 1927 by a distinguished committee under the chairmanship of Professor Morgan. Morgan et al., The Law of Evidence: Some Proposals for its Reform 63 (1927). With changes too minor to mention, it was adopted by Congress in 1936 as the rule for federal courts. 28 U.S.C. § 1732. A number of states took similar action. The Commissioners on Uniform State Laws in 1936 promulgated the Uniform Business Records as Evidence Act, 9A U.L.A. 506, which has acquired a substantial following in the states. Model Code Rule 514 and Uniform Rule 63(13) also deal with the subject. Difference of varying degrees of importance exist among these various treatments.

These reform efforts were largely within the context of business and commercial records, as the kind usually encountered, and concentrated considerable attention upon relaxing the requirement of producing as witnesses, or accounting for the nonproduction of, all participants in the process of gathering, transmitting, and recording information which the common law had evolved as a burdensome and crippling aspect of using records of this type. In their areas of primary emphasis on witnesses to be called and the general admissibility of ordinary business and commercial records, the Commonwealth Fund Act and the Uniform Act appear to have worked well. The exception seeks to preserve their advantages.

On the subject of what witnesses must be called, the Commonwealth Fund Act eliminated the common law requirement of calling or accounting for all participants by failing to mention it. United States v. Mortimer, 118 F.2d 266 (2d Cir.1941); La Porte v. United States, 300 F.2d 878 (9th Cir.1962); McCormick § 290, p. 608. Model Code Rule 514 and Uniform Rule 63(13) did likewise. The Uniform Act, however, abolished the common law requirement in express terms, providing that the requisite foundation testimony might be furnished by "the custodian or other qualified witness." Uniform Business Records as Evidence Act, § 2; 9A U.L.A. 506. The exception follows the Uniform Act in this respect.

The element of unusual reliability of business records is said variously to be supplied by systematic checking, by regularity and continuity which produce habits of precision, by actual experience of business in relying upon them, or by a duty to make an accurate record as part of a continuing job or occupation. McCormick §§ 281, 286, 287; Laughlin, Business Entries and the Like, 46 Iowa L.Rev. 276 (1961). The model statutes and rules have sought to capture these factors and to extend their impact by employing the phrase "regular course of business," in conjunction with a definition of "business" far broader than its ordinarily accepted meaning. The result is a tendency unduly to emphasize a requirement of routineness and repetitiveness and an insistence that other types of records be squeezed into the fact patterns which give rise to traditional business records. The rule therefore adopts the phrase "the course of a regularly conducted activity" as capturing the essential basis of the hearsay exception as it has evolved and the essential element which can be abstracted from the various specifications of what is a "business."

Amplification of the kinds of activities producing admissible records has given rise to problems which conventional business records by their nature avoid. They are problems of the source of the recorded information, of entries in opinion form, of motivation, and of involvement as participant in the matters recorded.

Sources of information presented no substantial problem with ordinary business records. All participants, including the observer or participant furnishing the information to be recorded, were acting routinely, under a duty of accuracy, with employer reliance on the result, or in short "in the regular course of business." If, however, the supplier of the information does not act in the regular course, an essential link is broken; the assurance of accuracy does not extend to the information itself, and the fact that it may be recorded with scrupulous accuracy is of no avail. An illustration is the police report incorporating information obtained from a bystander: the officer qualifies as acting in the regular course but the informant does not. The leading case, Johnson v. Lutz, 253 N.Y. 124, 170 N.E. 517 (1930), held that a report thus prepared was inadmissible. Most of the authorities have agreed with the decision. Gencarella v. Fyfe, 171 F.2d 419 (1st Cir.1948); Gordon v. Robinson, 210 F.2d 192 (3d Cir.1954); Standard Oil Co. of California v. Moore, 251 F.2d 188, 214 (9th Cir.1957), cert. denied 356 U.S. 975, 78 S.Ct. 1139, 2 L.Ed.2d 1148; Yates v. Bair Transport, Inc., 249 F.Supp. 681 (S.D.N.Y.1965); Annot., 69 A.L.R.2d 1148. Cf. Hawkins v. Gorea Motor Express, Inc., 360 F.2d 933 (2d Cir.1966); Contra, 5 Wigmore § 1530a, n. 1, pp. 391-392. The point is not dealt with specifically in the Commonwealth Fund Act, the Uniform Act, or Uniform Rule 63(13). However, Model Code Rule 514 contains the requirement "that it was the regular course of that business for one with personal knowledge * * * to make such a memorandum or record or to transmit information thereof to be included in such a memorandum or record * * *." The rule follows this lead in requiring an informant with knowledge acting in the course of the regularly conducted activity.

Entries in the form of opinions were not encountered in traditional business records in view of the purely factual nature of the items recorded, but they are now commonly encountered with respect to medical diagnoses, prognoses, and test results, as well as occasionally in other areas. The Commonwealth Fund Act provided only for records of an "act, transaction, occurrence, or event," while the

Uniform Act, Model Code Rule 514, and Uniform Rule 63(13) merely added the ambiguous term "condition." The limited phrasing of the Commonwealth Fund Act, 28 U.S.C. § 1732, may account for the reluctance of some federal decisions to admit diagnostic entries. New York Life Ins. Co. v. Taylor, 79 U.S.App.D.C. 66, 147 F.2d 297 (1945); Lyles v. United States, 103 U.S.App.D.C. 22, 254 F.2d 725 (1957), cert. denied 356 U.S. 961, 78 S.Ct. 997, 2 L.Ed.2d 1067; England v. United States, 174 F.2d 466 (5th Cir.1949); Skogen v. Dow Chemical Co., 375 F.2d 692 (8th Cir.1967). Other federal decisions, however, experienced no difficulty in freely admitting diagnostic entries. Reed v. Order of United Commercial Travelers, 123 F.2d 252 (2d Cir.1941); Buckminster's Estate v. Commissioner of Internal Revenue, 147 F.2d 331 (2d Cir.1944); Medina v. Erickson, 226 F.2d 475 (9th Cir.1955); Thomas v. Hogan, 308 F.2d 355 (4th Cir.1962); Glawe v. Rulon, 284 F.2d 495 (8th Cir.1960). In the state courts, the trend favors admissibility. Borucki v. MacKenzie Bros. Co., 125 Conn. 92, 3 A.2d 224 (1938); Allen v. St. Louis Public Service Co., 365 Mo. 677, 285 S.W.2d 663, 55 A.L.R.2d 1022 (1956); People v. Kohlmeyer, 284 N.Y. 366, 31 N.E.2d 490 (1940); Weis v. Weis, 147 Ohio St. 416, 72 N.E.2d 245 (1947). In order to make clear its adherence to the latter position, the rule specifically includes both diagnoses and opinions, in addition to acts, events, and conditions, as proper subjects of admissible entries.

Problems of the motivation of the informant have been a source of difficulty and disagreement. In Palmer v. Hoffman, 318 U.S. 109, 63 S.Ct. 477, 87 L.Ed. 645 (1943), exclusion of an accident report made by the since deceased engineer, offered by defendant railroad trustees in a grade crossing collision case, was upheld. The report was not "in the regular course of business," not a record of the systematic conduct of the business as a business, said the Court. The report was prepared for use in litigating, not railroading. While the opinion mentions the motivation of the engineer only obliquely, the emphasis on records of routine operations is significant only by virtue of impact on motivation to be accurate. Absence of routineness raises lack of motivation to be accurate. The opinion of the Court of Appeals had gone beyond mere lack of motive to be accurate: the engineer's statement was "dripping with motivations to misrepresent." Hoffman v. Palmer, 129 F.2d 976, 991 (2d Cir.1942). The direct introduction of motivation is a disturbing factor, since absence of motive to misrepresent has not traditionally been a requirement of the rule; that records might be self-serving has not been a ground for exclusion. Laughlin, Business Records and the Like, 46 Iowa L.Rev. 276, 285 (1961). As Judge Clark said in his dissent, "I submit that there is hardly a grocer's account book which could not be excluded on that basis." 129 F.2d at 1002. A physician's evaluation report of a personal injury litigant would appear to be in the routine of his business. If the report is offered by the party at whose instance it was made, however, it has been held inadmissible, Yates v. Bair Transport, Inc., 249 F.Supp. 681 (S.D.N.Y.1965), otherwise if offered by the opposite party, Korte v. New York, N.H. & H.R. Co., 191 F.2d 86 (2d Cir.1951), cert. denied 342 U.S. 868, 72 S.Ct. 108, 96 L.Ed. 652.

The decisions hinge on motivation and which party is entitled to be concerned about it. Professor McCormick believed that the doctor's report or the accident report were sufficiently routine to justify admissibility. McCormick § 287, p. 604. Yet hesitation must be experienced in admitting everything which is observed and recorded in the course of a regularly conducted activity. Efforts to set a limit are illustrated by Hartzog v. United States, 217 F.2d 706 (4th Cir.1954), error to admit worksheets made by since deceased deputy collector in preparation for the instant income tax evasion prosecution, and United States v. Ware, 247 F.2d 698 (7th Cir.1957), error to admit narcotics agents' records of purchases. See also Exception [paragraph] (8), infra, as to the public record aspects of records of this nature. Some decisions have been satisfied as to motivation of an accident report if made pursuant to statutory duty, United States v. New York Foreign Trade Zone Operators, 304 F.2d 792 (2d Cir.1962); Taylor v. Baltimore & O.R. Co., 344 F.2d 281 (2d Cir.1965), since the report was oriented in a direction other than the litigation which ensued. Cf. Matthews v. United States, 217 F.2d 409 (5th Cir.1954). The formulation of specific terms which would assure satisfactory results in all cases is not possible. Consequently the rule proceeds from the base that records made in the course of a regularly conducted activity will be taken as admissible but subject to authority to exclude if "the sources of information or other circumstances indicate lack of trustworthiness."

Occasional decisions have reached for enhanced accuracy by requiring involvement as a participant in matters reported. Clainos v. United States, 82 U.S.App.D.C. 278, 163 F.2d 593 (1947), error to admit police records of convictions; Standard Oil Co. of California v. Moore, 251 F.2d 188 (9th Cir.1957), cert. denied 356 U.S. 975, 78 S.Ct. 1139, 2 L.Ed.2d 1148, error to admit employees' records of observed business practices of others. The rule includes no requirement of this nature. Wholly acceptable records may involve matters merely observed, e.g. the weather.

The form which the "record" may assume under the rule is described broadly as a "memorandum, report, record, or data compilation, in any form." The expression "data compilation" is used as broadly descriptive of any means of storing information other than the conventional words and figures in written or documentary form. It includes, but is by no means limited to, electronic computer storage. The term is borrowed from revised Rule 34(a) of the Rules of Civil Procedure.

Note to Paragraph (7). Failure of a record to mention a matter which would ordinarily be mentioned is satisfactory evidence of its nonexistence. Uniform Rule 63(14), Comment. While probably not hearsay as defined in Rule 801, supra, decisions may be found which class the evidence not only as hearsay but also as not within any exception. In order to set the question at rest in favor of admissibility, it is specifically treated here. McCormick § 289, p. 609; Morgan, Basic Problems of Evidence 314 (1962); 5 Wigmore § 1531; Uniform Rule 63(14); California Evidence Code § 1272; Kansas Code of Civil Procedure § 60-460(n); New Jersey Evidence Rule 63(14).

Note to Paragraph (8). Public records are a recognized hearsay exception at common law and have been the subject of statutes without number. McCormick § 291. See, for example, 28 U.S.C. § 1733, the relative narrowness of which is illustrated by its nonapplicability to nonfederal public agencies, thus necessitating resort to the less appropriate business record exception to the hearsay rule. Kay v. United States, 255 F.2d 476 (4th Cir.1958). The rule makes no distinction between federal and nonfederal offices and agencies.

Justification for the exception is the assumption that a public official will perform his duty properly and the unlikelihood that he will remember details independently of the record. Wong Wing Foo v. McGrath, 196 F.2d 120 (9th Cir.1952), and see Chesapeake & Delaware Canal Co. v. United States, 250 U.S. 123, 39 S.Ct. 407, 63 L.Ed. 889 (1919). As to items (a) and (b), further support is found in the reliability factors underlying records of regularly conducted activities generally. See Exception [paragraph] (6), supra.

(a) Cases illustrating the admissibility of records of the office's or agency's own activities are numerous. Chesapeake & Delaware Canal Co. v. United States, 250 U.S. 123, 39 S.Ct. 407, 63 L.Ed. 889 (1919), Treasury records of miscellaneous receipts and disbursements; Howard v. Perrin, 200 U.S. 71, 26 S.Ct. 195, 50 L.Ed. 374 (1906), General Land Office records; Ballew v. United States, 160 U.S. 187, 16 S.Ct. 263, 40 L.Ed. 388 (1895). Pension Office records.

(b) Cases sustaining admissibility of records of matters observed are also numerous. United States v. Van Hook, 284 F.2d 489 (7th Cir.1960), remanded for resentencing 365 U.S. 609, 81 S.Ct. 823, 5 L.Ed.2d 821, letter from induction officer to District Attorney, pursuant to army regulations, stating fact and circumstances of refusal to be inducted; T'Kach v. United States, 242 F.2d 937 (5th Cir.1957), affidavit of White House personnel officer that search of records showed no employment of accused, charged with fraudulently representing himself as an envoy of the President; Minnehaha County v. Kelley, 150 F.2d 356 (8th Cir.1945); Weather Bureau records of rainfall; United States v. Meyer, 113 F.2d 387 (7th Cir.1940), cert. denied 311 U.S. 706, 61 S.Ct. 174, 85 L.Ed. 459, map prepared by government engineer from information furnished by men working under his supervision.

(c) The more controversial area of public records is that of the so-called "evaluative" report. The disagreement among the decisions has been due in part, no doubt, to the variety of situations encountered, as well as to differences in principle. Sustaining admissibility are such cases as United States v. Dumas, 149 U.S. 278, 13 S.Ct. 872, 37 L.Ed. 734 (1893), statement of account certified by Postmaster General in action against postmaster; McCarty v. United States, 185 F.2d 520 (5th Cir.1950), reh. denied 187 F.2d 234, Certificate of Settlement of General Accounting Office showing indebtedness and letter from Army official stating Government had performed, in action on contract to purchase and remove waste food from Army camp; Moran v. Pittsburgh-Des Moines Steel Co., 183 F.2d 467 (3d Cir.1950), report of Bureau of Mines as to cause of gas tank explosion; Petition of W___, 164 F.Supp. 659 (E.D.Pa.1958), report by Immigration and Naturalization Service investigator that petitioner was known in community as wife of man to whom she was not married. To the opposite effect and denying admissibility are Franklin v. Skelly Oil Co., 141 F.2d 568 (10th Cir.1944), State Fire Marshal's report of cause of gas explosion; Lomax Transp. Co. v. United States, 183 F.2d 331 (9th Cir.1950), Certificate of Settlement from General Accounting Office in action for naval supplies lost in warehouse fire; Yung Jin Teung v. Dulles, 229 F.2d 244 (2d Cir.1956), "Status Reports" offered to justify delay in processing passport applications. Police reports have generally been excluded except to the extent to which they incorporate firsthand observations of the officer. Annot., 69 A.L.R.2d 1148. Various kinds of evaluative reports are admissible under federal statutes: 7 U.S.C. § 78, findings of Secretary of Agriculture prima facie evidence of true grade of grain; 7 U.S.C. § 210(f), findings of Secretary of Agriculture prima facie evidence in action for damages against stockyard owner; 7 U.S.C. § 292, order by Secretary of Agriculture prima facie evidence in judicial enforcement proceedings against producers association monopoly; 7 U.S.C. § 1622(h), Department of Agriculture inspection certificates of products shipped in interstate commerce prima facie evidence; 8 U.S.C. § 1440(c), separation of alien from military service on conditions other than honorable provable by certificate from department in proceedings to revoke citizenship; 18 U.S.C. § 4245, certificate of Director of Prisons that convicted person has been examined and found probably incompetent at time of trial prima facie evidence in court hearing on competency; 42 U.S.C. § 269(b), bill of health by appropriate official prima facie evidence of vessel's sanitary history and condition and compliance with regulations; 46 U.S.C. § 679, certificate of consul presumptive evidence of refusal of master to transport destitute seamen to United States. While these statutory exceptions to the hearsay rule are left undisturbed, Rule 802, the willingness of Congress to recognize a substantial measure of admissibility for evaluative reports is a helpful guide.

Factors which may be of assistance in passing upon the admissibility of evaluative reports include: (1) the timeliness of the investigation, McCormick, Can the Courts Make Wider Use of Reports of Official Investigations? 42 Iowa L.Rev. 363

(1957); (2) the special skill or experience of the official, id., (3) whether a hearing was held and the level at which conducted, Franklin v. Skelly Oil Co., 141 F.2d 568 (10th Cir.1944); (4) possible motivation problems suggested by Palmer v. Hoffman, 318 U.S. 109, 63 S.Ct. 477, 87 L.Ed. 645 (1943). Others no doubt could be added.

The formulation of an approach which would give appropriate weight to all possible factors in every situation is an obvious impossibility. Hence the rule, as in Exception [paragraph] (6), assumes admissibility in the first instance but with ample provision for escape if sufficient negative factors are present. In one respect, however, the rule with respect to evaluative reports under item (c) is very specific: they are admissible only in civil cases and against the government in criminal cases in view of the almost certain collision with confrontation rights which would result from their use against the accused in a criminal case.

Note to Paragraph (9). Records of vital statistics are commonly the subject of particular statutes making them admissible in evidence, Uniform Vital Statistics Act, 9C U.L.A. 350 (1957). The rule is in principle narrower than Uniform Rule 63(16) which includes reports required of persons performing functions authorized by statute, yet in practical effect the two are substantially the same. Comment Uniform Rule 63(16). The exception as drafted is in the pattern of California Evidence Code § 1281.

Note to Paragraph (10). The principle of proving nonoccurrence of an event by evidence of the absence of a record which would regularly be made of its occurrence, developed in Exception [paragraph] (7) with respect to regularly conducted activities, is here extended to public records of the kind mentioned in Exceptions [paragraphs] (8) and (9). 5 Wigmore § 1633(6), p. 519. Some harmless duplication no doubt exists with Exception [paragraph] (7). For instances of federal statutes recognizing this method of proof, see 8 U.S.C. § 1284(b), proof of absence of alien crewman's name from outgoing manifest prima facie evidence of failure to detain or deport, and 42 U.S.C. § 405(c)(3), (4)(B), (4)(C), absence of HEW [Department of Health, Education, and Welfare] record prima facie evidence of no wages or self-employment income.

The rule includes situations in which absence of a record may itself be the ultimate focal point of inquiry, e.g. People v. Love, 310 Ill. 558, 142 N.E. 204 (1923), certificate of Secretary of State admitted to show failure to file documents required by Securities Law, as well as cases where the absence of a record is offered as proof of the nonoccurrence of an event ordinarily recorded.

The refusal of the common law to allow proof by certificate of the lack of a record or entry has no apparent justification, 5 Wigmore § 1678(7), p. 752. The rule takes the opposite position, as to Uniform Rule 63(17); California Evidence Code § 1284; Kansas Code of Civil Procedure § 60-460(c); New Jersey Evidence Rule 63(17). Congress has recognized certification as evidence of the lack of a record. 8 U.S.C. § 1360(d), certificate of Attorney General or other designated officer that no record of Immigration and Naturalization Service of specified nature or entry therein is found, admissible in alien cases.

Note to Paragraph (11). Records of activities of religious organizations are currently recognized as admissible at least to the extent of the business records exception to the hearsay rule, 5 Wigmore § 1523, p. 371, and Exception [paragraph] (6) would be applicable. However, both the business record doctrine and Exception [paragraph] (6) require that the person furnishing the information be one in the business or activity. The result is such decisions as Daily v. Grand Lodge, 311 Ill. 184, 142 N.E. 478 (1924), holding a church record admissible to prove fact, date, and place of baptism, but not age of child except that he had at least been born at the time. In view of the unlikelihood that false information would be furnished on occasions of this kind, the rule contains no requirement that the informant be in the course of the activity. See California Evidence Code § 1315 and Comment.

Note to Paragraph (12). The principle of proof by certification is recognized as to public officials in Exceptions [paragraphs] (8) and (10), and with respect to authentication in Rule 902. The present exception is a duplication to the extent that it deals with a certificate by a public official, as in the case of a judge who performs a marriage ceremony. The area covered by the rule is, however, substantially larger and extends the certification procedure to clergymen and the like who perform marriages and other ceremonies or administer sacraments. Thus certificates of such matters as baptism or confirmation, as well as marriage, are included. In principle they are as acceptable evidence as certificates of public officers. See 5 Wigmore § 1645, as to marriage certificates. When the person executing the certificate is not a public official, the self-authenticating character of documents purporting to emanate from public officials, see Rule 902, is lacking and proof is required that the person was authorized and did make the certificate. The time element, however, may safely be taken as supplied by the certificate, once authority and authenticity are established, particularly in view of the presumption that a document was executed on the date it bears.

For similar rules, some limited to certificates of marriage, with variations in foundation requirements, see Uniform Rule 63(18); California Evidence Code § 1316; Kansas Code of Civil Procedure § 60-460(p); New Jersey Evidence Rule 63(18).

Note to Paragraph (13). Records of family history kept in family Bibles have by long tradition been received in evidence. 5 Wigmore §§ 1495, 1496, citing numerous statutes and decisions. See also Regulations, Social Security Administration,

20 C.F.R. § 404.703(c), recognizing family Bible entries as proof of age in the absence of public or church records. Opinions in the area also include inscriptions on tombstones, publicly displayed pedigrees, and engravings on rings. Wigmore, supra. The rule is substantially identical in coverage with California Evidence Code § 1312.

Note to Paragraph (14). The recording of title documents is a purely statutory development. Under any theory of the admissibility of public records, the records would be receivable as evidence of the contents of the recorded document, else the recording process would be reduced to a nullity. When, however, the record is offered for the further purpose of proving execution and delivery, a problem of lack of firsthand knowledge by the recorder, not present as to contents, is presented. This problem is solved, seemingly in all jurisdictions, by qualifying for recording only those documents shown by a specified procedure, either acknowledgement or a form of probate, to have been executed and delivered. 5 Wigmore §§ 1647-1651. Thus what may appear in the rule, at first glance, as endowing the record with an effect independently of local law and inviting difficulties of an Erie nature under Cities Service Oil Co. v. Dunlap, 308 U.S. 208, 60 S.Ct. 201, 84 L.Ed. 196 (1939), is not present, since the local law in fact governs under the example.

Note to Paragraph (15). Dispositive documents often contain recitals of fact. Thus a deed purporting to have been executed by an attorney in fact may recite the existence of the power of attorney, or a deed may recite that the grantors are all the heirs of the last record owner. Under the rule, these recitals are exempted from the hearsay rule. The circumstances under which dispositive documents are executed and the requirement that the recital be germane to the purpose of the document are believed to be adequate guarantees of trustworthiness, particularly in view of the nonapplicability of the rule if dealings with the property have been inconsistent with the document. The age of the document is of no significance, though in practical application the document will most often be an ancient one. See Uniform Rule 63(29), Comment.

Similar provisions are contained in Uniform Rule 63(29); California Evidence Code § 1330; Kansas Code of Civil Procedure § 60-460(aa); New Jersey Evidence Rule 63(29).

Note to Paragraph (16). Authenticating a document as ancient, essentially in the pattern of the common law, as provided in Rule 901(b)(8), leaves open as a separate question the admissibility of assertive statements contained therein as against a hearsay objection. 7 Wigmore § 2145a. Wigmore further states that the ancient document technique of authentication is universally conceded to apply to all sorts of documents, including letters, records, contracts, maps, and certificates, in addition to title documents, citing numerous decisions. Id. § 2145. Since most of these items are significant evidentially only insofar as they are assertive, their admission in evidence must be as a hearsay exception. But see 5 id. § 1573, p. 429, referring to recitals in ancient deeds as a "limited" hearsay exception. The former position is believed to be the correct one in reason and authority. As pointed out in McCormick § 298, danger of mistake is minimized by authentication requirements, and age affords assurance that the writing antedates the present controversy. See Dallas County v. Commercial Union Assurance Co., 286 F.2d 388 (5th Cir.1961), upholding admissibility of 58-year-old newspaper story. Cf. Morgan, Basic Problems of Evidence 364 (1962), but see id. 254.

For a similar provision, but with the added requirement that "the statement has since generally been acted upon as true by persons having an interest in the matter," see California Evidence Code § 1331.

Note to Paragraph (17). Ample authority at common law supported the admission in evidence of items falling in this category. While Wigmore's text is narrowly oriented to lists, etc., prepared for the use of a trade or profession, 6 Wigmore § 1702, authorities are cited which include other kinds of publications, for example, newspaper market reports, telephone directories, and city directories. Id. §§ 1702-1706. The basis of trustworthiness is general reliance by the public or by a particular segment of it, and the motivation of the compiler to foster reliance by being accurate.

For similar provisions, see Uniform Rule 63(30); California Evidence Code § 1340; Kansas Code of Civil Procedure § 60-460(bb); New Jersey Evidence Rule 63(30). Uniform Commercial Code § 2-724 provides for admissibility in evidence of "reports in official publications or trade journals or in newspapers or periodicals of general circulation published as the reports of such [established commodity] market."

Note to Paragraph (18). The writers have generally favored the admissibility of learned treatises, McCormick § 296, p. 621; Morgan, Basic Problems of Evidence 366 (1962); 6 Wigmore § 1692, with the support of occasional decisions and rules, City of Dothan v. Hardy, 237 Ala. 603, 188 So. 264 (1939); Lewandowski v. Preferred Risk Mut. Ins. Co., 33 Wis.2d 69, 146 N.W.2d 505 (1966), 66 Mich.L.Rev. 183 (1967); Uniform Rule 63(31); Kansas Code of Civil Procedure § 60-460(cc), but the great weight of authority has been that learned treatises are not admissible as substantive evidence though usable in the cross-examination of experts. The foundation of the minority view is that the hearsay objection must be regarded as unimpressive when directed against treatises since a high standard of accuracy is engendered by various factors: the treatise is written primarily and impartially for professionals, subject to scrutiny and exposure for inaccuracy, with the reputation of the writer at stake. 6 Wigmore § 1692. Sound as this position may be with respect to trustworthiness, there is, nevertheless, an additional difficulty in the likelihood that the treatise will be misunderstood and misapplied without expert assistance and supervision. This difficulty is recognized in the cases demonstrating unwillingness to sustain findings relative to disability on the basis of judicially noticed medical texts. Ross v. Gardner, 365 F.2d 554 (6th Cir.1966); Sayers v. Gardner, 380 F.2d 940 (6th Cir.1967); Colwell v. Gardner, 386 F.2d 56 (6th Cir.1967); Glendenning v. Ribicoff, 213 F.Supp. 301 (W.D.Mo.1962); Cook v. Celebrezze, 217 F.Supp. 366 (W.D.Mo.1963); Sosna v. Celebrezze, 234 F.Supp. 289 (E.D.Pa.1964); and see McDaniel v. Celebrezze, 331 F.2d 426 (4th Cir.1964). The rule avoids the danger of misunderstanding and misapplication by limiting the use of treatises as substantive evidence to situations in which an expert is on the stand and available to explain and assist in the application of the treatise if desired. The limitation upon receiving the publication itself physically in evidence, contained in the last sentence, is designed, to further this policy.

The relevance of the use of treatises on cross-examination is evident. This use of treatises has been the subject of varied views. The most restrictive position is that the witness must have stated expressly on direct his reliance upon the treatise. A slightly more liberal approach still insists upon reliance but allows it to be developed on cross-examination. Further relaxation dispenses with reliance but requires recognition as an authority by the witness, developable on cross-examination. The greatest liberality is found in decisions allowing use of the treatise on cross-examination when its status as an authority is established by any means. Annot., 60 A.L.R.2d 77. The exception is hinged upon this last position, which is that of the Supreme Court, Reilly v. Pinkus, 338 U.S. 269, 70 S.Ct. 110, 94 L.Ed. 63 (1949), and of recent well considered state court decisions, City of St. Petersburg v. Ferguson, 193 So.2d 648 (Fla.App.1967), cert. denied Fla., 201 So.2d 556; Darling v. Charleston Memorial Community Hospital, 33 Ill.2d 326, 211 N.E.2d 253 (1965); Dabroe v. Rhodes Co., 64 Wash.2d 431, 392 P.2d 317 (1964).

In Reilly v. Pinkus, supra, the Court pointed out that testing of professional knowledge was incomplete without exploration of the witness' knowledge of and attitude toward established treatises in the field. The process works equally well in reverse and furnishes the basis of the rule.

The rule does not require that the witness rely upon or recognize the treatise as authoritative, thus avoiding the possibility that the expert may at the outset block cross-examination by refusing to concede reliance or authoritativeness. Dabroe v. Rhodes Co., supra. Moreover, the rule avoids the unreality of admitting evidence for the purpose of impeachment only, with an instruction to the jury not to consider it otherwise. The parallel to the treatment of prior inconsistent statements will be apparent. See Rules 613(b) and 801(d)(1).

Note to Paragraphs (19), (20) and (21). Trustworthiness in reputation evidence is found "when the topic is such that the facts are likely to have been inquired about and that persons having personal knowledge have disclosed facts which have thus been discussed in the community; and thus the community's conclusion, if any has been formed, is likely to be a trustworthy one." 5 Wigmore § 1580, p. 444, and see also § 1583. On this common foundation, reputation as to land boundaries, customs, general history, character, and marriage have come to be regarded as admissible. The breadth of the underlying principle suggests the formulation of an equally broad exception, but tradition has in fact been much narrower and more particularized, and this is the pattern of these exceptions in the rule.

Exception [paragraph] (19) is concerned with matters of personal and family history. Marriage is universally conceded to be a proper subject of proof by evidence of reputation in the community. 5 Wigmore § 1602. As to such items as legitimacy, relationship, adoption, birth, and death, the decisions are divided. Id. § 1605. All seem to be susceptible to being the subject of well founded repute. The "world" in which the reputation may exist may be family, associates, or community. This world has proved capable of expanding with changing times from the single uncomplicated neighborhood, in which all activities take place, to the multiple and unrelated worlds of work, religious affiliation, and social activity, in each of which a reputation may be generated. People v. Reeves, 360 Ill. 55, 195 N.E. 443 (1935); State v. Axilrod, 248 Minn. 204, 79 N.W.2d 677 (1956); Mass.Stat.1947, c. 410, M.G.L.A. c. 233 § 21A; 5 Wigmore § 1616. The family has often served as the point of beginning for allowing community reputation. 5 Wigmore § 1488. For comparable provisions see Uniform Rule 63(26), (27)(c); California Evidence Code §§ 1313, 1314; Kansas Code of Civil Procedure § 60-460(x), (y)(3); New Jersey Evidence Rule 63(26), (27)(c).

The first portion of Exception [paragraph] (20) is based upon the general admissibility of evidence of reputation as to land boundaries and land customs, expanded in this country to include private as well as public boundaries. McCormick § 299, p. 625. The reputation is required to antedate the controversy, though not to be ancient. The second portion is likewise supported by authority, id., and is designed to facilitate proof of events when judicial notice is not available. The historical character of the subject matter dispenses with any need that the reputation antedate the controversy with respect to which it is offered. For similar provisions see Uniform Rule 63(27)(a), (b); California Evidence Code §§ 1320-1322; Kansas Code of Civil Procedure § 60-460(y), (1), (2); New Jersey Evidence Rule 63(27) (a), (b).

Exception [paragraph] (21) recognizes the traditional acceptance of reputation evidence as a means of proving human character. McCormick §§ 44, 158. The exception deals only with the hearsay aspect of this kind of evidence. Limitations upon admissibility based on other grounds will be found in Rules 404, relevancy of character evidence generally, and 608, character of witness. The exception is in effect a reiteration, in the context of hearsay, of Rule 405(a). Similar provisions are contained in Uniform Rule 63(28); California Evidence Code § 1324; Kansas Code of Civil Procedure § 60-460(z); New Jersey Evidence Rule 63(28).

Note to Paragraph (22). When the status of a former judgment is under consideration in subsequent litigation, three possibilities must be noted: (1) the former judgment is conclusive under the doctrine of res judicata, either as a bar or a collateral estoppel; or (2) it is admissible in evidence for what it is worth; or (3) it may be of no effect at all. The first situation does not involve any problem of evidence except in the way that principles of substantive law generally bear upon the relevancy and materiality of evidence. The rule does not deal with the substantive effect of the judgment as a bar or collateral estoppel. When, however, the doctrine of res judicata does not apply to make the judgment either a bar or a collateral estoppel, a choice is presented between the second and third alternatives. The rule adopts the second for judgments of criminal conviction of felony grade. This is the direction of the decisions, Annot., 18 A.L.R.2d 1287, 1299, which manifest an increasing reluctance to reject in toto the validity of the law's factfinding processes outside the confines of res judicata and collateral estoppel. While this may leave a jury with the evidence of conviction but without means to evaluate it, as suggested by Judge Hinton, Note 27 Ill.L.Rev. 195 (1932), it seems safe to assume that the jury will give it substantial effect unless defendant offers a satisfactory explanation, a possibility not foreclosed by the provision. But see North River Ins. Co. v. Militello, 104 Colo. 28, 88 P.2d 567 (1939), in which the jury found for plaintiff on a fire policy despite the introduction of his conviction for arson. For supporting federal decisions see Clark, J., in New York & Cuba Mail S.S. Co. v. Continental Cas. Co., 117 F.2d 404, 411 (2d Cir.1941); Connecticut Fire Ins. Co. v. Ferrara, 277 F.2d 388 (8th Cir.1960).

Practical considerations require exclusion of convictions of minor offenses, not because the administration of justice in its lower echelons must be inferior, but because motivation to defend at this level is often minimal or nonexistent. Cope v. Goble, 39 Cal.App.2d 448, 103 P.2d 598 (1940); Jones v. Talbot, 87 Idaho 498, 394 P.2d 316 (1964); Warren v. Marsh, 215 Minn. 615, 11 N.W.2d 528 (1943); Annot., 18 A.L.R.2d 1287, 1295-1297; 16 Brooklyn L.Rev. 286 (1950); 50 Colum.L.Rev. 529 (1950); 35 Cornell L.Q. 872 (1950). Hence the rule includes only convictions of felony grade, measured by federal standards.

Judgments of conviction based upon pleas of nolo contendere are not included. This position is consistent with the treatment of nolo pleas in Rule 410 and the authorities cited in the Advisory Committee's Note in support thereof.

While these rules do not in general purport to resolve constitutional issues, they have in general been drafted with a view to avoiding collision with constitutional principles. Consequently the exception does not include evidence of the conviction of a third person, offered against the accused in a criminal prosecution to prove any fact essential to sustain the judgment of conviction. A contrary position would seem clearly to violate the right of confrontation. Kirby v. United States, 174 U.S. 47, 19 S.Ct. 574, 43 L.Ed. 890 (1899), error to convict of possessing stolen postage stamps with the only evidence of theft being the record of conviction of the thieves. The situation is to be distinguished from cases in which conviction of another person is an element of the crime, e.g. 15 U.S.C. § 902(d), interstate shipment of firearms to a known convicted felon, and, as specifically provided, from impeachment.

For comparable provisions see Uniform Rule 63(20); California Evidence Code § 1300; Kansas Code of Civil Procedure § 60-460(r); New Jersey Evidence Rule 63(20).

Note to Paragraph (23). A hearsay exception in this area was originally justified on the ground that verdicts were evidence of reputation. As trial by jury graduated from the category of neighborhood inquests, this theory lost its validity. It was never valid as to chancery decrees. Nevertheless the rule persisted, though the judges and writers shifted ground and began saying that the judgment or decree was as good evidence as reputation. See City of London v. Clerke, Carth. 181, 90 Eng.Rep. 710 (K.B. 1691); Neill v. Duke of Devonshire, 8 App.Cas. 135 (1882). The shift appears to be correct, since the process of inquiry, sifting, and scrutiny which is relied upon to render reputation reliable is present in perhaps greater measure in the process of litigation. While this might suggest a broader area of application, the affinity to reputation is strong, and paragraph [paragraph] (23) goes no further, not even including character.

The leading case in the United States, Patterson v. Gaines, 47 U.S. (6 How.) 550, 599, 12 L.Ed. 553 (1847), follows in the pattern of the English decisions, mentioning as illustrative matters thus provable: manorial rights, public rights of way, immemorial custom, disputed boundary, and pedigree. More recent recognition of the principle is found in Grant Bros. Construction Co. v. United States, 232 U.S. 647, 34 S.Ct. 452, 58 L.Ed. 776 (1914), in action for penalties under Alien Contract Labor Law, decision of board of inquiry of Immigration Service admissible to prove alienage of laborers, as a matter of pedigree; United States v. Mid-Continent Petroleum Corp., 67 F.2d 37 (10th Cir.1933), records of commission enrolling Indians admissible on pedigree; Jung Yen Loy v. Cahill, 81 F.2d 809 (9th Cir.1936), board decisions as to citizenship of plaintiff's father admissible in proceeding for declaration of citizenship. Contra, In re Estate of Cunha, 49 Haw. 273, 414 P.2d 925 (1966).

1974 Enactment

Note to Paragraph (3). Rule 803(3) was approved in the form submitted by the Court to Congress. However, the Committee intends that the Rule be construed to limit the doctrine of Mutual Life Insurance Co. v. Hillmon, 145 U.S. 285, 295-300 (1892), so as to render statements of intent by a declarant admissible only to prove his future conduct, not the future conduct of another person.

Note to Paragraph (4). After giving particular attention to the question of physical examination made solely to enable a physician to testify, the Committee approved Rule 803(4) as submitted to Congress, with the understanding that it is not intended in any way to adversely affect present privilege rules or those subsequently adopted.

Note to Paragraph (5). Rule 803(5) as submitted by the Court permitted the reading into evidence of a memorandum or record concerning a matter about which a witness once had knowledge but now has insufficient recollection to enable him to testify accurately and fully, "shown to have been made when the matter was fresh in his memory and to reflect that knowledge correctly." The Committee amended this Rule to add the words "or adopted by the witness" after the phrase "shown to have been made", a treatment consistent with the definition of "statement" in the Jencks Act, 18 U.S.C. 3500. Moreover, it is the Committee's understanding that a memorandum or report, although barred under this Rule, would nonetheless be admissible if it came within another hearsay exception. This last stated principle is deemed applicable to all the hearsay rules.

Note to Paragraph (6). Rule 803(6) as submitted by the Court permitted a record made "in the course of a regularly conducted activity" to be admissible in certain circumstances. The Committee believed there were insufficient guarantees of reliability in records made in the course of activities falling outside the scope of "business" activities as that term is broadly defined in 28 U.S.C. 1732. Moreover, the Committee concluded that the additional requirement of Section 1732 that it must have been the regular practice of a business to make the record is a necessary further assurance of its trustworthiness. The Committee accordingly amended the Rule to incorporate these limitations.

Note to Paragraph (7). Rule 803(7) as submitted by the Court concerned the absence of entry in the records of a "regularly conducted activity." The Committee amended this Rule to conform with its action with respect to Rule 803(6).

Note to Paragraph (8). The Committee approved Rule 803(8) without substantive change from the form in which it was submitted by the Court. The Committee intends that the phrase "factual findings" be strictly construed and that evaluations or opinions contained in public reports shall not be admissible under this Rule.

Note to Paragraph (13). The Committee approved this Rule in the form submitted by the Court, intending that the phrase "Statements of fact concerning personal or family history" be read to include the specific types of such statements enumerated in Rule 803(11). House Report No. 93-650.

Note to Paragraph (4). The House approved this rule as it was submitted by the Supreme Court "with the understanding that it is not intended in any way to adversely affect present privilege rules." We also approve this rule, and we would point out with respect to the question of its relation to privileges, it must be read in conjunction with rule 35 of the Federal Rules of Civil Procedure which provides that whenever the physical or mental condition of a party (plaintiff or defendant) is in controversy, the court may require him to submit to an examination by a physician. It is these examinations which will normally be admitted under this exception.

Note to Paragraph (5). Rule 803(5) as submitted by the Court permitted the reading into evidence of a memorandum or record concerning a matter about which a witness once had knowledge but now has insufficient recollection to enable him to testify accurately and fully, "shown to have been made when the matter was fresh in his memory and to reflect that knowledge correctly." The House amended the rule to add the words "or adopted by the witness" after the phrase "shown to have been made," language parallel to the Jencks Act [18 U.S.C. § 3500].

The committee accepts the House amendment with the understanding and belief that it was not intended to narrow the scope of applicability of the rule. In fact, we understand it to clarify the rule's applicability to a memorandum adopted by the witness as well as one made by him. While the rule as submitted by the Court was silent on the question of who made the memorandum, we view the House amendment as a helpful clarification, noting, however, that the Advisory Committee's note to this rule suggests that the important thing is the accuracy of the memorandum rather than who made it.

The committee does not view the House amendment as precluding admissibility in situations in which multiple participants were involved.

When the verifying witness has not prepared the report, but merely examined it and found it accurate, he has adopted the report, and it is therefore admissible. The rule should also be interpreted to cover other situations involving multiple participants, e.g., employer dictating to secretary, secretary making memorandum at direction of employer, or information being passed along a chain of persons, as in Curtis v. Bradley [65 Conn. 99, 31 Atl. 591 (1894); see, also, Rathbun v. Brancatella, 93 N.J.L. 222, 107 Atl. 279 (1919); see, also, McCormick on Evidence, § 303 (2d ed. 1972)].

The committee also accepts the understanding of the House that a memorandum or report, although barred under this rule, would nonetheless be admissible if it came within another hearsay exception. We consider this principle to be applicable to all the hearsay rules.

Note to Paragraph (6). Rule 803(6) as submitted by the Supreme Court permitted a record made in the course of a regularly conducted activity to be admissible in certain circumstances. This rule constituted a broadening of the traditional business records hearsay exception which has been long advocated by scholars and judges active in the law of evidence.

The House felt there were insufficient guarantees of reliability of records not within a broadly defined business records exception. We disagree. Even under the House definition of "business" including profession, occupation, and "calling of every kind," the records of many regularly conducted activities will, or may be, excluded from evidence. Under the principle of ejusdem generis, the intent of "calling of every kind" would seem to be related to work-related endeavors--e.g., butcher, baker, artist, etc.

Thus, it appears that the records of many institutions or groups might not be admissible under the House amendments. For example, schools, churches, and hospitals will not normally be considered businesses within the definition. Yet, these are groups which keep financial and other records on a regular basis in a manner similar to business enterprises. We believe these records are of equivalent trustworthiness and should be admitted into evidence.

Three states, which have recently codified their evidence rules, have adopted the Supreme Court version of rule 803(6), providing for admission of memoranda of a "regularly conducted activity." None adopted the words "business activity" used in the House amendment. [See Nev.Rev.Stats. § 15.135; N.Mex.Stats. (1973 Supp.) § 20-4-803(6); West's Wis.Stats.Anno. (1973 Supp.) § 908.03(6).]

Therefore, the committee deleted the word "business" as it appears before the word "activity". The last sentence then is unnecessary and was also deleted.

It is the understanding of the committee that the use of the phrase "person with knowledge" is not intended to imply that the party seeking to introduce the memorandum, report, record, or data compilation must be able to produce, or even identify, the specific individual upon whose first-hand knowledge the memorandum, report, record or data compilation was based. A sufficient foundation for the introduction of such evidence will be laid if the party seeking to introduce the evidence is able to show that it was the regular practice of the activity to base such memorandums, reports, records, or data compilations upon a transmission from a person with knowledge, e.g., in the case of the content of a shipment of goods, upon a report from the company's receiving agent or in the case of a computer printout, upon a report from the company's computer programmer or one who has knowledge of the particular record system. In short, the scope of the phrase "person with knowledge" is meant to be coterminous with the custodian of the evidence or other qualified witness. The committee believes this represents the desired rule in light of the complex nature of modern business organizations.

Note to Paragraph (8). The House approved rule 803(8), as submitted by the Supreme Court, with one substantive change. It excluded from the hearsay exception reports containing matters observed by police officers and other law enforcement personnel in criminal cases. Ostensibly, the reason for this exclusion is that observations by police officers at the scene of the crime or the apprehension of the defendant are not as reliable as observations by public officials in other cases because of the adversarial nature of the confrontation between the police and the defendant in criminal cases.

The committee accepts the House's decision to exclude such recorded observations where the police officer is available to testify in court about his observation. However, where he is unavailable as unavailability is defined in rule 804(a)(4) and (a)(5), the report should be admitted as the best available evidence. Accordingly, the committee has amended rule 803(8) to refer to the provision of [proposed] rule 804(b)(5) [deleted], which allows the admission of such reports, records or other statements where the police officer or other law enforcement officer is unavailable because of death, then existing physical or mental illness or infirmity, or not being successfully subject to legal process.

The House Judiciary Committee report contained a statement of intent that "the phrase 'factual findings' in subdivision (c) be strictly construed and that evaluations or opinions contained in public reports shall not be admissible under this rule." The committee takes strong exception to this limiting understanding of the application of the rule. We do not think it reflects an understanding of the intended operation of the rule as explained in the Advisory Committee notes to this subsection. The Advisory Committee notes on subsection (c) of this subdivision point out that various kinds of evaluative reports are now admissible under Federal statutes. 7 U.S.C. § 78, findings of Secretary of Agriculture prima facie evidence of true grade of grain; 42 U.S.C. § 269(b), bill of health by appropriate official prima facie evidence of vessel's sanitary history and condition and compliance with regulations. These statutory exceptions to the hearsay rule are preserved. Rule 802. The willingness of Congress to recognize these and other such evaluative reports provides a helpful guide in determining the kind of reports which are intended to be admissible under this rule. We think the restrictive interpretation of the House overlooks the fact that while the Advisory Committee assumes admissibility in the first instance of evaluative reports, they are not admissible if, as the rule states, "the sources of information or other circumstances indicate lack of trustworthiness."

The Advisory Committee explains the factors to be considered:

Factors which may be assistance in passing upon the admissibility of evaluative reports include: (1) the timeliness of the investigation, McCormick, Can the Courts Make Wider Use of Reports of Official Investigations? 42 Iowa L.Rev. 363 (1957); (2) the special skill or experience of the official, id.; (3) whether a hearing was held and the level at which conducted, Franklin v. Skelly Oil Co., 141 F.2d 568 (19th Cir.1944); (4) possible motivation problems suggested by Palmer v. Hoffman, 318 U.S. 109, 63 S.Ct. 477, 87 L.Ed. 645 (1943). Others no doubt could be added.

The committee concludes that the language of the rule together with the explanation provided by the Advisory Committee furnish sufficient guidance on the admissibility of evaluative reports.

Note to Paragraph (24). The proposed Rules of Evidence submitted to Congress contained identical provisions in rules 803 and 804 (which set forth the various hearsay exceptions), admitting any hearsay statement not specifically covered by any of the stated exceptions, if the hearsay statement was found to have "comparable circumstantial guarantees of trustworthiness." The House deleted these provisions (proposed rules 803(24) and 804(b)(6)[(5)]) as injecting "too much uncertainty" into the law of evidence and impairing the ability of practitioners to prepare for trial. The House felt that rule 102, which directs the courts to construe the Rules of Evidence so as to promote growth and development, would permit sufficient flexibility to admit hearsay evidence in appropriate cases under various factual situations that might arise.

We disagree with the total rejection of a residual hearsay exception. While we view rule 102 as being intended to provide for a broader construction and interpretation of these rules, we feel that, without a separate residual provision, the specifically enumerated exceptions could become tortured beyond any reasonable circumstances which they were intended to include (even if broadly construed). Moreover, these exceptions, while they reflect the most typical and well recognized exceptions to the hearsay rule, may not encompass every situation in which the reliability and appropriateness of a particular piece of hearsay evidence make clear that it should be heard and considered by the trier of fact.

The committee believes that there are certain exceptional circumstances where evidence which is found by a court to have guarantees of trustworthiness equivalent to or exceeding the guarantees reflected by the presently listed exceptions, and to have a high degree of prolativeness [sic] and necessity could properly be admissible.

The case of Dallas County v. Commercial Union Assoc. Co., Ltd., 286 F.2d 388 (5th Cir.1961) illustrates the point. The issue in that case was whether the tower of the county courthouse collapsed because it was struck by lightning (covered by insurance) or because of structural weakness and deterioration of the structure (not covered). Investigation of the structure revealed the presence of charcoal and charred timbers. In order to show that lightning may not have been the cause of the charring, the insurer offered a copy of a local newspaper published over 50 years earlier containing an unsigned article describing a fire in the courthouse while it was under construction. The court found that the newspaper did not qualify for admission as a business record or an ancient document and did not fit within any other recognized hearsay exception. The court concluded, however, that the article was trustworthy because it was inconceivable that a newspaper reporter in a small town would report a fire in the courthouse if none had occurred. See also United States v. Barbati, 284 F.Supp. 409 (E.D.N.Y.1968).

Because exceptional cases like the Dallas County case may arise in the future, the committee has decided to reinstate a residual exception for rules 803 and 804(b).

The committee, however, also agrees with those supporters of the House version who felt that an overly broad residual hearsay exception could emasculate the hearsay rule and the recognized exceptions or vitiate the rationale behind codification of the rules.

Therefore, the committee has adopted a residual exception for rules 803 and 804(b) of much narrower scope and applicability than the Supreme Court version. In order to qualify for admission, a hearsay statement not falling within one of the recognized exceptions would have to satisfy at least four conditions. First, it must have "equivalent circumstantial guarantees of trustworthiness." Second, it must be offered as evidence of a material fact. Third, the court must determine that the statement "is more probative on the point for which it is offered than any other evidence which the proponent can procure through reasonable efforts." This requirement is intended to insure that only statements which have high probative value and necessity may qualify for admission under the residual exceptions. Fourth, the court must determine that "the general purposes of these rules and the interests of justice will best be served by admission of the statement into evidence."

It is intended that the residual hearsay exceptions will be used very rarely, and only in exceptional circumstances. The committee does not intend to establish a broad license for trial judges to admit hearsay statements that do not fall within one of the other exceptions contained in rules 803 and 804(b). The residual exceptions are not meant to authorize major judicial revisions of the hearsay rule, including its present exceptions. Such major revisions are best accomplished by legislative action. It is intended that in any case in which evidence is sought to be admitted under these subsections, the trial judge will exercise no less care, reflection and caution than the courts did under the common law in establishing the now-recognized exceptions to the hearsay rule.

In order to establish a well-defined jurisprudence, the special facts and circumstances which, in the court's judgment, indicates that the statement has a sufficiently high degree of trustworthiness and necessity to justify its admission should be stated on the record. It is expected that the court will give the opposing party a full and adequate opportunity to contest the admission of any statement sought to be introduced under these subsections. Senate Report No. 93-1277.

Rule 803 defines when hearsay statements are admissible in evidence even though the declarant is available as a witness. The Senate amendments make three changes in this rule.

Note to Paragraph (6). The House bill provides in subsection (6) that records of a regularly conducted "business" activity qualify for admission into evidence as an exception to the hearsay rule. "Business" is defined as including "business, profession, occupation and calling of every kind." The Senate amendment drops the requirement that the records be those of a "business" activity and eliminates the definition of "business." The Senate amendment provides that records are admissible if they are records of a regularly conducted "activity."

The Conference adopts the House provision that the records must be those of a regularly conducted "business" activity. The Conferees changed the definition of "business" contained in the House provision in order to make it clear that the records of institutions and associations like schools, churches and hospitals are admissible under this provision. The records of public schools and hospitals are also covered by Rule 803(8), which deals with public records and reports.

Note to Paragraph (8). The Senate amendment adds language, not contained in the House bill, that refers to another rule that was added by the Senate in another amendment ([proposed] Rule 804(b)(5)--Criminal law enforcement records and reports [deleted]).

In view of its action on [proposed] Rule 804(b)(5) (Criminal law enforcement records and reports) [deleted], the Conference does not adopt the Senate amendment and restores the bill to the House version.

Note to Paragraph (24). The Senate amendment adds a new subsection, (24), which makes admissible a hearsay statement not specifically covered by any of the previous twenty-three subsections, if the statement has equivalent circumstantial guarantees of trustworthiness and if the court determines that (A) the statement is offered as evidence of a material fact; (B) the statement is more probative on the point for which it is offered than any other evidence the proponent can procure through reasonable efforts; and (C) the general purposes of these rules and the interests of justice will best be served by admission of the statement into evidence.

The House bill eliminated a similar, but broader, provision because of the conviction that such a provision injected too much uncertainty into the law of evidence regarding hearsay and impaired the ability of a litigant to prepare adequately for trial.

The Conference adopts the Senate amendment with an amendment that provides that a party intending to request the court to use a statement under this provision must notify any adverse party of this intention as well as of the particulars of the statement, including the name and address of the declarant. This notice must be given sufficiently in advance of the trial or hearing to provide any adverse party with a fair opportunity to prepare to contest the use of the statement. House Report No. 93-1597.

1987 Amendment
The amendments are technical. No substantive change is intended.

1997 Amendment
The contents of Rule 803(24) and Rule 804(b)(5) have been combined and transferred to a new Rule 807. This was done to facilitate additions to Rules 803 and 804. No change in meaning is intended.

GAP Report on Rule 803. The words "Transferred to Rule 807" were substituted for "Abrogated."

2000 Amendment
The amendment provides that the foundation requirements of Rule 803(6) can be satisfied under certain circumstances without the expense and inconvenience of producing time-consuming foundation witnesses. Under current law, courts have generally required foundation witnesses to testify. See, e.g., Tongil Co., Ltd. v. Vessel Hyundai Innovator, 968 F.2d 999 (9th Cir. 1992) (reversing a judgment based on business records where a qualified person filed an affidavit but did not testify). Protections are provided by the authentication requirements of Rule 902(11) for domestic records, Rule 902(12) for foreign records in civil cases, and 18 U.S.C. § 3505 for foreign records in criminal cases.

GAP Report--Proposed Amendment to Rule 803(6)

The Committee made no changes to the published draft of the proposed amendment to Evidence Rule 803(6).

Rule 804. Hearsay Exceptions; Declarant Unavailable

(a) Definition of unavailability. "Unavailability as a witness" includes situations in which the declarant--

(1) is exempted by ruling of the court on the ground of privilege from testifying concerning the subject matter of the declarant's statement; or

(2) persists in refusing to testify concerning the subject matter of the declarant's statement despite an order of the court to do so; or

(3) testifies to a lack of memory of the subject matter of the declarant's statement; or

(4) is unable to be present or to testify at the hearing because of death or then existing physical or mental illness or infirmity; or

(5) is absent from the hearing and the proponent of a statement has been unable to procure the declarant's attendance (or in the case of a hearsay exception under subdivision (b)(2), (3), or (4), the declarant's attendance or testimony) by process or other reasonable means.

A declarant is not unavailable as a witness if exemption, refusal, claim of lack of memory, inability, or absence is due to the procurement or wrongdoing of the proponent of a statement for the purpose of preventing the witness from attending or testifying.

(b) Hearsay exceptions. The following are not excluded by the hearsay rule if the declarant is unavailable as a witness:

(1) Former testimony. Testimony given as a witness at another hearing of the same or a different proceeding, or in a deposition taken in compliance with law in the course of the same or another proceeding, if the party against whom the testimony is now offered, or, in a civil action or proceeding, a predecessor in interest, had an opportunity and similar motive to develop the testimony by direct, cross, or redirect examination.

(2) Statement under belief of impending death. In a prosecution for homicide or in a civil action or proceeding, a statement made by a declarant while believing that the declarant's death was imminent, concerning the cause or

circumstances of what the declarant believed to be impending death.

(3) Statement against interest. A statement which was at the time of its making so far contrary to the declarant's pecuniary or proprietary interest, or so far tended to subject the declarant to civil or criminal liability, or to render invalid a claim by the declarant against another, that a reasonable person in the declarant's position would not have made the statement unless believing it to be true. A statement tending to expose the declarant to criminal liability and offered to exculpate the accused is not admissible unless corroborating circumstances clearly indicate the trustworthiness of the statement.

(4) Statement of personal or family history. (A) A statement concerning the declarant's own birth, adoption, marriage, divorce, legitimacy, relationship by blood, adoption, or marriage, ancestry, or other similar fact of personal or family history, even though declarant had no means of acquiring personal knowledge of the matter stated; or (B) a statement concerning the foregoing matters, and death also, of another person, if the declarant was related to the other by blood, adoption, or marriage or was so intimately associated with the other's family as to be likely to have accurate information concerning the matter declared.

(5) [Transferred to Rule 807]

(6) Forfeiture by wrongdoing. A statement offered against a party that has engaged or acquiesced in wrongdoing that was intended to, and did, procure the unavailability of the declarant as a witness.

ADVISORY COMMITTEE NOTES

1972 Proposed Rules
As to firsthand knowledge on the part of hearsay declarants, see the introductory portion of the Advisory Committee's Note to Rule 803.

Note to Subdivision (a). The definition of unavailability implements the division of hearsay exceptions into two categories by Rules 803 and 804(b).

At common law the unavailability requirement was evolved in connection with particular hearsay exceptions rather than along general lines. For example, see the separate explications of unavailability in relation to former testimony, declarations against interest, and statements of pedigree, separately developed in McCormick §§ 234, 257, and 297. However, no reason is apparent for making distinctions as to what satisfies unavailability for the different exceptions. The treatment in the rule is therefore uniform although differences in the range of process for witnesses between civil and criminal cases will lead to a less exacting requirement under item (5). See Rule 45(e) of the Federal Rules of Civil Procedure and Rule 17(e) of the Federal Rules of Criminal Procedure.

Five instances of unavailability are specified:

(1) Substantial authority supports the position that exercise of a claim of privilege by the declarant satisfies the requirement of unavailability (usually in connection with former testimony). Wyatt v. State, 35 Ala.App. 147, 46 So.2d 837 (1950); State v. Stewart, 85 Kan. 404, 116 P. 489 (1911); Annot., 45 A.L.R.2d 1354; Uniform Rule 62(7)(a); California Evidence Code § 240(a)(1); Kansas Code of Civil Procedure § 60-459(g)(1). A ruling by the judge is required, which clearly implies that an actual claim of privilege must be made.

(2) A witness is rendered unavailable if he simply refuses to testify concerning the subject matter of his statement despite judicial pressures to do so, a position supported by similar considerations of practicality. Johnson v. People, 152 Colo. 586, 384 P.2d 454 (1963); People v. Pickett, 339 Mich. 294, 63 N.W.2d 681, 45 A.L.R.2d 1341 (1954). Contra, Pleau v. State, 255 Wis. 362, 38 N.W.2d 496 (1949).

(3) The position that a claimed lack of memory by the witness of the subject matter of his statement constitutes unavailability likewise finds support in the cases, though not without dissent. McCormick § 234, p. 494. If the claim is successful, the practical effect is to put the testimony beyond reach, as in the other instances. In this instance, however, it will be noted that the lack of memory must be established by the testimony of the witness himself, which clearly contemplates his production and subjection to cross-examination.

(4) Death and infirmity find general recognition as grounds. McCormick §§ 234, 257, 297; Uniform Rule 62(7)(c); California Evidence Code § 240(a)(3); Kansas Code of Civil Procedure § 60-459(g)(3); New Jersey Evidence Rule 62(6)(c). See also the provisions on use of depositions in Rule 32(a)(3) of the Federal Rules of Civil Procedure and Rule 15(e) of the Federal Rules of Criminal Procedure.

(5) Absence from the hearing coupled with inability to compel attendance by process or other reasonable means also satisfies the requirement. McCormick § 234; Uniform Rule 62(7)(d) and (e); California Evidence Code § 240(a)(4) and (5); Kansas Code of Civil Procedure § 60-459(g)(4) and (5); New Jersey Rule 62(6)(b) and (d). See the discussion of procuring attendance of witnesses who are nonresidents or in custody in Barber v. Page, 390 U.S. 719, 88 S.Ct. 1318, 20 L.Ed.2d 255 (1968).

If the conditions otherwise constituting unavailability result from the procurement or wrongdoing of the proponent of the statement, the requirement is not satisfied. The rule contains no requirement that an attempt be made to take the deposition of a declarant.

Note to Subdivision (b). Rule 803, supra, is based upon the assumption that a hearsay statement falling within one of its exceptions possesses qualities which justify the conclusion that whether the declarant is available or unavailable is not a relevant factor in determining admissibility. The instant rule proceeds upon a different theory: hearsay which admittedly is not equal in quality to testimony of the declarant on the stand may nevertheless be admitted if the declarant is unavailable and if his statement meets a specified standard. The rule expresses preferences: testimony given on the stand in person is preferred over hearsay, and hearsay, if of the specified quality, is preferred over complete loss of the evidence of the declarant. The exceptions evolved at common law with respect to declarations of unavailable declarants furnish the basis for the exceptions enumerated in the proposal. The term "unavailable" is defined in subdivision (a).

Exception (1). Former testimony does not rely upon some set of circumstances to substitute for oath and cross-examination, since both oath and opportunity to cross-examine were present in fact. The only missing one of the ideal conditions for the giving of testimony is the presence of trier and opponent ("demeanor evidence"). This is lacking with all hearsay exceptions. Hence it may be argued that former testimony is the strongest hearsay and should be included under Rule 803, supra. However, opportunity to observe demeanor is what in a large measure confers depth and meaning upon oath and cross-examination. Thus in cases under Rule 803 demeanor lacks the significance which it possesses with respect to testimony. In any event, the tradition, founded in experience, uniformly favors production of the witness if he is available. The exception indicates continuation of the policy. This preference for the presence of the witness is apparent also in rules and statutes on the use of depositions, which deal with substantially the same problem.

Under the exception, the testimony may be offered (1) against the party against whom it was previously offered or (2) against the party by whom it was previously offered. In each instance the question resolves itself into whether fairness allows imposing, upon the party against whom now offered, the handling of the witness of the earlier occasion. (1) If the party against whom now offered is the one against whom the testimony was offered previously, no unfairness is apparent in requiring him to accept his own prior conduct of cross-examination or decision not to cross-examine. Only demeanor has been lost, and that is inherent in the situation. (2) If the party against whom now offered is the one by whom the testimony was offered previously, a satisfactory answer becomes somewhat more difficult. One possibility is to proceed somewhat along the line of an adoptive admission, i.e. by offering the testimony proponent in effect adopts it. However, this theory savors of discarded concepts of witnesses' belonging to a party, of litigants' ability to pick and choose witnesses, and of vouching for one's own witnesses. Cf. McCormick § 246, pp. 526-527; 4 Wigmore § 1075. A more direct and acceptable approach is simply to recognize direct and redirect examination of one's own witness as the equivalent of cross-examining an opponent's witness. Falknor, Former Testimony and the Uniform Rules: A Comment, 38 N.Y.U.L.Rev. 651, n. 1 (1963); McCormick § 231, p. 483. See also 5 Wigmore § 1389. Allowable techniques for dealing with hostile, double-crossing, forgetful, and mentally deficient witnesses leave no substance to a claim that one could not adequately develop his own witness at the former hearing. An even less appealing argument is presented when failure to develop fully was the result of a deliberate choice.

The common law did not limit the admissibility of former testimony to that given in an earlier trial of the same case, although it did require identity of issues as a means of insuring that the former handling of the witness was the equivalent of what would now be done if the opportunity were presented. Modern decisions reduce the requirement to "substantial" identity. McCormick § 233. Since identity of issues is significant only in that it bears on motive and interest in developing fully the testimony of the witness, expressing the matter in the latter terms is preferable. Id. Testimony given at a preliminary hearing was held in California v. Green, 399 U.S. 149, 90 S.Ct. 1930, 26 L.Ed.2d 489 (1970), to satisfy confrontation requirements in this respect.

As a further assurance of fairness in thrusting upon a party the prior handling of the witness, the common law also insisted upon identity of parties, deviating only to the extent of allowing substitution of successors in a narrowly construed privity. Mutuality as an aspect of identity is now generally discredited, and the requirement of identity of the offering party disappears except as it might affect motive to develop the testimony. Falknor, supra, at 652; McCormick § 232, pp. 487-488. The question remains whether strict identity, or privity, should continue as a requirement with respect to the party against whom offered. The rule departs to the extent of allowing substitution of one with the right and opportunity to develop the testimony with similar motive and interest. This position is supported by modern decisions. McCormick § 232, pp. 489-490; 5 Wigmore § 1388.

Provisions of the same tenor will be found in Uniform Rule 63(3)(b); California Evidence Code §§ 1290-1292; Kansas Code of Civil Procedure § 60-460(c)(2); New Jersey Evidence Rule 63(3). Unlike the rule, the latter three provide either that former testimony is not admissible if the right of confrontation is denied or that it is not admissible if the accused was not a party to the prior hearing. The genesis of these limitations is a caveat in Uniform Rule 63(3) Comment that use of former testimony against an accused may violate his right of confrontation. Mattox v. United States, 156 U.S. 237, 15 S.Ct. 337, 39 L.Ed. 409 (1895), held that the right was not violated by the Government's use, on a retrial of the same case, of testimony given at the first trial by two witnesses since deceased. The decision leaves open the questions (1) whether direct and redirect are equivalent to cross-examination for purposes of confrontation, (2) whether testimony given in a different proceeding is acceptable, and (3) whether the accused must himself have been a party to the earlier proceeding or whether a similarly situated person will serve the purpose. Professor Falknor concluded that, if a dying declaration untested by cross-examination is constitutionally admissible, former testimony tested by the cross-examination of one similarly situated does not offend against confrontation. Falknor, supra, at 659-660. The constitutional acceptability of dying declarations has often been conceded. Mattox v. United States, 156 U.S. 237, 243, 15 S.Ct. 337, 39 L.Ed. 409 (1895); Kirby v. United States, 174 U.S. 47, 61, 19 S.Ct. 574, 43 L.Ed. 890 (1899); Pointer v. Texas, 380 U.S. 400, 407, 85 S.Ct. 1065, 13 L.Ed.2d 923 (1965).

Exception (2). The exception is the familiar dying declaration of the common law, expanded somewhat beyond its traditionally narrow limits. While the original religious justification for the exception may have lost its conviction for some persons over the years, it can scarcely be doubted that powerful psychological pressures are present. See 5 Wigmore § 1443 and the classic statement of Chief Baron Eyre in Rex v. Woodcock, 1 Leach 500, 502, 168 Eng.Rep. 352, 353 (K.B.1789).

The common law required that the statement be that of the victim, offered in a prosecution for criminal homicide. Thus declarations by victims in prosecutions for other crimes, e.g. a declaration by a rape victim who dies in childbirth, and all declarations in civil cases were outside the scope of the exception. An occasional statute has removed these restrictions, as in Colo.R.S. § 52-1-20, or has expanded the area of offenses to include abortions, 5 Wigmore § 1432, p. 224, n. 4. Kansas by decision extended the exception to civil cases. Thurston v. Fritz, 91 Kan. 468, 138 P. 625 (1914). While the common law exception no doubt originated as a result of the exceptional need for the evidence in homicide cases, the theory of admissibility applies equally in civil cases and in prosecutions for crimes other than homicide. The same considerations suggest abandonment of the limitation to circumstances attending the event in question, yet when the statement deals with matters other than the supposed death, its influence is believed to be sufficiently attenuated to justify the limitation. Unavailability is not limited to death. See subdivision (a) of this rule. Any problem as to declarations phrased in terms of opinion is laid at rest by Rule 701, and continuation of a requirement of firsthand knowledge is assured by Rule 602.

Comparable provisions are found in Uniform Rule 63(5); California Evidence Code § 1242; Kansas Code of Civil Procedure § 60-460(e); New Jersey Evidence Rule 63(5).

Exception (3). The circumstantial guaranty of reliability for declarations against interest is the assumption that persons do not make statements which are damaging to themselves unless satisfied for good reason that they are true. Hileman v. Northwest Engineering Co., 346 F.2d 668 (6th Cir.1965). If the statement is that of a party, offered by his opponent, it comes in as an admission, Rule 803(d)(2) [sic; probably should be "Rule 801(d)(2)"], and there is no occasion to inquire whether it is against interest, this not being a condition precedent to admissibility of admissions by opponents.

The common law required that the interest declared against be pecuniary or proprietary but within this limitation demonstrated striking ingenuity in discovering an against-interest aspect. Higham v. Ridgway, 10 East 109, 103 Eng.Rep. 717 (K.B.1808); Reg. v. Overseers of Birmingham, 1 B. & S. 763, 121 Eng.Rep. 897 (Q.B.1861); McCormick, § 256, p. 551, nn. 2 and 3.

The exception discards the common law limitation and expands to the full logical limit. One result is to remove doubt as to the admissibility of declarations tending to establish a tort liability against the declarant or to extinguish one which might be asserted by him, in accordance with the trend of the decisions in this country. McCormick § 254, pp. 548-549. Another is to allow statements tending to expose declarant to hatred, ridicule, or disgrace, the motivation here being considered to be as strong as when financial interests are at stake. McCormick § 255, p. 551. And finally, exposure to criminal liability satisfies the against-interest requirement. The refusal of the common law to concede the adequacy of a penal interest was no doubt indefensible in logic, see the dissent of Mr. Justice Holmes in Donnelly v. United States, 228 U.S. 243, 33 S.Ct. 449, 57 L.Ed. 820 (1913), but one senses in the decisions a distrust of evidence of confessions by third persons offered to exculpate the accused arising from suspicions of fabrication either of the fact of the making of the confession or in its contents, enhanced in either instance by the required unavailability of the declarant. Nevertheless, an increasing amount of decisional law recognizes exposure to punishment for crime as a sufficient stake. People v. Spriggs, 60 Cal.2d 868, 36 Cal.Rptr. 841, 389 P.2d 377 (1964); Sutter v. Easterly, 354 Mo. 282, 189 S.W.2d 284 (1945); Band's Refuse Removal, Inc. v. Fairlawn Borough, 62 N.J.Super. 522, 163 A.2d 465 (1960); Newberry v. Commonwealth, 191 Va. 445, 61 S.E.2d 318 (1950); Annot., 162 A.L.R. 446. The requirement of corroboration is included in the rule in order to effect an accommodation between these competing considerations. When the statement is offered by the accused by way of exculpation, the resulting situation is not adapted to control by rulings as to the weight of the evidence, and hence the provision is cast in terms of a requirement preliminary to admissibility. Cf. Rule 406(a). The requirement of corroboration should be construed in such a manner as to effectuate its purpose of circumventing fabrication.

Ordinarily the third-party confession is thought of in terms of exculpating the accused, but this is by no means always or necessarily the case: it may include statements implicating him, and under the general theory of declarations against interest they would be admissible as related statements. Douglas v. Alabama, 380 U.S. 415, 85 S.Ct. 1074, 13 L.Ed.2d 934 (1965), and Bruton v. United States, 389 U.S. 818, 88 S.Ct. 126, 19 L.Ed.2d 70 (1968), both involved confessions by codefendants which implicated the accused. While the confession was not actually offered in evidence in Douglas, the procedure followed effectively put it before the jury, which the Court ruled to be error. Whether the confession might have been admissible as a declaration against penal interest was not considered or discussed. Bruton assumed the inadmissibility, as against the accused, of the implicating confession of his codefendant, and centered upon the question of the effectiveness of a limiting instruction. These decisions, however, by no means require that all statements implicating another person be excluded from the category of declarations against interest. Whether a statement is in fact against interest must be determined from the circumstances of each case. Thus a statement admitting guilt and implicating another person, made while in custody, may well be motivated by a desire to curry favor with the authorities and hence fail to qualify as against interest. See the dissenting opinion of Mr. Justice White in Bruton. On the other hand, the same words spoken under different circumstances, e.g., to an acquaintance, would have no difficulty in qualifying. The rule does not purport to deal with questions of the right of confrontation.

The balancing of self-serving against dissenting aspects of a declaration is discussed in McCormick § 256.

For comparable provisions, see Uniform Rule 63(10); California Evidence Code § 1230; Kansas Code of Civil Procedure § 60-460(j); New Jersey Evidence Rule 63(10).

Exception (4). The general common law requirement that a declaration in this area must have been made ante litem motam has been dropped, as bearing more appropriately on weight than admissibility. See 5 Wigmore § 1483. Item (i)[(A)] specifically disclaims any need of firsthand knowledge respecting declarant's own personal history. In some instances it is self-evident (marriage) and in others impossible and traditionally[not required (date of birth). Item (ii)[(B)] deals with declarations concerning the history of another person. As at common law, declarant is qualified if related by blood or marriage. 5 Wigmore § 1489. In addition, and contrary to the common law, declarant qualifies by virtue of intimate association with the family. Id., § 1487. The requirement sometimes encountered that when the subject of the statement is the relationship between two other persons the declarant must qualify as to both is omitted. Relationship is reciprocal. Id., § 1491.

For comparable provisions, see Uniform Rule 63(23), (24), (25); California Evidence Code §§ 1310, 1311; Kansas Code of Civil Procedure § 60-460(u), (v), (w); New Jersey Evidence Rules 63-23), 63(24), 63(25).

1974 Enactment

Note to Subdivision (a)(3). Rule 804(a)(3) was approved in the form submitted by the Court. However, the Committee intends no change in existing federal law under which the court may choose to disbelieve the declarant's testimony as to his lack of memory. See United States v. Insana, 423 F.2d 1165, 1169-1170 (2nd Cir.), cert. denied, 400 U.S. 841 (1970).

Note to Subdivision (a)(5). Rule 804(a)(5) as submitted to the Congress provided, as one type of situation in which a declarant would be deemed "unavailable", that he be "absent from the hearing and the proponent of his statement has been unable to procure his attendance by process or other reasonable means." The Committee amended the Rule to insert after the word "attendance" the parenthetical expression "(or, in the case of a hearsay exception under subdivision (b)(2), (3), or (4), his attendance or testimony)". The amendment is designed primarily to require that an attempt be made to depose a witness (as well as to seek his attendance) as a precondition to the witness being deemed unavailable. The Committee, however, recognized the propriety of an exception to this additional requirement when it is the declarant's former testimony that is sought to be admitted under subdivision (b)(1).

Note to Subdivision (b)(1). Rule 804(b)(1) as submitted by the Court allowed prior testimony of an unavailable witness to be admissible if the party against whom it is offered or a person "with motive and interest similar" to his had an opportunity to examine the witness. The Committee considered that it is generally unfair to impose upon the party against whom the hearsay evidence is being offered responsibility for the manner in which the witness was previously handled by another party. The sole exception to this, in the Committee's view, is when a party's predecessor in interest in a civil action or proceeding had an opportunity and similar motive to examine the witness. The Committee amended the Rule to reflect these policy determinations.

Note to Subdivision (b)(2). Rule 804(b)(3) as submitted by the Court (now Rule 804(b)(2) in the bill) proposed to expand the traditional scope of the dying declaration exception (i.e. a statement of the victim in a homicide case as to the cause or circumstances of his believed imminent death) to allow such statements in all criminal and civil cases. The Committee did not consider dying declarations as among the most reliable forms of hearsay. Consequently, it amended the provision to limit their admissibility in criminal cases to homicide prosecutions, where exceptional need for the evidence is present. This is existing law. At the same time, the Committee approved the expansion to civil actions and proceedings where the stakes do not involve possible imprisonment, although noting that this could lead to forum shopping in some instances.

Note to Subdivision (b)(3). Rule 804(b)(4) as submitted by the Court (now Rule 804(b)(3) in the bill) provided as follows:

Statement against interest.--A statement which was at the time of its making so far contrary to the declarant's pecuniary or proprietary interest or so far tended to subject him to civil or criminal liability or to render invalid a claim by him against another or to make him an object of hatred, ridicule, or disgrace, that a reasonable man in his position would not have made the statement unless he believed it to be true. A statement tending to exculpate the accused is not admissible unless corroborated.

The Committee determined to retain the traditional hearsay exception for statements against pecuniary or proprietary interest. However, it deemed the Court's additional references to statements tending to subject a declarant to civil liability or to render invalid a claim by him against another to be redundant as included within the scope of the reference to statements against pecuniary or proprietary interest. See Gichner v. Antonio Triano Tile and Marble Co., 410 F.2d 238 (D.C.Cir.1968). Those additional references were accordingly deleted.

The Court's Rule also proposed to expand the hearsay limitation from its present federal limitation to include statements subjecting the declarant to criminal liability and statements tending to make him an object of hatred, ridicule, or disgrace. The Committee eliminated the latter category from the subdivision as lacking sufficient guarantees of reliability. See United States v. Dovico, 380 F.2d 325, 327 nn. 2, 4 (2nd Cir.), cert. denied, 389 U.S. 944 (1967). As for statements against penal interest, the Committee shared the view of the Court that some such statements do possess adequate assurances of reliability and should be admissible. It believed, however, as did the Court, that statements of this type tending to exculpate the accused are more suspect and so should have their admissibility conditioned upon some further provision insuring trustworthiness. The proposal in the Court Rule to add a requirement of simple corroboration was, however, deemed ineffective to accomplish this purpose since the accused's own testimony might suffice while not necessarily increasing the reliability of the hearsay statement. The Committee settled upon the language "unless corroborating circumstances clearly indicate the trustworthiness of the statement" as affording a proper standard and degree of discretion. It was contemplated that the result in such cases as Donnelly v. United States, 228 U.S. 243 (1912), where the circumstances plainly indicated reliability, would be changed. The Committee also added to the Rule the final sentence from the 1971 Advisory Committee draft, designed to codify the doctrine of Bruton v. United States, 391 U.S. 123 (1968). The Committee does not intend to affect the existing exception to the Bruton principle where the codefendant takes the stand and is subject to cross-examination, but believed there was no need to make specific provision for this situation in the Rule, since in that event the declarant would not be "unavailable". House Report No. 93-650.

Note to Subdivision (a)(5). Subdivision (a) of rule 804 as submitted by the Supreme Court defined the conditions under which a witness was considered to be unavailable. It was amended in the House.

The purpose of the amendment, according to the report of the House Committee on the Judiciary, is "primarily to require that an attempt be made to depose a witness (as well as to seek his attendance) as a precondition to the witness being unavailable."

Under the House amendment, before a witness is declared unavailable, a party must try to depose a witness (declarant) with respect to dying declarations, declarations against interest, and declarations of pedigree. None of these situations would seem to warrant this needless, impractical and highly restrictive complication. A good case can be made for eliminating the unavailability requirement entirely for declarations against interest cases. [Uniform rule 63(10); Kan.Stat. Anno. 60-460(j); 2A N.J.Stats.Anno. 84-63(10).]

In dying declaration cases, the declarant will usually, though not necessarily, be deceased at the time of trial. Pedigree statements which are admittedly and necessarily based largely on word of mouth are not greatly fortified by a deposition requirement.

Depositions are expensive and time-consuming. In any event, deposition procedures are available to those who wish to resort to them. Moreover, the deposition procedures of the Civil Rules and Criminal Rules are only imperfectly adapted to implementing the amendment. No purpose is served unless the deposition, if taken, may be used in evidence. Under Civil Rule (a)(3) the Criminal Rule 15(e), a deposition, though taken, may not be admissible, and under Criminal Rule 15(a) substantial obstacles exist in the way of even taking a deposition.

For these reasons, the committee deleted the House amendment.

The committee understands that the rule as to unavailability, as explained by the Advisory Committee "contains no requirement that an attempt be made to take the deposition of a declarant." In reflecting the committee's judgment, the statement is accurate insofar as it goes. Where, however, the proponent of the statement, with knowledge of the existence of the statement, fails to confront the declarant with the statement at the taking of the deposition, then the proponent should not, in fairness, be permitted to treat the declarant as "unavailable" simply because the declarant was not amenable to process compelling his attendance at trial. The committee does not consider it necessary to amend the rule to this effect because such a situation abuses, not conforms to, the rule. Fairness would preclude a person from introducing a hearsay statement on a particular issue if the person taking the deposition was aware of the issue at the time of the deposition but failed to depose the unavailable witness on that issue.

Note to Subdivision (b)(1). Former testimony.--Rule 804(b)(1) as submitted by the Court allowed prior testimony of an unavailable witness to be admissible if the party against whom it is offered or a person "with motive and interest similar" to his had an opportunity to examine the witness.

The House amended the rule to apply only to a party's predecessor in interest. Although the committee recognizes considerable merit to the rule submitted by the Supreme Court, a position which has been advocated by many scholars and judges, we have concluded that the difference between the two versions is not great and we accept the House amendment.

Note to Subdivision (b)(3). The rule defines those statements which are considered to be against interest and thus of sufficient trustworthiness to be admissible even though hearsay. With regard to the type of interest declared against, the version submitted by the Supreme Court included inter alia, statements tending to subject a declarant to civil liability or to invalidate a claim by him against another. The House struck these provisions as redundant. In view of the conflicting case law construing pecuniary or proprietary interests narrowly so as to exclude, e.g., tort cases, this deletion could be misconstrued.

Three States which have recently codified their rules of evidence have followed the Supreme Court's version of this rule, i.e., that a statement is against interest if it tends to subject a declarant to civil liability. [Nev.Rev.Stats. § 51.345; N.Mex.Stats. (1973 Supp.) § 20-4-804(4); West's Wis.Stats.Anno. (1973 Supp.) § 908.045(4).]

The committee believes that the reference to statements tending to subject a person to civil liability constitutes a desirable clarification of the scope of the rule. Therefore, we have reinstated the Supreme Court language on this matter.

The Court rule also proposed to expand the hearsay limitation from its present federal limitation to include statements subjecting the declarant to statements tending to make him an object of hatred, ridicule, or disgrace. The House eliminated the latter category from the subdivision as lacking sufficient guarantees of reliability. Although there is considerable support for the admissibility of such statements (all three of the State rules referred to supra, would admit such statements), we accept the deletion by the House.

The House amended this exception to add a sentence making inadmissible a statement or confession offered against the accused in a criminal case, made by a codefendant or other person implicating both himself and the accused. The sentence was added to codify the constitutional principle announced in Bruton v. United States, 391 U.S. 123 (1968). Bruton held that the admission of the extrajudicial hearsay statement of one codefendant inculpating a second codefendant violated the confrontation clause of the sixth amendment.

The committee decided to delete this provision because the basic approach of the rules is to avoid codifying, or attempting to codify, constitutional evidentiary principles, such as the fifth amendment's right against self-incrimination and, here, the sixth amendment's right of confrontation. Codification of a constitutional principle is unnecessary and, where the principle is under development, often unwise. Furthermore, the House provision does not appear to recognize the exceptions to the Bruton rule, e.g. where the codefendant takes the stand and is subject to cross examination; where the accused confessed, see United States v. Mancusi, 404 F.2d 296 (2d Cir.1968), cert. denied 397 U.S. 942 (1907); where the accused was placed at the scene of the crime, see United States v. Zelker, 452 F.2d 1009 (2d Cir.1971). For these reasons, the committee decided to delete this provision.

Note to Subdivision (b)(5). See Note to Paragraph (24), Notes of Committee on the Judiciary, Senate Report No. 93-1277, set out as a note under rule 803 of these rules. Senate Report No. 93-1277.

Rule 804 defines what hearsay statements are admissible in evidence if the declarant is unavailable as a witness. The Senate amendments make four changes in the rule.

Note to Subdivision (a)(5). Subsection (a) defines the term "unavailability as a witness". The House bill provides in subsection (a)(5) that the party who desires to use the statement must be unable to procure the declarant's attendance by process or other reasonable means. In the case of dying declarations, statements against interest and statements of personal or family history, the House bill requires that the proponent must also be unable to procure the declarant's testimony (such as by deposition or interrogatories) by process or other reasonable means. The Senate amendment eliminates this latter provision.

The Conference adopts the provision contained in the House bill.

Note to Subdivision (b)(3). The Senate amendment to subsection (b)(3) provides that a statement is against interest and not excluded by the hearsay rule when the declarant is unavailable as a witness, if the statement tends to subject a person to civil or criminal liability or renders invalid a claim by him against another. The House bill did not refer specifically to civil liability and to rendering invalid a claim against another. The Senate amendment also deletes from the House bill the provision that subsection (b)(3) does not apply to a statement or confession, made by a codefendant or another, which implicates the accused and the person who made the statement, when that statement or confession is offered against the accused in a criminal case.

The Conference adopts the Senate amendment. The Conferees intend to include within the purview of this rule, statements subjecting a person to civil liability and statements rendering claims invalid. The Conferees agree to delete the provision regarding statements by a codefendant, thereby reflecting the general approach in the Rules of Evidence to avoid attempting to codify constitutional evidentiary principles.

Note to Subdivision (b)(5). The Senate amendment adds a new subsection, (b)(6) [now (b)(5)], which makes admissible a hearsay statement not specifically covered by any of the five previous subsections, if the statement has equivalent circumstantial guarantees of trustworthiness and if the court determines that (A) the statement is offered as evidence of a material fact; (B) the statement is more probative on the point for which it is offered than any other evidence the proponent can procure through reasonable efforts; and (C) the general purposes of these rules and the interests of justice will best be served by admission of the statement into evidence.

The House bill eliminated a similar, but broader, provision because of the conviction that such a provision injected too much uncertainty into the law of evidence regarding hearsay and impaired the ability of a litigant to prepare adequately for trial.

The Conference adopts the Senate amendment with an amendment that renumbers this subsection and provides that a party intending to request the court to use a statement under this provision must notify any adverse party of this intention as well as of the particulars of the statement, including the name and address of the declarant. This notice must be given sufficiently in advance of the trial or hearing to provide any adverse party with a fair opportunity to prepare to contest the use of the statement. House Report No. 93-1597.

1987 Amendments

The amendments are technical. No substantive change is intended.

1997 Amendments
Subdivision (b)(5). The contents of Rule 803(24) and Rule 804(b)(5) have been combined and transferred to a new Rule 807. This was done to facilitate additions to Rules 803 and 804. No change in meaning is intended.

Subdivision (b)(6). Rule 804(b)(6) has been added to provide that a party forfeits the right to object on hearsay grounds to the admission of a declarant's prior statement when the party's deliberate wrongdoing or acquiescence therein procured the unavailability of the declarant as a witness. This recognizes the need for a prophylactic rule to deal with abhorrent behavior "which strikes at the heart of the system of justice itself." United States v. Mastrangelo, 693 F.2d 269, 273 (2d Cir.1982), cert. denied, 467 U.S. 1204 (1984). The wrongdoing need not consist of a criminal act. The rule applies to all parties, including the government.

Every circuit that has resolved the question has recognized the principle of forfeiture by misconduct, although the tests for determining whether there is a forfeiture have varied. See, e.g., United States v. Aguiar, 975 F.2d 45, 47 (2d Cir.1992); United States v. Potamitis, 739 F.2d 784, 789 (2d Cir.), cert. denied, 469 U.S. 918 (1984); Steele v. Taylor, 684 F.2d 1193, 1199 (6th Cir.1982), cert. denied, 460 U.S. 1053 (1983); United States v. Balano, 618 F.2d 624, 629 (10th Cir.1979), cert. denied, 449 U.S. 840 (1980); United States v. Carlson, 547 F.2d 1346, 1358-59 (8th Cir.), cert. denied, 431 U.S. 914 (1977). The foregoing cases apply a preponderance of the evidence standard. Contra United States v. Thevis, 665 F.2d 616, 631 (5th Cir.) (clear and convincing standard), cert. denied, 459 U.S. 825 (1982). The usual Rule 104(a) preponderance of the evidence standard has been adopted in light of the behavior the new Rule 804(b)(6) seeks to discourage.

GAP Report on Rule 804(b)(5). The words "Transferred to Rule 807" were substituted for "Abrogated".

GAP Report on Rule 804(b)(6). The title of the rule was changed to "Forfeiture by wrongdoing." The word "who" in line 24 was changed to "that" to indicate that the rule is potentially applicable against the government. Two sentences were added to the first paragraph of the committee note to clarify that the wrongdoing need not be criminal in nature, and to indicate the rule's potential applicability to the government. The word "forfeiture" was substituted for "waiver" in the note.

Rule 805. Hearsay Within Hearsay

Hearsay included within hearsay is not excluded under the hearsay rule if each part of the combined statements conforms with an exception to the hearsay rule provided in these rules.

Rule 806. Attacking and Supporting Credibility of Declarant

When a hearsay statement, or a statement defined in Rule 801(d)(2)(C), (D), or (E), has been admitted in evidence, the credibility of the declarant may be attacked, and if attacked may be supported, by any evidence which would be admissible for those purposes if declarant had testified as a witness. Evidence of a statement or conduct by the declarant at any time, inconsistent with the declarant's hearsay statement, is not subject to any requirement that the declarant may have been afforded an opportunity to deny or explain. If the party against whom a hearsay statement has been admitted calls the declarant as a witness, the party is entitled to examine the declarant on the statement as if under cross-examination.

ADVISORY COMMITTEE NOTES

1972 Proposed Rules

On principle it scarcely seems open to doubt that the hearsay rule should not call for exclusion of a hearsay statement which includes a further hearsay statement when both conform to the requirements of a hearsay exception. Thus a hospital record might contain an entry of the patient's age based on information furnished by his wife. The hospital record would qualify as a regular entry except that the person who furnished the information was not acting in the routine of the business. However, her statement independently qualifies as a statement of pedigree (if she is unavailable) or as a statement made for purposes of diagnosis or treatment, and hence each link in the chain falls under sufficient assurances. Or, further to illustrate, a dying declaration may incorporate a declaration against interest by another declarant. See McCormick § 290, p. 611.

ADVISORY COMMITTEE NOTES

1972 Proposed Rules

The declarant of a hearsay statement which is admitted in evidence is in effect a witness. His credibility should in fairness be subject to impeachment and support as though he had in fact testified. See Rules 608 and 609. There are however, some special aspects of the impeaching of a hearsay declarant which require consideration. These special aspects center upon impeachment by inconsistent statement, arise from factual differences which exist between the use of hearsay and an actual witness and also between various kinds of hearsay, and involve the question of applying to declarants the general rule disallowing evidence of an inconsistent statement to impeach a witness unless he is afforded an opportunity to deny or explain. See Rule 613(b).

The principal difference between using hearsay and an actual witness is that the inconsistent statement will in the case of the witness almost inevitably of necessity in the nature of things be a prior statement, which it is entirely possible and feasible to call to his attention, while in the case of hearsay the inconsistent statement may well be a subsequent one, which practically precludes calling it to the attention of the declarant. The result of insisting upon observation of this impossible requirement in the hearsay situation is to deny the opponent, already barred from cross-examination, any benefit of this important technique of impeachment. The writers favor allowing the subsequent statement. McCormick § 37, p. 69; 3 Wigmore § 1033. The cases, however, are divided. Cases allowing the impeachment include People v. Collup, 27 Cal.2d 829, 167 P.2d 714 (1946); People v. Rosoto, 58 Cal.2d 304, 23 Cal.Rptr. 779, 373 P.2d 867 (1962); Carver v. United States, 164 U.S. 694, 17 S.Ct. 228, 41 L.Ed. 602 (1897). Contra, Mattox v. United States, 156 U.S. 237, 15 S.Ct. 337, 39 L.Ed. 409 (1895); People v. Hines, 284 N.Y. 93, 29 N.E.2d 483 (1940). The force of Mattox, where the hearsay was the former testimony of a deceased witness and the denial of use of a subsequent inconsistent statement was upheld, is much diminished by Carver, where the hearsay was a dying declaration and denial of use of a subsequent inconsistent statement resulted in reversal. The difference in the particular brand of hearsay seems unimportant when the inconsistent statement is a subsequent one. True, the opponent is not totally deprived of cross-examination when the hearsay is former testimony or a deposition but he is deprived of cross-examining on the statement or along lines suggested by it. Mr. Justice Shiras, with two justices joining him, dissented vigorously in Mattox.

When the impeaching statement was made prior to the hearsay statement, differences in the kinds of hearsay appear which arguably may justify differences in treatment. If the hearsay consisted of a simple statement by the witness, e.g. a dying declaration or a declaration against interest, the feasibility of affording him an opportunity to deny or explain encounters the same practical impossibility as where the statement is a subsequent one, just discussed, although here the impossibility arises from the total absence of anything resembling a hearing at which the matter could be put to him. The courts by a large majority have ruled in favor of allowing the statement to be used under these circumstances. McCormick § 37, p. 69; 3 Wigmore § 1033. If, however, the hearsay consists of former testimony or a deposition, the possibility of calling the prior statement to the attention of the witness or deponent is not ruled out, since the opportunity to cross-examine was available. It might thus be concluded that with former testimony or depositions the conventional foundation should be insisted upon. Most of the cases involve depositions, and Wigmore describes them as divided. 3 Wigmore § 1031. Deposition procedures at best are cumbersome and expensive, and to require the laying of the foundation may impose an undue burden. Under the federal practice, there is no way of knowing with certainty at the time of taking a deposition whether it is merely for discovery or will ultimately end up in evidence. With respect to both former testimony and depositions the possibility exists that knowledge of the statement might not be acquired until after the time of the cross-examination.

Moreover, the expanded admissibility of former testimony and depositions under Rule 804(b)(1) calls for a correspondingly expanded approach to impeachment. The rule dispenses with the requirement in all hearsay situations, which is readily administered and best calculated to lead to fair results.

Notice should be taken that Rule 26(f) of the Federal Rules of Civil Procedure, as originally submitted by the Advisory Committee, ended with the following:

" * * * and, without having first called them to the deponent's attention, may show statements contradictory thereto made at any time by the deponent."

This language did not appear in the rule as promulgated in December, 1937. See 4 Moore's Federal Practice ¶¶ 26.01[9], 26.35 (2d ed.1967). In 1951, Nebraska adopted a provision strongly resembling the one stricken from the federal rule:

"Any party may impeach any adverse deponent by self-contradiction without having laid foundation for such impeachment at the time such deposition was taken." R.S.Neb. § 25-1267.07.

For similar provisions, see Uniform Rule 65; California Evidence Code § 1202; Kansas Code of Civil Procedure § 60-462; New Jersey Evidence Rule 65.

The provision for cross-examination of a declarant upon his hearsay statement is a corollary of general principles of cross-examination. A similar provision is found in California Evidence Code § 1203.

1974 Enactment

Rule 906, as passed by the House and as proposed by the Supreme Court provides that whenever a hearsay statement is admitted, the credibility of the declarant of the statement may be attacked, and if attacked may be supported, by any evidence which would be admissible for those purposes if the declarant had testified as a witness. Rule 801 defines what is a hearsay statement. While statements by a person authorized by a party-opponent to make a statement concerning the subject, by the party-opponent's agent or by a coconspirator of a party--see rule 801(d) (2)(c), (d) and (e)--are traditionally defined as exceptions to the hearsay rule, rule 801 defines such admission by a party-opponent as statements which are not hearsay. Consequently, rule 806 by referring exclusively to the admission of hearsay statements, does not appear to allow the credibility of the declarant to be attacked when the declarant is a coconspirator, agent or authorized spokesman. The committee is of the view that such statements should open the declarant to attacks on his credibility. Indeed, the reason such statements are excluded from the operation of rule 806 is likely attributable to the drafting technique used to codify the hearsay rule, viz. some statements, instead of being referred to as exceptions to the hearsay rule, are defined as statements which are not hearsay.

The phrase "or a statement defined in rule 801(d)(2)(c), (d) and (e)" is added to the rule in order to subject the declarant of such statements, like the declarant of hearsay statements, to attacks on his credibility. [The committee considered it unnecessary to include statements contained in rule 801(d)(2)(A) and (B)--the statement by the party-opponent himself or the statement of which he has manifested his adoption--because the credibility of the party-opponent is always subject to an attack on his credibility]. Senate Report No. 93-1277.

The Senate amendment permits an attack upon the credibility of the declarant of a statement if the statement is one by a person authorized by a party-opponent to make a statement concerning the subject, one by an agent of a party-opponent, or one by a coconspirator of the party-opponent, as these statements are defined in Rules 801(d)(2)(C), (D) and (E). The House bill has no such provision.

The Conference adopts the Senate amendment. The Senate amendment conforms the rule to present practice. House Report No. 93-1597.

1987 Amendments
The amendments are technical. No substantive change is intended.

1997 Amendments
The amendment is technical. No substantive change is intended.

GAP Report. Restylization changes in the rule were eliminated.

Rule 807. Residual Exception

A statement not specifically covered by Rule 803 or 804 but having equivalent circumstantial guarantees of trustworthiness, is not excluded by the hearsay rule, if the court determines that (A) the statement is offered as evidence of a material fact; (B) the statement is more probative on the point for which it is offered than any other evidence which the proponent can procure through reasonable efforts; and (C) the general purposes of these rules and the interests of justice will best be served by admission of the statement into evidence. However, a statement may not be admitted under this exception unless the proponent of it makes known to the adverse party sufficiently in advance of the trial or hearing to provide the adverse party with a fair opportunity to prepare to meet it, the proponent's intention to offer the statement and the particulars of it, including the name and address of the declarant.

ADVISORY COMMITTEE NOTES

1997 Amendments

The contents of Rule 803(24) and Rule 804(b)(5) have been combined and transferred to a new Rule 807. This was done to facilitate additions to Rules 803 and 804. No change in meaning is intended.

GAP Report on Rule 807. Restylization changes in the rule were eliminated.

ARTICLE IX. AUTHENTICATION AND IDENTIFICATION

Rule 901. Requirement of Authentication or Identification

(a) General provision. The requirement of authentication or identification as a condition precedent to admissibility is satisfied by evidence sufficient to support a finding that the matter in question is what its proponent claims.

(b) Illustrations. By way of illustration only, and not by way of limitation, the following are examples of authentication or identification conforming with the requirements of this rule:

(1) Testimony of witness with knowledge. Testimony that a matter is what it is claimed to be.

(2) Nonexpert opinion on handwriting. Nonexpert opinion as to the genuineness of handwriting, based upon familiarity not acquired for purposes of the litigation.

(3) Comparison by trier or expert witness. Comparison by the trier of fact or by expert witnesses with specimens which have been authenticated.

(4) Distinctive characteristics and the like. Appearance, contents, substance, internal patterns, or other distinctive characteristics, taken in conjunction with circumstances.

(5) Voice identification. Identification of a voice, whether heard firsthand or through mechanical or electronic transmission or recording, by opinion based upon hearing the voice at any time under circumstances connecting it with the alleged speaker.

(6) Telephone conversations. Telephone conversations, by evidence that a call was made to the number assigned at the time by the telephone company to a particular person or business, if (A) in the case of a person, circumstances,

including self-identification, show the person answering to be the one called, or (B) in the case of a business, the call was made to a place of business and the conversation related to business reasonably transacted over the telephone.

(7) Public records or reports. Evidence that a writing authorized by law to be recorded or filed and in fact recorded or filed in a public office, or a purported public record, report, statement, or data compilation, in any form, is from the public office where items of this nature are kept.

(8) Ancient documents or data compilation. Evidence that a document or data compilation, in any form, (A) is in such condition as to create no suspicion concerning its authenticity, (B) was in a place where it, if authentic, would likely be, and (C) has been in existence 20 years or more at the time it is offered.

(9) Process or system. Evidence describing a process or system used to produce a result and showing that the process or system produces an accurate result.

(10) Methods provided by statute or rule. Any method of authentication or identification provided by Act of Congress or by other rules prescribed by the Supreme Court pursuant to statutory authority.

ADVISORY COMMITTEE NOTES

1972 Proposed Rules

Note to Subdivision (a). Authentication and identification represent a special aspect of relevancy. Michael and Adler, Real Proof, 5 Vand.L.Rev. 344, 362 (1952); McCormick §§ 179, 185; Morgan, Basic Problems of Evidence 378 (1962). Thus a telephone conversation may be irrelevant because on an unrelated topic or because the speaker is not identified. The latter aspect is the one here involved. Wigmore describes the need for authentication as "an inherent logical necessity." 7 Wigmore § 2129, p. 564.

This requirement of showing authenticity or identity falls in the category of relevancy dependent upon fulfillment of a condition of fact and is governed by the procedure set forth in Rule 104(b).

The common law approach to authentication of documents has been criticized as an "attitude of agnosticism," McCormick, Cases on Evidence 388, n. 4 (3rd ed. 1956), as one which "departs sharply from men's customs in ordinary affairs," and as presenting only a slight obstacle to the introduction of forgeries in comparison to the time and expense devoted to proving genuine writings which correctly show their origin on their face, McCormick § 185, pp. 395, 396. Today, such available procedures as requests to admit and pretrial conference afford the means of eliminating much of the need for authentication or identification. Also, significant inroads upon the traditional insistence on authentication and identification have been made by accepting as at least prima facie genuine items of the kind treated in Rule 902, infra. However, the need for suitable methods of proof still remains, since criminal cases pose their own obstacles to the use of preliminary procedures, unforeseen contingencies may arise, and cases of genuine controversy will still occur.

Note to Subdivision (b). The treatment of authentication and identification draws largely upon the experience embodied in the common law and in statutes to furnish illustrative applications of the general principle set forth in subdivision (a). The examples are not intended as an exclusive enumeration of allowable methods but are meant to guide and suggest, leaving room for growth and development in this area of the law.

The examples relate for the most part to documents, with some attention given to voice communications and computer printouts. As Wigmore noted, no special rules have been developed for authenticating chattels. Wigmore, Code of Evidence § 2086 (3rd ed. 1942).

It should be observed that compliance with requirements of authentication or identification by no means assures admission of an item into evidence, as other bars, hearsay for example, may remain.

Example (1). Example (1) contemplates a broad spectrum ranging from testimony of a witness who was present at the signing of a document to testimony establishing narcotics as taken from an accused and accounting for custody through the period until trial, including laboratory analysis. See California Evidence Code § 1413, eyewitness to signing.

Example (2). Example (2) states conventional doctrine as to lay identification of handwriting, which recognizes that a sufficient familiarity with the handwriting of another person may be acquired by seeing him write, by exchanging correspondence, or by other means, to afford a basis for identifying it on subsequent occasions. McCormick § 189. See also California Evidence Code § 1416. Testimony based upon familiarity acquired for purposes of the litigation is reserved to the expert under the example which follows.

Example (3). The history of common law restrictions upon the technique of proving or disproving the genuineness of a disputed specimen of handwriting through comparison with a genuine specimen, by either the testimony of expert witnesses or direct viewing by the triers themselves, is detailed in 7 Wigmore §§ 1991-1994. In breaking away, the English Common Law Procedure Act of

1854, 17 and 18 Vict., c. 125, § 27, cautiously allowed expert or trier to use exemplars "proved to the satisfaction of the judge to be genuine" for purposes of comparison. The language found its way into numerous statutes in this country, e.g., California Evidence Code §§ 1417, 1418. While explainable as a measure of prudence in the process of breaking with precedent in the handwriting situation, the reservation to the judge of the question of the genuineness of exemplars and the imposition of an unusually high standard of persuasion are at variance with the general treatment of relevancy which depends upon fulfillment of a condition of fact. Rule 104(b). No similar attitude is found in other comparison situations, e.g., ballistics comparison by jury, as in Evans v. Commonwealth, 230 Ky. 411, 19 S.W.2d 1091 (1929), or by experts, Annot., 26 A.L.R.2d 892, and no reason appears for its continued existence in handwriting cases. Consequently Example (3) sets no higher standard for handwriting specimens and treats all comparison situations alike, to be governed by Rule 104(b). This approach is consistent with 28 U.S.C. § 1731: "The admitted or proved handwriting of any person shall be admissible, for purposes of comparison, to determine genuineness of other handwriting attributed to such person."

Precedent supports the acceptance of visual comparison as sufficiently satisfying preliminary authentication requirements for admission in evidence. Brandon v. Collins, 267 F.2d 731 (2d Cir.1959); Wausau Sulphate Fibre Co. v. Commissioner of Internal Revenue, 61 F.2d 879 (7th Cir.1932); Desimone v. United States, 227 F.2d 864 (9th Cir.1955).

Example (4). The characteristics of the offered item itself, considered in the light of circumstances, afford authentication techniques in great variety. Thus a document or telephone conversation may be shown to have emanated from a particular person by virtue of its disclosing knowledge of facts known peculiarly to him; Globe Automatic Sprinkler Co. v. Braniff, 89 Okl. 105, 214 P. 127 (1923); California Evidence Code § 1421; similarly, a letter may be authenticated by content and circumstances indicating it was in reply to a duly authenticated one. McCormick § 192; California Evidence Code § 1420. Language patterns may indicate authenticity or its opposite. Magnuson v. State, 187 Wis. 122, 203 N.W. 749 (1925); Arens and Meadow, Psycholinguistics and the Confession Dilemma, 56 Colum.L.Rev. 19 (1956).

Example (5). Since aural voice identification is not a subject of expert testimony, the requisite familiarity may be acquired either before or after the particular speaking which is the subject of the identification, in this respect resembling visual identification of a person rather than identification of handwriting. Cf. Example (2), supra, People v. Nichols, 378 Ill. 487, 38 N.E.2d 766 (1942); McGuire v. State, 200 Md. 601, 92 A.2d 582 (1952); State v. McGee, 336 Mo. 1082, 83 S.W.2d 98 (1935).

Example (6). The cases are in agreement that a mere assertion of his identity by a person talking on the telephone is not sufficient evidence of the authenticity of the conversation and that additional evidence of his identity is required. The additional evidence need not fall in any set pattern. Thus the content of his statements or the reply technique, under Example (4), supra, or voice identification under Example (5), may furnish the necessary foundation. Outgoing calls made by the witness involve additional factors bearing upon authenticity. The calling of a number assigned by the telephone company reasonably supports the assumption that the listing is correct and that the number is the one reached. If the number is that of a place of business, the mass of authority allows an ensuing conversation if it relates to business reasonably transacted over the telephone, on the theory that the maintenance of the telephone connection is an invitation to do business without further identification. Matton v. Hoover Co., 350 Mo. 506, 166 S.W.2d 557 (1942); City of Pawhuska v. Crutchfield, 147 Okl. 4, 293 P. 1095 (1930); Zurich General Acc. & Liability Ins. Co. v. Baum, 159 Va. 404, 165 S.E. 518 (1932). Otherwise, some additional circumstance of identification of the speaker is required. The authorities divide on the question whether the self-identifying statement of the person answering suffices. Example (6) answers in the affirmative on the assumption that usual conduct respecting telephone calls furnish adequate assurances of regularity, bearing in mind that the entire matter is open to exploration before the trier of fact. In general, see McCormick § 193; 7 Wigmore § 2155; Annot., 71 A.L.R. 5, 105 id. 326.

Example (7). Public records are regularly authenticated by proof of custody, without more. McCormick § 191; 7 Wigmore §§ 2158, 2159. The example extends the principle to include data stored in computers and similar methods, of which increasing use in the public records area may be expected. See California Evidence Code §§ 1532, 1600.

Example (8). The familiar ancient document rule of the common law is extended to include data stored electronically or by other similar means. Since the importance of appearance diminishes in this situation, the importance of custody or place where found increases correspondingly. This expansion is necessary in view of the widespread use of methods of storing data in forms other than conventional written records.

Any time period selected is bound to be arbitrary. The common law period of 30 years is here reduced to 20 years, with some shift of emphasis from the probable unavailability of witnesses to the unlikeliness of a still viable fraud after the lapse of time. The shorter period is specified in the English Evidence Act of 1938, 1 & 2 Geo. 6, c. 28, and in Oregon R.S.1963, § 41.360(34). See also the numerous statutes prescribing periods of less than 30 years in the case of recorded documents. 7 Wigmore § 2143.

The application of Example (8) is not subject to any limitation to title documents or to any requirement that possession, in the case of a title document, has been consistent with the document. See McCormick § 190.

Example (9). Example (9) is designed for situations in which the accuracy of a result is dependent upon a process or system which produces it. X rays afford a familiar instance. Among more recent developments is the computer, as to which see Transport Indemnity Co. v. Seib, 178 Neb. 253, 132 N.W.2d 871 (1965); State v. Veres, 7 Ariz.App. 117, 436 P.2d 629 (1968); Merrick v. United States Rubber Co., 7 Ariz.App. 433, 440 P.2d 314 (1968); Freed, Computer Print-Outs as Evidence, 16 Am.Jur.Proof of Facts 273; Symposium, Law and Computers in the Mid-Sixties, ALI-ABA (1966); 37 Albany L.Rev. 61 (1967). Example (9) does not, of course, foreclose taking judicial notice of the accuracy of the process or system.

Example (10). The example makes clear that methods of authentication provided by Act of Congress and by the Rules of Civil and Criminal Procedure or by Bankruptcy Rules are not intended to be superseded. Illustrative are the provisions for authentication of official records in Civil Procedure Rule 44 and Criminal Procedure Rule 27, for authentication of records of proceedings by court reporters in 28 U.S.C. § 753(b) and Civil Procedure Rule 80(c), and for authentication of depositions in Civil Procedure Rule 30(f).

Rule 902. Admissibility of Duplicates

Extrinsic evidence of authenticity as a condition precedent to admissibility is not required with respect to the following: (1) Domestic public documents under seal. A document bearing a seal purporting to be that of the United States, or of any State, district, Commonwealth, territory, or insular possession thereof, or the Panama Canal Zone, or the Trust Territory of the Pacific Islands, or of a political subdivision, department, officer, or agency thereof, and a signature purporting to be an attestation or execution.

(2) Domestic public documents not under seal. A document purporting to bear the signature in the official capacity of an officer or employee of any entity included in paragraph (1) hereof, having no seal, if a public officer having a seal and having official duties in the district or political subdivision of the officer or employee certifies under seal that the signer has the official capacity and that the signature is genuine. (3) Foreign public documents. A document purporting to be executed or attested in an official capacity by a person authorized by the laws of a foreign country to make the execution or attestation, and accompanied by a final certification as to the genuineness of

the signature and official position (A) of the executing or attesting person, or (B) of any foreign official whose certificate of genuineness of signature and official position relates to the execution or attestation or is in a chain of certificates of genuineness of signature and official position relating to the execution or attestation. A final certification may be made by a secretary of an embassy or legation, consul general, consul, vice consul, or consular agent of the United States, or a diplomatic or consular official of the foreign country assigned or accredited to the United States. If reasonable opportunity has been given to all parties to investigate the authenticity and accuracy of official documents, the court may, for good cause shown, order that they be treated as presumptively authentic without final certification or permit them to be evidenced by an attested summary with or without final certification.

(4) Certified copies of public records. A copy of an official record or report or entry therein, or of a document authorized by law to be recorded or filed and actually recorded or filed in a public office, including data compilations in any form, certified as correct by the custodian or other person authorized to make the certification, by certificate complying with paragraph (1), (2), or (3) of this rule or complying with any Act of Congress or rule prescribed by the Supreme Court pursuant to statutory authority.

(5) Official publications. Books, pamphlets, or other publications purporting to be issued by public authority.

(6) Newspapers and periodicals. Printed materials purporting to be newspapers or periodicals.

(7) Trade inscriptions and the like. Inscriptions, signs, tags, or labels purporting to have been affixed in the course of business and indicating ownership, control, or origin.

(8) Acknowledged documents. Documents accompanied by a certificate of acknowledgment executed in the manner provided by law by a notary public or other officer authorized by law to take acknowledgments.

(9) Commercial paper and related documents. Commercial paper, signatures thereon, and documents relating thereto to the extent provided by general commercial law.

(10) Presumptions under Acts of Congress. Any signature, document, or other matter declared by Act of Congress to be presumptively or prima facie genuine or authentic.

(11) Certified Domestic Records of Regularly Conducted Activity.--The original or a duplicate of a domestic record of regularly conducted activity that would be admissible under Rule 803(6) if accompanied by a written declaration of its custodian or other qualified person, in a manner complying with any Act of Congress or rule prescribed by the Supreme Court pursuant to statutory authority, certifying that the record--

(A) was made at or near the time of the occurrence of the matters set forth by, or from information transmitted by, a person with knowledge of those matters;

(B) was kept in the course of the regularly conducted activity; and

(C) was made by the regularly conducted activity as a regular practice.

A party intending to offer a record into evidence under this paragraph must provide written notice of that intention to all adverse parties, and must make the record and declaration available for inspection sufficiently in advance of their offer into evidence to provide an adverse party with a fair opportunity to challenge them.

(12) Certified Foreign Records of Regularly Conducted Activity.--In a civil case, the original or a duplicate of a foreign record of regularly conducted activity that would be admissible under Rule 803(6) if accompanied by a written declaration by its custodian or other qualified person certifying that the record--

(A) was made at or near the time of the occurrence of the matters set forth by, or from information transmitted by, a person with knowledge of those matters;

(B) was kept in the course of the regularly conducted activity; and

(C) was made by the regularly conducted activity as a regular practice.

The declaration must be signed in a manner that, if falsely made, would subject the maker to criminal penalty under the laws of the country where the declaration is signed. A party intending to offer a record into evidence under this paragraph must provide written notice of that intention to all adverse parties, and must make the record and declaration available for inspection sufficiently in advance of their offer into evidence to provide an adverse party with a fair opportunity to challenge them

ADVISORY COMMITTEE NOTES

1972 Proposed Rules

Case law and statutes have, over the years, developed a substantial body of instances in which authenticity is taken as sufficiently established for purposes of admissibility without extrinsic evidence to that effect, sometimes for reasons of policy but perhaps more often because practical considerations reduce the possibility of unauthenticity to a very small dimension. The present rule collects and incorporates these situations, in some instances expanding them to occupy a larger area which their underlying considerations justify. In no instance is the opposite party foreclosed from disputing authenticity.

Note to Paragraph (1). The acceptance of documents bearing a public seal and signature, most often encountered in practice in the form of acknowledgments or certificates authenticating copies of public records, is actually of broad application. Whether theoretically based in whole or in part upon judicial notice, the practical underlying considerations are that forgery is a crime and detection is fairly easy and certain. 7 Wigmore § 2161, p. 638; California Evidence Code § 1452. More than 50 provisions for judicial notice of official seals are contained in the United States Code.

Note to Paragraph (2). While statutes are found which raise a presumption of genuineness of purported official signatures in the absence of an official seal, 7 Wigmore § 2167; California Evidence Code § 1453, the greater ease of effecting a forgery under these circumstances is apparent. Hence this paragraph of the rule calls for authentication by an officer who has a seal. Notarial acts by members of the armed forces and other special situations are covered in paragraph (10).

Note to Paragraph (3). Paragraph (3) provides a method for extending the presumption of authenticity to foreign official documents by a procedure of certification. It is derived from Rule 44(a)(2) of the Rules of Civil Procedure but is broader in applying to public documents rather than being limited to public records.

Note to Paragraph (4). The common law and innumerable statutes have recognized the procedure of authenticating copies of public records by certificate. The certificate qualifies as a public document, receivable as authentic when in conformity with paragraph (1), (2), or (3). Rule 44(a) of the Rules of Civil Procedure and Rule 27 of the Rules of Criminal Procedure have provided authentication procedures of this nature for both domestic and foreign public records. It will be observed that the certification procedure here provided extends only to public records, reports, and recorded documents, all including data compilations, and does not apply to public documents generally. Hence documents provable when presented in original form under paragraphs (1), (2), or (3) may not be provable by certified copy under paragraph (4).

Note to Paragraph (5). Dispensing with preliminary proof of the genuineness of purportedly official publications, most commonly encountered in connection with statutes, court reports, rules, and regulations, has been greatly enlarged by statutes and decisions. 5 Wigmore § 1684. Paragraph (5), it will be noted, does not confer admissibility upon all official publications; it merely provides a means whereby their authenticity may be taken as established for purposes of admissibility. Rule 44(a) of the Rules of Civil Procedure has been to the same effect.

Note to Paragraph (6). The likelihood of forgery of newspapers or periodicals is slight indeed. Hence no danger is apparent in receiving them. Establishing the authenticity of the publication may, of course, leave still open questions of authority and responsibility for items therein contained. See 7 Wigmore § 2150. Cf. 39 U.S.C. § 4005(b), public advertisement prima facie evidence of agency of person named, in postal fraud order proceeding; Canadian Uniform Evidence Act, Draft of 1936, printed copy of newspaper prima facie evidence that notices or advertisements were authorized.

Note to Paragraph (7). Several factors justify dispensing with preliminary proof of genuineness of commercial and mercantile labels and the like. The risk of forgery is minimal. Trademark infringement involves serious penalties. Great efforts are devoted to inducing the public to buy in reliance on brand names, and substantial protection is given them. Hence the fairness of this treatment finds recognition in the cases. Curtiss Candy Co. v. Johnson, 163 Miss. 426, 141 So. 762 (1932), Baby Ruth candy bar; Doyle v. Continental Baking Co., 262 Mass. 516, 160 N.E. 325 (1928), loaf of bread; Weiner v. Mager & Throne, Inc., 167 Misc. 338, 3 N.Y.S.2d 918 (1938), same. And see W.Va.Code 1966, § 47-3-5, trademark on bottle prima facie evidence of ownership. Contra, Keegan v. Green Giant Co., 150 Me. 283, 110 A.2d 599 (1954); Murphy v. Campbell Soup Co., 62 F.2d 564 (1st Cir.1933). Cattle brands have received similar acceptance in the western states. Rev.Code Mont.1947, § 46-606, State v. Wolfley, 75 Kan. 406, 89 P. 1046 (1907); Annot., 11 L.R.A.(N.S.) 87. Inscriptions on trains and vehicles are held to be prima facie evidence of ownership or control. Pittsburgh, Ft. W. & C. Ry. v. Callaghan, 157 Ill. 406, 41 N.E. 909 (1895); 9 Wigmore § 2510a. See also the provision of 19 U.S.C. § 1615(2) that marks, labels, brands, or stamps indicating foreign origin are prima facie evidence of foreign origin of merchandise.

Note to Paragraph (8). In virtually every state, acknowledged title documents are receivable in evidence without further proof. Statutes are collected in 5 Wigmore § 1676. If this authentication suffices for documents of the importance of those affecting titles, logic scarcely permits denying this method when other kinds of documents are involved. Instances of broadly inclusive statutes are California Evidence Code § 1451 and N.Y.CPLR 4538, McKinney's Consol.Laws 1963.

Note to Paragraph (9). Issues of the authenticity of commercial paper in federal courts will usually arise in diversity cases, will involve an element of a cause of action or defense, and with respect to presumptions and burden of proof will be controlled by Erie Railroad Co. v. Tompkins, 304 U.S. 64, 58 S.Ct. 817, 82 L.Ed. 1188 (1938). Rule 302, supra. There may, however, be questions of authenticity involving lesser segments of a case or the case may be one governed by federal common law. Clearfield Trust Co. v. United States, 318 U.S. 363, 63 S.Ct. 573, 87 L.Ed. 838 (1943). Cf. United States v. Yazell, 382 U.S. 341, 86 S.Ct. 500, 15 L.Ed.2d 404 (1966). In these situations, resort to the useful authentication provisions of the Uniform Commercial Code is provided for. While the phrasing is in terms of "general commercial law," in order to avoid the potential complications inherent in borrowing local statutes, today one would have difficulty in determining the general commercial law without referring to the Code. See Williams v. Walker-Thomas Furniture Co., 121 U.S.App.D.C. 315, 350 F.2d 445 (1965). Pertinent Code provisions are sections 1-202, 3-307, and 3-510, dealing with third-party documents, signatures on negotiable instruments, protests, and statements of dishonor.

Note to Paragraph (10). The paragraph continues in effect dispensations with preliminary proof of genuineness provided in various Acts of Congress. See, for example, 10 U.S.C. § 936, signature, without seal, together with title, prima facie evidence of authenticity of acts of certain military personnel who are given notarial powers; 15 U.S.C. § 77f(a), signature on SEC registration presumed genuine; 26 U.S.C. § 6064, signature to tax return prima facie genuine.

1974 Enactment
Note to Paragraph (8). Rule 902(8) as submitted by the Court referred to certificates of acknowledgment "under the hand and seal of" a notary public or other officer authorized by law to take acknowledgments. The Committee amended the Rule to eliminate the requirement, believed to be inconsistent with the law in some States, that a notary public must affix a seal to a document acknowledged before him. As amended the Rule merely requires that the document be executed in the manner prescribed by State law.

Note to Paragraph (9). The Committee approved Rule 902(9) as submitted by the Court. With respect to the meaning of the phrase "general commercial law", the Committee intends that the Uniform Commercial Code, which has been adopted in virtually every State, will be followed generally, but that federal commercial law will apply where federal commercial paper is involved. See Clearfield Trust Co. v. United States, 318 U.S. 363 (1943). Further, in those instances in which the issues are governed by Erie R. Co. v. Tompkins, 304 U.S. 64 (1938), State law will apply irrespective of whether it is the Uniform Commercial Code. House Report No. 93-650.

1987 Amendments
The amendments are technical. No substantive change is intended.

1988 Amendments
These two sentences were inadvertently eliminated from the 1987 amendments. The amendment is technical. No substantive change is intended.

2000 Amendments
The amendment adds two new paragraphs to the rule on self-authentication. It sets forth a procedure by which parties can authenticate certain records of regularly conducted activity, other than through the testimony of a foundation witness. See the amendment to Rule 803(6). 18 U.S.C. § 3505 currently provides a means for certifying foreign records of regularly conducted activity in criminal cases, and this amendment is intended to establish a similar procedure for domestic records, and for foreign records offered in civil cases.

A declaration that satisfies 28 U.S.C. § 1746 would satisfy the declaration requirement of Rule 902(11), as would any comparable certification under oath.

The notice requirement in Rules 902(11) and (12) is intended to give the opponent of the evidence a full opportunity to test the adequacy of the foundation set forth in the declaration.

GAP Report--Proposed Amendment to Rule 902

The Committee made the following changes to the published draft of the proposed amendment to Evidence Rule 902:

1. Minor stylistic changes were made in the text, in accordance with suggestions of the Style Subcommittee of the Standing Committee on Rules of Practice and Procedure.

2. The phrase "in a manner complying with any Act of Congress or rule prescribed by the Supreme Court pursuant to statutory authority" was added to proposed Rule 902(11), to provide consistency with Evidence Rule 902(4). The Committee Note was amended to accord with this textual change.

3. Minor stylistic changes were made in the text to provide a uniform construction of the terms "declaration" and "certifying."

4. The notice provisions in the text were revised to clarify that the proponent must make both the declaration and the underlying record available for inspection.

Rule 903. Subscribing Witness' Testimony Unnecessary

The testimony of a subscribing witness is not necessary to authenticate a writing unless required by the laws of the jurisdiction whose laws govern the validity of the writing.

ADVISORY COMMITTEE NOTES

1972 Proposed Rules
The common law required that attesting witnesses be produced or accounted for. Today the requirement has generally been abolished except with respect to documents which must be attested to be valid, e.g. wills in some states. McCormick § 188. Uniform Rule 71; California Evidence Code § 1411; Kansas Code of Civil Procedure § 60-468; New Jersey Evidence Rule 71; New York CPLR Rule 4537.

ARTICLE X. CONTENTS OF WRITINGS, RECORDINGS AND PHOTOGRAPHS

Rule 1001. Definitions

For purposes of this article the following definitions are applicable:

(1) Writings and recordings. "Writings" and "recordings" consist of letters, words, or numbers, or their equivalent, set down by handwriting, typewriting, printing, photostating, photographing, magnetic impulse, mechanical or electronic recording, or other form of data compilation.

(2) Photographs. "Photographs" include still photographs, X-ray films, video tapes, and motion pictures.

(3) Original. An "original" of a writing or recording is the writing or recording itself or any counterpart intended to have the same effect by a person executing or issuing it. An "original" of a photograph includes the negative or any print therefrom. If data are stored in a computer or similar device, any printout or other output readable by sight, shown to reflect the data accurately, is an "original".

(4) Duplicate. A "duplicate" is a counterpart produced by the same impression as the original, or from the same matrix, or by means of photography, including enlargements and miniatures, or by mechanical or electronic re-recording, or by chemical reproduction, or by other equivalent techniques which accurately reproduces the original.

ADVISORY COMMITTEE NOTES

1972 Proposed Rules

In an earlier day, when discovery and other related procedures were strictly limited, the misleading named "best evidence rule" afforded substantial guarantees against inaccuracies and fraud by its insistence upon production or original documents. The great enlargement of the scope of discovery and related procedures in recent times has measurably reduced the need for the rule. Nevertheless important areas of usefulness persist: discovery of documents outside the jurisdiction may require substantial outlay of time and money; the unanticipated document may not practically be discoverable; criminal cases have built-in limitations on discovery. Cleary and Strong, The Best Evidence Rule: An Evaluation in Context, 51 Iowa L.Rev. 825 (1966).

Note to Paragraph (1). Traditionally the rule requiring the original centered upon accumulations of data and expressions affecting legal relations set forth in words and figures. this meant that the rule was one essentially related to writings. Present day techniques have expanded methods of storing data, yet the essential form which the information ultimately assumes for usable purposes is words and figures. Hence the considerations underlying the rule dictate its expansion to include computers, photographic systems, and other modern developments.

Note to Paragraph (3). In most instances, what is an original will be self-evident and further refinement will be unnecessary. However, in some instances particularized definition is required. A carbon copy of a contract executed in duplicate becomes an original, as does a sales ticket carbon copy given to a customer. While strictly speaking the original of a photograph might be thought to be only the negative, practicality and common usage require that any print from the negative be regarded as an original. Similarly, practicality and usage confer the status of original upon any computer printout. Transport Indemnity Co. v. Seib, 178 Neb. 253, 132 N.W.2d 871 (1965).

Note to Paragraph (4). The definition describes "copies" produced by methods possessing an accuracy which virtually eliminates the possibility of error. Copies thus produced are given the status of originals in large measure by Rule 1003, infra. Copies subsequently produced manually, whether handwritten or typed, are not within the definition. It should be noted that what is an original for some purposes may be a duplicate for others. Thus a bank's microfilm record of checks cleared is the original as a record. However, a print offered as a copy of a check whose contents are in controversy is a duplicate. This result is substantially consistent with 28 U.S.C. § 1732(b). Compare 26 U.S.C. § 7513(c), giving full status as originals to photographic reproductions of tax returns and other documents, made by authority of the Secretary of the Treasury, and 44 U.S.C. § 399(a), giving original status to photographic copies in the National Archives.

1974 Enactment

Note to Paragraph (2). The Committee amended this Rule expressly to include "video tapes" in the definition of "photographs." House Report No. 93-650.

Rule 1002. Requirement of Original

To prove the content of a writing, recording, or photograph, the original writing, recording, or photograph is required, except as otherwise provided in these rules or by Act of Congress.

ADVISORY COMMITTEE NOTES

1972 Proposed Rules

The rule is the familiar one requiring production of the original of a document to prove its contents, expanded to include writings, recordings, and photographs, as defined in Rule 1001(1) and (2), supra.

Application of the rule requires a resolution of the question whether contents are sought to be proved. Thus an event may be proved by nondocumentary evidence, even though a written record of it was made. If, however, the event is sought to be proved by the written record, the rule applies. For example, payment may be proved without producing the written receipt which was given. Earnings may be proved without producing books of account in which they are entered. McCormick § 198; 4 Wigmore § 1245. Nor does the rule apply to testimony that books or records have been examined and found not to contain any reference to a designated matter.

The assumption should not be made that the rule will come into operation on every occasion when use is made of a photograph in evidence. On the contrary, the rule will seldom apply to ordinary photographs. In most instances a party wishes to introduce the item and the question raised is the propriety of receiving it in evidence. Cases in which an offer is made of the testimony of a witness as to what he saw in a photograph or motion picture, without producing the same, are most unusual. The usual course is for a witness on the stand to identify the photograph or motion picture as a correct representation of events which he saw or of a scene with which he is familiar. In fact he adopts the picture as his testimony, or, in common parlance, uses the picture to illustrate his testimony. Under these circumstances, no effort is made to prove the contents of the picture, and the rule is inapplicable. Paradis, The Celluloid Witness, 37 U.Colo.L.Rev. 235, 249-251 (1965).

On occasion, however, situations arise in which contents are sought to be proved. Copyright, defamation, and invasion of privacy by photograph or motion picture falls in this category. Similarly as to situations in which the picture is offered as having independent probative value, e.g. automatic photograph of bank robber. See People v. Doggett, 83 Cal.App.2d 405, 188 P.2d 792 (1948), photograph of defendants engaged in indecent act; Mouser and Philbin, Photographic Evidence--Is There a Recognized Basis for Admissibility? 8 Hastings L.J. 310 (1957). the most commonly encountered of this latter group is of course, the X ray, with substantial authority calling for production of the original. Daniels v. Iowa City, 191 Iowa 811, 183 N.W. 415 (1921); Cellamare v. Third Ave. Transit Corp., 273 App.Div. 260, 77 N.Y.S.2d 91 (1948); Patrick & Tilman v. Matkin, 154 Okl. 232, 7 P.2d 414 (1932); Mendoza v. Rivera, 78 P.R.R. 569 (1955).

It should be noted, however, that Rule 703, supra, allows an expert to give an opinion based on matters not in evidence, and the present rule must be read as being limited accordingly in its application. Hospital records which may be admitted as business records under Rule 803(6) commonly contain reports interpreting X-rays by the staff radiologist, who qualifies as an expert, and these reports need not be excluded from the records by the instant rule.

The reference to Acts of Congress is made in view of such statutory provisions as 26 U.S.C. § 7513, photographic reproductions of tax returns and documents, made by authority of the Secretary of the Treasury, treated as originals, and 44 U.S.C. § 399(a), photographic copies in National Archives treated as originals.

Rule 1003. Admissibility of Duplicates

A duplicate is admissible to the same extent as an original unless (1) a genuine question is raised as to the authenticity of the original or (2) in the circumstances it would be unfair to admit the duplicate in lieu of the original.

ADVISORY COMMITTEE NOTES

1972 Proposed Rules
When the only concern is with getting the words or other contents before the court with accuracy and precision, then a counterpart serves equally as well as the original, if the counterpart is the product of a method which insures accuracy and genuineness. By definition in Rule 1001(4), supra, a "duplicate" possesses this character.

Therefore, if no genuine issue exists as to authenticity and no other reason exists for requiring the original, a duplicate is admissible under the rule. This position finds support in the decisions, Myrick v. United States, 332 F.2d 279 (5th Cir.1964), no error in admitting photostatic copies of checks instead of original microfilm in absence of suggestion to trial judge that photostats were incorrect; Johns v. United

States, 323 F.2d 421 (5th Cir.1963), not error to admit concededly accurate tape recording made from original wire recording; Sauget v. Johnston, 315 F.2d 816 (9th Cir.1963), not error to admit copy of agreement when opponent had original and did not on appeal claim any discrepancy. Other reasons for acquiring the original may be present when only a part of the original is reproduced and the remainder is needed for cross-examination or may disclose matters qualifying the part offered or otherwise useful to the opposing party. United States v. Alexander, 326 F.2d 736 (4th Cir.1964). And see Toho Bussan Kaisha, Ltd. v. American President Lines, Ltd., 265 F.2d 418, 76 A.L.R.2d 1344 (2d Cir.1959).

1974 Enactment
The Committee approved this Rule in the form submitted by the Court, with the expectation that the courts would be liberal in deciding that a "genuine question is raised as to the authenticity of the original." House Report No. 93-650.

Rule 1004. Admissibility of Other Evidence of Contents

The original is not required, and other evidence of the contents of a writing, recording, or photograph is admissible if--

(1) Originals lost or destroyed. All originals are lost or have been destroyed, unless the proponent lost or destroyed them in bad faith; or

(2) Original not obtainable. No original can be obtained by any available judicial process or procedure; or

(3) Original in possession of opponent. At a time when an original was under the control of the party against whom offered, that party was put on notice, by the pleadings or otherwise, that the contents would be a subject of proof at the hearing, and that party does not produce the original at the hearing; or

(4) Collateral matters. The writing, recording, or photograph is not closely related to a controlling issue.

ADVISORY COMMITTEE NOTES

1972 Proposed Rules
Basically the rule requiring the production of the original as proof of contents has developed as a rule of preference: if failure to produce the original is satisfactorily explained, secondary evidence is admissible. The instant rule specifies the circumstances under which production of the original is excused.

The rule recognizes no "degrees" of secondary evidence. While strict logic might call for extending the principle of preference beyond simply preferring the original, the formulation of a hierarchy of preferences and a procedure for making it effective is believed to involve unwarranted complexities. Most, if not all, that would be accomplished by an extended scheme of preferences will, in any event, be achieved through the normal motivation of a party to present the most convincing evidence possible and the arguments and procedures available to his opponent if he does not. Compare McCormick § 207.

Note to Paragraph (1). Loss or destruction of the original, unless due to bad faith of the proponent, is a satisfactory explanation of nonproduction. McCormick § 201.

Note to Paragraph (2). When the original is in the possession of a third person, inability to procure it from him by resort to process or other judicial procedure is a sufficient explanation of nonproduction. Judicial procedure includes subpoena duces tecum as an incident to the taking of a deposition in another jurisdiction. No further showing is required. See McCormick § 202.

Note to Paragraph (3). A party who has an original in his control has no need for the protection of the rule if put on notice that proof of contents will be made. He can ward off secondary evidence by offering the original. The notice procedure here provided is not to be confused with orders to produce or other discovery procedures, as the purpose of the procedure under this rule is to afford the opposite party an opportunity to produce the original, not to compel him to do so. McCormick § 203.

Note to Paragraph (4). While difficult to define with precision, situations arise in which no good purpose is served by production of the original. Examples are the newspaper in an action for the price of publishing defendant's advertisement, Foster-Holcomb Investment Co. v. Little Rock Publishing Co., 151 Ark. 449, 236 S.W. 597 (1922), and the streetcar transfer of plaintiff claiming status as a passenger, Chicago City Ry. Co. v. Carroll, 206 Ill. 318, 68 N.E. 1087 (1903). Numerous cases are collected in McCormick § 200, p. 412, n. 1.

1974 Enactment
Note to Paragraph (1). The Committee approved Rule 1004(1) in the form submitted to Congress. However, the Committee intends that loss or destruction of an original by another person at the instigation of the proponent should be considered as tantamount to loss or destruction in bad faith by the proponent himself. House Report No. 93-650.

1987 Amendments
The amendments are technical. No substantive change is intended.

Rule 1005. Public Records

The contents of an official record, or of a document authorized to be recorded or filed and actually recorded or filed, including data compilations in any form, if otherwise admissible, may be proved by copy, certified as correct in accordance with rule 902 or testified to be correct by a witness who has compared it with the original. If a copy which complies with the foregoing cannot be obtained by the exercise of reasonable diligence, then other evidence of the contents may be given.

ADVISORY COMMITTEE NOTES

1972 Proposed Rules
Public records call for somewhat different treatment. Removing them from their usual place of keeping would be attended by serious inconvenience to the public and to the custodian. As a consequence judicial decisions and statutes commonly hold that no explanation need be given for failure to produce the original of a public record. McCormick § 204; 4 Wigmore §§ 1215-1228. This blanket dispensation from producing or accounting for the original would open the door to the introduction of every kind of secondary evidence of contents of public records were it not for the preference given certified or compared copies. Recognition of degrees of secondary evidence in this situation is an appropriate quid pro quo for not applying the requirement of producing the original.

The provisions of 28 U.S.C. § 1733(b) apply only to departments or agencies of the United States. The rule, however, applies to public records generally and is comparable in scope in this respect to Rule 44(a) of the Rules of Civil Procedure.

Rule 1006. Summaries

The contents of voluminous writings, recordings, or photographs which cannot conveniently be examined in court may be presented in the form of a chart, summary, or calculation. The originals, or duplicates, shall be made available for examination or copying, or both, by other parties at reasonable time and place. The court may order that they be produced in court.

ADVISORY COMMITTEE NOTES

1972 Proposed Rules
The admission of summaries of voluminous books, records, or documents offers the only practicable means of making their contents available to judge and jury. The rule recognizes this practice, with appropriate safeguards. 4 Wigmore § 1230.

Rule 1007. Testimony or Written Admission of Party

Contents of writings, recordings, or photographs may be proved by the testimony or deposition of the party against whom offered or by that party's written admission, without accounting for the nonproduction of the original.

ADVISORY COMMITTEE NOTES

1972 Proposed Rules
While the parent case, Slatterie v. Pooley, 6 M. & W. 664, 151 Eng.Rep. 579 (Exch.1840), allows proof of contents by evidence of an oral admission by the party against whom offered, without accounting for nonproduction of the original, the risk of inaccuracy is substantial and the decision is at odds with the purpose of the rule giving preference to the original. See 4 Wigmore § 1255. The instant rule follows Professor McCormick's suggestion of limiting this use of admissions to those made in the course of giving testimony or in writing. McCormick § 208, p. 424. The limitation, of course, does not call for excluding evidence of an oral admission when nonproduction of the original has been accounted for and secondary evidence generally has become admissible. Rule 1004, supra.

A similar provision is contained in New Jersey Evidence Rule 70(1)(h).

1987 Amendments
The amendment is technical. No substantive change is intended.

Rule 1008. Functions of Court and Jury

When the admissibility of other evidence of contents of writings, recordings, or photographs under these rules depends upon the fulfillment of a condition of fact, the question whether the condition has been fulfilled is ordinarily for the court to determine in accordance with the provisions of rule 104. However, when an issue is raised (a) whether the asserted writing ever existed, or (b) whether another writing, recording, or photograph produced at the trial is the original, or (c) whether other evidence of contents correctly reflects the contents, the issue is for the trier of fact to determine as in the case of other issues of fact.

ADVISORY COMMITTEE NOTES

1972 Proposed Rules
Most preliminary questions of fact in connection with applying the rule preferring the original as evidence of contents are for the judge, under the general principles announced in Rule 104, supra. Thus, the question whether the loss of the origi-

nals has been established, or of the fulfillment of other conditions specified in Rule 1004, supra, is for the judge. However, questions may arise which go beyond the mere administration of the rule preferring the original and into the merits of the controversy. For example, plaintiff offers secondary evidence of the contents of an alleged contract, after first introducing evidence of loss of the original, and defendant counters with evidence that no such contract was ever executed. If the judge decides that the contract was never executed and excludes the secondary evidence, the case is at an end without ever going to the jury on a central issue. Levin, Authentication and Content of Writings, 10 Rutgers L.Rev. 632, 644 (1956). The latter portion of the instant rule is designed to insure treatment of these situations as raising jury questions. The decision is not one for uncontrolled discretion of the jury but is subject to the control exercised generally by the judge over jury determinations. See Rule 104(b), supra.

For similar provisions, see Uniform Rule 70(2); Kansas Code of Civil Procedure § 60-467(b); New Jersey Evidence Rule 70(2), (3).

ARTICLE XI. MISCELLANEOUS RULES

Rule 1101. Applicability of Rules

(a) Courts and judges. These rules apply to the United States district courts, the District Court of Guam, the District Court of the Virgin Islands, the District Court for the Northern Mariana Islands, the United States courts of appeals, the United States Claims Court, and to United States bankruptcy judges and United States magistrate judges, in the actions, cases, and proceedings and to the extent hereinafter set forth. The terms "judge" and "court" in these rules include United States bankruptcy judges and United States magistrate judges.

(b) Proceedings generally. These rules apply generally to civil actions and proceedings, including admiralty and maritime cases, to criminal cases and proceedings, to contempt proceedings except those in which the court may act summarily, and to proceedings and cases under title 11, United States Code.

(c) Rule of privilege. The rule with respect to privileges applies at all stages of all actions, cases, and proceedings.

(d) Rules inapplicable. The rules (other than with respect to privileges) do not apply in the following situations:

(1) Preliminary questions of fact. The determination of questions of fact preliminary to admissibility of evidence when the issue is to be determined by the court under rule 104.

(2) Grand jury. Proceedings before grand juries.

(3) Miscellaneous proceedings. Proceedings for extradition or rendition; preliminary examinations in criminal cases; sentencing, or granting or revoking probation; issuance of warrants for arrest, criminal summonses, and search warrants; and proceedings with respect to release on bail or otherwise.

(e) Rules applicable in part. In the following proceedings these rules apply to the extent that matters of evidence are not provided for in the statutes which govern procedure therein or in other rules prescribed by the Supreme Court pursuant to statutory authority: the trial of misdemeanors and other petty offenses before United States magistrate judges; review of agency actions when the facts are subject to trial de novo under section 706(2)(F) of title 5, United States Code; review of orders of the Secretary of Agriculture under section 2 of the Act entitled "An Act to authorize association of producers of agricultural products" approved February 18, 1922 (7 U.S.C. 292), and under sections 6 and 7(c) of the Perishable Agricultural Commodities Act, 1930 (7 U.S.C. 499f, 499g(c)); naturalization and revocation of naturalization under sections 310-318 of the Immigration and Nationality Act (8 U.S.C. 1421-1429); prize proceedings in admiralty under sections 7651-7681 of title 10, United States Code; review of orders of the Secretary of the Interior under section 2 of the Act entitled "An Act authorizing associations of producers of aquatic products" approved June 25, 1934 (15 U.S.C. 522); review of orders of petroleum control boards under section 5 of the Act entitled "An Act to regulate interstate and foreign commerce in petroleum and its products by prohibiting the shipment in such commerce of petroleum and its products produced in violation of State law, and for other purposes", approved February 22, 1935 (15 U.S.C. 715d); actions for fines, penalties, or forfeitures under part V of title IV of the Tariff Act of 1930 (19 U.S.C. 1581-1624), or under the Anti-Smuggling Act (19 U.S.C. 1701-1711); criminal libel for condemnation, exclusion of imports, or other proceedings under the Federal Food, Drug, and Cosmetic Act (21 U.S.C. 301-392); disputes between seamen under sections 4079, 4080, and 4081 of the Revised Statutes (22 U.S.C. 256-258); habeas corpus under sections 2241-2254 of title 28, United States Code; motions to vacate, set aside or correct sentence under section 2255 of title 28, United States Code; actions for penalties for refusal to transport destitute seamen under section 4578 of the Revised Statutes (46 U.S.C. 679); actions against the United States under the Act entitled "An Act authorizing suits against the United States in admiralty for damage caused by and salvage service rendered to public vessels belonging to the United States, and for other purposes", approved March 3, 1925 (46 U.S.C. 781-790), as implemented by section 7730 of title 10, United States Code.

ADVISORY COMMITTEE NOTES

1972 Proposed Rules

Note to Subdivision (a). The various enabling acts contain differences in phraseology in their descriptions of the courts over which the Supreme Court's power to make rules of practice and procedure extends. The act concerning civil actions, as amended in 1966, refers to "the district courts * * * of the United States in civil actions, including admiralty and maritime cases. * * *" 28 U.S.C. § 2072, Pub.L. 89-773, § 1, 80 Stat. 1323. The bankruptcy authorization is for rules of practice and procedure "under the Bankruptcy Act." 28 U.S.C. § 2075, Pub.L. 88-623, § 1, 78 Stat. 1001. The Bankruptcy Act in turn creates bankruptcy courts of "the United States district courts and the district courts of the Territories and possessions to which this title is or may hereafter be applicable." 11 U.S.C. §§ 1(10), 11(a). The provision as to criminal rules up to and including verdicts applies to "criminal cases and proceedings to punish for criminal contempt of court in the United States district courts, in the district courts for the districts of the Canal Zone and Virgin Islands, in the Supreme Court of Puerto Rico, and in proceedings before United States magistrates." 18 U.S.C. § 3771.

These various provisions do not in terms describe the same courts. In congressional usage the phrase "district courts of the United States," without further qualification, traditionally has included the district courts established by Congress in the states under Article III of the Constitution, which are "constitutional" courts, and has not included the territorial courts created under Article IV, Section 3, clause 2, which are "legislative" courts. Hornbuckle v. Toombs, 85 U.S. 648, 21 L.Ed. 966 (1873). However, any doubt as to the inclusion of the District Court for the District of Columbia in the phrase is laid at rest by the provisions of the Judicial Code constituting the judicial districts, 28 U.S.C. § 81 et seq., creating district courts therein, id. § 132, and specifically providing that the term "district court of the United States" means the court so constituted. Id. § 451. The District of Columbia is included. Id. § 88. Moreover, when these provisions were enacted, reference to the District of Columbia was deleted from the original civil rules enabling act. 28 U.S.C. § 2072. Likewise Puerto Rico is made a district, with a district court, and included in the term. Id. § 119. The question is simply one of the extent of the authority conferred by Congress. With respect to civil rules it seems clearly to include the district courts in the states, the District Court for the District of Columbia, and the District Court for the District of Puerto Rico.

The bankruptcy coverage is broader. The bankruptcy courts include "the United States district courts," which includes those enumerated above. Bankruptcy courts also include "the district courts of the Territories and possessions to which this title is or may hereafter be applicable." 11 U.S.C. §§ 1(10), 11(a). These courts include the district courts of Guam and the Virgin Islands. 48 U.S.C. §§ 1424(b), 1615. Professor Moore points out that whether the District Court for the District of the Canal Zone is a court of bankruptcy "is not free from doubt in view of the fact that no other statute expressly or inferentially provides for the applicability of the Bankruptcy Act in the Zone." He further observes that while there seems to be little doubt that the Zone is a territory or possession within the meaning of the Bankruptcy Act, 11 U.S.C. § 1(10), it must be noted that the appendix to the Canal Zone Code of 1934 did not list the Act among the laws of the United States applicable to the Zone. 1 Moore's Collier on Bankruptcy ¶ 1.10, pp. 67, 72, n. 25 (14th ed. 1967). The Code of 1962 confers on the district court jurisdiction of:

"(4) actions and proceedings involving laws of the United States applicable to the Canal Zone; and

"(5) other matters and proceedings wherein jurisdiction is conferred by this Code or any other law." Canal Zone Code, 1962, Title 3, § 141.

Admiralty jurisdiction is expressly conferred. Id. § 142. General powers are conferred on the district court, "if the course of proceeding is not specifically prescribed by this Code, by the statute, or by applicable rule of the Supreme Court of the United States * * *" Id. § 279. Neither these provisions nor § 1(10) of the Bankruptcy Act ("district courts of the Territories and possessions to which this title is or may hereafter be applicable") furnishes a satisfactory answer as to the status of the District Court for the District of the Canal Zone as a court of bankruptcy. However, the fact is that this court exercises no bankruptcy jurisdiction in practice.

The criminal rules enabling act specified United States district courts, district courts for the districts of the Canal Zone and the Virgin Islands, the Supreme Court of the Commonwealth of Puerto Rico, and proceedings before United States commissioners. Aside from the addition of commissioners, now magistrates, this scheme differs from the bankruptcy pattern in that it makes no mention of the District Court of Guam but by specific mention removes the Canal Zone from the doubtful list.

The further difference in including the Supreme Court of the Commonwealth of Puerto Rico seems not to be significant for present purposes, since the Supreme Court of the Commonwealth of Puerto Rico is an appellate court. The Rules of Criminal Procedure have not been made applicable to it, as being unneeded and inappropriate, Rule 54(a) of the Federal Rules of Criminal Procedure, and the same approach is indicated with respect to rules of evidence.

If one were to stop at this point and frame a rule governing the applicability of the proposed rules of evidence in terms of the authority conferred by the three enabling acts, an irregular pattern would emerge as follows:

Civil actions, including admiralty and maritime cases--district courts in the states, District of Columbia, and Puerto Rico.

Bankruptcy--same as civil actions, plus Guam and Virgin Islands.

Criminal cases--same as civil actions, plus Canal Zone and Virgin Islands (but not Guam).

This irregular pattern need not, however, be accepted. Originally the Advisory Committee on the Rules of Civil Procedure took the position that, although the phrase "district courts of the United States" did not include territorial courts, provisions in the organic laws of Puerto Rico and Hawaii would make the rules applicable to the district courts thereof, though this would not be so as to Alaska, the Virgin Islands, or the Canal Zone, whose organic acts contained no corresponding provisions. At the suggestion of the Court, however, the Advisory Committee struck from its notes a statement to the above effect. 2 Moore's Federal Practice ¶ 1.07 (2nd ed. 1967); 1 Barron and Holtzoff, Federal Practice and Procedure § 121 (Wright ed. 1960). Congress thereafter by various enactments provided that the rules and future amendments thereto should apply to the district courts of Hawaii, 53 Stat. 841 (1939), Puerto Rico, 54 Stat. 22 (1940), Alaska, 63 Stat. 445 (1949), Guam, 64 Stat. 384-390 (1950), and the Virgin Islands, 68 Stat. 497, 507 (1954). The original enabling act for rules of criminal procedure specifically mentioned the district courts of the Canal Zone and the Virgin Islands. The Commonwealth of Puerto Rico was blanketed in by creating its court a "district court of the United States" as previously described. Although Guam is not mentioned in either the enabling act or in the expanded definition of "district court of the United States," the Supreme Court in 1956 amended Rule 54(a) to state that the Rules of Criminal Procedure are applicable in Guam. The Court took this step following the enactment of legislation by Congress in 1950 that rules theretofore or thereafter promulgated by the Court in civil cases, admiralty, criminal cases and bankruptcy should apply to the District Court of Guam, 48 U.S.C. § 1424(b), and two Ninth Circuit decisions upholding the applicability of the Rules of Criminal Procedure to Guam. Pugh v. United States, 212 F.2d 761 (9th Cir.1954); Hatchett v. Guam, 212 F.2d 767 (9th Cir.1954); Orfield, The Scope of the Federal Rules of Criminal Procedure, 38 U. of Det.L.J. 173, 187 (1960).

From this history, the reasonable conclusion is that Congressional enactment of a provision that rules and future amendments shall apply in the courts of a territory or possession is the equivalent of mention in an enabling act and that a rule on scope and applicability may properly be drafted accordingly. Therefore the pattern set by Rule 54 of the Federal Rules of Criminal Procedure is here followed.

The substitution of magistrates in lieu of commissioners is made in pursuance of the Federal Magistrates Act, P.L. 90-578, approved October 17, 1968, 82 Stat. 1107.

Note to Subdivision (b). Subdivision (b) is a combination of the language of the enabling acts, supra, with respect to the kinds of proceedings in which the making of rules is authorized. It is subject to the qualifications expressed in the subdivisions which follow.

Note to Subdivision (c). Subdivision (c) singling out the rules of privilege for special treatment, is made necessary by the limited applicability of the remaining rules.

Note to Subdivision (d). The rule is not intended as an expression as to when due process or other constitutional provisions may require an evidentiary hearing. Paragraph (1) restates, for convenience, the provisions of the second sentence of Rule 104(a), supra. See Advisory Committee's Note to that rule.

(2) While some states have statutory requirements that indictments be based on "legal evidence," and there is some case law to the effect that the rules of evidence apply to grand jury proceedings, 1 Wigmore § 4(5), the Supreme Court has not accepted this view. In Costello v. United States, 350 U.S. 359, 76 S.Ct. 406, 100 L.Ed. 397 (1965), the Court refused to allow an indictment to be attacked, for either constitutional or policy reasons, on the ground that only hearsay evidence was presented.

"It would run counter to the whole history of the grand jury institution, in which laymen conduct their inquiries unfettered by technical rules. Neither justice nor the concept of a fair trial requires such a change." Id. at 364. The rule as drafted does not deal with the evidence required to support an indictment.

(3) The rule exempts preliminary examinations in criminal cases. Authority as to the applicability of the rules of evidence to preliminary examinations has been meagre and conflicting. Goldstein, The State and the Accused: Balance of Advantage in Criminal Procedure, 69 Yale L.J. 1149, 1168, n. 53 (1960); Comment, Preliminary Hearings on Indictable Offenses in Philadelphia, 106 U. of Pa.L.Rev. 589, 592-593 (1958). Hearsay testimony is, however, customarily received in such examinations. Thus in a Dyer Act case, for example, an affidavit may properly be used in a preliminary examination to prove ownership of the stolen vehicle, thus

saving the victim of the crime the hardship of having to travel twice to a distant district for the sole purpose of testifying as to ownership. It is believed that the extent of the applicability of the Rules of Evidence to preliminary examinations should be appropriately dealt with by the Federal Rules of Criminal Procedure which regulate those proceedings.

Extradition and rendition proceedings are governed in detail by statute. 18 U.S.C. §§ 3181-3195. They are essentially administrative in character. Traditionally the rules of evidence have not applied. 1 Wigmore § 4(6). Extradition proceedings are accepted from the operation of the Rules of Criminal Procedure. Rule 54(b)(5) of Federal Rules of Criminal Procedure.

The rules of evidence have not been regarded as applicable to sentencing or probation proceedings, where great reliance is placed upon the presentence investigation and report. Rule 32(c) of the Federal Rules of Criminal Procedure requires a presentence investigation and report in every case unless the court otherwise directs. In Williams v. New York, 337 U.S. 241, 69 S.Ct. 1079, 93 L.Ed. 1337 (1949), in which the judge overruled a jury recommendation of life imprisonment and imposed a death sentence, the Court said that due process does not require confrontation or cross-examination in sentencing or passing on probation, and that the judge has broad discretion as to the sources and types of information relied upon. Compare the recommendation that the substance of all derogatory information be disclosed to the defendant, in A.B.A. Project on Minimum Standards for Criminal Justice, Sentencing Alternatives and Procedures § 4.4, Tentative Draft (1967, Sobeloff, Chm.). Williams was adhered to in Specht v. Patterson, 386 U.S. 605, 87 S.Ct. 1209, 18 L.Ed.2d 326 (1967), but not extended to a proceeding under the Colorado Sex Offenders Act, which was said to be a new charge leading in effect to punishment, more like the recidivist statutes where opportunity must be given to be heard on the habitual criminal issue.

Warrants for arrest, criminal summonses, and search warrants are issued upon complaint or affidavit showing probable cause. Rules 4(a) and 41(c) of the Federal Rules of Criminal Procedure. The nature of the proceedings makes application of the formal rules of evidence inappropriate and impracticable.

Criminal contempts are punishable summarily if the judge certifies that he saw or heard the contempt and that it was committed in the presence of the court. Rule 42(a) of the Federal Rules of Criminal Procedure. The circumstances which preclude application of the rules of evidence in this situation are not present, however, in other cases of criminal contempt.

Proceedings with respect to release on bail or otherwise do not call for application of the rules of evidence. The governing statute specifically provides:

"Information stated in, or offered in connection with, any order entered pursuant to this section need not conform to the rules pertaining to the admissibility of evidence in a court of law." 18 U.S.C.A. § 3146(f). This provision is consistent with the type of inquiry contemplated in A.B.A. Project on Minimum Standards for Criminal Justice, Standards Relating to Pretrial Release, § 4.5(b), (c), p. 16 (1968). The references to the weight of the evidence against the accused, in Rule 46(a)(1), (c) of the Federal Rules of Criminal Procedure and in 18 U.S.C.A. § 3146(b), as a factor to be considered, clearly do not have in view evidence introduced at a hearing under the rules of evidence.

The rule does not exempt habeas corpus proceedings. The Supreme Court held in Walker v. Johnston, 312 U.S. 275, 61 S.Ct. 574, 85 L.Ed. 830 (1941), that the practice of disposing of matters of fact on affidavit, which prevailed in some circuits, did not "satisfy the command of the statute that the judge shall proceed 'to determine the facts of the case, by hearing the testimony and arguments.' " This view accords with the emphasis in Townsend v. Sain, 372 U.S. 293, 83 S.Ct. 745, 9 L.Ed.2d 770 (1963), upon trial-type proceedings, id. 311, 83 S.Ct. 745, with demeanor evidence as a significant factor, id. 322, 83 S.Ct. 745, in applications by state prisoners aggrieved by unconstitutional detentions. Hence subdivision (3) applies the rules to habeas corpus proceedings to the extent not inconsistent with the statute.

Note to Subdivision (e). In a substantial number of special proceedings, ad hoc evaluation has resulted in the promulgation of particularized evidentiary provisions, by Act of Congress or by rule adopted by the Supreme Court. Well adapted to the particular proceedings, though not apt candidates for inclusion in a set of general rules, they are left undisturbed. Otherwise, however, the rules of evidence are applicable to the proceedings enumerated in the subdivision.

1974 Enactment
Note to Subdivision (a). Subdivision (a) as submitted to the Congress, in stating the courts and judges to which the Rules of Evidence apply, omitted the Court of Claims and commissioners of that Court. At the request of the Court of Claims, the Committee amended the Rule to include the Court and its commissioners within the purview of the Rules.

Note to Subdivision (b). Subdivision (b) was amended merely to substitute positive law citations for those which were not. House Report No. 93-650.

1987 Amendments
Subdivision (a) is amended to delete the reference to the District Court for the District of the Canal Zone, which no longer exists, and to add the District Court for the Northern Mariana Islands. The United States bankruptcy judges are added to conform the subdivision with Rule 1101(b) and Bankruptcy Rule 9017.

1988 Amendments

The amendments are technical. No substantive change is intended.

1993 Amendments

This revision is made to conform the rule to changes in terminology made by Rule 58 of the Federal Rules of Criminal Procedure and to the changes in the title of United States magistrates made by the Judicial Improvements Act of 1990.

Rule 1102. Amendments

Amendments to the Federal Rules of Evidence may be made as provided in section 2072 of title 28 of the United States Code.

ADVISORY COMMITTEE NOTES

1991 Amendments

The amendment is technical. No substantive change is intended.

Rule 1103. Title

These rules may be known and cited as the Federal Rules of Evidence.

Index

References are to pages.

✝